THE OXFORD ENCYCLOPEDIA OF
FOOD AND DRINK IN AMERICA

EDITORIAL BOARD

THE OXFORD ENCYCLOPEDIA

OF

FOOD AND DRINK

IN

AMERICA

Andrew F. Smith

Editor in Chief

VOLUME 1

A–J

OXFORD

UNIVERSITY PRESS

2004

OXFORD
UNIVERSITY PRESS

Oxford   New York

Auckland   Bangkok   Buenos Aires   Cape Town   Chennai
Dar es Salaam   Delhi   Hong Kong   Istanbul   Karachi   Kolkata
Kuala Lumpur   Madrid   Melbourne   Mexico City   Mumbai   Nairobi
São Paulo   Shanghai   Taipei   Tokyo   Toronto

Copyright © 2004 by Oxford University Press, Inc.

Published by Oxford University Press, Inc.
198 Madison Avenue, New York, New York, 10016
http://www.oup.com

Oxford is a registered trademark of Oxford University Press

Library of Congress Cataloging-in-Publication Data

Encyclopedia of food and drink in America / Andrew F. Smith, editor in chief.
p. cm.
ISBN 0-19-515437-1 (Set) – ISBN 0-19-517551-4 (Volume 1: alk. paper)
– ISBN 0-19-517552-2 (Volume 2: alk. paper)
1. Food–Dictionaries. 2. Cookery, American–Dictionaries.
3. Beverages–Dictionaries. I. Smith, Andrew F., 1946-
TX349.E45 2004
641.3'003–dc22

2003024873

9 8 7 6 5 4 3 2 1

Printed in the United States of America
on acid-free paper

EDITORIAL AND PRODUCTION STAFF

CONTENTS

THE OXFORD ENCYCLOPEDIA OF

FOOD AND DRINK IN AMERICA

LIST OF ARTICLES

PREFACE

Food is the first of life's essentials. It is connected with every aspect of our lives from birth to death. The quest for food has been a driving force underlying human history, and almost every major political, economic, religious, and social event or upheaval has had food dimensions or repercussions. For better and worse, humankind has reshaped the physical and biological world from before the Neolithic revolution to the genetic revolution.

Food has profoundly affected American history, beginning in prehistoric times, when Old World hunters came to the New World seeking big game, to modern times, in which American agriculture helps feed the world. Food has profoundly shaped our society: It has influenced population growth and migrations, dictated economic and political changes, expanded commerce, inspired poems and literature, and precipitated the evolution and invention of lifestyles. The desire for food served at particular times and in specific ways has caused the creation of new technologies, from the earliest canning efforts to microwave ovens. Food was at the core of American medicine in the nineteenth century, and dietary concerns remain an important component of medical practice. Food has been an important weapon in war. Well-fed armies usually defeat hungry ones, as illustrated by the Civil War; conversely, wars have altered our eating habits by introducing new foods and processes and by creating new uses for old foods. Food is inherent in America's class structure. Character and status often are judged by the foods on one's table and the style and rituals involved in serving and eating them. Food has symbolic value. Other peoples and American ethnic groups have frequently been pejoratively identified in terms of food with such names as "frog," "lime," "kraut," and "greaser." Food has always been important in moral and religious life. Where, what, and how one eats reflect spiritual and ethical values. Beyond nutritional value, food has psychological and emotional value. Consuming foods and beverages gratifies pleasure and relieves stress. Who acquires and prepares food has traditionally reflected gender and social status.

With whom one eats and under what conditions can be a family get-together, a romantic encounter, a business matter, a status enhancer, or a religious experience. Finally, food is security and power: Those who have it survive and thrive; those who lack it languish and die.

Food is America's most important business and its largest export. Never before in the history of the world has one group of people had so much influence over the culinary lives of others. American food surpluses have saved millions of lives in other nations, and American domestic farm subsidies and tariffs have caused economic havoc and political upheaval in Africa and Southeast Asia. Other countries are rapidly expanding their exports to the United States, and American food corporations are rapidly expanding abroad. American fast food companies are increasing their operations in other countries while they are contracting their operations in the United States. American food corporations are at the forefront of genetic engineering research and applications. As a consequence of this technology, the world may be on the verge of a great culinary revolution or perhaps a genetic catastrophe.

The idea of an "American cuisine" is not a new phenomenon. Although the dominant culinary style in the original thirteen colonies was English, Americans adapted to new environmental conditions by creating a new cuisine. English cookbooks were published in America beginning in 1742, but few recipes that appeared in these cookbooks reflected the culinary shifts under way in North America. When Amelia Simmons wrote the first cookbook published by an American, she titled it *American Cookery* (1796). Many recipes in the cookbook reflected English culinary traditions, but Simmons also included New World ingredients, and many of her recipes were unlike anything in British cookbooks. In the four centuries since the English colonies were established in North America, American cookery has been greatly modified by climatic and environmental conditions in the New World, the availability of new ingredients, and numerous adoptions and adaptations of the cookery of immigrants from numerous nations, cultures, and religions.

When the United States celebrated its one hundredth birthday with the Philadelphia Centennial Exposition in 1876, the notion of American culinary exceptionalism emerged. The Women's Centennial Committee posed the question: What is unique about American food? For answers, the committee queried women in all states and territories, requesting uniquely American recipes. The results were published in *The National Cookery Book* (1876), which was sold at the exposition. Despite 250 years of culinary drift in the New World, American cookery as reflected in the cookbook retained much of its English roots, and many recipes could be traced to their traditional British sources. The recipes demonstrated a range from slightly modified European dishes to highly unusual items, such as several from an Oneida "squaw," a dozen Jewish recipes, and several Florida recipes that demonstrated Spanish culinary heritage. Particularly interesting about the recipes in the *National Cookery Book* was that few survived into the twentieth century. Massive immigrations from central and eastern Europe and China, along with the industrialization of American food, greatly altered what and how Americans ate and drank, creating a bewildering kaleidoscope of changing patterns. American food has never stopped changing, and this constant innovation is perhaps its hallmark. The pace of culinary change in America and the world is accelerating, and it will likely continue to do so.

The self-evident significance of food in American history has been traditionally ignored by historians and other academicians. America's food history has been largely told by newspaper reporters, magazine writers, and television producers. Some writers have taken the easy way out and presented nice stories rather than spend the time and energy to discern significant underlying patterns. In the early 1980s it would have been difficult to write an encyclopedia of American food and drink. Not enough serious research had been conducted to warrant such a publication, and the audience for the book would have been limited. Research into topics related to American food and drink has increased; numerous articles have appeared in academic and popular journals; and serious books on culinary topics have proliferated. Academic interest in food, particularly American food, is expanding. What has emerged is the broad-based, eclectic, and electric field of culinary studies. The field involves academicians from diverse disciplines, such as history, sociology, anthropol-ogy, economics, food studies, women's studies, and culinary arts, but it also is peopled with museum curators, professional chefs, independent scholars, cookbook authors, food writers, librarians, and foodies. Although practitioners have approached their studies from different perspectives using different methods and different vocabularies, each has illuminated slices of America's real culinary past. When these diverse works are sifted and amalgamated, a fascinating tale of American food and drink emerges. It is action packed, peopled with home cooks and fancy restaurateurs, family farmers and corporate giants, captains of industry and street vendors, mom-and-pop grocers and massive food conglomerates, burger barons and vegetarians, the hungry and the affluent, hard-hitting advertisers and health-food advocates, those who make medical claims and home economists, slow-food advocates and fast-food consumers, and ethnic and religious groups of every flavor.

The intent behind this Encyclopedia is to pull the research together and introduce these novel findings to a wider audience. The objective is to make a major contribution by bringing together in one authoritative reference work the best scholarship on the history of American food. The 770 entries summarize knowledge on this large theme. The authors of the entries reflect the eclectic nature of the culinary history field. Considerable effort has gone into the planning of this project, which has drawn on the expertise of researchers with a variety of interests. The Encyclopedia has been designed in such a way as to combine historical, descriptive, and analytical articles with synthetic and interpretive essays. Although this Encyclopedia is organized alphabetically, there are several types of entries:

- Chronological surveys that look at American history during different time periods from the pre-Columbian era to the early twenty-first century. These entries are broad reviews of important events and trends.
- Product entries that focus on a specific food or drink, such as tomatoes, Manhattans, club sandwiches, and breakfast cereal.
- Contributions of ethnic, religious, cultural, and racial groups to American culinary life, such as those by African Americans, German Americans, Mexican Americans, Chinese Americans, Seventh-Day Adventists, Muslims, Catholics, and Jews.
- Biographies of important contributors to American food and drink, including chefs, corporate leaders, critics, food writers, cookbook authors, cookery bibliographers, and others whom the editors considered influences on American culinary life.

- Political and social movements, such as Temperance, Prohibition, and the drive for pure food.

The entries in the Encyclopedia are arranged in alphabetical order letter by letter. Composite entries gather together discussions of similar or related topics under one headword. For example, under the entry "Cooking Schools" the reader will find two subentries: "The Nineteenth Century" and "The Twentieth Century." A headnote listing the various subentries introduces each composite entry.

The nearly two hundred contributors have sought to write in clear language with a minimum of technical vocabulary. The articles give important foreign-language terms and titles in their original languages, with English translations when needed. A selective bibliography at the end of each article directs the reader who wishes to pursue a topic in greater detail to primary sources and to the most important scholarly works in any language plus the most useful works in English.

To guide readers from one article to related discussions elsewhere in the Encyclopedia, end-references appear at the end of many articles. There are cross-references within the body of a few articles. Blind entries direct the user from an alternate form of an entry term to the entry itself. For example, the blind entry for "Train Food" tells the reader to look under "Dining Car." Readers interested in finding all the articles on a particular subject (for example, categories of foods or ethnic cuisines) may consult the topical outline at the end of volume 2. A comprehensive index at the end of the same volume lists all the topics covered in the Encyclopedia, including those that are not headwords themselves.

The Encyclopedia includes nearly four hundred illustrations. At the end of volume 2 there are appendixes, a topical outline (which shows how articles relate to one another and to the overall design of the Encyclopedia), the directory of contributors, and the index.

This Encyclopedia is not intended to be comprehensive, and it does not include every possible topic. Because of the eclectic nature of American gastronomy, the Encyclopedia covers a wide range of topics, but it only scratches the surface of most topics. It is not intended as the final word on American food and drink. Extensive bibliographic resources are provided for most entries and in the appendixes to suggest directions for readers interested in knowing more about American gastronomy. This Encyclopedia is also intended to point the way to future research and growth. Because the study of American food and drink is rapidly expanding, it is anticipated that this Encyclopedia will be revised regularly to include new works and perspectives.

Many individuals could be singled out for their assistance in producing this Encyclopedia. I would like to thank especially Barry Popik, whose online research appearing in the archives of the American Dialect Society was used by many writers. He was always willing to answer questions and respond to inquiries.

Many thanks to those who contributed to the illustration program. Meryle Evans helped to plan and organize it. Meryle Evans, Kit Barry, Cathy Kaufman and the Institute for Culinary Education, and Barbara Kuck provided invaluable assistance in locating and gaining permission to use many illustrations in this Encyclopedia. Kit Barry, Rynn Berry, Steve Heller, Barbara Kuck, Georgia S. Maas, John C. Campbell, Howard Paige, Alice Ross, Bonnie Slotnick, and Mark H. Zanger, among others, allowed us to use images from their own collections. Joe Zarba took photographs in the New York area.

On a personal note, I would like to thank Bonnie Slotnick, who commented on all my entries and pointed out foolish mistakes of grammar as well as of content. I also thank the contributors who wrote the entries and the members of the editorial board for their thousands of hours of work on this Encyclopedia, designing and selecting entries, identifying and guiding authors, and reviewing and editing entries. It was a personal joy and professional pleasure to work with them all.

Finally, I thank the staff at Oxford University Press, especially Ralph Carlson, who helped launch the Encyclopedia; Beth Ammerman, who helped develop it; Mark Gallagher, Erica Pirrung, Georgia S. Maas, and Stephen Wagley, who helped produce it; Rebecca Seger, for promoting and marketing it; and especially Timothy J. DeWerff and Karen Day for their constant support. Without their encouragement, this Encyclopedia would never have been completed.

ANDREW F. SMITH

COMMON ABBREVIATIONS USED IN THIS WORK

AI, adequate intake

AID, Agency for International Development

AVA, American Viticultural Area

BATF, Bureau of Alcohol, Tobacco, and Firearms

B.C.E, before the Common Era (= B.C.)

BLT, bacon, lettuce, and tomato sandwich

CARE, Cooperative for American Relief Everywhere

C.E., Common Era (= A.D.)

DRI, dietary reference intake

EAR, estimated average requirement

FDA, Food and Drug Administration

GM, genetically modified

GMO, genetically modified organism

NAFTA, North American Free Trade Agreement

PL, Public Law

RDA, recommended dietary allowance

UNICEF, United Nations International Children's Emergency Fund

USFA, United States Food Administration

USDA, United States Department of Agriculture

WHO, World Health Organization

WTO, World Trade Organization

THE OXFORD ENCYCLOPEDIA OF
FOOD AND DRINK IN AMERICA

Additives, *see Chemical Additives*

Adulterations

Adulteration is the practice of adding unsafe amounts of chemical preservatives to foods and drinks, or adding color to conceal inferior or deteriorated food and drink products, or mixing inexpensive foods and drinks with expensive ones so as to reduce costs, or substituting inexpensive foods and drinks for expensive ones. Adulteration has played a large role in the history of American food and drink; the public's demand for federal protection from unscrupulous and dishonest producers and manufacturers at the beginning of the twentieth century led to the breakthrough passage in 1906 of both the Pure Food Act and the Meat Inspection Act.

Industrialization and Fraud

Although adulteration of American food and drink existed during the eighteenth century, it was not prevalent until the end of the nineteenth century, after dramatic changes had taken place in the nation's food industry. Before the end of the Civil War in 1865, most food was obtained locally: bread came from the town baker, meat from the local butcher, seasonal fresh fruits and vegetables from nearby farms, and milk from a neighbor's cow. Americans knew where their food was made and who made it. The distance between producer and consumer was usually the length of a handshake—a distance that ensured the quality of most food products by means of the producer's personal guarantee. Preservation of food was primitive; sophisticated forms of chemical preservation were unavailable and unnecessary. Most farms had a root cellar to store vegetables, and a springhouse—a small building constructed over a spring, in which cold springwater was collected—to keep milk and butter cool. Fresh fruits were dried in the sun, preserved by canning, or conserved in jams and jellies.

After the Civil War, as industry moved people from rural to urban areas, cities grew and Americans became distant from the producers and manufacturers of their food. By 1875 a national railroad system transported food from farms and ranches to centrally located urban processing locations; in turn, the railroads carried jarred, tinned, and paper-packaged food to distant consumers. America had developed a national commerce in food.

The distance food traveled and the time that elapsed between production and sale created significant problems with respect to preservation. Food producers hired chemists who addressed these problems by using various chemical additives to prevent decomposition, hide decay, restore natural color, and modify flavor. As the food industry grew and food became big business, few consumers knew how their food was produced, manufactured, or handled. Taking advantage of this situation, many food companies directed their chemists to develop inexpensive goods as fraudulent substitutes for more costly ones, thereby decreasing costs and increasing profits. For example, apple stock was jarred and sold as blackberry, currant, or plum jelly: the cores, skins, and rejected portions of apples along with whole rejected apples were made into an apple stock or juice, which was then artificially colored, flavored, and jellied.

Fraudulent suppliers would package and price inauthentic products as if they were the real thing. It was said, for example, that if every square foot of Vermont was planted with sugar maple trees, there would not have been enough trees to account for the amount of "Pure Vermont Maple Syrup" sold in America. American drinks were also adulterated. Caramel color was added to fresh raw whiskey in order to mimic the amber color of barrel-aged whiskey. Sugar and caramel color were added to make inexpensive young brandy look and taste like expensive aged brandy.

Over time, dishonest manufacturers were profitable, while many honest competitors failed. Consequently, by the end of the nineteenth century, most American food and drink was adulterated. Against this wave of corporate irresponsibility there arose in the United States a movement supporting a return to pure food. The leader of this effort was Dr. Harvey W. Wiley, the chief of the Department of Agriculture's Bureau of Chemistry. He was joined in the crusade for pure food by other chemists who had been hired by state governments to help enforce state pure food laws. These chemists had designed analytical tests to determine if a food product was pure. Their analyses proved that most of America's food was adulterated for producers' economic benefit. These chemists and their supporters concluded that the only solution to this widespread problem was a national law prohibiting adulteration.

For approximately twenty-five years, between 1879 and 1905, the pure food movement was unsuccessful in its attempts to get a national pure food law passed by Congress. During that period more than one hundred bills were introduced in Congress; all of them failed under lobbying pressure from big business in the form of food and liquor manufacturers.

Forces of Change

Just after the turn of the twentieth century, however, three significant events ultimately resulted in the enactment of a pure food law. First, adulteration of food became a hot topic at the St. Louis World's Fair of 1904. Although this seven-month event, which drew 20 million visitors, is important in American food history for the introduction and popularization of ice cream cones, iced tea, peanut butter, and cotton candy, there was an important pure food presentation at the fair as well.

In one of the exhibit halls, food companies set up impressive displays of their canned and bottled foods—but many of these foods were artificially colored. Chemists from the National Association of State Dairy and Food Departments opened a booth nearby with their own exhibit. They had extracted the dyes from many of the artificially colored foods on display and used those dyes to color pieces of wool and silk. They attached a certificate to each piece of cloth, documenting the properties of the dye and naming the food that contained the dye. The brightly colored cloths were disturbing to most visitors and became a vehicle for the chemists manning the booth to educate people about the need for a national pure food law.

The state chemists' exhibit attracted the attention not only of the general public but of legislators and newspaper and magazine writers. In the words of one of the state chemists, the exhibit "kindled a fire of public interest which no power on earth will be able to put out" (quoted in Sullivan).

The second significant event focusing attention on adulteration of food was Dr. Wiley's study of the effects of chemical preservatives on healthy people. Twelve young men volunteered to eat their meals at the Bureau of Chemistry in Washington, D.C. They agreed to eat pure food only; however, the volunteers also took capsules that contained increasing doses of chemical preservatives. For this reason, the press gave the volunteers the melodramatic title "the Poison Squad."

When Dr. Wiley testified before the House of Representatives in February 1906, he reported that the volunteers suffered various degrees of illness, including stomach pain, dizziness, nausea, and significant weight loss. Nine of the twelve had to drop out of the experiment because of illness. The "Poison Squad" experiments proved to many Americans that chemical preservatives were harmful to their health.

The third significant event was the publication of Upton Sinclair's novel *The Jungle* in February 1906. In *The Jungle*, Sinclair exposed the evils of immigrant victimization in Packingtown—the stockyards and slaughterhouses of Chicago. His fictional account shed light on the fact that immigrants from European countries were paid slave wages and required to work long hours in unsafe and unhealthy conditions.

Although Sinclair's novel was not about pure food, American readers focused their attention on the dozen or so pages of the book that described the evils of the meat-packing industry. Sinclair vividly portrayed the unsanitary conditions in the slaughterhouses, the limited scope of federal meat inspections, the ineffectualness of inspectors, the hush money paid to have diseased animals removed and processed elsewhere, the potted (canned) meats dyed to conceal spoilage or inferior quality, and the poisoned rats and poisoned bread ground with meat to make sausage.

At the time *The Jungle* was published, a pure food bill was in dire trouble in the House of Representatives. The bill had been introduced in the Senate in December 1905 after President Theodore Roosevelt recommended that Congress try again to enact a law "to regulate interstate commerce in misbranded and adulterated foods, drinks, and drugs." While the new bill was pending in the Senate and facing strong opposition, the American Medical Association notified the Senate leadership that America's physicians planned to ask their patients to pressure the Senate to pass the bill. Shortly thereafter, on February 21, 1906, the bill was brought to the floor and passed. The pure food bill was sent to the House, but the Republican leadership decided that the bill was too controversial and slated it to die quietly in committee without reaching the floor for a vote.

President Roosevelt read *The Jungle* in March 1906. Concerned about the impact of Sinclair's novel on American meat exports, Roosevelt sent investigators to Chicago; these investigators confirmed Sinclair's account of adulteration in the meatpacking plants. They found filthy conditions in the workrooms: meat contaminated by dirt, splinters, pieces of rope, rubbish, and the "expectoration of tuberculous and other diseased workers."

Roosevelt decided that a law was needed to increase the scope of meat inspections at the plants, so that federal inspectors would exercise complete control over the meatpacking process. A new law, solely focused on meat inspection, met with significant opposition in Congress, particularly in the House, but a compromise amendment ultimately passed, called the Meat Inspection Act. President Roosevelt signed it into law on June 30, 1906.

Meanwhile, although the pure food bill had nothing to do with the problems in the meatpacking industry, President Roosevelt obtained its release from committee, where it had been languishing. Pushed along by Roosevelt, the impetus of the meatpacking reform legislation, and the pure food reformers, the pure food bill finally passed Congress. It was signed into law on June 30, 1906.

The Pure Food Act prohibited the introduction into interstate commerce of any food that was adulterated or misbranded. The statutory definition of adulteration was broad. It included the addition of any substance that diminished the food's quality or reduced its strength; the use of a fraudulent substitute; the removal of any valuable part of the food; the concealment of any damage or inferiority by coloring, coating, or staining; the addition of any poisonous or deleterious ingredient; and the incorporation of any filthy, decomposed, or putrid animal or vegetable substance into the food.

Enforcement of the Pure Food and Drug Act of 1906 and its successor, the Federal Food, Drug, and Cosmetic Act of 1938, greatly decreased the adulteration of food during the twentieth century. Adulteration has not been eliminated, however. Some specific foods are recurring targets of this activity: honey and maple syrup adulterated with high fructose corn syrup, sugar beet syrup, or sugarcane syrup; chicory, cereal, or other fillers added to coffee; other food oils blended in with pure olive oil; synthetic vanillin substituted for real vanilla bean extract. In addition, uninspected imported food presents a significant risk of illness from unregulated, excessive amounts of chemical preservatives. In the early twenty-first century, it remains to be seen whether the federal government will muster sufficient resources to defeat the continuing problem of adulteration.

[*See also* Food and Drug Administration; Pure Food and Drug Act; Sinclair, Upton; Wiley, Harvey.]

BIBLIOGRAPHY

Sinclair, Upton. *The Jungle*. Introduction and notes by James R. Barrett. Urbana: University of Illinois Press, 1988.

Sullivan, Mark. *Our Times: The United States, 1900–1925*. Vol. 2, *America Finding Herself*. New York and London: Scribner's, 1927.

Wiley, Harvey W. *Foods and Their Adulteration: Origin, Manufacture, and Composition of Food Products; Infants' and Invalids' Foods; Detection of Common Adulterations*. 3rd ed. Philadelphia: P. Blakiston's Sons, 1917.

ROBERT W. BROWER

Advertising

When President Calvin Coolidge addressed a national advertising conference in 1926, he was pleased to report on the happy state of the nation. Unlike in countries where "the uncivilized make little progress because they have few desires," he explained, "the inhabitants of our country are stimulated to new wants in all directions" (Hill, p. 7). And indeed they were. The two generations that had preceded Mr. Coolidge's presidency had seen a country transformed in large part by the ubiquitous advertising that was stimulating America to buy Coke and Crisco, Chestertons and Chevrolets.

By the 1920s, most of the marketing and advertising techniques recognizable today were already in place. Newspapers and magazines survived almost exclusively as a function of their advertising revenue. Billboards cluttered country roads and railway lines. Promotional gimmicks, premium giveaways, and direct mail enjoined consumers to try something new, to switch brands, or just to keep on buying. Store displays beckoned to the harried shopper. Enticing packaging promised health, wealth, and motherhood. Experts, celebrities, cartoon characters, and even plain-Jane regular folk were enlisted to pitch everything from canned soup to fake lard. Today's techniques

Dairy Advertising. A late-nineteenth-century Sweet Clover Brand billboard dominates a pasture.

utilizing focus groups and psychological analysis had their origins then. By the end of the twenties, even the brand-new mass medium of radio had been enlisted to sell a reinvented American diet.

Early American Advertising

While advertising as we know it came of age hand in hand with the Industrial Revolution, the use of signs and symbols to advertise shops and services is likely as old as commerce itself. Archeologists have uncovered depictions of food in ancient Pompeii that once directed travelers to taverns, bakeries, and butcher shops. Using much the same technique, placards identifying a particular business had appeared in America by the mid-seventeenth century. (In the larger colonial towns, portrait artists frequently painted signs to make ends meet.) The most prominent of these signboards promoted inns, taverns, and coffeehouses, often with an iconic picture rather than text. This approach never died out; McDonald's golden arches are a direct descendant of this tradition of promotional signage.

By the early eighteenth century, print advertising was beginning to make inroads, first in the form of broadsides and leaflets that might be posted on trees, posts, and buildings and, somewhat later, as actual advertisements in newspapers. The tone of these was hardly promotional; rather the copy concentrated on the goods available and where they might be purchased. "We will sell low for CASH" or "Country Produce" was about all the enticement offered.

Regular newspaper ads began appearing around 1704, when the *Boston Newsletter* began publication. These straightforward notices mostly announced the sale of such imported goods as cloth and wine. In Philadelphia, the ever-inventive Benjamin Franklin started publishing his *Pennsylvania Gazette* in 1728, with a more robust strategy. To distinguish the promotional material from copy, Franklin introduced the use of large headlines; for the first time, separated (with a space) advertisements from editorial content; and, after 1750, even began illustrating some shipping notices. As in other contemporary publications, the "goods" advertised ranged from coffee to slaves. A notice from a 1735 issue advertised a product he himself sold: "VERY good COFFEE sold by the printer hereof." More typically, an importer would publicize his current stock: "CHOICE Double- and Single-refin'd Loaf-Sugar, Muscovado Sugar fit for Shop or Family Use, Sugar-Candy Mollasses, Bohea [a black tea] and Imperial TEAS, all at the cheapest Rates." Franklin did include more advertisements than any other colonial newspaper, but similar notices appeared in newspapers in New York, Boston, and Richmond. Most featured wine, cheese, chocolate, codfish, tea, coffee, and imported kitchen accoutrements such as glasses, silverware, and stoves.

The Revolutionary War disrupted the wheels of commerce in numerous ways, but after the interruption, newspapers returned to their prewar habits. In terms of day-to-day life, little had changed in the intervening years. In 1790 all but some 200,000 of the country's 4 million inhabitants still lived on farms, producing their own food, perhaps trading some bacon with their neighbors for a few eggs, and only occasionally splurging on a little molasses to sweeten their Sunday cake. Very little currency was actually exchanged. Even as the nation established itself, this culture of the land would persist up until the last decades of the nineteenth century, when the industrial economy created an altogether new way of food production and distribution and, with it, a new way of eating.

A Society Transformed

The era between the Civil War and World War I saw a country completely transformed in ways that made advertising, as we now know it, possible. The railroads united the country into one national market, while national magazines (made affordable by the invention of cheap, wood pulp–based newsprint) now reached into every home in the country. For the first time, the Shredded Wheat Company, located in Niagara Falls, New York, could promote their product to consumers in St. Louis by placing ads in the New York–based *Ladies' Home Journal*. Of course, a skyrocketing urban population could no longer grow its own supper, so a currency-based market for food as well as consumer goods exploded. Moreover, with the advent of a national transportation network and the efficiencies of mass production, the price of food fell dramatically, while per capita income actually increased. In America, even the poor could buy adequate quantities of food, and the burgeoning middle class had plenty of cash to spare. A little later, with the introduction of rural free delivery in 1896 and of parcel post in 1913, even the farming population was brought into the consumer economy.

The Industrial Revolution also ushered in a whole new religion, its twin canons a belief in science and faith in progress. From the vantage point of our own cynical age, it is hard to fathom how genuinely Americans were convinced that world history was evolving from worse to better. But they were. They mobbed the world's fairs celebrating modern technology and industrial achievement; they believed their labor organizations when they promised members a better future; they flocked to buy goods promoted as icons of progress.

Nevertheless, for the population at large, all this was also tremendously unsettling. At the end of the nineteenth century, an overwhelming majority of city dwellers had their roots in an agricultural civilization—whether in the valleys of Massachusetts or the hills of Calabria—that had hardly prepared them for an urban, industrial existence. Those who could now count themselves as middle class were no less displaced, albeit in a different way: many were the first generation in their family to join the middle class, with its attendant "servant problem" and strictly segregated gender roles. Whereas on the farm women were easily as productive as men, in the capitalist economy the husband was required to be the breadwinner while the wife was expected to be the consumer—and women had to be taught their new role in the marketplace. All the resulting insecurities led to a barrage of household manuals and women's magazines giving advice on everything from maid management to icebox maintenance. In this modern world, where people's roots were planted in quicksand, advertisers could lend a steadying hand, supporting and succoring the newborn consumer culture.

New Approaches to Advertising

As late as the 1880s, most advertisements still performed the traditional function of informing consumers about the availability, costs, and characteristics of products. Two product categories, however, pioneered a fresh approach that was more purely based on hype. The leading advertisers of the late nineteenth century had been the patent medicine sellers and soap manufacturers. (Food products came in third.) The soap ads made luxury, glamour, and wholesomeness as much a selling point as cleanliness, while the patent medicine notices promised bogus cures for everything from neuralgia to baldness. Coca-Cola, a drink concocted as a tonic by an Atlanta pharmacist in 1886, was first advertised like the patent medicine it was meant to be: "THE IDEAL BRAIN TONIC" ran an 1892 ad headline, "For Headache & Exhaustion." Not only soft-drink manufacturers but cereal makers as well copied techniques learned from the patent medicine sellers, placing notices full of testimonials in national magazines, advertising cures for all sorts of vague maladies, and even putting on public displays not unlike the fabled medicine shows.

Though healthfulness has been a recurrent theme throughout the life of American food advertising, never was it utilized as regularly, or as brazenly, as in the decades on either side of 1900. In part, this was the result of advertising's roots in the health claims of the patent

Magazine Ads. Advertisements from the November 1899 issue of *The American Monthly Illustrated Review of Reviews. Collection of Georgia Maas*

medicine industry; in part, it was fueled by the breakfast-cereal boom, which had its origins in various vegetarian and health food movements then popular. Certainly Kellogg's Corn Flakes, Post Grape-Nuts, and Quaker Oats were all originally promoted as health foods. Quaker Oats "supply what brains and bodies need . . . with more proteids [sic], more phosphorus, more lecithin than any other food." Post Grape-Nuts was advertised as an alternative to surgery for an inflamed appendix and recommended for consumption, malaria, and loose teeth. Even foods like chocolate and beer were hyped for their healthfulness. The first three-cent Hershey's milk chocolate bar billed itself as "a nutritious confection" and was supposedly "endorsed by physicians." In 1903, a full-page, back-cover *Harper's Weekly* ad for Schlitz showed a man consulting with his doctor while the copy listed the doctor's reasons for recommending Schlitz: "It is good for anybody. The hops form a tonic; the barley a food. The trifle of alcohol is an aid to digestion. . . . A great deal of ill-health is caused by a lack of it."

The focus of nutrition and health claims for products has varied as scientific and popular opinion latched on to the latest panacea. Thus, in the 1920s, vitamins were all the rage, even if their functions were barely understood. Sunkist oranges were promoted for their "vitamines and rare salts and acids."

In the 1970s, as an increasing number of dietary villains assumed media center stage, food as cure-all was the subject of a full-court advertising press. Various foods were hyped as lowering cholesterol, decreasing the incidence of various cancers, or being salt reduced, low fat, or sugar free. The trend got a further boost during the deregulatory climate of the 1980s and 1990s, when the government allowed advertisers much broader leeway in making health claims. In this new environment, Kellogg's All-Bran as well as Lipton Tea could be promoted as cancer fighters. By 2002, when carbohydrates had nudged out fats as enemy number one, Michelob beer introduced Ultra, a lower-carbohydrate beer with an ad campaign featuring athletic young adults with the headline "Lose the carbs. Not the taste. With fewer carbs, fewer calories and the same great Michelob taste, ULTRA is the ultimate reward for an active lifestyle."

Inventing Brands

The industrializing world of post–Civil War America created opportunities for growth and consolidation on the part of many food manufacturers, but it also presented them with a common obstacle as they expanded beyond their immediate territory: namely, how to differentiate their particular product from the competition. Until the end of the nineteenth century, almost all goods sold in stores were sold in bulk. Jobbers bought a product from the manufacturer and distributed it to neighborhood stores with nothing to identify the food's origin. Storekeepers had no interest in scooping out one company's flour instead of another. To create a demand for their particular product, manufacturers had to instill brand consciousness in consumers, so that a shopper would not only ask for, but demand, say, Purina flour and no other. Companies that sold basic commodities like bananas and baking powder faced the biggest challenge. The businesses that survived and prospered found their salvation in advertising their brand name in every way imaginable.

One of the earliest basic commodities to have a national brand identity was a cylindrical box of oatmeal. Henry Crowell, who had purchased the bankrupted Quaker Mill Company, was the first to register a trademark for a cereal in 1877. He began his campaign by packaging ordinary oatmeal in the familiar box, featuring a color image of a Quaker holding a bowl or box of oatmeal. Crowell went on to innovate an approach that would later be called saturation advertising. He had signs painted on barns; he ran special trains plastered with signs and filled with oatmeal; he invented the idea of premiums, such as bowls and saucers that came in the box; he created half-ounce boxes, which he gave away by the thousands. The cereal entrepreneur went so far as to festoon the White Cliffs of Dover with a sign extolling Quaker Oats. And, needless to say, his ads made all sorts of unsubstantiated medical claims. Later, when the company was producing ready-to-eat cereals, Quaker Puffed Rice was introduced at the 1904 St. Louis World's Fair by shooting it from eight bronze cannons. (It was later advertised as "the cereal shot from cannons.") Long after Crowell's passing, the wacky promotions went on. In 1955, in conjunction with the *Sergeant Preston of the Yukon* radio show, the company obtained land in Canada and promised purchasers a deed for one square inch of the Yukon Territory for every box purchased. The campaign resulted in some 35 million boxes sold.

Companies like Royal Baking Powder came to dominate their respective markets by means of massive promotional expenditures, spending $500,000 for advertising in 1893 alone. By 1900, the president of the company estimated that any potential rival would be forced to spend $15 million to capture Royal's market. While it would be difficult to quantify the resulting influence on national baking habits, the success of Royal's campaign may explain why many more American desserts use baking powder than is the habit in Europe.

An unintended by-product of advertising success was sometimes to inflate the competition's sales, since one result of an advertising blitz was often an increase in the total consumption of a given commodity. Because most retailers were as happy to sell one brand as another, advertisements often warned of some shopkeepers' nefarious ways. "LOOK OUT FOR FRAUDS," cautioned the headline of one 1897 ad for Franco-American soups.

The most effective way of bypassing bulk sales was to follow the Quaker example and ship your product in a convenient package that prominently displayed your name. It helped if the name was catchy. The National Biscuit Company was hugely successful with its Uneeda Biscuits brand. As the nature of retailing changed, packaging became even more critical in the overall marketing mix. By the 1920s, self-serve grocery stores with open shelves began to replace the old-fashioned shops where all the goods had been hidden away behind the shopkeeper and his counter. Increasingly, manufacturers had to vie for the customer's attention with brighter, larger, and more alluring packaging.

Initially, there had been a great deal of customer resistance to packaged foods that wary shoppers could not examine, smell, and taste. As late as 1912, a grocer's magazine claimed that "many people are afraid of canned goods because of sensational stories which are repeatedly printed about them." With patent medicines loaded with unspecified quantities of alcohol, cocaine, and opium and reports of flour being adulterated with chalk and sawdust, shoppers had good reason to worry. The large national manufacturers explicitly took advantage of these fears by promoting the purity, safety, and healthfulness of their brands in both their packaging and their print material. Royal Baking Powder always came with the tag line "Absolutely Pure." Jell-O was "Approved by the Pure Food Commissioners" in an ad from 1906. The copy goes on to warn: "Beware of dangerous imitations claiming to be just as good. They may undermine your health." The American Sugar Company, a "trust" that controlled virtually all white sugar production by the end of the century, found it useful to consolidate its market with a campaign denigrating brown sugar. Utilizing photo-

graphs taken through the newly perfected microscope, the ads showed the grotesque—but utterly harmless—microbes that might be found in unrefined sugar.

Another way the big companies promoted their brand-name products was through factory tours and ads that featured their state-of-the-art factories. Particularly popular was the Shredded Wheat factory in Niagara Falls, where honeymooners swelled the ranks of the visitors. By 1907, 100,000 were touring this "Palace of Light" annually and sending home postcards with copy that read, "The cleanest and purest of all cereal foods, made in the cleanest, most hygienic food factory in the world." Most other large manufacturers followed suit. Kellogg's even offered factory tours through 1986.

Reinventing the American Meal

The trouble with treating food as a commodity is that people can eat only so much. In fact, they are able to consume even less in an industrial society than if they are toting bales of hay. While the American food industry has managed to increase the actual quantity that Americans eat, especially in the later part of the twentieth century, this has not been their primary strategy. The best way of maximizing profits is to take raw food, process it to add "value," and then resell this new food at a higher price. The less expensive the input, the greater the potential for profit. And with the efficiencies of mass manufacturing bringing processing costs lower and lower, often the single largest component of an item's price is the marketing.

The pioneers in the field of packaging food that costs little and sells for a lot were the intrepid originators of breakfast cereal. In 1900, when a package of breakfast cereal cost about fifteen cents, a sixty-cent bushel of wheat could be transformed into a commodity selling for twelve dollars retail. Profuse advertising by companies like Post, Quaker, and, especially, Kellogg's actually persuaded America to change its breakfast dietary habits completely by eating food no one's mother had ever heard of. Will Kellogg once spent one-third of his funds on a single page in the widely circulated *Ladies' Home Journal* to promote his Corn Flakes. In 1912, he had erected a 50- by 106-foot sign—at that time the largest sign in the world—in Times Square. By 1942, Kellogg Company figures showed that they had spent approximately $100 million on advertising. It was probably the most successful new food introduction of all time; by the mid-twentieth century, 50 percent of Americans would be eating an ounce or so of cereal every day.

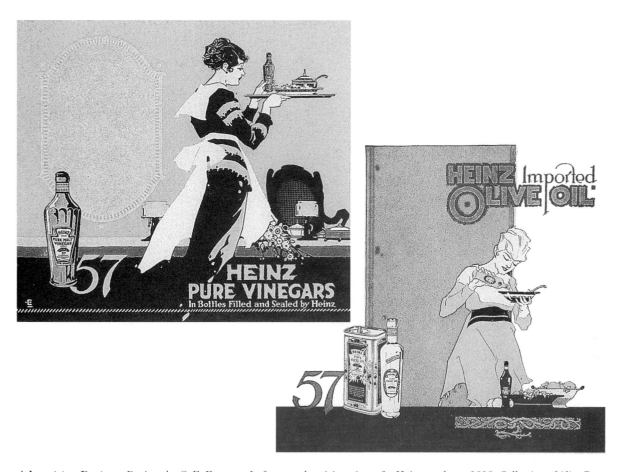

Advertising Designs. Designs by C. E. Emerson Jr. for two advertising pieces for Heinz products, 1918. *Collection of Alice Ross*

Many heretofore unheard-of foods have been introduced to the American consumer, with varying degrees of success. The taste and market for drinking chocolate had expanded dramatically in the post–Civil War years, in large part owing to the advertising efforts of companies like Baker's and Maillard, but the idea of eating chocolate was a novel concept. The demand for chocolate exploded only when companies, led by Hershey, started to sell and market their inexpensive candy bars. Milton Hershey did not limit himself to mere print ads; in 1903 he used a high-tech electrical truck emblazoned with the Hershey name to promote his ultramodern chocolate and cocoa, handing out free samples from town to town. To retail stores, the company provided unusually large polychrome dioramas depicting Hershey, Pennsylvania, and the chocolate factory, its two chimneys sporting the company name. In fact, the town, along with its amusement park, was used repeatedly to promote the chocolates. For many years, every Hershey's milk chocolate bar contained a "free" postcard depicting frolicking couples in Hershey Park; millions of these were printed and mailed to every corner of the nation. Even into the early 2000s Hershey Park, with its chocolate ride, Hershey kiss–shaped streetlights, and walking, talking Hershey bars is still part of the company's strategy.

Procter and Gamble unveiled another extremely successful "Absolutely New Product" in 1912: Crisco. The company's marketing onslaught, perfected through many years of selling Ivory Soap, largely succeeded in replacing lard as America's shortening of choice. Other new products were less successful. Some, like Nestlé's instant coffee, never lived up to their company's expectations. Others, like Swanson's TV Dinners, faded with changing eating fashions. But the great majority of new-product introductions, like the debacle the Coca-Cola Company had with New Coke in the 1980s, were utter failures in spite of the millions of advertising dollars spent.

New products, when introduced, have often needed to be explained. This was especially true for newfangled kitchen appliances—like toasters, blenders, microwave ovens, and food processors—that no one had used before.

In 1927, when Toastmaster first introduced the automatic pop-up toaster, they had not only to tell people that it existed but also to explain how it worked—even including step-by-step illustrated instructions. The copy is explicit in explaining: "1. Drop a slice of bread into the oven slot. 2. Press down the two levers. . . . 3. Pop! Up comes the toast automatically when it's done."

Premium Cookbooks

For educating the public about new food products, premium cookbooks were popular with manufacturers and consumers alike. An early pamphlet such as "The Vital Question Cook Book," published by the Shredded Wheat Company, was published in sixteen editions of 250,000 each by 1902. These promotional guides, cooked up in the test kitchens of companies who manufactured products like Tabasco hot sauce, Carnation condensed milk, Jell-O gelatin, Campfire marshmallows, Nestlé's chocolate, and Campbell's soup, influenced the cooking of several generations. The Campbell Soup Company alone sold more than a million books per year during the 1950s, with the result that sales of condensed soup destined for inclusion in these recipes increased to an estimated 1 million cans per day. Without Campbell's book *Cooking with Condensed Soup*, America may have never learned to cook Heavenly Ham Loaf or Green Bean Bake (green beans, cream of mushroom soup, and a can of french fried potatoes), to say nothing of Perfect Tuna Casserole.

Often, the recipes developed for these cookbooks migrated to the package itself. Nestlé first printed the recipe for Toll House cookies on the back of its chocolate bars. The company created chocolate chips only later, in response to the recipe's popularity. Other foods that originated as back-of-the-box recipes, like Rice Crispy squares, have become the comfort food of generations of Americans.

Women's Magazines

Advertisers found a ready audience for their products in women's magazines. The combination of a growing and increasingly literate and affluent population, cheap newsprint, and improved printing technology that allowed for color and photographs made the magazines a perfect vehicle for promoting all the new consumables of the age. As the economics of magazine publishing changed from a subscription-based model to one wherein almost all the revenue came from advertising, it became profitable to publish many more titles. Such magazines as *Ladies' Home Journal*, *Women's Home Companion*, and *Good Housekeeping* flooded the market with their combination of home advice and advertising. Between 1890 and 1905, the monthly circulation of American periodicals increased from 18 million to 64 million, and by 1900, magazines often exceeded one hundred pages of advertising an issue. Cyrus H. K. Curtis, the founder of *Ladies' Home Journal*, made the point explicit in an address to a gathering of manufacturers. "Do you know why we publish the *Ladies' Home Journal*?" he began. "The editor thinks it is for the benefit of American women. That is an illusion, but a very proper one for him to have. . . . The real reason, the publisher's reason, is to give you people who manufacture things that American women want and buy a chance to tell them about your products" (Norris, p. 36).

Advertisers found many ways to tell readers about their products. One way was to hire magazine editors to write their premium cookbooks. (So the *Ladies' Home Journal* editor Marion Harris Neil, for example, authored the 1913 edition of *The Story of Crisco*.) Another way was to place advertisements that consisted mostly of recipes. A copy of *Ladies' Home Journal* from the 1950s could easily feature more recipes in the advertisements than in the editorial pages of the magazine. Even more telling, the dishes developed at the magazines were barely distinguishable from those in the ads. In earlier decades even the recipes developed by the magazines' staff included advertisers' brands. By the mid-fifties this was no longer considered proper, but most ingredients still came from the factory pantry.

By the late twentieth century, advertisers had become more nuanced in their approach: inviting editors to judge (and feature in the magazine) such events as the Pillsbury Bake-Off, inundating the staff with free samples of their latest wares, and sending editors on all-expense-paid junkets to learn about Alaskan salmon or California strawberries. But mostly, advertisers advertise—with the goal of making sure that women pick their new, improved brands when they survey the grocer's shelf.

Advertising to Women

It is, of course, women who are the target of all this advertising. It has been estimated that, even as of the late nineteenth century, 85 percent of all manufactured consumer goods were purchased by women, and where food and kitchen product purchases are concerned, virtually all the decisions have historically been in women's hands. This was recognized as early as the 1880s, when advertisers began to make use of techniques thought to appeal especially to women. "Avoid the cold and unfeminine," counseled early twentieth-century advertising manuals. It was assumed that women desired "luxury and daintiness," which led to ads with delicate drawings, pastel colors, and serif typefaces.

Typically, food advertising was aimed at white, married, middle-class homemakers; the existence of working women and women of color was barely acknowledged until the late 1980s. It is hardly surprising that predominantly well-off male advertising executives would have a stereotypical view of a woman's role; but more fundamental economic considerations may have also been at play. As seen from Madison Avenue, the American consumer with the most available time and leisure was the affluent housewife, and women who did not fit this demographic were assumed to be aspiring to it.

Women have invariably appeared in advertising as wives, mothers, and homemakers. In an attempt to appeal to women's presumed maternal feelings, young children have often appeared in ads of every kind, from the Morton's Salt girl to the Campbell Kids. Men, on the other hand, have seldom been shown, except as contented consumers. When, in the 1990s, husbands began to make an appearance in the kitchen, it was usually as klutzy interlopers; women were flattered that they still ruled the domestic realm.

Men have also had occasional cameo roles as objects of desire. Sex, of course, has long been used to sell products, from Cool Whip to wine coolers. And while the full force of sexy, seminaked men invading print and broadcast media was not felt until the mid-1980s, earlier examples abound. As early as 1912, an ad for Nabisco Sugar Wafers featured an illustration of a shirtless Hiawatha with the demure Indian maiden Minnehaha seeking shelter behind his buff torso.

Repeatedly, advertising campaigns have played on women's insecurities. True, few food companies went as far as Hygeia Nursing Bottle Company in 1917, whose ad warned mothers that "Just one unclean bottle may bring fatal results." More subtle approaches have been just as successful, however. A Jell-O ad from 1959 played on the trepidation of a newly wed bride with an illustration of a husband seated before his plate of burnt food scraps while his wife proudly marches in with a towering gelatin mold. "Jell-O can't burn, can't fall and can't fail to delight the light of your life" the copy reads. "A would-be bride can use it to bait a date and a bride of a few years can use it to remind her mate how lucky he is."

Advertisers sought to educate women not only about how to seduce and keep a husband but also on the basics of child rearing and nutrition. Commercially prepared baby food first came on the market in the 1870s, and the campaign to convince mothers of its superiority knew no bounds. A 1901 ad for Imperial Granum baby food relied on the authority of an unspecified "surgeon general of one of the most important states of the union." He is quoted as saying: "I have four boys, all raised on IMPERIAL GRANUM exclusively, never having tasted mother's milk. One boy is center rush on his football team. . . . All very healthy, hearty boys."

In addition to their print ads, manufacturers of processed baby food often produced child-care guides with recipes. Since these guides were often authored by physicians, women came to trust the brand-name foods for which the pamphlets were produced. In the 1950s and 1960s, Gerber baby food ran ads formulated as advice columns under the title of "Bringing Up Baby." The ads featured "hints collected by Mrs. Dan Gerber, mother of 5" and included suggestions not only on nutrition but also on child rearing and safety around the house. By 2002, Gerber had updated their advice column ads to a website feature called the "Gerber Parents Resource Center," which promised "expert [infant care] advice anytime day or night," by e-mail or even by telephone.

Icons and Spokespeople

As appealing as advice from "experts" might be, food manufacturers have often sought to imbue their brand-name products with personality by using, or more often inventing, icons or spokespeople to hawk their wares. One of the earliest and most enduring of these was Baker's Chocolate's La Belle Chocolatiere, trademarked in 1836 and based on an eighteenth-century painting of a chocolate shop waitress carrying a tray of cups. In subsequent years she would be seen carrying a plate of brownies, a giant chocolate bar, and other similar confections. Many icons have been chosen more arbitrarily: the smiling African American chef that has graced Cream of Wheat packages since 1893 is there primarily because the original printer found a woodblock in his storeroom with that image.

An even more famous African American made the transition from icon to actual person. When Aunt Jemima pancake mix was first brought on the market in 1890, the character on the package was imaginary; but in 1893, when the company sought to promote its new product at

Yeast Advertisement. Magic Yeast advertisement. *Culinary Archives & Museum at Johnson & Wales University, Providence, R.I.*

the Columbian Exposition in Chicago, they hired the very real Nancy Green. Her flapjack demonstrations were so successful that more than fifty thousand merchant's orders for the mix were generated during her six-month tenure at the fair. Subsequent demonstrations, coupled with extensive advertising, made the image of Aunt Jemima famous. For decades, dolls representing her and her fictitious family were popular box-top premiums and, even when discontinued, highly sought-after collectibles. Finally, in the 1980s, it occurred to corporate headquarters that it might be inappropriate to use the image of a slave plantation cook to represent its brand, and so Aunt Jemima was replaced by a slimmer, more contemporary-looking black model, who discarded Aunt Jemima's gingham bandanna to don pearl earrings.

Many icons have undergone periodic updating, but perhaps none more prominently than Betty Crocker. The Gold Medal Flour spokeswoman was created in 1921 as a baking expert answering questions in the company's ads, but her fictional face did not debut until 1936. She was marketed so well that General Mills started receiving proposals of marriage for Betty in addition to requests for cooking advice. This, in turn, inspired a 1945 ad headlined "to the man who wanted to marry Betty Crocker." The copy took the form of a polite rejection letter in which the company explained that Betty was too busy baking to entertain such proposals. Up until the 1960s, Miss Crocker had the look of a middle-aged maiden aunt, but she then underwent several transformations that updated her style and made her younger with each passing decade. In 1996, an extensive ad campaign heralded her seventy-fifth anniversary incarnation, in which her new, contemporary look was supposedly created by blending the faces of seventy-five women.

Over the years, all sorts of creatures—real and imagined, human and animal, vegetable and even partially mineral—have been enlisted to sell brand-name foods. Children have always been popular, whether as the cartoon Campbell Kids who cavorted in Campbell's soup ads throughout the first half of the twentieth century or as the finicky little boy Mikey, who became a national celebrity in the 1980s by eating the supposedly "adult" Life cereal. Many actual celebrities have also been repeatedly enlisted as spokesmen and women. An early-twentieth-century ad for Hornby's Oatmeal featured an endorsement by James A. Garfield, the former president's son. At the end of the century, Sarah, the former wife of England's Duke of York, transformed her notoriety into commercials for Weight Watcher's diet foods.

Comic strip celebrities would do, too. In the midst of World War II, Lil' Abner was enlisted by Cream of Wheat to rid the country of spies while eating the cereal, all in a full-page comic. Other cereals have employed a whole menagerie of animal "spokesbeasts," including rabbits (General Mills's Trix), tigers (Kellogg's Frosted Flakes), and bears (Kellogg's Hunny B's). In keeping with the times, the Goya Company even created a commercial in the 1970s with a swinging single Coco Goya can, who was the life of the party.

Government Regulation

One cannot help admiring the astonishing outpouring of creativity that has gone into marketing and selling products for which people have no basic need. The enthusiasm of advertising professionals, however, has led them to go over the line more than once.

The first federal government effort to reign in deceptive labeling was passed into law in 1906 as the Pure Food and Drug Act. The 1912 Sherley Amendment broadened its reach by providing "that no package should make false or fraudulent claims pertaining to curative or therapeutic effects." Although much of the legislation was aimed at the excesses of the patent medicine companies and the often-dubious ingredients in canned foods, companies of all kinds were hauled into court on account of their creative excesses. As late as 1951, the Federal Trade Commission threatened the advertisers of Postum coffee substitute with action if they did not stop running ads claiming that drinking actual coffee discouraged marriage or that it resulted in "divorces, business failures, factory accidents, juvenile delinquency, traffic accidents, fire or home foreclosures."

The enthusiasm for regulating advertising has waxed and waned with the political climate in Washington. After efforts to stimulate sales during the Great Depression led to further excesses, the 1938 Wheeler-Lea amendments to the Federal Trade Commission Act were passed, giving the commission regulatory power over false advertising, with special attention given to food, drug, and cosmetic advertisements. Using actors to play scientists and physicians to promote food and drug products in an effort to give them (false) legitimacy was forbidden by the Television Code of 1967. On the other hand, the 1980s and 1990s have seen the legislative tide turn, particularly with passage of the 1994 Dietary Supplement Health and Education Act, which explicitly restrained the government from regulating many health claims.

The government has also occasionally entered into the business of advertising food itself, or at least promoting the way it should be eaten. At the time of the world wars, Washington pushed for the use of alternatives to the foods needed by the boys at the front. During World War I, for example, the U.S. Food Administration advanced a policy of "wheatless" and "meatless" days through traveling exhibitions and enlisted well-known cookbook authors and food companies to put out promotional cookbooks for the war effort.

In 1917, the U.S. Department of Agriculture published *How to Select Foods*, the first of many pamphlets intended to educate the public. By the 1990s, government efforts mostly focused on promoting a lower-fat, higher-carbohydrate diet that was illustrated as a food "pyramid," presumably to make consumer choices easier to make. The promotional attempt took the form of pamphlets, posters, and the occasional print ad. Not surprisingly, the results were lackluster, given that the entire $300 million annual educational budget of the USDA was not even half of what McDonald's alone was spending on print and broadcast ads at the same time.

Mass Media: Radio

While magazines were the first to create a national market for advertising in the waning decades of the nineteenth century, it was not until the arrival of radio that a truly mass audience could be created. Initially, radio was a toy for wealthy early adopters, but by the 1930s it had become ubiquitous. If anything, the Depression was actually *good* for radio. Advertisers, looking for the most exposure for the fewest dollars, increasingly chose radio over newspapers. By 1939, about 80 percent of Americans owned radios.

In the United States, the funding model for radio followed in the steps of magazine advertising. Advertising agencies jumped readily into the act of not only creating advertising messages for radio but—even before the establishment of networks—producing the actual programs. At first, the main form of advertising took the form of sponsorship, but soon spot ads became ubiquitous. The early commercials were woven directly into the programs—so that, for example, a musical variety show might have the star singing the sponsor's jingle, or in the course of a dramatic program's dialogue, the fictional characters would discuss the sponsor's product. Print ads drove home the connection between a particular program and its sponsor. Thus, Campbell, which sponsored the Burns and Allen show in the 1930s, ran ads featuring the Campbell Kids listening to the radio and exclaiming, "Oh, Wednesdays and Fridays / Are great nights for me, / With Campbell's broadcasting / Such laughter and glee!" *Kraft Music Hall*, *Maxwell House Showboat*, and other programs followed suit.

By the 1930s, daytime radio began to specifically target the female stay-at-home audience with serial melodramas, soon to be known as "soap operas" because they were usually sponsored by household product and food manufacturers. Radio's monopoly as a mass medium, however, was to last barely more than two decades before it was usurped by television in the 1950s.

Mass Media: Television

The two decades following World War II saw the biggest dislocation in living patterns since the end of the previous century, especially among the primary advertising audience: the white middle class. The new suburban lifestyle transformed not only the landscape but also shopping patterns, ways of eating, and even socializing rituals. The new jumbo-sized supermarkets required bigger, bolder packaging and eye-catching displays. The car culture created a demand for fast food and, in part because of the mobility that it made possible, a desire for predictable, standardized products from coast to coast. Perhaps more subtle was the effect on the women who moved to the Levittowns and Villa Serenas of the time. While her husband commuted to work, the model fifties housewife was left home alone to prepare meals with foods and devices unknown to her mother; she was often insecure about her cooking skills and isolated from the traditional community in which she had grown up. It is no wonder that Tupperware parties—where the plastic containers were marketed and sold—were such a popular form of social mingling.

Of course, the new houses springing up everywhere needed plenty of kitchen appliances, and advertisers were ready to educate the young homemakers about what was available. The most popular appliance, however, and the one with the greatest influence on consumption patterns was the television receiver. The growth of TV ownership by families skyrocketed in the 1950s, from 9 percent at the beginning of the decade to 50 percent in 1953 and some 90 percent by 1960. By that point, some 25 percent of the nation's population had moved to the suburbs, and television, with its steady stream of commercials, became many women's most faithful companion.

The early TV advertising model was pretty much the same as it had been for radio. Even the stars were often the same. *The George Burns and Gracie Allen Show*, sponsored by Carnation, would have the actors segue directly into a commercial. "I use Carnation, you know," Gracie would comment as she poured coffee in the midst of a comic routine.

Until the late 1950s, a single manufacturer frequently sponsored an entire program, but with rapidly rising costs, few companies could afford to purchase the time for an entire program. The presence of multiple advertisers meant that sponsors could no longer exert the direct influence they had once held over programming, but that hardly meant that the networks were deaf to their opinions.

Television continued to reflect a mostly contented world of aspiring consumers. Nevertheless, advertising did reflect the times, even if its products seemed almost always to be in the hands of a particularly upwardly mobile demographic. In the 1950s, the cold war could be enlisted to sell Ovaltine with spots featuring "Captain Midnight" in his high-tech bunker rallying his young "secret squadron members" to defend our shores while drinking "nourishing" Ovaltine. The contemporary infatuation with all things cowboy led Cheerios to create a cartoon character called the Cheerio Kid, who got his Indian-fighting "go-go-go-power" by eating the cereal. Roy Rogers, a singing cowboy who later gave his name to a chain of fast food outlets, was hired by the Nestlé Quik division to sing the praises of its products around televised campfires.

With the onset of the 1960s, peace and love, to say nothing of self-indulgence, became the dominant subtext, especially with respect to soft drinks and other products aimed at the youth culture. The youthful aspirations of the Vietnam War generation were probably best expressed in a 1971 Coca-Cola commercial in which a huge chorus sang, "I'd like to teach the world to sing / In perfect harmony. / I'd like to buy the world a Coke / And keep it company. / That's the real thing." Since the sexual revolution of the 1970s, sex has been used much more blatantly to attract viewers' attention with commercials that verge on soft porn. And by the end of the twentieth century, commercials even began to show a society that included working women and nonwhites.

A New Market: Kids

Television also brought a particularly malleable class of consumers to the marketplace: children. Not that weaning Americans on the corporate teat was particularly new, but television delivered a young audience in a way that radio or magazines just could not. In the 1950s, Howard M. List, then advertising manager of the Kellogg Company, was pleased to report: "With television, we can almost sell children our product before they can talk. . . . In the old days, children ate what their mothers bought; now the kids tell their mothers what to buy."

Commercials aimed at children have been carefully constructed to catch their attention; thus, such spots often feature other kids, fuzzy animals, and, especially, cartoon characters. A typical 1950s commercial for a particularly nutrition-free morning meal presented a parade of animated toddlers singing, "Cocoa Puffs for energy, Cocoa Puffs for fun, chocolate-flavored cereal, yum yum yum!" Some two generations later, in the 1990s, a survey of kids 6 to 14 reported that about 80 percent influenced the brand of cereal their families bought. The same study showed that about two-thirds exerted "some" influence to "a lot" on the family's choice of restaurants. No wonder that fast food restaurants have gone out of their way to make themselves attractive to children, with playgrounds and other kid-friendly amenities. Toy giveaways, usually cross-marketed with television or movie characters, have been a particularly popular promotional gimmick. Another, more subtle promotional technique has been to license a particular brand name to toy manufacturers, so that kids could, for example, flip "pretend" McDonald's burgers in their very own playrooms. Brands like Cheerios and Oreos have licensing arrangements with book publishers who create counting books whereby toddlers can learn to count by eating cookies. Pepsi, Dr Pepper, and 7Up sell the use of their designs for baby bottles; once the kids are old enough to go to school, logo-emblazoned soft-drink dispensers are ubiquitous.

In the 1990s, the Houston School system signed a contract with Coca-Cola worth more than $5 million over five years for exclusive pouring rights in the district's schools, giving the schools a direct monetary interest in increasing consumption of the product. And television itself, packed with commercials for snack foods and soft drinks, has been introduced into schools. Even before kindergarten, though, children have already been well primed; one 1991 study counted, in addition to all the toy ads, 222 junk food ads in just one Saturday morning's set of cartoon shows.

This phenomenon was noted with alarm as early as 1952, when Senator Estes Kefauver (D–TN) held the first of many congressional hearings on the subject. The Federal Trade Commission even made a futile effort to ban children's advertising in 1978. By 1990, more than 250 separate studies had been conducted on children's television, but the books that spell out how to market to kids have been almost as numerous.

Criticism has focused not only on advertising of products that children can legally buy, but also on the marketing of tobacco and alcohol in ways attractive to kids. In the 1990s, for example, Budweiser used a series of spots featuring amiable animated frogs croaking, "Bud-WEI-ser." In 1994, the American Academy of Pediatrics estimated that, each year, youngsters were exposed to two thousand television ads for beer and wine. The advertisers have clearly had some success: in a survey of 534 teens, 99 percent of them correctly identified the Budweiser frogs.

Fragmentation of the Mass Market

Since the 1970s, advertising has begun to appear on just about any medium that will accommodate it, from T-shirts and baseball caps to parking meters and public restrooms. Corporate sponsorship took over once countercultural rock concerts, with brands like Coke, Pepsi, and Bacardi Rum subsidizing tours. Movie producers began to charge for product placement in films—perhaps the most successful example being the use of Reese's Pieces candy in the movie *E.T.* (1982), which resulted in a sales increase of 85 percent. Even outer space was enlisted. A large sign inside Russia's Mir space station before it was destroyed said it all: "Even in Space . . . Pepsi Is Changing the Script." It has been estimated that in the early 1970s the daily number of ads targeted at the average American was 560; by 1999 this number had jumped to 3,000.

Television itself had been through a seismic change. The three networks, which until the 1970s had provided American manufacturers with one undifferentiated mass audience, were increasingly faced with competition from cable channels. First a few dozen and then hundreds of alternative venues began to vie for advertising dollars. These channels were designed around delivering a particular demographic to the advertisers, whether children, teenagers, women, African Americans, Hispanics, or any other niche market. In reaching out to these new audiences, the commercials for the first time actually depicted people of color without the early stereotypes. For those particularly interested in cooking and eating, the Food Channel delivered food manufacturers a particularly engaged viewership. And some stations, like the home shopping channels, even dispensed with programs altogether to dedicate themselves to commercials around the clock.

The idea of niche marketing was not new; magazines had always sought out particular audiences. When their medium was eclipsed by television, radio broadcasters found that if they catered to a specific audience they could target it with more finely tuned advertising. "Negro" radio, in particular, was an early success, showing how well a segmented market approach could work for that medium. In the last two decades of the twentieth century, though, not only were there thousands of venues, but American society itself was seen as much more atomized by gender, race, language, marital status, generation, and class, to name just a few variables. Magazines, perhaps even more than cable television, reflected this change. Thus, AdvantEdge, a chocolate-flavored nutrient shake, found just the right fit with *Shape* magazine; Coors beer was presented a ready readership in the men's magazine *Maxim*; Land O'Lakes "Dairy Ease" lactose-free milk knew it would find a receptive audience in the black publication *Essence*; and to Perrier-Jouet it was natural to promote its champagne in *Food & Wine*.

For the next generation, the Internet promises a future where "we can target not just demographic segments but individual households," as Edwin L. Artzt, the chief executive officer of Proctor and Gamble, foretold in a 1994 talk. He was referring to contemporary notions of interactive television; but as we are increasingly drawn into the digital age, his prognostications are proving even more true of the online world.

Advertising in These United States

The contemporary American diet is largely a result of the advertising and marketing that has nurtured it since the last decade of the nineteenth century. Our gulp-and-go lifestyle may have originated long before the advent of corn flakes and Gatorade, but it cannot be denied that the hundreds of billions spent each year on advertising have influenced our eating habits as in no other culture. In its earlier years, advertising had a unifying effect, cobbling together a common culture out of a multitude of displaced migrants and immigrants, all eating Campbell's soup and drinking Coke. Today, the homogenizing effect of advertising has weakened as each subgroup gets its own culturally specific product. Indeed, advertising may be one of the main contributors to the new multicultural society. Nevertheless, the unstated ideology of the United States, the creed of consumption, will continue to unite us, even if one chooses to fill his bowl with vanilla Häagen Dazs, and another, with dulce de leche.

[*See also* Advertising Cookbooklets and Recipes; Aunt Jemima; Baby Food; Budweiser; Campbell Soup Kids; Coca-Cola; Crisco; Film, Food in; Health Food; Hershey Foods Corporation; Jell-O; Kellogg Company; Nestlé; Politics of Food; Post Foods; Pure Food and Drug Act; Quaker Oats Man; Radio and Television; School Food; Toasters; World's Fairs.]

BIBLIOGRAPHY

Applegate, Edd. *Personalities and Products: A Historical Perspective on Advertising in America*. Westport, CT: Greenwood Press, 1998.
Carson, Gerald. *Cornflake Crusade*. New York: Rinehart, 1957.
The Chocolate Plant (Theobroma cacao) *and Its Products*. Dorchester, MA: Walter Baker, 1891.
Fox, Roy F. "Warning: Advertising May Be Hazardous to Your Health." *USA Today Magazine*, November 2001.
Goodrum, Charles, and Helen Dalrymple. *Advertising in America: The First 200 Years*. New York: Abrams, 1990.
Guber, Selina S., and Jon Berry. *Marketing to and through Kids*. New York: McGraw-Hill, 1993.
Hershey Chocolate Corporation. *The Story of Hershey, the Chocolate Town*. Hershey, PA: Hershey Chocolate Corporation, 1963.
Hill, Daniel Delis. *Advertising to the American Woman, 1900–1999*. Columbus: Ohio State University Press, 2002.
Krondl, Michael. *Around the American Table: Treasured Recipes and Food Traditions from the American Cookery Collections of the New York Public Library*. Holbrook, MA: Adams, 1995.
Levenstein, Harvey. *Paradox of Plenty*. New York: Oxford University Press, 1993.
Levenstein, Harvey. *Revolution at the Table*. New York: Oxford University Press, 1988.
Nestle, Marion. *Food Politics: How the Food Industry Influences Nutrition and Health*. Berkeley: University of California Press, 2002.
Norris, James D. *Advertising and the Transformation of American Society 1865–1920*. New York: Greenwood Press, 1990.
Pillsbury, Richard. *No Foreign Food: The American Diet in Time and Place*. Boulder, CO: Westview Press, 1998.
Strasser, Susan. *Satisfaction Guaranteed: The Making of the American Mass Market*. New York: Pantheon, 1989.

MICHAEL KRONDL

Advertising Cookbooklets and Recipes

Since the mid-nineteenth century, recipes have been used to sell products. At first, recipes were incidental to the products advertised. Publishers hoped that readers interested in the recipes would see and buy the advertised products. As the century progressed, advertisers became much more sophisticated, and recipes often called for the use of the products that were being advertised.

In many ways, advertising cookbooklets reflect the broader advertising industry that developed in the nineteenth century. During the 1850s advertising companies promoted products such as soap. As food processors became important toward the end of the century, the advertising profession turned its attention to selling brand-name foods and drinks, such as Quaker Oats and Coca-Cola. By the beginning of the twentieth century, advertising accounted for 25 percent of the total budget of many food processors.

Patent Medicine Cookbooklets

The first such recipes appeared in patent medicine cookbooklets and almanacs. The intent of these small pamphlets was to promote manufacturers' medical products to housewives. The booklets usually included descriptions of products or services and testimonials from satisfied customers. The recipes usually had little to do with the medical products being sold. Good examples include *Mrs. Winslow's Domestic Receipt Book*, published annually from 1862 to 1879, which promoted the medicines of Jeremiah Curtis and John I. Brown of Boston. An even longer series was the

Ransom's Family Receipt Book, published annually from 1868 to 1921, which promoted the medicines of David Ransom and Company of Buffalo, New York. Both annuals were thirty-six-page pamphlets that were about half recipes and half advertising and testimonials. Druggists distributed them free to customers, who saved them for future reference. Another famous patent medicine maker who also produced cookbooklets was Lydia Pinkham. Her Vegetable Compound for "female complaints" was widely advertised, and tens of thousands of copies of dozens of different cookbooklets were distributed by the company that bore her name. This genre declined after the Pure Food and Drug Act of 1906 knocked many patent medicines off the market.

Product Cookbooklets

After the Civil War another category of product-sponsored publications appeared. These publications promoted specific foods or culinary equipment. When the U.S. Patent Office began registering trademarks and slogans, the use of brand names and attractive labels grew. Around the same time, a drop in the price of paper and the invention of the rotary press made possible high-speed, low-cost printing. With major advances in color lithography and

Product Cookbooklet. *Food Surprises from the Mirro Test Kitchen* (c. 1920). *Collection of Bonnie Slotnick*

photography in the late 1800s, brand-name food manufacturers began advertising nationally by buying ad space in magazines and by publishing pamphlets. These pamphlets encouraged customers to request particular brand-name products at local grocery stores rather than to accept unbranded bulk goods. Local stores, in turn, were encouraged to purchase products directly from manufacturers. This system eliminated the need for middlemen or brokers and reduced prices for retailers and for customers. The recipes in these booklets usually featured the company's products, and these recipes were often reprinted in newspapers, magazines, and cookbooks.

Among the early producers of advertising cookbooklets were manufacturers of cookery equipment. In the 1870s Granite Iron Ware distributed cookery booklets that encouraged the use of the company's pots and pans. Granite Iron Ware was followed by Agate Iron Ware, whose cookbooklets were particularly attractive. Other manufacturers followed, including makers of meat grinders, stoves, and electrical appliances, such as refrigerators, freezers, bread machines, and microwave ovens.

Ingredient-Based Cookbooklets

In many cases, the advertised food products were simply the old generic commodities with new brand names. Because brand-name products required advertising and expensive packaging, they cost more than generic products. Manufacturers had to offer reasons why housewives should purchase their products rather than generic products. Hence, the "new and improved" shibboleth became commonly associated with food advertising campaigns. In addition, many products claimed health benefits.

Many food products, however, were new creations or inventions and had no generic equivalent. In these cases manufacturers had to create a demand for their products. Also, housewives had to be shown how to use these products. As these were showcase recipes, they were often developed by professionals. Two successful early examples include the Shredded Wheat Company and the Genesee Pure Food Company. The Shredded Wheat Company produced a series of advertising cookbooklets provocatively titled *The Vital Question* (1899), featuring dozens of creative uses of shredded wheat; the Genesee Pure Food Company published cookbooklets that included a wide variety of recipes incorporating Jell-O.

Early producers of advertising cookbooklets turned to well-known cookery experts. For instance, Fannie Farmer, the principal of the Boston Cooking School, first published *The Horsford Cook Book* (1895), an advertising booklet promoting the baking powder made by Rumford Chemical Works in Rhode Island. All recipes in the booklet were subsequently incorporated into the popular first edition of her *Boston Cooking School Cook Book* (1896). Sarah Tyson Rorer wrote advertising cookbooklets for the Marvelli Company (1900), the Liebig Company (1905), the Fairbanks Company (1910), and the Perfection Stove Company (1926). Janet MacKenzie Hill, the editor of the *Boston Cooking-School Magazine*, published dozens of advertising cookbooklets, such as *The Story of Crisco with Two Hundred Recipes* (1914) produced by Procter and Gamble.

Many early promotions claimed that their products saved consumers time and energy. Then the focus shifted to economy and nutrition. In 1931 *Favorite Recipes of the Movie Stars* suggested a new direction for advertising cookbooklets—using movie stars to push products. In 1933 General Mills published the cookbooklet *Betty Crocker's 101 Delicious Bisquick Creations As Made and Served by Well-Known Gracious Hostesses; Famous Chefs; Distinguished Epicures and Smart Luminaries of Movieland*, which included many recipes signed by Hollywood movie stars. Two years later, General Mills offered *Let the Stars Show You How to Take a Trick a Day with Bisquick as Told to Betty Crocker*. Of course, the "as told to Betty Crocker" tag is disingenuous as she was a fictional character invented by General Mills in 1922. Betty Crocker was not the first fictional character intended to sell food products. Probably the first was trademarked in 1877, and the image of a Quaker originally graced the label of a whiskey bottle. This image was more successfully used to sell Quaker Oats, one of the first cardboard-packaged foods in America. Other successful fictional characters, such as Aunt Jemima and Uncle Ben, were also created about the same time.

Children's fantasy characters emerged to promote the sale of particular products. America's sweetener during the nineteenth century was molasses. As the price of sugar decreased, sugar sales boomed, and molasses sales declined. By the 1920s molasses manufacturers had to advertise to attract customers. Brer Rabbit was borrowed from children's literature to sell molasses. The strategy did not work, and molasses has since been relegated to the position of a minor sweetener. Promotional cookbooklets targeted at children were common, such as *The Little Gingerbread Man* (1923), published by the Royal Baking Powder Company.

In addition to those booklets published by individual manufacturers to sell specific products, advertising cookbooklets were also produced by agricultural and business associations interested in promoting generic products. Calavo, an association of California avocado growers, published recipes encouraging consumers to incorporate avocados in many different dishes. Power companies published cookbooklets encouraging customers to use electrical kitchen appliances.

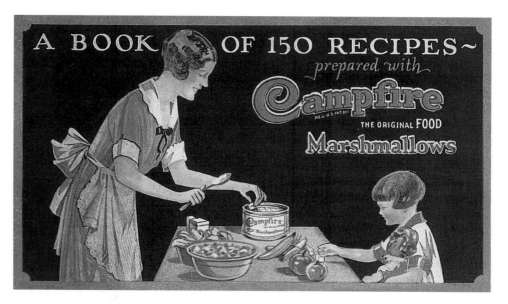

Ingredient-Based Cookbooklet. Promotional book of recipes distributed by Campfire Marshmallows.

The single descriptive characteristic of advertising cookbooklets is their diversity. Some were no more than small, one-page, folded brochures while others were actually full-fledged books with hard bindings. As all were intended to sell products, many were written by professionals. As the companies that manufactured the products needed to guarantee that the recipes worked, the recipes were excellent examples of how their products could be used. Hence the recipes in advertising cookbooklets were occasionally much better than those that appeared in regular cookbooks, as were the recipes that manufacturers placed on their labels or inserted into advertisements in newspapers and magazines.

Distribution

Companies circulated cookbooklets in a variety of ways. Some gave them away with their products by inserting them into boxes. Cookbooklets connected with cooking equipment, such as stoves, refrigerators, or choppers, took the form of instruction booklets, providing as a bonus recipes for foods that could be prepared or served using the equipment. Other companies distributed the booklets free through retail outlets. One of the most common ways of distributing booklets was to mention them in a magazine advertisement or on the product package. A cookbooklet would be sent to customers free or for the price of postage. This method gave manufacturers the customer's address, and that customer could then be targeted for future unsolicited product advertising.

In general, advertising cookbooklets were often enticing and usually included illustrations of products, of the foods produced by the recipes, of prizes the company had won at fairs and expositions, or occasionally of company headquarters or the factory, demonstrating its modernity and cleanliness. Early booklets were relatively simple, black-and-white affairs with few illustrations. As time progressed, these booklets became more colorful, elaborate, and attractive. Most were filled with lively anecdotes, engaging advice of the era, and amusing quotes praising the products. The booklets introduced new color processing techniques in drawings and photographs. Color was used as an eye-catcher to promote products and whet the appetite for the depicted meal or recipe. For instance, the Jell-O cookbooklets published by the Genesee Pure Food Company offer some of the best illustrations, including some by Norman Rockwell, who was more famous for his *Saturday Evening Post* covers.

Some cookbooklets were die cuts, shaped like the product or another image related to the product. The Campbell Soup Company, for instance, issued *Campbell's Condensed Tomato Soup* (1914) shaped partly like a tomato soup can. Penick and Ford published a cookbooklet promoting its molasses partly in the shape of Brer Rabbit.

Tens of thousands of advertising cookbooklets were published, and many have survived. Unfortunately, no comprehensive bibliography of advertising cookbooklets has been published. There are an estimated 100,000 cookery pamphlets and leaflets in known collections, and this estimate is probably low. While the success of advertising cookbooklets to sell products is difficult to determine, manufacturers obviously believe they are important. Many companies, including General Foods, General Mills, the Campbell Soup Company, and H. J. Heinz, continue to publish booklets, and it is likely that advertising cookbooklets will continue to be part of food manufacturers' advertising repertoire.

[*See also* Advertising; Cookbooks and Manuscripts, *subentries* From the Civil War to World War I, From World War I to World War II, From World War II to the 1960s; From the 1970s to the Present, Children's Cookbooks.]

BIBLIOGRAPHY

Cagle, William R., and Lisa Killion Stafford. *American Books on Food and Drink.* New Castle, DE: Oak Knoll Press, 1998.

Crumpacker, Bunny. *The Old-Time Brand-Name Cookbook: Recipes, Illustrations, and Advice from the Early Kitchens of America's Most Trusted Food Makers.* New York: Smithmark, 1998.

"Nicole Di Bona Peterson Collection of Advertising Cookbooks." Duke University. http://scriptorium.lib.duke.edu/eaa/cookbooks_dbinfo.html.

Norman, Sandra J., and Karrie K. Andres. *Vintage Cookbooks and Advertising Leaflets.* Atglen, PA: Schiffer, 1998.

Smith, Andrew F. "Advertising and Promotional Cookbooks." *The Cookbook Collectors' Exchange* (September–October 1999): 5–9.

ANDREW F. SMITH

African American Food

[This entry includes two subentries:

To the Civil War
Since Emancipation]

To the Civil War

There are multiple aspects to African American foodways, and a survey of them requires an examination of the homelands in Africa, where various aspects of African American culture originated; some of the foods of the seventeenth- to nineteenth-century African kitchen; the introduction of the African cook to what became the United States; the early African American cookbook authors; and the Big House cooks on southern plantations versus the field hand cooks.

Almost all present-day African Americans are descended from people originating from the tip of Senegal around the coast of West Africa, across the highlands of Cameroon to western Congo and northern Angola. The area includes such present-day coastal nations as Senegal, Gambia, Guinea-Bissau, Guinea, Sierra Leone, Liberia, Ivory Coast, Ghana, Togo, Benin, Nigeria, and the Cameroon, as well as inland areas from which people migrated or were brought to the coast.

These lands have been the setting for great African empires for more than fifteen hundred years, from Ghana in the fourth to thirteenth centuries to Ashanti and Dahomey in the seventeenth to nineteenth centuries. These empires had their own governments, courts, systems of highways, remarkable buildings, impressive arts, medicine, and unique foodways.

The various peoples of Africa grew their own staple crops, either millet, rice, sorghum (called "guinea corn" in early America), or yams. Around the edges of their staple crops, they planted black-eyed peas, sesame seeds, groundnuts, plantains, eggplant, okra, spinach, cabbage, and flavorings, such as *malagueta* pepper and palm oil. Yams were the staple crop of the Ashanti in the central region of Ghana and of the Yoruba and the Ibo of Nigeria; plantain (and later cassava) was favored by the tribes of the Congo and Angola; and it was rice or millet (and later maize) that pleased those of Sierra Leone, Ivory Coast, and the Grain Coast (now Liberia), so named because it was the source of *malagueta* pepper, known as "grains of paradise" in Europe.

African Kitchen

Some of the foods available to the West African kitchen of the seventeenth to nineteenth centuries are listed below. Some were indigenous to West Africa, such as okra, tamarind, ackee, watermelon, the Bambara groundnut, and some species of rice, millet, yams, cowpeas (black-eyed peas), sesame seeds, and sorghum. During the period from 1450 to 1650, referred to by some historians as the Age of Expansion or the Age of Discovery, European explorers introduced Asian bananas, cowpeas, and rices and American cassavas, maize, squashes, sweet potatoes, and peanuts into the region. Not all of

these foods were available to any one tribe, although all were to be found throughout the West African region at this time in history.

The West African cook made use of such vegetables as okra, kidney beans, pigeon peas, mushrooms, spinach, cabbages, rice, plantains, taros, cowpeas, pumpkins, squashes, eggplants (later known in the American South as "guinea squash"), onions, maize (Indian corn), tomatoes, mustard greens, collard greens, lima beans, cucumbers, sugarcane, ackees, yams, sweet potatoes, cocoyams, and hearts of palm. Some of their fruit choices were bananas, the oval fruit of the Baobab tree, lemons, mangoes, limes, guavas, peaches, sweetsops, figs, melons, coconuts, and watermelons. A wide variety of meats was available to the cook. These included small bush animals, large game, sheep, wild ducks, goats, pigs, chickens, guinea hens, cows, buffalo, and elephants. The streams, lagoons, and rivers offered a variety of fish and shellfish. The herbs, spices, and other seasonings at the cook's disposal included salt, *malagueta* (or guinea) peppers, pili-pili (chili peppers, also known as "peri-peri" or "piri-piri"), pimiento peppers, lemon juice, lime juice, coriander, ginger, saffron, thyme, sage, sweet basil, mint, parsley, onions, shallots, leeks, tomatoes, and curry mixtures. Nuts, seeds, and grain were also prominent in the African kitchen, including groundnuts and peanuts (*pindar* in West African languages, *nguba* in Bantu languages, which became "goober peas" in the United States), sesame seeds (benne seeds), watermelon seeds (called "egusi seeds" in Africa, they are often dried and ground or pulverized to be used as a paste to thicken soups and stews), cucumber seeds, hazelnuts, pistachios, kola nuts (the basis of American colas), millet, sorghum, and rice.

African Culinary Techniques

The West African cook employed a variety of methods and kitchen utensils to prepare enjoyable meals for her family. Iron working became a highly developed skill in Africa approximately two thousand years ago, so by the seventeenth to nineteenth centuries the average West African wife had at least one iron pot for preparing delectable hot soups and stews. The pots, either iron or earthen, were placed in the center of a fireplace made of three stones arranged into a triangle, or simply over three low clay mounds. If the pot were one of the smaller, earthen vessels similar to a double boiler, the cook could opt to steam her preparation. She would fill the bottom vessel with water and seasonings and place her vegetables, breads, puddings, or meat in the top vessel, with its perforated bottom.

If meat were from a large animal, most likely the cook would first tenderize it by wrapping it in the leaves of the papaya tree or boiling it with papaya fruit. Then she could impale it with sharp, thin strips of wood or iron rods and roast it over an open pit, saucing it with lime or lemon juice and her preferred peppers. For baking purposes, she could wrap her food in a multipurpose banana leaf and place it under hot cinders, or if she wanted it boiled, she could lower it into a pot of boiling water. For frying foods and seasoning vegetables, she had a variety of oils (some of which she extracted from shea nuts, coconuts, and peanuts), including the red oil of palm nuts—her most commonly used oil.

Two very useful kitchen utensils were the grating stone and the mortar and pestle. The former was used to pulverize rice and corn, the latter to pound yams, beans, millet, cassavas, seeds, and nuts. With these two useful instruments, the cook could make multiple preparations for her family. For example, boiled beans could be pounded into a paste to thicken soups and sauces, dried beans, pounded into flour to make bread, bean fritters, or bean cakes.

Foods were served in clay bowls, gourds, tightly woven little wicker bowls, wooden saucers, or banana leaves. The gourds, made from the hard shells enclosing the fruit of the calabash tree, were used as mixing bowls, jugs for carrying water, drinking cups, measuring cups, storage containers, and spoons.

Africans Come to America

There is some evidence for the presence of Africans in the Americas in pre-Columbian times. Among Christopher Columbus's crew in 1492 was Alonso Pietro, the pilot of the *Niña*, who was an African. African slaves were part of the early Spanish colonies in Florida and the Carolinas, and some probably escaped to join the Indians. What is generally not in dispute is that a Dutch man-of-war came into the river at Jamestown in 1619 and sold twenty "Negroes" into forced service.

It is possible that these first Virginia "Negroes" were indentured like the British undesirables, criminals, captured foreign soldiers, prostitutes, debtors, "ne'er-do-wells," kidnapped children, poor children put into service by their parents, gypsies, would-be farmers, unemployed soldiers, "restless souls," and adventurers who were in servitude for a contractual period before becoming free to advance in the colonies. But Virginia documents make clear that within two generations most "Africans" were in permanent slavery.

The manner in which West Africans were rounded up, put on European vessels, and shipped across the Atlantic to the colonies was more horrifying than what was experienced by indentured servants from Europe. But in the midst of their helpless condition, the enslaved Africans were able to hold onto an important aspect of their culture—their foodways. Africans on board the various slave vessels were resolute against eating foods with which they were not familiar. This meant that Africans from Ivory Coast, the Grain Coast, and Sierra Leone had to be given boiled rice and millet, while those from the Congo and Angola required cassava or plantain. The captives forced their captors to observe their food preferences, and in this way some of the foods of the West African kitchen of the seventeenth to nineteenth centuries, including okra, eggplants, taros, ackees, yams, plantains, melons, pigeon peas, guinea hens, cowpeas, sesame seeds, and watermelons, accompanied the Africans into the New World.

A review of the travails in the early days of all the European colonies shows a people poorly provisioned with their native foods—which they still preferred—and often starving, until the necessary adjustments were made in their food habits to secure their survival in their new world. It was within this nascent state of cookery in the colonies that the African cook first began to fuse her culinary traditions with America's developing cuisine, sometimes in farm homes in the New England colonies and the Middle Atlantic colonies, or as Big House cooks in the South.

African American cooks were engaged in cooking foods to please the palates of those who owned their service. Many of the foods common to the colonial table, such as squashes, pumpkins, tomatoes, white potatoes, corn, beans, peas, greens, carrots, and cabbage, were not too unlike the foods common to the table of the seventeenth- to nineteenth-century West African kitchen. The basic kitchen utensils and cooking techniques of the West African kitchen were also similar to those in the colonies: consider the West Africans' iron or earthen pots; their wooden spoons and multiple gourds; their technique of piercing meats with thin sticks of wood or iron to roast over open fires, or of wrapping meats in banana leaves and submersing them in boiling water; the use of grating stones to pulverize rice, beans, plantains, millet, cassavas, yams, and corn, or of mortar and pestle to pound them into flour for making bread or into paste for thickening sauces, soups, and stews.

Big House Cook

There are many written sources detailing the kinds of food that the Big House cook was required to prepare on the plantation. One interesting source is Frederick Douglass's *Life and Time of Frederick Douglass* (1845), which covers the period from his birth as a slave on Colonel Lloyd's plantation in February 1817 until his eventual escape in September 1838. Some of the wide range of foods that were found on Colonel Lloyd's table included preparations of fowl, such as Muscovy ducks, guinea fowls, turkeys, geese, peafowls, swans, black-necked wild geese, partridges, quails, pheasants, and pigeons; meats, such as beef, veal, mutton, and venison; and delectable dishes of rock perch, drums, croakers, trout, oysters, crabs, and terrapins. These dishes of fish and meat were garnished with fresh fruits and vegetables that the cook used directly from Colonel Lloyd's garden: tender asparagus, crisp celery, delicate cauliflowers, eggplants, beets, lettuce, parsnips, peas, French beans, early and late radishes, cantaloupes, and melons of all kinds. All of these foods were prepared for the most demanding and discriminating palates of not only the Lloyd family but also their many friends and guests, for Lloyd's plantation was like a pretentious quasi-nation, indulged and swollen in "the tide of high life, where pride and indolence lounged in magnificence and satiety" (p. 34).

Field Hand Cook

Foods common to the field hand's table were johnnycake, greens, cornmeal dumplings, cornmeal mush, hoecakes, corn dodgers, corn pone, cornbread, sweet potatoes, fried fowl, rice, fish, game, vegetables, and greens (turnips, cabbage, mustard, collards). From Christmas to New Year's, field hands on some plantations were given access to cakes, pies, tarts, cookies, fruits, nuts, molasses, peach cobblers, apple dumplings, whole hogs, sheep, beef, cheese, candy, coffee, wine and liquor, custards, tea cakes, and other fine foods.

The kind and amount of foods rationed to the slaves were not the same throughout the land but varied by place, based most often upon the foods common to that particular place, local food preference, custom (foods considered proper slave foods), and the season. The standard ration may have been a quart of cornmeal and half

a pound of salt pork per day for each adult, with less for children. This was supplemented by the foods the slaves grew on their own plots, the poultry and pigs they raised, the game caught or trapped in surrounding woods, and the fish netted or hooked in nearby lakes and streams.

Owners and white reporters tended to give an account of food allowances that were rather generous, whereas former slaves tended to depict one that was meager and inadequate. Perhaps this former slave's account from *The History of the American Negro, In Their Own Words* by Milton Meltzer (1964) is the most reliable and objective of all:

> Now you see, dar was good marsas an' bad marsas. Marsas what was good see dat slaves lived decent an' got plenty to eat. Marsas what was mean and skinflinty throw 'em scraps like dey feed a dog an' don' care what kind of shack dey live in. Warn't no law sayin' dey got to treat slaves decent. (p. 44)

African American Culinary Professionals

The shock of sudden displacement and cultural separation did not prevent West African cooks from performing culinary duties in the English colonies in America. Colonizers in the North and planters in the South took advantage of this fact, for West African slaves were used extensively as domestics throughout the colonies. Indeed, they were among the most prominent cooking practitioners of the time, interpreting and defining the recipes and food preparations of America's ever-evolving cuisine. This early culinary role of Africans in North America and their culinary separation from their homeland are evident in the early books on cookery matters by African American authors: *House Servant's Directory* by Robert Roberts (1827); *Hotel Keepers, Head Waiters, and Housekeepers Guide* by Tunis G. Campbell (1847); and *What Mrs. Fisher Knows about Old Southern Cooking* by Abby Fisher (1881). Their books all share one thing: a failure to trace any of the foods or recipes to the regions of West Africa. The important thing the books do offer, however, is a significant number of recipes that have been identified with African Americans since that early period.

For a glimpse into what some of these books offer, consider *The House Servant's Directory*, written by the freeman Robert Roberts and published thirty-one years after America's first cookbook, *American Cookery*, by Amelia Simmons (1796). The bibliographer Maxwell Whiteman writes that *The House Servant's Directory* was the "first book by a black American published by a commercial

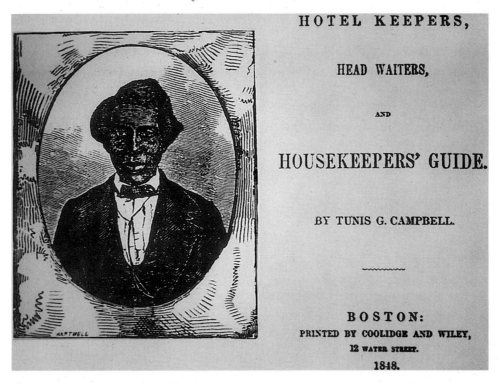

HOTEL KEEPERS,

HEAD WAITERS,

AND

HOUSEKEEPERS' GUIDE.

BY TUNIS G. CAMPBELL.

BOSTON:
PRINTED BY COOLIDGE AND WILEY,
12 WATER STREET.
1848.

Tunis G. Campbell. Portrait and title page of his *Hotel Keepers, Head Waiters, and Housekeepers' Guide* (Boston, 1848).

publisher." *The House Servant's Directory* provided excellent advice in all aspects of running a prominent home in the most efficient and proper way, from the performance of servants' work (including instructions on cleaning plates, brass, steel, glass, and lamps and for correctly burning Lehigh coal) to the art of waiting on tables. It also offered friendly advice to cooks and contained some useful recipes for the table, such as salad sauce, mustard, liquid currant jam, ginger beer, and several versions of lemonade. For Roberts, a prominent position in culinary trades brought with it community leadership: He sponsored and addressed national abolitionist meetings.

Hotel Keepers, Head Waiters, and Housekeepers Guide was written by the freeman Tunis G. Campbell and published December 14, 1847. Campbell's book was similar to Roberts's in that it contained advice to domestics for carrying out their various chores in prominent homes. He made his purpose abundantly clear on the very first page: "This work is intended for hotels and private families. As, truly, 'order is Heaven's first law,' it becomes our duty to aim at, if we cannot attain it, in all things." To presume that Campbell may have acquiesced to a subservient role in American society, or that he advocated such a role for others, would have been wrong in 1847, when he was

already an active abolitionist, and would have been proven utterly wrong during and after the Civil War, when he went south to organize freed slaves during Reconstruction. Campbell offered a wide range of recipes—a total of ninety-eight—covering hotel dinner dishes, sauces, and desserts, as well as early published recipes for such recognizable African American specialties as cornbread, buckwheat cakes, and dumplings.

The publications of Roberts and Campbell did include some recipes for food preparation, but they were not cooks, nor did they intend for their books to be regarded as cookbooks. The first cookbook authored by an African American and featuring foods from her own table, as well as from those of her white customers, is most likely the work of Mrs. Abby Fisher, *What Mrs. Fisher Knows about Old Southern Cooking*, published in 1881. It is probable that Fisher was born a slave and learned her profession in a plantation kitchen in South Carolina. There is no conjecture, however, about her culinary skills. In 1880, at the San Francisco Mechanics' Institute Fair, she was awarded two medals, one for her pickles and sauces and another for her jellies and preserves. Her book includes recipes for Maryland Beat Biscuits, Plantation Hoe Cake, Lamb or Mutton Chops, Pork Steak or Chops, Croquettes,

Sponge Cakes, Ginger Cookies, Sweet Cucumber Pickles and Pears, Apple Pie and Black Berry Rolls, Rice and Plum Puddings, Brandy Peaches and Strawberry Jam, Roast Beef and Lamb, Chicken and Crab Salads, Fish and Clam Chowder Soup, and Fricasseed and Fried Chicken, among the total of 152 recipes.

[*See also* Campbell, Tunis G.; Mortar and Pestle; Rice; Southern Regional Cookery.]

BIBLIOGRAPHY

Booth, Sally Smith. *Hung, Strung, and Potted: A History of Eating Habits in Colonial America.* New York, 1971.
Douglass, Frederick. *Life and Times of Frederick Douglass.* London: Collier Macmillan, 1892.
Franklin, John Hope. *From Slavery to Freedom: A History of Negro Americans.* New York, 1967.
Grosvenor, Vertamae. *The Americas' Family Kitchen.* San Francisco: Bay Books, 1996.
Hall, Robert L. "Savoring Africa in the New World." In *Seeds of Change,* edited by Herman J. Viola and Carolyn Margolis. Washington, DC: Smithsonian Institution Press, 1991.
Harris, Jessica. *African American Heritage Cooking.* New York: Simon and Schuster, 1995.
Herskovits, Melville J. *The Human Factor in Changing Africa.* New York: Knopf, 1958.
Hess, Karen L. *The Carolina Rice Kitchen: The African Connection.* Columbia: University of South Carolina Press, 1992.
Jones, Wilbert. *New Soul Food Cookbook.* New York: Kensington, 1996.
Lewis, Edna. *The Taste of Country Cooking.* New York: Knopf, 1996.
Longone, Janice B., and Daniel Longone. *American Cookbooks and Wine Books, from 1797–1950.* Ann Arbor, MI: University of Michigan, 1984.
Meltzer, Milton. *The History of the American Negro, In Their Own Words.* New York: Crowell, 1964.
National Council of Negro Women. *The Black Family Reunion Cookbook.* New York: Fireside, 1996.
Paige, Howard. *Aspects of Afro-American Cookery.* Southfield, MI: Aspects (23905 Plumbrooke Dr., Southfield, MI), 1987.
Randall, Joe. *A Taste of Heritage: The New African-American Cuisine.* New York: Macmillan, 1998.
Whit, William C. "Soul Food as Cultural Creation." Paper presented at the joint meetings of the Association for the Study of Food and Society and the Agriculture, Food, and Human Values Society, San Francisco, June 4–7, 1998.
White, Ann Terry. *Human Cargo: The Story of the Atlantic Slave Trade.* Champaign, IL: Garrard, 1972.
Zafar, Rafia. "Cooking Up a Past." Paper presented at the joint meetings of the Association for the Study of Food and Society and the Agriculture, Food, and Human Values Society, San Francisco, June 4–7, 1998.

HOWARD PAIGE

Since Emancipation

At the beginning of the Civil War, approximately 10 percent of African Americans were free. But as much as one-quarter of the free population were runaway slaves who had to live with a daily fear of being recaptured and returned to slavery, almost certainly with exemplary punishment. Their situation was perilous in both northern and southern states and worsened as tensions about slavery increased. Although slavery had ended in most northern states by 1840, rising tides of prejudice and the arrival of new groups of European immigrants pushed African Americans out of many trades. One sector that remained open to them was food service, whether in private homes or as independent caterers, street merchants, or cooks and waiters in commercial hotels and restaurants.

Catering and Food Service

The African American caterers in particular were comparatively well-to-do; they employed other members of their community, met with prominent white families, and were social leaders and noted abolitionists. In *The Philadelphia Negro*, W. E. B. Du Bois described the situation in 1840s Philadelphia, but there were similar developments in New York and Boston:

> The whole catering business, arising from an evolution shrewdly, persistently and tastefully directed, transformed the Negro cook and waiter into the public caterer and restaurateur, and raised a crowd of underpaid menials to become a set of self-reliant, original business men, who amassed fortunes for themselves and won general respect for their people.

Philadelphia caterers developed reputations for particular dishes, such as terrapin stew and chicken croquettes, which were seen both as African American specialties and prestigious foods on the tables of socially prominent white

African American Food. Hoe cakes and hush puppies. *Collection of Howard Paige*

families. By the 1850s the Philadelphia cookbook author Eliza Leslie was acknowledging that she had gathered recipes from southern cooks, including many "dictated by colored cooks of high reputation in the art, for which nature seems to have gifted that race with a peculiar capability" (*New Receipts for Cooking*, 1854). Here are both the positive and negative stereotypes of African Americans as fine but instinctive cooks that were to haunt American culinary literature for another 150 years, and perhaps still counting. White writers have praised African American cooks and food for most of that period but have also described their abilities as mysterious, innate, nonintellectual, untrained, and secretive. In deliberate contrast, African American food writers have described their multisensory approach to cooking and seasoning and presented careful measurements, from the first recipes published by Robert Roberts in 1827 on.

African Americans continued to dominate the catering business in northeastern cities into the 1890s and competed notably in Chicago, Washington, D.C., and even as far west as San Francisco after the Civil War. African American caterers also held positions of respect in southern cities throughout the era of segregation.

The Civil War, Slave Cooks, and Emancipation

The coming of the Civil War did not end all the perils of the black community in the North, as was tragically illustrated by the 1862 New York draft riots, in which eleven were lynched and dozens more beaten. However, the outbreak of war did reduce the danger of being returned to slavery and opened some economic opportunities and, eventually, military service. The Civil War also helped spread African American culinary art and its reputation. Northern soldiers were welcomed into the homes of free people of color in the border states and parts of the South, where they enjoyed relief from hardtack and salt pork. Southerners were deprived of imported foods by the Union naval blockade, but they were pleasantly surprised by what their remaining slave cooks could create out of locally grown produce—foods like sweet potatoes, black-eyed peas, hoppin' John, collard greens, and hoecakes, which had been staples for centuries down in the slave quarters. The stereotype of the slave cook as mistress of the Big House kitchen has been backdated from the late nineteenth century, but its basis in fact arose only during the Civil War. Prior to that time, the role of slave cook was more often to prepare imported delicacies from recipes dictated by the mistress of the house.

Few slaves outside the kitchen crew had tasted fine Anglo-American foods, except during the week between Christmas and New Year's. However, after emancipation, and even after migration north or west, the memory of those annual feasts persisted in the African American enjoyment of tea cakes and fancy desserts.

The case of fried chicken is more complicated. Both slaves and free African Americans were active raisers of poultry wherever possible, and in the Chesapeake area slaves were at times allowed to dominate the local poultry market. The taste for chicken goes back to Africa, as may pan-frying in iron pots. However, chicken was more expensive than pork was for much of the nineteenth century, and where slaves were compelled to eat rationed foods, chickens had to be stolen and fried surreptitiously. During the Civil War fried chicken was regarded as a food that kept well and could be sent from home to the soldiers. Thus fried chicken was a food about which freed African Americans felt both ownership and prestige. It was often a dish for Sunday supper. Only in the twentieth century did the mainstream stereotypes about watermelon and fried chicken lead some African Americans to identify these foods with country or backward people, or refuse to eat them at mixed social events.

Since emancipation, economic opportunities for African Americans have varied, but food service has almost always been a possibility, and sometimes the only possibility. For African American males, the railroads provided service employment, including positions as high as head chef. Several railroad chefs went on to write cookbooks, from Rufus Estes at the turn of the twentieth century to Leonard E. Roberts in the 1960s, whose *Negro Chef Cookbook* sold hundreds of thousands of copies, almost entirely in the African American community. The food served was necessarily simplified for the tiny kitchens of dining cars, but eventually railroads competed on the basis of their dinners and invited comparison to fine urban restaurants. African Americans were also chefs in restaurants, even, and perhaps especially, segregated restaurants. African American men were regarded as the masters of all schools of slow-cooked barbecue and were sought-after cooks at wealthy estates and hunting camps.

Free African Americans continued their prewar efforts as street vendors despite increasing immigrant competition. They were identified with Creole breakfast fritters called "callas" in New Orleans, with Nagadoches meat pies in northern Louisiana, with pepper pot soup and peanut brittle in Philadelphia, and with "hot tamales" (fresh and warm, not spicy) all through the southern states. They sold peanuts, pralines, produce, seafood, and groceries door to door.

A Layering of Hungers

Within the African American community, tastes persisted for African foods like yams, black-eyed peas, okra, and guinea hens. But there was also a hunger for foods of slavery times made from pork and cornmeal, as well as for the fancier southern foods, such as peach pie and tea cakes, and for the small game of the South, such as raccoons, opossums, and snapping turtles. Special effort was made for Sunday dinners and church suppers, with competing pies, potato salads, fried chicken, and barbecue. This layering of hungers reflects the zigzag progress of African Americans through Reconstruction, the imposition of segregation, the period of the second Ku Klux Klan with its widespread lynching and race riots, the migrations north and west, the Great Depression, the opportunities of World War II, the civil rights era, and the retreats and advances since.

The African American community was always multicultural, with clear differences between the Gullah-Geechee rice table of the Carolina lowlands and sea islands (harking back perhaps most to Sierre Leone, Senegambia, and Liberia) and the Creole dishes of Louisiana (with more apparent influences from present-day Togo, Benin, and Nigeria). Distinctive mixed-race ethnic groups, such as the Cape Verdean American community of southern Massachusetts, the Cane River Creoles of Louisiana, and the Lumbee Indians of North Carolina, have existed at the edges of black and white America since the American Revolution, or long before. (The 1970 U.S. Census, the only one to survey mixed-race ancestry groups as such, enumerated some two hundred groups of "tri-racial isolates.") Many of these groups identify with specific foods, and some of these foods have spread into neighboring African American or Native American communities.

But the community became even more multicultural with the addition of African Caribbean immigrants in the 1920s. West Indian immigrants, especially in New York City but also in other eastern ports, took prominent social and political roles in the African American community, initially in the Garveyite nationalist movement and the Harlem Renaissance, but also in food service and local politics.

With the civil rights movement, "soul food" became an interest for white liberal cooks, although segregationists in the South had enjoyed a modified version for more than a century. (The term "soul" for essential blackness

Soul Food. Sylvia's, a noted soul food restaurant in Harlem, New York City. *Photograph by Joe Zarba*

THE HERITAGE OF SOUL FOOD

The expression "soul food" is a term grafted from the expression "soul music," which in the 1960s referenced black artists noted for their soulful blues and rhythmic music. The term "soul" was applied also to artists noted for their culinary skills, particularly to field-hand cooks in antebellum America, who performed culinary miracles with foods then thought to be too common for the master's table. These included the South's cheapest staples, such as black-eyed peas, yams or sweet potatoes, collard greens, dandelion greens, turnip greens, chitterlings (the small intestines of hogs), hog maws (the stomach of the hog), ham hocks, trotters (the feet of the hog), hog jowl (the cheek of the hog), cornbread, and so on.

The numerous African American authors who wrote soul food cookbooks in the 1960s (and even in the twenty-first century) invariably listed a wide range of foods, many of which were made from corn, such as cornbread, spoon breads, corn muffins, hot corn cakes, crackling bread, hush puppies, griddlecakes, batter cakes, corn dodgers, corn on the cob, grits, hominy, corn pudding, fried corn, or stuffing for poultry. Other dishes included beaten biscuits, buttermilk biscuits, salmon croquettes, fried oysters, frogs legs, fried shrimp, fried or stewed catfish, codfish balls, crab cakes, conch salad, country-fried chicken, smothered and chicken, chicken and dumplings, chicken salad, and chicken feet soup. Preparations were made from practically all parts of the hog except the squeal—thus fried tripe, barbecued pig feet, fried ham with cream gravy, salt pork and cream gravy, hog's-head cheese, fried or smothered pork chops, neck bones and rice, salt pork and black-eyed peas, fried spareribs, spareribs and lima beans, ham hocks and beans, ham hocks and turnip greens, pig snouts, and pig tails. The list goes on with peanut cookies, tea cakes, fried or smothered steak, hamburger meat pie with red bean sauce, beef and rutabaga, beef gumbo, pot roast of beef, short ribs of beef, candied yams, fried sweet potato cakes, apple fritters, rice custards, sweet potato pie, lemon meringue pies, chess pie, pecan pie, egg custard pies, molasses pies, fried fruit pies, old-fashioned pound cakes, bourbon pecan cakes, coconut cakes, marble cakes, hash brown potatoes, fried green tomatoes, baked corn and tomatoes, baked eggplant, butter beans, succotash, fried grits, jambalaya, hoppin' John, smothered cabbage, okra gumbo, brussels sprouts, okra and tomato soup, and oxtail soup.

Because African Americans played such a prominent role as the cook-practitioners of the South, interpreting and imposing their preferences in the kitchen on their own and other people's foodways, it is reasonable to view the boundaries between soul food and so-called southern food as extremely blurred; and one is most cautious in saying, if one must, that "'soul food' is more a determinant based on who cooked it than what was cooked."

HOWARD PAIGE

seems to date from the 1930s, whereas printed references to soul food date from 1964, although the term was probably used in conversation earlier.)

Within the African American community, pan-Africanism renewed the old yearning for the sense of homeland. The ethnic revival of the 1980s, set off in part by the television miniseries *Roots*, inspired all Americans to search out the foods of their ancestors, and many African American families produced a West African peanut-chicken stew for school events. In the 1990s a more sophisticated feeling for the African diaspora developed, and many families added Caribbean or Brazilian foods, or found jerk chicken or Dominican fried chicken or Trinidadian roti in restaurants catering to African Caribbean immigrants. Large immigrant communities from Nigeria, Ethiopia, Eritrea, Egypt, Haiti, the Dominican Republic, Cuba, Honduras, and Guyana have also enriched the common pot, the church buffet, the school potluck, the restaurant table, and urban street food. Urban markets now sell goat meat and Caribbean seafoods as well as tropical roots, plantains, African cowpeas, and prepared Jamaican meat pies. The pan-Africanist holiday of Kwanzaa has become widely popular, with its New Year's Eve feast incorporating African and diaspora dishes.

Another phenomenon within the African American community since the 1970s has been an interest in dietary reform. This might be traced to the unusual food rules of the Nation of Islam (which add to orthodox Islam strictures against fried food, hot bread, most cornbread, and piecrust), or to the fasting and vegetarian diets promoted by the comedian and civil rights activist Dick Gregory. A much wider circle more casually rejects pork, and urban barbecue establishments in African American neighborhoods generally offer beef ribs as an alternative to pork ribs. In addition, wide publicity of diet-related health problems has led to a general effort from chefs and homemakers at substituting smoked turkey for bacon as a flavoring in many dishes and at reducing sugar and salt in traditional soul food.

Some African American foods march on without African American cooks. The African kola nut remains the key flavoring in American soft drinks enjoyed by all Americans and marketed around the globe. African-style soups thickened with peanuts were served by slave cooks to George Washington and other early Americans but are now made most often by white colonial reenactors.

[*See also* Appalachian Food; Aunt Jemima; Barbecue; Caribbean Influences on American Food; Carver, George Washington; Chesapeake Bay; Communal Gatherings; Dining Car; Kwanzaa; Muslim Dietary Laws; Rastus; Rice; Southern Regional Cookery; Street Vendors; Train Food; Uncle Ben.]

BIBLIOGRAPHY

Du Bois, W. E. B. *The Philadelphia Negro: A Social Study*. New York: Lippincott, 1899. Online at http://www2.pfeiffer.edu /~lridener/DSS/DuBois/pnchiv.html. Chapter 4 discusses the role of caterers in the early nineteenth century. Later chapters discuss the status of Negro servants and culinary workers in the 1890s.

Jacobs, Donald M., ed. *Courage and Conscience: Black and White Abolitionists in Boston*. Bloomington: Indiana University Press, 1993.

Roberts, Leonard E. *The Negro Chef Cookbook*. New York: Vantage, 1969.

Roberts, Robert. *The House Servant's Directory*. Boston: Munroe and Francis, 1827. Facsimile, Waltham, MA: Gore Place Society, 1977.

MARK H. ZANGER

Airplane Food

United Airlines, a pioneer in the industry, was the only airline to serve meals on trays from the beginning of commercial aviation. While other airlines had copilots passing out sandwiches to passengers, United employed uniformed stewardesses to serve cold chicken. Many airplane travelers in the early days of the aviation industry's food service complained of how often chicken was served; American Airlines was even nicknamed "the fried chicken airline." Passengers derided chicken as a cheap food option; industry professionals found that chicken's versatility responded well to the demands of in-flight food service.

By 1936, American Airlines stewardesses were filling service trays with food from very large thermoses containing hot food prepared in advance, usually by the airport café—and offering real dishware and flatware to boot. Food would stay hot in the containers for about one to two hours, with no need for reheating. The thermoses approach was succeeded by a system of using large casseroles, which provided the advantage of loading meals already plated and hot. Food often stayed heated for many hours with this system; however, food quality suffered, along with menu choices. Then, around 1945, Pan American worked together with Clarence Birdseye and the Maxson Company to create the convection oven, which would allow frozen foods to be heated on board the aircraft. Maxson called the first convection oven it designed the Whirlwind Oven: it had a heating element in front of a fan and held six meals. Soon afterward, the microwave oven was developed; it has since become the industry standard in aircraft food service preparation.

The first meal trays were served on pillows on passengers' laps, until trays had been developed with lids that would serve to elevate the food in front of the passengers. Finally, foldout service trays were installed in the seat backs. The three-course meal that has become the standard for airplane food trays grew out of the creation by United Airlines in 1937 of the first functional airplane kitchen, conceived in an effort to improve the quality of food offered during flight. United brought in managers and chefs from hotels to redesign their food service. Don Magarrell, one such hotel manager hired by United, began to supervise the preparation of gourmet meals in the airline's kitchen facilities on the ground and is responsible for the design of the standard three-course airline meal, a design devised to comport with the dimensions of the meal trays:

> In the center of [Magarrell's] twenty-four-by-thirty-inch mock-up was a twelve-inch depression—that was for the main dish. Laid on at the right were coffee, cream, and sugar. Salad in a paper cup took the upper center, dessert the upper left corner, and appetizer the upper right, and there were little holes for salt and pepper shakers. What then emerged from the atelier of Industrial Designers, Incorporated, was a flat, rigid artifact of pressed pulp, light and disposable, but strong enough to hold things in place in choppy air. A cunningly shaped cover, in matching white with blue and buff stripes, fitted over it. (Solberg, *Conquest of the Skies*, p. 220)

The first successful frozen three-course meal fitting the tray's specifications—consisting of meat, potatoes, and vegetables—was marketed by the Maxson Company; the meals were sold to Pan American Airways in 1946.

As the twentieth century progressed, two elements affected the continuing development of airplane food: America became more tolerant of a diversity of eating habits, and a greater diversity of people began using airplanes as a means of travel. To respond to these trends, airlines began offering a greater variety of types of meals that responded to religious, ethnic, or health requirements with respect to food. As of 1995, a trade journal reported that American Airlines offered all of these food options for their in-flight service: "children's meal . . . bland/soft (suitable for those with ulcers); diabetic; gluten-free (no wheat, rye, barley, oats, which people with celiac disease cannot digest); low calorie; lactose-free (no milk products); low carbohydrate; low fat and low cholesterol; low sodium; Moslem; Hindu; Kosher; vegetarian; and strict vegetarian (excludes milk products and eggs)" (cited in Gottdeiner, *Life in the Air*, p. 103).

During the late 1990s and early 2000s, airlines began doing away with meal service on their flights so as to reduce the price of their tickets; some offered cold meals in packs that passengers picked out of coolers as they boarded the aircraft. Passengers grumbled at the bag of peanuts or pretzels served as a snack in place of a real meal, but the market for cheaper tickets remained strong. Many passengers began bringing food on board, most often from the fast food restaurants in airports. Now a few discount airlines sell meals to passengers on board their flights. The sale of airplane meals for profit is perhaps one of the most significant changes in the history of airplane food.

[*See also* Birdseye, Clarence.]

BIBLIOGRAPHY

Fairechild, Diana. *Jetsmart*. Berkeley, CA: Celestial Arts, 1992.

Gottdeiner, Mark. *Life in the Air: Surviving the New Culture of Air Travel*. Lanham, MD: Rowman and Littlefield, 2001.

Haynes, Karla, ed. *Sky Chefs: From the Beginning*. Arlington, TX: Sky Chefs, 1992.

McCool, Audrey C., Fred A. Smith, and David L. Tucker. *Dimensions of Noncommercial Foodservice Management*. New York: Van Nostrand Reinhold, 1994.

McCool, Audrey C. *Inflight Catering Management*. New York: Wiley, 1995.

Parrott, Philip J. *The History of Inflight Food Service*. Miami Springs, FL: International Publishing Company, 1986.

Solberg, Carl. *Conquest of the Skies: A History of Commercial Aviation in America*. Boston: Little, Brown, 1979.

LYNN MARIE HOUSTON

Alaska

A line of salmon tails sticking out of the dirt is an appetizing sight to an Alaskan, especially if the tails come off easily in his hand. This means the fish have ripened into an enigmatic dish known as "stink fish," eaten raw. The line of tails is the fast food version of the dish. The more time-consuming version, meant to be harvested months later, is a cache pit, lined with wild celery leaves and then filled with salmon or salmon heads. Beauty is in the tastebuds of the eater, or, as Cervantes put it in *Don Quixote*, "Hunger is the best sauce." A whale grounded on the beach meant good eating to early Alaskans.

Finding food is crucial to survival. Thus, in prehistoric Alaska, villages or seasonal camping spots were often named after resources. For example, the Taku River derives its name from the Tlingit word meaning "where geese gather." The Athabascan village of Telida gets its name from the fall run of whitefish or *telia*; *Telia-da* means "place of whitefish."

Fifteen to forty thousand years ago, Asian people walked across a land bridge to the place later called "Alaska." Their long migration was a natural extension of their following herds of grazing mammals, which they ate. Those who made Alaska their permanent home gradually evolved into separate cultures. They became the four major anthropological groups of the state: Eskimos, Aleuts, Athabascans, and Northwest Coast Indians (Tlingit, Haida, and Tsimshian, fishermen of the coast and hunters of the rain forest).

Until Russian and European explorers made contact in the 1700s, Alaskan natives ate what was at hand. Eskimos chowed down on bowhead whale, walrus, and seal, along with seabird eggs. Aleuts searched tide pools for shellfish, octopus, and seaweed; they speared seals from kayaks and downed birds with arrows. Athabascans dined on moose, caribou, bear, beaver, muskrat, geese, ducks, and fish. Tlingit, Haida, and Tsimshian consumed steelhead, salmon, herring, halibut, and venison. Menus were seasonal, depending on the migration of caribou, the nesting of birds, and the spawning of fish.

Greens and edible roots supplemented meals. Depending on the habitat, natives enjoyed greens like rosewort, beach asparagus, goosetongue (*Plantago maritima*), pink plume (*Polygonum bistorta*), and king's crown (*Sedum rosea*). They brewed hot drinks from evergreen shrubs, such as Labrador tea (*Ledum* species). Food was eaten raw, frozen, fermented, smoked, dried, or boiled. Hundreds of variations are possible by combining methods. Half-dried salmon, for example, is an Aluutiq dish; salmon is simmered with wild onions before it is ready to store.

Clay cooking pots were known to only a few Eskimo groups; most Alaskans roasted their food on spits or boiled it in baskets. Cooking baskets were woven of split spruce roots; those roots swell when wet, making the baskets watertight. Rocks heated in the fire were added and the contents stirred until the food was done. Tongs removed cooled rocks and added new, hot ones.

Preservation of food for the lean months of winter was paramount. Food was dried or smoked; if that was impossible, blubber or whale roasts were frozen in "ice cellars," holes dug in the permafrost. The Tlingit packed berries into wooden forms to make "bricks," and strung dried clams on willow withes. The Tsimshian preserved wild crab apples in the rendered fat of eulachon or candlefish. Sealskins were hollowed out like gourds to form "pokes," skin bottles in which willow leaves or small birds were stored with oil, which tenderized them. At Barrow during winter months, one can still see haunches of caribou perched frozen on the roof, safe from dogs, and mallards hanging by their necks from front-porch railings.

Celebrations meant Eskimo ice cream or *aguduk*. The Eskimo cook whips seal oil until it is creamy and then folds in freshly fallen snow and tundra roots. The Athabascan version is whipped caribou-leg marrow, cooked meat flakes, and berries. Aguduk was served on festive occasions, such as a young man's first successful polar bear hunt or a wedding. Oil from hooligan, seal, or whale was a diet staple, used to soften dried foods and add vitamins, along with a taste something like that of anchovy dip.

Russian fur hunters and settlers introduced new foods— barley, rice, buckwheat, Chinese tea, and flour—as well as a new kitchen tool, the oven. The Aleuts quickly mastered piecrust and began baking *pirog*, a "fish pie" of salmon, hard-boiled eggs, rice, and onion, enclosed in pastry. The Russians also introduced rudimentary agriculture, with crops like cabbage, radishes, turnips, and potatoes. Walrus stew slowly changed from a simple pot of meat and broth to something complicated, with potatoes and macaroni.

After the United States purchased Alaska in 1867, paddle wheelers began regular journeys up great inland rivers with supplies like dried beans, sugar, oranges, apples, and canned milk. Gold rush prospectors survived mostly on beans and biscuits, often cooked by novices. The author Rex Beach, on a trip to Candle near Nome, where gold was discovered in 1901, wrote in his autobiography *Personal Exposures* (1940), "If the weather wasn't bad it promised to become so and we talked about little else except that, and indigestion."

To avoid the curse of underdone beans along the gold rush trail, portable soup became the savior of the hour. Beans and bear grease were stewed to tenderness on the stove; then the kettle was allowed to freeze. Next, the soup was dumped from the pot in a lump and stored in a burlap sack. When dinner was needed an ax was applied to the lump, and a few chunks were thawed and heated.

Holidays were celebrated with feasts of roast ptarmigan, sourdough bread, canned pineapple, plum duff, and spaghetti concocted of moose rump roast, goose grease, and dried soup vegetables. Prospectors who lingered to become settlers learned to adapt local ingredients to recipes of the lower forty-eight states. They made ketchup with currants or cranberries, piecrust with black-bear lard, butter with caribou marrow, and mincemeat with moose. Alaskan cuisine continues to evolve, but it is easy to glimpse its roots when a friend brews rose hips with whole cloves for tea, or when mason jars of hooligan oil sit side by side with beadwork on bazaar tables.

[*See also* Russian American Food.]

BIBLIOGRAPHY

Beck, Mary Giraudo. *Potlatch: Native Ceremony and Myth on the Northwest Coast.* Anchorage, AK: Alaska Northwest Books, 1993.
Chandonnet, Ann. *The Alaska Heritage Seafood Cookbook.* Anchorage, AK: Alaska Northwest Books, 1995.
Emmons, George T. *The Tlingit Indians.* Seattle, WA: University of Washington Press, 1991.
Kari, Priscilla Russell. *Tanaina Plantlore, Dena'ina K'et'una: An Ethnobotany of the Dena'ina Indians of Southcentral Alaska.* Fairbanks, AK: Alaska Native Language Center, 1987.
Nelson, Edward William. *The Eskimo about Bering Strait.* Washington, DC: Smithsonian Institution, 1983.
Qawalangin Tribe of Unalaska. *Unalaaskam Qaqagan Qasudaa, "Good Unalaska Food" Cookbook.* Unalaska, AK, 1998.
Paul, Frances Lackey. *Kahtahah.* Rev. ed. Anchorage, AK: Alaska Northwest Books, 1996.
Wallis, Velma. *Two Old Women.* Fairbanks, AK: Epicenter Press, 1993.
Wilder, Edna. *Once Upon an Eskimo Time.* Anchorage, AK: Alaska Northwest Books, 1987.

ANN CHANDONNET

Alcohol and Teetotalism

At the time of European exploration and settlement of the United States, Native Americans had few alcoholic beverages and drank fresh water, herb tea, *sofkee* (hominy porridge), and soup. (Caribbean natives knew how to grow and ferment the juice of pineapples, and there may have been a little weak corn beer in what are now the southwestern states.) The native beverages surprised the Europeans, who at home and on ship drank ale, wine, or (regionally) cider with every meal—men, women, children, and babies. In Europe most urban water sources were dangerously polluted, and people who drank plain water became ill.

Alcoholism is hard to describe in a society in which everyone drinks all the time, every day. But the colonies had laws against public drunkenness and quickly attempted to pass laws about trading liquor to the Indians. The latter were notoriously unsuccessful, and the Indians seemed to get drunker faster than colonists did, whether this was due to a genetic difference in metabolizing alcohol or a lack of cultural experience with drugs other than tobacco and yaupon.

Among themselves, the early colonists fined public drunks and sometimes put them in the stocks or had them whipped. The definition of a drunk sharpened in Plymouth in 1646 to "a person that lisps or falters in his speech by reason of overmuch drink, or that staggers in his going or that vomits by reason of excessive drinking, or that cannot follow his calling," as noted in *The Times of Their Lives: Life, Love, and Death in Plymouth Colony* by James Deetz and Patricia Scott Deetz (2000).

The phrase "that cannot follow his calling" shows the difficulty in the precarious colonial economy of disciplining every infraction. Indeed, Deetz and Deetz point out several cases of convicted drinkers who subsequently held important offices in the colonies and note that because colonial governments in the seventeenth century also depended on the income of liquor regulation, they were less apt to prosecute offenders.

Alcoholic beverages took different forms in the New World. Apple trees were more reliable than barley was, so cider replaced beer for many American families. Drinks were also brewed from molasses, maple syrup, and corn.

Eighteenth-Century Drinking and Temperance

Problems with alcohol increased in the eighteenth century, as inexpensive spirits became more common in commerce. Rum was produced for trade in Boston and Philadelphia. Pennsylvania Dutch and Scotch-Irish immigrants put their brewing and distilling know-how to American corn and rye, creating the first American whiskeys.

While the American colonies did not often see the widespread alcoholism of Hogarth's London, there were enough problems to produce the first American temperance movements toward the end of the century. In some cases these were branches of temperate British denominations, such as the Methodists, but a nondenominational temperance movement began around the time of the American Revolution, with a 1788 convention that suggested using only beer and cider, under the slogan "Despise Spiritous Liquors as Anti-Federal." People who did not want to use fermented beverages at all could drink water, tea, coffee, sweet cider in season, diluted fruit vinegars, and milk—more popular in the colonies than in England or even Holland. Sweet cider is mentioned as a substitute for wine in mince pie in *American Cookery* by Amelia Simmons (1795), suggesting that this temperance movement recipe was already in use. Alcohol was an important preservative in mincemeat, and sweet cider would not have been used except as an effort at temperance.

In the Early American period temperance became associated with a series of reform issues that also included abolition of slavery, women's suffrage, public education, healthier food, and religious revival. One might specifically give up rum, because sugar was harvested by slaves. Or one might, like Sylvester Graham and the Alcott family, give up leavened bread, because yeast produces alcohol in the action of "putrefaction."

It is significant that almost all of the new religious denominations that began in America took up aspects of temperance or dietary reform: Seventh-Day Adventism and the Mormon Church, both founded in Early American times, avoid alcoholic beverages and caffeinated drinks. The Shakers, who appeared during this period, experimented with vegetarianism and temperance, sometimes dividing into dining tables of vegetarians versus meat eaters. Christian Science, drawing on Adventist ideas of health food, discourages alcohol, and some Scientists also avoid caffeine, although Peet's coffee is served in the café in the Boston Mother Church complex. (Mary Baker Eddy had been a temperance lecturer before founding Christian Science, although she observed of the many health food regimens of the nineteenth century that the experimenters were often ill.)

By the 1840s Catharine Esther Beecher knew of three schools of temperance:

> One class consider it to be a sin *in itself*, to take anything that contains the intoxicating principle. Another class . . . engage not to use intoxicating

drinks *as a beverage*. . . [and] to *avoid the appearance of evil*, they will not employ it in *cooking*, nor keep it in their houses. The third class . . . think it proper to use wine and brandy in cooking, and occasionally for medicinal purposes, and suppose that the cause of temperance will be best promoted by going no farther. (Beecher, *Mrs. Beecher's Receipt-Book*)

Beecher put herself in the third group. In her cookbook she produces the first nonalcoholic, noncaffeinated recipes for children, indeed some of the first published recipes designated for children in America.

Mrs. Horace Mann probably would have classed herself with Beecher, judging by Mann's recipe for "Innocent Plum Pudding," which has cooked-in wine, but none of the usual brandy sauce, according to Mann's *Christianity in the Kitchen: A Physiological Cook Book* (1857). Although prohibition was enacted in a few states for short periods of time before the Civil War, early temperance was a matter of individual conscience.

Given that early American cookbooks use wine and spirits in almost every recipe, including cakes and cookies, it is possible to follow the idea of temperance when sweet cider or vinegar is included as a substitution in mincemeat, syllabub, cakes, or summer drinks. Baking powder was promoted by some temperance enthusiasts as a replacement for demon yeast in breads and cakes. Temperate travelers or students could stay at Grahamite boardinghouses and hotels, which were both vegetarian and yeast free. Dr. R. W. Trall was the Julia Child of later temperance cooks with his *New Hydropathic Cookbook*, published and republished from 1854 through the 1870s. Trall's lacto-ovo vegetarianism would not be out of place in the twenty-first century; he rejected chemical baking powders, brought back yeast for breads, and gave recipes for pie crust and Christmas pudding without alcohol or suet, substituting cream.

Historical statistics suggest a spike in alcohol consumption around 1860, with levels of consumption not reached again until the period from 1906 to 1915. After the Civil War the reform coalitions began to diverge, but temperance and women's rights were still strongly connected. A wave of direct attacks on saloons in the early 1870s relaunched temperance as a militant movement. The Women's Christian Temperance Union, founded in 1874, pressed not only for temperance but also for prohibition, as well as women's suffrage, and reached out to rural and religious women. Mrs. Annie Wittenmyer, who

had written a cookbook for Civil War hospitals, was an early leader. One of the few prominent female "wets" was the labor leader Mary "Mother" Jones.

Prohibition was a women's issue that made men nervous in the 1870s, as shown by the widespread public mockery of Mrs. Rutherford B. Hayes as "Lemonade Lucy" after she banned liquor from White House receptions. By 1890 the temperance position was respectable enough for a temperance punch to be included in *Statesmen's Dishes and How to Cook Them*, a recipe book putatively edited by Mrs. Benjamin Harrison. The movement began to focus on beverages, and toward the end of the nineteenth century there are fewer recipes for temperance cake and more for temperance punch and unfermented grape juice—the communion wine of dry denominations, promoted by Thomas Welch of Vineland, New Jersey.

It is also in the last quarter of the nineteenth century that the British term "teetotaler" (coined in the 1830s) entered American discourse. Early American temperance advocates had often opposed stimulating beverages as well.

Twentieth-Century Prohibition and Repeal

The emphasis on individual and family temperance became political in the early 1900s with the collection of tens of thousands of circulating pledge cards on which young people signed an oath never to drink. The numbers of these pledge cards were communicated to politicians, and candidates found themselves polarized between "wets" and "dries." Among the wets were working-class immigrants, especially German and Irish Americans for whom the saloon or pub was a community institution.

National prohibition did not take effect until 1919 and was repealed in 1933. "Near beer" with .5 percent alcohol was permitted, as was home brewing and limited commercial wine making for religious use. Prohibition also marked the introduction of oversalted cooking wine. Cookbooks of the 1920s have alcohol-free recipes for drinks, often with a winking reference to how much wine or bourbon had been used in former times. Illegal imported liquor turned American tastes to blended Scotch and Canadian whiskeys. Cocktails, blending often crude spirits with wines, juices, and flavorings, proliferated and remained part of American taste through the 1960s. Many local breweries never reopened after Prohibition, and numerous American vineyards were replanted with fruit trees. American wines did not again become nationally popular until the 1970s. This was followed by a revival of craft brewing in the mid-1980s and a revival of retro-cocktail drinking in the 1990s.

Some localities retained prohibition after 1932. But most anti-alcohol activism since has used the individual-recovery model of Alcoholics Anonymous (founded in 1935). Contemporary recipes in which the usual alcohol has been removed—mostly for faux cocktails—can be found in cookbooks published by those religious denominations that do not use alcohol. The failure of Prohibition and the hardships of the Depression and World War II produced a tacit pro-alcohol culture in the 1950s and 1960s, with many cookbooks published on how to use wine and spirits in every course and manuals entirely on how to mix drinks. Suburban homes included a bar in the basement, so one could have a kind of saloon in one's own home. Government statistics suggest a spike in alcohol consumption in 1946, with a general rise through the 1950s and 1960s to unprecedented levels in the 1970s and 1980s.

Political opposition to alcohol revived in the 1990s with movements for more severe punishments for drunk driving, but the liquor industry countered with widely supported "designated driver" programs and warnings to "drink responsibly." There has been some overall decline in alcohol consumption by Americans age fourteen and over since 1992. Some surveys indicate that about one-fourth of all American adults are lifelong abstainers, 60 percent drink at times, and between 5 and 20 percent are binge drinkers or alcoholics. Youth surveys are less reliable, but there is some evidence that by the early 2000s Americans were starting to drink at a younger age.

The identity politics of the 1970s led to focused anti-alcohol programs on Native American reservations, and the Islamic strictures against alcohol were and are part of the prestige of Islam and the American Nation of Islam in the African American community. African American churches have criticized the number of billboards advertising alcoholic beverages in minority areas. Scientific backing for the moderate use of wine as protection against heart disease has reversed the nineteenth-century health dictates of Graham and Trall, who would be surprised by the range of organic wines and beers sold in health food supermarkets.

[See also Alcoholism; Beecher, Catharine; Graham, Sylvester; Prohibition; Temperance.]

BIBLIOGRAPHY

Oliver, Sandra L. *Saltwater Foodways*. Mystic, CT: Mystic Seaport Museum, 1995. Based on the records of actual inhabitants of historic buildings relocated to the museum, two of whose families were temperance activists in the 1840s and 1850s.

Zanger, Mark H. *The American History Cookbook*. Bridgeport, CT: Greenwood, 2003. Chapter on temperance recipes from 1837 to 1931, with emphasis on Early American nonalcoholic substitutions. (This book was originally commissioned for school libraries.)

MARK H. ZANGER

Alcoholism

Alcoholism, also known as Alcohol Dependence Syndrome, is a general term describing many types of alcohol abuse and alcohol dependence. The National Council on Alcohol and Drug Dependence defines alcoholism as a "chronic disease . . . characterized by a continuous or periodic impaired control over drinking, preoccupation with the drug alcohol, use of alcohol despite adverse consequences, and distortions in thinking, most notably denial." Other authorities contend that alcoholism is not actually a disease, but rather a symptom of other physical and psychological disorders. Despite moral, medical, or philosophical disagreements about the problem, alcoholism is understood to be an individual's compulsive craving for and overconsumption of alcohol.

Both the recognition and condemnation of alcoholism date back through thousands of years of recorded history. Though most cultures around the world used alcohol for recreation, religious ceremony, and medicine, virtually all created taboos against its overuse and dependency. Ancient Greek, Hebrew, and early Christian writings celebrated the role of wine in sacred worship, while consistently warning against the evils of the overindulgence in alcohol. In his Analects, Confucius even spoke about "trouble with alcohol." Throughout world history, each culture defined its own acceptable parameters for alcohol consumption and devised sanctions against chronic or excessive drunkenness. Nevertheless, some individuals in almost every society continued to habitually abuse alcohol, despite ridicule, punishment, and deteriorating health. The excessive drinking of gin became so rampant in England that Parliament in 1751 imposed exorbitant taxes on all hard liquor to stem consumption.

In early America, Protestant religious groups often stressed sobriety, usually allowing moderate alcohol use, but meting out harsh punishments for those who remained persistently drunk. Puritan New Englanders condemned chronic alcohol abuse both as a moral evil itself, and even more practically as an economic burden on the resources of their community. Puritans prized productivity and personal virtue and often severely punished chronic drunkards who could not work to provide for themselves or their families. Over the years, controversy over appropriate alcohol use continued in American society, frequently pitting newly arrived Catholic immigrants against native-born Protestant groups, who differed in their definitions of what constituted alcohol abuse. In essence, alcoholism was often culturally defined, with one group's idea of chronic drunkenness simply being another's idea of recreation. Social and political movements continued to attack excessive drinking throughout the late eighteenth and early nineteenth centuries, eventually culminating in an unsuccessful national prohibition of alcohol from 1920 to 1933.

Despite varying cultural perspectives, the concept of alcoholism—that some members of every society just could not control their drinking—was clearly understood for thousands of years. Alcoholism became only formally identified as a serious health problem in the late nineteenth century, as physicians scientifically defined categories of diseases and dysfunction. In an 1879 study, H. Maudley first described "alcoholic insanity," "chronic alcoholism," and "dipsomania," which he defined as "well-marked mental degradation, if not actual mental derangement which shows itself in a fierce morbid craving for alcoholic stimulants and is greatly aggravated by indulgence." Debates raged throughout the twentieth century about the possible physiological or psychological roots of alcoholism; whether alcoholism was a single problem or, rather, numerous disassociated problems. All of these same controversies still exist in the early 2000s, but a notable consensus quickly formed around E. M. Jellinek's 1960 study, *The Disease Concept of Alcoholism.* In this study, Jellinek identifies five categories of alcoholics, each with their own unique physiological origins, patterns of drinking, and adverse health effects. Most important, Jellinek's work reinforced both the medical diagnosis and the popular understanding that alcoholism was a real physical and psychological problem, or disease, instead of an avoidable moral failing. Other medical and psychological research continues, however, which advances still more differing theories about the nature and manifestations of alcoholism, with many studies focusing on the role of genetic predisposition.

Treatment for alcoholism is as varied as the theories explaining it. Severely addicted alcoholics experience intense and often dangerous withdrawal symptoms when detoxified. Treatment often includes a month-long hospital stay. Physicians prescribe drugs to alcoholics that either deter the craving for alcohol or cause unpleasant physical effects, such as nausea, when alcohol is consumed. In the late twentieth century, physicians began to use a variety of new antidepressant medications to treat underlying chemical imbalances in the brain that may cause the alcoholic to drink. The clinical assumption behind this course of treatment adheres to the argument that alcoholism is more symptomatic of other ills than a disease in itself.

By far the most popular treatment program for alcoholism is Alcoholics Anonymous. Self-described as a worldwide fellowship of men and women who help each other to stay sober, it is a mutual help program for recovering alcoholics. Alcoholics Anonymous was founded in 1935 by the stockbroker and alcoholic Bill Wilson. Wilson envisioned a network of small support groups to aid other alcoholics. Today, over 100,000 of these groups meet worldwide. Laying out a twelve-step recovery program, Alcoholics Anonymous stresses the importance of taking responsibility for past behavior, staying anchored in the reality of the present moment, and relying both on other alcoholics and a spiritual "higher power" to achieve continued sobriety. While among the first to acknowledge the disease nature of alcoholism, Alcoholics Anonymous places its emphasis on member spirituality and self-determination rather than on medical solutions.

Alcoholism remains a pervasive and expensive problem in the United States. The National Institute on Alcohol Abuse and Alcoholism says that alcohol abuse costs about $166.5 billion each year. Research continues in an effort to discover the sources of alcoholism and to find ways to minimize problem drinking. Despite now being securely defined medically as a disease, alcoholism still carries with it a stigma of immorality, deviance, or character flaw.

[*See also* Alcohol and Teetotalism; Prohibition; Temperance.]

BIBLIOGRAPHY

Dodes, Lance M. *The Heart of Addiction: A New Approach to Understanding and Managing Alcoholism and Other Addictive Behaviors.* New York: HarperCollins, 2002.

Edwards, Griffith. *Alcohol: The World's Favorite Drug.* New York: St. Martin's, 2002.

Harrison, Larry, ed. *Alcohol Problems in the Community.* New York: Routledge, 1996.

Hartigan, Frances. *Bill W: A Biography of Alcoholics Anonymous Cofounder Bill Wilson.* New York: Thomas Dunne/St. Martin's, 2000.

Jung, John. *Psychology of Alcohol and Other Drugs: A Research Perspective.* Thousand Oaks, CA: Sage, 2001.

Lender, Mark Edward, and James Kirby Martin. *Drinking in America: A History.* Rev. ed. New York: Free Press, 1987.

Milam, James Robert, and Katherine Ketcham. *Under the Influence: A Guide to the Myths and Realities of Alcoholism.* Seattle: Madrona Publishers, 1981.

Olson, Nancy. *With a Lot of Help from Our Friends: The Politics of Alcoholism.* Lincoln, NE: Writers Club Press, 2003.

DAVID GERARD HOGAN

Ale Slipper

The ale slipper, also known as an ale boot, or less commonly an ale shoe, is a boot-shaped vessel with a pouring spout, a handle, and sometimes a hinged cover that is used to heat beverages in hot coals. Ale slippers are made of tin-lined copper, tin, or cast iron and were in use in the British Isles by the sixteenth century. They came to the New World with early colonists and were used to heat mulled wine, ale, and cider, as well as caudles, possets, and gruels. Ingredients were combined in the ale slipper and then the toe was pushed into glowing embers. The heated drink was poured into a mug or cup before being consumed.

Ale slippers were common equipment in taverns and possibly in homes. Nineteenth-century American cookbooks indicate that the same hot ale preparations were being prepared at home, but in "pots," suggesting that the ale slipper had become obsolete as the fireplace gave way to the cookstove.

[*See also* Cider; Hearth Cookery; Pots and Pans.]

BIBLIOGRAPHY

Franklin, Linda Campbell. *From Hearth to Cookstove.* 5th ed. Iola, WI: K. P. Krause, 2003.

Seymour, John. *Forgotten Household Crafts: A Portrait of the Way We Once Lived.* New York: Knopf, 1987.

ROBERT SIMMONS

Almonds

The almond (*Prunus amygdalus*) is botanically related to the cherry, peach, plum, and apricot. It probably originated in Asia Minor and has been consumed since prehistoric times. Almonds were particularly important during the Middle Ages; at that time, marzipan, a sweet almond-paste confection, was introduced by Arabs into Western Europe. Recipes using almonds appear in Medieval English cookery manuscripts. Almonds were first planted in coastal California by Franciscan missionaries in the eighteenth century, but the growing conditions were not suitable. In the 1850s, almond trees were successfully cultivated in California's Central Valley.

Almonds are the most important and the most versatile of all tree nuts and have the largest share of the world's tree nut trade. In addition to being a popular and nutritious snack, almonds are used for making flavorings, macaroons, marzipan, salads, baked goods, and confections, such as coconut-almond and chocolate-almond candy bars. All commercial American almonds are grown in California, which also supplies more than 70 percent of all the almonds consumed in the world.

[*See also* California; Candy Bars and Candy; Nuts.]

ANDREW F. SMITH

American Chop Suey

American food culture was formed in an environment that was resource-rich and labor-poor. There has always been a premium on one-pot sautés or quick stews, and these have sometimes acquired fanciful names like

PRINCE PREPARED FOODS

Hurry-up days usually mean hurry-up meals! That's why Prince offers you a variety of heat-and-serve dishes that can be ready to enjoy in minutes. Pick your happy heat-and-eat choices for buon appetito: Square Spaghetti in Sauce, Rigatoni in Sauce, Meat Ravioli in Sauce, Cheese Ravioli in Sauce, Shells in Sauce, and Prince's newest triumph, American Chop Suey — an appetizing blend of beef, macaroni, tomato, celery, and green pepper, gently seasoned.

American Chop Suey. One of a line of "happy heat-and-eat choices for buon appetito" from *Prince Treasury of Italian Recipes,* 1960s. *Collection of Mark H. Zanger*

slumgullion (perhaps from Salmagundi), or mulligan stew (perhaps from slumgullion), or Finnish American *mojaka* (perhaps from mulligan stew). In old New England, a random collection of smothered meat and potatoes was known as potato bargain or necessity mess. A quasi-Italian casserole from Columbus, Ohio, spread across the country as Johnny Mazzetti with numerous variations. During the Great Depression, the names of foreign mixed dishes, such as goulash, hodgepodge (perhaps from *hachepôt*), or chop suey, were applied to quick assortments of meat, vegetables, and potatoes, and sometimes even to desserts with mixed ingredients.

American chop suey, however, eventually became somewhat standardized, especially in institutional catering, as a stew or casserole of beef, celery, and macaroni—none of which seems especially Chinese. Chinese restaurant chop suey was itself a poorly defined American invention and basically another mixed stew. A likely origin for American chop suey is the recipe for Chop Suey Stew in the 1916 *Manual for Army Cooks,* an urtext for many institutional foods of the twentieth century. The army recipe could be made with either beef round or pork shoulder, beef stock, barbecue sauce, and salt. By 1932, the Navy's cookbook had added cabbage and green peppers. *Practical Home Economics* (1919) has a recipe entitled Chop Suey that adds tomatoes and parsley and omits the onions and cabbage.

All these early recipes leave out soy sauce, but suggest serving the stew over rice. More recent recipes simplify the service by dropping the rice and mixing in cooked macaroni, but they tend to restore some amount of soy sauce unless using Italian tomato sauce. As distinct from Chinese restaurant chop suey, American chop suey in the early twenty-first century is usually made with beef instead of pork; the vegetables are usually restricted to celery and onions; and macaroni often replaces rice.

MARK H. ZANGER

Amusement Parks

The roots of today's amusement parks date back to the 1500s, when so-called pleasure gardens began opening on the outskirts of major European cities. In addition to primitive rides, these gardens featured shows, fireworks, and numerous concession stands selling food and novelties. While there is little written about the food that the pleasure gardens served, most likely it was simple to store and to prepare and easy for customers to consume while walking around enjoying the other attractions. These traits continue to guide amusement park food choices to this day.

As America became increasingly urbanized in the mid-1800s, people began clamoring for ways to escape the crowded, dirty conditions that characterized cities of the time. Entrepreneurs responded by opening American versions of the European pleasure gardens. These amusement parks tended to develop in two major forms: seaside resorts and picnic parks. Seaside resorts were best embodied by Coney Island in Brooklyn, New York, which was the heart and soul of the amusement park industry during the late 1800s and early 1900s and featured three major amusement parks and dozens of smaller attractions.

According to legend, Charles Feltman invented the hot dog, a staple of amusement park food, at Coney Island in 1867. Feltman went on to open a large, elaborate restaurant at the resort, ceding the hot dog business to other concessionaires—including Nathan Handwerker, who opened Nathan's at Coney Island in 1916. It quickly became the most popular stand at Coney Island by selling hot dogs for a nickel, half the price of its competitors. Nathan's remains a popular Coney Island institution.

Picnic parks were popularized by trolley companies, which sought a way to generate ridership on evenings and weekends. Although most customers brought a picnic lunch to enjoy in the park's groves, concession stands were plentiful as well. The most popular items included hot dogs and hamburgers; popcorn, peanuts, and Cracker Jack; lemonade; and ice cream. Most of these stands were operated by independent concessionaires who leased space from the park owners.

Another popular item throughout the industry, particularly in areas with a large German population, was beer, which was served in elaborate beer gardens. In fact, many early amusement parks were developed by brewers like Schlitz and Pabst.

After peaking at fifteen hundred in 1919, the number of amusement parks in the United States entered a period of decline in the 1930s and the 1940s and was reduced to fewer than four hundred. But the complexion of the industry was forever changed in 1955 when Disneyland opened in Anaheim, California, kicking off the theme park era. With Disneyland's tightly controlled themed environments and high levels of maintenance, the nature of food service changed. To maintain standards, control shifted from concessionaires to the park operators themselves. While a few once-popular items like roasted peanuts fell by the wayside, as the mess they created did not meet standards of cleanliness, customers continued to seek out food that could be quickly served and easily consumed, and many of the traditional favorites remained.

Theme parks being an all-day destination, however, most include some sort of cafeteria or restaurant offering full meal service, although alcohol was typically forbidden. The popularity of such dining facilities is generally limited—with a few exceptions, such as Epcot Center at Walt Disney World, Florida, where fine dining is a key part of the experience.

As of the early twenty-first century, there are approximately six hundred parks in the United States attracting over 300 million visitors, who spend approximately $11 billion annually. Food accounts for approximately one-fourth of park revenues, and approximately 80 percent of a park's food revenue typically comes from 20 percent of the products. On average, parks tend to have between fifteen and twenty food outlets.

Amusement parks have continued to add new items to reflect changing customer habits. Ethnic items such as nachos, pizza, and egg rolls can be found in many amusement parks, along with more healthful alternatives, such as salads and frozen yogurt, although traditional fare such as hot dogs, hamburgers, ice cream, funnel cakes, and cotton candy still dominate.

Parks have also become much more focused on offering greater value to customers. Some, such as Cedar Point in Sandusky, Ohio, feature all-you-can-eat buffets, and many places have combo meals, much like fast food restaurants. In 2000, Holiday World in Santa Claus, Indiana, set a new industry standard when it offered free soft drinks to their patrons.

Another dominant trend in amusement park food service has been the addition of branded foods. Parks not only promote particular food brands such as Coke and Pepsi; increasingly, they incorporate entire fast food franchises. While some parks—like Paramount's Kings Island in Kings Island, Ohio, near Cincinnati—emphasize local chains, others—such as Dorney Park in Allentown, Pennsylvania—feature national franchises.

[*See also* Beer; Beer Gardens; Cracker Jack; Fast Food; Hot Dogs; Lemonade; Peanuts; Popcorn.]

BIBLIOGRAPHY

Adams, Judith A. *The American Amusement Park Industry: A History of Technology and Thrills.* Boston: Twayne, 1991.
Amusement Business. "Food and Drink: 1992 Annual Survey." May 29, 1992.
Amusement Business. "Branding Is Key to Path Per Cap Increases." May 11, 1992.
Samuelson, Dale. *The American Amusement Park.* St. Paul, MN: MBI, 2001.

JAMES FUTRELL

Anadama Bread

This yeast bread made with cornmeal and molasses originated on the North Shore of Boston. The Cape Ann towns of Rockport and Gloucester are among those that claim to have invented it. According to competing popular legends, a farmer—or a local fisherman—grew tired of eating the cornmeal-and-molasses porridge that his wife incessantly prepared for him. He dumped flour and yeast into the bowl and threw it in the oven, grumbling, "Anna, damn her!" Others say it was Anna who got so fed up with her husband that she left him; returning home, her distraught husband threw random ingredients into her unfinished cornbread, muttering, "Anna, damn her!" More appreciative versions claim that Anna's spouse pronounced his defining epithet with pride as he munched thick slices of her tasty bread, or that Anna's tombstone fondly read, "Anna was a lovely bride, but Anna, damn 'er, up and died." The bread is also known as Amadama bread, allegedly derived from the irate husband who cried, "Where am 'er, damn 'er?" when his wife was away.

These stories, traceable in written form only to the nineteenth century, are repeated by local restaurants and bakeries that serve Anadama bread. The bread's varying legends reveal a simple, home-cooked regional food. Whether created by a colonial settler, who added flavorful indigenous ingredients to an English yeast bread, or by a post-Revolutionary housewife, in a community whose cuisine harked back to seventeenth-century English cooking, Anadama bread embodies the fierce local pride and deep English roots of the North Shore of Boston. The Arnold Bread Company produced a commercial variety until the late twentieth century; Klink's Baking Company in South Hamilton, Massachusetts, still distributes it to local grocery stores.

[*See also* Bread.]

BIBLIOGRAPHY

The American Heritage Cookbook and Illustrated History of American Eating and Drinking. New York: American Heritage; distributed by Simon and Schuster, 1964.

Bowles, Ella Shannon, and Dorothy S. Towle. *Secrets of New England Cooking*. New York: Barrows, 1947.

CAROLIN C. YOUNG

Appalachian Food

Traditional Appalachian foods include the many-layered dried-apple stack cake; soup beans or pinto beans boiled with pork; chicken and slick dumplings served with gruel; white half-runner green beans boiled for long periods with salt pork or pork side meat; and feather-light biscuits covered with white-sausage gravy. Traditional Appalachians take pride in preparing apple butter, deviled eggs, pork barbecue, and fried apple pies, and they speak reverently about their eggs scrambled with poke, their fried morel mushrooms or dryland fish, and their white lightning or moonshine, a high-alcohol-content drink poured from quart-sized canning jars. The corn that yields moonshine is also the source of cornbread, roasted ear corn, fried corn, hominy, and grits. This list of diverse Appalachian foods could go on for hundreds of items, including the wild, garliclike green ramps dug from the ground in March and the highly perfumed tropical pawpaw fruits that fall from small trees in September. It would also have to include wild meats such as bear, venison, squirrel, and turtle.

This discussion of Appalachian food is limited to the central and southern highlands of the Appalachian region, a mountainous area that stretches from the Maryland panhandle through southwestern Ohio, West Virginia, eastern Kentucky and Tennessee, western Virginia and North Carolina, and northeastern portions of Georgia. It is an area of extreme beauty, with small valleys, precipitous mountains, and slow-moving rivers. Because of the region's generous rains and warm climate, the growing season may last nine months, with many areas planting peas at the beginning of February and some sweet corn being ready for harvest in early July.

The distinctive nature of the region's food evolved by word of mouth and was preserved in recipe files, notebooks, and blank pages in the front of national cookbooks. Mountain food is home cooked, and the cookware is cast iron. This food did not develop in commercial test kitchens, cookbook writers' homes, or cooking schools. It is food from the soil, hearth, and home.

Pre-Columbian Period

A nomadic people, likely arriving from Asia, settled the Appalachian region some twelve thousand or more years ago, and they developed food traditions that continued until the Industrial Revolution. They ate mastodon and giant tortoise. They hunted, fished, and gathered. Then the earth warmed, the mastodon and tortoise died off, and their diet changed. About ten thousand years ago, native Appalachians ate white-tailed deer, turkeys, squirrels, and raccoons. They also enjoyed hickory nuts, black walnuts, acorns, grapes, berries, and persimmons.

The most prominent Native American foods of this region are corn, beans, pumpkins, and squash, but these became important much later, when they were grown rather than gathered. For example, domesticated squash dates back five thousand years, while corn was not raised as a crop until about one thousand years ago, and the common bean arrived here some eight hundred years ago.

Once Europeans settled the region, native food habits began to change. In the 1950s, the Museum of the Cherokee Indian in Cherokee, North Carolina, sponsored Indian feasts that illustrated the mixture of native and European foods that had become characteristic of the region. For example, dinners featured boiled corn mush, baked cornbread loaves or pones, fresh young-ear gritted cornbread, thick and salty cornmeal gravy, rolled flat-flour dumplings boiled with dry beans or chicken, succotash of lima beans and corn, butter beans boiled with onions, flavorful dried leather breeches (green beans) boiled with side meat, fresh ramps, fried crease greens, watercress, and squirrel gravy served over biscuits. Also included were dishes with wild blackberries, dewberries, huckleberries, raspberries, elderberries, plums, cherries, crab apples, ground cherries, persimmons, fox grapes, muscadine grapes, opossum grapes, and gooseberries. The mix of foods served at these dinners illustrates that although Europeans influenced Appalachian food, native Appalachians had an even greater impact on European habits.

Frontier Period

From the beginning of the nineteenth century and until the coming of railroads and industry about eighty years later, European settlers were often isolated and independent, receiving some help from Indians in Appalachia. To survive in the Appalachian frontier, they cleared fields, built cabins, and cooked with cast-iron cookware. In early mountain cabins, the fireplace and open hearth provided heat for both the house and the cooking.

A grand dinner during this period might include elk backstrap steaks, venison stew, greens fried in bear grease, and ashcakes. Ashcakes are a cornbread rolled in ashes and baked, not in a pan but near the coals on the hearth. Corn on the cob, Irish potatoes, and sweet potatoes were cooked in the same fashion. After a dessert of fruit pie or sweet cake, a bottle was passed and a shot of whiskey taken. Appalachian settlers prided themselves on quality foods, and occasionally the table was set in high fashion and the meal served with hot biscuits, fresh butter, honey, strawberry preserves, mixed pickles, rich milk, cream, tea, and coffee.

For emergencies and hunting trips, settlers made jerky and hardtack, a hard biscuit made with flour and water. Popular food storage methods were salting and pickling, with dried foods taking a lesser role. Frontier folk also stored dry foods such as corn, flour, and beans aboveground, and in cool underground storage areas they saved potatoes, beets, turnips, carrots, and parsnips. From this period, dried apples, peach leather (a sheet of dried fruit purée), and shuck beans have remained popular.

From native Appalachians, settlers learned to use wild greens—and some of these, including creases, dandelions, dock, fiddleheads, lambs-quarters, poke, purslane, ramps, shepherd's purse, spring beauty, and watercress, are well known today. But during this period, wild meat and animal fats were more important than greens. Settlers ate buffalo, bear, elk, deer, razorback hogs, turkey, fox, raccoon, and the meat of many more wild animals. Pork and beef were raised to supplement wild game. As evidenced by the Hatfield-McCoy feud, an interfamily battle that started in 1878 and is often associated with a stolen pig, pork was an essential frontier food. Mature pigs, laden with lard, were killed in late fall or winter. The fat was boiled off for use in cooking and soap making. The hams were dry-cured, side meats were salted, bacon was cured and sliced, bones were boiled to make souse, and pigs feet were boiled for soup. The pork lard that was so highly valued on the frontier dominated mountain cooking until the end of the twentieth century, and pork remains a favorite meat in the region. Cattle were raised for meat and milk, and the milk was used to make cheese, buttermilk, butter, and cream.

Industrial Period

The impact of industrialization on Appalachia was uneven, with some communities modernizing quickly and others maintaining traditional ways long into the twentieth century. Although electricity reached some rural areas in the 1930s, other areas were not electrified until the 1950s and 1960s. In some areas one- and two-room schools were the norm until the late 1950s, and a rural lifestyle was dominant. Those living in the country often worked in mines and factories but continued to raise livestock, with chickens and new vegetable varieties such as sweet corn becoming new frontier traditions. They canned meats, fruits, and vegetables. During this period the glass canning jar and walk-in can house became the dominant method of food storage; freezing required electricity. While families in the Deep South often survived on cornmeal, fatback, and molasses, this diet was not complete and they sometimes suffered from pellagra. The Appalachian diet, however, was more diverse and pellagra was not a problem.

During this period, families were large and close. Life was centered on meals, and there was often a division of work among family members. In some settings women prepared the food, served it to the men, and ate later; children fed pigs, hoed the garden, and carried water. Much of this has changed, but families still find value in family meals. Some come together for church and family reunions; others enjoy Sunday dinner at the home of "mamaw and papaw." Families celebrate births, graduations, weddings, and retirements as they mark funerals—with food. Holidays such as Christmas, Easter, the Fourth of July, and Labor Day weekend are occasions for large gatherings at which home-cooked covered-dish dinners are served.

Such dinners, while family oriented, are diverse, reflecting the varied nationalities of immigrants to Appalachia—whose population comprises people from Croatia, Germany, Greece, Hungary, India, Ireland, Italy, Mexico, Poland, Russia, Scotland, Serbia, Slovenia, Ukraine, and Wales. Appalachia during the late frontier and industrial periods did not have a homogeneous style of eating or cooking, and this fact is illustrated again and again in community-based cookbooks. Poles, for example, came to Appalachia to work in the mines and mills. When they settled, they prepared pierogi, crullers, and pickled herring. Russians brought sweet nut and poppy seed breakfast rolls. Italians cooked gnocchi and stromboli. Croatians prepared *sarma*, or stuffed cabbage. Germans brought to the region orange cookies and sauerkraut salad. Lamb soup, Greek salad, and braised string beans were borne to the region by Greek settlers, while from the Scots, Appalachia acquired shortbread, scones, and oatcakes. Many of these recipes, while associated with particular ethnic groups, are now widely known throughout Appalachia.

Appalachian Recipes. *Appalachian Mountain Country Cookin',* cookbooklet issued by Christian Relief Services, Vernon, Va., 1992. *Collection of Andrew F. Smith*

An example of a complex recipe that has remained popular in Appalachia is the stack cake, also called the dried-apple stack cake. This traditional cake is delicate, highly flavored, and low in fat, and it comports well with today's dietary and lifestyle needs. It stores well, slices thin, and looks classy, comprising six to twelve ginger-flavored layers covered with a spicy apple sauce; the sauce soaks into the cake, softening it and allowing the flavors to mingle.

Current Trends in Appalachian Food

In the last quarter of the twentieth century, Appalachian food changed to include both more commercial food and fine restaurant foods. The fastest fast food in Appalachia is purchased along with gasoline at self-serve stations: drinks, snacks, candies, and sandwiches; fried foods such as potatoes and chicken; and, of course, for the sleepy driver, coffee, both hot and cold. The cookies, beverages, and coffee are brand-name all-American; this is part of the food of Appalachia because it is sold there, but it is not typical of food identified with Appalachia. Packed in plastic, this food is so removed from the farm and garden that for those who grew up long ago, it yields little in the way of personal satisfaction.

Another style of food that is, again, far removed from the garden, home, and frontier work ethic is upscale chef food. Such dishes are created in large kitchens with foods from around the globe, from across the country, and from down the road. Appalachian chefs, like others, do not work in a vacuum; rather, their "invented" food is often inspired by ethnic and regional traditions. Hence, today's Appalachian fine dining is distinctively Appalachian. Years ago, for example, the Terrace Restaurant of Grove Park Inn in Asheville, North Carolina, offered an appetizer of fried bean cakes. For more than one hundred years, mountain cooks have been using leftover soup beans or boiled pintos to make bean cakes, but at the Grove Park Inn the bean cakes were inspired. The beans were black, pinto, and white; the cakes were tiny; and the garnishes were extensive. Sour cream, chowchow, fox grapes, raisins, and chives adorned the plate. The simple bean cake was transformed, in the manner of haute cuisine, into a multilayered, complex, mixed-texture dish with an artistic presentation. Today, talented Appalachian chefs are successful in cities from Pittsburgh to Charlotte because they are inspired by Appalachian home-style traditions.

Appalachian food continues to be a mix of slow home cooking, simple restaurant food, complex chef creations, and new ethnic influences. As new ethnic groups arrive, the food landscape, though influenced by the past, changes again. Traditional foods such as pure sorghum, fried greens, squirrel gravy, and boiled groundhog are important, but for most Appalachians they are no more than a memory. Just as the mastodon and giant tortoise died out because of a change in climate, some Appalachian foods have disappeared because of a change in culture.

[*See also* Canning and Bottling; Cookbooks and Manuscripts, *subentry on* Community Cookbooks; Dumplings; Game; Hardtack; Moonshine; Native American Foods, *subentry* Before and After Contact; Pawpaw; Pickling; Ramps; Salt and Salting; Southern Regional Cookery.]

BIBLIOGRAPHY

Dabney, Joseph E. *Mountain Spirits: A Chronicle of Corn Whiskey from King James' Ulster Plantation to America's Appalachians and the Moonshine Life.* New York: Scribners, 1974.

Dabney, Joseph E. *Smokehouse Ham, Spoon Bread, and Scuppernong Wine: The Folklore and Art of Southern Appalachian Cooking.* Nashville, TN: Cumberland, 1998. A comprehensive book of history and lore. that includes an excellent oral history, 300-item bibliography, and complete index.

Farr, Sidney Saylor. *More than Moonshine: Appalachian Recipes and Recollections.* Pittsburgh, PA: University of Pittsburgh Press, 1983. A family memoir, with about 250 recipes that really work.

Farr, Sidney Saylor. *Table Talk: Appalachian Meals and Memories.* Pittsburgh, PA: University of Pittsburgh Press, 1995. About twenty first-person accounts that focus on family stories and favorite recipes.

Lambert, Walter N. *Kinfolks and Custard Pie: Recollections and Recipes from an East Tennessean.* Knoxville: University of Tennessee Press, 1988.

Page, Linda Garland, and Eliot Wigginton. *The Foxfire Book of Appalachian Cookery: Regional Memorabilia and Recipes.* New York: Dutton, 1984.

Sohn, Mark F. *Mountain Country Cooking: A Gathering of the Best Recipes from the Smokies to the Blue Ridge.* New York: St. Martin's, 1996. A personal, yet regional book with three hundred kitchen-tested Appalachian recipes given in traditional and updated healthful forms.

Steelesburg Homemakers Club. *Appalachian Heritage Cookbook.* Radford, VA: Commonwealth, 1984.

Taylor, Joe Gray. *Eating, Drinking, and Visiting in the South: An Informal History.* Baton Rouge: Louisiana State University Press, 1982.

MARK F. SOHN

Appetizers

Appetizers and hors d'oeuvres—the latter literally meaning "outside of the work"—assume a wide variety of forms in American dining. Late-twentieth-century dictionaries treat appetizers and hors d'oeuvres—popularly understood to be bite-sized finger foods offered at cocktail parties and receptions—as synonyms. Americans also use "appetizer" to indicate the first course eaten when seated at table in a three-course (appetizer, main course, dessert) meal.

Hors d'Oeuvres in History

Virtually all cultures have indulged in preprandial morsels designed to whet the appetite for more substantial fare, and there is remarkable consistency across cultures in offering salty foods as stimulants. The ancient Greeks and Romans sampled bits of fish, seasoned vegetables, cheeses, and olives, while the Renaissance Italian writer Platina recommended thin rolls of grilled veal to stimulate the appetite for food and drink. Wealthy Frenchmen picked at *hors d'oeuvre* throughout fancy meals from the late seventeenth through the mid-nineteenth centuries, when little plates

and their suggested contents—ranging from oysters, stuffed eggs, and pâtés to slices of beef tongue or braised quails—were shown on table layouts illustrating dinners served *à la française*. Those Americans who emulated that French model made a variety of hors d'oeuvres (the plural is used only in English) part of the American table and offered them throughout the meal as a palate refresher until the desserts were served.

Styles of service changed radically in the nineteenth century, evolving to the successive, multicourse structure of formal contemporary meals. The role of hors d'oeuvres in the structure of a meal changed as well. Although simple hors d'oeuvres, such as olives, radishes, celery, and nuts, remained on the table throughout the meal, by the late nineteenth century, more complicated hors d'oeuvres, sometimes called "dainty dishes"—such as small pastry cases filled with bits of meat in creamy sauce—had

Hors d'Oeuvres. Recipe booklet issued by Canapé Parade, Scarborough, New York, 1932. *Collection of Andrew F. Smith*

become a separate course after the soup was served. The term "appetizer" seems to have appeared nearly simultaneously in England and America in the 1860s simply to provide an Anglophone equivalent for the French *hors d'oeuvre*.

By the 1890s both appetizers and hors d'oeuvres could appear within the same elegant menu. Abby Buchanan Longstreet's *Good Form Dinners, Ceremonious and Unceremonious, and the Modern Methods of Serving Them* (1896) describes appetizers as an optional first course, preceding soup, that is set on the table prior to a party's entering the dining room. These appetizers were most often raw oysters or clams, but they might be small canapés, such as caviar on toast. Mrs. Longstreet assumed that celery, salted nuts, and the like would fill the table throughout the meal, and she directed the host to place these "various *hors-d'oeuvres* within reach of each guest, these appetizers serving to fill in the time between courses."

The Americanization of Hors d'Oeuvres: The Cocktail Hour and Streamlined Menus

The introduction of the pre-dinner cocktail hour in the early twentieth century changed Americans' view of hors d'oeuvres. Before World War I, guests at a dinner party were presumed to arrive punctually and to proceed almost immediately into the dining room. If cocktails were served, they opened the dinner, accompanying a plated appetizer, once everyone was seated at the table. This custom had changed by the 1920s, when racy hostesses served hors d'oeuvres as "accompaniments for the liquid refreshment that dodges prohibition conscientiously and yet is flavorsome enough to make the quarter hour before dinner less solemn and uninteresting than it sometimes proves" (Eaton, p. 124). After the repeal of Prohibition, the modern cocktail party burst on the scene, with a slew of recipes for hors d'oeuvres to help absorb the liquor.

Until about 1940, "fine dining" restaurant menus tended to use French terminology in organizing the successive courses—at least for those courses that did not have a handy English translation, such as *hors d'oeuvre*, *entrée*, and *entremets*. But a simpler model for a "proper" meal was emerging from the 1920s on, consisting of only three courses. A term being needed to pigeonhole the many types of dishes being offered, the generic category "appetizers" began to appear, denoting the first of three courses. Appetizers broadly included soups, salads, and savory pastries, all of which had appeared as separate courses—although in smaller portions—in nineteenth-

and early twentieth-century meals. Middle-class cookbooks, such as Alice Bradley's *Menu-Cook-Book* (1936), also began to suggest "a first course or appetizer for every dinner, as it seems to add much pleasure to the meal. . . . This course may be omitted if it seems to be the extra item that means too much work."

Influences beyond the French

Americans who have not assimilated the Anglo-French style of dining have different appetizer traditions. Perhaps most familiar is the Italian antipasto, meaning "before the meal." The dishes serving as the antipasto vary with the cook's budget and regional heritage; they may be modest grilled vegetables or rich cured meats. The eastern Mediterranean and Middle Eastern *mezze* (derived from the Persian for taste or relish), found wherever Greek and Arab populations settled, typically present baba ghanoush, *tzanziki*, hummus, and *taramasalata*, all scooped with bits of flat breads. The Scandinavian-inspired *smörgåsbord* ("table of buttered bread") groans under small, open-faced sandwiches covered with herring, salmon, and other fishes and may serve as a meal in itself. Authentic Russian *zakuska* can be found in Brighton Beach, Brooklyn, where plates brimming with smoked and cured fishes, pickled and stuffed vegetables, meat-filled pastries, and the omnipresent caviar vie for table space among frosty bottles of vodka. The tapas bar is at home in cities with a Spanish population, allowing patrons to snack on small plates of marinated vegetables and seafood and the signature chorizo and *jamón*, while imbibing sherry, sangria, or cocktails. Chinatowns bustle with dim sum ("so close to my heart") trolleys delivering little baskets of dumplings, spareribs, and the like, which can be eaten for breakfast or lunch, but never dinner.

The universal appeal of a variety of little "tastes" coupled with a relaxing drink has encouraged "grazing" as a restaurant trend, beginning in the late twentieth century: diners compose a meal from dishes offered in appetizer-sized portions. Appealing primarily to a youthful, urban clientele, these grazing bars often fuse diverse cultural influences in their menus and offer more "tastes" than a traditional three-course meal.

[*See also* Dining Rooms, Table Settings, and Table Manners; French Influences on American Food.]

BIBLIOGRAPHY

Beard, James. *Hors D'Oeuvre and Canapés, with a Key to the Cocktail Party.* New York: Barrows, 1940. A good general collection of recipes, this book is divided into chapters for different categories (hot, cold, sandwiches, canapés, first courses), each of which is introduced by a brief essay on the different functions served by hors d'oeuvre.

Burros, Marion. "The Small-Plate Club." *New York Times*, March 20, 2002. A report on the contemporary "appetizers-as-dinner" phenomenon.

Eaton, Florence Taft. "Varied Hors d'Oeuvres." *Delineator* 109, no. 31 (November 1926): 31, 124. A very interesting article addressed to the middle class, which includes recipes and techniques and explains the multiple functions of hors d'oeuvres.

CATHY K. KAUFMAN

Applejack

Applejack, an American type of apple brandy, was widely produced during the colonial period of American history. In New England, applejack was the most commonly consumed brandy. It was made by placing hard cider in wooden barrels and exposing them to freezing temperatures during winter. The water in the hard cider froze on the top of the barrel and was removed, leaving a stronger fermented concentrate in the barrel, along with other residues. In the middle colonies and the upper southern colonies, where temperatures were not cold enough to use the freezing method, applejack was made by distilling hard cider. It competed with peach and other brandies.

Applejack had a reputation for its strong kick, which was illustrated by its many colloquial names, such as "cider oil," "essence of lockjaw," and, because New Jersey produced large quantities of it, "Jersey Lightning." George Washington enjoyed apple brandy, and Abraham Lincoln served it in his tavern in Springfield, Illinois. The consumption of applejack declined during the nineteenth century and almost disappeared during the twentieth century. The major reason for the decline was that the freezing method retained unpleasant apple residue and oils.

The alcoholic content of applejack has varied greatly through the years, depending on the method used to make it. By the early twenty-first century, all commercial applejack was made through distillation, which produces a product that is about 70 proof. It is usually aged for two years before consumption; other apple brandies are aged for a much longer period. For instance, French Calvados is frequently aged about twenty years. The major commercial producer of applejack, Laird and Company of Scobeyville, New Jersey, which began making the brandy in 1780, uses the distillation method. The company has published a cookbook, *AppleJack: The Spirit of Americana*, filled with recipes using applejack in food and drinks.

[*See also* Brandy; Cider, Hard.]

BIBLIOGRAPHY

Laird and Company. *AppleJack: The Spirit of Americana*. Brick, NJ: Strand Printery, 1992.

Watson, Ben. *Cider Hard and Sweet: History, Traditions, and Making Your Own*. Woodstock, VT: Countryman Press, 1999.

Weiss, Harry B. *The History of Applejack or Apple Brandy in New Jersey from Colonial Times to the Present*. Trenton: New Jersey Agricultural Society, 1954.

ANDREW F. SMITH

Apple Pie

The typical American pie made from uncooked apples, fat, sugar, and sweet spices mixed together and baked inside a closed pie shell descends from fifteenth-century English apple pies, which, while not quite the same, are similar enough that the relationship is unmistakable. By the end of the sixteenth century in England, apple pies were being made that are virtually identical to those made in America in the early twenty-first century.

Apple pies came to America quite early. There are recipes for apple pie in both manuscript receipts and eighteenth-century English cookery books imported into the colonies. Amelia Simmons's *American Cookery* (1796) contains two different recipes for apple pie, one flavored with rose water or wine. The anonymous *New American Cookery*, published in 1805, contains a recipe for dried-apple pie.

Apple pies can vary in many ways: the type of sweetener used, if any; the type of fat; the type of crust, whether solid or made of crumbs; the use of such extra ingredients as raisins, lemon juice, or almonds; and the choice of spices. While the most common apple pie in America is the two-crust pie, there are other versions as well, including one-crust pies and pies with bottom crusts and crumb toppings. One-crust pies have been found in the United States since at least 1820. Mary Randolph's *The Virginia House-Wife* (1824) contains a recipe for Baked Apple Pudding, which is an apple pie variant that has already-baked apples, butter, sugar, eggs, and lemon rind baked further in a one-crust pie shell.

Apple pies rapidly became an iconic part of the American culture, witnessed by the cliché "as American as apple pie." In Louisa May Alcott's *Little Men* (1886), one of the first things Jo teaches her niece Daisy to cook is an apple pie. Even imitation ones were devised. In the

1930s, a mock apple pie recipe, which used Ritz crackers instead of apples, was printed on Ritz cracker boxes. In 1968, McDonald's added an apple pie dessert to its menu.

Apple pies have been eaten not only as a dessert. In the nineteenth century, apple pie was also a common breakfast food among Yankees and people in rural communities, prompting Ralph Waldo Emerson's alleged comment, "Well, what is pie for?" The use of pie as a breakfast food had declined by the end of the nineteenth century.

Although homemade apple pies were most common through the early twentieth century, bakeries and grocery stores in urban settings started offering apple pies for sale in the nineteenth century. In the early twentieth century, a woman by the name of Mrs. Smith, who baked pies which her son then marketed, turned her pie company, Mrs. Smith's Pies, into a mass-market industry, still in existence in the early twenty-first century. By the mid-twentieth century, frozen apple pies became available.

Apple pies are often served with a topping. The two most common are vanilla ice cream, first served with the title "à la mode" in the 1890s, and cheese. The poet Eugene Field in the late nineteenth century praised the latter combination in a poem asking "the Lord to bless me with apple pie and cheese."

[*See also* Apples, Apple-Preparation Tools; Desserts; Pie-making Tools; Randolph, Mary; Simmons, Amelia.]

BIBLIOGRAPHY

The American Heritage Cookbook. New York: Simon and Schuster, 1964.

Booth, Sally Smith. *Hung, Strung, and Potted: A History of Eating in Colonial America.* New York: Clarkson N. Potter, 1971.

Hechtlinger, Adelaide. *The Seasonal Hearth.* Woodstock, NY: The Overlook Press, 1977.

Simmons, Amelia. *American Cookery.* Hartford, CT: Hudson and Goodwin, 1796.

JUDY GERJUOY

Apple-Preparation Tools

As eighteenth-century American apple orchards expanded throughout the colonies, demand increased for mechanical aid in preparing the seasonal harvest for cider, preserves, and drying. By the 1780s or 1790s, belt-driven, bench-mounted wooden devices made paring quicker. Seated astride the bench, with one hand the operator cranked a shaft with an apple on its pronged tip while pressing a sharp-bladed shaver against the fruit. The first parer patent, in 1803, was for a simple wood and

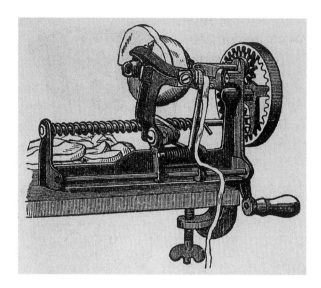

Apple Parer. Illustration from *The Housewife's Library* (Philadelphia, 1883), p. 290.

iron device clamped to a tabletop. Homemade adaptations during the next forty years led to mass-produced cast-iron peelers with replaceable, bolted-together parts, gears that increased the apple's turning speed, and blades held firmly against the fruit with a spring. A simple lathe-type apple parer, "The White Mountain," first patented in 1880, is still made in the early 2000s.

Improvements to several geared parers added the ability to core, segment or slice, and ultimately eject an apple in less than three seconds. Large and small versions satisfied both commercial and home canners.

Before the mid-nineteenth century, corers were made of carved bone or wrought iron. Tin corers took their place, some with wooden knobs that protected the user's palm. Tin coring and segmenting (usually quartering) tools with sharp edges were used by pushing against an apple on a cutting board.

[*See also* Applejack; Apple Pie; Apples.]

BIBLIOGRAPHY

Franklin, Linda Campbell. *Three Hundred Years of Kitchen Collectibles.* Iola, WI: Krause Publications, 2003.

Thornton, Don. *Apple Parers.* Moss Beach, CA: Thornton House, 1997.

LINDA CAMPBELL FRANKLIN

Apples

Apples are in the family Rosaceae and constitute the genus *Malus.* It is speculated that the cradle of the apple is in

Apple Picking. *Culinary Archives & Museum at Johnson & Wales University, Providence, R.I.*

Asia Minor and that the fruit resulted from a millennia-old evolutionary cross of an Asiatic crab apple and a European crab apple. The science and study of the apple is "pomology," a word that also applies to the study of fruit in general.

Malus pumila, the domestic apple we know from supermarket shelves, is not a native fruit of America. A few native crab apples, notably *M. augustifolia* and *M. coronaria*, were found by the colonists. Seeds, buds, and small plants of the apples of the British Isles and Europe trickled into the temperate zones of the New World to establish the apple as a food commodity. By the middle of the seventeenth century, there were apple orchards with thousands of trees, planted not for eating but for cider production.

Every seed in every apple is a new variety; thus, the planting of the seeds out of a named variety from abroad in the rich soil of the colonies would produce many different varieties. Trueness to name was unimportant, because the purpose of the apple in new America was exclusively to produce juice for cider. Production was so successful that by 1820 cider not only was the national beverage but also became a currency, a major commodity for barter.

From the great cider orchards of America, where tens of thousands of trees were planted from the random seeds collected from the cider presses, a tree occasionally would produce a fruit with desirable eating qualities. Cider seedling orchards were the natural breeding laboratories

for the selection of more pleasing apple varieties for eating and for culinary purposes. Buds from the acclimated varieties were grafted to unknown-variety seedlings; when they had been established for a few years in the first American fruit tree nurseries, orchards with named apple selections were planted for the first time in America.

By 1850, thousands of named apple varieties for fresh eating, cooking, drying, pickling, and making cider, apple butter, applesauce, vinegar, wine, and even livestock food were listed in nursery catalogs. There was considerable diversity of varieties in New England, the Middle Atlantic, the upper Midwest, and the Northwest, and there were even a few adapted to the warmer regions of the Deep South. In 1905, W. H. Ragan's *Nomenclature of the Apple: Catalog of Known Varieties Referred to in American Publications from 1804–1904* listed seventeen thousand apple varieties grown in America.

In the first half of the twentieth century, because of developments in transportation and fruit-storage facilities as well as the disappearance of the diversity once found on family farms and orchards, thousands of varieties were abandoned. In the 1920s and 1930s, alcohol prohibition, the proliferation of pests and diseases, and the emergence of the soft-drink industry furthered the decline of the golden age of the apple in America.

The agricultural skill of fruit propagation by grafting disappeared with the orchards, as marketing and sales came under the control of larger and larger nurseries focused on fewer and fewer varieties. The dozen or so commercial varieties marketed in the second half of the twentieth century were chosen by producers for high volume and trouble-free bearing, low mechanical damage, long shelf life, and, above all, cosmetic impact. The approaching monoculture solidified with the appearance of the Red Delicious and its three hundred look-alike strains. The stereotypical apple had emerged, and it would dominate the apple industry until the 1960s, when other commercial varieties from abroad began to be introduced.

Apples: The Immigrant Fruit

History repeated itself in the "re-appleing" of America. New varieties from Japan, New Zealand, and Australia, notably Gala, Braeburn, Pink Lady, and Fuji, trickled in to begin the fragmentation of the Delicious monoculture. The consumer demanded apples with better flavor. In the development of new varieties, research stations began to consider taste as a major characteristic. Apple varieties of the past, like the Newtown Pippin, Roxbury Russet, Grimes Golden, Northern Spy, and Arkansas Black, returned to commerce, at least on a small scale.

Thirty-five states grow apples commercially, with the largest production in Washington, New York, Michigan, California, Pennsylvania, and Virginia. In 2002, the total bearing acreage in the United States was 404,950 acres. The sale value exceeded $1.3 billion. The most popular apple variety harvested is still the Red Delicious, though its market share is shrinking steadily. The Golden Delicious remains in second place. Some other prominent commercial varieties are Braeburn, Cortland, Empire, Fuji, Gala, Ginger Gold, Goldrush, Granny Smith, Honeycrisp, Jonagold, Jonathan, McIntosh, Mutsu, Pink Lady, Rome, Suncrisp, Winesap, and York. One hundred or more other varieties have lesser commercial value; many are popular regionally, among them the Baldwin, Grimes Golden, Macoun, Newtown Pippin, Stayman, Gravenstein, and Wealthy.

Physical characteristics of apples vary considerably, with skin colors that range from all hues of whites to reds, greens, browns, and yellows. Striping, mottling, and speckling can cover all or just a small area of the skin surface. The shapes are enormously diverse, and sizes may range from that of a small pea to that of a large grapefruit. Inside, the flesh can be very dense or open grained. Seeds may be white, green, yellow, brown, tan, or red. The stems vary from chunky to threadlike, and they can be just long enough to hold the fruit to the stem or up to two inches in length. When the apples are mature, the flavors may range from extremely bitter to saccharine sweet and contain varying amounts, singly or in combination, of acid, tannin, and sugar as well as trace elements. A medium-sized dessert apple has about eighty calories.

The apple is a portable fruit that can be conveniently stored from a few days to many months under a controlled environment. Some varieties exude a natural coating, often described as greasy or waxy, that protects the fruit from desiccation. The wood of the apple is used for heating, flavoring meats by its smoke, and furniture making. The versatile fruit continues to be consumed in a variety of forms.

[*See also* Applejack; Cider; Myths and Folkore, *sidebar on* Johnny Appleseed.]

BIBLIOGRAPHY

Beach, S. A. *The Apples of New York.* Albany: New York Agricultural Experiment Station, 1905.
Browning, Frank. *Apples.* New York: North Point Press, 1998.
Burford, Thomas. *Apples: A Catalog of International Varieties.* Rev. ed. Monroe, VA: Burford Brothers, 2003.
Manhart, Warren. *Apples for the 21st Century.* Portland, OR: North American Tree Company, 1995.
Morgan, Joan, and Allison Richards. *The New Book of Apples: The Definitive Guide to Apples, Including over 2,000 Varieties.* 2nd ed. London: Ebury Press, 2002.
Ragan, W. H. *Nomenclature of the Apple: Catalog of Known Varieties Referred to in American Publications from 1804–1904.* Washington, DC: United States Department of Agriculture, Bureau of Plant Industry, 1905.

THOMAS BURFORD

Apricots

The apricot (*Prunus armeniaca*), once thought to be native to Armenia, is actually indigenous to China, where it has been cultivated for at least four thousand years. Its culture spread through Asia by ancient travelers along the Silk Road and reached the Mediterranean during Roman times. In America, Thomas Jefferson set out apricot trees in his orchard at Monticello as early as 1778, and the British explorer George Vancouver found apricot trees growing at the Spanish mission of Santa Clara, California, in 1792. The apricot, with its early-blooming habit, flourishes in the soil and climate of California. There, after the gold rush, the world's largest apricot industry developed in areas relatively free of spring frosts, which is the limiting factor for commercial production east of the Rockies.

In the early years, most of California's production was dried or preserved by canning. Major varieties included Royal Blenheim and Moorpark. These traditional varieties were considered the most delectable of fruits, with soft, juicy, aromatic flesh; rich flavor; and a delicate balance of sweetness and acidity. In the 1970s and 1980s, growers shifted to apricots with firmer flesh, both for the fresh market and processing; thus, the Castlebrite and Patterson varieties, which have larger, firmer fruit but more acidic flavor, began replacing the older varieties. Urbanization of older growing districts, reliance on varieties of lesser quality, and foreign competition led to a steady decline in California's apricot industry, as Turkey overtook California in dried apricot production and Spain and Greece took the lead in canned apricots. Since the late 1990s, newer varieties like Tomcot, Goldensweet, and Robada, which combine rich flavor with good shipping qualities, are increasingly being planted in California and the Northwest.

The apricot is truly a versatile fruit. It is consumed fresh, canned, conserved, and dried. It is very high in vitamins C and A, containing as much as one hundred times more vitamin A than is found, on average, in most other fruits. The rich sweet-tart flavor of apricots makes them a favorite filling for old-fashioned fried pies, a comfort food and dessert staple in the southern United States for generations.

[*See also* California; Fruit.]

BIBLIOGRAPHY

"The Apricot." In *Fourth Biennial Report of the State Board of Horticulture of the State of California for 1893–1894*, 29–55. Sacramento, CA: California State Board of Horticulture, 1894.

Rubin, Cynthia, and Jerome Rubin. *Apricot Cookbook*. Newton, MA: Emporium Publications, 1974.

Wickson, E. J. *The California Fruits and How to Grow Them*. 6th ed. San Francisco: Pacific Rural Press, 1926.

ANDREW MARIANI

Arab American Food, *see Middle Eastern Influences on American Food*

Arbuckles

Creating a business requires courage, determination, and imagination. John Arbuckle, a Pittsburgh grocer, had them all. In 1860, Arbuckle entered the wholesale grocery business McDonald and Arbuckle, begun by his brother Charles, his uncle Duncan McDonald, and his friend William Roseburg. The uncle and friend left the business, and John and Charles assumed charge. By 1868, John Arbuckle's formula for a tasty roasted coffee and his keen business expertise had revolutionized the coffee industry. William Ukers, writing in *All about Coffee*, calls Arbuckle "the original national-package-coffee man" (p. 447).

Until the mid-nineteenth century, people purchased green coffee beans, which had to be roasted and ground before the drink could be brewed. Although a few firms advertised that they sold ground coffee "guaranteed to retain its strength and flavor for years" (as advertised in the *St. Louis Missouri Republican*, March 30, 1850), the product did not live up to the promise. Unscrupulous manufacturers often mixed chicory, sawdust, or bran with the coffee. Moreover, successful roasting was difficult, because freshly roasted beans quickly lost the volatile oils that give coffee flavor and aroma. A good cup of coffee meant daily roasting until 1868, when Arbuckle perfected a glutinous mixture made of Irish moss, gelatin, isinglass, white sugar, and eggs for preserving the freshness of roast coffee. Subsequent formulas contained only sugar and eggs. Arbuckle packaged the beans in one-pound "little paper bags like peanuts" (Fugate, p. 30). In 1873, Arbuckle combined hearty Rios and Santos beans to produce a blend called Ariosa. It was the first successful national brand of packaged coffee in the United States. The trademark, a drawing of an angel floating in the air, became famous.

To persuade consumers to purchase his brand, Arbuckle hired an army of agents to write orders. The coffee was publicized with colored folksy handbills, trading cards, and coupons redeemed for premiums. The coupons printed on the package had a cash value of one cent. As consumers began sending in coupons and collecting premiums, such as silverware, china, towels, and curtains, houses, especially in the West, took on an "Arbuckles" decor. The catalog describing the gifts was a "wish book" for many. Ahead of his time, Arbuckle had the catalog printed in Spanish so that Spanish-speaking aficionados could order their gifts.

Westerners, mainly cowboys and Indians, had a particular fondness for Ariosa coffee. They liked the convenience that eliminated roasting, the light weight of the packages compared with large bags of beans, and the guarantee of a consistently good cup of coffee.

Arbuckles' was so successful that in the 1880s, the company established branches in New York, Kansas City, and Chicago as well as ports in Brazil and Mexico. The company acquired its own fleet of seagoing vessels to transport coffee beans from field to factory and entered the sugar-refining business. Thirty-five years after developing a successful roasting process, John Arbuckle improved his own method by patenting a coffee roaster that used hot gases to suspend coffee beans in superheated air.

In 1937, the General Foods Corporation acquired a number of Arbuckle Brothers brand names, including Yuban, which had been served only to dinner guests by John Arbuckle. Having disappeared from the market by 1944, the Ariosa brand, the "Coffee That Won the West"—packaged with a stick of peppermint, a favorite premium—was resurrected in 1993.

[*See also* Coffee.]

BIBLIOGRAPHY

Fugate, Francis L. *Arbuckles: The Coffee That Won the West*. El Paso: Texas Western Press, 1994. A history of how one man and one company set about solving the task of making a consistently good cup of coffee. Includes extensive photographs and illustrations.

Ukers, William H. *All about Coffee*. New York: Tea and Coffee Trade Journal Company, 1935. A comprehensive history of the coffee industry. Includes a coffee chronology, coffee dictionary, and a bibliography of more than two thousand authors and titles.

JACQUELINE BLOCK WILLIAMS

Archer Daniels Midland

With 275 processing plants worldwide, 22,000 employees, and official sales of more than $20 billion at the end of the millennium, the Archer Daniels Midland Company (ADM) is one of the world's leading agribusinesses. Headquartered in Decatur, Illinois, the self-styled "Supermarket to the World" processes soybeans, wheat, corn, peanuts, rice, barley, and various oil seeds and converts cocoa into "value-added products" for human and animal consumption. The company is also a world leader in nutraceuticals (vitamins E and C, choline, soy isoflavones, and others) and bioproducts, especially ethanol fuels. It is a thoroughly modern company that grew because of innovation, business prowess, and the close links it forged with government policymakers at home and abroad.

The union of two flaxseed-crushing companies founded in the nineteenth century, Archer Daniels joined with Midland Linseed in 1923 to become America's largest producer of linseed oil. It was a conservative company located in Minneapolis, Minnesota, but it broke from usual milling company practices when it established a research laboratory in the 1930s. From it came the first edible soy protein and soy lecithin, the main emulsifier in many food products. After World War II, ADM grew to be the leading soybean producer, selling some seven hundred items to industries ranging from food to printing, gasoline, pharmaceuticals, and even a cake mix called Airy Fairy.

Archer Daniels Midland took on its modern form beginning in 1966, when Dwayne and Lowell Andreas, and eventually other members of their family, were invited to take control of the company. Raised on a farm in Iowa, the Andreas brothers were already highly successful in the growing agribusiness industry. Dwayne Andreas came to head the company, moved it to Decatur, and led it to its preeminent position as the leader in soybean oil, high fructose corn syrup (a critical ingredient of many processed foods, especially soft drinks); and textured soy protein. A percipient businessman, Andreas saw market demands and was able to adjust the company's products to meet them. These products range from chicken and cattle feeds to pasta, hydroponic vegetables, meat substitutes (the Boca Burger line), soy milk, pet foods, and low-calorie sweeteners.

With its mission "to unlock the potential of nature to improve the quality of life," (admworld.com) ADM has been a leader in the use of co-generated, environmentally friendly power and the development of products that have the potential to fight disease and world hunger. The image of good corporate citizen was tarnished in the 1990s by scandals that were all too common in American business at the time. Seeming to reflect the company's culture, a former president is reported to have said, "Our competitors are our friends. Our customers are the enemy" (Lieber, 2000).

In the late 1990s, ADM was fined a record $100 million for price-fixing. Several company officials were found guilty of other acts of price-fixing in federal court and sentenced to heavy fines and jail sentences. The company has also been accused of lavishing gifts and campaign funds on politicians—presidents, senators, and members of Congress—who, in turn, have protected ADM's interests. Sugar subsidies and ethanol production are two policy areas most often mentioned. ADM remains a corporate powerhouse with strong political connections. Like other agribusiness entities, it will doubtless grow ever larger in the twenty-first century.

BIBLIOGRAPHY

Kahn, E. J., Jr. *Supermarketer to the World: The Story of Dwayne Andreas, CEO of Archer Daniels Midland.* New York: Warner Books, 1991.

Lieber, James B. *Rats in the Grain: The Dirty Tricks and Trials of Archer Daniels Midland.* New York: Four Walls Eight Windows, 2000.

Archer Daniels Midland. http://www.admworld.com. Corporate website.

BRUCE KRAIG

Armour, Philip Danforth

Born in 1832 on a farm in Stockbridge (now Oneida), New York—close to the Erie Canal—Philip Danforth Armour was uniquely prepared to recognize and capitalize on the integration of agriculture, technology, and transportation systems. His foresight and entrepreneurial zeal made him a prototype for modern agribusiness, and, along the way, changed the way Americans eat.

As a young man, Armour went to California in search of gold. He used the capital he acquired to open his first meat-packing plant, in Milwaukee in 1859. Business acumen was an essential part of Armour's success. He sold barrels of salt pork to the Union armies during the Civil War—until he saw that the war was coming to an end. At that point Armour sold all his inventory at forty dollars a barrel, watched the market collapse, and then bought it back for five dollars a barrel. In 1879 Armour purchased 150,000 barrels of pork intended for foreign markets at eight dollars a barrel and then resold it in the United States for fourteen dollars a barrel. Armour learned early on to control the flow of key materials, and he became a major speculator in grain futures. Recognizing that the Union Stockyards and the Chicago rail hub (which had opened in 1865 and 1870, respectively) made Chicago's location pivotal in the transfer of goods from the Great Plains to the markets of the East, Armour relocated his operations there in 1875.

Armour's use of emerging technologies, in both processing and transportation, was among his most important contributions. Armour was one of the first to develop a processing line (a precursor of Ford's assembly line—or, in Armour's case, a disassembly line) to prepare the carcasses of hogs. Armour was an early proponent of canning and sold huge quantities of canned meats. In 1886 his company was the first in the packing industry to hire a full-time chemist—Dr. Herman B. Schmidt—for the purpose of finding profitable uses for all the waste products

Armour Advertising. Advertising card for Armour Star meats. *Collection of Alice Ross*

of the plant. Soap, glue, upholstery, stuffing, and fertilizer were produced and marketed. It was said at the time that Armour had a use for "everything but the squeal" (Geib, "Everything but the Squeal").

Armour's early plants made use of natural ice, but by the 1880s artificial ice (already in use in Milwaukee's breweries) was the standard. A decade later all Armour plants were refrigerated. Armour was mistaken in his belief that his brother Joseph was the first to develop refrigerated railroad cars (Gustavus Swift did so, in 1879), but he made good use of them.

Armour, the consummate meat monopolist, was pitted against the railroad monopolists. The railroad companies preferred to ship live cattle, because profits were dependent on the volume, not the market value, shipped. The railroads also were reluctant to accept the added complications of keeping refrigerated cars iced. In 1889 Armour was successful in persuading the railroads to ship dressed beef. By the end of his life, in 1901, more than six thousand refrigerated cars carried the Armour logo.

[*See also* Canning and Bottling; Pig; Swift, Gustavus Franklin; Transportation of Food.]

BIBLIOGRAPHY

Geib, Paul. E. "Everything but the Squeal: The Milwaukee Stockyards and Meat-packing Industry." *Wisconsin Magazine of History* 78 (1994): 2–23.

Leech, Harper, and John Charles Carroll. *Armour and His Times.* New York and London: Appleton-Century, 1938.

Sinclair, Upton. *The Jungle.* New York: Heritage Press, 1965.

GARY ALLEN

Artichokes

The globe artichoke *(Cynara scolymus)*, which originated in the Mediterranean basin, is a member of the thistle family. Artichokes were eaten by the ancient Greeks and Romans, who served them in a sauce of honey and vinegar. North African Arabs improved the artichoke during Europe's Dark Ages and introduced the new version into Muslim-controlled parts of southern Italy. During the Renaissance, the improved artichoke became highly prized, first in Italian and later in French cookery. Artichokes were also introduced into England at this time, and recipes for them appear in British cookbooks. Martha Washington's *Booke of Cookery,* a manuscript once owned by George Washington's wife, contains a seventeenth-century recipe titled "To Make Hartichoak Pie."

Globe artichokes, also called French artichokes or green artichokes, were grown in Virginia as early as the 1720s and in New England around the time of the Revolutionary War, when they may have been introduced by allied French soldiers. Instructions for growing artichokes regularly appeared in gardening books beginning in 1806. Early American cookbooks occasionally published recipes with artichokes as ingredients. N. K. M. Lee's *The Cook's Own Book* (1832), for example, featured five recipes, including two for boiling and dipping the leaves in butter and two for preserving artichoke hearts.

Before the Civil War, artichokes often appeared on the tables of wealthy Virginia planters. After the war, artichoke recipes frequently appeared in American cookbooks. In 1868, *quartiers d'artichauts lyonnaise* were featured on the menu of a Delmonico's banquet honoring Charles Dickens.

Artichokes were grown in California and Louisiana in the eighteenth century but were not a successful commercial crop. In the 1890s, Italian farmers in northern California's Half Moon Bay planted the crop, and beginning in 1904 boxcar loads of artichokes were sent east from California to supply the needs of artichoke lovers on the East Coast—at that point, mainly Italian immigrants. The first American pamphlet published about artichoke canning was prepared by A. W. Bitting in the 1920s.

The first American artichoke cookbook was R. E. Scammell's *Thistle Eaters Guide* (1969), and it has been succeeded by several others, including Patricia Rain's *The Artichoke Cookbook* (1985) and A. C. Castelli's *The Sensuous Artichoke* (1998). Fresh artichokes are usually boiled or steamed and served with a butter-based sauce for dipping. Artichoke hearts—fresh, canned, or frozen—are served on their own and used in salads, casseroles, and pizzas.

In 1922, Italian farmers began cultivating artichokes in the Salinas Valley of California. Castroville, home to artichoke growers, packers, and processors, calls itself "the Artichoke Capital of the World" and celebrates this claim with an annual artichoke festival. Today, all artichokes produced commercially in the United States are grown in California.

[*See also* Canning and Bottling; Italian American Food.]

BIBLIOGRAPHY

Bitting, A. W. *The Artichoke.* Baltimore: Canning Trade, n.d.

Castelli, A. C. *The Sensuous Artichoke: Magic of the Artichoke.* Riverdale, NY: A. C. Castelli, 1998.

Hooker, Richard J. *Food and Drink in America: A History.* Indianapolis, IN: BobbsMerrill, 1981.

Rain, Patricia. *The Artichoke Cookbook.* Berkeley, CA: Celestial Arts, 1985.

Scammell, R. E. *Thistle Eaters Guide.* 6th ed. Lafayette, CA: Floreat, 1970.

ANDREW F. SMITH

Aseptic Packaging

The first invention was likely a device for carrying food. Hunters and gatherers needed to lighten the burden of bringing food back to a central camp. These early camps were undoubtedly located near water, because the means of transporting liquids was still a long way off. As populations grew and were forced to move farther away from a secure source of water, the need to carry liquids became urgent. Skins and shells, followed by pottery and ceramics and then glass, metals, and plastics, became the materials needed for storing, preserving, and transporting liquids. In 1989, the Institute of Food Technologists, an organization of food scientists devoted to improving the production and distribution of food, selected aseptic packaging as "the most significant food science innovation of the past fifty years" (Mermelstein, 2000). Most consumers do not recognize the term "aseptic packaging," but they instantly recognize this packaging concept as the familiar "juice box." This revolutionary packaging system first appeared in U.S. supermarkets in the 1970s. Aseptic packaging is defined as "the filling of a commercially sterile product into sterile containers under aseptic conditions and sealing of the containers so that reinfection is prevented" (Robertson, p. 51). Aseptic packaging is more than just a container; it is a system that allows food manufactures to fill a sanitized package with a sterile food product in a hygienic environment. The word "aseptic" means that unwanted organisms have been eliminated from the packaging system.

Ruben Rausing in Sweden reportedly conceived the concept for holding milk in a container made from a paperboard composite. The original package had a tetrahedral shape and was called a Tetra Pak. This new technology was married to aseptic technology, and a new industry was born. The box-shaped package that is so widely available is a laminate of six layers of three materials: paperboard, 70 percent; polyethylene, 24 percent; and aluminum, 6 percent. Each layer of material serves a specific purpose. The single layer of paperboard provides mechanical rigidity. The aluminum foil layer acts as a gas and light barrier. The outer polyethylene layer protects the ink layer and enables the package flaps to be sealed. Two inner layers of polyethylene provide a liquid barrier, and another layer binds the aluminum to the paperboard. When it is sealed, the container can preserve milk, soy beverages, juice, soup, sauce, wine, tea, and many other products for months without refrigeration or artificial preservatives.

Aseptic processing is not limited to retail food items. Aseptic bulk storage and transportation systems that can hold up to 1 million gallons of products such as orange juice have been designed. These large commercial systems allow food manufactures to harvest fruit and vegetables at optimum growing periods, partially process the food, and store it for final processing at a later time. Innovations in plastic technology and plasma-discharge silica-coating technology offer the promise that more foods will be packaged in efficient aseptic packages during the twenty-first century.

[*See also* Containers; Material Culture and Technology, *subentry on* The Technology of Cooking Containers; Packaging.]

BIBLIOGRAPHY

Brody, Aaron L. "Thinking outside the Box: Tetra Pak's Past and Future." *Food Technology* 56, no. 11 (November 2002): 66–68.
Mermelstein, Neil H. "Aseptic Bulk Storage and Transportation." *Food Technology* 54, no. 4 (April 2000): 107–109.
Robertson, Gordon L. "The Paper Beverage Carton: Past and Future." *Food Technology* 56, no. 7 (July 2002): 46–52.

JOSEPH M. CARLIN

Asparagus

This perennial garden vegetable (*Asparagus officinalis*) is a member of the lily family. Native to the East Mediterranean area, the name is derived from the Persian word *asparag*, meaning "sprout." Originally, asparagus was quite tall and spindly, resembling contemporary wild asparagus, but by the eighteenth century fatter-stemmed varieties had evolved. The cultivated form of this plant has been developed through selective breeding to produce a number of varieties that shade from white to purple.

For centuries, the British have known the vegetable as "sparrow grass," a term that English and Dutch colonists to New England brought in their cookbooks in the 1700s along with their asparagus seeds. Amelia Simmons in her *American Cookery* (1796) considers the asparagus an "excellent vegetable" and recommends the largest available. Her cooking instructions include the lovely refinement to "tie them up in small even bundles . . . and boil them up quick; but by overboiling they will lose their heads." Miss Eliza Leslie's *Directions for Cookery* (1828) advised cooks that ham should always be accompanied by a green vegetable, such as asparagus. Virtually all nineteenth-century cookbooks recommend serving asparagus on toast, accompanied by melted butter and usually lemon or orange slices. More contemporary

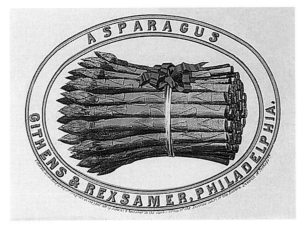

Asparagus. Githens & Rexsamer advertisement. *Warshaw Collection of Business Americana, Archives Center, National Museum of American History, Behring Center, Smithsonian Institution*

THE SMELL OF ASPARAGUS

Asparagus has been known for centuries to cause what the French scholar Louis Lemery called in 1702 a "filthy and disagreeable Smell in the Urine." The odor comes from methylmercaptan, which is excreted in the urine of anyone who eats asparagus, but its detection depends on whether a person is genetically able to smell it. Not every creature is offended by the smell, and this fact may have been put to patriotic use in World War II, when the United States was rumored to have included spears of asparagus in spy kits. Agents allegedly were instructed to eat the delicacy and urinate into oceans or rivers and lakes, thereby allowing the mercaptans to attract fish, making them easier to catch.

SARA RATH

recipes for asparagus feature it either as a hot side dish (minus the toast) or as a cold salad, although asparagus has found its way into soups, sauces, pickles, and such nouvelle cuisine conceits as asparagus ice cream.

Asparagus has been a kitchen garden crop since colonial times but has also been readily naturalized in sandy soils along riverbanks, lakeshores, and seacoasts. Commercial cultivation took off only in the nineteenth century, with improved plants and means of transporting the perishable vegetable to urban markets. Among the most popular variety was Conover's Colossal Asparagus, a fat-stemmed asparagus developed in New York that is recommended to home gardeners as an "heirloom" variety in the twenty-first century.

California has grown asparagus since the 1850s; the white asparagus first used for canning came entirely from that state. In the early 2000s, California led the nation in asparagus production with a harvest of over 50,000 metric tons annually, or 70 percent to 80 percent of the annual total. Most of this is marketed as fresh asparagus. The remainder of the major U.S. commercial asparagus crop is raised in Washington and Michigan where the crop is often frozen or canned.

[See also Heirloom Vegetables; Leslie, Eliza; Simmons, Amelia; Vegetables.]

BIBLIOGRAPHY

Cornell University. *Department of Horticulture at Cornell University.* http://www.hort.cornell.edu. The vegetable research and extension program provides agricultural producers and the general public with current science-based information and production practices.

Michigan Asparagus Advisory Board. *Welcome to Asparagus Online.* http://www.asparagus.org. This site has the answer to almost any asparagus-related question, including details on the National Asparagus Festival.

Moss, Kay, and Kathryn Hoffman. *The Backcountry Housewife.* Vol. 1, *A Study of Eighteenth Century Foods.* Gastonia, NC: Shiele Museum of Natural History, 1985.

SARA RATH

Aunt Jemima

Aunt Jemima pancake flour, the first nationally distributed ready-mix food and one of the earliest products to be marketed through personal appearances and advertisements featuring its namesake, was created by combining advances in manufacturing and distribution with popular nostalgia for the antebellum South.

The self-rising pancake flour was created by a pair of speculators, Chris Rutt and Charles Underwood, in St. Joseph, Missouri, in 1889. The duo had purchased a bankrupt mill and planned to make it successful by developing a new product that would spur demand for their flour. Despite their lack of culinary expertise, or perhaps because of it, the two settled on developing a foolproof and less labor-intensive pancake batter that would require only the addition of water. They experimented with a variety of recipes in the summer of 1889 before settling on a mixture of wheat flour, corn flour, lime phosphate, and salt.

The product was originally named "Self-Rising Pancake Flour" and sold in bags. In the fall of 1889, Rutt was inspired to rename the mix after attending a minstrel show, during which a popular song titled "Old Aunt Jemima" was performed by men in blackface, one of whom was depicting a slave mammy of the plantation South. The song, which was written by the African American singer, dancer, and acrobat Billy Kersands in 1875, was a staple of the minstrel circuit and was based on a song sung by field slaves.

Rutt and Underwood sold their milling company to a larger corporation owned by R. G. Davis of Chicago. He transformed the local product into a national one by distributing it through a network of suppliers and by creating a persona for Aunt Jemima. Davis hired Nancy Green, a former Kentucky slave and cook in a Chicago kitchen, to portray Aunt Jemima in that city's 1893 Columbian Exposition. She served pancakes from a booth designed to look like a huge flour barrel and told

"I'se in town, Honey!"
Reg. U. S. pat. off.

America's most famous recipe

New ways in which millions of women are using it to make delicious pancakes, waffles and muffins

Aunt Jemima. Recipe pamphlet issued by the Quaker Oats Company, mid-twentieth century. *Collection of Andrew F. Smith*

stories of life as a cook on an Old South plantation. Her highly publicized appearance spurred thousands of orders for the product from distributors. Davis also commissioned a pamphlet detailing the "life" of Aunt Jemima. She was depicted as the actual house slave of one Colonel Higbee of Louisiana, whose plantation was known across the South for its fine dining—especially its pancake breakfasts.

The recipe for the pancakes was a secret known only to the slave woman. Sometime after the war, the pamphlet said, Aunt Jemima was remembered by a Confederate general who had once found himself stranded at her cabin. The general recalled her pancakes and put Aunt Jemima in contact with a "large northern milling company," which paid her (in gold) to come north and supervise the construction of a factory to mass-produce her mix. This surprisingly durable fable formed the background for decades of future Aunt Jemima advertising.

The Advertising Campaign

The basic story was fleshed out and brilliantly illustrated through an advertising campaign in North American women's magazines during the 1920s and 1930s. The ads were the work of James Webb Young, a legendary account executive at the J. Walter Thompson advertising agency in Chicago, and N. C. Wyeth, the well-known painter and illustrator of such books as *Treasure Island* and *The Last of the Mohicans*. The full-page color advertisements ran regularly in *Ladies' Home Journal*, *Good Housekeeping*, and the *Saturday Evening Post* and told tales of the leisure and splendor of the plantation South, complete with grand balls, huge dinners, and visitors dropping in from across the region. Not too subtly, Aunt Jemima Pancake Mix, a labor-saving product, was marketed with comparisons to a time and place when some American white women had access to the ultimate labor-saving device: a slave. A line from a 1927 product display read, "Make them with Aunt Jemima Pancake Flour, and your family will ask where you got your wonderful southern cook."

After Aunt Jemima's debut in 1893, her character was played by dozens of women in radio and, eventually, television commercials and in appearances at schools and county fairs. After Nancy Green, the original actress, died in 1923, she was replaced as Aunt Jemima by Anna Robinson, a darker-complected and heavier (at 350 pounds) woman. The image on the box and in ads was adjusted to resemble her more closely. Later, the actresses Aylene Lewis and Edith Wilson portrayed the mammy in some advertisements. Lewis also played the role at Aunt Jemima's Pancake House in Disneyland, which opened in 1957.

However, the advertising icon, always a source of criticism in African American newspapers, came under increasing scrutiny in the 1950s and 1960s as first the civil rights movement and then the black power movement reached their respective crests. Local chapters of the National Association for the Advancement of Colored People began pressuring schools and fair organizers not to invite Aunt Jemima to appear. In 1967, Edith Wilson became the last woman to play Aunt Jemima in advertisements when the Quaker Oats company, which had owned the product since 1925, fired her and canceled its television campaign. Quaker Oats also took Aunt Jemima's name off the Disneyland restaurant in 1970; Aylene Lewis was the last woman to portray Aunt Jemima on the company's behalf.

Revising the Image

Throughout the 1960s, Quaker Oats lightened Aunt Jemima's skin and made her look thinner in print images. In 1968, the company replaced her bandanna with a headband, slimmed her down further, and created a somewhat younger-looking image. She still appeared in print advertisements but without the heavy reliance on the southern plantation settings and largely without a speaking role. In 1989, Quaker Oats made the most dramatic alteration yet to Aunt Jemima's appearance, removing her headband to reveal a head full of graying curls and adding earrings and a pearl necklace. The company said it was repositioning the brand icon as a "black working grandmother."

In 1993, Quaker Oats debuted a series of television ads for the pancake mix featuring the singer Gladys Knight as a spokeswoman and using Aunt Jemima's face only sparingly. The ads had a very short run, and Aunt Jemima continues to hold a low profile in the advertising world, even though she consistently ranks as one of the most recognizable trade names in North America. Aunt Jemima pancake mix and syrup remain market leaders in the United States, and in the 1990s Quaker Oats even licensed the use of her name and image for a line of frozen breakfast products manufactured by another firm. Despite the controversy surrounding her image in the late twentieth century, Aunt Jemima remains one of the most successful advertising icons of our time.

[*See also* Advertising.]

BIBLIOGRAPHY

Kern-Foxworth, Marilyn. *Aunt Jemima, Uncle Ben, and Rastus: Blacks in Advertising, Yesterday, Today, and Tomorrow.* Westport, CT: Greenwood Press, 1994.

Manring, M. M. *Slave in a Box: The Strange Career of Aunt Jemima.* Charlottesville: University Press of Virginia, 1998.

Marquette, Arthur F. *Brands, Trademarks, and Good Will: The Story of the Quaker Oats Company.* New York: McGraw-Hill, 1967.

Quaker Oats, Advertisement Tear Sheets and Proofs, 1927. J. Walter Thomson Company Archives. John W. Hartman Center for Sales, Advertising, and Marketing History, Duke University. Durham, NC.

M. M. MANRING

Automats

Before McDonald's, there was the Horn and Hardart Automat. On December 22, 1888, Joe Horn and Frank Hardart opened their first lunchroom at 39 South Thirteenth Street in Philadelphia, opposite Wanamaker's Department Store. Customers flocked to their lunchroom to sip their "gilt-edge" coffee, prepared in the French-drip method made popular in New Orleans, Louisiana.

At the turn of the twentieth century, the company learned about a new Swiss invention called the "waiter-less restaurant" or the "automatic." The first machine they purchased was manufactured in Germany and installed at 818 Chestnut Street in Philadelphia on June 9, 1902. In 1912 John Fritsche, the chief engineer for Horn and Hardart, designed a more efficient machine with rectangular glass doors that could be opened by a knob. The customer would walk down a wall of these windows, select a hot or cold item, insert a nickel, and turn the knob; the door would then spring open to reveal the food. Behind the bank of glass doors an efficient team of women kept the slots filled with food.

The company opened its first Automat in New York City in 1912. Horn and Hardart commissioned the glass sculptor Nicola D'Ascenzo, who had designed the windows for the Cathedral Church of St. John the Divine in New York City, to create a stained-glass window two stories high. The ceiling contained elaborate carvings, and the customers sat at tables topped with Carrara glass. At the time there was probably no other place in the United States where a person could have a nickel cup of coffee and a nourishing meal in that much splendor. Forty-two Automats were operating in New York City by 1932, and another forty-six had opened in Philadelphia.

All food was prepared in a central commissary and delivered to the Automats daily. To meet the demands of their customers, retail stores were opened in 1922 so that people could have their favorite Horn and Hardart prepared food at home.

The Oxford Dictionary of Word Histories defines "fast food" as "food served in catering outlets where it is kept hot or semi-prepared ready to serve quickly." Based on this definition alone, Horn and Hardart can be credited with starting the fast food revolution in America.

To promote the Automat in the late 1930s, the company started *The Horn and Hardart Children's Hour* on WCAU radio in Philadelphia, with the slogan "less work for mother." It became one of the longest-running shows on radio and television. Bernadette Peters, Frankie Avalon, Eddie Fisher, and Bobby Rydell got their starts on this program.

Joe Horn and Frank Hardart understood the need of customers for a familiar and clean environment and a quick meal at low cost, with no tipping. What they did not expect was that the Automat would be a rendezvous for celebrities and a cultural icon immortalized in both song and movies. The image of two children inserting nickels into the slots under cakes and pies, as their chauffeur held their coats, graced the February 26, 1938, cover of the *New Yorker.* Doris Day is pictured standing next to a bank of Automat glass doors in the movie *That Touch of Mink* (1962). Other scenes filmed in Automats are in *Affair with a Stranger* (1953), with Victor Mature and Jean Simmons, and *Just This Once* (1952), with Peter Lawford and Janet Leigh.

In the 1980s most Horn and Hardart Automats were converted to Burger Kings. The last Automat closed in Philadelphia on May 12, 1990, and nearly a year later the last Automat in New York City closed on April 8, 1991.

Before the Automat disappeared entirely, a thirty-five-foot section of an ornate Automat with mirrors, marble, and marquetry was installed in the Smithsonian's National Museum of American History.

[*See also* Luncheonettes; New York Food.]

BIBLIOGRAPHY

Crowley, Carolyn Hughes. "Meet Me at the Automat." *Smithsonian Magazine*, August 2001.
Diehl, Lorraine B., and Marianne Hardart. *The Automat: The History, Recipes, and Allure of Horn and Hardart's Masterpiece.* New York: Potter, 2002.

JOSEPH M. CARLIN

Avocados

The avocado *(Persea americana)* originated in the broad geographical area stretching from the eastern Mexican highlands to the Pacific Coast of Central America. In pre-Columbian times avocados were disseminated to other places in Central America and Peru. Its seeds have been found in archaeological sites in Mexico dating to 6000 B.C.E. The Aztecs consumed avocados in a variety of ways, one of which was to make a sauce base called *ahuaca-mulli* or "guacamole," which consisted of mashed avocados with chopped tomatoes and New World onions.

Three distinct avocado subspecies have emerged: Mexican, Guatemalan, and Antillean (or lowland). Lowland avocados were disseminated to the Caribbean region soon after the Spanish conquest of Central America and were subsequently introduced into Southeast Asia. The avocado was introduced into the region that became the United States from three directions: from Hawaii early in the nineteenth century (the fruit was common on Oahu by 1855); from Florida before 1850, probably from Cuba; and from California before 1856, perhaps by a gold rush participant who traveled through Central America. By the end of the nineteenth century, avocados had become popular, and an extensive avocado trade had bloomed between the Caribbean region and East Coast cities.

To compete with companies importing avocados, Floridians in the early twentieth century planted the first American commercial avocado orchards. But it was in California that the avocado industry flourished. Eleven years after avocados were first grown commercially in Altadena, California, by Carl Schmidt in 1911, growers

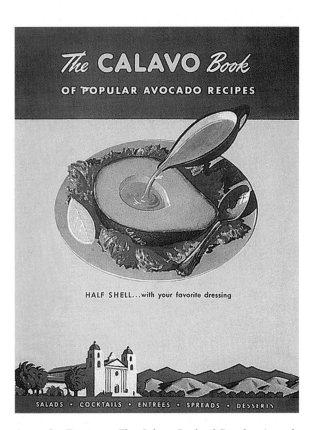

Avocado Recipes. *The Calavo Book of Popular Avocado Recipes,* published by Calavo Growers of California (Los Angeles, 1949). *Collection of Andrew F. Smith*

formed a cooperative association called Calavo, which eventually dominated the industry. California produces 95 percent of the avocados grown in the United States.

Soon after its formation, Calavo published an advertising booklet that contained recipes and encouraged readers to consume avocados in diverse ways. Calavo subsequently published numerous such works. Many of the recipes were later published in noncommercial sources, including magazines, newspapers, and cookbooks. Avocados were used mainly in salads, sandwiches, and cold soups, because avocado pulp becomes bitter when heated.

Avocado cuisine flowered beginning in the 1920s. The 1933 *Sunset All-Western Cook Book* featured twenty-eight avocado recipes. From that date on, avocado recipes were published in almost all mainstream American cookbooks. The first noncommercial cookbook to focus entirely on avocado cookery was Judy Hicks and Mims Thompson's *The Alluring Avocado: Recipes Hot and Cold* (1966). A great diversity of avocado recipes were published, including unusual ones for guacamole, avocado candy, avocado ice cream, and even cooked avocados.

The Fuerte avocado, which matures in winter, is the green-skinned variety that built the industry, but the summer-ripening Hass dominates production, because it holds up better in shipping, is high in oil, and turns black when ripe. By 2002, an estimated 43 percent of all U.S. households were purchasing avocados annually. Consumption increased in part because of the growing popularity of guacamole, a dish featured in Mexican American cookery. The United States produced 225,000 tons of avocados in 2002 and was the second-largest avocado producer in the world after Mexico. Despite record production, importation of avocados from Caribbean countries and South America is common in the United States in the early twenty-first century.

[*See also* Advertising Cookbooklets and Recipes; Dips; Mexican American Food.]

BIBLIOGRAPHY

Calavo. *Introducing the Calavo*. Los Angeles: Calavo Growers of California, 1927.

Hicks, Judy, and Mims Thompson. *The Alluring Avocado: Recipes Hot and Cold*. New York: Walker, 1966.

Rolfs, P. H. *The Avocado in Florida: Its Propagation, Cultivation, and Marketing*. Bulletin no. 61. Washington, DC: Bureau of Plant Industry, U.S. Department of Agriculture, 1904.

Whiley, A. W., B. Schaffer, and B. N. Wolstenholme, eds. *The Avocado: Botany, Production and Uses*. New York: CABI International, 2002.

ANDREW F. SMITH

B

Baby Food

Historically, babies, were fed with breast milk, provided by their own mothers or wet nurses. Solid foods were usually not introduced until the fourth month or later. The norm at the beginning of the twentieth century was for an infant to be nourished with mother's milk through the first year. A small percentage of infants were dry-nursed with formulas, called pap, made of boiled flour or sugar and water, tea, or animal's milk. In the United States, however, the decades from the mid-nineteenth to mid-twentieth centuries saw a shift in feeding patterns for infants, as bottled formula was introduced to be followed as early as six weeks after birth by manufactured baby foods. The rise of industrialism and consumerism transformed the practice of infant feeding, and the increased use of commercial formula and baby food was accompanied by lively public discourse over the meaning of motherhood, child rearing, and nutrition.

Milk, Industrialization, and Ideology

Changing practices of infant feeding were brought about in part by industrialization, which led to innovations in the mass production and distribution of canned goods. Industrialization also led to a rise in the number of women in the workforce, including mothers of young children and infants. By the late nineteenth century, the growth in advertising, made possible by increased circulation of books, newspapers, and magazines, helped promote the rapid introduction of new food products to the American consumer.

These changes were accompanied by shifting ideologies of motherhood. Before the early twentieth century, many believed that so-called "natural motherhood" and proper child development favored breast milk as the best food for babies. Through the mid-nineteenth century, breast-feeding on demand was the norm, and ministers and others valorized white nursing mothers as the highest form of womanhood. At the turn of the century, most child-rearing texts advocated that supplemental foods were to be plain and natural because they affected the development of the infant. Writers cautioned that feeding infants with "stimulating" foods that were spicy, rich, salty, or sugary would lead to irritable and nervous adults. In particular they suggested that overstimulation through food could damage future character and intellect.

At the same time, nineteenth-century physicians and reformers believed that some babies were malnourished because of nutritional deficiencies in their mother's milk. However, babies that were deprived of breast milk were also endangered, because cow's milk alone could transmit disease when it passed through many hands; sterilization through heat was often recommended as a solution to contaminated milk. Dr. A. V. Meigs in 1884 analyzed human and cow's milk to determine the relative amounts of water, fat, sugar, inorganic matter, and protein in each, developing a protocol that imitated human milk, which was widely adopted by food manufacturers.

By the late nineteenth century, various combinations of cow's milk or nonmilk products were marketed as substitutes for mother's milk. In 1867, the Swiss merchant Henri Nestlé invented the first artificial infant food, and in 1873, 500,000 boxes of Nestlé's Milk Food were sold in the United States as well as in Europe, Argentina, and the Dutch East Indies. By the late 1880s, several brands of mass-produced foods, mostly grain mixtures to be mixed with milk or water, were on the market. These included Liebig's Food, Carnrick's Soluble Food, Eskay's Albumenized Food, Imperial Granum, Wagner's Infant Food, and Mellin's Food. Mellin's was perhaps the most widely used. Developed by the English chemist Gustav Mellin in the late 1860s, Mellin's Food was manufactured in the United States by the early 1880s and consisted of a "milk modifier" to be diluted in milk and water. There was also Borden's condensed milk, invented by Gail Borden as a remedy for poor infant health, which consisted of milk preserved by the addition of sugar. In 1924, Moores and Ross Milk Company created a milk-based infant formula known as Franklin Infant Food. Its name was changed to Similac in 1927. By the 1930s, other companies producing infant formula included Abbott, Bristol-Myers, and American Home Products.

Scientific Motherhood, Bottle-Feeding, and Formula

The adoption of these formulas was reinforced by the growth of the belief in so-called "scientific motherhood," which emphasized the importance of medical and scientific expertise in all areas of mothering and favored bottle-feeding over breast-feeding. Mothers were to follow the advice of experts and adhere to rigid feeding schedules. Maternal instinct was considered old-fashioned and unsound; doctors were to "prescribe" breast-feeding or bottle-feeding to mothers.

Advice manuals, such as Frederic Bartlett's *Infants and Children: Their Feeding and Growth* in 1932 and Benjamin Spock's *The Pocket-Book of Baby and Child Care* first published in 1946, encouraged mothers to practice elaborate methods of infant feeding. They were to feed their babies on precise schedules and weigh them before and after feeding. In addition, mothers were to follow elaborate procedures for preparing formula using powdered, evaporated, or whole milk and to sterilize bottles, nipples, and bottle caps conscientiously. If breast-feeding their babies, mothers were to wean them to formula by three to seven months of age. The advice manuals also advocated the early introduction of solid foods. Bartlett, for example, recommended the introduction of cereal by three months of age, vegetables by five months, and bacon by eight months. Spock suggested that the early introduction of solids provided nutrients unavailable in milk, such as iron. Commercially canned vegetables, he advised, were as good as fresh vegetables strained at home. Many of the companies producing baby food and formula, including Gerber, Mellin's, and Bordens, circulated free booklets on child care emphasizing scientific approaches to infant feeding. The U.S. Children's Bureau, through the publication of the booklet, *Infant Care*, similarly emphasized the scientific nature of motherhood to millions of readers beginning in 1914.

The notion that infant formula was equal to if not superior to mother's milk took hold in America. Where 80 percent of American infants had been breast-fed before 1920, by 1948 only 38 percent of babies were breast-fed at one week of age. By 1956, the incidence of infants breast-feeding at one week of age had declined to 18 percent. At the same time, the age at which solid foods were introduced dropped from about seven months of age in 1920, to four to six months during the 1930s, to four to six weeks by the 1950s. As a result, of course, the market for both infant formula and baby food expanded rapidly.

The decline in breast-feeding and the increased use of infant formula and early introduction of solids were not universal. Some women resisted the move toward scientific expertise in motherhood and urged a return to more natural forms of child rearing. Those interested in a return to what were considered to be natural mothering practices included the members of the La Leche League, a voluntary association of women promoting "good mothering through breast-feeding" that was founded in Elmhurst, Illinois, in 1956. By the mid-1980s, the La Leche League claimed over four thousand breast-feeding support groups in forty-eight countries, and by that time the incidence of breast-feeding by new mothers had risen to about 60 percent. Yet while the La Leche League advocated that babies be breast-fed as long as possible—at least a year, and preferably longer—in practice most American women who breast-fed did so for short periods. There were striking differences among racial and ethnic populations. For example, by the end of the twentieth century, when 67 percent of all infants were breast-fed in the days after birth, only 17 percent still breast-fed at one year. Of these infants, a smaller proportion was African American and a slightly higher proportion was Hispanic.

Commercial Baby Food

By the late 1920s, commercially canned baby food was introduced and quickly adopted by American consumers. Conditions were favorable: advertising had become widespread, the cost of canned foods had fallen, and experts recommended the addition of fruits and vegetables to the infant diet. The Gerber Company initiated this revolution in infant feeding by expanding the scope of the canned foods industry. According to the Gerber company history, in 1927 Dorothy Gerber laboriously hand-strained vegetables for her seven-month-old daughter, Sally, and urged her husband, Daniel, to consider manufacturing strained baby food at the Gerber family's Fremont Canning Company. The next year, the company introduced strained peas, prunes, carrots, and spinach to the market. The Gerbers launched an advertising campaign featuring a sketch of an infant known as the Gerber Baby that ran in such publications as *Good Housekeeping*, the *Ladies' Home Journal*, the *Journal of the American Dietetics Association*, and the *Journal of the American Medical Association*. The

Gerber Baby icon, drawn by Dorothy Hope Smith, became the company's official trademark in 1931. Within a year, Gerber baby foods were distributed nationwide. By 1932, over 2 million cans had been sold. In 2002, the company manufactured some 190 food products labeled in sixteen languages and distributed in eighty countries. Gerber dominated the U.S. market.

Beech-Nut, a company that had been formed in 1891 to market ham and bacon, entered the baby food industry in 1931, introducing thirteen varieties of strained baby foods in glass jars, an innovation in an industry in which competitors sold foods in tin cans. That same year, Heinz, a company begun in 1869 to manufacture horseradish, added baby food to its product line.

Additives and Advocacy

Public concerns with food additives developed by mid-century. The American Medical Association declined to approve the addition of vitamins and minerals to canned baby food during World War II. Debates over additives during the 1960s focused on corporate practices driven by market concerns. The consumer advocate Ralph Nader appeared before the U.S. Senate in 1969 to testify that the food industry flavored baby food with salt, sugar, starches, and monosodium glutamate not to enhance the nutrition of babies but to please the palates of the mothers tasting the food. He proposed laws for food labeling as well as funding for food research. Later reformers argued that the addition of sugar to baby food contributed to the obesity and poor food habits of adults.

Another tension developed in 1977 as a result of the widespread use of infant formula. A consumer boycott against the Nestlé Corporation was launched in the United States by the Infant Formula Action Coalition to protest Nestlé's promotion of infant formula and bottle-feeding in developing countries that lacked the technology to use formula effectively. This boycott had spread to ten countries by 1983. It was suspended the next year after Nestlé agreed to adhere to the International Code of Marketing of Breastmilk Substitutes, adopted in 1981 by the World Health Organization and UNICEF.

By the beginning of the twenty-first century, baby food in the United States was a $1.25 billion a year industry. Multinational corporations purchased the three largest baby food brands. Squibb Inc. acquired Beech-Nut in 1968. The brand was then purchased by Nestlé of Switzerland in 1979. In 1994, the Swiss drugmaker Sandoz bought Gerber for $3.7 billion and then merged

with Ciba-Geigy to form Novartis. Heinz sold its U.S. baby food businesses to Del Monte Foods Company in 2002.

In an effort to expand the market further and respond to consumer criticism of processed food, Gerber developed niche flavors, such as apple-mango-kiwi for Hispanics, and in 1997 initiated a Tender Harvest label for organically grown foods. In 2002, Gerber began to convert its packaging from the familiar glass jars to plastic tubs. Beech-Nut altered its baby food through the 1980s and 1990s, removing refined sugar, added salt, and chemically modified starch. In 2002, Beech-Nut added fatty acids, which were found naturally in breast milk and were thought to enhance an infant's visual and mental development, to its First Advantage baby foods. Infant formula producers, such as Ross Products of Abbott Laboratories, also added fatty acids to their products.

In 2002, Gerber held a 77 percent market share among mass retailers of baby food, with rivals Beech-Nut and Heinz following far behind at 11 percent of market share apiece. Smaller companies, such as Earth's Best and Growing Healthy, accounted for less than 3 percent of baby food sales. Only 15 percent of American families prepared their own baby food at home.

[*See also* Beech-Nut; Milk; Nestlé; Nutrition.]

BIBLIOGRAPHY

Apple, Rima. *Mothers and Medicine: A Social History of Infant Feeding, 1890–1950.* Madison: University of Wisconsin Press, 1987.
Bartlett, Frederic. *Infants and Children: Their Feeding and Growth.* New York: Farrar and Rinehart, 1932.
Bentley, Amy. "Inventing Baby Food: Gerber and the Discourse of Infancy in the United States." In *Food Nations: Selling Taste in Consumer Societies,* edited by Warren Belasco and Philip Scranton, 92–112. New York: Routledge, 2002.
Levenstein, Harvey. *Paradox of Plenty: A Social History of Eating in Modern America.* New York: Oxford University Press, 1993.
Spock, Benjamin. *The Pocket Book of Baby and Child Care.* New York: Pocket Books, 1950.
Van Esterik, Penny. *Beyond the Breast-Bottle Controversy.* New Brunswick, NJ: Rutgers University Press, 1989.
Weiner, Lynn. "Reconstructing Motherhood: The La Leche League in Postwar America." *Journal of American History* (March 1994): 1357–1391.

LYNN WEINER

Bagels

A bagel is a round yeast roll with a hole in the middle. A true bagel is completely plain and is made with white

Assorted Bagels. La Bagel Delight, Brooklyn, New York. *Photograph by Joe Zarba*

wheat high-gluten flour, then boiled in water and baked. Boiling the dough reduces the starch content and gives the bagel its outer sheen and hard crust. The word "bagel" possibly derives from *beigen,* German for "to bend," or the Middle High German *bougel* or *buegel,* meaning a twisted or curved ring or bracelet.

In ancient Egypt, there was a hard cracker with a hole in the middle called *ka'ak* that can be seen as an ancestor of the bagel. From Egypt, ancestry can be traced to classical Rome and to what is now Italy and then to France where there is a boiled and baked anise-flavored bread, similar to a bagel. Eventually, precursors of the bagel made their way to Russia and Poland. The first Jewish community in Poland, established by invitation and charter in the thirteenth century, probably brought with them *biscochos,* a ring-shaped cookie or cracker, dating from the Roman period.

It is in Poland where some say the present-day bagel was born. Mentioned as early as 1610 in the community regulations of Kraców, Poland, bagels—symbolic of the endless circle of life—were given as a gift to women in childbirth. There is another theory tracing bagels to 1683 Vienna, where bakers created stirrup-shaped buns in honor of their deliverance from the Turks by the Polish King John Sobieski; *buegel* is the Austrian word for stirrup. Yet another theory is that bagels were invented as an economical food for poor people because the hole saved on ingredients.

The Beigel family of Kraców, Poland, bread bakers for centuries, tells a story that may explain why the bagel is boiled. Eastern European Jews were particularly careful about their meats, fish, and breads, allowing only Jewish bakers to bake for them. Most Jews earned their living as peddlers and when traveling the countryside could not eat bread, the most holy of foods, because it had not been blessed. Jewish dietary laws dictated that bread could not be eaten until after hands were washed and a blessing said. But because clean water was rarely available when they were traveling, the men had to go hungry. By having their dough boiled first, rather than baked, bagels fell outside the category of traditional bread. Consequently, the ritual hand washing and blessing was not required before eating for a time.

Many bagel bakers came to the United States with the mass of eastern European Jewish immigrants at the turn of the twentieth century. The hole in the center of the bagel enabled bakers to sell their wares on the streets of the Lower East Side of New York by threading dozens of bagels on long sticks that they could carry to customers. By 1907, the International Beigel Bakers' Union was created joining together 300 bagel bakers. Only sons of union members could be apprenticed to learn the secrets of bagel baking in order to safeguard the culinary act. Until the late 1950s, bagels were handcrafted in small two- or three-person cellar bakeries on New York's Lower East Side. The oven was built so low that a pit two or three feet deep had to be dug in front of it for the person working the oven. To remove the bagels, they used a twelve-foot *shalivka,* which was a board with a knifelike edge that slid under the bagel and helped toss them into a chute.

By the mid-1920s, the number of bagel bakeries had begun to decline as Jews turned away from their old folk customs. Then in 1951, a Broadway comedy, *Bagels and Yox,* put the word "bagel" into mainstream magazines such as *Time.* That same year, *Family Circle* included a recipe for bagels. This was also the time when bagels were paired with toppings like cream cheese, sweet butter, and smoked salmon. Although bagels had always been a food reserved for Sunday mornings and were thought of as a Jewish dish, this new recognition in major magazines began popularizing them throughout America.

When Murray Lender joined his father's bagel business in 1955, he began expanding the business and making bagels a mainstream food item by packaging bagels to sell in supermarkets. He also began to experiment with bagels flavored with onions, egg, and pumpernickel flour. In 1962, Lender's bought and made operational the first bagel-making machine and began freezing bagels, which they marketed nationally under the Lender's brand.

In the twenty-first century, bagels have been completely assimilated into American food culture and can be found everywhere in supermarkets and national bakery chains, such as Dunkin' Donuts, Einstein's Bagels, and Bruegger's Bagel shops. Bagels are mostly steamed and are offered in every conceivable flavor, from the more traditional pumpernickel or onion to the sweetened blueberry or chocolate chip versions, as well as many other flavors in between. Of all Jewish foods, the bagel has become the most mainstream, enjoyed not only by people in the United States but also worldwide.

[*See also* Bialy; Jewish American Food; Jewish Dietary Laws.]

BIBLIOGRAPHY

Da Silva, Cara. "Cookbook of Dream Recipes: A Collection from a Tragic Past." *Newsday*, April 15, 1991.

Fabricant, Florence. "Cooking a Pot Roast: Four Well-Spent Hours." *The New York Times*, December 5, 1990.

Heinze, Andrew R. *Adapting to Abundance*. New York: Columbia University Press, 1990.

Kirshenblatt-Gimblett, Barbara. *Getting Comfortable in New York: The American Jewish Home, 1880–1950*. New York: Jewish Museum, 1990.

Nathan, Joan. *Jewish Cooking in America*. Updated Edition. New York: Random House, 2001.

Nathan, Joan. *Jewish Holiday Baker*. New York: Schocken, 1997.

Nathan, Joan. *Jewish Holiday Kitchen*. New York: Schocken, 1985.

O'Neill, Molly. "Where Seltzer Once Thrived, Few True Fizzes Remain." *The New York Times*, July 11, 1991.

JOAN NATHAN

Bakeries

Bread bakeries heralded the dawn of civilization. Often government-run or regulated because of the importance of a reliable supply of this staple food, bakeries flourished in Egypt, Mesopotamia, and the Greco-Roman world as well as throughout medieval and early modern Europe. Indeed, wherever villages grew to a critical mass, bakers made and sold fresh, perishable bread. Within a generation of the establishment of successful colonies in America, commercial bakeries had opened in Plymouth, Massachusetts (no later than 1640), New Amsterdam (by 1645), and New Haven, Connecticut (by 1650). However, most baking in America was done at home until the mid-twentieth century, when the balance shifted to favor store-bought products.

Typically the village baker ran a one-man operation reminiscent of his European forefathers. His living quarters adjoined his oven and workspace, with only a small retail area, because colonial bakeries tended to produce to order. From the mid-seventeenth through the mid-nineteenth centuries, many local authorities regulated bakers through assizes of bread that established quality and price controls.

The baking industry grew slowly through the mid-nineteenth century: in 1700, Philadelphia boasted seven bakers serving a population of 4,500, probably the densest concentration of bakers then in America, and 150 years later, the *Census of Manufacturers of 1850* reported a paltry 2,027 bakeries in the entire United States, employing fewer than seven thousand workers to produce the country's commercial supply of breads, sweet and savory pastries, and crackers. Most bakeries remained small, constrained by limited urban markets, the practical difficulties of distributing a perishable product, and arduous preindustrial production techniques that had changed little since the Roman Empire and kept the price of bakery goods relatively high. The convenience of store-bought breads and pastries was a luxury unavailable to the estimated 85 percent of the population living rurally in 1850. Moreover, even when the commercial product was available, Americans generally preferred home-baked goods, especially the South's oven-warm breads and biscuits.

Notable exceptions to the one- or two-person bakeshops were the ship bread (or hardtack) bakers, who produced dry, unleavened, nearly imperishable breads that fed the colonial merchant fleets, the overland western expansion, and the armies (especially during the Civil War). These crackerlike commodities had no tradition of home production, did not stale, and were easier to produce and distribute than leavened breads, sparking the first larger-scale American baking operations virtually from their inception as adjuncts to flour milling. The ship bread was purchased in large volumes by wholesalers, who resold the product to ships' operators, pioneering expeditions, and grocers; ship bread manufacture, combined with flour milling, was second in economic importance only to tobacco in the middle and southern colonies. These bakers evolved into the behemoth modern cookie and cracker industry.

Changes in ovens and the introduction of mechanical mixers and dough shapers brought an industrial efficiency and uniformity to the bakers of perishable goods, starting in the late nineteenth century and continuing through the twentieth. Furthermore, by 1900 approximately 40 percent of the population lived in cities, easing distribution issues. Servantless housewives had less time to devote to the perceived drudgery of baking, especially breads. The 1890s hygienic innovation of wrapping loaves individually in waxed paper for transporting from factory to store also led to greater acceptance of commercial loaves. As incomes rose in the early twentieth century, so did the consumption of purchased bakery goods: by 1930 as much as 60 percent of all bread was purchased, although many housewives still preferred to bake their cakes and pastries. The Great Depression temporarily interrupted the growth in the baking industry, which revived during and after World War II, when most bread and, increasingly, pastries were purchased either directly from small-scale bakeries or from grocery stores retailing products from wholesale operations.

Bakeries have played a role in perpetuating ethnic foodways, creating new ones (for example, blueberry bagels), and defining class norms. Wherever significant immigrant populations congregated, mom-and-pop bakeries produced distinctive old-country breads and pastries to satisfy the physical and emotional needs of recent arrivals and to maintain ethnic identities in subsequent generations. At the opposite end of the spectrum are the French bakeries that appeared in the early Federal period, especially in Washington, D.C., serving the transient diplomatic trade. These bakeries and their counterparts in other cities allowed an aspiring or upper-class clientele in the nineteenth century to demonstrate what was viewed as urbane taste. In the last quarter of the twentieth century, the revival of interest in artisanally produced foods encouraged many small-scale bakers to penetrate urban and affluent areas. Exquisitely handcrafted loaves and specialty pastries of astounding variety come at a price:

by the early twenty-first century, in major metropolitan markets well-heeled clients were paying pay five dollars or more for their daily bread.

[*See also* Bread; Cakes; Crackers; Hardtack; Pastries.]

BIBLIOGRAPHY

Leslie, Eliza. *Seventy-five Receipts for Pastry, Cakes, and Sweetmeats.* Boston: Munroe & Francis, 1828.
Glezer, Maggie. *Artisan Baking across America.* New York: Artisan, 2000.
Panschar, William G. *Baking in America: Economic Development.* Evanston, IL: Northwestern University Press, 1956.

CATHY K. KAUFMAN

Baking Powder, *see Chemical Leavening*

Bananas

Bananas are tropical or subtropical plants of the genus *Musa* that bear clusters of long yellow or reddish fruit. There are sixty-seven species and more than two hundred varieties of bananas. Cultivated as early as 1000 B.C.E. in the rain forests of Southeast Asia, bananas were taken to the Near East and Africa by Arab traders in the seventh century. In 1516 the Catholic missionary Friar Tomas de Berlanga landed on the island of Hispaniola (Haiti and the Dominican Republic) and planted bananas as the least expensive and most satisfactory food for the growing African slave population. When he became bishop of Panama, Friar Tomas took banana plants with him to the mainland. Bananas spread rapidly through Central America, Mexico, and southern Florida, so rapidly that later observers believed the banana to be native to the New World.

The first English colonists of Roanoke Island, off the coast of what became North Carolina, brought banana stocks with them from the Caribbean islands, but the bananas did not thrive in the nontropical climate. Bananas were growing on the Hawaiian Islands when the islands were visited by Captain James Cook in 1799, and the fruit became an export crop in the nineteenth century. Despite several attempts in Florida and California, commercial banana plantations on the mainland United States have not been successful.

Before the 1880s most residents of the United States had never seen or eaten a banana. Although they found

Bakery. Interior of a bakery at Homestead, Iowa, 1920s. *Amana Restoration*

a ready market in schooner days, bananas remained a luxury item until the introduction of steamships, the extension of the railroad throughout the United States, and the availability of refrigeration. These innovations made it possible to cut the time in transit and to keep the fruit at a constant temperature to slow the ripening process. By the mid-1880s consumers could find red and yellow bananas in the markets of New York, Philadelphia, and Boston. At the end of the nineteenth century, bananas were available in many parts of the United States, although they were expensive and considered a luxury outside the port cities of the East Coast. Fruit importing companies knew that they had a profitable item if they could only find a consistent supply of the fruit abroad and expand their markets at home.

American fruit companies taught Americans to eat bananas and encouraged the people of the Caribbean basin to grow bananas on a commercial basis. Local banana growers in Jamaica, Cuba, and elsewhere expanded cultivation of bananas in response to the increasing North American demand for the fruit. The United Fruit Company was the first to achieve a constant, year-round flow of bananas to North American cities. By 1920 United Fruit had become one of the largest enterprises in the United States. The company had a vertically integrated network of plantations, refrigerated steamships, and railroad cars to produce, transport, distribute, and market bananas.

The large banana companies set up marketing divisions and education programs to persuade Americans that bananas were an essential item to be eaten every day. Bananas lost their status as a luxury food and were transformed through low price, year-round availability, and abundance into comfort food for children and the elderly and health food for athletes and dieters. The fruit that had been introduced to the Americas as a food for slaves and became an exotic luxury for wealthy and well-traveled North Americans in the nineteenth century entered the twentieth century as an inexpensive food for the poor as well as a food of the health-conscious middle and upper classes.

Bananas became widely available in the United States at roughly the same time that discoveries were being made concerning calories, germs, and vitamins. Changing notions about sanitation, diet, and disease led to incorporation of the newly available fruit into American medicine. Bananas were advertised successfully as the fruit in the germproof wrapper, as full of

Chiquita Banana. Chiquita Banana was a trademark of the United Fruit Company. Recipe book, 1950.

essential vitamins, and as a diet food. In the 1930s bananas were promoted for use in the treatment of diarrhea, ulcers, colitis, tuberculosis, diabetes, obesity, malnutrition, fertility problems, celiac disease, scurvy, and gout. The American Medical Association approved bananas for general promulgation to the public in 1931.

In the nineteenth century bananas were served raw with dessert, but by 1900 American cooks were experimenting with bananas to produce a variety of dishes, including deep-fried banana fritters, baked bananas served with meat, and banana ice cream. In 1910 an advertisement showed a bowl of sliced bananas with a small amount of cereal being spooned over it. Soon it became more common to add sliced bananas to a bowlful of breakfast cereal. On cereal is perhaps the most common way in which Americans at the beginning of the twenty-first century consume bananas, despite decades of effort by fruit companies to include the fruit in all meals and between-meal snacks.

Latrobe, Pennsylvania, is credited with being the home of the banana split, which was first served in 1904. Banana splits became widely popular soda fountain treats in the 1920s and remain popular. Banana bread is said to have been invented by a Depression-era housewife in search of a way to make extra money at home. Banana pudding with vanilla cookies embedded in it has also become an American staple and is often found at diners, supermarket salad bars, and restaurants featuring "home cooking."

Banana puree was first produced commercially in 1966 and is used to flavor sherbet, ice cream, eggnog, yogurt, and cottage cheese. It is also used in banana bread, cake, tarts, muffins, doughnuts, icing, and cream pie and is found in a variety of baby food products. Banana powder is used in dry mixes and crunch toppings, and banana extract is used to flavor beverages, dairy products, and bakery products. Bananas are included in commercial products such as barbecue and other sauces, glazes, gravy, soups, and salad dressings as a flavor builder and thickening agent.

Imported bananas have been one of the least expensive fruits in the grocery store for more than a century. Bananas also are the most widely consumed fruit in the United States. Per capita consumption of bananas increased from 21 pounds in 1979 to 28.4 pounds in 2000, representing a triumph of distribution, advertising, and marketing.

[See also Baby Food; Breakfast Foods; Caribbean
    Influences on American Food; Cereal, Cold; Desserts;
    Fruit; Hawaiian Food; Health Food; Homemade
    Remedies; Puddings; Transportation of Food; Twinkies.]

BIBLIOGRAPHY

Abella, Alex. *The Total Banana: The Illustrated Banana—Anecdotes, History, Recipes, and More!* New York: Harcourt, Brace, Jovanovich, 1979.
Gowen, S. R., ed. *Bananas and Plantains.* London: Chapman and Hall, 1995. The most comprehensive reference.
Jenkins, Virginia Scott. *Bananas: An American History.* Washington, DC: Smithsonian Institution Press, 2000.
Langley, Lester D., and Thomas Schoonover. *The Banana Men: American Mercenaries and Entrepreneurs in Central America, 1880–1930.* Lexington: University Press of Kentucky, 1995.
Robinson, J. C. *Bananas and Plantains.* Wallingford, U.K.: CAB International, 1996.
Stover, R. H., and N. W. Simmonds. *Bananas.* 3rd ed. London: Longman, 1987. The classic work of botany and horticulture includes a substantial historical chapter.
United States Department of Agriculture, Economic Research Service. *Food Consumption per Capita Data System.* http://ers.usda.gov/data/foodconsumption.

VIRGINIA SCOTT JENKINS

Barbecue

Barbecue is a method of slow-cooking meat over coals, also known as barbeque, bar-b-q, BBQ, or simply 'cue. Although backyard grilling in general is called barbecuing by most English-speaking peoples, only the traditional American slow-cook barbecue first popularized in the American South will be discussed.

Most authorities agree that both the word "barbecue" and the cooking technique derive from the Taino and Carib peoples of the Caribbean and South America. The Spanish conquistadores reported natives of Hispaniola roasting, drying, and smoking meats on a wooden framework over a bed of coals, called a *barbricot*, which the Spaniards pronounced *barbacoa*. The derivation from the French *barbe à queue*, literally "from beard to tail," has been discounted.

Europeans had of course been cooking meat over fires for thousands of years. It was the low heat of the coals and the consequent slowness of the process that set the New World method apart. One early French explorer reported: "A Caribbee has been known, on returning home from fishing fatigued and pressed with hunger, to have the patience to wait the roasting of a fish on a wooden grate fixed two feet above the ground, over a fire so small as sometimes to require the whole day to dress it."

The Europeans in the New World quickly adopted this novel method of slow cooking, discovering fairly early that hogs made great barbecue. So popular was pork in North Carolina that in 1728 William Byrd of Virginia wrote, "these people live so much upon swine's flesh that . . . many of them seem to grunt rather than speak in their ordinary conversation." Barbecue parties featuring whole hogs became fashionable enough by the late 1600s that Virginia passed a law banning the discharging of firearms at barbecues. The Founders were fond of barbecue parties as well: In a 1773 diary entry George Washington says that he attended a "Barbicue [sic] of my own giving at Accatinck."

The barbecue as a social occasion has been well documented. It was and is popular for community or church get-togethers or fund-raisers, and it has been used by politicians ever since George Washington as a means of drawing voters, initially in the South, then nationally. Sam Houston gave a speech at the Great American Barbecue in 1860; in the 1960s President Lyndon B. Johnson was famous for his Texas barbecues; and a victory barbecue in 1961 for South Carolina's Governor

Russell was the first integrated political event there since the days of Reconstruction.

Styles of Barbecue

The oldest form of American open pit barbecue is practiced all along the flat coastal plain of the southeastern United States where the English colonists originally settled. What is called the "pit" is constructed either by digging a hole in the ground or by making a wide, shallow container, and placing a rack on top. A whole dressed hog is split and placed on the rack. Hardwood logs are burned down to coals in a separate fireplace and then these hot coals are continuously shoveled under the meat, which cooks anywhere from eight to fourteen hours, depending on the fire and the pitmaster. It is an extremely laborious process. No sauce is used on the meat nor is the meat basted while it cooks, although some pitmasters will allow a dry-seasoning rub before the meat goes on the rack to cook. When the meat is so tender that it is ready to fall off the bone, the pig is taken off the rack, the meat is "pulled" into shreds or chopped fine, then splashed with a thin, sharp sauce of vinegar and red pepper. This barbecue will sometimes be served as is, but it is most often topped with some coleslaw and additional sauce and sandwiched into a soft, white bun. Sweetened iced tea is the preferred beverage, and hush puppies are a typical side dish.

Whole-hog barbecues with a simple vinegar sauce can still be found in the rural areas of Georgia and South Carolina, but in the urban areas shoulder and rib barbecues are more common. South Carolina is famous for its unusual yellow mustard–based barbecue sauce, but Georgia's sauce, while tomato-based, also has a distinct mustard component. South Carolina is also known for serving Brunswick stew with its barbecue, along with sweetened iced tea.

Mississippi, Tennessee, and Alabama also have the occasional whole-hog barbecue, but again shoulder and ribs are more common. It is in Kentucky that the first real break from the pork barbecue tradition takes place, for Kentucky is the home of barbecued mutton. There are a number of theories as to why mutton is so popular there. One theory suggests that because of the Wool Tariff of 1816, raising sheep became profitable in Kentucky at about the same time the sheep-loving Welsh were migrating into the area. Yet even before that Kentuckians were eating mutton. A guest at the wedding of Thomas Lincoln and Nancy Hanks in Kentucky in 1806 said, "We had . . . a sheep barbecued whole over coals of wood burned in a pit, and covered with green boughs to keep the juices in." Every May over twenty-thousand pounds of mutton is barbecued at the International Bar-B-Q Festival in Owensboro, Kentucky. Barbecue in Kentucky is likely to be served with sweetened iced tea and burgoo, a traditional squirrel and corn stew.

In Oklahoma, Missouri, Kansas, and Texas, beef becomes the meat of choice for barbecue, and the style of cooking changes as well. Although there are many theories as to how barbecue migrated into these western states, there is no doubt that several influences converged. An important factor was that blacks, both free and slave, moved into the area from the Southeast and brought a love of barbecue with them. In the early twenty-first century, most of the western barbecue restaurants that specialized in pork were owned by African Americans. Another factor was the influence of the Mexican *barbacoa*, a pre-Columbian technique of slow-cooking pieces of meat wrapped in leaves in earth-covered pits. Added to this, nineteenth-century cowboy cooks found that long cooking over coals turned tough beef from range cattle into edible meat. Lastly, the German and Eastern European immigrants who came to Texas in the 1800s brought with them a liking for certain cuts of meat and sausage and these cuts were quickly incorporated into western-style barbecue.

All of these differing influences met in Texas and the West and combined to create a new style of barbecue using beef, as well as such other available meats as goat. Western-style barbecue tends to be "closed pit," in which the cooking container is covered, using indirect heat rather than live coals under the meat, and features a great deal more smoke than the older southeastern style. It is in closed pit barbecue that the telltale smoke ring appears. This is a pinkish ring just inside the meat that forms as part of a chemical reaction between the smoke and the moisture in the meat. This is considered a good thing in the West but a sign of over-smoking on the Eastern seaboard.

In parts of Texas, the very smoky beef is cooked and served without any sauce at all. Side dishes are different, as well: crackers, Texas toast (Texas-size garlic bread), and beans are common accompaniments. In Kansas and Missouri, where beef brisket "burnt ends" are a favorite, a very spicy tomato-based barbecue sauce is common. Side dishes are likely to include spicy barbecued beans. Western barbecue is served with either iced tea or beer, depending on the locale and the attendees.

African Americans brought barbecue with them to the far West and the North during the great post-Emancipation migrations. Chicago is one of the few areas outside the South that has developed its own unique barbecue culture, featuring heavily smoked pork ribs, shoulders, and other cuts, served with a spicy tomato-based sauce. In other urban centers, such as New York, Los Angeles, and Seattle, fairly authentic African American–owned barbecue "joints" may be found, but these areas have not yet developed their own styles of barbecue.

The Future of Barbecue

The future of authentic slow-cooked barbecue in the United States is not clear. Old-fashioned barbecue cookery is labor intensive and time consuming, many of its prime practitioners are nearing retirement, and few younger people are willing to take their places. Environmental and safety regulations in many parts of the country make it difficult for barbecue restaurants to continue to operate their wood-burning pits. However, at the beginning of the twenty-first century, interest in old-fashioned barbecue was at an all-time high. One of the reasons was the growing popularity of barbecue contests. Two of the biggest contests were the American Royal Barbecue Contest in Kansas City and the Memphis in May Contest, which started in the 1980s as relatively small, local barbecue cook-offs. By the beginning of the twenty-first century, each of these contests was drawing crowds of over 100,000. Most of the contestants were nonprofessional cooks who competed on teams, many of them with such colorful names as Elvis Porksley's Greaseland Porkers, The Pit and the Pigulum, or Tangled Up in 'Que, to name but a few examples.

In addition, the rising popularity of the study of American culinary history has sparked an interest in indigenous and historical cooking methods, such as barbecue. As a result, several universities have begun research into the complex roots of American barbecue, and the number of books published about barbecue had grown from virtually none prior to 1990 to well over thirty by the early 2000s. It can only be hoped that such a unique and fascinating, not to mention delicious, method of cooking will be preserved and will prosper.

[See also Communal Gatherings; Cooking Techniques; Fund-Raisers; Hearth Cookery; Meat; Southern Regional Cookery; Southwestern Regional Cookery.]

BIBLIOGRAPHY

Browne, Rick, and Jack Bettridge. *Barbecue America: A Pilgrimage in Search of America's Best Barbecue*. Alexandria, VA: Time-Life, 1999.

Elie, Lolis Eric. *Smokestack Lightning: Adventures in the Heart of Barbecue Country*. New York: Farrar, Straus and Giroux, 1996. A very personal, entertaining, yet factual exploration of barbecue across the country.

Garner, Bob. *North Carolina Barbecue: Flavored by Time*. Winston-Salem, NC: John F. Blair, 1996. Scholarly and accessible.

Schlesinger, Chris, and John Willoughby. *The Thrill of the Grill*. New York: Morrow, 1990.

Thorne, John, and Matt Lewis Thorne. *Serious Pig*. New York: North Point Press, 1996.

Walsh, Robb. *Legends of Texas Barbecue Cook Book*. San Francisco: Chronicle, 2002.

SYLVIA LOVEGREN

Barley

A grass in the genus *Hordeum,* barley is cultivated mostly for animal feed and as a key ingredient in beer. Barley is also used in private kitchens in the making of soup, cereal, and gluten-free bread. Archeologists studying Sumeria in southern Mesopotamia discovered remnants of wild barley, *Hordeum spontaneum,* dating to approximately 8000 B.C.E. Resembling oatmeal, barley grains were used as a basic unit in the Sumerian measuring system. Cultivated barley was important to the Egyptians dating to 5000 B.C.E. Barley bread and beer made from fermented barley were everyday nourishment for Egyptian slaves who built the pyramids. Much later, the medieval English used barley bread as a trencher, which served as a platter, bowl, plate, and serving dish.

Ancient Hebrews revered barley as one of seven special species along with wheat, grapes, figs, pomegranates, olives, and date honey. In 2800 B.C.E., the Chinese held barley to be one of five sacred plants along with rice, wheat, millet, and soybeans. At the beginning of the common era, wheat became the favorite grain of the rich. Wheat was popular because it contained more gluten than other grains, affording lighter and moister bread. The poor continued to eat barley bread. By 1602, barley was being planted in North America. Pennsylvania settlers added limestone water to barley; once fermented, the concoction was distilled and made into whiskey.

In the making of beer, whole, unrefined barley is soaked until it sprouts. During soaking, proteins within the bran convert to enzymes that change starches to sugars. Next the barley is dried to prevent further sprouting and is lightly cooked. The resulting malt is crushed and combined with warm water, and the conversion of starch to sugar begins. Addition of yeast to malt leads to fermentation, which results in alcohol. In beer production, hops are added to the barley malt.

In the twenty-first century, dominant producers of barley are Australia, Russia, and Canada. The United States ranks fourth and is followed by France. Barley grows in three varieties: two-rowed and six-rowed and an irregular type found in Ethiopia. Because it is drought resistant, barley can be sown in spring and fall. In countries with severe climates, such as Tibet, only one crop a year is possible.

Rich in carbohydrates and containing protein, barley is low in fat and contains no cholesterol. Barley also supplies potassium, calcium, iron, B vitamins, and fiber. Hull-less barley contains the most protein, is chewier, and has a richer flavor than other forms. Pearled barley has had the husk, bran, and germ removed and is used widely as flour, grits, powder, groats, and flakes. Patent barley, which is ground from pearl barley, is used commercially to make thickener and baby cereal.

Barley is a central part of the diet of many cultures. In Britain, ale berry or barley berry is a favorite dessert. Stale barley bread is boiled in mild ale until quite thick, sweetened with honey, and served with cream. In the mountains of France, *boulon* is served as a hard bread with a soupy casserole for dunking. Tibetan monks prepare *tsampa*, a porridge of toasted barley ground into flour and blended with yak butter and boiling tea.

[*See also* Beer; Bread; Distillation; Whiskey.]

BIBLIOGRAPHY

Bumgarner, Marlene Anne. *The New Book of Whole Grains: More than 200 Recipes Featuring Whole Grains, Including Amaranth, Quinoa, Wheat, Spelt, Oats, Rye, Barley, and Millet.* New York: St. Martin's Griffin, 1997.

Wood, Rebecca. *The Splendid Grain: Robust, Inspired Recipes for Grains with Vegetables, Fish, Poultry, Meat, and Fruit.* New York: Morrow, 1997.

MARTY MARTINDALE

Bars

Bars, taverns, saloons, pubs, taprooms, clubs, cafés, and cocktail lounges all fall within the larger context of what can be called "commercial leisure spaces." The definition for each of these different drinking places is not precise, and the elements that distinguish them blur at the boundaries.

One element found in all of these places is the bar. The bar is generally as a wooden counter, longer than it is wide, over which alcoholic beverages or other refreshments are served. The person who pours the drinks or pulls the tap is the bartender; the woman who carries drinks to the table is the barmaid or cocktail waitress. Almost anything that comes in contact with the wooden counter picks up the prefix of "bar." The bowls of peanuts and pretzels on the bar are called bar mixes or bar snacks. Patrons sit upon bar stools and if they spill their drink, the towel used to wipe it up is called a bar mop.

Another universal element is that bars are nocturnal establishments, places where people go to drink and eat, generally after work. Drinking during daylight hours has a negative image to many Americans. The idea of a three-martini lunch signifies excess and waste.

Nightclubs (1940s and 1950s), go-go clubs (1960s), and discos (1970s) were also nocturnal drinking establishments. When they flourished, they were viewed as places to visit after dinner or the theater, even after bar hopping, to continue drinking and dancing. Bars that operated illegally during Prohibition (1920 to 1934) were called speakeasies. They were everything your neighborhood pub or bar was not.

Colonial taverns dispensed expensive distilled liquors, imported wines, and bowls of punch from a small room called a bar or cage bar. This bar was generally constructed in one corner of the main room. It was open on two sides except for wooden bars that ran from the top of the counter to the ceiling. A small section of the obstructing grate could be lifted or lowered from within the cage. The tavern keeper entered the enclosed space from a back door. In this small space he mixed the punches, decanted wine, and measured out spirits into tankards and mugs while at the same time protecting his investment from breakage or theft. Patrons did not drink at this bar but carried their drinks to a table.

The modern bar and saloon, along with the concept of the hotel and restaurant, slowly evolved out of the inns and taverns that served the needs of the colonies for food, drink, and lodging during the seventeenth and eighteenth centuries. These public arenas were copied from British inns and taverns that had been part of the social structure since medieval times. Taverns were places where people came to socialize and interact. Just as they were necessary then to provide shelter, food, and entertainment for the traveler, they exist in the twenty-first century for the same reasons.

With the explosion in the number of Americans traveling abroad in the second half of the nineteenth century, bars modeled after English and Irish pubs became

Bartender. Bartender preparing for customers at the Park Slope Ale House in Brooklyn, New York. *Photograph by Joe Zarba*

popular in American cities. "Pub," short for "public house," was the British designation for a casual neighborhood bar. The signboard hanging outside to identify it as a drinking place might be the only outward indication that it was not a private house.

In some cities, particularly Philadelphia, neighborhood bars were called taprooms and catered mostly to blue-collar workers. Many of these neighborhood institutions started off as private homes. When retrofitted for serving food and drink, the first floor was divided into taproom, public parlor, bar, and kitchen. Private living quarters were located on the second and third floors. Male patrons entered the bar directly from the main street but women entered the public parlor from a side door. Above this door might be a sign that read Ladies Entrance or Ladies Invited.

Bar proprietors competed with each other by putting out elaborate repasts to attract so-called barflies and beer hounds. During the early part of the twentieth century and the second half of the nineteenth century the free lunch was not limited exclusively to bars and saloons. The Waldorf, Knickerbocker, Biltmore, and Plaza hotels in New York also provided a free lunch, but the ten-cent mugs of beer in these establishments were out of reach of the working class. At these upscale hotels the lunch counter might offer chicken salad, lobster Newburg, melted cheese on toast, cold corned beef, or sliced Virginia ham.

At bars that catered to the working class with five-cent beers, patrons could choose from tomatoes, scallions, beans, radishes, or sausages. Some offered a complete New England boiled dinner and two beers, all for the price of a dime. Barkeepers kept a close eye on what customers were eating. It was an unwritten law that patrons invest at least fifteen cents in beers if they were going to partake of the free lunch. Bouncers kept a close eye on hungry drinkers.

Before Prohibition took effect in the 1920s, it seemed to some that there was a bar on every corner. After Prohibition, bars did not return in the same numbers because soda fountains, drugstores, and even cigar stores gobbled up the spots vacated by the barrooms. The stores that replaced the bar were more profitable because drugstore customers, except when they stopped for a malted milk at the soda fountain, did not linger. In contrast, saloons made money only when their customers stayed to drink.

The triangular martini glass with an olive in it is internationally recognized as the symbol for "bar."

[*See also* Alcohol and Teetotalism; Alcoholism; Beer Halls; Microbreweries; Prohibition; Roadhouses; Saloons; Taverns; Temperance; Wine-Tasting Rooms.]

BIBLIOGRAPHY

Ryder, Bethan. *Bar and Club Design*. New York: Abbeville, 2002.
Rector, George. *The Girl from Rector's*. Garden City, NY: Doubleday, Page & Co., 1927.

JOSEPH M. CARLIN

Batidos

Batidos are tropical fruit shakes consisting of crushed ice, fruit, a sweetener, and milk or water. The ingredients can be blended with ice or served over crushed ice. Typical fruits include banana, guava, mamey, pineapple, sweetsop, papaya, mango, passion fruit, and tamarind. Derived from the Spanish word meaning "to beat," these light, frothy drinks originated as thirst quenchers in tropical climates. In the early twenty-first century batidos are becoming popular in the United States wherever there are large Latin American and Caribbean immigrant communities.

Two modern devices have aided the popularity of batidos: the blender and the refrigerator. Before blenders, all ingredients except ice were beaten by hand, and the resulting mixture was poured over crushed ice. Freezers make ice storage possible and allow milk, a primary ingredient, to stay fresh in warm climates. Before the widespread availability of refrigerators, sweetened, condensed milk—a dairy product needing no refrigeration—was often used in batidos.

[*See also* Blenders; Caribbean Influences on American Food; Fruit; Milkshakes, Malts, and Floats.]

BIBLIOGRAPHY

Farrell-Kingsley, Kathy. "Florida Fusion." *Vegetarian Times* 228 (August 2001): 42–46.
Raichlen, Steven. *Miami Spice: The New Florida Cuisine*. New York: Workman, 1993.

JENNIFER MINNICK

Bayless, Rick

He refers to himself as a "gringo from Oklahoma," yet Rick Bayless has become one of America's leading emissaries of Mexican cuisine thanks to his odyssey as an award-winning chef, restaurateur, author, TV personality, salsa manufacturer, and teacher. Bayless was born in Oklahoma City in 1953 into the fourth generation of a family of restaurateurs and food people. His great-grandparents were the first grocers in the state of Oklahoma, and his parents ran the family barbecue restaurant. Bayless demonstrated his own culinary bent when, on his tenth birthday, he asked his parents to buy him Julia Child's *Mastering the Art of French Cooking*.

Although without Mexican roots, Bayless has said he had felt a spiritual connection to Mexico from childhood. He began studying Spanish when he was twelve and organized a family vacation to Mexico when he was fourteen. On arrival there, he said he felt as if he had come home. He pursued an undergraduate degree in Spanish language and literature and Latin American culture at the University of Oklahoma and a master's degree in linguistics at the University of Michigan. He had nearly completed his doctorate in anthropological linguistics at Michigan, when he decided to leave academia and devote himself full time to teaching cooking classes, running a catering business, and hosting *Cooking Mexican*, his first PBS show in 1979.

In the early 1980s, Bayless began a five-year, 35,000-mile grassroots exploration of Mexico's diverse regional cuisine. He visited local markets, home kitchens, and street vendors, taking notes with a scholar's zeal. In 1987, with his treasure chest of recipes, Bayless published with his wife, Deann, *Authentic Mexican: Regional Cooking from the Heart of Mexico*. Considered a classic, the book is still in print in the early 2000s. Immediately following the book's publication, Bayless opened Frontera Grill, a casual seventy-seat restaurant near downtown Chicago that he decorated with festive, contemporary Mexican art.

Bayless chose Chicago because of its large Mexican population and excellent Mexican markets. Working closely with local farmers and purveyors, Bayless showcased the bold, vibrant flavors of authentic Mexican cuisine, such as complexly spiced moles, light citrus marinades, grilled quail, smoky chilies, and cilantro-enhanced dishes, not the soft, heavy food, covered with melted cheese, which he said the majority of Americans mistakenly believed was true Mexican. Frontera Grill was an immediate success. In 1989, Bayless opened Topolobampo, a seventy-five-seat fine-dining restaurant, adjacent to Frontera.

As he came to prominence, Bayless began winning numerous awards, including the 1995 James Beard Award as Outstanding Chef in the United States. He appeared as a guest on Julia Child's *Cooking with Master Chefs*. He was a founder, and later chairman, of the Chef's Collaborative, a nationwide group that promotes sustainable agriculture. He started his own company,

Frontera foods, which produces sauces and salsas from regional recipes. In the early 2000s, he had launched his second PBS series *Mexico—One Plate at a Time* and had authored his fourth cookbook. He was also teaching at professional chefs training schools throughout the world. Bayless says he intends to continue his crusade to make authentic Mexican cuisine accessible to the home cook and to help Americans appreciate Mexican food for the world-class cuisine it is.

[*See also* Child, Julia; Mexican American Food.]

BIBLIOGRAPHY

Davis, Dawn. *If You Can Stand the Heat: Tales from Chefs and Restaurateurs.* New York: Penguin, 1999.
Dornenburg, Andrew, and Karen Page. *Dining Out: Secrets from America's Leading Critics, Chefs, and Restaurateurs.* New York: Wiley, 1998.
Shore, Debbie, Catherine Townsend, and Laurie Roberge. *Home Food: 44 Great American Chefs Cook 160 Recipes on Their Night Off.* New York: Clarkson N. Potter, 1995.

SCOTT WARNER

Beans

Beans and bean products are diet staples worldwide. The history of beans in the Americas in general and the United States in particular is highly colorful—including, with a great deal of crossover, brown pintos, black beans, red beans, black-eyed peas, navy beans, and soybeans. Most varieties of beans are grown in the United States, whether or not they are indigenous.

Taxonomy

Beans are of the order Fabales and the family Leguminosae, or Fabaceae, known as legumes or pulses—terms applicable both to the plants as a whole and to their edible pods and seeds. Beans inhabit several genera, but the most important for culinary study are *Phaseolus, Vigna, Vicia,* and *Glycine.* In these genera are almost all the most familiar species. For example, among beans not native to the Americas are *Glycine maximus,* the soybean so crucial to the Asian diet, which along with *Vigna radiata,* the mung bean, is the main source of bean sprouts; *Vigna angularis,* the small, red adzuki bean also of Asia; *Vigna unguiculata,* the African cowpea, known more widely in the United States as the black-eyed pea; and *Vicia faba,* the European broad bean or fava bean, which arrived in America with the colonists. American species generally belong to the genus *Phaseolus,* such as *Phaseolus coccineus,* the runner or scarlet bean; *Phaseolus lunatus* (also called *Phaseolus limensis),* the lima or butter bean; and *Phaseolus vulgaris,* whose many varieties fall under the umbrella term "haricot bean." (That the fame of haricot beans would spread across the world with a French name stemmed from the chance resemblance of "haricot" to the Aztec word, *ayacotl* or *ayecotl.) Phaseolus* includes black (turtle) beans, white (cannellini) beans, green (snap, French, or string) beans, navy (pea) beans, kidney beans, pinto beans, flageolets, and more (these terms sometimes overlap).

The differences between beans go beyond appearance. For one thing, the varieties of beans exhibit distinct growth patterns. Some grow on vines, in which case they are pole or garden beans; others, called bush or field beans, grow on low-growing plants. For another, beans vary with respect to flavor at maturity. Some, like green beans, are best eaten young, fresh, and in the pod; some, like flageolets, require maturation and shelling before consumption; and still others, such as black beans, must be dried well. Age also tends to determine cooking time: the older the bean, the longer it takes to cook properly.

Beans. Low's New Champion bush bean, from Aaron Low's Illustrated Retail Seed Catalogue and Garden Manual, 1887, p. 13.

History

Archaeological evidence shows that beans were among the world's first domesticated plants. It is estimated that Amerindian tribes began cultivating bean crops anywhere from 7000 to 3000 B.C.E. For centuries, in both North and South America, beans were, and sometimes still are, among a handful of foods that constituted daily fare—the others being corn, which forms a complete protein in combination with beans; squash; and, from Mexico southward, tomatoes and chilies.

In *America's First Cuisines*, Sophie D. Coe explores the cookery of the ancient empires of North and South America—Aztec, Maya, and Inca. Whereas the Incan repertoire was generally limited to lima beans (which ultimately lent their name to the Peruvian capital), the Aztecs and Mayans developed customs and created dishes involving beans that are recognizable as part of U.S. culinary heritage, such as Tex-Mex and southwestern cuisine. The Mesoamerican Mayans were partial to the black bean or *buul*. They boiled the beans with chilies and then paired the mixture with squash seeds or greens, such as epazote. An especially important companion to *buul* was corn. Stone-ground, stone-griddled tortillas were filled with the beans, whole or in a paste, and cornmeal was used as a thickener for bean stew. The Aztecs did likewise with myriad *P. vulgarius* specimens, for instance, adding them to the potable pulp of corn boiled in water and lime they called *atolli*. And the Aztec predilection for mashed beans foretold of *frijoles refritos*.

The culinary traditions of what would later be called Latin America contributed to some extent to the evolution of bean cookery in what would be Anglo America. But the indigenous peoples of the latter also had an influence. Tribes that were particularly committed to husbandry, such as the Hopi in the southwest and the Iroquois in the northeast, grew several varieties of beans—and even worshipped them in ceremonial bean dances or festivals. The Iroquois developed a mythology around beans, corn, and squash in which these plants were known as the "three sisters." The southwestern Papagos acquired the nickname "the bean people" for their agricultural work. Haricot beans entered into many pre-Columbian foodways that fed into mainstream postcolonial U.S. foodways. The most important bean of North American origin, however, the tepary bean of the species *Phaseolus acutifolius*, has been rendered all but extinct.

The first step in the preparation of beans often was drying, a process to which beans were especially amenable. Even green beans, usually eaten fresh, could be hung out to dry to make what the Cherokees called "leather britches." Subsequent cooking was a leisurely affair, involving simmering, stewing, and baking. Two dishes in particular found lasting popularity with natives (across tribal lines) and colonists alike: succotash and baked beans. Just as the name "succotash" is a simplification of a number of similar-sounding Indian names for the dish, the dish itself, still common in the South, is often boiled down (literally) to two ingredients—lima beans and corn—from its original hodgepodge of ingredients. Baked beans, meanwhile, underwent a metamorphosis to become a hallmark of culinary Americana. Natives taught settlers how to cook beans with maple sugar and bear fat in a pit filled with hot stones or ashes. Settlers replaced the pit with a pot, the maple sweetener with molasses, and the bear fat with hog fat—and finally ignored altogether the origins of the dish, instead crediting Bostonians with the invention, who did in fact adopt and adapt it as a Sabbath specialty with such fervor that the city earned the moniker "Beantown." Toward the end of the nineteenth century, baked beans began a new life as one of the most popular canned items in history. By that time, navy beans were the variety of choice, and mustard and tomato sauce had made their way into the recipe. Industry pioneers included Burnham and Morrill (B&M) and Van Camp's, brands still in use in the early twenty-first century.

Usage

Third world poverty continues to guarantee the stature of beans as part of a plant-based diet. The wealth of first world nations, however, especially the United States, has led to carnivorous excesses that have generated medical, ecological, and ethical crises. Beans are an important part of attempts to mitigate the effects of the excesses with a return to healthful eating habits. Ever-changing patterns in U.S. immigration and their effect on the multicultural revolution of the late twentieth century have encouraged the introduction of a variety of bean products and bean dishes as well as a heightened receptivity to them. To the huge repertoire of Italian and French recipes, for example, have been added Tuscan *ribollita* (a stew of cannellini, or white beans, greens, and stale bread, perhaps not so different from the aforementioned Mayan stew) and the Provençal *soupe au pistou* with green beans and flageolets. Meanwhile, the cuisines of modern Latin America, especially Brazil and Cuba, have made increasing headway in the United States. Newly visible are specialties such as Brazilian *feijoada completa*—a festival stew of black beans and an assortment of meats—and the staple black beans and rice from Cuba.

Americans' exposure to Asian foods broadened considerably in the late twentieth century. With increased exposure came greater tolerance, if not appreciation, of soybean-based items that—unlike the quickly assimilated soy sauce—once seemed alien. Tofu, or bean curd, is the most prominent example. Used extensively in Japanese, Chinese, and other Asian cuisines, tofu has proven an efficient meat substitute. *Chi*, the salty fermented black bean paste used in Chinese sauces, is found on the shelves of many supermarkets. That the relatively novel adzuki bean has met with comparatively less resistance in the United States is probably due to the fact that it is found primarily in sweets, such as mooncakes (filled with a paste made from the beans) and ice cream.

But the bean dishes most representative of American cuisine are probably not those that have been borrowed, however enthusiastically, from one or another culture, but those that have been fused together from several cultures at once. Tex-Mex cookery is, as the expression goes, full of beans, which are indispensable for dishes such as burritos, enchiladas, tamales, and tacos, be they refried with lard or simply boiled (although chili con carne, a Texas original, has historically been bean free). Farther west, New Mexico offers similar foods, although the beans are as likely to be black as they are mottled pink—and the corn with which they are served may be blue rather than yellow, thanks to the agricultural experiments of the Pueblo Indians, with whom the Hispanic population has lived side by side for centuries. Similarly, celebrated dishes containing beans abound at the Cajun-Creole intersection that is Louisiana, criss-crossed by the descendants of French-Canadian settlers, African slaves, and Native Americans. Limpin' Susan, for example, also known as red beans and rice, is traditionally prepared on Mondays, flavored with the bone from Sunday's ham. It has a companion in hoppin' John, a combination of black-eyed peas and rice flavored with pork and traditionally reserved for a particular occasion—in this case, New Year's Day, when it is thought to bring good luck. (The derivation of the name remains a mystery, though John Thorne concurs with many historians who suspect that it is an anglicization of the French term for the similarly used pigeon pea, *pois à pigeon*. These authorities point to a triangulation of culinary influences borne of the slave trade among Africa, the French Caribbean, and the American South.)

Widespread culinary usage goes hand in hand with widespread linguistic usage—often humorous. As a slang term for "head," "bean" can be prefixed to the word "pole" to refer to a thin person. "Bean" also can be used as a verb to describe hitting someone square in the cranium. "Bean" also signifies pluralities, sums—as in the phrase "you don't know beans"—and, by extension, money, leading to the slightly derisive term "bean counter," meaning "accountant." Meanwhile, beans have plenty of colorful nicknames of their own, such as Boston, Mexican, or prairie strawberries, whistle berries, and even bullets or ammunition—the last three terms alluding to beans' propensity for causing flatulence.

[*See also* African American Food; Cajun and Creole Food; Caribbean Influences on American Food; Chinese American Food; Japanese American Food; Mexican American Food; Native American Foods; Rice; Soybeans.]

BIBLIOGRAPHY

Coe, Sophie D. *America's First Cuisines*. Austin: University of Texas Press, 1994. Coe is an authority on the little-known cookery of the ancient Americas.

Cox, Beverly, and Martin Jacobs. *Spirit of the Harvest: North American Indian Cooking*. New York: Stewart, Tabori and Chang, 1991. A cookbook with meticulous head notes.

Davidson, Alan, ed. *The Oxford Companion to Food*. New York and Oxford: Oxford University Press, 1999. Useful for general concepts. Provides excellent sources for further reading; see "Bean," "Black Bean," "Cowpea," and "Soybean."

Fussell, Betty. *I Hear America Cooking: The Cooks and Recipes of American Regional Cuisine*. New York: Penguin, 1997. Fussell's recipe histories are well balanced between anecdote and research findings.

Root, Waverly, and Richard de Rochemont. *Eating in America: A History*. New York: Ecco, 1981. A classic, well-written text for students of American foodways.

Tannahill, Reay. *Food in History*. New York: Stein and Day, 1973. A classic, succinct overview of food in world history.

Thorne, John, with Matt Lewis Thorne. *Serious Pig: An American Cook in Search of His Roots*. New York: North Point Press, 2000. Contains Thorne's oft-noted, poignant essay "Rice and Beans: The Itinerary of a Dish."

RUTH TOBIAS

Beard, James

Often referred to as the father of American gastronomy, James Beard (1903–1985) crusaded for appreciation of American cuisine, no matter how humble. Through cookbooks, a cooking school, personal appearances, and groundbreaking television programs, Beard popularized the art of home cooking in general and American cooking in particular.

Born on May 5, 1903, in Portland, Oregon, to Elizabeth and John Beard, James Beard learned about Oregon's natural bounty during summers at the beach and by haunting local food markets. In 1923, Beard was expelled from Reed College, in Portland, and he began to pursue his first love, the theater. He lived abroad for several years, studying voice and acting. Beard returned to the United States in 1927, intent on a theatrical career. To supplement his earnings, he began a catering business and with friends in 1937 opened a small shop called Hors d'Oeuvre Inc.

Writing was Beard's strength. Throughout his career, he contributed articles and columns to *Woman's Day, Gourmet,* and *House and Garden,* among others, encouraging readers to appreciate their American roots. Beard wrote twenty-seven cookbooks, many of which were best-sellers. *Hors d'Oeuvre and Canapés* (1940) was followed by *Cook It Outdoors* (1941). Reflecting Americans' migration to the suburbs, the latter offered plans for a build-it-yourself barbecue pit. After World War II, Beard wrote *Fowl and Game Cookery* (1944), *The Fireside Cookbook* (1949), *Paris Cuisine* (1952), *James Beard's Fish Cookery* (first edition published in 1954 under the title *Fish Cookery*), *How to Eat Better for Less Money* (1954; with Sam Aaron, of the Sherry-Lehmann wine store), *The Complete Book of Outdoor Cookery* (1955; with Helen Evans Brown), and *The Casserole Cookbook* (1968).

Beard made television history in 1946 when he hosted television's first cooking show, NBC's *Elsie Presents James Beard in "I Love to Eat,"* Elsie being the Borden cow. Beard's national exposure led to commercial endorsements for Birds Eye, Green Giant, and Planters. Beard advised the food service giant Restaurant Associates for many years beginning in 1954, when it opened innovative themed restaurants such as the Latin American La Fonda del Sol (1960) and the Forum of the Twelve Caesars (1957), an opulent re-creation of ancient Rome. Both demonstrated Beard's "food as theater" philosophy.

In New York in 1955, the James Beard Cooking School opened in Beard's home in Greenwich Village. Beard taught cooking for the rest of his life there as well as at a branch of his home school, in Seaside, Oregon, at women's clubs, at other cooking schools, and at civic clubs around the United States. To a country just becoming aware of its culinary heritage, Beard advocated good food passionately prepared with fresh, wholesome ingredients. *The James Beard Cookbook* (1959), a paperback originally priced at seventy-five cents and positioned at cash registers, introduced millions to classic American and international dishes. *James Beard's American Cookery* (1972) reflected Beard's encyclopedic knowledge of American cuisine. Beard's joyous approach to food and cooking is epitomized in *James Beard's Theory and Practice of Good Cooking* (1977), in which he writes, "Cooking is primarily fun and . . . the more [people] know about what they are doing, the more fun it is" (p. vii). When he died at age eighty-two on January 21, 1985, James Beard left a legacy of American culinary authenticity to home cooks and professional chefs.

[*See also* Brown, Helen Evans; Celebrity Chefs; Cookbooks and Manuscripts, *subentry* From World War II to the 1960s; Cooking Schools, *subentry* Twentieth Century; Radio and Television.]

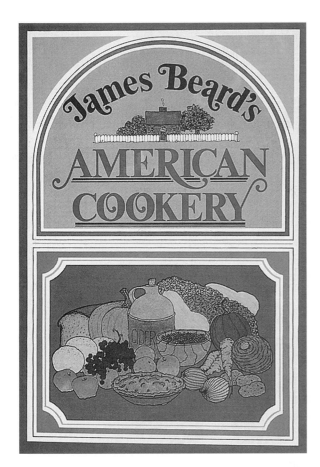

A James Beard Cookbook. Cover of James Beard's American Cookery, 1972. *Culinary Archives & Museum at Johnson & Wales University, Providence, R.I.*

BIBLIOGRAPHY

Beard, James. *Delights and Prejudices.* New York: Atheneum, 1964.

Beard, James, in collaboration with José Wilson. *James Beard's Theory and Practice of Good Cooking*. New York: Knopf, 1977.

Clark, Robert. *The Solace of Food: A Life of James Beard*. Hanover, NH: Steerforth, 1996.

Jones, Evan. *Epicurean Delight: The Life and Times of James Beard*. New York: Simon and Schuster, 1990.

PHYLLIS ISAACSON

Beatrice

George Haskell, a bookkeeper with the Fremont Butter and Egg Company, purchased the company's Nebraska plant when the company folded in 1891. He renamed it the Beatrice Creamery Company. In 1901 the company adopted the trademark Meadow Gold for its butter.

From an early date, Beatrice was a leader and innovator in the dairy business. It is reported to have been the first company to package butter in sealed cartons. The company pioneered the use of aluminum foil milk caps and was an early innovator in the marketing of homogenized milk. In 1931 Beatrice was the first company to advertise its ice cream products nationally.

In an attempt to expand its product line, the company purchased La Choy, a producer of Asian foods, in 1943. La Choy was founded in 1922 by Wally Smith and Ilhan New, who met while attending the University of Michigan. New, a Korean by birth, and Smith, a grocery store owner in Detroit, set out to sell bean sprouts packaged in glass jars.

In a new round of acquisitions Beatrice purchased the Krispy Kreme doughnut chain in 1975 and added sandwiches, a retail mix that failed. A group of investors, led by one of the chain's most successful franchisees, purchased the company in the 1980s.

In 1984 Beatrice Food purchased Hunt-Wesson, Inc., a large food products company in California. By 1985 Beatrice in turn was purchased in what was then the largest leverage buyout in history. Beatrice, along with Hunt-Wesson and La Choy, was sold to ConAgra, Inc. Besides being a case study in acquisition and diversification within the food industry, Beatrice has become a slimmer and more focused company in the early 2000s.

[*See also* ConAgra; Dairy Foods; Dairy Industry; Krispy Kreme; Milk Packaging.]

BIBLIOGRAPHY

International Directory of Company Histories. 55 vols. Chicago: St. James Press, 2003.

JOSEPH M. CARLIN

Beecher, Catharine

Catharine E. Beecher (1800–1878) was a social innovator who helped to reshape women's roles in the mid-nineteenth century and whose writings continued to guide an idealized image of middle-class urban women for decades to come. Beecher's authority derived from her membership in a famous family of activists and reformers and from her own extensive pioneering of education for single professional women and married women at home. Beecher wrote and lectured widely on women's issues, intermingling what was sometimes extreme conservatism with far-seeing change.

In *Treatise on Domestic Economy* (1841), Beecher expanded on the inherited Calvinist belief that women's true destiny was marriage and home. She encouraged women to develop their presumed gender-specific talents for religiosity, morality, esthetics, and nurturing, areas in which women were considered superior to men. Beecher saw in the female "profession" of homemaking a role parallel to and balancing that of urban men in factories, shops, and offices. Women were thus charged with creating a beautiful, serene, and smoothly run home, a haven for husbands distressed by the anxiety-filled business world. Expected to display her husband's success at moneymaking, a woman was to create a stylishly decorated home, to dress modishly, and to set a fashionable table. This "glorification" of women separated them from the public sphere and consequently was a rejection of women's suffrage.

Although its framework was conventional, the *Treatise* included a number of food-related innovations. With an eye to efficiency, Beecher discussed health, kitchen fires, and care of the kitchen, cellar, and storeroom. Cookery was a major arena. Beecher's cookbook (*Domestic Receipt Book*, 1846) emphasized basic traditional cooking, baking, and preserving but tempered them with modernizing innovations, such as the new cookstove, cream of tartar, and the home ice cream maker. Beecher included many more regional recipes than was usual at the time, perhaps because of her wide-flung lecture circuit. On one page alone she lists Pennsylvania flannel cakes, Kentucky corn dodgers, and Ohio corn cakes. Beecher's recipe for birthday pudding (a layered bread pudding with apples) encouraged the new rituals and elaboration of birthday celebrations, and her "temperance drinks" represented an early voice in what would become a major movement.

Much ahead of her time, Beecher detailed efficient work routines for the kitchen, furnishing plans and recommendations for cooking utensils. Beecher included lengthy chapters on dining etiquette, such as table setting, food presentation, servant training, and service (the *service à la française* buffet style).

In 1869, Catharine collaborated with her sister Harriet Beecher Stowe in writing an update of the *Treatise*, titled *The American Woman's Home*. Among other topics, *Home* offered expanded plans for kitchen efficiency and recommended new factory-made furnishings and utensils.

Despite her strong voice for married women's place in the home, Catharine Beecher never married. Her own life's example of the independent single woman working professionally to improve the lot of others (in part through food, in part through education) may seem to be a contradiction but nevertheless figured in the creation of the new range of choices opened to twentieth-century women.

[*See also* Alcohol and Teetotalism; Home Economics.]

BIBLIOGRAPHY

Beecher, Catharine. *Domestic Receipt-Book: Designed as a Supplement to Her Treatise on Domestic Economy.* New York: Harper, 1846.
Rugoff, Milton. *The Beechers: An American Family in the Nineteenth Century.* New York: Harper and Row, 1981.
Sklar, Kathryn Kish. *Catharine Beecher: A Study in American Domesticity.* New York: Norton, 1976.

ALICE ROSS

Beech-Nut

Between 1891 and 1946 the Beech-Nut Packing Company grew from a regional business to a nationally significant corporation because of its diverse product line and innovative marketing techniques. It tried to portray itself as a small company appealing to women, children, and families, and it frequently succeeded in doing so.

The Beech-Nut Packing Company was founded in 1891 as a meatpacking plant in Canajoharie, New York. Most of the initial investment came from two local families, the Lipes and the Arkells. When the board of directors chose the officers for the new company, then known as the Imperial Packing Company, Bartlett Arkell was designated president and Walter Lipe chosen to be vice president. The company was named after the hotel in New York where Arkell lived at that time. From the start,

Imperial Packing produced bacon, sliced ham, and beef under two brand names, Erie and Beech-Nut. In 1898 Imperial Packing reincorporated as Beech-Nut Packing Company. Informal corporate histories suggest that the change occurred after the executives held a contest at the plant to select a less formal, more national name for the company.

At the time the company was founded, New York State had the strictest laws in the country for regulating the food-processing industry. The company emphasized food purity and lack of adulteration in its products, in both advertising campaigns and packaging. The public was allowed and encouraged to visit the plant, and most of the early products were packed in glass jars so that customers could see the products they were buying.

The plant expanded at a single location in Canajoharie for the first ten years of its existence, until a fire in 1903 destroyed the smokehouse. The rebuilding of the company in 1903–1905 also saw the expansion of the product line to include chewing gum, hard candy, jams and jellies, coffee, peanut butter, ketchup, and mustard, all made before World War I. (See the table for specific dates of product manufacture.)

Growth of the Company between the Wars

By 1900 Beech-Nut not only was vacuum packing most of its food products in glass jars but also was including, as a seal, a rubber gasket it had patented that year. This ensured a very long shelf life for the company's products.

BEECH-NUT PRODUCTS AND DATES OF MANUFACTURE

Product name	First produced	Last made
Baby food	1931	Present
Bacon	1891	1942
Beans (baked)	1906	1940
Beef (sliced)	1891	1942
Biscuits (cookies)	1926	1940
Candy (hard)	1908	1956
Candy (Life Saver)	1956	Present
Candy (gum)	1911	Present (limited amounts)
Ketchup	1908	1939
Coffee	1911	Present
Jams and jellies	1903	1939
Macaroni	1919	1939
Mustard	1913	1935
Peanut butter	1904	1956
Tomato juice	1931	1939

Beech-Nut. Beech-Nut advertisement, 1905. *Collection of Kit Barry*

Although there have been improvements in the manufacturing methods and materials used to seal glass jars since that time, the basic canning process remains similar.

By 1910 a single building was too small for the company's manufacturing needs, and a second plant was built in Canajoharie. By 1920 Beech-Nut was also making gum and coffee at the Bush Terminal Building in Brooklyn, New York, and had acquired a plant in San Jose, California, to make jams and jellies. In 1924 the company added a plant in Rochester, New York, for coffee and tomato juice.

In 1919 a fire at the Equitable Life Building at 120 Broadway in New York City all but destroyed the Beech-Nut offices and corporate records. Most of the company executives moved to Canajoharie, although Bartlett Arkell maintained a New York City office on Broadway at Fortieth Street for the rest of his life. In the 1920s and 1930s the company was at its most adventurous in terms of advertising. The use of commercial artists such as Norman Rockwell and Cushman Parker established the company's association with women and families. Celebrities such as Chef Oscar of the Waldorf Astoria, the aviator Amelia Earhart, and the boxer Jack Dempsey also were involved in advertising promotions for the company. Radio spots were used on the program *Chandu the Magician.* Lifestyle spots advertised that Beech-Nut offered "everything for breakfast but the eggs."

At about this time Beech-Nut sued the Lolliard Tobacco Company, a Virginia firm, for copyright and trademark infringement. Lolliard used a very similar logo and the name "Beechnut" for one of its brands of chewing tobacco. The case, which reached the U.S. Supreme Court in 1924, determined that two companies could use almost identical trademarks as long as the products were different. The finding, which is a major, and still valid, legal precedent with respect to trademarks, was a setback for Beech-Nut.

In 1932, after two years of test marketing, Beech-Nut introduced a line of strained baby food for younger children and a line of junior foods for older ones. Company brochures from the 1930s suggest that the products were marketed for convenience and to replace home-strained food at about the time that mothers had traditionally introduced foods other than milk to their infants' diets. Packing this type of food in glass jars eased consumer worries about the purity of the product. Along with candy, baby food is Beech-Nut's best-known product line and the only one still manufactured in Canajoharie.

Between the World Wars, Beech-Nut salesmen generally tried to sell as many different products as they could to small, family-owned groceries, offering free window displays, better discounts, and racks to store owners who took the entire company line. Federal Trade Commission efforts to fine and discontinue this practice failed in court. Although Beech-Nut had to close its San Jose plant and discontinue some product lines, the company remained stable during the Depression, surviving mostly on gum and candy sales. Not every product the company introduced at this time was successful. It made soda for just three years and oyster sauce for only two.

World War II and Later Years

The Beech-Nut company had to alter some of its lines to fulfill government contracts during World War II. Most of the extra wartime production involved the making of K Ration—a packaged line of emergency foods developed for the armed services. All but the chewing gum was produced elsewhere and shipped to Canajoharie, where the various parts were assembled into a finished meal. Beech-Nut Gum was added to each meal prior to shipping. A small machine shop and freeze-drying plant were added to Beech-Nut's regular manufacturing facilities as well.

In 1946 Bartlett Arkell passed away, and within ten years the company was sold to Life Saver. Its focus became more specialized, and it made fewer and fewer products. By 1960 baby food and candy were the two main products; coffee was a distant third. A baby-food plant, which opened in San Jose in 1947, was the only new plant built after the war, before the Life Saver merger.

The 1956 acquisition of Beech-Nut by Life Saver brought about a short-lived boom for the company. It expanded aggressively in the 1960s, buying several additional businesses and building a large plant in Michigan. By 1967 the company was in serious financial trouble, and that year it sold its holdings to Squibb. Since that time, Squibb has divested all of the various divisions, which are each owned by several other national and international companies.

[*See also* Baby Food; Pure Food and Drug Act.]

BIBLIOGRAPHY

"Beech-Nut Packing." *Fortune*, November 1936, 85–93.
Hughes, Lawerence. "Beech-Nut Keeps the Kettle Boiling." *Sales Management*, August 1950.

JAMES CRAWFORD

Beer

With the desire to form settlements, rather than remaining nomadic and gathering crops where they grew wild, early humans developed the practice of agriculture, and civilization was born. There is some debate as to whether grain was first cultivated specifically for use in brewing beer or baking bread. However, there is no doubt that the earliest days of farming took place around 8000 B.C.E., in the Middle East, between the Euphrates and Tigris rivers.

Even before that civilization, the fruits of fermentation were considered gifts from the gods and were offered back to them. Wine may have been a happy accident that happened after someone left fruit juice uncovered for a day or two and noticed the foamy froth that began to appear on the surface of the juice, and it has been suggested that the original beer was discovered when prehistoric ancestors let their bowl of grain mush sit for a day or so and sipped the frothy liquid that rose to the surface.

Civilizations establish complex systems of social order. At the top of early social orders were the priests. They got the best of the harvest, as well as the responsibility of ensuring that fermented fruit juice (wine) and fermented grain mush (beer) were made especially to please the gods. Artifacts have been recovered that place beer at the tables of the priests of Ninkasa, the Sumerian goddess of brewing, and Isis, the Egyptian goddess of fertility.

Ancient texts indicate that beer became a more egalitarian beverage. The Sumerians, circa 3000 B.C.E., used straws made from reeds to draw off the liquid from special containers of fermented grain and water. This grain-based beverage played an important part in Sumerian culture and was consumed by men and women from all social classes. The Sumerian version of beer parlors received special mention in the Code of Hammurabi in the eighteenth century B.C.E. Stiff penalties (death by drowning)

Drinking Beer. A bar in New York City in 1919. *Prints and Photographs Division, Library of Congress*

were dealt out to owners who overcharged customers or who failed to notify authorities of criminals in their establishments. In the Sumerian and Akkadian dictionaries being studied in the early 2000s, the word for beer is listed in sections relating to medicine, ritual, and myth.

When this grain beverage found its way to Egypt, it was considered a drink for only the royal. This beer was made of grain, ginger, and honey, sweetened with date sugar. To lengthen the drinkable life of the beverage, its alcohol content was raised through the addition of more date sugar.

As civilization spread north, across the Mediterranean, so did beer. The Greeks called the Egyptian beer a barley wine and introduced it to the Romans, who passed it to other civilizations as they traveled through Europe. In northern Europe, where grain grew in abundance, the preference for beer was a result of agricultural whim. Where grapes grew in abundance, wine was the beverage of choice. Beer and brewing took hold and flourished where grains were a staple for survival. The Mediterranean area produced wine, and the rich breadbasket of Europe became the cradle for the development of beer.

Evidence of the early history of brewing in Europe is meager but reveals that brewing was done by women as part of maintaining a proper household. Grains unsuited for baking were crushed and made into a thin porridge. Sweet liquid was drained from the porridge and the grain then fed to livestock, while the liquid was helped to ferment either through the addition of starters from previous brews (similar to starters for sourdough bread) or by leaving the liquid open to the influence of ambient yeast and airborne flora. The entire family drank fermented beverages made from grain. They were nutritious and not nearly as dangerous as drinking the contaminated waters found near most towns and villages.

After the Holy Roman Empire fell apart, the monasteries of Europe were the sole providers of healers, teachers, preachers—and beer. Monasteries were the way stations for pilgrims going from one shrine to another or travelers seeking refuge on long journeys. All visitors were offered refreshment and a place to rest. The monks and priests were dedicated to religious pursuits that included humility, poverty, waging the Crusades, studying nature, illuminating books, and brewing beer as a subsistence beverage. Some religious groups had such strict dietary restrictions that so-called liquid bread was the foundation of their existence. Beer, brewed by the members of the religious community, was the beverage offered to the visitors. Some monasteries also provided beer for trade, sale, or barter with their neighbors.

The first recorded mention of hops in relation to brewing is in the twelfth-century writing of Hildegard, the Benedictine nun who was abbess of Rupertsberg, near Mainz, Germany. She specifically suggested that hops retarded spoilage of beer. This knowledge was important to every monastery and brewing guild that wanted to expand its market. Hops made it possible for beer to endure long trips from the brewery to the consumer. With the growth of cities and the greater use of roads, sea-lanes, and caravan routes, the market for beer became intercontinental.

In the beginning, beer was brewed for almost immediate consumption by the monks, families, or manor folk who lived near the brewing site. It was fermented in wood casks, but not long enough for the wood to impart any significant flavor. Once opened, the cask of beer was usually consumed at one session, and the quality of the beer depended very much on the ability of those present to finish the keg. Beer could be further aged, or "lagered" (from the Old High German *leger*, bed), in pitch-lined casks. A beer brewed to almost 12 percent alcohol by volume, and liberally hopped, could last for a number of years.

How Beer Is Made

Beer is made in a brew house. The traditional brew house consists of a gristmill, a mash tun (a large vessel where the grist and hot water are combined to make a porridge, or mash), a copper (a large boiler, traditionally made of copper because of its ability to conduct heat, in which the liquid, or wort, from the mash tun is flavored with hops), and a fermenter (a large vessel in which the first fermentation takes place), fermenting tanks (used if the brew is to be aged or lagered), conditioning tanks (vessels that contain the fermented and carbonated brew), and a kegging or bottling line—unless, as in a brewpub, the beer is drawn to the tap directly from the conditioning tanks.

The traditional brewery, which is the building containing the brew house, was built on at least three levels to allow gravity to do much of the work of moving the grain, grist, mash, wort, and spent grains. It was also important that the fermenting and conditioning tanks be in cellars where the temperature was optimum for fermenting and conditioning the beer. Ale can be fermented and conditioned at higher temperatures than lager, but both need cool, stable temperatures to yield the best product.

Grist The first step in making beer is crushing barley that has reached germination and dried (malted) into grist by rolling it between metal rollers set so that the grain is not ground into flour. This is a process that allows grain to germinate until its protein is converted to a starch that natural enzymes found in the grain can in turn convert to sugar during the mash process. The coarse grind of the grist allows for optimum extraction of the fermentable sugars when hot water (called liquor) is added to the grist in the mash tun to create the mash. The crushing of the grist also leaves the husk of the grain intact, which forms a bed at the bottom of the mash tun that aids in filtration. When as much of the starch has been converted to sugars and fermentable substances as desired, the liquid in the mash tun is drained through the bed of husks and spent grain in the bottom of the mash tun and transferred to the copper. This sweet liquid is now called wort.

The Boil The wort is piped into the copper where it is boiled with the hops until the residual proteins are extracted from the wort and the essential oils are extracted from the hops. The hopped wort is then quickly chilled to around 60°F and piped into fermenting tanks.

Fermentation The fermenting tanks, which are traditionally open in a clean room, are filled with the cool wort. Yeast is pitched (added) and fermentation takes place as the yeast metabolizes the sugar in the wort with the resulting by-products of ethyl alcohol and carbon dioxide being released into the brew. The brew is then bottled, kegged, or, in the case of pub-breweries, drawn by taps in the bar and served to customers.

Early Colonial Brewing

The earliest settlers in the Virginia colony began using maize, native to North America, to brew beer, because

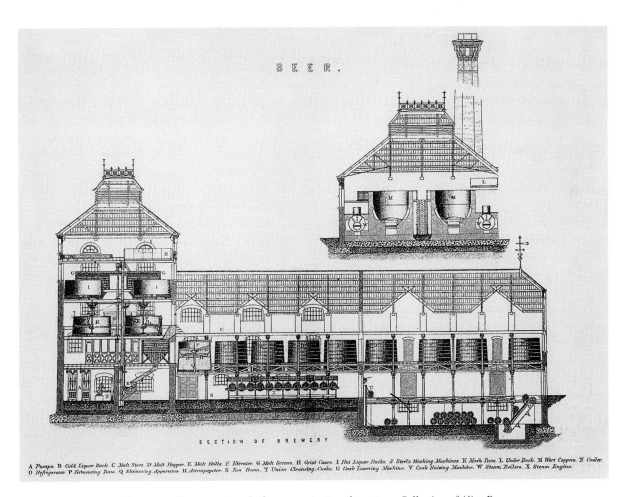

Brewery. Cross-section of a brewery, nineteenth century. *Collection of Alice Ross*

the cost of shipping the raw ingredients for English-style beers was prohibitive. By the late 1500s their efforts were successful enough that in 1609 the administrators of the colony were advertising in the London newspapers for the services of qualified brewers.

Three years later Adrian Block and Hans Christiansen established the first commercial brewery in the growing trading center of New Amsterdam. It was in this brewery in 1614 that Jean Vigne was brought into the world. Eighteen years later he would open his own brewery not far from where he had been born.

The arrival of the *Mayflower* at Plymouth Rock in 1620 was not intended. The ship's original destination was what was then called Hudson's River, but because of less-than-perfect navigation and other problems while crossing a less-than-friendly Atlantic Ocean, the vessel found itself off the coast of Cape Cod. The captain and crew of the *Mayflower* insisted that the passengers disembark there, because if more time were spent looking for another site, there would not be enough beer to supply the crew for the trip back to England. Beer was the only potable beverage available to the crew. The Pilgrims had no choice but to settle where they landed.

While the New England Pilgrims struggled to build their settlement, the colonists of Virginia were getting very good at brewing beer out of maize. Their beer was good enough to have a visitor from England remark that he much preferred it to English beer.

For the next twenty years the brewing done in the American colonies was subsistence brewing. The brew was made from whatever was at hand. The grains were malted and then ground and added to cauldrons of hot water. From then on any resemblance to modern beer disappears. The resulting sweet water from the grains being immersed in the heated water was allowed to naturally ferment and the beer produced was mildly alcoholic and almost without effervescence. Consumed almost as soon as it was finished fermenting, it remained a popular daily beverage.

In 1630, after being licensed by the General Court, held in Newton, Massachusetts on November 20, 1637, Captain Robert Sedgwick opened the first of the New England breweries in Charlestown, now part of greater Boston. In nearby Cambridge, home of Harvard University, Nathaniel Eaton was dismissed as president in 1639 when he failed to maintain the students' beer supply.

By now the port of New Amsterdam was host to the businesses and industry that supported sea traders. In 1632, the West India Company opened a brewery on Brouwers (Brewers) Straet in lower Manhattan. In less than a year Jean Vigne opened his brewery on the same street, a short distance from where he had been born in the brewery of Block and Christiansen.

The business of brewing was taking hold in the New England colonies as well. In 1634 the city officials in Boston awarded the first brewery license to Samuel Cole.

One year later they presented the aforementioned Captain Robert Sedgwick a license to brew in the city of Boston. He must have been quite successful. Three years later the colony itself awarded him a brewing license.

New Amsterdam was rivaling Boston as a seaport and center of commerce, but it was not until 1653 that a city hall was established in what had been the Stadts Herbergh or City Tavern. Four years later the number of breweries on Brouwers Straet discharging their effluent into the street made it necessary to pave it with cobblestones and change its name to Stone Street.

When the English took control of what they called New York in 1664, the duke of York immediately issued a proclamation that restricted commercial brewing to professionals. Three years later in Massachusetts the colonial administrators instituted a list of regulations designed to ensure the quality of beer brewed there.

In 1734, two years after Benjamin Franklin began publishing *Poor Richard's Almanack*, May Lisle of Philadelphia took over the running of her family's brew house. She was known as the first brewster (woman brewer) in the colonies. It remained in operation until 1751.

The breweries of colonial North America were primarily urban and supplied nearby taverns and the inhabitants of the town with potable beverages that ranged from small beer, a barely alcoholic brew to full-strength brews of between 6 and 7 percent alcohol by volume.

The French and Indian War redrew the map of North America and put such a crimp in colonial commerce that the brewers suffered. From the end of the French and Indian War in 1763 until after the American Revolution in 1783, North American brewers were most influential in their willingness to lend their taverns as meeting places for the various organizations that would become the government of the new nation.

On September 17, 1787, following the final day of deliberations at the Constitutional Convention in Philadelphia, George Washington records in his diary: "The business being closed the members adjourned to the City Tavern." In 1789, George Washington, now president, declared that he would only buy beer brewed in the United States. That same year Massachusetts followed by passing legislation designed to encourage local production of beer. The beers brewed in Philadelphia drew the praise of the British consul there in 1789, when he reported home that although the porter in that city was not as good as the porter from Bristol, the reason was that they drank it too soon.

The Industrial Revolution

While the new nation was being created, the industrial revolution was ushering in the use of steam machines in the factories of Europe and would soon change the way breweries were run. No longer small and under the hand of a single brewmaster, his assistant, and family, the breweries of the new generation were more like factories.

With the Industrial Revolution came the rise of the clipper ships and the opportunity to bring lager yeast to the United States. Lager (anaerobic) yeast could not survive the long sea voyage from Europe to North America. If it was not used soon after being transferred from active fermentation, or proper propagation, it was rendered useless. Ale (aerobic) yeast, a far hardier organism, was, and is, less fragile. When lager beer reached the market in the United States in the nineteenth century, it was regarded for some time as little more than a novelty. With the development of industrial refrigeration that could produce it and with the immigration of central Europeans, Germans, and Czechs, who had a thirst for it, lager beer soon eclipsed traditional ale. The novelty was fast becoming the norm.

John Wagner began brewing lager beer in Philadelphia in 1840. He is credited with being the first American to produce lager beer. Later that year in St. Louis, Adam Lemp also began brewing lager beer. Four years later, in 1844, Jacob Best established a brewery in Milwaukee. The brewery later changed its name to Pabst.

Prohibition in the Nineteenth Century

A doctor named William Clark organized the Union Temperance Society of Moreau and Northumberland. On April 30, 1808, in the upstate New York town of Saratoga, the first organized temperance meeting in the United States was held. Eighteen years after that first temperance meeting in Saratoga, in 1826, citizens in Boston formed the American Society for the Promotion of Temperance. Over the next three years it would gain more than 100,000 members. It was considered the country's first significant temperance group. In 1836, Saratoga once again hosted the national temperance union meeting. During this session the concept of total abstinence

was first proposed. Prior to that, abstention did not include beer. Ten years later, in their first victory of note, the forces of temperance succeeded in bringing prohibition to the state of Maine.

While the temperance movement was gaining momentum, in 1849, August Krug went into business with the Milwaukee Brewery. Later it would become Schlitz and grow to be the largest in the world in the 1960s. In 1849 there were 421 breweries operating under license in the United States. Three years later in St. Louis, Missouri, George Schneider established a brewery that, when acquired by Eberhard Anheuser in 1852, would become the cornerstone of Anheuser-Busch. That same year, 1852, state prohibition laws were enacted in Vermont, Massachusetts (repealed 1868), Rhode Island (repealed 1863), and Minnesota. One year later they were joined by Michigan. Two years later Connecticut had a statewide prohibition law on the books. By 1855, New York (repealed 1867), New Hampshire, Delaware, Indiana, Iowa (repealed 1867), and Nebraska had gone dry.

The Civil War and the Growth of Commerce

From 1861 through 1865, the demand for machinery and raw materials during the Civil War sapped resources. But the rebound of industry can be seen when, in 1867, there were 3,700 breweries in operation in the United States producing 6 million barrels of beer. Two years later, with the completion of a transcontinental railroad, the market for goods and the ability to provide mass-produced packaged goods would propel the industry forward until, in 1873, breweries in the United States numbered 4,131 and were turning out 9 million barrels of beer annually. One year later the Woman's Christian Temperance Union was founded.

In Europe, the Franco-Prussian War had halted the German beer supply to France. In 1875, Louis Pasteur developed the process (named for him) of keeping wine and beer from spoiling because of the need to put the French brewing industry on a level with the German. Under pressure to keep the home front, and the troops, happy, he carried out experiments that proved that bacteria caused the spoilage of fermented liquids. Ergo, yeast free of bacteria produces a fermented beer that will not spoil. Pasteur found out that by steaming the finished product he could kill all harmful bacteria. This process, pasteurization, consisted of putting filled, well-corked bottles into a water bath that was gradually heated through the use of steam to 170°F. This temperature was sufficient to kill all yeast and bacteria in the solution. It supposedly had little effect on the flavor of the beverage.

Pasteurization helped the commercial producers of beer. The process not only prevented spoilage, it was also easier to control the amount of carbonation when it was forced into the beer after pasteurization. With pasteurized beer, brewers needed only to create an extensive distribution network and they were capable of becoming national brands. The beginning of bottled beer dates from the introduction of pasteurization.

In addition, in 1883 Emil Christian Hansen, a Danish biochemist, proved that certain yeasts were harmful in the fermentation process. He worked to produce an absolutely pure culture that would be best suited for the manufacture of beer. In November 1883, he produced a pure yeast culture at the Carlsberg Brewery. The discoveries of Pasteur and Hansen are of significant importance in the development of bottled beer.

The Internal Revenue Department records for 1880 indicate 2,830 ale and lager breweries were in operation. During the next twenty years the number of breweries in the United States began to decline because improved methods of production and distribution meant that fewer breweries could make more beer. By 1910 the number of breweries had dropped to around 1,500 as breweries consolidated.

Through the efforts of Fred Pabst, on June 18, 1890, the Internal Revenue Act was changed to allow "the construction of pipelines from storage cellars to bottling houses." The beer was run through a gauge, and a tax collector was on hand to see that the appropriate amount of revenue was collected. This method remained in effect up to Prohibition.

Meanwhile, the instability in Europe created a wave of immigrants. In 1892 the immigration center on Ellis Island in New York harbor received its first arrivals, many of whom were daily beer drinkers. That same year William Painter of the Crown Cork and Seal Company of Baltimore invented the crown cap. It provided the finishing touch for the bottled-beer industry.

War, Depression, and Prohibition

In 1900 the Woman's Christian Temperance Union member Carrie Nation challenged the public imagination when she allegedly took a hatchet and proceeded to chop at the bar of the Carey Hotel in Wichita, Kansas. Four years later a resolution to prohibit liquor through a constitutional amendment lost narrowly in the House of Representatives. The beer, spirits, and wine producers were hampered in forming a cohesive front against the prohibitionists by the outbreak of hostilities in Europe. The identification of the beer industry with Germany was part of the reason that the beverage alcohol producers never mounted an answer to the prohibitionist challenge.

In 1914, the secretary of the Navy, Josephus Daniels, ordered prohibition of alcohol on navy ships and naval installations. By 1916 twenty-three states had gone dry. In 1917 the United States entered World War I, and the District of Columbia passed its own prohibition legislation. With the onset of war, all distilleries were closed by the Food Control Law and the brewing industry was also restricted. On the eleventh hour of the eleventh day of the eleventh month of 1918, World War I ended. Just over two months later, on January 16, 1919, the Eighteenth Amendment to the United States Constitution was ratified. Prohibition began one year later.

To survive Prohibition, many breweries shifted production to "near beers" (containing less than one half of 1 percent of alcohol by volume) with names such as Pablo (Pabst), Famo (Schlitz), Vivo (Miller), Lux-O (Strohs), and Bevo (Anheuser-Busch). In 1920, brewers produced more than 300 million gallons of near beer.

Repeal

Prohibition began to recede into history in March 1933, in the depths of the Great Depression, when the Cullen Bill was passed, allowing states that did not have state prohibition laws to sell 3.2 percent beer and placing a five-dollar per barrel tax on that beer. Then, on April 17, 1933, the legalization of beer took effect with the passage of the Twenty-first Amendment—as of the early 2000s the only amendment to the Constitution of the United States ratified to nullify another amendment.

On December 3, 1933, U.S. citizens took their first legal drinks in fourteen years. Of the 1,568 breweries in operation in 1910 (brewing over 63 million barrels a year), only 750 reopened when Prohibition was ended in 1933. Production in that year was just over 2 million barrels. By the end of June, 31 breweries were back in full operation. One year later, 756 breweries were meeting the demands of a thirsty nation. The brewing industry recovered gradually, reaching production of just over 55 million barrels when World War II broke out.

The recovering breweries' efforts to expand market share involved product delivery. Shipping weight was a major problem in transporting beer any significant distance. Canned beer, significantly lighter than traditional bottled beer, was introduced on June 25, 1935, by the American Can Company and Krueger Brewing Company of Newark, New Jersey, and became the most economical way to ship beer. That same year, the Schlitz Brewing Company introduced a cone-top can made by the Continental Can Company. Five years later beer production reached pre-Prohibition levels with half the number of breweries in operation.

After World War II

As with most other nonmilitary industries, the breweries fit into the wartime economy. In 1943, all breweries were required to allocate 15 percent of production for military use. After the war, beer was available in three forms: on draft, in bottles, and in cans. (Canned beer had been perfected on a grand scale to provide beer to the armed forces during the war.) News was also available in three forms: newspapers, radio, and television (actually four; there were still barbershops). Both cans and media were to affect the brewing and appreciation of beer in the United States.

The postwar years were a time of prosperity for most North Americans. There was an optimistic belief that there was no limit to the expansion of science, technology, democracy, or economy. The economy of size was undeniable. Larger size meant lower overhead cost per item and ease of production. Gradually the small, local breweries that survived Prohibition had to close because they could not compete with the cans of beer distributed across the country by national brewers and sold for half the price of locally bottled beer. Then regional brewers folded under the onslaught of nationwide advertising on radio and television, designed to create a demand for national products. It came down to fewer than one hundred breweries in the United States—and Anheuser-Busch, Miller, Schlitz, and Pabst owned three-quarters of them.

In 1953, Anheuser-Busch of St. Louis built a new brewery in Newark, New Jersey, its way of announcing that it could produce a standard brew anywhere it wanted to. This started a trend of production expansion for the most powerful brewing companies. In 1954, the Schlitz Brewing Company introduced the first sixteen-ounce can of beer. Nevertheless, three years later, Anheuser-Busch knocked Schlitz out of first place in the U.S. brewing industry. The Coors Brewing Company of Golden, Colorado, introduced the first aluminum beer can in 1959. More new packaging innovations followed in 1962 with the introduction of the tab-top can by the Pittsburgh Brewing Company. Ring-pull cans arrived in 1965, stan-

dardizing packaging among the major forces in the brewing industry. By 1969 canned beer outsold bottled beer.

The year 1969 was also a turning point for the small, local brewery that had a reputation, a good product, but no more money. That year, Fritz Maytag, of the family better known for home appliance manufacturing, took ownership of the Anchor Brewing Company in San Francisco. It was not obvious at the time, but a brewing revolution had begun.

Microbreweries

The giants continued to battle when, in 1971, Philip Morris absorbed the Miller Brewing Company as part of a series of acquisitions. By 1978 Miller had passed Schlitz and Pabst to take second place, but Anheuser-Busch triumphed, becoming the first brewer to sell 40 million barrels a year. Soon the two top brewers were producing over 50 percent of the beer sold in America, largely at the expense of smaller, independent breweries. (While the brewing industry was churning out billions of bottles and cans of beer, the challenge of what to do with the empty containers was first addressed in 1972 when Oregon became the first state to enact a bottle and container deposit law.)

After the small wineries of California had caught the attention of the Europeans, and young Americans were beginning to demand quality rather than quantity in their beverage alcohol, Jack McAuliffe sold a pint of ale in 1973 that had been brewed at the New Albion Brewery in Sonoma, California, the first "microbrewed" beer since Prohibition. It was a time when many young people had the chance to travel and discover the classic brews of Europe, and McAuliffe's ale was brewed to challenge the mass-produced pale lager-style beverage that seemed on the verge of taking over the entire beer market.

The New Albion Brewery would only last five years, from 1977 to 1982. But it would take less than twenty years for the microbrew industry to grow to more than 2,500 breweries and brewpubs offering more than 10,000 different beers.

[See also Alcohol and Teetotalism; Alcoholism; Ale Slipper; Bars; Beer, Corn and Maple; Beer Barrels; Beer Cans; Beer Gardens; Beer Halls; Beer Mugs; Birch Beer; Boilermaker; Bottling; Budweiser; Canning and Bottling; Coors Brewing Company; Fermentation; Microbreweries; Miller Brewing Company; Prohibition; Root Beer; Stout; Taverns; Temperance; Yeast.]

BIBLIOGRAPHY

Arnold, John Paul. *History of the Brewing Industry and Brewing Science in America.* Chicago: [n.p.], 1933.

Baron, Stanley Wade. *Brewed in America: A History of Beer and Ale in the United States.* Boston: Little, Brown, 1962.

Baum, Dan. *Citizen Coors: An American Dynasty.* New York: Morrow, 2000.

Burrows, Edwin G., and Mike Wallace. *Gotham: A History of New York City to 1898.* New York: Oxford University Press, 1999.

Downard, William L. *Dictionary of the History of the American Brewing and Distilling Industries.* Westport, CT: Greenwood, 1980.

Jackson, Michael. *Michael Jackson's Beer Companion: The World's Greatest Beer Styles, Gastronomy, and Traditions.* Philadelphia: Running Press, 1993.

LaFrance, Peter. *Beer Basics: A Quick and Easy Guide.* New York: Wiley, 1995.

Lathrop, Elise. *Early American Inns and Taverns.* New York: Arno Press, 1977.

Lender, Mary Edwards, and James Kirby Martin. *Drinking in America: A History.* New York: Free Press, 1982.

Merchant, W. T., comp. *In Praise of Ale.* London: G. Redway, 1888.

Plavchan, Ronald Jan. *A History of Anheuser-Busch 1852–1933.* New York: Arno Press, 1969.

Rice, Kym S. *Early American Taverns: For the Entertainment of Friends and Strangers.* Chicago: Regnery Gateway, 1983.

Ronnenberg, Herman. *Beer and Brewing in the Inland Northwest, 1850–1950.* Moscow, ID: University of Idaho Press, 1993.

Salem, Frederick William. *Beer: Its History and Its Economic Value as a National Beverage.* Hartford, CT: F. W. Salem & Co., 1880.

Sklinik, Bog. *The History of Beer and Brewing in Chicago, 1833–1978.* St. Paul, MN: Pogo Press, 1999.

Smith, Gregg. *Beer in America: The Early Years, 1587–1840: Beer's Role in the Settling of America and the Birth of a Nation.* Boulder, CO: Siris Books, 1998.

Thomann, Gallus. *American Beer: Glimpses of Its History and Description of Its Manufacture.* New York: United States Brewers' Association, 1909.

United States Brewers' Foundation. *Beer and Ale in Old New York and Its Environs.* New York: United States Brewers' Foundation, 1961.

Vaizey, John. *The Brewing Industry, 1886–1951: An Economic Study, for the Economic Research Council.* London: Pitman, 1960.

Van Wieren, Dale P. *American Breweries II.* West Point, PA: East Coast Breweriana Association, 1995.

PETER LAFRANCE

Beer, Corn and Maple

Pre-Classic Maya farmers were probably the first people to brew beer from maize, doing so around 2600 B.C.E. The Maya used fermentation as one method of releasing vital amino acids stored in the grain. Other indigenous North American peoples fermented maize to make it more nutritious and used it as leavening and flavoring for maize breads, gruels, "soft" drinks, and broths. In 1587, English colonists at Roanoke made beer from maize, most likely the first brewed in what is now the United States. Beer was the beverage of choice in seventeenth-century America, a habit and technology inherited from a mother country whose drinking water supply was chronically contaminated. By 1620, Virginia boasted European brewhouses, which produced maize beer for local consumption.

Imports of beer and barley crops for beer freed "corn mash" for distillation into bourbon whiskey, but corn beer continued to be used during shortages and emergencies. In the Civil War, Union soldiers brewed corn beer in Confederate prison camps to augment rations and prevent scurvy. Corn was widely used as an additive in the commercial beers that came to dominate the North American brewing industry in the late nineteenth century. Corn helps to produce the distinct flavor of mass-marketed American beers.

Southeastern Native Americans used the sap of the sugar maple tree to flavor "sagamite," or wood ash hominy, and to increase yeast production in fermented maize dishes. Europeans were quick to appreciate maple as a sweetener and as a fermenting agent. Alone or combined with maize, maple made a beer of variable potency, and fermented with native persimmons it made a sweet fruit wine. Maple beer is brewed as a regional New England specialty. Like maize, maple is used as a flavoring and fermenting agent in the microbrewery renaissance.

[*See also* Beer; Corn; Distillation; Maple Syrup.]

BIBLIOGRAPHY

Alström, Jason, and Todd Alström. *BeerAdvocate.com.* http://www.beeradvocate.com. All about beer by people who love it.

Fussel, Betty. *The Story of Corn: The Myths and History, the Culture and Agriculture, the Art and Science of America's Quintessential Crop.* New York: North Point Press, 1992. A social and scientific history of corn combined with a family history and memoir. The author describes a worldwide pursuit of "corn culture." The use of corn in the American South is mentioned briefly.

ESTHER DELLA REESE

Beer Barrels

It is likely that the barrel of ironbound wooden staves used to hold beer during its secondary fermentation originated with the "beer pails" of the Vikings. A barrel is a thirty-six-gallon cask made from metal by machines or out of white oak by a "tight cooper," a craftsman who specializes in making casks that will hold liquid. Stainless steel and aluminum barrels first came into use in the United States in the 1930s, almost completely replacing oak casks by the 1970s.

Although lighter and more efficient in production of a uniform brew suitable for the mass market, metal barrels do not impart the flavor that cask conditioning does. To compensate, commercial brewers use additives to imitate the natural carbonation and unique body imparted by oak. The success of "traditional method" microbreweries has encouraged a return to oak-cask fermentation both commercially and by home brewers. Cask-conditioned beers are called "real ales."

[See also Brewing.]

BIBLIOGRAPHY

American Brewery History Page. http://www.beerhistory.com. Excellent reference for the history of beer in America.
Glover, Brian. *The World Encyclopedia of Beer.* Lanham, MD: Lorenz Books, 2001. A good general resource concerned mostly with cataloging currently available beers. Contains a comprehensive historical introduction to beer and beer brewing.
Smith, Larry D. *The Cooper.* 2001. http://www.motherbedford.com/cooper.htm. A visually informative website about the craft of coopering in early America.

ESTHER DELLA REESE

Beer Cans

Attempts to can beer before 1930 were unsuccessful. What made canning beer difficult was that the beer can had to be able to withstand pressures over eighty pounds per square inch (psi). Food products require between twenty five and thirty psi. A greater challenge was finding a can lining to protect the beer from what brewers called "metal turbidity," a chemical reaction that ruined the beer. The American Can Company developed a breakthrough in 1934 when it produced the flat, or punch-top, can with a lining made from "Vinylite," a Union Carbide product. The package was trademarked as "Keglined" on September 25, 1934.

On January 24, 1935, in Richmond, Virginia, the first twelve-ounce cans of Krueger Special Beer went on the market. The Gottfried Krueger Brewing Company of Newark, New Jersey, supplied the beer, and the American Can Company provided the technology. That first year of beer in cans ended with over 200 million cans having been sold. By then, twenty-three brewers had begun using cans. The competition soon included the Continental Can Company, which introduced the "cone-top" can in an effort to fill the need of brewers who wanted to use can technology on their bottling lines. The cone-top beer can all but disappeared during the 1950s.

In July 1935, it was announced that Pabst Export Beer would be canned. One month later G. Heilemann Brewing Company of La Crosse, Wisconsin; Berghoff Brewing Company of Fort Wayne, Indiana; and Bridgport Brewing Company of Albany, New York, were also canning their beer. During World War II, rationed metal was directed toward the war effort, forcing brewers to package their beer almost entirely in bottles. The exception was beer packaged especially for the overseas troops. Many of the cans exported overseas for the war effort were painted in the army's traditional olive drab color. Even the can tops and bottoms were painted this color, to avoid reflecting light at night and possibly giving an easy target to the enemy.

From the beginning, the beverage can was made from three pieces of metal: a sleeve with separate top and bottom. It was not until 1959 that Coors introduced the first all-aluminum beverage can and launched a recycling program, offering a penny for every returned can. The Schlitz Brewing Company offered the next significant development when it introduced the pull-tab can to the market in March 1963. This inventive package was later made safer for the beer drinker and more ecologically friendly by the development of the stay-tab, introduced in the mid-1970s.

[See also Beer and Coors Brewing Company.]

BIBLIOGRAPHY

Baron, Stanley. *Brewed in America.* Boston: Little, Brown & Company, 1962.
Ronnenberg, Herman. *Beer and Brewing in the Inland Northwest, 1850–1959.* Moscow: University of Idaho Press, 1993.
Skilnik, Bob. *The History of Beer and Brewing in Chicago, 1833–1978.* St. Paul, MN: Pogo Press, 1999.

PETER LAFRANCE

Beer Gardens

Beer gardens were introduced to the United States by German immigrants, who also brought with them lager beer, the familiar light-colored, effervescent beverage. In the days before refrigeration, brewers planted trees to cool the ground above the cellars where aging lager was kept cold. In good weather, beer was sold to the public in the "garden." The Germans believed that beer was best enjoyed in social settings, preferably with food, fresh air, and music. They gathered in outdoor venues planted with groves of trees and filled with rows of tables. Beer gardens were places where people from all social classes could mix on an equal basis. Everyone was welcome, including women, children, and non-Germans. Prices were kept low to allow even those of modest means to visit often.

America's first beer gardens were opened in the middle of the nineteenth century by breweries seeking to attract more customers. Over the years, beer gardens grew increasingly elaborate. The largest offered entertainment such as Wild West shows, dance halls, menageries, and lavish nighttime light displays. Beer gardens such as the Schlitz Palm Gardens and Pabst Park, both in Milwaukee, Wisconsin, are considered the forerunners of theme parks. In some cities with large German populations, especially New York, huge, parklike indoor establishments were built that offered lager beer and live entertainment year round. As a result, the term "beer garden" came to be interchangeable with "beer hall." Outdoor beer gardens offering traditional food and entertainment are found in a number of communities with German American populations. Blob's Park in Jessup, Maryland, claims to have introduced Oktoberfest to America, staging the nation's first such celebration in 1947.

[See also Amusement Parks; Beer Halls; German American Food.]

BIBLIOGRAPHY

Gabaccia, Donna R. *We Are What We Eat: Ethnic Food and the Making of Americans.* Cambridge, MA: Harvard University Press, 1998.

Mariani, John. *America Eats Out: An Illustrated History of Restaurants, Taverns, Coffee Shops, Speakeasies, and Other Establishments That Have Fed Us for 350 Years.* New York: Morrow, 1991.

Oldenberg, Ray. *The Great Good Place: Cafes, Coffee Shops, Bookstores, Bars, Hair Salons and Other Hangouts at the Heart of a Community.* 3rd ed. New York: Marlowe, 1999.

Smith, Gregg, and Carrie Getty, eds. *The Beer Drinker's Bible: Lore, Trivia and History: Chapter and Verse.* Boulder, CO: Brewers, 1997.

PAUL RUSCHMANN

Beer Halls

Throughout history, people have gathered in public places to drink beer and converse. But in post–Revolutionary War America, the beer hall, both the term and the institution, fell into disfavor. It became unfashionable for large numbers of people to drink beer socially, and beer was associated with idleness. That all changed in the middle of the nineteenth century, when waves of German immigrants arrived. Beer and a place to drink it were essential to their community life. The towns in which Germans settled soon

had breweries and, later, beer halls similar to those in which they had drunk back home. The Germans were uncomfortable in "American" taverns, by which they usually meant Irish bars: dark establishments patronized exclusively by men. Germans viewed drinking places as extensions of the home. Their beer halls were well lit and filled with large tables where groups, often working-class families, drank together and ate traditional food, such as sausages, sauerkraut, Bismarck herring, rollmops, and sauerbraten.

The beer Germans brought with them was different from the dark, rich, English-style ales Americans had consumed since colonial times. German beer was a light colored—and less potent—beverage called lager, so named because it required long fermentation in a cool place (the word is derived from *lagern*, meaning "to store"). Americans, especially the young, quickly took a liking to lager. Beer hall proprietors, many of whom were German, catered to the newfound taste for lager. In some cities they built establishments with high ceilings and filled them with trees and plants in an effort to capture the atmosphere of an outdoor park—even in winter. Although they were roofed and enclosed, these establishments were commonly referred to as "beer gardens." After the Civil War, there were an estimated three to four thousand beer halls in New York City alone. The largest, such as the Atlantic Beer Garden, entertained customers with shooting galleries, billiard rooms, and bowling alleys in addition to music and dancing.

Americans considered beer halls more wholesome than taverns because the halls had gemütlichkeit, an atmosphere of intimacy and comfort. Men brought their wives and children; patrons drank slowly; the practice of buying rounds was unheard of; beer only was served; and, most important, violence was not tolerated. Some observers promoted beer as a beverage of moderation and held up the Germans as examples of temperance. Nevertheless, the presence of children in beer halls and the practice of drinking on Sundays offended many Americans. Prohibition, wartime hostility toward Germans and their culture, and the assimilation of German Americans into mainstream culture led to the near extinction of beer halls.

Even though it adopted German beer, over time the United States dropped the amenities associated with German beer halls. After the repeal of Prohibition, most drinking establishments were modeled after the Irish bar. The concept of the beer hall survived, however, especially in the Midwest. Beer halls of the early twenty-first century include the Brauhaus, in Chicago; the Dakota Inn Rathskeller, in Detroit, Michigan; and the Essen Haus, in Madison, Wisconsin. A number of small breweries, such as the Pennsylvania Brewing Company, in Pittsburgh, and the Weeping Radish, in Maneto, North Carolina, offer modern versions of the German beer hall. The world's most famous beer hall, the Hofbraühaus, of Munich, has a location in the Cincinnati, Ohio, area, and the Kaltenberg Castle Brewery, of Bavaria, has a beer hall in Vail, Colorado.

[*See also* Beer Gardens *and* German American Food.]

BIBLIOGRAPHY

Gabaccia, Donna R. *We Are What We Eat: Ethnic Food and the Making of Americans.* Cambridge, MA: Harvard University Press, 1998.
Mariani, John. *America Eats Out: An Illustrated History of Restaurants, Taverns, Coffee Shops, Speakeasies, and Other Establishments That Have Fed Us for 350 Years.* New York: Morrow, 1991.
Oldenberg, Ray. *The Great Good Place: Cafes, Coffee Shops, Bookstores, Bars, Hair Salons, and Other Hangouts at the Heart of a Community.* 3rd ed. New York: Marlowe, 1999.

PAUL RUSCHMANN

Beer Mugs

Beer mugs are lidless, handled drinking containers made of materials that include glass, earthenware, pewter, and stoneware. Before the development of sturdy glass and stoneware, wooden and earthenware mugs were used. In the late seventeenth century in England, strong, leaded glass was developed, but throughout Europe, pewter and German stoneware remained the materials of choice. In England in the mid-nineteenth century, pressed glass technology and lifting of the glass excise tax led to the creation and acceptance of the modern glass beer mug.

Colonial Americans imported mugs from Germany and England and produced them at local pottery and pewter factories. As were all drinking vessels of the time, these mugs were marked according to official capacity standards to ensure that the drinker received the measure of drink paid for. Around the time of the Revolutionary War, with the breakdown of communication between America and England, pewter fell out of use because tin could no longer be imported. In the early twenty-first century mugs are made predominately of stoneware and glass but are also made with other materials, such as plastic. Both the temperature and the material of a mug can affect the fla-

vor of the beer. Some beer drinkers enjoy drinking beer from room-temperature stoneware mugs, whereas others prefer icy-cold plastic mugs.

[*See also* Beer; Beer Barrels; Beer Cans; Beer Gardens; Beer Halls.]

BIBLIOGRAPHY

Kirsner, Gary. *The Beer Stein Book: A 400 Year History.* Coral Springs, FL: Glentiques, 2000.
Noël Hume, Ivor. *Here Lies Virginia: An Archaeologist's View of Colonial Life and History.* Charlottesville: University Press of Virginia, 1994.
Stratton, Deborah. *Mugs and Tankards.* London: Souvenir, 1975.

JENNIFER MINNICK

Benne, *see Fats and Oils*

Berries, *see Blackberries; Blueberries; Fruit; Raspberries; Strawberries*

Betty Crocker

One of the most famous Americans who never lived, Betty Crocker was "born" in 1921, a child of necessity. The Washburn-Crosby Company, makers of Gold Medal flour, had run a promotional contest, and along with thousands of entries came hundreds of baking questions. Previously, a small staff had answered consumer correspondence over their own signatures, but the onslaught of queries called for the creation of a fictional spokeswoman to sign the letters. Company directors chose the names Betty ("one of the most familiar and most companionable of all family nicknames"), and Crocker (surname of recently retired director William G. Crocker). Betty's "signature" was developed from samples submitted by female employees.

In 1924, Washburn-Crosby began broadcasting the *Betty Crocker Cooking School of the Air* on its Minneapolis radio station, WCCO. Later aired nationally, the program was written (and originally hosted) by Marjorie Husted. In 1951, Adelaide Hawley, an actress, was the first to portray Betty Crocker on television. A number of actresses took the role when the *Betty Crocker Magazine of the Air* was broadcast nationally in the 1950s.

The first product to bear the Betty Crocker name was a soup mix, in 1941. The first Betty Crocker cake mix was introduced in 1947. The *Betty Crocker Cook Book of All-Purpose Baking*, a soft-cover promotional item, was published in 1942. The comprehensive *Betty Crocker's Picture Cook Book*, one of the most successful and beloved American cookbooks, was published in 1950, and more than a million copies were in print by 1951. So began a dynasty of Betty Crocker books, booklets, and other publications. Keeping up with the times, the Betty Crocker website, launched in 1997 and retooled in 2001, offers recipes, advice, product information, cookbooks, kitchen equipment, tableware, and gifts.

Beginning in the 1920s, Betty Crocker had been depicted in print ads by various artists. In 1936, Neysa McMein, a prominent painter, was commissioned to create an official portrait. According to General Mills, the image was not a portrait of an individual but was an artful composite of the staff of the home service department. The Betty Crocker making her debut on the Softasilk cake flour box in 1937 was a severe young matron with a distant gaze, slightly pursed lips, and crisp white ruching at the neck-

Betty Crocker. The original Betty Crocker, painted by Neysa McMein, 1936. She first appeared on packaging in 1937. *Courtesy of General Mills*

line of her red dress. The portrait has been updated seven times since 1955. In 1957, a touch of gray appeared at Betty's temples, rendering her sweetly motherly. The 1965 incarnation was distinctly younger, reminiscent of Jacqueline Kennedy. The 1996 seventy-fifth-anniversary Betty Crocker, painted by John Stuart Ingle, is an olive-skinned career woman who might be part Asian, Latin, or African American. The watercolor, based on the digital "morphing" of photographs of seventy-five American women chosen by General Mills as embodying the characteristics of Betty Crocker, was engineered for broad demographic appeal. The Betty Crocker red spoon, a symbol first used on packages in 1954, has all but supplanted the Betty Crocker image on products and in advertising.

In 1945, Betty Crocker was identified by *Fortune* as the second most popular woman in America (after Eleanor Roosevelt). She was named one of the top ten advertising icons of the twentieth century by *Advertising Age*. Betty Crocker products, adapted for the tastes of local markets, are sold in Canada, the United Kingdom, Europe, Australia, the Middle East, and Asia.

[*See also* General Mills.]

BIBLIOGRAPHY

Betty Crocker. http://www.bettycrocker.com. Information about Betty Crocker food products, books and other publications, and catalogs of home products.
General Mills. http://www.GeneralMills.com. Corporate history, information on products, and frequently asked questions.
Inness, Sherrie A., ed. *Kitchen Culture in America*. Philadelphia: University of Pennsylvania Press, 2001.
Smallzreid, Kathleen Ann. *The Everlasting Pleasure*. New York: Appleton-Century-Crofts, 1956.

BONNIE J. SLOTNICK

Bialy

The bialy is a type of bread roll, consumed as an alternative to the bagel. Typically three to four inches in diameter, it has a depressed center and a doughy, chewy circular rim flecked with chopped onions. The dough is made with high-gluten flour, fresh baker's yeast, salt, and water. Both bialys and bagels are associated with Jewish American culinary traditions. However, the awareness and popularity of bagels have reached a national level, while bialys remain virtually unknown.

Bialys differ from bagels in four significant ways: ingredient content, manufacturing process, general appearance, and flavor. Unlike bagel dough, bialy dough does not have added sugar or sweeteners. Bialys are baked, whereas bagels are kettle-boiled and then baked. Bialys have a signature depression, but never a hole. And bialys are always doughy and have the taste of onion, while bagels are available in a variety of flavors.

The bialy originated in the city of Bialystok, in what is now northeastern Poland, although no one can definitively claim its creation or give the date when it was first made. Before World War II, Bialystok was a thriving city with a majority Jewish population, one of the largest in Poland. The word "bialy" is derived from the Yiddish *bialystoker kuchen*—*kuchen* referring to a baked good such as a cake. Jews from the Bialystok area were nicknamed *bialystoker kuchen fressers*, or prodigious *kuchen* eaters. Bialys were baked primarily by Jewish bakers and were a staple of the Jewish diet. They were commonly spread with butter or soft farmer cheese, either on top or on the bottom. They were never cut. Children often ate them with halvah, a sweet sesame paste. The original bialys were large—roughly six to nine inches in diameter—with a wider and crisper indent and a generous topping of chopped fresh onions and poppy seeds. Bakers used special rolling pins to create the depressed center.

Pogroms and the Holocaust dispersed the remaining European Jews throughout the world. Many immigrated to New York City's Lower East Side. From the 1920s on, *bialystoker* bakers set up numerous bialy productions in that area; only one, Kossar's, survived into the twenty-first century. Bialys are no longer made or known in Poland. To *bialystokers* around the world, the bialy is more than just a lost bread; it has come to represent a lost culture.

[*See also* Bagels; Jewish American Food; Polish American Food.]

BIBLIOGRAPHY

Eskin, Leah. "Exploring Some of the Cultural-Religious Roles of Food." *Chicago Tribune*, April 29, 2001.
Sheraton, Mimi. *The Bialy Eaters: The Story of a Bread and a Lost World.* New York: Broadway Books, 2000.
Wi'sniewski, Tomasz. *Jewish Bialystock and Surroundings in Eastern Poland.* Translated by Lucyna Aleksandrowicz-Pedich. Ipswich, MA: Ipswich Press, 1998.

IZABELA WOJCIK

Biotechnology

Biotechnology, seemingly a modern concept, has been used for thousands of years. Grain was turned into beer and bread, and grapes were made into wine and vinegar. Milk and salted vegetables were turned into products that did not spoil readily. With human observation and ingenuity, many foods were preserved and stored against lean times. Taste and appearance often changed drastically, but these foods, unlike spoiled foods, caused no illness.

With biotechnology, living organisms or biological processes are used to generate useful or desirable products. Yogurt and beer seem unrelated, but both are formed through the agency of live microorganisms (bacteria in yogurt, yeast in beer). Some medicines, such as antibiotics (produced by molds), also are products of biotechnology.

One aspect of biotechnology has generated more public attention than did the industrial production of yogurt or penicillin: recombinant DNA (rDNA) technology, also known as genetic engineering. Before protests at the 1999 World Trade Organization meeting in Seattle, Washington, many Americans had not heard the words "frankenfoods," "biopiracy," and "genetically modified organism," or "GMO." Few had known before those protests that they were eating foods that were the result of genetic engineering. In September 2000 news was made again when a major U.S. food manufacturer recalled taco shells that included genetically modified (GM) corn not approved for human consumption. The corn had been mixed with other lots of non-GM corn. The GM corn had not been found toxic or even allergenic but had been approved only for use as animal feed. Many Americans were surprised to learn that such crops were regulated.

Biotechnology in food production is controversial. American farmers who plant GM crops with the intention of increasing productivity and profit often find it difficult to export those crops. Some countries are not convinced of the safety or need for GM foods and choose not to import them. Some have increased the amount of acreage allotted to GM crops, and some accept imports from the United States. Some American food manufacturers use GM ingredients; others have banned them. Organic farmers are worried about contamination from nearby altered crops, because organic certification cannot be granted if a GM crop becomes mixed with the organic crop. Multinational biotechnology companies have been accused of arrogance in promoting GM crops. Their defense is that they believe they are trying to feed the world. Seeds for GM crops are not sold outright, and farmers are not permitted to save GM seed for the next season. In the early twenty-first century Americans are starting to take more notice of biotechnology and how it affects their food supply. It is not easy, however, for consumers to know what they are buying, because GM foods are not labeled as such in the United States. Consumer education will have a great deal of influence on how the biotechnology industry proceeds.

Genetic Engineering

Early agriculturalists learned that their crops and animals made copies of themselves. A tall variety of grain usually produced tall plants, and sheep with a particular coat color or length usually produced more of the same. Oddities occurred and sometimes were exploited, such as Jacob's spotted sheep (Gen. 30: 32–43). New varieties thus were produced by selective breeding. Parent plants or animals were chosen for desired characteristics and were bred. Offspring with those characteristics were bred again until the trait "bred true" generation after generation with few surprises.

The mechanism of selective breeding was unknown until the mid-nineteenth century. In 1856 Gregor Mendel, a Moravian monk, started to examine the pea plants growing in the garden of his Brno (in what was to become the Czech Republic) monastery. Mendel was able to establish that heredity followed specific patterns and that certain outcomes could be predicted. The offspring, as a group, would exhibit a particular trait in definite ratios. The trait would be inherited as though it were a fixed unit. However, Mendel could not identify the unit with the technology of his time.

The "fixed unit" of heredity became known as a "gene." Each gene is a recipe or set of instructions for producing a particular molecule, usually a protein. These instructions are strung along structures known as "chromosomes." Genes and chromosomes are made of DNA (deoxyribonucleic acid). Cells use DNA and its relative, RNA (ribonucleic acid), to store the information needed to run the cell and produce the next generation.

DNA has only four components, which are assembled in varying linear arrangements (sequences) to make every gene in a cell. Modern technology allows genetic engineers to isolate or synthesize desired sequences and then to "cut and paste" them into the DNA of another organism. If this procedure is properly done, the new piece of DNA, usually a complete gene, works in its new location. The recipient organism need not be related to the donor of the DNA. The host organism uses the inserted DNA to make the protein specified by the foreign gene. Genetic engineers can purchase kits containing all the components needed to make a functional gene insert.

All that need be added is the desired gene (such as one that confers pesticide resistance, obtained from petunias or bacteria) and a host (soybeans, for example) will take up the DNA.

Taking up DNA is only the first step. The DNA must enter the nucleus of the cell and slip into the existing DNA there. Modern methods make this process increasingly less random. If the inserted DNA breaks up an existing gene, the cell may not function properly or may die. The next step is to identify and select appropriate cells that have taken up and incorporated the new DNA. Selection is usually done by "markers" that are attached to the inserted DNA. However, a trait such as pesticide resistance can be identified by growing the cells in the presence of the pesticide. Cells that survive have most likely integrated the required gene. Common markers are antibiotic-resistance genes, although these are being phased out because of concerns about the transference of resistance to disease-causing bacteria.

The final stage is producing a complete organism. With bacteria and other single-cell organisms, DNA uptake and production of more organisms are simpler than with plants or animals. However, under the right conditions, plants regenerate from single cells taken from the parent plant. Obtaining whole animals from engineered cells is more complicated, but the procedure has been developed. Organisms so altered are called "transgenic." Another popular name is "genetically modified organism." Plants or animals bred by conventional methods are genetically modified relative to their wild ancestors, but they are not considered transgenic. These organisms would not normally carry genes from an unrelated species.

Purpose of Genetic Engineering

Early farmers noticed that some characteristics in their crops and animals were more desirable than others. With a careful choice of breeding stock, those traits could be reinforced or improved in successive generations. But the process was slow. Yields of grain or milk were not fully apparent until the season was well along or the cattle had reached maturity and were bred again. Later, plant and animal breeders crossed and recrossed to obtain "improved" varieties, taking years to establish a new line. Although a spectacular new flower or high-yielding grain could make a large amount of money for a breeder when released, the cost of the process could make overall profits small. A method of accelerating the process would have been welcomed. Enter genetic engineering, in which traditional breeding methods are short circuited and the time required for a new crop variety to be marketed is reduced. With traditional methods a new seed type can take ten years or more to reach consumers. With direct gene transfer and selection this time can be halved.

Traditional methods involve uncertainty. Several characteristics are transmitted to offspring, whether or not all are wanted. Genetic engineering allows for selection of a single trait, although in theory more than one gene can be transferred. Specific combinations of traits can be obtained that would take too long to be profitable with other methods.

Another attraction of gene transfer is the ability to add novel traits to organisms that would not gain them otherwise. Bt (*Bacillus thuringiensis*), a bacterial insecticide long used by organic gardeners, has been engineered into some commercial crops. Human insulin is produced by engineered bacteria. Farm animals can be engineered to carry genes for useful pharmaceuticals and produce them in their milk. Novel foods can be generated by rDNA technology. Flavors, colors, and nutrients can be inserted into foods lacking them. An example is "golden rice," which has been engineered to produce a vitamin A precursor not normally present in rice. It may also be possible to use engineering techniques to remove undesirable molecules, such as allergens in peanuts or nicotine in tobacco. Any combination, such as the notorious "fish genes" in tomatoes, is possible, but not all combinations are of commercial interest. The final product must be useful to producers, acceptable to consumers, and present no harm. Products of transferred genes remain in crops, so there are risks of toxicity and allergenicity. In the 1990s a soybean developed for animal feed carried a gene for a Brazil nut protein to enhance levels of a particular amino acid. However, the protein was found to be an allergen in humans, and the beans were never commercialized. Careful screening can minimize risks.

A goal of genetic engineering of plants is nitrogen fixation. Certain bacteria can use otherwise inert atmospheric nitrogen directly, converting it into ammonia and then into the amino acids needed to make proteins. The most familiar examples are the bacteria that live in the root nodules of leguminous plants, such as beans, peas, and clover. The root nodules provide the bacteria with the needed environment for nitrogen fixation. Engineering this trait into other plants, so that they also become hospitable to the necessary bacteria, could save farmers the use of huge quantities of synthetic nitrogen fertilizer. However, nitrogen fixation is a multigene trait, and not all of the genes have been identified.

Regulation of Biotechnology

Three government agencies regulate transgenic organisms in the United States: the Department of Agriculture (USDA), the Environmental Protection Agency (EPA), and the Food and Drug Administration (FDA). Each agency oversees a different aspect of biotechnology, although there is some overlap. A product may be regulated by more than one agency.

U.S. Department of Agriculture Founded in 1862 to provide support to farmers and ranchers, the USDA also regulates transgenic plants and animals. The division responsible is the Animal and Plant Health Inspection Service (APHIS), which is charged with protecting American agriculture from pests and diseases. Importation and introduction of organisms or products with "pest potential" are regulated, and a company must obtain permission before importing or releasing such organisms. The regulations include field trials of transgenic crops and animals.

Producers can apply to have their crops or products considered "nonregulated." APHIS then determines the safety of the crop or product, usually on the basis of information provided by the producer. If nonregulated status is granted, no further permission is needed for release or importation. A crop or product is then considered "safe to grow," or no threat to agriculture.

The National Organic Program, established in 2002, is administered by the USDA. The technology of rDNA falls under "excluded methods." No transgenic plant or animal can be certified as organic, however raised subsequently.

U.S. Environmental Protection Agency Pesticides (chemical or biological), new uses for pesticides, and novel microorganisms are the responsibility of the EPA. This agency sets tolerance limits for pesticide residues in the environment and on (or in) crops and foodstuffs. Transgenic plants and microorganisms that produce pesticidal compounds (such as Bt) must meet these tolerances. Because they represent new uses of existing pesticides, herbicide-resistant crops are regulated by the EPA. Plants engineered for disease resistance also must be approved. Resistance acquired by weeds would present environmental problems.

Transgenic bacteria modified to break down pollution and then released into the natural environment fall under the Toxic Substances Control Act. Regulation is meant to prevent damage to the environment caused by possible contamination of wild organisms by engineered counterparts. Bacteria and other microorganisms kept contained in structures, as in research and development centers, and never released live into the environment are exempt. Researchers in those facilities usually must document compliance with other regulations, such as those of the U.S. National Institutes of Health. Producers must seek approval from the EPA for field trials of plants or microorganisms. The agency bases decisions on information supplied by producers.

U.S. Food and Drug Administration Ensuring that foods, medicines, health-care products, and ingredients are safe falls to the FDA. The responsible division is the Center for Food Safety and Applied Nutrition. Novel ingredients in foods and medicines must be proved safe by the manufacturer, on the basis of the manufacturer's own results of research and trials. The FDA reviews the information in an initial consultation and bases judgment on existing regulations.

Inserted DNA falls under the concept of "generally recognized as safe" (GRAS), because all living cells contain DNA. However, the FDA has advised food developers to avoid using marker genes that encode resistance to clinically important antibiotics. It is not certain that such genes can never be transferred to bacteria and spread that resistance. The resulting protein (generally an enzyme) is not normally considered novel, because it existed previously in another organism. The consultation process determines whether a bioengineered food is generally recognized as safe. If there are doubts, the manufacturer must apply for full approval, as it does for new colorings or flavorings. Food crops that produce pesticides are regulated by the EPA. If the EPA has granted approval, the FDA has no further involvement; the enzymes inducing pest resistance are considered generally recognized as safe. Similarly, herbicide-resistant food crops are first regulated by the EPA rather than the FDA.

The FDA sets rules for food labeling. Foods that are the result of biotechnology need not be labeled as such, provided there are no hidden hazards, such as potential toxins or allergens. The presence of allergens or toxins must be mentioned on the label. The source of these substances does not have to be mentioned. Use of the term "genetically modified" or "GM" on labels is not allowed. The FDA considers that all foods are genetically modi-

fied from their wild-type ancestors and that to label foods as such is "misleading" ("Guidance for Industry," http://www.cfsan.fda.gov/~dms/biolabgu.html). Results of research with FDA focus groups, however, indicate that consumers want such information on labels. Almost all participants said that bioengineered foods should be labeled as such, as is done in the European Union and some other countries.

Obtaining approval for a transgenic foodstuff can be a lengthy and expensive process. Only the largest companies can afford to complete the process and remain profitable. In addition, approval in the United States does not ensure approval overseas. American companies must obtain similar approvals from any country to which they wish to export a biotechnology product.

Biotechnology on the Farm

The first genetically engineered vegetable grown and released for sale in the United States was the Flavr Savr tomato. Developed by Calgene (later a division of Monsanto), the tomato was approved by the USDA in 1992 and commercialized in 1994. The engineering consisted of insertion of a gene back to front, which delayed softening of the tomatoes as they ripened. In theory the tomatoes could be left to ripen longer on the plant without becoming too soft for packing and shipping. The Flavr Savr tomato was withdrawn from the market in 1996. Crop yields had been low, and there was not enough consumer interest.

The first commercially successful GM crop in the United States was the Roundup Ready soybean, sold by Monsanto. Government approval was granted in 1994, and the first commercial fields were planted in 1996. The beans are engineered to resist a widely used herbicide, glyphosate, originally patented by Monsanto as Roundup. The resistance also was engineered into corn, cotton, sugar beets, rapeseed (canola), and wheat, although not all of these crops have been commercialized. Other herbicides have been paired with resistant crops. Farmers can spray the chosen herbicide on fields at any time with little or no damage to crops. Approximately 70 percent of the soybeans grown in the United States in 2002 were engineered to be herbicide resistant. Most of the canola oil used by Americans comes from engineered varieties grown in Canada and approved for use in the United States. Little herbicide-resistant canola is grown in the United States.

Another pest-resistance strategy is to engineer plants to produce their own pesticide, such as Bt, a group of toxins originating in bacteria. The molecules are toxic to many insects and have been used by organic as well as conventional growers as a spray. Bt has been engineered into corn, cotton, soybeans, potatoes, tomatoes, and other crops. Not all have been approved for commercial production. GM potatoes with Bt and virus-protection genes were never commercially important in the United States and were discontinued by the developers (Monsanto) in 2001. Approximately 30 percent of the corn grown by U.S. farmers in 2002 was of an engineered variety. Most of that corn was Bt producing; herbicide-resistant and combination varieties also were grown.

Cotton also is engineered in the United States— approximately 70 percent of the crop in 2002. About half this amount was herbicide resistant; the other half was divided between Bt-producing cotton and a combination of the two traits. Although cotton is grown primarily for fiber, cottonseed oil is a by-product used in the food industry. Most engineered corn, soybeans, and cottonseed oil are used in animal feed and in processed foods. Engineered and conventional varieties are not segregated by wholesalers and processors. Disease resistance to specific plant viruses also has been engineered into papaya, squashes, and potatoes. As much as 50 percent of Hawaiian papayas are genetically modified in this way. Although most of those papayas do not reach mainland U.S. markets, some may be sold on the West Coast. The squashes are grown by few farmers. The virus resistance is limited to two or three types, whereas numerous infections are common.

Another aspect of biotechnology linked to farming is production of transgenic plants and animals for substances used in medicine. This practice is known colloquially as "pharming." Living organisms produce biochemicals more efficiently than do most industrial processes. Although yeast and bacteria often are used in this way, these organisms cannot form many human or animal proteins properly. Inserting genes for the production of biochemicals into common crop plants and farm animals can result in abundant "manufacture" of those protein molecules at low cost. Ruminants, such as cows or sheep, often are used, because the biochemicals can be excreted in milk. In some cases no purification is needed. Milk can be drunk as is, or a fruit can be consumed as usual. An example is the GM banana system being designed to deliver vaccines. The bananas can be eaten raw, and vaccines produced in them may not be as perishable as conventional vaccines.

Development of pharming has been slow. PPL Therapeutics, in Scotland, owners of the technology that produced Dolly the sheep, has been unable to bring a single pharmed product to commercial production in ten years of effort. The U.S. company Genzyme also has had no success. Pharmed products must meet the standards for any drug being brought to market. Development has been slowed further by concerns about mixing of pharmed products with conventional products. All milk and all bananas or other crops of a given type look very much the same. Should pharming become commercially viable, care must be taken that such pharmaceuticals not end up on consumers' plates without their consent. At the beginning of the twenty-first century no widespread mechanisms are in place in the United States to segregate GM from non-GM products.

Biotechnology at the Supermarket

The average American supermarket contains many foods with ingredients of GM origin. Consumers may be unaware of what is or is not genetically modified, because such labeling is voluntary. The first product of genetic engineering in the U.S. food supply was Chy-Max chymosin, developed by Pfizer and approved by the FDA in 1990. It is a version of vegetarian rennet, used to make some kinds of cheese.

The presence of animal rennet (derived from the stomach tissue of calves) makes many cheeses undesirable for vegetarians and for those observing certain religious dietary bans. The gene for chymosin (the main molecule involved in rennet-induced milk coagulation) is either isolated from calf tissue or synthesized in a laboratory and inserted into bacteria or certain fungi. The chymosin produced is reliable in its clotting properties, making it cost effective for cheese makers. Approximately 60 percent of all U.S. cheeses are produced with GM chymosin from various companies. Some cheeses may be labeled "vegetarian," but most supermarket hard cheeses are made with these chymosins. Those same cheeses may be made with milk from cows that have been given recombinant bovine somatotropin (rBST), sometimes called recombinant bovine growth hormone (rBGH), a protein hormone. Approximately one-third of U.S. dairy cattle are given rBST to increase milk production 10 to 15 percent. The rBST is indistinguishable from BST, or natural bovine somatotropin, and is mostly destroyed by pasteurization.

By far the most common biotechnology products in American supermarkets are obtained from GM soybeans and corn. Processed foods, such as bakery products, heat-and-serve meals, textured vegetable protein, confectionery products, salad dressings, and breakfast cereals all contain a variety of corn- and soybean-derived ingredients. Although most corn grown in the early twenty-first century is not genetically modified, GM corn is mixed with conventional corn after harvest.

Items such as cornmeal or soybean flour can be readily identified as genetically modified, not genetically modified, or a combination of the two (more usual). Many other ingredients, such as sugars, vitamins, and amino acids, have been further refined or processed and no longer retain any corn or soybean identity. Because the FDA considers various ingredients isolated from GM soybeans and corn to be "substantially equivalent" to their non-GM counterparts, no labeling of the origins of the products is required.

Cottonseed oil, a by-product of cotton crops, is common in processed foods. It is often listed in generic vegetable oils or fats as "vegetable shortening (partially hydrogenated soybean and/or cottonseed oil)." Most cottonseed oil in the United States is derived from GM cotton varieties. Canola oil, whether bottled oil or generic vegetable fat, is mostly genetically modified and is imported from Canada. One variety, high-laurate oil, is labeled as such because its nutritional characteristics are altered. This oil is produced primarily for the manufacture of soaps and detergents rather than for food use. Research is being conducted to engineer vegetable oils to be more heart-friendly and to have a better shelf life and industrial characteristics. The nutritional characteristics will be changed relative to those of conventional oils, and the GM oils must be labeled as being altered in composition.

Genetically engineered fruits and vegetables are extremely rare on market shelves, because few have been approved for commercialization in the United States. As of 2002 cantaloupes, potatoes, radicchio, squash, papaya, sugar beets, corn, soybeans, and tomatoes were the only fruits and vegetables given FDA approval. The only engineered potatoes approved in the United States, Monsanto's New Leaf varieties, were discontinued in 2001, and no further seed has been supplied to farmers. Cantaloupes are not yet being marketed by their developer (Agritope, bought by Exelixis). The radicchio was withdrawn by the Dutch developer Bejo Zaden. Few engineered squashes reach American consumers, and most of the papayas in mainland supermarkets are not the GM varieties grown in Hawaii. The sugar beets are not yet planted commercially.

The fresh corn on the cob, canned and frozen corn, and popcorn sold directly to consumers are unlikely to be biotechnology versions. Only a small percentage of U.S.

engineered corn is sweet corn, and no popcorn varieties have been approved. Americans rarely use fresh soybeans, other than as the snack *edamame*, popular since the late 1990s. The frozen beans one finds in Asian shops are not likely to be genetically modified and are often marked "not genetically engineered."

Production of genetically engineered tomatoes and tomato products has been discontinued in the United States. The Flavr Savr tomato did not survive the transition to commercial status. The tomato did not look or taste better than other tomatoes and was not less expensive. A different modified tomato was developed by Zeneca for the processing industry and was grown in California. Production of the Zeneca tomato was discontinued in 1999 because of lack of consumer demand, although sales of the paste produced were initially good. Research into improving the ripening, nutritional, and processing properties of tomatoes is ongoing. Consumer preferences are geared toward taste, however, and research in that direction is not being emphasized.

Future Foods or Food Fights?

American food production has traditionally been centered on quantity. The typical goal is to produce as much as possible per acre, regardless of surpluses and low prices to farmers. Surplus food is exported as part of complicated trade agreements with other industrialized nations or is used to aid famine-stricken countries. Most farms in the United States are small and family owned, but they do not always provide a living for their owners. In 1997 approximately 70 percent of farms brought in less than fifty thousand dollars, whereas the average cost of production was approximately seventy thousand dollars. Between 1992 and 1997 total cropland and the number of farms decreased approximately 1.5 percent nationwide, with regional differences (for example, in California the decline was approximately 5 percent). To maintain supply, more food must be grown in less space and by fewer growers. Intensive farming, however, is known to deplete soil. Chemical additives cause pollution at sites of application and of manufacture. Irrigation causes problems such as salinization of soil and water-table depletion.

Traditional agriculture has developed methods and crops for dealing with marginal land, but yields are often low and variable. Genetically engineered crops can be a tool for increasing production on a decreasing amount of farmland. In theory, crops can be developed for conditions previously considered unsuitable for agriculture. Yields presumably can be manipulated by manipulation of the genes responsible for yield. Nutritional factors can be inserted into crops lacking these factors. Use of disease-resistant plants may reduce losses in the field. Cloned animals may provide tailor-made nutrition, maturation times, and pharmaceuticals. Biotechnology can be considered a route to "cleaner," less-polluting agriculture. Research is being conducted to develop plants that can survive in polluted soil and to develop bacteria to clean up such soil. Herbicide- and pest-resistant crops should require less spraying. The nitrogen-fixing crops envisioned would require less nitrogen-containing fertilizer.

When the first large-scale commercial biotechnology crops were planted in the United States in 1996, the "agrobiotechnology" companies were confident that their products would completely revolutionize farming and the food industry. Many of those companies started corporate life as chemical and pharmaceutical concerns that had developed reputations as polluters. During the last part of the twentieth century, companies such as Monsanto, DuPont, and Dow became interested in genetic engineering. Biotechnology was seen as a new way to improve or maintain profitability while boosting public relations. These companies learned that although everyone needs to eat, not everyone wants to eat engineered food. Abundant food production is a good thing, but "dumping" surpluses can disrupt farming in poor countries. The chemical-companies-turned-"life-science"-companies were often caught off guard by consumer attitudes toward their products. Biotechnology companies have tended to present their patented, licensed, genetically engineered crops as the only solution to world hunger. Factors such as politics, poverty, and trade regulations have been ignored. Marketing overseas has often been conducted with the assumption that what is good for Americans is good for the world. The companies have realized that this attitude does not work and are attempting to win over consumers.

For protection of intellectual property rights, GM seeds are not sold outright to farmers. Only the final crop belongs to the grower. No seed may be saved for another season or exchanged with another grower. Growers must sign documents and usually pay a licensing fee, often factored into the price of the seed. For a time licenses from Monsanto prohibited the use of any brand of glyphosate herbicide other than its own Roundup. That restriction was overturned in the courts. Agrobiotechnology companies inspect farms, looking for license violations. Farmers have been prosecuted when their fields were found to contain GM plants, even when no such seed was bought or planted. Factors such as pollen drift and seed adherence to hired equipment are discounted. This policy does not set well with many farmers. Poor farmers worldwide may find it difficult to deal with complicated licenses and then find themselves bound to third parties who will. In the process these farmers could lose their self-sufficiency.

GM crops have not always performed well in less-than-ideal conditions, and farmers have sued for compensation. Local weeds and insects have developed herbicide and pesticide resistance where GM crops are grown worldwide. Continual production of resistance factors seems to shorten the time needed for local pests and weeds to adjust. In an effort to slow development of resistance, growers may plant non-GM "reserves" to allow a susceptible population of plants to remain.

American farmers sometimes find that their GM crops are not welcome in all countries. Importers have begun paying premiums to growers for non-GM crops. In addition, laws regarding labeling of engineered foodstuffs vary among countries. Consumers in many countries expect GM foods to be labeled as such, whereas a large percentage of American producers (not consumers, however) object to such labeling. This discrepancy can lead to trade disputes.

The "rediscovery" of regional American cooking with local ingredients will have long-term influence on how biotechnology affects food in the United States. Most biotechnology research benefits producers and processors rather than consumers. Herbicide resistance is unlikely to be a selling point at the supermarket; taste and appearance are more important. The organic food industry has benefited from biotechnology in an oblique way. The National Organic Program does not allow GM foods to be certified as organic. Consumers who do not want to eat GM foods can choose organic foods. Thus, the production of organically raised foods is increasing in the United States.

Many farmers can readily sell GM crops. Food-processing companies use biotechnology ingredients along with conventional ingredients. Many U.S. consumers do not have an opinion about factory farming and biotechnology as long as the food produced is low cost and attractive. Various food scares, however, have caused American consumers to wonder about what they eat and how it is produced. Biotechnology has a role to play in world food production, if it is managed sensibly and is responsive to consumer demand.

[*See also* Department of Agriculture, United States; Food and Drug Administration; Politics of Food.]

BIBLIOGRAPHY

Ag BioTech InfoNet. http://www.biotech-info.net. Digests of press releases and newspaper and journal articles mostly relating to the agricultural aspects of biotechnology. Sponsored by scientific, environmental, and consumer organizations.

Animal and Plant Health Inspection Service. http://www.aphis.usda.gov.

Charles, Daniel. *Lords of the Harvest: Biotech, Big Money, and the Future of Food*. Cambridge, MA: Perseus, 2001. A general account of the biotechnology industry, players, and politics.

Cooper, Ann, with Lisa M. Holmes. *Bitter Harvest: A Chef's Perspective on the Hidden Dangers in the Foods We Eat and What You Can Do About It*. New York: Routledge, 2000. Presents common concerns about the food supply in the United States, including biotechnology. Not antibiotechnology as such but in favor of sustainable local agriculture.

Cornell University Public Issues Education Project. http://www.geo-pie.cornell.edu. Introduction to genetically engineered organisms and concerns.

Council for Biotechnology Information: http://www.whybiotech.com. An industry-sponsored website covering all aspects of biotechnology.

Cummins, Ronnie, and Ben Lilliston. *Genetically Engineered Food: A Self-Defense Guide for Consumers*. New York: Marlowe, 2000. Against GMO, this book promises to "Help protect you from the risks posed by genetically engineered food." Contains many misconceptions about GMOs and little good scientific information.

Durant, John, Martin W. Bauer, and George Gaskell. *Biotechnology in the Public Sphere*. London: Science Museum, 1998. One of the first assessments of European public opinion on biotechnology.

Gaskell, George, and Martin W. Bauer, eds. *Biotechnology 1996–2000: The Years of Controversy*. London: Science Museum, 2001. Accounts of the state of public opinion, regulatory issues, and media coverage about biotechnology in the United States, Canada, and fourteen European countries.

Lambrecht, Bill. *Dinner at the New Gene Café: How Genetic Engineering Is Changing What We Eat, How We Live, and the Global Politics of Food*. New York: St. Martin's, 2001. Emphasis on the people involved in the story of GM foods and consumer reactions to these foods. Little technical content. Mostly neutral.

Lurquin, Paul F. *High Tech Harvest: Understanding Genetically Modified Food Plants*. Boulder, CO: Westview, 2002. Explains technology for nonscientists. Mostly neutral.

Martineau, Belinda. *First Fruit: The Creation of the Flavr Savr Tomato and the Birth of Biotech Foods*. New York: McGraw-Hill, 2001. An account of how the Flavr Savr tomato was developed and brought to market and why it failed. Written by a member of the Calgene team that originated the project.

McHughen, Alan. *Pandora's Picnic Basket: The Potential and Hazards of Genetically Modified Foods*. Oxford and New York: Oxford University Press, 2000. A good basic explanation of how GM foods are derived and of consumer concerns. Primarily in favor of GM. Readers are told that there are no good reasons to reject biotechnology foods.

Organic Trade Association. http://www.ota.com. An industry-sponsored site promoting organic agriculture. Against genetic engineering.

Pence, Gregory E. *Designer Food*. Lanham, MA: Rowman and Littlefield, 2002. Concentrates on the controversies over biotechnology and food. Mostly in favor of GM.

U.S. Department of Agriculture Statistics. http://www.nass.usda.gov/census.

U.S. Environmental Protection Agency. http://www.epa.gov.

U.S. Food and Drug Administration. http://vm.cfsan.fda.gov.

U.S. Food and Drug Administration. "Guidance for Industry: Voluntary Labeling Indicating Whether Foods Have or Have Not Been Developed Using Bioengineering." http://www.cfsan.fda.gov/~dms/biolabgu.html.

Wilmut, Ian, Keith Campbell, and Colin Tudge. *The Second Creation: Dolly and the Age of Biological Control*. New York: Farrar, Straus, and Giroux, 2000. An account of how Dolly the sheep and other cloned animals came into being by the team who produced them. Includes ethical implications of cloning and other concerns.

ASTRID FERSZT

Birch Beer

Birch beer, a beverage made with the sap of birch trees, first became popular in America in the 1880s and 1890s, during the temperance movement. Many soft drinks, including ginger ale, sarsaparilla, spruce beer, root beer, cherry smash, and Coca-Cola, were developed and mass-marketed during this time. Because they contained no alcohol, these beverages were billed as family drinks. That some of these sodas were said to have healing properties helped spur sales. For example, ginger ale was supposed to cure nausea and help digestion; sarsaparilla was said to be a blood purifier; and early versions of Coca-Cola were billed as hangover and headache cures. By the late 1800s, many sodas were being bottled for mass distribution. The crimped metal cap was patented in 1892, enabling more than one hundred bottles per minute to be easily sealed.

The first birch beers were homemade, brewed without a standard recipe. All contained at least some portion of sap from birch trees, also called birch water. The trees, usually sweet birch or black birch, were tapped in the early spring, around the end of February or beginning of March, similar to the way maples are tapped to make maple syrup. A hole was drilled in the tree, and a spile (tube) was inserted to let the sap run into a bucket. Although it did not contain much flavor, the raw sap was used to replace plain water in drink recipes.

Early versions of birch beer contained yeast and were left to ferment, making them alcoholic. Birch wine was made with birch sap that was boiled down, fermented, and stored in casks stopped with bungs. Other ingredients in birch beer varied but could include sassafras, honey, juniper, and vanilla. Birch bark or small birch twigs sometimes were added to give the brew a stronger birch flavor.

Birch beer is similar to root beer but typically is less sweet and less carbonated. The natural flavor of birch sap and twigs is similar to wintergreen. Modern formulas for birch beer usually include flavor extracts as well as benzoate of soda as a preservative. Because sassafras root was a suspected carcinogen, the U.S. government banned use of the root in the 1960s. Sassafras extract is permitted as a flavoring. Food coloring is sometimes added to birch beer to make it red. White birch beer is a clear, colorless variation.

Birch beer never gained the cult following of other temperance drinks, such as Moxie and Dr Pepper. Birch beer is a regional specialty, sold mostly in the Mid-Atlantic states and New England. It is especially popular in the Pennsylvania Dutch country. Companies that have been making birch beer since the late nineteenth century include the Kutztown Soda Co. in Pennsylvania, and Boylan's in New Jersey. Birch beer is experiencing a comeback because several beverage companies are reviving old-fashioned American sodas.

[*See also* Bottling; Root Beer; Sarsaparilla; Sassafrasses; Soda Drinks.]

BIBLIOGRAPHY

Brown, John Hull. *Early American Beverages*. Rutland, VT: Tuttle, 1966.
Cresswell, Stephen. *Homemade Root Beer, Soda and Pop*. Pownal, VT: Storey, 1998.
Devito, Carlo. *The Everything Beer Book*. Holbrook, MA: Adams, 1998.
Witzel, Michael Karl, and Gyvel Witzel-Young. *Soda Pop!* Stillwater, MN: Town Square, 1998.

CLARA SILVERSTEIN

Birdseye, Clarence

Clarence Birdseye, the inventor and pioneer in frozen foods, was born in Brooklyn, New York, on December 9, 1886. Until he died on October 8, 1956, Birdseye never came in from the cold. According to family legend, an ancestor saved the life of an English queen by shooting an attacking hawk through the eye, thereby earning the name "Birds Eye." Clarence Birdseye attended Amherst College but was forced to leave school for lack of money. As a struggling student, Birdseye recounted the day he passed a spring hole and saw thousands of small frogs. He wondered what the frogs were good for, so he sold them to the Bronx Zoo for $115. This ability to look at the familiar and see opportunity was a creative trait Birdseye never lost.

Birdseye went to Labrador, Canada, to work as a fur trapper and to conduct a fish and wildlife survey as a field naturalist for the U.S. government. On August 21, 1915, on a visit to Washington, D.C., Birdseye married Eleanor Garrett, whose father was a founder of the National Geographic Society. The Birdseyes and their newly born son, Kellogg, returned to Labrador to live in a remote shack. While Clarence traveled by dogsled to acquire furs, Eleanor tended the winter traps.

In Labrador, Birdseye discovered that foods frozen quickly in the frigid Artic air kept their flavor. He experimented by putting cabbages in his baby's bath pan, adding salt water, and exposing the pan to the frigid winds. As a result, the family had green food all winter.

Upon returning to the United States, Birdseye took a job as assistant to the president of the U.S. Fisheries Association. It disturbed him to see fish in melted ice water, a medium that promoted bacterial growth. In September 1922 Birdseye began development of a commercial method for quickly freezing food. His tools were primitive—an electric fan, buckets of brine, and ice. Birdseye moved to Gloucester, Massachuetts, in 1925 to be near a supply of fresh fish and founded the General Seafoods Corporation to produce "frosted foods." His method of quick freezing produced small ice crystals that did not damage the structure of food. When thawed, the food retained its original flavor, texture, color, and taste. After Birdseye sold the company it was renamed General Foods Corporation. Birdseye stayed with General Foods to supervise its frozen foods laboratory. Over his career Birdseye was granted almost three hundred patents.

Birdseye was very modest about his accomplishments. "I did not discover quick-freezing. The Eskimos had used it for centuries, and scientists in Europe had made experiments along the same lines I had. What I accomplished . . . was merely to make packaged quick-frozen food available to the public" (Nickerson). Birdseye was also an early pioneer in the area of food dehydration. He called his new food processing method "anhydration" and the product "waterless foods."

An inventor in the mold of Benjamin Franklin and Thomas Edison, Birdseye was an adventurer, explorer, scientist, promoter, and naturalist. His contributions revolutionized the way food was marketed, not only in the United States but also throughout the world. Without Birdseye's creative thinking, there would have been no TV dinners in the 1950s.

[*See also* Birds Eye Foods; Frozen Food; General Foods.]

BIBLIOGRAPHY

Nickerson, Jane. "News of Food: New and Better Way to Process Food by Anhydration Announced by Birdseye." *New York Times,* November 14, 1945.

JOSEPH M. CARLIN

Birds Eye Foods

Freezing food for later consumption was not a new idea in twentieth-century America. English philosopher-statesman Francis Bacon had long ago experimented with stuffing chickens with snow. Clarence Birdseye, while working in Labrador, Canada, observed that foods frozen quickly at low temperatures had superior quality. Upon returning to the states, he perfected a method for rapid freezing that did not destroy the cellular structure of foods.

Birdseye founded the Birdseye Seafood Company in 1919 in New York City, where he began processing fish fillets at a facility near the Fulton Fish Market. In 1925, Birdseye founded the General Seafoods Corporation in Gloucester, Massachusetts, to be closer to a steady supply of fresh fish. His successful technique was to pack fresh fish in five-inch by three-inch by two-inch retail cartons and to place the cartons between two metal plates in contact with calcium chloride brine flowing at a very low temperature. The frozen cartons were packaged in cellophane. Birdseye was one of the first people to use cellophane as a moisture-vapor seal to prevent dehydration of frozen food. By 1928, he was able to apply this technique to meat, poultry, and shellfish in commercial quantities. Birdseye's success coincided with the development of home refrigeration and freezing units.

A major influence on Clarence Birdseye and the future of frozen food was Marjorie Merriweather Post, daughter of the founder of the Postum Company. Post is reported to have enjoyed eating frozen goose aboard her yacht when it tied up in Gloucester for provisioning. Her chef told her that the goose had been frozen for several months. Post urged her second husband, Edward F. Hutton, to talk to the inventor of this frozen goose. Impressed, Post persuaded the board of directors of

the Postum Company to purchase Birdseye's company. The deal was made in 1929, when Postum together with the Goldman Sachs Trading Corporation bought Birdseye's patents and trademarks for $22 million. The new company was called the General Foods Corporation. The Birdseye name was kept as a corporate trademark but split into two words: "Birds Eye."

The first sale of frozen foods—Birdseye preferred to call his invention "quick-frozen foods"—to the public took place on March 6, 1930, in Springfield, Massachusetts, at Davidson's Market and Bakery. This step was bold because at the time consumers thought frozen foods were low grade. Another problem faced by retailers was the high cost of freezer cabinets and the electric current needed to run them. By 1933, there were only 516 retail outlets for frozen foods in America.

The Birds Eye brand has been owned by a number of companies over the years. It is now owned by Birds Eye Foods Inc., which was called Agrilink Foods Inc. until 2003.

[*See also* Birdseye, Clarence; General Foods; Post Foods.]

BIBLIOGRAPHY

Guinane, Joseph E. "I Remember 'Bob' Birdseye." *Quick Frozen Foods* (March 1960): 317–320.

JOSEPH M. CARLIN

Birthdays

Birthdays are milestones in the evolution of an individual or a group. In ancient times, they occasioned feasting and entertainment, through solely among the upper echelons of societies. Birthday cakes were not then part of the celebrations, although special sweets abounded. Centuries would pass before celebrations of birthdays and saints' days would find a place in popular culture, a result of the medieval church's new practice of recording births. Subsequently, local European birthday rituals developed according to national cultural differences and were brought by various ethnic groups to colonial America, where they eventually merged into a new form.

The dominant English culture in America shaped birthday patterns for some time. Colonial birthdays were enjoyed by privileged adults, who feasted well, or, at the very least, shared a glass of wine and a small slice of fruitcake with friends. Children's parties echoed the adult formats. After the Revolutionary War, patriots honored the

Founding Fathers on their birthdays. George Washington's birthday, for example, was celebrated locally in many communities, and the special foods served were either those known as his favorite dishes or others named for him. This kind of birthday-holiday survives in the commemorations of Abraham Lincoln and Martin Luther King Jr.

In the new age of democracy, birthdays did not remain class-limited. As the nineteenth century progressed, a number of factors reshaped the events. The growth of industry, elevated urban material standards, and emerging middle-class culture made more elaborate birthday celebrations increasingly attractive. Changing notions of the nature of childhood stimulated a new style of young people's parties. Enterprising manufacturers saw great financial possibilities in the accoutrements of birthdays, such as special room and table decorations, foods, entertainments, party favors, and hats. Typical was the early twentieth-century party game of "pin the tail on the donkey," requiring the purchase of colorful paper accessories. This game was almost as necessary as blowing out candles and making secret wishes, cutting the formulaic cake and serving it with ice cream, and receiving gifts.

Ice cream and cake became defining elements, whether after a meal or as the centerpiece of a party. By the late 1800s, ice cream had become available to those of almost all income levels and was featured at any festivity. Fancy ice cream shops delivered their frozen wares to birthday parties, while some people cranked ice cream churns at home to make their own. After the turn of the twentieth century, a number of confectioneries stocked small pewter ice cream molds of varied patterns and themes. Beautifully hand-colored, molded ice creams could be ordered to suit the guest list, such as military and patriotic themes for boys and dolls and flowers for girls.

Birthday Cake. Card published by L. Prang, 1886. *Collection of Alice Ross*

The Candles

Small, colored candles became an integral part of the American birthday cake. An American style guide of 1889 directed, "At birthday parties, the birthday cake, with as many tiny colored candles set about its edge as the child is years old, is, of course, of special importance." The modern use of candles on a special cake may be connected to the German tradition of *Kinderfest,* dating from the fifteenth century, a time when people believed that on birthdays children were particularly susceptible to evil spirits. Friends and family gathered around protectively, keeping the cake's candles lit all day until after the evening meal, when the cake was served.

The candles were thought to carry one's wishes up to God. This German observance was brought to colonial Pennsylvania and was later reinforced by the influence of British-German fashions from Queen Victoria's court.

The British contribution to American birthdays was the model of dramatic Christmas pudding presentations. Almost identical to the Cratchit family's ritual in Dickens's *A Christmas Carol*, the iconic American cake is aflame with candles instead of brandy and makes the same entrance into a darkened dining room, promising to fulfill anticipations of sugared delight. Ultimately candles would be made in novel shapes, sizes, and colors, and would add to the cake's decor.

The Cake

Although fruitcakes and rich, yeasted cakes were the traditional English festive cakes, the modern form of the

Cutting the Cake. Cutting the birthday cake after the candles have been blown out. *Photograph by Glen H. DeWerff*

birthday cake originated in American kitchens in the mid-nineteenth century. In contrast to their European counterparts, American women were active home bakers, largely because of the abundance of oven fuel in the New World and the sparsity of professional bakers. By the later 1800s, home bakers were spurred further by several innovations. The cast-iron kitchen stove, complete with its own quickly heated oven, became standard equipment in urban middle-class homes. Women in towns had more discretionary time, compared to farmwomen, and they had an expanding social life that required formal and informal hospitality. Sugar, butter, spice, and flour costs were dropping. Improved chemical leavening agents, baking powder among them, enabled simpler and faster baking and produced a cake of entirely different flavor and texture. A cake constructed in layers, filled and frosted, became the image of the standard birthday cake. One observer of the early 1900s compared bubbly soap lather to "the fluffiness of a birthday cake" and snowy, frost covered hills to iced birthday cakes.

Ornamentation

Writing on birthday cakes began with professional bakers and caterers, who were proliferating in growing cities. The cakes of the late 1800s were decorated with inscriptions like "Many Happy Returns of the Day" and the celebrant's name, a tradition that continues into the twenty-first century. Sometimes the cake was home-baked but then decorated by a specialist. A typical inscription might read, "Mabel Smither July 8th 1885 from Dick and Lizzie." The phrase "Happy Birthday" did not appear on birthday cake messages until the popularization of the now-ubiquitous song "Happy Birthday to You" (1910).

Cookbook authors began to recommend decorating with birth dates and names and offered instruction on how to make colored frostings with such ingredients as parsley and beets. Some taught home bakers to make their own pastry bags, which were used to dispense the decorative frostings. By 1958, A. H. Vogel had begun to manufacture preformed cake decorations. Inexpensive letters, numbers, and pictorial images, such as flowers or bows, with matching candleholders were standard supermarket offerings.

The Twentieth-Century Birthday Industry

In the course of the twentieth century, the homemade birthday cake depended increasingly on purchased cake mixes. The use of mixes was reinforced by such guides as *The Cake Mix Doctor*. Available in white, spiced, and devil's food flavors, these mixes made suitable birthday cakes. In the twenty-first century, many adults thought of cake mixes when they remembered the so-called "homemade" birthday cakes of their childhoods.

Commercial novelty cakes found a new direction. In the late 1930s Carvel, combining traditional party ice cream with cake, developed ice cream cakes often made in cartoon character shapes. Cakes of unusual size were newsworthy, for example the 128,238-pound cake honoring the one-hundredth birthday of Fort Payne, Alabama. In the early 2000s, the American emphasis on individualism found expression in vegetarian or vegan cake recipes, special interests, favorite flavors of cakes, or even life-size portraits in cake, increasing the province of professional party designers. Cakes are often made in a format or with designs expressing the celebrant's interests, such as golf, football, or gardening. Despite the attractions of the new professionalism in the birthday industry, numbers of how-to publications such as *The Birthday Cake Book* and *Colette's Birthday Cakes* seemed to indicate that baking from scratch and homemade birthday parties were still alive in American culture.

[*See also* Bakeries; Cakes; Crisco; Ice Cream and Ices; Washington's Birthday.]

BIBLIOGRAPHY

Byrn, Anne. *The Cake Mix Doctor*. New York: Workman, 1999.
Dooven, K., and Camille Den. *The Master Baker and His Work*. Boston: 1928.
Lewis, Percy, and A. G. Bromley. *The Victorian Book of Cakes*. New York: 1903. Reprint, New York: Random House, 1991.
Rorer, Sarah Tyson. *Mrs. Rorer's Cakes, Icings, and Fillings*. Philadelphia: Arnold, 1905.

LIZA JERNOW

Biscuit Cutters

Biscuits that were no longer hard, like sea biscuits or beaten biscuits, appeared with the early nineteenth-century use of homemade potash, pearl ashes, and subsequent commercial baking sodas and powders. It was customary from the 1840s or so to the mid-twentieth century for farm housewives and family cooks to make fresh biscuits for at least one meal a day. An inverted tumbler twisted against the dough can cut a biscuit, but it pinches the edge and keeps the biscuit from rising fully. A sharp-edged cutter did not have to be twisted. Until the 1870s, biscuit cutters were either pieced tin or carved wood circles, with or without a handle, similar to cookie cutters.

The ideal of quickly cutting as many biscuits as possible out of each rolled-out sheet of dough spurred inventors. By the late nineteenth century, two types of multiple cutters were in use. Rolling types of tin or aluminum (looking somewhat like toy lawnmowers), which would cut at least two biscuits with each revolution of the wheel, to which the cutting edges were attached, were made from the 1880s to the 1930s. A tin and wood rocker type that cut four biscuits with one rocking movement across the dough was manufactured in the late 1880s and 1890s by the inventor and manufacturer Henry Sidway, who also made rolling types.

BIBLIOGRAPHY

Franklin, Linda Campbell. *300 Years of Kitchen Collectibles*. 5th ed. Iola, WI: Krause Publications, 2003.

LINDA CAMPBELL FRANKLIN

Bison, *see Buffalo*

Bistros

The original French incarnation of bistros is that they feature *cuisine de grand-mère*, or grandmother's cooking. Bistro foods and wines are robust, rustic, and plentiful. Bistros serve simple dishes, presented simply and priced inexpensively, as would be expected in neighborhood restaurants that cater to nearby residents. Bistros in France still preserve their social center feeling.

No one is certain where the name "bistro" came from. There are several apocryphal tales to explain it, but none is convincing. One theory says that Russians occupying Paris in 1815 shouted "bistrot," meaning faster, while they waited for food, and the French adopted the term. The only problem with that idea is that "bistro" did not enter written French until the 1880s, and the variant "bistrot" did not enter the language until the 1890s.

Others suggest that the name comes from *bistrouille*, which refers to eau-de-vie, or from the verb *bistrouiller*, which means to make a sort of cobbled-together "wine" from alcohol, water, and other ingredients. Most lexicographers do not accept any of these explanations.

Ignoring the source of the name, another idea is that bistros were originally *café-charbons*, or shops that sold coal and firewood. They were places where locals could meet for a glass of wine or a cup of coffee. After a time, owners began to serve family-style dishes to their guests, according to the legend.

Irrespective of the origins of the name, early in the twentieth century the concept of neighborhood restaurants serving plain but good foods and wines was well established in France. The spirit of French bistro life is generosity, simplicity, and earthy lustiness. Portions are liberal and are often served in large bowls or on platters family-style for all at the table to help themselves. Menus change infrequently in French bistros, and the plat du jour is often the same thing on corresponding days each week.

In the United States there was not that same sort of cultural push to create the bistro in the French style. The diversity that immigrants brought pushed casual dining in a completely different direction. The American parallels to the idea of the French bistro have two major incarnations of the style in the United States—one rather sophisticated and one much more homey.

The urban bistro is less a social center than a casual restaurant emphasizing sophisticated food and drink. Urban bistros often feature fancier service ware and presentations than their French namesakes, and they have a more variable menu. Menus in the upscale bistros generally change to suit the seasons, and specials are usually changed more frequently. Offerings reflect adventuresome preparations using a wide variety of raw materials and techniques.

The other variation is home-style restaurants that would never be called bistros. Their hallmark is that they offer inexpensive food in casual settings. They include a wide range of restaurant concepts, from country operations in rural areas with a homey feel to places featuring foreign cuisines. Typically, service is very informal, portions are large, and prices are low.

Like "trattoria" and "pub," "bistro" has become as much a marketing term as a designation of a type of restaurant. It became fashionable in the 1980s to so name restaurants for the social cachet to be gained.

[*See also* Restaurants; Taverns.]

BIBLIOGRAPHY

Mariani, John. *America Eats Out: An Illustrated History of Restaurants, Taverns, Coffee Shops, Speakeasies, and Other Establishments that Have Fed Us for 350 Years.* New York: Morrow, 1991.
Wells, Patricia. *Bistro Cooking.* New York: Workman, 1989. Well-researched and comprehensive source of anecdotal information and recipes.

BOB PASTORIO

Bitting, Katherine

Katherine Golden (1869–1937) was born in Canada, but her family later immigrated to the United States. She received her bachelor's degree from the State Normal School in Salem, Massachusetts; studied bacteriology at the Massachusetts Institute of Technology in Cambridge; and received an M.S. from Purdue University in Lafayette, Indiana. While completing her master's thesis, she worked at the Purdue Agricultural Extension Station, and in 1893 she became an assistant professor, teaching biology, structural botany, and bacteriology. At Purdue, she met and married Arvil Bitting, who had previously served as veterinarian for the Agricultural Experiment Station in Florida for three years. He received a doctorate in veterinary medicine from Iowa State College in 1895. After graduation, he began teaching veterinary medicine at Purdue University while studying medicine at the Indiana Medical College. He received his M.D. in 1900 but never practiced medicine.

The marriage between Arvil Bitting and Katherine Golden launched a successful personal and professional partnership that lasted four decades. In 1906, Arvil Bitting became a special agent for the U.S. Department of Agriculture, stationed at Lafayette. The following year he became an inspector for the Bureau of Chemistry. In September 1907, Katherine Bitting was appointed to the position of microbotanist in the bureau and was assigned to work with her husband. Their first joint project was to determine how to make ketchup without the use of added preservatives.

The Bittings established a laboratory and a model ketchup factory in their home in Lafayette. In all, they analyzed more than sixteen hundred bottles of ketchup. In addition, they visited dozens of factories that made tomato pulp and twenty ketchup factories. As homemade ketchup stayed fresh for a much longer period after opening than did their experimental ketchup, the Bittings began collecting ketchup recipes from magazines, journals, cookbooks, and other sources and testing them in their laboratory. In 1907, after numerous experiments, the Bittings devised a method for producing preservative-free ketchup that would keep almost indefinitely under normal household conditions; their system became the standard for making ketchup. The method increased the amount of sugar and vinegar in the ketchup, thus creating a thick and sweet product. In January 1909, Arvil Bitting published their initial findings, *Experiments on the Spoilage of Tomato Ketchup.* Six years later, the Bittings published two additional monographs bound together: Arvil Bitting's *Ketchup: Methods of Manufacture* and Katherine Bitting's *Microscopic Examination.*

In the 1920s, the Bittings left the Bureau of Chemistry to work for the National Canners Association, Arvil as a food technologist and Katherine as a micro-analyst. She later worked as a biologist with the Glass Container Association. Based on their knowledge of the canning process, Arvil published his major work, *Appertizing; or, The Art of Canning,* in 1937.

From their early years the Bittings collected food-related books. Their collection grew over the years to include the French edition of Nicolas Appert's *L'art de conserver les substances animales et végétales (1810),* which Katherine Bitting translated into English as *The Book for All Households; or, The Art of Preserving Animal and Vegetable Substances for Many Years* and published in 1920. During the 1930s, she began assembling a bibliography of their collection. She died before it saw print, but her husband published her *Gastronomic Bibliography* posthumously in 1939. It has endured as a major American culinary resource. Even more significant, the Bittings donated their extensive cookbook collection to the Library of Congress, and it is a significant legacy accessible to researchers.

[*See also* Canning and Bottling; Ketchup.]

BIBLIOGRAPHY

A file on Katherine Golden Bitting and "Notes on Arvil W. Bitting" are held in Special Collections, Purdue University Library, Lafayette, Indiana.
Appert, Nicolas. *The Book for All Households; or, The Art of Preserving Animal and Vegetable Substances for Many Years.*

Translated by K. G. Bitting. Chicago: Glass Container Association of America, 1920.

Bitting, A. W. *Appertizing; or, The Art of Canning: Its History and Development.* San Francisco: Trade Pressroom, 1937.

Bitting, A. W., and K. G. Bitting. *Ketchup: Methods of Manufacture and Microscopic Examination.* Lafayette, IN: Murphey-Bivins, 1915.

Bitting, Katherine. *Gastronomic Bibliography.* San Francisco: Halle-Cordis Composing Room and Trade Freeroom, 1939.

Smith, Andrew F. *Pure Ketchup: The History of America's National Condiment.* Columbia: University of South Carolina Press, 1996.

ANDREW F. SMITH

Blackberries

The blackberry of common speech is not one, but some two dozen species of plants in the genus *Rubus*, native to America, Europe, and Asia. All have in common a fruit composed of drupelets (small, round, juicy parts) arranged upon a pithy central core. It is this core, which detaches intact from the fruit stem, that distinguishes blackberries from the other group of bramble species, the raspberries; in blackberries, the adherence of drupelets to the core gives the fruit a solidity lacking in raspberries. Since blackberries do not decompose when heated, they are suitable for cooking.

In horticultural terms, blackberries are divided between upright and running types. Upright-growing blackberries are found east of the Rocky Mountains; attain a height of seven feet; and, in the wild, form dense, impen-

Blackberries. Label for preserved blackberries. *Warshaw Collection of Business Americana, Archives Center, National Museum of American History, Behring Center, Smithsonian Institution*

etrably thorny clumps. Modern breeders have produced thornless forms, which have made blackberry culture more popular in the eastern states. Formerly, blackberry fanciers and the markets relied on wild-collected berries. By the early twenty-first century, certain states— Arkansas, in particular—had a considerable cultivated blackberry industry. Blackberries, no longer limited to rural availability at farm stands, have become an article of long-distance commerce. Modern varieties are large and durable, with a long shelf life; however, they often lack the characteristic "wild" flavor sought by many.

Running blackberries, known as dewberries in the lower South, are a group of species, chiefly of Pacific Coast origin, that trail along the ground. Olallieberry and Himalayan ("Theodor Reimers"), which runs wild in the West, are typical, but there exist many other forms, often hybridized with the raspberry, such as boysenberry, youngberry, marionberry, loganberry, and Lucretia. The parent species are all susceptible to winter cold and most are intolerant of great heat, so commercial culture is limited to the West and lower South. These species, with their rich, acid flavor, provide the frozen blackberries of commerce. Preserved berry juices as a beverage, formerly an article of commerce, are now uncommon. Blackberries, often strained of their large seeds, are used in conserves and in cooked desserts, such as pies.

[*See also* Fruit; Pacific Northwestern Regional Cookery.]

BIBLIOGRAPHY

Daubeny, Hugh A. "Brambles." In *Fruit Breeding.* Volume 2: *Vine and Small Fruits,* edited by Jules Janick and James N. Moore, 109–190. New York: Wiley, 1996.

Galetta, Gene J., and David G. Himelrick. *Small Fruit Crop Management.* Englewood Cliffs, NJ: Prentice Hall, 1990.

C. T. KENNEDY

Blenders

The modern blender, a familiar electric appliance that blends, chops, grates, purees, and liquefies foods, was invented by Stephen Poplawski in 1922 to make soda fountain drinks. In 1935, the popular bandleader Fred Waring teamed up with the inventor Frederick Osius to improve the appliance, marketing the Waring Blender (originally Blendor) as a revolutionary bartending tool. By the 1950s, blender manufacturers' cookbooks contained recipes for everything from soups and canapés to cakes and ice creams and, in a sign of the times, more than a few recipes for gelatin desserts and molded salads. *The Blender Cookbook* of 1961 promised to revolutionize Americans' cooking habits with "exciting new ideas, short cuts, and magic recipes that will take the drudgery out of cooking and make it a pleasure."

That same year, in *Mastering the Art of French Cooking*, Julia Child, Louisette Bertholle, and Simone Beck taught millions of Americans how to make emulsions like mayonnaise and hollandaise with the electric blender, though of the latter they warned that "the blender variety lacks something in quality . . . perhaps because of complete homogenization." But, they continued, "as the technique is well within the capabilities of an 8-year-old child, it has much to recommend it."

The emergence of the food processor later threatened the supremacy of the blender, but cooks soon realized the blender's superiority for certain tasks, such as liquefying solids, pureeing solids with liquids, and preparing smoothies and frozen drinks. The standard blender consists of a covered jar (usually glass or, for bar use, metal) fitting securely on top of a motorized base, with four sharp blades that make thousands of rotations per minute. While modern blenders often come with electronic touch-pad controls, sleek new jar designs, and a multitude of speeds, one test by *Cook's Illustrated* found that basic, old-fashioned models outperformed newer designs. Newer handheld immersion blenders, some of which even crush ice, are also growing in popularity.

[*See also* Food Processors.]

BIBLIOGRAPHY

Child, Julia, Louisette Bertholle, and Simone Beck. *Mastering the Art of French Cooking.* New York: Knopf, 1961.
Church, Ruth Ellen. *Mary Meade's Magic Recipes for the Electric Blender.* New York: Bobbs-Merrill, 1952.
Reid, Adam. "Basic Blenders Beat Upscale Rivals." *Cook's Illustrated*, May 2000.
Schur, Sylvia, ed. *New Ways to Gracious Living: Waring Blendor Cook Book.* Winsted, CT: Waring Products, 1957.
Seranne, Ann, and Eileen Gaden. *The Blender Cookbook.* Garden City, NY: Doubleday, 1961.
340 Recipes for the New Waring Blendor. New York: Waring Products, 1940.

MERYL S. ROSOFSKY

Bloody Mary and Virgin Mary

The Bloody Mary is a cocktail made with vodka, tomato juice, lemon juice, Worcestershire sauce, cayenne pepper, and salt. Folklore attributes the origin of the Bloody Mary to Ferdinand "Pete" Petiot, a bartender at Harry's Bar in Paris. Petiot purportedly first mixed vodka with tomato juice in 1921. After Prohibition ended in 1933, Petiot moved to the United States and became a bartender at the King Cole Bar at New York's St. Regis Hotel, where he added Worcestershire sauce and pepper to the recipe. Petiot named the drink either after a girlfriend called Mary or after Mary Tudor, the mid-sixteenth-century Catholic queen of England, who killed many Protestants during her reign. In any case, the Bloody Mary was born—or so the story goes.

While the story is plausible, it is unlikely. An essential Bloody Mary ingredient is tomato juice, which was not available commercially until 1929. Decades earlier, chefs had experimented unsuccessfully with juicing tomatoes. When juiced, tomato solids quickly separate and settle at the bottom of a can or glass. This problem was not solved until John Kemp and his son Ralph, of Frankfort, Indiana, began experimenting with breaking tomato pulp into minute particles that floated in the juice. They did this with a viscolizer, a machine used in making ice cream. After four years of work, the Kemps finally succeeded in 1928, and the following year they began manufacturing the first commercial tomato juice. Tomato juice was an instant hit with the American public. The H. J. Heinz Company and the Campbell Soup Company moved into high gear to produce and promote their own brands of tomato juice, and by 1935 more than eight million cases of tomato juice were sold in America.

It may never be known who first paired tomato juice with vodka, but two other claims have some plausibility. The first is that it was invented in the 1930s at New York's 21 Club by a bartender named Henry Zbikiewicz, who was charged with mixing Bloody Marys. A second claim attributes its invention to the comedian George Jessel, who frequently visited the 21 Club. The first known recipe for the Bloody Mary was published in Lucius Beebe's *Stork Club Bar Book* (1944). Beebe, a columnist for the *New York Herald Tribune*, mentioned the Bloody Mary in December 3, 1939: "George Jessel's newest pick-me-up which is receiving attention from the town's paragraphers is called a Bloody Mary: half tomato juice, half vodka."

Six months later, Beebe again associated the Bloody Mary with Jessel. Jessel knew John G. Martin, a member of the Heublein family, which owned G. F. Heublein and Company. The company acquired Smirnoff Vodka after

Vladimir Smirnoff's death in 1939. The Bloody Mary made its national debut in a magazine advertisement that appeared in late 1955 featuring George Jessel, who declared that he had invented the cocktail. Whether or not Jessel invented the Bloody Mary, his advertisement popularized the Bloody Mary nationwide, and the cocktail was on the road to stardom. To exploit the interest, Bloody Mary bars have been launched by restaurants, permitting customers to construct their own cocktail with various garnishes. It is one of the few cocktails drunk at breakfast or brunch.

By the beginning of the twenty-first century, the Bloody Mary was America's most popular cocktail, which has contributed to an increase in the sale of vodka. By the 1970s, vodka was outselling bourbon in most states. For those unable or unwilling to make their own Bloody Marys, commercial mixes have been manufactured, such as McIlhenny's Tabasco Bloody Mary Mix, which claims to use the original 1934 recipe. For those who prefer their Bloody Mary's without the vodka, the Virgin Mary has been served since the 1970s.

[*See also* Vodka.]

BIBLIOGRAPHY

O'Hara, Christopher B. *The Bloody Mary: A Connoisseur's Guide to the World's Most Complex Cocktail.* New York: Lyons Press, 1999.
Smith, Andrew F. *Souper Tomatoes: The Story of America's Favorite Food.* New Brunswick, NJ: Rutgers University Press, 2000.

ANDREW F. SMITH

Blueberries

The blueberry is a fruit native to America, whose popularity has soared since its domestication began in the early twentieth century. At that time, a scientist for the U.S. Department of Agriculture, Frederick Coville, working in conjunction with a grower, Elizabeth White of Whitesbog, New Jersey, began studying the conditions required by the plant and selecting and breeding varieties. Despite its small size, the blueberry is not a berry but a pome, as are apples and pears.

Three types are grown commercially. Lowbush blueberries, *Vaccinium angustifolium,* are native to the northeastern United States. The plants spread by underground stems and grow only about a foot high; they are small, sweet, and often powdery blue. The bulk of the commercial crop is destined for canning and pie fillings. These blueberries are harvested mostly from tamed wild stands. Highbush blueberries, *V. corymbosum,* which are native to the East Coast, grow as six- to ten-foot-high bushes. So-called southern highbush blueberries are adapted to areas with mild winters and provide the earliest harvests. The latest-ripening blueberries, rabbit eyes (*V. asheii*), are native to the Southeast and are borne on fifteen-foot-tall bushes.

Blueberry plants' unusual soil requirements have limited their commercial cultivation to where they are native or where soil is otherwise naturally suited. Blueberries require soils that are very acidic, very high in humus, and consistently moist and well aerated. Important production areas include New Jersey, North Carolina, Michigan, Maine, and the Canadian Maritime Provinces. Production also has spread to California, where early-season harvests are possible in soils amended to suit the plants.

[*See also* Fruit.]

BIBLIOGRAPHY

Eck, Paul, and Norman F. Childers, eds. *Blueberry Culture.* Piscataway, NJ: Rutgers University Press, 1966.
McClure, S., and L. Reich. *Rodale's Successful Organic Gardening: Fruits and Berries.* Emmaus, PA: Rodale Press, 1996.
Reich, Lee. *Uncommon Fruits for Every Garden.* Portland, OR: Timber Press, 2004.

LEE REICH

Boardinghouses

Throughout history, people have needed to live apart from their families for a variety of reasons. Colonial travelers traditionally resorted to taverns, inns, and, since the nineteenth century, to hotels. However, during the nineteenth and twentieth centuries, industrialization and the growth of American cities stimulated a considerable movement of people, rich and poor. Many were relocating from farms to industrial centers; others were immigrants from abroad in search of work. The sudden demand for inexpensive housing was unprecedented and contributed to the development of the boardinghouse. Usually the province of women, keeping a boardinghouse was one of the first cash-economy jobs considered suitable for women.

The boardinghouse institution began as a middle ground between the financial need of a married, middle-class woman and the prevalent "doctrine of separate spheres" that forbade her to work in the public marketplace. Sometimes the extra income enabled a young family to meet mortgage payments on a house; at other times it meant survival for a widow with no business training or the skills for succeeding in the male business world. Taking in lodgers allowed women to support themselves with the only capital they had—a house with empty bedrooms and domestic skills. Ideally, women provided boarders with a bed (sometimes shared), ample meals, laundry, and a degree of personal assistance, although standards varied widely.

Types of Boardinghouses

One of the earliest forms of boardinghouses in nineteenth-century America evolved in frontier towns that were developing rapidly into small cities. Lodgers coming from farms for jobs in town were often absorbed into the keeper's family routines and treated like distant relatives. They attended church with their host families and socialized together, partaking in meals that were much like the farm cuisine of their own families.

In contrast, company boardinghouses were organized by large mills, as exemplified by the textile mills of Lowell, Massachusetts, begun in the 1820s. Their experimental arrangements were far more ambitious and impersonal than the small family operations. Built as part of the mill complex, they accommodated between twenty and forty lodgers each, often six in a room. Although at this time women did not usually leave home for careers, mill owners sought to attract young farm girls of good families by instituting a series of rules and curfews; the presumably safe and moral environment was presided over by salaried boardinghouse keepers. Keepers were allotted limited budgets for expenses, based on the numbers of lodgers they had, and they competed for boarders on the reputation of their tables, a situation that sometimes resulted in financial distress. For example, Lucy Larcom, the daughter of a Lowell boardinghouse keeper, described in her memoirs her mother's inability to compromise her fine culinary taste with the company's allocations and her constant difficulties in supporting her children.

Keepers bought their provisions from local shops and vendors, many of whom maintained delivery routes. Boardinghouse cuisine was typical of New England and of necessity leaned heavily on inexpensive staples, such as potatoes and beans, and on seasonal products merchandized by nearby farmers and fishermen. Local salmon was cheap and readily available and was overused to the point that keepers were forced to promise their boarders not to

serve it more than once a week. Many staples, including flour, sugar, salt cod, and fresh and preserved meats, were shipped from Boston to meet the large demand.

Meal schedules accommodated the Lowell Mill bell system. Work began seasonally with sunrise, and a half hour was allotted to breakfast. The noon bell announced the dinner break, during which time the girls literally ran across the street to their boardinghouses (intentionally placed nearby to save time), where a hot family-style meal awaited. Girls ate as fast as they could before the work bell rang again, only forty-five minutes later. A simple evening supper, the most relaxed meal of the day, provided the only time to linger over desserts and tea.

Other kinds of small, job-related boardinghouses were established for the convenience of employers and their tenants, sometimes because of the lack of appropriate nearby accommodations. Under the master-journeyman-apprentice system, the master's wife boarded her husband's young trainees. Apprentices did not pay directly for such services, but boarding was considered part of their reimbursement for labor. In addition, a master boatbuilder might take in one of his unmarried craftsmen, or a milliner might offer room and board to a female assistant for whom there were few housing alternatives. Keeping hired hands on ranches and farms and boarding itinerant "mechanics" (artisans) of the countryside fell into this arrangement. Cuisine in such cases was entirely regional and was often abundant, standard fare.

Throughout the nation, ethnic boardinghouses developed to accommodate the succeeding waves of immigration and were a factor in the survival of cultures. Immigrant families living in the tenements of large coastal cities rented some of their meager space to "greenhorns" from home. The lodgers were sometimes family members or friends from home who boarded temporarily until they could learn the language and find their way in the job market. A boarder might have slept in a temporary bed in the corner of an already crowded kitchen and shared the family's familiar ethnic cooking, thereby maintaining cultural prescriptions and taboos. The landlady bought her ingredients at food shops, open markets, or pushcarts run by immigrants. Thus, a kosher Jew could purchase food in compliance with the dietary laws of *kashruth* (keeping kosher) and could also maintain such traditional foods as salt herring and potatoes; Italians could find the fixings for *pasta e fagiole* (pasta and beans); Asians could buy special kinds of rice; blacks in the North could cook the okra or black-eyed peas they had been used to eating in the South; and western Basques could make and eat their own sourdough breads and lamb shanks.

Another kind of urban boardinghouse of the mid-nineteenth century was dedicated to groups with special orientations or professions. One could find accommodations specifically for actors, sailors, artists, spiritualists, medical students, and others, and sometimes the menu was essential. For example, Graham boardinghouses were tailored to the needs of the often famous advocates of Sylvester Graham's dietary theories, serving the requisite vegetarian diet and avoiding stimulants of all kinds (red meat, spices, sugar, spirits, and caffeine).

With an entirely different focus, expensive and luxurious urban boardinghouses sheltered wealthier people of all ages. Young married couples of means sometimes preferred the carefree life of this kind of lodging, as it offered freedom from domesticity, a pleasant interlude before "taking up housekeeping." The keepers of these establishments, who were also from privileged backgrounds and aware of fashion, set a stylish tone with their furnishings, table appointments, and menus. The food was often extravagant and may have boasted a French influence. The new *"service à la russe,"* which required ostentatious place settings and servants, was de rigueur. Such boardinghouses were later replaced by residential hotels.

Before the end of the nineteenth century, summer boardinghouses in the countryside or at the waterfront hosted people escaping the heat and discomfort of the cities. Visitors may have been working people with one week a year for vacation, or an entire family of more means enjoying a three-month stay. Their meals were based on the wholesome and fresh yield of the keeper's barnyard, orchard, and garden, and they were entertained by such bucolic entertainments as fishing, berry picking, and ice-cream making. A seasonal vacation boardinghouse demanded intensive work from the keeper's entire family, but many earned enough to carry them through the winter and secure their children's futures.

By the turn of the twentieth century, certain boardinghouse keepers with a high priority on cuisine had developed their own natural aptitudes or had hired talented cooks. Their fine meals were in high demand, and dinners were offered on a subscription basis to others in the community. They were among the first kinds of restaurants for middle-class and rural diners, who were otherwise limited to meals at home. Their influence sometimes spread far beyond their locales. For example, Craig Claiborne, the cookbook author and first and long-time food editor of the *New York Times,* absorbed the high standards of his mother's southern boardinghouse kitchen, and James Beard, the influential cooking educator and author from the West Coast, similarly learned and disseminated the elements of fine cooking and new Asian influences prevalent where he lived.

The American boardinghouse has largely disappeared, a victim of affluence, more varied job choices for women, increasing mobility, the rise of motels, the wide availability of fast food, and the growth of good middle- and working-class restaurants. Only a few echoes of its once common culture remain in folklore—as, for example, in the phrase "boardinghouse reach" to describe unmannerly conduct at the dining table, the repeated lampooning of squalid or pretentious boardinghouses in such 1930s comics as "Our Boarding House," and this song of the Great Depression:

> In the boarding-house where I live, everything is green with mold.
> Grandma's hair is in the butter, silver threads among the gold.
> When the dog died, we had hot dogs, when the cat died, catnip tea,
> But when the landlord kicked the bucket, oh, that was too much for me.
> (I don't like hash).

[*See also* Graham, Sylvester.]

BIBLIOGRAPHY

Claiborne, Craig. *A Feast Made for Laughter: A Memoir with Recipes.* New York: Holt, Rinehart and Winston, 1983.

Dublin, Thomas. *Women at Work: The Transformation of Work and Community in Lowell, Massachusetts, 1826–1860.* New York: Columbia University Press, 1979.

Echeverria, Jeronima. *Home away from Home: A History of Basque Boarding Houses.* Reno: University of Nevada, 1999.

Gunn, Thomas Butler. *The Physiology of New York Boarding Houses.* New York: Mason Brothers, 1857.

Ryan, Mary. *The Cradle of the Middle Class: The Family in Oneida County, 1790–1865.* New York: Cambridge University Press, 1981.

ALICE ROSS

Boilermaker

A boilermaker is a shot of whiskey with a beer chaser, although it may also be a glass of beer with a shot of whiskey in it—sometimes dropped in, shot glass and all. (The latter version is also known as a Depth Charge.) Some aficionados say that the drink is meant to be imbibed all in one slug, but this practice is unusual. The particulars vary by region, bar, and bartender.

The Boilermaker originated in the 1890s in the mining camps of Butte, Montana, as the "Sean O'Farrell." The powerful, ten-cent "Sean O'" was served only as miners came off their shifts. Bartenders all over the United States imitated the drink, dubbing it the Boilermaker for reasons that remain unknown. The name may have come from the "head of steam" feeling that the drink generates, or perhaps it was a favorite drink of men who worked as boilermakers. The U.S. heavyweight boxing champion from 1899 to 1905, James Jackson Jeffries, was nicknamed "the Boilermaker," and perhaps the drink name stems from a similar tough, manly sense of the word. (Purdue University's football team has had the name "Boilermakers" since 1891.)

The main purpose of this workingman's drink is to take a great deal of alcohol into one's system as quickly as possible. It is not a drink only for men, though—Myrna Loy's character in the movie *Airport 1975* drinks a few to take her mind off a hair-raising flight. Recipes for boilermaker barbecue sauce, baked beans, jambalaya, and the like incorporate whiskey and beer with the more usual ingredients.

[*See also* Beer; Whiskey.]

BIBLIOGRAPHY

Reynolds, Edward B., and Michael Kennedy. *Whistleberries, Stirabout, Depression Cake: Food Customs and Concoctions of the Frontier West.* Helena, MT: Three Forks, 2000.

JESSY RANDALL

Borden

At one time the Borden company was America's largest dairy business. Gail Borden Jr., the founder of the Borden Condensed Milk Company, was born in Norwich, New York, in 1801. He died in 1874, leaving behind a thriving business, two sons, and a host of inventions and patents.

Borden worked as a surveyor during the 1820s and moved to Texas in 1829. For a time he edited the *Telegraph and Texas Register,* a newspaper founded by his brother and another partner to serve as the voice of

Borden. Advertising piece in the shape of a milk-delivery van, c. 1890. *Collection of Kit Barry*

ELSIE THE COW

Elsie, the world-famous "spokesbovine" of the Borden Milk Company, first began appearing in newspaper and radio advertisements in the 1930s. In these early appearances Elsie is clearly a cow. She stands on all fours; she does not wear clothes, except for a garland of daisies around her neck; and her face is squarish and cowlike, with a broad mouth and big eyes.

At the New York World's Fair of 1939–1940 Borden's enormous and enormously successful exhibit featured the Rotolactor, a turntable device on which cows rode while attached to milking machines. Many fairgoers asked the guides which cow was Elsie. It was in response to these inquiries that the Borden Company decided to choose the handsomest Jersey cow at the fair and introduce her as Elsie. The company put Elsie herself on display, and in the second year of the fair an exhibit entitled "Elsie in Her Boudoir" became part of the Borden exhibit.

Over the years Elsie became less of a cow and more of a girl. Her udder was last seen in 1940. Her face became narrower and more human and her eyes more heavily lashed. In 1941 Elsie stood up on her hind legs and began wearing dresses or aprons with a cinched waist that gave her an enviable hourglass figure (for a cow). Andy Warhol chose Elsie, along with Marilyn Monroe, as the subject for one of his paintings of American icons.

BIBLIOGRAPHY

Miller, I. C. "What Makes a World's Fair Exhibit Click?" *Food Industries* (January 1940): 44-48; (February 1940): 55–59.

EVE JOCHNOWITZ
SPECIAL THANKS TO CHRISTINE IADOROSA

the government of Texas when it was still a republic. Some claim that Borden wrote the famous headline "Remember the Alamo." He turned his creative mind to inventing and soon came up with ideas for the lazy Susan and the prairie schooner, a sail-powered wagon. But the invention for which he is best known is a process using a vacuum evaporator to kill bacteria in fresh milk. He is reported to have committed himself to finding a safe milk product after witnessing several children die aboard ship after drinking contaminated milk. He borrowed the idea for using a vacuum evaporator from the Shakers, who used this technology to preserve fruit. Charles Page and Henri Nestlé also used vacuum evaporators to start their companies. In time, both of these companies would combine to form the Nestlé Company. Borden called his unique product "condensed milk."

In 1857 Borden established a small company to produce his new product. Borden received financing from Jeremiah Milbank, and in 1858 they formed a partnership called the New York Condensed Milk Company. The product came on the market at the same time national magazines were condemning "swill milk" produced under unsanitary conditions in city dairies.

Borden's first major orders came from the U.S. government, which used condensed milk to feed the troops during the Civil War. In a patriotic spirit Borden adopted the American bald eagle as his trademark. In 1930 Borden introduced Elsie the Cow as the company's mascot and brand identity. Elsie went on to become one of the best-loved trademarks in the country.

In 1919 the company changed its name to the Borden Company and throughout the twentieth century purchased a number of smaller companies to capture supermarket shelf space. Many of the companies acquired have remained regional brands, but others have catapulted into national brands, including Snow's seafood chowders, Wyler's bouillon, RealLemon lemon juice, Cracker Jack candied popcorn, Pennsylvania Dutch egg noodles, Drake Bakeries, and Campfire marshmallows.

In 1929 the company acquired a small company that made glue from casein, a by-product of skim milk. From this initial beginning in the adhesives business the company's specialty chemicals businesses grew. In 2001 Borden sold its domestic and overseas food businesses to become Borden Chemical, Inc.

[See also Cracker Jack; Dairy Foods; Dairy Industry; Milk; Milk Packaging; Nestlé.]

BIBLIOGRAPHY

International Directory of Company Histories. 55 vols. Chicago: St. James Press, 2003.

JOSEPH M. CARLIN

Elsie's Magic Recipes. Cookbooklet published by the Borden Company (New York, 1942). *Collection of Andrew F. Smith*

Boston Cooking School

The Boston Cooking School began as a charitable endeavor by the Women's Educational Association to teach cooking to poor women. Begun with seven students, it widened its scope to include homemakers, and by 1882 there were nearly 400 students.

Volunteer women ran the school, but the beginning teaching staff consisted of experienced teachers. Joanna Sweeney, who had given cooking classes in Boston, and Maria Parloa, a noted cooking authority and author, were the first two teachers. They trained Mary Lincoln, who then became another teacher. She became well known for her *Mrs. Lincoln's Boston Cook Book* written as a text book for her classes. Fannie Farmer, who became principal in 1894, was first a pupil and then an assistant principal.

MISS FARMER'S SCHOOL OF COOKERY

30 HUNTINGTON AVENUE, BOSTON, MASSACHUSETTS

MISS ALICE BRADLEY, Principal

Courses of Four and Eight Weeks from April to November

JULY SUMMER COURSE

Plain and Advanced Cookery; Table Service; Marketing; Food Values; Balanced Menus; Household Administration; Cooking for Profit

Open All the Year   Bulletin on Request

Farmer's Cooking School. Advertisement in *American Cookery,* June–July 1917. *Collection of Alice Ross*

The school offered a First Course (Plain Cooking), a Second Course (Richer Cooking), and a Third Course (Fancy Cooking), as well as twelve lessons for nurses. The school also became well known for its sickroom cookery classes and taught Harvard Medical School students for many years.

The school had considerable influence on cooking through these classes; it also trained teachers of cooking. Parloa taught the first course for prospective teachers. The school received many invitations for graduates of its training course to open cooking schools in other cities.

The Boston Cooking School Magazine spread ideas about cooking to the general public. Fannie Farmer's *The Boston Cooking-School Cook Book* became very popular, going through several revisions and reprintings.

Despite its many successful ventures, the Boston Cooking School taught its last course in 1903. Farmer had opened her own school in 1902, and the older school was unable to compete. However, though in existence for only some twenty years, the Boston Cooking School had a wide influence on American cooking.

[*See also* Cooking Schools, *subentry* Nineteenth Century; Farmer, Fannie; Lincoln, Mrs.; Parloa, Maria.]

BIBLIOGRAPHY

Lincoln, Mary J. *Mrs. Lincoln's Boston Cook Book*. Boston: Roberts Brothers, 1893. Contains a listing of the foods taught in the twelve lessons of each of the courses of instruction at the Boston Cooking School.

Schlesinger, Elizabeth Bancroft. "Fannie Farmer." In *Notable American Women 1607–1950*, edited by Edward T. James. Cambridge, Mass.: Belknap Press, 1971.

Shapiro, Laura. *Perfection Salad: Women and Cooking at the Turn of the Century*. New York: Farrar, Straus, and Giroux, 1986.

MARY MOONEY-GETOFF

Bottling

Historic finds indicate that the art of making glass bottles was well known throughout the ancient world when the Egyptians were producing them in 1400 B.C.E. Their glass was made in much the same ways as it is in the twenty-first century, by heating a mixture of sand, lime, and other minerals to a temperature of 2500°F. Naturally occurring glass, such as obsidian and rock crystal, had been used for art in the Stone Age. By 300 B.C.E., the Syrians had perfected the blowpipe, and blown-glass bottles were common. Rapid progress in bottling followed the early Renaissance introduction of standard-size corks to fit glass bottles. In the mid-sixteenth century, bottles fitted with wax seals were status symbols for the nobility of Europe, with every family marking their private bottles with its own seal. The first American glass house began producing blown-glass bottles in Jamestown, Virginia, in 1608. By 1650, adaptations introduced from England, including flanged bottlenecks and screw-on metal caps sealed with resin or pitch, improved the seal, enabling bottlers to maintain carbonation in beer.

Demand for bottled products by the late 1700s led to glass shortages, and customers were asked to bring glass of any kind back to glass production houses. While customers were still often expected to bring bottles back to the bottler for refilling, large-scale glass recycling had begun. The debut of the modern champagne bottle in 1757, with a flared cork affixed in a flanged bottle top with wire webbing, made possible the bottling of much higher-pressure contents than ever before. This opened the door to commercial packaging of sparkling mineral waters and beers, although results were inconsistent and leakage was a problem.

The introduction of the porter bottle, commonly known as a beer bottle, in 1820 standardized packaging shape. Bottles had to be stored on their sides to keep their corks from drying out and leaking. Around the same time, carbonated water sold as a health tonic and sometimes flavored with fruit juice was introduced by Townsend Speakman under the name Dr. Physick's Soda Water. Popularity of flavored soda water grew over the next forty years, spreading across America until nearly every city could claim its own soda fountain. Root beer, a descendant of colonial birch beer, made its appearance in the 1840s and achieved national renown when Charles E. Hires introduced bottled Hires Root Beer in 1870. Numerous capping methods were in use in the late 1800s, including marbles tied into the necks of bottles and the Hutchinson closure, an internal stopper held in place by the pressure of a carbonated beverage, which was opened by pushing the stopper inward.

The invention of the crown cork cap by William Painter in 1892 revolutionized the bottling industry. His single-use, cork-lined metallic cap eliminated problems that had plagued the bottling industry for centuries, including leakage and contamination. He patented his process, which is widely used one hundred years later, and formed the Crown Cork and Seal Company. His 1898 invention, the Crown Soda Machine, which mixes sodas, fills bottles, and caps them in one integrated process, is the standard equipment used by modern bottlers.

Cans had been used for food products since the mid-1800s but were not sturdy enough to package liquids under pressure. Prior to Prohibition, breweries like Anheuser-Busch and Pabst had experimented with canning. But contact with metal spoiled the beer, a condition known as metal turbidity. The idea was shelved until better can liners were brought to the market by the American Can Company in 1934 in the form of a Union Carbide product called Vinylite, a plastic. The can had obvious advantages over glass bottles in terms of surface area available for advertising. Punch-top cans, requiring a special opener, were eclipsed for a time by cap-sealed, or cone-top cans, which could be used with existing bottling infrastructure. Crown Cork and Seal, after purchasing the Acme Can Company of Philadelphia in 1936, introduced the most advanced cone-top model, known as the Crowntainer, which consisted of a well-sealed two-piece structure, capped with the same crown cap as the company used on its glass bottles. Opinions flared into battles between adherents of glass or metal packaging,

with can fans pointing out the deleterious effects of light on beer and bottle believers arguing that metal made beverages taste skunky. The shipping and storage advantages of flattop cans spelled the end of the cone-top era by the early 1950s. The cans have become highly prized collectibles.

The advent of the zip-tab can in 1962 rejuvenated can sales by eliminating the need for a special can opener. Environmental concerns about litter and the danger of the sharp tabs to children led to the development of push-top cans in the late 1970s, in which the tab remains attached to the container after opening. While glass bottles remain popular among beer drinkers, the introduction of cheaper disposable plastic bottles in the late 1970s eclipsed glass in the packaging of soft drinks.

[See also Aseptic Packaging; Canning and Bottling; Can Openers; Corks; Mason Jars; Milk Packaging; Seltzer; Water, Bottled; Wine Bottles.]

BIBLIOGRAPHY

American Society of Mechanical Engineers. "The Crown Cork Cap and Crown Soda Machine 1892 and 1898." May 25, 1994.
Bates, Paul W. "History of the Beverage Can." Millersville, TN: Museum of Beverage Containers and Advertising, 1996.

JAY WEINSTEIN

Bourbon

Bourbon, a style of whiskey that can legally be made only in the United States, must be distilled from a mash containing a minimum of 51 percent corn and aged in new, charred, oak barrels for a minimum of two years. It gained its name from Bourbon County, Kentucky, where, in the late 1700s, flatboats were loaded with barrels of local whiskey that were then transported to cities in the South. There, it became known as whiskey from Bourbon and, eventually, bourbon whiskey.

Although the Whiskey Rebellion against taxes introduced on spirits in 1791 took place in Pennsylvania, it is pertinent, since it drove some distillers into Kentucky, where bourbon was born. In 1794, after numerous riots resulting in tax collectors being tarred and feathered and their houses burned, President George Washington, for the first time in the history of the United States, mustered troops to fight their own countrymen and quell the uprising. The rebellious distillers lost the battle without a great deal of violence; those who agreed to pay taxes were pardoned, and others were imprisoned until they settled their debts.

One drink that is usually associated with bourbon is the mint julep (although the original base spirit of this classic was, in all probability, peach brandy), a drink described in 1803 as "a dram of spirituous liquor that has mint in it, taken by Virginians of a morning." Another famous bourbon-based cocktail is the old-fashioned, a drink said to have been created at the Pendennis Club in Louisville, Kentucky, and introduced to New York at the old Waldorf-Astoria by Colonel James E. Pepper, a Kentucky whiskey distiller, in the late 1800s.

Ulysses S. Grant was known to have been enamored of bourbon, and during the Civil War, when it was brought to President Abraham Lincoln's attention that Grant might be drinking too much, Lincoln reportedly asked what brand of whiskey Grant drank, so that he could send some to his other generals. After becoming president, though, Grant was once again connected to bourbon when Benjamin Helm Bristow, secretary of the treasury, initiated an investigation into what became known as the Whiskey Ring, a group of people, including Grant's secretary, General Orville E. Babcock, who were accused of keeping for themselves a percentage of the taxes paid by bourbon distillers.

Grant himself testified at Babcock's trial, and Babcock was acquitted, but General John McDonald, a regional supervisor of the Internal Revenue Service, was found guilty of the crime and sentenced to three years in prison and a fine of five thousand dollars. Upon his release, McDonald accused Grant, in a book, *Secrets of the Great Whiskey Ring*, of being directly involved with the Whiskey Ring, and the scandal was said to have been largely responsible for Grant's loss of the next election.

Various other scandals have plagued the bourbon industry, and legal pressure in the late 1800s brought down what was known as the Whiskey Trust, a conglomerate of sorts that sought to control the whole industry. Also, because unscrupulous profiteers offered adulterated whiskey bearing "bourbon" labels, Colonel Edmund Haynes Taylor Jr., a reputable distiller, teamed up with John G. Carlisle, then secretary of the treasury, to lobby for the Bottled-in-Bond Act, which was passed in 1897. The act stipulated that bonded whiskey must be aged for at least four years in government-supervised warehouses and bottled at 50 percent alcohol by volume, thus giving legitimate bourbon producers a way to differentiate their whiskey from those not made to high standards. Further standards of identity that clarified the definition of true bourbon were enacted in acts of Congress in 1907 and 1909.

Although some bourbon distilleries remained in business during the years of Prohibition (1920–1933) by keeping pharmacists supplied with what was known as medicinal whiskey, available by prescription only, the majority of American whiskey producers went out of business. During this time, a great quantity of blended whisky from Canada was smuggled into America, and when Prohibition was repealed, the American public had grown used to these lighter products.

Although it was once again legal to distill bourbon, this change in taste, coupled with the fact that the newly distilled whiskey had to be aged before it could be sold, gave the public even more time to grow used to lighter whiskeys. Also, many people switched to rum and gin—both spirits that had increased in popularity during Prohibition. Hence, bourbon sales declined and remained low, to a large extent, right up until the 1980s.

During the last two decades of the twentieth century, relatively high priced single-malt scotches became popular, partly because the American public had reduced its intake of distilled spirits. Instead, many Americans spent their money on small quantities of high-quality, expensive products. In the late 1980s, the bourbon industry took note of this phenomenon and began to introduce more premium whiskeys of its own; in this way, bourbon once again became popular with the American public. The

Bourbon. Advertisement for Hunter's Own Bourbon. *Warshaw Collection of Business Americana, Archives Center, National Museum of American History, Behring Center, Smithsonian Institution*

market in the early twenty-first century boasted more bottlings than at any time since the onset of Prohibition.

Along with the influx of these new, bolder bourbons came descriptive phrases used to market them. "Single-barrel" bourbon, meaning whiskey that is from a single barrel (most bourbons are the product of mingling together whiskeys from many barrels) had been around prior to Prohibition, but the term was not used after repeal until 1984, when Blanton's Bourbon was introduced. Other companies followed the trend, and more single-barrel bourbons appeared in a relatively short time.

The first "small-batch" bourbon, Booker's, was released in 1988, and this was a term that would cause some controversy. The Jim Beam Brands company, which issued Booker's bourbon, defined the term as "rare and exceptional bourbons married from a cross-section of barrels in the rack house" and went on to explain that the whiskey was picked from certain spots in their aging warehouses where bourbon seemed to mature better than in other places. Master distillers from other companies agreed that this phenomenon existed, but not all companies that started to use the phrase "small-batch" stuck to Beam's definition. Maker's Mark, for example, claimed that, since it distilled in smaller quantities than any other distillery at the time, its bourbon was a true small-batch whiskey, and other companies followed suit, creating their own definitions of the term. Most bourbon aficionados agree that whiskeys bearing the "small-batch" designation on their label are high-quality products but that an age statement, showing how long the bourbon had spent in the barrel, is far more important as a guide to high quality.

In 2002, America's bourbon distilleries numbered ten: Barton, Jim Beam, A. Smith Bowman, Buffalo Trace, Early Times, Four Roses, Heaven Hill, Labrot and Graham, Maker's Mark, and Wild Turkey. The A. Smith Bowman plant is in Virginia, and all the rest are based in Kentucky. Jack Daniel's and George Dickel whiskeys, though commonly mistaken for bourbons, are Tennessee whiskeys, both produced in Tennessee. These whiskeys are differentiated from bourbons by a filtration through sugar-maple charcoal before aging, which adds a distinctive "sooty sweetness" to the final products.

[See also Distillation; Prohibition; Whiskey.]

BIBLIOGRAPHY

Barr, Andrew. *Drink: A Social History of America.* New York: Carroll and Graf, 1999.
Harwell, Richard Barksdale. *The Mint Julep.* Charlottesville: University Press of Virginia, 1985.
Marrison, L. W. *Wines and Spirits.* Baltimore: Penguin, 1957.
Murray, Jim. *Classic Bourbon, Tennessee, and Rye Whiskey.* London: Prion, 1998.

GARY AND MARDEE HAIDIN REGAN

Brady, Diamond Jim

The phrase "Gilded Age" appears in histories of the later nineteenth century and is often accompanied by pictures of obese, bearded men, their bulging stomachs covered in white and black evening clothes stuck through with diamond pins and draped with gold chains. Captains of industry and finance, they are often seated at saturnalian tables, symbols of an age of coarse materialism, massive corruption, and unbridled greed. Of them all, none was more emblematic than the grand gourmand of his, and perhaps any, age, Diamond Jim Brady.

James Buchanan Brady, the son of an immigrant Irish saloon keeper, was born on the Lower East Side of Manhattan in 1856. Raised in the slums of New York City and without much formal education, the plump lad left home at age eleven for a bellhop job at the St. James Hotel. Always jovial, smart, and hungry, he learned how to ingratiate himself with wealthy patrons and how to behave among them. Hired by the New York Central Railroad at age fifteen, Brady rose to become a salesman for a railroad equipment company, thus beginning his career as America's first "supersalesman." Through sharp dealing, a keen business sense, and financial tips from his many well-placed friends, Brady made (and spent) millions and entered the ranks of America's newly rich.

Diamond Jim's feeding bouts are the stuff of legend, especially when he dined with his great (platonic) friend, the incomparable American beauty Lillian Russell. Breakfasts consisted of several dozen oysters, chops, steaks, eggs, and pancakes, all washed down with quarts of milk and orange juice. Twelve-course dinners always consisted of balanced food groups—fish and fowl; oysters and clams; canapés; turtle soup; several lobsters; roasted meats; refreshing sherbet; and a course of canvasback duck, terrapin, and fresh asparagus followed by mousses, cakes, pies, and fruit topped off with two to five pounds of his favorite chocolates. Russell could and sometimes did match him dish for dish, after shedding her corset.

Like the aristocracy of medieval and early modern Europe, Brady's eating was a spectator sport. He held court at Rector's and the other great New York restaurants, sharing gargantuan meals and demanding every new dish that he had heard about. At Chicago's Columbian Exposition in 1893, watching Brady and Russell eat mountains of fresh corn at Rector's Marine Café was as popular an event as any on the celebrated midway, according to the press.

Conspicuous consumption was the mark of the man; diamonds, he reckoned, were a salesman's best friend. To sell high-priced goods, one had to look the part, both in bearing and attire. Of his twenty thousand diamonds and six thousand other precious stones, he said, "Them as has 'em, wears 'em." The same explanation held for his three hundred plus pounds. Still, he was the soul of generosity, constantly giving lavish gifts. He founded the nation's first urological institute (where he had had surgery for kidney stones) and, upon his death in 1917, left almost all his wealth to charities. While the Vanderbilts and Rockefellers built dynasties, Diamond Jim became the model and caricature of a society built upon eternal salesmanship and never-ending consumption.

BIBLIOGRAPHY

Burke, John. *Duet in Diamonds: The Flamboyant Saga of Lillian Russell and Diamond Jim Brady in America's Gilded Age.* New York: Putnam, 1972.

Jeffers, H. Paul. *Diamond Jim Brady: Prince of the Gilded Age.* New York: Wiley, 2001.

Rector, George. *The Girl from Rector's.* Garden City, NY: Doubleday, 1927.

BRUCE KRAIG

Brandy

From bucks to fixes, flips to fizzes, smashes to sours and slings, Americans have taken the venerable Old World spirit known as brandy and turned it into something all their own—a cocktail-hour favorite. The word "brandy" derives from the Dutch *brandewijn*, or "burnt wine," a reference to the heat-based distillation process that yields spirit from a fermented mash of fruit—primarily grapes, though apples, berries, and some stone fruits yield notable variations. The reasonable consensus among historians is that brandy originated with the Dutch, who were trading in it by the sixteenth century, although the French managed within decades to take the concept and run with it, all the way to Cognac. Today, French brandies set the standard, while several other European countries, Spain foremost, dabble in its manufacture as well—not only as an end product but as an additive, whereby it fortifies wines like port, sherry, and Madeira; the long-standing practice both preserves and boosts the alcohol content of such wines, which were thus highly popular in the era of maritime trade.

Although there are now several domestic brands, even imported brandy could always be counted on to help put the "spirit" in "American spirit." For instance, one much disputed, but no less beloved bit of folklore finds Manhattan being baptized in brandy, as the beverage with which the English explorer Henry Hudson plied the Delaware Indians he met there in 1609; in honor of the hilarity that ensued, Hudson's new associates named the spot Manahachtanienk, which translates roughly as "the place where we got drunk." Thus did the Big Apple spring from grapes. True or not, brandy was undeniably a factor in the shaping of convivial customs that were a literal and symbolic departure from those overseas. For Europeans, brandy is inherently postprandial, best served neat in snifters as a digestif; in the United States, however, it functions as often as not as an ingredient in mixed drinks—which themselves form the nucleus around which our drinking culture revolves. In the colonial and Revolutionary War eras, taverns served brandy-based toddies and sweetened punches such as shrub to warm tummies and kindle republican ardor.

In modern times, from the cocktail lounge to the cocktail party, Americans have mixed company in conjunction with drinks, whose supposedly salubrious effects become irrelevant compared with their socially lubricating effects.

Brandy. Jarvis Medicinal Blackberry Brandy label. *Warshaw Collection of Business Americana, Archives Center, National Museum of American History, Behring Center, Smithsonian Institution*

In fact, it may even be possible to draw a link between the appearance of the cocktail and the disappearance of alcohol, brandy included, from the American doctor's kit bag—the frivolity of the one being incommensurate with the sobriety, so to speak, of the other as a restorative.

At any rate, among brandy's more illustrious cocktail credits are the orange-tinged sidecar (said, oddly enough, to be an invention of Harry's New York Bar—in Paris); the crème de menthe–spiked stinger; the sweetly spiced brandied coffee known in New Orleans as *café brûlot;* the brandy Alexander, which incorporates heavy cream and crème de cacao in an appeal to dainty tastes; and even the original mint julep (in which, however, it was ultimately replaced by bourbon).

The United States—as represented by California, where the stateside industry resides almost exclusively—also differs from Europe (as represented by France) with respect to modes of production. While under penalty of law, the French must use only white grapes (and the Cognacais only certain types thereof), Californians have access to any state-grown grape, although Thompson seedless and flame Tokay predominate. And whereas the most celebrated French brandies must undergo a laborious double-distillation process in copper pot stills or alembics, California makers have contented themselves, by and large, with the continuous or patent still, the results being both more expedient and more consistent—hence, one might say, more in keeping with American values. (There are exceptions among top-tier producers, such as Germain-Robin and Jepson.) Relatively painless government regulations include minimums on the duration of oak aging (two years) and the percentage of alcohol (30 percent, or 60 proof), which most respected producers not only meet but, in fact, exceed.

The U.S. brandy industry has not always, however, enjoyed such freedom from federal interference. Its birth and early growth in the 1850s and 1860s—with which the French émigré Jean-Louis Vignes, the German immigrants Charles Kohler and John Frohling, and the Hungarian-born Colonel Agoston Haraszthy are all associated, although Spanish missions had long been doubling as private distilleries—was hobbled by prohibitive taxation and exacting fines, the latter often leveled against those who engaged in fraudulent labeling practices precisely in order to evade the former. Such shenanigans on both sides dogged the industry for decades. Eventual tax repeals, however, and the Pure Food and Drug Act of 1906 undid some of the early damage. By the early years of the twenty-first century, with the insult and injury of Prohibition all but forgotten, California brandies were slowly earning a vastly improved reputation.

[*See also* Brandy Alexander; Cocktails; Sherry.]

BIBLIOGRAPHY

Carosso, Vincent P. *The California Wine Industry: A Study of the Formative Years.* Berkeley and Los Angeles: University of California Press, 1976.
Grossman, Harold J. *Grossman's Guide to Wines, Beers, & Spirits.* 7th rev. ed. New York: Wiley, 1983.
Pinney, Thomas. *A History of Wine in America: From the Beginnings to Prohibition.* Berkeley and Los Angeles: University of California Press, 1989.

RUTH TOBIAS

Brandy Alexander

The brandy Alexander, which rose to popularity as a Prohibition-era after-dinner drink, consists of brandy, crème de cacao, and cream, shaken with ice and sometimes garnished with nutmeg. It was originally known as the Alexander cocktail, made with gin in place of brandy. Perhaps the most notorious "girl drink," the brandy Alexander is cloyingly sweet, like a chocolate milkshake. (The nonalcoholic, "mocktail" version of the brandy Alexander is a blend of milk, chocolate syrup, and soda water—in other words, a chocolate egg cream.)

A 1934 issue of *Esquire* included the Alexander on its list of the ten worst cocktails of the preceding decade, with other "pansies" like the pink lady and the clover club. The drink has survived, however, into the twenty-first century: the international chain restaurant T.G.I. Friday's serves it in hot, cold, and "frozen" versions, the last with ice cream, whipped cream, and chocolate shavings. The flavor has also endured in the form of brandy Alexander pie, invented in 1933, when Prohibition was repealed and people could go back to using liqueurs in foods. The pie is a blend of crème de cacao, brandy, whipped cream, and chocolate in a graham-cracker or cookie-crumb crust.

[*See also* Brandy *and* Cocktails.]

BIBLIOGRAPHY

Lanza, Joseph. *The Cocktail: The Influence of Spirits on the American Psyche.* New York: St. Martin's Press, 1995.

JESSY RANDALL

Brazil Nuts

Brazil nuts (*Bertholletia excelsa*) originated in the tropical forests of Brazil, Bolivia, Peru, Colombia, and Venezuela. The Brazil nut tree has hardly been domesticated, and hence nearly all nuts are harvested by hand from wild trees. Indigenous peoples in South America ate Brazil nuts from their forests. Europeans first encountered them in the sixteenth century. The earliest known shipment of Brazil nuts to the United States occurred in 1810, when a small quantity was exported to New York. Larger quantities were imported after the Civil War. By 1873, 3 million pounds of Brazil nuts were imported into the United States. Large, meaty Brazil nuts, which are very high in fat, are eaten raw, roasted, and salted and are an important component in mixed nuts. They are used in bakery and confectionery.

[*See also* Candy Bars and Candy; Nuts.]

ANDREW F. SMITH

Bread

The history of bread in America is complex, encompassing the traditions of Native Americans and of myriad immigrant groups, each of whom brought to the American table their own breads, such as tortillas, pumpernickel, focaccia, matzo, and pita. Many of these traditional breads have been modified, and new types or unique variations of bread, such as Anadama bread, have emerged in the United States. Finally, American entrepreneurs have commercialized many types of bread and have changed the breads in the process.

The main grain cultivated by Native Americans in pre-Columbian times was corn. They removed the tough outer covering from the kernels by soaking them in lye ash and water, and then ground the kernels in mortars and pestles. From this ground hominy, Native Americans made bread by patting the dough into flat disks and cooking them on heated rocks; or they wrapped the dough in leaves and buried it in hot ashes. This way of making bread was almost universal throughout the world, whether it was made with corn in the Americas, wheat in ancient Mesopotamia, barley in ancient Palestine, or oats in the British Isles.

The best bread is made from grains rich in glutanin and gliadin, two proteins that, when moistened and stirred or kneaded, combine to create gluten. Gluten gives dough a plastic quality that allows it to entrap the air bubbles created by yeast or other leavening; these bubbles cause the dough to rise as the heated air expands. When the dough is baked, the walls of these tiny air pockets become rigid, so the bread retains its inflated form after the trapped air has cooled again. Wheat flour develops far more gluten than flour made from other grains, so it is preferred in much of the world for baking bread. Wheat-flour dough can be shaped, braided, or molded into myriad shapes. Wheat flour can also be combined with other flours, such as oat or rye, that do not develop enough gluten to be used on their own.

Early English colonists brought Old World grains, including barley, oats, rye, and wheat, but, as many colonists were ill equipped for and unskilled in farming, their first crops were generally unsuccessful. Had it not been for the active assistance of the Native Americans, the first settlers would probably not have survived. The Native Americans taught the colonists to grow corn and prepare it for the table by grinding the corn in a hollowed or burned-out tree stump, using a log as a pestle, and baking the meal into so-called ash cakes. These techniques eventually produced corn pone, johnnycake, and cornbread.

Rye thrived in New England, and it was mixed with cornmeal to produce a dark, dense bread called "Injun 'n' Rye"; this local staple later evolved into Boston brown bread. Primitive corn-and-rye and corn-and-barley breads were flatbreads, as neither rye nor barley develops much gluten. While the breads were heavy and sustaining, they did not satisfy the bread hunger of British and European immigrants, who traditionally ate wheat bread.

Home Baking

In colonial times, bread was baked in ovens made of brick, clay, or stone; they could be either inside or outside the house. Inside the house, separate ovens might be built into

---

SOURDOUGH BREAD

Sourdough breads have been consumed since antiquity. The word "sourdough" goes back to Middle English, and recipes for such breads appear in English cookbooks beginning in the seventeenth century. Sourdough bread is made with wild yeast and bacteria that give a slight sour taste to the bread. As yeasts and bacteria vary with location, sourdough breads differ as well. San Francisco has become famous for its sourdough bread.

the fireplace. First, they were placed at the back of the fireplace, but later they were built into the wall next to the fireplace opening. Bread was also baked in Dutch ovens, covered pots that were placed directly in the fireplace among the coals. Although at this time the equipment and methods of home bakers were similar to those used by commercial bakers, the homemade loaf was generally regarded as superior to baker's bread. Indeed, making a good loaf of bread was considered a test of a homemaker's skill.

Professional Bakers

A few commercial bakeries were in operation in the colonies by the mid-seventeenth century, especially in New Amsterdam, and several communities were supporting professional bakers by the end of the century. Colonial bakers were similar to their European counterparts. Many had immigrated to America from Europe and taught the baking trade to apprentices in their new home. Bakeries were usually one-man operations. At this time most bakers used the sponge method, which put water, yeast, and flour into a large bowl, then added only enough of the remaining flour to make a thick mass called a sponge, which was later added to the remaining flour to help fermentation and the production of gluten. The sponge method produced a light bread. In the main, bread was retailed at the bakery, but sometimes bakers delivered bread to their customers' homes. Bread was sold unwrapped over the counter and later in paper bags.

By most accounts, baker's bread was considered inferior to homemade bread until the twentieth century. Home bakers made bread in relatively small batches with the best ingredients they could afford. But commercial bakeries were subject to market forces: local laws controlled the price and characteristics of baker's bread. To make a profit, bakers cut costs by altering ingredients and methods and occasionally through using adulterations, such as powdered chalk or plaster to make the bread whiter and heavier.

Demographics, however, were on the side of commercial bakers. As urbanization and real income increased, home baking decreased. Urban life required a different allocation of women's time. Well-to-do women spent more time at churches, schools, and social organizations. They could easily afford to purchase their bread rather than spend tedious hours baking at home. Less affluent women, who worked in sweatshops and at other grueling jobs, had less time for baking bread, and they did not teach their daughters how to bake.

PARKER HOUSE ROLLS

Parker House rolls originated during the 1870s at Boston's Parker House Hotel, which opened in 1856. They are made by folding a butter-brushed round of dough in half; when baked, the roll has a pleasing abundance of crusty surfaces. Recipes for Parker House rolls first appeared in cookbooks during the 1880s.

Urbanization also created the concentration of potential customers that made the mass distribution of bread financially viable. Bakers could sell their goods retail, or they could distribute their bread to grocery stores. City dwellers were able to pay for the ease and convenience of buying baker's bread; and women's tasks shifted from making things to buying things.

Sylvester Graham

By the 1820s, many gristmills were bolting flour (sifting out the bran) to produce a finer, whiter product. Not everyone was happy with these changes. One person who was particularly upset was Sylvester Graham, who had begun his career in 1830 as a temperance lecturer. Two years later he delivered a series of lectures reflecting on broader topics, such as vegetarianism and the use of whole wheat bread. He was an impassioned speaker who attracted large audiences, and his lectures were published beginning in 1832. These struck a responsive chord among many Americans. Beginning in 1833, "Graham" boardinghouses were established in New York and Boston, which attempted to institutionalize his culinary views. Graham advocated the use of coarse, unbolted flour for bread, which was to form a large part of his prescribed diet. He was so popular that bread made in this way—the same way that it had been made for centuries—was called "Graham bread" by 1834. Whole wheat flour is still known as Graham flour in some areas of the United States.

Graham collected his thoughts about bread and published them in his *Treatise on Bread and Bread-Making* (1837), which was the first book published in America solely focused on the subject. He criticized the way wheat was grown, objecting to the use of fertilizers. Graham stated that he could smell the difference between bread made with unfertilized wheat and wheat that had been fertilized. Graham also expressed his concerns about milling—that the wheat was not cleaned properly before it was ground, and that bolting largely eliminated the healthful bran from the flour. Graham considered the superfine white flour that was increasingly being produced in mills to be unwholesome.

Graham was also concerned with the adulteration of bread, but he was not the first to publish such opinions. An Englishman, Henry Jackson, wrote the first book-length attack on British bread making in *An Essay on Bread* (1758). By the late eighteenth century, English cookbooks included directions for determining whether flour or bread was contaminated. The German-born chemist Frederick Accum reported in his *Treatise on Adulterations of Food, and Culinary Poisons* (1820) that bread made by bakers was frequently adulterated with alum, subcarbonate of ammonia, and carbonate of magnesia, in addition to ground beans, peas, and potatoes. Although Accum was writing about bread making in London, these are the same charges that Graham leveled in America. The reason for adulteration, according to Accum, was that such a small profit attached to baking bread because of the laws regulating it, and therefore bakers used cheap, poor-quality wheat. Hence, chemicals were needed to remove odors and off colors. Accum's book generated excitement throughout Europe and America and was cited regularly during the following decades in books dealing with adulteration of foods. In 1821 Accum published a *Treatise on the Art of Making Good and Wholesome Bread of Wheat, Oats, Rye, Barley, and Other Farinaceous Grain*, which gave clear directions on how to make good bread. It is extremely likely that Graham had read Accum's work, but he clearly read reports with similar charges, which he quoted in his *Treatise on Bread and Bread-Making*.

Sylvester Graham believed that only the housewife should bake bread, as he was concerned with the quality and wholesomeness of baker's bread. Even if bakers used good grain, did not use adulterations, and prepared the dough properly, Graham believed they would still not turn out a good, healthful loaf. He suggested that every family grind their own wheat with a hand mill to ensure that the process was done properly.

Shortly after his *Treatise* was published, Graham spoke to large crowds in New York and New England, inveighing against bakers and the bread they produced. On at least three occasions, he was assaulted by angry bakers in the crowd. The furor died down in 1839, and fewer people attended Graham's lectures. Graham, believing himself to be a failure, retired from public life in 1839. But his concerns outlived him. Many of his ideas were adopted by the proponents of hydropathy or the water cure, and later by Seventh-Day Adventists.

Recipes for Graham bread were published in most American cookbooks until the early twentieth century. The first person known to sell Graham flour was R. T. Trall, a hydropath and vegetarian, whose New York institute began selling Graham flour during the 1850s. Trall was followed by James Caleb Jackson, who established a water-cure facility near Danville, New York, in 1859. Using Graham flour, Jackson produced Granula, the first commercial cold cereal. Hence, Graham's ideas contributed to the rise of the modern American breakfast cereal industry.

Leavenings

According to Cletus P. Kurtzman and Jack W. Fell's *The Yeasts: A Taxonomic Study* (2000), there are over fifty genera, 678 species, and thousands of strains of yeast. Different strains produce different flavors and textures in bread, and require different rising times. Until the mid-nineteenth century, both commercial and home bakers used wild yeast, which grows naturally when moistened flour is left exposed to the air. One common way of maintaining yeast was by saving a portion of yeast-filled dough for use in the next batch. Wild yeasts are unpredictable—new strains could find their way into the dough when it was being stored or handled—so it was difficult to turn out a consistent product.

Although bakers and brewers knew the effects of yeast, it was not until 1680 that Antoni van Leeuwenhoek, the Dutch lens grinder who made the first microscope, observed yeast. But its importance was not understood until 1855, when Louis Pasteur (and others working independently) proved that yeast caused fermentation. From these discoveries, others learned how to isolate single yeast cells and select pure cultures with particular characteristics. The end result was compressed yeast (*Saccharomyces cerevisae*), which was predictable, tolerant of temperature variations, and inexpensive to manufacture.

PUMPERNICKEL

Pumpernickel is a dense, slightly sour traditional dark rye bread brought to the United States by German immigrants. Commercial pumpernickel is usually made from refined rye flour and wheat flour, colored with caramel or other additives.

Commercial compressed yeast was first manufactured by German bakers in 1825. Compressed yeast was a more consistent product in high concentration. The yeast-making businesses began to flourish, particularly in the Austro-Hungarian Empire, where the best grain was also produced. Charles Fleischmann, a Hungarian who was born in Budapest and educated in Vienna, learned how to make compressed yeast. In 1866, he and his brother Maximilian immigrated to the United States, where they set up a compressed-yeast factory, the first in America.

Yeast was not the only leavening agent used in bread; various forms of what we now call baking powder evolved over the course of the nineteenth century, including saleratus (bicarbonate of potash); tartaric acid, a by-product of wine making, which when refined into a powder is called cream of tartar; and bicarbonate of soda. These were used to leaven cakes and breads. Commercial baking powders appeared around 1850. Eben Norton Horsford, a Harvard professor who was one of the founders of the Rumford Chemical Works of Providence, Rhode Island, urged in his *Theory and Art of Bread-making* (1861) that sodium bicarbonate and lime phosphate be used to leaven bread. As no fermentation was necessary, the dough was ready for the oven in minutes rather than hours.

Vienna Bread

In the mid-nineteenth century Vienna was renowned throughout Europe for its peerless baked goods. Norton Horsford discovered fine Viennese bread at the International Exposition in Vienna in 1873; while in central Europe, he visited Hungarian wheat fields and mills, the source of the flour used by Viennese bakers. When Horsford returned home, he wrote a *Report on Vienna Bread* (1875) that was published by the U.S. government. Horsford's report encouraged the use of compressed yeast and the construction of new mills, on the Hungarian pattern, in the United States. Vienna bread was such a sensation in the United States that those planning the Centennial Exposition in Philadelphia decided to include a working Viennese-style bakery. The bakery and the Fleischmann's yeast used there were tremendous successes.

Loss of Taste

Traditional flour milling released the oils from the wheat germ, which quickly turned rancid, a process that was exacerbated by the heat generated by high-speed roller mills used during the 1880s. So millers installed blowers

---

SODA BREAD

Soda bread is a light loaf leavened with bicarbonate of soda. Soda bread was made in America during the 1830s. It had become known as Irish soda bread by the latter part of the nineteenth century.

---

and other devices to rid the flour of bran and germ. Previously, the consumer simply bought only as much freshly ground flour as was convenient. But the flour manufactured by the new system created bright white flour that had a long shelf life. In the process, the flour was robbed of much of its nutrition and flavor.

Traditionally, in America, as in France and England, everyday white bread was made of flour, water, salt, and yeast. To compensate for the loss of flavor in bread, bakers began to change their formulas. Beginning in the last two decades of the nineteenth century, they increased the amount of sugar used in the dough; and standard recipes came routinely to call for milk, rather than water, as well as shortening. A dense, chewy crust was one of the casualties of these changes, and commercial bread became softer, sweeter, moister, and whiter.

Freshly ground wheat contains small amounts of carotene, a plant pigment that gives it a yellowish tinge. Over time, the pigment oxidizes and the flour turns off white. But in milling, time is money, and millers began to use an improved bleaching process using chlorine. J. N. Alsop, the founder of the Alsop Process Company, St. Louis, patented the chlorine bleaching process for flour in 1904.

Cookbook Bread

For millennia, the art of cookery was passed down orally from mother to daughter, and little of this wisdom was written down. Early bread recipes recorded and published by Americans often reflect local commodities and conditions. For instance, Harriot Pinckney Horry's "Receipt Book" (1770) includes two recipes for rice bread, which reflects the importance of rice and the high cost of wheat in South Carolina during the eighteenth century. Amelia Simmons's *American Cookery* (1796), the first cookbook authored by an American, includes recipes for cornbread, which she calls Johny Cake or Hoe Cake, and Indian Slapjack, which reflects the dominance of corn-based breads in New England at the end of the eighteenth century.

JOHNNYCAKE

Johnnycake has its origin in an oaten bread called jannock (later bannock) in parts of England. These names evolved into "johnnycake" and later to "journey cake" in England. In America, johnnycakes were made from whatever grain, such as corn, rice, wheat, or oats, was available. Since they could be made on any hot surface and did not require an oven, johnnycakes became a common food among the poor.

While so-called white bread recipes appeared in English cookbooks in the eighteenth century, the earliest American recipe is found in *The Virginia House-wife* (1824) by Mary Randolph, who calls for a loaf made of flour, water, salt, and yeast. It was baked directly on the floor of a wood-fired brick oven, a method virtually unchanged from those used centuries earlier in England. It differed only in minor detail from that given for making "your best and principall bread . . . manchet" by Gervase Markham in *The English Hus-wife* (1615), a work that was brought to America by English colonists. A number of recipes for such bread later appeared in English cookbooks that were widely circulated in America in the eighteenth and early nineteenth centuries, some coming out in American editions, such as Hannah Glasse's *The Art of Cookery* (1805) and Maria Eliza Rundell's *A New System of Domestic Cookery*, first published in 1806.

Diverse recipes for bread began appearing in the late nineteenth century. One of the earliest references to Graham bread in a cookbook was published in Sarah Josepha Hale's *The Good Housekeeper* (1841), which offered a recipe for Brown or Dyspepsia Bread. In the recipe, Hale notes that, "This bread is now best known as 'Graham bread'—not that Doctor Graham invented or discovered the manner of its preparation, but that he has been unwearied and successful in recommending it to the public." Directions on how to make Graham or dyspepsia bread were published in cookbooks through the nineteenth century and well into the twentieth century.

Breads made from corn, rye, rice, and oats regularly appeared in American cookbooks. Recipes for wheat breads containing other ingredients, such as potatoes, squash, beans, and pumpkin, which had probably been in use for centuries, appeared in print beginning in the 1840s, as did recipes for rolls. About the same time, recipes using buttermilk and sour milk as well as soda and other leavenings were also published. Toast had been eaten for centuries, but recipes for milk toast, cream toast, water toast, fried toast, and others using toasted bread, such as croutons, stuffings, sauces, omelets, soups, and puddings, became common during the mid-nineteenth century.

As the flour produced by roller mills began to dominate the marketplace, cookbook authors revised their recipes. In *Mrs. Lincoln's Boston Cook Book* (1883), Mary Johnson Lincoln called for a tablespoon of sugar to six cups of flour in bread making, but she was defensive about it: "Many object to the use of sugar in bread," she wrote. "Flour in its natural state contains sugar; this sugar is changed in fermentation. Just enough sugar to restore the natural sweetness, but not enough to give a really sweet taste, is necessary in fermented bread." The addition of sugar vitiates fermented bread, encouraging puffiness, a flaccid crumb, and a soft crust, and gives the bread a sweet taste. Mrs. Lincoln was playing the role of the new domestic scientist who was enthusiastic over the "new" flours. She described them and their milling in considerable detail. More than a decade later Fannie Merritt Farmer, whose *Boston Cooking-School Cook Book* (1896) was the successor to Mrs. Lincoln's publications, included sugar as standard practice. By the 1915 edition of Farmer's work, she had doubled the amount of sugar in the basic bread recipes.

The first American cookbook focused solely on bread baking was published by Sarah Tyson Rorer, *Bread and Bread-making* in 1889. Mrs. Rorer discusses the change

BREAD SLICERS

Since colonial times, Americans have used toasters that held slices of bread upright near an open fire, at first on open hearths and later in wood and coal stoves. At the beginning of the twentieth century, electric toasters began to be sold, and their popularity led to the development of the bread slicer. The problem with slicing bread mechanically was not how to cut the bread, but how to hold the slices together until the bread was wrapped. Many devices were tried, including rubber bands, string, and wire pins. These were abandoned in favor of a device developed in 1928 by Gustav Papendick, a St. Louis baker, which provided for a collapsible cardboard tray. With Papendick's device, the loaf was fitted into the tray and held firmly while being sliced, and then the entire unit, slices and tray, were wrapped together.

in flour, including its loss of nutrients, and offers dozens of recipes for making bread, from the traditional types, such as those titled Boston Brown Bread, Oatmeal Bread, Sally Lunn, and Graham Bread, to Dodgers, Puffs, Pop Overs, Cinnamon Buns, and French Rolls.

During the late nineteenth and early twentieth centuries, recipes for sandwiches became common in virtually all cookbooks. As the sandwich became more important, breads were modified to meet new needs. Hot dogs, hamburgers, and hot sandwiches required thicker and more solid types of bread. Submarines or po'boys needed long rolls. Tea sandwiches called for thin, delicate slices.

Other types of bread were developed in the United States based on culinary traditions from other countries, such as the bagel and bialy, which were based on eastern European traditions. Challah is the bread eastern European Jews traditionally eat on the Sabbath and on holidays. Portuguese sweet bread (*pao doce*), which is similar to Hawaiian sweet bread, became popular during the mid-twentieth century, as did tortillas from Mexico and pita from the Mediterranean, which became part of American culinary traditions during the twentieth century, although they did not become mainstream until after World War II.

Commercial Bread Baking

After the Civil War commercial bakeries grew in number, especially in cities with large immigrant populations who brought their own breads and baking techniques. But the trend toward whiter, softer bread continued. Whole wheat bread (also called middling bread, which referred to the larger particles of whole wheat in it) came to be considered coarse and common, while white bread signified purity and refinement.

As home bread baking declined, commercial bakeries thrived. By the end of the nineteenth century, only about one quarter of all bread was still made in the home, and this would decline further in subsequent years. After 1900, large-scale commercial baking required new types of flour, which were different from those traditionally used in the home. Commercial flours were adapted to high-speed mechanical mixers and needed to be dependable for quick fermentation.

Commercial baking thrived during World War I, despite wheat shortages. The United States needed to ship vast loads of wheat to its European allies and the U.S. military. As part of the wartime food conservation efforts, Mondays and Wednesdays were declared "Wheatless Days," and home bakers were asked to use

---

HOT DOG AND HAMBURGER BUNS

The production of commercial hot dog buns, long, soft rolls tailored to the size of the popular sausage, began during the early 1870s. The hot dog bun is frequently credited erroneously to Charles Feltman, a baker who opened a restaurant at Coney Island about 1874. Billy Ingram, who started the White Castle hamburger chain in 1921, is usually identified as the inventor of the commercial hamburger bun. He maintained standardization among the different chains by centralizing bun-baking operations.

"mixed flours" made of 75 percent wheat and 25 percent corn, rye, oats, or barley. Wheat flour was less available at retail stores, but bakers continued to be supplied with it. By the end of the war, most Americans were buying their bread rather than baking it at home.

Sliced bread is widely (if jokingly) acknowledged as one of civilization's greatest achievements, but bakers were slow to adopt bread slicers because sliced bread went stale much faster than bread in uncut loaves. Wrapping machines were improved, and, later, preservatives were added to keep bread fresh. Bread wrappers offered a bonus in that the baker could advertise on the wrapper, and bread sliced and wrapped by machine was handled less by bakery employees. The first wrapping machine appeared in 1911; it used a wax seal to close the ends of the paper. Three years later, a new machine used waxed paper, folding the paper around the loaf and sealing it by means of a heating plate. This process was not perfected until 1930, during the Depression, and since the cost of the new equipment raised the price of bread, many bakers did not install bread slicers until the late 1930s.

The bread symbolic of this period is Wonder Bread. This originally unsliced bread was first baked by the Taggart Baking Company of Indianapolis about 1920. Taggart was acquired by Continental Baking Company in 1925. Wonder Bread was first sold sliced in 1930, and during the decade extensive promotion was carried out on its behalf. Wonder Bread was produced at a full-scale bakery at the New York World's Fair in 1939 and was the sponsor of popular radio programs. In 1941 Wonder Bread was advertised as "enriched" with vitamins and minerals and was advertised on children's radio and television programs, such as *Hopalong Cassidy* and *Howdy Doody*. During the 1950s, the tag line "Wonder Bread Builds

TOAST

Bread becomes toast in the course of a complex series of chemical reactions to dry heat that includes the caramelization of sugars and the breakdown of starches, known collectively as the Maillard reaction. The ancient Egyptians are credited with the discovery of yeast leavening, and they are assumed to have been the first to brown the resulting loaves in a fire—that is, to make toast. The English have made the most extensive use of the practice in their cookery. In medieval times, toast frequently appeared at the table in the form of sops and sippets—relatively small pieces of toast used for dipping, mopping, and topping with various meats and sauces. In the Victorian era "toast water" was used as a folk tonic. Although it is a dish unto itself at breakfast and tea time, toast plays a supporting role in classics of home cooking such as creamed tuna or chipped beef on toast, the restorative milk toast, fricassee or stew, and in the shape of garnishing points or croutons.

As the heirs to such tradition, Americans rely on toast as a mealtime staple. Historically, crops such as corn and oats eclipsed wheat in terms of availability, yielding breads with a crumb not generally associated with toast. In the nineteenth century wheat and wheat products began to dominate. A traditional American breakfast of bacon or sausage and eggs almost inevitably includes toast with butter and jelly. Common alternatives range from cinnamon toast (an English hand-me-down) to Texas toast, which is served in grilled slabs rather than slices and is topped with gravy or honey. French toast, which technically is not toast at all, is day-old bread dipped in egg, sautéed in butter, and sprinkled with powdered sugar. At lunchtime, toasted bread is the key to many sandwiches, including the club sandwich; bacon, lettuce, and tomato; peanut butter and jelly; and grilled cheese. Hamburger and hot dog buns are properly browned as well.

If the taste for toasting is Anglo-bred, it was the typically American thirst for convenience spurred by the revolutionary invention of the electric toaster at the turn of the twentieth century that ensured toast's place at the table. Before that time, the world, the English in particular, made do with hearth implements such as long-handled forks and ornate swiveling irons that held the bread upright. Tin and wire racks served the same function on early wood-burning stovetops. Then, between 1904 and 1909, the first electric models were patented and put on the market with varying degrees of success. General Electric had the most models, although Hotpoint and Simplex were also industry pioneers. Note that "electric" doesn't necessarily mean "automatic." The early toasters were manual, meaning the user was no less responsible than before for determining doneness by empirical observation. In 1926 toasters became fully automatic. A bell heralded the end of the toasting cycle, and there was a mechanism for dislodging the toast. This "pop-up" toaster led to the development of sliced, packaged bread. As electricity entered more homes, this method of toasting became a way of life in American kitchens.

RUTH TOBIAS

Rolls. Rolls fresh from the oven at the Institute of Culinary Education, New York.

Strong Bodies 8 Ways," came into use. In the 1960s, when a backlash arose against overly refined food products, Wonder Bread became a prime target for criticism.

Health Issues

Beginning in the 1880s, wheat milling removed the bran, germ, and oil from the flour, and then the flour was bleached. This created a bright white flour that appealed to consumers and extended the flour's shelf life, which pleased grocers. That this white flour and the bread made from it lacked important nutritional components was a concern by the end of the nineteenth century. Nutrition experts began to object to removing the germ and bran and urged consumption of whole wheat bread. During the 1940s, the Federal Drug Administration encouraged commercial bakeries to enrich white bread. In 1943, the War Foods Administration temporarily required enriched

Bread Counter. Part of the bread selection at Zabar's, New York City. *Photograph by Joe Zarba*

bread. This restriction was later lifted, but most commercial white flour continues in the early twenty-first century to be enriched with B vitamins, such as thiamine (vitamin B_1), riboflavin (B_2), and niacin (B_3), as well as iron, folate, and calcium.

Modern commercial bakeries incorporated other additives into their breads. Some bleaching agents, as well as other substances, including malted flours, called "improvers," increase the dough's fermentation period, enabling bakers to make better bread from otherwise substandard flour. The list of additives in commercial breads includes chemicals that retard staling and inhibit mold, as well as emulsifiers, flavor enhancers, dough conditioners, yeast stimulants, stiffeners, and many more.

Developments since the 1970s

After World War II, large commercial bakers produced the greatest proportion of the bread eaten in America. It was not until the 1970s that a backlash developed against the bland, standardized flavor and texture and limited nutritional value of commercial bread. Home bread baking enjoyed a renaissance, and since the 1970s many communities have enjoyed the products of small artisanal bakeries. One group supporting this trend has been the Bread Bakers Guild of America, which has also attempted to raise the standards of artisanal bread

CROISSANTS

The croissant is a crescent-shaped breakfast roll made from a very buttery dough resembling puff pastry. It is said to have been created by Viennese bakers or by Budapest bakers to celebrate the late seventeenth-century defeat of the Turks, whose symbol was the crescent. No primary evidence has surfaced to support these contentions. It became part of French culinary traditions in the mid-nineteenth century. The first known introduction of croissants into the United States was not until after World War I; croissants became increasingly popular beginning in the 1960s, and in the 2000s stuffed croissants are served as breakfast sandwiches by fast food outlets.

baking. Artisanal bakers have been particularly interested in "identity preserved" (IP) wheat. Most commercial wheat is stored in silos, creating a blend of wheats. Blends make it difficult to determine how flour will perform, as different types of wheat have different properties. Flour made from IP wheat is composed of a single type of wheat, thus giving bakers greater control over the qualities of their bread.

American supermarkets, reflecting the diversity of the nation's population, stock corn and flour tortillas, Italian focaccia, Armenian lavash, Indian naan and chapatis, British scones, and French baguettes as well as fiber-rich whole grain breads and sturdy European-style loaves.

[*See also* Anadama Bread; Bagels; Bakeries; Bialy; Bread Machines; Bread, Sliced; Bread-Making Tools; Chemical Leavening; Cornbread Baking Pans; Dutch Ovens; Farmer, Fannie; Fermentation; Graham, Sylvester; Lincoln, Mrs.; Matzo; Pillsbury; Randolph, Mary; Rorer, Sarah Tyson; Sally Lunn; Sandwiches; Simmons, Amelia; Stoves and Ovens; Toasters; Waxed Paper; Yeast.]

BIBLIOGRAPHY

Bishai, David, and Ritu Nalubola. "History of Food Fortification in the United States: Its Relevance for Current Fortification Efforts in Developing Countries." *Economic Development and Cultural Change* 51 (2002): 37–53.

Burnett, J. A., R.W. Payne, and D. Yarrow. *Yeasts: Characteristics and Identification.* 3rd ed. New York: Cambridge University Press, 2000.

David, Elizabeth. *English Bread and Yeast Cookery*, with an introduction by Karen Hess. New York: Viking, 1980.

Dupaigne, Bernard. *The History of Bread.* New York: Abrams, 1999.

Hamper, Karol Redfern. *A Romance with Baking: A Millennium Dedication to the American Flour Milling Industry.* n.p.: K. R. Hamper, 2000.

Hess, Karen. "A Century of Change in the American Loaf: Or, Where Are the Breads of Yesteryear?" Paper delivered at the Smithsonian Institution, April 29–30, 1994.

Ingram, Christine, and Jennie Shapter. *The World Encyclopedia of Bread and Bread Making.* New York: Lorenz, 1999.

Jacob, H. E. *Six Thousand Years of Bread: Its Holy and Unholy History.* Garden City, NY: Doubleday, Doran, 1944.

Kurtzman, Cletus P., and Jack W. Fell, eds. *The Yeasts: A Taxonomic Study.* 4th ed. New York: Elsevier, 2000.

Panschar, William G. *Baking in America.* Evanston, IL: Northwestern University Press, 1956.

Pyler, E. J. *Baking Science and Technology.* 3rd ed. Merriam, KS: Sosland, 1988.

Rorer, Sarah T. *Bread and Bread-making.* Philadelphia: Arnold, 1889.

Storck, John, and Walter Dorwin Teague. *A History of Milling Flour for Man's Bread.* Minneapolis: University of Minnesota Press, 1952.

Wood, Ed. *World Sourdoughs from Antiquity: Authentic Recipes for Modern Bakers.* Berkeley, CA: Ten Speed Press, 1996.

ANDREW F. SMITH

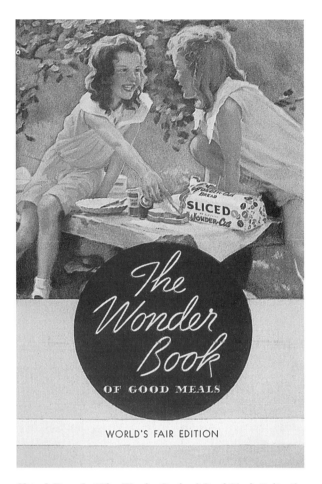

Sliced Bread. "The Wonder Book of Good Meals," distributed by the Continental Baking Company at the Century of Progress Exposition, Chicago, 1933–1934. *Collection of Andrew F. Smith*

Bread, Sliced

The earliest barley bread appeared in about 10,000 B.C.E. It was a flatbread less than one inch thick and required no slicing. Later, wheat, rye, and leavening agents were introduced, making much larger loaves that needed to be torn by hand or sliced with a knife. At the beginning of the twentieth century, an Iowa-born inventor, Otto Frederick Rohwedder, recognized that the slicing of entire loaves would be helpful. He struggled for twenty-six years before his machine went on the market in Battle Creek, Michigan, in 1928, earning him the title "Father of Sliced Bread." During the process, Rohwedder knew that slicing the bread was not his only goal. He needed to devise a way to hold the slices next to one another for portability and longer-lasting freshness. First, he tried hat pins, which joined several slices to each other. He soon discovered that this method was not practical. His final solution was to create a slicing machine that also wrapped all the slices together.

Wonder Bread placed the first commercially sliced bread on the market in 1930. Within five years North Americans were consuming more sliced than unsliced bread. This popularity helped increase the demand for Charles Strite's spring-loaded, pop-up toaster, invented in 1926, which went along with the popularity of the lunch counter, with its grilled cheese sandwiches, BLTs, and club sandwiches. Later, a St. Louis baker, Gustav Papendick, improved on Rohwedder's design by devising a cardboard tray, which he placed between the bread and the wrapper to stabilize the loaves. Presliced bread was still considered a dispensable luxury in 1943, when the U.S. secretary of agriculture banned the manufacture of metal bread-slicing machines to release materials for use in World War II.

[*See also* Bread; Toasters.]

BIBLIOGRAPHY

Jacob, H. E. *Six Thousand Years of Bread: Its Holy and Unholy History.* Translated by Richard and Clara Winston. 1944. Reprint, New York: Lyons and Burford, 1997.

MARTY MARTINDALE

Bread Machines

Long considered a twentieth-century marvel, the automatic bread-making machine debuted at the end of the nineteenth century. Created by a Massachusetts inventor named Joseph Lee, the prototype of the modern bread maker mixed and kneaded ingredients with commendable speed. But in the late twentieth century, the Japanese—not traditionally bread-eating or bread-making people—further developed the concept: Zojirushi Corporation marketed the Home Baker in 1988, an all-in-one bread-making appliance that proofs, mixes, kneads, rises, shapes, and bakes the bread dough within hours. This appliance enables amateur cooks to create their own gourmet loaves without the manual labor and guesswork characteristic of making bread.

Several manufacturers have competed with Zojirushi to capture the home bread-baking market. Despite slight variations, machines operate similarly and generally include a nonstick loaf pan—sizes and shapes may vary from manufacturer to manufacturer—a kneading paddle, heating coil, and timer. The cook has only to select the appropriate bread recipe, measure and add the ingredients to the loaf pan, set the timer, and push a switch. After several hours, the bread has baked and is ready for cooling, slicing, and eating. Success depends on following the manufacturer's detailed instructions carefully and on other factors outside the machine's control, such as the quality of ingredients, humidity, and air temperature.

With practice, cooks may confidently develop their own recipes, but several bread-making cookbooks offer recipes suitable for all brands of bread machines. While most machines generally work equally well with quick breads and yeast breads, some of the more expensive and sophisticated models include instructions on making jams, cakes, and pizzas.

BIBLIOGRAPHY

Hensperger, Beth. *The Bread Lover's Bread Machine Cookbook.* Boston: Harvard Common Press, 2000.
Vance, Glenna, and Tom Lacalamita. *Bread Machines for Dummies.* New York: Hungry Minds, 2001.

ALEXANDRA GREELEY

Bread-Making Tools

From earliest civilizations, the technology of bread baking has been relatively simple. European colonists brought a tradition of unleavened flatbreads, adapted to New World ingredients, and baked in the fire's embers as ash cake. Alternatively, cornmeal johnnycakes used hearth griddles over coals and wrought iron turners. More complex European yeasted breads depended on large brick ovens, covered bake kettles, or Dutch ovens heated with flames or glowing embers. Their overnight risings required large, wooden, lidded dough troughs and bowls or earthenware containers with cloth coverings. Heavy tin (actually tinned sheet iron) bowls made with close-fitting but ventilated lids became available before the Civil War.

Although loaves were traditionally "cast" directly on the oven floor, cast-iron bread pans saw occasional use during the eighteenth century. Nineteenth-century cookstoves required bread pans, first manufactured in earthenware and tin. By the 1880s, enameled tin (agate ware, for example) had eliminated problems of breakage, rust, and cleaning (though not chipping); this was followed by twentieth-century improvements in aluminum and, later, Pyrex.

The real change came when inventors in the third quarter of the nineteenth century patented tin and cast-iron dough "machines" that used hand-turned, geared cranks to move paddles through the dough as it was manipulated in a semblance of hand-mixing and kneading. When thoroughly combined, the paddles were withdrawn and the container (which came in a range of sizes to make one loaf or several) was covered and set in a warm place for rising. These machines were called dough mixers, dough brakes, bread mixers, and bread machines. By the 1930s, large electric countertop or stand mixers were available with attachments for mixing and kneading bread dough. Since the 1990s, electric bread makers have accomplished the mixing, rising, and baking of bread, while their automatic timers can start and finish the process at any time of day or night.

Commercial neighborhood bread bakeries thrived in colonial cities almost from their start. After the Civil War, they proliferated, with evolving assembly-line and moving-belt production, ovens, and improved bread slicers, providing the forerunners of the familiar packaged, sliced, and airy loaves sold in modern times.

[*See also* Bread Machines.]

BIBLIOGRAPHY

Franklin, Linda Campbell. *300 Years of Kitchen Collectibles*. 5th ed. Iola, WI: Krause, 2003.

LINDA CAMPBELL FRANKLIN

Breakfast, *see Meal Patterns*

Breakfast Drinks

At the beginning of the twentieth century a growing number of patent-medicine peddlers exploited customers who wanted to lose weight regardless of their health. They began selling the forerunners to liquid diets and instant breakfast drinks. These patent medicines ranged from the harmless Jean Down's Get Slim mixture of pink lemonade to less benign remedies, such as the 1930s Helen's Liquid Reducer Compound, which encouraged dieters to gargle away their fat with a mixture of peppermint, bleach, and hydrogen peroxide. Dr. Stoll's Diet Aid was the first of these new diet drinks that got their start in the 1930s and have been reincarnated in each subsequent decade.

Liquid diets replaced patent medicines when science became more sophisticated and the Food and Drug Administration (FDA) became more powerful, clamping down on hucksters and their useless remedies. Breakfast drinks marketed as liquid diets at the turn of the twenty-first century included Carnation Instant Breakfast, Ensure, Herbalife, Naturslim, Metrecal, Sustacal, Resource, Boost, Nutrament, Sweet Success, Nutrilite, Nutrasoy, Go Lean, and Slim-Fast. Resembling milkshakes, the liquid diets are powders or canned drinks that include protein, vita-

mins, minerals, and other dietary supplements. While powders are combined with water, juice, milk, or other liquids, canned drinks require no preparation.

These beverages were first developed as a way for sick and weak patients to get some nutritional sustenance, and they were recommended by doctors and dietitians. Metrecal was one of the early beverages created for people trying to gain weight and was introduced to the public in 1959 as one of the first high-energy, high-protein drinks. It became popular as a meal replacement for dieters, known as the "Metrecal for Lunch Bunch." Trying to rekindle interest in similar products in the late 1960s, Mead Johnson Nutritionals also created Nutrament, promoted as a recovery drink for athletes, and Boost, a meal replacement or snack for healthy adults and for weight gain in cases of illness or surgery.

Introduced about twenty-five years ago, Slim-Fast now promotes their product with a plan that promises weight loss. According to researchers, Slim-Fast is effective in "long-term weight loss and weight maintenance" (Chernitsky, 1999). But staying on the Slim-Fast plan or other liquid diets longer than a couple of weeks may deprive the body of necessary nutrients found only in food. Many of these vitamins, minerals, fiber, phytonutrients, fat, and carbohydrates are contained only in whole foods.

Two-income households, longer workweeks, and a faster pace of life have become the American norm, leaving less time and requiring more energy for meal preparation. The drink manufacturers take advantage of baby boomers' worry about age-related slowing down, by equating healthful eating with their products and touting their nutritional benefits. Convenience is another selling point—portable cans or cartons are easily tucked into a briefcase, purse, or athletic bag. The old adage "breakfast is the most important meal of the day" partly explains why American adults continue to turn to simple solutions such as breakfast drinks. Whatever the concern—diet, health, or convenience—the market for breakfast drinks remains strong.

[*See also* Breakfast Foods; Diets, Fad.]

BIBLIOGRAPHY

Chernitsky, Laura. "Slim-Fast® and Weight Loss." 1999. http://www.vanderbilt.edu/AnS/psychology/health_psychology/healthpsych.htm. Evaluates the Slim-Fast® Company's plan for weight loss and weight management, reviewing research studies and concluding that the plan is an effective method.
Ditschuneit, Herwig H., et al. "Metabolic and Weight-Loss Effects of a Long-Term Dietary Intervention in Obese Patients." *American Journal of Clinical Nutrition* (1999): 198–204.

Pilcher, Jeffrey M. "Food Fads." In *The Cambridge World History of Food*, edited by Kenneth F. Kiple and Kriemhild Coneè Ornelas, vol. 2, 1492–1493. New York: Cambridge University Press, 2000.

Schwartz, Hillel. *Never Satisfied: A Cultural History of Diets, Fantasies, and Fat.* New York: Free Press, 1986.

ELISABETH TOWNSEND

Breakfast Foods

A twenty-first-century American might find a typical Pilgrim breakfast of cider, cornmeal mush, and maple syrup a bit spartan, but it would be recognizable. However, to a Pilgrim, a twenty-first-century breakfast of corn flakes with sliced banana, a toaster pastry, and a glass of orange juice would be almost incomprehensible. How we went from one to the other is the story of breakfast in America. And like the stories of many American foods, it involves a new continent, a mixture of scientific discoveries, vast waves of immigration from around the globe, with the addition of the Industrial Revolution and the American propensity for advertising and marketing.

Breakfast Food. Advertising flier issued by the Shredded Wheat Co., Niagara Falls, New York, 1916. *Collection of Andrew F. Smith*

The First Colonists

When the first colonists arrived in the New World from Europe, one of the things they quickly discovered was that the foods they were used to were no longer available. Wheat for bread and porridge was difficult to grow. The pigs and hens that might provide breakfast meats and eggs were scarce. Milk cows were few and far between. Coffee and tea were simply too expensive and exotic to be imported. What the colonists did find in the new land was a new grain: Indian corn, or maize. And though at first they longed for their Old World wheat, they found that maize could be baked into bread, cooked into porridge, and prepared in many new ways, demonstrating that maize not only staved off hunger, it was also an appealing food.

The Native Americans showed the colonists not only how to grow the corn but also how to prepare it and grind it, how to cook it into cakes and pones, and how to stew it into what the Europeans had called porridge but which became known by the American term "mush." Cornmeal mixed with water and a little salt and cooked into cakes or into mush was a typical breakfast throughout the early settlements. When fat was available, pieces of mush could be fried to an appealing crispness. As soon as the colonists had sweeteners—once they learned how to extract syrup from maple trees and once the beehives imported from Europe were producing honey—they used them to add interest and calories to their corn-based preparations.

In the new American colonies, the breakfast drink of choice for most was either hard cider or low-alcohol beer. Although the idea of starting the day with an alcoholic drink seems strange to us, at that time it made a great deal of sense: water contained no nutrients and was very often polluted; milk was considered a drink only for babies; and coffee and tea were expensive or nonexistent. But hard cider and beer, if drunk in moderation, were not high enough in alcohol content to be debilitating. They were cheap to make from easily available ingredients and, because of their natural yeasts and ferments, were rich in essential nutrients.

Early New England

As the colonies took hold and grew richer, the diets of the colonists improved and expanded. In New England, cornmeal mush—known as hasty pudding—was still popular, served with maple syrup or, later, with molasses. But with prosperity, the colonists added coffee and tea to their breakfasts. Breads, meat, and fruit pies became part of the breakfast menu as well. The breads were often cornmeal mixed with other grains, such as "rye 'n' injun" (hearth-baked corn-and-rye bread) or brown bread (steamed bread made with rye, corn, and wheat). The meat was likely to be salt pork. Exactly why fruit pies came to be such popular breakfast items in early American life has never been studied, but the answers are not difficult to guess: a pie made the day before could sit overnight without spoiling and was readily available to eat upon demand in the morning, with no further cooking. It was filling and relatively nutritious—containing fruit, sweetener, fat, and grain—and it tasted good. Breakfast in New England was typically an early affair, partaken when the farmers rose to begin their chores.

Early South

In the southern colonies, the settlers added tea and coffee to their cornmeal breakfasts, rounding them out more luxuriously than their northern cousins with eggs, meats, fruit, breads, and cheese. As slavery and the plantation system grew, the difference between northern and southern eating habits grew as well. The southern plantation owner would rise early to survey his holdings, perhaps breaking his fast with a julep—because the drink was supposed to protect against malaria—but his first real meal would be eaten later in the morning. With servants or slaves to help with the cooking, the southern kitchen became famous for its breakfasts: grits lavishly dappled with butter, succulent pieces of fried ham and redeye gravy, spoon bread or hominy soufflé, eggs and toast, grilled chicken or game, fried shrimps or oysters, and as many different types of sweet breads as the cook could imagine. When chocolate became known in the late 1700s, the expensive hot drink became another part of the sumptuous feast.

While the New England colonies had been settled by Protestants from England, whose frugal attitudes were reflected in their foods, the southern colonies were settled by widely differing groups. There the English colonists were often from wealthy families, and they proudly tried to duplicate the hunt breakfasts and landed-gentry style of the old country. Protestant refugees from France, known as Huguenots, also settled the area, adding a French touch to the emerging local cooking. Slaves from Africa and the West Indies not only added more elements to the southern cuisine, they provided leisure time for the slave owners to enjoy lavish meals.

Early Mid-Atlantic Region

In the Mid-Atlantic colonies the early settlers were the common-sense, middle-class Dutch and Swedes, followed by English settlers, who tended to be much more moderate than their northern neighbors and more middle class than their southern counterparts. The English colonists welcomed settlers from other lands, and soon the Mid-Atlantic areas filled up with Welsh, Irish, and Germans. Like their neighbors north and south, this very practical group of people ate cornmeal mush and cornbreads washed down with beer or cider, but they also brought with them a number of new foods that became identified with American breakfasts. The best known of these foods was the Dutch waffle.

Although in Europe waffles were primarily a dessert and feast food—dusted with powdered sugar or lavished with whipped cream—in America they were treated like many other quick breads and were served for breakfast garnished with syrup, either maple or the molasses that was appearing as a result of the slave trade in the West Indies. Waffles also became popular as a sort of bread, served topped with creamed items such as chicken or chipped beef.

Oliebollen (oil balls)—doughnuts without the hole—were another Dutch food that became common Mid-Atlantic breakfast fare. The New England doughnut with the hole in the middle was the one that became a regular part of American breakfasts, but some theorists believe that the Pilgrim settlers became fond of doughnuts during their stay in Holland and brought them to the New World. Dutch cooks also introduced deep-fried crullers sprinkled with powdered sugar.

Buckwheat pancakes were popular in the middle Atlantic region as well as in New England. Traditionally, they were made with a slightly sour yeast starter, and the batter had to be mixed at least twenty-four hours before the pancakes were cooked. Because the pancakes were considered heating to the system and the buckwheat grain was not harvested until late in the year, raised buckwheat pancakes were a winter breakfast dish. They were enormously popular throughout the United States in the eighteenth and nineteenth centuries, so much so that the English traveler George Makepeace Towle said in 1870, "It is hard for the American to rise from his winter breakfast without his buckwheat cakes" (Mariani, 1983). However, by the middle of the twentieth century buckwheat cakes had become something of an anachronism.

Breakfast in the Developing Nation

As the colonies developed into a nation, immigrants continued to enrich the American breakfast table. The Moravians settled in Pennsylvania, Georgia, and North Carolina, bringing with them a sweet, yeast-raised coffee cake, known as Moravian sugar cake. In Philadelphia, where Ben Franklin was defending the American breakfast of coffee and corn cakes to mocking Englishmen, the yeast-raised Philadelphia sticky—or cinnamon—bun, a specialty of the Swiss and Germans, became a breakfast staple.

In the South, the breakfast tradition of lavish hot breads continued. Beaten biscuits—so called because the dough was literally beaten with a rolling pin for thirty minutes or more—were the sure sign of a genteel, and slave-filled, kitchen. With the advent of chemical leavens at the end of the 1700s, the popularity of quick breads accelerated. Biscuits, pancakes, and waffles (which had formerly been raised with either yeast or beaten egg whites), chemically raised cornbreads, and cakes all became popular breakfast fare.

When Louisiana became part of the growing country in 1803, another rich contribution was made to the breakfast table. With its exotic mix of French, Indian, Spanish, French Acadians (or Cajuns), and free and enslaved Africans, Louisiana's unique cuisine gave us French doughnuts, or beignets; *calas* (deep fried rice cakes dusted with powdered sugar); and *pain perdu* (French toast), all served up with Louisiana-style café au lait enriched with bitter chicory. The Louisiana breakfast table was also likely to feature pork sausage, grits and grillades (braised beef or veal with gravy), biscuits, and eggs. Another interesting dish was called *coush coush*, a kind of cornmeal mush enriched with eggs and served with molasses.

To visiting Europeans, the lavish American breakfasts were quite startling. One Scotsman reported on a visit he made to a humble backwoods home in the United States in 1811:

> "Have you any eggs?" said I. "Yes, plenty," replied she. . . . "Well," said I, "just boil an egg, and let me have it, with a little bread and tea, and that will save you and I a great deal of trouble." She seemed quite embarrassed, and said she never could set down a breakfast to me like that. . . . She detained me about half an hour, and at last placed upon the table a profusion of ham, eggs, fritters, bread, butter and some excellent tea. (Melish, John, *Travels in the United States of America* [1811], quoted in Mariani [1983])

Breakfast in the Old West

As restless Americans and newcomers moved west, away from the Eastern Seaboard, new challenges and new situations helped to develop new foods. Bishop's bread, a kind of crumb coffee cake, was supposed to have been invented on the Kentucky frontier one Sunday morning when the circuit preacher dropped in unexpectedly for breakfast (although a similarly named sweet bread existed in Europe). But not everything was as appetizing as bishop's bread. The Englishman Sir Richard Burton commented on a meal he was served in pioneer Nebraska:

> Our breakfast was prepared in the usual prairie style: First the coffee—three parts burnt beans—which had been duly ground to a fine powder and exposed to the air, lest the aroma should prove too strong for us. . . . Then the rusty bacon, cut into thick slices, was thrown in the fry-pan. . . . Thirdly, antelope steak, cut off a corpse suspended for the benefit of flies outside, was placed to stew within influence of the bacon's aroma. Lastly came the bread, which of course should have been cooked *first*. (Graber, 1974)

Not all prairie breakfasts were as dismal as Burton's, of course, but pioneering offered many challenges to the cook. Coffee was scarce and expensive, so substitutes such as parched corn, carrots, or okra were used. At first, wheat would not grow, so corn again became the primary grain. Corn mush or hasty pudding was common, and the leftovers were fried and served with sweetener of some sort. Cornmeal and pork scrapple also became a typical breakfast item. Molasses and honey were difficult to obtain, but pioneer cooks devised a type of syrup from corncobs, and some enterprising (or desperate) cooks even boiled down watermelon or pumpkin juice to make syrup for breakfast. Fresh fruit was hard to find on the trail west, but dried apples were plentiful, so dried apple pies became standard breakfast fare in the Midwest during the 1800s. Butter was scarce, but Native Americans taught the settlers to make butter from crushed green hickory nuts to spread on their corn bread.

Most of the new immigrants moving into the newly opened West were northern and middle Europeans from Germany, Austria, Switzerland, Bavaria, and Bohemia and, a little later, Scandinavians from Sweden, Norway, and Denmark. These countries all had strong baking traditions, and the immigrants brought those traditions to their new land. As the western territories were settled and the homesteads began to prosper, these cooks produced Swedish coffee cakes; Danish pastries; Austrian apple strudels; Bohemian *kolaches* (little pastry turnovers) filled with apples, prunes, poppy seeds, or cheese; Alsatian sour-cream cakes; Czech potato pancakes; and German puffed pancakes (*Pfannekuchen*) and jelly-filled doughnuts (also called Bismarcks).

Pork was a favorite meat in the new territories, but fish was often eaten for breakfast as well. Fresh-caught trout, rolled in cornmeal and fried to a turn in bacon fat, was a western trail item that found a permanent home in the new territories. Creamed salt or smoked fish—particularly cod or mackerel—was also popular, the creamy savory gravy being a perfect complement to bland potatoes or crisp toast.

In Texas and Oklahoma, beef was often the most commonly available meat, but in the 1800s beef came from tough, range-fed, and driven cattle. Chicken-fried steak—a leathery piece of beef that has been pounded to tenderness and then dredged in seasoned flour and fried like chicken—was the creative cook's answer to that problem. Served with coffee, cream gravy, and biscuits or potatoes, chicken-fried steak made a filling, if slightly indigestible, breakfast.

Land of Plenty

The rich land and prosperous farms gave Americans the wherewithal to make huge breakfasts, the only limit being the cook's imagination. With wheat joining corn as a widespread crop, with cows and their cream and butter plentiful, with chickens laying endless supplies of eggs, and with sugar becoming inexpensive enough to join honey, maple syrup, and molasses as a sweetener, cooks had at hand everything they needed for producing bounteous meals. They rose to the challenge.

Breakfast breads seemed to come pouring out of American ovens. Sally Lunn—a sweet, cakelike, yeast bread—was very popular, as were other sweetened breads made with yeast doughs, such as cinnamon rolls and sticky buns. Toast, of course, was common, but it was served not just spread with butter and preserves but also as milk toast (hot buttered toast dipped in hot milk) or even what was called buttered toast—which meant toasted bread dipped in a sort of butter gravy. Bread could also be made into French toast or Mennonite toast (deep-fried French toast).

Biscuits were popular throughout the United States, some made with sour milk and soda and others with sweet milk and baking powder. They were as likely to be served with butter and preserves as they were to be split and covered with creamed chipped beef, a northern specialty, or fried chicken with gravy in the South. Beaten biscuits continued to find favor in the South, where there were slaves or servants, and biscuits enriched with sweet potato were also common.

At first, "muffins" meant what we call English muffins—yeast bread cooked in a ring on a griddle before being split and toasted. The sweet, cupcakelike quick bread we know as muffins were called "gems" in the 1800s—although, confusingly enough, gems could also be a sort of eggless popover. Gems or muffins offered endless opportunities for variation to the cook and were made with blueberries or cranberries in New England and enriched with cornmeal or whole-wheat flour in the Midwest or huckleberries in the Northwest. Popovers—a sort of individual Yorkshire pudding—usually served with butter and preserves, seem to have made their appearance in the mid-1800s.

Waffles and pancakes of every stripe were made, but except for yeast-raised buckwheat pancakes, most were leavened with egg white, soda, or baking powder, earning them quick-bread status. In the 1800s, waffles and pancakes were much more prevalent than they were in later years and were ready vehicles for the creative cook's talents. Rice and cornmeal were frequently used to make them up, as were bread crumbs that had been soaked overnight in buttermilk. An interesting recipe for snow pancakes was fairly familiar in northern climates—freshly fallen snow took the place of eggs in the batter, using the air trapped in the snow crystals to leaven the dough. Snow fritters, deep-fried batter made with snow, were also enjoyed, as were fritters made with everything from apples to tomatoes to corn to oysters. Some cooks served sweet fritters dusted with powdered sugar, while others passed syrup or molasses and butter.

To go along with the hot breads, hearty meats were served. Bacon, salt pork, sausages, and ham were perhaps the most widely eaten breakfast meats, but there were others, depending on the region of the country, that graced the breakfast table: in New England, corned beef hash or codfish balls; in the Mid-Atlantic region, creamed chipped beef or a Porterhouse steak; in the South, fried chicken or chicken hash; and in the Midwest and West, pan-fried fish, broiled oysters, liver and bacon, or lamb chops.

To top it all off, a few eggs (sunny-side up, over easy, scrambled, or soft- or hard-boiled), potatoes in many different guises (sometimes boiled, but often hashed), fruit in compotes or in sparkling jellies or preserves, and even a mild vegetable or two, along with pies or doughnuts and, in many places, cookies, would make a hearty meal. Coffee, tea, or hot chocolate would round out the repast.

Land of Plenty . . . of Stomachaches

When most of the population was performing heavy labor on farms, the huge breakfasts that Americans consumed made some sense. But as people moved into the city and took up a more sedentary life, yet still ate as though they were working on the farm, there was trouble. It was no wonder that dyspepsia became one of the most common complaints of the 1800s. To the rescue of suffering dyspeptics came Sylvester Graham, who had learned about the gastric benefits of whole wheat from the Shakers. Graham's work made what would come to be known as "Graham" flour a common item in the nineteenth-century pantry. Although graham crackers would be his most lasting contribution, Graham gems, Graham muffins, and Graham bread made with his flour all became common breakfast fare in the 1800s.

Graham crackers and apples made up the breakfast diet of John Harvey Kellogg before he took over the new Seventh-Day Adventist sanitarium in Battle Creek, Michigan, in 1876. At first, the "San," as it was called, served porridge, milk toast, and boiled rice for breakfast, but Dr. Kellogg was anxious to find something that would be quick to prepare and would vary the patients' diet. His first invention was called Granula and consisted of twice-baked graham cracker nuggets that had to be soaked in milk overnight to make them edible. Next came the real breakthrough: Dr. Kellogg and his brother, Will Keith Kellogg, had the idea of running softened boiled wheat through a rolling machine and then baking the flattened product. The result was the first flake cereal. The Kellogg Company marketed its first Toasted Corn Flakes in 1906, the foundation for what would become the largest manufacturer of ready-to-eat cereals in the world.

One of Dr. Kellogg's patients at the San was Charles William Post—who became convinced that healthy breakfast foods could make him rich. After leaving the sanitarium, he set up business in Battle Creek, where he developed an ersatz coffee based on toasted wheat and molasses, not unlike the "coffees" used by the pioneers, which he called Postum. Following Postum's success as a noncaffeinated alternative to coffee, Post tried again with another grain beverage. Although Grape-Nuts did not take off as a coffee substitute, it was a huge hit as a breakfast cereal.

With Post and Kellogg making big profits, other cereal entrepreneurs tried their hands as well, many of them moving into Battle Creek for the magic of the name. One of them came up with a celery-flavored hot cereal called Tryabita which, needless to say, failed. Still, many others did not, and the American breakfast table was changed forever.

Manufactured Food

At the close of the 1800s, a combination of events was taking place that would bring industry into the kitchen, especially to the breakfast kitchen. The Industrial Revolution had made factories and factory life a commonplace; transcontinental railroads transported factory products coast to coast; although many Americans still lived on farms, the cities were beginning to take over as population centers; the United States Department of Agriculture and the home economics movement were promoting scientific cooking as the cleanest and the best; and women were just starting to work outside the home. The race was on to find the products that would simplify the American woman's life, while giving her family quick, nutritious meals.

Kellogg and Post, of course, offered their ready-to-eat cereals, but they were by no means the only bringers of change. In 1889, Aunt Jemima pancake mix went on the market, only a year after Log Cabin syrup was first sold. The Quaker Oats Company started selling their breakfast oats in 1891, followed two years later by the first box of Cream of Wheat. Industry came even more

Manufacturing Breakfast Foods. Labeling and inspecting at the Quaker Oats Factory, Cedar Rapids, Iowa, mid-twentieth century. *Prints and Photographs Division, Library of Congress/Theodor Horydczak*

visibly to the breakfast table in the form of the electric toaster in 1908 and the mechanical refrigerator—which could keep cold the additional milk that families were using as an unintended side effect of increased cereal consumption—in 1918.

The march of new products continued, with malt-flavored Malt-O-Meal hot cereal in 1919 and the first packaged, sliced bacon in 1924. Wheaties, the "Breakfast of Champions," also was introduced in 1924, followed in 1928 by Rice Krispies, which made noises described as "snap, crackle, pop," and, in 1930, by two biscuit mixes, Jiffy and Bisquick. The latter two were considered almost miracle products by many cooks, who could whip up biscuits, pancakes, waffles, coffee cakes, and muffins with little fuss and at the drop of a hat.

Exotic imported bananas had been the rage—for breakfast as well as for other meals—in the 1890s, but canned fruits became popular at the end of the century as well, with canned pineapple becoming particularly fashionable in the 1920s. Fruit juices had never been particularly appreciated, at breakfast or any other time, but with the rising popularity of canning, the interest in healthful foods and in the newly discovered vitamins, and, strangely enough, the advent of Prohibition in 1920, canned fruit juice came to be considered an elegant addition to the breakfast table. One of the most common of the juices was grape, which was sold "as is" by desperate vineyards that could no longer sell wine. Sunsweet prune juice and tomato-based V8 both debuted in 1933, just as Prohibition was ending—but by then Americans had become used to drinking fruit juices at all times during the day as a substitute for alcoholic drinks. The crowning achievement, of course, in fruit juice history and perhaps a defining moment in the American breakfast came with the development of frozen orange juice after World War II.

New Immigrants—From Breakfast Doughnut to Breakfast Bagel

Industrialization and the move to cities were not the only things changing the face of American breakfast habits. The new immigrants flooding into the country in the early part of the twentieth century were having a profound impact as well. Bagels and blintzes were two breakfast staples contributed by Eastern European Jews; though, at first, these items would be most associated with New York City, by the latter half of the twentieth century both would be thoroughly Americanized. Bagels with lox (a type of smoked salmon) and cream cheese was a deli-

cious and original combination developed by American Jews in New York City, according to *The Dictionary of American Food and Drink.* Frozen bagels made by large agribusinesses are available across the country, but bagel connoisseurs agree that nothing beats a freshly made bagel from the corner deli.

Blintzes are less common than bagels, but these thin pancakes wrapped around a cheese filling and usually garnished with fruit compote were popular enough that they became a regular breakfast item at such chains as International House of Pancakes and Denny's. Challah bread and potato pancakes (latkes) are two other Jewish specialties that have become part of the American breakfast table.

On the West Coast, Chinese cooks made the egg-vegetable cakes known as egg foo yong a popular breakfast dish. Later in the twentieth century, the Chinese restaurant breakfast and brunch specialties known as dim sum became extremely fashionable. The Italian omelet called the frittata, also made with vegetables, became another West Coast specialty, particularly in San Francisco. An Italian savory bread pudding, called cheese strata, started turning up in community cookbooks all through the 1960s and 1970s.

Throughout the Southwest, rancher-style eggs, or huevos rancheros, became a standard breakfast dish, usually served with refried beans and tortillas. The Denver omelet—an omelet folded over a mix of ham and peppers—became a breakfast staple as well, and it, like blintzes, was soon found on chain-restaurant breakfast menus. The Mexican influence in the Southwest was also felt with the introduction of the breakfast burrito—a

---

AVENA

"Avena" means "oats" in both Latin and Spanish. It is also the name of a gruel consumed as a breakfast drink in Latin America and by Latinos in the United States. Rolled oats or oat flour is steeped or boiled in milk, fruit juice, or water and often sweetened with sugar or honey. Crushed fruit and spices, especially cinnamon, may be added. The drink is served either hot or cold in the same manner as corn-based *atole* and pinole, which have been staples in the Central American diet since before the introduction of oats from Europe.

ROBERT SIMMONS

tortilla wrapped around eggs, salsa, sausages, chiles, and other garnishes. For many years this dish was confined to the Southwest, but it has become popular as far away as New York City.

There is a great deal of controversy over who introduced one of the most enduringly popular of twentieth-century breakfast items, eggs Benedict. Whether it was the Creoles of New Orleans or restaurateurs in New York City, the dish has been a standard for fancy breakfasts for nearly one hundred years, as well as a constant at brunch.

Modern Breakfast Tables

If the end of the 1800s signaled a new era in the American breakfast, with the invention of ready-to-eat packaged cereals, the 1960s heralded the modern age with a vengeance. The decade opened with a bang with the release of Coffee Rich, an instant nondairy creamer, followed by the competing brands Coffee-mate and Cremora, all of which were perfect to stir into the instant coffee that became so popular after World War II. In 1964 Kellogg introduced Pop-Tarts, the first successful toaster pastry (Post had tried six months earlier with Country Squares, which failed). And in 1965 the space age orange juice substitute Tang took the kid's breakfast market by storm, accompanied that same year by the breakfast-in-a-glass drink for young moderns in a hurry: Carnation Instant Breakfast. Suddenly a complete—or at least filling—breakfast could be assembled from packaged products, with no work or dirty dishes.

Restaurants were quick to notice this hurry-up trend in American breakfasts. Both the International House of Pancakes and the southern chain, the Waffle House, got their start in the mid-1950s, specializing in breakfast served any time of the day. In the mid-twentieth century, diners and truck stops—located near the newly built highways and freeways—served dishes like "Adam and Eve on a raft with some joe" (poached eggs on toast with coffee) to the thousands of Americans on the move. Breakfast "on the go" got a boost when 7-Eleven stores started selling takeout coffee in 1964, along with a variety of packaged coffee cakes and sweet breads. The 7-Eleven model was so effective that gas station mini-marts were soon catering to the traveler with little time to stop for a restaurant breakfast, with coffee, packaged donuts, Danish pastries, and coffee cakes. McDonald's restaurants, the ubiquitous purveyors of lunchtime and dinnertime hamburgers, decided to offer three meals a day with the introduction of the Egg McMuffin in 1972. In a move to catch up to McDonald's, which has average annual breakfast sales of more than $400,000 per store, Burger King experimented with offering hamburgers for breakfast, with a resultant rise in their breakfast sales of 4 to 7 percent.

Another modern breakfast trend has been for super-sweet cereals. During the 1940s, cereal companies introduced a few mildly sweetened cereals aimed squarely at the children's market, but that push accelerated greatly in the 1950s, particularly with the advent of children's television programming and its accompanying commercials. Kellogg introduced Frosted Flakes in 1952 and Fruit Loops in 1963, General Mills gave us chocolate-flavored Cocoa Puffs in 1958, and Post brought Fruity Pebbles and Cocoa Pebbles to the market in 1971, both tie-ins with *The Flintstones* cartoon program. Each year it seemed as though children's cereals became sweeter, so that by the time Post debuted Oreo O's in 1998 many cereals hardly seemed to be food any longer, but were simple sugary snacks.

There was some rebellion against the highly sugared breakfast offerings of the big companies, particularly in the 1960s, with the advent of a strong organic health food movement. Whole-grain granolas became popular during this period, and in the early 1970s a number of natural bakeries, including Barbara's in California, started producing alternative cereals and baked goods. Ironically, one of the health food movements' biggest sellers was the granola bar. Kellogg and General Mills picked up on that trend very quickly and were soon selling their own brands of cereal bars, promoted as the perfect breakfast on the go. In 2000, General Mills introduced perhaps the ultimate quick-breakfast item (short of a pill)—the Milk 'n Cereal Bar, which was billed as just as good and nutritious as a real bowl of cereal with milk. It has been a huge hit. Technology has also given us microwaveable instant hot cereal, some already in its own plastic breakfast cup. Cold cereal in a cup is also available in a refrigerated cereal kit, which includes cereal in a plastic bowl with a container of milk and a plastic spoon.

The American breakfast table has indeed changed in the nearly four hundred years since the Pilgrims first landed. Many Americans eat no breakfast at all, while others have a quick breakfast of cereal, coffee, and perhaps fruit. The growing numbers of people who are too pressed for time to fix a sit-down breakfast instead fuel up on instant convenience foods. The lavish breakfasts of the 1700s and 1800s have been almost completely relegated to special occasions or to rare, leisurely brunches.

[See also Aunt Jemima; Bagels; Breakfast Drinks; Cereal, Cold; Doughnuts; Dutch Influences on American Food; Fruit Juices; Kellogg Company; Maple Syrup; Orange Juice; Post Foods; Puddings, sidebar on Hasty Pudding; Sally Lunn; Scrapple; Tang; Waffle, Wafer, and Pizelle Irons.]

BIBLIOGRAPHY

Graber, Kay, ed. *Nebraska Pioneer Cookbook*. Lincoln: University of Nebraska Press, 1974. A compilation of nineteenth-century sources.

Jones, Evan. *American Food: The Gastronomic Story*. Woodstock, NY: Overlook Press, 1990.

Mariani, John F. *The Dictionary of American Food and Drink*. New Haven, CT: Ticknor and Fields, 1983. An essential resource.

Smith, Andrew, ed. *Centennial Buckeye Cook Book*. Columbus: Ohio State University Press, 2000. Reprint of the 1876 cookbook.

Weaver, William Woys. *Pennsylvania Dutch Country Cooking*. New York: Abbeville Press, 1993. Fascinating overview of Pennsylvania German cooking and history.

Weaver, William Woys. *Sauerkraut Yankees: Pennsylvania Dutch Foods and Foodways*. Mechanicsburg, PA: Stackpole Books, 2002. A look at the foodways of early Pennsylvania Germans.

SYLVIA LOVEGREN

Brewing

Fermentation happens when yeast attacks a solution of sugar dissolved in water. Yeast eats sugar, gives off alcohol and carbon dioxide, and creates chemicals called esters, which are volatile flavor compounds. Being volatile means that esters evaporate easily and, in doing so, make themselves available to the sense of smell. Esters derive from the combination of organic acids and the alcohols formed during fermentation. Most of the fruity aromas of beer (and, indeed, many of the fruity aromas of fruit) come from esters. In bread making, the alcohol evaporates during baking; in wine making, the carbon dioxide is released into the air; and in beer making, both products are preserved.

Barley is starchy, and before it can be fermented, the starch has to be converted to sugar. The conversion involves a bit of deception. First, the grain is warmed and dampened. In an environment that mimics spring, the barley sprouts. This sprouting, or "malting," as it is known in the trade, converts the barley's hard starch into a soft, soluble one. It also develops useful enzymes. These sprouts are then baked, and the heat of baking kills the sprout. A short, cool kilning makes pale, light-flavored malt; longer, hotter roasting adds a toasty flavor and darker color to the grain.

To convert the soft starch to fermentable sugar, the roasted grain is then crushed and soaked in water, and the water is heated to about 150°F in a process called "mashing," which occurs in huge copper kettles called "mash tuns." The heating activates enzymes that make vitamins for the yeast and contribute to the beer's head. It also kick-starts the enzymes that will convert the soft starch into fermentable sugar. The fermentable sugar dissolves into the hot water.

This sugary water, called "wort," is moved to a new kettle and boiled with hop flowers. The hop plant grows all over the beer-making world in dozens of different varieties. Hops may be added at any time after the boil is complete, in a process called dry-hopping. The hops in the boiling beer contribute bitterness through the extraction of alpha acids and also act as a preservative. The cooler temperatures preserve the aroma of the hops without extracting any more alpha acids. Each variety of hops has a distinctive aroma and capacity to impart bitterness, and a beer may contain more than one kind of hops. The wort is then cooled, inoculated with yeast, and fermented.

All these various choices in the brewing create different recipes of beer. If a wine's flavor is the product of the soil and climate where the grape is grown, a beer's flavor is the product of its recipe. Some of these recipes are very similar to one another, and among the cognoscenti these families of recipes and their beers are each called a beer style. Beer styles commonly produced in the United States include lagers, pilsners, pale ales, and stouts.

[See also Barley; Beer; Beer, Corn and Maple; Yeast.]

LYNN HOFFMAN

Bridge Luncheon Food

Although the roots of the card game of bridge go back at least to the early sixteenth century, the game itself, a variant of whist, did not come into being until the end of the nineteenth century. When and by whom the first bridge luncheon was given is not known, but it is probable that bridge's rapid rise in popularity at the turn of the twentieth century, in combination with the emerging club movement, made it a natural way for a middle-class woman to entertain her female friends.

One of the earliest mentions of a luncheon featuring bridge occurred in Mary E. Wilkins Freeman's *The Winning Lady*, published in 1909. By 1922 Emily Post's

Etiquette included advice on how long a guest was expected to stay at a bridge luncheon. Since bridge luncheons were almost always strictly feminine affairs, the food and drink tended to be light and dainty. A typical menu from a 1933 cookbook was cream of mushroom soup, frozen cheese salad with fruit mayonnaise, pocket rolls or ginger muffins, coconut cake or cherry angel food, coffee, and chocolate peppermints. The book noted "a smart bridge luncheon may be served easily" on the card tables (*All About Home Baking*, 1933). Some hostesses served small sandwiches, biscuits, or cookies cut out in club, heart, diamond, or spade shapes, while others had special sets of table linens decorated in card-suit themes or even similarly decorated bridge luncheon plate-and-cup sets designed to fit comfortably around the small tables. Manufacturers also obliged the hostess with bridge mix, candy, and nut assortments, in this period.

By the end of the 1990s, bridge luncheons were perhaps not as ubiquitous as they had been from the 1920s to the 1960s, owing to the card game's declining popularity and the rise in the numbers of women working outside the home, yet they could still be a popular way to entertain. A 2002 symphony orchestra bridge luncheon fund-raiser featured an updated menu of wild mushroom tartlets, roasted red pepper soup, lobster salad with mini-croissants, pear tart, and champagne cocktails.

[*See also* Gender Roles.]

BIBLIOGRAPHY

Adams, Joan. *Foodarama Party Book.* New York: Kelvinator Institute, 1959. Distributed by E. P. Dutton.

Editors, General Foods Corporation. *All About Home Baking.* New York: General Foods Corporation, 1933. A fascinating look at middle-class entertaining and cooking.

MacDougall, Alice Foote. *Coffee and Waffles.* Garden City, NY: Doubleday, Page & Co., 1926. Contains a large section of seasonal bridge luncheon menus and recipes.

SYLVIA LOVEGREN

Broccoli

Broccoli is paradoxical. It is identified in American consumer surveys as the vegetable most often eaten to promote good health, yet it is these same protective factors (particularly glucosinolates) that make broccoli bitter tasting and widely disliked. Unopened flower heads on thick stalks form broccoli (*Brassica oleracea*), which is botanically undifferentiated from cauliflower and is similar to

cabbage sprouts. It is also related to brussels sprouts, turnips, and other cool-weather vegetables, all members of the Cruciferae family. Although its origins are lost to history, broccoli has long been associated with Italy. It was prized by the Romans, and the term "broccoli" is derived from the Italian word *brocco*, meaning "little branches." The sprouting type, often called Italian broccoli, is most common, though a strain with a cauliflower-like head is also available.

Colonists introduced broccoli to the United States in the early eighteenth century. It was mentioned in *A Treatise on Gardening by a Citizen of Virginia*, written by a Williamsburg resident, John Randolph, around 1765. Broccoli was also planted in Thomas Jefferson's garden at Monticello. Recipes for broccoli appear in a number of cookbooks found in America in the eighteenth and nineteenth centuries, such as Hannah Glasse's *The Art of Cookery Made Plain and Easy* (both in the original 1747 English edition and the 1805 American edition). Lettice Bryan's *Kentucky Housewife* (1839) contains recipes for both sprouting and head broccoli. Broccoli did not gain widespread availability, however, until the 1920s, when the first commercial crops were grown by Italian immigrants in California.

The popularity of broccoli increased in the late 1970s, when the health benefits of cruciferous vegetables were reported. An excellent source of vitamin C, beta-carotene, folate, potassium, calcium, and dietary fiber, broccoli also contains numerous phytochemicals, such as sulforaphane, which are considered potent cancer-fighting compounds. American broccoli consumption rose by more than 900 percent in the last quarter of the twentieth century, nearing eight pounds per person annually.

[*See also* Vegetables.]

BIBLIOGRAPHY

Drewnowski, Adam, and Carmen Gomez-Carneros. "Bitter Taste, Phytonutrients, and the Consumer: A Review." *American Journal of Clinical Nutrition* 72 (2000): 1424–1435.

Lucer, Gary. "Broccoli: Super Food for All Seasons." *Economic Research Service USDA Agricultural Outlook* (April 1999): 8–12.

PAMELA GOYAN KITTLER

Brown, Helen Evans

Helen Evans Brown (1904–1964) was an internationally known food expert and a prolific author not only of magazine articles, some as contributing editor to *Sunset Magazine*, but also of cookbooks. Helen Brown's most stunning literary achievement was the classic book on Pacific coast food, *West Coast Cook Book* (1952). *West Coast Cook Book* documented and collected the best recipes of the Pacific states and employed tools not widely used in food writing at that time: historical detail, bibliographic reference, and social commentary. The book awakened Americans to the rich bounty of the Pacific coast and bridged the gap between the earlier chatty, nonscholarly voice in such American cookery books as *Joy of Cooking* (1931) and the later, more authoritative voice heard in books like James Beard's *American Cookery* (1972).

Helen Brown's reputation as a cooking and food expert dated from the middle 1930s. The excellent food and hospitality of her Pasadena home attracted publishers, authors, and food experts from all over the world. Brown's husband, Philip, a rare-book dealer, acted as her typist, taster, and editor. He was also the librarian who built her extensive and eventually famous culinary library.

At the height of her career, Brown was known to New York foodies as "the West Coast food establishment." She was a well-connected member of the food community. Her professional associations included Julia Child, Albert Stockli, Craig Claiborne, and Helen McCully, but Brown's most famous associate was James Beard. Beard and Brown formed a friendship when he wrote her a fan letter after reading *West Coast Cook Book*. The two had a lifelong association. They wrote each other twice weekly about matters culinary and otherwise, took trips together to enjoy food, and spent evenings at the Brown house socializing over food and cookbooks. Brown's name appears in the dedication to Beard's treatise *American Cookery*, and they cowrote a book on outdoor cookery. Brown was an assertive, intelligent woman who shared Beard's enthusiasm for American cuisine. Beard was deeply attached to her. She functioned somewhat as an older sister. She was unerringly supportive in his professional endeavors and was concerned especially about his health and professional reputation. Hers was the voice of reason he would listen to. The two of them championed the burgeoning reputation of American regional cuisine until Brown died suddenly in 1964, her life cut short by cancer.

[*See also* Beard, James; California; Pacific Northwest Regional Cookery.]

BIBLIOGRAPHY

Beard, James. *Love and Kisses and a Halo of Truffles: Letters to Helen Evans Brown*. Edited by John Ferrone. New York: Arcade, 1994.

JANET JARVITS

Brownies

Brownies are bar cookies, usually chocolate, baked in square or rectangular cake pans. Although in the early 2000s some brownies seemed as rich and dense as fallen chocolate cakes, the original brownie recipes by Fannie Farmer were based on her cookie recipes, and she initially baked them in fluted marguerite molds or "small, shallow, fancy cake tins" as individual cakes. The original brownies had no leavening, except for an egg or two, and little flour, but were so rich with butter and melted chocolate that they baked up softer than other cookies, a distinction that is sometimes lost among the many soft or underbaked cookies of the twenty-first century. Fannie Farmer's first brownie recipe, published in 1896, produced a confection that was colored and flavored with molasses. Each brownie had a nut placed at its center. All early brownies contained chopped nuts as well.

Brownies took their name from the mobs of nocturnal "little people," or Brownies, who were the subjects of Palmer Cox's cartoons and poems, which began appearing in the early 1880s. Cox's Brownies also inspired elf-shaped chocolate candies sold in the 1897 Sears catalog, an 1898 marble cake fiddled with straws (the cook used hay straws to pull the darker batter into lines) to make the image of an elf in every slice, and eventually Eastman Kodak's comparatively elfin portable cameras, as well as the younger level of the Girl Scouts called Brownie Scouts (1916).

The first chocolate brownie recipe was also published by Fannie Farmer in her 1905 revision of the *Boston Cooking-School Cook Book*. The proportions are similar to her 1896 chocolate cookie recipe, except that she radically reduced the amount of flour. In the chocolate recipe she specified a "7-inch square pan." As her assistant Janet M. Hill had remarked earlier of the molasses brownies, "The mixture is rather stiff, but spreads in baking." In fact, if you follow the 1907 directions of Maria Willett Howard [Hilliard] to "spread on buttered sheets and bake ten to fifteen minutes," the batter is apt to drip over the edge of the sheets.

Howard, who had been trained by Fannie Farmer, was then employed by the Walter Lowney chocolate company. She enriched Farmer's chocolate brownie recipe with an extra egg, creating Lowney's Brownies. She then varied the recipe by adding an extra square of chocolate and named them Bangor Brownies. This last recipe apparently started the idea that brownies had been invented by housewives in Bangor, Maine. The leading advocate of the Bangor theory of brownie origin was Mildred Brown Schrumpf, aptly nicknamed "Brownie," born in Bangor in 1903. Unfortunately, Mrs. Schrumpf's best piece of evidence that brownies began in Bangor was a *Girl's Welfare Cook Book* published there in 1912. This is not only seven years post-Farmer, but the recipe contributed by Marion Oliver for Chocolate Brownies to that cookbook is almost exactly the same as the two-egg recipe for Lowney's Brownies, not Bangor Brownies. Oliver also contributed a recipe for Molasses Brownies evidently taken from the Farmer cookbook. *The You-and-I Cook Book*, published in Bangor in 1905, has no brownies in it at all, although "A.M.T." provided a version of Fannie Farmer's chocolate cookies.

Maria Howard may have considered the Bangor Brownies, which were to be baked in a cake pan (unlike her Lowney's Brownies), to be descended from a recipe for Bangor Cake in Maria Parloa's *Appledore Cook Book* (1872), which was a white sheet cake. Another explanation for the myth that brownies began in Maine may be that "Bangor Brownies" was a mistake for "Brockton Brownies." The September 1906 *Brockton* [Mass.] *Hospital Cook Book* anticipates one of Howard's recipes. But the Brockton women's recipe used a second egg, as did Lowney's Brownies, whereas the Bangor Brownies used one egg, and three ounces of chocolate. And Brockton, then the shoe capital of New England, failed to produce a Brownie Schrumpf.

In fact, the two-egg Lowney's Brownies was the recipe most often reprinted in New England community cookbooks before 1912. It was renamed Brownies II in Cora Perkins's 1915 revision of the Fannie Farmer cookbook. In 1908, Maria Parloa, one of Farmer's teachers, developed a three-egg version with a little baking powder, called Fudge Squares, for Walter Baker and Company, a Boston chocolate manufacturer in competition with Lowney's. Ruth Wakefield slightly reduced the flour in her *Toll House Tried and True Recipes* (1936).

Molasses brownies persisted in commerce at least as late as the third edition in 1926 of *Baker's Weekly Recipes*, but chocolate and nuts endure as the basic brownie. Spices, raisins, and molasses were combined in an early Philadelphia hybrid recipe, but only tentatively were the nuts replaced by chocolate chips (first marketed in 1939), candies, or raisins. By the 1950s, butterscotch or vanilla brownies were described as "blonde brownies," underscoring the primacy of chocolate. Recipes were categorized as "fudgey" or "chewy," a difference produced mainly by fiddling with baking times and temperatures. "Cakey" brownies require more flour and leavening, such as the reaction of buttermilk and baking soda, or are made from commercial cake mixes with added butter and eggs.

Contemporary brownies vary considerably. One Internet site listed 569 different recipes in late 2003. Flavor variations include chocolate mint, white chocolate, mocha or coffee, peanut butter, raspberry truffle, and even ginger-chocolate. Mix-ins, beyond or replacing the original walnuts, include almonds, apricots, cherries, chocolate chips (or butterscotch or vanilla chips), coconut, currants, dates, hazelnuts, macadamia nuts, orange peel, peanuts, raisins, and candies, such as brickle bits, chocolate-covered espresso beans, Heath bars, miniature marshmallows, M&Ms, or whole Snickers bars.

Attempts to make brownies more healthful include substituting carob for cocoa; using applesauce, prune butter, bananas, pumpkin, or zucchini to replace butterfat; and mixing in fiber in the forms of bran, cornmeal, oatmeal, or raisins. Some recipes substitute honey or caramel candies for the sugar or brown sugar; James Beard tried maple syrup.

Modern nonchocolate variations include Amish apple brownies, "beige" or praline brownies (made with brown sugar), cinnamon (also added to chocolate), and carrot-bran. Common color contrasts are marble brownies (usually with vanilla cheesecake) or "black and white" brownies (often layered with coconut).

By analogy, any bar cookie with a chocolate layer can be described as a brownie, such as frosted brownies (sometimes vanilla frosting on chocolate or vice versa), and banana, orange, or vanilla cream brownies. Brownie recipes clearly not for children include Black Russian brownies made with vodka and coffee liqueur.

Perhaps the most extreme commercial variation is a brownie pizza promoted in the 1990s by Kraft foods. This is a round, thin brownie shell covered with sliced fruit like a fruit tart. The official illustration shows kiwi and strawberry slices—a long reach from Fannie Farmer's elfin cakes, each with its walnut half placed delicately at the center.

[*See also* Boston Cooking School; Chocolate; Cookies; Farmer, Fannie; Parloa, Maria.]

BIBLIOGRAPHY

Brockton Hospital Ladies' Aid Association. *The Brockton Hospital Cook Book*. Brockton, MA, 1906. Anticipates Howard's two-egg brownies by a few months.

Dennett, Mabel Freese, ed. *Girl's Welfare Cook Book: Containing Practical Recipes and Favorite Dishes*. Bangor, ME: Press of the Furbish Printing Company, 1912. First documented Bangor, Maine, brownies.

Farmer, Fannie Merritt. *The Boston Cooking-School Cook Book*. Boston: Little, Brown, 1896. A facsimile of the first edition by Hugh Lauter. Westport, CT: Levin Associates, 1996. First recipe for brownies.

Farmer, Fannie Merritt. *The Boston Cooking-School Cook Book*. Boston: Little, Brown, 1905. Addition of chocolate brownies.

Hill, Janet M. "Seasonable Recipes." *Boston Cooking School Magazine* 7, no. 9 (April 1904). Brownies or Marguerites illustrated with both individual tins and a molded sheet of twelve. Recipe same as Farmer's 1896 recipe with slightly more flour.

Howard, Maria Willett. *Lowney's Cook Book*. Boston: Walter M. Lowney, 1906. Farmer's former assistant produced two more-chocolatey brownies for this chocolate company and started the Bangor controversy.

The Ladies of the Church of the Epiphany, Danville, Va. *Key to the Pantry*. Danville, VA, 1898. Brownie Cake, contributed by Miss Augusta Yeates.

Walter Baker and Company Limited. "Choice Recipes." Dorchester, MA, 1908.

MARK H. ZANGER

Brunch, *see Meal Patterns*

Bubble Tea

Invented by street vendors in Taiwan in the early 1980s, bubble tea was originally a mix of tea, milk, and ice shaken to produce frothy bubbles. It became popular with children, and fruit flavors and purees were added to the mix. Finally, vendors included marble-sized dark tapioca pearls, which are now considered characteristic of true bubble tea. Bubble tea, also called *boba* drink, is usually served in a clear cup, showing off the dark tapioca bubbles, with a fat straw wide enough to suck up the chewy tapioca. Flavors range from the original tea with milk to mango, coconut, peach, peppermint, red bean, papaya, watermelon, and every common or exotic flavor sellers can devise. Bubble tea has spawned variants such as Thai bubble tea, made with sweetened condensed milk, and bubble coffee. Bubble tea first appeared in the United States in California in the mid-1980s, but by the year 2000, the fad was spreading across the country.

BIBLIOGRAPHY

Bubble Tea Supply. http://www.bubbleteasupply.com

SYLVIA LOVEGREN

Budweiser

The most popular beer in the world, Budweiser is the flagship brand for the Anheuser-Busch Companies Inc. A lager beer of very mild flavor, Budweiser helped set industry standards for American brewing, became one of the most identifiable brands among all consumer products, and dominated beer marketing for over a century.

Budweiser is part of a long brewing tradition. In 1860, the German immigrant Eberhard Anheuser bought a struggling St. Louis brewery and, with his son-in-law Adolphus Busch, made it a thriving company. Under primarily Busch's leadership, the Bavarian brewery strove to serve a national market, an unusual idea in an era of local and even neighborhood breweries. In 1863, for example, there were 2,004 breweries operating in the United States, collectively making 2 million barrels of beer. To facilitate creating such a national brand and shipping it great distances, Busch devised a network of roadside icehouses to cool railcars filled with his beer. Years later he would pasteurize his product and invest in a fleet of refrigerated freight cars.

Upon creating this system to cool barrels of beer while in transit, Busch and his friend Carl Conrad developed a new brand of beer in 1876 to be shipped nationally. Naming it Budweiser, Busch made his new beer a rather light amber lager, a bottom-fermenting brew, using the yeast strain *Saccharomyces uvarum*. Brewed cooler and fermented longer than either ales or stouts, his Budweiser and other lagers were clearer and lighter, appealing more to the American palate.

Busch's Budweiser was an immediate success, soon selling well in cities throughout the Midwest. As Busch changed his company's name to the Anheuser-Busch Brewery in 1879, his Budweiser was already competing with the other burgeoning national brands, especially rival Pabst Brewing Company's Blue Ribbon Beer. For the remainder of the nineteenth century, Anheuser-Busch and Pabst competed to be the dominant "shipper," the slang term of the era for nationally shipping brewers.

National expositions and fairs featured elaborate pavilions funded by both companies, and taste-judging contests often dissolved into bitter disputes. In 1896, Busch introduced another national brand, Michelob, which he described as a "draught beer for connoisseurs," and by 1901 was brewing a combined total of 1 million barrels of beer each year (Smith, 1995).

Despite Adolphus Busch's death in 1913, his company's growth continued unabated until 1920, when the temperance movement's political efforts culminated in a national prohibition of alcoholic beverages. His son, August A. Busch Sr., assumed the helm, pivoting production over to a line of nonalcoholic items, including carbonated soft drinks, corn syrup, ice cream, and baker's yeast—a product that became an enormously profitable industry leader and continued in the Anheuser-Busch line until 1988. These diverse consumer products sustained profitability until Prohibition ended in 1933, when the company immediately resumed beer production. To celebrate the return to brewing, Busch included a team of matching Clydesdale workhorses as part of Budweiser's marketing campaign. These huge horses would come to symbolize the Budweiser brand, and Anheuser-Busch constantly maintained a herd of over two hundred for public display and enjoyment in parades and fairs.

Budweiser remained a national leader throughout the century, earning the status in 1957 of being the world's best-selling beer. The advent of television closely tied the brand name Budweiser with American sports, largely because of Anheuser-Busch's sponsoring of thousands of televised events and games. This strategic use of television advertising confirmed the popular perception of Budweiser as America's "national beer." Its continued success spawned Bud Light in 1982, a lower-calorie version brewed with a different ratio of malt and hops, targeted at health- and weight-conscious consumers.

Bud Light's subsequent success as the second-best-selling beer in the United States, trailing only its parent, led to the introduction of additional Budweiser spin-offs twelve years later, Bud Ice and Bud Ice Light. This expanded Budweiser family extended the beer market even further; by 2002, the company was producing more than 100 million barrels per year and collectively accounting for over 20 percent of all beer sold in the United States. The brand continues to become more and more ingrained in American culture, its Clydesdales a traditional feature of many community events and its Super Bowl advertising an annual event in itself.

[*See also* Advertising; Beer.]

BIBLIOGRAPHY

Hernon, Peter, and Terry Ganey. *Under the Influence: The Unauthorized Story of the Anheuser-Busch Dynasty.* New York: Simon and Schuster, 1991.

Plavchan, Ronald. *A History of Anheuser-Busch, 1852–1933.* New York: Arno Press, 1975.

Price, Steven D. *All the King's Horses: The Story of the Budweiser Clydesdales.* New York: Viking Press, 1983.

Smith, Gregg. *Beer: A History of Suds and Civilization from Mesopotamia to Microbreweries.* New York: Avon, 1995.

DAVID GERARD HOGAN

Buffalo

The scientific name of buffalo is *Bos bison*, commonly known as bison, which in turn is used interchangeably with American buffalo, or buffalo for short. The largest terrestrial mammals on the North American continent, buffalo were the center of life for the Plains Indians. These majestic animals provided them with food, clothes, and shelter, and they served as a basis for the Indians' spiritual life.

When the Europeans arrived, they found buffalo on the plains in awesome numbers, their estimated total varying from 30 to 70 million. Pushing west to find a way to the Pacific coast, members of the Lewis and Clark expedition reported that upon reaching the heart of buffalo country, they encountered buffalo in such numbers that the animals were beyond counting. Other reports record that during the "running season," buffalo herds congregated into such masses as literally to blacken the prairies for miles.

However, by 1800 the herds east of the Mississippi River were nearly gone, most likely having been killed to protect the newly developed homesteads in that region. With westward expansion of the American frontier, systematic reduction of the plains herds began around 1830, when unregulated buffalo hunting became the chief industry of American migrants to the plains. Organized groups of hunters killed buffalo for hides, meat, or trophy. By 1900, fewer than one thousand buffalo remained.

Thanks to the efforts of a handful of dedicated conservationists, the federal government finally stepped in to help save the noble beast from extinction. Budding ranchers discovered that the genetically strong buffalo are able to thrive year-round anywhere there is adequate forage, water, and space. Efficient grazers, buffalo eat only top grass and do not damage the ecosystem the way cattle do, making buffalo the ideal environmentally correct animal for the twenty-first century. Buffalo herds are being farm-raised in nearly every state of the nation. In addition, about fifty-one Native American tribes are actively engaged in restoring the American bison to its rightful range.

Bulls weigh up to 2,200 pounds, and cows weigh up to 1,000 pounds. Despite their size, buffalo have amazing mobility and are able to sprint at great speed. Male and female are characterized by an overdeveloped front portion and tapered hindquarters. Their huge head and hump, covered with dark brown, woolly hair, contrasts sharply with their small hips. Buffalo cows travel in herds of related animals while the mature males either roam alone or in small groups. The cows are very protective of their young and will become aggressive if they are threatened. Newborn calves are tawny to buff colored and darken over time.

Roaming free, raised without growth hormones or antibiotics, buffalo is a splendid source of red meat. High in protein and low in fat, tasty buffalo is the meat of choice of a large number of consumers and is featured in many fine American restaurants. Frozen buffalo meat is available in many supermarkets or may be ordered from one of the specialty mail order houses, many of which are owned by dedicated ranchers who are bent on restoring the balance of nature.

[*See also* Frontier Cooking of the Far West; Midwestern Regional Cookery; Native American Foods, *subentry* Before and After Contact.]

BIBLIOGRAPHY

Intertribal Bison Cooperative. http://www.intertribalbison.com.
National Bison Association. http://www.bisoncentral.com.

HELEN H. STUDLEY

Bully Beef

The name "bully beef" was used primarily by British and British colonial soldiers for canned corned beef. Most sources indicate that the name came into use during World War I when troops noticed the words *bouilli boeuf* (French for "boiled beef") on the cans. However, an Australian source says the term derived from the canned salt beef supplied from Booyoolee Station to men working in the outback in the 1870s. The workers called this ration "Booyoolee beef," which was shortened to bully beef.

Although references to bully beef turn up chiefly in British, South African, Australian, Jamaican, New Zealand,

and Canadian sources, American soldiers also used the term. In 1932, a group of World War I veterans formed the Last Buddies' Bully Beef Club, whose symbol was a bottle of cognac and a can of bully beef. During World War II, one Michigan soldier wrote that the only rations that survived a supply-plane drop were the cans of bully beef.

[*See also* Combat Food; Corned Beef.]

BIBLIOGRAPHY

American Heritage Dictionary of the English Language. 4th ed. New York: Houghton Mifflin, 2000.
"Bully Beef on Thanksgiving." *The Holland Sentinel.* November 27, 1997.

SYLVIA LOVEGREN

Burger King

In 1954, James W. McLamore and David Edgerton founded Burger King of Miami Inc. in Miami, Florida. The company, which had 11,450 restaurants in fifty-eight countries by the early twenty-first century, played an important role in shaping the fast food industry, standardizing its practices, and developing task-specific machinery, such as the "Miracle Insta Machine," which broiled hamburgers and toasted buns.

Burger King's first restaurant, which was located in Miami, sold eighteen-cent hamburgers and eighteen-cent milkshakes, along with twelve-ounce and sixteen-ounce sodas. Three years later, the best-selling Whopper sandwich was introduced for thirty-seven cents. In 1958, the company turned to advertising, and the campaign featuring the memorable tagline "Home of the Whopper®" was launched. Seen as an alternative to McDonald's hamburgers, which were fried, the Whopper was touted as superior because it was "flame-broiled."

From the recognition gained from the ad campaign, McLamore and Edgerton secured national and international franchising rights. The first stores to open outside the continental United States were in Puerto Rico in 1963. The company's growth caught the attention of Pillsbury Company, which in 1967 acquired Burger King as a subsidiary for $18 million. In 1988, Grand Metropolitan PLC acquired Pillsbury and its subsidiaries, including Burger King, for $5.79 billion. The following year, Grand Metropolitan acquired Wimpy restaurants, two hundred of which were converted to Burger King franchises by mid-1990. In 1997, Grand Metropolitan merged with Guinness to create a new company called Diageo PLC. In December 2002, Diageo sold its Burger King holdings for $1.5 billion to the buying consortium of Texas Pacific Group, Bain Capital, and Goldman Sachs Capital Partners.

For almost thirty years, Burger King's menu remained unchanged until, in an attempt to keep pace with competitors and food trends, the company began offering new food items, such as the Bacon Double Cheeseburger (1982); salad bars (1983); breakfast featuring the Croissan'wich (1985), French Toast Sticks (1986), and Cini-minis (1998); Chicken Tenders (1986); Bagel Sandwiches (1987); Chicken International sandwiches (1988); the BK Broiler (1990), a flame-broiled chicken sandwich; spicier, crisper french fries (1997); the Chicken Club sandwich (1999); and the first Whopper line extension, the Chicken Whopper (2002).

Since the 1990s, criticism has been leveled at Burger King by nutrition experts, citing the company's encouragement of poor eating habits in adults and especially children. The critics considered Burger King's food too high in saturated fat. The company responded by switching to 100 percent vegetable oil for frying french fries, 1 percent low-fat milk, and reduced-fat mayonnaise in its ingredients list. The launch of the 2002 BK Veggie®, a nonmeat alternative that boasts Burger King's signature flame-broiled flavor, was another attempt to cater to modern tastes.

One criticism that Burger King and other fast food companies have not been able to counter is that the inexpensiveness of its products, the ubiquitousness of its stores, and the ease of purchase, made especially convenient by drive-through windows, have contributed to altering—and, some have said, eroding—the tradition of the American family dinner.

[See also Fast Food.]

BIBLIOGRAPHY

Burger King. http://www.burgerking.com. A company website that highlights products, lists career opportunities, and includes a detailed history of the company and a complete list of press releases from the past six years.

Schlosser, Eric. *Fast Food Nation: The Dark Side of the All-American Meal.* New York: HarperCollins, 2002.

DAVID LEITE

Butchering

The word "butcher," from the French *boucher*, dating back to the thirteenth century, is synonymous with slaughtering and meatpacking. Butchering entails dismembering animals and fowl and salvaging their parts for sale or consumption.

As evidenced by 300,000-year-old artifacts in Tornalba, Spain, Cro-Magnons pioneered butchering tools. The first butchering tools discovered in America belonged to the Clovis culture of ancient New Mexico (11,000 B.C.E.). Early natives butchered primarily bison and turkey as diet staples until cattle were introduced in the 1500s by the Spanish and then by the British.

Different animals were butchered according to the seasons, such as spring lamb or autumn pigs. In rural communities, much of the operation was concentrated in the late fall and early winter, as farmers slaughtered animals that would strain limited winter pasturage and feed stores and whose flesh could be preserved through such techniques as salting and smoking. Butchery was a year-round activity in urban markets where, through the nineteenth century, quadrupeds were either "walked" or shipped by rail and slaughtered on premises. Skilled artisan butchers slaughtered and dressed fresh meats for consumers; some accounts estimate eleven minutes to slaughter and dress an entire ox.

Large-scale commercial butchering started in the Chicago stockyards in the nineteenth century, setting standards on quality and innovation for the rest of the world. Kansas City, Kansas, served by major cattle trails, became the next major player. In the 1850s the meat mogul Philip Armour organized slaughterhouses in both cities and introduced high-speed mass butchering technologies to serve dinner tables and pioneered the use of

Butchering Turkeys. Nineteenth-century print. *Culinary Archives & Museum at Johnson & Wales University, Providence, R.I.*

by-products for glue, fertilizer, lard, gelatin, and margarine production.

Butchering practices profited tremendously when technology and standardization of processes improved efficiency and reduced reliance on expensive skilled workers. In the late 1800s ice-cooling and refrigerated railroad cars facilitated yearlong butchering activities, shipping products instead of live animals to distant markets. Overhead rails, power lifts, and assembly-line production compartmentalized the work of slaughtering thousands of animals daily and enabled the Armour, Cudahy, Merrell, and Swift companies profitably to introduce canned meats for consumer meal preparations. World War I and World War II introduced American standards and enhanced global butchering practices.

Meat inspection, essential to butchering, was first documented in the Hebrew Bible as part of Mosaic law. Federal enforcement was enacted in 1891. Owners applied questionable and often dangerous techniques for profits and circumvented meat inspection laws. To instigate more effective regulations, Upton Sinclair published *The Jungle* in 1906, exposing the appalling conditions of meat production and slaughterhouse workers. The Meat Inspection Act (1906) and the Pure Food and Drug Act (1906) were passed to protect consumers, but butchering practices improved only when President Lyndon B. Johnson signed the Wholesome Meat Act (1967) and the Wholesome Poultry Products Act (1968), which mandated federal standards for butchering practices.

Before 1938, slaughterhouse owners adopted tactics that isolated butchers, minimized communication for any coordinated reaction, and shielded from the public the appalling conditions of meagerly paid workers. Subsequently, the United Packinghouse Workers Union emerged to defend workers. The titans retaliated by distancing themselves from unions into rural environs, where cattle were fed and housed. Kansas, with access to feedlots, railroad tracks, and rivers, emerged as the butchering industry leader.

At the beginning of the twenty-first century, the butchering industry was comprised of low-paid immigrants operating high-tech plants in rural areas for such conglomerates as Iowa Beef Processing (IBP), Smithfield, Armour-Swift, ConAgra, and Tyson. In addition to immigrant workers, skilled butchers were operating service counters in independent stores and meat departments of large chain grocers in urban and suburban areas. Relatively few independent butcher shops still exist where the customer can request a special cut or watch steaks being trimmed from a primal quarter, and these shops tend to be found in affluent communities and ethnic neighborhoods.

[*See also* Armour, Philip Danforth; ConAgra; Meat; Pig; Sinclair, Upton; Swift, Gustavus Franklin.]

BIBLIOGRAPHY

"How New York Is Fed." *Scribner's Monthly*, October 1877. Reprint, *Journal of Gastronomy* 4 (spring 1988): 62–80.

Rixson, Derrick. *The History of Meat Trading*. Nottingham, UK: Nottingham University Press, 2000.

Toussaint-Samat, Maguelonne. *A History of Food*. Translated by Anthea Bell. Cambridge, MA: Blackwell Reference, 1993.

U.S. Department of Agriculture. *Official United States Standards for Grades of Slaughter Cattle*. Washington, DC: Agricultural Marketing Service, 1989.

KANTHA SHELKE

Butter

Americans are not known for eating prodigious amounts of butter. In 2001, they consumed an average of 4.9 pounds of butter per person, almost five four-stick packs. While this is much more than is eaten by residents of Latin American and Asian countries, it is far less than the quantity eaten by most Western Europeans. German consumption that year averaged almost three times that of Americans, and French consumption, the highest in the world, was almost four times as high.

Moderate and declining butter consumption has been a long-standing trend. In 1937, when margarine consumption was quite low and butter was still produced on many farms, the average American ate 16.7 pounds of butter a year. This total is much higher than the 2001 figure, but rates in other English-speaking countries, such as New Zealand, Canada, and the United Kingdom were even higher.

Americans may not eat as much butter as most Europeans, but the United States has a large butter industry that produced over 1 billion pounds a year by 2000. Almost all of this production takes place off-farm, in large factories. For much of the history of the nation, however, butter making was a farm activity. Butter was generally made from leftover cream during the summer months, when milk production was high. While some of this butter was marketed, much of it was used on the farm. The first creameries (butter factories) appeared in upstate New York in the late 1850s and early 1860s.

These were small plants that generally contained a springhouse, filled with pans for separating cream from skim milk, and a churning area.

Industrial Butter Production

The industrialization of butter production truly took off in the last decade of the nineteenth century, promoted by the invention of the mechanical cream separator. Earlier, the size of creameries had been constrained by the time needed to wait for the cream to rise to the top of the separating vats. The mechanical cream separator allowed cream to be separated out from whole milk in a matter of minutes rather than days, and creameries could start butter production with cream rather than whole milk.

Factory production of butter rose from 29 million pounds in 1879 to 627 million in 1909 to over 1 billion in 1921. With this rise, dominant brands appeared. In the nineteenth century, butter was marketed mainly in tubs and portioned out by the grocer to individual buyers. In 1898, the first packaged butter was marketed by Beatrice Creamery Company, the predecessor of Beatrice Foods. Aside from Beatrice, many of the early leaders in packaged butter were meatpacking companies, such as Swift and Armour, who entered the business through their production of margarine. There were few differences in the packaging of butter and margarine, so these companies attempted to control sales of both products.

The hold of these companies over the market was lessened in the 1920s with the passage of the Capper-Volstead Act, which awarded farm cooperatives antitrust protection. Dairy cooperatives, in particular, Minnesota-based Land O'Lakes, began to market their products aggressively, directly to consumers. Their butter was produced from "sweet cream," rather than sour. Using soured cream was thought to be essential in creating flavorful butter, but it also increased perishability. Making butter from sweet cream quickened production and extended the distance from the manufacturing plant that butter could be sold, but it also may explain the charges of tastelessness that are often levied against American butter. Most butter by this time was made from pasteurized milk and also iced in transit. These and other innovations in hygiene allowed less preservative salt to be added.

The butter that Land O'Lakes sold in the 1920s, lightly salted in one-pound containers with four prepackaged bars, differed little from their product sold by the end of the twentieth century. Land O'Lakes also asked the federal government to send an inspector directly to their plants to certify that their butter met the highest standards. Previously, butter had been scored at the mercantile exchanges. The company included in its packages a certificate of inspection from the U.S. butter inspector. A race to promote quality followed, and soon premium butter of 93 score or higher, from pasteurized milk with few defects in taste, became the standard for retail marketing.

Butter and Margarine

Since that time, consumption and production of butter in the United States have fallen, primarily owing to rising consumption of margarine. Margarine was developed in the nineteenth century, but consumption paled compared with that of butter, partly as the result of home butter production by farmers but also because of taxes and regulations on margarine. Margarine consumption rose quickly during World War II because of quotas on butter and truly took off following the war. Margarine production surpassed that of butter in 1958 and nearly doubled butter production in 1969. Total butter production peaked in 1940 at over 2.2 billion pounds a year but dropped to less than half this amount by 1975.

Margarine outsold butter because it was cheaper, usually costing about one-quarter to one-half the price of butter. During the 1980s, margarine was also promoted as healthier than butter. Questioning of this theory by researchers in the late 1990s may help account for a consequent modest rise in butter consumption. Nevertheless, Americans consume about one-third as much butter per capita as they did in 1940. Several innovations have been introduced. Margarine-butter "blends" have appeared. Premium quality butters, including American artisan and imported European products, are sold at specialty stores. In general, however, the appearance and packaging of American butter have been amazingly stable since the period of innovation that ended in the 1920s. Perhaps as a result, consumers often tie butter to a less industrialized age of food production.

[*See also* Beatrice; Dairy Foods; Fats and Oils; Margarine.]

BIBLIOGRAPHY

Hunziker, Otto Frederick. *The Butter Industry*. 3rd ed. LaGrange, IL: Otto Frederick Hunziker, 1940.
International Dairy Foods Association. *Milk Facts*. Washington, DC: Milk Industry Foundation, 2002.
Riepma, S. F. *The Story of Margarine*. Washington, DC: Public Affairs Press, 1970.
Selitzer, Ralph. *The Dairy Industry in America*. New York: Dairy and Ice Cream Field and Books for Industry, 1976.

Wiest, Edward. *The Butter Industry in the United States: An Economic Study of Butter and Oleomargarine.* New York: Columbia University Press, 1916.

DANIEL R. BLOCK

Butter-Making Tools and Churns

Butter is made by agitating cream until it emulsifies. The high fat content of cream makes butter possible. This agitation is best accomplished with a churn, which until the mid-nineteenth century was typically a vessel of wood or glazed ceramic. Later in the century, churns were sometimes metal. Churns could hold as little as three pints of cream or as much as sixty gallons. Churns also had different designs. Some worked by moving a perforated dasher up and down through the cream for hours until it emulsified. Others had a turbinelike dasher that was cranked. Sometimes the whole churn rocked or revolved, rather like a washing machine. After 1900, small, glass tabletop churns with hand-cranked gears were introduced. These prepared butter for at most a few days' use. Dairies, on the other hand, used huge churns that required external power sources, such as windmills or treadmills using animals, to move the dasher.

After the butter had formed in the churn, it needed to be removed and "worked" to remove the last traces of buttermilk and to mix in salt if desired. A wooden butter fork or spade transferred the butter from the churn to either a wooden bowl where it was worked with a butter ladle, or to a butter worker, which was a traylike device with a corrugated or flat wooden arm that was moved back and forth over the butter.

Butter Molds. *Culinary Archives & Museum at Johnson & Wales University, Providence, R.I.*

When the butter was ready for serving, a pair of corrugated wooden paddles could be used to form fancy butter balls. The butter might also be pressed into carved molds that produced a design, which could even include advertising, on the top. Plain molds existed that made a simple rectangular log of butter. Levered iron and wire butter slicers were patented after 1900 to slice pats from stick butter.

[*See also* Butter; Buttermilk; Dairy Foods; Dairy Industry; Milk.]

BIBLIOGRAPHY

Franklin, Linda Campbell. *Three Hundred Years of Kitchen Collectibles.* 5th ed. Iola, WI: Krause, 2003.
Kindig, Paul E. *Butter Prints and Molds.* West Chester, PA: Schiffer, 1986.
Van Vuren, Robert E., and Barbara S. Van Vuren. *Molds and Stamps: A Guide to American Manufacturers with Photo Identifier.* Napa, CA: Butter Press, 2000.

LINDA CAMPBELL FRANKLIN

Buttermilk

Despite its name, buttermilk lacks butter. Traditionally, buttermilk was the liquid left over after fat had been separated out of cream for making butter. It has a distinct, lightly sour flavor. Buttermilk has been drunk and used in American cooking since colonial times. Dutch settlers in New York had it with their breakfasts. In the early 1800s, New York City peddlers sold buttermilk at three cents a quart. It was sometimes resold as pot cheese, a combination of buttermilk, butter, salt, and sometimes sage.

Buttermilk was important to early farmers because it was an economically valuable by-product of the cheese- and butter-making process. In the early twentieth century another by-product use was created when a process was developed to make cultured buttermilk by adding lactic acid bacteria to skim milk. At the time, skim milk was relegated primarily to feeding farm hogs.

Today, buttermilk is used in the United States mainly as an ingredient in cooking. Buttermilk pancakes and biscuits connote wholesomeness and old-time cooking. Buttermilk consumption figures show that this old-fashioned label is not incorrect. In 1909, the average American consumed over seven gallons of buttermilk a year. In the early 2000s, Americans consumed less than one gallon annually. This trend is ongoing. Buttermilk sales halved between 1975 and 2002. Buttermilk's downfall may be its name. Although it is usually fat-free, declines in consumption have paralleled those for whole milk, as consumers increasingly avoid fatty foods. In addition, buttermilk consumption may be falling as Americans find less time for cooking homemade biscuits and pancakes.

[*See also* Butter; Dairy Foods; Dairy Industry; Milk.]

BIBLIOGRAPHY

Selitzer, Ralph. *The Dairy Industry in America*. New York: Dairy and Ice Cream Field and Books for Industry, 1976.

DANIEL R. BLOCK

Cabbage

Native to Europe, wild cabbage is a parent plant of many cultivated vegetables, including broccoli, brussels sprouts, cabbage, cauliflower, collards, kale, and kohlrabi. The domesticated cabbage (*Brassica oleracea capitata*) consists of large leaves that form a compact globular head. There are three major types of cabbage. The most popular in the United States are the smooth-leaved green (sometimes so pale that is almost white) and red (magenta to purple) cabbages. The third type, Savoy, which has finely crimped leaves that form a looser head, is less common.

The earliest European settlers on North America's eastern shores brought cabbage seeds with them, and cabbage was a general favorite throughout the colonies. The Dutch who founded New Netherland (New York State), for instance, grew cabbage extensively along the Hudson River. They served it in their old-country ways, often as *koolsla* (shredded cabbage salad). This dish became popular throughout the colonies and survives as coleslaw. In New Jersey and Pennsylvania, German immigrants grew cabbage to make their traditional sauerkraut.

By the 1880s, cabbage and its cousins had fallen from favor with the upper class because of the strong sulfurous odors these vegetables give off when cooking. Marion Harland, hoping to change public opinion, offered a dish she called "Ladies' Cabbage"—finely chopped boiled cabbage baked in a rich, creamy sauce. American fiction writers often described lower-class homes as smelling objectionably of cabbage. But this sturdy and versatile vegetable never disappeared from middle-class kitchens.

Later immigrants to American shores brought different cabbage varieties and diverse recipes with them. For instance, stuffed cabbage, sweet-and-sour red cabbage, and cabbage soups came from central and eastern Europe. Wisconsin produces more cabbage than any other state; the crop is used mainly in the production of sauerkraut. Florida is the leading state for winter and spring production of fresh market cabbage.

BIBLIOGRAPHY

Dalton, Dennis E. *Sauerkraut Cook Book: One Nation under Sauerkraut.* St. Petersburg, FL: privately printed, 1980.

Cabbage. Cabbages offered in a seed catalog, from *Aaron Low's Illustrated Retail Seed Catalogue and Garden Manual,* 1887, p. 51.

Turgeon, Charlotte Snyder. *Of Cabbages and Kings Cookbook: An Uncommon Collection of Recipes Featuring That Family of Vegetables Which Includes Broccoli, Brussels Sprouts, Cauliflower, Collards, Turnips, Kale, and Kohlrabi*. Indianapolis, IN: Curtis Publishing, 1977.

Weaver, William Woys. *Sauerkraut Yankees: Pennsylvania German Foods and Foodways*. Philadelphia: University of Pennsylvania Press, 1983.

ANDREW F. SMITH

Cabbage Cutters and Planes

A wooden plank with a hole cut into it for an adjustable steel blade is called a cabbage plane or cabbage cutter. In America, it dates back at least to the eighteenth century. Sometimes, the planks were carved with a date, a fancy cutout hanging hole, initials, or even a heart at one end. Such a tool is much safer to use than a chopping knife when slicing and shredding a large, unwieldy, and heavy head of cabbage. In fact, many were made with a box enclosure for the cabbage, to use in passing it back and forth over the very sharp blade.

Shredded cabbage was used for making Dutch slaw, German sauerkraut, or Irish "bubble and squeak," a sort of casserole of boiled, then fried, beef, potatoes, and cabbage. When making sauerkraut, the cabbage plane could be set up directly over the storage keg or small barrel, ready for adding salt for the fermenting. Small planes with an adjustable blade have long been used for slicing cucumbers, squash, and root vegetables.

[*See also* Cabbage.]

BIBLIOGRAPHY

Franklin, Linda Campbell. *300 Years of Kitchen Collectibles*. 5th ed. Iola, WI: Krause, 2003.

LINDA CAMPBELL FRANKLIN

Cactus

Most botanists think that the family of plants called Cactaceae is native to the New World. Those cactus species indigenous to the southwestern United States were used for food by the original inhabitants, but only one, *Opuntia ficus-indica*, plays a significant role in American commerce. The fruits, once known as tunas or prickly pears, are mostly marketed to North Americans as cactus pears; they come in many colors, but the leading commercial variety,

grown near Salinas, California, and harvested in fall and winter, has a greenish-red peel and red pulp. The spines are rubbed off before sale. The flesh, which contains numerous seeds, is juicy, with a mild flavor reminiscent of watermelon. The fruits are generally eaten fresh; traditionally, they were also juiced and made into a sweetened paste, called *queso de tuna* in Spanish. In addition, the thick, fleshy cactus pads, called *nopalitos*, are stripped of their spines and used as a vegetable in salads, egg and meat dishes, soup, and pickles. Since about the year 2000, several California growers have established plantings of another species, *Hylocereus undatus*, known as *pitahaya*, *pitaya*, and dragon fruit, which has large, spineless, flaming pink fruit with white flesh and small seeds.

BIBLIOGRAPHY

Nobel, Park S., ed. *Cacti: Biology and Uses*. Berkeley, CA: University of California Press, 2002.

DAVID KARP

Cafeterias

In its heyday, the American cafeteria was a sociological as well as a culinary phenomenon. Although it was christened with the Spanish word for "coffee shop," it is rather a buffet—a self-service operation on a relatively large scale. Efficient and economical, it provided a solution to various logistical problems arising in the transition between a primarily agrarian and an essentially urban-industrial society: as fewer and fewer people worked on either their own land or their own time, and scheduled lunch breaks made midday commutes home impractical, the need for eateries that were conveniently located within commercial districts and streamlined for speed—as well as thrift—increased. This need was first met in the 1880s with the opening of the Exchange Buffet in New York City (met, that is, for men, to whom the place catered exclusively). It gained credence across the country in the next decade, boosted by an exhibition at the 1893 Chicago World's Fair—where the term "conscience joint" was coined in a nod to the honor system by which patrons settled the check—and by the efforts of such entrepreneurs as the brothers Samuel and William Childs, who are credited with introducing the system of lines and trays that defines the modern cafeteria.

Where expedience in a restaurant is a virtue, food preparation and selection are sure to be mere formalities—or informalities, for that matter. Cafeteria fare generally resembles that of any other casual American-style eatery, from coffee shop to truck stop. Cheap, hearty (but seldom heart-healthy) quick fixes abound, from snack items like burgers, fries, and malts to entrées like fried chicken or spaghetti and meatballs. These meals come complete with starchy sides, the occasional boiled vegetable, and a bowl of Jell-O or a slice of pie for dessert. As for beverages, soda, juice, coffee, and the like are typical; alcohol is less so.

Like the bland food, the cafeteria setting is instantly recognizable in its very anonymity. Granted, this was not always the case; in the first half of the twentieth century, cafeterias were distinguished (from other genres, if not from one another) by their swanky, or at least imitation swanky, interiors. As the ethic and aesthetic of the fast food franchise began to affect the restaurant industry as a whole, however, the look changed. By the end of the twentieth century, vast dining rooms, identically decorated and awash in oranges, beiges, and browns, were filled with vinyl booths and booster chairs negotiated by busboys and waitstaff with more or less limited duties, such as seating, filling drink orders, or transacting payment. Diners line up at long counters or steam tables fitted with sneeze guards and slide rails, lading their trays as they go; the level of counter service varies, but the standard practice is to station employees at the hot buffet while keeping cold items, such as salads and desserts, within customers' own reach.

Still, if sameness in the sense of homogeneity has always been the name of the cafeteria game, sameness in the sense of stagnation has not. Spin-offs have periodically thrived, from the vending-service "automats" of the early twentieth century to the smorgasbords of the 1960s to the salad bars of the 1970s and 1980s; cafeteria chains have also flourished, beginning with the Childs brothers' New York–based operations at the turn of the century and eventually migrating south and west. In fact, while the original urban model has all but disappeared in the shuffle of fast food establishments, its roadside offspring have fared comparatively well in those areas of the country where automobility is a necessity, offering as they do a somewhat more formal, yet still affordable, alternative to the burger chains (hence their folkloric popularity with churchgoing crowds on Sunday). Indeed, according to Ruth Kedzie Wood (Jakle and Sculle, p. 33), California was known for a time as the "Cafeteria Belt," while the Deep South to this day fairly teems with Morrison's, Furr's, Piccadillys, and Luby's. Although these places command only a small share even of these regional markets, they continue to attract certain segments of the pop-

ulation steadily, namely, retirees and middle- to lower-middle-class families.

Of course, the rise of the automobile spurred a steady exodus of individuals, and the industries that service them, from city centers to rapidly forming bedroom communities; but the commercial cafeteria's shift from urban, worker-oriented environs to suburban, family-oriented ones may be linked even more specifically to its development and image in noncommercial sectors. Initially, the impersonal, assembly-line nature of the cafeteria was deemed disruptive to the family unit, breaching the sanctity of the sit-down dinner hour, at the same time that it was conducive to productivity in its emphasis on rapid lunch-hour turnover. Granted, from a managerial standpoint, the root of the problem—the midday scattering of employees from the workplace itself, regardless of the length of the lunch break—had yet to be addressed. But since the advantages of the cafeteria system—relatively low costs and, hence, a potentially superb cost-benefit ratio—were not in question, the solution, it seemed, was simply to install it onsite. Thus did the company lunchroom evolve, becoming commonplace by the 1920s. Of course, its commercial counterpart in the vicinity waned accordingly, and the owners of such establishments were forced to rethink the nature of their enterprise.

Meanwhile, cafeterias were proving effectual in another unexpected context—schools. Concerns about child malnutrition around the turn of the twentieth century had prompted various philanthropic organizations to set up shop within schools to furnish students with balanced lunches; eventually, the schools themselves became legally responsible for such provisions and the cafeteria-style facilities proper to them. Their success in this venture is highly debatable; time-honored children's jokes about mystery meat and fish sticks have given way to much more serious misgivings regarding corporate takeovers of school lunchrooms, whereby students have on-campus access to the same junk food they have long gravitated toward off campus.

Still, for much of the twentieth century, cafeterias were equated vis-à-vis school-lunch programs with wholesomeness. For that matter, they are probably the type of eatery most closely connected with social services in general and with the moral commitment presumably required to coordinate them, from hospitals to armed service camps to soup kitchens. The patina of charity and even patriotism thus covering cafeterias further explains the steadfastness of their reputation among many Americans in those areas of the country where a belief in hospitality and a bent for conservatism coexist.

[See also Automats; Roadside Food; School Food.]

BIBLIOGRAPHY

Bryan, Mary de Garmo. *The School Cafeteria*. New York: F. S. Crofts, 1936.

Jakle, John A., and Keith A. Sculle. *Fast Food: Roadside Restaurants in the Automobile Age*. Baltimore: Johns Hopkins University Press, 1999. Thoroughly scholarly without being overly academic.

Levenstein, Harvey A. *Paradox of Plenty: A Social History of Eating in Modern America*. New York: Oxford University Press, 1993.

Mariani, John. *America Eats Out: An Illustrated History of Restaurants, Taverns, Coffee Shops, Speakeasies, and Other Establishments That Have Fed Us for 350 Years*. New York: Morrow, 1991. Smart and entertaining both as a written and as a pictorial document.

National Industrial Conference Board. *Industrial Lunch Rooms*. New York: National Industrial Conference Board, 1928.

Pillsbury, Richard. *From Boarding House to Bistro: The American Restaurant Then and Now*. Boston: Unwin Hyman, 1990. Judicious use of statistical data balances out the distracting anecdotal sidebars.

RUTH TOBIAS

Cajun and Creole Food

Although it is fashionable in America's beau monde restaurants to spotlight seasonal ingredients purchased from local growers and small distributors, there were times and places in our nation's history when relying on the goods and produce closest at hand was a matter of necessity, even survival. Take the Gulf Coast region of the United States, which for more than three hundred years has beckoned immigrants and inspired, if not demanded, ingenuity at the table. Although it was traversed by explorers in the sixteenth century, this vast area spanning the Gulf of Mexico and eventually known as the Louisiana Territories was not permanently settled by outsiders until 1699, when French colonists first touched its shores. Since then, peoples from Europe, Africa, Asia, and Latin America have left their mark on the region's history and culture and inspired not one, but two, original culinary traditions: the Creole cuisine of New Orleans and the Cajun food of the surrounding bayous and prairies.

Creole and Cajun food, both tracing their roots to France, offer hard proof of Louisiana's long love affair with eating. They share a commitment to practicing economy in the kitchen, using the freshest products available, and making do with what is on hand. They even share many of the same recipes, including gumbo (a rich seafood soup) and jambalaya (a hearty rice dish), to name just two. Nevertheless, Cajun and Creole foods extend from different traditions, each possessing its own history and touting its own creations. How they became a part of America's unique culinary landscape is a story—and distinction—worth knowing.

From *Criollo* to Creole

Proper use of the term "Creole" has sparked countless discussions and debates among residents and historians of Louisiana alike. The word is derived from the Spanish word *criollo*, which means "native to the place," and was probably first used in the sixteenth century to describe pure-blooded Spanish children born in Spain's South American and West Indian colonies. In Louisiana, the term was used in the same manner to identify the children of French, and later Spanish, colonists who settled there in the seventeenth and eighteenth centuries. Over time, "Creole" would also distinguish slaves born in Louisiana from those brought to the colony, describe children born of both African and European lineage, and, in its broadest meaning, designate anyone from New Orleans. Creole also refers to the original cuisine of New Orleans, which finds its roots in classical French recipes and techniques that have been adapted and shaped for more than three hundred years by the diverse peoples who have passed though the city's ports.

In 1682, while on expedition to the mouth of the Mississippi, the French explorer René-Robert Cavelier, sieur de La Salle, claimed the lands of the entire river valley for his country and called the territory Louisiana in honor of his king, Louis XIV. More than a decade later, in 1699, Pierre Le Moyne, sieur d'Iberville, an officer in the French Canadian navy, established the first Louisiana settlement at Biloxi, which later became part of the state of Mississippi.

When the first settlers arrived in Louisiana, they surely relied on traditional French cooking techniques and any foodstuffs that had survived the long voyage. In a short time, though, the challenges of colonial life forced adaptation at the table and a reliance on local Indian nations, such as the Choctaws and Chitimachas. From native groups like these, the early colonists learned to mine the fresh- and saltwaters of the Gulf Coast region for seafood and fish, to hunt the area's forests for meat and fowl, and to till the soil for fresh vegetables such as corn and squash. The profusion of local plants and animals was key to the early colonists' survival.

Women, indentured servants, and, eventually, African and Indian slaves no doubt were responsible for the cooking, and a small uprising in New Orleans by young French wives is often touted as the official birth of Creole cuisine. In 1722, just four years after the city's founding, fifty women, at their wits' end over the meager quantity of traditional foods and the unsavory quality of the dishes they were able to prepare, are said to have staged a protest at the mansion of the colonial governor, Jean-Baptiste Le Moyne, sieur de Bienville. For effect, they banged frying pans with spoons as they marched.

To quiet the Petticoat Rebellion, as the uprising was wistfully named, Bienville ordered his housekeeper, Madame Langlois, to teach the ladies about the ingredients and cooking techniques she had learned from the Choctaw Indians and adapted to French recipes. Among the Choctaw's lasting contributions to Creole cuisine were the introduction of filé (dried and powdered sassafras leaves) as a flavoring and thickening agent in soups and stews and the substitution of ground corn for wheat flour in bread.

As this quaint story indicates, though, the transformation of French cooking had begun even before the Petticoat Rebellion. It is almost certain that in addition to the Indians, African slaves were already influencing the flavors of the pot. The first slave ships arrived in Louisiana in 1719, and records show that rice seed and slaves who knew how to cultivate it may have been onboard. What is clear is that rice was being grown in abundance within a few years and that Louisiana owes a debt to Africa for the development of its rice culture.

Likewise, Louisiana was already becoming home to Europeans other than the French. A small group of Germans, for example, was lured to the New World by the promises of freedom and prosperity touted by John Law, a Scotsman who served as the French minister of finance. Law also headed the Company of the Indies, which had an exclusive deal with the French Crown to settle and develop the colony. When the venture failed, the Germans, who had served Law as indentured workers, received their own land grants and established farms that became key suppliers of corn, rice, and other vegetables to New Orleans.

Gumbo, Quintessential Creole Classic

It should come as no surprise, then, that gumbo, New Orleans's most famous Creole creation, has a rather complex pedigree. *The Oxford English Dictionary* traces the

Creole Cookbook. *Mme. Begue and Her Recipes: Old Creole Cookery. Culinary Archives & Museum at Johnson & Wales University, Providence, R.I.*

word "gumbo" to the Angolan term *kingombo*, which means "okra" (also an African word). Although some historians have speculated that the word may derive from the Choctaw word *kombo*, which means "sassafras," the African origin is the most accepted. The term also refers to a French patois spoken in the West Indies and a separate French dialect used in Louisiana (also called Black Creole), but gumbo has come to signify for Americans the rich soup for which Louisiana is famous.

Although some aficionados of Louisiana cuisine consider gumbo an adaptation of bouillabaisse, there are problems with this theory. First, the cooking time for bouillabaisse is just minutes, but gumbos simmer on the stove for an hour or more. Second, early Creole cookbooks distinguish clearly between bouillabaisse and gumbo, some putting gumbo in a category of its own. The *Picayune's Creole Cook Book*, first published in 1901 in New Orleans as a collection of time-honored recipes gathered from housekeepers and black cooks, even declares that gumbo cannot be described as having evolved, but rather must be considered a sui generis creation of New Orleans cooks. The bouillabaisse served in New Orleans, though, was indeed a variation on the original, substituting Gulf Coast fish like red snapper and redfish for the usual rascasse, whiting, and other fish from the Mediterranean. It was so good, in fact, that, according to the *Picayune's Creole Cook Book* and other sources, it inspired the writer William Makepeace Thackeray to declare that "in New Orleans you can eat a Bouillabaisse, the like of which was never eaten in Marseilles or Paris." Third, and perhaps most important, bouillabaisse is strictly a seafood dish. Gumbos, however, often contain an unusual mixture of seafood (shrimp, crab, and fish) and meat (poultry, pork, and game, but never beef). African, Spanish, West Indian, and Native American cooking all make similar combinations.

Culinary historians suggest many other influences on gumbo's recipe. The Choctaws, for example, may have shared a recipe for boiled seafood that influenced the early development of gumbo, and it is well documented that their sassafras became an important additive in the soup. Gumbo may bear its strongest resemblance to a host of African and West Indian okra soup recipes, which undoubtedly were on the stove wherever slaves could be found in large numbers. In time, though, gumbo soup took on a more generic meaning and could refer to various soups made with or without the actual vegetable. Gumbo also benefited from Spanish-, West Indian-, and African-inspired infusions of red peppers and other pungent seasonings.

The endless varieties of gumbo make clear that this dish is intended to maximize economy in the kitchen. As such, preparation begins with the cook's surveying the kitchen for enough leftover bits of meat like chicken, ham, turkey, crab, or shrimp to make a complete meal when tossed in the same pot. Cookbooks contain recipes for popular combinations, such as chicken and ham with oysters, shrimp with okra, and chicken or turkey with okra, but these are only a few samples of the endless possibilities. New Orleans is perhaps best known for its seafood gumbo, which typically contains shrimp, oysters, and crabmeat. Cajun varieties tend to include more game.

The unusual *gumbo z'herbes* calls for a veritable garden of greens. One Creole recipe lists the greens of cabbage, radish, turnip, mustard, spinach, watercress, and parsley, which are boiled, strained, chopped, and added to a browned mixture of onion, veal, and ham. Other recipes might include lettuce, collard greens, radish tops, kale, or carrot tops. Although *gumbo z'herbes* bears a resemblance to the French *potage aux herbes*—a more delicate vegetarian soup containing sorrel, watercress, chervil, and pimpernel and thickened with a smashed potato—it was probably modified by the African cooks who prepared it in New Orleans homes. Indeed, some sources show that *gumbo z'herbes* actually may have ties to a Congolese dish that itself was a twist on the French original. A meatless *gumbo z'herbes* has long been a popular Lenten dish and symbol of good luck in New Orleans.

To prepare a traditional gumbo, one first must make a roux, a mixture of equal parts flour and fat cooked slowly, usually in a cast-iron pot, until it reaches a rich, dark mahogany color. Although a roux is as indispensable to Creole and Cajun sauces and gravies as it is to traditional béchamel and velouté sauces, the French sauces are typically prepared with a white roux (cooked only long enough to eliminate the flour's raw flavor) or a pale roux (removed from the heat just as the mixture begins to change color). French cooking does rely on a so-called brown roux for its famous brown sauces, but the color is still lighter than the Creole and Cajun varieties. In addition, whereas French sauces like these are prepared as accompaniments to a dish, a roux in Louisiana recipes provides the foundation for one-pot creations that marry entrée and sauce before they ever meet the plate.

When the roux for a gumbo reaches the proper color (the darker the roux, the deeper and more complex the flavor), it is seasoned with onions, garlic, green pepper, and herbs such as parsley, bay leaves, and thyme. Then the main ingredients are stirred into the mix; covered with water, stock, or oyster liquor (for a seafood gumbo); and simmered for an hour or more; when done, the gumbo is served over white rice. (Filé, the Choctaw's inspiration, finds its way into the dish as a thickener only when okra is not added.)

Spain Acquires a Neglected Colony

In 1762, in the infamous Treaty of Fontainebleau, Louis XV of France secretly granted New Orleans and the area of Louisiana west of the Mississippi to his cousin Charles III of Spain. By the time Louisiana was handed over to Spain, the colony was in trouble. For decades colonists, many lured by the promises of prosperity, had struggled to survive floods and famine and the general neglect of the colony by the French crown. Through improved management and the encouragement of settlement, the Spanish transformed New Orleans into a growing seaport and commercial hub. Despite a period of rebellion by French loyalists, Louisiana remained under Spanish control until 1800.

The recipe for jambalaya, a highly seasoned rice casserole, has long been considered a Spanish contribution to Creole menus. Numerous sources contain theories on the derivation of the term "jambalaya" from the Spanish word for ham, *jamon*. They also trace the recipe's inspiration to paella, a signature dish of Valencia that combines rice with vegetables (green beans, butter beans, and tomatoes), seasonings (olive oil, paprika, saffron, salt, and pepper), and meat (chicken, rabbit, and pork) in a shallow, iron pan of the same name.

Later scholarship, particularly that of culinary historian Karen Hess, contradicts the Spain theories by asserting that jambalaya is closer to the rice dishes of Provence, France, called pilau (more commonly known as pilaf in English). Although the recipes for paella and pilau both ultimately trace their roots to Persia, the subtle but important differences in the two may suggest a closer link of pilau with jambalaya. For example, recipes for both call for long-grain rice, which is added to a seasoned, boiling broth. The traditional Valencian paella uses short-grain rice, which is sautéed in oil before the cooking liquid is added. Some of the seasonings for a Creole jambalaya compare more closely with paella, however. Where paella calls for paprika, for example, jambalaya will usually feature chili pepper and cayenne. Likewise, French pilaus characteristically do not contain both seafood and meat—a combination that is common in both jambalaya and paella and typical of African and West Indian cooking as well.

In the preparation of classic Creole jambalaya, ham and pork sausage are combined with butter, onions, thyme, parsley, ground cloves, and bay leaves and brought to a boil with water or broth. To this mix, rice is added, along with salt, black pepper, and cayenne pepper to taste. The combination is cooked until the liquid has been absorbed and the rice is tender. The Cajuns, who also claim jambalaya as a staple recipe, might include game, such as quail, or a spicy pork sausage called andouille in their renditions of the classic dish.

A no-nonsense and highly nutritious concoction called red beans and rice is another example of how Spanish tastes influenced early Creole cooking. Specifically, *Moros y Cristianos*, a Spanish dish of highly seasoned black beans and plain white rice, is often cited as the inspiration for the New Orleans classic. As with jambalaya, though,

there is debate on this point, as some scholars look more to the African roots of the women who prepared the dish for clues to its origins. It is likely that both theories are correct to some degree. For example, the popular New Orleans dish bears many similarities to bean-and-rice dishes from Haiti, Cuba, and other Caribbean islands that were influenced by the tastes of Spanish colonists, African slaves, and native populations.

Traditionally, red beans and rice was served on Mondays in New Orleans and seasoned with Sunday's ham bone. Since Monday was wash day, African cooks could leave the beans unattended on the stove for hours while they engaged in the laborious and time-consuming chore of cleaning clothes. Red beans and rice still appears on the tables of elegant restaurants, neighborhood dives, and private homes alike. While the dish's origins may remain in question, its exalted place in Louisiana's culinary history is beyond dispute.

Despite decades of Spanish influence on the economics, politics, and culture of New Orleans, the city retained a distinctively French personality—and does so to this day. This is true in large part because the Castilians, eager to establish Louisiana as a bulwark against British incursions into its Mexican and Caribbean territories, opened Louisiana's gates wide to new settlers, including members of the French nobility who escaped the revolution of 1789 and French refugees who fled the crown's colony at Saint Domingue (Haiti) in the 1790s during an uprising by black slaves. Both groups made their way to New Orleans with a passion for good food and drink intact. The members of the French nobility were accompanied by skilled French cooks. The refugees from Saint Domingue were accompanied by slaves and free blacks who helped instill in New Orleans cooking a distinctive Afro-Caribbean flair. French Acadians whom the British expelled from Canada in 1755 also made their way to Louisiana during this period.

Antoine Amédée Peychaud, an apothecary in New Orleans and himself a French refugee from Saint Domingue, is credited with the invention of the cocktail. In 1793, as the legend goes, at his shop on Royal Street in the French Quarter, Peychaud introduced a tonic of cognac and bitters that he served in a French egg cup, or *coquetier*. It was an instant hit with customers: Peychaud is said to have sold enough of his healing elixir to inspire a bit of slurring in the words of those who imbibed, thereby securing the cocktail's place forever in the English lexicon.

Like wine at dinner or café noir (strong black coffee, usually made with chicory) at the close of a meal, the cocktail became ingrained in the social and eating customs of New Orleans. Although it is similar to a brandy toddy, Peychaud's potion was unique in its use of bitters and, over the next century, would inspire other famous Crescent City drinks. The Sazerac cocktail, first served at the Sazerac Coffee House in 1870 and later exclusively at the Roosevelt Hotel's Sazerac Bar, is a mixture of sugar, water, bitters, whiskey, and absinthe or absinthe substitute. The Ramos gin fizz, created by the barman Henry Ramos in the 1880s, is a creamy beverage that combines gin, lemon juice, orange-flavored water, sugar, an egg white, and milk or half-and-half. Like New Orleans restaurants that became famous for their specialty dishes (oysters Rockefeller at Antoine's, shrimp Arnaud at Arnaud's, and shrimp Clemenceau at Galatoire's, to name a few), barmen and drinking establishments were known for their signature cocktails—and remain so to this day.

Cajuns

In 1755, the French Acadians, who first settled in Canada in the seventeenth century, fell victim to the colonial struggle for control of North America and the Mississippi River and were ordered by the British to leave Canada. Thousands returned to France, while others wandered the Eastern Seaboard in search of a welcoming place. The first Acadians arrived in Louisiana around 1765. Over the

Brer Rabbit. Advertisement for Brer Rabbit molasses, from a cookbooklet issued by Pennik and Ford, New Orleans, 1930s. *Collection of Alice Ross*

next forty years, several thousand settlers would make the colony home, many having passed through Saint Domingue on their way. Some scholarship suggests that about half of Louisiana's Acadians can trace their roots to coastal areas of France, such as Brittany and Normandy.

Although some Acadians put down roots in New Orleans, the majority settled on nearby lands granted to them by the Spanish. In time, they could be found on farms and settlements across the bayous and prairies of southern Louisiana and down to the marshlands of the Gulf of Mexico. Already accustomed to colonial living, the Acadians adjusted to their new home and set about making good use of native plants and animals not only for their own food and livelihood but also for shipment and sale in New Orleans. Along the Mississippi the Acadians planted diverse crops, including rice, corn, peaches, apples, squash, peppers, beans, and potatoes. Along the coast they gathered oysters, shrimp, crabs, and fish. In the kitchen they let virtually nothing go to waste.

The term "Cajun," a corruption of "Acadian," came into use during the nineteenth century. Although the two words are used interchangeably, historians like Carl A. Brasseaux suggest an important distinction between the two. Following the sale of Louisiana to the United States in 1803, Anglo-Americans began streaming down the Mississippi River into New Orleans. According to Brasseaux, these English-speaking migrants used "Cajun" to refer, perhaps in a derogatory manner, to anyone of French descent or poor economic means—whether Creoles, Acadians, recent French immigrants, or even Anglos.

The Americans' melding of various groups into a single classification does not stray far from a process of cultural amalgamation that had been occurring since the Acadians' arrival in Louisiana. Like the first French settlers, the Acadians relied on native Indians for information about indigenous foods and techniques for growing or catching them. Over time, they also interacted with the Spanish, the French Creoles, and an array of new immigrants who arrived in Louisiana during the nineteenth century from places like Italy, Ireland, Yugoslavia, Greece, and China. The Acadians also intermingled with Africans, both slave and free.

Just as "Cajun" refers to a blended cultural group, it also designates a cuisine that reflects hundreds of years of adaptation. Although many of the best-known Cajun dishes are nearly identical to Creole favorites, general distinctions are often made between seasonings and presentation. Cajun cooking might use pungent flavorings, such as garlic and cayenne pepper, with more abandon than its Creole counterpart, but it is not the stereotypical mouth-blistering cuisine that was popularized in the 1980s. Cajun cuisine is also generally less formal in its presentation than Creole cooking, relying more on one-pot dishes that can be cooked over long periods of time and extended easily with the addition of water or stock. The New Orleans Creole table has always been more likely to display simple dishes like gumbo with sophisticated creations inspired by the finest French recipes and cooking techniques.

The humble crawfish (known more widely as crayfish) owes its rise to stardom to the Cajuns. This petite crustacean is plentiful in the freshwaters of Louisiana's bayous and lakes and resembles a lobster in general appearance. However, the crawfish's meat is more flavorful than that of its larger saltwater counterpart, with its yellowish fat cherished for the richness it imparts to any dish. Considered delicacies in France and Scandinavia, crawfish have had a place on elegant French menus for centuries, whether in their shells, as a mousse, or in aspic. Although they have appeared in similar manner on the menus of French and Creole restaurants in New Orleans, crawfish are much more strongly identified with the Cajuns, who consume and market them with near equal passion.

When crawfish are in season from the late winter through early summer, they are abundant on tables in southern Louisiana. At large outdoor parties, for example, it is popular to boil crawfish whole in a spicy broth, along with red potatoes and corn on the cob. The cooked and drained ingredients are then dumped onto long newspaper-topped tables and served with nothing more than a roll of paper towels and ice-cold beer. The crawfish boil is wonderful in its simplicity, and the slow pace required to peel and eat these piping-hot critters allows maximum time for socializing and good conversation with family and friends. The city of Breaux Bridge, located in the area of southern Louisiana officially designated by the state's legislature as Acadiana, proudly calls itself the crawfish capital of the world.

While crawfish find their way into myriad dishes, they are perhaps most notably identified with étouffée. Literally meaning "smothered," étouffée in Cajun parlance is a one-pot stew that spotlights a single main ingredient, such as crawfish or shrimp. An étouffée may or may not begin with a roux—that is the cook's choice—but it will always start off with basic seasoning vegetables, such as green peppers, onions, and celery sautéed in the pan. Peeled crawfish tails and either water or stock are added to the mix, which is covered with a lid and cooked down in the pot until the main ingredient becomes tender. It is served over rice. Crawfish bisque, a rich soup containing stock prepared by boiling the heads, is another beloved recipe. After boiling, the heads are stuffed with a mixture of onions, garlic, parsley, bread crumbs, and tail meat and served with the soup over rice.

While étouffée is considered a unique Cajun creation, the lineage of many other popular recipes is slightly more confused. Take court bouillon, which has solid roots in French cooking and appears in its traditional form as a simple poaching liquid for fish, eggs, and vegetables in early Creole cookbooks. However, variations on the original are more appealing to modern tastes. For example, the *Picayune's Creole Cook Book*, contains two modifications: one called court bouillon à la Creole and another called Spanish court bouillon.

Unlike the traditional poaching liquid, these recipes both start with a roux, contain a considerable amount of tomatoes, and call specifically for redfish or red snapper. They differ mainly in their use of herbs and spices, particularly in the Creole version's addition of cayenne pepper and allspice. Although the *Picayune's Creole Cook Book* presented these recipes as Creole concoctions, southern Louisiana's version of court bouillon is identified more closely with Cajun cooking and bears resemblance to spicy, tomato-based dishes from the Caribbean and rich West African stews.

Similar one-pot dishes in New Orleans are described simply as "à la Creole," meaning that they are prepared with a dark roux-based sauce, usually containing onions, celery, garlic, and green peppers. Shrimp Creole is a particular southern Louisiana favorite. Water (or stock), tomatoes (or tomato paste), salt, pepper, and a selection of herbs (typically thyme, bay leaves, and parsley) are added to the roux, and the dish is simmered for an hour or more. Just before serving the shrimp are stirred in. Chicken or fish may be substituted.

American Influence

A major turning point in the history of Louisiana came in 1803, when the United States, under the presidency of Thomas Jefferson (a self-avowed Francophile and devotee of French cuisine), purchased Louisiana from France. The incorporation of Louisiana into the Union precipitated a flood of American influence, including the arrival in 1812 of the first steamer to navigate the Mississippi River down to New Orleans. The resulting boom in river trade ushered in a golden era of commerce, wealth, and migration that forever changed the region. The increased trade also spiked the demand for slave labor, which was needed to sustain the plantations and a burgeoning agricultural sector. Many slaves became part of a community of female cooks whose talent for mixing diverse cultures and tastes on a single plate was considered unsurpassed. Even after the end of slavery, many remained in charge of kitchens throughout New Orleans and continued to perfect the melding of African, French, Spanish, English, Latin American, and other tastes that crossed the city's path.

During this period, black women called *pralinieres* could be found on the streets of New Orleans selling confections like the Creole praline to earn a bit of extra money. Bearing the name of César duc de Choiseul, comte Du Plessis-Praslin, the French marshal and diplomat who served Louis XIII and took credit for creating the praline (his cook was more likely the inventor), the traditional French confection is simply a sugared almond. Ursuline nuns who arrived in New Orleans in the 1700s are sometimes credited with introducing Louisiana to the French praline. Another explanation is that a New Orleans plantation owner returned from Paris with the confections and asked his cook to recreate the recipe. The cook, no doubt a slave, substituted pecans for the almonds and used Louisiana cane sugar to produce a small, round patty.

The Louisiana praline, which also calls for butter and cream, actually bears little resemblance to the French version and is thought to compare more closely to Spanish-inspired candies and patties from Mexico, South America, and the Caribbean. The Mexican *cajeta*, for example, is a popular caramel candy similar in consistency to fudge that is made of sugar and goat's milk. Fruit and nuts are sometimes added. Pralines are still hawked in the shops of the French Quarter, though more as a novelty for tourists than a delightful morsel for the city's locals.

Despite Louisiana's withdrawal from the Union during the American Civil War, a process of assimilation and Americanization continued throughout the late nineteenth and early twentieth centuries. Still, the Gulf Coast region of Louisiana, so deeply entrenched in French culture, never lost its distinctively Gallic flair. In Cajun country, where the use of the French language was once suppressed in schools, a council was established in 1968 to promote its use. Likewise, the efforts of Louisiana chefs like Paul Prudhomme ignited a craze for Cajun in the 1980s and cast an international spotlight on the region's food and culture.

New Orleans became known as the Paris of America in the nineteenth century. There, in private homes and elegant restaurants, the best of French and Creole cooking could be found on the table. Some of the same restaurants remain open to this day and continue to offer delicious reminders of the city's unusual past and its insatiable love affair with food.

Menu cards at the famous French Quarter restaurant called Arnaud's (established in 1918) still carry the founder's festive missive: "At least once a day, preferably in the cool and quiet of the evening, one should throw all care to the wind, relax completely and dine leisurely and well." Conveying more than their author's philosophy on dining, Arnaud Cazenave's words also express a timeless philosophy for living and being in New Orleans. Likewise, in the bayou country, where a survivor mentality continues to reign, the Cajuns have preserved their traditions of living and eating simply but well. Together, Cajun and Creole food constitute something much more than a collection of old recipes whose flavors can be parsed into their countries of origin. Instead, they represent a blurring of cultural lines and a marriage of flavors that have produced something uniquely and unmistakably American.

[*See also* African American Food, *sidebar* The Heritage of Soul Food; Casseroles; Cocktails; French Influences on American Food; Herbs and Spices; Okra; Native American Foods; Prudhomme, Paul; Rice.]

BIBLIOGRAPHY

Ancelet, Barry Jean, Jay D. Edwards, and Glen Pitri. *Cajun Country*. Jackson: University Press of Mississippi, 1991. See especially chapter nine on Cajun foodways.

Brasseaux, Carl A. *Acadian to Cajun: Transformation of a People, 1803–1877*. Jackson: University Press of Mississippi, 1992.

Brasseaux, Carl A., Keith P. Fontenot, and Claude F. Oubre. *Creoles of Color in the Bayou Country*. Jackson: University Press of Mississippi, 1994.

Clark, Morton G. *French-American Cooking: From New Orleans to Quebec*. New York: Funk and Wagnalls, 1967.

Feibleman, Peter S., and the editors of Time-Life Books. *American Cooking: Creole and Acadian*. New York: Time-Life Books, 1971.

Guste, Roy F., Jr. *Antoine's Restaurant Cookbook*. New Orleans: Carbery-Guste, 1978.

Gutierrez, C. Paige. *Cajun Foodways*. Jackson: University Press of Mississippi, 1992.

Hall, Gwendolyn Midlo. *Africans in Colonial Louisiana: The Development of Afro-Creole Culture in the Eighteenth Century*. Baton Rouge: Louisiana University Press, 1992.

Hellman, Lillian, and Peter S. Feibleman. *Eating Together: Recipes and Recollections*. Boston: Little, Brown, 1984. See chapter 2 on New Orleans.

Hess, Karen. *The Carolina Rice Kitchen: The African Connection*. Columbia: University of South Carolina Press, 1992. See chapter 3 for its discussion of jambalaya.

Jones, Evan. *American Food: The Gastronomic Story*. New York: Vintage, 1981. See chapters two and three about French and Spanish influences on American cooking.

Mitcham, Howard. *Creole Gumbo and All That Jazz: A New Orleans Seafood Cookbook*. Reading, MA: Addison-Wesley, 1978.

The Original Picayune Creole Cook Book. New Orleans: Times-Picayune, 1966. First published in 1901.

Prudhomme, Paul. *Chef Paul Prudhomme's Louisiana Kitchen*. New York: Morrow, 1984. This cookbook was instrumental in giving Cajun cooking gourmet status in America.

AMANDA WATSON SCHNETZER

Cakes

From the beginning of the nineteenth century through the middle of the twentieth, cake was the reigning passion of American women, and the cakes that American women devised, in all their glorious tastes and textures, stunning colors, and imposing forms, constituted a world-class repertoire.

The Early English Roots of American Cake

Cake came to America with the first English settlers primarily as "great cake," a lightly spiced, lightly sweetened, fruited bread something like today's "raisin bread" baked in the large, or "great," size of approximately fifty pounds. In England great cake was brought forth at weddings, christenings, funerals, and festivities marking religious and secular holidays. In colonial America, great cake was particularly associated with harvest festivals, thanksgiving feasts, university commencement days, and, above all, with election day, the day on which local representatives to the colonial courts were chosen. Election day great cakes survived beyond America's independence. *American Cookery*, published in 1796, contains a recipe for a gargantuan election cake weighing more than one hundred pounds. Much smaller versions of the cake, meant to be served at election day teas, remained part of American cookbook literature through the time of Fannie Farmer (1857–1915). Even today, recipes continue to be published in local newspapers across the United States during the election season.

Around the turn of the eighteenth century, a different sort of great cake evolved in England and quickly became fashionable among the colonial American gentry. This new great cake was not as large as its predecessor, but it was much richer and sweeter, its basic components being roughly equal weights of flour, sugar, butter, and eggs, with about half the weight of fruit to batter. Crucially, this

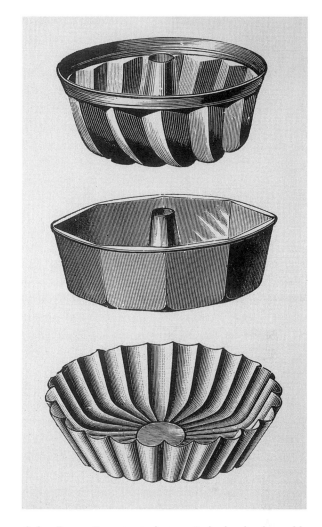

Cake Pans. *From top to bottom*, Turks head cake mold, octagon cake mold, and scalloped cake pan. From the 1922 catalog of the Crandall Pettee Co., New York.

new great cake, rather than being raised by yeast, was raised by beating air into the batter. The process was laborious—recipes give beating times in hours—but, for weddings, the prime occasions for the cake, the effort seemed worthwhile. A recipe for a great cake of this kind survived among the papers of Martha Washington, who most likely had the cake baked for family weddings. Gentry women of Washington's day placed smaller versions of the cake, iced white, surmounted by porcelain figurines, and festooned with paper or foil leaves, in the center of party tables for Christmas and Twelfth Night. These smaller fruited cakes were commonly called "plum cakes," plum being an old English term for raisins and currants.

Although yeast-raised great cake was the most characteristic, most broadly familiar of seventeenth-century

English cakes, it was not the only one. Those seventeenth-century English settlers of America wealthy enough to "banquet," that is, to enjoy an elaborate course of sweets, also knew "Portugal cake" and "bisket." By the eighteenth century, as the banquet gave way to dessert, these cakes became known as "queen cake" and "biscuit." In terms of composition and technique, Portugal cake and queen cake were similar to the new plum cakes of the eighteenth century, but they differed in size. Both were small individual cakes baked in fancy pans—heart shapes were characteristic for queen cake—as all cakes served at banquets and at dessert were.

Biscuit was an early form of sponge cake. Unlike Portugal cake and queen cake, which seem to have been uniquely English inventions, biscuit came to England via Italian and French sources, the latter predominating after 1700 and prompting the shift from the English "bisket" to the French "biscuit." Biscuit was baked either in small individual pans, typically square or rectangular, or as dropped cakes. Through the eighteenth century biscuit often was dried until crisp after baking, as many European sponge biscuits still are. Around 1840 Americans began calling slender rectangular biscuits, much in use for charlottes, "lady fingers."

During the eighteenth century, in both England and America, dessert was joined by two new entertainments that also called for cake. One was tea, which originated in the early part of the eighteenth century as a small, late-afternoon meal but became, by the middle of the century, a fancy-dress early-evening party that particularly featured cakes. The other entertainment was the so-called evening party, an affair of socializing and dancing that culminated, at eleven o'clock or later, in a buffet-like "supper" of mixed savory and sweet dishes. Although only individual-sized cakes customarily were served at dessert, tea tables and evening-party tables were set with large, decorative cakes baked in broad, deep, round or square pans or in turban molds and sometimes iced. These large cakes were of two basic types, pound cakes and sponge cakes, offshoots of the seventeenth-century Portugal cake and bisket, respectively.

The American Fine Cakes of the Early Nineteenth Century

In *American Notes*, published in 1842, Charles Dickens wrote that he could discern no difference between English and American evening parties. But the great English novelist was missing something. At English evening parties of the early nineteenth century, cake played a relatively minor role. At American evening parties, in contrast, cake was a principal attraction. The long supper table covered with a white cloth typically bore a row of different "fine cakes" down the center. These cakes were iced with a dried meringue similar to, but more tender than, today's royal icing and decorated in various ways: with colored icings applied by a syringe, with colored "sugar sand," with filigree sugar devices purchased at confectioners' shops, or with real or artificial flowers and leaves. In *The Kentucky Housewife*, published in 1839, Lettice Bryan, a wealthy planter's wife turned cookbook author, described the iced, decorated cakes served at elite evening parties in the antebellum South. "If you wish a splendid table," Bryan wrote, you should "dress," that is, ice and decorate, "all your fine cakes in different attire, suitable to the names and materials of which they are made, and arrange them handsomely upon the table, that the company may see the different kinds of cake."

By the time Bryan penned her remarks, the three "fine cakes" of the English eighteenth-century tradition—plum cake, pound cake, and sponge cake—had been revised along uniquely American lines and spun into new cakes of uniquely American pedigree. Plum cake became known as "black cake," the new name reflecting its new color. Americans darkened the cake with molasses—"Molasses makes it dark colored, which is desirable," wrote the cookbook author Lydia Maria Child in 1832 of her wedding fruitcake—with brown sugar, with large amounts of spice, or with all three. This fashion was English in origin, and it was copied in another English colonial outpost, Jamaica, where a very dark black cake is still made. Americans took the fashion for dark cake to a greater extreme than the English. Lettice Bryan, for example, described a black cake made not only with molasses, brown sugar, and spice, but also spiced with one pound of fresh blueberries. It is the darkest fruitcake imaginable.

Meanwhile, American women developed two vividly colored cakes out of pound cake, causing pound cake itself to lose its status as a standard fancy party cake. As Eliza Leslie, the most popular and influential American cookbook author of the second quarter of the nineteenth century, declared in a cookbook of 1848, "Common pound cakes are now very much out of use. They are considered old-fashioned." The usurpers of pound cake were lady cake, also known as "silver cake," and golden cake.

Lady cake was essentially a pound cake made with egg whites rather than whole eggs—as many as two dozen egg whites in some particularly extravagant recipes—and hauntingly flavored with bitter almonds pounded to a paste with rose water. The cake was not only dazzlingly white but also downy soft. Golden cake was a pound cake made with a combination of whole eggs and egg yolks and highly flavored with orange juice and zest. It was deep yellow, and, according to Leslie, it would "when cut, perfume the table." At particularly elegant evening parties two pairs of lady cakes and golden cakes would be present on the supper table, one pair at each end. On dessert tables another fancy convention prevailed. Women would bake silver cake and golden cake in separate square pans, cut each cake into individual squares, and then, as Leslie instructed, "pile" the differently colored squares "alternately" on the same plate, "handsomely arranged."

American women also developed white and yellow sponge cakes, the white made only with egg whites, and the yellow solely with egg yolks. Bryan warned her readers that these cakes were difficult to make, particularly the white, which she said would be "tough" unless the flour was stirred in "very lightly and gradually." Still, the cake was worth the pains taken because it was so special. Bryan told her readers to "ice it very white and smooth; and if it is for a fine supper, place round the edge some very small gilded leaves, which is a common decorament on such occasions with some of the most fashionable people in America."

The final member of the early American family of colored cakes was the jelly cake, composed of a number of round cakes stacked together with brightly colored jelly or jam spread lavishly between the layers. Jelly cake sometimes was iced and sometimes not. Leslie suggested that when jelly cake was iced, the top be decorated with wedges of differently colored sugar sand. In the earliest recipes, jelly cake was prepared with pound cake batter baked in numerous very thin layers on a griddle. In later recipes the batter is baked in an oven in four to six layers, a procedure that Leslie called "less troublesome," and sponge cake, silver cake, or golden cake sometimes were used in place of pound cake. One particularly ambitious recipe, from the Georgia cookbook author Annabella Hill, called for stacking thin silver and golden cake layers alternately—"very beautiful," said Hill. Whatever the basic cake material, the goal was the same: a cake that when cut, revealed vivid stripes of color.

The Cakes Served at Tea in the Early Nineteenth Century

Around 1800 two new sorts of teas came to the United States from England, both of which, like the fancy-dress evening tea party (which remained in vogue), called for cake. These new teas were sit-down meals. One tea quickly replaced supper and often was called supper in the homes of farm families and working people, the largest portion of the American population. This tea consisted of leftovers from the noonday dinner (then the main meal of the day), perhaps a simple hot dish or two, great platters of thickly buttered bread slices, and as many hot breads, griddle cakes, doughnuts, gingerbread, and other cakes as a housewife could muster, all washed down with tea and coffee. The other new tea was an entertainment staged at various times but most typically in the early evening. It featured only breads and cakes, particularly the latter, along with their typical accompaniments, such as butter, jelly, jam, fruit butters, lemon jelly (or curd), and quince cheese (or paste). In the homes of ordinary Americans, where dinner parties, evening tea parties, and evening parties were unknown, this tea was the most common means of entertaining company.

In some homes, expensive, difficult, time-consuming "fine cakes," particularly plain pound cake and sponge cake, were served at teas for company, at least on important occasions. In most households, however, women opted for less expensive, quicker, easier cakes to serve at tea. These cakes fell into two major groups. First were various cakes similar to pound cake but made with less butter and fewer eggs, the two most expensive cake ingredients in period American kitchens. These cakes were flavored with spice, and most were made with raisins and currants. Some were quite rich, whereas others were extremely plain, although the plainness was misleading. At tea, most cakes, even pound cake and sponge cake, were commonly eaten with butter, much to the consternation of the cookbook author Sarah Hale, who declared in a cookbook in 1841 that such practice was "a sin." The richer, nicer spiced, fruited cakes served at tea were named for American patriots (Washington, Madison, Harrison, Jefferson) or American cities (Boston, Rutland, Dover) or were given highfalutin names such as "composition cake" and "French cake." American women obviously considered these cakes uniquely theirs.

The second type of cake served at tea was most commonly called "cup cake" but also was called "measure cake" or "number cake." This cake proved to be one of the most important cakes in American cake-baking history. Like the spiced, fruited cakes, cup cake was a sort of less expensive pound cake, but it was a plain cake, containing little or no spice and no fruit. The name was something of a play on words. The cake was a cup cake both because, contrary to convention, its ingredients were measured by the cup rather than weighed (ingredients for cake were always weighed at the time) and because it was baked in cups, which, depending on the household, might be tea cups, small pattypans (similar to today's tartlet molds), or the cups of so-called puff pans (broadly similar to today's cupcake pans). But beneath the play on words was serious business. The reason the ingredients of the cake were measured rather than weighed was to save time. And the reason why the cake was baked in cups was that, paradoxically, this was a very convenient way in the hearth-era kitchen. Large cakes took an extremely long time to bake, whether in a fireplace oven (or "beehive oven") or in a Dutch oven, a covered pot nestled in the embers of the fireplace, and had to be checked often. And even with conscientious checking, large cakes were prone to burning. But cakes baked in small cups baked rapidly and rose properly even when made inexpensively and quickly. Lydia Maria Child made the point succinctly: "Cup cake is about as good as pound cake, and is cheaper."

The American inventions in cakes served at tea occurred in the context of a major technological development. Toward the end of the eighteenth century, Americans had begun to leaven molasses gingerbread with pearl ash, a type of baking soda derived from wood ashes, a trick almost certainly learned from Dutch American settlers in New York. Since the evolving tea cakes were deficient in butter and eggs, women often made them with pearl ash and milk, which provided the lift, tenderness, and moisture that butter and eggs ordinarily supplied. By the 1830s women had come to realize that cup cake, when made with pearl ash, did not have to be baked in cups but could instead be baked in a single large pan, and by the 1840s this practice had become prevalent. The formula now most commonly used for cup cake was the one that was simplest to remember: one cup of butter, two cups of sugar, three cups of flour, and four eggs plus one cup of milk and one spoonful of soda (not necessarily pearl ash at this point; other alkalis were in use). Recalling this crucial transition in a cookbook of the 1890s, the cookbook author Marion Harland, promoting a brand of baking powder (a development of

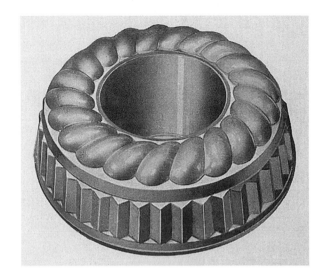

Cake Pan. Cepeco sandtorte pan. From the 1922 catalog of the Crandall Pettee Co., New York.

the 1850s), wrote, " 'One cup of butter, two of sugar, three of flour, and four eggs.' Thus ran the formula that fixed the proportions of 'one, two, three, and four cake' in our grandmothers' minds. When we add a cupful of milk and a heaping teaspoonful of Cleveland's Baking Powder we better the recipe." This simple formula became known as one-two-three-four cake.

The New Cakes of the Stove Era

Throughout the hearth era, the American "fine cakes"—black cake, pound cake, lady cake, golden cake, jelly cake, and the various sponge cakes—remained a thing apart from the cakes baked for tea, their ingredients still weighed rather than measured and their batters still raised exclusively by butter and/or eggs and strenuous beating, without the aid of chemical leavening. But times were changing. By 1850, most American households had forsaken the ancestral kitchen hearth in favor of the enclosed iron stove. Because the stove oven was much easier to manage than the fireplace oven and Dutch oven, cake-baking became more accessible to ordinary middle-class women. Middle-class women, however, found the hearth-era recipes for fine cakes too expensive, time-consuming, and labor-intensive for their means. Cookbook authors responded to their plight. By the 1850s, cookbook authors outlined many thriftier, simplified recipes for fine cakes, the ingredients measured rather than weighed, butter and eggs reduced to modest quantities, the beating process shortened and streamlined, and, crucially, the batter raised with chemical leavening.

In a cookbook of the 1850s, Eliza Leslie addressed the use of chemical leavening in fine cakes. Leslie's concern was that some of her readers, in an effort to make their golden cakes more golden and to make use of the yolks left over from silver cake, were making golden cakes with egg yolks only, rather than with a combination of yolks and whole eggs, and then puffing up the batter with soda. "Do not attempt to make this cake with yolk of egg only by way of improving the yellow color. Without any whites, it will assuredly be tough and heavy," Leslie admonished her readers. Then she homed in on her main point: "If you use soda, saleratus, hartshorn, or any of the alkalis, they will entirely destroy the orange flavor, and communicate a bad taste of their own." But the eighteenth-century gentry taste principles that Leslie had been taught in her youth no longer held sway. Middle-class women would have fine cake, and chemical leavening was their indispensable means of acquiring it.

By the end of the Civil War a new American cake age had dawned. There were now essentially three American cake families. First, there were the traditional cakes of the pound-cake type, namely, pound cake itself and black cake, typically called fruitcake, which remained the favorite American celebration cake. Neither was immune to the broader period trends in American cake baking. Recipes calling for diminished quantities of butter and eggs and chemical leavening were outlined in a number of cookbooks published in the 1860s and thereafter. The big news of the 1860s was the arrival of a new cake family, the family that is today referred to as "butter cakes." The leading member of this family was cup cake, or one-two-three-four cake, which now appeared in cookbooks in innumerable slightly modified forms—that is, with two or three eggs rather than four, with four cups of flour instead of three, and so on—and under many names. The other members of this family were the previous generation's silver cake, golden cake, and various spiced, fruited cakes baked for tea, all of which were now revised as modified cup cakes. The basic formula for silver cake now ran one cup of butter, two of sugar, three of flour, and six or eight egg whites, with a cup of milk and a spoonful of chemical leavening added. The basic formula for gold cake was similar, except that six or eight egg yolks were used. There had been many spiced, fruited cakes in the hearth-era kitchen, and there remained many in the stove kitchen, but the new cakes, unlike the old, all hewed to the same basic one-two-three-four formula. A number of fancy spiced, fruited cakes now appeared on the scene, all of them fashionably dark in color. So-called spice cakes were made with large amounts of cinnamon and cloves and, generally speaking, either brown sugar or molasses. "Coffee cakes," made with coffee instead of milk, became a rage. And in the South, "jam cakes," typically made with blackberry jam, the darkest of all preserves, bloomed.

Finally, there were the sponge cakes. Although traditional egg-rich formulas for plain sponge cake persisted in cookbooks, most recipes were inexpensive and quick, calling for only two or three eggs and, of course, chemical leavening. White and yellow sponge cakes were an entirely different matter. White sponge cake, commonly called "angel cake," became much lighter and moister and much more difficult to make than it had been in Lettice Bryan's day. Angel cake required precise beating of the egg whites and a dexterous hand in folding. To rise, the cake had to be baked in a specialized tube pan, which was never to be greased, and in order not to collapse after baking, the cake had to be hung upside down until cold, a procedure that invited a range of disasters, as period cookbooks attested. How Victorian American women developed the complicated techniques that angel cake requires remains mysterious. The new yellow sponge cakes of the stove era were neither as innovative nor as difficult as angel cake, but they were nonetheless extravagant cakes by the standards of the age. They required many eggs (in most recipes, a combination of whole eggs and egg yolks) and a great deal of beating, and they were never made with chemical leavening. Generally called "sunshine cake" or "moonshine cake," these cakes, although fairly fashionable through the mid-twentieth century, were never as popular as angel cake.

The New Cake Forms of the Stove Era

The cookbook evidence suggests that Victorian American women served cake in the same basic ways that their mothers and grandmothers had. For desserts, women generally baked cake in square pans or "in sheets" and served it in cut squares on cake plates or in pierced-silver cake baskets. Meanwhile, for parties, including afternoon tea parties, a new fashion set in part by Queen Victoria, large, showy cakes remained fashionable. However, the party cakes of the early nineteenth century would no longer do. No matter how skillfully iced and fancifully decorated, they were, at bottom, simply large "loaves." America had entered its legendary Gilded Age, when grandiloquent Frenchified styles of cooking, dining, and entertaining were in vogue among the wealthy, styles that were imitated, albeit on a humbler scale, by middle-class women. Much grander party cakes were required for this new age, and they promptly materialized.

First was the marble cake, a logical extension of the American fascination with cake color. When marble cake first appeared, its dark swirls were produced through the addition of molasses, spice, and, in some recipes, raisins or currants. The simpler recipes were prepared using a single whole-egg batter, half of it darkened, but more ambitious recipes produced a more dramatic effect by making use of separate silver and gold batters, the latter darkened. Other bicolored cakes soon entered the scene. Hard-money cake was made by swirling silver and gold batters. Watermelon cake called for lining a cake pan with a silver batter and then filling in the center with a red-tinted batter flecked with chopped raisins to simulate seeds. Some bakers cinched the conceit by baking the cake in a melon mold (at the time standard kitchen equipment, at least in well-heeled households, for producing molded French ice cream) and covering the cake with green-tinted icing. Red velvet cake, the successor of watermelon cake, seems plain in comparison.

Equally grand were two reconfigurations of the old jelly cake. One, the "roll jelly cake," later known as the "jelly roll," was a conflation of the jelly cake with the fashionable French roll cakes of the day. The other was a completely American notion: the layer cake. The earliest layer cake recipes were outlined in southern cookbooks published immediately after the Civil War. Most often called "white mountain cake," the cakes typically consisted of four to six layers of yellow or white butter cake filled and frosted with meringue icing. Grated fresh coconut often was included between the layers and over the cake. In her cookbook of 1871, Mrs. M. E. Porter included step-by-step instructions for the new cake, which, she wrote, "is very nice indeed, particularly for weddings and parties. . . . Bake [the cake] like jelly cake, four in number; frost the first cake on top, lay on another and frost in like manner, and in like manner the other two; when all are done, even the edges with a knife and frost the sides, and the 'White Mountain' is finished." For this new cake a new sort of frosting was required: a soft frosting. Porter made the point explicit: "Do not put the cake by the fire to harden the frosting." Porter described a frosting prepared in the old way, by simply whisking up raw egg whites with sugar, but experiments with cooked meringue frostings, which were smoother and more stable, were already under way and soon gave rise to boiled icings.

By the 1880s the vogue for layer cakes had spread across the United States, and new layer cakes developed. The most popular were white or yellow layer cakes mortared with "jellies" that were actually rich stovetop custards made with eggs, sugar, and butter. Many of the lemon and orange cakes of the day fell into this group, their custardy jellies made with citrus zest and juice. Almost as popular were layer cakes filled with "caramel," a glossy, sticky-chewy cooked syrup made with brown sugar, milk, butter, and, in some recipes, chocolate. Caramel fillings were succeeded in the 1890s by fudge filling and frosting, which were similar to caramel except that the syrup was beaten after cooking and so became soft and creamy.

In a category of their own were the various sponge layer cakes, which called for a different roster of fillings and frostings. The most fashionable sponge layer cakes were the cream cakes, filled with either whipped cream or pastry cream and generally left unfrosted. Southern bakers served Robert E. Lee cake, a sponge layer cake filled and frosted with a moist icing of sugar and orange juice. The most historically important sponge layer cake was the mocha cake, a French-inspired dessert typically filled and frosted with coffee-flavored confectioners' sugar butter cream. This cake introduced butter cream frosting to American kitchens.

The longtime American fascination with dark-colored cake found expression in the new layer cakes. A favorite conceit entailed sandwiching a dark cake layer between two yellow or, better, white layers. Such was the plan behind ribbon cake, metropolitan cake, Neapolitan cake, Prince of Wales cake, Dolly Varden cake, Jenny Lind cake, and others. Cakes composed entirely of dark layers also were prized, and these were no longer darkened exclusively with spice, molasses, and fruit. Caramel cakes, colored with either brown sugar or caramel syrup, now appeared and, more important, so did cakes darkened with chocolate. Americans did not embrace chocolate cake overnight. In the original 1896 edition of Fannie Farmer's *Boston Cooking-School Cook Book*, for example, there were only two chocolate cakes, and both were exceedingly pale. In the 1914 edition, however, there were four chocolate cakes and two devil's food cakes, one of which was far more chocolatey than the most intensely chocolate devil's food cakes made today. Farmer's cookbook also contained recipes for chocolate Vienna cake, chocolate sponge cake, and chocolate fruitcake. Farmer even added four squares of chocolate to one of her wedding fruitcakes in order to darken it.

The Cakes of the Twentieth Century

By the 1930s marketing forces increasingly ruled American kitchens and steered the course of American cake. American homemakers were using cake recipes found in newspaper and magazine advertisements, on box tops and product inserts, and in booklets published by companies that produced flour, sugar, vegetable shortening, baking powder, chocolate, nut meats, flavoring extracts, dried fruits, and other products. One of their favorite cookbook authors, Betty Crocker, was actually the fictional face of General Mills, producer of Gold Medal flour and Softasilk cake flour. Most real-life cookbook authors endorsed even more products than Betty did. Some of these products, such as vegetable shortening, turned out to be successes, whereas others, such as dates, proved to be passing phenomena. But the truly important consequence of marketing in American kitchens had nothing to do with products. It was that the preparation of all dishes, including cakes, became less

Cake Recipes. Cookbooklet issued by Kraft. *Culinary Archives & Museum at Johnson & Wales University, Providence, R.I.*

expensive, quicker, easier, and more approachable. The goal of marketers was to reach as broad an audience as possible. This is not to say that the new cake recipes of the mid-twentieth century were bad. On the contrary, they were generally excellent, particularly recipes produced by corporate test kitchens and by magazine conglomerates such as *Good Housekeeping* and *Better Homes and Gardens*. The decline in quality came later, when "cheaper, quicker, easier" came to mean mix-made cakes glommed together with canned frosting, packaged pudding mix, synthetic whipped toppings, artificially flavored gelatin, and glutinous canned fruit filling.

The layer cake remained the most characteristic American cake at mid-century. However, it was now as often baked for family as for company, and it was customarily quite simple: a single kind of cake, typically yellow, white, or chocolate butter cake filled and frosted with a single preparation, typically boiled meringue icing or confectioners' sugar butter cream. "Snack cakes" baked in square or rectangular pans, tube pans, or brick-loaf bread pans also proliferated. The two favorites were chocolate cake and, harking back to the previous century, various cakes made with spices and raisins. From the spice-raisin group emerged snack cakes in which applesauce, mashed bananas, or mashed cooked prunes or dates replaced some or all of the customary buttermilk. Chopped walnuts, now heavily promoted by the California producers, joined or replaced raisins in many recipes. One test-kitchen employee discovered that this kind of cake could even be made with canned condensed tomato soup.

When the occasion was fancy, American women gravitated toward either roll cakes or angel cake, which some particularly ambitious bakers hollowed out and filled with gelatinized mousse and frosted with whipped cream. Angel cake was difficult to prepare, and American bakers were grateful when Betty Crocker unrolled, with great fanfare, a brand-new cake that was every bit as moist and tender and every bit as tall as angel cake but was much easier to make. It was the chiffon cake, invented in the 1920s by Harry Baker, a Los Angeles insurance salesman turned Hollywood caterer. Baker sold the formula to General Mills in the 1940s. The secret of Baker's formula was cooking oil, a then unheard-of ingredient in cake.

While Baker was perfecting chiffon cake, the large food companies were simplifying the mixing of butter cakes. The standard procedure was to "cream" (that is, soften and aerate) the butter and sugar, to beat in the eggs one at a time, and then to add the dry ingredients (flour, leavening, and salt) in increments alternating with the milk. A General Foods baking booklet of the 1930s described a quicker, easier way, often called the "muffin method," in its recipe for busy day cake, a yellow butter cake. As the booklet explained, "All the dry ingredients are sifted together, the liquids are combined and added with the softened butter, and the batter beaten vigorously." This was a good way to mix a butter cake, and by the 1940s the major flour mills were publishing many recipes for cakes mixed this way (and also, by the way, making use of the same principles in devising the first cake mixes). But American women did not embrace the muffin method, most likely because, working with a spoon or rotary egg beater, as most women then still did, they were unable to beat the batter sufficiently to achieve good results. The muffin method, now called the two-stage method (dry, then wet), is better known in the early 2000s due in large measure to Rose Levy Beranbaum's *The Cake Bible* (1988), a highly popular cookbook in which it was featured. Using electric mixers, Beranbaum's readers can be assured of success.

A less effective version of the muffin method was also abroad by the 1930s. It entailed the use of melted rather than softened butter, and no matter how hard the batter was beaten, the result was a low-rising, crumbly, coarse-textured cake that indeed resembled a muffin. Ruth Wakefield, in *Toll House Tried and True Recipes* (1940), called her melted-butter muffin cake "slop-over cake"—not exactly a mouth-watering title. From melted butter it was only one small step to cooking oil, already familiar in American cake baking owing to chiffon cake. Faux butter cakes made with cooking oil and mixed slop-over style appeared sporadically in cookbooks in the 1950s. Such recipes were not widely used, however, until the introduction of carrot cake in the 1960s. Carrot cake was an oil cake that blended the old American predilection for spiced, raisin-studded cake with the health consciousness of the late twentieth century. It was a tremendous hit. By the 1980s there were uncountable recipes for oil cakes in cookbooks. Many of these cakes were made with fruits or vegetables, such as applesauce, bananas, pumpkin, and chopped pineapple (as in hummingbird cake), but some were simply yellow cakes or chocolate cakes. These so-called dump-and-mix cakes not only were extremely quick and easy to make, but, just as important, they also were moist, at least if sufficient oil was used. Truly dry cake has never been liked. Eliza Leslie inveighed against dry cake in cookbooks of the 1830s and 1840s. But Leslie would be surprised by the degree of moistness expected from cake in the twenty-first century. "Dump-and-mix" has not entirely conquered American cake baking. Rich pound cakes and Bundt cakes, which often are soaked in syrup to give them the sought-after moistness, are much in vogue.

Fine European cakes started filtering into mainstream American cookbooks in the early twentieth century. The first arrivals were middle European tortes, which were further popularized by successive editions of *The Joy of Cooking*, a cookbook with German American roots. Since the 1950s French chocolate cakes of various kinds have come into fashion, giving rise to intensely chocolate mud cake, chocolate truffle cake, chocolate soufflé cake, and individual molten chocolate cakes. The temperamental French sponge cake genoise has been popular on and off in the United States since the 1960s, although home cooks seem now to be giving up on it. Reflecting the current romance with Italy in the early 2000s, various "polenta cakes" and semolina cakes are fashionable, some of these made with olive oil.

But notwithstanding the appearance of these fancy new cakes, ours is not an age of cake. Cake is not really all that difficult, but decades of reliance on store-bought cakes and cake mixes have rendered American home bakers, particularly younger ones, helpless before even the simplest recipes. When people no longer know what softened butter is, nor even how to soften it, the game is fairly well up. Furthermore, cakes, or at least grand cakes, are the sort of thing one brings forth on a footed cake stand and serves with a certain degree of ceremony—on dessert plates with dessert forks and accompanied by coffee and tea. This does not sound like America at the opening of the twenty-first century.

[*See also* Advertising Cookbooks and Recipes; Betty Crocker; Child, Lydia Maria; Desserts; Farmer, Fannie; Jelly Rolls; Ladyfingers; Leslie, Eliza; Simmons, Amelia.]

BIBLIOGRAPHY

All About Home Baking. New York: General Foods, 1933.

Beranbaum, Rose Levy. *The Cake Bible*. New York: William Morrow, 1988.

Bryan, Lettice. *The Kentucky Housewife*. Facsimile of the original 1839 edition. Columbia: University of South Carolina Press, 1991.

Child, Lydia Maria. *The American Frugal Housewife*. Facsimile of the twelfth edition, 1832. Bedford, MA: Applewood Books [n.d.].

Dickens, Charles. *American Notes*. Reprint of the 1842 edition. New York: Penguin, 2000.

Farmer, Fannie Merritt. *The Boston Cooking-School Cook Book*. Facsimile of the original 1896 edition. New York: Weathervane Books [n.d.].

Farmer, Fannie Merritt. *The Boston Cooking-School Cook Book*. Boston: Little, Brown, 1914.

Hale, Sarah Josepha. *The Good Housekeeper*. Facsimile of the 1841 edition. Mineola, NY: Dover, 1996.

Harland, Marion. *National Cookbook*. New York: Scribners, 1896.

Hill, Annabella. *Mrs. Hill's New Cook Book*. Facsimile of the 1872 edition. Columbia: University of South Carolina Press, 1995.

Leslie, Eliza. *Directions for Cookery, in Its Various Branches*. Philadelphia: Cary and Hart, 1837. Facsimile of the 1848 edition, New York: Arno, 1973. Facsimile of the 1851 edition, Mineola, NY: Dover, 1999.

Leslie, Eliza. *Miss Leslie's New Cookery Book*. Philadelphia: T. B. Peterson, 1857.

Leslie, Eliza. *Miss Leslie's New Receipts for Cooking*. Philadelphia: T. B. Peterson, 1854.

Porter, Mrs. M. E. *Mrs. Porter's New Southern Cookery Book*. Reprint of the 1871 edition. New York: Promontory Press, 1974.

Rombauer, Irma S. *The Joy of Cooking*. New York: Bobbs-Merrill, 1943.

Simmons, Amelia. *American Cookery*. Facsimile of the 2nd edition, 1796. Bedford, MA: Applewood Books, 1996.

Wakefield, Ruth. *Toll House Tried and True Recipes*. New York: M. Barrows, 1940.

STEPHEN SCHMIDT

California

California's geography—its rivers, valleys, deserts, gorges, lakes, streams, forests, marshlands, estuaries, fertile Central Valley, and extensive coastline—supports an overwhelming variety of flora and fauna, which for thousands of years has shaped the diet of those who lived in what is today California. Historians' best estimates suggest that nomadic groups of peoples originating in Asia first visited what is today California beginning in about 12,000 B.C.E. These groups were followed by successive waves of peoples, some of whom settled permanently. Their diets reflected the local climate and ecology. In the northwestern California rain forest, salmon and trout were the major protein source, while groups living along the coast hunted sea mammals and gathered shellfish. For those living east of the Sierras, the staple food was the pine nut, especially the nut of the piñon pine. In the southern deserts, mesquite beans and the leaves of the century plant provided food. California Indians living along the lower Colorado River in southeastern California practiced agriculture, and raised corn, beans, and squashes.

Using bows and arrows, nets, and throwing sticks, most California Indians hunted large and small game, including deer, elks, antelopes, aquatic birds, and rabbits. They supplemented the game with the local wild plant foods—

Gathering Seeds. A Coast Pomo gathers seeds with a seed beater and basket, 1924. *Prints and Photographs Division, Library of Congress/Edward S. Curtis*

seeds, nuts, berries, leafy plants, roots, and bulbs. Oak trees and shrubs covered large portions of California, and the acorn was a very important food. In autumn, women gathered, dried, and hulled the acorns, then pounded them into flour. Water was poured over the flour to leach out the tannic acid. The flour was made into mush or baked into unleavened bread. Piñon (pine nuts) were a staple for groups living east of the Sierras. These nuts were harvested in the late summer or very early autumn as the pinecones began to drop. The cones had to be beaten or roasted near a fire in order to open them up, so the nuts could be removed. Once roasted, the shells were lightly cracked on a metate, or mortar, and the kernels were removed. Pine nuts could be eaten raw but were commonly ground into a fine meal and cooked into mush.

Some Indians ate insects, such as grasshoppers and wasps. Along the coast and waterways, they fished with hooks, nets, and spears. By 7000 B.C.E., Native Americans had built small boats able to travel great distances, as archaeological sites on the Channel Islands off the California coast attest.

Most California Native Americans cooked over open fires. They also mastered pit-cooking, which was done by digging a hole, lining it with rocks, and building a wood fire at the bottom. When the flames subsided, the coals were spread out and food was placed on top and covered with leaves, earth, and sometimes rocks to seal in the heat. Basket making was highly developed; very tightly woven baskets served as cooking pots and water containers. The baskets could not be placed over a fire, so instead hot rocks were dropped into a water-filled basket, and the food was cooked in the heated water.

Spanish and Mexican Period

Beginning in 1769, Spain supported the establishment of twenty-one Franciscan missions, military strongholds, and small civilian colonies from San Diego to north of San Francisco. The Spanish, Mexican, and Mexican Indian colonists brought with them many plants and domesticated animals from Mexico, including almonds, apples, apricots, bananas, barley, beans, cherries, chickpeas, chilies, citrons, dates, figs, grapes, lemons, lentils, limes, maize, olives, nectarines, oranges, peaches, pears, plums, pomegranates, quinces, tomatoes, walnuts, and wheat, as well as chickens, cows, donkeys, goats, horses, sheep, and domesticated turkeys. The colonists supplemented their fare with most of the same types of game hunted by the Native Americans. The colonists made corn tortillas, as the wheat varieties that they brought with them were not easily cultivated in California. When wheat became more abundant, it was used to make tortillas on special occasions. The Spanish established the first flour mill in 1786.

The role of the missions was to Christianize the California Indians. Many Indians did convert to Christianity and relocated around the Spanish settlements, which resulted in a shift in their diet. They had been accustomed to eating vegetables, fish, and game, but mission agriculture and husbandry brought them a monotonous diet of *atole*, a gruel made from ground, leached acorns or other nutlike seeds, and pinole, a flour made by grinding seeds. Many Native Americans became ill and died because of this limited, nutrient-poor diet.

Spanish settlements in California were isolated from Mexico, and the Spanish communities remained small. Mexico gained its independence in 1821 and during the following decade began to secularize the Franciscan missions. At the time, the missions had an estimated 14,500 horses and 151,000 cows. Mexican colonists sacked the buildings and took possession of the grounds, vineyards, cattle, horses, and stores. The main foods consumed during California's Mexican period were beef, frijoles (beans), and tortillas. These foods were supplemented with *picadillo* (hash), stuffed chilies, stuffed onions, *estofado* (a type of stew), Spanish rice, and tamales, which consisted of beans, beef, pork, or chicken encased in corn dough, wrapped and tied with cornhusks, and boiled or steamed.

After secularization, the economy of California was entirely based on ranchos—large ranches that had started as land grants to retired soldiers who had protected the missions. The missions provided the ranchos with seeds, plants, horses, and cattle. After secularization, many ranchos controlled thousands of acres. They were generally cattle-raising operations, and hides and tallow became a medium of exchange. As the ranchos expanded and settlement in California increased, the hunting grounds for the California Indians fast disappeared. Many California Indians were forced into cattle raiding or peonage on the ranchos. Failing these, they starved.

Americanization

For the United States, Mexico's independence in 1821 meant the beginning of overland travel to the Pacific: American trappers and traders traversed the Rocky Mountains and visited California. Trade between California and the United States began in the 1840s. Although there were only a few hundred Americans living in California at the time, they controlled the trade. When war erupted between Mexico and the United States in 1846, American soldiers supported by local Mexicans quickly seized California from Mexican authorities.

When gold was discovered in 1848, thousands of prospectors headed for California's gold mining regions. About 75 percent came from the eastern United States and the remaining 25 percent were Europeans, Chinese, Japanese, Australians, and Hawaiians. These groups overwhelmed the small Spanish Mexican population of California and brought their own culinary ideas with them. Ever since, California has been one of the major conduits for foreign culinary influences in America.

To meet the needs of the diverse immigrants flooding in, modest hotels and boardinghouses were opened in northern California. Restaurants, at first crude, became increasingly elaborate. Meals were hearty, such as a breakfast composed of beefsteak, flapjacks, bacon, stewed apples, rolls, butter, and coffee. As the gold rush brought new wealth to the region, San Francisco restaurants became particularly significant. The Poule d'or, which opened in

1849, was founded by a French chef from New Orleans. Later renamed the Poodle Dog, it was famous for its frogs legs and other French delicacies. Other early restaurants included Tadich Grill and the New World Coffee Stand. The Chinese immigrant Norman Asing opened America's first Chinese restaurant, the Macao and Woosung. San Francisco's first brewery opened in 1850.

Lacking a similar infusion of wealth to spur rapid growth, southern California grew more slowly. Its population was small by comparison to northern California and its culinary achievements were limited. In 1852 the first bakery in Los Angeles opened, as did the first restaurant. According to a contemporary account, La Rue's had a mud floor and half a dozen wooden tables covered with dirty tablecloths; the food was poorly cooked but generously portioned. About the same time, the first lager beer, imported from San Francisco, was offered for sale in Los Angeles.

During the late nineteenth and early twentieth centuries, northern California's restaurants continued to improve. In San Francisco, Tadich Grill, which had been a saloon originally, was converted to a respectable restaurant and thrived, as did the Poodle Dog. After the 1906 San Francisco earthquake and fire, restaurants had to be rebuilt. The Poodle Dog reopened, newly named Jack's. The European Hotel, which later became the elegant San Francisco landmark Ernie's, opened in 1907. *Bohemian San Francisco,* a restaurant guide published in 1914, lists French, Spanish, German, Italian, Mexican, Chinese, and Japanese establishments, as well as fish restaurants and hotel restaurants. By the end of World War II, Jack's and Tadich Grill still flourished, as did Ernie's. The Blue Fox was another favorite.

With its population growing because of the construction of railroads and a man-made harbor, Los Angeles also began to develop several good restaurants. Some, such as the Brown Derby, which opened in 1926, catered to movie stars. Although the restaurant is long gone, its Cobb salad remained an important item on American menus in the early 2000s. Other restaurants, such as Perino's and LaRue, targeted the culinary elite; although both of these establishments were Italian-owned, they both served classic French food.

Agriculture and Canning

During the gold rush, the main problem confronting early agriculture in northern California was how to grow food fast enough to meet the demands of miners and immigrants. Supplying the growing population was a difficult task. Flour and canned goods had to be shipped from the East Coast, unloaded at Panama, carted over the isthmus, reloaded onto ships on the Pacific side, and then shipped north to San Francisco. The only alternative was the arduous and much longer trip around the tip of South America. This was an expensive venture and it was not financially feasible for many products to be shipped this way. Beans and dried fruits were imported from Chile and yams from the Sandwich Islands (Hawaii). Turtles' eggs and seagulls'

California Product. Sun-Maid raisin recipe booklet issued by the California Associated Raisin Co., Fresno, 1921. *Collection of Andrew F. Smith*

eggs from the Farallon Islands in the Pacific off the San Francisco coast were collected and sold. Hunters supplied snipes, plover, cranes, ducks, curlews, and other wildfowl, as well as elks, black-tailed deer, and grizzly bears. Salmon and salmon trout were caught in California rivers. Vegetables were extremely hard to obtain during the first years and their price extremely high (a one-and-one-half-acre vegetable plot was estimated by one source to generate the equivalent of eighteen thousand dollars in income). As a result, scurvy and other diseases caused serious problems for the miners.

While gold was the reason immigrants poured into California in the late 1840s and 1850s, agriculture was the reason many remained. California's climate and soil were ideal for a variety of crops, particularly fruits, vegetables, and nuts, and for raising cattle, poultry, and sheep. California's agriculture rapidly expanded during the 1850s.

The astronomical price of food during the gold rush made it profitable for canneries to open in California. But even with the vast immigration, California was too small a market for major canneries. Until the completion of the transcontinental railroad in 1869 (and the opening of the Panama Canal in 1914), California canners reached out to overseas markets, which were more accessible and profitable. Before long, California's canned goods were dispatched to China, Japan, the Sandwich Islands (Hawaii), Mexico, Central and South America, Russia, and Australia.

The California canning industry was strengthened when silver was discovered in Nevada, and the miners had to be supported from California. The transcontinental railroad permitted food grown or canned in California to be shipped quickly to the rest of the United States. Hundreds of small canneries opened. By 1875 California was a net exporter of canned goods. With the invention of the refrigerated railroad car in the 1880s, fresh produce could be shipped east.

Some of America's largest food companies were launched in California. Joseph and William Hunt opened a small preserving business in Santa Rosa, California, in 1890. The Hunt Brothers Fruit Packing Company eventually produced an extensive line of canned fruits and vegetables, many of which were still sold in the early 2000s under the Hunt label. The California Fruit Canners Association was initially a cooperative of eighteen canners. Its premier brand was Del Monte, which packed a vast array of products, including peaches,

baked beans, coffee, berries, olives, squashes, sweet potatoes, peppers, tuna, and cranberries, as well as dried fruit, jams, and jellies.

Fish, particularly salmon, was canned in California until the rivers were fished out. Southern California fish canning was in its infancy as the nineteenth century ended. The California Fish Company in East San Pedro caught and canned halibut, rock cod, and sardines. In 1908 it began canning tuna. Mexicans, Mexican Americans, and Japanese Americans had long eaten tuna, but it was not a familiar food to Anglo-Americans. California canned tuna was aggressively marketed as "chicken of the sea," and demand for tuna accelerated throughout the United States. The tuna canning industry thrived in California until the 1950s when the industry began to relocate to other parts of the world.

Fruits and Vegetables

Tomatoes were grown in California by Franciscan priests well before California became part of the United States. California has the right climate for growing tomatoes, with adequate water in the Central Valley and farms large enough to make it economically attractive to invest in the major equipment associated with tomato farming. At the beginning of the twenty-first century, 90 percent of all American processed tomatoes were grown in California.

Old World fruit and citrus trees had also been introduced into California by the Franciscans, but many groves were neglected after the missions were secularized. New groves were planted shortly after the American conquest of California in 1846, and California's fruit and citrus industry was launched. At first these groves only fed Californians, but as soon as the transcontinental railroad was completed a cascade of fruits poured forth from California. California fruit growers received great publicity at the 1893 Columbian Exposition in Chicago, where the state's exhibit housed a grove of twenty lemon trees and thirty orange trees and a tower of oranges and lemons. Grapefruit culture began in California in the 1880s. The discovery of the value and sources of vitamin C gave a huge boost to the market for citrus. Sales increased threefold by World War II. California also produces many other tree fruits. For instance, the California Prune and Apricot Growers Association, founded in 1917, marketed the crops of its members under the brand name Sunsweet. As the twenty-first century opened, Sunsweet was the world's largest handler of dried tree fruits: prunes, apricots, peaches, pears, and apples.

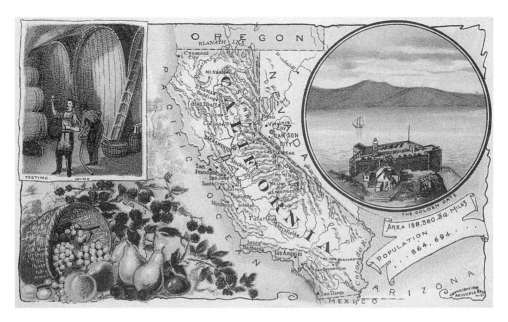

California Cornucopia. Premium card distributed with Arbuckles' Ariosa Coffee, late 1880s. *Collection of Alice Ross*

Salad plants grew easily in California. It is no surprise that California has been considered the "land of salads" since the late nineteenth century. With the development of early varieties of sturdy head lettuce in the 1890s, it became possible to ship California-grown lettuce across the nation. The first California cookbook entirely devoted to salads was published in 1897. In the early 2000s, California and Arizona raised about 80 percent of America's lettuce.

During the early twentieth century, America's new devotion to salads led a California canner to market diced fruits for salads, and canned fruit cocktail was born. California was also the birthplace of a great number of famous salads, such as green goddess and Cobb salads. While Caesar salad was created in Tijuana, Mexico, it was popularized in the 1930s by Hollywood stars. California is the place where the salad came into its own as a main dish—a trend that continues nationwide.

Olives had been introduced to California by Franciscans, and attempts had been made to manufacture olive oil as early as 1872. Olives, however, did not become an important commercial crop until the end of the nineteenth century. At that time, Californians cured green olives in brine, creating a unique flavor. For more than a decade these olives were known only to Californians. By 1901 olives were being canned and shipped eastward. At the beginning of the twenty-first century, almost all commercial American olives were grown in California.

California has become the center for many other fruits and vegetables. All commercial artichokes grown in the United States are grown in California, about 80 percent of them in Monterey County, home to the annual Artichoke Festival. (The 1947 Artichoke Queen was Norma Jean Baker, soon to be known as Marilyn Monroe.) In 1978, the people of the town of Gilroy proclaimed it the garlic capital of the world. The Gilroy Garlic Festival was drawing eighty thousand people annually by the early 2000s. The town of Fresno considers itself the raisin capital, Fallbrook calls itself the avocado capital, and the Coachella Valley is known as the date capital of the world.

Spanish missionaries had also introduced almonds and walnuts to California in the eighteenth century, but climatic conditions along the coast were not suitable for their cultivation. In the 1850s, almonds were planted in California's Central Valley and these orchards were successful. During the late nineteenth century, massive walnut groves were established throughout the state. The first pistachio seeds were planted in California in 1854, but they did not thrive. Renewed efforts to establish a pistachio industry in California commenced in the 1970s. In 1976, the first commercial crop was harvested in California. In the early 2000s, virtually the entire commercial crop of American walnuts, almonds, and pistachios came from California.

California Wine

Franciscan missionaries planted vineyards in California, but commercial production of wine did not begin until the missions had been secularized. Later, immigrants from France and Germany established the first commercial vineyards with vines they brought from their home countries. Agoston Haraszthy de Mokcsa, born in Hungary, worked in California vineyards and published his experiences in *Grape Culture, Wines and Wine-Making* (1862), the first American wine book to discuss California wine production. Thomas Hart Hyatt's *Hand-Book of Grape Culture* (1867) was the first wine book actually published in California. California wine was sold at Philadelphia's Centennial Exposition in 1876 and was again marketed at the Columbian World's Fair in 1893, but these promotional campaigns did not create much of a response. Despite the rapid development of the wine industry in the state, there was little demand even in California. America was not a wine-drinking country, and the wine industry almost disappeared during Prohibition and the Depression. This changed beginning in the 1930s, when Frank Schoonmaker, an American wine authority, began publicizing the best California wines, especially those of Napa and Sonoma counties. Previously California wines had been marketed with French names. Schoonmaker urged winemakers to call the wines by the varietal names of the grapes, such as Zinfandel and Cabernet Sauvignon. Some vintners earned excellent reputations, and by the 1980s California wines were competing successfully with the best French wines.

Early California Cookbooks

In addition to its Hispanic and immigrant culinary heritages, California's cuisine was influenced by foods, recipes, and traditions brought by Americans from the eastern United States. California's first cookbooks were written mainly by Americans from the eastern states. The first cookbook published in California was B. F. Barton and Company's *Peerless Receipt Book*, published around 1870. It was an advertising cook-booklet promoting Peerless Baking Powder. During the next few years, several California cookbooks were published, some as fund-raisers, including *The Sacramento Ladies Kitchen Companion* (1872), compiled for the benefit of Grace Church. After 1875, California cookbooks proliferated. Among the more interesting early cookbooks were Abby Fisher's *What Mrs. Fisher Knows about Old Southern Cooking* (1881), which was the first California cookbook written by an African American. The second was *El Cocinero Español* (1898), the first Spanish-language cookbook printed in California. Its author, Encarnación Pinedo, came from a prominent California family, and her recipes represented sophisticated Mexican cooking in nineteenth-century California. She was not impressed with English cooking traditions, stating (as translated by Dan Strehl) that there was "not a single English cook who knows how to cook well, and the food and style of seasoning is the most insipid and tasteless as can be imagined."

At the turn of the twentieth century, California restaurant chefs began writing cookbooks. Victor Hirtzler, chef of the Hotel Saint Francis in San Francisco during the late nineteenth and early twentieth centuries, published the *Hotel St. Francis Book of Recipes* in 1910. This substantial tome demonstrated a wide range of dishes from classical French to typical American food. The Los Angeles chef A. C. Hoff published a series of cookbooks that featured the best chefs in America and Europe.

California home cooking was also developing in the first half of the twentieth century, as reflected in recipes submitted by readers of the "Kitchen Cabinet" section of *Sunset: The Magazine of Western Living;* the recipes were collected in books beginning in 1929. "Kitchen Cabinet" dishes reveal a distinctive California cuisine in formation, with recipes using dates, figs, artichokes, avocados, chilies, grenadillas, ripe olives, and tangerines, as well as creations with Chinese, Japanese, and Mexican influences. Genevieve Callahan's *California Cook Book for Indoor and Outdoor Cooking*, first published in 1946, stressed quintessentially Californian main-dish salads, local seafood and wildfowl, and grilling and barbecuing, and it supplied recipes for guava, youngberry, and persimmon jams. Helen Evans Brown, a friend and occasional collaborator of James Beard, published her *West Coast Cook Book* in 1952. Salads and local ingredients are proudly featured, and the book also surveyed foreign contributions to California cookery, from Chinese and Japanese to French, Italian, and Spanish.

Mexican and Other Ethnic Food

Of all the foreign influences on California's foodways, the Mexican contribution is the most important. Taco recipes appeared in California cookbooks beginning in 1914. Bertha Haffner-Ginger's *California Mexican-Spanish Cook Book: Selected Mexican and Spanish Recipes* (1914) described tacos as being "made by putting chopped cooked beef and chili sauce in tortilla made of meal and flour; folded, edges sealed together with egg; fried in deep fat, chile sauce served over it." Another Californian, Pauline Wiley-Kleemann, featured six taco and taquito (small taco) recipes in her *Ramona's Spanish-Mexican Cookery* (1929). During the twentieth century, a distinctive so-called Cal-Mex cookery evolved. A dish from Los Angeles, dated 1905, consisted of avocado chunks, olive oil, and minced onion served on a bed of lettuce. This very basic guacamole was elaborated upon as the years went by, and by the early 2000s had become one of the signal dishes of Cal-Mex cuisine. The stuffed tortilla called a burrito, which means literally "little burro," first appeared on a menu in Los Angeles's famed El Cholo Spanish Café in the 1930s. Perhaps unique to the Cal-Mex tradition is the seafood taco.

Victor J. Bergeron, proprietor of Trader Vic's restaurant in Oakland, California, was a popularizer of Mexican and other foreign cuisines beginning in the 1930s. In 1951 Bergeron opened the San Francisco Trader Vic's that became the launching pad for a string of Polynesian-inspired restaurants (staffed by Chinese cooks) throughout the world. Bergeron was a fan of Mexican food. He was particularly taken with the manner in which it was, as he said, "fabricated and put together," but he believed that Mexican food was "primitive." As commonly served, he felt, it was "greasy, hot, and not well prepared." Bergeron thought he could do better. To learn how to make good Mexican food, he spent a week in Texas, where he collected recipes. He made up other dishes, giving them a self-described Mexican slant. Bergeron taught his Chinese cooks how to make this food and opened his first Señor Pico restaurant in San Francisco in 1964 and another in Los Angeles three years later. The Señor Pico menu popularized Mexican food, and many other so-called Mexican restaurants that appealed to mainstream American tastes soon followed.

During the twentieth century, ethnic food from around the world became common California fare as immigrant groups moved into the state, including Italians, Basques, Japanese, Chinese, Koreans, and more recently Southeast Asians. M. F. K. Fisher, who was born in Whittier, California, proclaimed that California had the most thoroughly relaxed cookery in America and that California cookery was filled with ethnic diversity.

Fast Food

By the mid-twentieth century, California food was ready to explode onto the national scene. One of the ways it did so was through fast food. Many fast food establishments sprang up in California in the 1930s. Bob's Big Boy opened in Glendale during that decade; its signature dish was the double-patty burger. As Bob's Big Boy franchised its operation, it expanded throughout California and then across the United States. In-N-Out Burger was founded by Harry and Esther Snyder in Baldwin Park, California, in 1948. Although this chain of West Coast hamburger restaurants had grown to more than 140 outlets, control remained in the hands of the Snyder family at the beginning of the twenty-first century. In 1951 a businessman named Robert O. Peterson opened the first Jack in the Box restaurant in San Diego. Jack in the Box was the nation's first major drive-through hamburger chain. In the 1950s Glen Bell decided to experiment with the fast-food preparation of tacos. After several attempts, in 1962 he launched Taco Bell in Downey, California, and by the early 2000s Taco Bell was a national chain.

The most important fast-food operation, however, was launched by Richard and Maurice McDonald, who had moved to southern California to seek their fortune in 1930. In 1948 the brothers opened a hamburger drive-in in San Bernardino, California, that applied assembly-line efficiency to the restaurant business. The McDonald brothers franchised their operation and later sold it. McDonalds has become a worldwide enterprise.

The California Culinary Revolution

Although California had little French immigration, French cuisine greatly influenced California cookery. M. F. K. Fisher and Julia Child, Californians who went on to join the ranks of America's most prominent culinary authors, both studied in France. In the 1970s, San Francisco, already an important restaurant town, became the capital of French-inspired California cuisine. In 1971 Alice Waters launched her restaurant Chez Panisse in a Victorian brownstone in Berkeley. Like Fisher and Child, Waters had spent time in France, and at first she served simple French food with a particular emphasis on the traditions of Provence. As time went on, she began experimenting with local ingredients. She changed her menu daily, focusing on the freshest and best seasonal ingredients; her preparations flattered the food without overwhelming it. *Gourmet* magazine discovered Chez Panisse in October 1975, and subsequently James Beard and many other food writers wrote about Alice Waters, raising Chez Panisse to national prominence.

Chez Panisse served a number of dishes that came to be identified with California cuisine, such as grilled fish and vegetables, green salads topped with grilled meat or warm goat cheese, and grilled pizza with nontraditional toppings. Many of these innovations have been attributed to Jeremiah Tower, one of the first chefs at Chez Panisse. Waters hired Paul Bertolli as chef in 1982. He was a native Californian who had worked in restaurants in Florence, Italy. Bertolli brought Italian flavors, such as roasted garlic, olive oil, and red peppers, to the Chez Panisse table. Alice Waters was one of the first American restaurateurs to partner with local farmers, ensuring them a market for the finest produce they could grow, and as the twenty-first century opened she had become an outspoken advocate of sustainable agriculture, a key factor in the continued success of California cuisine. In collaboration with chefs at Chez Panisse, Waters published several cookbooks, beginning with *The Chez Panisse Menu Cookbook* (1982).

Chefs from Chez Panisse went out on their own and made many additional contributions to American culinary life. Jeremiah Tower launched Stars in San Francisco. His first book, *New American Classics* (1986), popularized California-style cooking, while his *California Dish* (2003) described the California culinary revolution and its impact on America. The former Chez Panisse chef Mark Miller launched the Coyote Café in Santa Fe, New Mexico, and two years later published his cookbook, *Coyote Café*, which popularized southwestern cuisine.

Many other innovators contributed to the California culinary revolution. Wolfgang Puck, Austrian-born, became famous as the chef at Ma Maison in Los Angeles in 1981. He subsequently opened Spago in Hollywood and had restaurants in many cities in the early 2000s. Puck became known for his California-style brick-oven pizza, which was topped with unusual ingredients such as golden caviar or duck sausage. During the 1990s Puck marketed frozen versions of his California-style pizzas as well as other gourmet specialties. His cookbooks include *Modern French Cooking for the American Kitchen* (1981) and *The Wolfgang Puck Cookbook* (1996).

California's culinary revolution has been encouraged by cultural organizations and universities. The American Wine and Food Institute, which published the *Journal of Gastronomy* beginning in 1984, has contributed to a better understanding of the importance of the nation's food and wine. While the *Journal of Gastronomy* ceased publication in the early 1990s, *Gastronomica*, published by the University of California Press, offered a forum for

scholarly writing on culinary matters in the early 2000s. Copia, the American Center for Wine, Food, and the Arts in Napa Valley, opened in November 2001. Both public and private universities have also contributed greatly to California's revolution. The University of California, Davis, has had one of the nation's strongest programs on viticulture and enology, and the Culinary Institute of America (CIA) opened a West Coast campus at the former Christian Brothers winery in Napa Valley.

At the beginning of the twenty-first century, the California culinary style continued to embrace inventive cooking methods that showcased the highest quality fresh, seasonal, and native ingredients.

[*See also* Almonds; Artichokes; Avocados; Brown, Helen Evans; Celebrity Chefs; Child, Julia; Citrus; Del Monte; Drive-Ins; Fast Food; Fisher, M. F. K.; Garlic; Grapes; Hunt's; Lettuce; McDonald's; Mexican American Food; Olives; Periodicals, *sidebar* Gastronomica; Pinedo, Encarnación; Pinole; Puck, Wolfgang; Taco Bell; Tomatoes; Walnuts; Waters, Alice; Wineries; Wine, *subentry on* California Wines.]

BIBLIOGRAPHY

Balls, Edward K. *Early Uses of California Plants.* Berkeley and Los Angeles: University of California Press, 1962.

Bitting. A. W. *Appetizing or the Art of Canning.* San Francisco: Trade Pressroom, 1937.

Brenner, Leslie. *American Appetite: The Coming of Age of a Cuisine.* New York: Avon, 1999.

Brown, Philip S. "Old California Cook Books." *Quarterly News Letter* 20 (Winter 1954): 4–12.

Hooker, Richard J. *A History of Food and Drink in America.* Indianapolis, IN, and New York: Bobbs-Merrill, 1981.

Kuh, Patric. *The Last Days of Haute Cuisine: America's Culinary Revolution.* New York: Viking, 2001.

Linsenmeyer, Helen Walker. *From Fingers to Finger Bowls: A Sprightly History of California Cooking.* San Diego: Union-Tribune Publishing, 1972.

Muscatine, Doris. *A Cook's Tour of San Francisco.* New York: Scribners, 1963.

Pinedo, Encarnación. *The Spanish Cook: Selected Recipes from El Cocinero Español.* Edited and translated by Dan Strehl. Pasadena, CA: Weather Bird Press, 1992.

Reardon, Joan. *M. F. K. Fisher, Julia Child, and Alice Waters.* New York: Harmony Books, 1994.

Smith, Andrew F. "Tacos, Enchiladas and Refried Beans: The Invention of Mexican-American Cookery." In *Cultural and Historical Aspects of Foods*, edited by Mary Wallace Kelsey and ZoeAnn Holmes, 183–203. Corvallis: Oregon State University, 1999.

Strehl, Dan, ed. *One Hundred Books on California Food and Wine.* Los Angeles: Book Collectors, 1990.

Vaught, David. *Cultivating California: Growers, Specialty Crops, and Labor, 1875–1920.* Baltimore and London: Johns Hopkins University Press, 1999.

ANDREW F. SMITH

Camas Root

Two species of camas, the common *Camassia quamash* and the less common *C. leichtlinii*, grew profusely in the grassy meadows of the Pacific Northwest. Explorers such as Meriwether Lewis noted that the bulb resembled an onion and had a sweet taste. A member of the lily family, the edible camas is an herbaceous perennial with large, glutinous bulbs covered with a membranous brown skin. It was a staple food of the Indians, who considered camas plots valuable personal property.

To distinguish the blue-flowering edible camas from the white-flowering death camas, which grows in the same areas, Indian women harvested the bulbs during or soon after flowering. A three- or four-foot-long hardwood stick, sharpened at one end and fitted with an antler horn handle, was their digging tool. After gathering a large quantity, the women layered a rock-lined steaming pit with branches of such plants as salal, moss, camas, and dirt. Water poured into a hole furnished the steam. When cooked, the camas was soft, blackish, and sweet. It could then be molded into cakes and baked in the sun or on heated stones to preserve it for later use. This prolonged cooking process, one to three days, depending on the quantity, breaks down the long-chain sugar inulin and makes the bulbs more digestible. A communal feast celebrated the camas harvest.

[*See also* Native American Foods; Pacific Northwestern Regional Cookery.]

BIBLIOGRAPHY

Pojar, Jim, and Andy MacKinnon. *Plants of the Pacific Northwest Coast: Washington, Oregon, British Columbia, and Alaska.* Edmonton, Canada: Lone Pine Publishing, 1994.

Thwaites, Reuben Gold, ed. *Original Journals of the Lewis and Clark Expedition, 1804–1806.* Reprint. New York: Antiquarian Press, 1959.

JACQUELINE BLOCK WILLIAMS

Campbell, Tunis G.

In *The Philadelphia Negro*, W. E. B. Du Bois praised the African American caterers of the 1840s, who "aided the Abolition cause to no little degree." Although the caterers assumed a subservient manner, they were independent businesspeople of means who led their community toward liberation. No individual more successfully embodied this duality than Tunis Campbell (1805–1891). Born in New Jersey, and educated in a Long Island Episcopal school where he was the only black student, Campbell became an African Methodist Episcopal Church elder, headwaiter, temperance preacher, baker, abolitionist, author of the second cookbook published by an African American, and was elected leader of three predominantly African American Georgia counties for eleven years. In the 1840s, he had preached equality and self-help on lonely New York street corners, and he went on to organize among newly freed slaves on the Carolina Sea Islands in the 1860s and in Georgia into the late 1870s.

Campbell's *Hotel Keepers, Head Waiters, and Housekeeper's Guide* was published in Boston in 1848, with supporting letters from the owners of Howard's Hotel in New York and the Adams House Hotel in Boston. In it, he honored the tradition—begun by Robert Roberts—of teaching African American servants how to succeed through polite service. At the same time, he outlined a style of dining room organization on military models, to make "an entire change in hotel-keeping and waiting." In light of Campbell's career, it is impossible to overlook such comments as, "Men should be instructed to hold themselves erect, and upon a squad drill they should be taught a regular step, the same as a military company."

Recipes fill more than half the book to enable waiters to increase their versatility and employability. Most of the recipes are for the kinds of game dishes and sauces served in early American hotels; however, a dish of stewed gizzards and the opening recipe for cornbread—with carefully detailed proportions that refute the stereotype of African American cooks never measuring—may be the first instances of published recipes for African American food, to be used by African Americans.

During the Civil War, Campbell was an active partner in Davies and Company, Unfermented Bread Manufacturers in what is now Manhattan's East Village. At that time, temperance activists were concerned about the yeast and alcohol in conventional bread. Temperance was part of a group of reform issues that included the abolition of slavery and advocacy for women's suffrage. Unable to enlist in the army, Campbell eventually secured a commission to organize freed slaves to farm, attend school, and serve in militia companies in the Carolina Sea Islands.

Campbell's work continued under military auspices after the Civil War. He eventually had to relocate hundreds of people to the Georgia mainland, where he was able to register them to vote, secure land titles, and rebuild schools and churches. He was elected to the Georgia constitutional convention, state senate, state legislature, and more enduringly as justice of the peace in three counties. He lobbied in Washington for Congressional reconstruction, the Fifteenth Amendment, and the Ku Klux Klan Act.

In 1876, white authorities imprisoned him over malpractice in two county legal cases in which he had sentenced white offenders, and he served a year in prison on a chain gang. He was made to eat hard corn cakes and undercooked bacon but later was able to obtain better meals from an Atlanta Hotel and cakes from his wife.

He left Georgia, but he returned briefly to aid the losing Republican cause in the 1882 election. He died in Boston in 1891.

[*See also* African American Food; Cookbooks and Manuscripts, *subentry* From the Beginnings to 1860; Dining Rooms, Table Settings, and Table Manners; Hotel Dining Rooms; Temperance.]

BIBLIOGRAPHY

Campbell, Tunis Gulic. *Freedom's Shore: Tunis Campbell and the Georgia Freedmen.* Athens: University of Georgia Press, 1986.

Campbell, Tunis Gulic. *Hotel Keepers, Head Waiters, and House keepers' Guide.* Boston: Coolidge and Wiley, 1848. Posted on the Michigan State University website *Feeding America: The Historic American Cookbook Project.* For a transcript, http://digital.lib. msu.edu/cookbooks/hotelkeepers/hote.xml. For page images, http://digital.lib.msu.edu/cookbooks/image.cfm? TitleNo=6&image=001.

Campbell, Tunis Gulic. *Sufferings of the Rev. T. G. Campbell and Family in Georgia.* Washington, DC: Enterprise Publishing, 1877. Excerpted in *First Person Past: American Autobiographies*, edited by Marian J. Morton and Russell Duncan, vol. 2. St. James, NY: Brandywine Press, 1994.

MARK H. ZANGER

Campbell Soup Company

Joseph Campbell, born in Bridgeton, New Jersey, joined Abraham Anderson as a partner in a tomato canning and preserving firm established in Camden in 1869. Beginning with canned peas and asparagus, the two men added many other kinds of canned and preserved foods. One of their more important products was the beefsteak tomato, which they aggressively advertised using the trademarked image of a gigantic tomato carried upon the shoulders of two men. In 1876, Anderson and Campbell received a medal for their preserving at the Philadelphia Centennial Exposition. When difficulties arose between the partners, Campbell bought Anderson out and acquired new partners. One was

Arthur Dorrance from Bristol, Pennsylvania. In 1891, Dorrance and Campbell incorporated in New Jersey as the Joseph Campbell Preserve Company, which canned and bottled preserves, jellies, meats, fruits, sauces, vegetables, and other goods.

The company grew and flourished, even in the five depression years from 1892 to 1897. It advertised its canned goods as the "best in the world." If a local grocer did not stock Campbell's products, the company supplied samples directly to the consumers in the area, putting pressure on local retailers. By the 1890s, the company produced more than two hundred products, one of which was canned ready-to-serve soup. Arthur Dorrance's son, John T. Dorrance, a chemist trained in Germany, was hired at Campbell's Camden laboratory in 1896 to improve the quality of soup. He concentrated on producing condensed soups. Within a few months of his arrival, he had come up with five condensed soups: tomato, chicken, oxtail, vegetable, and consommé, which were released in 1897.

The following year, the company adopted the famous red-and-white labels. The uncluttered design prominently displayed the name of each Campbell's condensed soup. The condensed soups were successful, and Dorrance expanded his work, conducting experiments to determine how best to maintain uniformity of flavor and how to reduce waste caused by can spoilage. In the year that John Dorrance arrived at Campbell, the company had lost sixty thousand dollars. One year after the introduction of condensed soups, the firm became profitable. The soup division expanded, while the other sectors declined in importance. Most of Campbell's other products were phased out, and the major effort focused on condensed soup. In recognition of its importance, the company changed its name in 1921 to the Campbell Soup Company.

Initially, Campbell's soup retailed for ten cents a can. It was sold to retailers at the same price, leveling the playing field for smaller operations that did not warrant volume discounts. The profit generated for the Campbell Soup Company was less than a quarter-cent per can. For larger stores, it meant that Campbell soup was a loss leader; that is, stores sold it at a loss to bring in customers who bought other items at a profit for the store. Campbell raised the price of a can to twelve cents in 1925—a price that remained constant for decades.

Advertising

There were many reasons for Campbell's rapid and consistent growth, but, most important, the company knew how to advertise and market its products. Newspaper and streetcar advertising was initially used, followed by magazine advertising, which gave Campbell's much broader exposure. Its major advertising image was the Campbell Kids, created by Grace Drayton in 1904. The company advertised extensively in newspapers and magazines and on radio and television when the Depression hit in the 1930s, and the company's advertising budget shot up to $3.5 million. During the 1930s, the Campbell Soup Company introduced the jingle "M'm! M'm! Good!"

Another very effective way of advertising was through regular offerings of cookery pamphlets and cookbooks emphasizing how soups could be enhanced or used as ingredients to make other dishes. Campbell's published its first advertising cookbooklet in 1910 and has subsequently put out dozens of such items. The recipes that appear in these booklets frequently were reprinted in newspapers, magazines, and cookbooks. In 1994, the Campbell Soup Company was inducted into the Marketing Hall of Fame. It is one of the leading advertisers in the United States.

Globalization and Diversification

The Depression had profound effects on Campbell. While the company had exported its soup abroad for decades, many countries put up protectionist barriers to help local manufacturers during the Depression. For instance, Canada protected its manufacturers from American competition by increasing the import rate for duties on canned goods in 1930. Campbell responded by organizing a subsidiary in Canada, the Campbell Soup Company Limited. For similar reasons, Campbell's Soups Limited was organized in the United Kingdom in 1933 and quickly became one of the United Kingdom's greatest suppliers of tomato and other soups. These first subsidiaries in other countries were followed, after World War II, by many more. In addition, the Campbell Soup Company has acquired companies in other countries, such as Liebig in France and Erasco in Germany.

The Campbell Soup Company's first major diversification was into tomato juice, which reversed the sole focus on soup making. Shortly after World War II ended, the company made another logical addition when it purchased V8 juice from Standard Brand. Campbell has been diversifying ever since. Its other American food brands are Swanson, V8 and V8 Splash juices, Pace Mexican sauces, Prego pasta sauces, Godiva chocolates, and Pepperidge Farm, which makes Gold Fish crackers

and Chocolate Chunk and Milano cookies. Although the company is still headquartered in Camden, it closed its manufacturing operation at that site in 1900. Its main tomato-processing operations are located in California. Soup remains Campbell's flagship product, and the company is still the largest soup manufacturer in the world.

[*See also* Advertising; Campbell Soup Kids.]

BIBLIOGRAPHY

Collins, Douglas. *America's Favorite Food: The Story of Campbell Soup Company.* New York: Abrams, 1994.
Packaged Facts. *The International Soup Market.* New York: Packaged Facts, 1996.
Smith, Andrew F. *Souper Tomatoes: The Story of America's Favorite Food.* New Brunswick, NJ: Rutgers University Press, 2000.

ANDREW F. SMITH

Campbell Soup Kids

During the early twentieth century, the Joseph Campbell Company, forerunner to the Campbell Soup Company, began to advertise its products nationally. They were advised to market their products to women through "child appeal." Theodore Wiederseim, an employee of Ketterlineus Lithographic Manufacturing Company in Philadelphia, was asked for suggestions. He recommended the services of his wife, Grace Drayton, a staff artist for the *Philadelphia Press and Evening Journal* and a freelance illustrator of children's books. She had been sketching little round-faced, rosy-cheeked children for years, and she adapted them for the company's purposes, creating what would become known as the Campbell Kids.

The Campbell Kids first appeared on streetcar advertisements in early 1905. Along with the illustrations appeared light and sometimes humorous advertising verses. The Kids were so successful that the company used them in black-and-white magazine advertisements in the September 1905 issue of *Ladies' Home Journal* and later in the *Saturday Evening Post*. The company added a touch of red to their artwork in 1906 and commenced full-color advertising in the 1920s.

The Campbell Kids were first sold as dolls in 1910, under license to the E. I. Horseman Company. They were subsequently marketed by other companies, including Montgomery Ward and Sears. Dolls were one of the first of numerous products to bear the Campbell Kids' likeness: the Kids appeared on balloons, bells, bridge tallies, calendars, canisters, cards, clips, clocks, cookbooklets, cookie jars, cutting boards, dolls, games, can covers, decals, die-cuts, dishes, figurines, hats, jewelry, lamps, lapel buttons, lunch boxes, markers, mugs, music boxes, napkins, ornaments, pails, playing cards, pins, planes, plaques, plates, posters, puzzles, salt and pepper shakers, silverware, T-shirts, thermometers, thermoses, timers, toys, waste cans, watches, and water bottles, to name a few.

Until 1921, the Kids appeared in almost every Campbell advertisement. Thereafter, they were downplayed in Campbell's advertising. They appeared in fewer than 10 percent of the company's ads by the early 1950s. In 1954, this trend was reversed as Campbell's commemorated the Kids' fiftieth birthday. Campbell's licensed thirty-four companies to manufacture Kids products, which appeared on beach balls, doll carriages, rubber stamps, paper napkins, toy vacuum cleaners, wallpaper, and yo-yo's. This campaign commenced with a seven-page advertisement in a November 1954 issue of *Life* magazine and climaxed with the release of over half a million Campbell Kids dolls. Simultaneously, the Campbell Kids were featured on television promotions.

Over the years, the Campbell Kids were updated and modernized. Their clothes kept pace with changing fashion. The thousands of products featuring the Campbell Kids are eagerly sought by collectors, and some are quite valuable. By any standard, the Campbell Kids are one of the most successful American advertising icons.

[*See also* Advertising; Campbell Soup Company.]

BIBLIOGRAPHY

Collins, Douglas. *America's Favorite Food: The Story of Campbell Soup Company.* New York: Abrams, 1994.
Smith, Andrew F. *Souper Tomatoes: The Story of America's Favorite Food.* New Brunswick, NJ: Rutgers University Press, 2000.
Young, David, and Micki Young. *Campbell's Soup Collectibles: A Price and Identification Guide.* Iola, WI: Krause, 1998.

ANDREW F. SMITH

Candy Bars and Candy

Early Candy

Sweetmeats—comfits, candied nuts, and preserved fruits—came to America in the eighteenth century, imported from Britain and France. A few colonists skilled in the European arts of "sugar work" were able to offer their delectable wares to the rich, who were the only ones able to afford such treats. "Sugar candy" was first advertised in the 1730s by refiners, who sold many other grades of sugar along with this item, a hard, crunchy confection. Made from crystallized sugar, rock candy was the easiest kind of candy to produce and could be found in dry-goods stores, groceries, and spice shops. But because sugar was such a rarity in the eighteenth century, even this crude form of sugar candy counted as a luxury.

Beginning in the 1830s, refined sugar was becoming cheap and plentiful enough in America to reach a larger market than only the elite consumer. Inspired by druggists' use of hard sugar coatings for medicated lozenges, people realized the potential profitability of producing hard sugar candies without the medicine, making the word "treat" a noun instead of a verb. By the early 1840s candy men, who sold the cheaper hard candies to children, became more common than fine confectioners, whose luxurious products had until then monopolized the trade. In the process, the businessmen trading in confectionery began a trend that radically altered the American diet, as candy shifted from a rarity to a necessity.

Making hard candies required few ingredients and little skill, and manuals aimed at the professional candy man began appearing by mid-century. A typical recipe called for mixing together sugar, water, flavoring essences, and coloring agents in a pan or copper kettle and then heating the liquid to 300–310°F, the "hard crack" stage for sugar. The molten mass was poured out of the pan and left until it was cool enough to handle; then it would be kneaded to form stiff dough. Having shaped the mass into individual pieces by hand—rods, balls, lozenges, or tablets—the candy man would leave them to cool and harden.

In 1847 the candy press (also called a "toy" machine) was invented, making it possible not only to produce multiples of the same candy shapes at once but also to increase the variety of those shapes by changing the rollers on the press through which the molten sugar passed. A lozenge-cutting machine, patented in 1850, made producing multiples even more efficient. By 1851 confectioners were using the revolving steam pan to facilitate the sugar-boiling process. This device was a great innovation because the candy man no longer had to stir the bubbling vats of boiling sugar constantly. Since the pan's surface heated more uniformly, the hot sugar mass was less likely to burn. These technological developments all aided the production of confectionery, allowing a single businessman alone, or with an assistant, to run a modest, successful operation.

PENNY CANDY

Penny candies, the first goods children spent their own money on, were also the first confections to reach a mass audience in America. By the late 1830s sugar's increasing availability and decreasing price enabled confectioners to profitably produce sugary drops without the medicine typically found in druggists' stocks. Unlike exclusive confections marketed to elite adults, these "penny candies," often sold ten to a dozen for a penny, were aimed at the palates of working-class children, for whom a penny was in reach. By the early 1850s individual candy men could readily obtain the machinery and raw materials necessary to profit from making batches of candy in greater quantities. Revolving steam pans enabled boiling sugar and water to reach the correct molten consistency without burning, and candy "presses" shaped and separated the saccharine masses into a marketable product. Because they did not need to be as skilled as fine confectioners, candy men could therefore run successful, if modest, neighborhood businesses.

Penny candies introduced nineteenth-century children to the world of consumption by teaching them how to be good future consumers; they were the bane of the period's reformers, who feared that a taste for candy inculcated in the young would lead to intemperate behavior as adults. Brightly colored and often displayed in shop windows in glass jars, penny candies (also called "toys") often came in the shape of familiar consumer products, such as shoes, boats, hats, and purses; confectioners also offered candies shaped as cigars, cigarettes, and even gin bottles.

From the beginning, candy store operators, who depended on narrow profit margins and a capricious audience, relied on novelty to entice their customers, presaging later marketing techniques aimed at children. "Prize packages," popular after the Civil War, sensationally promised an often chintzy item in every box of candy, a technique used in the twentieth century to sell Cracker Jack and sugar-laden cereals. Cardboard and glass candy containers—themselves shaped like popular material objects—also enticed children but were often too costly for the poor.

By the early 1870s penny candies were ubiquitous, appearing not only in candy shops but also in tobacco stores and five-and-dimes, and at newsstands and movie theaters. By the mid-twentieth century the penny candy as such no longer existed except as more expensive nostalgic root beer barrels, cinnamon-hot fireballs, and flavored candy sticks. But later candy manufacturers continued to use marketing techniques established in the nineteenth century. Sweets aimed at young people continued to stress novelty; some candies featured tie-ins to the mass media, referencing popular cartoon characters or action heroes.

Like their nineteenth-century counterparts, candies of the late twentieth century also tapped into children's desire to be more adult and often came in forms imitating desirable adult goods. Bright candy lipstick and jewelry, for example, allowed little girls to imitate their mothers. And cigarettes made of chocolate and bubble gum were popular throughout the twentieth century until concern about tobacco effectively removed them from store shelves.

BIBLIOGRAPHY

Woloson, Wendy. *Refined Tastes: Sugar, Consumers, and Confectionery in Nineteenth-Century America.* Baltimore: Johns Hopkins University Press, 2002.

WENDY A. WOLOSON

The chief customers for these new candies were not upper-class adults who purchased the expensive nougats and pralines of fine confectioners, but working-class children, for whom it was relatively easy to obtain a penny. Penny candies were the first things American children spent their own money on, and these treats introduced the practice of consumption to a generation who would grow up to become buyers of more substantial products. To maintain the continued interest of fickle children, candy men focused on novel candies, often making sweet imitations of adult consumer products, such as boats, shoes, and lamps. As a result, the candy shop became the institution that taught children how to be discerning consumers. For the price of a penny, children gained entrée into the corner store, where they spent hours with friends. Gleaming glass jars and display cases full of brightly colored hard candies and piles of nuts enticed children, who could often purchase many pieces of candy for one cent.

Mass-produced candies were not desired just by children, however. Many confectioners identified distinct consuming audiences, and adults, who preferred more subtly colored and flavored candies, such as chocolates and bonbons, figured into their commercial repertoire as well.

Candy Advertisement. Advertisement for Heide's candies, 1901. *Collection of Kit Barry*

In 1847 the English firm Joseph Fry and Son successfully developed a way to mix cocoa powder, sugar, and cacao butter with water to make a paste that could be molded. Two other innovations, both from 1879, also improved chocolate production. Henri Nestlé produced the first milk chocolate bar, and Rudolphe Lindt invented a mechanized "conching" process to improve the texture of solid chocolate, making it much less gritty. With these three innovations, the ability to produce in quantity a solid chocolate fit for eating became a reality. But until Milton Hershey, solid chocolates in America were produced mostly by skilled French immigrants for a luxury market, and chocolate itself was available only as a pulverized powder and either incorporated in baked goods or reconstituted with sugar and warm milk to make a beverage.

Solid chocolates often came packaged in ornate, handmade, imported containers and appealed to Americans' fascination with Europe as the center of refinement and civility. Men involved in romantic relationships often gave boxes of these fine confections to their lovers, a practice that began after the Civil War. Tokens of affection, boxes of chocolates were symbolically loaded gifts whose exchange was highly circumscribed by cultural mores. More expensive than shelf candy, midline boxed chocolates and bonbons, which began to appear at the turn of the century, became common gifts that expressed platonic sentiment and were given among friends and family. The Stephen F. Whitman Company, founded in 1842, was the first to manufacture such confections on a large scale. The company introduced its trademark "Sampler," an assortment of chocolate-coated candies, around 1912. Other similar brands appealing to adults and the elderly have included Brach's (specializing in caramels and founded in 1904) and Fannie May Candies (established in 1920).

Although (or perhaps because) consumers embraced newly democratized confections, the treats became the target of criticism. Reformers opposed treats marketed to children and adults alike, objecting to them on both physical and moral grounds. Many people believed that penny candies, in order to be profitable, were filled with adulterated ingredients; indeed, many of the dyes used to color the candy itself and to print the wrappers were made from harmful chemicals. In addition, reformers believed that penny candies could entice vulnerable children toward other, more dangerous vices. They feared that a taste for sweets would lead to smoking, gambling, drinking, and other transgressions. Candy men did little to discourage these charges and instead tried to please their customers by producing, among their lines, candies in the shapes of cigars, cigarettes, and even gin bottles. Black licorice was a perennial favorite of boys, who enjoyed chewing it and expelling the dark spit in imitation of their fathers' chewing tobacco. Mothers, too, were blamed for weakening their children by appeasing them with sweets from infancy, a practice that reformers also decried.

Women's own consumption of confectionery was also not exempt from the critiques of reformers, who feared that a woman's custom of eating bonbons, like a child's habit of consuming penny candies, might lead to other more serious vices. Victorians often equated eating with sex and viewed both, involving bodily processes, as practices to engage in with as much detachment as possible. Buying fancy candies for oneself was akin to other forms of self-pleasure to which women were especially prone. It was against a woman's culturally prescribed gender role to purchase luxuries, such as confectionery, for herself, and because soft candies, such as chocolates and bonbons, possessed sensual qualities, this was an even more controversial practice. Authorities beyond religious reformers, including doctors and etiquette advisers, cautioned women against making such purchases for their own fulfillment, as it constituted both improper and unhealthy behavior.

Expanding Candy Markets

Yet small and large candy enterprises alike enjoyed a great deal of success at the end of the nineteenth century. By this time both adults and children possessed a well-developed sweet tooth. Individually owned businesses thrived because, like comparable enterprises, they limited their operations to a few easily produced candy lines and a local distribution. In some instances, candy became reflective of and identified with regional tastes. For example, although saltwater taffy—made of sugar, corn syrup, water, corn starch, butter, and salt—was a common staple by the 1870s at midwestern fairs, it became most closely linked to the Atlantic City boardwalk beginning in the 1880s, as the quintessential souvenir item from a trip to the Jersey Shore. Similarly, Goo Goo Clusters (1913), the first bars to combine marshmallow, milk chocolate, caramel, and peanuts, became associated with southern culture.

Many candy companies popular throughout the twentieth century began as small family enterprises. The Austrian immigrant Leo Hirshfield first made Tootsie Rolls (the first penny candies to be individually wrapped in paper) in 1896 and gave them his daughter's nickname. David L. Clark, who opened a small business in 1886, developed his Clark Bar as a confection for soldiers during World War I; the Clark Company's Zagnut first appeared in 1930. Peter Paul Halajian and five friends founded Peter Paul Candy Manufacturing Company in 1919, producing the Mounds Bar—coconut covered with bittersweet chocolate—in 1922 and Almond Joy in 1948.

All these companies grew not only because of the continuing popularity of candy but also because of technological developments such as steam power and electricity. Implementing vertical integration, some companies produced their own packaging as well. Aiding candy operations were trade organizations, such as the National Confectioners Association, Chocolate Manufacturers Association, and Retail Confectioners International. Treats formerly confined to specific regions became popular nationally as they could be mass-produced and transported in bulk quickly and safely across the country.

Some people in the business became powerful corporate magnates who changed how Americans thought about candy. By being the first to democratize edible chocolate in America, Milton Hershey became the most successful

Making Candy. A taffy pull. From a promotional booklet issued by the Franklin Sugar Refining Co. *Collection of Bonnie Slotnick*

candy maker in the country. Born in rural Pennsylvania in 1857, Hershey began as a failed candy man, yet he succeeded in establishing a thriving company town that not only supported the factory but also was able to finance benevolent institutions through the Hershey Trust. In 1893 he installed state-of-the-art chocolate-making equipment in his factory in Lancaster, Pennsylvania, which he used to coat his caramels. Hershey was able to sell off one arm of his operation, the Lancaster Caramel Company, in 1900. Retaining his chocolate-making equipment, he began manufacturing affordable edible chocolates for a mass market that was eager to consume them.

The key to Hershey's achievement was his revolutionary ability to mass-produce milk chocolates, whose milder flavor better suited the palates of the American public and whose detachment from a direct association with the darker chocolates (which were considered exotic and sexually charged) made them more appropriate products for children's consumption. The Hershey's Chocolate Bar became the most popular candy bar in America. Although its size fluctuated over the years, it cost five cents until 1970. Hershey's other early and enduringly popular products included the Hershey's Almond Bar, which first appeared in 1894, and Kisses, which the company introduced in 1907.

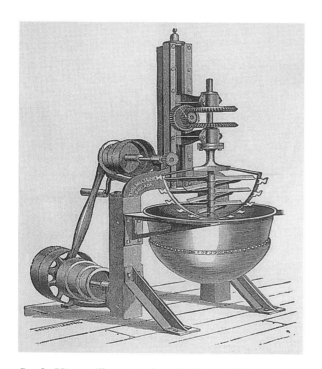

Candy Mixer. Illustration from the Thomas Miller and Bro. catalog, 1930.

The Mars Company became Hershey's chief competitor in the twentieth century. Frank Mars, founder of the family company, finally began turning a profit in 1923, after many failed attempts at being a confectioner. Among other products, the company manufactured the Milky Way bar (introduced to the market in 1924), Snickers (1930), 3 Musketeers (1932), and the Mars bar (1936). Frank's son, Forrest E. Mars, Sr., founded M&M Ltd. in 1940 and manufactured M&M's, candy-coated chocolate bits (1941), and Peanut M&M's (1954). Dominating the American chocolate industry, Mars and Hershey's together controlled 75 percent of the retail candy market by the late twentieth century.

Other chocolate-coated candy bars developed in the first half of the twentieth century grew into enduringly popular brands. (According to the National Confectioners Association, about 65 percent of candy brands in existence at the beginning of the twenty-first century had been around for more than fifty years.) The Swiss company Nestlé Inc. introduced its Milk Chocolate Bar and one with almonds in 1919, added crisped rice to produce the Crunch bar in 1938, and first started making its $100,000 Bar in 1966. Other popular chocolate bars included Oh Henry! (1920), Charleston Chew! (1922), the Heath bar (1932), and Chunky (mid-1930s).

The wide variety of confections on the market, besides chocolate bars, showed not only the ingenuity of producers and marketers but also the sheer material versatility of refined sugar and the things with which it could be combined. Chewing gum—sugar mixed with a gum base and flavorings—was first popularized in America by William Wrigley Jr., who introduced Juicy Fruit gum and Wrigley's Spearmint gum in 1893. Recalling sugar's medicinal use, the first LifeSavers, appearing in 1912, were chalky in texture and peppermint flavored and came stacked in a foil-wrapped roll. In 1924 the company began making rolls of boiled candy in single flavors that included lemon, lime, and orange. Red Hots, brought to the market in 1932 by the Ferrara Pan Candy Company (which, in the 1960s, began producing Lemonheads), were, like larger Atomic Fire Balls, flavored with cinnamon and spicy hot. Other popular candy lines included Smarties (1949), small pastel-colored discs, and SweeTARTS (1963), which combined a sweet and sour flavor. The tooth-sized candy blocks called PEZ, short for *Pfefferminz* (peppermint), were invented in 1927 by the Austrian Eduard Haas. PEZ became popular with children after the introduction of the PEZ dispenser, a plastic container topped with various heads of popular culture characters.

Gelatin-based sugar candies had also become staples of the confectionery business by the first half of the twentieth century. Jelly beans, an Easter favorite by the 1930s, were derived from a Middle Eastern confection dating back to biblical times, called Turkish Delight. They became popular penny candies after the "panning" process was used to coat the gelatin centers with a hard outer layer of sugar. Henry Heide Inc.'s Jujubes and Jujyfruits were both first marketed in 1920. Just Born, Inc.'s Mike and Ike, fruit-flavored jellied capsules, were on the market in 1940, and Hot Tamales (cinnamon flavored) came a decade later. Jelly Belly jelly beans, considered "gourmet" candies and first introduced in 1976 by the Herman Goelitz Candy Company, came in many flavors, from the sweet to the savory, and could be combined to make more complex flavors. They were a favorite treat of President Ronald Reagan, who was said always to have a bowl on his desk. Gummi bears and gummi worms, brightly colored gelatin-based candies shaped as critters and also manufactured by the Goelitz Candy Company, became popular in America in the 1980s.

Candy companies produced a wide variety of confections by using sugar-based coatings to cover other small edibles. Cracker Jack, first marketed in 1893 by F. W. Rueckheim, was a mixture of caramel-coated popcorn and peanuts. Beginning in 1912 Jack and Bingo, the candy's signature sailor boy and companion dog, promised a toy inside every box, a marketing strategy that borrowed from the techniques of earlier shop owners who offered miniature toys with every purchase. (Like glass candy containers, bonbon boxes, and PEZ dispensers, Cracker Jack toys became highly sought-after collectors' objects in their own right.) Other popular coated candies included Goobers, chocolate-coated peanuts (1925), and Raisinets, chocolate-covered raisins (1927).

Holiday Candy

Candy has become big business in America, and manufacturers recognize both distinct consuming groups and consuming seasons (some of which they have been instrumental in creating). Trick-or-treating has made Halloween the largest candy holiday, overtaking Easter in 1995. The National Confectioners Association recorded 2001 American Halloween candy sales of almost $2 billion. In the mid-twentieth century, it was common for people to give to costumed children not only candies but also related treats, such as caramel-coated apples, wax lips, and chocolate cigarettes. Parental anxieties about food tampering has led to the practice of handing out prepackaged confections, such as cellophane packets of hard candies and individually wrapped miniature candy bars.

Although it is as highly commercialized as Halloween, Easter—the second largest candy holiday ($1.8 billion in sales in 2001)—has a longer tradition linking the holiday to confectionery. Borrowing from traditional folk symbolism of fertility, abundance, and nature, chocolate bunnies and marshmallow-centered eggs have been central to the holiday's celebration since the late nineteenth century, although the folktale that the Easter rabbit laid colorful eggs was brought to America in the eighteenth century by the Pennsylvania Dutch. The continuation of this tradition can be seen in rural Pennsylvania, where people still pride themselves on their homemade chocolate-covered coconut eggs.

Candy not only helped maintain the tradition of celebrating Easter but also secularized and homogenized its iconography. Instrumental to this process in the twentieth century was Just Born Inc. Founded in 1923, the company began making the sugar-coated marshmallow confection "Peeps," shaped as chicks, in 1953 and have added other holiday-related goods, such as jack-o'-lanterns, bunnies, and Christmas trees. As the largest manufacturer of marshmallow "novelties," Just Born produced more than 4.2 million marshmallow treats each day in 2001.

To a lesser extent, candy has figured into American Christmas celebrations, accounting for about $1.5 billion in 2002 sales. Historically, at a time when sugar was still a rarity, cakes, imported candy, sweetmeats, and fruit were staples of Christmas and New Year's celebrations. During the nineteenth century, sugar-coated almonds, rock candy, and fresh and candied fruits were often stuffed into brightly colored printed "horns" (paper cones) and hung from the Christmas tree or placed in stockings. The children in the famous poem "The Night before Christmas" (1822) had "visions of sugarplums" dancing in their heads, for example. Both the confections and their containers, often imported from Europe, were prized gifts that graced the hearths of only the very wealthy.

When sugar became available to the masses, such confections were largely replaced by cookies and pies, although gold foil–covered chocolate coins are still given as Hanukkah gelt. One exception has been candy canes, which are thought to have first decorated an American Christmas tree in the late 1840s. While red-and-white

JELLY BEANS

Jelly beans are a combination of the Middle Eastern fruit-gum candy Turkish Delight and the seventeenth-century method of coating Jordan almonds. The production of jelly beans has changed little since the candy was first developed in the late nineteenth century. The interior portion is formed first by filling starch molds with the gum jelly, which is then allowed to dry and become firm. After the centers are removed from the molds they are placed in a rotating chamber, where the hard outer shell is formed by flavored sugar syrup showering the candies while they tumble. The final step is the polishing of the bean-shaped confection. Even with modern technology, the entire procedure takes five to seven days. While the jelly beans are still in the rotating chamber they are sprayed with confectioner's glaze. The shiny coat is produced as the candies tumble and the glaze dries.

The date of the introduction of the jelly bean is in dispute, but the earliest known published mention of the candy was October 2, 1898, in the *Brooklyn Daily Eagle*. By the turn of the century, jelly beans were popular, selling for nine to twelve cents per pound, and by the 1930s they had become associated with Easter. President Ronald Reagan increased their year-round popularity when he stocked candy dishes in his White House office and his presidential airplane with Jelly Belly beans. He is credited with the statement, "You can tell a lot about a fellow's character by his way of eating jelly beans."

BIBLIOGRAPHY

Jelly Belly Candy Company. *Jelly Beans, An American Original.* http://jellybelly.com/Cultures/en-US/About+Jelly+Belly/Company+History.htm. Describes the process of making jelly beans.
Wolke, Robert L. "How Beans Are Born." *Washington Post,* May 3, 2000.

VIRGINIA MESCHER

---

stripes were typical for peppermint stick candies by the turn of the century, candy canes as such were not made until the 1920s—credited to a Georgia man who made them by hand for his friends and family. After automation, they were introduced nationally in 1950 by Bob's Candy Canes and have become a perennial favorite for Christmas celebrations and an icon of the winter holidays in general.

Edible solid chocolates in fancy boxes became the preferred Valentine's Day gift by the last quarter of the nineteenth century, and they continue to be popular. Chocolate boxes, three-dimensional versions of paper Valentines, were often elaborately shaped and covered with chromolithographic prints, crushed velvet, paper doilies, and colorful foils. Objects of conspicuous consumption, boxed bonbons and chocolates conveyed personal sentiment and symbolized economic status. Candy manufacturers aggressively pursued the Valentine's Day trade starting in the 1890s, capturing with cheaper goods a more widespread market than could be had with fine confections made and sold by independent retailers alone. One Valentine's candy, "conversation hearts," bite-sized pastel-colored chalky candies first produced by the New England Confectionery Company (NECCO) in 1866, bore such printed expressions as "Be true," "Be kind," and "Be mine" and tended to appeal to the younger market. The practice of giving confectionery on Valentine's Day has only increased. By 2001 candy sales for the holiday reached over $1 billion.

Other holidays were wholly devised by the candy industry to generate revenue. "April fool candy," made of sugar-coated cotton laced with cayenne pepper, was sold by candy men in the late 1890s. Candy Day was invented by the National Confectioners Association around 1916 and celebrated on the second Saturday in October. When it lost popularity because of its transparent commercial aims, it was renamed Sweetest Day and continues to be celebrated, mostly in the Midwest, on the third Saturday of October. Although Sweetest Day is a manufactured holiday, people continue to believe its origins are more organic. Common lore has it that, during the Depression, a man who thought people should do a generous deed for someone in need was responsible for its founding, and the myth continues to circulate in popular culture.

Candy in Popular Culture

For a commodity that was relatively rare in the early 1800s, candy enjoyed such a degree of popularity one hundred years later that Americans considered it a staple food—a necessity. It was thought so essential to the American life and diet that chocolate bars made up part of soldiers' rations during the two world wars of the twentieth century. In addition, candy became an integral part of American leisure pursuits. Pink clouds of spun-sugar cotton candy were consumed at baseball games and local fairs. Bite-sized sugary morsels, such as Jujubes, Junior Mints, and M&M's, were part of the entertainment experience at movie theaters. Merchandising of certain goods in the twentieth century went hand in hand with sugar. Children's products, such as baseball cards, came packaged with sticks of bubble gum. And saccharine products such as cereal, borrowing from the legendary caramel-coated popcorn Cracker Jack, were often accompanied by small premiums meant for children, borrowing from merchandising strategies in the penny candy days.

As cultural artifacts, confections reflected their times. Because they rely so heavily on novelty, they often express existing cultural preoccupations. For example, candies and their containers were made in the images of popular adult products. At the beginning of the twentieth century these included boxes shaped as cars and candies shaped as phonographs—expressions of the commodities produced by new technologies. Similarly, candies of the early twenty-first century have come packaged in plastic containers molded in the form of cell phones or computers, or they are made to look like popular characters from television and movies. Candy cigars and cigarettes, once wildly popular among children, were censored in the late twentieth century, owing to growing antitobacco sentiment and were available only from companies producing "nostalgia" candies, which also capitalized on the backward-looking preoccupations of the baby-boomer generation.

The diet fads of the late twentieth century inspired more "healthy" sweet alternatives, such as the granola bar, introduced in 1975 by General Mills, and the supposedly high-energy fitness bars popular since the 1990s. Confections were also marketed as having no fat, although their calorie content remained the same. Boutique confections—fancy, handmade chocolates and hard candies that recalled the elite nineteenth-century trade—also became popular and were marketed in upscale urban areas, while traditionally expensive chocolates, such as Godiva, began being mass-distributed to department stores and local shops.

Candy's ubiquity has infiltrated cultural forms beyond the diet. When the tennis player Billy Jean King defeated Bobby Riggs in a 1973 match that was highly publicized as a battle of the sexes, Riggs presented King with a giant version of a Sugar Daddy. Roald Dahl's 1964 book *Charlie and the Chocolate Factory* was made into the movie *Willy Wonka and the Chocolate Factory* (1971) and made tie-in confections such as Everlasting Gobstoppers extremely popular. Sammy Davis Jr. rerecorded one of the movie's songs, "The Candy Man," which became the biggest hit of the singer's career. In 1982 the movie alien E.T. was famously lured out of the woods by the boy Elliot with Reese's Pieces, making them instantly popular.

At the beginning of the twentieth century the confectionery business still consisted primarily of small-scale, regionally based operations run by families. By century's end only about half of the three hundred confectionery companies were still family owned and operated. Large companies have increasingly bought up smaller enterprises and the prime store shelf space their goods occupied. For example, in 1993 the E. J. Brach Corporation bought Brock Candy Company. Also in 1993 Russell Stover Candies Inc. bought out Stephen F. Whitman to become the last American company selling mid-priced boxed chocolates.

The candy giant Hershey Foods Corporation purchased Peter Paul in 1988. The company bought out Leaf North America in 1996, gaining ownership of Good & Plenty, Jolly Rancher, Whoppers, Milk Duds, Heath, and PayDay. In the late 1990s it acquired family-owned Henry Heide Inc. (est. 1869), taking over Jujyfruits and Wunderbeans in the process. Hershey and other confectionery companies not only expanded candy lines but also established subsidiaries, making them conglomerates selling dog food, pasta, and rice, among other products.

It is difficult for modern-day Americans to imagine a time when candy was not freely available and affordable. In fact, because mass-produced confections are so ubiquitous, many grocery stores have "no candy" aisles for parents who want to dissuade their children from reaching for it. It has become a necessary part of the American diet and of American business enterprise, as statistics bear out: estimated American consumption for 2001 totaled 7 billion pounds of confectionery (including gum, chocolate, and nonchocolate candies), equaling $15.7 billion in wholesale prices.

[See also Chocolate; Christmas; Cracker Jack; Easter; Halloween; Hershey Foods Corporation; Mars; Nestlé; Saltwater Taffy; Valentine's Day.]

BIBLIOGRAPHY

Brenner, Joël Glenn. *The Emperors of Chocolate: Inside the Secret World of Hershey and Mars.* New York: Random House, 1999.
Broekel, Ray. *The Great American Candy Bar Book.* Boston: Houghton Mifflin, 1982.

Coe, Sophie D., and Michael D. Coe. *The True History of Chocolate*. London: Thames and Hudson, 1996.

Lopez, Ruth. *Chocolate: The Nature of Indulgence*. New York: Abrams, 2002.

National Confectioners Association. http://www.candyusa.org.

Schmidt, Leigh Eric. *Consumer Rites: The Buying and Selling of American Holidays*. Princeton, NJ: Princeton University Press, 1995.

Woloson, Wendy. *Refined Tastes: Sugar, Consumers, and Confectionery in Nineteenth-Century America*. Baltimore, MD: Johns Hopkins University Press, 2002.

WENDY A. WOLOSON

Canning and Bottling

The marvels of modern canning and bottling operations are the result of millennia of humankind's efforts. From prehistoric times, humans have tackled the problem of how to preserve surplus foods for use in times of want. Numerous ways were developed, from drying food in the sun to salting food in containers. Other early preserving techniques included smoking, sugaring, and freezing food in ice or snow. These techniques were employed for hundreds of years with little alteration.

This state of affairs changed in the early nineteenth century. In 1795 the French government offered a prize for an improved method of conserving food. Nicolas Appert began experiments on different methods of preserving food. The best technique, he concluded, was boiling and sealing food in a container without air. Appert packed fruits, vegetables, meats, and other foods into wide-mouthed glass bottles and then heated them for various lengths of time in a bath of boiling water. The openings were sealed with a stopper made of cork tightly wired to the bottle. He wrote up his conclusions, which were published in France in 1810 and two years later in England and the United States as *The Art of Preserving*. The British built on Appert's methods, choosing tin for containers rather than glass.

American Bottles and Cans

In the United States commercial bottling operations did not commence until the arrival of experienced English canners. The first was William Underwood, an English pickler, who landed in New Orleans in 1817 and decided to trek across the country on foot. Two years later he arrived in Boston, where he launched the firm later known as the William Underwood Company. Underwood canned luxury goods and ships' provisions, including oysters, lobsters, fish, meats, soups, fruits, and a few vegetables. By 1821 he was shipping plums, quinces, currants, barberries, cranberries, pickles, ketchup, sauces, jellies, and jams packed in glass to South America. During the next thirty years many small bottling factories were launched from Maryland to Maine, but the three major canning areas were Baltimore, New York, and Portland, Maine.

Another early packing firm was operated by Ezra Daggett and his son-in-law, Thomas Kensett, who packed salmon, lobsters, and oysters in New York City starting in about 1819. In 1825 they applied for a tin canning patent, the first in the United States. Canning with tin was difficult and expensive. These operations were labor intensive, for everything was made entirely by hand. The food was placed in the can, and the lid was soldered in place. The can was then placed in a water bath for five hours, a hole in the lid providing a means for the steam to escape. When the bath was finished, the hole was soldered, and the can was sealed airtight. These techniques were not well understood, and problems emerged, including bursting cans and contamination, which often resulted in illness or death to those consuming the contents. The American public was leery both of the high price of canned goods and their high spoilage rates and health threats. As canning in tin and bottling in glass were two very different processes, requiring different machinery and raw materials, specialization developed by the mid-nineteenth century.

Civil War

By 1860 canned goods were an expensive specialty item consumed by few Americans. In the following year American canners greatly sped up the processing of food by heating cans in a solution of calcium chloride and reduced the time the cans remained in a water bath. This and other innovations caused the canning industry to leap ahead during the Civil War. The federal government began purchasing small amounts of canned goods in 1863; this action primed the pump, and canneries sprang up across northern states. The quality of these operations improved, as did their efficiency, which lowered costs. The result was that millions of Americans were exposed to canned goods, including Confederate soldiers, who often raided Union supply trains. The demand for canned goods grew after the war, and the upward spiral continued. Where 5 million cans were put up annually in 1860, the figure was six times greater a decade later. By the 1880s, canned foods were commonly available in most grocery stores throughout the nation.

HOME CANNING

Food preservation was not new when Mason invented his "fruit jar" (1858), but it had never achieved the relatively safe and durable vacuum seals of home canning. Incidentally timed to coincide with the new availability of inexpensive sugar, it offered average homemakers their first opportunity (economically) to put up a year's supply of summer products for winter use. In addition, the process was simplified by the use of the popular cookstove and such adjunct implements as canning kettles, racks, wide-mouth funnels, and lifters.

Home canning surpassed the earlier preservation methods of salting or drying. Out-of-season fruits and vegetables, far less expensive than comparable commercially canned foods, could be eaten with much greater frequency and brought great improvement in nutritional health. Home-canned foods were the closest thing to fresh fruits and vegetables, which were not yet distributed nationally out of season. Year-round meals were more likely to include additional vegetable courses, sweet desserts of fruits in their syrups, cakes and pies with berry fillings, and flavored beverages, homemade beers, and soda pop. In addition, seasonally butchered or hunted meats and fish were sometimes put up in large canning jars, albeit most frequently on farms.

"Putting up" became a major concern of women, whether on farms or in towns or cities. Preserved foods were judged at local fairs for color, texture, (sometimes flavor), and pleasing arrangements within the jar, and good results earned high status for a woman. Cookbooks began to include entire chapters on home canning, and eventually the process became the sole focus of such works as Mrs. Rorer's *Canning and Preserving* (1887).

The large job of home canning required expanded spaces in while to do the work. Summer kitchens were now built to accommodate the heavy summer and fall undertakings, while at the same time distancing the increased and excessive heat from the house. Some were added to the house itself as a second kitchen, but sometimes they were little more than free-standing lean-tos in the yard. They were fueled by means of cast-iron cookstoves, which were simply moved from the winter kitchen, and sometimes by oil stoves—small kerosene burners that were intended to handle canning demands.

ALICE ROSS

Home Canning

At the end of the summer, many farmers and gardeners found themselves with a glut of fruit and vegetables. Canning with tin was difficult for individuals, and bottling was complicated and often unsuccessful. The need for easier means of preserving food in the home led to new techniques and devices for home canning. One important innovation was devised by New Jersey-born John L. Mason, who had set up a metalworking shop in New York. On November 30, 1858 Mason patented the glass jar and zinc lid. The screw-on lid pressed down on a rubber gasket and sealed out air. It greatly simplified home bottling and made it possible to reuse glass jars, thus revolutionizing fruit and vegetable preservation in the home. As the jars were relatively inexpensive, their popularity soared, and by 1860 mason jars were shipped throughout the United States. Home canning was important through the mid-twentieth century. Because of the low cost of canned and bottled commercial foods and a busy urban way of life, most Americans have forgotten the art of home canning.

Canning and Bottling Revolutions

Canning technology took a major leap forward with the invention of the "sanitary can" in the early twentieth century. It built on previous inventions, such as the double-seamed cans first manufactured in 1859, and was used in Europe for canning food shortly thereafter. A thick rubber gasket similar to those used on mason jars was placed between the end and body, and the end was crimped to the body by rollers. This method was demonstrated at the Columbian Exposition in 1893 in Chicago. But the rubber ring was cumbersome and costly. Charles M. Ams lined the edge of the can end with rubber cement, greatly reducing the amount of rubber used and simplifying the sealing process. It was dubbed the "sanitary can." Ams continued to improve the process and by 1903 had developed a line of commercial machines that revolutionized the canning industry.

In the late nineteenth century bottling manufacturers faced serious problems related to glass and capping technology: heating filled bottles to temperatures above 200°F resulted in enormous breakage, but if the contents were

Home Canning. Canning instructions and recipes issued by the Burpee Can Sealer Co., early twentieth century. *Collection of Andrew F. Smith*

Challenges and Opportunities

Despite the spectacular success and rapid expansion of the bottling and canning industry, all was not well in the food-packaging world. Since the industry's inception, contamination and adulteration had been alarming problems. These afflictions became more menacing and more visible as the industry expanded. Fly-by-night manufacturers filled cans and bottles with low-quality products or toxic ingredients, and illness and death resulted. These abuses spurred on the movement to enact pure food laws in states and attempts to pass legislation in Congress beginning in 1876. Federal efforts were not successful until June 1906, when Congress passed the Pure Food and Drug Act. While passage of the act did not immediately end all abuses, serious problems sharply declined subsequently.

By 1900 most middle-sized communities in America were home to one or more canners. The Pure Food and Drug Act required food processors engaged in interstate trade to adhere strictly to proper health and safety procedures. This made it more difficult for small and medium-sized canners to survive, and many closed or were bought out. Slowly the canning and bottling industry has been consolidating into large conglomerates, such as the H. J. Heinz Company, Campbell Soup, Del Monte, Kraft Foods, PepsiCo, and Coca-Cola. Smaller canners and bottlers have survived, and many thrive in niche or regional markets.

Larger canning operations have advantages of scale. They can invest in state-of-the-art equipment, ensuring maximum efficiency at the lowest possible price. Some

not heated above this temperature, they were not sterilized. The contents had to be heated first and then poured into the bottles and corked. As the contents cooled, the corks were unable to maintain the vacuum. Air was sucked through and around the cork, and spoilage commenced. In the early part of the twentieth century researchers developed improved glass bottles that were shatter proof at higher temperatures. Researchers also concluded that vacuum-sealed bottles were absolutely essential. Hence, corks were covered with a metal cap that effectively sealed the bottle from contact with outside air. This type of bottle was especially important in the soda industry. Another major advance was the development of the screw cap, which enabled consumers to open bottles and reseal them for subsequent use.

Canning. Home-canned fruits and vegetables, Box Elder County, Utah, 1940. *Prints and Photographs Division, Library of Congress*

large plants are able to manufacture millions of cans or bottles daily. Large canners can also invest in national distribution networks and extensive advertising campaigns, which have greatly increased sales of canned and bottled goods. Finally, large conglomerates have the ability to expand to markets in other countries.

[*See also* Jams and Jellies; Mason Jars; Preserves; Pure Food and Drug Act.]

BIBLIOGRAPHY

Bitting, A. W. *Appertizing; or, The Art of Canning: Its History and Development*. San Francisco: California Trade Pressroom, 1937.

Collins, James H. *The Story of Canned Foods*. New York: Dutton, 1924.

Keuchel, Edward F., Jr. "The Development of the Canning Industry in New York State to 1960." Ph.D. diss., Cornell University, 1970.

May, Earl Chapin. *The Canning Clan: A Pageant of Pioneering Americans*. New York: Macmillan, 1937.

Sim, Mary B. *Commercial Canning in New Jersey: History and Early Development*. Trenton: New Jersey Agricultural Society, 1951.

Smith, Andrew F. *Souper Tomatoes: The Story of America's Favorite Food*. New Brunswick, NJ: Rutgers University Press, 2000.

ANDREW F. SMITH

Canola, *see Fats and Oils*

Can Openers

The earliest can openers were not like those we know, with revolving cutting blades. Early cans, from the 1830s to the 1870s, had filling holes over which caps were soldered or cemented tight after boiling. Until the 1850s, cans were opened by chiseling a new hole in their tops.

The first patented opener in the United States dates from 1858. It has a piercing bar that is hammered into the tin to make a starter hole into which a rocking cutter blade is inserted. The simplest can openers work the same way in the twenty-first century. Because cans came in so many sizes and shapes, it was useful to be able to adjust the distance between piercing bar and cutting blade; many patents were designed this way. A rocking-blade "sardine opener" was made to open boxy sardine cans and had a relatively small blade, which allowed it to go around the corners. Powerful metal-cutting shears called sardine shears, with small, sharp blades, could be used for sardine cans, corned beef cans, or even

stovepipes. In the 1880s and 1890s, openers with round frames and rotating blades were made for the increasingly more standardized, cylindrical, commercial cans. The major collector of can openers in the United States has over five thousand different designs. Obviously, consumers have never thought their can openers worked perfectly.

[*See also* Canning and Bottling.]

BIBLIOGRAPHY

Franklin, Linda Campbell. *Three Hundred Years of Kitchen Collectibles*. 5th ed. Iola, WI: Krause, 2003.

LINDA CAMPBELL FRANKLIN

Caribbean Influences on American Food

The Caribbean influence on American food has been continual for hundreds of years, initially in coastal areas of similar climate, from Texas to the Carolinas. The early Spanish involvement in the Caribbean brought Caribbean foods to Europe and Africa, from whence they quickly returned to North America. Spanish gold shipments attracted other Europeans to the area and brought about the colonization of eastern North America. Cheap Caribbean sugar, coffee, cocoa, and spices have influenced the palates and tables of all Americans. The peoples of the Caribbean islands have developed multicultural cuisines that have been affecting American cooking at all levels since colonial times.

Influence of the Caribbean on contemporary American food may predate Columbus, because there is some possibility that Caribbean Indians reached Florida and introduced tropical tubers, or chilies. The chain of influence began in 1492, as the varieties of maize, beans, chilies, squash, peanuts, and cassava collected by the Spanish expeditions to the Caribbean would return to North America with every European visitor and with African slaves as early as the abortive Spanish settlement of South Carolina in the 1520s. (That colony ended with internal dissension, including a slave revolt. It is likely that the Africans fled and joined nearby Indian nations. They may have brought some Caribbean or African foodstuffs with them, because in the 1580s British explorers of the same area reported finding cassava and natives who knew it by that name.)

Preparing Caribbean Food. Brawta Café in Brooklyn, New York. *Photograph by Joe Zarba*

Much of the sixteenth-century settlement of North America was actually directed at protecting or capturing the annual Spanish treasure convoys bringing silver and gold out of the Caribbean via the harbors of Cartagena, Colombia, and Havana, Cuba. By 1565 the Spanish had set up forts from Saint Augustine, Florida, to Cape Fear, North Carolina—largely to forestall French, British, and Dutch rivals. In the process, the Spanish introduced European, Caribbean, and African foods, including pigs, chickens, watermelons, peaches, oranges, coconut palms, and sweet potatoes, all of which remained with Native Americans, African Americans, and European settlers of the Southeast and Gulf coasts. Watermelons and peaches were adopted so rapidly by Native Americans that later Spanish explorers found them in remote areas and assumed that they were native species.

French Huguenots attempted two settlements of coastal Georgia in the 1560s, the later of which was massacred by a Spanish expedition. In Virginia, English settlements at Roanoke and Jamestown were periodically endangered by the desertion of ships and men to Caribbean treasure seeking. But Caribbean captures, including slaves and food, were sometimes added to the English North American mix, perhaps as early as Sir Francis Drake's relief of Roanoke in 1586. As the English, French, and Dutch established or conquered

Caribbean colonies in the early 1600s, trade between the Caribbean and North American colonies increased, and the Spanish expanded and fortified Saint Augustine. Contrary to schoolbooks that say the first slaves reached the future United States in 1619, African slaves were used to build the first military fortifications of Saint Augustine.

By the late 1600s, New England's economy had become organized around supplying food and forest products to the British sugar planters in the Caribbean, engendering the development of New England cod fisheries and saltworks, plantation maize production by slaves in Rhode Island, rum and sugar refineries in Massachusetts, the triangular slave trade, and the periodic appearance of chocolate (from British Jamaica), coconuts, oranges, and pineapples on the tables of wealthy Anglo-American merchants.

Sugar and Slaves

One of the lasting legacies of the sugar trade with the Caribbean was the American sweet tooth—cheap sugar was as much an emblem of American freedom and prosperity as cheap meat. British efforts to control and tax the New England trade were the cause of tensions from the 1680s to the Revolution. The by-product of the refineries—molasses—flavored Boston baked beans, Indian pudding, and hermit cookies. Under the table, New England–based ships also traded for or pirated cheaper French and Spanish sugar and slaves. In the Caribbean, salt cod from New England and Newfoundland was a staple slave food, though centuries would pass before delicious codfish fritters returned to New England with Caribbean immigrants.

The slave trade is widely understood to have brought African foods and techniques directly to North America. The British slave trade used the island of Barbados as a sorting, training, and trading center. Thus many slaves were traded north to the British American colonies and the early United States after some period in the Caribbean. Barbadian planters established the North American colony of South Carolina. Cuba played the same role in the Spanish slave trade, and the French equivalent was Saint Domingue (Haiti and the present-day Dominican Republic). The initial shipment of African slaves that landed in Jamestown in 1619 had been captured from the Spanish in the Caribbean by a Dutch warship.

Thus many of the American slaves who founded African American cooking did so after some experience with African Caribbean cooking, whether in British, French, or Spanish kitchens.

In the U.S. Civil War, Confederate soldiers made a fried cornmeal mush they called "coush" or "coush coush." This is quite similar to a Barbadian dish of cornmeal and okra called "coo-coo," which is in turn likely named for African couscous. Barbadian planters established the British South Carolina colony and brought their slaves with them to found its rice plantations.

Another African Caribbean food established early in the United States is hoppin' John, served throughout the southern states on New Year's Day for good luck. It is also called by that name in the Bahamas, and the same dish brings the same New Year's good luck as *arroz con gandules* in Puerto Rico.

Native Caribbeans, not entirely exterminated as is widely believed, were mixed in with African slaves and shipped north, sometimes in exchange for Native American slaves from the British colonies. Native Caribbeans (and probably some South American natives as well) were referred to as "Spanish Indians" in the British colonies. Tituba, the original Salem witch, was a native Caribbean slave. A community on John's Island in the Bahamas has recently reconnected with Wampanoag and Narragansett Indians in the United States.

Caribbean Foods and Cooks in the British Colonies

In 1765 the British took over Florida, and most of the Spanish returned to Havana. Enough stayed, however, to preserve some local foodways, such as the use of the fiery datil chili, a variety of *habanero* localized in Saint Augustine and taken up by the newly settled Catalan-speaking Minorcans (whose Mediterranean home island had been acquired by Britain at the same time). During much of the British rule over Florida, the Spanish were officially in charge of Louisiana and the Gulf Coast ("West Florida"), increasing the influence of such Caribbean foods as mirlitons and possibly jambalaya in New Orleans, Louisiana.

Mirlitons are a tree fruit used as a vegetable; they are similar to summer squash. They can be stuffed and baked, diced and steamed, or sautéed. They are also known as chayote, or *tayote* in the Spanish Caribbean (and in American bodegas), as *cho-cho* in Jamaica, and sometimes as "alligator pears."

West Indian immigrants such as Alexander Hamilton were prominent in the American Revolution, but some were also cooks, such as the mixed-race innkeeper Samuel Fraunces. Fraunces exported American pickled oysters back to the West Indies from his base at the foot of Manhattan, New York, and eventually served George Washington as presidential chef. Someone like Fraunces probably developed the Philadelphia version of Jamaica pepper pot stew at about the same time. From the 1840s another African Caribbean immigrant, Peter Augustin (or Augustine), was a leading caterer in Philadelphia, famous for chicken croquettes that may have been based on African Caribbean–style bean or codfish fritters.

The United States Looks South

In the early nineteenth century, the United States acquired the Louisiana Territory, Florida, and the Gulf Coast areas (West Florida), with their Caribbean-style foods and their newly assimilated cooks from Haiti. The Haitian Revolution had sent French colonists, free "Creoles of color," and their slaves primarily to Francophone New Orleans but also as far north as Philadelphia, where the Haitian Creoles are thought to have introduced peanut brittle.

Although the legal slave trade ended in 1807, the short leg of the triangular trade continued as the United States supplied the Caribbean islands with salt cod and other foodstuffs for slaves and contract laborers in exchange for raw sugar and tropical fruit. The illegal slave trade, in which New Orleans is especially implicated, also tended to run through the Caribbean, because slavery remained legal in Cuba into the 1880s. The increasing tensions in Spanish Cuba produced some of the earliest Caribbean migrations to the United States in the form of Cuban cigar factories and their workers, established in Tampa and Key West, Florida, and East Harlem by the 1890s. Puerto Ricans went to Hawaii as sugar workers in the 1890s; some remain, contributing *pasteles* (plantain tamales wrapped in banana leaves), fried plantains, and fried pork rinds to Hawaiian "local food." Others relocated to San Francisco. At about the same time, Bahamians migrated to Florida, especially to Key West and Miami.

The United States took over Cuba and Puerto Rico at the end of the nineteenth century, although Cuba was returned to a semblance of local control. The building of the Panama Canal to connect the Caribbean with the Pacific also brought North Americans into more direct contact with Caribbean foods and people, if only through the century-long military presence in the Canal Zone. The canal brought large numbers of Caribbean islanders to Panama as workers, some of whom then migrated to the United States. The United States took over part of the Virgin Islands during World War I. To protect American sugar and banana companies, the United States frequently intervened throughout the twentieth century in the governments of many of the Caribbean nations. All of these developments increased migration of Caribbean peoples to the United States, especially of African Caribbeans to the eastern states, where they became cultural and political leaders in the wider African American community. (Black American tourism, immigration, and a wider appreciation since the 1970s of the African diaspora concept brought African Caribbeans to the celebration of Kwanzaa and their dishes to the Kwanzaa *Karamu*, or feast.) The domestic science movement of the early twentieth century promoted Caribbean-grown but corporate-distributed foods like bananas, pineapples, and coconuts in home economics classes and in radio broadcasts.

Increasingly in the twentieth century, Florida and the Caribbean islands became accessible to North American tourists. Miami vacationers and retirees encountered tropical fruits from early in the century and by the 1970s could wander into Cuban American restaurants. If they went on to Key West, they might encounter Cuban or Bahamian dishes in casual restaurants. Those who sailed or flew on to Cuba or Puerto Rico brought back tourist-trade cocktails, such as the daiquiri and rum punch, and later the Cuba libre and piña colada (invented in 1948 at the San Juan Hilton and still served there). While a Cuban-style black bean soup or a Puerto Rican–derived arroz con pollo were still exotic dishes at 1950s North American dinner parties, they had arrived and were especially popular among military families.

World War II opened some Gulf Coast port jobs to Caribbean people, who replaced Americans (and Puerto Ricans) who had gone to war. In the concentrated migration of Puerto Ricans to the United States in the 1950s, many immigrants came to New York City and the northeastern states. Although some Puerto Rican rice and bean dishes became known outside the community, there was more mainstream culinary interest in the 1960s wave of Cuban refugees, who established more restaurants serving black bean soup, roast fresh ham, fried plantains, sandwiches made with three kinds of pork, and other Cuban Creole dishes. The South Beach scene has become an international Latin restaurant row, with a generation of innovative chefs developing an haute cuisine with Caribbean flavors.

With the opening of immigration laws in the late 1960s, substantial immigrant communities of Jamaicans, Dominicans, Trinidadians, Guyanese, Honduran and Belizan Garifuna, and others joined the Cubans and Puerto Ricans in American port cities from Houston, Texas, to Boston. Along with the worldwide popularity of reggae music, there was a confluence of interest in Jamaican meat pies and jerk barbecue, Trinidad-style roti, fried plantains, and every national variety of rice and beans. By the 1990s Caribbean dishes could be found in relatively authentic versions in immigrant neighborhoods, in upscale or "nuevo Latino" versions by enterprising (and often Anglo) chefs, and in reduced-spice form in more casual restaurants, especially in African American communities.

The hot sauce vogue of the 1990s renewed interest in the Caribbean *habanero* pepper, one of the hottest of all chilies, which originally came to North American notice in Jamaican sauces made from the local variety, called "Scotch bonnet." Specialty stores and mail-order catalogs feature dozens of *habanero* sauces that most North Americans must use drop by drop or risk serious discomfort.

Urban markets now offer plantains; Caribbean-style, espresso-ground coffee; tropical roots; low-fat Caribbean avocados; Jamaican Ugli tangelos; sour oranges; and sometimes more localized specialties, such as canned Jamaican akee, frozen Puerto Rican *pasteles* or *alcapurrias*, *recao* (a native herb that smells like cilantro), Dominican cassava bread, Haitian mushrooms, and canned Barbadian chutneys.

These immigrant foods so far from home close a circle, for when Columbus first made contact with Caribbean Taino Indians on Hispaniola (the present Dominican Republic), he was given chilies, which the Spanish heard described as "axi." In any Dominican bodega in New York City, they are still there, labeled "achies."

[*See also* Cajun and Creole Food; Cuban American Food; Hawaiian Food; Iberian and South American Food; Mexican American Food; Native American Foods, *subentry* Before and After Contact; Puerto Rican Food; Rice; Southern Regional Cookery; Southwestern Regional Cookery.]

BIBLIOGRAPHY

Cook, Evelyn, comp. *West Kauai's Plantation Heritage: Recipes and Stories for Life from the Legacy of Hawaii's Sugar Plantation Community.* Edited by Elizabeth Hahn. Waimea, HI: West Kauai Community Development Corporation, 2002.

Lauber, Almon Wheeler. *Indian Slavery in Colonial Times within the Present Limits of the United States.* New York: Columbia University, 1913. Still the definitive survey, with many allusions to "Spanish Indians" in various contexts.

Steele, Ian K. *Warpaths: Invasions of North America.* New York: Oxford University Press, 1994. Colonial America from the Native American point of view, with a fine history of early Saint Augustine, Florida.

Weber, David J. *The Spanish Frontier in North America.* New Haven, CT: Yale University Press, 1992.

Wright, Louis B., ed. *The Elizabethans' America.* Cambridge, MA: Harvard University Press, 1965. Excellent collection of original documents on visits from 1565 to 1630.

MARK H. ZANGER

Carrots

The carrot (*Daucus carota*) most likely originated in Afghanistan as a yellow or purple root. Its earliest dispersal, possibly via the Greeks, is uncertain, but there is some evidence that colorful central Asian varieties were cultivated in the Hellenistic Mediterranean, becoming extinct after Rome's fall. The vegetable spread (or was reintroduced) to the Middle East, Europe, India, and China by the Arabs, starting in the eleventh century. The Dutch crossed the old Afghani varieties in the late seventeenth century creating the brilliant orange root that is associated with most modern carrots, botanically subgrouped as *D. carota sativus*.

Adding to the confusion of early carrot history is the wild white carrot (also classed *D. carota*) that is native to Europe and was subsequently naturalized in America. Now popularly known as Queen Anne's lace, and most famous for its ornamental flower, the woody root has been used interchangeably with its visually similar cousin, the parsnip (both are members of the Apiaceae family). The late-fourth-century Roman cookery book of Apicius lists recipes suitable for either carrots (presumably wild and cultivated) or parsnips, advice repeated nearly fifteen hundred years later in Lettice Bryan's *The Kentucky Housewife* (1839) that "carrots may be cooked in every respect like parsnips."

English carrots were the first to be introduced into the colonies, accompanying colonists to Jamestown in 1609 and early Pilgrims to Massachusetts no later than 1629, where they grew "bigger and sweeter" than anything found in England. Dutch Mennonites brought orange and scarlet carrots with them into Pennsylvania, from whence they slowly spread through the rest of the colonies. Amelia Simmons's *American Cookery* (1796) describes yellow, red, and orange carrots, preferring the yellow of "middling siz'd, that is, a foot long and two inches at the top end." Carrots were easily transported, and they became popular vegetables with truck farmers, who brought them into urban markets from outlying areas by the end of the colonial period.

All parts of the carrot have culinary uses. The roots are most commonly eaten raw or pickled, in salads and as hors d'oeuvres; boiled, roasted, fried, or mashed as vegetable side dishes; pureed or chopped for soups and stews; extracted into juices; or baked into sweet cakes and puddings. Considered an aromatic (along with onions and celery), carrots add subtle sweetness to stocks and sauces. The lacy green leaves can be used in salads and as an herb, while the aromatic seeds function as a spice. Carrots traditionally were ascribed tonic properties, thought to be good for the stomach. Teas made from wild carrots have been used for bladder and kidney ailments. During World War II, carrots were dehydrated, treated with carbon dioxide or nitrogen, and shipped to troops overseas to supply dietary carotene. Pennsylvania folk medicine prescribed the wild seeds as a postcoital contraceptive.

Most of the carrots in contemporary markets are orange descendants of the two varieties introduced by the Mennonites. Specialized carrots, including the gourmet baby sizes, have been developed through selective breeding. Shapes range from small spheres through stumpy cylinders to long tapers, and colors shade from pale whites to deep violet; some are variegated. Although fresh carrots form the largest segment of the American market, with California and Colorado the leading producers, carrots also withstand canning and freezing reasonably well.

[*See also* Homemade Remedies; Kitchen Gardening; Simmons, Amelia; Vegetables.]

BIBLIOGRAPHY

Facciola, Stephen. *Cornucopia II: A Source Book of Edible Plants.* Vista, CA: Kampong, 1998.

Hedrick, U. P. *A History of Horticulture in America to 1860.* New York: Oxford University Press, 1950.

Hedrick, U. P., ed. *Sturtevant's Edible Plants of the World.* New York: Dover, 1972. Reprint of *Sturtevant's Notes on Edible Plants.* Albany, NY: J. B. Lyon, 1919.

Purdue University, Department of Horticulture and Landscape Architecture. http://www.hort.purdue.edu/rhodcv/hort410/carrot/carrot.htm.

Weaver, William Woys. *Heirloom Vegetable Gardening.* New York: Henry Holt, 1997.

CATHY K. KAUFMAN

George Washington Carver. *Prints and Photographs Division, Library of Congress*

Carver, George Washington

George Washington Carver's early life is shrouded in myth and legend. He was probably born in the spring of 1865 in a one-room cabin on a farm in Newton County, Missouri. His mother had been a slave; his father was unknown to him. The owners of the farm were Moses and Susan Carver, German immigrants. Along with his mother, George was abducted as an infant by night riders who carried him off to Arkansas. Moses Carver found George and traded a horse valued at three hundred dollars for him—or so legend relates.

Carver never saw his mother again, and the childless Carvers became his foster parents. George was sickly as a child, so he was assigned household chores and learned to read. The Carvers encouraged him to get an education. He worked his way through high school and then enrolled in Simpson College in Indianola, Iowa. In 1891 he transferred to Iowa State College of Agriculture and Mechanical Arts at Ames. Working his way through college, Carver received a bachelor's degree in 1894, after which he was given faculty status while pursuing graduate work. He received a master of agriculture degree in 1896. Carver was particularly interested in botany and mycology, but he also painted.

In 1896, Booker T. Washington offered Carver a position at the Tuskegee Institute in Alabama. Washington wanted Carver to head the new agriculture department. Carver accepted the position and spent the remainder of his forty-six years at the institute. During the first twenty years he focused his research on a variety of food plants, including tomatoes, sweet potatoes, and cowpeas. Carver's work earned him election to membership in Great Britain's Royal Society of Arts in 1915.

Carver paid little attention to peanuts during his early years at Tuskegee. The minor exception was a small experiment he conducted in 1903, using peanuts as swine feed. However, in late 1915 Carver decided to publish a bulletin on peanuts. The boll weevil had destroyed Alabama's cotton crop, and many farmers had begun to convert to peanuts. Peanuts had several distinct advantages over other potential cash crops, especially for sharecroppers. If the peanuts could not be sold, sharecroppers would at least have something nutritious to eat during the winter. Shortly after the publication of the bulletin, Carver began conducting experiments and developing products from peanuts.

When Congress held hearings on a peanut tariff, Carver was asked to testify. He performed well, and his national popularity soared. He continued to develop peanut products, reportedly more than three hundred items, including chili sauce, candy, salad oils, oleomargarine, cheese, instant coffee, beverages, paint, cattle feed, and milk substitute. Carver was criticized at the time for his failure to commercialize his peanut discoveries, and few were ever converted to practical uses.

Carver died on January 3, 1943. Although America was again embroiled in a world war, newspapers, magazines, and Americans of all races paused to show their respect for him. He has been portrayed as an African American role model ever since in school textbooks and in children's books, many of which have stressed Carver's connection with the peanut.

[*See also* Peanuts.]

BIBLIOGRAPHY

Holt, Rachham. *George Washington Carver: An American Biography*. Garden City, NY: Doubleday, Doran, 1944.
McMurry, Linda O. *George Washington Carver: Scientist and Symbol*. New York: Oxford University Press, 1982.
Smith, Andrew F. *Peanuts: The Illustrious History of the Goober Pea*. Urbana: University of Illinois Press, 2002.

ANDREW F. SMITH

Cashews

Cashews (*Anacardium occidentale*) are native to tropical South America. The Portuguese introduced cashews to East Africa, Indonesia, and India, where they quickly spread to the Malabar coast and southwestern India. The Spanish introduced cashews to their colonies in the Caribbean, Central America, and the Philippines. Cashews were first imported into the United States shortly after the Civil War. Although their origins are in the New World, cashews are not a major crop in any country of the Americas. In the early twenty-first century, India led the world in production. Raw or roasted, salted or not, cashews are favorites for snacking, and they are the most important dessert nut after almonds. Cashews are lower in fat than other commonly consumed nuts.

[*See also* Almonds; Brazil Nuts; Nuts.]

ANDREW F. SMITH

Cassava

Most North Americans know cassava only in the form of tapioca pudding, but it is an American domesticate that

is a staple for an estimated 500 million people in ninety-two countries, mostly in tropical Africa and Asia as well as South America. Cassava (also known as manioc or yucca) is the tuber of a large shrub, *Manihot esculenta*. The word "cassava" comes from the Taino Indian word for cassava bread, a stiff flatbread offered to Columbus by the Taino Indians on Hispanola. Cassava bread is still produced in the Dominican Republic and is widely available in urban bodegas in New York and other East Coast American cities. The original domestication was probably in Brazil, where cassava meal, "farinha," is still part of every meal. Cassava was a staple of the Mayan empire and had reached Peru and Argentina before the arrival of Columbus. The Taino preferred it to maize, and their other name, "Arawaks," means "eaters of meal." Cassava is an unusual domesticate, in that the raw roots of most varieties contain fatal amounts of prussic acid. Thus the Indians had to devise methods of grating, soaking, pressing, boiling, drying, and roasting to produce edible starches and syrups. (Some inferior varieties can be peeled and boiled like potatoes.) Cassava became a slave staple in Brazil and was disseminated by the Portuguese to central Africa, by the Dutch to Indonesia, and by the Spanish to the Philippines. Cassava was probably grown in parts of Florida, the Carolinas, and Virginia to feed slaves, but the written record is unclear. The earliest reference in English is Thomas Harriot's account of 1585–1586; he described the food of the Indians of the outer banks of the Carolinas: "*Coscúshaw*, some of our company tooke to bee that kinde of roote which the Spaniards in the West Indies call *Cassauy*, whereupon also many called it by that name." If this was true cassava, it might have been brought there by far-ranging Tainos or, more likely, by the Spanish Carolina colonists of 1526, whose one hundred African slaves rebelled and joined the Indians near the Pee Dee river.

Thomas Jefferson's 1787 *Notes on the State of Virginia* lists cassava as a domestic plant but gives the Latin name of an entirely different species. The last and northernmost reference is Mary Randolph's 1824 description in *The Virginia House-Wife* of a rice johnnycake "nearly as good as cassada [sic] bread." It is thus possible that Virginia plantations had been quietly growing and processing cassava for more than two hundred years, but, more likely, Randolph's cassava bread was imported from the West Indies. The durable flatbreads had become a ship's supply and conquistador marching ration as early as the 1500s.

Manioc starch (Brazilian arrowroot) was used as a pudding thickener in colonial and early America, and pearl tapioca, primarily from Indonesian plantations, became a popular thickener for puddings and pies in the United States in the mid-nineteenth century. Since the 1950s, cassava has reentered the United States as a boiled or fried root (yucca) with migrant populations from Puerto Rico, refugees from Cuba, and immigrants from Brazil (mandioca) and the Dominican Republic. Honduran and Belizan Garifuna (descendants of Africans and indigenous peoples of the West Indies) in Los Angeles, New Orleans, and Brooklyn, New York, use cassava to thicken stews and toast breads. Cassava syrup, *cassareep*, is the crucial ingredient in Jamaican pepper pot, and Brazilian farinha is sold to Nigerian Americans as well as Brazilian immigrants.

[*See also* Caribbean Influences on American Food; Native American Foods.]

BIBLIOGRAPHY

Randolph, Mary. *The Virginia House-Wife*. With historical notes and commentary by Karen Hess. Columbia: University of South Carolina Press, 1984.

MARK H. ZANGER

Casseroles

The name for the food comes from the container in which it is cooked. A casserole (from a Greek word meaning "cup," a Latin word meaning "ladle" and "pan," and an Old French word *casse*, which eventually evolved into *cassole*) is a cooking vessel made of ovenproof material. Ceramic or metal, the casserole usually has a lid and is suitable for long, slow cooking in an oven; it holds at least two ingredients that are subjected to a constant temperature and continuous basting. The typical casserole container is round, may vary in depth, and, if decorative, may be placed on the buffet or dining table when the meal is served. It is also a favorite at American potluck suppers, summer picnics, and anywhere a "hot dish to pass" is requested of guests.

Casserole cookery has been around since prehistoric times, when it was discovered that cooking food slowly in a tightly covered clay vessel softened fibrous meats and blended succulent juices. It is an unsophisticated method and can withstand a bit of neglect. If the casserole is not removed from the oven immediately, it will not be ruined.

With the addition or subtraction of leftovers or inexpensive cuts of meat, the casserole is flexible and economical in terms of both ingredients and effort. The classic casserole, a French dish, was originally made with a mound of cooked rice. Fannie Merritt Farmer's *Boston Cooking-School Cook Book* (1896) had one casserole recipe, for Casserole of Rice and Meat, to be steamed for forty-five minutes and served with tomato sauce.

In the twentieth century, casseroles took on a distinctive American identity. During the depression of the 1890s, the economic casserole provided a welcome way to stretch meat, fish, and poultry. Certain items were also scarce during World War I and leftovers were turned into casserole meals. The same was true during the Great Depression of the 1930s, when busy housewives and small kitchens eventually made the casserole convenient fare.

For many, the cherished comfort foods of childhood include the ubiquitous tuna–potato chip casserole bound together with Campbell's Cream of Mushroom Soup (an absolute boon for housewives when it was introduced in 1934), a Tater Tot casserole (cook's choice of creamed soup, plus hamburger and Tater Tots) or the good old green bean casserole (green beans, cream of mushroom soup, and french fried onion rings), a Thanksgiving dinner requirement almost as necessary as pumpkin pie.

To prepare food *en casserole* initially denoted culinary sophistication to American cooks, but immigrants brought their own casserole recipes to the New World in the nineteenth century, and favorite ethnic and regional classics evolved. The New England cookstove often held a simmering casserole of baked beans and molasses. In the southern United States, jambalaya was popular. Ethnic influences and regional tastes adapted the Greek or Turkish moussaka with acceptable modifications. In South Carolina and Georgia, rice plantations and an abundance of shrimp brought about a casserole that combined both. Yankee oyster pie, a casserole native to the northeastern coast of the United States, layers oysters and oyster crackers with plenty of cream, butter, and Worcestershire sauce. Hungarian goulash is enjoyed everywhere. A truly original concoction, the King Ranch casserole, with chicken, cheese, tortilla chips, and cream of mushroom and cream of chicken soup is, according to the magazine *Texas Monthly*, "the clubwoman's contribution to Texas cuisine."

[*See also* Advertising Cookbooklets and Recipes; Campbell Soup Company; Cooking Techniques; Pots and Pans.]

BIBLIOGRAPHY

Kaufman, William I. *The Art of Casserole Cookery*. New York: Doubleday, 1967.

Swartz, Mimi. "King Ranch Casserole." *Texas Monthly* (January 1989).

Vilas, James. *Crazy for Casseroles*. Boston: Harvard Common Press, 2003.

SARA RATH

Cauliflower

Cauliflower (*Brassica oleracea botrytis*) is one of the cultivated varieties of the cabbage plant. The vegetable is picked in the bud stage, before it blossoms, and only the florets are consumed—these are the small, tightly packed buds that make up the head. Cauliflower is a close relative of broccoli, but unlike the leaves of broccoli, cauliflower's leaves cover the flower head as it grows, keeping the florets from producing chlorophyll and turning green.

Cauliflower may have originated in the Middle East, and it has been grown in Italy since the fifteenth century. It was subsequently distributed to other parts of Europe and was cultivated in North America by the late 1600s. By the late eighteenth century, recipes were published in American cookbooks for boiling, frying, or stewing cauliflower; early recipes were also offered for pickling, and pickled cauliflower was served when fresh vegetables were unavailable and as a condiment. In the nineteenth century, cauliflower cookery expanded. Sometimes boiled in milk to gentle its flavor, cauliflower was sauced, usually with a butter or white sauce, and served as a side dish with meats; it was also sieved to make creamy soups.

Cauliflower was baked and browned in a cheese sauce, folded into omelets, and served (cooked, chilled, and dressed with mayonnaise or vinaigrette) as a salad. Raw cauliflower, fairly tough on the digestive system, became a component of crudités platters served with dips during the late twentieth century. The first cauliflower cookbooklet was published by Arthur A. Crozier in 1891, and cauliflower has been featured in later cookbooks, such as Charlotte Snyder Turgeon's *Of Cabbages and Kings Cookbook* (1977).

White cauliflower is more abundant in the United States, but orange and purple cauliflowers are sold, and some markets stock a cauliflower-broccoli hybrid called the broccoflower, which is light green in color and milder and sweeter in flavor than either of its parents.

Cauliflower. Cauliflower seed advertisement.

BIBLIOGRAPHY

Crozier, Arthur A. *How to Cook Cauliflower*. Ann Arbor, MI: published privately, 1891.

Turgeon, Charlotte Snyder. *Of Cabbages and Kings Cookbook: An Uncommon Collection of Recipes Featuring That Family of Vegetables Which Includes Broccoli, Brussels Sprouts, Cauliflower, Collards, Turnips, Kale, and Kohlrabi*. Indianapolis, IN: Curtis Publishing, 1977.

ANDREW F. SMITH

Celebrity Chefs

Celebrity chef is the title given to people who are famous for cooking in public. Although the term did not gain widespread use until the 1990s, it is generally applied to all well-known cooks and chefs of the past and present. It is a role characterized by status, rather than a particular function, in a culture in which food has become a form of popular entertainment. There are many types of celebrity chefs—from restaurateur-activists to cooking-show host-authors—and, collectively, they appeal to a broad spectrum of American society. Popularized through the mass multimedia, including twenty-four-hour television programming, cookbooks, consumer magazines, and the Internet, they have become prominent public figures in our culture.

Postwar to 1970s

Chefs, Hollywood celebrities, and radio personalities were in the public eye before the mid-twentieth century, their images publicized through cookbooks, advertising pamphlets, and other food-product endorsements. But the phenomenon of the celebrity chef stems from two cultural forces of the post–World War II era: the emergent food consciousness in America and the development of the mass media. The watershed event in the rise of the celebrity chef was the debut of Julia Child as *The French Chef* in 1962. From its first local broadcast, the show rapidly became a national sensation, and she became universally recognized by her given name, Julia, and her sign-off, "Bon appétit." When her image appeared on the cover of *Time* magazine (November 25, 1966), the accompanying article read, "Julia Child's TV cooking shows have made her a cult from coast to coast and put her on a first-name basis with her fans."

Julia Child's broad fan base was made up of a generation of new consumers of a gourmet culture that developed from the economic boom and increased social and physical mobility after World War II. Affluence, automobiles, and new restaurants across the country gave the middle class newfound access to eating out as a leisure activity, while increased air travel put international dining within reach of more Americans. Popular cookbooks, general interest and food magazines, and radio and television programs also widely promoted the idea of food as a source of pleasure for the average American. Julia Child captivated the nation's attention because she reconceived haute cuisine as an affordable luxury for the general public. French cuisine, the order of the day in the finest restaurants, was what socially mobile people aspired to eat in and outside of the country. The allure of French food was further heightened by the glamour surrounding the Francophile First Lady Jacqueline Kennedy, whose hiring of the French chef René Verdon in 1961 made front-page news.

Julia Child was not the first television cooking teacher. For example, James Beard, a successful cookbook author, instructor, *Gourmet* magazine contributor, and product spokesperson, had starred in *Elsie Presents*

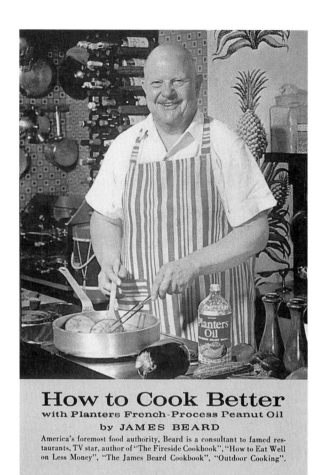

Celebrity Chef. James Beard on the cover of a recipe booklet issued by Planters Peanuts, 1961. *Collection of Andrew F. Smith*

James Beard in "I Love to Eat" from 1946 to 1947 on the NBC network. His and other early programs introduced cooking shows to the television audience. By the 1960s, with televisions in many more American homes, *The French Chef* revolutionized the cooking program as a form of entertainment.

Although Julia Child was an unlikely television star, she quickly rivaled the popularity of the best-known food personality in America of the period, the fictional character Betty Crocker. Child's onscreen persona tempered her patrician background with a disarming lack of pretense. She reassured her audience while demonstrating the pleasures of cooking and eating well. Her wit and unedited goof-ups on the program made *The French Chef* not only educational but also engaging and funny. The mass media played a pivotal role in turning the television cook Julia Child into a national superstar. Her successful cookbook, *Mastering the Art of French Cooking*, which had been published in 1961, further bolstered her public image. In turn, sales of the book surged. Publicity only increased with the publication of a second volume in 1970, which coincided with a new *French Chef* series. From *TV Guide* to *House and Garden* to the *New Yorker*, it was the rare magazine that did not feature her. Likewise, newspapers across the country ran articles, especially when she was in the area for book tours, cooking demonstrations, honorary dinners, and charity events.

The media attention showered on Julia Child, which expanded her influence and status, is one of the hallmarks of the celebrity chef. For her part, Child wrote companion cookbooks to *The French Chef* series, granted countless interviews in her homes in Cambridge, Massachusetts, and Provence, France, and contributed to national publications. It is also significant that although Child never endorsed specific products, her publicity inspired waves of purchasing, cooking, and eating behaviors, which accelerated the gourmet food trend throughout the country.

1970 to the Twenty-first Century

With the success of *The French Chef*, public television expanded its offerings of cooking programs. Some of them included other ethnic cuisines popular in the 1970s, notably Chinese and Italian. Joyce Chen, a Chinese immigrant restaurant owner, and Margaret and Franco Romagnoli, Italian cookbook authors and restaurateurs, hosted their own programs. They were exceptional because they were chefs in the classical sense, that is, they were the heads of kitchens, as well as public figures. But audiences have never recognized a distinction between chefs and nonchefs. Television cooking stars, such as Graham Kerr of *The Galloping Gourmet*, and cookbook authors, such as the *New York Times*'s Craig Claiborne, are all considered celebrity chefs.

Social changes through the late 1970s and into the 1980s further entrenched the status of food in American culture. More full-time working women put a premium on cooking at home, while more cookbooks were published each year. Dining out continued to connote status, and new magazines, such as *Food and Wine*, spurred the public passion for the next dining trend. Health concerns spawned vegetarian cookbooks, including *The Moosewood Cookbook*, and diet-conscious magazines, such as *Cooking Light*. The paradox of the predominant interest in food in general society is that while it steadily increased, the number of home-cooked meals decreased—a trend that has continued.

The 1980s is the period often noted as the food revolution in the United States. It is also significant for the widespread name recognition accorded to American chefs for the first time. Two California chefs in particular, Alice Waters and Wolfgang Puck, received major media coverage when the West Coast became the focus of national culinary interest. As attention turned to the country's other regional cuisines, working chefs, including Paul Prudhomme, Larry Forgione, and Mark Miller gained prominence. *Cooking with the New American Chefs*, published in 1985, profiled these three chefs, along with twenty others. Although they were not yet called "celebrity chefs," the enhanced status of the American-made chef contributed significantly to the celebrity chef phenomenon. Organizations within the culinary profession, several of which were founded during the 1980s, also spotlighted chefs by publicly honoring them. The annual James Beard Foundation awards, for example, are called "the Oscars of the food world."

The creation of the Food Network in 1993 was the final breakthrough in the era of the celebrity chef. It not only capitalized on the entertainment value of cooking on television but also firmly established food as pop culture. Cooking, which once had been a common, private activity, became public performance. And those who cooked had become a new brand of cultural hero to a wide range of classes, age groups, and tastes in America.

Emeril Lagasse, one of the first stars created by the Food Network, is a model of the celebrity chef. Like Julia Child, Lagasse is widely recognized by first name only, as is his catchphrase, "Bam!" In addition to his many television series, he manages a conglomeration of commercial and media enterprises that includes restaurants and cookbooks, cookware lines, a website, primetime television programs, documentaries, guest appearances, and charity events. He is one of many cult figures in the large and growing pantheon of celebrity chefs.

[*See also* Beard, James; Child, Julia; Claiborne, Craig; Lagasse, Emeril; Prudhomme, Paul; Puck, Wolfgang; Radio and Television; Waters, Alice.]

BIBLIOGRAPHY

Brenner, Leslie. *American Appetite: The Coming of Age of a National Cuisine.* New York: HarperCollins, 1999.

Fitch, Noël Riley. *Appetite for Life: The Biography of Julia Child.* New York: Doubleday, 1997.

Kuh, Patric. *The Last Days of Haute Cuisine.* New York: Viking Penguin, 2001.

LYNNE SAMPSON

Celery

The crisp, mild-flavored celery eaten in the early twenty-first century is a descendent of a bitter wild celery (*Apium graveolens*), called smallage, that is indigenous to Europe, the Middle East, and South Asia. In the ancient Mediterranean, the seeds and roots of this plant were used by the Greeks and Romans, mainly as spices and flavorings. In the seventeenth century, the bitterness was bred out, and the stalks and leaves began to be served in salads and as cooked vegetables in Europe. This improved variety was grown in England by 1644 but was not introduced into America until the following century.

Celery became an important food in America by the early nineteenth century. Four varieties were noted in Bernard M'Mahon's *The American Gardener's Calendar* (1806). Celery stalks were used for a variety of culinary purposes: fried or stewed and sauced and served as a vegetable, added to soups and sauces (the latter used especially for turkey and other fowl), and immersed in seasoned vinegar for pickles. Celery glasses, serving pieces that held celery stalks, became important during the first two decades of the nineteenth century. These pieces were made from glass or silver and initially took a variety of urn shapes. Around the 1890s the flatter plate or dish became popular, supplanting glasses, stands, and vases for celery.

By the late nineteenth century, raw celery stalks were served as appetizers and as an ingredient in salads, such as Waldorf salad. Celery seeds and leaves were used as a flavoring. Celery salt, consisting of dried, pulverized celery stalks mixed with salt, was added to America's spice shelf by the 1870s. In the twentieth century, celery became still more popular. By midcentury, a succession of diet fads made the crisp stalks a favorite food for weight watchers, and a false rumor circulated that celery had "negative calories" (that chewing it burned more calories than the celery supplied to the body). Lengths of celery stalks filled with cream cheese became a popular appetizer during the 1950s. Filled with peanut butter and topped with a row of raisins, celery stalks became "ants on a log," a children's favorite. In the 1960s, a celery stalk became a requisite garnish for a Bloody Mary cocktail. Celery sticks are also a standard accompaniment to Buffalo wings.

The main variety of celery consumed in the United States is Pascal, which was first cultivated in 1874 in Michigan. California is the largest celery producer, followed by Florida. Celery seed for seasoning is generally imported from Asia.

[*See also* Bloody Mary and Virgin Mary; California; Health Food; Peanut Butter; Pickles; Pickling; Poultry and Fowl; Salads and Salad Dressings; Vegetables.]

BIBLIOGRAPHY

Beattie, William Renwick. *Celery Culture: A Practical Treatise of the Principles Involved in the Production of Celery for Home Use and for Market.* New York: Orange Judd, 1907.

Bitting, A. W. *Appertizing or the Art of Canning.* San Francisco: Trade Pressroom, 1937.

ANDREW F. SMITH

Central Asian Food

Central Asian culinary influences in the American diet are historically minor but are starting to grow as Americans travel to Central Asia and as more and more Central Asians settle in the United States. Central Asian or Turkestani (mainly from former Soviet Central Asia and China's Xinjiang, or Sinkiang, province) immigrant communities have existed in the United States, mainly in Brooklyn and New Jersey, since the Russian Revolution in 1917. Many of these early Central Asian immigrants fled the Russian empire, first spending time in Afghanistan, Iran, China, and Turkey before immigrating to the United States. Since the 1930s steadily growing numbers of Turks, Persians, and Afghans have come to the United States following the flight of Soviet Jewry (mid-1970s), the Iranian Revolution (1979), and the Soviet invasion of Afghanistan (1980). Substantial Turkish immigration to the United States followed World War II. It can be further divided into eras and classes: the first wave, mainly through the mid-1970s, comprised typical immigrants seeking a better life and less repressive states. Since the 1970s Turks coming to America typically have been young and accomplished professionals, people demanding higher-quality and more authentic restaurant culture.

The heart of former Soviet Central Asian culinary culture lies in New York—mainly the boroughs of Brooklyn and Queens. Most but not all of the clientele remain first-generation Central Asians, predominantly Bukharan Jews, Tajiks, and Uzbeks. Los Angeles and Seattle also boast a number of Central Asian eateries with a wider multiethnic appeal. Southern California is home to greater numbers of Iranians and Afghans than Central

Asians, but similarities in culinary lifeways mutually reinforce one another. Since the 1970s Seattle has had a sister-city relationship with Tashkent, the capital of Uzbekistan, and the University of Washington has had a very active Central Asian studies program, which has brought many Central Asians to Seattle.

Probably the most widely accepted and enjoyed Central Asian food in America is yogurt (a Turkish word; in Turkish the "g" is not pronounced). Of course, the consumption of yogurt is so widely spread throughout Europe that it is easy to forget its origins as a product of the Eurasian steppe. One yogurt drink is slowly catching on in large cities, such as Chicago and Los Angeles, and in large university towns that support Near Eastern or Central Asian communities. The drink is *airan* (Turkish) or *doh* (Persian), and it is a watered-down yogurt drink, sometimes served with salt, ice, and herb flavorings, such as basil or cilantro. It is available not only in restaurants but also as a packaged good in specialty ethnic groceries. On hot days in Iran, Turkey, or Uzbekistan, *doh* or *airan* stands are ubiquitous.

Pilafs, generally available since the end of World War II in American supermarkets in the form of packaged dry mixes, are widely obtainable throughout the Near East and Central Asia, where they are known as *palov* or *osh*. These hearty rice stews—which typically include copious amounts of carrots, mutton and mutton fat or beef and vegetable oil, cumin, and garlic—are served in Central Asian eateries on the coasts and in Chicago.

Increasingly, the Uzbek and Tajik variety of bread, known as *obi* or *patir non* (or naan), is gaining a wider audience, owing to its wonderful textures, aroma, and flavor. It resembles some of the best types of naan found in Indian or Pakistani restaurants but tends to have an even crisper and firmer crust. Bread lovers in coastal cities such as New York and Los Angeles are becoming familiar with this world-class bread.

Curiously, some of the best foodstuffs in Central Asia, including soups, noodle dishes, and large dumplings, seem to have their origins in western China—Xinjiang to be exact. Whereas in Central Asia the status of Uyghur cooks is legendary, Americans are just barely learning of the various ethnic cum national distinctions extant in Central Asia. It will probably be some time before localized Central Asian culinary traditions become better known in North America.

Afghan dishes, themselves an interesting fusion of northern Indian and Iranian ingredients with many local variants, have been attracting Americans to dining establishments since the 1970s. Renewed interest in Afghan cuisine accompanies the "War on Terror." Breads, kebabs, yogurt sauces, and vegetarian dishes, including those made with eggplant, okra, and squashes, tend to be among the favorites.

Most Central Asians are Muslims, so pork does not appear on their tables. Lamb and mutton are often the basis for cherished dishes. Americans on the whole do not consume large quantities of lamb, much less mature mutton and certainly not the famous fat-tailed sheep beloved of the Central Asian homeland. For that reason, among others, authentic Central Asian cuisine has been and will remain a niche cuisine. No doubt, clever restaurateurs will modify their menus for American tastes and, like their Greek counterparts, emphasize beef and poultry dishes.

Overall, the influence of Central Asian culinary types in American gastronomy mainly operates through restaurants and cookbooks. Since journalism seems to be the primary vehicle by which discussion of relatively unknown cuisines is spread in America, people who try such foods often do so after reading restaurant reviews. Others who are getting out the word and slowly helping influence mainstream eating patterns are the increasingly popular chowhound-type organizations, which make use of the Internet to spread the news.

[*See also* Lamb and Mutton.]

BIBLIOGRAPHY

Algar, Ayla E. *Classical Turkish Cooking: Traditional Turkish Food for the American Kitchen.* New York: HarperCollins, 1991.

Shaida, Margaret. *The Legendary Cuisine of Persia.* London: Grub Street, 2000.

Visson, Lynn. *The Art of Uzbek Cooking.* Hippocrene Books, 1999.

RUSSELL ZANCA

Cereal, Cold

Ready-to-eat (or cold) cereal, an American invention, developed as a result of the health reform movement in the late 1800s. Sanatoriums, often with religious affiliations, sprang up to offer food regimens for those suffering with dyspepsia, the chronic digestion problems that afflicted many Americans because of their high-protein diets. The grain-based cereals that were invented to offer abdominal relief to the sufferers became one of the first modern convenience foods—easy to serve, sanitary, and long lasting. Breakfast cereals are eaten throughout the world, and a few of the companies that were built by the original cereal inventors have grown into several of the largest American food conglomerates.

Granula, a predecessor of modern cereals, was created in 1863 by Dr. James C. Jackson at his sanitorium in Dansville, New York. Whole-wheat "Graham" flour (developed by Sylvester Graham) was mixed with water and baked into thin sheets, which were then broken into chunks, ground into bean-sized pieces, rebaked, and reground. The resulting coarse nuggets had to be reconstituted with liquid for a minimum of twenty minutes or, preferably, overnight before they were eaten.

During the late 1880s and early 1890s, as demand grew, several independent, ready-to-eat cereal types developed. At his sanitorium in Battle Creek, Michigan, Dr. John Harvey Kellogg (1852–1943) created a product

Cold Cereals. Advertisement for American Breakfast Cereals.

similar to Dr. Jackson's that was also called Granula, although it was made of wheat flour, cornmeal, and oatmeal. Renamed Granola in 1881, after a lawsuit brought by Dr. Jackson, by 1889 Kellogg's Sanitas Food Company was selling approximately two tons of Granola per week. Experimenting with other grains, Dr. Kellogg and his brother, W. K. (Will) Kellogg (1860–1951), developed a process that pressed boiled wheat through rollers, forming flakes that crisped when baked, creating the first flaked breakfast food, Granose Flakes, in 1895.

Henry Perky (1843–1906) filed patents in the early 1890s for machines that squeezed boiled wheat between two rollers, one with a groove cut into it, extruding long strands, which could be shaped and then baked. Perky sold the Shredded Wheat biscuits door to door in Denver, Colorado, before expanding east in 1895, when he built a factory in Worcester, Massachusetts. In 1902 he moved his "Palace of Light" factory to Niagara Falls, New York, taking advantage of a newly constructed electrical plant. The immaculately clean factory with thirty thousand lights became a major tourist attraction, from which each visitor went home with a free sample of Shredded Wheat. Dr. Kellogg passed up an offer in 1894 from Perky to buy Shredded Wheat, a decision he later regretted.

In 1898 the Kellogg brothers devised a flake made from corn called Sanitas Toasted Corn Flakes. Unfortunately, the dull-tasting cereal spoiled quickly, a problem finally overcome in 1902. W. H. Kellogg then added sugarcane to the flakes, over his brother's strong objections, and sales of the newly named Kellogg's Toasted Corn Flakes soared. After working for his brother for twenty-two years, W. H. separated the cereal company from the sanitorium in 1906, forming the Battle Creek Toasted Corn Flake Company, which became the Kellogg Company in 1925.

Charles (C. W.) Post (1854–1914), who had once been sickly, opened a sanatorium in 1897, also in Battle Creek. There, in 1898, he created Grape-Nuts cereal, a granulated, twice-baked nugget, for his Postum Cereal Company (renamed General Foods in 1929). Post, an innovative advertiser, used national ad campaigns, coupons, premiums, and samples to make Grape-Nuts a success. He also included a booklet, "The Road to Wellville," in each box of Grape-Nuts, outlining his theories on good health. His next product was a flaked corn cereal originally called Elijah's Manna; forced to change its name to Post Toasties in 1908 by outraged clergy, it also became a sensation thanks to Post's advertising genius.

Dr. Alexander P. Anderson (1862–1943) spent years trying to perfect a technique to create puffed rice. He solved the problem in 1902 when he shot rice kernels from a Spanish American War cannon. He sold his patented process to the Quaker Oats Company, which introduced Puffed Rice cereal in 1905, followed by puffed wheat and other whole grains.

During this period Battle Creek became a magnet for cereal makers, attracting more than forty breakfast food companies in the early 1900s. In 1902 there were thirty wheat flake companies, and by 1911, 107 brands of corn flakes were being produced there. What really sold the often similar-tasting cereals were the advertising and promotions, of which C. W. Post was the major innovator and W. K. Kellogg a close second.

New cereal brands sprouted up during the next two decades, many with short shelf lives. Kellogg introduced All-Bran, labeled "a natural laxative cereal," in 1916 and Rice Krispies in 1928. Bran flakes were created when cooked bran porridge spilled on a hot stove; the Washburn Crosby Company (later General Mills) perfected the flakes, creating Wheaties in 1921. The first singing radio commercial, which touted Wheaties, aired on Christmas Eve in 1926. By 1929 a national radio ad campaign, directed toward children, was launched. The "Breakfast of Champions" connection to sports began in 1933, when radio ads ran during a minor league baseball game. Later, Wheaties campaigns included such major baseball figures as Babe Ruth, Joe DiMaggio, and Jackie Robinson.

In 1937 General Mills unveiled Kix, a puffed cereal of corn, malted barley, and sugar, coated with vitamins, and in 1941 Cheerioats, the O-shaped oat cereal whose name was shortened to Cheerios in 1946. Post's Raisin Bran appeared in 1942, duplicating another cereal, the 1928 Skinner's Raisin Bran. The first presweetened cereal, Ranger Joe Popped Wheat Honnies, came out in 1939, in Chester, Pennsylvania. Versions from the big cereal companies followed—Post's Sugar Crisp, a sugar-coated wheat puff, in 1949; Kellogg's Sugar Corn Pops in 1950, a newly sweetened version of the 1930s Corn Pop; and Frosted Flakes in 1952. General Mills entered the sugar sweepstakes in 1954 with Trix, which at that time contained more than 46 percent sugar, and Cocoa Puffs, a chocolate-covered corn puff, in 1958. Quaker Oats' Cap'n Crunch, a corn-oat kernel with a butterscotch sugar shell, debuted in 1963.

Quaker Oats introduced Quisp, a saucer-shaped corn cereal in 1965. Although it was successful in the early 1970s, it was soon removed from national distribution and made available in only a few select cities. But nostalgic customers helped revive Quisp, ordering boxes from the few grocers that carried it. Quaker created a website for the cereal in 1997, building a "virtual" national brand on the Internet.

Television opened up a new medium for cereal advertising, launching the relationship between television characters and cereal promotions. By the early 1950s Kellogg was sponsoring television shows for children about outer space and the Old West and variety shows geared toward adults. The other cereal manufacturers soon followed. The animated characters on cereal boxes began to have their own cartoon series, until 1969, when the Federal Communications Commission ruled that characters, real or animated, associated with a product could not appear on children's television shows. By 1976, 43 percent of all the Saturday morning commercials were promoting high-sugar breakfast cereals. A ten-year legal battle started in 1972, when the Federal Trade Commission (FTC) accused Kellogg, General Mills, General Foods, and Quaker Oats of having an illegal monopoly on cereal sales. The FTC charged that overpricing, false advertising, and deceptive practices denied competition, but the case was dismissed when the charges could not be proved.

Consumers experienced a renewed interest in health, particularly the benefits of high-fiber diets, in the 1970s and 1980s. Granola, available in health food stores, entered the mainstream with Heartland Nature Cereal in 1972; other brands, such as Quaker 100% Natural, followed suit. Kashi, a cereal mix of several grains, developed in 1984, began appearing in supermarkets in the 1990s. Kellogg acquired the Kashi Company in 2001. By 1996, sales of store-brand cereals were growing as consumers began to buy cereals by price, not by taste, causing the major cereal companies, led by Post, to slash prices by as much as 28 percent.

The late 1990s and early 2000s found consumers' interest shifting toward whole grains, soy, and organic foods. In 1999 General Mills introduced Sunrise, the first mainstream organic cereal. Smaller organic cereal companies, like Arrowhead Mills and Cascadian Farms (owned by General Mills), began to infiltrate the supermarket shelves. Multi-ingredient fortified cereals, such as Kellogg's Smart Start, which had first appeared in 1998, added a soy version in 2000, and cereals targeted expressly toward women, such as General Mills's Harmony, also introduced in 2000, contained calcium, soy, antioxidants, and folic acid.

Cereal advertising to children in the early 2000s extended beyond television; both Kellogg and General Mills published counting and play books featuring their cereals. Interactive cereal websites, often merging the cereal's animated characters with the content, offered a new medium for games, prizes, and promotions.

Although ready-to-eat cereal still accounted for approximately 35 percent of all American breakfasts, the 2001 sales of the $8.5-billion cereal industry had begun a slight decline. Hoping to maintain cereal's dominance, all the major cereal manufacturers introduced breakfast bar versions of their cereals and some, following new eating trends, had repackaged their cereals into containers that could be eaten on the go.

[See also Breakfast Foods; General Mills; Graham, Sylvester; Kellogg, John Harvey; Kellogg Company; Post Foods.]

BIBLIOGRAPHY

Bruce, Scott, and Bill Crawford. *Cerealizing America: The Unsweetened Story of American Breakfast Cereal.* Boston: Faber and Faber, 1995.

Carson, Gerald. *Cornflake Crusade.* New York: Rinehart, 1957. Available at http://memory.loc.gov/cgi-bin/query/r?ammem/lhbumbib: @field (TITLE+@band (Cornflake+crusade++)

General Mills. http://www.generalmills.com/corporate/. The Company History section of the website includes a timeline of product introductions, a history of Wheaties, and a history of their radio and television advertising.

JOY SANTLOFER

Chafing Dish

"Chafing dish" derives from the French *chauffeur*, meaning "to heat." The chafing dish's history goes back at least as far as classical times, when Cicero described a "kind of saucepan of Corinthian brass. . . . This simple and ingenious vessel possesses a double bottom, the uppermost one holds the light delicacies . . . and the fire is underneath" (Lovegren 1995). It was used in medieval times as well, for delicately warming foods and medicines.

In 1720 a wealthy American ordered six small brass chafing dishes to be sent from England for his daughter's wedding gift, but it is likely that the implement, common in Europe, had been brought to American shores long before that date. By the early 1800s the chafing dish had taken its modern form of an elegant silver-plated dish set

Chafing Dish. Three-pint nickel-plated chafing dish.

over a spirit lamp. It went through a period of great popularity during the 1890s, when the renowned Waldorf-Astoria hotel served after-theater chafing dish suppers to such celebrities as J. P. Morgan and Lillian Russell. The Gay Nineties chafing dish fad was so strong that special sets of tablecloths and matching napkins became popular, and a great number of American cookbooks were written on the subject.

After losing steam during the 1920s and 1930s, the chafing dish again became chic after World World II, owing to the rise of informal entertaining, the lack of servants, and the desire to add a touch of glamour to everyday life. Popular dishes included beef Stroganoff, Swedish meatballs, crêpes suzette, cherries jubilee, cheese fondue, and sukiyaki.

BIBLIOGRAPHY

Hess, Karen, ed. *Martha Washington's Booke of Cookery.* New York: Columbia University Press, 1981.

Kinsley, H. M. *One Hundred Recipes for the Chafing Dish.* New York: Creative Cookbooks, 2001. Reprint of the 1894 edition.

Lovegren, Sylvia. *Fashionable Food: Seven Decades of Food Fads.* New York: Macmillan, 1995.

SYLVIA LOVEGREN

Champagne

Champagne is a wine produced only within the region of France of that name, and made only as specified and delimited by the *Appellation d'Origine Contrôlée* (AOC) laws. It is a sparkling wine, the overwhelming majority of which is white, made exclusively from three legal grapes: Pinot Noir, Pinot Meunier, and Chardonnay. Champagne has had a long presence in America; it was shipped through English wine merchants and brokers into the colonies starting in about 1735, coinciding with the very beginning of the international Champagne trade. By the 1850s, vintners in Ohio were making the first American sparklers.

Champagne must be made by the *méthode champenoise*, meaning that the second fermentation, which produces the bubbles, must occur in the same bottle that is sold to the consumer. Producers of Champagne have gone to great lengths to protect the name "Champagne" from imitators making sparkling wines outside the official AOC zone, and many countries both within and outside of Europe have signed international trade agreements not to use the term "Champagne" (or for that matter, *méthode champenoise*) on their labels or in their advertising.

The United States and Champagne

The United States is not a signatory to these agreements. Although not alone in its refusal to recognize the patrimony of Champagne as geographically and historically French, membership in that group is shrinking. The United States is by far the most powerful wine-producing nation that does not acknowledge that true Champagne is unique. Indeed, in the United States "Champagne" is a generic but legal label term for any wine with bubbles. This state of affairs has led to great confusion in the American wine market, which appears to be exactly what the Champagne imitators had in mind when they adopted the name of a famous wine-producing region to describe a style of wine.

The use of "Champagne" as a generic label is no different from calling any white swill-in-a-box "Chablis" or any red wine from a jug "Burgundy." Since the end of Prohibition in 1933 and until 1997 (when for the first time, varietal label wines accounted for a greater proportion of sales than generics), the American wine industry was built on popular, mostly drinkable, inexpensive wines with generic labels. True Chablis, the glorious unoaked Chardonnay made from grapes grown on chalk soils in the coolest climate in Burgundy, is still a tough sell in the American wine market because of the image of Chablis as a cheap jug wine. The image problem for Champagne is even worse.

Undrinkable wines made from excess Thompson seedless grapes, and nearly undrinkable wines made from excess Chenin Blanc, are subjected to the Charmat bulk process, first employed around 1913 in Ohio, California,

and New York. Although interrupted by Prohibition, Charmat bulk processing resumed in the 1930s, with various technical improvements. In the processing of the early 2000s, the wine is sealed in an anaerobic tank and pumped up with carbon dioxide, forming bubbles as large as those in ginger ale. A flavoring dosage is added and the wine is bottled under continuous pressure. This finished product, often featuring a plastic stopper, will sell extremely cheaply. The label will of course include the name of the producer (often a wholly fictitious French winegrower, whose name may be Jean or André), and the product name "Champagne." Most domestically produced sparklers are this Charmat plonk.

Many Americans will complain that Champagne gives them a headache or stomach trouble. When asked if they have ever tried true Champagne, they respond with a blank look because quite a few neophyte wine drinkers have limited their consumption of sparkling wines to cheap imitations of Champagne. Often these wines are consumed at catered events, where they are drunk out of modified sherbet glasses, or coupes, that are also used to create the popular "Champagne Fountain."

Champagne vs. Sparklers

The informed American consumer can at least choose from wines made from a better selection of grapes, and a wine that is hopefully made by the transfer method, not Charmat bulk processing. In the transfer method, the second fermentation does indeed happen in a bottle, but then thousands of bottles of this bubbly wine are poured into a tank, a dosage is added, and the wine is poured back into bottles. Wines labeled as "fermented in the bottle" are made by this process, which was developed in Germany for its *Sekt* sparklers. The American versions of these wines are drinkable, even enjoyable, but despite their label, they are not, and will never be, true Champagne.

It is important to note that some good, inexpensive Champagne alternatives without misleading labels have flooded the American market, led by Cava from northeastern Spain, which is made by the actual *méthode champenoise*, most often in a true brut style, from white Macabeo, Xarell-lo, and Parellada grapes. Cavas outsell Champagne in the American market and are the single largest sparkling import. Fruity and refreshing Prosecco from Veneto, Italy, is a pleasing Charmat-produced alternative. The French have joined the American domestic production, making sparklers in California's North Coast

American Viticultural Area (AVA). Domaine Chandon is owned by Moët, Domaine Carneros by Taittinger, Mumm Cuvée Napa by Mumm, Pacific Echo by Veuve Clicquot, and Roederer Estate (the finest of the five) by Louis Roederer.

Méthode champenoise Wines

Excellent vintage-dated, estate-bottled *méthode champenoise* wines are made, in the early 2000s, by American-owned Iron Horse in the Green Valley of Sonoma County. The artisan Milla Handley in the Anderson Valley of Mendocino also makes fine sparklers. Schramsberg of Napa Valley labels at least some of their fine wines as "Napa Valley Champagne." The late Jack Davies, who with his wife, Jamie, founded Schramsberg in 1965 as the first sparkling-wine producer in the Napa Valley, originally created the label to needle the neighboring French interlopers, and that label stands in the early twenty-first century.

Argyle sparklers (although owned by Petaluma of Australia) come from Oregon's Willamette Valley. Washington State's Domaine Ste. Michelle produces thousands of cases of fine *méthode champenoise* wines. In New Mexico, Gruet produces quality sparklers and North Carolina's Biltmore Estate Brut is justifiably famous. In New York State's Finger Lakes, Glenora makes extraordinary sparkling wines by the classic method (so does Konstantin Frank Vinifera Winery, but it is labeled "Champagne"). Americans generally do not successfully export their sparklers, and market share for American *méthode champenoise* wines is less than 10 percent of the domestic market for sparklers.

Perhaps the last word on this touchy subject should be left to the son of an American mother who loved true Champagne so much that Pol Roger named its *cuvée de prestige* in his honor: Sir Winston Churchill. In 1918, as World War I was coming to a close, he proclaimed, "Remember, gentlemen, it's not just France we are fighting for, it's Champagne!"

[*See also* Wine; Wineries.]

BIBLIOGRAPHY

Adams, Leon. *The Wines of America.* New York: McGraw-Hill, 1990.
Blue, Anthony Dias. *American Wine.* New York: Doubleday, 1985.
Brennan, Thomas. *Burgundy to Champagne: The Wine Trade in Early Modern France.* Baltimore: Johns Hopkins University Press, 1997.
Faith, Nicholas. *The Story of Champagne.* New York: Facts on File, 1989.
Guy, Koleen M. *When Champagne Became French: Wine and the Making of a National Identity.* Baltimore: Johns Hopkins University Press, 2003.
Haraszthy, Arpad. *Wine-Making in California: 1871–72.* San Francisco: Book Club of California, 1978.
Johnson, Hugh. *Wine.* New York: Simon and Schuster, 1987.
Lapsley, James T. *Bottled Poetry.* Berkeley: University of California Press, 1996.
Pinney, Thomas. *A History of Wine in America: From the Beginnings to Prohibition.* Berkeley: University of California Press, 1989.
Simon, André. *The History of Champagne.* New York: Octopus Books, 1971.
Stevenson, Tom. *World Encyclopedia of Champagne and Sparkling Wine.* San Francisco: Wine Appreciation Guild, 2003.
Sutcliffe, Serena. *Champagne: The History and Character of the World's Most Celebrated Wine.* New York: Simon and Schuster, 1989.
Teiser, Ruth, and Catherine Harroun. *Winemaking in California.* New York: McGraw-Hill, 1983.
Wait, Frona Eunice. *Wines and Vines of California.* San Francisco: Bancroft Co., 1889.

STEVEN KOLPAN

Cheese

This entry includes two subentries:
Historical Overview
Later Developments

Historical Overview

There is no evidence that any of the Native American tribes milked animals. In 1611, "six good shippes, men, provisions and cattle" arrived to replenish the Jamestown, Virginia, colony, which had been chartered in 1606. Farther north the Massachusetts colonists were joined in 1623 by the ship *Anne,* which contained both goats and cattle. It is unlikely that any of the "Holland Cheeses" listed as provisions on the *Mayflower* remained when the ship reached shore, but it is purported that fresh goat and cow cheeses were made early in Plymouth Plantation.

In the history of early immigrations to the Americas, agricultural skills that included cheese making were among the assets brought by settlers from their native countries to the New World. Whether they were Spanish missionaries moving north from Mexico into California, Netherlanders settling "Nieuw Amsterdam," or part of the subsequent flows of Italians, French, Russians, and other nationals, each group craved the foods, including cheeses, that were specific to its traditional ethnicity.

Big Cheese in the White House. Admirers of President Andrew Jackson presented him with a 1,400-pound wheel of cheese shortly before he left the White House in 1837. Jackson invited members of the public to eat the cheese; it was disposed of within two hours. *Culinary Archives & Museum at Johnson & Wales University, Providence, R.I.*

In the colonial period cows gave low yields of milk, and most cheese production was a family affair. Cheddar was the style of choice for both New Englanders and New Yorkers. Taking its name from England's Cheddar Gorge, "cheddaring" was a method of milling or cutting curd, enhancing the drying process as well as acidification. Cheddar cheeses are made worldwide and represent a large percentage of U.S. cheese production.

Cheese production expanded in the mid-nineteenth century. Credit is given the Williams family of Rome, Oneida County, New York, for the organization of a farmers' milk cooperative. The cooperative's cheddar plant began production in 1851. In the late nineteenth century a factory in Verona, New York, started shipping cheeses to England. The Crowley cheese plant of Vermont claims to have the longest operating history in the United States.

Although Wisconsin is known as America's Dairyland, it was not until 1841 that Anne Pickett opened the first cheese factory in that state. By 1864 Chester Hazen of Ladoga, Wisconsin, was using the milk of three hundred cows for cheese making, and in 1886 the University of Wisconsin offered short courses for dairy farmers and cheese makers. Both the American Dairy Association and the Wisconsin Dairymen's Association were formed in the late nineteenth century.

In 1921 Wisconsin was the first state to adopt an official cheese-grading program. Approximately fifteen hundred Wisconsin cheese plants produced more than 500 million pounds of cheese annually in the mid-twentieth century. In the early twenty-first century milk from approximately seventeen thousand Wisconsin dairy farms, 90 percent of which is used to make approximately 2 billion pounds of cheese annually, represents almost one-fourth of annual U.S. cheese production. Wisconsin traditionally had small dairy farms that milked twenty to one hundred cows each. A national pattern starting in the late twentieth century, however, is toward the large-scale economy of highly automated milking herds, numbering as many as one thousand or more high-yield cows. By 2003 California dairy farms had surpassed Wisconsin farms in annual milk production.

Only a few cheeses originated in America. Among those varieties are Wisconsin brick and colby. Wisconsin is the only state with a master cheese maker certification program. In the early 2000s, one of those masters was Joe Widmer, the third-generation proprietor and maker of Widmer's brick cheese in the small town of Theresa. The name "brick" is not a description of the cheese's shape; it refers to the building bricks used as weights to press the liquid whey from the cheese curds. Widmer continues to use the bricks used by his grandfather and father. The Widmer family also has maintained the "washed rind" bacterial culture used to produce the characteristic pungent and aromatic flavors that develop as brick cheese is aged.

Colby is the name of a Wisconsin city and the name of a cheese type made since 1885. In that year a cheddar maker named Joseph Steinwand varied his normal procedure by washing the curds with cold water. The result was a more open-textured, granular, moister cheese, which Steinwand named after the nearby city. Colby quickly gained popularity as a milder, economically produced variety of cheddar. Both colby and brick cheeses are mass marketed under these generic labels.

In the twentieth century advances in the technology of cheese production made possible the construction and operation of ever larger and more automated plants. James Kraft, like many cheese sellers, was troubled by the perishability of his product. Kraft experimented, grinding up cheddar, adding emulsifying salts, heating the mixture, and then pouring the results into forms. In 1917 Kraft sold the first canned processed cheese to the U.S. Army. From then on the Kraft Cheese Company developed a full line of processed cheese products, Velveeta (1928) and Cheez Whiz (1952) among them, that culminated in the individually wrapped slice.

In the early twenty-first century, processed cheese competes with mozzarella for the largest annual sales numbers. Distinct from the classic cooked and stretched *pasta filata* Italian mozzarella, the cheese produced in the United States is mostly a brined product used to make ever-increasing quantities of fresh and frozen pizza. A cheese anomaly is the term "American cheese." This term refers to a type of cheese akin to cheddar and includes American processed varieties, the irony being that much of this processed food is made from imported products.

An increase in the growth of small specialty cheese making began in the late twentieth century in the United States. The American Cheese Society counts approximately two hundred farms and plants engaged in so-called artisanal activity. Many of these cheese makers buy milk from farmers or cooperatives, but quite a few make "farmstead cheese" a term used somewhat loosely to mean cheese made of cow, goat, or sheep milk from the farm where the cheese is made. Beginning with the early settlements, most cheese in America carried the names of European varieties, but Cypress Grove Humboldt Fog, Cowgirl Creamery Mount Tam, and Capriole Wabash Cannonball demonstrate a trend of naming new American cheeses for American regions. Oregon Tillamook, dating to the first years of the twentieth century, is an early example.

In the 1970s annual per person cheese consumption reached eighteen pounds. Early in the twenty-first century Americans consume more than thirty pounds of cheese per person per year. Travel abroad, attention from the news media, the interest of hotel and restaurant chefs, and the spread of specialty food outlets have contributed to this increase, but the most important factor has been the interest of consumers in the quality and variety of a national product.

[*See also* Cheese, Moldy; Cheese-Making Tools; Dairy Foods; Dairy Industry; Kraft Foods; Milk; Pizza.]

BIBLIOGRAPHY

Cheese Importers Association of America. *Cheese Importers Association of America Yearbook, 2003–2004.* New York: CIAA, 2004.

Eekhof-Stork, Nancy. *The World Atlas of Cheese.* Edited by Adrian Bailey. London and New York: Paddington Press, 1976.

Selitzer, Ralph. *The Dairy Industry in America.* New York: Dairy and Ice Cream Field and Books for Industry, 1976.

GERD STERN

Later Developments

The artisan cheese movement in the United States is a recognized phenomenon in the broader food renaissance that also encompasses new vineyards, microbreweries, chocolate, coffee and tea, and many other specialty foods whose dominant characteristics are quality of flavor and handcrafted methods of production. Cheese making by ethnic communities had become moribund by the end of World War II, replaced by industrial practices and mass marketing. But in the late 1970s and early 1980s, a countermovement began that was similar to the practices of small-farm production which had continued in England, reemerged in Ireland, and never disappeared in the Mediterranean countries, where cheese had always been a dietary staple.

Growth and the Small Farmer

For many years, the small dairies producing farmstead cheeses in the United States found a limited market. While this is still somewhat true in the early 2000s, certain trends have emerged that will facilitate the growth of these products and enable them to secure a larger role in American foodways. The first of these trends is the prevalence of small farmers who want to make these cheeses. Where once a handful of (mostly) entrepreneurial women produced small quantities of fresh goat cheese, which was often sold at local markets or found in the new cuisine just beginning to emerge from the Bay Area in the 1970s, in the early 2000s there was an explosive growth in farmers who produced all varieties of goat, sheep, and cow milk cheeses and brought them to market in a number of ways. In 1993, the American Cheese Society, which holds an annual competition, received fewer than a hundred submissions in all categories; in 2003, the number reached over seven hundred submissions from virtually every region of the country.

The restaurant cheese board, or cheese course, patterned on the European model, serving a selection of fine cheese after the entrée, had by the end of 2003 become common place in any restaurant with a claim to serving fine food (except for certain ethnic restaurants, particularly Asian, that serve few or no dairy products). Moreover, the cheeses were being served not only as traditional cheese courses but could also be found throughout the menu. Indeed, the use of cheese as an ingredient in appetizers and desserts was a major trend in the early 2000s, and the farm names were often listed on the menu.

At the same time, the American taste for fuller flavors is just beginning to replace the traditional preferences for bland, boring, tasteless, and processed, in cheese especially. Once goat cheese had become established, the fuller flavors of bloomy rind cheeses, washed rinds, and blues began to seduce the American palate. Today, the United States boasts as many varieties of fine blue cheese as any country other than France. Along with a greater range of cheese types, the emergence of a taste for aged cheese with its fuller flavors has also emerged. The mouth-puckering appeal of fine, aged cheddars, goudas, and asiagos, all made domestically, has spurred interest in the many uses such cheeses have in cooking, whether grated, shaved, or crumbled.

The interest in fuller flavors has led to an interest in unpasteurized cheeses, which have a complexity gained from milk that has not had many of its flavor components

Cheese Case. Park Slope Food Coop, Brooklyn, New York. *Photograph by Joe Zarba*

destroyed by heat. Many Americans were able to sample these cheeses in France and other European countries as travel became more commonplace. Restaurateurs and retail purveyors of fine cheese in the United States responded to consumers' developing taste for cheese. Because U.S. law allows only raw milk cheeses that have been aged at least sixty days, many of the younger cheeses were available only as contraband. The illegal nature of these cheeses made them even more desirable than they would have been if left quietly alone. However, the post–September 11 bioterrorism act has focused on all imports into the United States, and more difficulty in finding them in the nation's shops can be predicted. At the same time, unpasteurized milk cheeses aged more than sixty days are being developed and may be expected to fill a larger niche in the years ahead.

Cheese is a growth category, with specialty cheeses growing more quickly than other kinds, and expected to grow 25 percent from 2000 to 2005 alone. Part of this increase can be attributed to the rehabilitation of traditional fats, once taboo, such as cream, butter, and egg yolks. Certain diet plans, most notably Atkins, sought to limit the intake of carbohydrates and increased consumption of protein and fats. Here, specialty cheese may seem to be an ideal food source, as it generally contains nothing but milk, rennet, and salt, and supplies not only protein but also many other nutrients including the essential mineral calcium. Calcium requires Vitamin D, abundant in whole milk cheese, to be absorbed. Cheese is a high-quality, nutrient-dense snack food. It stores and travels reasonably well, can be made into many shapes and forms, and can be packaged in an unlimited number of ways. Specialty cheese, with its perception of value, will continue to lead the growth in cheeses. In addition to a growing desire for whole foods regarded as healthy, consumers show a strong interest in ecological farming methods. With an increasingly sophisticated clientele, farmers, cheese makers, retailers, and chefs market cheeses as "grass-fed"—the traditional and ideal way to raise dairy cattle. Grass-fed cheese is not only higher in omega-3 fatty acids and conjugated linoleic acid (an anticancer nutrient) than dairy from grain-fed animals; it is also substantially more complex and satisfying in flavor.

Distribution Trends

One of the trends aiding specialty cheese consumption in the United States has been the development of alternative means of distribution. While industrial production is well established and the food supply lines entrenched, the ability to find and purchase artisan cheese has been severely limited. Since it is often perceived to be a healthy, or natural, product, most health food stores have followed the lead of gourmet stores (indeed, in the Whole Food chain, the two concepts have merged) in stocking cheese. Huge displays of hitherto unknown cheeses are more common in suburban markets, where before they had been found only in urban specialty or ethnic markets. The rise of farmers' markets as places to find natural, wholesome, local foods is also significant. Many farmers' market organizers, having previously neglected dairy and other animal foods, now actively recruit farmstead cheese makers.

Distribution remains one of the main impediments to wider consumption of specialty cheese in the United States. The small production, the high cost of marketing, and the vast distances in the continental United States all pose problems for growth and wider availability. Most specialty cheeses are shipped from point to point using express freight services, which greatly adds to their cost. A few local distributors have begun carrying these products, but these same distributors may not have the product movement necessary to justify taking up precious warehouse space, nor the skills in handling products that may still be unfamiliar to most Americans, even those in the cheese business.

Cost of the product itself remains an issue and will remain so in the near future at least. U.S. society is geared for massive scale and agribusiness, and small farms are dying out across the country at an ever-increasing pace. In New York State alone, Cornell University projects that six thousand dairies will be lost. The cost of animal care, feed, machinery, and equipment, combined with adherence to

A Selection of Cheeses. D'Vine Taste International Gourmet in Brooklyn, New York. *Photograph by Joe Zarba*

health regulations and other state and federal food production guidelines make domestic cheeses far more expensive than their European counterparts, which despite new trade laws are still heavily subsidized and in any event have a lower cost of production and distribution, along with greater sales. Not until better distribution methods are developed will the artisan cheese movement reach its full potential. Still, it must be noted that a few new distributors have begun operations that specialize in American cheeses only; there may be more of them in the future.

As with most successful products in modern capitalism, branding is important. The few pioneers that have survived two or three decades are becoming more widely known to the public. Some have begun to put their mark on cheese they do not produce. Often these cheeses are imported from abroad. It may be that in the future some of the most successful among the pioneers will have neither herds of animals nor dairies.

The rise and Americanization of ethnic markets have brought growth in the specialty realm. The rapid rise of the Hispanic market has seen a corresponding boom in cheese from Mexico, the Caribbean islands, and Central America. The absorption of other cuisines, particularly Italian, into the American food mainstream has made Parmesan, asiago, and mozzarella among the biggest beneficiaries of the cheese boom. Although most of these cheeses are factory-made, more small farms and cheese makers are utilizing milk from their own herds to make them, as well as brie, emmenthal, gruyere, and blue cheese.

Conclusion

As Americans experience farm cheeses, they are reluctant to return to plastic-wrapped or spray-can cheeses and are willing to pay more for better products. A 2004 survey by the California milk advisory board found that 83 percent of one hundred Napa and Sonoma valley restaurants served cheese in their appetizer course, up from 19 percent in 2001. More cheeses are identified by producer and region on menus, a practice also becoming common in retail shops that carry these products. More shops are springing up that carry these cheeses. Young people, including young chefs, are more frequently seeking careers in the specialty cheese business; some are returning to make cheese themselves on the farm. Taken as a whole, specialty cheese in the United States may be analogous to the wine industry in the 1980s, although no one predicts it will be as large a market.

Also like wine, cheese needs educated consumers: classes in cheese making, production, selection, and serving are becoming routine in the nation's restaurant schools. And cheese and wine classes are becoming readily available to consumers. Books on cheese are being published in the early 2000s, and some specialize in American farmstead cheeses. The media continues to highlight both the movement itself and various players within the industry. Artisan cheeses are entering the American food mainstream as bagels and espresso did before them.

[*See also* Cheese, Moldy; Cheese-Making Tools; Dairy; Dairy Industry; French Influences on American Food; Velveeta.]

BIBLIOGRAPHY

Baboin-Jaubert, Alix. *Handbook of Cheese.* London: Hachette Illustrated, 2003.
Boisard, Pierre. *Camembert: A National Myth.* Translated by Richard Miller. Berkeley: University of California Press, 2003.
Fiori, Giacomo. *Formaggi Italiani.* Verolengo: EOS Editice, 1999.
Freeman, Sarah. *The Real Cheese Companion: A Guide to the Best Handmade Cheeses of Britain and Ireland.* London: Time Warner, 2003.
Graham, Peter. *Classic Cheese Cookery.* London: Grub Street, 2003.
Jenkins, Steven. *Cheese Primer.* New York: Workman, 1996.
Michelson, Patricia. *The Cheese Room.* London: Penguin, 2001.
Sardo, Piero, et al., eds. *Italian Cheese.* Bra, Italy: Slow Food Editore, 1999–2000.

ROBERT KAUFELT

Cheese, Moldy

Like wine and truffles, moldy cheeses are products of the damp, dark underworld. Legend has it that the first moldy cheese was discovered thousands of years ago when an absent-minded shepherd left his curds and bread in a cave while he was off chasing sheep. The shepherd returned to find a moldy sandwich but was so hungry he ate it anyway. Since then, moldy cheeses such as Roquefort, Gorgonzola, English Stilton, and Danish blue have been developed by Europeans into gourmet fare. Government licenses assure a cheese is the genuine article. Aficionados of moldy cheese have included Pliny the Elder, Charlemagne, and Casanova, who considered the cheeses an aphrodisiac.

People who love the earthy zest of moldy cheeses—primarily called blue cheeses—crumble the cheese over salad, stir it into scrambled eggs, melt it on hamburgers, use it in pasta and on pizza, and eat it as is with a stack of water crackers. Few cheeses offer as many menu possibilities, from a sliced apple and Stilton appetizer to an elegant, not too sweet dessert mousse. Not all blue cheeses are smelly, crumbly lumps; some are mild, creamy, and even sweet.

The aroma and taste of moldy cheeses depend on the intensity of the cure and the type of mold. The shape, size, and surface of the cheese, and the microclimate of the curing cellar also affect the outcome. The type of milk used to make the cheese is an important factor. For example, sheep provide the milk for Roquefort, and a red sheep is imprinted on the wrapper. Milk from Holstein cows is used for most moldy cheese made in the United States.

The earliest makers of blue cheese used bread to begin production of the distinctive mold and then waited patiently for the veins of mold to grow and spread naturally between the curds. In later times mold growth is often induced with penicillium spores (related to the mold that produces the antibiotic penicillin but not known to cause the allergic reaction penicillin can). White-hatted "cheese ripeners" still use bread to inoculate wheels of Roquefort with mold spores. After repeated salting by hand during the first three to five days of preparation (to make the cheese firm on the outside), the cheese is pricked so that oxygen essential to mold growth can penetrate the wheel. Veins of mold range in color from pale blue to deep green. Roquefort is aged for three months in neat rows on oak benches in limestone caves in Combalou, in southwestern France. The caves have a constant temperature, high humidity, and optimal air circulation.

Maytag blue is the most famous of the American-born moldy cheeses. It was developed at Iowa State University in 1941 from the Holstein cows on the family farm of Fritz Maytag, an early-twentieth-century settler who became known as an appliance king. An Iowa State professor who helped develop the cheese had worked in the dairy industry in Denmark, where Saga blue cheese was developed. Maytag blue is a dense, crumbly cheese with a spicy and creamy flavor. It is handmade in small batches in Newton, Iowa, and aged for six months in caves on the side of a hill where the natural molds and yeast live. Some of the Holsteins that produce the milk for Maytag blue cheese are direct descendants of the original 1919 prizewinning herd.

Another cave-produced cheese was developed in the early 1940s in an old railroad tunnel that cut through Stumphouse Mountain in South Carolina. The abandoned tunnel caught the attention of a professor in the dairy department of Clemson Agricultural College of South Carolina (later Clemson University) who began experimenting with a Roquefort-style cheese made with milk from the Clemson herd of 680 Holsteins. World War II and scarce milk supplies interrupted production, but Operation Blue Cheese resumed in 1953. The cheese was manufactured on campus and cured in the tunnel, which was thirty miles away. Production was directed by a graduate of Iowa State University.

Clemson blue cheese is an artisan cheese, made the old-fashioned way. Each 288-gallon vat holds a batch of approximately 240 pounds, which is salted, waxed, and aged for six months. When the cheese is ready, each hoop is scraped and packaged by hand. Eventually the college duplicated the conditions of the cave on campus, so the need to transport cheese to the tunnel and back ended, and the tunnel became a tourist site. Other small artisan moldy cheeses are made where the breeds of cows needed are available, such as the Colorado foothills and Minnesota.

Although they vary in color from white to creamy yellow, moldy cheeses should never be brown. The veining ranges from the palest blue to dark hues of green. If the veining looks gray or dusty, the cheese is past its prime. Whether a creamy or a dry variety, the cheese should be firm. Cheese that looks cracked, mushy, or weepy should not be purchased.

Consumers need to ask for a taste before buying moldy cheese. A good blue is always flavorful but is never sour or harsh. The older the cheese, the more pungent is the flavor and the more dense the veining. Roquefort, for example, sometimes is overly salted for the export market, so consumers sensitive to sodium need a taste. The riper the cheese, the more difficult it is to slice. Cheese is easier to cut when cool. A knife used to serve cheese should be dipped in hot water to melt the cheese fat. A cheese wire is the better tool. Roquefort-style cheeses simply crumble. Pressing the cheese through a strainer and combining it with cream, lemon juice, and oil produces the famous Roquefort salad dressing.

Like an aromatic, full-bodied red wine—its most worthwhile accompaniment—moldy cheese needs to breathe, because the mold is a living thing, and the cheese continues to ripen. If the cheese is wrapped in plastic, the wrapping must be changed often. Moldy cheeses can be refrigerated for several weeks, but they taste better when allowed to warm to room temperature.

[*See also* Cheese; Cheese-Making Tools; Dairy; Milk.]

BIBLIOGRAPHY

Betancourt, Marian. "Singing the Blues." *Philadelphia*, August 1991.

Department of Food Science and Human Nutrition, Clemson University. www.clemson.edu.

MARIAN BETANCOURT

Cheesecake

Tarts, pies, and pastries filled with various types of cheese have been common throughout Europe and the Middle East since ancient times. The English and other European colonists introduced their versions of cheesecake into North America, and cheesecake recipes were included in colonial cookery manuscripts, such as those used by the William Penn family in Pennsylvania, dated about 1694, and that of Harriot Pinckney Horry in South Carolina, dated 1770. The family recipe book used by Martha Washington beginning in 1794 contained three cheesecake recipes, two of which call for making fresh curds using new milk and rennet. The third thickens cream with eggs and butter.

Immigrants from southern and eastern Europe introduced their cheesecake traditions into the United States in the late nineteenth and early twentieth centuries. Italian cheesecake, for instance, is made with ricotta cheese. Russian *pashka* is a molded dessert—a pyramid of sweetened creamy cheese—served at Easter. Eastern European cheesecakes are made with cottage cheese or farmer cheese, and some are baked in yeast-dough crusts.

America's favorite, New York–style or "Jewish-style" cheesecake, relies for its dense richness on cream cheese, which became available toward the end of the nineteenth century. The New York City restaurants Lindy's and Junior's became famous for their cheesecakes, and restaurants nationwide followed suit with similar cakes. The classic is made of cream cheese sweetened with sugar, enriched with eggs and cream, flavored with vanilla, and baked in a crumb, cookie dough, or sponge-cake crust. It is sometimes dressed up with fruit toppings—cherry, blueberry, strawberry, pineapple—and new variations are constantly appearing: chocolate swirl, mocha, pumpkin. An unbaked "icebox" cheesecake with a gelatin-thickened filling is a convenient shortcut; and there are yogurt cheesecakes for the fat-conscious and tofu cheesecakes for the vegan.

[*See also* Cakes; New York Food.]

BIBLIOGRAPHY

Benson, Abraham, ed. *Penn Family Recipes: Cooking Recipes of William Penn's Wife Guielma.* Edited by Evelyn Abraham Benson. York, PA: G. Shumway, 1966.

Bovbjerg, Dana, and Jeremy Iggers. *The Joy of Cheesecake.* Woodbury, NY: Barron's, 1980.

Hooker, Richard J., ed. *A Colonial Plantation Cookbook: The Receipt Book of Harriott Pinckney Horry, 1770.* Columbia: University of South Carolina Press, 1984.

Pappas, Lou Seibert. *Cheesecake: Thirty-One Fantastic Recipes.* San Francisco: Chronicle Books, 1993.

Ultimate Kraft Philadelphia Cream Cheese Cheesecakes: Featuring Our Philly Cream Cheese 3-Step Cheesecakes. Lincolnwood, IL: Publications International, 1995.

Zisman, Larry, and Honey Zisman. *The 50 Best Cheesecakes in the World: The Recipes That Won the Nationwide "Love That Cheesecake" Contest.* New York: St. Martin's Press, 1993.

ANDREW F. SMITH

Cheese-Making Tools

Soft and hard cheeses are made after curd, which is solid, is separated from whey, which is liquid. Cheese baskets or cradles have been used for centuries to drip off whey. These devices were woven of natural materials, usually strips of oak splint. Cheese drainers were colander-like vessels of ceramic and later of punctured sheet metal. Some cheese drainers had a weighted lid that rested on top of the curds. A large cheese press was needed to apply great pressure to make a large, hard cheese. The cheese press resembled a sawhorse to which was attached a round wooden container that had holes in the bottom and a long wooden lever that pushed a presser against the curds in the container. The first U.S. patent for a cheese press was granted in 1812, and many patented and homemade presses followed. Fancy tin egg cheese and cottage cheese strainer molds in heart and other shapes were made in the 1850s to 1870s in Pennsylvania. Long, thin, flexible steel cheese knives and whips have been used since the middle of the nineteenth century to break curds into large or small pieces for soft cheeses. The knives are used in the making of hard cheeses to mix in thickening and curdling agents, such as rennet, as well as salt and coloring and to break up the curds to make the cheese smooth.

[*See also* Cheese.]

BIBLIOGRAPHY

Franklin, Linda Campbell. *300 Years of Kitchen Collectibles.* 5th ed. Iola, WI: Krause Publications, 2003.

LINDA CAMPBELL FRANKLIN

Chefs and Cookbooks, *see Celebrity Chefs; Radio and Television*

Chemical Additives

Extra ingredients have been added to foods for millennia to make preparation easier, to preserve, to enhance appearance and scents, to thicken, to improve nutritive value, to create intoxicants, and to add apparent social value (as gold leaf on foods). Many additives have been beneficial or at least harmless, but others have been toxic, like mercuric compounds painted on foods to make them white and pretty, and bits of brass added to the cooking water of vegetables to brighten the color. Others have been added inadvertently, as lead from Roman drinking goblets or American colonial pewter tableware, and have resulted in illness or death.

According to the American governmental agency responsible for additives, the Food and Drug Administration (FDA) in the Department of Health and Human Services, a food additive is "any substance the intended use of which results or may reasonably be expected to result—directly or indirectly—in its becoming a component or otherwise affecting the characteristics of any food." This definition includes any substance used in the production, processing, treatment, packaging, transportation, or storage of food.

Anything added deliberately to food is called a direct additive. Indirect additives become part of the food in trace amounts from packaging, storage, or other handling materials. A food color additive is any dye, pigment, or other substance that can impart color when added or applied to a food.

Food additives are employed in both home and commercial food production to address any of five issues. They are, briefly stated, to maintain consistency from preparation to preparation, to improve or maintain finished nutritional value, to maintain desirable palatability and wholesomeness, to provide leavening or to control pH (acidity or alkalinity), and to enhance basic flavors or impart desired color. These five issues are most often considerations of mass-marketed foods produced and packaged in industrial facilities.

In addition to commercial uses, food additives are incorporated into home cooking for flavor, color, and other desirable characteristics. Few chemical additives were in wide use until relatively recent times. With increased population, migration from rural to urban areas, modern chemistry, technological sophistication, and cultural changes, more foods are being processed than ever before, and with that growth, more additives are being created and used, directly and indirectly. The FDA lists more than six thousand additives that can be deliberately or coincidentally added in production, handling, and packaging. The various lists are available on the FDA's rather complex website or in hard copy from the U.S. Government Printing Office.

Several FDA online databases facilitate finding information about chemical food additives. The science and chemistry that become obvious with just a cursory glance at these lists show that food production has become a very sophisticated industry using the newest technologies.

Directly Added Food Additives

The more than three thousand total substances directly added to food comprise an inventory often referred to as "Everything Added to Food in the United States" (EAFUS). The EAFUS database, administered by the FDA, contains administrative, chemical, and toxicological information on more than two thousand substances directly added to food, including those regulated by the FDA, in the following categories: direct, secondary direct, color additives, generally recognized as safe (GRAS), and prior-sanctioned substances. The database also contains administrative and chemical information

Baking Powder. Advertisement for Hecker's Perfect Baking Powder, 1890s. *Collection of Kit Barry*

(but no toxicological data) on several hundred more such substances. It can be found on the FDA website.

Indirect Additives Used in Food Contact Substances

The Federal Food, Drug and Cosmetic Act (FFDCA) of 1938 defines a food contact substance as "any substance intended for use as a component of materials used in manufacturing, packing, packaging, transporting, or holding food if such use is not intended to have any technical effect in such food." A database of indirect additives is maintained by the FDA Center for Food Safety and Applied Nutrition (CFSAN) under an ongoing program known as the Priority based Assessment of Food Additives (PAFA). It contains administrative and chemical information on more than three thousand substances.

The database includes adhesives and components of coatings, paper and paperboard components, polymers, and adjuvants and production aids. In general, these are substances that may come into contact with food as part of packaging, handling, or processing equipment but are not intended to be added directly to food. The database of indirect additives can be found on the FDA website.

Premarket Notifications

"Premarket notification" means that manufacturers and users must advise the FDA if they plan to use something that will contact food but has not been approved before and is not on the database of indirect additives. The process for premarket notification requires that the manufacturer or user provide information which demonstrates that the product is safe for the application intended. The premarket notification for food contact substances is the primary method by which the FDA authorizes the use of food additives that are food contact substances. There are several hundred substances in the inventory, with new ones being posted to the FDA website as appropriate.

Color Additives

Certifiable color additives are man-made, with each batch being tested by the manufacturer and the FDA. This process, known as color additive certification, assures the safety, quality, consistency, and strength of the additive. Nine color additives are certified for use in food in the United States. Color additives that are exempt from certification include pigments derived from natural sources, such as vegetables, minerals, or animals, and man-made counterparts of natural derivatives.

Certifiable color additives are available for use in food as either dyes or lakes. Dyes dissolve in water and are manufactured as powders, granules, liquids, or other special purpose forms. They can be used in beverages, dry mixes, baked goods, confections, dairy products, pet foods, and a variety of other products. Lakes are the water insoluble form of the dye. Lakes are more stable than dyes and are ideal for coloring products containing fats and oils or items lacking sufficient moisture to dissolve dyes. Typical uses include coated tablets, cake and doughnut mixes, hard candies, and chewing gum. Certifiable colors include FD&C Blue No. 1 (Dye and Lake), FD&C Blue No. 2 (Dye and Lake), FD&C Green No. 3 (Dye and Lake), FD&C Red No. 3 (Dye), FD&C Red No. 40 (Dye and Lake), FD&C Yellow No. 5 (Dye and Lake), FD&C Yellow No. 6 (Dye and Lake), Orange B, and Citrus Red No. 2. Orange B and Citrus Red No. 2 are restricted to specific uses.

Colors that are exempt from certification include annatto extract, B-Apo-8' carotenal, betacarotene, beet

Artificially Colored. An advertisement for Aurora brand macaroni notes that it is artificially colored.

powder, canthaxanthin, caramel color, carrot oil, cochineal extract (carmine), cottonseed flour (toasted partially defatted, cooked), ferrous gluconate, fruit juice, grape color extract, grape skin extract (*enocianina*), paprika and paprika oleoresin, riboflavin, saffron, titanium dioxide, turmeric and turmeric oleoresin, and vegetable juice. Some substances, such as B-Apo-8' carotenal, ferrous gluconate, grape color extract, grape skin extract, and titanium dioxide, include GRAS and prior sanctioned substances as well as food additives.

History of Chemical Food Additives

Salt was probably the first important chemical food additive. Because its use began in prehistory, no dating can be ascribed to it. In primitive cultures with no refrigeration, salt was an important commodity for flavoring, for health, and as a preservative. There are suggestions that spices were being used in the Middle East as early as 5000 B.C.E., and certainly they were in use in Egypt as part of the mummification process as far back as 3000 B.C.E. Pliny the Elder, in the first century C.E., mentions wine (which he diluted with eight parts water, as was the custom then), making *garum* or *liquamen* (a fermented condiment made from fish) and cabbage preserved with a salt brine. Interestingly, in the Americas salting was an unknown technique until Europeans arrived.

Recognizing human nature, Hammurabi (ca. 1792–1750 B.C.E.) included in his code of laws (ca. 1780 B.C.E.) the conditions that tavern owners must observe in serving beer with very severe penalties for violations. While not directly concerned with ingredients, Hammurabi's code demonstrates that the issues of commercial fairness surrounding eating and drinking have long been at the fore of human society.

Additives are mentioned in the Bible in reference to leavened bread, wine, and salted meat. Yeast is an additive because it has the function of changing the characteristics of the food to which it has been added. As beer and bread are both made from essentially the same ingredients, it has been conjectured that either could be a by-product of the other. They existed side by side in ancient Egypt, and beer was recorded in China as early as 5000 B.C.E. The Metropolitan Museum of Art in New York City has a clay tablet that lists some of the ancient Babylonian beers, including dark beer, pale beer, red beer, three-fold beer, beer with a head, beer without a head, and others.

Wine was made from dates and grapes earlier than 3000 B.C.E. Greek grape wines did not keep well since they were stored in porous ceramic storage containers. Winemakers created additives to help with preservation and to disguise the diminished quality. One such concoction included herbs and spices combined with concentrated seawater and aged for years before use. Another approach mixed liquid resin with burned vines and added them to the juice before fermentation. Wines were often stored in lofts where meats were smoked, adding a lightly smoky flavor.

Solomon's temple, described in the Old Testament, had a courtyard called a "molten sea," which was said in legend to have held two thousand baths for salting meat. Many contemporary religions, such as Judaism and Islam, continue the ancient ritual slaughter and salting of meats as a component of their practices.

The English food law of King Henry III called the Assizes of Bread (1266) dictated ingredients and pricing to be used by bakers. The loaf price was fixed, but the weight was permitted to vary according to an official table that balanced the price of wheat and the extent of "bolting," or sifting, to separate out the bran to make a more refined product.

Around 1365, the poem *Piers Plowman* was written by a Londoner who chronicled much of daily living. Because of adulteration of foods, people were suffering, he said, and it was the job of English officials

> To punish . . .
> Brewers, bakers, butchers and cooks;
> For these be the men on earth who do most harm
> To the poor people who buy piece-meal.
> They poison the people secretly and most often.

But regulations were more stringent in other parts of Europe, with adulterants specifically forbidden. A decree was proclaimed in 1165 in Augsburg, Germany, where a penalty was declared for dispensing "bad" beer. In 1487 in Munich, Germany, Duke Albrecht IV proclaimed a regulation establishing a uniform beer price. From that time on, each brewer was required to swear a brew oath before the ducal treasurer, whereby he would "use only barley, hops and water for the beer, knowledgeably simmer it and add nothing else nor allow anyone else to add anything." This regulation was originally decreed only for Munich, but it influenced what was to come. The *Reinheitsgebot* (German Purity Law) was adopted in Bavaria in 1516 and is the oldest provision still enforced to protect consumers. It dictated ingredients, processes, and prices for beer, and it was ultimately adopted for the whole nation, with additional provisions to help brewers, in the German Beer Tax Law.

Two and a half centuries later in England, with the publication of Tobias Smollett's *Expedition of Humphrey Clinker* in 1771, the complaints about food in London persisted and intensified. Says Matthew Bramble, a character in the book, "As to . . . wine, it is a vile, unpalatable, and pernicious sophistication, balderdashed [mixed] with cyder, corn-spirit and the juice of sloes. . . . The bread . . . is a . . . paste, mixed up with chalk, alum and bone-ashes; insipid to the taste, and destructive to the constitution."

Milk was made from "faded cabbage leaves and sour draff" (spoiled milk usually fed to pigs), "lowered with hot water, frothed with bruised snails, carried through streets in open pails. . . . The tallowy rancid mass, called butter, is manufactured with candle-grease and kitchen-stuff."

As bad as the food was, something else was even worse, Clinker says, as he goes on in sarcastic indignation: "Now, all these enormities might be remedied with a very little attention to . . . civil regulation; but the wise patriots of London have taken it into their heads, that all regulation is inconsistent with liberty." There were few regulations, and the ones that did exist were not enforced with any regularity. Unscrupulous brewers added coriander, red pepper, tobacco, opium and other narcotics, licorice, ginger, linseed, molasses, and some kinds of hazardous metal salts to improve the foam on beers.

Around 1600, sugar was discovered to be a preservative and an additive. The demand for sugar grew rapidly, and the demand for honey, the only other important sweetener, declined abruptly. When the method of making jam with sugar was developed (around 1730), it forced a still greater demand. Sugar preservation of fruit introduced a new additive to European and American foods.

Smoke is also a chemical food additive and is one of the oldest of the historically developed additives, dating from prehistory and in use around the world. While smoking foods was a well-known process in Europe, New World natives had taken the process further, creating the forerunners of barbecue (*barbacoa*) and jerky (*charqui*). The next wave of additives would be synthetic or processed and would take place with the advent of the Industrial Revolution and more extensive food processing.

Chemical Food Additives in American History

It is against this backdrop of chicanery that all through the history of the United States there have been crusaders who tried to persuade the government to create and administer regulations about food sanitation, purity, and adulteration.

In the early 1800s, the first stirrings of a movement to codify and regulate medicines began. From this beginning, more and more consideration was given to food safety and purity, and in 1862 President Lincoln created the Bureau of Chemistry, which would later become the Food and Drug Administration. Out of that public concern and the prompting of people in the Bureau of Chemistry, around 1880 serious legislative proposals began to reach the floor of Congress. Not many were passed initially.

But the tide for reform and control was cresting, and it resulted in the first federal efforts to define and supervise safe food production. Muckraking novels like *The Jungle* by Upton Sinclair, which portrays the horrors of the meatpacking industry, and lurid newspaper stories inflamed public indignation and helped set the stage for congressional action. Common use of toxic preservatives and dyes in foods as well as quack claims for worthless and dangerous patent medicines were the triggering issues. In 1906, the Food and Drug Act was passed. The Meat Inspection Act was enacted on the same day. The next year, certified color regulations were promulgated to standardize colors and make sure the ones used were safe.

Through the next three decades, small steps were taken to deal with the issues of food safety. In 1930, the Bureau of Chemistry became the Food and Drug Administration and was given broader authority. In 1933, the FDA proposed a drastic updating of the Food and Drug Act, and the negotiations and congressional floor battles went on for five years. In 1938, the Federal Food, Drug, and Cosmetic Act (FFDCA) was passed, and the modern era of food safety definition and oversight began.

In 1949, the FDA published guidance for the industry for the first time. Titled *Procedures for the Appraisal of the Toxicity of Chemicals in Food* (and informally called Guidance to Industry), it came to be known as the "black book" in the food production industry. In 1958, the Food Additives Amendment was enacted, and the list of "Generally Recognized as Safe" food additives was published. In the late 1960s, the agency was given additional responsibility for sanitation standards for handling milk, shellfish, food service, and interstate travel facilities, and for preventing poisoning and accidents.

Common Uses of Additives

Different types of food products call for different types of additives. Many foods include more than one additive to address the multiple considerations that consumers expect, and many additives perform more than one

function. Often two or more additives serve the same general purpose but have slightly different characteristics that, when combined, create a synergistic effect, modifying or amplifying each other's effects. Looking at the five applications of food additives in some detail gives a sense of the process whereby foods are designed or adapted to modern industrial opportunities.

1 To impart or maintain desired consistency in the finished product Both manufacturers and consumers have preferences and expectations about food. Consumers say that baked goods and mixes should be able to reach the table with a sense of freshness and moisture. Salad dressings, ice cream, and processed cheeses are expected to be smooth and emulsified (nonseparating). Consumers expect coconut to stay moist on the shelf. Foods are expected to have a good "mouthfeel." Table salt has to pour freely to be used easily.

Food gums, like alginates, carrageenan, pectin, guar gum, and xanthan gum, can thicken and gel foods, adding viscosity to beverages and helping to solidify puddings and other spoonable desserts. Ingredients like maltodextrin can also help provide thickness and body in liquids and help retain moisture in baked goods. Such emulsifiers as lecithin, monoglycerides, and diglycerides help hold oil and water combinations together, as in salad dressings and cheeses, but they can also help foods retain moisture and are antifoaming agents.

Sweetened, flaked coconut has a combination of additives to keep it tasting and feeling fresh, including sugar, water, propylene glycol (to preserve freshness and give a moist mouthfeel), salt, and sodium metabisulfite (a preservative to maintain whiteness). Sodium aluminosilicate is added to salt to keep it free pouring, but it is also used with whole, broken, or flaked grain, including rice, other sugars and syrups (such as brown sugar or maple syrup), herbs, spices, seasonings (including salt substitutes), and condiments (such as seasoning for instant noodles).

2 To improve or maintain the nutritive value of the food Many foods are enriched by the addition of minerals and natural and synthetic vitamins. Sometimes foods are enriched to replace nutrients lost in processing; at other times additives are included to improve the nutrient profile, as, for example, when vitamins A and D are added to milk. Products containing added nutrients must be so labeled. Additives can be found in wheat products, including flour, bread, biscuits, breakfast cereals, and pasta. These additives include niacin, reduced iron, thiamine mononitrate, riboflavin, and folic acid, all essential nutrients. Cornmeal products are often enriched with the same additives that are found in flour.

Margarine is a complex formulation made up in great measure of additives. The following are ingredients in a typical margarine product: partially hydrogenated soybean oil (to make the product solid), liquid soybean oil (to keep it spreadable), water (to approximate butter), salt (for flavor and a slight degree of preservation), whey (from milk, for flavor), soy lecithin (to emulsify the oil and water), vegetable monoglycerides and diglycerides (to help emulsify), sodium benzoate (as a preservative), citric acid (as a preservative and a flavoring agent), artificial flavor, vitamin A (palmitate), and beta-carotene (for color). Iodized salt is enriched with iodine to prevent goiter in the general population. The condition has virtually disappeared since the introduction of the product.

3 To maintain palatability and wholesomeness of packaged foods

Several families of chemical additives help retain freshness and retard spoilage in processed foods (caused by mold, air, bacteria, fungi, or yeast), and they are not interchangeable, even when chemically similar. Propionic acid and its salts are a good example: Although both calcium propionate and sodium propionate are equally effective antimicrobial agents, calcium propionate is used throughout the world as a preservative in bread production. It can act as a calcium enricher, contributing to total calcium in the diet, and its use in preference to sodium propionate will result in slightly lower sodium levels in the bread. By contrast, sodium propionate is favored over calcium propionate in cake production because added calcium can interfere with the leavening, or rising action, of the cake.

Ascorbic acid is vitamin C, which can act as a preservative while also providing flavor.

Butylated hydroxyanisole (BHA) and butylated hydroxytoluene (BHT) are antioxidants and preservatives in food, food packaging, animal feed, and cosmetics. They are added to edible fats and fat-containing foods for their antioxidant properties, preventing food from becoming rancid and developing objectionable odors, and for their carry through and stabilizing effects on commercial fried foods. They are added to butter, lard, meats, cereals, baked goods, sweets, beer, vegetable oils, potato chips, snack foods, nuts and nut products, dehydrated potatoes, and flavoring agents. They are also used in sausage, poultry and meat products, dry mixes for beverages and desserts,

glazed fruits, chewing gum, active dry yeast, defoaming agents for beet sugar and yeast, and emulsion stabilizers for shortenings.

4 To produce a light texture or to control pH (acidity or alkalinity)

Leavening agents cause baked goods to rise by releasing carbon dioxide gas, whether from live organisms, like yeast, or chemicals, like baking soda or baking powder. Yeast digests carbohydrates to create the gas while leavening chemicals combine acids and alkalis to release it. Governing acidity or alkalinity offers better control of the conditions used in processing foods and helps maintain food quality and safety in canned or bottled goods. That balance is also an important element of taste since a slight acidity is generally appealing to most people, particularly in sweet foods and beverages. Some of the additives frequently used for these purposes include yeast, sodium bicarbonate (baking soda), citric acid, fumaric acid, phosphoric acid, lactic acid, and tartrates. Foods formulated with these additives include yeast breads, cakes, cookies, quick breads, crackers, soft drinks, and spoonable desserts, such as gelatins and puddings.

5 To enhance flavor or impart a desired color

The first group of flavor additives to consider is the oldest—herbs and spices, such as cloves, ginger, cinnamon, and nutmeg as well as fruit flavors derived from the flesh or peels (for example, limonene, an oil from the skins of citrus fruit). Some herbs and spices provide both flavor and color (to varying degrees), such as turmeric, saffron, and annatto seeds.

In addition to the four basic tastes that have been considered the standards (sweet, sour, bitter, salt), a recent addition to that list, still being debated, is umami, or a savory taste, to some extent both provided and bolstered by monosodium glutamate (MSG), mainly with meats and seafoods.

The various sugars found in nature, including fructose, lactose, sucrose, and others, are often used in ranges from light seasonings in savory foods to major components in dessert foods. Cooked and otherwise processed sugars as caramel are also used both for flavor and color, adding shades of browns to finished foods. Synthetic sweeteners, such as aspartame, sucralose, acesulfame-potassium, saccharin, and others, have become important in reduced-calorie formulations to replace caloric sugars.

It is difficult to find a processed food that has not had some enhancement of flavors and color. Foods ranging as far and wide as spice cake and gingerbread, soft drinks, yogurt, soup, candies, baked goods, cheeses, jams, and chewing gum all contain flavor enhancers, and most will also have some color added.

Additives in Action

The ingredient list from a commonly available cherry-flavored, sugar-free, gelatin dessert mix includes the following ingredients, in descending order of quantity:

Gelatin, which is a naturally derived gelling agent.

Adipic acid, which promotes rapid setting, provides tartness, and protects against quality loss. It is also used in beverages, condiments, relishes, dairy product analogs, fats and oils, frozen dairy desserts, puddings, gravies, meat products, and snack foods.

Disodium phosphate, which controls acidity and adds body.

Maltodextrin, which is made from cornstarch and is slightly sweet. It is a diluent to keep gelatin granules separated during home processing to help prevent lumping and unpleasant textures, and it also adds body. It replaces sugar in traditional gelatin dessert mixes but at a much lower volume.

Fumaric acid, which improves flavor stability and lengthens shelf life because it is not hygroscopic (does not absorb moisture from the atmosphere). It maintains noncaking and free flowing qualities and increases gel strength, so food processors may reduce normal gelatin content by about 2 percent. It is slightly bacteriostatic.

Aspartame, which is a synthetic sweetener that reduces caloric content with equivalent sweetness and acceptability to sugar. It may enhance certain flavors.

Artificial flavor, which can be any of the many approved flavors.

Acesulfame potassium, which is a synthetic sweetener. Since sweeteners have different characteristics, a blend can help overcome limitations of each as well as minimizing aftertaste.

Salt, which is primarily a flavoring agent since gelatin has very little flavor of its own. It also contributes nutrients.

FD&C Blue No. 1, which is one of eighteen permitted colors.

FD&C Red No. 40, which is one of eighteen permitted colors. In combination with the blue, it creates a color in the finished product that users will accept as looking like cherry should.

[See also Chemical Leavening; Flavorings; Herbs and Spices; Honey; Preserves; Salt and Salting; Sugar; Sweeteners; Vitamins.]

BIBLIOGRAPHY

Food and Drug Administration. http://www.fda.gov/. A complex website with exhaustive information about food additives in America.

"Food Timeline." http://www.gti.net/mocolib1/kid/food.html. A survey of food from prehistory through modern times with many links to other authoritative sites.

McGee, Harold. *On Food and Cooking: The Science and Lore of the Kitchen.* New York: Scribners, 1984. Well-researched and well-written analyses of science, technology, and culture that influence all aspects of dealing with food.

Tannahill, Reay. *Food in History.* Rev. ed. New York: Crown Publishers, 1989. A broad sketch of the evolution of foods and cultures from prehistory through the end of the twentieth century.

BOB PASTORIO

Chemical Leavening

North American predilection for speed and innovation spurred the nineteenth-century adoption of chemical leavenings in common baking and so laid the groundwork for prepackaged mixes. A flurry of experimentation through the 1800s with combinations of chemicals known to work as leavening agents resulted in the most common and popular modern types. Along the way, there was much controversy and confusion about the dangers of using the agents and charges and countercharges of ingredient adulteration.

Chemical leavenings replaced yeast and beaten egg whites. A blending of acid and alkali creates the gas required to raise batter or dough, usually accomplished by introducing an alkali to acid ingredients in the batter or by adding both an acid and an alkali to the ingredients. Since basic principles of chemistry were understood by the late eighteenth century, conscious product development led to the use of these products.

The use of pearlash was in all likelihood one of the professional secrets of European bakers. Peter Rose, historian of colonial Dutch American culinary practices, theorizes that in mid-eighteenth-century Albany, New York, the practice leaked out from bakers to home cooks. The first recorded mention of pearlash use in America was in Amelia Simmons's *American Cookery*, published in 1796, though the practice was surely established by that time.

Pearlash is potassium carbonate, refined from potash, which was derived from plant material ashes—in

England from pea and bean stalks and in America usually from wood. Potash, widely used in wool manufacturing, was made by boiling lye leached from ashes. Subjected to intense heat in an oven or reverberatory furnace, carbon was burned away from potash, leaving the lighter-colored alkaline pearlash. For pearlash to work in baking, it had to be combined with an acid ingredient, usually molasses, or milk (sometimes sour milk), wine, or lemon, and required thorough mixing.

Saleratus (from *sal*, meaning salts, and *aeratus*, meaning aerating) was a term in use from the 1830s through the early twentieth century to describe a variety of products, including potassium bicarbonate and sodium bicarbonate, used as rising agents. There were plant and, increasingly, mineral sources for saleratus, particularly as methods were developed for using sea salt as a source.

The term "baking soda" occurs in cookery books in the 1850s, referring to sodium bicarbonate, which formerly had been called saleratus and was a by-product of salt or, in some cases, was refined from naturally occurring alkalis. It, too, had to be used with sour milk, buttermilk, or molasses. Some of the earliest products easily clumped in dampness, so they had to be stored dry and carefully powdered before use.

Cream of tartar is bitartrate of potassium, an acid product used in combination with the alkalis to aerate batters. Originally derived from the lees of wine, it was expensive until nonorganic sources were developed. Its costliness accounted for much adulteration of the product in the later nineteenth century.

Baking powder was developed as a self-contained, pre-mixed acid-and-alkali combination product. For the last half of the nineteenth century, cookbooks called for both baking soda and cream of tartar in baking and by the 1850s occasionally referred to "yeast powders" (baking soda and cream of tartar wrapped separately but sold together), an early form of baking powder. Recipes continued to call for baking soda and cream of tartar even into the 1900s, but increasingly baking powder is specifically mentioned.

To make baking powder, the acid and alkali ingredients were typically mixed in proper proportion with a starch filler to prevent lumping. The nature of the acid determined the type of baking powder. Phosphate powders were made with calcium phosphate, tartrate powders with cream of tartar, and alum powders from a calcined double phosphate of aluminum.

There were many confusing, sometimes alarmist, claims made by competing baking powder companies,

Horsford Bread Preparation. America makes breads for the world. From *The Horsford Cook-book*, published by the Rumford Chemical Works, Providence, R.I., late 1870s.

which proliferated in the last two decades of the nineteenth century and the first decade of the twentieth century. Unscrupulous manufacturers fluffed out baking powders with inert or poor-quality ingredients. Various claims were made about healthfulness, purity, reliability, and digestibility. Most modern baking powders have their origins in the last half to last quarter of the 1800s, including Rumford, Davis, and Clabber Girl.

Besides these basic rising agents, there were other types in use during the 1800s. Most, but not all, of them have largely fallen out of use, including baking ammonia, Rochelle salts, powdered alum (used with baking soda), and hartshorn. With the favored acids and alkalis all coming from various sources, and used in various combinations with each other and other ingredients, the chemical leavening picture between 1850 and 1880 still can be very confusing, as it must have been to the cooks of the era as well. Nevertheless, they were widely adopted as a cheap and easy alternative to eggs or yeast, and the harm to flavor seems not to have been much regretted.

[*See also* Cakes.]

BIBLIOGRAPHY

The best historical information about baking powders comes from grocer's manuals and descriptions of manufacturing processes.

Corriher, Shirley O. *Cookwise: The Hows and Whys of Successful Cooking.* New York: Morrow, 1997. The scientific processes behind basic cooking and baking techniques and the use of various ingredients, including baking powders.

De Voe, Thomas F. *The Market Assistant, Containing a Brief Description of Every Article of Human Food Sold in the Public Markets of the Cities of New York, Boston, Philadelphia, and Brooklyn; Including the Various Domestic and Wild Animals, Poultry, Game, Fish, Vegetables, Fruits &c., with Many Curious*

Incidents and Anecdotes. Detroit: Gale Research, 1975. Reprint of the 1867 first edition.

Felker, Peter H. *The Grocer's Manual, Containing the Natural History and Process of Manufacture of All Grocer's Goods*. Claremont, NH: Claremont Manufacturing, 1878.

Sandra L. Oliver

Cherries

Wild forms of both the sweet cherry (*Prunus avium*) and the sour cherry (*P. cerasus*) grow along the eastern Mediterranean, especially in southeastern Europe and Asia Minor, the regions of origin for both species. The species name for sweet cherry, *avium*, refers to birds, the agents largely responsible for the distribution of the seed and therefore the spread of both species. Hybrids of the two species, commonly called Duke cherries, are also cultivated to a limited extent but are not significant commercially in the United States.

The sweet cherry apparently was first domesticated in ancient Greece. Although it has been cultivated for more than two thousand years, for much of that time it remained a plant for the home garden, not one cultivated for the market. Both sweet and sour cherries were introduced to America by early settlers in the Northeast and later were distributed into states such as Virginia and Carolina and then expanded into the Midwest and, finally, to the Pacific Coast. There, in Oregon, the Lewelling family introduced the Bing cherry. This popular, firm-fleshed variety, together with improvements in transportation and the advent of refrigeration, helped establish the modern sweet cherry industry by making it possible to ship fresh cherries to distant markets.

Sweet cherries are classified into two general groups. One type, a class of soft, juicy cherries, is called a heart cherry or a gean, and the other is called a *bigarreau*, a French term that initially referred to the variegated color of the fruit but now applies to any sweet cherry with firm flesh, regardless of color. A typical heart is Black Tartarian, a soft, richly flavored cherry, very delicate when ripe and suitable only for nearby markets. The *bigarreau* type includes the crisp-textured Bing and Rainier cherries, which account for most of the nation's sweet cherry production, concentrated in the Northwest and California. Sweet cherries are also grown in New York and Pennsylvania.

The bane of sweet cherry growers even in the more arid parts of the West is rainfall at harvest, which can be devastating, inducing fruit of susceptible varieties like Bing to crack. Sweet cherries also are traditionally harvested with their stems, and this is accomplished only by costly hand labor, thus making sweet cherries one of the most expensive fresh fruits on the market. While the Bing is the mainstay of the industry, there are new varieties maturing earlier and later than Bing, thus extending the marketing season; there are also new self-fertile types and others with some resistance to rain cracking. The Rainier is a light-fleshed but highly blushed sweet cherry growing in popularity as a high-quality dessert fruit.

Sweet cherries are primarily sold for fresh consumption, but they are also used in cherries jubilee, a classic dessert made of a saucy cherry flambé poured over ice cream. Maraschino cherries, used in fruit cocktail, drinks, and fruit cakes, are made of sweet cherries that are artificially flavored and colored, mostly of the Royal Ann variety.

The tart, or sour, cherry industry began in the mid-nineteenth century and is centered in Michigan. The Montmorency is the primary variety and can be harvested mechanically. Used mostly for culinary purposes, tart cherries are excellent for cherry pies and preserves; however, a new, sweeter variety from Hungary, the Balaton cherry, shows great potential for fresh market and juice. Both species of commercial cherries are relatively high in vitamin C and antioxidants and appear to provide both antigout and anti-inflammatory benefits.

[*See also* Fruits; Pacific Northwestern Regional Cookery.]

BIBLIOGRAPHY

Hedrick, U. P. *The Cherries of New York*. Albany, NY: J. B. Lyon, 1915. The classic pomology of cherry varieties, giving their history and botany.

Janick, Jules, and James N. Moore, eds. *Fruit Breeding*, Volume 1: *Tree and Tropical Fruits*. The section on cherries is a thorough treatment of cherry variety history, botany, and prospects for continued breeding.

Webster, A. D., and N. E. Looney, eds. *Cherries: Crop Physiology, Production, and Uses*. Wallingford, U.K.: CAB International, 1996. A comprehensive review covering all aspects of cherry production and research.

Andrew Mariani

Cherry Bounce

Cherry bounce is best known as an American cordial that is homemade at all socioeconomic levels. Wild black cherries or cultivated sour cherries are crushed together with their pits, sugar, and the alcohol of choice and the mixture is then allowed to mature. The well-to-do colonial New Englander or Virginian opted for rum or brandy; other southerners preferred whiskey. Modern-day Louisiana Cajuns accept only bourbon, while cherry-rich Wisconsin claims vodka as the spirit of choice.

In late-seventeenth-century England, "cherry-bouncer" might refer to any "mingled" drink or punch. By the mid-1700s cherry bounce was often indistinguishable from cherry brandy (although it was sometimes spiced with cinnamon or nutmeg). Indeed, it is probable that the name "bounce" was intended to foil tax collectors: in the eighteenth and nineteenth centuries (and in early twentieth-century rural Maryland) one meaning of "bounce" was to lie or swindle. Before its near-synonymous association with cherries, "bounce" sometimes also referred to other fruit-flavored cordials (e.g., blackberry brandy) and to an eighteenth-century combination of spruce beer and wine drunk by some New Hampshire fishermen.

[See also Cordials; Cordials, Historical; Ratafia.]

ROBIN M. MOWER

Cherry Pitters or Stoners

Cherry pies can be enjoyed fully only when the eater is confident that there are no pits to break the teeth. Homemade pronged sticks were used to push a pit through a cherry. In 1863 a cherry pitter was patented in the United States. The device was a cast iron, horseshoe-shaped frame with three legs, a hopper, and a crank. Cherries were poured slowly into the hopper while the user turned a crank to move a ribbed wheel that rubbed the stones out and away while the mangled fruit was channeled into a bowl. A cherry pitter patented in 1870 was a box and frame that held twenty cherries. The device was fitted with a hinged presser and twenty wooden dowels that pushed out the twenty stones at the same time. Later patents generally followed the 1863 concept. By 1890 handheld stoners with a spring-action prong were being used to push stones from one cherry at a time. This type continues to be manufactured in the early 2000s.

[See also Cherries.]

BIBLIOGRAPHY

Franklin, Linda Campbell. *300 Years of Kitchen Collectibles*. 5th ed. Iola, WI: Krause Publications, 2003.

LINDA CAMPBELL FRANKLIN

Chesapeake Bay

The Chesapeake Bay is America's largest tidal estuary, bordered by Maryland and Virginia. The bay watershed extends north to Cooperstown, New York, and west to West Virginia, but the Chesapeake region is restricted to the Tidewater on the west and the Delmarva Peninsula (or the Eastern Shore) to the east. The bay is two hundred miles long, with a combined shoreline, indented by numerous rivers and creeks, of about four thousand miles. The major cities in this region are Norfolk, Virginia; Washington, D.C.; and Baltimore, Maryland.

The region has a temperate climate that favors vegetable and fruit growing. The Chesapeake Bay is rich in seafood, and salt marshes provide food and winter quarters for migrating birds and waterfowl. Shad and herring spawn in the rivers in the spring. Native Americans grew corn, sweet potatoes, melons, and a variety of squash and beans. They harvested strawberries, blackberries, persimmons, acorns, hickory nuts, and black walnuts and hunted deer, turkeys, and small game. They also ate large quantities of oysters, crabs, and fish. English explorers established Jamestown, Virginia, the first European settlement in this area, in 1607. St. Mary's City, the first capital of the Maryland colony, was founded in 1634. The new settlers added domesticated animals, such as cattle, sheep, pigs, and chickens, and European grains, fruits, and vegetables. They enjoyed native sassafras tea and sent tons of the root to England as a cash crop.

The Colonial Era

The colonial-era tobacco plantation society that grew up around the bay was noted for its tradition of lavish hospitality. This was also a time of African slavery, and black cooks combined the foods of America, Europe, and Africa to create a regional cuisine that became famous throughout the United States. Virginia and Maryland fried chicken (served with cream gravy) may have had its origins in Africa. Sweet potato biscuits are in the Indian tradition of bread made from sweet potatoes, chestnuts, beans, and corn. Peanuts, black-eyed peas, okra, and watermelon came from Africa. Corn pudding, spoon bread (batter bread in Virginia), unsweetened white corn bread, hominy, grits, and sweet potato and pumpkin pies are all adaptations using local ingredients. (White potato pie is found on the Eastern Shore.) Brunswick stew (made with squirrel and onions) originated in Brunswick

County, Virginia. Later additions included chicken, lima beans, corn, okra, and tomatoes.

Pork is a common ingredient in Chesapeake regional cooking. Ham, bacon, fatback or salt pork, scrapple, and lard are ubiquitous. Vegetables and game, such as stewed muskrat, are cooked with salt pork. Piecrusts and biscuits frequently are made with lard as shortening. Stuffed fresh hams are a traditional Easter dish, cooked with spring greens packed into slits cut in the meat.

Mid-eighteenth-century Eastern Shore farmers switched from growing tobacco to growing wheat, and the Delmarva Peninsula became America's primary grain-growing region, known as the breadbasket of the Revolution. A few wealthy landowners owned fishing nets, used to catch herring in the spring spawning runs on the rivers. The fish were preserved by salting as food for slaves and the poor. Not until the mid-nineteenth century were fish caught in quantity for the growing urban markets. Planked shad is a Virginia specialty, and an annual shad festival is held on the Nanticoke River in Maryland. Rockfish, known elsewhere as striped bass, is a very popular dish, often stuffed and baked.

Cider was made in Maryland and Virginia, and peach brandies and fruit cordials were distilled from local fruits. Rye whiskey production centered in Maryland and Pennsylvania, where Scotch-Irish immigrants settled and borrowed rye grain from their German neighbors, who had used it to produce schnapps and vodka at home in northern Europe. Rye whiskey was for many years America's most popular spirit and was produced by George Washington and Thomas Jefferson. Rye remained the dominant whiskey type in Maryland and southern Pennsylvania well into the twentieth century.

The Nineteenth Century

In the early nineteenth century Maryland and Virginia passed laws barring nonresident harvesting and fishing in the bay, as northern harbors became polluted and local oyster beds were exhausted. Many New Englanders moved to the Chesapeake region to take advantage of the abundance of oysters. The New Yorker Thomas H. Kensett II established an oyster packinghouse in Baltimore in 1834 and was the first to use hermetically sealed tin "canisters" (giving us our word "can") for shucked oysters, fruits, and vegetables. The canning industry in Baltimore grew rapidly, and the number of oysters shipped west more than quadrupled, to over 3 million pounds, between 1848 and 1860.

In the nineteenth century Baltimore, with a deep harbor on the Patapsco River, developed as an industrial center and became the second most important port of entry for European immigrants to the United States. The nation's

Raking for Oysters in Chesapeake Bay. From George Augustus Sala, *America Revisited,* 3rd edition (London, 1883), vol. 1, facing p. 97.

first railroad was built from Baltimore and connected with the Ohio River by 1853, providing new markets for the products of the Chesapeake region. Market hunting sent wild geese and other waterfowl to the restaurants and markets of New York and other big cities. Canvasback ducks, fed on wild celery in Chesapeake marshes, were internationally acclaimed as one of America's great wild foods. Trappers caught muskrat for their fur, but the local people esteemed the flesh as well. As the region was cleared for farming and urban areas grew, white-tailed deer disappeared, but they later returned in large numbers.

In 1860 Baltimore was the third-largest American city, feeding the nation with seafood and locally grown fruits and vegetables. Thirty-four Baltimore companies responded to demand for canned goods for the Union army during the Civil War and the technological developments that allowed for greater production. The principal products were oysters, peaches, tomatoes, and corn. By 1868 there were eighty oyster packinghouses in Baltimore. Raw oysters were a popular between-meal snack, and oyster stew was eaten across the nation. Fried oysters, oyster stew, scalloped oysters, oyster fritters, and ham-and-oyster pie remain common dishes in the region.

The bay's oyster catch peaked at 14 million bushels in 1874 and then began a long, steady decline. Baltimore in 1880 packed more oysters than any other city in the world and more than all the other packing points in Maryland and Virginia combined. When refrigerated railroad cars made it possible to distribute fresh Chesapeake Bay seafood throughout the United States, factories made up for the decrease in volume of canned oysters by processing increasing varieties and quantities of fruits, vegetables, and fish, including shad and herring roe.

With its mild climate, the Eastern Shore prospered, growing peaches, melons, tomatoes, and all sorts of vegetables. Produce was sent by steamboat, sailing vessel, and railroad to Baltimore canneries. Eastern Shore canneries were important contributors to both world wars of the twentieth century. Maryland was the leading tomato-canning state in the nation until the 1940s, when the canning industry moved west to California and farmers shifted their efforts to raising poultry and growing corn and soybeans for poultry feed. The Delmarva Peninsula became one of the most highly concentrated poultry-raising areas in the world, and the first Delmarva Chicken Festival, with an annual chicken-cooking contest, was held in 1947. Delmarva farmers still grow melons, tomatoes, sweet corn, pumpkins, strawberries, and peaches.

Nineteenth- and early twentieth-century travelers looked forward with pleasure to meals on board the Chesapeake Bay steamboats and the food served at local hotels and boardinghouses. Competition led to elaborate menus featuring local delicacies. Coddies (small codfish cakes served on crackers) were a favorite with budget travelers. Victorian opulence and glamour faded by the Great Depression of 1930s, but the food has continued to attract visitors to the Chesapeake region.

On the fishing boats of the bay, all-male crews developed a tradition of good eating with inexpensive ingredients, often prepared by black men. The custom of melting sharp cheese in hot coffee both lightened the coffee when there was no fresh milk and provided melted cheese for hard biscuits. Watermen relished salt fish for breakfast, cooked with potatoes, onions, and salt pork. Bean soup with hot biscuits or fry bread and molasses was a staple midday meal. Many people around the bay still enjoy stewed chicken or dried lima bean soup with slick dumplings or cornmeal dumplings known as dodgers.

German immigrants settling in Maryland brought with them a taste for sauerkraut. In Baltimore sauerkraut is a necessary complement to Thanksgiving turkey (with oyster stuffing), and sauerkraut salad is a popular dish. Sauerbraten, or sour beef, is another regional favorite. German settlers also brought a taste for beer, and there were more than two dozen breweries in Baltimore alone in the 1890s. German breweries also operated in Washington, D.C., and Norfolk, Virginia, until Prohibition in 1920 closed most of them. After Prohibition, National Bohemian Beer was brewed in Baltimore with the slogan "From the Land of Pleasant Living." The last big brewery in Maryland closed in about 1980. Beer is served with steamed crabs, crab cakes, soft-shell crabs, oysters, fried fish, and barbecued foods. It is also used by local cooks for steaming shellfish and fish and as a braising agent for meats, cabbage, sausages, and sauerkraut.

The Twentieth Century

In the twentieth century blue crabs took the place of oysters in the economy and cuisine of the Chesapeake region. Crabmeat dishes have always been popular, but out-of-state markets for this perishable product were limited. With declining oyster harvests and scares over polluted shellfish and typhoid outbreaks in the 1920s, many watermen and packinghouse owners shifted their focus to the harvesting and marketing of blue crabs. The seafood industry was shaken during the Great Depression and nearly died in response to low consumer demand, but seafood consumption increased in the late 1930s and was boosted during World War II, as seafood was not included in government food rationing.

In the late 1940s, Fletcher Hanks invented a hydraulic dredge to harvest soft-shell clams in deep water. The vast majority of these clams, both fresh and frozen, were sent to New England markets. Maryland state agencies promoted local consumption of soft-shell clams (known as maninose or manos, from the Algonquian *mananosay*) with a festival in 1971, but overharvesting and a hurricane that buried the remaining clam beds in silt defeated their efforts. Hard-shell clams from southern Virginia waters are found in chowders and stews. Eels, the second-largest commercial finfish catch in Maryland, are not eaten locally; most of the catch is exported to Europe and Asia.

Advances in frozen-food technology after World War II provided stimulus to the seafood industry, which could process seafood harvested around the world on the Eastern Shore and sell seafood (in the form of fish cakes, fish sticks, fillets, and soups) prepared in Maryland and Virginia worldwide. Some 90 percent of Maryland crabs are sold live for crab feasts to restaurants around the Chesapeake Bay. A good cook knows at least twenty ways to prepare crabs, including crab cakes, crab soups, deviled crabs, crab Imperial, crab Norfolk, and crab salads. Soft-shell crabs are fried and served whole in sandwiches. Local supplies have not been able to keep pace with rapid population growth in the metropolitan corridor between Norfolk and Boston and growing consumer demand for crabmeat and soft-shell crabs. Maryland and Virginia companies import crabs and crabmeat from eastern Asia and Mexico as well as Texas, Louisiana, and the Carolinas.

Desserts have changed very little since the eighteenth century. Puddings made from rice, bread, and crackers are still favorites, as are custard pies (baked pudding in a pie shell). Elegant dessert jellies favored in the eighteenth and nineteenth centuries have been replaced by Jell-O. Chess pies (originally containing cheese) are a Virginia specialty, filled with a mixture of butter, sugar, raisins, eggs, and black walnuts or hickory nuts. Pecan pies, a variant of chess pies, are popular farther south. Ginger cookies and gingerbread date back to colonial days. Peach cobbler and strawberry-rhubarb pie are favorites on Maryland tables. Regional cakes include Kossuth cake, created to honor the visit of the Hungarian patriot General Lajos Kossuth to Baltimore in 1851; Lady Baltimore cake, also claimed by Savannah, South Carolina; Lord Baltimore cake; and Smith Island seven-layer chocolate-frosted cakes.

[*See also* Brewing; Canning and Bottling; Clams; Crab Boils; Game; Oysters; Pies and Tarts, *sidebar on* Chess Pie; Scrapple; Seafood; Stuffed Ham.]

BIBLIOGRAPHY

Booth, Letha, comp. *The Williamsburg Cookbook: Traditional and Contemporary Recipes*. Williamsburg, VA: Colonial Williamsburg Foundation, 1975.

Carson, Jane. *Colonial Virginia Cookery: Procedures, Equipment, and Ingredients in Colonial Cooking*. Williamsburg, VA: Colonial Williamsburg Foundation, 1985.

From a Lighthouse Window: Recipes and Recollections from the Chesapeake Bay Maritime Museum, St. Michaels, Maryland. St. Michaels, MD: Chesapeake Bay Maritime Museum, 1989.

Jones, Evan. *American Food: The Gastronomic Story*. Woodstock, NY: Overlook Press, 1990.

Root, Waverley, and Richard de Rochemont. *Eating in America: A History*. Hopewell, NJ: Ecco, 1995.

Shields, John. *Chesapeake Bay Cooking with John Shields*. New York: Broadway Books, 1998.

Stieff, Frederick Philip. *Eat, Drink and Be Merry in Maryland: An Anthology from a Great Tradition*. New York: Putnam, 1932.

Walter, Eugene, and the editors of Time-Life Books. *American Cooking: Southern Style*. New York: Time-Life Books, 1971.

Warner, William W. *Beautiful Swimmers: Watermen, Crabs, and the Chesapeake Bay*. Boston: Little, Brown, 1976.

VIRGINIA SCOTT JENKINS

Chestnuts

In the nineteenth century in the eastern part of the United States the chestnut was everyone's free food. Chestnuts fell in profusion from the branches of 4 billion trees and were there on the forest floor for the taking. Farmers allowed their pigs to roam free to fatten on the mast of the forest, the edible nuts and fruits that fall from the trees and bushes. The American chestnut (*Castanea dentata*) was also an important source of quality lumber for construction and furniture making. In Europe and Asia cousins of the American chestnut played a similar role in the lives of the people.

In the first half of the twentieth century a blight that came to America with imported Asian trees virtually destroyed the American chestnut. In Europe there was a similar blight, although it was not nearly as savage. The Asian varieties were much more resistant and escaped major damage. Today's typical chestnuts roasted on an open fire are probably from Asian chestnut trees—either trees from Asia or Asian trees planted in America. The Asian trees do well in orchards but because they are short and bushy they do not do well in forests of tall straight trees.

The American Chestnut Foundation has been having some success in breeding the blight resistance of the Asian tree into the surviving American chestnut trees.

The chestnut is not an ordinary fat-laden tree nut. It has much less oil than pecans, walnuts, and almonds and much more carbohydrate. Sometimes called "the bread of the mountain," the chestnut was often ground into flour for cooking. And in northern Italy, before explorers brought corn from the New World, ground chestnuts were the key to the early polenta. The chestnut, once free for the taking, is today a luxurious treat. The sweet-soaked marrons of France and Italy are a sought-after treasure at holiday time. The wonderfully fragrant roasting chestnuts that are sold on the streets of Milan or Lyon or New York City are coveted by buyers willing to pay whatever it takes to get a bagful.

[See also Nuts.]

BIBLIOGRAPHY

Bhagwandin, Annie. *The Chestnut Cook Book: Recipes, Folklore, and Practical Information regarding the Most Diverse of Culinary Nuts.* Onlaska, WA: Shady Grove Publications, 1996.

Griffith, Linda, and Fred Griffith. *Nuts: Recipes from around the World That Feature Nature's Perfect Ingredient.* New York: St. Martin's Press, 2003.

Rosengarten, Frederic, Jr. *The Book of Edible Nuts.* New York: Walker, 1984.

LINDA AND FRED GRIFFITH

Chicken

Charles Darwin identified the wild jungle fowl of Southeast Asia, *Gallus gallus*, as the biological forerunner of the domestic chicken, *Gallus domesticus*. These ancestral birds still exist both in their native areas and as escapees from domesticated and cockfighting flocks. As discomforting as cockfighting may seem to most Americans in the twenty-first century, it remains widespread among many cultures, having been called the most popular sport ever known to man (and it is almost exclusively a masculine pastime). There is a school of thought that domesticating birds for cockfighting predated the development of the chicken and the egg as food and facilitated the birds' original adoption as a staple of the table.

The time of the chicken's domestication is lost in prehistory, but no doubt it was relatively early in the history of agriculture. Chickens apparently spread from Southeast Asia through cultural diffusion and as a trade item. Whether moved as cargo on beasts of burden, or carried below decks as part of the virtual barnyard on merchant and naval ships to provide meat and eggs for the captain's table, chickens spread to Egypt and ports throughout the world, including Europe, England, and eventually the Americas.

In Egypt, references to chickens are attributed to the Second Dynasty in the early fourteenth century B.C.E. Egypt was a technologically advanced and highly inventive society, adapted to the mass production and distribution of food. The Egyptians built incubators of clay brick, in which the attendants kept the incubation temperature correct with constantly burning fires, using their own skin to judge the warmth, about 105 degrees Fahrenheit. These incubators, one of the most remarkable inventions of the time, could hatch ten or fifteen thousand chicks at once. It is only in recent years that production of this magnitude was approached in the West.

The Chicken Reaches America

The worldwide migration of the chicken was hugely successful. The birds' compact size and obvious utility on and off ships made them ideal immigration partners with the earliest Spanish and English colonists in the sixteenth and seventeenth centuries, although some contend that chickens reached the New World, specifically South America, through earlier contacts. By virtue of their adaptability to a variety of environments, chickens are now found throughout America, from the blustery shores of Maine to the warmth of Baja California. They also thrive on the islands of Hawaii. It is amazing to observe them scratch at the poorest soil, somehow finding enough sustenance not only to stay alive but also to raise their chicks and to help provide for the family table. Although chickens are not generally found on the boulevards of cities or the manicured streets of suburbia, it is not uncommon to find them kept as pets in city apartments.

In the eighteenth and early nineteenth centuries, the general public began to take an interest in science, becoming a part of the so-called scientific revolution. From the mid-nineteenth through the early twentieth centuries, American amateur agriculturalists developed different breeds by selecting the birds that showed desirable characteristics and, through brother-sister mating, establishing a line that eventually bred true. Setting aside the difficult techniques of genetic engineering, this is very much the same method in use in the early 2000s. The popularity of selective breeding, coupled with the exchange of particular chickens between individual breeders, produced some truly beautiful and quite astonishing birds. This fad, dubbed "Hen Fever" by one of its proponents, led to shows where the public could inspect these unusual birds—one 1849 exhibition brought together 1,023 breeds and attracted thousands of enthusiastic viewers. The newspapers contained accounts of "rare and curious and inexpressibly beautiful examples of poultry." Others of these special breeds were selected for their fighting abilities, as cockfighting continued to be a popular sport, particularly in the American South.

The Industrial Chicken

The urbanization of the population in America in the late nineteenth century led to "improvements" in the production of birds for meat and eggs. With every American consuming an average of eighty pounds of chicken per year, with an estimated total value of $40 billion, the chicken industry became more centralized and vastly more efficient. Hens, in the twenty-first century, can be housed in buildings containing 250,000 birds. In many cases the buildings have no windows, so the birds are denied the pleasure of even a bit of sunlight. Each hen shares a cage with six or seven others. The cages, themselves, are stacked six to seven on top of each other, and each is so scandalously small that a hen cannot do that most natural act in the class Aves—spread her wings, flutter them a bit, and relax contentedly.

In most cases when eggs are selected for hatching they are placed on a mechanical contrivance that rotates them regularly while maintaining the optimum temperature for hatching. Nature, of course, does it quite differently. Biologists now understand that "broodiness," nesting on eggs until they hatch in favor of laying new ones, is the result of an increased production of the pituitary hormone prolactin.

Nutritional Value

Nutritionally the chicken and egg are almost certainly the most readily and universally available source of food in both industrialized and emerging areas. The flesh of the chicken has no known special nutritional qualities that distinguish it from other sources of meat. The most striking feature of the chicken is its white breast meat, characterized by the absence of the oxygen-binding protein, myoglobin. The myoglobin gives the flight muscles the ability to scavenge oxygen from the blood with greater efficiency. Chickens do not migrate and are not well adapted

for long flights, their activities being mainly terrestrial during the day. By contrast, in birds that migrate long distances and for which endurance is an essential survival characteristic, such as ducks and geese, the breast is dark because of its high content of myoglobin. The chicken's white breast has the sprinter's advantage, however, being characterized by very powerful "fast twitch fibers" that are capable of launching even a heavy-bodied bird into a tree or onto a roost for the night. There is no significant nutritional difference between the two types of flesh, beyond the larger amount of iron present in the myoglobin-rich dark meat.

The egg is virtually a complete food, used as the main source of materials and energy during the chick's embryonic development. Compared to most other eggs, particularly those of mammals, it is huge. The ova needed to produce several thousand elephants would fit comfortably within even a small hen's egg. This size is another reason the chicken's egg is such a good source of nutrition.

There are interesting cultural differences with respect to what a proper egg should look like when cracked open. The yolk from a local U.S. franchise-type restaurant has a pale yellow color. Overseas, yolks with much deeper coloring are found, deriving from the yellow pigment carotene. The carotene can come from marigolds, which are often one of the components of chicken feeds, or from green plants, such as grasses, which account for the beautiful color of eggs from free-range chickens. Similar feed manipulations are used to vary the skin tones of industrially produced chickens, from creamy white to more golden hues.

[*See also* Chesapeake Bay; Chicken Cookery; Eggs; Kentucky Fried Chicken; Poultry and Fowl; Sanders, Colonel.]

BIBLIOGRAPHY

Burnham, George. *The History of the Hen Fever*. Boston: James French, 1885.
Cobb, Ernest. *The Hen at Work: A Brief Manual of Home Poultry Culture*. New York: G. P. Putnam's, 1919.
Jull, M. A. "The Races of Domestic Fowl." *National Geographic* (April 1927): 379–452.
Kligender, Francis. *Animals in Art and Thought to the End of the Middle Ages*. Edited by Evelyn Antal and John Harthan. Cambridge, MA: MIT Press, 1971.
Morse, Hosea Ballou. *The Chronicles of the East India Company: Trading to China, 1635–1834*. 5 vols. Taipei: Ch'eng-wen, 1966–1969.
Scott, George Rypley. *The History of Cockfighting*. 2nd ed. Hindhead, U.K.: Triplegate, 1983.
Smith, Page, and C. W. Daniel. *The Chicken Book*. Boston: Little Brown, 1975.

CHARLES DANIEL

Chicken Cookery

Seventeenth- and eighteenth-century descriptions of colonial foodways ignored the chicken for the most part. In the earliest manuscripts to enter America there are, of course, chicken recipes for roasts, stews, and pies, and none other than Governor William Byrd II was dining on the iconic southern dish of fried chicken at his Virginia plantation by 1709. But most culinary descriptions praise the abundant wild game that so caught visitors' eyes and make scant mention of the barnyard fowl. Nor do platters of chicken occupy prestigious spots on the meticulously diagrammed table layouts; these, too, were reserved for wild birds and game. This is not to suggest that chickens were not widely eaten; virtually every colonial American archaeological site shows evidence of chicken consumption. Chicken merely suffered an image problem, possibly attributable to its husbandry.

Unlike the manly and aristocratic hunting of game, tending, slaughtering, and cleaning barnyard chickens was work for women and children. A few imported English books offered advice on raising chickens, but little appears domestically until C. N. Bement's *American Poulterer's Companion* (1843). The common chicken was known by the unappetizing moniker "Dung-hill" fowl. Amelia Simmons's *American Cookery* (1796) judged the ubiquitous dunghill only "tolerable," and she then cryptically noted that *"chickens,* of either [unspecified] kind are good, and the yellow leg'd the best, and their taste the sweetest." N. K. M. Lee's *Cook's Own Book* (1832) disagreed, preferring the black-legged fowls for roasting.

By the nineteenth century, cookbook authors assumed that many of their readers would purchase poultry rather than raise their own. Shoppers were advised to differentiate between young and old chickens by the softness of the breastbone, the stiffness of the feet, and the color and smoothness of the legs and comb, all relevant indicia at a time when selections could be poked and heads and feet still came attached. Even with a market chicken, the cook faced the tedious task of cleaning it by picking out the pinfeathers and singeing the flesh to remove the last delicate down.

For those raising and slaughtering their own fowl, Sarah Josepha Hale's *The Good Housekeeper* (1841) recommended hanging the poultry to tenderize it before cooking: one night in summer, while "in cold weather it may be kept a much longer time to advantage."

Preservation was only a modest issue in the days before ice boxes. Unlike larger animals, chickens could be consumed without waste promptly after slaughter. If a chicken started to "become musty before you want to cook it," Mrs. Hale recommended placing a skinned onion or a bit of charcoal in the cavity.

Recipes recommended different sizes and ages of chickens for particular preparations. Capons, or castrated young roosters, were particularly prized for their generous size and fatty flesh. Roasting times seem short by contemporary standards and may be attributable to the intense heat of hearth cookery and the scrawnier eighteenth- and nineteenth-century free-range birds, compared with the industrially produced broiler chickens available in the twenty-first century. The stewing recipes resemble current practices.

One of the most common recipes for chicken from the eighteenth through the mid-twentieth centuries was the fricassee, a white or brown stew of small chickens lightly bound with egg yolks, and, by the nineteenth century, often enriched with milk or cream. In a nod to increasing delicacy (an elegant term for Victorian squeamishness) at table, later nineteenth-century hostesses would remove the head and, less frequently, the feet before serving roasted birds; in the earlier nineteenth century, cooks were instructed that the head of roasted fowls "should be turned under the wing, like a turkey." Southern tables were noted for pilafs, chicken cooked with rice; the dish spread throughout the country in the nineteenth century and remains popular. Among the most diverse and interesting chicken recipes through the first half of the nineteenth century are those found in Lettice Bryan's *The Kentucky Housewife* (1839).

In the later nineteenth century, the emerging railroad networks eased the transportation of chickens to hatcheries and markets, helping launch an incipient poultry industry. The number of chickens in America more than doubled in the decade between 1880 and 1890, from 102 million birds to over 250 million, although much of the industry focused on egg-layers rather than table birds. "How-to" poultry manuals proliferated and cookbooks offered proportionately more chicken recipes, as the availability of game birds declined in the late nineteenth and early twentieth centuries. The United States Department of Agriculture (USDA) encouraged home rearing of chickens during both World Wars, viewing a small flock of ten hens as an efficient recycler of table scraps, producer of many dozen eggs per year, and supplier of meat to a country severely strained by wartime shortages.

CHICKEN A LA KING

There's nothing royal about Chicken à la King, which is an entrée of cubed cooked chicken breast in a cream sauce that is dotted with pimento and mushrooms and often flavored with Madeira or a similar wine. An early claim for its invention appeared in 1915 in the obituary of William King, who had worked as a cook at Philadelphia's fashionable Bellevue Hotel around 1895. King included truffles and red and green peppers in his recipe.

Under the more pedestrian name "creamed chicken," similar recipes appeared in cookbooks beginning in the late nineteenth century. Peas are often added to the sauce in these recipes, and the sauced chicken is served over hot toast, biscuits, or waffles. The first located recipe titled "Chicken à la King" appeared in Paul Richards's *The Lunch Room* (1911). The name quickly became popular, and the dish became a standard menu item in all kinds of restaurants, upscale and down, especially tearooms that catered to women, since this dish could be eaten in a most ladylike way without picking up a knife.

BIBLIOGRAPHY

New York Tribune, March 5, 1915, p. 9.

BARRY POPIK AND ANDREW F. SMITH

But market chickens remained dear, generally costing more than beef through World War II, because chicken flocks could be devastated by disease and parasites. One mark of the chicken's enhanced status and relative expense was Herbert Hoover's 1928 campaign promise of prosperity that would be measured by "a chicken in every pot." Working with the USDA in breeding experiments, poultry farmers in the 1930s began raising broiler chickens (ranging up to five pounds) for the commercial market, culminating in the "Chicken of Tomorrow" contest in 1948, designed to engineer a meatier, faster-growing bird. The experiments were successful, but the size of commercial chicken farms would be limited until growers could control diseases and parasites with the introduction of the first effective drugs in the 1950s.

Drugs, coupled with higher-protein and vitamin-enriched feeds, inaugurated large-scale chicken production,

most famously by Tyson Foods and Perdue Farms. Chicken became an inexpensive, year-round staple. The smaller nuclear family of the mid-twentieth century made the chicken an ideally sized roast. Butchered chickens, sold prepackaged as breasts, wings, legs, or thighs, further eased the housewives' burden. Pierre Franey's "60-Minute Gourmet," a nationally syndicated column from the 1970s and 1980s, depended heavily on the widely available, quick-cooking breast to put tasty dishes on the table in what was then considered record time.

Chicken maintains a prominent place in American cookery, shown by the huge number of chicken recipes found in cookbooks, including a number of "365" books that offer a different chicken preparation for each day of the year. Consumers concerned with food safety, especially the *salmonella* bacteria associated with chickens and eggs, and gourmands looking for perceived deeper flavor, have encouraged smaller, free-range production of chickens, harking back to the preindustrial production of the nineteenth century. Like those in the nineteenth-century market, these chickens are significantly more expensive than their industrial counterparts.

[*See also* Chicken; Kentucky Fried Chicken; Poultry and Fowl; Sanders, Colonel.]

BIBLIOGRAPHY

Ellis, William. *The Country Housewife's Family Companion* [1750]. Prospect Books, 2000.

Florea, J. H. *ABC of Poultry Raising: A Complete Guide for the Beginner or Expert*. Chicago: Nelson-Hall, 1954.

Levenstien, Harvey. *Paradox of Plenty: A Social History of Eating in Modern America*. New York and London: Oxford University Press, 1993.

Percy, Pam. *The Complete Chicken: An Entertaining History of Chickens*. Stillwater, MN: Voyageur Press, 2002.

Smith, Andrew F. *The Saintly Scoundrel: The Life and Times of Dr. John Cook Bennett*. Champaigne, IL: University of Illinois Press, 1997.

Trager, James. *The Food Chronology*. New York: Henry Holt, 1995.

CATHY K. KAUFMAN

Chickpeas

The chickpea (*Cicer arietinum*) is a legume or pulse. It is one of the oldest foods known to humankind, having been among the first crops cultivated—along with wheat and barley—in the Fertile Crescent (modern Iraq) around 4000 B.C.E. The chickpea is a large, round seed, slightly pointed at one end, and grooved down the center. It is a larger relative of the garden pea, but there is only one to a pod. Because of its taproot system, the chickpea can withstand drought conditions by extracting water from deep in the soil. This allows it to thrive in dry climates. Although the color varies widely when grown in the Mediterranean, in the United States it is almost always light brown when ripe.

The chickpea was first brought to the New World by the Spanish and Portuguese conquerors and has become one of the basic ingredients of Mexican cooking. It is known in the southwestern states as the garbanzo bean from the Spanish for "chickpea," *garbanzo*. However, the chickpea also reached the United States with later immigrants, chiefly from Italy (where chickpeas are known as *ceci*), the Middle East, and the Indian subcontinent (where two varieties are grown: *besan* and the smaller variety, *channa*).

The chickpea prefers a relatively cool, dry climate so it is a useful winter crop to alternate with cereals. Half of the chickpeas eaten in the United States are grown in California. The rest come from eastern Washington State, Idaho, and Montana.

The chickpea is extremely versatile, hence its popularity. When ground into flour and mixed with olive oil and tahini, it is known as hummus, a Middle Eastern dish that has become a universally popular appetizer. In Mexican cooking, chickpeas are added to stews, such as *ropas viejas* and *cocido*, and they are used similarly in Spain, India, and France. Common uses in the United States are in soups, vegetable combinations, or as a component of salads.

The chickpea is highly nutritious—containing about 20 percent protein, 5 percent fat, and 55 percent carbohydrate, as well as malic and oxalic acid—and it has become a favorite among health-conscious Americans.

Chickpeas. Chickpeas and other dried vegetables and seeds, Sahadi's Middle Eastern foods, Brooklyn, New York. *Photograph by Joe Zarba*

[*See also* Beans; Middle Eastern Influences on American Food; Peas.]

BIBLIOGRAPHY

"Grain Legumes as Alternative Crops." 1987. Proceedings of a symposium sponsored by the Center for Alternative Crops and Products. University of Minnesota, July 23–24, 1987.

Grains, Pasta, and Pulses. Alexandria, VA: Time-Life Books, 1978.

McMahan, Jacqueline Higuera. *California Rancho Cooking.* Lake Hughes, CA: Olive Press, 1983.

McNair, James. *James McNair's Beans and Grains.* San Francisco: Chronicle Books, 1997.

South Dakota State University. *Chickpeas: A Potential Crop for the Midwest.* Bulletin 698. Brookings, SD: Agriculture Experiment Station, 1986.

JOSEPHINE BACON

Child, Julia

Julia Child (1912–2004) became the most celebrated American cook and an important cultural figure in a public career spanning more than forty years. Her appealing blend of education and entertainment in the groundbreaking television series *The French Chef* introduced classical cooking techniques, exotic ingredients, and specialty equipment to mainstream America in the 1960s and 1970s. As a popular television personality, cookbook author, and mentor, Child elevated the status of cooking, shaped modern notions of food, and contributed to the development of the culinary profession throughout the second half of the twentieth century.

Child's success as a media star is often attributed to her charming wit and uninhibited nature. The oldest daughter of a well-to-do family, Julia McWilliams was born in Pasadena, California, and graduated from Smith College in Northampton, Massachusetts, in 1934. A position with the Office of Strategic Services during World War II took her to posts in Asia, where she met her husband, Paul Child, who later became her collaborator. Her culinary career began at the age of thirty-seven, when the Childs moved to Paris and she enrolled in the Cordon Bleu cooking school.

Child's first cookbook, *Mastering the Art of French Cooking*, was the product of her collaboration with two Frenchwomen, Simone Beck and Louisette Bertholle. The three were partners in a Paris cooking school called L'École des Trois Gourmandes, and its insignia decorated the blouse Child later wore on *The French Chef*. The book's long route to publication is part of publishing lore.

Julia Child. *Culinary Archives & Museum at Johnson & Wales University, Providence, R.I.*

1963 to 1973, created the celebrity called "Julia" and institutionalized the televised cooking show.

Her role as an educator was paramount to the show's success and popularity. She approached haute cuisine with a sense of fun and fearlessness and emphasized simplicity over snobbery. Although she strayed from French cooking in successive series, she remained devoted to teaching home cooks the pleasures of preparing a meal—and to public television. She was also instrumental in the development of the American Institute of Wine and Food and the International Association of Culinary Professionals. She became a mentor to many chefs and was a role model for women in the field.

Soon after receiving the French Legion of Honor and just before her ninetieth birthday, Child left her home in Cambridge, Massachusetts, and the famous kitchen that was the set for her last three cooking shows to return to Southern California. In recognition of her role in American social history, the Smithsonian Institution acquired her original kitchen with nearly all of its contents, including the pegboard wall of pans and the Garland stove, and reinstalled it in the National Museum of American History in 2002.

[*See also* Celebrity Chefs; Cookbooks and Manuscripts, *subentries* From WWII to the 1960s *and* From 1970s to the Present; Radio and Television.]

Ten years in the making and rejected by Houghton Mifflin, its contracted publisher, *Mastering the Art of French Cooking* was ultimately published by Knopf in 1961 to great acclaim. The best-selling cookbook was the first to popularize the principles of French cooking to a broad-based American audience. Thorough instructions and consideration of available ingredients set a new standard in cookbook writing, a model for the many cookbooks on ethnic cuisines that followed in the 1970s.

Child achieved her greatest influence through television. Although it was initially broadcast on a Boston public television station, *The French Chef* quickly became a national sensation, watched by men and women, noncooks and cooks, and won the first of its five Emmy Awards in 1965, a landmark event for educational television. Its popularity was due in part to Child's sense of humor and the mistakes she handled with aplomb. Statuesque, with an unmistakable warbling voice, her manner and gaffes were frequently exaggerated and widely parodied. *The French Chef*, which aired from

BIBLIOGRAPHY

Beck, Simone, Louisette Bertholle, and Julia Child. *Mastering the Art of French Cooking*. New York: Knopf, 1961.
Child, Julia. *Cooking with Master Chefs*. New York: Knopf, 1993.
Child, Julia. *The French Chef Cookbook*. New York: Knopf, 1968.
Child, Julia. *From Julia Child's Kitchen*. New York: Knopf, 1975.
Child, Julia. *Julia Child's Menu Cookbook*. New York: Wings Books, 1991.
Child, Julia. *The Way to Cook*. New York: Knopf, 1989.
Child, Julia, with Nancy Barr. *In Julia Child's Kitchen with Master Chefs*. New York: Knopf, 1995.
Child, Julia, and Simone Beck. *Mastering the Art of French Cooking*. Vol. 2. New York: Knopf, 1970.
Child, Julia, with David Nussbaum. *Julia and Jacques: Cooking at Home*. New York: Knopf, 1999.
Child, Julia, with David Nussbaum. *Julia's Kitchen Wisdom: Essential Techniques and Recipes from a Lifetime of Cooking*. New York: Knopf, 2000.
Child, Julia, with E. S. Yntema. *Julia Child and Company*. New York: Knopf, 1978.
Child, Julia, with E. S. Yntema. *Julia Child and More Company*. New York: Knopf, 1979.
Fitch, Noël Riley. *Appetite for Life: The Biography of Julia Child*. New York: Doubleday, 1997.
Greenspan, Dorie. *Baking with Julia*. New York: Morrow, 1996.

LYNNE SAMPSON

Child, Lydia Maria

The daughter of a baker known for his Medford Crackers, Lydia Maria Francis was born near Boston in 1802 and grew up to become part of that city's intellectual scene. She eventually married David Child, a dedicated reformer. Mrs. Child also became an ardent reformer and was known especially for writing the antislavery book *An Appeal in Favor of That Class of Americans Called Africans* (1833). To support herself and her impractical husband, Child lived by her pen, and in 1829 she published one of the most popular and successful domestic books of the nineteenth century, *The Frugal Housewife*. Retitled *The American Frugal Housewife* when it was sold in England and Germany, the book does not give an accurate image of its author, who projected herself as a middle-aged housewife with a brood of children. In fact, Child was only twenty-six when the book was published, remained childless throughout her marriage, and lived a public life at a time when women were expected to confine themselves to domestic pursuits.

Child's theme of frugality clearly appealed to her reading public; by 1832 *The Frugal Housewife* had gone into seven editions. The book has a sober, cheeseparing tone, with recommendations to feed the family with scraps that otherwise would have been directed to the garbage pail and careful instructions for cooking the cheapest cuts of meat. "Calf's head should be cleansed with very great care," Child explains. "It is better to leave the wind-pipe on, for if it hangs out of the pot while the head is cooking, all the froth will escape through it." Her memorable aphorisms include admonishments such as, "Look to the grease pot, and see that nothing is there which might have served to nourish your own family or a poorer one." The book is an extended lecture on the morality of parsimony.

The money she earned from writing popular books was used to fund projects that the Childs hoped would correct social injustices. To this end, David Child, who knew nothing about farming, set off to Northampton, Massachusetts, to start a sugar beet farm. Like other antislavery reformers of their day, the Childs believed that if sugar beets could be grown throughout the United States, then the Caribbean sugarcane plantations—major incentives for perpetuating slavery—could be made obsolete. Unfortunately, David Child's attempt at farming only put him further into debt, causing his wife to work even harder by writing novels, children's books, magazine articles, and poems in addition to political treatises.

At the time of Child's death in 1880, the poet John Greenleaf Whittier wrote, "Wherever there was a brave word to be spoken, her voice was heard, and never without effect." While her zealous opposition to slavery should define her legacy, she is most remembered for a line from her poem "A Boy's Thanksgiving Day," published in *Flowers for Children*, volume 2 (1844): "Over the river, and through the wood, to Grandfather's house we go," which is sung by schoolchildren all over America each November.

[*See also* Cookbooks and Manuscripts, *subentry* From the Beginnings to 1860; Sugar Beets.]

BIBLIOGRAPHY

Clifford, Deborah Pickman. *Crusader for Freedom: A Life of Lydia Maria Child*. Boston: Beacon Press, 1992.
Karcher, Carolyn L. *The First Woman in the Republic: A Cultural Biography of Lydia Maria Child*. Durham, NC: Duke University Press, 1994.
Yellin, Jean Fagan. *Women and Sisters: The Antislavery Feminists in American Culture*. New Haven: Yale University Press, 1989.

BARBARA HABER

Chili

Chili is a dish consisting of meat (usually beef, coarsely ground or finely cubed) cooked in fat and then slowly simmered with red chilies (hot-spicy *Capsicum* peppers, fresh or dried, or both), a liquid such as water or meat stock, and seasonings such as cumin, garlic, oregano, salt, and sometimes other spices. Its consistency is halfway between a thick soup and a stew. Although other ingredients (onions and tomatoes, for example) can be added, chili's primary constituent is meat. Chili as we know it originated in the American Southwest, most likely in the region that became the state of Texas. Before the arrival of Europeans in the Western Hemisphere, similar dishes of meats stewed with peppers and herbs were no doubt prepared by Native Americans in those areas where peppers grew wild. Historians seeking the more modern roots of the specific dish called "chili" trace its origin to several possible sources: chuck wagon cooks on cattle drives, prospectors from the Southwest en route to the California gold rush, military field kitchens in the West, the kitchens of Texas prisons, immigrants from other countries who substituted local American ingredients in their own traditional recipes for highly spiced meat stews, and even a Spanish nun to whom the recipe

Chili. Jalapeño peppers. *Culinary Archives & Museum at Johnson & Wales University, Providence, R.I.*

Chili has always been especially associated with the state of Texas, where it is such a common and well-loved dish that it has come to be known simply as "a bowl of red"—a term popularized by the writer Frank X. Tolbert in his classic book titled *A Bowl of Red*. And in 1997, in recognition of chili's long-standing and deep-rooted connection with the state, the Texas legislature declared chili to be the "Official Texas State Dish."

In Texas, chili is a one-dish meal, traditionally served in a plain, heavy bowl and eaten with a spoon. Beef is by far the preferred meat in Texas chili, although game (especially venison) is also sometimes used. Purists insist that Texas chili should never contain beans—and some refuse to use tomatoes and onions too—but many Texans like their chili with beans (usually pinto beans), either added to the dish itself or served in a separate small bowl beside the chili. Sometimes soda crackers are crumbled over the serving of chili, adding more salt to the flavor and soaking up the layer of fat that often rises to the top of a bowl of Texas red. Occasionally chopped raw onions or fresh or pickled jalapeño peppers—or both onions and jalapeños—are used as a garnish as well. Regardless of its ingredients, however, spicy-hot Texas chili is usually washed down with plenty of iced tea or cold beer, although some people drink strong hot coffee with their chili.

Beyond the Lone Star State

In the late 1800s chili's popularity also began spreading to other parts of the United States, as visitors to Texas carried back home their newfound taste for this regional dish and as Texans themselves transported chili recipes with them throughout the country. At the Chicago World's Fair in 1893 thousands of people sampled Texas chili at the San Antonio Chili Stand. By the 1920s "chili parlors" or "chili joints"—which originated in Texas—were opening across America. Typically small, inexpensive, hole-in-the-wall diners located in industrial districts and working-class neighborhoods, these chili parlors not only served cheap bowls of chili but also became gathering places for men from various parts of the community, as the eating of chili expanded across social, economic, and ethnic lines. Although the number of chili parlors declined in the United States during World War II, more chili parlors began to open again in the 1950s, only to be eventually replaced by the inexpensive hamburger chains that were also being built around the country. One of the most famous purveyors of chili was Chasen's restaurant in Beverly Hills, founded in 1936, a classic California dining

for a chili-like dish was supposedly revealed in a vision. Whatever its origin, historians agree that chili began as a peasant dish prepared by poor people using cheap, inferior cuts of meat cooked together with other inexpensive, readily available ingredients, primarily peppers and onions. They also agree that chili is an American, not Mexican, dish—although chili is associated closely with the Mexican population in Texas, and dishes similar to chili can be found in Mexico, particularly in the north.

The city first associated with chili was San Antonio, Texas, where the cooking of a chili-like dish was documented in the 1820s. By the 1880s Mexican women dressed in embroidered peasant blouses and full skirts were selling homemade chili, tamales, enchiladas, and beans from individual stands set up around San Antonio's Military Plaza, a bustling, open-air municipal market in the heart of the city. A colorful part of San Antonio's history, these vendors, known as "chili queens," continued selling their spicy foods on the streets until 1943, when public health regulations finally forced them out of business, putting an end to one of the city's culinary traditions.

emporium that served chili to movie stars and film studio executives for almost six decades until it closed in 1995.

As the popularity of chili spread throughout America, recipes for this dish evolved to reflect the ingredients and taste preferences of local cooks in different parts of the country. From a simple Texas stew of meat and hot peppers, served in a bowl, chili also developed into a kind of topping for a number of other foods: rice, spaghetti, macaroni, corn chips, hamburgers, and hot dogs. The list of possible ingredients expanded too, so that you can find dishes called "chili" that are made with pork, bacon, sausage, lamb, mutton, or poultry; bell peppers, carrots, celery, corn, potatoes, turnips, or beans (lima, navy, pinto, kidney, and black); tomato juice, coffee, beer, whiskey, or tequila; thickeners such as flour, *masa harina*, or cracker meal; sugar, nuts, or unsweetened cocoa or chocolate (used for adding depth to the flavor); and such garnishes as sour cream, diced avocados, shredded cheese, and snipped chives. There are even vegetarian versions of chili, usually made with several kinds of beans to provide the protein. Chili recipes are reinterpreted and reinvented every time a cook sets foot in the kitchen to stir up a pot of this spicy stew.

Outside Texas some regional versions of chili have attained recognition in their own right. In Cincinnati, Ohio, in the early 1920s, two Macedonian immigrant brothers named Kiradjieff opened a restaurant, where they began serving a layered chili dish that came to be characteristic of that city. And in the 1940s the Greek Lambrinides family opened the first in their own chain of restaurants serving this particular dish. Cincinnati's famous "five-way chili" is composed of a layer of spaghetti on a shallow oval plate, topped with a layer of chili sauce made with ground beef seasoned with spices such as cinnamon, cardamom, allspice, and cloves. This is covered with a layer of kidney beans, followed by a layer of chopped raw onions and one of shredded cheddar cheese. (Sometimes the beans are served as the bottom layer.) "Two-way," "three-way," and "four-way" versions are eaten as well, which are merely the same dish with fewer layers of ingredients, always starting with a base of spaghetti and a topping of chili sauce. Oyster crackers are the traditional garnish for this special Cincinnati dish.

In some parts of the Midwest any chili served with pasta is called a "chili mac." In Kansas City, Missouri, and Chicago, Illinois, a "chili mac" consists of chili served over cooked macaroni; in some other places the macaroni is mixed with the chili before serving. And

chili even turns up as a filling for Cornish miner chili pasties in Michigan's Upper Peninsula.

The state of New Mexico lays claim to its own dish, called "*chile*," which is made primarily of red or green peppers stewed with onions, garlic, other herbs and spices, and water or meat stock. The consistency of a thick sauce, New Mexico *chile* can be eaten on its own, used as a sauce to garnish other dishes, or included as an ingredient in other recipes. New Mexico's *chile verde* (green *chile*) can be made with any of several varieties of New Mexican green peppers, which have first been roasted and peeled. These processed green peppers are then used fresh, frozen, or canned. *Chile colorado* (red *chile*) is made with dried, ripe New Mexican red peppers—whole, crushed into flakes, or ground into powder. These types of processed green and red New Mexican peppers are also major ingredients in *chile* stews containing meats such as pork, beef, lamb, mutton, or poultry as well as starches such as garbanzo beans, corn, or *posole* (hominy).

Chili Products

The commercial development of chili powder spice mixtures made chili easier to prepare and helped spread the popularity of this dish to other parts of America, particularly to those regions where dried red peppers (whole or powdered) were not as commonly available as in the Southwest. The first commercial chili powders were manufactured and marketed in Texas. In the early 1890s DeWitt Clinton Pendery established his Mexican Chilley Supply Company in Fort Worth and began selling his brand of "Chiltomaline" powder to cafés and hotels in the state, while also touting the healthful properties of his product. At about the same time, William Gebhardt of New Braunfels, Texas, began packaging and selling his own chili spice mixture, and in 1896 he built a factory in San Antonio to produce "Gebhardt's Eagle Chili Powder." Both the Pendery and Gebhardt companies were still making chili powders at the beginning of the twenty-first century.

Chili powders—commercial or homemade—are a pungent blend of spices, including powdered dried red peppers (mild, medium, or hot, or any combination of these) mixed with ground cumin, dried Mexican oregano, garlic powder, and salt. Other spices can be included too. Powdered *ancho* peppers are usually the primary ingredient, and cumin gives all chili powder mixtures their characteristic taste. Several varieties of chili powder are marketed in the United States, each with its own particular flavor based on the type of peppers used, the other spices added, and the proportions in which they are combined.

By the early 1900s commercially canned chili (meat with peppers and sometimes beans) was being produced in several places, including Texas, Oklahoma, and Missouri. This new convenience food in a can also helped spread the popularity of chili around the country, although many cooks still consider canned chili to be greatly inferior to the homemade variety. By 1980 chili was one of the best-selling canned foods in America; in the early twenty-first century most of the chili eaten in the United States comes out of a can. Commercial frozen chili is also available.

Chili Cook-offs

Chili cook-offs are culinary competitions that have become so widespread in the United States that they are part of the country's culture. Thousands of cook-offs are held every year, many of them under the auspices of the Chili Appreciation Society International (CASI) or the International Chili Society (ICS). Both organizations sponsor official chili cook-offs at the local, state, regional, and national levels, in which cooks compete for cash prizes (at ICS cook-offs) or trophies (at CASI cook-offs) and millions of dollars are raised for charity.

The first official championship chili cook-off, sanctioned by CASI, was held in 1967 in the remote old mining town of Terlingua, Texas. Since that time, official chili cook-offs have been staged throughout the country, during every month of the year, and in many foreign countries as well. At CASI cook-offs the chili is judged on aroma, consistency, color, taste, and aftertaste. No beans, macaroni, rice, hominy, or other similar ingredients are permitted. At ICS cook-offs there are three categories of competition: red chili, made with any kind of meat cooked with hot red peppers, various spices, and other ingredients (but no beans or pasta); green chili, made with meat (usually pork or chicken), fresh green peppers (such as Anaheims, *poblanos*, and jalapeños), and other green ingredients (such as tomatillos and cilantro); and salsa. The two types of chili are judged on their flavor, texture of meat, consistency, blend of spices, aroma, and color. Despite their required entry fees, specific rules, and official judges, these chili cook-offs are fun for everyone—culinary events that bring together people of many different ages, professions, social classes, races, and ethnic groups from locations all over America.

[*See also* Cincinnati Chili; Mexican American Food; Southwestern Regional Cookery.]

BIBLIOGRAPHY

Bridges, Bill. *The Great Chili Book*. New York: Lyons and Burford, 1994.
Butel, Jane. *Chili Madness: A Passionate Cookbook*. New York: Workman, 1980.
Cooper, Joe E. *With or without Beans*. Dallas, TX: W. S. Henson, 1952.
DeWitt, Dave, Mary Jane Wilan, and Melissa T. Stock. *Hot and Spicy Chili*. Rocklin, CA: Prima, 1994.
Hudgins, Sharon. "Red Dust: Powdered Chiles and Chili Powder." In *Spicing Up the Palate: Studies of Flavourings—Ancient and Modern*, edited by Harlan Walker. Proceedings of the Oxford Symposium on Food and Cookery 1992. Totnes, U.K.: Prospect Books, 1993.
Jameson, W. C. *The Ultimate Chili Cookbook: The History, Geography, Fact, and Folklore of Chile*. Plano, TX: Republic of Texas Press, 1999.
O'Hara, Christopher B. *The Ultimate Chili Book*. Guilford, CT: Lyons Press, 2001.
Stern, Jane, and Michael Stern. *Chili Nation: The Ultimate Chili Cookbook with Recipes from Every State in the Nation*. New York: Broadway Books, 1998.
Tolbert, Frank X. *A Bowl of Red*. Garden City, NY: Doubleday, 1966.

SHARON HUDGINS

Chinese American Food

Food and eating have long occupied the Chinese in both the intellectual and sensual realms. While Chinese culinary art developed slowly over millennia, it did absorb and retain past experiences as it incorporated foreign customs and commodities. A defining principle among the very early Chinese was that those who ate raw or uncooked food and did not eat appropriate amounts of grain were regarded as non-Chinese. Another was adherence to the *fan-cai* (*fan-tsai*) principle, *fan* being rice and other grains, and *cai* (*tsai*) being vegetables, meats, and other foods. This philosophy mandated the combination of both to prepare a balanced meal. In addition to these principles, Chinese food differs from the foods of the Western world because it aims at creating and enjoying outstanding dishes at all levels of society. All Chinese meals should incorporate all of the basic flavors, which the Chinese believe are acid, salt, sweet, bitter, and pungent.

Chinese food has always incorporated a theory of elemental forces: the duality of *yin* and *yang*, in terms of food, preparation, and eating styles. To the contemporary Chinese, food is more than just nourishment; it plays a part in preventing and treating disease. Chinese food is consumed, metabolized, and then transformed into *Qi*, or life's energy. Different dishes are selected to maintain bodily harmony.

Chinese Immigration

China, known to its inhabitants as the Middle Kingdom, is a vast land of 3.7 million square miles, and by the beginning of the twenty-first century it had become the most populous nation in the world, with more than 1.2 billion people living in China and 57 million more outside of their homeland. U.S. census figures suggest that fewer than 5 million Chinese were living in the United States in 2000. The first American census to count Asian populations, in 1830, determined that the number of Chinese in the United States was three. Chinese have since become the largest group among Asian immigrants to the United States. Most are legal immigrants, but there are large numbers of undocumented residents. No matter how and when they came, those who remain several generations tend to behave and eat differently than do their newer immigrant compatriots.

Changing Chinese Immigrant Food Habits

Some immigrants seek the American dream and try Western food when they first arrive in the United States. Frequently those with children in school do so at first and then realize that they want their offspring to know about their own heritage. A few years after arriving in the United States, Chinese-born parents typically revert to serving traditional Chinese meals. They do so at least at dinnertime and almost always at festivals and life-cycle events, such as birthdays, weddings, and funerals. When immigrant families go back to eating more Chinese food, they use foods of the region from which they came. If they did not come directly from China, they eat their Chinese food with touches of the places from which they came.

First-generation American-born Chinese (ABCs) and their children eat more American foods in American ways at breakfasts and lunches during the week. They eat more Chinese food on weekends. Those who live in proximity to parents or large Chinese populations eat more Chinese breakfasts and sometimes eat American food only at lunch. Immigrants and ABCs mostly eat Chinese-tasting dinner-type foods. Immigrants living in areas with few Chinese families, while they eat somewhat Western style, still make their main meals with Chinese-tasting foods. Subsequent generations, particularly those living away from Chinatown areas, also eat more Western-style foods, even at their dinner meals. However, they do continue to maintain their Chinese eating habits, preparing many foods with Chinese tastes, particularly at festivals and family gatherings and at meals celebrating life-cycle events.

Men and women of mixed marriages, including some 72,000 military wives who immigrated from 1966 to 1981, Westernize their food behaviors faster than do families in which both spouses are Chinese. According to the 2000 U.S. census, more than 5 million children under the age of five are of mixed racial heritage, many of these part Chinese. Those who are, and other families with one Chinese parent or an adopted Chinese child, eat some or a lot of Chinese food at meals to continue customary food tastes of one or more family members; however, they do add a few Western food items. Some eat meals in which foods of their old and new homelands are mixed. Besides food differences, there are others in these multiracial homes; some of the immigrants speak one or more Chinese dialects at home, and they learn to or already do speak English. The more Chinese is spoken in these homes, the greater the Chinese food influences, but in mixed marriages, it is more common that only English is spoken, unless a Chinese parent lives with the family.

Early and Later Chinese Immigrants

As the first Asian group to come to the United States in significant numbers, the Chinese were mostly from the south of their country. By the end of 1852 about twenty thousand male immigrants had come at their own initiation, many needing money, to what they called *gum san*, or "Golden Mountain." They gave this name to America because they planned to pan for gold and return home rich. In 1865 more Chinese men came, this time to help build the transcontinental railroad. The Central Pacific Railroad Company initiated their coming, hiring thousands of Chinese men. Prior to these immigrations, perhaps only one hundred or so Chinese lived in the United States.

Over the following two dozen years, between 150,000 and 250,00 Chinese came to the United States. The Chinese Exclusion Act of 1882 made it illegal for more Chinese laborers to enter the United States, and it prohibited naturalization of those already here. After 1882 additional laws restricted more immigration. Many Chinese returned to their native land. It is estimated that between 1890 and 1920 the Chinese population in the United States fell to about sixty thousand. The number of Chinese in the United Sates did not increase much immediately thereafter, though some Chinese men did go to Hong Kong to get brides. The exclusion acts were repealed in 1943; from then until the early 1960s, fewer than 200,000 additional Chinese came to the United States.

Chinese Kitchen. Nineteenth-century print. *Culinary Archives & Museum at Johnson & Wales University, Providence, R.I.*

Early Chinese Food in the United States

When mining and railroad work were no longer available and discrimination against the Chinese was at its peak, many Chinese men found work as cooks and later opened restaurants. These eateries served primarily foods of their native land to other Chinese patrons. Later they served much the same fare to those willing to try Chinese food. As early as the 1860s in California and the 1870s in Louisiana, Chinese immigrants became involved in fishing and farming, producing food for Asian restaurants and markets. Dried shrimp were produced for export to China while importers began to provide Chinese foods in the United States.

Rare among those who opened these Chinese eateries was a trained cook. Even more rare was someone from China who had a lot of experience eating fine food in restaurants. The immigrants were poor working-class men who cooked and served the foods they remembered eating before they left southern China. At first, they cooked with neither familiar ingredients nor any knowledge about the finer aspects of their own cuisine. What they knew best was hunger and satiating it by eating lots of grain foods, mainly rice and noodles. To them, meat meant pork; chicken was a luxury; beef was rarely encountered; and lamb was virtually unknown. Therefore, when they cooked for others in the United States, they prepared improvisations of foods remembered. But, for their non-Chinese customers, they quickly learned that those in the United States liked beef, chicken, and other meats. So the early Chinese restaurant cooks made southern Chinese food with more animal protein than they would eat themselves. Chinese restaurants still emphasize meats and serve fewer vegetables than are commonly served in China.

Changing Chinese Food Availability

Immigrants from elsewhere in China did not arrive in large numbers until after Congress rescinded Chinese exclusion acts. Therefore, before the 1940s, almost all Chinese food in the United States was Cantonese as the earliest immigrants were from the southern province then called Canton (now Guangdong). After 1965, major immigration restrictions eased, and the Chinese population grew to about 500,000 men and women. Many of the newer immigrants came from regions other than southern China. When immigration restrictions eased even more in 1981 and 1987, additional immigrants came from all over China, Taiwan, and Hong Kong, as well as Vietnam and elsewhere in Southeast Asia, and a few came from Cuba and Latin America. By the beginning of the twenty-first century, there were about 3.5 million legal Chinese immigrants and many undocumented residents.

Since changes in the law, Chinese immigrants have not only arrived in increasing numbers, but they have also increased in diversity. Their economic status and occupations are also more diverse, as are the Chinese cuisines available to them and others in Chinese restaurants. Foods of many of China's more than twenty provinces and three major urban jurisdictions (Beijing, Guangzhou, and Shanghai)—and those of many of China's minority populations, such as Muslims, Mongols, and Hakka—are served in Chinese restaurants. Diverse Chinese cuisines are also served in many Chinese homes.

Chinese Food in Homes

With more women among the immigrants, particularly since the 1960s, there is more emphasis on Chinese family life. The diversity of immigrant occupations has also expanded into industries not related to food. Chinese immigrants, particularly those with more disposable income, are now maintaining more traditional eating habits. They are also maintaining close family and friendship rituals that revolve around food as well as traditional practices that include incorporating food and participating in other food-related Chinese social customs. For example, many Chinese families go to a nearby Chinatown or Chinese restaurant once a week for a Chinese meal after they buy Chinese groceries. They particularly like going early in the day and ending their trip by having dim sum (which means "dot the heart"), those small dishes that are common in southern China.

Chinese food has become more widely available in the United States. Imported foods that were popular in the 1950s and 1960s include bamboo shoots, Chinese sausages, cuttlefish, dried bean curd, pressed duck, dry fruit, dried oysters, fresh and preserved ginger, mushrooms, oranges, pomelos, preserved duck eggs, greater amounts and varieties of rice, slab sugar, many kinds of soy sauces, sweetmeats, and yams. More recent imports include arrowroot, bean sauces, birds' nests, chestnut flour, dried duck kidneys and other organ meats, dried persimmons and other dried fruits, fish fins (including sharks' fins), fresh and dried lily buds, sea cucumber, various seaweeds, tamarind, and taro root. Also coming in are native fresh and preserved greens, bamboo ware, cleavers, chopsticks, and other tableware. An increasing network of American farmers is producing fresh Chinese vegetables and herbs for Chinatown supermarkets; and

live fish, exotic seafood, and even turtles raised on American farms are for sale.

Chinese Foods and Food Behaviors

In the United States as in China, the importance of food to the Chinese cannot be overemphasized. To the Chinese, nothing is more important than eating. What the Chinese cook and eat can depend on availability, geography, trade, and the family's economic condition; however, no matter the food, the staple of the diet is one or another of many grain foods, primarily those made with rice or wheat. Pork is the most commonly consumed meat, though eaten in small amounts, and dairy products are rarely part of the Chinese diet. The Chinese eat vegetables in large quantities, and they enjoy beautiful large fruits, usually shared at a meal's end.

Chinese Americans often attempt to make everything taste Chinese, even if they are using locally available ingredients that are not Chinese. As the Chinese population in the United States grows, so do the number and size of their restaurants, which have become the second most popular ethnic cuisine (after Italian) among those who eat out. One-third of the ethnic restaurants in the United States are Chinese, and most are family run.

Merchants are importing more of China's own foodstuffs for the Chinese and for Westerners. They are servicing the increasing number of Asian markets and large American supermarkets that sell more Chinese ingredients than ever before. Large American supermarkets sell more than one kind of soy sauce and bean curd, snow peas, Chinese greens, fresh ginger, sesame oil, various bean sauces, rice wines and vinegars, Asian noodles, and often frozen dumplings that some call "Peking ravioli."

Chinese American Food in the Future

While Chinese families still maintain the central role of food in their lives, this practice is diminishing in successive generations. About half of all Chinese immigrants own their own homes and cook Chinese and Western meals at home. Those who can afford to do so eat more and more meals away from home, usually in coffee shops or restaurants.

In the United States, many Chinese Americans still enjoy family and banquet meals with a whole fish to represent prosperity. They still celebrate Chinese New Year and at that time find their greatest attachment to their roots. While many have dropped some traditional food practices, theirs is a society that mirrors practices back in

China, which has begun to allow many Western fast food eateries. The first American-born generation is changing considerably, as are the younger generations of Chinese in China and in other countries. They are consuming more fast food out as well as lots of carbonated soda, and they are bringing these and other foods into their homes.

It is interesting to note that families of professionals are becoming more acculturated than are the less affluent, many of whom cannot afford to move away from a Chinatown. Another change is that they purchase more and more Chinese frozen foods and Chinese take-out foods, and do less cooking; so do most Americans. As Chinese Americans become more Americanized, they tend to eat more red meat and larger amounts of all meats. They drink more coffee and less tea, and they consume more sugar and fat than their ancestors did when living in China. They exhibit many other Western ways. They do not cut their foods into small pieces before cooking them, and they are beginning to add salt and pepper at the table, a practice never popular in China. They are also ordering fewer dishes with fish maw, duck or chicken feet, tripe and other offal, and they are eating fewer "thousand-year eggs" (which are actually processed for about one hundred days).

Main Meals

At lunches and dinners, the Chinese in the United States still prefer their grain food in individual bowls. They eat lots of rice or noodles at main meals, and they put their *cai,* or meat and vegetable accompaniment dishes, in bowls or on platters in the center of the table. The Chinese in the United States still eat celebration or banquet meals one main dish at a time and at ordinary meals put all the dishes on the table at the same time.

Most Chinese people still eat three meals daily, and they almost always combine a little meat with one or more vegetables or unripe fruit when making a *cai* dish. Many Chinese people in the United States snack two or three times each day, a practice in which Chinese in their native land rarely indulge. They still consider meals eaten with family ordinary while special meals are occasions to be shared with guests. These special meals are often eaten away from home because the younger Chinese do not have the time, do not know how, or do not want to prepare these special foods. While Chinese Americans still eat less meat than typical Americans, they now eat lots of ice cream, candy, pizza, and pastries, all items that were never part of the Chinese diet.

Those Chinese who adopt more American food and other behaviors are sometimes called "bananas," meaning that they are yellow on the outside and white on the inside. Others call them "bamboo sticks," indicating lack of roots in either culture. An interesting change is taking place among many second- and later-generation Chinese. They are increasingly concerned with transmitting their cultural heritage to their children and grandchildren. They are buying them Chinese cookery and holiday books and subscribing to Chinese food magazines such as *Flavor and Fortune*. More and more American-born Chinese who neither speak, read, nor write Chinese are starting to follow some Chinese customs, such as eating more Chinese food and celebrating more Chinese festivals with their children.

Immigrants are changing the Chinese food scene by virtue of their numbers and their varied food behaviors. With fewer extended families, the lack of elders at home to cook for the children is one reason immigrants are changing their food habits quickly and eating more American fast and prepared food. Young adults in high school or college, particularly those living away from their elders, are also exposed to more Western and fast foods, and they, too, are eating very differently from their parents.

In spite of this assimilation, the extensive interest in food that is characteristic of Chinese culture does continue in the United States. Chinese Americans spend a larger proportion of their income on food than do other Americans. They still maintain respect for the elderly, though less than before. They still allow their elders at the table to have the best food at the table. The Chinese still ask, when greeting another person, "Have you eaten?" And they still observe many diet and health practices from their mother country and region.

Regional Differences

While Chinese foods maintain cultural continuity, there are some regional differences. Some say that Shanghai food is sweet though bland, that Sichuan is spicy, and that Cantonese is somewhere in the middle. These are oversimplifications, as are most regional differences. For all Chinese, no matter where they came from, main meals revolve around a staple carbohydrate food that accounts for 60 to 80 percent of their calories. This staple is rice or rice noodles in all areas except the North, where wheat and other grains are the major staple foods. Breakfast and lunch throughout China can be similar, or lunch and the evening meal can resemble each other. In the South it is more of the former; in the North, more of the latter. Main meals mean a large amount of grain food, called *fan* in the South and *mi* in the North. Other dishes are called *tsai* or *cai*, respectively, to flavor the grains. *Fan* means rice, and it can stand for the word "meal." In the North and South *chifan* or *mi* also means meal.

Southern Chinese Food The foods of the South, really of Guangzhou (Canton) and the entire Guangdong province, were those first known in the United States. Here fresh foods are available year-round and are served mild, their ingredients often cooked quickly to show off their distinct individual characteristics. There is a large selection of foods from land and sea, many foods naturalized from outside of China, such as sweet potatoes and tomatoes. Southern Chinese like roast pork and poultry, and rich chicken broths; a minimum of soy and other sauces. Few herbs are used except for medicinal reasons.

One of the primary cooking techniques is stir-frying. All regions stir-fry, but not so often, and everywhere the Chinese also steam, steep, boil, roast, red-cook (cook in soy sauce), clear-simmer, stew, deep-fry, blanch, cold-mix, salt, smoke, and pickle their foods. The South is best known for dishes with birds' nests and sharks' fins, particularly at banquet and life-cycle meals, and for fried rice and dim sum dishes (called *dian xin* in the North).

Eastern Chinese Food Shanghai foods tend to be a little sweeter than those of other Chinese regions, and they have a rich flavor and some delicacy. Many are red-cooked and simmered or stewed with a variety of soy sauces. Shanghai foods are also cooked with vinegar and with added sweetness from regular or slab brown sugar. Foods of this region also include those from other provinces, including those of Gansu and Zhejiang as well as foods from the southern province of Fujian, the ancestral home of many Chinese who immigrated to Southeast Asia and to the United States. Meals from Fujian come with two or more soups as well as stewed and red dishes. Their color comes from the red wine lees left after making wines based on red rice. This region is known for its red-cooked pork and its use of superior soy sauce.

Western Chinese Food Foods from the western region are primarily from the provinces of Sichuan and Hunan and surrounding areas. They are often spicy, incorporating lots of black and Sichuan peppercorns (of the genus *Xanthoxylum*), which are popularly known as fagara and also often call for hot chilies and piquant bean sauces.

Many of the dishes whose origins come from this western region are oily; some are double cooked and made hot and spicy, though banquet foods rarely are. Others incorporate smoky tea flavors. Many dishes incorporate nuts, cloud ear mushrooms, and chicken fat. This region is known for its hot and sour soup, twice-cooked pork, and Yunnan ham.

Northern Chinese Food The cooking of the northern region is associated with China's capital, Beijing. The northern Chinese use more wheat and other grains as their staple foods, making them into steamed breads, pancakes, and noodle dishes. Onions, garlic, and scallions are used in most dishes, except by Buddhist monks, who avoid these foods, as they are believed to increase sexual energy. Peking duck, usually a banquet dish, is roasted and served with bread made as a bun or a pancake. It is spread with a dollop of hoisin sauce and topped scallions, with or without cucumber strips. This adds coolness to the crisp skin of the duck, the only part served first. The meat and bones are made into one or more other dishes served at the same Peking duck banquet. Foods of this region can be cooked with lots of wine, and they can have many strong flavors. Quite a few come laced with ground white pepper and are salty; some are smoked. Lamb, rarely eaten in the rest of China, is grilled or stir-fried often in this region, as are many Muslim, Mongol, or other minority population foods. Popular dishes include sweet and sour fish, steamed buns, chicken velvet, and dumplings.

Chinese Food and Health

Chinese people are not only interested in the foods they eat, but they also try to balance these foods at meals to maintain optimum health. This philosophic balance, or duality, involves always having some grain, or yin, at every meal, with some *cai* (*tsai*), or yang, foods. *Yin* is considered cold, mild, and bland while *cai* (*tsai*) is yang, or hot, rich, strong, and spicy. Foods and conditions or illnesses are classified by the duality of yin or yang. When one has a yin condition, the Chinese recommend eating a yang food, and vice versa. In the United States, immigrant Chinese cannot always verbalize which disease or which food belongs to one or the other of these dualities, yet they use many traditional pairings.

Besides adherence to this duality, there are related cultural traditions that are also observed in the Chinese humoral theory of food. For example, the Chinese do not serve their elders cold foods, such as bean sprouts and white turnips. They know that older people already have weak blood, and these foods would weaken it further. Rather, they give them hot foods, such as ginger, to strengthen the heart, which is a yang organ. They also give new mothers lots of hot foods for thirty days postpartum, including eggs, chicken soup, liver, and gingerroot. They encourage new mothers to avoid most fruits and vegetables because they are considered philosophically cold.

Chinese Americans in the United States

The Chinese assimilate less rapidly than most other ethnic groups. Low-income Chinese and those of all incomes who live in or near a Chinatown maintain their traditional health practices and have a lower incidence of alcohol abuse than do second- and third-generation Chinese Americans.

Many cookbooks have been published about Chinese food, quite a few with Americanized Chinese recipes. However, few food books have been published in English about Chinese food behaviors, as have very few research articles. Publications confirm earlier research which shows that in the twenty-first century soup is still the beverage of choice, special foods are still being purchased for the elderly, and special foods are still very popular for life-cycle events and at banquets.

California and New York have the largest Chinese populations and the largest number of Chinese eateries and markets for Chinese food. In 2001 California had about 1.5 million Chinese residents; New York had about half that number; and Hawaii had less than a quarter of those who lived in New York. The next most populous states are, in decreasing order, Texas, New Jersey, Massachusetts, Illinois, and Washington.

Chinese Restaurant. Mr. Wonton, a Chinese restaurant in Brooklyn, New York. *Photograph by Joe Zarba*

Chinese food is changing in China, in the United States, and everywhere. The newer immigrants are coming with still different variations of Chinese food. The advantages they have in maintaining their traditions are greater availability of Chinese food as well as more Chinese and non-Chinese who know, understand, accept, and practice food habits similar to their own.

They and non-Chinese people in the United States will continue to change what they think is Chinese food and what they eat that is called Chinese food. The Chinese American population is projected to triple by 2020 to about 10 percent of the U.S. population. What Chinese food will be popularly consumed then is unknown because different cultural values will continue to effect Chinese food. In the past, the Chinese have traditionally exhibited resistance to assimilation, even in their food habits, often the last behavior to be acculturated. No one knows if those Chinese not yet part of the American mainstream will continue to retain some cultural affiliation.

[*See also* Duck; Dumplings; Rice; Soy Sauce; Soybeans.]

BIBLIOGRAPHY

Anderson, E. N. *The Food of China.* New Haven, CT: Yale University Press, 1988.

Ang, Catharina Y. W., KeShun Liu, and Yao-Wen Huang, eds. *Asian Foods, Science, and Technology.* Lancaster, PA: Technomic Publishing Company, 1999.

Buchanan, Keith, Charles P. Fitzgerald, and Colin A Ronan. *China: The Land and the People.* New York: Crown, 1981.

Chang, K. C. *Food in Chinese Culture: Anthropological and Historical Perspectives.* New Haven, CT: Yale University Press, 1977.

Chinese America: History and Perspectives. San Francisco: Chinese Historical Society of America, 1987.

Huang, H. T. *Fermentations and Food Science.* Vol. 6, pt. 5 of *Science and Civilization in China,* edited by Joseph Needham. Cambridge, UK: Cambridge University Press, 2000.

Jing, Jun, ed. *Feeding China's Little Emperors: Food, Children, and Social Change.* Stanford, CA: Stanford University Press, 2000.

Koo, Linda Chih-ling. *Nourishment of Life: Health in Chinese Society.* Hong Kong: Commercial Press, 1982.

Meiselman, Herbert L., ed. *Dimensions of the Meal: The Science, Culture, Business, and Art of Eating.* Gaithersburg, MD: Aspen Publishers, 2000.

Miscevic, Dusanka, and Peter Kwong. *Chinese Americans: The Immigrant Experience.* Southport, CT: Hugh Lauter Levin Associates, 2000.

Newman, Jacqueline M. *Chinese-American Foods, Customs, and Culture.* Beijing, China: Chinese Dietetic Culture Society, 1998.

Newman, Jacqueline M. *Chinese Cookbooks: An Annotated English-Language Compendium/Bibliography.* New York: Garland, 1987.

Newman, Jacqueline M. *Food Culture in China.* Westport, CT: Greenwood Press, 2004.

Newman, Jacqueline M. *Melting Pot: An Annotated Bibliography and Guide to Food and Nutrition Information for Ethnic Groups in America.* 2nd ed. New York: Garland, 1993.

Pan, Lynn, ed. *The Encyclopedia of the Chinese Overseas.* Cambridge, MA: Harvard University Press, 1999.

Roberts, J. A. G. *China to Chinatown in the West.* London: Reaktion, 2002.

Simoons, Frederick J. *Food in China: A Cultural and Historical Inquiry.* Boca Raton, FL: CRC Press, 1991.

Tachiki, Amy, E. Wolf, F. Odo, and B. E. Wong, eds. *Roots: An Asian American Reader.* Los Angeles: Continental Graphics, 1971.

Tchen, John Kuo Wei. *New York before Chinatown: Orientalism and the Shaping of American Culture, 1776–1882.* Baltimore: Johns Hopkins University Press, 1999.

Wilkinson, Endymion. *Chinese History: A Manual.* Cambridge, MA: Harvard University Asia Center, 1998.

Wittwer, Sylvan, Youtai Yu, Han Sun, and Lianzheng Wang. *Feeding a Billion: Frontiers of Chinese Agriculture.* East Lansing: Michigan State University Press, 1987.

Wong, Benita. *Food Habits and Customs of the Han and Six Dynasties Era.* Ann Arbor, MI: Chinese Association for Folklore, 1982.

Wu, David Y. H., and Chee-beng Tan. *Changing Chinese Foodways in Asia.* Hong Kong: Chinese University Press, 2001.

Wu, David Y. H., and Sidney C. H. Cheung. *The Globalization of Chinese Food.* Honolulu: University of Hawaii Press, 2002.

Zhou, Zhao, and George Ellis. *The Healing Cuisine of China: 300 Recipes for Vibrant Health and Longevity.* Rochester, VT: Healing Arts Press, 1998.

JACQUELINE M. NEWMAN

Chipped Beef

Chipped beef, or dried beef, is made from the lean cuts of top round, bottom round, or sirloin tip or knuckle. The beef is brined, then dried and sometimes smoked to preserve the meat, before being shaved—or chipped—into thin pieces. The end product's light weight and resistance to decay have made it the ideal food for wayfarers for centuries, as well as the perfect ration for soldiers and sailors. Creamed chipped beef on toast was served so often in U.S. military mess halls during World War II that it came to be known by the earthy name "shit on a shingle."

[*See also* Combat Food; Meat; Ship Food.]

BIBLIOGRAPHY

Chapman, Robert L., ed. *Dictionary of American Slang.* 3rd ed. New York: HarperCollins, 1995.

Lovegren, Sylvia. *Fashionable Food: Seven Decades of Food Fads.* New York: Macmillan, 1995.

Miller-Cory House Museum and the New Jersey Historical Society. *Pleasures of Colonial Cooking.* Newark, NJ: The Society, 1982.

SYLVIA LOVEGREN

Chocolate

This entry includes two subentries:
Historical Overview
Later Developments

Historical Overview

Chocolate, a product derived from the fruit of the cacao tree (*Theobroma cacao*), originated in the New World. In pre-Columbian times, the Olmec and Maya peoples of Central America figured out how to bring out the rich flavor of cacao beans through a complicated process that involved fermenting and roasting. Christopher Columbus encountered the cacao bean—which he mistook for a type of almond, noting that it was highly prized by the natives—on his fourth voyage in 1502, on the island of Guanaja, off Honduras. Hernán Cortés, during his invasion of Mexico in 1519, found the Aztec emperor and nobles consuming vast quantities of cacao in the form of a dense, frothy beverage thickened with cornmeal and flavored with chilies, vanilla, spices, and other additions. Cacao beans were introduced before 1585 into Spain. A beverage made from ground beans combined with sugar, vanilla, and water became a favorite drink of kings and nobles. This beverage was disseminated from Spain throughout Europe, reaching England by 1657.

Colonial Americans acquired large quantities of cacao beans from the West Indies, and drinking chocolate was served as a hot beverage by the late seventeenth century. Since it was also a popular drink in Mexico, cacao beans were imported into the Spanish possessions in California, Florida, Louisiana, and the Southwest prior to these lands being acquired by the United States. As in Mexico and Europe, chocolate was consumed mainly in beverage form, although consumption never reached the levels later attained by tea or coffee in America.

The processing of cacao beans in America did not begin until the mid-eighteenth century. One early chocolate manufacture was Dr. James Baker, who in 1780 began operating a small mill in Dorchester, Massachusetts. His son, Walter Baker, continued to expand the business, which eventually became Walter Baker and Company. It was sold to General Foods in 1927; a number of products, notably solid baking chocolate, are still sold under the Baker name in the early 2000s.

Attempts were first made to convert cacao into a solid in the late eighteenth century, but the result was a dry,

Bitter Chocolate. Hershey's advertisement, early twentieth century.

brittle bar. In 1815, the Dutch chemist Coenraad Van Houten developed a process to make chocolate easier to mix with water in order to make a beverage. He pressed out most of the fat and then put the resulting dry cocoa through an alkalizing process. His cocoa powder, patented in 1928, became known as Dutch chocolate; it was darker in color and milder in flavor. Dutch cocoa powder changed the way hot chocolate was prepared and also simplified the manufacture of chocolate in solid form.

American cookbooks throughout the nineteenth century included an expanding array of recipes made with chocolate. Although early chocolate cakes were made to serve with drinking chocolate, rather than containing the ingredient themselves, chocolate was the dominant flavor in blancmanges, creams, cream pies, custards, éclairs, jellies, jumbles, macaroons, puddings, soufflés, syrups, and tarts. In addition to its use in hot beverages, it was also used to make frappes, chocolate ice water, and even wine with a chocolate flavor. Chocolate ice cream became

popular, as did chocolate syrups for soda-fountain creations. Chocolate icing for yellow or white cakes was among the first uses of chocolate in cake baking, but subsequently cocoa or solid chocolate became an important ingredient in cakes and cookies themselves. Chocolate was used extensively in home candy making; fudge, chocolate drops, dipped bonbons, and chocolate-coated nuts were popular. Although the price of chocolate declined throughout the nineteenth century, chocolate was frequently adulterated and extended with peanuts, oats, or powdered rice, or colored with annatto.

Chocolate candies and the techniques that made them were imported from Europe, particularly from England, France, Switzerland, and Austria during the late nineteenth century. As European chocolate-making discoveries filtered into the United States during the nineteenth century, chocolate manufacturing rapidly expanded. Confectioners began coating candy with chocolate. By the 1870s, chocolate-covered candy and chocolate caramels were important American businesses.

Walter M. Lowney, a candy maker from Boston specializing in handmade chocolates, exhibited his wares at Chicago's Columbian Exposition in 1893. Milton S. Hershey, a caramel maker from Lancaster, Pennsylvania, visited Lowney's exhibit, and at the exposition Hershey also viewed the chocolate-making machinery manufactured by Lehmann and Company of Dresden, Germany. He ordered the machinery and, early in 1894, created the Hershey Chocolate Company as a subsidiary of his caramel business. In addition to chocolate coatings, the company produced breakfast cocoa, sweet chocolate, and baking chocolate. In 1900, Hershey sold the Lancaster Caramel Company, but retained the chocolate-manufacturing equipment and the rights to manufacture chocolate. In 1903, he moved to the heart of Pennsylvania's dairy country and began to build the world's largest chocolate-manufacturing plant, which opened two years later. Hershey's success pointed the way for other manufacturers, and many followed during the early twentieth century. Over the past one hundred years, more than forty thousand different candy bars have been manufactured in the United States. The most successful have contained chocolate.

Most Americans identify chocolate as their favorite flavor, and cookbooks featuring chocolate recipes are perennial best sellers. High on America's homemade chocolate hit parade are devil's food cake, fudge cake, German chocolate cake, brownies, and Toll House cookies.

[*See also* Brownies; Candy Bars and Candy; Chocolate Drinks; Combat Food; Cookies; Desserts; Frappes; Fudge; Halloween; Hershey Foods Corporation; Ice Cream and Ices; Ice Cream Sodas; Mars; Milkshakes, Malts, and Floats; Valentine's Day.]

BIBLIOGRAPHY

Bloom, Carole. *All About Chocolate: The Ultimate Resource to the World's Favorite Food.* New York: Macmillan, 1998.

Brenner, Joël Glenn. *The Emperors of Chocolate: Inside the Secret World of Hershey and Mars.* New York: Broadway Books, 2000.

Broekel, Ray. *The Chocolate Chronicles.* Lombard, IL: Wallace-Homestead, 1985.

Coe, Sophie D., and Michael D. Coe. *The True History of Chocolate.* New York: Thames and Hudson, 1996.

Morton, Marcia, and Frederic, Morton. *Chocolate: An Illustrated History.* New York: Crown, 1986.

ANDREW F. SMITH

Later Developments

Throughout the twentieth century, chocolate was mostly eaten in America in the form of highly sweetened, mass-produced candy, often bought in individually wrapped bars from vending machines or corner stores, and later, supermarkets. Among the most important manufacturers were Hershey's and Mars. Chocolate in several forms (bitter, bittersweet, or sweet, in tablets or chips) was also manufactured on a large scale for cooking purposes, the most popular producer being the old New England firm of Walter Baker. Drinking chocolate was generally made with cocoa powder, the solid component of cacao from which the fat has been extracted.

The taste preferences that American chocolate was meant to meet were simple and unadventurous. The cacao beans themselves (predominantly of the hardy *forastero* type, from plantations in West Africa or Brazil) were chosen, roasted, and processed for consistent, mild, sweet candies. When Americans wanted elegant, high-end eating chocolate, they generally thought of imported Swiss brands, such as Lindt.

The situation began to change in the 1970s and 1980s, when American consumers showed interest in darker chocolate (often Belgian or French) as both cooking ingredient and candy. But it was not until the 1990s that Americans started to explore European *couvertures*—high-quality chocolates made with greater percentages of cacao and less sugar—and become fascinated with chocolate's new-world roots and the baroque flavor combinations linked to its pre-Columbian past.

Trends and Innovations in Chocolate Making

There are several issues with which American consumers became concerned with respect to chocolate quality:

The quality and origin of the cacao itself, with a rediscovery of so-called flavor beans belonging to the superior *criollo* and *trinitario* strains or certain unusual *forasteros*

The fermentation and roasting processes, which develop deep and refined chocolate flavors while modulating the bitterness and astringency of raw cacao

The highest possible proportion of cacao to other ingredients, especially sugar. In the new paradigm, the aim was to preserve as much pure, natural cacao flavor as possible, unmasked by oversweetening, overroasting, or the common alkalization process that manufacturers used to suppress unwanted bitterness, astringency, and acidity in bulk beans

Possibly spurred by the examples of the influential French manufacturer Valrhona and the Venezuelan Chocolates El Rey (the latter having been introduced in the United States in 1995), artisanal American chocolatiers began producing chocolate with such selling points as beans of carefully selected origin, sometimes single-variety or single-estate from Venezuela (South America's premier producer of quality beans); high cacao content; and a lack of the alkalis or added "fillers" and artificial flavors common in mass-produced commercial chocolate. Beginning in the late 1990s firms such as the tiny San Francisco–based Scharffen Berger and Guittard Chocolates, an established San Francisco firm founded in the late nineteenth century, began manufacturing boutique lines of chocolate products made from custom blends of flavor beans and high cacao content. The success of these efforts and the continuing influence of innovative European manufacturers have inspired at least half a dozen other small producers to experiment with high-cacao artisanal chocolates from select beans. Some have gone even further, reaching back into chocolate's pre-Columbian and European past to devise such products as complexly spiced drinking chocolates inspired by Aztec or colonial Spanish recipes, chili-laced balls of ground cacao like those used for grating in parts of Latin America, or unusual perfumed combinations.

There are only two important modern innovations in chocolate technology—a trend toward crushing the cacao beans into coarse fragments, or "nibs," before, rather than after, roasting them and a switch to faster, more powerful conching machines to agitate the semiliquid ground chocolate to improve the final flavor and texture. There are more changes in store. The American chocolate industry is absorbing the impact of a new breed of premium chocolates along with other culinary and social developments. Although the industry as a whole began moving toward greater consolidation in the early years of the twenty-first century, with major processing operations (for example, nib roasting and grinding) in the hands of only nine American companies, a few of the major manufacturers are either considering or taking steps toward launching boutique-style high-cacao-content chocolates with select beans or chocolates with higher cacao content. Other issues that transcend technology are certain to affect American chocolate.

Other Concerns

Organic farming and sustainable agriculture have become a focus of interest. Certified organic cacao is being raised by growers in several Latin American and African countries, in response to demand from concerned consumers. The integrated use of renewable resources in tropical forest habitats is an allied issue that U.S. companies such as Mars and cacao organizations such as the World Cacao Foundation have sought to address through experimental projects in several producing countries.

There is also the question of human rights abuses. In response to exposés of harsh labor conditions (among them, forced exposure to toxic pesticides) and the coercive use of child labor in Ivory Coast and other cacao-growing West African nations, the major American chocolate companies have begun monitoring conditions on plantations that supply them. The international lobbying group the Fair Trade Federation began pressuring manufacturers to buy cacao only from sources that guarantee plantation workers safe working conditions and a minimum wage that is not dependent on speculator-driven market price fluctuations. Artisanal manufacturers and organic chocolate companies are leading the campaign to certify cacao produced under fair and humane conditions.

Chocolate's effects on health are the subject of much study. Reacting to people's interest in comparatively high-fat, low-carbohydrate weight-maintenance diets and the related issues of epidemic obesity and diabetes, the major American manufacturers have worked to develop products made with reduced sugar content (a trend that was anticipated by the makers of high-end boutique chocolates) or with other noncaloric sweeteners tested for flavor, safety, and suitability for use in cooking.

At the same time, an increasingly sophisticated medical understanding of the origins of cardiovascular disease is yielding surprising insights into the therapeutic properties of chocolate. With support from Mars, chocolate came under intense study as a strikingly rich source of compounds known as flavonoids. Two subclasses of these compounds, flavanols and procyanidins (present in large amounts in some dark chocolates and cocoa powder made with beans that have not been overly fermented, alkalized, or roasted at high temperatures), demonstrate antioxidant and anticlotting activity, along with an ability to improve arterial blood flow. At least one major company (Mars) is switching to cacao beans processed with a proprietary method that retains high concentrations of these beneficial substances; products made with these beans bear the trademark "Cocoapro" (from cacao and procyanidins). The ongoing research on chocolate's health benefits is bound to change the way chocolate is manufactured, marketed, and consumed for years to come.

[See also Candy Bars and Candy; Hershey Foods Corporation; Mars.]

BIBLIOGRAPHY

Brenner, Joel. *The Emperors of Chocolate: Inside the Secret World of Hershey and Mars.* New York: Broadway Books, 2000.

Coe, Sophie D., and Michael D. Coe. *The True History of Chocolate.* New York: Thames and Hudson, 1996.

Lopez, Ruth. *Chocolate: The Nature of Indulgence.* New York: Abrams, 2002.

Presilla, Maricel. *The New Taste of Chocolate: A Natural and Cultural History of Cacao with Recipes.* Berkeley, CA: Ten Speed Press, 2001.

Young, Allen M. *The Chocolate Tree: A Natural History of Cacao.* Washington, DC: Smithsonian Institution Press, 1994.

MARICEL PRESILLA

Chocolate Drinks

The Olmec civilization made a beverage, *chocolatl*, from the roasted and ground seeds of *Theobroma cacao* (cocoa tree) as early as 1600 B.C.E. The Maya and Aztec continued the practice, instructing Spanish conquistadores on how to process the raw cacao beans. In 1528 Hernán Cortés brought cacao to the Spanish court, where the Mesoamerican delicacy quickly was adopted. The royal physicians praised it as a food and medicine, and King Philip successfully kept cacao away from the rest of Europe until 1655, when Great Britain took control of his cacao plantations in Jamaica. By 1657 the first of many chocolate houses had opened its doors in London.

American colonists took quickly to the fashionable *chocolatl*. Beans imported from the West Indies were roasted and ground into a liquid paste. Spices like vanilla and nutmeg and aromatics like ambergris were added to the cocoa as it was ground. The resulting liquor was mixed with water, spirits, or milk and sweetened with sugar. After heating, the drink was skimmed to remove cacao butter and then beaten to a froth to lighten the remaining fat and mitigate any bitterness from faulty fermentation.

Hand grinding often resulted in chocolate-lover's elbow, a complaint that may have brought the money-making potential of cacao to the attention of Dr. James Baker of Dorchester, Massachusetts. In 1764 Baker opened the first successful American chocolate business in partnership with the Irish immigrant chocolate maker John Hannon. Baker's hot chocolate sustained pioneers on the Oregon Trail and bolstered the morale of Union troops in the Civil War, becoming so ubiquitous that its name is still confused with a type of chocolate rather than a brand.

Domenico Ghirardelli arrived in San Francisco for the gold rush in 1849, but instead struck a chocolate bonanza. In 1865 Ghirardelli's factory discovered cacao butter would separate from the roasted beans if they were left hanging in a bag in a warm room; the remaining solids were ground into powder. This technique, called broma processing, remains in common use. At the end of the Civil War, Americans were drinking three different chocolate drinks: cocoa, made from Dutched cacao and sold in cakes or powdered; hot chocolate, made from Baker's chocolate bars; and Broma.

America's relationship with chocolate was changed forever when, in 1893, the successful caramel manufacturer Milton Hershey saw a demonstration of the new Swiss conche machine and other European innovations at the World's Columbian Exposition in Chicago. By 1900 Hershey's milk chocolate candy bar had begun the industry that would make Americans think of chocolate as something to eat—preferably while drinking a chocolate soda.

In 1832 pharmacies began selling carbonated artificial mineral water as a therapeutic drink. Pharmacists soon added herb and fruit syrups to increase its healthfulness and marketability. The first use of chocolate syrup with soda water is unknown, but the earliest nationally recognized chocolate soda was the turn-of-the-century New York egg cream, made with Fox's U-Bet chocolate syrup, milk, and seltzer.

Consumers wanted soda water available in their own kitchens, and entrepreneurs raced to be the first to accommodate them. By the early 1920s the bottling industry had advanced sufficiently that manufacturers and retailers could offer homepaks, the forerunner of the six-pack. Many of the bottles were filled with noncarbonated Yoo-hoo chocolate drink. Popular through the early 1970s, Yoo-hoo and other nostalgia sodas are enjoying a new popularity.

In 1926 Hershey capitalized on the soda fountain and ice cream parlor boom by marketing cocoa syrup, renamed chocolate syrup in time to compete with Bosco Chocolate Syrup for the hearts and wallets of the baby boomers of the post–World War II generation. By 1956 Hershey was helping tuck children in at night with instant hot cocoa, a happy amalgamation of cocoa powder, milk powder, and sugar.

International producers began influencing the American market in 1930, when the Swiss-owned Ovaltine began sponsoring the popular radio adventure

Drinking Chocolate. From an advertisement for Bournville Cocoa, early twentieth century.

Little Orphan Annie. The Nestlé company followed in 1948 with the introduction of Nestlé Quik.

In the 1970s individual servings of chocolate-flavored soy milk began to appear in the American market, providing an alternative for the health conscious and lactose intolerant. Convenience drove the market in the 1980s, and beverage manufacturers obliged with off-the-shelf chocolate milk and powdered breakfast drinks for those on the go. In the 1990s chocolate diet drinks appeared along with energy-boosting drinks, which took a leaf from the pharmaceutical marketing slogans of the 1890s.

Current trends resemble the customized mixtures of cacao beans of the eighteenth and early nineteenth centuries. Inspired by the success of boutique coffees, restaurants and chocolate makers are producing gourmet chocolate for a new generation's drinking pleasure.

[*See also* Chocolate *subentry* Later Developments; Egg Cream; Hershey Foods Corporation; Nestlé; Soda Drinks.]

BIBLIOGRAPHY

Coe, Sophie D., and Michael D. Coe. *The True History of Chocolate.* New York: Thames and Hudson, 1996. This is the definitive history of *Theobroma cacao,* covering its botanical, historical, social, economic, and religious impact on the cultures of the world. Sophie D. Coe, an accomplished writer and food historian, died before she could finish writing this book. Her husband, Michael, one of the premier Maya scholars in the world, completed the work. Highly recommended for its depth of information as well as its readability.

ESTHER DELLA REESE

Chopping Knives and Food Choppers

Chopping knives have been used to cut everything from raw vegetables to chunks of meat. There are a few types, but all have relatively wide or deep blades, unlike a paring knife, for example. A few look like cleavers, with the blade and handle on the same horizontal plane, but most have handles on top, to utilize vertical force. Handles are either T-shaped with one tang or have a grip with two tangs—one at each end of the blade, for more control. Some chopping knives have two or even three blades, often curved along the bottom, giving them the nineteenth-century moniker "rug cutters," a nickname shared by rocking chairs. In the 1920s one was made with a spring-action T-handle, adding force. Chopping knives were used with cutting boards or wooden cutting bowls. Early nineteenth-century ones may be fancy and made with figural cutouts in the deep blade.

Chopping Knife. *Culinary Archives & Museum at Johnson & Wales University, Providence, R.I.*

Mechanical food choppers date from the 1860s on. Forerunners of food processors, they often had a set of blades for different purposes. Basically, there is a cast-iron frame with cranked gears that move the chopping blades up and down while the geared container (with wooden bottom) revolves. Used for vegetables and meat, they were often called "hashers."

[*See also* Food Processors.]

BIBLIOGRAPHY

Franklin, Linda Campbell. *300 Years of Kitchen Collectibles.* 5th ed. Iola, WI: Krause Publications, 2003.
Lasansky, Jeannette. *To Draw, Upset, and Weld: Work of the Pennsylvania Rural Blacksmith, 1742–1935.* Lewisburg, PA: Oral Traditions, 1980.

LINDA CAMPBELL FRANKLIN

Chorizo

Chorizo, Spain's ubiquitous sausage, is usually made of chopped pork, sweet or hot paprika, crushed red peppers, and garlic. It is available in two forms: a soft variety for cooking and a cured, hard variety that is sliced and served as a tapa. Spanish chorizo differs significantly from the plumper, juicier Mexican chorizo, which is made of freshly ground pork and a chili-spice blend, and from Portuguese *chouriço,* which contains less paprika and more garlic and includes wine. In America, Spanish chorizo is popular in areas with large Hispanic populations. It has caught the attention of top chefs and often is used as a bold flavor counterpoint, especially in fusion cuisine.

[*See also* Sausage; Southwestern Reginonal Cookery.]

BIBLIOGRAPHY

Davidson, Alan. *The Oxford Companion to Food.* Oxford: Oxford University Press, 1999.

DAVID LEITE

Christmas

For most Americans, Christmas rivals Thanksgiving for indulgence. Unlike Thanksgiving, however, Christmas is more than a single meal. Specialty Christmas foods permeate the month-long holiday season. Titles such as *Old-Fashioned Christmas Cookbook* and *Twelve Days of Christmas Cookbook* recall Christmases past, and gingerbread men, plum puddings, and cookies are part of culinary tradition. Homemakers have covered Christmas tables in red and green since the late nineteenth century, and holiday dishes bearing the image of Santa Claus or evergreens have been marketed since the 1930s.

All this would stun a time traveler from the early nineteenth century. When Philadelphia's *Democratic Press* asked in 1810, "Shall we have Christmas?" the question was not merely rhetorical. The answer depended on one's religion and ethnicity and ranged from a resounding "No!" through modest acknowledgement of the day to a patchwork of holidays. Starting with the feasts of Saint Lucy and Saint Nicholas in early December and continuing through Twelfth Night on January 6, many disparate threads have now been woven into a season-long American Christmas mantle. Yet it was only in the midnineteenth century that December 25 became a widespread, governmentally sanctioned holiday. At that same time, a formulaic Christmas dinner swept the nation that would last through the end of the nineteenth century, only to fade in the twentieth. Unlike the iconic Thanksgiving comestibles, which anchor that singularly American holiday regardless of one's ethnicity, there is nothing originally American about Christmas except Santa Claus and candy canes. Christmas's multicultural roots have meant that Americans of different regions, classes, and ethnic groups celebrate with different foodstuffs.

Christmas before the 1840s

English, Dutch, and German colonists approached the December holidays differently. Even among the English

Christmas Delivery. *Yard of Poultry,* advertising card issued by the William G. Bell Co., manufacturers of canned spiced seasoning, late nineteenth century. *Collection of Alice Ross*

expatriates, attitudes toward Christmas varied according to religious sect. William Bradford, the Puritan governor of Plymouth Colony, in 1621 chastised non-Puritans for their revelries on "the day they call Christmasday." Because nothing in the Bible identified December 25 as Christ's birthday, Puritans viewed that date as simply another workday. There were no special foods, church services, or commemorations, an attitude shared by many Protestant denominations well into the nineteenth century. Puritans railed against mincemeat pie as "idolatrie in a crust." The spices in the pie were believed to signify the luxuriously exotic gifts of the magi and to evoke popery. From 1659 to 1681, it was illegal to celebrate Christmas in Massachusetts, there being a five-shilling penalty for doing so. Analogous penalties were threatened against Dutch colonists who celebrated Saint Nicholas Day on December 6. In the seventeenth century, the Reformation government in Amsterdam tried to squelch the perceived disorder that arose from people congregating in public with "any kind of candy, eatables or other merchandise." Most of the early Dutch settlers in America celebrated nonreligious New Year's Day open houses, but there were only pockets of private Saint Nicholas observances.

Some early colonists in America did welcome Christmas. In the eighteenth century, German colonists in Pennsylvania brought branches, precursors of the evergreen Christmas tree, into the house and then decorated them with wafers, honey cakes, gingerbreads, cookies, apples, and marzipan. Descriptions (including criticism from Quakers, who shared the Puritans' attitude) abound of Philadelphians' extravagant early-nineteenth-century Christmas balls. Elegant collations fortified weary dancers with cold meats, terrapin, oysters, and pyramids of sweetmeats and creams. The celebrations were lavish, but the foods served were not distinctively associated with Christmas.

Southern colonists were largely Anglican with a few French Huguenots. Their Christmas festivities focused more on revelry than on food, Christmas hunts and games being the main entertainment. Outdoor parties adjourned to plantation homes for copious dinners, but these were "no otherwise than common," given the luxurious standards of the households. In 1709, the guests of the Virginia governor William Byrd II sat down to a typical southern spread of "turkey and chine, roast apples and wine, tongue and udder" as well as many other meats and seafood. Holiday observances might extend through Epiphany with "great pyes" and Twelfth Night cakes but little else to distinguish the tables.

Heavy drinking and gifts of liquor marked colonial and frontier celebrations. At wealthy plantations, eggnog often was drunk in bed on Christmas morning. Christmas in the South coincided with completion of the harvest. With the exception of the cooks and a few essential house workers, many (but by no means all) slaves were relieved of their labors and given a Saturnalian break for feasting, drinking, and revelry. This celebration followed the custom of the English country gentry who were the forebears of Anglican southerners. In England, the local squire hosted a Christmas feast for the extended community that contributed, directly or indirectly, to the running of the household. Through the Civil War, the plantation owner often prepared his personal concoction for eggnog in a large punch bowl and then distributed a cup to each guest and plantation dependent in much the same spirit as the wassail bowl had been passed in England.

Christmas Dinner in the Mid-Nineteenth Century

In the mid-nineteenth century, cultural changes in America led to a fundamental shift in the nature of Christmas observances, from bawdy and rowdy public frolics to sentimental Victorian domesticity. Popular literature such as *The Sketch-Book of Geoffrey Crayon, Gent.* (1819) by Washington Irving and the 1823 poem "A Visit from Saint Nicholas" piqued an antiquarian interest in Christmas. Christmas demanded a dinner with family that was special but within the economic reach of most Americans. Because no single cultural Christmas tradition monopolized American foodways, the unifying model for the American Christmas dinner of the middle to late nineteenth century was supplied by Charles Dickens in *A Christmas Carol* (1843).

Although Dickens did not invent the idea of serving turkey at Christmas (it had always been one of many foods on festive American tables), his extraordinarily popular novella was a remarkable case of life imitating art. Most American food writers in the late nineteenth and early twentieth centuries prescribed a Christmas dinner of roast turkey with gravy, mashed potatoes, sage and onion stuffing, and plum pudding. Unlike the controversial mincemeats, the plain menu described by Dickens largely lacked religious connotations and thus assuaged sectarian differences. Civil War diaries brimmed with descriptions of efforts to procure the "Christmas turkey." These accounts were matched by mid-nineteenth-century Minnesotans' careful recording of the prices of Christmas turkeys imported by sleigh from Iowa and Illinois. Those who could not afford turkey (a relatively expensive bird in the late nineteenth century) could follow the advice to the frugal offered by Marion Harland (the pseudonym of Mary Virginia Hawes Terhune) in *Breakfast, Dinner and Supper* (1897) that they enjoy the less expensive boiled goose. The charitable gesture whereby the character Ebenezer Scrooge sends the largest turkey in the poulterer's window to replace a scrawny goose was allegedly emulated by a Vermont factory owner on hearing Dickens read *A Christmas Carol* in Boston in 1867. This man reportedly was so moved that he broke with his Puritan tradition of opening his factory on Christmas Day. The following year,

Christmas Dinner. A charitable dinner held for the newsboys and girls of New York, 1876. The scrawny children come in for turkey and leave as corpulent, contented junior citizens. The newsboys were mainly drawn from the Irish population, explaining why the well-fed newsboy turns up his nose at a sign advertising corned beef. From *Harper's Weekly*, 15 January 1876, p. 53. *Collection of Cathy K. Kaufman*

the factory owner instituted the tradition of giving a holiday turkey to each employee. By the 1880s, the concept of a proper Christmas dinner for all led charities to host Christmas dinners for the urban poor, especially orphans, and for immigrants cloistered on Ellis Island. All served turkey as the main, "Americanizing" course, a tradition that continues in holiday soup kitchens.

Christmas Dinner in the Twentieth Century

By the late nineteenth century, some cookery writers tentatively suggested alternatives for those who wanted something out of the ordinary. Although roast turkey remained a popular centerpiece, turkey farmers such as Horace Vose found that the Christmas market demanded much smaller birds than the Thanksgiving market. Food writers suggested that other meats might supplement or even supplant the American bird. Terhune, writing for a more affluent readership in *House and Home* (1889), recommended a "noble" saddle of venison in lieu of the "provincial" turkey that must appear on Thanksgiving. She wrote that Christmas turkey was required only if "your culinary conscience or the family appetite demand the sacrifice of the Bird of Plenty." Other writers suggested steak, meatloaf, and veal curry. Even the somewhat conservative Good Housekeeping Institute by the late 1920s suggested crown roast of pork as an alternative to turkey.

As the importance, although not necessarily the form, of Christmas dinner was being established, newly invented dishes emulated the secular symbols of the holiday. Alice Bradley, the principal of Fannie Farmer's cooking school, in 1936 described Christmas pear salad. The recipe called for cutting a pear into the shape of a Christmas tree, dressing it with green mayonnaise, decorating it with slivered almond "candles," and then garnishing the result with cubes of cream cheese "presents" and with "ribbons" painted with food coloring. Others cooks used grapefruit salad to mimic wreaths by coating the edges of grapefruit shells with tinted green sugar and garnishing the fruit cup with maraschino cherry "poinsettias." Later cookbooks often incorporate red and green foods into Christmas menus.

Regional and ethnic influences tailor Christmas foods to local preferences, so it is impossible to identify a universal American Christmas. In the South, barbecue and chili are added to the Christmas table, and in the Southwest tamales are served. Italian Americans may eat a seven-course fish dinner on Christmas Eve. French

Christmas Recipes. From *Woman's Day* magazine, "Holiday Cakes & Cookies." *Collection of Andrew F. Smith*

Americans have imported the "thirteen desserts," said to represent each participant in the Last Supper. New Orleans continues to specialize in yeasted Twelfth Night cake, and many Japanese Americans serve white rice with turkey. Cookie exchanges, parties for the purpose of swapping homemade cookies, are becoming a tradition. Once-common foods such as mincemeat are now specifically associated with the holiday.

Although the modern Christmas menu is mutable, there lingers an undercurrent of nostalgia for the ancient feast described by Irving in the chapter in *The Sketch-Book* titled "The Christmas Dinner." The feast at Bracebridge Hall, complete with boar's head and wassail bowl, was knowingly anachronistic when Irving wrote and was too opulent to be mimicked on most American tables. Yet affluent Americans have patterned entertainments after this "medieval" feast since the mid-nineteenth century, children's dress-up pageants paying homage to the traditional foods. Adults also have indulged in the fantasy: Since 1927, the Ahwahnee Hotel in Yosemite National Park, in California, has held Bracebridge dinners at Christmas. Tickets are assigned by lottery, averaging fifteen thousand entries for three hundred spots. The photographer Ansel Adams was the original pagentmeister for the costumed fete that loosely adapts Irving's dinner to contemporary tastes—tenderloin of pork and fillet mignon stand for the aristocratic boar's head and baron of beef.

[See also Eggnog; New Year's Celebrations; Thanksgiving; Turkey.]

BIBLIOGRAPHY

Bauer, John E. Christmas on the American Frontier, 1800–1900. Caldwell, OH: Caxton, 1961.

Bigham, Shauna, and Robert E. May. "The Time O' All Times? Masters, Slaves, and Christmas in the Old South." Journal of the Early Republic 18 (1998): 263–288.

Foster, Don. Author Unknown. New York: Holt, 2000.

Golby, J. M., and A. W. Purdue. The Making of the Modern Christmas. London: B. T. Batsford, 1986.

Kaufman, Cathy. Nurturing a Holiday: Christmas Foods in Eighteenth and Nineteenth Century America. In The Proceedings of the Oxford Symposium on Food and Cookery 2003, edited by Richard Hosking. Forthcoming.

Marling, Karal Ann. Merry Christmas! Celebrating America's Greatest Holiday. Cambridge, MA: Harvard University Press, 2000.

Masumoto, David Mas. "Holiday Meals." In A Slice of Life: Contemporary Writers on Food, edited by Bonnie Marranca, 49–54. Woodstock, NY, and London: Overlook Duckworth, 2003.

Nissenbaum, Stephen. The Battle for Christmas. New York: Random House, 1996.

Rawlings, Kevin. We Were Marching on Christmas Day. Baltimore: Toomey, 1995.

Restad, Penne. Christmas in America. New York: Oxford University Press, 1995.

Reinecke, George F. "The New Orleans Twelfth Night Cake." Louisiana Folklore Miscellany 2 (April 1965): 45–54.

Rodgers, Rick. Christmas 101: Celebrate the Holiday Season from Christmas to New Year's. New York: Broadway, 1999.

Shoemaker, Alfred L. Christmas in Pennsylvania. Kutztown: Pennsylvania Folklife Society, 1959.

Terhune, Mary Virgina (Hawes). House and Home: A Complete Housewife's Guide. Chicago: Ziegler, 1889.

Vose, Horace. Turkey Secrets from the Experience of Horace Vose of Westerly, R.I. Edited by Michael K. Boyer. Philadelphia: W. Atkinson, 1912.

Weaver, William Woys. The Christmas Cook: Three Centuries of American Yuletide Sweets. New York: HarperCollins, 1990.

CATHY K. KAUFMAN

Chuck Wagons

The invention of the chuck wagon is attributed to the legendary rancher Charles "Chuck" Goodnight. In 1866, he designed a four-wheeled wagon of wide gauge for transporting supplies and preparing food. The notable feature of the chuck wagon is a cabinet or "chuck box" in the rear, filled with small supplies and bearing a fold-down table for food preparation. The chuck wagon was a significant development not only in forming and institutionalizing the "cowboy cuisine" of fact and lore but also in enabling, in part, the grand cattle drives of the cowboy heyday in the American West.

Ranching and Driving in Context

The short but colorful heyday of the American cowboy began after the Civil War and ended gradually with the privatization and fencing in of the West from the 1880s until the early twentieth century. It is estimated that in Texas alone in 1860 there were some 3.5 million wild cattle grazing the unfenced land, the descendants of a few ancestors brought to the Americas by conquistadors and settlers. After the Civil War ended, freed slaves; former soldiers already hundreds of miles from home; other men with marital, legal, or financial problems; and young boys looked to the American West for their fortunes or at least for a good steak dinner cut from one of the millions of wild cattle.

The fortune, if there was to be one, was found in rounding up these wild cattle, claiming them, and leading them to a major city where they could be sold and consumed or shipped by rail to another population center. These early cowboys, working alone or in small groups, typically cooked for themselves a meal of beef, coffee, and perhaps some pinto beans ("frijoles"); if they were wealthy enough, they might have a Mexican or black hired hand to handle the cooking and other chores.

As was true throughout American agricultural history, the independent cowboy with a small herd of cattle could not be financially successful compared with the owners of what is considered the "ideal herd size" by economies of scale. The larger outfits were orchestrated by entrepreneurial ranchers like Goodnight who had the capital and political clout to buy off or kill potential enemies on

Chuck Wagon. Cowboys near Spur, Texas, serving themselves at the chuck wagon, May 1939. *Prints and Photographs Division, Library of Congress/Russell Lee*

the trail. Furthermore, they could guarantee wages despite the volatility of beef prices, which could change dramatically over the months-long cattle drive. All of these early ranching outfits had the need for a mobile commissary to feed their staffs during the long cattle drives. While the idea of having a victual wagon with a designated cook traveling along the trail was a natural development, it was Goodnight's modifications to a traditional wagon that institutionalized the chuck wagon.

Coosie and the Chuck

Goodnight's wagon soon became the standard across the West, and a cook could move from one outfit to another without noticing significant changes in the commissary or the food system. In the wagon, often under a canvas roof, were stored the nonperishable foods and the men's bedrolls. The typical larder included frijoles (usually dried pinto or navy beans), coffee beans (usually Arbuckle's brand, which came with a peppermint candy awarded to the man who volunteered to grind), molasses, flour, dried fruit, and canned tomatoes. Under the wagon

in a hide attached to the bottom, called a "coonie" (from the Spanish *cuña*, or "cradle"), were stored firewood, pots, and Dutch ovens, and aging beef wrapped in canvas. In the chuck box one could find small items like spices, flatware (called "eating irons"), a bottle of whiskey for medicinal use, medicines, matches, and other incidentals.

With this wagon developed the cuisine of the cowboy, which revolved around the "three B's"—beef, beans, and bread. The beef, cowboys agreed, should preferably be steaks from the hindquarter of a heifer, fried in tallow until well done; the beans, pintos or navy; the bread, sourdough biscuits (the starter well coddled by the cook and also accredited to Goodnight, who is said to have picked up the knack from his mother). With this meal the men drank strong, boiled black coffee. If the cook was in a pleasant mood and feeling ambitious, there might have been a dessert, such as a cobbler or stewed dried fruit. "Chuck" was used to indicate any sort of meal, and colorful nicknames were ascribed to nearly every ingredient and preparation: sinker (biscuit), lick (molasses), mop (gravy), calf slobber (icing), alkali water (coffee), moonshine (rice), skunk eggs (onions), and music roots (sweet potatoes, said to cause flatulence).

The most famous distinctly cowboy food was "son of a bitch stew," almost ceremoniously prepared whenever a calf was slaughtered. While the muscle meat was best aged for a few days in the coonie, the organs—namely, brain, sweetbreads, liver, heart, tripe, and the key ingredient, marrow gut (or margut, a four-foot tube that connects the cow's stomachs and contains a milky fluid of partially digested grass)—would spoil immediately and so were cooked into stew with tomato, onion, and chilies.

Linked inextricably with the story of the chuck wagon is the tale of the stereotypical camp cook, often dubbed "Coosie," from the Spanish *cocinero*. Coosie was notoriously temperamental, often in trouble with the law, and of dubious culinary skill. A good cook was a treasure on the trail and a major perquisite. The men would go out of their way to keep a good cook happy by cleaning his dishes, gathering firewood, and, most important, respecting the cook's domain, the chuck wagon. A good cook could lure cowboys to work for the tastier outfits. Even a bad cook, though, was respected on the trail, as a cowboy complaining about the food or inciting the cook to quit would be promptly rewarded with his apron and "gouch hook" (pothook) and asked to demonstrate how things should be done. Both derisively and lovingly called "old woman" or "old lady," (Adams, *Come an' Get It*, p. 54) the cook "was doctor, dentist, and older brother, and it was he who dosed the cowboys when they were ill, heard them when they were depressed, or amused them when they were bored" (Durham and Jones, *The Negro Cowboys*, p. 50).

Although a diet based on the "three B's" may seem monotonous to our modern culinary sensibilities, cowboy cuisine as a whole became distinct and unified and reduced from its nuances in history and lore. Like Coosie and the foods themselves, the chuck wagon has become institutionalized as an icon of the American West.

[*See also* Arbuckles; Beans; Chili; Frontier Cooking of the Far West; Slang, Food.]

BIBLIOGRAPHY

Adams, Ramon F. *Come an' Get It: The Story of the Old Cowboy Cook.* Norman: University of Oklahoma Press, 1952.

Beckstead, James H. *Cowboying: A Tough Job in a Hard Land.* Salt Lake City: University of Utah Press, 1991.

Cano, Tony, and Ann Sochat. *Chuck Wagon Heyday: The History and Color of the Chuck Wagon at Work.* Canutillo, TX: Reata, 1997.

Durham, Philip, and Everett L. Jones. *The Negro Cowboys.* New York: Dodd, Mead, 1965.

Hughes, Stella. *Chuck Wagon Cookin'.* Tucson: University of Arizona Press, 1974.

Linck, Ernestine Sewell, and Joyce Gibson Roach. *Eats: A Folk History of Texas Food.* Fort Worth: Texas Christian University Press, 1984.

JONATHAN DEUTSCH

Cider

In America the word "cider" most often means juice right out of the apple, sweet juice. With the growing interest in fermenting sweet juice to develop an alcoholic drink, the products are being redefined. Buyers are often confused, because in the American marketplace cider has for many years meant a sweet, unfermented juice.

Besides fermented apple juice, there are several drinks with an apple base that have quenched the thirst of Americans for centuries. Low-quality sweet cider paved the way for the emergence of the soft drink industry. Before regulation, this roadside jugged juice often was not only watered down but also made from apples that had fallen from the tree, poorly washed or not washed at all, and pressed from a single variety that does not make a tasty cider, especially the Red Delicious. Many small orchardists take great pride in blending apples with the elements of acid, tannin, and sugar for a quality sweet cider.

Ciderkin is made by overnight soaking of the pomace, the residue left after most of the juice is removed from the apple, and then re-pressing it and fermenting this "wash" in the traditional way. It is very delicate, with a light apple taste, and is sometimes called cider wash or cider water. It was often served to children and, frequently, spices were added to elevate the flavor.

Scrumpy was made occasionally by colonists who came to America from England. It is a rough, strong, dry cider, ready for consumption after a few months of fermentation. There are recipes that add raisins and raw meat to the juice.

[*See also* Applejack; Apples; Cider, Hard.]

BIBLIOGRAPHY

Orton, Vrest. *The American Cider Book: The Story of America's Natural Beverage.* New York: Farrar, Straus and Giroux, 1973.

Proulx, Annie, and Lew Nichols. *Cider: Making, Using, and Enjoying Sweet and Hard Cider.* Pownal, VT: Storey Communications, 1997.

Watson, Ben. *Cider Hard and Sweet: History, Traditions, and Making Your Own.* Woodstock, VT: Countryman Press, 1999.

THOMAS BURFORD

Cider, Hard

The word "cider" has its roots in ancient Hebrew. *Sheker*, which means "strong drink," was translated into the Greek *sikera*, the Latin *sicera*, and then the French *cidre*. The English called it *cyder* or cider.

Hard cider has been produced since at least 1200 C.E., owing, in part, to the ease with which it can be made. Because of the natural yeasts that exist on apples, apple juice, will ferment if left at room temperature. This is one reason why grocery stores keep fresh apple juice chilled—to prevent it from turning into hard cider. Cider probably began as a farmer's drink. Apples were knocked from trees or, in the case of *scrumpy* (*scrump* originally meant "shriveled"), old, overripe apples were gathered off the ground. Traditionally, the apples are milled into a pulp (or pomace) from which the juice is pressed.

The Normans brought cider to England. By the seventeenth century it was so beloved that the English wrote poems and songs about cider. On Old Twelfth Night (January 17) field laborers would quaff cider and dance around the best apple trees, exhorting them to grow good apples. The English carried hard cider to America. It became very popular in the northeastern colonies, where apple trees were plentiful. Americans considered cider a health booster and a safer beverage than available water, so they consumed it throughout the day. From field laborers to American presidents, nearly everyone drank cider.

In the mid-nineteenth century, beer and then spirits and wine gained popularity, and cider consumption declined. Hard cider saw a resurgence in the 1980s, making way for dozens of new brands. They are more refined and variegated, and some have added flavors like cranberry. Cider also can be found on tap in many bars and in bottles at numerous retailers.

[*See also* Applejack; Apples; Cider.]

BIBLIOGRAPHY

Dunkling, Leslie. *The Guinness Drinking Companion.* New York: Lyons and Burford, 1995.

Watson, Ben. *Cider, Hard and Sweet: History, Traditions, and Making Your Own.* Woodstock, VT: Countryman Press, 2000.

KEVIN R. KOSAR

Cincinnati Chili

A popular fast food found principally in the region around Cincinnati, Ohio, Cincinnati chili is made of ground beef cooked in a tangy, tomato-based sauce. It is served over spaghetti and dressed with beans, onions, and cheese. Cincinnati chili was developed in the early 1920s in Cincinnati by a Macedonian immigrant, Athanas "Tom" Kiradjieff, and his brother, John, and served at their small restaurant, which became known as Empress Chili owing to its location next door to the Empress burlesque house.

The Kiradjieff brothers originally served their uniquely spiced sauce over steamed frankfurters on buns, in imitation of the style popularized at New York's Coney Island amusement park in the early part of the twentieth century. Their frankfurters were known as coneys and, sometimes, chili dogs. When grated cheddar cheese is added to the sandwich, it becomes a cheese coney. Raw chopped onions are another garnish, and hot sauce is often applied at the table.

The Kiradjieffs' sauce became popular and was soon served by itself in a bowl rather than as a topping for frankfurters. Embellished by combinations of condiments, Cincinnati chili spawned a unique chili jargon. A one-way is plain chili with oyster crackers on the side. Chili served over a plate of spaghetti becomes a two-way. Add grated cheddar cheese to the spaghetti and sauce to create a three-way. Raw chopped onions or kidney beans make a four-way chili. Spaghetti, cheese, onions, and kidney beans add up to a five-way. Experienced diners order by nickname.

SKYLINE CHILI
Carry Out Menu

	1/2 PINT	PINT
Chili Plain	1.30	2.25
Chili Spaghetti	1.15	1.95
Chili Beans	1.15	1.95
3-Way-Chili - Spaghetti, Cheese	1.55	2.35
4-Way-Chili - Spaghetti, Onions, Cheese	1.70	2.50
5-Way-Chili - Spaghetti, Onions, Beans, Cheese	1.75	2.55
Extra Chili	.15	.30
Extra Crackers		.10

* * * * *

Coney Islands	.65
Coney Islands with Cheese	.75
Order of Cheese	.40
Order of Onions	.15

* * * * *

Ice Tea	.35 & .45 & .50
Soft Drinks	.35 & .45 & .50
Coffee & Hot Tea	.35 & .40
Sanka	.35
Hot Chocolate	.35 & .45
Milk	.45 & .70 & .90

• **BY PHONING YOUR ORDER THERE'S NO WAITING** •
U.S. GOVT. INSPECTED MEATS, EST. 1691

Take-Out Menu. Skyline Chili, Cincinnati, 1980s.

A distinguishing characteristic of Cincinnati chili is that the beef is simmered directly with the other ingredients rather than undergoing a preliminary browning, although recipes vary. Unlike western and Texas-style chili, Cincinnati chili does not rely on whole chilies for heat, finding its warmth from cayenne, commercial chili powder, or cumin instead. It has a sweeter, more subdued flavor that is spicy but not hot. The Kiradjieff brothers drew from the familiar seasonings of their native Macedonia when they created Cincinnati chili. In addition to oregano and bay leaf, the sauce hints of allspice and cinnamon, seasonings frequently used in Balkan and other eastern Mediterranean cuisines. There is also an exotic whiff of chocolate.

Others adopted the idea of the original Empress Chili line, notably Greek immigrant Nicholas Lambrinides, who began Skyline Chili in the late 1940s. While there remains a brisk rivalry among chili brands, Skyline has become the dominant name in chili throughout the region. Recipes for each clan's spice blends are closely guarded secrets passed down to family members, and chili devotees are fiercely loyal to their favorite brand.

Cincinnati chili traditionally is served in chili parlors, small, utilitarian restaurants devoted almost exclusively to selling chili. Most Cincinnati chili parlors are owned by leading chains such as Empress or Skyline, although there are several independent restaurants. Frozen or canned chili produced by the major brands is available in supermarkets, and dried seasoning packets of the secret spice blends are also sold in area stores.

[See also Cooking Contests; Chili.]

BIBLIOGRAPHY

Bridges, Bill. *The Great American Chili Book.* New York: Rawson, Wade, 1981.
DuSablon, Mary Anna. *Cincinnati Recipe Treasury: The Queen City's Culinary Heritage.* Athens, OH: Ohio University Press, 1989.

MARY SANKER

Citrus

The many forms of commercial citrus all descend primarily from three original species native to Asia: citron (*Citrus medica*), an ancestor of the lemon; pummelo (*C. grandis*), a giant parent of the grapefruit; and mandarin (*C. reticulata*), which includes tangerines and similar fruits. Citrus cultivation in the area that would become the United States dates from the Spanish exploration and settlement of Florida in the sixteenth century; it reached Louisiana around 1700 and California with the arrival of Franciscan friars in 1769. Since most citrus cannot tolerate temperatures more than a few degrees below freezing, open-air cultivation has generally been limited to warmer areas, but until the second half of the nineteenth century it was not uncommon for the wealthy to grow oranges and lemons in greenhouses.

With the advent of steam transportation in the mid-nineteenth century, citrus was imported from Mexico, the West Indies, and Italy. Large-scale commercial cultivation began in Florida and California in the 1870s and 1880s, when the extension of railroads allowed fresh fruit to be shipped to major eastern and midwestern markets. Railroads and land promoters helped fashion a romantic image of citrus in the popular imagination, symbolizing sunshine, health, and elegance, to lure settlers to Florida and California. To sell their crops profitably, growers formed marketing cooperatives, such as Sunkist, founded as the Southern California Fruit Exchange in 1893. The major growing areas all experienced booms and busts, punctuated by devastating freezes such as the Great Freeze of 1894–1895 in Florida. The development of practical methods for concentrating and freezing orange juice just after World War II provided the basis for the explosive growth of the citrus-processing industry in the following decades.

In 2002 the United States ranked second to Brazil among citrus-producing nations, with more than one million bearing acres, of which Florida had 727,600; California, 268,000; Texas, 29,100; and Arizona, 28,600. These plantings yielded 16.4 million tons, of which 73.8 percent went to processing, mostly for juice; the total value of the crop was $2.6 billion. Per capita consumption of citrus fruits, both fresh and processed, amounted to 112.1 pounds in 2000, including 85.1 pounds of oranges, 13.1 pounds of grapefruit, 7.7 pounds of lemons, 4.4 pounds of tangerines and tangelos, and 1.8 pounds of limes.

At first, growers planted many seedling trees, which are easy to propagate but take up to a decade to come into bearing and are not always true to the type of the parent. In the second half of the nineteenth century nurserymen and growers imported scores of varieties, which they grafted onto rootstock (such as sweet or sour orange seedlings) selected for adaptation to the soil, resistance to disease, and productivity; this vegetative propagation shortened the wait for a crop to three to five years and made possible the marketing of true citrus varieties. Many of the major citrus varieties grown by the early years of the twenty-first century, such as navel and Valencia oranges and Eureka and Lisbon lemons, were imported, selected, or first commercially propagated in the 1870s and 1880s, as farmers found them to be superior in such attributes as size, appearance, flavor, and quantity of fruit produced.

The sweet orange (*C. sinensis*), believed by scientists to be a natural hybrid of pummelo and mandarin, is the leading citrus fruit in the United States, which produces three classes of oranges in commercial quantities: common oranges, a large and diverse group that includes Valencia and Florida juice oranges; navel oranges, which have small, rudimentary secondary fruits embedded in the blossom (bottom) end and are usually seedless; and blood oranges, pigmented with anthocyanins, which impart a distinctive red coloration and berry flavor to the flesh.

The Valencia, the most widely grown orange variety in the United States and the world, was sent from England to California in 1876 and to Florida the next year. Several characteristics account for its popularity: it is well colored and flavored and very late in season, maturing in late spring through autumn of the year after it flowers. By 2002 Florida grew 82 percent of the nation's Valencia crop on 300,500 bearing acres, but 97 percent of its harvest went to processing; California grew most of the rest, but in the same year 82 percent of its harvest went to the fresh market.

Juice oranges, such as Hamlin and Pineapple, are early and midseason varieties, maturing from late September into February. Florida grows most of the nation's crop on an estimated 267,235 acres (as of 2002); the vast majority goes to processing. Early fruits tend to be pale in color and insipid in flavor, but by January, Florida juice oranges are richer in color and taste.

The navel orange, imported from Brazil to Washington, D.C., in 1870 and sent to Riverside, California, several years later, is the nation's leading fresh citrus variety. Large, seedless, and easy to peel, the navel at its best has a smooth, deep-orange rind and intense, sweet-tart flavor, unsurpassed among oranges. In 2002 California had 127,500 bearing acres, mostly in the San Joaquin Valley, and accounted for 86 percent of the nation's crop; the rest came from Florida, Arizona, and Texas. California-grown navels, at peak from January to March, offer high levels of sugar and acidity, a proper balance between the two, and rich aromatics. The navel reaches perfection in the Riverside-Redlands district east of Los Angeles, where fruits ripen more slowly and have finer flavor than San Joaquin Valley fruits. But because of urbanization, bearing acreage of navels in Southern California dropped from 56,000 in 1945 to 7,500 in 2002. By comparison, Florida-grown navels, available from November to January, are larger, paler, and thinner skinned, with juicier but relatively insipid pulp.

Blood oranges first came to prominence and are most popular in the Mediterranean region. In America there were 436 bearing acres by 2002 in California, the major producing state, where chilly nights in late fall and winter produce ruddy pigmentation in the fruits' peels and flesh. Although increased interest in unusual produce has made blood oranges more popular since the 1980s, they are largely a specialty item. In addition to being consumed fresh and as juice, oranges are used in salads, savory dishes, and desserts such as cakes and ices.

Surprisingly recent in origin for a supermarket staple, grapefruit (*C. paradisi*) arose in the seventeenth century in the West Indies, as a hybrid of sweet orange and pomelo. All modern grapefruit—supposedly named for growing in clusters like grapes—derive from seeds or plants brought to Florida in 1809. Early varieties, notably Duncan, had whitish flesh and rich flavor, but many seeds; Marsh, a nearly seedless mutation discovered in about 1860, long dominated Florida's commercial shipments, which began in the 1880s. In the early twentieth century, growers in Florida and Texas discovered pink-fleshed, seedless mutations such as Ruby, which, along with later red-fleshed varieties, such as Rio Red and Star Ruby, dominate production. Most of the remaining white grapefruit goes for processing.

America, which had 138,300 bearing acres of grapefruit in 2002, is by far the world's largest producer of the fruit. The best growing areas, Florida and the lower Rio Grande valley of Texas, have humid conditions and high total heat units during the growing season. Peak quality is found in fruit that matures in late December to early March. Grapefruit is also grown in California, where it is harvested in spring and summer. Grapefruit is primarily consumed as a fresh fruit, in juice, and in fruit salad.

America is the world's second-largest producer of lemons, after Argentina. Of the nation's citrus crops, the lemon (*C. limon*) ranks second in value but third in bearing acreage, at 64,300 in 2002, virtually all in California and Arizona. The two main varieties, Eureka and Lisbon, both came to prominence in the 1870s; they are similar and are marketed interchangeably. The Meyer lemon, probably a hybrid of lemon and orange, is lower in acidity and more aromatic than regular lemons. It is a backyard favorite and is grown commercially on a small scale in California, southern Texas, and Florida.

In coastal California, lemon trees flower and fruit year-round, but overall lemon production peaks in winter, as for most citrus. Since demand increases in summer—for lemonade and for wedges to squeeze in alcoholic beverages—packinghouses have mastered the science of storing lemons, which are picked green and held for months in climate-controlled rooms. When market conditions are right, packers treat the fruits with heat, humidity, and ethylene gas to turn them yellow.

Mandarins, popularly often called tangerines, have thin skin and delicate pulp. They were introduced in the 1840s to Louisiana, but they have always been a secondary crop in America. There were 38,600 bearing acres in 2002, of which Florida had the majority and California and Arizona the rest. The classic Florida "Christmas tangerine," Dancy, has superb aroma and flavor and an edible rind, but it was replaced toward the end of the twentieth century by Fallglo and Sunburst, which are brightly colored but of mediocre eating quality. Satsumas, early-season, seedless varieties, are grown in California and along the Gulf Coast. Starting in the 1980s imported Spanish clementines, also seedless, claimed a significant share of the American market; in the late 1990s California growers planted several thousand acres. Most mandarins are eaten fresh. There are also substantial plantings of tangelos (grapefruit-mandarin hybrids, such as Minneola) and tangors (mandarin-orange hybrids, such as Temple). Florida has 14,400 bearing acres and California has 3,800 of these two types.

The two chief varieties of lime (*C. aurantifolia*) both have greenish, acid pulp and are usually sold with green rinds, although they turn yellow when fully ripe. The Mexican, or Key, lime, is small, round, and seedy; the Persian, or Bearss, lime is larger and seedless. Florida had 800 bearing acres in 2002, and California had 475, mostly of the Bearss type. Florida's plantings were drastically reduced in the late 1990s as canker, a devastating disease, struck the southernmost districts of the state, the traditional growing area for limes, which are the most cold sensitive of citrus fruits. Limes are used to flavor sweet items such as sorbet; to "cook" fish with its acid in seviche dishes; to add zest to soft and alcoholic drinks; and in a dessert classic, Key lime pie.

[*See also* Fruit; Fruit Juices; Orange Juice.]

BIBLIOGRAPHY

Jackson, Larry K., and Frederick S. Davies. *Citrus Growing in Florida.* 4th ed. Gainesville: University Press of Florida, 1999.

McPhee, John. *Oranges.* New York: Farrar, Straus and Giroux, 1967.

Reuther, Walter, Herbert John Webber, and Leon Dexter Batchelor, eds. *The Citrus Industry.* 5 vols. Berkeley: University of California, 1967–1989.

Saunt, James. *Citrus Varieties of the World.* Norwich, U.K.: Sinclair International, 2000.

Walheim, Lance. *Citrus: Complete Guide to Selecting and Growing More Than 100 Varieties.* Tucson, AZ: Ironwood Press, 1996.

DAVID KARP

Claiborne, Craig

Food editor, restaurant critic, cookbook author, and gracious host, Craig Claiborne (1920–2000) was instrumental in leading millions of meat-and-potato Americans to the table of fine cuisine. As food editor of the *New York Times* and the country's foremost restaurant critic, he introduced gastronomically sheltered Americans to the greatest chefs of France, Italy, and Asia and, through his recipes and more than twenty books, encouraged home cooks to broaden their culinary horizons.

Born in Mississippi, Claiborne graduated from the University of Missouri in 1942, where he studied journalism. Aided by the GI Bill after discharge from the navy, he fulfilled his lifelong dream and entered the prestigious École Hôtelière near Lausanne, Switzerland, to study classic French cooking.

He started his culinary journey as a receptionist at *Gourmet* magazine and eventually moved up to become one of its editors. In 1957 he broke journalistic ground by landing the position of food editor at the *New York Times*, a post traditionally held by women. He was the first restaurant critic with a solid background in food

Craig Claiborne. *Culinary Archives & Museum at Johnson & Wales University, Providence, R.I.*

preparation, rating a restaurant rigorously on its food. Known for his gentlemanly authoritarian manner, he showed a hitherto unfamiliar respect for chefs and restaurateurs. He hated pretension and sloppy or overbearing service, and his eye for detail could make even tough restaurateurs wince. In 1972 he gave up restaurant criticism for the *Times* to start a short-lived newsletter with his colleague Pierre Franey, whom he had known since 1959, when Franey was a chef at Henri Soulé's celebrated Le Pavillon. When Franey left Le Pavillon, he began accompanying Claiborne on his restaurant rounds and developed recipes for Claiborne's food columns.

Claiborne's most notorious caper was an American Express–sponsored unlimited-expense dinner for two. Reporting on the thirty-one-course, four-thousand-dollar dinner that he and Franey consumed at Paris's Chez Denis restaurant made headline news and brought thousands of letters of protest. Claiborne returned to the *Times* in 1974 to concentrate on writing about food and chefs. The cooking took place in the enormous kitchen of his East Hampton home, with Franey developing recipes for the *New York Times Magazine* and later for the Living Section. Their collaboration led to seven books for the *Times*, among them *Classic French Cooking*, *Veal Cookery*, *Craig Claiborne's "The New York Times" Cookbook*, and *Craig Claiborne's Gourmet Diet*, written after his doctor advised him to limit his salt and fat intake.

An avid traveler, Claiborne had a knack for identifying fresh talent and frequently bolstered a young chef's career by giving him or her exposure in the *Times*. Among those who benefited from his foresight were French chefs like Paul Bocuse, Roger Vergé, Alain Ducasse, Jean Troisgros, and Gaston Lenotre, as well as the Italian cookbook writer Marcella Hazan and the Cajun chef Paul Prudhomme.

A Feast Made for Laughter chronicles the dining and cooking adventures encountered along the way. At heart a Francophile, he was open to other cuisines, including those of Brazil, Mexico, and China. He had a talent for demystifying the formality of cooking and made it accessible to all, as in *The Chinese Cookbook*, written with Virginia Lee. *Memorable Meals* is his collection of meals shared with his wide range of friends, including his nearly legendary New Year's Eve dinners. Among other books are *Craig Claiborne's Kitchen Primer*, *Elements of Etiquette*, and *Craig Claiborne's Southern Cooking*, in which he pays homage to his southern roots.

[*See also* Celebrity Chefs; Cookbooks and Manuscripts, *subentry* From 1970s to the Present; Prudhomme, Paul.]

BIBLIOGRAPHY

Claiborne, Craig. *A Feast Made for Laughter*. New York: Henry Holt, 1983.

HELEN H. STUDLEY

Clambake

Generations of historians incorrectly record that the New England clambake is the survival of a native custom learned by the first English colonists. Archeological and historical evidence supports clam eating by Native Americans, but not by the newcomers, who identified them with "savagery." Clams were a starvation ration to the Europeans, who used the abundant shellfish to feed pigs.

The clambake myth arose from the social and political changes brought about by American independence. The new nation needed an icon of its unique cultural identity, and an "ancient ritual" featuring indigenous food provided it. It is no accident that the popularity of the clambake exploded after the Civil War, when a new national myth was again created. Plymouth replaced Jamestown as the cradle of America, and the "New England" clambake became an American institution.

The advent of mass transportation in the late nineteenth century gave businessmen the opportunity to turn the clambake into a tourist industry. Rhode Island entrepreneurs were so successful that the first printed recipe for a "clambake" gives that state credit for the custom. Clambake "pavilions" quickly spread across New England. Often combined with equally popular picnics, clambakes worked especially well as fund-raisers and political rallies, a role they continue to fill.

No longer exclusive to New England, clambakes seem to require only that the clams be cooked by steam. A "traditional" clambake occurs in a pit dug in the sand of the beach where the clams are gathered. The pit is lined with rocks, and a fire is built over them. When the rocks are white hot, they are covered with layers of seaweed, clams, and other foods. A wet tarp is laid over all until the food is cooked. Items typically included on the menu are lobster, corn, white potatoes, clam chowder, and cold beer.

[*See also* Clams; New England Regional Cookery; Picnics.]

BIBLIOGRAPHY

Neustadt, Kathy. *Clambake: A History and Celebration of an American Tradition.* Amherst: University of Massachusetts Press, 1992. Perhaps the definitive work on the clambake, its true history, and its meaning in American society.

ESTHER DELLA REESE

Clams

The poor clam has taken a back seat to the regal oyster. While oysters starred as oysters Rockefeller at city restaurants, clams either were used as bait or served fried at roadside clam shacks. While clams lack the regal image of the oyster, they still represent a valuable fishery product. Five species of clams make up the bulk of the U.S. commercial harvest: surf clam (*Spisula solidissima*), ocean quahog (*Arctica islandica*), hard-shell clam (*Mercenaria mercenaria*), soft-shell clam (*Mya arenaria*), and Manila clam (*Tapes philippinarum*).

Before Europeans arrived in America, Native Americans harvested clams. Huge piles of clamshells or kitchen middens identify old Indian campsites. Native Americans used the hard-shell clam, also known as a quahog, as a source of food and medium of exchange and for sealing friendships. The purple part of the shell, along with the white part of periwinkle shells, were fashioned into beads, strung on sinew, and made into belts called wampum. For a time during the colonial period, individual beads and ornamental wampum belts were used as money.

Surf clams and ocean quahogs are dredged from the ocean depths and represent by far the largest harvest. The hard-shell clams—also called littleneck, cherrystone, or chowder depending on the size—are consumed raw or minced for use in chowders. Hard-shell clams are harvested by hand with tongs or by dredging. Soft-shell clams are gathered at low tide by spading with a fork. It is a slow and laborious process, but clamming provides an important source of income for some New England coastal residents.

Understanding the names under which clams are sold is like untangling a fishnet. *M. arenaria*, the eastern soft-shell clam, is served as fried clams at roadside clam shacks throughout New England. Some cookbooks refer to this clam as the common clam, longneck, long clam, sand gaper, old maid, maninose (nannynose), belly clam, or squirt clam. Since the nineteenth century it has been listed on restaurant menus as the Ipswich clam after Ipswich Bay, with its highly productive clamming flats. Ipswich, Massachusetts, is a commercial center for clam processing and wholesale distribution. Since 1935 tourists have made the pilgrimage to Ipswich to eat fried clam bellies at the Clam Box.

Chowder Party. Illustration of a chowder party on Fire Island, Long Island, by John Worth, published in *Harper's Weekly,* 23 August 1873. *Collection of Alice Ross*

When East Coast production falls behind demand, clams are shipped from Washington State, where small amounts of soft-shell clams are harvested. It is estimated that most soft-shell clams are consumed "within five miles of the coast from Boston to Bar Harbor, Maine." The first canneries in the United States were established along the coast, and marine products made up a substantial part of what was canned. Burnham and Morrill opened the first clam cannery about 1870 at Pine Point, Maine.

On the West Coast, early pioneers found a host of new clam species to duplicate the chowders, bisques, clam pies, and fritters they remembered from New England. They had a group of small clams called the butter clam (*Saxidomus giganteus*), Pismo (*Tivela stultorum*), the western jackknife clam (*Tagelus californianus*) and the horse clam (*Tresus nuttallii*). They also had the giant geoduck (*Panopea abrupta*), pronounced "gooey-duck," a Nisqually Indian phrase meaning "to dig deep." Genevieve A. Callahan's *Sunset All-Western Cook Book: How to Select, Prepare, Cook, and Serve All Typically Western Food Products* (1933) describes this clam as a "legless, headless duck, the shells forming the wings and the wrinkled, mottled skin representing the down on the neck and breast." With this abundance of Pacific Coast clams, traditional New England recipes take on new names such as Pacific Coast Clam Chowder and Oregon Clam Bisque.

[*See also* Clambake; Fish, *subentry on* Saltwater Shellfish; New England Regional Cookery; Seafood.]

BIBLIOGRAPHY

Davidson, Alan. *North Atlantic Seafood.* New York: Viking, 1979.
Dore, Ian. *Shellfish: A Guide to Oysters, Mussels, Scallops, Clams, and Similar Products for the Commercial User.* New York: Van Nostrand Reinhold, 1991.
Peterson, James. *Fish & Shellfish.* New York: Morrow, 1996.

JOSEPH M. CARLIN

Clarifying

To "clarify" means to clear a liquid of solid particles. The purpose of clarifying is to make a liquid clear, preserve food, or remove a taste. Early recipes for clarifying sugar, butter, molasses, stocks, jellies, beer, and wine demonstrate various techniques. Typically, recipes involve introducing some sort of clarifying agent, frequently egg whites, and careful straining to filter impurities. While modern production techniques and changing tastes have eliminated the need to clarify most foods, a few, such as butter and stock, are still clarified for particular culinary applications.

Martha Washington's *Booke of Cookery and Booke of Sweetmeats*, written in the days before white sugar was common (probably between 1550 and 1625; the text is based on an old manuscript passed down to Washington), opens with a recipe for clarified sugar. "Take a pinte of faire water & beat ye white of an egg . . . put a pound of sugar in to it & let it boyle. . . . There will rise a black scum . . . take it off until it is very clear, & then streyne it through A Jelly Bag or wet cloth" (p. 225). Similar recipes appeared throughout the mid-nineteenth century in works such as Catharine Beecher's *Domestic Receipt-Book* (1858).

Recipes for "calf 's-feet jelly" require egg whites to clarify the stock. Typical is Eliza Leslie's recipe in *Seventy-five Receipts for Pastry, Cakes, and Sweetmeats* (1832), in which the whites and small bits of eggshell are mixed with stock. Leslie instructs the reader to "boil it hard for five minutes, . . . pour it hot into the bag (made of white flannel) and let it drip through into the dish" (p. 539). Broths for aspic and consommé are still clarified by a similar process.

Selected Receipts of a Van Rensselaer Family, 1785–1835 offers several clarifying techniques, including using milk to clear spiced wine, adding a piece of burned chalk to keep a barrel of beer "brisk and clear" (p. 42), and preserving butter (for up to a year) by melting it with an onion and letting the particles settle to the bottom. Modern cooks still clarify butter to extend its shelf life and increase its smoke point by melting it to remove the fragile milk solids.

[*See also* Butter; Cooking Techniques.]

BIBLIOGRAPHY

Kellar, Jane Carpenter, Ellen Miller, and Paul Stambach. *Selected Receipts of a Van Rensselaer Family, 1785–1835.* Albany, NY: Historic Cherry Hill, 1976.
Leslie, Eliza. *Seventy-five Receipts for Pastry, Cakes, and Sweetmeats.* Bedford, MA: Applewood Books, 1989. Reprint of the original 1832 edition.
Washington, Martha. *Martha Washington's Booke of Cookery and Booke of Sweetmeats.* Transcribed and edited by Karen Hess. New York: Columbia University Press, 1995.

ALEXA VAN DE WALLE

Club Sandwich

The club sandwich typically is composed of three slices of toast, spread with mayonnaise, that separate a filling of sliced turkey, ham, or chicken along with sliced tomato, strips of crispy fried bacon, and lettuce. The origin of the sandwich is unknown. The first recipe appears as Club-House Sandwiches in Sarah Tyson Rorer's *Sandwiches* (1894). In the late 1890s it was a popular item at the casino owned by Richard Canfield, "America's Greatest Gambler," in Saratoga Springs, New York. The casino's dining room was known for its fine cuisine and for its gambler's buffet, which provided delicious food for those who wanted minimum interruption of their gaming pursuits. By 1896 the club sandwich appeared on the menus of such New York City establishments as the Waldorf-Astoria Hotel and the Windsor Hotel. The club sandwich remains a ubiquitous item on restaurant luncheon menus.

[*See also* Sandwiches.]

BIBLIOGRAPHY

Mercuri, Becky. *Sandwiches That You Will Like*. Pittsburgh, PA: WQED Multimedia, 2002.
Rorer, Sarah Tyson. *Sandwiches*. Philadelphia, PA: Arnold and Company, 1894.

BECKY MERCURI

Cobbler, *see Pies and Tarts*

Coca-Cola

Invented in 1886 by an Atlanta pharmacist, John S. Pemberton, Coca-Cola is the second-best-known term on earth (after "OK") and is the most widely distributed single product in the world. As a symbol of the American consumer lifestyle, the drink has significance and power far beyond its fizzy sugar-water contents.

Coca-Cola evolved from Pemberton's French Wine of Coca, a cocaine-laced wine beverage sold in imitation of the extremely popular Vin Mariani. When Atlanta voted in November 1885 to go "dry" the following year, Pemberton revised his formula, removing the wine and adding an assortment of essential flavoring oils, caramel for color, and a large amount of sugar. Along with coca leaf and kola nut extract—the respective sources of cocaine and caffeine and the origin of the drink's name— these ingredients made up Coca-Cola syrup, which was then mixed with carbonated water to make a popular drink in an era of resplendent soda fountains offering a wide variety of flavors.

Coca-Cola Advertisement. Advertising card, c. 1905. *Collection of Kit Barry*

But Coca-Cola was also a patent medicine, a popular "nerve tonic" to cure neurasthenia, a mythical disease supposed to afflict high-strung housewives and businessmen. The beverage was also touted as a headache and hangover cure. When Pemberton died in 1888, a fellow Atlanta pharmacist, Asa Candler, who believed that Coca-Cola helped his migraines, secured the rights to the formula in a convoluted, somewhat shady series of transactions. Frank Robinson, who had worked for Pemberton, had named the drink, and had written the flowing script for the logo, marketed the drink for Candler and wrote most of the advertising. By 1899 it was a national soda fountain drink, with branches and syrup factories in Dallas, Chicago, Los Angeles, Philadelphia, and New York.

Up to that time Coca-Cola was only a soda fountain drink. Fearful of spoilage and spillage, Candler saw no future in bottles, so in 1899 he gave away the bottling rights to Benjamin Thomas and Joseph Whitehead, two lawyers from Chattanooga, Tennessee, with the stipulation that they buy syrup only from The Coca-Cola Company. These "parent bottlers" established a successful network of Coca-Cola bottlers, and the drink became available everywhere to everyone, including African Americans, who in those days were excluded from soda fountains.

By the turn of the century Coca-Cola's cocaine content, though very small, was causing problems, because the supposed wonder drug of 1886 was then seen as an addictive scourge. Owing to racism, it was also blamed for unrest among southern blacks. Bowing to social pressure, Candler took the cocaine out of Coca-Cola in 1903, though coca leaf extract with its cocaine content removed remains in the formula.

With missionary zeal, Coca-Cola salesmen and bottlers pushed the beverage as a magical elixir. With equal fervor, food faddists and temperance women fought against Coca-Cola, claiming that its caffeine was bad for children and adults. Candler survived a 1911 government lawsuit prompted by Dr. Harvey Wiley, head of the U.S. Food and Drug Administration, but the company stopped using children under the age of twelve in its advertising and cut the caffeine content in half.

As Candler grew older, he gave most of the company stock to his children, who sold the company in 1919 for $25 million to a consortium of bankers headed by the Atlanta wheeler-dealer Ernest Woodruff. In the inflationary post–World War I period, the price of sugar soared, throwing the company into crisis and conflict with its independent bottlers, whose contract called for a fixed syrup price. When Woodruff attempted to abrogate the contract, a protracted lawsuit ensued. It was finally settled with a sliding price for the sugar content.

The Woodruff Era

Robert Woodruff, Ernest's charismatic thirty-three-year-old son, took over as president in 1923. Known as "the Boss," he ruled the company, passing on every major decision until his death in 1985 at the age of ninety-five. Woodruff forbade negative, defensive advertising and, with the help of Archie Lee's "Pause That Refreshes" slogan and Haddon Sundblom's Coca-Cola Santa Claus paintings, he made Coca-Cola an all-American drink. By the time of World War II, it had become a symbol of the American way of life. During the war, Coca-Cola for the military was exempted from sugar rationing, and Coke employees were given pseudo-military status in order to bottle the drink behind the lines. This gave Coca-Cola an invaluable foothold for international expansion following the war.

Meanwhile, Pepsi-Cola emerged as a major contender. It had thrived during the Depression as a cheap alterna-

tive to Coke, but that had given it a lower-class stigma. In the 1950s and 1960s Pepsi sought a more vital, upscale image, focusing on the baby boom generation. The conservative Woodruff refused to respond for a long time, but in 1955 he permitted the introduction of King Size Coke to match Pepsi ounce for ounce, and in the 1960s the company began selling alternate drinks, such as Sprite, Tab, and Fanta.

Because of its symbolic weight and ubiquity, Coca-Cola was particularly subject to political forces. In the postwar world, Communists spread rumors that the drink caused health problems and that a German Coca-Cola plant was a secret atom bomb factory. When the company rejected an Israeli franchise in 1966, American Jews protested. After the company rushed to correct the problem, the Arabs boycotted Coke products. The company was politically well connected in the United States, however. Woodruff had helped elect President Dwight Eisenhower, who shared ownership in Latin American bottling plants, and a later president, Jimmy Carter, relied heavily on the Coca-Cola Company's expertise for inside information in foreign countries.

Goizueta's Changes

By the time the Cuban expatriate Roberto Goizueta took over as chief executive officer in 1981, Coca-Cola was widely perceived as a sleeping giant, a conservative company living largely on its past accomplishments. Pepsi was making inroads. Goizueta announced that there would be no sacred cows, no sacred formulas. For the first time, the company took on debt. Goizueta violated tradition by having the company assume equity positions in bottlers around the world; approving the introduction of Diet Coke, with its previously forbidden use of the main drink's name; and, finally, in 1985, daring to change the formula of Coca-Cola itself. New Coke turned out to be a disaster, but even that blunder worked out well in the end, when the market share of the reintroduced Coca-Cola Classic increased.

By the time Goizueta died of cancer in 1997, the revitalized company's market share had exploded from $4.3 billion when he took over to $145 billion, and Coke products accounted for half of the world's soft drink sales. Since then, the company has had problems, largely owing to a troubled world economy. During his brief, stormy tenure as CEO, Doug Ivester mishandled a health scare in which the company had to withdraw its supposedly contaminated drinks in Belgium and other European countries, although independent scientists concluded that the panic, nausea, and dizziness—classic symptoms of psychosomatic illness—were probably caused by mass hysteria. Ivester resigned in 1999 and was replaced by an Australian, Douglas Daft. In the twenty-first century, the drink Coca-Cola remains extremely important, but the company is shifting with the times to offer a wider variety of noncarbonated beverages, such as Fruitopia and its bottled water, Dasani.

[See also Advertising; Cola Wars; Soda Drinks.]

BIBLIOGRAPHY

Allen, Frederick. *Secret Formula: How Brilliant Marketing and Relentless Salesmanship Made Coca-Cola the Best-Known Product in the World.* New York: HarperBusiness, 1994. Good history, focusing on Atlanta and Robert Woodruff.

Greising, David. *I'd Like the World to Buy a Coke: The Life and Leadership of Roberto Goizueta.* New York: Wiley, 1998. A good business biography, published just after Goizueta's death.

Oliver, Thomas. *The Real Coke, the Real Story.* New York: Random House, 1986. A good account of the New Coke fiasco, written by an Atlanta reporter.

Pendergrast, Mark. *For God, Country, and Coca-Cola: The Definitive History of the Great American Soft Drink and the Company That Makes It.* 2nd ed. New York: Basic Books, 2000. Scholarly and comprehensive.

MARK PENDERGRAST

Cocktails

Cocktails are shaken or stirred, rolled or muddled; they are dry or sweet, creamy or frozen. They are perfect or dirty; they are up or over. But one thing they are not is weak. There is an hour reverentially dedicated to them. Parties are named after them. Thousands of designers have created vessels exclusively to showcase them or shake them. They are truly American, a gift to the beverage culture of the world.

> Cocktails are sexy and sleek
> But seldom are they ever weak
> When taken to excess
> We can no longer express
> Or even remain on our feet

The Old World alcoholic beverage traditions are neat and settled, with thousands of years of history behind them. Port has its place after dinner, and whiskey is taken neat with a little water. Before dinner a bitter aperitif is served to stimulate the appetite, and, of course, there is a wine for nearly every cuisine. The French were appalled at the idea of a cocktail before dinner. The English were astonished to see juleps served on mountains of snow ice.

It was this diversity of culture that came with the successive waves of immigrants to America that played the largest part in the development of the mixed drink known as the cocktail. All the groups brought with them long-established beverage traditions, like wine, brandy, grain spirits, or liqueurs. All of these traditions got mixed together, and they ended up in one glass called the cocktail—a composite drink for a composite people.

The New World was too big and too wild to be confined in a sherry glass. America was not about tradition; it was about adventure, leaping forward and taking chances on all fronts. What other country could produce the zombie, sex on the beach, the Alabama fogcutter, and the stinger? Even classics in the beverage tradition are mind-numbing doses of spirits called the martini and the Manhattan.

It did not take long for the early colonists to begin experimenting with the raw materials at hand in the New World. All manner of vegetables were fermented and distilled, including spruce and birch beers as well as turnip and rhubarb wines; and even corn, the New World staple, was distilled by the clever Scottish and Irish distillers into a spirit that would become the distinctive American bourbon whiskey. Sugarcane, arriving with Columbus on his second voyage west to create a sugar supply for the Old World, was quickly perverted into a new, thriving industry for colonial America—rum distilling. Old World vines planted in South America by the Spanish to produce wine were distilled into a rough brandy called pisco. Agave, the base of a native fermented drink called pulque, became the raw material for a potent New World spirit—tequila.

The first recorded definition of the cocktail appeared on May 13, 1806, in *The Balance and Columbian Repository,* published in New York City. In a comical letter written to the editor, a reader inquired about which "species of refreshment" a cocktail consisted of and whether the name was "expressive of the effect which the drink has on a particular part of the body." The editor replied:

> Cocktail is a stimulating liquor composed of spirits of any kind, sugar, water, and bitters—that is vulgarly called bittered sling and is supposed to be an excellent electioneering potion, inasmuch as it renders the heart stout and bold at the same time that it fuddles the head. It is said also to be of great use to a Democratic candidate; because, a person having swallowed a glass of it is ready to swallow anything else.

The one ingredient that differentiated the cocktail from other mixed alcoholic drinks that preceded it was the emergence of a new product called bitters. Made from distilled spirits infused with spice, fruit, and botanical ingredients, bitters are highly concentrated flavor additives. Although bitters contain as much as 40 percent alcohol, they are designated as a food additive and in the nineteenth century were sold as medicinal tonic, a designation that allowed the purveyors to avoid the high tax on spirits. The two most widely used bitters are Angostura and Peychaud's.

Many factors led to the emergence of the cocktail and the cocktail culture in the early 1800s. One of the biggest was the Industrial Revolution. New technology and the explosion of immigration greatly changed the American way of life in the beginning of the nineteenth century. In forty years America went from an agrarian to an urban society.

Immigration

Driven by the potato famine in the British islands and the disastrous economy of the post-Napoleonic Wars on the Continent, waves of immigrants flocked to the cities of the Northeast, and they brought strong communal drinking traditions with them—the pubs of the British islands and the beer halls of Germany.

Ghettos in the cities were soon filled with illegal drinking establishments and social clubs called "blind pigs." The enormous potential for a political power base in these ghettos did not go unnoticed by the political machines of the day. Many of these illegal operations were later turned into bars and saloons funded by the big-city political machines like Tammany Hall in New York City to gain control of the voting population in the Irish and German ghettos. Some blocks in Manhattan had as many as six bars, and it was in these bars that the business of the political precincts and wards was done. It was in these bars that the cocktail culture of the latter half of the nineteenth century was born.

Taxation

Fermented and distilled beverages were a tremendous source of revenue for the young republic. Alexander Hamilton paid off the war debt to the French after the Revolutionary War with an excise tax on whiskey and rum. The War of 1812 was also paid for by taxation; however, in 1817, after the war debt was settled, a forty-five year hiatus of virtually no taxation accounted for an explosion of growth in the spirits and beer industry.

After the two wars with England, a high increase in taxes drove the small farm distillers of Pennsylvania and Maryland to the frontier territories that would become Tennessee, Kentucky, and Indiana, where they produced corn whiskey on a subsistence basis. Unable to cross the mountains to sell their whiskey in the big cities of the Northeast, many farmers floated their barrels of whiskey downriver on flatboats to New Orleans, Louisiana. The French in New Orleans were brandy drinkers, so the price for whiskey was low. That situation changed with the arrival of the Industrial Revolution. The first big change was the steam engine, which was outfitted to push flatboats upstream. Overnight the small farm distillers gave way to large businesses that were able to take advantage of the newly invented steam engine to move their whiskey north against the current to the big markets of the Northeast. With the opening of the Erie Canal, big-city markets were open to the big river systems of Middle America.

Technology

The soul of the American cocktail is ice. Ice was a luxury enjoyed only by the wealthy early in the nineteenth century, so the artificial ice machines were especially important to cocktail development. By the 1880s artificial ice was affordable at even modest drinking establishments.

In the 1830s another development that dramatically changed the distilling industry was the invention of the Coffey, or column, still in Ireland. This permitted distillers to produce spirits faster and more cheaply than ever before. This new technology precipitated the emergence of the large commercial distiller.

On the retail side of the business, restaurants and gentlemen's drinking establishments were growing as fast as the population. The newly rich industrialists were catered to in the most luxurious fashion in their drinking salons with elaborate oyster bars and cigar counters. The appointments were worthy of royalty, with marble and fine wood bar cabinets augmented by more technological wonders, such as artificial ice machines, gas-driven beer taps, and water with gas bubbles for sparkling beverages—all tended by skilled craftsmen in their starched white jackets and diamond stickpins.

Recipe

In 1862, in the middle of this growth, a colorful figure named Jerry Thomas entered the scene with a book and a mission. The book was *How to Mix Drinks; or, The Bon Vivant's Companion*. It was a compilation of recipes from around the country and Europe, using spirits and wines in many categories of mixed drinks. The mission was to popularize the sprit-based mixed drinks Thomas had dedicated his life to compiling. Buried in the pages of this groundbreaking book with the flips and sangarees was a small category called "Cocktails and Crustas." The cocktail, true to the definition of fifty years before in *The Balance and Colombian Repository*, was a strong spirit, a sweet ingredient, and bitters. Only thirteen cocktails and crustas were listed in the book along with 223 other concoctions, so it was a relatively small category. By the end of the nineteenth century, however, the word "cocktail" had become the generic word for all mixed spirit drinks.

A similar phenomenon occurred with the word "martini." The martini cocktail, narrowly defined, is a combination of gin, vermouth, and an olive or a twist of lemon. Actually the martini cocktail has gone through substantial evolution as well, from a much sweeter version in the nineteenth century, with additional ingredients like bitters, to the vodka martini of the late twentieth century. Among a younger group of drinkers, "martini" describes any drink served with alcohol in the classic V-shaped martini glass.

Products from Europe figured prominently in early cocktail recipes, and some actually defined the classic cocktails that still reign as the superstars of the category. The two most widely known and classic of the cocktails from the nineteenth century are the martini and the Manhattan; both use vermouth, which was originally formulated in the late eighteenth century in Turin, Italy. Curaçao, from the Bols distillery, was an important sweet ingredient in the earliest cocktails even before vermouth was available in America, and some of the raw materials for both curaçao and vermouth were from the New World. The bitter oranges of Curaçao and the spices from South America and the Caribbean are ingredients that made the round trip and became the cornerstones of the cocktail culture.

Word Origin

In England the word "cocktail" was used to describe a horse of mixed breed but high quality that had a docked tail to distinguish it from thoroughbreds. In the early nineteenth century the word was used as slang to refer to soldiers who exhibited unsoldierlike or cowardly behavior, as a soldier faced with danger "turning cocktail." An intriguing quote attributed to Samuel Johnson would predate all previous stories of the origin of "cocktail" as a word for a mixed alcoholic drink: "To mix spirits to wine

smacks of our alcoholic hyperbole. It would be a veritable cocktail of a drink."

Antoine Amédée Peychaud, who created Peychaud's bitters at his apothecary shop in New Orleans, served cognac and bitters to guests in his shop in two-sided eggcups called *coquetiers*. The word sounds similar to the word "cocktail" in English.

There is the colonial story of Betsy's Tavern in Halls Corner, New York, where American and French soldiers were dining on stolen British pheasants and downing Betsy's bracers when a soldier exclaimed, "Here's to the divine liquor which is as delicious to the palate, as the cock's tails are beautiful to the eye." The French replied, "Vive le cocktail!"

The stories are too numerous to recount here, and it is doubtful that the mystery of why "cocktail" became the word to describe this American beverage will be solved.

[*See also* Alcohol and Teatotalism; Alcoholism; Bars; Bloody Mary and Virgin Mary; Boilermaker; Bourbon; Brandy; Brandy Alexander; Collins; Cuba Libre; Gin; Grasshopper; Highball; Irish Coffee; Mai Tai; Manhattan; Margarita; Martini; Mimosa; Mint Julep; Old-Fashioned; Rum; Sazerac; Stills; Taverns; Tequila Sunrise; Vermouth; Vodka; Whiskey; Whiskey Sour; Zombie.]

BIBLIOGRAPHY

Barr, Andrew. *Drink: A Social History of America*. New York: Carroll and Graf, 1999.

Brown, John Hull. *Early American Beverages*. Rutland, VT: Tuttle, 1966.

Farmer, J. S., and W. E. Henley. *Slang and Its Analogues*. New York: Arno Press, 1970.

DALE DEGROFF

Coconuts

Probably natives of tropical Asia or Melanesia, coconut palms (*Cocos nucifera*) flourish in tropical areas where their stately trunks (sometimes averaging one hundred feet in height) and their swaying, rustling leaves have become synonymous with beach holidays. The palm's hard, brown nut reportedly earned its name when Spanish and Portuguese explorers likened the three eyes of the coconut shell to the face of a smiling goblin, or *coco*. Cited in Samuel Johnson's 1775 *Dictionary of the English Language*, the word was once spelled "cocoanut," but over time the "a" was dropped, possibly to avoid confusion with the word "cocoa."

Credit for the coconut palm's global dispersal belongs to ancient traders, explorers such as Marco Polo, and seafarers who carried along the coconut as a source of both food and beverage. But the coconuts themselves may have played a role in their migration. The durable nut readily floats and can easily travel along ocean currents to land on tropical beaches miles away from its point of origin.

Just when the coconut palm appeared on American shores is open to debate, but some accounts tell that on southern plantations coconut meat was used for making the holiday dessert, ambrosia. In the late 1860s, a Pennsylvania farmer traveling along the Florida coast spotted three coconut palms growing wild on the shores of what is now Miami Beach and decided to relocate there to try growing and harvesting coconuts. A decade later, accounts state that Florida's Palm Beach received its name when the vessel *Providencia* bound from Havana to Europe, washed ashore with its load of coconuts in 1878.

Although all coconut palms look generally alike, numerous cultivars do exist and are distinguished by differences in size, color, meat and liquid content, and shape of the nut. The nut is probably the most valuable aspect of the coconut palm and has multiple uses. It can provide a cooling, clear liquid to quench thirst (including the alcoholic drink, toddy, derived from the sap); a firm, white flesh to enhance savory or sweet dishes; an oil for frying and conversion into such industrial products as soaps and fuel; a coarse husk for cooking fuel; and a hard outer shell for household items like kitchen utensils and hair ornaments. No wonder John F. Kennedy felt gratitude for the

hard-shelled nut. Stranded in the Pacific during World War II, Kennedy scratched a plea for rescue on a coconut shell, which natives found and took to the Americans. That coconut later became part of Kennedy's White House collection.

Coconut milk, extracted from the nut's mature meat, plays a significant role in the cuisines of several countries, including India, Southeast Asia, the Caribbean, and coastal Africa. For all its seeming blandness, versatile coconut milk offers its own culinary alchemy. It smoothes out flavors in fiery dishes, adds a subtle sweetness, and can double as cream, milk, or thickener. Because of its high fat content, thick coconut cream, which is the liquid produced from the first pressing of coconut meat, can also be used as an oil for frying.

Coconut milk should not be mistaken for the slightly opaque liquid that sloshes around in a young or immature coconut's cavity. This watery fluid can be extracted by cracking open the coconut's top and then sipping the coconut water with a straw or pouring it into glasses. Coconut water quenches thirsts in hot climates, and according to at least one old wives' tale, drinking it may help prevent skin from aging.

Although rarely an ingredient in north Asian or other northern kitchens, coconut milk is a staple in most tropical countries where natives understand its properties and worth. Southeast Asian and southern Indian cooks find coconut milk almost indispensable, using it in every course from soups and curries, to salads, beverages, and

Coconut Recipes. Cookbooklet issued by the Franklin Baker Co., 1923. *Collection of Andrew F. Smith*

desserts. Its widespread use in the American kitchen may be traced to the foresight of the Philadelphian Franklin Baker, who in the late 1890s processed the meat from a bulk shipment of coconuts, giving both home and professional cooks access to dried, shredded coconut for use in confections and other dishes.

Beyond the nut itself, the entire tree yields useful resources. Its roots and fibers provide herbal remedies; its trunk furnishes timber for building; and its dried fronds, or leaves, form thatching for buildings. No wonder Sanskrit writings describe the coconut palm as *kalpa vriksha*, or "the tree which gives all that is necessary for living."

[*See also* Candy Bars and Candy; Caribbean Influences on American Food; Fats and Oils; Indian American Food; Southeast Asian American Food.]

BIBLIOGRAPHY

Davidson, Alan. *The Penguin Companion to Food.* New York: Penguin Books, 2002.

Passmore, Jacki. *The Encyclopedia of Asian Food and Cooking.* New York: Hearst, 1991.

Stobart, Tom. *The Cook's Encyclopedia: Ingredients and Processes.* Edited by Millie Owen. New York: Harper & Row, 1981.

ALEXANDRA GREELEY

Coffee

Americans are addicted to two black energy-promoting liquids. Oil is the most valuable legal traded commodity on earth, fueling our vehicles and heating our homes until we find a better alternative. Coffee is the second most valuable, and it has been the beverage of choice to jump-start Americans on the go.

On the mountainsides of Ethiopia, the native understory coffee tree grows to twenty or thirty feet in the dappled shade of the rain-forest canopy. There are many species of coffee plant, but only two have proved to be commercially viable. *Coffea arabica*, the original Ethiopian species, considered superior in taste, accounts for 75 percent of world consumption. It grows best in mild tropical climates between three thousand and six thousand feet above sea level. *Coffea canephora*, also known as *Coffea robusta*, has twice the caffeine, is more disease resistant, endures hotter temperatures, and has a more bitter taste. It was discovered in the Congo in the late nineteenth century.

No one is sure when humans first used the coffee tree, which produces the alkaloid caffeine as a natural pesticide. The drug laces coffee leaves and berries, called cherries as they ripen and turn red. Rhazes, an Arabian physician, first mentioned coffee in print in a tenth-century medical text, emphasizing its positive properties. The raw seeds were ground and mixed with animal fat, the leaves brewed, and the dried husk made into a drink, until someone roasted and ground the pits and then steeped the grounds in hot water to produce the drink we know as coffee, probably in the fifteenth century.

By the sixteenth century, Arab coffeehouses were popular meeting places featuring gaming, erotic rendezvous, and seditious poetry. The governor of Mecca banned the coffeehouses in 1511, but he was countermanded by the Cairo sultan, a coffee drinker. For many years, the Arabs held a monopoly on coffee, exporting only parboiled, infertile beans from Yemen, where coffee trees were cultivated. As coffee achieved popularity in Europe in the seventeenth century, however, the Dutch broke the monopoly, growing coffee in Java and Ceylon (Sri Lanka). The French, too, began to grow coffee in the Caribbean, the Spanish in Central America and Colombia, and the Portuguese in Brazil. Today coffee grows in a girdle around the earth between the Tropics of Cancer and Capricorn.

Coffee in America

Although the American colonists drank some coffee, like their British cousins they preferred tea until the Boston Tea Party of 1773, after which it became a patriotic duty to switch to coffee. "Tea must be universally renounced," John Adams wrote to his wife, "and I must be weaned, and the sooner the better" (Pendergrast, p. 15). American coffee consumption grew in the first half of the 1800s, particularly after the War of 1812 temporarily shut off access to tea. By that time Brazilian coffee was cheaper and closer anyway.

The Civil War in the mid-nineteenth century increased the American desire for coffee on both sides of the conflict. Union soldiers received an annual allotment of thirty-six pounds of green coffee beans, which they roasted over campfires. "It was coffee *at* meals and *between* meals," wrote the former Massachusetts artilleryman John Billings in his 1887 book, *Hardtack and Coffee*, "and men going on guard or coming off guard drank it at all hours of the night" (Pendergrast, p. 49). Meanwhile, Confederate soldiers had no coffee, resorting to roasting acorns, dandelion roots, peanuts, chicory, and a number of other unsatisfactory substitutes. Real coffee was most welcome in the Reconstruction South.

Two inventions spurred by coffee demand during the Civil War helped spawn the postwar coffee industry. Paper bags for peanuts were created in 1862. In 1864 Jabez Burns invented the self-emptying roaster. The brothers John and Charles Arbuckle, Pittsburgh wholesale grocers, bought a Burns machine and began to sell preroasted coffee with an egg–sugar glaze in one-pound paper bags. Until then, most American coffee was unevenly roasted on home stovetops. "Oh, I have Burnt my Coffee again," a frustrated housewife cried in one advertisement. "Buy Arbuckles' Roasted, as I do, and you will have no trouble," her friend advised (Pendergrast, p. 52).

Arbuckle Brothers' main coffee brand, Ariosa, was wildly successful. In 1871 John Arbuckle, an aggressive marketing genius, opened a branch in New York. In the 1880s the company established branches in Kansas City, Missouri, and Chicago. Customers could clip Arbuckle Brothers' coupons and redeem them for everything from guns to jewelry. In the West, cowboys took pride in boiling it until it was "condensed panther," and the wooden crates in which the coffee was packed were recycled as both cradles and coffins (Pendergrast, p. 53). Meanwhile, John Arbuckle ventured to Brazil to establish green bean exporting offices and created his own shipping fleet.

Early Coffee Brands

The late nineteenth century, with its steam engines to power boats and trains and electricity to run factories and printing presses, was the spawning ground for modern industrial capitalism, mass marketing, and advertising. Coffee became an international commodity, and speculation in coffee beans made and lost fortunes. After an oversupply of Brazilian coffee ruined speculators in 1880, a coffee exchange was opened in New York. It provided a way to hedge and bet on coffee futures, but it did nothing to prevent speculation and attempts to corner the market.

This was the beginning of the boom-bust cycle that has plagued the coffee industry ever since. When prices are high, farmers plant more trees, which take four years to produce a good crop. Then there is too much coffee, and the price plummets. Farmers cannot just rip up coffee trees and plant corn, so they continue to harvest, but they neglect fertilizing and pruning. Over time the glut subsides, the price goes up, and the cycle starts over again.

Other coffee roasters challenged Arbuckle Brothers or grew in virgin territory on the West Coast. James Folger, who arrived in San Francisco in 1850 at the age of fourteen, roasted coffee for gold prospectors and eventually founded J. A. Folger and Company. San Francisco also provided a home for two other major roasters. Austin and Reuben Hills sold groceries as Hills Brothers and then purchased the Arabian Coffee and Spice Mills in 1881, subsequently focusing solely on coffee. Under the leadership of Mannie Brandenstein, MJB Coffee also thrived. In Boston, Caleb Chase and James Sanborn founded Chase and Sanborn in 1878, expanding with branches in Chicago and Montreal within four years. Joel Cheek, a Kentucky traveling salesman who moved to Nashville, Tennessee, created a blend he called Maxwell House Coffee, named after a prestigious Nashville hotel, in 1892.

All of these new coffee brands used increasingly sophisticated advertising to sell their products. MJB's ads in local newspapers always included the bold, mysterious tagline "Why?" to intrigue readers and identify the brand. A Chase and Sanborn ad showed an elderly woman peering into a coffee cup to read the fortune revealed in the grounds. "What vision, dear Mother, in your cup do you see?" asked the caption. "The whole world drinking Chase & Sanborn Coffee & Tea," she replied. Maxwell House, by its very name, used snob appeal, and its slogan, "Good to the last drop," supposedly derived from Teddy Roosevelt's appreciative comment (Pendergrast, pp. 55, 133).

Hills Brothers ads claimed that their product was "THE FINEST COFFEE in the WORLD," and in 1900 they pioneered an advanced technology, packing coffee in a vacuum can, which promised to "KEEP FRESH FOREVER IF SEAL IS UNBROKEN" (Pendergrast, p. 125). This was not completely true. Coffee is a notoriously fragile product. Once roasted, it stales quickly if exposed to oxygen. But it cannot be sealed in an airtight container immediately because the beans must degas carbon dioxide produced by the roast. Thus, it could not have been fresh when it was packed in the vacuum can, or the can would have burst. So with the mass production and retailing of preroasted (and often preground) coffee, something was both gained and lost. The product was uniform, likely to contain real coffee (as opposed to fraudulent adulterants), and easy to use. But it was also stale, unlike home-roasted beans.

Twentieth-Century Developments

As coffee consumption swelled around the turn of the twentieth century, health faddists such as John Harvey Kellogg preached that caffeine was harmful. C. W. Post, a former patient at Kellogg's Sanitarium in Battle Creek, Michigan, manufactured Postum, a grain-based coffee substitute, in 1895, claiming that "coffee is an alkaloid poison and a certain disintegrator of brain tissues"

(Pendergrast, p. 101). In response, coffee firms offered defensive ads that frequently made matters worse.

The coffee firms also had to contend with two new competitors: price-cutting chain stores and door-to-door peddlers. Under the direction of John Hartford, the Great Atlantic and Pacific Tea Company, otherwise known as the A&P, cut out wholesalers and in 1913 began to offer coffee in its "economy stores," which sold high-quality foods at low prices. A&P owned the American Coffee Corporation, with buyers in Brazil, Colombia, and elsewhere, purchasing for Eight O'Clock Coffee and its other brands. Meanwhile, the premium peddlers at Jewel Tea Company hooked coffee consumers on their home-delivered beans and the premiums they gave out *before* the required coffee. That way, customers were committed to purchasing coffee to earn the gift.

World War I boosted American coffee consumption, as soldiers in the trenches valued the caffeine hit and the warmth of the 29 million pounds of coffee beans requisitioned by the quartermaster-general in 1917 alone. The following year much of the military coffee came in the form of G. Washington's Refined Coffee, one of the first instant brands. In the Roaring Twenties, Prohibition advanced coffee as a nonalcoholic alternative, and coffeehouses proliferated, particularly in American cities. Alice Foote MacDougall, one of the first women to make a successful career in coffee, opened a chain of romantic pseudo-Italian coffeehouses in New York. Those brands that advertised widely—often hiring professional agencies such as J. Walter Thompson—did well, but Arbuckle Brothers refused to mount a national campaign and went into decline, despite its successful introduction of Yuban, an upscale brand.

Many family businesses gave way to corporations as the decade came to a close. Chase & Sanborn became a part of Standard Brands, while General Foods snapped up Maxwell House Coffee, which was ironic, since it also owned Postum, which continued to malign coffee with a cartoon campaign about Mr. Coffee Nerves, even as Maxwell House promised to be good to the last drop.

While the Depression put Alice Foote MacDougall out of business, the automat, with its robotic fresh-brewed nickel cup, appealed to frugal consumers, and coffee, promoted as an affordable luxury, continued to sell. Radio gave coffee advertising a vital new medium. The Maxwell House Show Boat, which debuted in 1932, featured sounds of a paddle wheel and steam whistle, with favorite characters clinking cups and smacking lips. Many people wrote to request tickets for the mythical boat, and it was the top-rated show in the country. Chase & Sanborn countered with Major Bowes Amateur Hour, followed by Edgar Bergen and his smart-aleck dummy, Charlie McCarthy.

Cheapened Blends and the Rise of Specialty Coffee

As had happened during the previous conflict, World War II increased the use of instant coffee overseas, this time with improved Nescafé from Swiss-based Nestlé, followed by American brands. After the war, instant coffee sales took off in the era of the TV dinner and Minute Rice, even though its taste only remotely resembled good coffee. Because taste was not really an issue, the company used inferior robusta beans (by then growing in Africa and Brazil as well as the East Indies) in instant coffee. As coffee roasters engaged in price-cutting wars in the supermarkets, they also cheapened their regular blends, adding robusta to them. Not surprisingly, consumers responded by brewing weak coffee and reducing consumption. Coffee lost the baby boomers to Coke and Pepsi.

In 1966 the Dutch immigrant Alfred Peet opened Peet's Coffee and Tea in Berkeley, California, inspiring a new generation of small, grassroots batch roasters (as opposed to mass continuous roasting) and sparking the modern "specialty coffee" movement, exemplified by Starbucks Coffee, founded in 1971 in Seattle. The Specialty Coffee Association of America became a large, inclusive, dynamic organization, while the older National Coffee Association primarily served the bigger roasters.

By 2001 coffee consumption in America had stabilized at 8.8 pounds per capita, far below the 1946 high of 19.8 pounds per person. Many people buy high-quality arabica beans from places like Kenya, Ethiopia, Sumatra, New Guinea, Guatemala, Jamaica, or Hawaii, grinding them at home for a superior cup. They can purchase fresh-roasted beans from a local coffee roaster or buy coffee in one-way valve bags, which allow beans to degas without admitting oxygen. Such connoisseurs brew their coffee using two tablespoons per six ounces, either with a drip method or a plunger pot, and many have home espresso machines to make the Italian coffee, produced in thirty seconds under high pressure through finely ground coffee.

Others go to Starbucks or the many other specialty coffeehouses that have sprung up around the United States, where consumers willingly pay several dollars for a cappuccino or latte, popular espresso-and-milk drinks. But the majority of coffee is still sold in cans by the four largest coffee companies: Maxwell House is owned by Philip Morris and Folgers by Procter and Gamble, while Nestlé owns

Taster's Choice, Hills Brothers, Chase and Sanborn, and other smaller brands. Sara Lee owns the Dutch firm Douwe Egberts and produces a great deal of institutional coffee.

The Modern Coffee Crisis

The world entered a "coffee crisis" at the dawn of the twenty-first century, with the worst and most prolonged bust cycle in history. From 1962 to 1989 the United States was a signatory to the International Coffee Agreement, a quota system that, while unsatisfactory and often violated by smugglers, helped stabilize the price of coffee. With the cold war ending, the United States pulled out of the agreement, and it collapsed, along with coffee prices.

In the 1990s Vietnam—which had never been a major player—began growing a great deal of cheap robusta and, in the process, dispossessed and persecuted the indigenous Montagnards in the central highlands of the country. By 2000 Vietnam had surpassed Colombia to become the world's second-largest coffee producer. As a result of this oversupply, coffee prices dropped well below the cost of production, with resulting dislocations and starvation throughout coffee-growing regions.

Despite increased awareness of social issues involved with coffee and much publicity for fair trade beans, which guarantee a decent price to certified coffee cooperatives of smallholders, the situation deteriorated in coffee-growing regions, even as the major roasters further cheapened their blends and reaped record profits. Although they used some of those profits for programs to aid the producers, it was not enough to solve the problem. In 1950 the Colombian coffee representative Andrés Uribe, testifying before the U.S. Senate, said: "When you are dealing with coffee, you are not dealing only with a commodity, a convenience. You are dealing with the lives of millions of people" (Pendergrast, p. 238). He was correct, and his words still ring true.

[*See also* Arbuckles; Coffeehouses; Coffee Makers, Roasters, and Mills; Coffee Substitutes; Coffee, Decaffeinated; Coffee, Instant; Combat Food; Folgers; Irish Coffee; Maxwell House; Middle Eastern Influences on American Food; Nestlé.]

BIBLIOGRAPHY

Allen, Stewart Lee. *The Devil's Cup: Coffee, the Driving Force in History.* New York: Soho, 1999. A quirky, funny travelogue with worthwhile information.

Bates, Robert H. *Open-Economy Politics: The Political Economy of the World Coffee Trade.* Princeton, NJ: Princeton University Press, 1997. Dry and academic, but useful.

Bersten, Ian. *Coffee Floats, Tea Sinks: Through History and Technology to a Complete Understanding.* Sydney, Australia: Helian Books, 1993. Written by an Australian collector and coffee expert.

Dicum, Gregory, and Nina Luttinger. *The Coffee Book: Anatomy of an Industry from Crop to the Last Drop.* New York: New Press, 1999. Focused primarily on social issues and fair trade.

Heise, Ulla. *Coffee and Coffee Houses.* Translated by Paul Roper. West Chester, PA: Schiffer, 1987. Coffee-table book with good history.

Illy, Francesco, and Riccardo Illy. *The Book of Coffee: A Gourmet's Guide.* Translated by Pamela Swinglehurst. New York: Abbeville Press, 1992. The Illy family is famed for its espresso blends.

James, Jack E. *Understanding Caffeine: A Biobehavioral Analysis.* Thousand Oaks, CA: Sage Publications, 1997. On the health effects of caffeine, leaning toward caution.

Kummer, Corby. *The Joy of Coffee: The Essential Guide to Buying, Brewing, and Enjoying.* Shelburne, VT: Chapters Books, 1995. Good general guide.

Pendergrast, Mark. *Uncommon Grounds: The History of Coffee and How It Transformed Our World.* New York: Basic Books, 1999. Comprehensive business and social history.

Weinberg, Bennett Alan, and Bonnie K. Bealer. *The World of Caffeine: The Science and Culture of the World's Most Popular Drug.* New York: Routledge , 2001. On the health effects of caffeine, leaning toward the positive.

MARK PENDERGRAST

Coffee, Decaffeinated

From its earliest history, there were health concerns regarding coffee and its effects. In 1511 the Arab governor of Mecca closed the coffeehouses, partly on medical advice that, like wine, coffee contained a harmful drug. In 1679 a French doctor asserted in a pamphlet that coffee produced "general exhaustion, paralysis, and impotence" (Pendergrast, p. 9).

Caffeine was first isolated from green coffee beans in 1820 and proved to consist of three methyl groups around a xanthine molecule; among other things, it mimics the neurotransmitter adenosine, which aids sleep. When a caffeine molecule gets to a receptor first, it prevents adenosine from doing its job, thus keeping people awake longer. Caffeine affects some people more than others, and excessive coffee consumption can lead to lack of sleep and irritability, which explains the appeal of decaffeinated coffee.

Ludwig Roselius was convinced that his father, a professional coffee taster in Bremen, Germany, had died prematurely because of his excessive caffeine intake. Roselius steamed green coffee beans and then flooded them with benzol; he patented this decaffeination process in 1906, selling Kaffee Hag in Germany, Sanka ("sans caffeine") in France, and Dekafa in the United States.

In the early 1980s coffee was implicated as a possible cause of birth defects, benign breast lumps, pancreatic cancer, and heart disease. Sales of decaffeinated coffee rose dramatically. The standard method of decaffeination used methylene chloride, which left virtually no chemical on the roasted bean, but a new "Swiss water process" appealed to the health conscious, as did treatment with carbon dioxide. While the taste was not equal to that of regular coffee, it had improved substantially.

Health fears about caffeine gradually subsided as the early epidemiological studies failed to be replicated. Most doctors give the nod to moderate consumption of regular coffee, but for those people who react badly to caffeine or who do not wish to become addicted and suffer withdrawal headaches or who want to drink coffee just before bedtime, decaffeinated coffee provides an alternative.

[*See also* Coffee; Coffee, Instant; Coffee Substitutes; Middle Eastern Influences on American Food.]

BIBLIOGRAPHY

James, Jack E. *Understanding Caffeine: A Biobehavioral Analysis.* Thousand Oaks, CA: Sage Publications, 1997. On the health effects of caffeine, leaning toward caution.

Pendergrast, Mark. *Uncommon Grounds: The History of Coffee and How It Transformed Our World.* New York: Basic Books, 1999. Comprehensive business and social history.

Weinberg, Bennett Alan, and Bonnie K. Bealer. *The World of Caffeine: The Science and Culture of the World's Most Popular Drug.* New York: Routledge, 2001. On the health effects of caffeine, leaning toward the positive.

MARK PENDERGRAST

Coffee, Instant

There are many possible claimants for maker of the first soluble coffee. In 1771 the British granted a patent for a "coffee compound," and in the late nineteenth century a Glasgow firm invented Camp Coffee, a liquid "essence." In 1900 the Tokyo chemist Sartori Kato made a version of instant coffee, as did the St. Louis roaster Cyrus Blanke with his Faust Instant Coffee in 1906 and, independently and simultaneously, the German-Guatelaman Federico Lehnhoff Wyld. In 1910 a Belgian named George Washington refined coffee crystals from brewed coffee, calling it G. Washington's Refined Coffee, which was very popular with soldiers during World War I.

All of these early instants used the "drum method," in which brewed coffee was boiled down to crystals. In 1938 Nestlé launched Nescafé, made by spraying coffee liquid into heated towers, and this produced a better cup. Although still lacking the body, aroma, and flavor of real coffee, it helped a new generation of soldiers survive

World War II. After the war, instant coffee became popular in America, prompting an increase in the growth of inferior robusta beans for the cheap blends used for soluble coffee. Aggressive advertising—millions of tiny "flavor buds" supposedly released with Maxwell House Instant Coffee—pushed sales.

In 1964 freeze-dried coffee provided a superior instant coffee, and in subsequent years more arabica beans have been used for instant coffees of higher quality. In the early 1990s a highly successful Taster's Choice (made by Nestlé) television ad campaign featured a serial soap opera approach in which Tony wooed Sharon with the right freeze-dried brand. Nonetheless, no instant coffee can compare to a fresh-brewed cup.

[*See also* Coffee; Combat Food; Maxwell House; Nestlé.]

BIBLIOGRAPHY

Pendergrast, Mark. *Uncommon Grounds: The History of Coffee and How It Transformed Our World.* New York: Basic Books, 1999. Comprehensive business and social history.

MARK PENDERGRAST

Coffeehouses

Beginning with the *kaveh kanes*, as fifteenth- and sixteenth-century Arab establishments were known, coffeehouses have provided a place for people to socialize over a cup of coffee and a bite to eat. The coffeehouse combined with café has a longer European pedigree, but the American Revolution was planned in Boston's Green Tavern, a coffeehouse that also served ale. In the 1950s smoky, atmospheric coffeehouses in cities such as San Francisco and New York fueled hipsters and beatniks. In the Vietnam War era, GI coffeehouses outside army bases promoted antiwar sentiments. By the end of the twentieth century, the coffeehouse boom based on espresso-milk drinks had given Americans an appreciation for safe places to meet or sip nonalcoholic beverages in contemplative solitude.

[*See also* Coffee; Middle Eastern Influences on American Food; Starbucks.]

BIBLIOGRAPHY

Pendergrast, Mark. *Uncommon Grounds: The History of Coffee and How It Transformed Our World.* New York: Basic Books, 1999. Comprehensive business and social history.

MARK PENDERGRAST

Coffee Makers, Roasters, and Mills

Harvested coffee beans are roasted to bring out the flavor. The first U.S. coffee roaster patent was granted in 1833 and the next in 1840, followed by about seventy-five more during the next thirty years, all of sheet metal or cast iron. Roasters were of two basic types: revolving drums with a side crank or stirring pans with a lid crank. All had stir-ring wings or fingers to agitate the berries constantly. Most roasters were used atop ranges, but one from 1866 was a cast-iron, round-bottom "kettle" with three peg legs and a crank in the lid, set over coals or hearth embers. A few were portable and came mounted on their own little stoves.

Coffee Pots. *Left, from top,* tin tea pot, tin coffee boiler, tin mess can; *right, from top* tin French coffee filter biggins, and heavy tin coffee biggins, with faucet. From the Duparquet, Huot, & Moneuse Co. catalog (Boston, 1915), p. 172.

After roasting, coffee beans are ground—to a consistency from coarse to fine—to make coffee in a coffee boiler, percolator, or biggin (drip style). Early mills may have been cylindrical brass mills, like spice mills, originating in the Middle East. The first U.S. coffee mill patent was granted in 1798, eight years after the patent office's establishment—it was the twenty-sixth patent granted. It was not until 1832 that another mill was patented, and that by a company—Parker Brothers—that made coffee mills until 1932. Mills proliferated as inventors tried to make one that would not grind the beans twice.

Box or lap mills were smallish boxes, with hoppers and cranks on top. Grounds fell into a drawer below. A side mill was rather like half a hopper mounted to a board or cupboard so as always to be ready to use. Canister-top mills held beans in a closed container and were usually wall mounted. Countertop mills had heavy cast-iron frames, one or two side wheels turned by a crank, and large closed hoppers on top. The largest were for stores. All coffee mills had screw adjustments to set fineness of grounds. Electric mills appeared in the 1930s as attachments to stand mixers. Also in the 1930s grocery stores had electric mills with adjustable settings for customers to grind bags of selected roast coffee beans. Small electric mills are still the most popular, but old-style box mills are sold to customers who shun electricity.

The method of coffee making is considered as important as grinding and is as hotly contested as it was during the nineteenth and twentieth centuries. Biggins—the original drip maker that was invented about 1800 in Paris by Mr. Biggin—were made in the United States for seventy to eighty years; some were arranged to drip hot water slowly through a fine strainer holding fine grounds and, later, a cloth and then a paper filter. Percolators were common by about 1910; in these coffee makers boiling water roiled up a tube and drained down through coarse grounds. The flavor was stronger, because the coffee kept boiling. In coffee boilers—large, lighthouse-shaped kettles in which coarse grounds were boiled directly in water—the coffee was "cleared" with eggshells to take away the muddiness and poured off after settling. This type is seen around the campfire in old Western movies. Many so-called coffeepots are actually serving pieces and may be fancy tin, enameled iron, silver plate, or china.

[*See also* Coffee; Middle Eastern Influences on American Food.]

Universal Coffee Percolator. From the Duparquet, Huot, & Moneuse Co. catalog (Boston, 1915), p. 173.

BIBLIOGRAPHY

Franklin, Linda Campbell. *300 Years of Kitchen Collectibles*. 5th ed. Iola, WI: Krause Publications, 2003.

Fumagalli, Ambrogio. *Coffeemakers. Macchine da Caffe, 1800–1950, American and European*. San Francisco: Chronicle Books, 1995. Vintage instruments from tin pots to fancy machines.

Kvetko, Edward, and Douglas Congdon-Martin. *Coffee Antiques*. Atglen, PA: Schiffer, 2000.

MacMillan, Joseph E. *The MacMillan Index of Antique Coffee Mills*. Marietta, GA: published by author, 1995. Definitive, lengthy book primarily about patent history, with biographies and copious illustrations and photographs.

White, Michael L., and Judith A. Sivonda. *Antique Coffee Grinders: American, English, and European*. Atglen, PA: Schiffer, 2001.

White, Michael L., and Derek S. White. *Early American Coffee Mills: Patent History and Guide for Collectors*. Yardley, PA: WhiteSpace Publishing, 1994.

LINDA CAMPBELL FRANKLIN

Coffee Substitutes

Wartime blockades, taxes, temperance movements, religions, health-food adventists, and the very great expanse and rough terrain of the country itself (leading to high transportation costs) have all challenged Americans' access to coffee. Chicory ("coffeeweed") roots, roasted and ground, had long been used to extend or adulterate coffee in Europe as well as in America. But ingenuity stepped up to adversity. Americans had found substitutes—some better than others—in barley, sweet potatoes, acorns, beets, grains (rye, barley, cornmeal, millet, and grain sorghum), figs, seeds (the Kentucky coffee tree, grape, locust, persimmon, okra, and cotton), parsnips, field peas, walnuts, crushed walnut shells, pumpkin shells, corn, corn cobs, and soybeans.

Advertisers began to brand coffee in the late 1860s, but by the end of the nineteenth century, coffee's commoditization had left it open to unscrupulous adulteration. Prodded by popular concern about just what it was that they were drinking, as well as by critical attitudes (many saw coffee as an "evil drug"), some people believed that the time was ripe for introducing a "pure food" commercial substitute. But these businessmen advertised against the odds: memories of "war coffee" remained strong.

One successful businessman, Charles William (C. W.) Post, prevailed. During a brief stay at Dr. John Harvey Kellogg's Sanitarium in Battle Creek, Michigan, in 1891, Post was served Caramel Cereal Coffee (which the doctor himself described as "a very poor substitute for a very poor thing," made from bran, molasses, and burned bread crusts). In 1895 C. W. introduced his own coffee substitute, Postum Cereal Food Coffee ("Postum"). By 1900 a half-dozen rival "healthy" coffee substitutes included Grain-o and Graino, but C. W. Post out-advertised them all, to build Postum into an enduring brand.

[*See also* Coffee; Coffee, Decaffeinated; Post Foods.]

ROBIN M. MOWER

Cola Wars

The so-called cola wars began shortly after Coca-Cola was invented in 1886 by Dr. John S. Pemberton, an Atlanta pharmacist, although two popular regional drinks—Moxie in Massachusetts and Dr Pepper in Texas—actually preceded Coke by a year. In the 1894 corporate report for the Coca-Cola Company, Asa Candler, who made a success of the beverage after Pemberton died, complained of various "bogus substitutes" (Pendergrast, p. 62). The imitators were led by J. C. Mayfield, a former Pemberton partner, who sold Yum Yum and Koke, and his former wife, Diva Brown, who sold My-Coca. Each claimed to have the original Coca-Cola formula.

By the turn of the century, eighty cola drinks were trying to ride on Coca-Cola's successful coattails, including Afri-Kola, Chero-Cola, Dope (a nickname for Coca-Cola, because of its former cocaine content), Kaw-Kola ("Has the Kick"), Pepsi-Cola, Vani-Kola, and Wise-Ola. Encouraged by the passage of the Trademark Law of 1905, Coca-Cola's lawyer Harold Hirsch began to sue imitators, in the process practically creating modern American trademark law while filing an average of one case per week. He won most of his cases, based on a competitor's similar label, script, or name. To help differentiate the Coca-Cola bottle from all others, in 1916 the company adopted a trademark "hobble skirt" bottle, with a slim waste and bulging top and bottom.

Of all the imitators, the most tenacious was Pepsi-Cola, developed in 1894 in New Bern, North Carolina, by the pharmacist Caleb Bradham. By World War I the drink had achieved modest success, with franchised bottlers in half the states. Caught in the wildly swinging sugar market of 1920, however, Bradham went bankrupt. The firm was purchased by a Wall Street speculator named Roy Megargel, who failed to make it thrive. Twice Coke refused to purchase the troubled Pepsi remains. In 1931 Charles Guth, who owned a chain of candy stores with soda fountains, became infuriated that Coca-Cola would not sell him its syrup at discount. He bought most of the ownership of Pepsi and began selling it in his stores. In 1934 he began to sell Pepsi in recycled twelve-ounce beer bottles for a nickel, the same price Coke charged for a 6.5-ounce drink. Sales boomed, particularly among poor people.

Guth lost the company over a lawsuit, and the canny businessman Walter Mack took over in 1939. Mack approved a lilting bit of doggerel that became the first smash-hit radio jingle. "Pepsi-Cola hits the spot / Twelve full ounces, that's a lot / Twice as much for a nickel, too / Pepsi-Cola is the drink for you."

John Sibley, the frustrated Coca-Cola lawyer who took over from Hirsch, sued in the United States and elsewhere. Pepsi countersued. Finally, in 1941 Coca-Cola's president, Robert Woodruff, cut a deal with Walter Mack, recognizing

Pepsi's trademark in the United States. Sibley felt betrayed and quit as Coca-Cola counsel soon afterward.

During World War II, Coca-Cola aced Pepsi by securing an exemption from sugar rationing for all Coke served to the military. Coca-Cola men were designated "technical observers," whose work behind the lines setting up bottling plants was deemed vital to the war effort. Although Walter Mack complained bitterly, Pepsi did not receive the same treatment. In response, Mack set up three huge Pepsi-Cola Servicemen's Centers in Washington, San Francisco, and New York, where soldiers could find a free Pepsi and other services.

In 1949 the former Coca-Cola executive Al Steele joined Pepsi and, under his leadership in the 1950s, Pepsi began to shed its lower-class image, with perky Polly Bergen singing "Pepsi-Cola's up to date" on television spots. Steele also reformulated the oversweetened drink to make it taste more like Coke. As Pepsi gained ground, Coca-Cola's boss Robert Woodruff refused to match Pepsi ounce for ounce at the same price, and no one inside Coke headquarters in Atlanta ever spoke the "P" word, referring to Pepsi only as the "Imitator" or the "Competition." Finally, in 1955, Woodruff allowed King Size Coke to match Pepsi.

The wars between Coca-Cola and Pepsi produced some of the most entertaining television advertisements of the modern era. Pepsi came up with "Come Alive, You're in the Pepsi Generation," attempting to claim the baby boomers. Coke responded with "Things Go Better with Coca-Cola" and then, in a simultaneous appeal to tradi-

tion and hippies, "It's the Real Thing." In 1971 Coca-Cola's Hilltop Commercial, filmed on an Italian hill, featured young people from around the world singing about buying the world a Coke and living in perfect harmony.

In 1975 in Dallas, Pepsi held a miserable 4 percent of the soft-drink market, behind native Dr Pepper and Coke. In desperation, Pepsi launched "the Pepsi Challenge," showing candid shots of die-hard Coke consumers astonished to discover that they preferred Pepsi in blind taste tests. The ads outraged Coca-Cola and, when secret blind taste tests inside company headquarters revealed that a slim majority *did* prefer Pepsi, Coke chemists began to work on a revised formula.

Meanwhile, the pattern for Coca-Cola and Pepsi ads was set. "Coke Is It," which made its debut in 1981, featured Coca-Cola itself as the star of the ads, fueling all-American good times at pep rallies and other wholesome events. Pepsi relied more on celebrity endorsements, lifestyle ads, and edgy humor, hiring the pop singers Michael Jackson and Madonna to push the drink.

No matter what ads Coke ran, the market share of Coca-Cola continued a slow decline. In 1985 Coke's chief executive officer, Roberto Goizueta, approved a new formula that beat Pepsi in taste tests. Pepsi's president, Roger Enrico, declared victory, saying, "The other guy just blinked," and proclaiming a companywide holiday (Pendergrast, p. 351). New Coke was a media and business disaster, as many consumers refused even to taste it, horrified that the symbol of America was being changed. When Coke brought back Coca-Cola Classic three months later, however, it *gained* market share on Pepsi.

Since the New Coke debacle, Coca-Cola has struggled to come up with an effective advertising campaign, while Pepsi continues to hammer at youthful, hip-hop, in-your-face themes. Nonetheless, Coca-Cola is still number one, and Pepsi is the perennial we-try-harder number two, particularly in the international market. Other drinks, such as Royal Crown Cola, may beat both of them in taste tests, and nouveau Virgin Cola may try to grab market share, but Coke and Pepsi remain the two top-of-mind drinks in the cola wars.

[*See also* Advertising; Coca-Cola; Dr Pepper; Pepsi-Cola; Radio and Television.]

BIBLIOGRAPHY

Allen, Frederick. *Secret Formula: How Brilliant Marketing and Relentless Salesmanship Made Coca-Cola the Best-Known Product in the World.* New York: HarperBusiness, 1994. Good history, focusing on Atlanta and Robert Woodruff.

Cola Wars. Coca Cola and Pepsi products in separate retail cases, La Bagel Delight, Brooklyn, New York. *Photograph by Joe Zarba*

Enrico, Roger, with Jesse Kornbluth. *The Other Guy Blinked: How Pepsi Won the Cola Wars*. New York: Bantam, 1986. Pepsi executive's gloating account of the New Coke fiasco.

Oliver, Thomas. *The Real Coke, the Real Story*. New York: Random House, 1986. A good account of the New Coke disaster, written by an Atlanta reporter.

Pendergrast, Mark. *For God, Country and Coca-Cola: The Definitive History of the Great American Soft Drink and the Company That Makes It*. 2nd ed. New York: Basic Books, 2000. Scholarly and comprehensive.

Stoddard, Bob. *Pepsi: 100 Years*. Los Angeles: General Publishing Group, 1997. Solid history of Pepsi-Cola.

MARK PENDERGRAST

Colanders, *see Sieves, Sifters, and Colanders*

Colas, *see Soda Drinks*

Collins

A Collins is a drink made with strong spirits, carbonated water, sugar, lemon juice, and ice. There are two different Collins drinks that appear in the classic recipe books: the Tom Collins and the John Collins. The John Collins was traditionally made with Holland gin, and the Tom Collins was made with Old Tom sweetened gin.

John Collins was a headwaiter at Limmer's Hotel and Coffee House on Conduit Street in London and is credited with the invention of the Collins. Limmer's Hotel is mentioned in *Reminiscences of Captain Gronow . . . Being Anecdotes of the Camp, the Court, and the Clubs, at the Close of the Last War with France*, written in 1814, and was clearly open for most of the nineteenth century, but it is unclear when John Collins worked at Limmer's. An early mention of the drink in print, possibly the first, was in the *Australasian Newspaper* from Victoria, Australia on February 24, 1865. This was in reference to "that most angelic of drinks for a hot climate—a John Collins (a mixture of soda water, gin, sugar, lemon, and ice)."

The John Collins is commonly prepared with American whiskey. Since Old Tom gin has not been produced since the 1960s, the Tom Collins is now made with London Dry Gin. The category of Collins drinks has grown to include the Michael Collins with Irish whiskey, the Pedro Collins with rum, and the Pierre Collins with cognac or brandy. One guess is that the Collins, which

requires carbonated water, would have gained popularity around the mid-nineteenth century, when machinery for producing carbonated water dispensed from a soda fountain became affordable to the average merchant.

Generally, the preparation of a Collins is fairly simple: sugar and lemon juices are dissolved together, and a shot of gin is added. The drink is served over ice in a tall chimney or Collins glass and topped with soda water. The Collins differs from a gin fizz in that the latter calls for a fruit garnish and is served in a taller chimney glass.

[*See also* Cocktails; Gin.]

BIBLIOGRAPHY

Farmer, J. S., and W. E. Henley. *Slang and Its Analogues*. New York: Arno Press, 1970.

Kappeler, George. *Modern American Drinks: How to Mix and Serve All Kinds of Cups and Drinks*. Akron, OH: Saalfield Publishing, 1895.

Mew, James, and John Ashton. *Drinks of the World*. New York: Scribner and Welford, 1892.

SaskyCom. http://www.sasky.com. A guide to alcoholic and nonalcoholic drinks.

DALE DEGROFF

Combat Food

At the beginning of the Revolutionary War, individual colonies fed their own militias. As the army increased in size, it soon became apparent that it would have to develop a system to feed itself. The first legislation fixing the components of the military ration came with the passage of a resolution by the Continental Congress on November 4, 1775, calling for such things as one pound of beef, three pounds of pork, or one pound of salt fish per day, along with three pints of peas or three pints of beans per week or the equivalent portion of vegetables, figured at one dollar per bushel for beans or peas. The ration also called for milk, rice or Indian meal, and spruce beer or cider.

Firecakes and Deprivation

The ration was not bad on paper but in reality commonly fell far short of what it was supposed to be. Items like vegetables and milk disappeared often and for long periods of time. Moreover, the ration was issued uncooked, and it was up to the individual soldier or small groups of soldiers to prepare their own food. The many stories of deprivation, starvation, and remarkable determination were a major legacy of the Revolutionary War. A particularly low point was reached during the winter of 1777–1778 at Valley

Forge, Pennsylvania, where George Washington's army came close to starvation. Albigence Waldo, a Connecticut surgeon, wrote about the fare at the encampment:

> What have you for our Dinners, Boys? Nothing but Fire Cake & Water, Sir. At night . . . What is your Supper, Lads? Fire Cake & Water, Sir. What have you got for Breakfast, Lads? Fire Cake & Water, Sir. The Lord send that our Commissary of Purchases may live on Fire Cakes & Water. (Dickson, *Chow*)

Fire cakes were simple to make and terrible to eat. To prepare them, the soldiers' flour ration was mixed with water to create a paste that was spread on a flat stone and stood up next to the fire. When sufficiently charred on the outside, the fire cake was peeled off the stone and eaten. Invariably, these crude cakes were doughy inside and unappetizing.

Contractors and Untrained Chefs

In 1790, after the war, Congress revised the ration, first turning it over to private contractors and then, in 1790, taking out vegetables and other perishables and replacing them with two ounces (raised to four ounces in 1798) of rum, brandy, or whiskey. This kind of thinking set the tone for the next hundred years. Dr. Benjamin Rush, noted army surgeon of the Revolutionary War, wrote of the new ration, "Fatal experience . . . has taught . . . that a greater proportion of men have perished with sickness in our armies than have fallen by the sword. . . . The diet of soldiers should consist chiefly of vegetables" (Dickson, *Chow*).

When war with Great Britain was declared on June 18, 1812, an army was in the field again and was soon having trouble getting fed. The contractor system established at the end of the Revolution was still in force, and from the very beginning of hostilities, contractors failed to deliver supplies. At Buffalo and Fort Niagara, New York, for example, came this report from a colonel in November 1812: "We are literally starving on this end of the line for bread; and unless the supply is more abundant, the contractors will be answerable for consequences more fatal to their country than treason" (Dickson, *Chow*). Attempting some kind of ration reform in 1832, President Andrew Jackson by executive order removed the rum ration and replaced it with coffee and sugar.

By the time of the Civil War, the Union Army ration was still a meat-and-bread diet, usually consisting of twelve ounces of pork or bacon and twenty ounces of fresh or salted beef, with eighteen ounces of flour or twenty ounces of cornmeal. Hardtack, a baked mixture of flour and water, was often soaked in cold water overnight and fried in grease for breakfast. Fresh beef was generally supplied on the hoof to armies in the field, the cattle being driven with the armies in such numbers as required. Beans or rice formed the vegetable component of the ration. Desiccated potatoes and desiccated mixed vegetables—forerunners of the dehydrated foods used in World War I—were substitute items. In addition to coffee (or tea) and sugar, the ration included salt, vinegar (to ward off the danger of scurvy), and small quantities of soap and candles.

The Civil War ration included too much salted meat, and the lack of vegetables often led to scurvy (despite the provision of vinegar). The meals were also commonly cooked by untrained men, so that even when good food became available, it was ruined during preparation. There was little innovation and improvement during the course of the war, though an army bakery was established in the basement of the U.S. Capitol. Troops also occasionally received condensed milk, reaping the benefit of Gail Borden's condensing process, invented in 1856.

Confederate troops suffered from a constant and critical lack of provisions, a situation caused primarily by a sparse, one-crop economy and a federal blockade. Arthur M. Schlesinger commented on this ever-present factor of hunger in the military and civil life of the Confederacy: "It can hardly be doubted that this circumstance contributed to the South's ultimate defeat" (Dickson, *Chow*).

Analysis and Deadly Failure

The major development of the period between the Civil War and the Spanish-American War was the growing realization that even the full army ration had deficiencies. In 1875 at Fort Leavenworth, Kansas, an analysis was made of the food that startled many by concluding that the American ration was below that of the English ration in the critical area of energy value. The report went on to say that the American ration was particularly lacking in fresh vegetables and milk, which led to the physical deterioration of the men.

In 1898, when the Spanish-American War was triggered by the sinking of the warship *Maine* in Havana's harbor, it was widely assumed that advances in canning, refrigeration, and other areas of food technology would keep the American army provided with fresh and nutritious food. Despite this initial optimism, the situation quickly turned nightmarish, with disastrous consequences. Ironically, canning and refrigeration were, in large part, to blame. A major problem was beef. To meet the needs of the war, large amounts of canned fresh beef and corned beef were ordered and rushed to Tampa, Florida, and other ports of embarkation for Cuba. Meat that had never been inspected by packers, in their haste to get it shipped, piled up at the docks in the blazing tropical sun, and cans that had been improperly sealed or not thoroughly sterilized went from bad to worse. Tremendous amounts of bad beef were served to the troops—so much that the Rough Rider Theodore Roosevelt estimated that not a tenth of the meat that arrived in Cuba was fit for human consumption. Predictably, many men became ill. Vegetables, whether fresh or canned, spoiled before making it to the troops, and many units were forced to live on a diet of coffee, hardtack, and fatty bacon for weeks at a time.

At the end of the fighting, the government reported that 345 men had been killed in battle or from battle wounds but that a stunning 2,485 had succumbed to sickness and disease. Only a handful of these deaths could be directly blamed on the rations, but the bad food and limited diet certainly lowered the resistance of the men to the malaria, typhoid, and yellow fever that took so many American lives in Cuba. In the period after the war, the federal government saw the need for vast improvement before Americans were again sent into combat. In 1905 the first school for cooking and baking was established at Fort Riley, Kansas, acknowledging the need for a professional approach to food preparation.

Doughboys Get Their Fill

The military did all right by the American doughboy of World War I. The most immediately noticeable food-related improvement was in the quality and variety of the ration itself. In addition to improved versions of standard ration items like beef and beans, the overseas ration of the American Expeditionary Forces included a wider assortment of canned goods, among them, soups, condensed milk, butter, cheese, sweet potatoes, spices, candy, and cigarettes. By the end of the war, the American army was being called the best fed on earth both at home and abroad. A few of the many improvements included the ability to better handle and process perishable food in the field, successful and widespread use of dehydrated vegetables (80 million pounds were sent overseas), and the creation in France of an official garden service to supply the men with fresh provisions. In addition, there was increasing use of scientific experts, nutritional survey teams, and inspectors to improve and ensure the quality of the food. There was also growing interest in new processes. The army, for example, took one little-known product, soluble coffee, and helped foster the growth of an instant-coffee industry that continued to serve civilians after the war.

This is not to say that mistakes did not happen, but most of them did not cause harm. In his book *The Doughboys: The Story of the AEF, 1917–1918*, Laurence Stallings tells of a full shipload of matzo arriving in Bordeaux, France, presumably because someone in the U.S. government had an incorrect notion of the number of Jewish holy days. It was issued all over the war zone with canned beef as a field ration and mixed into a palatable matzo-meat hash. But an oversupply of matzo or any other item (a common occurrence) was hardly a serious problem when compared with the fatal mistakes of the Spanish-American War. For the first time in history Americans at war could actually enjoy their food. It was also the first time that men commonly made jokes about their food rather than fearing its effects:

1st Doughboy: Sure looks like rain.

2nd Doughboy: I know, but the mess sergeant insists it's coffee. (Dickson, *Chow*)

The army's food bill for 1917–1918 was immense compared with the sum for earlier wars—a whopping $727,092,430.14 for the two years—but at war's end nobody was seriously questioning the amount paid for the food itself or for extra costs, such as that spent for stationing government agents in packing plants to ensure the quality and wholesomeness of the food. While there was nothing lavish about the food, it was as if the nation was finally willing to allow its army to eat fairly well and fight on a full stomach.

New Foods and Combat Rations

World War II marked major departures in the feeding of troops; special food packs became available for specific situations, and there was a much wider variety of food and a new concern for quality; a concerted attempt was made to go beyond just feeding the troops to feeding them well. Thousands of soldiers were trained as cooks—more than fifty thousand officers and men came out of the army's cooking and baking schools in 1943 alone—and much attention was given to recipes, menus, and even garnishes. The intent was well expressed in the opening to Training Manual 10-405, *The Army Cook*, published during the war:

> There is no limit to what can be done to improve a mess by thought and care and seasoning, attractive serving, and inventing new combinations and mixtures of foods. The pleasant task of cooking becomes doubly interesting to the cook who is not satisfied with merely cooking well, but takes advantage of every opportunity of finding new and pleasant ways to prepare food. To him cooking is not just a task—it is a pleasure (Dickson, *Chow*).

A result of this new approach to food preparation was that many Americans were exposed to new food and food ideas. They hardly sound exotic or out of the ordinary, but in 1942 a young American from a small town who had grown up on a limited diet was likely to be quite dazzled by the likes of tamales, lamb curry, goulash, New England clam chowder, ravioli, Yorkshire pudding, or shirred eggs—all items from Training Manual 10-412, *Army Recipes*. It has been suggested that the national taste for such things as chipped beef on toast and chili con carne stem from this period.

Of all the developments, none could overshadow the various combat rations—usually designated by a single letter—that will forever be associated with that war. The C ration, with a caloric value of 3,700, was intended for operational needs of three to twenty-one days under combat conditions. Billed as the "balanced meal in a can," Cs were bulky and came in packs of six twelve-ounce cans; three were meat concoctions and three contained bread. Sugar, instant coffee, and candy were also included. Although attempts were made to vary the meat portion late in the war, very few GIs ever saw anything other than the "big three"—meat and beans, meat-and-vegetable stew, and meat-and-vegetable hash.

The D ration was intended exclusively for survival. A "quick energy" emergency pack to be used for very short periods of time, when nothing else was available, it consisted of three four-ounce, nearly unpalatable chocolate candy bars. (The development of this item was based on the theory that an emergency ration should not be palatable lest it be consumed before an emergency arose. This concept was later dropped, though many GIs would argue to the contrary.) This "confection" was artificially flavored and fortified with sucrose, skim milk, cacao fat, and raw oatmeal flour. Each bar was wrapped in a tough, gas-proof wrapper and was able to withstand temperatures up to 120°F without melting.

K Rations. The dinner (lunch) unit included biscuits, a cheese product, a confection, lemon juice powder, sugar, chewing gum, and cigarettes. There were also a breakfast unit and a supper unit. *Collection of John U. Rees/Photograph by Timothy F. Thompson*

The K ration, with a content of 2,700 calories, was designed for a maximum of fifteen meals. Beyond doubt the most famous and well remembered of the World War II emergency rations, it was developed under the leadership of Dr. Ancel Keys (hence the "K") of the University of Minnesota. It was initially designed as a lightweight, nutritional blitz ration for paratroopers, tank soldiers, and others who needed something more substantial than a D or less bulky than a C ration.

Despite improvements in these emergency rations during the course of the war, no one seemed to miss them when they were able to get back to eating regular army food, which by this time was quite good. As the cartoonist Bill Mauldin put it in his book *Up Front*: "The main trouble with K and C rations was their monotony. I suppose they had all the necessary calories and vitamins but they didn't fill your stomach and you got awfully tired of them" (quoted in Dickson, *Chow*).

Expanded Research and Repertoire

The size and complexity of wartime food operations had an impact on civilian postwar America that transcended individual inventions and refinements in areas like canning and freezing. A veritable army of well-trained cooks and bakers came into the workforce and began working for such institutions as summer camps, cafeterias, schools, fraternity houses, and student unions. Whether or not they are aware of it, very few Americans born in the second third of the twentieth century have not sampled the cooking of army- or navy-trained cooks.

Following the war, the army projected a special pride in what it had accomplished and what it was doing. There were more than 650 recipes in the army repertoire, and service technicians were discovering new ways to dehydrate and condense. By the time of the Korean War, matters had continued to improve. Men in forward combat areas were usually given two hot meals a day, rolls and pastries were being baked close to the front lines, and combat-area cooks did so well preparing dehydrated potatoes that the men found they preferred them to the mashed variety made from fresh, whole potatoes.

If any development typified the period between the Korean and Vietnam Wars, it was a shift toward greater levels of coordinated research into such concerns as preservation, the decreased weight of combat rations, and new equipment. The army's Natick Laboratories in Natick, Massachusetts, accomplished much of this work. These laboratories, which have been in operation since the early 1950s, perform research for all branches of the military. The coordination that led to the Natick operation also resulted in the creation in 1968 of the Armed Forces Recipe Service, which did away with separate cookbooks for the various services, replacing them with an initial selection of 975 recipes. The file has continued to grow through a number of revisions.

Fresh Food and Lightweight Rations

During the initial period of American involvement in Vietnam, the provisioning of troops was on a par with that of the Korean War, but as the war intensified and U.S. buildup continued, the ability to feed the men became so sophisticated that it almost seemed incongruous for wartime conditions. Refrigerated vans and helicopters darted around, moving fresh fruit, vegetables, and eggs. Trucks that had been loaded with food were driven onto Sea-Land ships in the United States and driven off in Vietnam. During one stretch of the war that began in October 1967, 2,600 trucks—480 refrigerated and 2,120 dry-cargo vans—were unloaded every fifteen days. In addition, there was major food processing going on in Vietnam. At one point there were no fewer than forty small ice cream plants in the country for the benefit of American forces. The result of this massive effort was that soldiers at fire-support bases could begin their day with fresh eggs cooked to order and end it with a double-dip ice cream cone.

Sometimes, however, weather, hostile action, or terrain made it impossible to get these hot, freshly prepared meals to units in the field. At such times there were combat rations, the two most important being the MCI (for Meal, Combat, Individual), which was a more nutritionally balanced descendant of the C Ration of World War II and Korea, and the new Long Range Patrol Ration (dubbed "Lurp"), a remarkably lightweight, compact ration that could be flexibly packaged because it had no cans. The key components were eight precooked, freeze-dried entrees (such as chicken stew or beef hash) that could be turned into hot meals with the addition of hot water. But this ration could also be eaten cold with cold water or dry, like popcorn. The Lurp also came with a sweet, cereal, coffee, cream, sugar, toilet paper, matches, and a plastic spoon; it was found to be highly acceptable to the men who lived on it for as long as ten days at a time. Former GIs often wrote to Natick Laboratories after the war, attempting to buy these rations for their own use on camping trips. (Freeze-dried foods much like those in the Lurp packages began showing up in catalogs and stores selling to campers and backpackers in the 1970s.)

The staple ration of the Gulf War was the Meal, Ready-to-Eat (MRE), which in the early 1980s replaced the MCI and the Lurp as the standard individual military operational ration. The book-sized MRE is a self-contained, flexibly packaged meal for U.S. soldiers and marines in the field. It is used by the services to sustain individuals during operations that preclude organized food-service facilities but when resupply is established or planned. In early 2003, as the United States once again prepared for armed conflict in the Middle East, MREs cost six to eight dollars and contained up to 2,400 calories. Research and development breakthroughs have made these MREs lightweight, compact, and easily opened; they can withstand a parachute drop from 1,250 feet or a drop from a helicopter (with no parachute) at 100 feet, endure inclement weather, and survive temperature extremes from minus 60°F to 120°F. They must have a minimum shelf life of three years at 80°F and last for six months at 100°F. Over time the number of MRE menus increased from twelve to twenty-four, including a vegetarian option. By 2003 four vegetarian meals were available.

[*See also* Candy Bars and Candy; Coffee, Instant; Hardtack.]

BIBLIOGRAPHY

Dickson, Paul. *Chow: A Cook's Tour of Military Food.* New York: New American Library, 1978.

PAUL DICKSON

Communal Gatherings

America has always been a country of banquets. From the Pilgrims' 1621 feast with the Native Americans to latter-day spaghetti nights at local fire stations, social gatherings centered around a meal have been and remain an essential component of American life.

The earliest communal gatherings grew from the country's settlement period when, in exchange for much-needed help in building homes and completing farm tasks, even the poorest households were expected to offer a well-dressed table. These practical gatherings fostered an important sense of community among groups of settlers, encouraged integration, and, later in U.S. history, promoted a spirit of national unity. Outsiders were incorporated into the fold, news was shared, problems were solved, and laws and communal standards were formed and devised.

All kinds of events provided an excuse to meet around the table: market and court days were high points of early town life, for both news gathering and socializing, and often incorporated bake sales and cakewalks to benefit some local need; the long trip back home after the end of church services made hearty breakfasts nearly essential. Colonial diaries are filled with reports of arduous work being rewarded with such high-flinging socials as barn raising, corn husking, apple drying, and apple butter parties. Southern traditions such as cemetery and church cleanings always brought people out for a noon meal. Quilting bees were held indoors and mainly among women. Hog killing was a particularly inclusive affair: men did the butchering; women cleaned the entrails and rendered lard; children helped scrape the hair off the

Community Dinner. Putting out the food for dinner at community sing, Pie Town, New Mexico, 1940. *Prints and Photographs Division, Library of Congress/Russell Lee*

hides and prepare the feet and ears. Afterward, everyone sat down to a feast.

Communal dinners also hold a long-honored and important civic role. From the first democratic election, American politicians understood their best chance to capture an audience was to give them a meal. Perhaps the most famous of these political feasts was the barbecue thrown by the newly elected governor of Oklahoma, Jack Callaway Walton, on January 8, 1923. Proclaimed as the largest barbecue of its day, Walton's party lasted three days and the more than 250,000 guests consumed a railcar-full each of Alaskan reindeer, cattle, chickens, rabbits, and buffalo.

Many American gatherings developed a regional flavor. Indeed, individual traditional gatherings, even within a state, may vary widely in character, with almost ironclad rules that have been passed down and govern everything from the food preparation to presentation. Two of the most common examples of these variations may be seen in the recipes for clam chowder and Brunswick stew. For traditional chowder, cooks along the northern Atlantic coast add cream to the broth, in the mid-Atlantic stir in tomatoes, and below the Mason-Dixon Line scorn both. In Georgia, Brunswick stew includes pork or beef as the base, while in Virginia squirrel, rabbit, or chicken are the only proper meats at any self-respecting Brunswick party.

BIBLIOGRAPHY

The main source for this piece was the Federal Writers' Projects America *Eats!* papers in the Library of Congress.

PAT WILLARD

Community-Supported Agriculture

Community-supported agriculture (CSA) connects farmers with local consumers in a mutually beneficial agreement that creates a sense of community. To start a CSA collective, a group of buyers in an urban setting forms an association with a local farm, usually organic, and agrees to buy shares of the farm's crop for the growing season. The buyers pay in advance for their shares (or futures) to cover the farmer's costs; then during the harvest season the farmer delivers whatever was cut that week to a designated pickup point in the city.

The benefits of CSA for the farmer are that the buyers pay in advance and agree to accept a portion of the risks and benefits of the growing season. For example, if there is a failure in the pumpkin crop, the buyers get fewer (or no) pumpkins. If there is a bumper crop of tomatoes, they get extra tomatoes. Having sold the entire crop before the farming season, the farmer is free to concentrate on the work of farming and land stewardship. The benefits of CSA for the buyers are that each week through the summer and fall they receive a selection of the freshest and ripest produce at costs significantly below the market price. They also get the benefit of connecting directly with the land on which their food is grown. Many CSA farmers include a letter with the week's supply of vegetables explaining the harvest and how the weather has affected the crop. Some organize outings on which sharers visit the farm or volunteer a day's work harvesting.

Teikei (partnership) ventures originated in 1965 in the Kanagawa prefecture in Japan when a group of two hundred homemakers organized to ask a local family farm about providing milk at reduced prices if they pledged to pay in advance. This cooperative grew into the Seikatsu Club, which by the late twentieth century connected more than 20 million Japanese consumers with local producers. In 1985 Robyn Van En, the owner of the Indian Line Farm in western Massachusetts, organized the first such collective in the United States and named the venture "community-supported agriculture." By the early twenty first century, there were more than one thousand independent organic farms in the United States that were supported by CSA collectives. Organizations such as Just Food in New York City and the Hartford Food Collective in Connecticut connected farms with buyers, as well as arranging for sliding-scale systems of payment, food stamps, and the distribution of uncollected produce to local food banks.

[*See also* Cooperatives.]

BIBLIOGRAPHY

Nabhan, Gary Paul. *Coming Home to Eat: The Pleasures and Politics of Local Foods.* New York and London: Norton, 2001.
Van En, Robyn. "Eating for Your Community." *In Context: A Quarterly of Humane and Sustainable Culture* 42 (Fall 1995): 29–32.

EVE JOCHNOWITZ

ConAgra

Healthy Choice, Banquet, Armour, Blue Bonnet, Parkay, La Choy, Butterball, Slim Jim, Chef Boyardee, and Orville Redenbacher are brand names for some of America's most recognized food products. But few Americans outside the food industry know that they are all produced by ConAgra Foods, the second-largest food processing company in terms of retail sales.

This food processing giant started out in 1919, when Alva Kinney bought four grain milling companies in central Nebraska. He operated them successfully as Nebraska Consolidated Mills (NCM) until he retired in 1936. His successor, R. S. Dickinson, followed the example of other midwestern millers, such as General Mills and Pillsbury, and expanded into prepared foods, made profitable by the postwar boom. Company research led to the successful development of a cake mix. In 1953 NCM entered into an agreement with Hines-Park Foods to market the cake mix under the Duncan Hines label.

In 1971 the company changed its name to ConAgra, meaning "in partnership with the land," to better reflect the new direction of the company. In 1980 ConAgra acquired Banquet Foods Company to expand the market for chicken produced in its Georgia-based Dalton Poultry Company, which ConAgra had purchased in 1963.

During the 1980s the company aggressively moved into the frozen seafood and red meat markets by acquiring the Taste O' Sea brand and by purchasing the Armour Food Company. ConAgra expanded under the leadership of its next president, Michael Harper, but the job took its toll on him. Harper suffered a heart attack in 1985. During his recovery his wife prepared him a bowl of low-fat but spicy chili made from turkey. It came to him in a flash that healthy food can also taste good. After four years of development, the line of Healthy Choice products was announced—one of the most successful food brands introduced by an American food company since the 1960s.

During the 1990s ConAgra bought a slew of companies, including Beatrice in 1990 as well as the Slim Jim brand of meat snacks, Fleischmann's margarine, and Egg Beaters egg substitute, all in 1998. In 2000 ConAgra added Chef Boyardee pasta products, PAM cooking spray, Gulden's mustard, Bumble Bee seafood, and Jiffy Pop popcorn to its long list of brand name products.

Average American consumers may not recognize the name ConAgra, but they have one or more of the company's products in their kitchens.

[*See also* Beatrice.]

BIBLIOGRAPHY

International Directory of Company Histories. 55 vols. Detroit: St. James Press, 2003.

Encyclopedia of Consumer Brands. 3 vols. Edited by Janice Jorgensen. Detroit: St. James Press, 1994.

JOSEPH M. CARLIN

Condiments

The term "condiment" originally meant pickled or preserved foods. By the beginning of the twenty-first century, it was broadly applied to a variety of substances that enhance, intensify, or alter the flavor of other foods. Condiments can enhance delectable foods and make bland or unsatisfying foods palatable. Condiments have been used by Americans since colonial times, but they have changed over the centuries. The earliest condiments were salt, pepper, seeds, and herbs. In colonial times only the middle and upper classes could afford many condiments and the ones that were used were simple: salt, pepper, butter, jams, jellies, mustard, sugar, and molasses.

During the nineteenth century the use of table condiments such as ketchup and mayonnaise became common, as did opposition to the use of condiments. The food reformer Sylvester Graham in his *Lectures on the Science of Human Life* (1839) banned condiments, including mustard, ketchup, pepper, cinnamon, and salt, because they were "all highly exciting and exhausting." In 1835, William Alcott launched a campaign against condiments, which he defined as substances used "to season or give relish to dishes which would be otherwise less agreeable to the taste." In addition to banning the condiments cited by Graham, Alcott also opposed spices (ginger, fennel, cardamom, mace, nutmeg, and coriander) and flavorings (molasses, garlic, cucumbers, pickles, gravies, sauces, lettuce, and horseradish). Alcott considered them to be disgusting and indecent "powdered drugs." Dio Lewis, a Harvard-trained physician, campaigned around the country against the use of condiments. In his *Chastity; or, Our Secret Sins* (1874), he proclaimed, "Everything which inflames one appetite is likely to arouse the other also. Pepper, mustard, ketchup and Worchestishire [sic] sauce—shun them all. And even salt, in any but the smallest quantity, is objectionable; it is such a goad toward carnalism."

Graham, Alcott, and Lewis lost their campaign, and the use of condiments grew dramatically in the twentieth century as their cost to consumers decreased. Condiments became classified in several nonexclusive categories: salt and spices, such as pepper and cinnamon; bread spreads, such as butter, jellies, jams, and honey; table sauces, such as ketchup, mayonnaise, and mustard; vegetables, such as pickles, onions, and horseradish; beverage sweeteners and flavorings, such as sugar and cream; salad dressings, such as vinegar and oil; dips, such as french onion dip; and ethnic condiments, such as soy sauce, Japanese horseradish or wasabi (*Eutrema wasabi*), and chutney.

Salt and Spices

Historically, the two most common condiments in America have been salt and pepper. Salt was the early colonists' most important condiment and was used as a preservative and a seasoning on a wide range of foods. In early colonial times domestic production did not meet demand, and salt was imported from England, France, Spain, and the West Indies. In the early eighteenth century, salt deposits were located in the British North American colonies. During the American Civil War, northern armies controlled the major salt deposits and the South was cut off from them, causing severe problems in the preservation of food and the making of gunpowder.

Black pepper (*Piper nigrum*), a product of Asia, was expensive in colonial America. It was imported as early as 1629 and was commonly used by the middle and upper classes. Pepper was not available to the masses until improved production techniques and less expensive transportation made it an affordable condiment in the late nineteenth century.

Tabasco. Advertisement for Tabasco products. *Culinary Archives & Museum at Johnson & Wales University, Providence, R.I.*

Red pepper (*Capsicum*), a product of the Americas, was commonly employed in dried form in making ketchup, sauces, and pickles beginning in the nineteenth century. It was less expensive than black pepper until the twentieth century and it was more pungent. Condiments made from chilies, such as Tabasco sauce and crushed red pepper flakes, had become popular table condiments by the beginning of the twenty-first century.

Other spices, such as nutmeg, mace, cloves, ginger, and cinnamon, were imported into America and integrated into American cookery. Curry powder, a diverse combination of spices, also was used in American recipes by the nineteenth century. These spices mainly were used in cooking and not as table condiments; the exceptions were cinnamon, which was shaken on toast, and nutmeg, which was sprinkled on eggnog and other beverages.

Bread Spreads

Butter, jellies, jams, preserves, conserves, fruit butters, and honey were used by Europeans on their bread, toast, and pastries well before they immigrated to the Americas; these condiments were used regularly in America from colonial times. In North America, the Europeans found a new sweetener—maple sap—which was converted into syrup by boiling. By 1664 maple syrup was being used on flapjacks, pancakes, waffles, and other foods.

Table Sauces

By the beginning of the twenty-first century, the major table condiments were ketchup, mustard, hot sauce, and mayonnaise. Mustard seeds arrived with European colonists and were converted into powdered form and sold in stores by the eighteenth century. Ketchup became an important condiment in America during the late eighteenth and early nineteenth century, but mayonnaise did not emerge until the last decade of the nineteenth century. The use of all three condiments increased as they became interconnected with the rise of fast foods, particularly hot dogs, hamburgers, and french fries.

Other table condiments entered America during the nineteenth century, including A1 Steak Sauce, Harvey's Sauce, The Gentleman's Relish, and Worcestershire sauce, all of which were British imports, and Tabasco sauce, which was produced after the Civil War by the McIlhenny family on Avery Island, Louisiana. In the twentieth century, commercial barbecue sauce became a table condiment in many restaurants.

Horseradish (*Armoracia rusticana*) was integrated into English cookery before the arrival of English colonists in America, and was used regularly as a seasoning and condiment in colonial times. Horseradish was commercialized and made into a table condiment in the nineteenth century. The most prominent manufacturer of horseradish was the H. J. Heinz Company.

Vegetables

Vegetables historically have been converted into condiments, including pickled cucumbers, onions, ginger, horseradish, sauerkraut, piccalilli, and a variety of relishes. In addition, fresh vegetables came to be served as condiments, including sliced tomatoes and sliced or diced onions, which frequently were employed on sandwiches.

Beverage Sweeteners and Flavorings

After salt and pepper, the most popular condiment at the end of the twentieth century was sugar. However, sugar was expensive in colonial America and honey and molasses were used more commonly. As sugar prices declined during the nineteenth century, it was used in greater quantity in a greater diversity of cookery, such as baking. As a condiment, sugar was particularly important added to bitter beverages, such as tea, coffee, and chocolate. Sugar and honey also were employed in making other condiments such as jams, jellies, preserves, and marmalades. Likewise, milk, cream, and lemon were used to flavor beverages.

Salad Dressings

In colonial times, vinegar and oil was the most prevalent salad dressing. As salads became more important as the nineteenth century ended, salad dressings increased in diversity. By 1900 dozens of different dressings were employed on various salads. Beginning in the late nineteenth century, salad dressings were commercialized and seven major salad dressings emerged: russian, italian, blue cheese, thousand island, french, caesar, and ranch.

Dips

People have been dipping food into sauces for millennia, but the commercial category of dips can be traced to the 1950s, when Lipton began a promotional campaign to combine their french onion soup mix with sour cream or cream cheese as dips for potato and corn chips. Since then, hundreds of commercial dips have been manufactured; by far, salsa has been the most important. While it had been made in America since the early nineteenth century, its use exploded during the 1980s and continued to increase during the following decade. By the mid-1990s salsa outsold ketchup. Although it slipped subsequently in its ratings, in the early 2000s salsa remained as one of America's most important condiments.

Ethnic Condiments

During the second half of the twentieth century, ethnic sauces greatly changed the world of American condiments. These sauces were purveyed by restaurants and cookbooks, and promoted by their American manufacturers. A short list of common ethnic condiments includes: soy sauce, duck sauce, pickled ginger, oyster sauce, wasabi paste, guacamole, chutney, curry, and Vietnamese and Thai fish sauces. Dozens of other ethnic condiments are commonly available throughout America.

Continued Use of Condiments

In the twentieth century, the use of condiments in America expanded mainly due to their decrease in cost. The downside of the widespread dissemination of certain condiments was standardization. This loss of diversity was offset by the infusion of new condiments generally introduced by immigrants. Gradually, ethnic condiments became part of the culinary mainstream. American condiments have greatly influenced the world as many have been transported into other cuisines through American fast food establishments.

[*See also* Butter; Dips; Herbs and Spices; Honey; Ketchup; Maple Syrup; Mayonnaise; Molasses; Mustard; Pepper, Black; Pickles; Salads and Salad Dressings; Salsa; Salt and Salting; Sugar.]

BIBLIOGRAPHY

Alcott, William. "Abuse of Condiments." *Moral Reformer and Teacher on the Human Constitution* 1 (May 1835): 155–157.

Costenbader, Carol W. *Mustards, Ketchups, and Vinegars: Making the Most of Seasonal Abundance.* Pownal, VT: Storey Communications, 1996.

Hooker, Richard J. *Food and Drink in America: A History.* Indianapolis, IN: Bobbs-Merrill, 1981.

Itrich, Jeffree Wyn. *Spice It Up! The Art of Making Condiments.* Albuquerque, NM: Border Books, 1993.

Rinzler, Carol Ann. *The New Complete Book of Herbs, Spices, and Condiments.* New York: Checkmark Books, 2001.

Smith, Andrew F. *Pure Ketchup: A History of America's National Condiment, with Recipes.* Columbia: Washington, DC: Smithsonian Institution, 2001.

Solomon, Jay. *Condiments! Chutneys, Relishes, and Table Sauces.* Freedom, CA: Crossing Press, 1990.

Thudichum, J. L. W. *The Spirit of Cookery: A Popular Treatise on the History, Science, Practice, and Ethical and Medical Import of Culinary Art.* London: Frederick Warne, 1895.

ANDREW F. SMITH

Coney Island, *see Amusement Parks*

Containers

Most food before and after preparation has to be kept in a container to protect it from insects, rodents, or just the moisture in the air. In particular, staples—flour, sugar, salt, ground meal, spices, coffee, and tea—historically were stored in bulk in close-fitted containers. Tea and some spices were so expensive in the eighteenth and early nineteenth centuries that the small containers in which they were stored were kept locked. The earliest American food containers were barrels, baskets, boxes, canisters, and ceramic crocks or jugs. The first American patent for any kind of container was issued in 1811, for barrel staves and lids.

Barrels and kegs were made by coopers out of wooden staves, usually oak or cedar, which were bound by bentwood straps and later metal hoops. They were airtight enough to store dry foods such as flour or fresh foods such as apples packed in straw. The wood swelled when wet, so coopered wares were also watertight and leakproof for foods such as sauerkraut or cider. Various coopered wood containers, from buckets and firkins to barrels and hogsheads, also were used as dry or liquid measures; the more or less standard capacities differed based on the contents. A hogshead, for example, held 63 liquid gallons or 7.2 firkins.

Baskets were made of wood splints, especially oak or hickory, or of reeds, rushes, willow, or other plant materials that could be bent and woven. Sizes ranged from a half-pint, a quart, and a peck (8 quarts) to a bushel (32 quarts).

Boxes first were made of wood in the United States. Some had joined corners like case furniture drawers and some were bentwood—nailed or pegged to wood bases and lids, and oval or round. Shakers made the most notable bentwood boxes, in sizes from tiny for dried herbs or pastilles to quite large for cheeses. Often these boxes were painted.

By about 1810 tin boxes, which had been imported from Wales, began to be made on a large scale in the

United States. They were varnished or japanned with special coatings to keep them from rusting. Thirty years later square and round tins with lids were used to sell food, especially staples. By the 1880s decorated tin canisters were sold in sets. At the turn of the century, glass and ceramic canisters were made in sets for spices, sugar, salt, flour, meal, and soda. Matching sets of canisters, decorated and with the stenciled name of the food contents, became popular in the 1920s when the idea of a decorated kitchen, instead of just a functional kitchen, was touted in women's magazines. Color schemes such as red and yellow or green and cream could be echoed by colorful canisters. In the twentieth century, figural cookie jars made in the shape of animals, people, or houses became popular.

Crocks of stoneware (heavy ceramic with a salt glaze, created by throwing salt into the kiln during firing) were used for storing butter and soft cheese in the springhouse or cellar. Draped with a wet cloth, which cooled as the water evaporated, such crocks effectively stored foods at low temperatures before the advent of iceboxes and refrigerators. Salt glaze is impervious to acids, so such crocks were used widely for pickled foods. Jars, jugs, and bottles of glass and various ceramics (stoneware, earthenware, redware) were used by the eighteenth century for storing liquids and also dry staples. Corks, carved wooden plugs, and even corncobs were used to stopper jars and jugs throughout the nineteenth century.

Spice cabinets made like fine furniture, with many drawers and locked doors, were used in the eighteenth and early nineteenth centuries. These cabinets evolved by the 1880s into wooden wall-mounted little chests of drawers with a drawer for each spice. They were mostly made of oak, and reproductions imported from Germany were made at least until the 1950s. Similar tin spice chests also were used. Compartmentalized tin containers called spice boxes were popular in the 1800s. Round or rectangular, they were japanned inside and out and had hinged lids with a hasp for a lock and a carrying handle. Inside there were either sectional divisions or small lidded cans for at least four, and usually six to eight, necessary spices: allspice, cloves, nutmeg, ginger, cinnamon, mustard seeds, peppercorns, and mace. Usually there was a small nutmeg grater built in or detachable from the lid. By 1880 tin boxes sometimes included room for bottled extracts. Also by then commercially prepared and ready-to-use spices and flavorings were sold in small tins (later in cardboard and tin boxes, to store on shelves or wall-hung racks).

These were chromolithographed with decorative images so that housewives would keep the container in use and be reminded of the brand.

[*See also* Mason Jars; Material Culture and Technology.]

BIBLIOGRAPHY

Franklin, Linda Campbell. *300 Years of Kitchen Collectibles.* 5th ed. Iola, WI: Krause Publications, 2003.

Hine, Thomas. *The Total Package: The Evolution and Secret Meanings of Boxes, Bottles, Cans, and Tubes.* Boston: Little, Brown, 1995.

Lasansky, Jeannette. *Central Pennsylvania Redware Pottery, 1780–1904.* Lewisburg, PA: Union County Oral Traditions Project, 1979.

Lasansky, Jeannette. *Made of Mud: Stoneware Potteries in Central Pennsylvania, 1834–1929.* Lewisburg, PA: Union County Oral Traditions Project, 1977.

Lasansky, Jeannette. *To Cut, Piece, and Solder: The Work of the Rural Pennsylvania Tinsmith, 1778–1908.* Lewisburg, PA: Union County Oral Traditions Project, 1982.

Leybourne, Douglas M., Jr. *The Collector's Guide to Old Fruit Jars.* North Muskegon, MI: Altarfire Publishing, 2000.

Leybourne, Douglas M., Jr. *The Fruit Jar Works.* 2 vols. North Muskegon, MI: privately published, 1996.

McCann, Jerry, comp. and ed. *The Guide to Collecting Fruit Jars: Fruit Jar Annual.* Chicago: Phoenix Press, 1996–.

Nichols, Harold. *McCoy Cookie Jars: From the First to the Last.* 2nd ed. Ames, IA: Nichols Enterprises, 1991.

Roerig, Fred, and Joyce Herndon Roerig. *The Collector's Encyclopedia of Cookie Jars.* 3 vols. Paducah, KY: Collector Books, 1991–1998.

LINDA CAMPBELL FRANKLIN

Cookbooks and Manuscripts

This entry includes seven subentries:

From the Beginnings to 1860
From the Civil War to World War I
From World War I to World War II
From World War II to the 1960s
From the 1970s to the Present
Community Cookbooks
Children's Cookbooks

See also Advertising Cookbooklets and Recipes.

From the Beginnings to 1860

"I greatly suspect that some of the Pilgrim Fathers must have come over to this country with the Cookery book under one arm and the Bible under the other." There is a kernel of truth in this observation by an English visitor to America in 1836; early settlers carried manuscript and

AMERICAN COOKERY,

OR THE ART OF DRESSING

VIANDS, FISH, POULTRY and VEGETABLES,

AND THE BEST MODES OF MAKING

PASTES, PUFFS, PIES, TARTS, PUDDINGS,
CUSTARDS AND PRESERVES,

AND ALL KINDS OF

CAKES,

FROM THE IMPERIAL PLUMB TO PLAIN CAKE.

ADAPTED TO THIS COUNTRY,

AND ALL GRADES OF LIFE.

By Amelia Simmons,

AN AMERICAN ORPHAN.

PUBLISHED ACCORDING TO ACT OF CONGRESS.

HARTFORD;

PRINTED BY HUDSON & GOODWIN.

FOR THE AUTHOR.

1796.

American Cookery. Title page of the 1796 edition. Simmons's book was the first printed representative collection of the English-American cuisine in common usage in the eighteenth to early nineteenth century. *Culinary Archives & Museum at Johnson & Wales University, Providence, R.I.*

printed cookbooks with them to the New World. American archives contain hundreds of manuscript cookery books, which have yet to be thoroughly examined and cataloged.

Once the immigrants arrived in the New World, they purchased and collected European—especially English, Dutch, and German—cookbooks. The contributions of the foodstuffs and cooking techniques of the indigenous population, although ubiquitous, most often went unrecorded and unacknowledged in culinary archives. Native Americans' culinary contributions during this period must be gleaned from exploration and discovery literature and from letters and diaries.

Early American Cookbooks

America came late to cookbook publishing. Europeans and Africans had been preparing meals in America for more than one hundred years before the first cookbook was printed in the English colonies. The first formal cookbook of American imprint was Eliza Smith's *The Compleat Housewife; or, Accomplished Gentlewomen's Companion* (1742), published by William Parks, the printer at Williamsburg, Virginia. Smith's book was reprinted from the fifth London edition (original edition 1727) and became very popular on both sides of the Atlantic throughout the eighteenth century. Even prior to 1742, however, serving suggestions and recipes for foods and beverages had appeared in American books of more general practical information or in etiquette manuals. These books and manuals usually were reprinted or adapted from English works.

During the last half of the eighteenth century, Smith's book and other English works were reprinted in Boston, New York City, and Philadelphia. Notable publications include two editions of Susannah Carter's *The Frugal Housewife; or, Complete Woman Cook*, the first of which (1772) had plates on carving engraved by Paul Revere, and Richard Briggs's encyclopedic *The New Art of Cookery, according to the Present Practice* (1792).

When Parks printed *The Compleat Housewife*, he made some attempt to fashion the English cookbook to American tastes and circumstances by deleting certain recipes, "the ingredients or materials for which are not to be had in this country." However, no cookbook seriously attempted to reach an American audience for another fifty years.

Twenty years after the American Revolution, in Hartford, Connecticut, Amelia Simmons published her *American Cookery; or, The Art of Dressing Viands, Fish,*
Poultry, and Vegetables, and the Best Modes of Making Pastes, Puffs, Pies, Tarts, Puddings, Custards, and Preserves, and All Kinds of Cakes, from the Imperial Plumb to Plain Cake, Adapted to this Country, and All Grades of Life (1796). *American Cookery* is considered to be the first cookbook written by an American and published in the United States. Despite the passage of more than two hundred years, inquiry and speculation have provided little information on Simmons beyond her own avowal that she was "an American orphan."

While Simmons remains an enigma, her book speaks for itself. Although many of the recipes in *American Cookery* are outright borrowings from British cookery books of the period, especially Carter's work, it also contains new and distinctly American recipes. Its originality lies in its recognition and use of truly American produce. There are five recipes using cornmeal (corn is indigenous to America): three for Indian pudding, one for johnnycake or hoecake, and one for Indian slapjacks. These are among the earliest appearances of these recipes in any printed cookbook. Other American innovations were the use of corncobs for smoking bacon, the suggestion of cranberry sauce as an accompaniment to roast turkey (both cranberries and turkey are indigenous to the New World), and the use of watermelon rind to make American citron. Perhaps the most far-reaching innovation was the introduction of pearlash (similar to potash), a well-known staple in the colonial American household, as a chemical leavening in dough. This practice eventually resulted in the compounding of modern baking powders.

Development of American Classics

Two conflicting trends became evident during the sixty years following the publication of *American Cookery*. English works, including the major contemporary classics by Elizabeth Raffald, Maria Rundell, Hannah Glasse, W. A. Henderson, Frederick Nutt, William Kitchiner, Alexis Soyer, and Eliza Acton, still were being reprinted regularly in the United States, often with special sections or adaptations for the American audience. At the same time, Pennsylvania German publishers were printing or reprinting works in German for their ethnic constituencies. But increasingly, cookbooks written by Americans for Americans were capturing the market.

In the early decades of the 1800s, pirated and reprinted editions of Simmons's book continued to appear (a dozen by 1830). The next major U.S. cookbook after

American Cookery was Mary Randolph's *The Virginia House-Wife* (1824), printed in Washington, D.C. This first regional American cookbook was extremely popular, with at least nineteen printings prior to the Civil War, and is still in print. It includes recipes for truly regional items such as Ochra Soup, Catfish Soup, Barbecued Shote ("This is the name given in the southern states to a fat young hog"), Curry of Catfish, Gumbo ("A West India Dish"), Chicken Pudding ("A Favourite Virginia Dish"), Field Peas, and Apoquiniminc Cakes (a form of beaten biscuits).

In the 1820s the earliest cookery works of Eliza Leslie and Lydia Maria Child were first issued and became American classics. They exemplified a major trend of the nineteenth-century American cookbook publishing scene: the domination of the field by an influential and remarkable group of women who were not only recognized culinary authorities but also were active in all the major cultural and societal concerns of their day.

For example, Child, whose book *The Frugal Housewife* (1829) superseded *American Cookery* as the most popular cookbook of its day, was best known for her work in the cause of abolition. She was also a writer and journalist and the founder of *Juvenile Miscellany*, the first monthly periodical for children in America. Leslie wrote works on etiquette and homemaking, novels, short stories, and books for juveniles. She was the editor of *The Gift*, an annual designed primarily for young women, and authored numerous magazine articles in addition to her cookbooks. Leslie's *Directions for Cookery* (1837) was among the most popular cookery books of the nineteenth century. All of her cookery works were deservedly successful as they have fine recipes and evidence a concern for quality and integrity.

During the 1830s cookbooks by the American and English authors cited above were printed and reprinted in Boston; New York City; Philadelphia; Hartford; Baltimore; New Haven, Connecticut; Cincinnati, Ohio; Newark, New Jersey; Concord, New Hampshire; Woodstock, Vermont; Hamilton, Ohio; and several upstate New York communities including Watertown, Cortland, Bath, and Albany. The works of Randolph, Child, and Leslie clearly dominated this decade.

In the 1840s and 1850s cookbooks began to be published in new cities, including more in the Midwest and the South. In addition, new culinary authorities, almost all American women, emerged: Sarah Josepha Hale, Catharine Beecher, Mary Hooker Cornelius, Mrs. T. J. Crowen, Mrs. A. L Webster, Esther Allen Howland,

Mrs. L. G. Abell, Mrs. Bliss, and Mrs. J. Chadwick. Beecher was another of the cookery authorities who also contributed in many other areas. She was active in encouraging female education, founding the influential Hartford Female Seminary in 1827 and the American Women's Educational Association in 1852. Her works on cookery and household management, *A Treatise on Domestic Economy, for the Use of Young Ladies at Home, and at School* (1841) and *Miss Beecher's Domestic Receipt-Book* (1846), often were reprinted. They were of great import in influencing the development of scientific kitchen planning, which blossomed after the Civil War.

Trends in Topics and Authors

Certain trends and themes appear in the published cookbooks of the first half of the nineteenth century. Among these are a preoccupation with sweets and desserts, economy and frugality, management and organization, diet and health, vegetarianism, and regional American cooking. These trends are evident in such influential works as Leslie's *Seventy-five Receipts for Pastry, Cakes, and Sweetmeats* (1828), Child's *The Frugal Housewife* (1829), H. L. Barnum's *Family Receipts; or, Practical Guide for the Husbandman and Housewife* (1831), Sylvester Graham's *A Treatise on Bread, and Bread-Making* (1837), and William Alcott's *Vegetable Diet: As Sanctioned by Medical Men, and by Experience in All Ages, including a System of Vegetable Cookery* (1849; second edition, but first with recipes).

Following Randolph's 1824 work on Virginia cooking, many other regional American cookbooks appeared: Lettice Bryan's *The Kentucky Housewife* (1839), Phineas Thornton's *The Southern Gardener and Receipt Book* (1840), Philomelia Hardin's *Every Bodys Cook and Receipt Book: But More Particularly Designed for Buckeyes, Hoosiers, Wolverines, Corncrackers, Suckers, and All Epicures Who Wish to Live with the Present Times* (1842), Howland's *The New England Economical Housekeeper, and Family Receipt Book* (1844), Sarah Rutledge's *The Carolina Housewife; or, House and Home* (1847), Anna Maria Collins's *Mrs. Collins' Table Receipts: Adapted to Western Housewifery* (1851), and Mrs. P. H. Mendall's *The New Bedford Practical Receipt Book* (1859). Regional recipes abound in these works. For example, Hardin's book, which was published in Cleveland, Ohio, contains many locale-specific recipes: Buckeye Dumplings (Ohio), Wolverine Junket (Michigan), Hoosier Pickles (Indiana), and Corncrackers' Pudding (Kentucky). Rutledge's book, which was published in Charleston, South Carolina, has

THE

HOUSE SERVANT'S DIRECTORY,

OR

A MONITOR FOR PRIVATE FAMILIES:

COMPRISING

HINTS ON THE ARRANGEMENT AND PERFORMANCE OF

SERVANTS' WORK,

WITH GENERAL RULES FOR

SETTING OUT TABLES AND SIDEBOARDS

IN FIRST ORDER;

THE ART OF WAITING

IN ALL ITS BRANCHES; AND LIKEWISE HOW TO CONDUCT

LARGE AND SMALL PARTIES

WITH ORDER;

WITH GENERAL DIRECTIONS FOR PLACING ON TABLE

ALL KINDS OF JOINTS, FISH, FOWL, &c.

WITH

FULL INSTRUCTIONS FOR CLEANING

PLATE, BRASS, STEEL, GLASS, MAHOGANY;

AND LIKEWISE

ALL KINDS OF PATENT AND COMMON LAMPS:

OBSERVATIONS

ON SERVANTS' BEHAVIOUR TO THEIR EMPLOYERS;

AND UPWARDS OF

100 VARIOUS AND USEFUL RECEIPTS,

CHIEFLY COMPILED

FOR THE USE OF HOUSE SERVANTS;

AND IDENTICALLY MADE

TO SUIT THE MANNERS AND CUSTOMS OF FAMILIES

IN THE UNITED STATES.

———

By ROBERT ROBERTS.

———

WITH

FRIENDLY ADVICE TO COOKS

AND HEADS OF FAMILIES,

AND COMPLETE DIRECTIONS HOW TO BURN

LEHIGH COAL.

═══

BOSTON,

MUNROE AND FRANCIS, 128 WASHINGTON-STREET.

NEW YORK,

CHARLES S. FRANCIS, 189 BROADWAY.

1827.

House Servant's Directory. Title page of the 1827 edition. *Culinary Archives & Museum at Johnson & Wales University, Providence, R.I.*

about two dozen recipes for rice-based breakfast breads and cakes, plus recipes for a rice soup, several pilafs, and many rice desserts, and includes detailed instructions for preparing and boiling rice.

By the mid-nineteenth century women were writing the majority of American cookbooks. Several works by male professional chefs and caterers and male medical doctors were the exception. Representative works by male chefs are J. M. Sanderson's *The Complete Cook* (1843) and Parkinson's *The Complete Confectioner* (1844), published in a combined edition in 1851. Early cookbooks by a mix of English and American physicians include Kitchiner's *The Cook's Oracle: Containing Receipts for Plain Cookery on the Most Economical Plan for Private Families* (1822), Colin Mackenzie's *Five Thousand Receipts in All the Useful and Domestic Arts* (1825), and Russell T. Trall's *The New Hydropathic Cook-Book: With Recipes for Cooking on Hygienic Principles* (1854).

Two works by African American authors also were published prior to the Civil War: Robert Roberts's *The House Servant's Directory; or, A Monitor for Private Families, Comprising Hints on the Arrangement and Performance of Servants' Work . . . and Upwards of 100 Various and Useful Receipts Chiefly Compiled for the Use of House Servants* (1827) and Tunis Campbell's *Hotel Keepers, Head Waiters, and Housekeepers' Guide* (1848). Although each has recipes, these are not simply cookbooks, but rather manuals written by professional men to teach others how to manage large private households or hotel and restaurant dining rooms.

Popular Publishing Forms

Large compendiums, usually in encyclopedia form, were very popular in this early period of American culinary imprints. They present a wide variety of information, including recipes as well as advice on household management, medical cures, food preservation, beverage and dairy production, farming and laundry chores, etiquette, home furnishings, and child care. The earliest of these culinary encyclopedias, which were compiled from British, Continental, and American sources and often were reprinted, include Mrs. N. K. M. Lee's *The Cook's Own Book* (1832), Thomas Webster's *An Encyclopaedia of Domestic Economy* (1845), and Elizabeth Ellet's *The Practical Housekeeper: A Cyclopaedia of Domestic Economy Embracing Domestic Education* (1857). Ellet's book covers the house and its furniture, duties of the mistress and the servant, the storeroom and marketing, "domestic manipulation," bills of fare, perfumery and toilet, infusions and cosmetics, pomades, vinegars, and soaps, and provides a family medical guide as well as

"five thousand practical receipts and maxims"; it is illustrated with five hundred wood engravings.

In addition to recipe books and culinary encyclopedias, many works on gastronomy were published prior to the Civil War, including the first English-language translation of Brillat-Savarin's French classic, *The Physiology of Taste; or, Transcendental Gastronomy* (1854). Translations from the French and reprints of noted English works on French cookery also were printed with some regularity. Louis Ude's *The French Cook* appeared in 1828; Leslie's *Domestic French Cookery* in 1832. In 1846 three major French cookery books were published: Madame Utrecht-Friedel's *The French Cook*, Charles Elmé Francatelli's *French Cookery: The Modern Cook; A Practical Guide to the Culinary Art in All Its Branches, Adapted as Well for the Largest Establishments as for the Use of Private Families*, and Louis-Eustache Audot's *French Domestic Cookery*. In 1850 Soyer's *The Modern Housewife* was added to the books on the classic French repertoire easily available to the American public. German cookbooks, both in English and in translation, continued to be published in the Pennsylvania Dutch community.

Recipes for the housewife also were available in sources other than printed cookbooks, especially in the new women's magazines such as *Godey's Lady's Book* (founded in 1830) and in the ubiquitous and popular almanacs. *Godey's* influential editor, Sarah Josepha Hale, was the arbiter of national taste for forty years and was one of the great nineteenth-century culinary authorities. In addition to editing *Godey's* and writing many cookbooks, she wrote fiction, biographies, articles, and poetry. She was also a leading voice in supporting women's education and in alleviating the drudgery in women's work in the household by sponsoring and popularizing such laborsaving devices as the sewing and washing machines. The almanacs were of a multitude of kinds; some were agricultural, some were in support of causes, especially of temperance, and some were simply gift books. Examples are Turner's *The House-Keeper's Almanac; or, The Young Wife's Oracle, for . . .* (1842), *The Lady's Annual* (1842), and Fisher's *Temperance House-Keeper's Almanac* (1843).

Additional Sources

Although the early years of American cookbooks were dominated by the themes and names already cited, there are other books that are part of U.S. heritage and deserve to be recognized. One, *The Cook Not Mad; or, Rational Cookery; Being a Collection of Original and Selected*

Receipts . . . (1830), is a small book that appeared anonymously in Watertown, New York. It is worthy of note not so much for its insistence on its American origin and viewpoint, but because it was reprinted in Canada in 1831 and became Canada's first known printed cookbook. The only difference between the two printings appears to be the substitution of the word "Canadian" for "American" on the title page.

Another group of books, also not well known but of importance in early America, concerns milk, cheese, and dairying. Although most dairying and milk processing chores were the housewife's responsibility, all of these books and pamphlets were written by American or British male authorities. The books are practical how-to guides on home dairy management, stressing the importance of cleanliness and consistency of technique for the production of increased and better quality product. An excellent example is Joshua Johnson's twelve-page pamphlet called *The Art of Cheese-Making, Reduced to Rules, and Made Sure and Easy, from Accurate Observation and Experience* (1801). There are about a dozen similar early works on dairying recognized in the relevant bibliographies.

Most of the early trends in American cookbook publishing continued after 1860, although whole new genres of cookbooks increasingly became available.

[*See also* Beecher, Catharine; Campbell, Tunis G.; Cooking Manuscripts; Graham, Sylvester; Leslie, Eliza; Randolph, Mary; Simmons, Amelia.]

BIBLIOGRAPHY

Beck, Leonard N. *Two Loaf-Givers; or, A Tour through the Gastronomic Libraries of Katherine Golden Bitting and Elizabeth Robins Pennell*. Washington, DC: Library of Congress, 1984.

Bitting, Katherine Golden. *Gastronomic Bibliography*. San Francisco: privately published, 1939.

Brown, Eleanor, and Bob Brown. *Culinary Americana: Cookbooks Published in the Cities and Towns of the United States of America during the Years from 1860 through 1960*. New York: Roving Eye Press, 1961.

Cagle, William R., and Lisa Killion Stafford. *American Books on Food and Drink: A Bibliographical Catalog of the Cookbook Collection Housed in the Lilly Library at the University of Indiana*. New Castle, DE: Oak Knoll Press, 1998.

DuSablon, Mary Anna. *America's Collectible Cookbooks: The History, the Politics, the Recipes*. Athens: Ohio University Press, 1994.

Hooker, Richard J. *Food and Drink in America: A History*. Indianapolis, IN: Bobbs-Merrill, 1981.

Longone, Jan. *American Cookery: The Bicentennial, 1796–1996*. Ann Arbor, MI: Clements Library, 1996. Exhibition catalog published in conjunction with "An Exhibition of 200 Years of American Cookbooks" shown at the Williams L. Clements Library, University of Michigan.

Longone, Janice Bluestein, and Daniel T. Longone. *American Cookbooks and Wine Books, 1797–1950*. Ann Arbor, MI: Clements Library, Wine and Food Library, 1984. Exhibition catalog published in conjunction with an exhibition from the collections of the William L. Clements Library, University of Michigan.

Lowenstein, Eleanor. *Bibliography of American Cookery Books, 1742–1860*. 3rd ed. Worcester, MA: American Antiquarian Society, 1972.

Pennell, Elizabeth Robins. *My Cookery Books*. Boston: Houghton Mifflin, 1903.

Schlesinger, Arthur M. *Learning How to Behave: A Historical Study of American Etiquette Books*. New York: Macmillan, 1946.

Theophano, Janet. *Eat My Words: Reading Women's Lives through the Cookbooks They Wrote*. New York: Palgrave, 2002.

Theophano, Janet. *Household Words: Women Write from and for the Kitchen*. Philadelphia: University of Pennsylvania, 1996. Exhibition catalog published in conjunction with an exhibition of the Esther B. Aresty Collection of Rare Books on the Culinary Arts at the Van Pelt-Dietrich Library, University of Pennsylvania.

Wilson, Mary Tolford. "An essay." In *American Cookery*, by Amelia Simmons. A facsimile of the first edition, 1796. New York: Oxford University Press, 1958.

JANICE BLUESTEIN (JAN) LONGONE

From the Civil War to World War I

Many societal changes influenced the history of American cookbooks after 1860: the Civil War, the Industrial Revolution, the change from a rural to an urban society, large waves of immigration, the westward expansion, the changing role of women, and the increasing knowledge of and interest in scientific diet and nutrition. Although many of the pre–Civil War trends in cookbook publishing continued, new and major cookbook explosions occurred after the war that had effects throughout the twentieth century and still influence cookbook publishing.

New Postwar Publishing Forms

The first change was a legacy of the Civil War, when women's charitable organizations compiled and sold cookbooks to raise funds to aid war victims. When the war ended, these organizations turned their charitable attentions to other causes. The first known charity cookbook, *A Poetical Cook-Book* (1864), was published to benefit a sanitary fair in Philadelphia. What began as a trickle of charity cookbooks in the 1860s and 1870s became a flood in the following decades; from 1864 to the beginning of World War I more than five thousand such books were published, and by the early 2000s hundreds to thousands of such books were being published annually. These community cookbooks offered recipes for regional American cooking as well as insights into both the increasing diversity of women's activities outside of the home and the growth of advertising as a way of reaching the consumer. Working on these cookbooks taught women organizational skills and was one way for them to participate in the greater public life of the nation. The national movements capturing women's energies were reflected in cookbooks like *The Woman's Christian Temperance Union Cuisine* (1878); *The Creole Cookery Book* (1885), published by the Christian Woman's Exchange of New Orleans, Louisiana; and the *Woman Suffrage Cook Book* (1886). By 1880 charity cookbooks had been published in twenty-eight states and in nearly every state by the turn of the century. The proceeds benefited diverse causes, including suffrage, temperance, orphanages, schools, libraries, missionary work, hospitals, churches (Protestant and Catholic) and synagogues, women's exchanges, granges, the Young Men's Christian Association (YMCA) and Young Women's Christian Association (YWCA), and organizations to benefit children, veterans, and business and professional women. This genre of volunteer publications, essentially amateur and regional, remains an underutilized resource for the study of American culinary history.

Another major explosion in post–Civil War cookbooks was the growth of promotional and advertising literature. The new national food and equipment companies began publishing millions of copies of pamphlets and hardcover books (culinary ephemera) that provided instructions, hints, recipes, illustrations, and general diet and nutrition advice to convince the formerly self-sufficient farmer's wife to switch her allegiance to packaged, brand-name products. The success of this technique was phenomenal. The companies frequently hired home economists, famous food writers, celebrities, artists, and entertainers to help with their publications—anyone who could help sell their product. The illustrations and artwork in these ephemera enhance their historical value by providing vivid details of both U.S. advertising and printing history. There exist few more profitable avenues for an investigation of American culinary history than tracing, for example, one hundred years of advertising by all companies offering baking ephemera (flour, baking powder, baking soda, yeast, chocolate, baked goods); or Jell-O gelatin; or stoves (wood, coal, fireless, gas, electric) to the American public.

Another voluminous body of culinary literature made its debut in the postwar era. Federal, state, and local governments began publishing practical materials on all aspects of agriculture, diet and nutrition, and cooking.

Thousands of such pamphlets were issued and could be found in most rural and farm homes. Federal government pamphlets were issued by various departments, especially the U.S. Department of Agriculture, and were available free of charge from congressional offices. The pamphlets covered an enormous range of subjects, from basic utilitarian themes, such as Maria Parloa's *Canned Fruit, Preserves, and Jellies* (1905) and *Preparation of Vegetables for the Table* (1906), to more esoteric topics, such as *Use of Whale Meat for Food* (1918) and *Frogs: Their Natural History and Utilization* (1920).

Effects of Cooking Schools and Home Economics

Still another major development was the growth of the domestic economy, home economics, and cooking school movements. In the decades following the Civil War, several influential cooking schools were established throughout the Northeast; the schools' founders and instructors became prolific publishers and influenced students who went on to found local schools of their own and to work professionally in a variety of educational institutions and hospitals. The cooking schools often became involved with the movement for home economics education in public and private schools and colleges.

In 1865 Pierre Blot, a French émigré, opened the first cooking school in New York City. He taught at the school and in Brooklyn and traveled far and wide throughout the Northeast, teaching and lecturing. His activities were covered extensively in the press, turning Blot into one of America's first celebrity chefs. He wrote many lengthy, much-discussed articles for magazines in addition to his two major cookbooks, *What to Eat and How to Cook It* (1863) and *Hand-Book of Practical Cookery* (1867). In his time Blot was an anomaly, as most of the influential cooking schools were founded and run by women.

Parloa, Juliet Corson, Sarah Tyson Rorer, Mary Lincoln, Fannie Farmer, Marion Harland, and Janet McKenzie Hill continued in the footsteps of the great culinary authorities of the pre–Civil War era. Their books were published in numerous printings and editions, and they reached millions of households with their classes, articles, books, and travels. They also shared their earlier sisters' proclivities toward reform and social, cultural, and educational work. They were teachers, writers, poets, philosophers, editors, and businesswomen.

Corson, the founder of the New York Cooking School, was particularly interested in feeding the poor. She authored a number of influential pamphlets such as *Fifteen Cent Dinners for Workingmen's Families* (1878) and *Twenty-five Cent Dinners for Families of Six* (1878). She distributed many pamphlets free of charge to those in need, including both new immigrants and men out of work because of the economic upheaval following the 1877 railroad strike. In contrast to the pamphlets, her magnum opus, *Miss Corson's Practical American Cookery* (1885), is a large, glorious paean to American cooking. It was the result of a nationwide appeal by the author for information about local dishes. The appeal was sent to the U.S. commissioner of education and circulated by him throughout the country. Corson explained that she undertook to write the book "to verify [her] assertion that genuine American cookery is both wholesome and palatable and has lost none of the traditional excellence which characterized it in our grandmothers' days." The book is a fascinating mixture of French recipes (Foie Gras with Truffles) and regional American dishes (New England Style Rhubarb Pie, Philadelphia Ice Cream, Succotash from Dried Samp and Beans, Apple Pan Dowdy, and Virginia Verder or Bottled Milk Punch).

Rorer, the founder of the Philadelphia Cooking School, published more than one hundred books and pamphlets. She was the part owner of *Table Talk*, a gastronomic monthly, and was the domestic editor of the *Ladies' Home Journal* for fourteen years. Lincoln, in addition to her work at the Boston Cooking School and on many books, traveled tirelessly to every corner of the country giving lectures and demonstrations. She was the culinary editor of the *American Kitchen Magazine* and active in many educational clubs and organizations. Farmer, of the Boston Cooking School and Miss Farmer's School of Cookery, taught and lectured throughout the United States and became the best known of the nineteenth-century cooks. From its first publication, Farmer's *The Boston Cooking-School Cook Book* (1896) went on to become one of the all-time best sellers in the field, with more than 4 million copies printed in numerous editions. She edited a cooking page in the *Woman's Home Companion* and authored several other cookbooks. She was most proud of the book *Food and Cookery for the Sick and Convalescent* (1904), which reflected her interest in cooking for invalids. She supplied lectures on that subject to training schools for nurses nationwide and lectured on nutrition at the Harvard Medical School.

Marion Harland (Mary Virginia Terhune) was a popular southern writer whose special interest was the role of women and American home life. Her many books on cookery, etiquette, and household management were best-sellers in their day. She edited or ran departments in such periodicals as *Babyhood* and the *Home-Maker*. Janet McKenzie Hill, a graduate of the Boston Cooking School, founded the *Boston Cooking School Magazine* in 1896 and was its editor until shortly before her death in 1933. She was a prolific culinary author, editing a variety of promotional pamphlets for various food companies and was a leader in the evolving relationship between food companies and trained domestic servants.

Postwar interest in scientific cooking, eating, and homemaking added to the general diet and nutrition literature of an earlier period. New scientific discoveries became intermingled with the work of the cooking schools and the home economics movement. One of the most influential books of this genre was authored by Catharine Beecher and her sister Harriet Beecher Stowe, the author of *Uncle Tom's Cabin* (1852). Their book, *The American Woman's Home* (1869), was a pioneering effort in scientific kitchen planning. Their innovative delineation of specific work areas for preparation and cleanup, as well as descriptions of continuous work surfaces and standardized built-in cupboards and shelves, were all ideas taken for granted a century later.

Consumer issues, adulteration, and agitation for pure food and drug laws all produced a voluminous body of writing authored by doctors, politicians, civic authorities, and the public. Hundreds of books and pamphlets, as well as many of the major magazines of the day, entered the fray. There was an increased interest in vegetarianism, resulting in a growing body of literature. Representative books include Ella Ervilla Kellogg's *Science in the Kitchen* (1892), David Chidlow's *The American Pure Food Cook Book* (1899), and the *Vegetarian Cook Book* (1915), published by the Los Angeles Lodge of the Theosophical Society.

Immigration and Ethnic Recipes

The great waves of immigration, mostly from Europe but also from Asia and the Middle East, that transformed America during the late nineteenth century naturally broadened American eating habits and cookbook publishing. The new immigrants needed to know how to cook with American equipment using American ingredients and satisfying American tastes, as well as how to cook foods and recipes from their original homelands. This body of cookery literature is usually difficult to find. Prior to 1920 the American housewife could purchase books on the cuisine of dozens of other cultures, sometimes in English, sometimes in the original language, and sometimes with bilingual text. The books contained American recipes or ethnic recipes or, in many cases, both. In addition to British, Dutch, German, and French works, books from the following cultures were available: Chinese, Japanese, Jewish, Bohemian, Austro-Hungarian, Polish, Lithuanian, Central American, Mexican, South American, Italian, Spanish, Greek, Norwegian, Danish, Finnish, Belgian, Russian, Armenian, Turkish, Syrian, and Hindu. These works include the first Jewish cookbook published in America, Esther Levy's *Jewish Cookery Book* (1871); the charity cookbook *St. Paul's Bazaar-Kochbuch und Geschaeftsfuehrer* (1892); the bilingual *Svensk Amerikansk Kokbok* (1895); May E. Southworth's *One Hundred and One Mexican Dishes* (1906); Sara Bosse and Onoto Watanna's *Chinese-Japanese Cook Book* (1910); Ardashes H. Keoleian's Armenian and Turkish *The Oriental Cook Book* (1913); Mina Walli's Finnish bilingual *Suomalais-Amerikalainen Keittokirja* (1914); George Haddad's Syrian *Mount Lebanon to Vermont* (1916); and K. D. Shastri's *Hindu Dietetics* (1917). According to its introduction, this last book was made possible by "the influence of Hindu thought on the life of the American people since the Columbian Exposition held in Chicago in 1893."

Foreign and ethnic foods, foodways, and recipes were further introduced to American housewives by countless articles in women's magazines. Every culture and country was represented, from ancient Greece and Rome to the Azores, Cuba, Lithuania, Japan, Persia, the Orient, and South America. In addition, charity cookbooks often introduced the ethnic contributions of their communities. One such work, *The Landmarks Club Cook Book* (1903), was written to raise funds to preserve the California missions and contained a chapter of the "most famous Old California and Mexican dishes."

Professional Publications

The growing culinary professional and trade organizations began publishing their own books and magazines in the postwar era. The Hotel Monthly Press of Chicago produced an enormous variety of practical professional guides in many editions following the turn of the century. These guides include Jessup Whitehead's *Steward's Handbook* (1889), John Tellman's *Practical Hotel Steward* (1900), Frank Rivers's *Hotel Butcher, Garde Manger, and Carver* (1916), Paul Richard's *Pastry Book* (1907), and

three influential works by Charles Fellows: *Menu Maker* (1910), *Chef's Reminder* (1895), and *Culinary Handbook* (1904). The Hotel Monthly Press also issued a popular and oft-reprinted series of vest-pocket guides to sauces, pastry, eggs, fish, and oysters. In addition it published several of the classic compendia of fine dining in America, written by the most renowned chefs of the era: from Delmonico's restaurant in New York City, Charles Ranhofer's *The Epicurean* (1894); from Chicago, Arnold Shircliffe's *Edgewater Beach Hotel Salad Book* (1926); and from San Francisco, Victor Hirtzler's *Hotel St. Francis Cook Book* (1919). *The Epicurean* offers the best picture of fine restaurant dining in Victorian America. It is a massive compendium (almost twelve hundred pages, with four thousand recipes) and was the distillation of Ranhofer's life's work and knowledge. There are sixty pages of menus of the great banquets and dinners held at Delmonico's in the nineteenth century, including those for Charles Dickens, the financier Diamond Jim Brady, and General William Tecumseh Sherman. It was said that many professional chefs were furious that Ranhofer had given away all of their professional secrets. Another large, splendid volume was published about this time: *The Cook Book by "Oscar" of the Waldorf* (1896) by Oscar Tschirky, the maître d'hôtel of the Waldorf-Astoria in New York City.

Fairs and Expositions

As Americans began to travel by train or car, books on camping as well as guides to hotels and restaurants appeared. Among the most popular destinations were the many fairs and expositions held in all parts of the country. A remarkable cookbook came out of the fair held in Philadelphia to celebrate America's Centennial in 1876: *The National Cookery Book*, issued by the Women's Centennial Committee, is a splendid picture of regional American cookery at that time. It was written to answer the question, "Have you no national dishes?" The answer was a resounding "yes!" The recipes affirm the national presence of uniquely American dishes and include: To Roast Oysters along the Shore in Maryland; A Michigan Receipt for Making Shortcake in Camp and One for Cooking Brook Trout in Camp; A Kansas Poor Man's Pudding in Grasshopper Times; An Old Time Boston Cake for an Election Day; Idaho Miner's Bread, Which Is Baked in a Gold Pan in Which He Washes His Gold Dirt; A Philadelphia Receipt for Cooking Terrapins; and Poke Melia—A Russian Pickle (This Receipt Was Given to Benjamin Franklin on His Departure from Paris in 1785 by a Russian). There are also recipes for New Orleans Gumbo, Rhode Island Chowder, Virginia Tomato Ketchup, Baltimore Oyster Pie, Gundinga (A Florida Dish), New England Bean Porridge, Wisconsin Breakfast Eggs, Pacific Biscuits, South Carolina Rice Johnny Cakes, Georgia Ash Cake, Palo Alto Pudding, Kentucky Boiled Custard, and Mississippi Cream. A chapter on game features recipes for many species, some no longer available (reed birds, venison, grouse, canvas-back duck, wild duck, woodcock, snipe, partridge, pigeons, squab). There are a surprising number of Jewish dishes, including many for holiday celebrations.

By the turn of the century, fairs and expositions were being held from California to New York and from Chicago to Atlanta, Georgia. They had immediate and long-lasting effects on American eating habits and produced fascinating cookbooks. The World's Columbian Exposition held in Chicago in 1893 to commemorate the four-hundredth anniversary of Christopher Columbus's first voyage of exploration was the greatest public amusement of the nineteenth century. The fair was a phenomenal success, attracting almost 28 million visitors and the participation of more than one hundred states, territories, countries, and colonies, as well as thousands of concessionaires, from individual entrepreneurs to the largest companies. The sheer scope of food operations at the fair was staggering. Guidebooks were written describing Chicago's one thousand restaurants, along with the one hundred hotels and fifteen thousand rooms and boardinghouses available for fairgoers to patronize. New and exotic foods from every part of America and the world were introduced to the visiting public, along with the most modern cooking equipment and techniques. Many exhibits gave away recipe and instruction booklets. Hundreds of items of culinary literature were generated at and by the exposition. One of the most interesting was Mary Green's *Food Products of the World* (1895), in which the doctor estimated that the most complete and cosmopolitan array of food products ever displayed had been gathered at the Chicago fair. Green's book offers invaluable insights into the then-current knowledge of culinary botany, food chemistry, and nutrition. Another important work was *Favorite Recipes: A Columbian Autograph Souvenir* (1893), which collected three hundred autographed recipes and twenty-three portraits contributed specially by the fair's Board of Lady Managers. The recipes include Jambolaya [sic] (Louisiana), Tamales de Chile (New Mexico), Pilauf (South Carolina), Wild Duck in Maryland, Old Virginia

Slap Jacks, North Dakota Sponge Cake, and Connecticut Election Cake.

Several of the cookbooks produced for other fairs became classics. From the Cotton States and International Exposition held in Atlanta in 1895 came the *Tested Recipe Cook Book*, which was compiled by Mrs. Henry Lumpkin Wilson and attempted to preserve old southern traditions. It contains recipes for Creole Gumbo, Ground-pea Soup, Pickled Figs, Dixie Waffles, Green Tomato Pie, and Jeff Davis Pudding. From the Panama-Pacific International Exposition held in San Francisco in 1915, two books emerged that captured the international character of that city: Linie Loyall McLaren's *Pan-Pacific Cook Book*, which has recipes from sixty countries from Algeria to Venezuela, and Joseph Charles Lehner's *World's Fair Menu and Recipe Book: A Collection of the Most Famous Menus Exhibited at the Panama-Pacific International Exposition*. For the Louisiana Purchase Exposition held in Saint Louis in 1904, Sarah Tyson Rorer published the *World's Fair Souvenir Cook Book*.

Children's Cookbooks

Prior to this historical period, few books for children had been published except those relating to religion, morality, and etiquette. After the Civil War, books on feeding children and educating children about food, as well as cookbooks for children's use, began to emerge. Some have hints on housekeeping or manners and etiquette; many have fine illustrations. The books include Ella Farman Pratt's *The Cooking Club of Tu-Whit Hollow* (1876); Elizabeth Stansbury Kirkland's *Six Little Cooks* (1877); *A Little Book for a Little Cook*, published by Pillsbury (1905); Olive Hyde Foster's *Cookery for Little Girls* (1910); and Jane Fryer's *The Mary Frances Cook Book* (1912). This last is among the most beautiful and nostalgic of all children's cookbooks, with the kitchen utensils coming alive and explaining their purpose and use to the young Mary Frances. The character is enchanted by this bit of magic, learns well how to prepare a meal, and wants to share what she has learned with other children. These early works formed the basis of the large and competitive children's cookbook industry that developed later in the twentieth century.

Pre–Civil War Trends

All these newer trends in post-1860 cookbook publishing did not replace the earlier, prewar literature and publishing trends. Books on economy and frugality, management and organization, and sweets and desserts were still being published in large numbers. Corson's pamphlets on frugality, mentioned earlier, are just two examples from the hundreds of such works printed. Management and organization subjects were well covered by books issued by those in the cooking school, domestic economy, and home economics movements. A prominent example of the continuing interest in sweets and desserts is the comprehensive *The Art of Confectionery* (1866). Its forty-four chapters in 346 pages cover every aspect of the subject, with recipes from Almond Paste and Bonbons to Iced Beverages Called Graniti and Psyche's Kisses. Baking, candy, and confectionery works, for and by both the professional and the amateur, continued to appear in great numbers. Henry J. Wehman's *Confectioner's Guide and Assistant: A Complete Instruction in the Art of Candy Making* (1905) indicated that it was expressly aimed at both the professional and amateur candy maker. It begins with advice on how to start a retail candy business, has hundreds of quantity recipes, and was popular enough to be in print for thirty years.

As in the earlier 1800s, books by doctors continued to be popular. For example, the many editions of works by the medical doctor Alvin Wood Chase of Ann Arbor, Michigan, sold more than 4 million copies. The publishing of almanacs and pamphlets touting a wide variety of patent medicines also increased astronomically. These concoctions included worthless nostrums—sometimes helpful, sometimes poisonous—that were peddled at fairs and door-to-door by salesmen and quacks. They often had intriguing names, such as Kickapoo Indian Oil, Botanic Cough Balsam, Dr. Drake's Great Tonic Medicine, Perry Davis's Pain Killer, Castoria, Cardui Women's Tonic, and Black-Draught Liver Medicine. Some American carbonated beverages got their start as patent medicines. Many other types of almanacs were published in all parts of the country.

Culinary encyclopedias also continued to be issued in great numbers. Representative are Mrs. E. F. Haskell's *The Housekeeper's Encyclopedia . . . in All Branches of Cookery and Domestic Economy* (1861), Henry Hartshorne's *The Household Cyclopedia of General Information Containing Over Ten Thousand Receipts* (1871), and Artemas Ward's compilation of *The Grocer's Encyclopedia* (1911). This last is an exhaustive and "informative compendium of useful information concerning foods of all kinds. How they are raised, prepared and marketed. How to care for them in the store and home. How best to use and enjoy them." Ward was formerly the editor of *The National Grocer*, and he published this volume for use by grocers and general storekeepers. The first entry is on Abalone and the last on Zwetschenwasser (the German form of slivovitz). The book is illustrated with eighty spectacular color plates of foodstuffs and many black-and-white photographs. Numerous huge compendia with advice by contributing experts were published in great quantities in the last twenty years of the nineteenth century. These books deal with matters relating to health and medicine, nutrition and diet, child rearing, etiquette and morals, dealing with servants, gardening, embroidery and needlework, household management, furnishings and equipment, exercise and sports, and cooking.

Manuscript cookbooks continued to be composed during and after the Civil War. However, the handwritten script increasingly was intermingled with clippings from magazines and newspapers, where articles on cooking were becoming ubiquitous. The increasing availability of published cookbooks and culinary ephemera lessened the need for mothers to write family recipes to hand down to their daughters. This trend has been reversed with the twenty-first-century availability of desktop publishing. Now, the daughters and granddaughters are collecting family culinary history and recipes for their descendants.

Women's Magazines

Newly formed general women's magazines, such as *The Woman's Home Companion* (founded 1873), *Ladies' Home Journal* (1883), and *Good Housekeeping* (1885), all carried articles on cooking and entertaining. They also published many cookbooks and pamphlets. In addition to these more general magazines, a new genre arose: periodicals devoted specifically to cookery and gastronomy. These included *The Table* (1873), *The Caterer and Household* (1882), *Table Talk* (1886), *Hotel Monthly* (1893), *The Cooking Club* (1895), *The Boston Cooking School* (later called *American Cookery*) (1896), and *What To Eat: The National Food Magazine* (1896). Some of these magazines were short-lived; others ran for more than fifty years. Beginning in the 1870s, newspapers in all parts of the country also began conducting recipe contests and issuing cookbooks. The latter included books by the *Los Angeles Times*, *Daily News of Chicago*, *Detroit Free Press* (Michigan), *Albany Journal* (New York), *New York Press*, and *Picayune of New Orleans*. This era's admixture of cookbook publishing and the media, as represented by newspapers and magazines, was soon to be joined by radio and later by tie-ins with movie, music, and television celebrities.

Food Markets

In the pre–Civil War era, many cookbooks had a few pages on marketing and how to select seasonal food. Interest in these subjects intensified after 1860. Two excellent books, both by Thomas De Voe, offered invaluable information on the history of public markets in New York City: *The Market Book* (1862), and on all articles of food sold there, *The Market Assistant* (1867). *The Cook*, a short-lived (1885–1886) but informative weekly magazine, offered columns describing exactly what was currently available in the markets of New York City, Philadelphia, and Boston. It contained insightful stories about the markets and their foods, with prices, and suggested menus and recipes. This magazine presents an excellent picture of the culinary life of middle- to upper-class families in the Northeast in the 1880s.

Gastronomic Literature

Gastronomic literature continued to appear after 1860. Most of the authors were male, both American and English, and their books often were published in both countries. While the number of these books is not large, compared to the volume of cookery books, they are an important part of the archive. They interested many people in preserving the older literature, and many great culinary collections were formed at this time. Representative volumes include George H. Ellwanger's *The Pleasures of the Table* (1902) and Elizabeth Robins Pennell's *My Cookery Books* (1903). The latter is an effusive description and enumeration of the early cookery books collected by Pennell and later bequeathed to the Library of Congress, helping to form its unparalleled culinary collection. Pennell's book is a handsomely printed limited edition of 330 numbered copies with tipped-in plates of facsimiles of title pages and illustrations of the books treated.

Regional and Sectarian Cookbooks

The burst of regional American and sectarian cookbooks continued unabated. The South, which has America's most enduring cookery heritage, added glorious cookbooks to those available before the Civil War. Some of the books can be classified as Reconstruction literature and were written to teach southern homemakers how to keep their traditions alive in the "altered" postwar circumstances of loss of slaves and servants in the home. More importantly, these works reflected southern pride in the regional culinary history; other books were written simply to preserve the old recipes and traditions. This splen-

did body of literature includes: Annabella P. Hill's *Mrs. Hill's Southern Practical Cookery and Receipt Book* (1867), Mrs. M. E. Porter's *Mrs. Porter's New Southern Cookery* (1871), Theresa C. Brown's *Modern Domestic Cookery* (1871), Jane Grant Gilmore Howard's *Fifty Years in a Maryland Kitchen* (1873), M. L. Tyson's *The Queen of the Kitchen, Old Maryland Receipts* (1874), Marion Cabell Tyree's *Housekeeping in Old Virginia* (1879), Mary Stuart Smith's compilation of the *Virginia Cookery-Book* (1885), Mary Jane Carlisle's *Mrs. John G. Carlisle's Kentucky Cook Book* (1893), Mrs. Samuel G. Stoney's *Carolina Rice Cook Book* (1901), Célestine Eustis's *Cooking in Old Creole Days* (1903), Minnie C. Fox's compilation of *The Blue Grass Cook Book* (1904), Martha McCulloch-Williams's *Dishes and Beverages of the Old South* (1913), and Frances Barber Harris's *Florida Salads* (1914–1915), in addition to the Atlanta Exposition and New Orleans books mentioned earlier.

The rest of the country contributed its shelves of regional cookbooks. From the Northeast, these publications include Lucia Gray Swett's *New England Breakfast Breads* (1891) and *Aunt Mary's New England Cook Book* (1881), "by a New England Mother." Works on how to cook and run your household without a servant also appeared. Many of the cooking school and home economics books previously cited reflect a New England and northeastern character.

From the Midwest emerged a number of classic regional charity cookbooks. The popular *Buckeye Cook Book* (1876) went through many editions, printings, and title changes after its first appearance as a charity cookbook by the women of the First Congregational Church of Marysville, Ohio. All printings after the first were privately published for profit. In contrast, *The Settlement Cook Book* (1901), edited by Lizzie Black Kander at first to benefit the Jewish Settlement House in Milwaukee, Wisconsin, continued to raise money for charities for about seventy-five of the more than one hundred years it has been in print. Both of these books reflect the northern, central, and eastern European communities of the Midwest and are still in print. For the extensive German population in the Midwest, the most popular work was Henriette Davidis's *Praktisches Kochbuch für die Deutschen in Amerika* (1879). It was first published in Germany and was printed and reprinted in the United States in both German and English. Other classic works, both published for charities, include *The Kansas Home Cook-Book* (1874) and *The Trans-Mississippi Home Maker* (1898).

The West produced a voluminous literature during this period. Hundreds of charity cookbooks were published reflecting the region's unique geographic and ethnic characteristics. These include *Good Housekeeping in High Altitudes* (1888); *Eureka: A Book of Proven Recipes* (1901), by "Women Living One Mile above Sea Level"; and *The Progressive Cook* (1901), which includes a short and rather potted one-page chapter of purported Chinese recipes. From north to south in California, communities were publishing charity cookbooks with titles such as *California Recipe Book* (1872), *The California Practical Cook Book* (1882), *Cookery in the Golden State* (1890), *How We Cook in Los Angeles* (1894), and *How We Cook in East Santa Cruz* (1900). One of the several charity cookbooks whose proceeds were to benefit victims of the 1906 San Francisco earthquake has the poignant title of *The Refugees' Cook Book*, "compiled by one of them" (Hattie P. Bowman).

It was also in this period that rail transportation, and then refrigerated freight cars, made it possible for fruits, vegetables, and meat to be transported from California and the West to the rest of the United States. Culinary ephemera showing how to use these products were issued in astonishing number and variety by the newly formed trade organizations and cooperatives. Two other renowned regional books emanating from California were Clarence E. Edwards's *Bohemian San Francisco* (1914), elegantly printed by the renowned Paul Elder and Company, and *Grandma Keeler's Housekeeper* (ca. 1903), which was offered to its readers by the *Los Angeles Examiner*. The first book contains vignettes of famous restaurants and their recipes; the second, recipes and ads for California, Mexican, and Italian products including olives, olive oil, wine, and chilies.

Complementing the Creole cookbooks already mentioned are a number of other historic works on that unique American mix. *La Cuisine Creole* (1885) appeared anonymously but is now attributed to Lafcadio Hearn. Its subtitle, *A Collection of Culinary Recipes from Leading Chefs and Noted Creole Housewives, Who Have Made New Orleans Famous for Its Cuisine*, accurately reflects its contents. Mrs. Washington's *The Unrivalled Cook Book* (1886) offers two hundred heirloom Creole recipes from a collection in the hands of a friend's family for more than a century. These recipes include Daddy Jim's Barbecued Rabbit, Madame Eugene's Puree of Snipe à la Creole, Old Humphrey's Orange Ginger Snaps, and Dinah's Spice Cake.

African American authors were represented in greater numbers after the Civil War. These publications include two scarce items authored by African American women. The earliest, Malinda Russell's *A Domestic Cook Book* (1866), was written by a free woman of color. The second, Abby Fisher's *What Mrs. Fisher Knows about Old Southern Cooking* (1881), was by an emancipated slave who left the South after the Civil War to make a new life in California. Two major works were written by African American professional men who followed in the footsteps of Robert Roberts and Tunis Campbell. Rufus Estes, the author of *Good Things to Eat* (1911), was born a slave and persevered to become one of the best-known chefs in Chicago and a renowned Pullman private car attendant. Tom Bullock, the author of *The Ideal Bartender* (1917), also was born a slave and rose to become a legendary bartender in clubs in Louisville, Kentucky; St. Louis, Missouri; Cincinnati, Ohio; and Chicago.

Several of America's sectarian communities contributed their own literature in this period. Elizabeth E. Lea's *Domestic Cookery* (1845) was deservedly popular and was in print for twenty-five years. It presents cookery as practiced by the Quakers of Pennsylvania, blending elements of the Tidewater South, Anglo-American, and Pennsylvania Dutch traditions. Edith May Bertels Thomas's *Mary at the Farm and Book of Recipes* (1915) is an invaluable document of the life, foodways, and recipes of the Pennsylvania Germans. Its authentic recipes include Frau Schmidt's Molasses Snaps, Aunt Sarah's German Crumb Cakes, Honig Kuchen, Rot Pfeffers Filled with Cabbage, and Wunderselda Marmalade.

In the years between 1860 and World War I, the ferment of culinary publishing mirrored the dramatic changes and innovations characterizing all areas of American life, both in breadth and intensity. The eddies and currents of the diverse cultural, societal, and scientific movements made this one of the most exciting and seminal periods in American cookbook history. Cookbook publishing in the twenty-first century is beholden to this formative era.

[*See also* Advertising Cookbooklets and Recipes; Cooking Manuscripts; Cooking Schools; Home Economics; World's Fairs.]

BIBLIOGRAPHY

Beck, Leonard N. *Two Loaf-Givers; or, A Tour through the Gastronomic Libraries of Katherine Golden Bitting and Elizabeth Robins Pennell*. Washington, DC: Library of Congress, 1984.
Bitting, Katherine Golden. *Gastronomic Bibliography*. San Francisco: privately printed, 1939.

Bower, Anne L., ed. *Recipes for Reading: Community Cookbooks, Stories, Histories.* Amherst: University of Massachusetts Press, 1997.

Brown, Eleanor, and Bob Brown. *Culinary Americana: Cookbooks Published in the Cities and Towns of the United States of America during the Years from 1860 through 1960.* New York: Roving Eye Press, 1961.

Cagle, William R., and Lisa Killion Stafford. *American Books on Food and Drink: A Bibliographical Catalog of the Cookbook Collection Housed in the Lilly Library at the University of Indiana.* New Castle, DE: Oak Knoll Press, 1998.

Cook, Margaret. *America's Charitable Cooks: A Bibliography of Fund-Raising Cook Books Published in the United States (1861–1915).* Kent, OH: privately printed, 1971.

DuSablon, Mary Anna. *America's Collectible Cookbooks: The History, the Politics, the Recipes.* Athens: Ohio University Press, 1994.

Hooker, Richard J. *Food and Drink in America: A History.* Indianapolis, IN: Bobbs-Merrill, 1981.

Longone, Jan. *American Cookery: The Bicentennial, 1796–1996.* Ann Arbor, MI: Clements Library, 1996. Exhibition catalog published in conjunction with "An Exhibition of Two Hundred Years of American Cookbooks" shown at the Williams L. Clements Library, University of Michigan.

Longone, Janice Bluestein, and Daniel T. Longone. *American Cookbooks and Wine Books, 1797–1950.* Ann Arbor, MI: Clements Library, Wine and Food Library, 1984. Published in conjunction with an exhibition from the collections of the Williams L. Clements Library, University of Michigan.

Pennell, Elizabeth Robins. *My Cookery Books.* Boston: Houghton Mifflin, 1903.

Schlesinger, Arthur M. *Learning How to Behave: A Historical Study of American Etiquette Books.* New York: Macmillan, 1946.

Theophano, Janet. *Eat My Words: Reading Women's Lives through the Cookbooks They Wrote.* New York: Palgrave, 2002.

Theophano, Janet. *Household Words: Women Write from and for the Kitchen.* Philadelphia: University of Pennsylvania, 1996. Exhibition catalog published in conjunction with an exhibition of the Esther B. Aresty Collection of Rare Books on the Culinary Arts at the Van Pelt-Dietrich Library, University of Pennsylvania.

Janice Bluestein (Jan) Longone

From World War I to World War II

At the start of World War I, few American households owned more than one or two cookbooks and these were not central to most kitchen activity. The Boston area still retained an importance in instructional food writing inherited from the early days of the New England Kitchen and the Boston Cooking School. The best-known American cookbook was *The Boston Cooking-School Cook Book* (1896) by Fannie Farmer, who had died in 1915. Its very fine predecessor and rival, *Mrs. Lincoln's Boston Cook Book* (1884) by Mary J. Lincoln, went out of print after 1919. Revisions of the Farmer book were overseen until 1930 by her sister, Cora Perkins, and thereafter by Perkins's daughter-in-law, Wilma Lord Perkins. A few

other veterans of the nineteenth-century New England scientific cookery movement—notably Janet McKenzie Hill, the longtime editor of *The Boston Cooking School Magazine*, and Alice Bradley, Farmer's successor as the principal of Miss Farmer's Cooking School—continued to publish widely for several decades, but their books seldom aimed for universal manual status or stressed claims of scientific method. Despite the huge prestige of dietetics at this time, too much emphasis on the subject was coming to mark a cookbook as stuffy and dated. By the early 1940s, even Wilma Lord Perkins was trying to make *The Boston Cooking-School Cook Book* match current preferences with dashes of added warmth, personality, and attention to new products or fashions.

New Classics and Niches

By the 1920s, New York City was the main hub of food-writing activity. Enterprising service or shelter magazine publishers and home economics institutes, both there and elsewhere, set about creating encyclopedic, up-to-date, all-purpose manuals to challenge *Boston* as the nation's preeminent kitchen bible. Efforts of this kind include Ida C. Bailey Allen's *Mrs. Allen's Cook Book* (1917) and *Mrs. Allen on Cooking, Menus, Service* (1924), which was reissued in 1932 as *Ida Bailey Allen's Modern Cook Book*; Isabel Ely Lord's *Everybody's Cook Book* (1924), a work developed at the Pratt Institute in Brooklyn; *America's Cook Book* (1937), compiled by the Home Institute of the *New York Herald Tribune*; *The American Woman's Cook Book* (1938), edited by Ruth Berolzheimer and produced at the Culinary Arts Institute in Chicago; *The New American Cook Book* (1941), edited by Lily Haxworth Wallace; an enormous revision of *The Good Housekeeping Cook Book* (1942); and the *Woman's Home Companion Cook Book* (1942). The most serious competitors to Fannie Farmer, however, were productions by midwestern amateurs. From 1936 through the late 1990s, Irma Rombauer's *Joy of Cooking* was issued by one of the few remaining midwestern publishers, Bobbs-Merrill. The many reissues of *The Settlement Cook Book* (1901), compiled by Mrs. Simon Kander, remained based in Milwaukee, Wisconsin, until 1954. With its strong German Jewish emphasis, *Settlement* was probably the most important cookbook for many American Jews during this period.

While the big kitchen manuals duked it out, cookbook publishers began exploiting specialized marketing niches. Works devoted to particular corners of a subject now seen as vast and complex multiplied. An audience developed for food-related books meant as bedtime reading or gift ideas rather than answers to concrete domestic needs. Some authors applied themselves to one specialty subject after another; among the best known were the tireless Ida Bailey Allen and the mother, daughter-in-law, and son team of Cora, Rose, and Bob Brown.

The following list is by no means a complete roster of the numerous subcategories that developed:

Books directed to special needs or circumstances like wartime food rationing, financial straits, dietary limits, two-person households, cramped kitchenettes, or working women's schedules. Some of the best known are *Cooking for Two* by Janet McKenzie Hill (1909; frequently reissued until 1968), *Macy's Cook Book for the Busy Woman* (1932) by Mabel Claire (published under different titles for distribution through several department stores and newspapers), and *How to Cook a Wolf* (1942) by M. F. K. Fisher (inspired by World War II shortages).

Books for cooks/readers and nostalgia buffs, with or without recipes. These sprang from an increasing sense of food as something to be not just cooked and eaten but recalled, contemplated, discussed, and dreamed of. The strong breaks with an earlier America represented by World War I and Prohibition helped create an audience for evocations of the past, including *The Girl from Rector's* (1927) and *The Rector Cook Book* (1928) by George Rector, *Peacock Alley* (1931) by James R. McCarthy, and *The Old-Time Saloon* (1931) by George Ade. A taste developed for other forms of vicarious culinary experience: food mavens' anthologies like *The Bed-Book of Eating and Drinking (1943)* by Richardson L. Wright, culinary reminiscences like the charming *The Country Kitchen* (1936) by Della T. Lutes, and protean food-for-thought musings like M. F. K. Fisher's *Serve It Forth* (1937), *Consider the Oyster* (1941), and *The Gastronomical Me* (1943).

Media tie-ins and celebrity cookbooks. *Feeding the Lions: An Algonquin Cookbook* (1942) by Frank Case of New York City's Algonquin Hotel was an agreeable instance of the latter. Several of the former were sparked by radio shows, including *One Hundred Four Prize Radio Recipes* (1924) by Ida Bailey Allen, *Aunt Sammy's Radio Recipes* (1926; several reissues) by the U.S.D.A. Bureau of Home Economics, and *The Mystery Chef's Own Cook Book* (1934) by John MacPherson, an industrial engineer who moonlighted as radio's "Mystery Chef."

Books on parties and entertaining. The best of this genre was the sophisticated *June Platt's Party Cookbook* (1936) by the popular *House Beautiful* columnist.

Works devoted to a single ingredient or class of ingredients, cooking appliance, menu category, theme, or gimmick. Notable single-subject books included *Ida Bailey Allen's Wine and Spirits Cook Book* (1934), *Herbs for the Kitchen* (1939) by Irma Goodrich Mazza, *Hors d'Oeuvres and Canapés* (1940) by James Beard, and *Casserole Cookery* (1941) by Marian and Nino Tracy.

Works on foreign cuisines and haute cuisine. A sprinkling of these appeared in the 1920s; interest gathered in the next decade, perhaps reflecting a Depression-fed yearning for luxury and cosmopolitan adventure. Books on particular cuisines or geographical areas include *Good Food from Sweden* (1939) by Inga Norberg, the still-insightful *South American Cook Book* (1939) by the Browns, *Cook at Home in Chinese* (1938) by Henry Low, and the extraordinarily illuminating *How to Cook and Eat in Chinese* (1945) by Buwei Yang Chao. Among the globe-trotting anthologies published between the wars, *The Questing Cook* (1927) by Ruth A. Jeremiah Gottfried was the most perceptive and the *World Wide Cook Book* (1939) by Pearl V. Metzelthin the most ambitious. Works evincing a growing American taste for epicurean flourishes and fanfare include the Nero Wolfe mysteries of Rex Stout (beginning in 1934 with *Fer-de-Lance*), *The Art of Good Living* by André Simon (first American edition 1930), *Cooking à la Ritz* (1941) by Louis Diat, *Gourmet Dinners* (1941) by G. Selmer Fougner (the *New York Sun*'s wine columnist), and an English translation of Escoffier's *Guide Culinaire* (1941).

Explorations of America's culinary heritage. The post–World War I vogue for both automobile and armchair tourism, aided by surges of popular interest in colonial and pioneer history as well as American folk culture, found expression in many cookbooks. Because cookbooks were largely irrelevant to the cooking of African Americans, recent immigrants, rural women, many of the elderly, and poor people in general, this flowering generally sheds little light on their experience. There are, however, some valuable documents of regional cooking, including *Southern Cooking* (1928; first trade edition 1941) by Henrietta Dull, *The Savannah Cook Book* (1933) by Harriet Ross Colquitt, *Good Maine Food* (1939) by Marjorie Mosser, *Hawaiian and Pacific Foods* (1940) by Katherine Bazore, *Mrs. Appleyard's Kitchen* (1942) by Louis Andrews Kent, *Cross Creek Cookery* (1942) by Marjorie Kinnan Rawlings, and several *Sunset* magazine recipe collections by Genevieve A. Callahan culminating in *The California Cook Book for Indoor and Outdoor Eating* (1946). The most illuminating coast-to-coast surveys of the time are *The National Cook Book* (1932) by Sheila

Hibben, which appeared in a revised version in 1946 as *American Regional Cookery; Through the Kitchen Door* (1938) by Grace and Beverly Smith and Charles Morrow Wilson; and *New York World's Fair Cook Book: The American Kitchen* (1939) by Crosby Gaige (a remarkable state-by-state compilation of recipes collected by each state's home economists).

[*See also* Boston Cooking School; Beard, James; Farmer, Fannie; Fisher, M. F. K.; Prohibition; Rombauer, Irma.]

BIBLIOGRAPHY

Clark, Robert. *The Solace of Food: A Life of James Beard.* South Royalton, VT: Steerforth Press, 1996.
Hooker, Richard J. *Food and Drink in America: A History.* Indianapolis, IN: Bobbs-Merrill, 1981.
Lovegren, Sylvia. *Fashionable Food: Seven Decades of Food Fads.* New York: Macmillan, 1995.
Levenstein, Harvey A. *Paradox of Plenty: A Social History of Eating in Modern America.* New York: Oxford University Press, 1993.
Levenstein, Harvey A. *Revolution at the Table: The Transformation of the American Diet.* New York: Oxford University Press, 1988.
Mendelson, Anne. *Stand Facing the Stove: The Story of the Women Who Gave America the Joy of Cooking.* New York: Scribner, 2003.

ANNE MENDELSON

World War II to the 1960s

Between 1945 and 1969 the United States underwent economic, technological, and social changes that had a profound impact on how Americans ate and cooked. While the finest-quality meat and produce were readily available, manufacturers continually introduced new processed convenience foods. At the same time, Americans discovered U.S. regional cooking and the cuisines of other countries and wanted to enjoy those same foods at home. As women increasingly entered the workforce, families had more disposable income but less time to cook the foods they desired. Social issues and environmental concerns also played a role in the evolution of American cooking during this period.

Through it all, writers of culinary literature found an enthusiastic audience and publishers issued a steady stream of cookbooks that responded to Americans' growing interest in food and cooking. Some publications served as guides to basic cooking, while others launched the cook on an exciting adventure to foreign lands and flavors. Among the thousands of cookbooks that rolled off the presses over the twenty-five-year period following World War II, several stand out based on the quality of the writing, the clarity and ease with which recipes and techniques are presented, and the inclusion of social and cultural information that clearly explains foodways in time and place. The result is a representative body of classical culinary literature that exemplifies the diversity of the period.

1945 to 1949: A Culinary Awakening

With the end of World War II in 1945, Americans—having suffered the rigors of rationing—hastily abandoned the thriftiness of the wartime economy. Beef, pork, and dairy products were consumed in abundance. But urban women, who had supported the war effort by working in factories, were not about to give up their newly discovered freedom from the kitchen. Victory gardens, canning, and preserving were forsaken in favor of convenient canned and frozen fruits and vegetables.

Among a host of general cookery manuals used throughout the period from 1945 to 1970, Irma Rombauer's *The Joy of Cooking* (1931) was one of the most popular. Rombauer, a well-known hostess from St. Louis, Missouri, delivered her eminently practical recipes in a personable, chatty style that resulted in a classic manual destined to sell more than 15 million copies.

The robust economy of the postwar years meant Americans could indulge in luxuries like automobiles and vacations. Travel to other parts of the country resulted in an awakening interest in America's diverse regional cookery, based in large part on food products indigenous to a particular area or on heritage foods popularized by distinct ethnic groups; publishers and food writers responded in kind. America's fascination with California, home to a burgeoning population made up, in large part, of former servicemen and their families, was rewarded with Genevieve Callahan's *The California Cook Book for Indoor and Outdoor Eating* (1946). California's bountiful produce was showcased, and Americans were reminded of the tantalizing dishes that could be prepared on outdoor grills, a concept that had been touted by James Beard in *Cook It Outdoors* (1941) on the eve of America's entry into World War II.

African Americans had long influenced the cookery of America, first as slaves in the kitchens of the South and later as caterers or employees in hotel kitchens and on railroad dining cars. Following the end of the Civil War, African Americans made new lives for themselves throughout the country and contributed to regional cuisines beyond the South. Little credit was given to the

African American influence on American cookery until the publication of Freda De Knight's classic *A Date with a Dish: A Cook Book of American Negro Recipes* (1948). De Knight dispensed with the stereotypical mammy in the southern kitchen and clearly illustrated the culinary diversity and accomplishments of African American cooks.

Americans also were becoming more worldly and sophisticated, increasingly looking beyond their own culinary borders. World War II provided a positive catalyst in furthering Americans' interest in foreign cuisines. While serving in distant lands, U.S. troops developed a taste for local foods and sought to reproduce these favorite dishes upon returning home. Dione Lucas, the founder of the New York City branch of Le Cordon Bleu cooking school, was teaching Americans to cook classic French recipes; in 1947 her compilation *The Cordon Bleu Cook Book* was published. Those looking for guidance in Chinese cooking turned to Buwei Yang Chao's *How to Cook and Eat in Chinese* (1945), one of the earliest Chinese American cookbooks. It was recognized for its clarity and authenticity, and Americans learned the technique of stir-frying.

The brightest flower in America's postwar culinary bouquet was M. F. K. Fisher, whose passion, wit, and sensuality toward food made her the nation's first lady of food writing. It was through her work that Americans began to appreciate food as more than simple sustenance. *Here Let Us Feast: A Book of Banquets* (1946) presents a deliciously whimsical argument for celebrating life's great moments with fine food and drink. *An Alphabet for Gourmets* (1949) lays out Fisher's version of a dictionary, which traces and celebrates food's connections with all aspects of life.

Dichotomy of the 1950s

The 1950s reflected a culinary dichotomy. An increasingly affluent middle class meant travel to foreign countries, elegant dining out, and an increased interest in gourmet cooking. On the other hand, working mothers and suburban housewives wanting to escape the drudgery of the kitchen eagerly embraced the advantages of time-saving appliances and foods like TV dinners, which were introduced by Swanson in 1954. Consumers also welcomed canned soups and the growing array of prepackaged products stocked by supermarkets. Cookbook writers and manufacturers' advertising catered to both camps and cooks were free to choose their own path.

Americans in search of culinary guidelines and recipes for international cooking frequently turned to *Bouquet de*

France: An Epicurean Tour of the French Provinces (1952) and *Italian Bouquet: An Epicurean Tour of Italy* (1958), both by Samuel Chamberlain. These volumes, accompanied by maps and photos, led American readers through France and Italy, province by province, providing an appreciation for the culture, history, food, and wine of each country. The accompanying recipes for regional dishes provided a glimpse into European foodways previously unknown to most Americans and contributed to the movement toward a more cosmopolitan American diet.

The 1950s also saw the publication of important new cookbooks dedicated to the exploration of regional American cooking. *The Southern Cook Book* (1951) was the result of Marion Brown's efforts to compile a representative selection of southern recipes culled from charitable cookbooks, old manuscripts, private individuals, and professional cooks. Her commentary throughout the book provided an understanding of the many cultures that affected the evolution of southern cooking, including reference to that of African Americans; Brown's book was recognized as a landmark study of a single American regional cuisine.

African Americans continued to make headway in their efforts to record black heritage and food culture. In 1958 the National Council of Negro Women, under the direction of the editor Sue Bailey Thurman, compiled *The Historical Cookbook of the American Negro*. Recognizing the powerful role that food plays in life, Thurman designed a format based on a calendar of major African American historical events followed by recipes for celebratory dishes. The cookbook, comprised of recipes from throughout the United States, represented a major advancement in the documentation of African American foodways.

Gourmet Era of the 1960s

Throughout the 1960s America was buffeted by the winds of change from both a social and a culinary perspective. The economy was booming, Americans were in a hurry, and the world was becoming smaller. Affordable commercial jet travel meant people were on the move. By the beginning of the decade, almost two-thirds of American women were working outside the home, resulting in increased disposable family income. Despite the rosy surface, serious issues were brewing relative to civil rights and there was a growing concern about the environment.

Two-income households necessarily limited time spent by parents in the kitchen. Frazzled wives hurried home from jobs and guiltily prepared dinners based on convenience products. Women who found themselves trapped in an endless whirlwind of domestic chaos thus greeted the publication of Peg Bracken's *The I Hate to Cook Book* (1960) with relief. Based on the message that women did not need to be subservient to husband and family or feel guilty about not spending endless hours in the kitchen, Bracken's work was an overnight success and represented a turning point in both cookbooks and the traditional familial role of women.

On the other hand, a prosperous economy and greater disposable income prompted homemakers to enroll in cooking schools, invest in fancy cooking utensils, and buy cookbooks from the vast array that were being published during the 1960s, launching what would become known as the gourmet era. The publication of *Mastering the Art of French Cooking* (1961) by Simone Beck, Louisette Bertholle, and Julia Child turned out to be a culinary landmark. The American-born Child single-handedly revolutionized American home cooking with her precise instructions that taught Americans how to prepare French cuisine. The overriding message was that if Child could cook those dishes, so could others. On weekends American women headed to their kitchens and duplicated recipes for *boeuf bourguignon* and coq au vin, basking in praise for their efforts and enjoying themselves in the process. Child's television debut in 1963 clearly reinforced the fact that cooking could be fun. By the time her second book, *The French Chef Cookbook*, was released in 1968, Americans had been converted to the delights of French cooking.

In 1968 Time-Life Books launched its seminal twenty-seven-volume *Foods of the World* series. Authored by the top food writers of the time, each volume is an in-depth, well-researched exploration of the culture and history of a particular cuisine accompanied by authentic recipes. Americans, hungry for knowledge as well as for food, toured the United States and the world from the comfort of home and duplicated international dishes from the sanctity of their kitchens. Notable volumes published in 1968 include *American Cooking* by Dale Brown, *The Cooking of Provincial France* by M. F. K. Fisher, *The Cooking of Italy* by Waverley Root, and *The Cooking of Vienna's Empire* by Joseph Wechsberg.

Amid the racial strife of the 1960s, African Americans demonstrated renewed pride and interest in the documentation of their recipes and foodways. In 1962 the *Ebony* magazine columnist Freda De Knight's cookbook was republished as *The Ebony Cookbook: A Date with a Dish; A Cookbook of American Negro Recipes*. During the

For Noncooks. *Appendix to the I Hate to Cook Book* (New York, 1966). *Culinary Archives & Museum at Johnson & Wales University, Providence, R.I.*

late 1960s, the term "soul food" appeared to describe traditional African American food, and there was great interest in the study of African culture and cooking. Amid a flurry of new African American cookbooks, the first commercial use of "soul food" in a title appeared in *Soul Food Cookery* (1968) by Inez Yeargan Kaiser. A revised edition, also published in 1968, carried the title *The Original Soul Food Cookery*, perhaps to distinguish Kaiser's work from other similarly named volumes.

The American social conscience relative to the pollution of the environment was ignited by the publication of *Silent Spring* (1962) by Rachel Carson, a marine biologist who documented the deaths of songbirds resulting from spraying the pesticide DDT. This sparked the health food movement, much of which was initiated in hippie communes, which advocated back-to-nature living and cooking. The first food-related book in this vein was

Euell Gibbons's *Stalking the Wild Asparagus* (1962). The idea of foraging for food caught on, and it was incorporated into the natural food and vegetarian movements. Young people raised on Wonder bread and canned vegetables were baking their own bread and learning to garden, and by 1969 they had their first cookbook. The *Alice's Restaurant Cookbook*, written by Alice May Brock, advocates improvisation and creativity by cooking with fresh, natural foods on a daily basis.

By 1969 Americans had traveled through a decade that began with the romance and glamour of Julia Child and French cooking and ended with the comparative austerity of the natural food movement. Even a quick glance back to 1945 provides ample proof that an enormous array of new foods and cooking techniques, as well as a new culinary sophistication, had been embraced by the end of the 1960s. America's endless curiosity, a rapacious appetite, and the arrival of new immigrant groups from Asia promised that even more diversity and change would come in the following decades.

[*See also* African American Food; Beard, James; Child, Julia; Fisher, M. F. K.; French Influences on American Food; Gibbons, Euell; Health Food; Rombauer, Irma.]

BIBLIOGRAPHY

Anderson, Jean. *The American Century Cookbook*. New York: C. Potter, 1997.

Leite, David. "Dining through the Decades: 100 Years of Glorious American Food." *Chicago Sun-Times*, December 29, 1999. http://www.leitesculinaria.com/features/dining.html.

Lovegren, Sylvia. *Fashionable Food: Seven Decades of Food Fads*. New York: Macmillan, 1995.

Neuhaus, Jessamyn. "The Way to a Man's Heart: Gender Roles, Domestic Ideology, and Cookbooks in the 1950s." *Journal of Social History* 32, no. 3 (spring 1999).

BECKY MERCURI

From the 1970s to the Present

The last third of the twentieth century brought a proliferation of cookbooks so dramatic that few could keep count and even fewer wanted to try. National publishers churned them out by the hundreds. The momentum grew through the decades to the year 2000, when about one thousand cookbooks were published. In 1998, 37.5 million cookbooks were sold.

It seemed that authors could not possibly think up a new food topic to tackle—and yet they continued to do so. Whether buyers were really cooking from all of these tomes was open for debate. Some shoppers confessed to buying cookbooks merely for bedtime reading, as a way to escape to culinary destinations without lifting a spatula.

Americans' fascination with food continues and, indeed, seems to be growing. Cookbooks feed this fascination. They are at once mirrors into cultures as well as practical guides to getting a meal on the table. They can be memoir or blueprint, history lesson or primer. Cookbooks have changed as American lifestyles have changed.

As the 1970s began and America shrugged off the swinging sixties, one holdover from that previous decade continued to capture the imaginations of cooks around the country. Television's Julia Child brought French cooking to the masses of American cooks who were ready to graduate from the restrictions of Clarence Birdseye's frozen convenience foods, Kraft's macaroni and cheese from a box, and the basic cookery texts, such as Irma Rombauer's *The Joy of Cooking* (1931). After the success of Child's *Mastering the Art of French Cooking* (1961), which she wrote with Simone Beck and Louisette Bertholle, Child continued her mission of educating American cooks by writing a series of books in the following years. These included *The Way to Cook* (1989) and *Cooking with Master Chefs* (1993), the latter based on another of her popular television series in which she invited well-known chefs into her kitchen in Cambridge, Massachusetts, to cook up their specialties. Viewers and readers alike soaked it up and started cooking.

Cooking from Child's books was not easy. One suspects that as many would-be gastronomes were put off by the lengthy, detailed recipes as were converted to the cause. Recipes often ran for pages. But there is no denying it: cooks learned from Child's meticulous recipes.

French Cuisine Reigns

Americans embraced all things French throughout the 1970s. Gourmet dinner parties morphed into gourmet cooking clubs. A certain amount of one-upmanship crept into the dinner parties of the time. Who could recreate Child's pot-au-feu with finesse? Or do her daube without mishap? Talking and thinking about food no longer seemed a puritanical taboo. Cooking classes picked up new converts.

While Child may have introduced many Americans to French cuisine, it was Craig Claiborne who further spread the Gallic gospel through his books and weekly columns. Claiborne, the influential food editor and critic for the *New York Times*, wrote *Classic French Cooking* (1970) with the chef Pierre Franey for Time-Life Books, following the success of the *New York Times Cook Book*

(1961), which Claiborne edited. Trained at the École hôtelière de Lausanne in Switzerland, Claiborne knew the ins and outs of classical French preparations. But he approached the subject with straightforward writing, which simplified the process for his readers. His recipes were concise, yet comprehensive enough for American cooks to duplicate the traditional dishes of France, from hearty pâtés to airy quenelles. Claiborne, with his writing and cooking partner, Franey, continued influencing American cooks for the next three decades.

Richard Olney brought another view of French food to the American table. An expatriate living in Provence, Olney began writing about the earthy, country dishes of the south of France. In *The French Menu Cookbook: The Food and Wine of France—Season by Delicious Season—in Beautifully Composed Menus for American Dining and Entertaining by an American Living in Paris and Provence* (1970) and *Simple French Food* (1974), he described a more casual approach to French cooking, which appealed to Americans. His books attracted new converts to traditional Provençal pots, full of olives, herbs, eggplants, lamb, and seafood from the Mediterranean. Olney's cooking inspired many, including Alice Waters who opened the restaurant Chez Panisse in Berkeley, California. Waters offered a menu of the simple country dishes championed by Olney and then went on to influence American tables in her own way.

Along with learning what went into those French cooking pots, Americans also discovered the best ways to chop, mince, julienne, and whip those ingredients into shape, thanks to Jacques Pépin, a transplanted French chef with the charm to lead armies of cooks. His groundbreaking *La Technique: The Fundamental Techniques of Cooking; An Illustrated Guide* (1976) focuses on the how-tos of cooking, complete with step-by-step photographs and directions. With *La Technique* and *La Methode: An Illustrated Guide to the Fundamental Techniques of Cooking* (1979), Pépin helped take the fear out of cooking for his readers. As an educator who traveled the U.S. cooking school circuit, Pépin earned a loyal following who scooped up his books by the thousands. *The Making of a Cook* (1971) added the singular views of Madeleine Kamman, another transplanted French citizen and cooking teacher, to the cookbook world. Her book appealed to many Americans with its passion, strong point of view, and clearly written recipes. Kamman continued her mission with *When French Women Cook: A Gastronomic Memoir* (1976) and *In Madeleine's Kitchen* (1984).

The French way of cooking introduced Americans to the possibilities in the kitchen—that cooking was fun and satisfying. Despite the "fancy food" impression many had of French food, cooking a French meal often was more economical than buying the frozen TV dinners of the day. Cooks were thinking about economizing, as a number of events in the 1970s drove them to look more closely at what foods cost. Poor harvests in Russia and India raised the demand and thus the price for wheat and soybeans. Beef production fell. Then in 1973 oil prices rose and, as a result, food costs spiraled higher.

Books on supermarket shopping, bargain foods, and the virtues of hamburger (365 ways!) filled bookstore shelves. The editors of *Family Circle* magazine introduced *Great Meals on a Tight Budget: More than 250 Recipes and Dozens of Tips to Save You Money* (1984). William J. Hincher wrote the ever-practical *The Day before Payday Cookbook* (1985). In the previous decade, Perla Meyers had finished *The Seasonal Kitchen: A Return to Fresh Foods* (1973), a book preaching the economies and the fresh flavors inherent in cooking with foods during their peak harvest times. With an emphasis on Mediterranean dishes with hearty flavors, it became one of the most popular books of 1973 and beyond and a forerunner of future cookbooks emphasizing farmers' markets, sustainable farming, and natural foods.

Food for Health

Budgeting for meals was not the only concern for cooks of the 1970s and early 1980s. As nutritional research made advances, scientists, the government, and consumer watchdog groups began issuing recommendations about what to feed the family. An onslaught of books on diet regimens, food additives, and healthful eating lined bookstore shelves, a process that continues. *Diet for a Small Planet* (1971) examined the American system of food production and found it lacking. The author, Frances Moore Lappé, warned against America's wasteful process of raising meat for food while many in the rest of the world starved. Vegetarian cookbooks appeared, including the popular series by Mollie Katzen based on the recipes at the Moosewood Restaurant in Ithaca, New York. Health food stores stocked brown rice, tofu, and sprouts.

As knowledge of nutritional and food science expanded, authors turned new discoveries into printed versions of nutritional elixirs. Calories and fat sneaked onto the country's radar as enemies to be destroyed. Americans jumped onto this health bandwagon, beginning the long-

Vegetarian Cookbook. Cover of the *Moosewood Cookbook* by Mollie Katzen (1977).

running dichotomy of enjoying their newfound pleasures of the table—à la Child—while worrying about the correctness of what they were eating. The *Weight Watchers Cookbook* (1978) edited by Pamela Dixon, *The Beverly Hills Diet* (1981) by Judy Mazel with Susan Shultz, and *The Pritikin Program for Diet and Exercise* (1980) quickly capitalized on the public concern over weight loss. *The Supermarket Handbook: Access to Whole Foods* (1973), by Nikki and David Goldbeck, was a more balanced attempt to lead readers to a healthier, smarter lifestyle.

Regional Pride

Meanwhile, a growing pride in America's food heritage captured the imagination of several writers. Foremost among them was James Beard, the New York City author and cooking teacher, who often was called the father of American cooking. Beard had written cookbooks in the 1950s and 1960s, but his most impressive work, *James Beard's American Cookery*, was published in 1972. Part history lesson, part cookbook, it brought his fresh down-to-earth approach to regional and national foods such as potpies, cheeseburgers, and potatoes O'Brien. The popular author continued a run of best sellers with *Beard on Bread* (1973) and, in collaboration with José

Wilson, *James Beard's Theory and Practice of Good Cooking* (1977).

Time-Life Books turned to America and her regions, from New England to the Northwest, in a series that evocatively wove together culture and cuisine with the help of writers familiar with each area. *The Time-Life American Regional Cookbook*, a one-volume distillation of the series, appeared in 1978. Evan Jones set out to write a more historical account of American cooking in his landmark *American Food: The Gastronomic Story* (1975). With help from his wife, Judith, an editor at Knopf Publishing who worked on the recipes for the book, Jones captured the transformation of American regional cookery to a more national uniformity.

American cooking was coming of age. By the 1980s Judith Jones felt it was time to focus on America's uniqueness. She introduced the *Knopf Cooks American* series, which included the best of regional cooking from around the country. Judith and Evan Jones wrote the *L. L. Bean Book of New New England Cookery* (1987). Then Judith edited Bill Neal's *Biscuits, Spoonbread, and Sweet Potato Pie* (1990), Janie Hibler's *Dungeness Crabs and Blackberry Cobblers: The Northwest Heritage Cookbook* (1991), and *Savoring the Seasons of the Northern Heartland* (1994) by Beth Dooley and Lucia Watson.

Jane and Michael Stern shared their reporters' views of what Americans were eating from coast to coast in the appealing *Square Meals: A Cookbook* (1984), followed by *Real American Food: From Yankee Red Flannel Hash and the Ultimate Navajo Taco to Beautiful Swimmer Crab Cakes and General Store Fudge Pie; Jane and Michael Stern's Coast-to-Coast Cookbook* (1986). More regional flag waving appears in Anne Lindsay Greer's *Cuisine of the American Southwest* (1983), Marcia Adams's *Cooking from Quilt Country: Hearty Recipes from Amish and Mennonite Kitchens* (1989), Sarah Leah Chase and Jonathan Chase's *Saltwater Seasonings: Good Food from Coastal Maine* (1992), John Sarich's *Food and Wine of the Pacific Northwest* (1993), and *Jasper White's Cooking from New England: More than 300 Traditional Contemporary Recipes* (1998).

One regional cuisine captured the imagination of American cooks and restaurant chefs in the 1980s and 1990s like no other. The love affair began with the publication of *Chef Paul Prudhomme's Louisiana Kitchen* (1984). Prudhomme, who was the chef at the legendary Commander's Palace before opening his own K-Paul's Louisiana Kitchen in New Orleans, did more for spreading the Cajun gospel than any other culinary preacher before or since. From Cajun martinis to scorchingly hot, blackened redfish, his versions of Louisiana victuals found their way to countless restaurants and home kitchens around the country.

The South has brought forth more cookbooks' births than most other regions. The Web-based amazon.com bookstore offers more than one thousand listings for southern cooking books. Worthy examples include *Craig Claiborne's Southern Cooking* (1987), John Egerton's *Southern Food: At Home, on the Road, in History* (1987), *Bill Neal's Southern Cooking* (1985), John Martin Taylor's *Hoppin' John's Lowcountry Cooking: Recipes and Ruminations from Charleston and the Carolina Coastal Plain* (1992), and *Nathalie Dupree's Southern Memories: Recipes and Reminiscences* (1993).

The doyenne of southern cooking and the African American influence on it was Edna Lewis. She was a chef who wrote *The Taste of Country Cooking* (1976), a mouthwatering book that sets forth the traditions of raising and cooking food on her family's farm in Freetown, Virginia, a town founded by former slaves after the Civil War. A respect for country traditions and foods fresh from the land permeates the book. Lewis followed her first book with *In Pursuit of Flavor* (1988) with Mary Goodbody, in which she shares ways for getting the best from any food.

Soul food became synonymous with good country cooking in the 1970s, when more urban restaurants appeared advertising the ribs, grits, and fresh peach cobbler of the South. African Americans began setting their recipes down on paper, often combining practical tips with memories of home and relatives. These books include Vertamae Smart-Grosvenor's *Vibration Cooking; or, The Travel Notes of a Geechee Girl* (1970), Pearl Bailey's *Pearl's Kitchen: An Extraordinary Cookbook* (1973), Norma Jean and Carole Darden's *Spoonbread and Strawberry Wine: Recipes and Reminiscences of a Family* (1978), Sylvia Woods and Christopher Styler's *Sylvia's Soul Food: Recipes from Harlem's World Famous Restaurant* (1992), and Jessica Harris's *The Welcome Table: African-American Heritage Cooking* (1995).

Perennial Classics

While new regional cookbooks were popping up as fast as corn kernels in hot oil, general cookbooks also continued selling well. In the 1970s new editions of *The Better Homes and Gardens Cookbook, The Joy of Cooking,* and *The Fannie Farmer Cookbook* appeared. Considered the best of the basic cookbooks, they became stalwarts in the kitchens of a whole new generation of newlyweds and young cooks. Two food-company cookbooks also resonated with new cooks, who may have seen earlier editions of them in their mothers' kitchens: *Betty Crocker's Cookbook* (1969) and *The Pillsbury Cookbook* (1989). The huge *The Doubleday Cookbook: Complete Contemporary Cooking* by Jean Anderson and Elaine Hanna began its bid for classic status in 1975, rivaling *The Joy of Cooking* for its excellent scope of American and international recipes.

Women's magazine publishers also churned out collections of recipes. *Ladies' Home Journal, Good Housekeeping, McCall's, Woman's Day, Family Circle,* and others turned out books. Regional lifestyle magazines followed suit, including *Sunset* magazine, long a supplier of excellent recipes in the casual California style, and the Alabama-based *Southern Living.* Later, as more food magazines came on the scene, the logic of reformatting recipes in annual books became clear to their editors and publishers. *Gourmet, Bon Appétit, Food and Wine, Saveur,* and *Cook's Illustrated* produced countless books of well-tested recipes that their loyal readers added to their collections of the magazines themselves.

Beyond America

Although French cuisine remained a popular topic for books, Americans' tastes were expanding in the 1970s and 1980s with every visit overseas or every meal at the new ethnic restaurants in their neighborhoods. They turned to cookbooks to duplicate the exciting flavors from China, Italy, Spain, Morocco, Greece, Russia, Hungary, Mexico, Thailand, and Vietnam. The groundbreaking series *Foods of the World* from Time-Life Books answered the need for international recipes in the late 1960s and early 1970s. The series, written and edited by such experts as Claiborne, M. F. K. Fisher, Franey, Michael Field, Peter S. Feibleman, and Joseph Wechsberg impressively captured the cultures of many countries. Beautifully illustrated with photographs, the books quickly became collectibles.

The classically trained Claiborne was one of the first to move beyond the Gallic influence and embrace other cultures and their foods. While numerous Chinese cookbooks had been available to the public for years, his *The Chinese Cookbook* (1972), written with the cooking teacher Virginia Lee, became a popular and accessible source of information on techniques and ingredients.

Claiborne also "discovered" the author Diana Kennedy, after he wrote about her extensive knowledge of Mexican food in the *New York Times*. Kennedy had been living part-time in Mexico for years. When her *The Cuisines of Mexico* debuted in 1972, it was considered to be the ultimate reference to the country's ingredients and classic dishes. While most U.S. cooks were familiar with the Tex-Mex cooking of the American Southwest, few knew about Mexico's wide range of regional dishes. Kennedy's book led them by the hand to sample moles, chilies, and seviches. Later, the book was combined with two of Kennedy's other efforts, *The Tortilla Book* (1975) and *Mexican Regional Cooking* (1984), to form the comprehensive *The Essential Cuisines of Mexico* (2000).

Elisabeth Lambert Ortiz wrote a definitive guide to South American dishes in *The Book of Latin American Cooking* (1979). Other experts followed Kennedy and Ortiz in defining Latin American cooking in the 1980s and 1990s, including the Chicago chef Rick Bayless. He and his wife, Deann Groen Bayless, wrote *Authentic Mexican: Regional Cooking from the Heart of Mexico* (1987) and, with JeanMarie Brownson, *Rick Bayless's Mexican Kitchen: Capturing the Vibrant Flavors of a World-Class Cuisine* (1996).

Couscous and Other Good Food from Morocco (1973) was Paula Wolfert's first book, and it opened America's eyes to the exotic dips, stews, and desserts of that North African country. Wolfert later became an authority on Mediterranean cooking. In *The Cooking of South-West France: A Collection of Traditional and New Recipes from France's Magnificent Rustic Cuisine, and New Techniques to Lighten Hearty Dishes* (1983) and *The Cooking of the Eastern Mediterranean: 215 Healthy, Vibrant, and Inspired Recipes* (1994), Wolfert successfully tracked down dishes from regional cooks and translated them in detail for Americans, while still keeping their authenticity. Readers learned about delicious pomegranate syrup and Aleppo peppers, bitter wild greens, and preserved lemons.

Italian Wave

In much the same fashion, the cooking teacher Marcella Hazan introduced Americans to the simple joys of Italian food when she wrote *The Classic Italian Cook Book: The Art of Italian Cooking and the Italian Art of Eating* (1973), followed by *More Classic Italian Cooking* (1978). With recipes that clearly led even amateur cooks to successful results, the books soon earned their titles, becoming classics. Hazan introduced readers to then little-known ingredients such as balsamic vinegar, sun-dried tomatoes, and extra-virgin olive oil. It was the beginning of an Italian love affair that American cooks have embraced ever since.

Giuliano Bugialli boosted Italian cuisine further with a series of excellent, historically authentic cookbooks, beginning with *Giuliano Bugialli's Classic Techniques of Italian Cooking* (1982). Like Hazan, Bugialli spent parts of each year teaching cooking in New York City and in Italy. His main aim was to teach readers the true Italian cuisine, not the Italian American concoctions found in so many U.S. restaurants. He continued his mission with the glossy *Giuliano Bugialli's Foods of Italy* (1984) and *Bugialli on Pasta* (1988).

Carol Field and Lynne Rossetto Kasper followed Hazan's and Bugialli's paths, writing excellent books that captured the Italian style with its emphasis on cooking with the seasons, simplicity, and, above all, respect for the freshest of ingredients. Field's *The Italian Baker* (1985) and *Italy in Small Bites* (1993) took a journalist's approach to discovering true Italian methods and dishes. Kasper's *The Splendid Table: Recipes from Emilia-Romagna, the Heartland of Northern Italian Food* (1992) captured the region's cooking style in a well-researched book that won the best cookbook award from the James Beard Foundation for that year.

Gadget Age

As the economy grew in the late 1980s, people had more disposable income. In addition to buying cookbooks, they enhanced their kitchens with an increasing number of appliances and gadgets: microwave ovens, slow cookers, food processors, blenders, toaster ovens, and woks. As their countertops became more crowded, their bookshelves did, too. New cookbooks soon appeared to help readers learn how to use these tools to make cooking quicker and easier.

An emphasis on grilling grew as Americans bought ever-larger grills and took to their backyards and balconies to cook. Beard was one of the first to publish a grilling book, but in the 1980s and 1990s a new group of grill-meisters appeared on the scene. Chris Schlesinger and John Willoughby wrote *The Thrill of the Grill: Techniques, Recipes, and Down-Home Barbecue* (1990). Steven Raichlen's *The Barbecue! Bible* (1998) spawned his series of barbecue titles. Cheryl Alters Jamison and Bill Jamison's *Smoke and Spice* (1994) and *Born to Grill: An American Celebration* (1998) continued the education of backyard chefs. Basic grilling manuals soon were followed by books on more specialized topics, such as outdoor smoking and cooking pizza, fish, and vegetables on the grill. Men, especially, took up grilling as their private cooking domain, a trend soon reflected in television commercials and movies.

As the end of the 1980s neared, the revolutionary bread machine swept the cookware shops. Authors took up the cause and baking was given new life with this amazing gadget that could proof, knead, and bake almost like grandma used to do.

Armed with new gadgets, American cooks could entertain with a measure of ease. One of the most popular books of the decade was *The Silver Palate Cookbook* (1982), written by Julee Rosso and Sheila Lukins with Michael McLaughlin. Rosso and Lukins, the owners of a Manhattan take-out food shop, had a great flair for creating simple yet appealing dishes for entertaining. Their recipes for chicken marabella and chili for a crowd became some of the most requested party dishes of that time; more than 2.5 million copies of their first book are in print. The duo went on to write *The Silver Palate Good Times Cookbook* (1985), with Sarah Leah Chase, and *The New Basics Cookbook* (1989). *Entertaining* (1982) by Martha Stewart continued what Rosso and Lukins began, with a do-it-yourself mantra that appealed to so many cooks.

Meanwhile, a new way of cooking arrived, courtesy of the French. It was called nouvelle cuisine. A group of young chefs had been experimenting with a restaurant cuisine that spurned the heavy-handed sauces and preparation techniques of classical French cuisine à la Auguste Escoffier. They lightened their presentations (and often their portions) and announced their new cuisine to the world. *Michel Guérard's Cuisine Minceur* (1976) was the most influential cookbook to come from the movement. Soon American chefs were mimicking the style, but it also freed them to start thinking about their own ways of creating dishes. While critics blasted the tiny portions, baby vegetables, precious preparations, and high prices, nouvelle cuisine influenced cooking in America for a decade or more.

Twinkling Chefs

The boom times of the last quarter of the twentieth century also allowed consumers to leave their kitchens. Eating out became big business. Forsaking their new gadgets, cooks took to trendy restaurants like kittens to catnip. Moving from one glitzy spot to the next, the foodies created a new diversion: eating out as entertainment. With their enthusiasm, they cooked up a new star: the chef.

From New York City to Los Angeles, city diners embraced the new temples of gastronomy. As competition grew between restaurants, their owners and chefs turned to marketing themselves as never before. Every chef of note needed to write a cookbook, as much to keep his or her name in the forefront of the food press as to please loyal customers who wanted to duplicate the recipes at home. Never mind that restaurant cooking is a far cry from home cooking.

The era of the television chef, which began with Child in the 1960s, really blossomed when chefs began to be perceived as celebrities. The recipes demonstrated on air found their way into matching cookbooks. While early television cooks like Jeff Smith, "the Frugal Gourmet," and Graham Kerr had their shows and books, the momentum gained speed as more and more chefs and cooks appeared on the small screen: Pépin, Wolfgang Puck, Bayless, Charlie Trotter, Stewart, Mario Batali, Emeril Lagasse, Bobby Flay, and more.

With gorgeous color photography and pages-long recipes, many of the chef or restaurant cookbooks rested more comfortably on the coffee table than on the kitchen counter. In many cases, fellow chefs found more to use within their pages than did amateur cooks. Nevertheless, the public devoured books by nationally known chefs. Two of the first impressive efforts were *The Wolfgang Puck Cookbook: Recipes from Spago, Chinois, and Points East and West* (1986) and *Jean-Louis, Cooking with the Seasons* (1989) by Fred J. Maroon with recipes by Jean-Louis Palladin. Others who picked up the pen included Charlie Palmer and Daniel Boulud in New York City; Trotter and Bayless in the Midwest; Joyce Goldstein, Thomas Keller, and Waters on the West Coast; and Stephan Pyles, Dean Fearing, Mark Miller, and Norman Van Aken in the South and Southwest. The trend continues.

As publishers realized that the public seemed to be reading and looking at cookbooks as much as cooking from them, they spent more and more money on design and photography. Large formats, gorgeous color photography, and enticing stories became common. Prices rose. Cookbooks as gifts, as something to display on the coffee table, became a growing business. One of the most successful of the oversized genre was a series of "beautiful" books from HarperCollins. The books focus on traditional dishes of different countries and states, including the Scotto sisters and Gilles Pudlowski's *France, the*

Beautiful Cookbook: Authentic Recipes from the Regions of France (1989), Lorenza de' Medici and Patrizia Passigli's *Italy, the Beautiful Cookbook: Authentic Recipes from the Regions of Italy* (1989), Susanna Palazuelos and Marilyn Tausend's *Mexico, the Beautiful Cookbook: Authentic Recipes from the Regions of Mexico* (1991), and Patsy Swendson and June Hayes's *Texas, the Beautiful Cookbook: Authentic Recipes from the Regions of Texas* (1995).

Specialized shops devoted only to cookbooks began appearing in the 1980s and 1990s. Small stores, some with actual kitchens for visiting authors to demonstrate their recipes, opened in Los Angeles, New York City, Chicago, and Portland, Oregon, and in the Canadian cities of Toronto and Vancouver. Larger bookstores such as Barnes and Noble increased the shelf space allotted to cookbooks and promoted authors with popular cookbook signings and recipe tastings.

Bibles of Food

While a fascination with cooking and chefs continued, a new generation of noncooks came of age in the 1980s. Mother and grandmother no longer were able or had the time to teach cooking to their offspring. Most parents worked full-time. If cooking was done in most households, it was not the from-scratch variety. Eating out became easier than cooking in. Little surprise, then, that food professionals became concerned and began writing books to help the new generation get a grip. A new run of cookbooks began that took amateurs by the hand and in complete detail gave them the basics to master any dish. Many of these books had the word "bible" in their titles; *The Cake Bible* (1988) by the pastry chef Rose Levy Beranbaum may have been the first of these. It soon was followed by titles such as *The Cheese Bible* (1998) by Christian Teubner, *The Dessert Bible* (2000) by Christopher Kimball, *The Bread Bible* (2003) by Beranbaum, and the previously mentioned *The Barbecue! Bible*.

While Time-Life's *The Good Cook* series presented simple, straightforward information about basics including salads, poultry, pasta, and meats, the 1990s also brought the denigrating *Cooking for Dummies* (1996) by Bryan Miller and Marie Rama. "Dummies" cookbooks nevertheless became a popular concept, with similar titles including *Desserts for Dummies* (1997) by Bryan Miller and Bill Yosses, *Grilling for Dummies* (1998) by Marie Rama and John Mariani, and *Cookies for Dummies* (2001) by Carole Bloom.

More Global Outreach

"Fusion" became a buzzword in the 1990s as restaurant chefs experimented, mixing many cultures on the plate or in the pot. Asian greens appeared with increasing frequency in French-inspired entrées. French goat cheese found its way into macaroni and cheese. Italian polenta mixed with Mexican salsas. The international approach was not limited to fusion cuisine. Americans were traveling beyond the usual European nations to Asia, and Pacific Rim foods became sought after. Notable books from this trend include Yamuna Devi's *The Art of Indian Vegetarian Cooking: Lord Krishna's Cuisine* (1987), Elizabeth Andoh's *An Ocean of Flavor: The Japanese Way with Fish and Seafood* (1988), and Nicole Routhier's *The Foods of Vietnam* (1989). The impressive *Hot, Sour, Salty, Sweet: A Culinary Journey through Southeast Asia* (2000) won that year's best cookbook award from both the International Association of Culinary Professionals and the James Beard Foundation. Building on their winning formula of travel, research, and photography, Jeffrey Alford and Naomi Duguid created a picture of Southeast Asia that few authors had managed before.

As the global emphasis continued in cookbook publishing, a secondary trend began to emerge, perhaps as a backlash, in the mid- to late 1990s. Restaurant chefs and cookbook authors focused on food closer to home. All-American dishes of the past reemerged, including homey fare such as pot roast, mashed potatoes, macaroni and cheese, and roast chicken. This change reflected a society frustrated with the stresses of everyday working life. The terrorist attacks on the United States on September 11, 2001, only bolstered the need for a return to nostalgic dining. Everyone needed a comfort meal to set things right. *Recipes from Home* (2001) by David Page and Barbara Shinn, the owners of the Manhattan restaurant of the same name, revealed recipes based on the past but shaped by modern techniques. *Back to the Table: The Reunion of Food and Family* (2001) by Art Smith, the talk show host Oprah Winfrey's personal chef, highlighted the importance of a return to family dinners.

Nothing is more comforting than baked goods, so dessert cookbooks also gained ground as popular sellers. The classic *The Simple Art of Perfect Baking* was revised by Flo Braker in 1992. *In the Sweet Kitchen: The Definitive Baker's Companion* (2001) by Regan Daley took bakers by the hand with its extensive directions. Chocolate cookbooks answered the growing obsession with this indulgent ingredient. Cakes, pies, brownies,

Cookbook Selection. Cookbook shelves at Park Slope Food Coop, Brooklyn, New York. *Photograph by Joe Zarba*

puddings, tarts, and even cupcakes earned their star turn as cookbook topics.

The growth of farmers' markets in the 1990s also made cooks more aware of ingredients and the importance of freshness. Buying local became a mantra of urban chefs around the country. Farmers at last were getting recognition for their crucial role in American cuisine. Waters continued the crusade with books on fruits and vegetables, following her earlier works, *The Chez Panisse Menu Cookbook* (1982) and the *Chez Panisse Café Cookbook* (1999). Deborah Madison's *Local Flavors: Cooking and Eating from America's Farmers' Markets* (2002) also focused on fresh ingredients.

A transplanted movement from Italy called slow food embellished on the "return to fresh, local cooking" trend. Begun as a protest against fast food, the Slow Food group (founded as Slow Food Arcigola in 1989 by Carlo Petrini) called for a return to traditional cooking, using local ingredients with respect. It established a list of endangered foods such as breeds of turkeys or species of potatoes and worked to restore them to their former numbers. It set up an international food show to display the best of artisan foods. The group's goals were set forth in *The Pleasures of Slow Food: Celebrating Authentic Traditions, Flavors, and Recipes* (2002) by Corby Kummer.

Sustainable farming and organic foods became more important as consumer groups called for more of them and the U.S. government struggled to define them. Natural foods and vegetarian foods crept closer to the consciousness of mainstream America. Ever since Lappé's *Diet for a Small Planet* in 1971, perhaps a book before its time, Americans had heard about how organic farming was better for the environment. More than two decades later, supermarket chains such as Whole Foods, Fresh Fields, and Trader Joe's opened nationwide and devoted their aisles to more healthful foods.

The mid-1990s also saw a number of retro-revival cookbooks, as publishers updated some of their old titles to appeal to younger cooks who missed out on the originals. *The Boston Cooking-School Cook Book*, first written in 1896 by Fannie Farmer, was revised almost one hundred years later by Marion Cunningham as *The Fannie Farmer Cookbook* (1990). Olney's *French Menu Cookbook* (1970) was back in print in 2002. The still popular *Joy of Cooking* went through a massive update, in which the chapters of the original work by Irma Rombauer and Marion Rombauer Becker, her daughter, were totally rewritten by food professionals around the country, much to the dismay of many *Joy* fans. Others applauded the new 1997 edition as a comprehensive work and an impressive accomplishment despite the loss of the Rombauer "voice." *The Better Homes and*

Gardens New Cook Book (2002), a new anniversary edition of the red-and-white-checked classic, updated recipes to match modern tastes (lower fat content, for example) and added new recipes that reflected Americans' growing appreciation of ethnic foods. An updated series of M. F. K. Fisher's acclaimed books brought her art to a new generation.

Changing American Culture

Through more than thirty years, cookbooks have become more eclectic, reflecting the changing American culture and our love affair with food. They reflect all that Americans find appealing, from classic preparations to silly fads, from nutritious and wholesome produce to decadent desserts, from fifteen-minute meals to weekend ethnic stews. Whatever dish or cuisine a cook desires, he or she can find it in a cookbook.

However, with the economic downturn of 2001 and 2002, there were signs that the cookbook boom was coming to an end. Fewer cookbooks were getting published because of a consolidation of book publishers. With money tight, demand for expensive cookbooks softened. But plenty of customers still flocked to book signings by ever-increasing numbers of star chefs and television personalities who helped keep the cookbook market alive. The proliferation of recipes found in cyberspace also seemed to show signs of affecting the cookbook business.

For cooking enthusiasts, it may be hard to imagine following recipes from Web printouts: no glossy pages to protect from stains or crumbs, no favorite recipes marked by folded-down page corners, and no battered, but coveted, books to hand down to the next generation of cooks.

[*See also* Barbecue; Bayless, Rick; Beard, James; Cajun and Creole Food; Celebrity Chefs; Child, Julia; Claiborne, Craig; Farmers' Markets; French Influences on American Food; Fusion Food; Health Food; Nouvelle Cuisine; Organic Food; Puck, Wolfgang; Slow Food Movement; Southern Regional Cookery; Stewart, Martha; Trotter, Charlie; Vegetarianism.]

BIBLIOGRAPHY

Anderson, Jean. *The American Century Cook-Book.* New York: C. Potter, 1997.

Barile, Mary. *Cookbooks Worth Collecting.* Radnor, PA: Wallace-Homestead, 1994.

Fussell, Betty. *Masters of American Cookery—M. F. K. Fisher, James Andrews Beard, Raymond Craig Claiborne, Julia McWilliams Child.* New York: Times Books, 1983.

Haber, Barbara. *From Hardtack to Home Fries: An Uncommon History of American Cooks and Meals.* New York: Free Press, 2002.

Lovegren, Sylvia. *Fashionable Food: Seven Decades of Food Fads.* New York: Macmillan, 1995.

Tannahill, Reay. *Food in History.* New York: Crown, 1989.

Theophano, Janet. *Eat My Words: Reading Women's Lives through the Cookbooks They Wrote.* New York: Palgrave, 2002.

Trager, James. *The Enriched, Fortified, Concentrated, Country-Fresh, Lip-Smacking, Finger-Licking, International, Unexpurgated Foodbook.* New York: Grossman, 1970.

Trager, James. *The Food Chronology: A Food Lover's Compendium of Events and Anecdotes from Prehistory to the Present.* New York: Henry Holt, 1995.

CAROL MIGHTON HADDIX

Community Cookbooks

Recipe collections published to support a charitable cause are known variously as community, charity, regional, and fund-raising cookbooks. The form evolved during the American Civil War in conjunction with sanitary fairs, fund-raisers largely orchestrated by women to raise money for medical corps. Cookbooks to benefit northern and southern veterans, widows, and war orphans followed, and the form was quickly adopted by religious and philanthropic groups. In early community cookbooks (CCBs), recipe donors were usually part of a local or regional community, but a number of later books include recipes contributed by women from across the United States sympathetic to a particular cause. Most nineteenth-century CCBs were created and printed locally, although women's groups adapted each other's designs at times. Commercial companies that assisted women in compiling, publishing, distributing, and often, sadly, standardizing their cookbooks came on the scene in the 1930s.

CCBs have always been valued as sources of practical recipes reflecting what people "really eat" (as opposed to the idealized representations of what people should eat found in commercial cookbooks); keepsakes that link individuals to their ancestors, institutions, and communities; and souvenirs of visits to particular regions. The McIlhenny Company of Avery Island, Louisiana, the maker of Tabasco products, celebrates CCBs via its annual Community Cookbook Awards; the Walter S. McIlhenny Hall of Fame recognizes CCBs selling more than 100,000 copies.

However, community cookbooks were not taken seriously until feminist scholarship gave them academic attention in the second half of the twentieth century. Margaret Cook authored the first bibliography of CCBs and delved into their origin (1971). Since then, culinary historians and academics in many fields have argued that these cookbooks reveal much about the women who put them together: the values that prompted women's involvement in charitable and reformist causes; their attempts to assimilate into or differentiate themselves from mainstream American society; their class affiliations and aspirations; their interests in forming and maintaining community; and their abilities to use the cookbook genre to tell history, demonstrate creativity, and promote female agency.

Early Developments

Protestant church women were the most frequent publishers of early CCBs, although synagogue sisterhoods and women in other denominations soon followed suit. By the early 1900s, CCBs were being published all over the country, and the form had been adapted by business and professional women's groups, chapters of the Woman's Christian Temperance Union, homes for orphans and widows, schools, women supporters of veterans' groups, suffrage proponents, the Daughters of the American Revolution (DAR), Young Men's Christian Association (YMCA), and Young Women's Christian Association (YWCA), granges, expositions and fairs. The well-known *Creole Cookery* was put out in 1885 by the Christian Women's Exchange of New Orleans. Jewish women in San Francisco published the *Council Cook Book* in 1909, with recipes for Passover as well as for tamales, ravioli, mulligatawny, and many seafood dishes. These older recipe collections usually contain prefatory matter attesting to the "tried-and-true" nature of the dishes included but frequently also contain caveats concerning a book's modest goals or its authors' lack of professional culinary training.

At the same time, the compilers often assert the importance of the homemaker role or, to use Catharine Beecher's and Harriet Beecher Stowe's famous phrase from *The American Woman's Home* (1869), the centrality of woman as the "prime minister of the family state." The *Centennial Buckeye Cook Book*, put out by the First Congregational Church of Marysville, Ohio, is dedicated to "the plucky housewives of 1876, who master their work instead of allowing it to master them" (Smith, p. 4). With the adoption of the domestic science movement and its notion that home management was just as important as the public work of men, the women contributing to and compiling charity cookbooks proposed that the kitchen could serve as a power base from which to wield influence in spheres beyond the home. For example, the editor of the *Centennial Buckeye Cook Book*, Estelle Woods Wilcox, in conjunction with her publisher husband, saw

this book through many editions and adaptations, including an 1887 German edition published in Minneapolis and four editions of the *Dixie Cookbook* (1883–1893).

Some early CCBs, such as the *Ladies' Handbook and Household Assistant* (published in the 1880s "In Behalf of the Old South Church, Windsor, Vermont"), were organized quite loosely, without any real table of contents. On one page, a table showing the capacity of various churches appears along with advice for preserving fuel when boiling water. As with many books of this era, the *Ladies' Handbook* is only partly a cookbook, containing rules for "Religious and Table Etiquette" and "Rules, Tables, and Suggestions of Infinite Value in Every Household." Other cookbooks, even when containing diverse information, were organized more efficiently, as with the *Buckeye Cook Book*, which featured a full table of contents in its first edition and, in later editions of the 1880s, included a detailed index. Special sections for menus and for "foreign foods" were also components of some books.

The advertisements included in most early CCBs indicate that women had a central economic role as consumers. Ads for everything from foodstuffs, furniture, hotels, restaurants, clothing, and groceries to business schools, office supplies, fuel, and auto repair provide insights into the commercial world in which the women lived. For many nineteenth- and early twentieth-century women, soliciting such ads, along with seeing a cookbook to publication and then marketing it, provided an introduction to the life of business and industry.

Some women took bolder steps within the pages of their cookbooks to assert their rights and values. For example, the *Woman Suffrage Cook Book* published in Boston in 1886, includes recipes by Lucy Stone and other leading suffragists, words of advice from Julia Ward Howe, and a section on "Eminent Opinions on Woman Suffrage," containing quotations from Plato, Louisa May Alcott, Ralph Waldo Emerson, Abraham Lincoln, and others. Similarly, the *Washington Women's Cook Book* (1909), published by the Washington Equal Suffrage Association, used recipes, quotations from women activists, and humorous cartoons to forward its cause.

Changing Styles and Values

As more women entered public life, CCBs' recipes, along with their prefatory and discursive passages, revealed the ways women negotiated their sometimes conflicting roles. While older CCBs often include everything from how to bake a cake to how to black a stove, prepare foods for invalids, cut up a side of beef, and store various food-stuffs, later cookbooks usually concentrate on food preparation and preservation. Ready-made products clearly relieved women of certain duties. But other changes occurred as more women entered the workforce. A book like *Who Says We Can't Cook!*, from the National Women's Press Club (1955), stresses women's professional roles as journalists, while proclaiming (in the fore-word) that many of the women are noted hostesses and have created "short-cut scoops" to produce fine dinners. A number of the recipes use canned foods or items such as "1 roll prepared snappy cheese" (p. 38), and recipe titles often indicate speed or efficiency, as with "Angel in a Hurry" and "Favorite Quick and Easies."

Some mid-twentieth-century CCBs assert the desire for traditional values, even as they incorporate canned soup and Jell-O gelatin into recipes. *Virginia Cookery—Past and Present*, published in 1957 by the Women's Auxiliary of Olivet Episcopal Church, emphasizes continuity with past traditions of life and cookery through its prefatory material, as well as chapter introductions that refer to historical characters and events (with titles like "Virginia Breads: The Great Tradition"). The book also includes, at the beginning of the volume, a manuscript cookbook from the Lee and Washington families. *Virginia Cookery's* final section contains excerpts from "Old Virginia" cookbooks. Thus this 1957 cookbook is framed by the past: the book's form as well as its content attest to its authors' desires to maintain their regional history and foodways.

Other CCBs reflect women's class struggles as well as their changing roles. A number of nineteenth-century cookbooks contain etiquette sections or even are part etiquette manual, as with the *Ladies' Handbook and Household Assistant*, mentioned earlier. It provides sample dinner invitations, dress codes, and directions for servants, all of which reveal the hoped-for status of the community being addressed. Certain guidelines imply, however, that not everyone being addressed is a well-established middle-class member. For example, the book admonishes readers: "Never apologize to a waiter for asking for anything. . . . Never pick the teeth at the table or in the presence of ladies after a meal" (p. 13). Late twentieth-century cookbooks continue to demonstrate class consciousness, with illustrations of table settings, menu arrangements, and elegant recipes that many will aspire to but few will actually prepare. Elaborate Junior League cookbooks like *Stop and Smell the Rosemary* (1996) combine sophisticated format and photographs, a cosmopoli-

tan assortment of recipes, and introductory material that stresses the role of gracious entertaining and models upper-class behavior.

Fund-raising cookbooks also demonstrate their women authors' attitudes toward assimilation into mainstream American society, or their need to distinguish and honor their particular heritage. Before World War II, emphasis on a particular ethnicity occasionally occurred in both commercial cookbooks and CCBs. In the first half of the twentieth century, groups of women turned to CCBs to assert their communal identity, whether to preserve it from the incursions of mainstream American culture or to proclaim their right to their own heritage even as they integrated socially into their towns and cities. *As the World Cooks: Recipes from Many Lands*, published in 1938 in Lowell, Massachusetts, by "women interested in the International Institute of Lowell" (which aided immigrants), provided sections in which residents of different backgrounds could display the culinary arts of their homelands—Italy, Spain, Syria, Great Britain, Armenia, Germany, Poland, Albania, Russia, and China.

Books stressing one ethnicity also appeared. *Woman's Glory: The Kitchen*, issued in 1953 by the Slovenian Women's Union of America to celebrate its silver anniversary and published in Chicago, announces in the preface that one of its purposes is to "serve as an instructor to the Slovenian women of today who wish to include in their homemaking dishes for which their mothers have always been famous." Jewish CCBs began in the nineteenth century; one of the most famous, the *Way to a . . . Man's Heart* (1903), later published as the *Settlement Cook Book*, had enduring popularity. The book contains typical German Jewish fare and includes recipes using shrimp, bacon, and other items Orthodox Jews do not eat; it is assimilationist in tone. In contrast, *At Home on the Range*, published in 1937 by the Westchester Ladies' Auxiliary in support of the United Home for Aged Hebrews, New Rochelle, New York, contains a section on foods for the Jewish holidays, including brief discussions of the seder meal and service, along with short introductions to Rosh Hashanah, the Day of Atonement, Succoth, Hanukkah, and Purim. The preservation and proclamation of Jewish identity was vital to these women compilers.

With the social upheavals and changes of the mid-twentieth century, from World War II to women's liberation and the civil rights movement, community cookbook authors took new approaches to their genre, in both content and form. Groups around the country proudly presented recipes for their national specialties, often with background information about special holidays, foods, and history. Cookbooks like *Espanola Valley Cookbook: Recipes from Three Cultures, Spanish, Anglo, Indian*, published in 1974 by the women of the Espanola Hospital Auxiliary, became more common. In such CCBs the women authors take on the role of cultural historians, using the book's foreword and explanatory sections within food categories to educate their readers on different food traditions. African American women also have created CCBs featuring aspects of their historical backgrounds; an early example is the National Council of Negro Women's *Historical Cookbook of the American Negro* (1958), followed in the 1990s by four more recipe collections based on African American and African traditions.

In the later twentieth century CCBs also were put together by both children's and men's groups. *Out of Our Kitchen Closets: San Francisco Gay Jewish Cooking* (1987) demonstrates the adaptability of the CCB form for community building and outreach. At the beginning of the twenty-first century, CCBs were still reliable as fundraisers and repositories of beloved dishes, and also had become valued as part of America's material culture, telling the stories of the books' authors—their ways of life, their changing food preparation and consumption patterns, and the values they associate with their food traditions and innovations.

[*See also* Beecher, Catharine; Cooking Manuscripts; Etiquette Books; Fund-Raisers.]

BIBLIOGRAPHY

Beecher, Catharine E., and Harriet Beecher Stowe. *The American Woman's Home*. A new edition, edited and with an introduction by Nicole Tonkovich. New Brunswick, NJ: Rutgers University Press, 2002; copublished with the Harriet Beecher Stowe Center, Hartford, CT. Originally published in 1869 as *The American Woman's Home; or, Principles of Domestic Science; Being a Guide to the Formation and Maintenance of Economical, Healthful, Beautiful, and Christian Homes*. Provides a strong sense of white, middle-class, nineteenth-century sensibilities about women and domesticity.

Bower, Anne L. "Bound Together: Recipes, Lives, Stories, and Reading" and "Cooking Up Stories: Narrative Elements in Community Cookbooks." In *Recipes for Reading: Community Cookbooks, Stories, Histories*, edited by Anne L. Bower, 1–14, 29–50. Amherst: University of Massachusetts Press, 1997. This volume contains thirteen articles analyzing community cookbooks and related texts and events from varying perspectives.

Cook, Margaret. *America's Charitable Cooks: A Bibliography of Fund-Raising Cook Books Published in the United States (1861–1915)*. Kent, OH: privately printed, 1971. The first bibliography of community cookbooks.

Ireland, Lynne. "The Compiled Cookbook as Foodways Autobiography." *Western Folklore* 40 (1981): 107–114.

Kirshenblatt-Gimblett, Barbara. "Kitchen Judaism." In *Getting Comfortable in New York: The American Jewish Home, 1880–1950*, edited by Susan L. Braunstein and Jenna Weissman Joselit, 75–105. New York: Jewish Museum, 1990.

Kirshenblatt-Gimblett, Barbara. "Recipes for Creating Community: The Jewish Charity Cookbook in America." *Jewish Folklore and Ethnology* 9 (1987): 8–20. Includes a 201-item bibliography of Jewish community cookbooks, mostly from the 1960s to the 1980s.

Shapiro, Laura. *Perfection Salad: Women and Cooking at the Turn of the Century*. New York: Holt, 1986. Links the nineteenth-century domestic science movement to both reformism and literary sentimentalism.

Smith, Andrew F. Introduction to *Centennial Buckeye Cook Book*, edited by Estelle Woods Wilcox. 1876. Reprint, Columbus: The Ohio State University Press, 2000.

Theophano, Janet. *Eat My Words: Reading Women's Lives through the Cookbooks They Wrote*. New York: Palgrave, 2002. Sympathetic analyses of English and American women's cookbooks (many of them unpublished) explore class and gender issues, along with the cultures and histories surrounding the women.

Westbrook, Virginia M. Introduction to *Buckeye Cookery and Practical Housekeeping*, edited by Estelle Woods Wilcox. 1876. Reprint, Saint Paul: Minnesota Historical Society Press, 1988.

ANNE L. BOWER

Children's Cookbooks

The European cookbook tradition brought by settlers to the first American colonies did not include children's cookbooks. This literary genre is a relatively recent phenomenon that originated in the late nineteenth century, a time when domestic training for girls was reinforced by social ideals, increased leisure time and affluence among the middle class, and the new home economics movement. The first juvenile cookbooks were written in entertaining and sometimes fanciful styles to secure children's interest, teach cookery, and sugarcoat a substantial measure of morality, manners, obedience, religion, and social responsibility. As in the late 1800s, children's cookbooks continue to reflect contemporary social issues and child-rearing philosophies.

Using the ploy of fictionalized stories for girls, the first cooking instructions for children were set into the plot as the action dictated. Recipes appeared as conversations between young friends or mothers and daughters. As exemplified by Ella Farman Pratt's volume *The Cooking Club of Tu-Whit Hollow* (1885), standard recipes such as those for soft cake or fruitcake were presented following the traditional anecdotal style everyone used to teach cooking skills to the next generation.

Child's Cookbook. Frontispiece to *The Mary Frances Cook Book* by Jane Allen Boyer (Philadelphia, 1912). *Collection of Alice Ross*

The use of fictional settings in children's cookbooks continued for some decades, although the balance between story content and recipes shifted. Jane Eayre Fryer's *Easy Steps in Cooking, or, the Mary Frances Cookbook, or, Adventures among the Kitchen People* (1912) keeps a story line but stresses cookery. Anthropomorphized kitchen utensils in cartoonlike drawings verbalize the cooking hints.

By the 1920s, home economics had found a place in public school curricula. Clara Ingram Judson wrote a series of children's cookbook texts, among them, *Cooking without Mother's Help* (1920). Judson's *When Mother Lets Us Cook* (1919) was a straightforward collection of recipes with only the occasional diversion of presenting basic rules in poetry form. As her series of texts progressed, the illustrations became more educational, and Judson adapted the new emphasis on science by presenting recipes in modern form (utensils, ingredients, and processes listed separately).

By the 1930s, simple cookbooks had become more accessible both financially and instructionally. Louise

Price Bell's paperback *Kitchen Fun: Teaches Children to Cook Successfully* (1932) used large-format pages, print, and measurements; she diagrammed measuring cups and spoons for ease in fractional amounts and produced a book of simple recipes that a young reader could handle alone or in school. Under the combined influence of ongoing immigration and new melting pot theories, Gertrude I. Thomas's *Foods of Our Forefathers in the Middle Colonies, 1614–1776* (1941) offered a text on American cultural history through recipes.

Increasing commercialism prompted the publication of free or giveaway promotional cookbook pamphlets. In 1905 Pillsbury issued *A Little Book for a Little Cook* by L. P. Hubbard. After World War II, Westinghouse offered schools its text *Sugar an' Spice and All Things Nice* (1951) by Julia Kiene. In 1957 the classic *Cook Book for Boys and Girls* by Betty Crocker began its long series of reprints and revisions, all sprinkled with advertisements.

In the 1970s a new emphasis on creativity brought books like the award-winning Tomie de Paola's *Pancakes for Breakfast* (1978), extended the readership of children's cookbooks to preschoolers, and raised the publication of cookbooks to an art form. Newer cookbooks ask children to see food in larger contexts: survival basics, science in the kitchen, ethnicity, holidays, health, vegetarianism, and just plain fun.

[*See also* Home Economics.]

ALICE ROSS

Cookie Cutters

After cookie dough is rolled out, cookie cutters sometimes are used to shape the dough before baking. At their simplest, cookies cutters are round and indistinguishable from biscuit cutters. At their fanciest, they cut an outline and impress a design on the top, for example, leaf-shaped cutters with veins. Tin cutters, which, according to folklore were fashioned from scraps by traveling tinkers, have been made since the 1840s; they may have been made earlier in Pennsylvania by European immigrants with a cookie-shaping heritage. The first U.S. patent for a cake cutter (cookies were called "cakes" in the 1800s) was issued in 1857. Early cookie cutters usually were made of tin, or occasionally of wrought iron or copper. They were one-of-a-kind creations until about 1870, when mass-produced sets were made in the United States or imported, particularly from Germany. Housewives often kept a dozen or more strung on a cord, ready for use.

Tin cutters may have flat backs to strengthen the thin bent outline, with airholes to easily release the dough. Simple outlines may be braced only with strips of tin. Backed or backless cutters may have strap handles. By the 1880s rolling cutters, which cut several designs with one turn, were made. Stamped aluminum cutters came next. The first plastic cookie cutters were made in the 1940s and had the same features as tin ones: a strap handle, bracing, airholes, and even the interior shallow impression lines.

The shapes of cookie cutters have long reflected changing popular culture—people, flowers, everyday objects, animals, holiday characters such as Belsnickel (an early German version of Santa Claus), geometrics, playing card suits, and patriotic symbols. In the twentieth century, a multitude of commercial figures based on cartoons came out. The huge variety of available cookie cutters has encouraged housewives to buy new sets and singles.

[*See also* Biscuit Cutters; Cookies.]

BIBLIOGRAPHY

Franklin, Linda Campbell. *300 Years of Kitchen Collectibles*. 5th ed. Iola, WI: Krause Publications, 2003.
Lasansky, Jeannette. *To Cut, Piece, and Solder: The Work of the Rural Pennsylvania Tinsmith, 1778–1908*. Lewisburg, PA: Union County Oral Traditions Project, 1982.
Wetherill, Phyllis Steiss. *Cookie Cutters and Cookie Molds: Art in the Kitchen*. Exton, PA: Schiffer, 1985.

LINDA CAMPBELL FRANKLIN

Cookies

Cookies are a favorite American sweet, made from a dough of flour and sugar that contains a relatively high ratio of fat, such as butter, vegetable shortening, or margarine. The dough typically is flavored with various combinations of spices, extracts, chocolate, fruits, and nuts and is baked in the form of small, thin cakes. Categories include cookies rolled and cut in shapes, bar cookies, drop cookies, molded or stamped cookies, pressed cookies, and sliced refrigerator cookies. America's oldest and most beloved homemade cookies include macaroons, jumbles, and apees, as well as gingerbread, oatmeal, peanut butter, and chocolate chip cookies; commercially produced favorites include Fig Newtons, Animal Crackers, Lorna Doones, and Oreos. Although cookies are eaten year-round as snacks or dessert, they are especially popular at Christmas, when they often are made from heirloom recipes.

Origin and Evolution of Cookies

Cookies have an ancient heritage, dating back to the time of the pharaohs in Egypt, when they were made with honey. In the Middle East, cookies later were sweetened with sugar, which was cultivated in seventh-century Persia. The Venetians, who imported sugar from Alexandria as early as the fifteenth century, commonly used sugar to sweeten all manner of desserts, including cookies, and they are thought to be the original refiners of sugar in Europe. The macaroon is one of the earliest of cookies still known in modern times. A reference to the French "macaron," a word that comes from the Italian "maccarone," dates at least to 1611, most likely indicating that the French adopted the cookie from their Italian neighbors. From there the cookie spread to Holland and crossed the channel to England, where references to "mackroons" and other cookies, such as "jumbals," are to be found in seventeenth-century family manuscripts, including *Martha Washington's Booke of Cookery*.

Early English and Dutch immigrants first introduced the cookie to America in the 1600s. While the English primarily referred to cookies as small cakes, sweet biscuits, or tea cakes, or by specific names, such as jumbal or macaroon, the Dutch called them *koekjes*, a diminutive of *koek* (cake). The original Dutch colony was New Amsterdam (later New York City), and on New Year's Day it was the custom to hand out *Nieuwjaar koeken*, a practice adopted by other groups of the time. Etymologists note that by the early 1700s, *koekje* had been Anglicized into "cookie" or "cookey," and the word clearly had become part of the American vernacular.

Following the American Revolution, people from other parts of the country became familiar with the cookie when visiting New York City, the nation's first capital, a factor that resulted in widespread use of the term. *American Cookery* (1796), the first American cookbook, originally was published in Hartford, Connecticut, and later that year the second edition was published in Albany, New York, a region also settled by the Dutch. The author, Amelia Simmons, gave recipes for both "Cookies" and "Another Christmas Cookey." The terms "cake," "cookie," and "tea cake" were used interchangeably until the late nineteenth century, when "cookie" became the preferred term, most likely because it had long been in the American vernacular. Although cookie recipes inherited from the English were used predominantly throughout the eighteenth and nineteenth centuries, other immigrants later added their own recipes to America's growing repertoire.

America's First Homemade Cookies

During the seventeenth, eighteenth, and nineteenth centuries most cookies were made in home kitchens. They mainly were baked as special treats because of the cost of sweeteners and the amount of time and labor required for preparation. The most popular of these early cookies still retain their prize status. Recipes for jumbles, a spiced butter cookie, and for macaroons, based on beaten egg whites and almonds, were common in the earliest American cookbooks. Simmons provided a recipe for "Tumbles" in *American Cookery,* and recipes for both "Jumbals" and "Macaroone" are included in Mary Randolph's *The Virginia House-Wife* (1824).

A recipe for apees, a rolled cutout cookie made with caraway seeds, sometimes called "seed cakes," first appeared in Eliza Leslie's *Seventy-five Receipts for Pastry, Cakes, and Sweetmeats* (1828). Another version, known as "apeas," was based on German *Anis Plätchen* (anise cookies), and Philadelphia bakers commonly sold them on the streets. Apeas became associated with Ann Page, a popular baker who stamped her initials, A. P., on the cookies. Anise is still a common flavoring used in a variety of cookies, ranging from old recipes for apeas to simple cutout cookies and ethnic specialties like German *Springerles,* which are imprinted by using carved boards or rolled out with a decorative rolling pin.

Because it was relatively inexpensive and easy to make, gingerbread was one of the most popular early cookies and remained so in subsequent centuries. In cookie form it is often called "hard" gingerbread to distinguish it from the softer cake version. There are two basic types of gingerbread cookies: shortbreadlike cookies made with molasses, which originated in Scotland, and the German type, called *Lebkuchen,* which are made with honey as a sweetener. Gingersnaps are a variation of molasses-flavored gingerbread, and they quite likely got their name because of their crispy texture and tops that crinkle when baked. An early version, called "Gingerbread Nuts," appears in Leslie's *Seventy-five Receipts for Pastry, Cakes, and Sweetmeats. Housekeeping in Old Virginia* (1877), edited by Marion Cabell Tyree, refers to the cookie as "Ginger Snaps."

Fannie Merritt Farmer included what may be the first printed recipe for oatmeal cookies in *The Boston Cooking-School Cook Book* (1896). The Quaker Oats Company is credited with popularizing the cookie by including various recipes on oatmeal packages over the years. Later additions to the basic recipe include raisins, nuts, and chocolate chips.

As kitchen technology improved in the early 1900s, most notably in the ability to regulate oven temperature, America's repertoire of cookie recipes grew, and one new cookie included peanut butter. Manufacturers of the product sponsored cookbooks with peanut butter cookie recipes after it was introduced at the 1904 St. Louis World's Fair, but those recipes used very little of the ingredient, and the cookies were rolled and cut. What may be the first recipe for peanut butter cookies as they are known in modern form appears in *Ruth Wakefield's Toll House Tried and True Recipes* (1937). Wakefield's instructions call for rolling peanut butter–flavored dough into nut-sized balls and pressing them with a fork in crisscross fashion.

Chocolate, which was discovered in Mexico by early Spanish explorers, was consumed as a popular drink in chocolate houses throughout Europe in the seventeenth and eighteenth centuries. It was first manufactured in 1765 in America, where it also was consumed primarily as a beverage until candy bars were created in the mid-nineteenth century. The Industrial Revolution introduced the mass production of chocolate, and its subsequent popularity grew further with the lifting of import duties in 1853. But baking chocolate, also called "unsweetened chocolate," did not make an appearance until 1893, when Milton Hershey, using new manufacturing technology, first produced it in Pennsylvania. Chocolate was no longer a luxury, and chocolate cookies soon became popular; one of the first recipes appears in Farmer's *Boston Cooking-School Cook Book.*

Baking chocolate was melted before its incorporation into cookie dough until the 1930s, when Wakefield, the owner of the Toll House Inn in Whitman, Massachusetts, created the "Toll House Chocolate Crunch Cookie," which later became known as the chocolate chip cookie. Her original recipe, from *Toll House Tried and True Recipes,* calls for cutting bars of Nestlé semisweet chocolate into very small pieces, which are then added to a basic butter cookie dough. When sales of semisweet chocolate soared in New England, Nestlé investigated, and the company began producing scored chocolate bars packaged with a small chopper. In 1939 the company introduced semisweet chocolate morsels and signed a contract with Wakefield allowing the company to print her recipe on every package. The shortcut formula for adding chocolate to cookies was a big success, and the chocolate chip continues its reign as America's favorite homemade cookie.

Sweetening of America

Americans inherited their well-known sweet tooth from the English, and even the first colonists had sweetening agents. They used honey and molasses, and Native Americans taught them to use maple sugar, which was less expensive and more plentiful than imported sugar. Nevertheless, America's first cookies called for conservative amounts of sugar compared with what was to come.

The discovery of America by Europeans had its roots in explorers seeking faster routes to the Far East, the heart of the lucrative spice trade, but it soon was discovered that highly prized sugarcane could be grown successfully in the Caribbean. New England became pivotal in the triangular trade of the day, turning sugarcane, which was shipped from the West Indies, into molasses. Rum was then produced with the molasses and used to buy slaves in West Africa for deployment in the cane fields of the Caribbean. Because refined white sugar remained expensive, American cooks supplemented it with molasses and sorghum.

The Industrial Revolution brought additional changes to American food. In the 1840s new milling processes increased flour production but removed the wheat germ and nutrients, resulting in a white, starch-laden product. The advent of chemical leavens around 1850 eased both time and labor in the preparation of baked goods, but they also imparted a bitter, metallic taste. In an effort to compensate for loss of flavor and to disguise the taste of leavens, Americans increased their use of sugar, and by the mid-nineteenth century they consumed the second-largest amount of sugar in the world, surpassed only by the English.

Then, in 1868, a new method of sugar refining that reduced the processing time from three weeks to eight days was patented in San Francisco. This was followed by the removal of American sugar tariffs in the 1880s, making sugar an affordable commodity. It was not long before American consumption of sugar became the largest in the world. By the turn of the century sugar was a dominant ingredient in American cooking, most notably in sweets such as cookies. Americans still consume prodigious amounts of sugar and sweets in comparison to other countries.

Commercialization of the Cookie

The increasing popularity of cookies, accompanied by affordable sugar and new technologies, caught the attention of manufacturers, who began mass production of many of America's most popular cookies around the turn of the twentieth century. The commercial sale of cookies became especially viable when, in 1899, the National Biscuit Company introduced the "in-er-seal," a method of packaging that ensured product freshness. This innovation resulted in the transition from selling bulk goods shipped in barrels, boxes, and tins to smaller, more individualized packaging. The commercialization of cookies was aided by two other factors. As more women entered the workplace, they had less time to bake and yet were expected to ensure that their husbands and children were well and happily fed. At the turn of the twentieth century women were taught domestic science, which relied heavily on technological advances in the kitchen as well as on the processed foods that were making their way into the marketplace, supported by advertising based on clever, enticing slogans. America's commercial cookie production, aided by technology, the availability of inexpensive sugar, and a large ready market, assumed an early position of dominance relative to variety and sheer production numbers worldwide.

The Fig Newton, a soft cookie filled with fig jam, was one of the first commercially baked products in America. The Kennedy Biscuit Company of Massachusetts began manufacturing Fig Newtons in 1891. The company used a cookie recipe purchased from Charles M. Roser, an Ohio-born cookie manufacturer, along with technology developed by James Henry Mitchell, who invented a machine that supported mass production of the filled cookie. Kennedy Biscuit Works commonly named its products after towns in the Boston area, and the new fig cookie was named for the community of Newton.

During the late 1800s cookies shaped like animals were imported from England, and it was not long before small American bakeries began to imitate the product, which they called "circus crackers" or "animals." In 1898 several of those regional bakeries merged to form the National Biscuit Company (later Nabisco). In 1902 the company renamed the cookies "Barnum's Animals," and because packaging was fundamental to successful national marketing, the product was released for the Christmas holidays in a box designed as a circus wagon complete with a string for hanging on the tree. Children were enchanted with the gimmick, and Animal Crackers, as they later became known, still are sold in the famous box.

The year 1912 saw the National Biscuit Company's introduction of two other popular American cookies: the Lorna Doone and the Oreo. Home cooks had long favored shortbread cookies, so it was a natural for commercial production. Because shortbread commonly was identified with Scotland, the company named its new cookie the "Lorna Doone," probably after the Scottish heroine of the 1869 novel of the same name by R. D. Blackmore.

Originally introduced as the "Oreo Biscuit," the Oreo cookie consists of two rounds of chocolate sandwiched together with a rich cream filling. It is unknown how the confection, now officially called the "Oreo Chocolate Sandwich Cookie," got its name. Oreos were created in response to the Hydrox cookie, which was launched in 1908 by Sunshine Biscuits. Backed by superior marketing and distribution, and a name that was more felicitous, Nabisco's Oreos became the leader of the chocolate sandwich cookie category and the largest-selling cookie in the world. According to Nabisco, more than 450 billion have been produced for worldwide consumption since the cookie's introduction in 1912.

Commercial Cookie Production Diversifies

Manufacturers eventually added cookie mixes to their product lines. In 1947 General Mills introduced its first "Betty Crocker GingerCake Mix," and two years later it reappeared as "GingerCake and Cooky Mix." In 1953 Pillsbury introduced its "Chocolate Chip Cookie Mix."

Homemade cookie dough formed into rolls and refrigerated for slicing and baking at a later time, called "icebox cookies," first appeared in the 1930s, coincident with the widespread use of electric refrigerators in American homes. By the 1950s prepared foods were fashionable, and in 1957 Pillsbury introduced its refrigerated cookie dough, called "Ice Box Cookies," in three flavors: butterscotch nut, crunchy peanut, and coconut. Chocolate chip and sugar cookies soon followed, and Americans eventually could choose from a broad range of both refrigerated and frozen cookie dough.

With more women working outside the home and an increased clamoring for freshly baked goods, the 1970s saw the rise of the cookie entrepreneur. Chocolate chip cookies reigned as the most popular cookie in America, and enterprising cookie bakers moved in to capitalize on it, each claiming to have the ultimate chocolate chip cookie. Wally Amos introduced his Famous Amos version in 1975, followed by Debbi Fields's launch of her first Mrs. Fields Chocolate Chippery cookie boutique in Palo Alto, California, in 1977, a move that led to a nationwide chain of cookie stores. In 1979 the chef David Liederman opened a small cookie shop in New York City that rapidly expanded to more than 250 locations.

Baked goods, including cookies, have long been sold to raise money for charities and other organizations, and several cookbooks have been written featuring bake sale cookie recipes. A new twist was added in the early 1990s, when cookie dough, packed in tubs for refrigeration or freezing, was added to the fund-raising product roster.

Thousands of recipes, hundreds of cookie cookbooks, and dozens of commercially baked cookies attest to the continued popularity of this sweet, all-American snack. Billions of cookies, both homemade and commercially made, are consumed annually by more than 95 percent of American households. The cookie is honored every October, which is designated as National Cookie Month.

[*See also* Chocolate; Desserts; Dutch Influences on American Food; Nabisco; Sugar.]

BIBLIOGRAPHY

Anderson, Jean. *The American Century Cook-Book*. New York: C. Potter, 1997.
Brenner, Leslie. *American Appetite: The Coming of Age of a Cuisine*. New York: Bard, 1999.
Hess, John L., and Karen Hess. *The Taste of America*. Urbana: University of Illinois Press, 2000.
Weaver, William Woys. *The Christmas Cook: Three Centuries of American Yuletide Sweets*. New York: HarperPerennial, 1990.

BECKY MERCURI

Cooking Contests

Cooking contests are an American pastime, annually attracting thousands of participants. The culinary equivalent of sporting events, they fall into three categories: those held as part of fairs and festivals; those sponsored by food manufacturers as promotional events, such as the Pillsbury Bake-Off Contest; and those that celebrate distinctive, all-American foods. Many cooking contests feature monetary prizes, while others benefit charity. The most famous American cook-offs include several state fair and food festival cooking competitions and major league events like the Pillsbury Bake-Off Contest and barbecue and chili competitions.

Cooking Competitions at State Fairs and Food Festivals

America's agricultural fairs, which can be traced back to the medieval fairs of Europe, were established in the early 1800s. They facilitated the exchange of information and technology required for Americans to develop and maintain a self-sufficient agrarian economy. Because fairs provided a communal venue for the entire family, there was a natural expansion from activities involving farming implements, crop exhibitions, and animal husbandry into the domestic arts. These fairs sponsored America's oldest cookery competitions, based on home canning and preserving, showcasing vital skills for housewives of the time. Baking contests, featuring breads and pies, soon were added, and the winners received ribbons in recognition of their prowess in the kitchen. As fairs spread throughout the country on both a county- and statewide basis, cooking exhibits and contests also proliferated.

One of the earliest cookbooks containing recipes for winning fair entries is Abby Fisher's *What Mrs. Fisher Knows about Old Southern Cooking, Soups, Pickles, Preserves, etc.* (1881). Fisher's pickles and preserves earned numerous awards at California exhibitions and fairs, including a diploma from the 1879 Sacramento State Fair. With assistance from many of her patrons, Fisher documented and published her recipes, producing what is considered to be the first African American cookbook.

Nearly two centuries after the establishment of agricultural fairs, Americans still compete in fair cooking contests; the most prestigious are those held by state fairs. From the New York State Fair's pie competition to the pickling and preserves contest at the California State Fair, the domestic arts are celebrated. Various new categories, such as Tex-Mex and heart-healthy cooking, have been added along with divisions for various age groups. Major food manufacturers sponsor many of the contests, and cash prizes often are awarded in addition to ribbons. Many of the fair organizations periodically publish cookbooks featuring winning recipes.

Food festivals, held in ever-increasing numbers throughout the United States, typically pay tribute to a regional crop, a food product, or even a special ethnic dish. Many of America's food festivals originated around the turn of the twentieth century, with hundreds having

been added over the years. They often feature cooking contests that showcase special foods or ingredients.

At the Wild Blueberry Festival in Machias, Maine, the state's Wild Blueberry Commission sponsors a cooking contest for the best overall entry in a wide variety of categories featuring Maine's favorite berry. Oysters take center stage at the National Oyster Cook-Off, held as part of the St. Mary's County Oyster Festival in Leonardtown, Maryland. The innovative use of cornmeal, a southern staple, is rewarded with handsome cash prizes at the National Cornbread Festival and World Championship Cornbread Cook-off in South Pittsburg, Tennessee. America's heartland features the country's favorite dessert at Pie Day in Braham, Minnesota, where flaky-crusted pies are entered in a contest designed to ensure that pie making does not become a lost art. In Gilroy, California, the annual Garlic Festival includes the Great Garlic Cook-Off, one of America's most famous festival cooking contests. Hundreds of amateur chefs from all over the country enter recipes ranging from appetizers to desserts in the hope of winning both cash and the ritual crown of garlic. Many festival organizations also publish cookbooks containing winning recipes, and these books serve as popular souvenirs.

Pillsbury Bake-Off Contest

The Pillsbury Bake-off Contest, the premier manufacturer-sponsored cooking contest in America, was first held in 1949. Known initially as the Grand National Recipe and Baking Contest, it debuted at the Waldorf-Astoria Hotel in New York City; it was held annually (except for 1965) until 1976 and then subsequently every two years. The media christened Pillsbury's event the "Bake-Off Contest," and the company soon adopted the name; in 1971 the term "Bake-Off" was trademarked.

Thousands of recipe submissions are reviewed to ensure compliance with Pillsbury's entry rules and to confirm that the recipes are the unique creations of the contributors. Selected recipes are tested, and one hundred finalists are chosen to prepare their recipes for judging by a panel of food experts. The grand prizewinner receives $1 million.

Over the years, winning Pillsbury Bake-Off Contest recipes have reflected the evolution of Pillsbury's products as well as America's tastes. Early recipes primarily were for baked goods, made from scratch and based on the company's flour. Convenience products soon were incorporated, simplifying recipes and reducing preparation time. Nutrition and healthy eating, the use of time-saving appliances, and America's interest in ethnic cuisine have become hallmarks of more recent recipes.

The Pillsbury Bake-Off Contest's first winning recipe was for rolls called "No-Knead Water-Rising Twists," created by Theodora Smafield of Rockford, Illinois. In 1996 the $1 million grand prize was awarded for the first time to a man. Another first was marked in 2002, when the winning recipe was for a sandwich, "Chicken Florentine Panini."

In 1999 Pillsbury created the Bake-Off Hall of Fame, a collection of the most popular winning recipes, such as "Dilly Casserole Bread," "French Silk Chocolate Pie," "Peanut Blossom Cookies," and "Tunnel of Fudge Cake." Pillsbury donated the collection, which includes contest materials and memorabilia, to the Smithsonian Institution's National Museum of American History. Annual Pillsbury Bake-Off Cookbooks are highly sought by collectors.

Competition Barbecue

Cooking meat slowly over hot coals, known as barbecuing, has been done in America since colonial days. It is characterized by a high-spirited competitiveness based on distinct regional preferences relative to pork versus beef, the best type of firewood, and what concoctions should be used to marinate, rub, mop, and baste the meat. True aficionados of the art of barbecue have marshaled that competitive spirit into formal barbecue cook-offs, which have grown from a few dozen in the mid-1980s to more than five hundred annual events attended by some five million people. The pinnacle of serious all-American barbecue is represented by three major competitive events known as MiM, the Royal, and the Jack.

The granddaddy of the big three is the World Championship Barbecue Cooking Contest, held in Memphis, Tennessee, as part of a month-long celebration known as Memphis in May (MiM). Billed as the "Superbowl of Swine, where the big pigs come to play," MiM is the largest annual pork barbecue competition in the world, with more than thirty-nine tons of pork served each year.

Since 1980 the American Royal Barbecue has been held as part of the annual American Royal Livestock, Horse Show, and Rodeo in Kansas City, Missouri. Renowned for great American barbecue, the area is also home to the Kansas City Barbecue Society (KCBS), which established the de facto standard judging rules for barbecue cook-offs. The Royal, also known as the "World Series of Barbecue," is officially sanctioned by the KCBS. Barbecue categories include brisket, pork ribs, chicken, and pork shoulder or Boston butt.

The tiny town of Lynchburg, Tennessee, is home to the Jack Daniel Distillery and the Jack Daniel's World Championship Invitational Barbecue. A comparative cook-off newcomer, the Jack began in 1988, but it quickly established itself as a serious barbecue event. To win the Jack's championship title, teams are required to demonstrate expertise in four of the following categories: whole hog, pork ribs, pork shoulder, chicken, and beef brisket.

Chili Wars

American chili cooking competition is as heated and volatile as the debate surrounding the origin of chili and what constitutes a proper "bowl of red." Such debates sparked the first chili cook-off, which was held in 1967 in the abandoned mining town of Terlingua, Texas. Over the years, the original organization that sponsored Terlingua split into three separate camps, resulting in the three major chili championships.

The Terlingua International Chili Championship is staged annually during the first weekend in November at Rancho CASI de los Chisos. It is sponsored by the Chili Appreciation Society International (CASI), an organization formed after the first Terlingua cook-off in 1967. CASI lost the right to use the title "World's Championship Chili Cookoff" in 1974 when Carroll Shelby, one of the original organizers, trademarked the term; soon thereafter CASI adopted the title "International Chili Championship."

Terlingua hosts a second cook-off that also is held the first weekend of November: the Original Terlingua International Frank X. Tolbert–Wick Fowler Memorial Championship Chili Cookoff, which takes place four miles away from CASI's cook-off. It is held "behind the store," referring to Terlingua's single provisioning emporium. The event is named for two of CASI's original founders, who split off to form their own organization in 1983. "The Cookoff," as it is commonly known, celebrates authentic Texas chili.

Although Shelby grabbed the right to use the title "World's Championship Chili Cookoff," he subsequently lost the fight to use the CASI trademark and logo, so he established the International Chili Society (ICS). The ICS cook-off is held annually during the first weekend of October, and entrants compete in divisions for traditional red chili and *chile verde*.

America's interest in cook-offs continues to grow. Perhaps it is because of the good-natured competitiveness of these contests; perhaps it is because of pride in events that celebrate favorite American dishes like barbecue and chili. Or possibly, it is because Americans simply love cooking and eating delicious food. Whatever the reason, the cook-off is a uniquely American institution that has become deeply ingrained in our social culture and foodways.

[*See also* Barbecue; Chili; Food Festivals; Pillsbury Bake-Off.]

BIBLIOGRAPHY

Barbecue America. http://www.barbecueamerica.com. This website provides an overview of barbecue and statistics related to *Barbecue America: The American Public Television Series*.

Mercuri, Becky. *Food Festival, U.S.A.: Red, White, and Blue Ribbon Recipes from All 50 States*. San Diego, CA: Laurel Glen, 2002.

Pillsbury Bake-Off. http://www.bakeoff.com. This website contains Pillsbury Bake-Off Contest history, registration information, and winning recipes.

Warnock, Kirby F. "Terlingua Chili Cookoff." *Big Bend Quarterly* (Fall 1998).

BECKY MERCURI

Cooking Manuscripts

Every person who cooks has a manuscript cookbook. It may not be a tidy copybook written in a fine Spenserian hand, as so many early American manuscripts were. Scribbles and indecipherable notes may decorate the pages. It could be a file folder stuffed full of clippings and handwritten recipes from friends. Or, in the early 2000s, the computer may be the family cookbook. Whatever the system, a cookbook is highly personal, revealing much of the cook's taste, family preferences, and skills, and it frequently opens a window on the life of the author.

In early America, female literacy was not a priority, so few written records by women are extant. But those books that survive, each one unique, say a great deal about the life of American women from the seventeenth century through the twenty-first.

Handwritten Cookbooks

Many British women emigrating to the New World brought along perhaps their most precious possession, a personal cookbook, often a wedding gift, almost certainly passed down through the family, with recipes frequently written in more than one hand. Some surviving manuscripts contain an interesting combination of English and American recipes that often require detective work in order to discover the provenance. Some eighteenth-century manuscripts at first glance appear to be English, but recipes for American ingredients, such as Indian meal and cranberries, give away their true origins.

Frequently the recipes share space with other enterprises, such as an account book of either household expenditures or a family business. Polly Lathrop, who lived in Saybrook and Norwich, Connecticut, from 1779 until 1817, kept meticulous accounts of her boardinghouse roomers ("Mr. Ezra L. Hommedieu came to bord [sic] October 10, 1804), as well as her income as a seamstress ("Maid [sic] a gingham frock for Mary 47 cents"). Hattie A. Sachs, the recording secretary of the National American Woman Suffrage Association, kept detailed minutes of the proceedings at the group's annual convention in Akron, Ohio, but only half of her notebook contains association business. On the back of almost every page are menus for elaborate dinners and more modest luncheons, along with many recipes, including sweet-and-sour fish, horseradish sauce, and maple parfaits.

Common Characteristics

Although each cookbook is an individual record of some aspects of a woman's life, many have characteristics in common. The manuscript is often anonymous: no date, no name, no town, simply a collection of kitchen wisdom compiled by a woman whose major priority was taking care of her family. These books have been well used, pages stained, brown with age and spilled food, some frayed at the edges. In the center of a worn copybook a child has scribbled a mysterious drawing. A neatly bound nineteenth-century volume includes a calendar from a farmer's almanac pasted inside the front cover. Handwritten comments are attached to some recipes: "Very nice," "Tried and didn't like it," "Add more milk."

These books reveal what was important to the housewife and her family. The vast majority of manuscripts, at least until the early 1900s, include medical information. Women, especially on the frontier, were often without benefit of what medical help existed at the time. It is no wonder that they collected numerous and often bizarre prescriptions for ailments ranging from mad dog bites to cures for cancer; new treatments for cholera and scarlet fever clipped from newspapers; and handwritten notations on cures for whooping cough, rattlesnake bites, indigestion, consumption, nausea, and a host of other ailments.

Appended to some is the brave declaration, "Never fails." Likewise, household hints abound: how to clean kid gloves, mend a black satin dress, make a yellow dye, deflea a pig, remove wine stains from a carpet, make liquid shoe blacking, mend broken china, bleach bed linens, banish bedbugs.

Because many women in the early days of the Republic were educated poorly, if at all, words were often spelled phonetically. Thus it is not uncommon to find "plumb pudding," "warfels," "cramburys," "linnen," "blomong (blanc mange)," and "flat-jacks."

Until the mid-twentieth century, directions are skimpy, if given at all, and measurements are far from accurate, usually requiring a teacup of this or a handful of that. A list of ingredients for a cake or cookies may omit flour entirely, since the experienced housewife supposedly knew that she must add a sufficient amount of flour to make a proper batter. Cooking times are rare, and the overwhelming number of recipes in early manuscripts are for sweets—candy, pie and cake, pudding and jelly—with far fewer directions for everyday meat and vegetables.

Tucked between the Pages

Manuscript cookbooks are full of surprises. Many display newspaper clippings pasted in, but not always of recipes. Poems, prayers, household hints, almanacs, and farm information abound, as well as scribbled recipes on torn sheets of note paper tucked into the pages, waiting to be properly entered at another time. Pressed flowers drop out; checks, knitting directions, letters, menus, grocery lists—the accumulation of a housewife's hours. A newspaper clipping of a poem, "To My Brother," tucked into the 1833 Pittsburgh copybook of Mrs. Boggs asks him to think of her in times of trouble, and is pasted beside a newspaper story about the battleship *Sumpter*. A poem, "On the Loss of a Child in Infancy," begins, "Our beauteous child we laid among the silence of the dead."

Sources

Fortunately, culinary historians, such as Karen Hess and Janet Theophano, have recognized the importance of these manuscripts and rescued many from oblivion, editing and publishing them to present a picture of the person and her time. In her edition of *Martha Washington's Booke of Cookery*, Hess not only provides recipes but also digs deeply into genealogical mysteries, giving us a rich picture of the Washington household. Many important manuscripts are available to scholars, housed in special collections in universities and historical societies. Those interested in family cookbooks should search the attic or garage for these tattered journals that were once considered of no value. Now they deserve a second look, an irretrievable part of America's history.

[*See also* Advertising Cookbooklets and Recipes; Cookbooks and Manuscripts; Homemade Remedies; Library Collections.]

BIBLIOGRAPHY

Many universities, historical societies, and libraries have excellent collections of manuscript cookbooks. Some of the most outstanding include the Joseph Downs Collection, Winterthur Library; the Esther B. Aresty Collection, University of Pennsylvania; Johnson Wales Culinary Archives Museum, Providence, Rhode Island; Old Sturbridge Village Library; New York Public Library; and Boston Public Library.

Hess, Karen. *Martha Washington's Booke of Cookery*. New York: Columbia University Press, 1981.

Theophano, Janet. *Eat My Words: Reading Women's Lives Through the Cookbooks They Wrote*. New York: Palgrave, 2002.

VIRGINIA K. BARTLETT

Cooking Schools

This entry includes two subentries:
Nineteenth Century
Twentieth Century

Nineteenth Century

Four different types of cooking schools emerged in America during the nineteenth century. The first was an expansion of the pastry lessons offered by experts during the eighteenth century. The shift between private lessons and public courses was made by Elizabeth Goodfellow, who opened a pastry shop in Philadelphia in 1808. She subsequently offered lessons, which turned into formal classes offered to the public, and thus established America's first cooking school. Goodfellow never published a cookbook, but her course of study is known through her students. One of her pupils, Eliza Leslie, collected Goodfellow's recipes and published them as *Seventy-Five Receipts for Pastry, Cakes, and Sweetmeats* (1828). After Goodfellow's death in 1851, the cookbook *Cookery as It Should Be* (1853) was compiled by an unidentified "pupil of Mrs. Goodfellow." Despite Leslie's complaints that many of the book's recipes had not come from Goodfellow, the cookbook went through at least four editions.

Celebrity Chef Cooking Schools

The second type of cooking school was a European import. Its proponent was Pierre Blot, a Frenchman who immigrated to the United States about 1855. Claiming to have been the editor of *Almanac Gastronomique* in Paris, he lectured on the culinary arts. In 1863 he published his first book, *What to Eat, and How to Cook It; Containing over One Thousand Receipts*. Two years later, he launched a cooking school called the Culinary School of Design and called himself the professor of gastronomy. Blot's second book, *Hand-Book of Practical Cookery*, first was published in 1867, and he followed it up with a series of articles on culinary topics in *Galaxy* magazine, which gave him great visibility. With the financial assistance of Commodore Vanderbilt's daughter, Blot opened the New York Cooking School, which was America's first French cooking school. It mainly catered to the wealthy and lasted only a few years, but

Cooking School Kitchen. The British traveler George Augustus Sala commented in the 1880s on the "schools of cookery for young ladies" that were springing up in American cities. From *America Revisited*, 3rd edition (London, 1883), vol. 1, p. 178.

the celebrity chef cooking school reemerged during the twentieth century.

Cooking Schools for Working-Class Women

In addition to offering classes for middle-class women who wanted to learn the latest cooking techniques, Juliet Corson also targeted unemployed working-class women, with the hope that after taking cookery courses they might find employment as domestics. Beginning in 1872, she began lecturing on cooking at charitable institutions in New York City. In November 1876 she launched the city's second New York Cooking School, which offered a series of twelve lessons. Based on her lectures, Corson wrote *The Cooking Manual of Practical Directions for Economical Every-Day Cookery* (1877) and *Cooking School Text Book and Housekeepers' Guide to Cookery and Kitchen Management: An Explanation of the Principles of Domestic Economy Taught in the New York Cooking School* (1879), which became the textbook for subsequent cooking schools. Her establishment was so successful that she received inquiries from many cities around the nation, including Philadelphia and Boston, on how to start and manage cooking schools.

In Philadelphia, the New Century Club invited Matilda Lees Dods, a graduate of the South Kensington Cooking School in London who had taught at the Culinary College in Edinburgh, to lecture on cooking. Her lectures were so successful that the New Century Club decided to open a cooking school. Elizabeth Devereaux agreed to teach courses, and one of her star pupils was Sarah Tyson Rorer. When Devereaux left in 1880 over a contract dispute, Rorer, who was a cousin of the school's founders, replaced her. The course of study consisted of twenty-four demonstration lectures. After three years of running the New Century Cooking School, Rorer left to establish the Philadelphia Cooking School, which flourished from 1882 until 1903. *Mrs. Rorer's Philadelphia Cook Book: A Manual of Home Economics* (1886) was largely based on her courses offered at the school.

Events similar to those in Philadelphia were underway in Boston. In 1878 the Boston Cooking School was launched under the auspices of the Women's Education Association. Maria Parloa was the first teacher. The program consisted of three private lessons and three group lessons each week. Twenty-four lessons constituted a course. One of Parloa's pupils was Mary J. Lincoln. When Parloa resigned from the school to write a book, Lincoln became the principal, a position she retained until 1885. Lincoln's books, the *Boston Cooking-School Cook Book* (1884) and *Boston School Kitchen Text-Book, Lessons in Cooking for the Use of Classes in Public and Industrial Schools* (1887), were used by other cooking schools and were cited extensively by leaders of the home economics movement.

One of Lincoln's students was Fannie Merritt Farmer, who became the assistant principal and later the principal when Lincoln left. Farmer's *Boston Cooking-School Cook Book* (1896), a revision of Lincoln's book, became one of the most popular cookbooks ever published in the United States. Graduates of the Boston Cooking School included Lucy Allen, Alice Bradley, and Janet McKenzie Hill, who also went on to become successful authors. Many graduates also contributed editorial columns to the *Boston Cooking School Magazine*. Farmer left the school and in 1902 opened Miss Farmer's School of Cookery, which survived her death in 1915 and continued until 1944.

Collegiate Programs and Schools

The final type of cooking school to emerge during the nineteenth century was based at colleges and universities. The interest in cooking schools also influenced college programs. These originally were intended to prepare women for life as homemakers and later were vocationally directed. The first known cookery program at a college was at Iowa Agricultural School at Ames (later Iowa State University); in 1876 the school offered a course in domestic economy, which included cooking. The teacher was Mary B. Welch, who convinced the college administration that the school should offer cookery courses. A kitchen was constructed and in 1878 Welch began teaching the course using Corson's *Cooking Manual* as a text. About this time, many other collegiate cooking programs were begun, including ones at Kansas State Agricultural College at Manhattan (later Kansas State University) and the Illinois Industrial University, which started a School of Domestic Science in 1878. Its course of study included dietetics, household science, chemical structure of bread making, and many other topics. Many graduates of these college programs taught in public schools, and many became leaders of the home economics movement in America.

[*See also* Boston Cooking School; Cookbooks and Manuscripts, *subentries* From the Beginnings to 1860 *and* From the Civil War to World War I; Farmer, Fannie; Home Economics; Leslie, Eliza; Lincoln, Mrs.; Parloa, Maria; Rorer, Sarah Tyson.]

BIBLIOGRAPHY

Longone, Jan. "Professor Blot and the First French Cooking School in New York." *Gastronomica* (Spring 2001): 65–70 and (Summer 2001): 53–59.

Rorer, Sarah Tyson. "Early Dietetics." In *Essays on History of Nutrition and Dietetics*, compiled by Adelia M. Beeuwkes, E. Neige Todhunter, and Emma Seifrit Weigley. Chicago: American Dietetic Association, 1967.

Shapiro, Laura. *Perfection Salad: Women and Cooking at the Turn of the Century*. New York: Holt, 1987.

Shircliffe, Arnold. "American Schools of Cookery." In *Essays on History of Nutrition and Dietetics*, compiled by Adelia M. Beeuwkes, E. Neige Todhunter, and Emma Seifrit Weigley. Chicago: American Dietetic Association, 1967.

Weaver, William Woys. "Mrs. Goodfellow." In *Encyclopedia of Food and Culture*, edited by Solomon H. Katz. 3 vols. New York: Scribner, 2003.

Weigley, Emma Seifrit. *Sarah Tyson Rorer: The Nation's Instructress in Dietetics and Cookery*. Philadelphia: American Philosophical Society, 1977.

ANDREW F. SMITH

Cooking Instruction. Class at the Institute of Culinary Education, New York. *Courtesy of the Institute of Culinary Education*

Twentieth Century

In the first half of the twentieth century, cooking schools for housewives and their domestics continued in much the same vein as nineteenth-century schools. But at the mid-century point, cooking schools changed fundamentally as the market for cookery instruction expanded into three new territories. First was the truly revolutionary emergence of vocational schools for training cooks for professional kitchens. Second, hobbyist-cooks who wanted more than the basics began exploring an astonishing diversity of culinary instruction that went beyond the Anglo-French techniques and nutritional knowledge that had marked so much of late-nineteenth-century cooking schools. Third, celebrity chef demonstrations and cooking-school vacations became a new form of entertainment for affluent, curious cooks.

Vocational Instruction

Prior to 1946, no one in America went to school to learn to be a restaurant chef. What little culinary training existed in America through the first half of the twentieth century was either conducted haphazardly on the job, which accounted for the vast majority of native cooks and bakers, or given in a rarefied, academic context. The latter instruction, such as the Cornell University Department (now School) of Hotel Administration, was designed to give budding hospitality executives a passing familiarity with cookery that would enable them to supervise, rather than actually toil in, professional kitchens.

This lack of American cooking schools was meaningless, given most Americans' view of cooking as a vocation. In the nineteenth and early twentieth centuries, at least at the more elegant establishments, kitchens were staffed by European men trained through arduous apprenticeship, a course of practical education, governed by contract, which for centuries had been the way that culinary knowledge was transmitted. Although a few apprenticeships could be found in America, complaints were rife that Americans generally would not submit to the grueling, hierarchical training. Low-level cooking jobs might be held by undereducated American workers, but Americans saw cooking as a low-status vocation, falling somewhere between manual labor and a trade, or as something uniquely appropriate to foreigners (especially the French and the Germans).

The emergence of culinary trade unions, such as the International Hotel Workers Union, founded in 1911, planted the first seeds of formal culinary education on American soil. Touting cooking as a "profession" rather than as mere "slavish drudgery," such culinary activists as Joseph Dommers Vehling (a German immigrant and a product of several European apprenticeships) stressed the need to educate cooks formally. Unions offered enrichment cooking classes to their members (many of whom continued to be immigrant workers) as early as the 1910s, and union newspapers were littered with testimonials from cooks about the classes' value. The downside was that the classes were sporadic, without overarching curricula, and one needed to be a working cook and union member to take advantage of these opportunities: they were not an entry path to professional cooking.

The issue of training professional cooks heated up during Prohibition, as the economics of running restaurant kitchens without the lubricant of alcoholic beverage profits brought increasing attention to a chef's managerial as well as culinary talents. The American Culinary Federation, founded in 1929 for the purpose of advancing the culinary profession, urged the adoption of an apprenticeship system, ideally one that would "sandwich" hands-on experience with theoretical classroom instruction. The Great Depression and World War II intervened, moving culinary education to the back burner.

One consequence of World War II was the opening in 1946 of the first American cooking school for professionals. The New Haven Restaurant Institute in Connecticut benefited from the GI Bill's education boom for returning veterans and also encompassed modern concepts: first, that postsecondary education should be widely available; second, that culinary workers needed theory and management training in addition to hands-on cooking; and third, that vocational cooking could be a respectable, middle-class career path. Later known as the Culinary Institute of America (CIA), the school relocated to an impressive campus in Hyde Park, New York, in 1970. The CIA became the first degree-granting culinary institution, awarding associate's degrees in occupational studies and applied science; since 1993, it has awarded four-year baccalaureates in professional studies, with students majoring in either culinary or pastry arts management. For the first decade, these bachelor's degrees were valuable only in the culinary world, because accrediting agencies did not recognize the credits as transferable to more traditional academic pursuits. This situation changed in 2002, when the CIA was granted initial academic accreditation by the Middle States Association and Commission on Higher Education. Generally considered the preeminent, and certainly the pioneer, professional cooking school in America, the CIA faced plenty of competition by 2003, with nearly five hundred American programs in different aspects of the hospitality industry. Many programs copy significant parts of the CIA curriculum or use its frequently revised textbook, *The Professional Chef*. So great is the CIA's cachet with the general public that passionate amateurs devour its home cook's version, *Cooking Secrets of the CIA*.

The training of cooks for professional kitchens is constantly evolving and reflects changing attitudes. Some culinary associations support structured apprenticeships

in lieu of, or in addition to, classroom study. Some schools have expanded their offerings to include separate programs for cookery, pastry, and baking, and for business-oriented management skills, maintaining a more traditional distinction between the front of the house and the kitchen. These management programs compress the college and university studies forged at places such as Cornell into short, bare-bones instruction for small-business owners and budding restaurateurs who may not have the luxury of spending four years pursuing a bachelor's degree. Most interesting of all is the language chosen to describe culinary training programs: many call themselves "vocational," whereas others employ the more prestigious label of "professional" or "career." Some of the vocational programs involve secondary school instruction that supplants college preparatory classes, perpetuating the more traditional view of cooking for money as a trade. In the early twenty-first century, tuition costs at many private postsecondary culinary schools exceeded $25,000; those institutions marketed their training as "professional." This nomenclature chasm illustrates the centuries-old debate about the precise status of cookery—art, science, craft, or labor.

Finally, the study of cookery has entered academia at Boston University in its graduate-level master of liberal arts in gastronomy and at New York University in its Department of Nutrition, Food Studies, and Public Health, which awards bachelor's and graduate degrees. Although neither program is designed to train restaurant cooks, both programs take an interdisciplinary approach to the study of food in society that includes fine cookery and related topics.

Recreational Cooking Classes

Whether as adult education adjuncts to secondary schools and colleges, private schools set up to teach cooking exclusively, or add-ons to restaurant and hotel kitchens, cooking classes reached unprecedented cadres of eager students in the second half of the twentieth century. The catalyst was television, with such luminaries as James Beard and Julia Child, who popularized "cooking as fun" to the increasingly affluent, post–World War II generation. Hobbyist-cooks seeking ways of perfecting their craft could turn to a burgeoning assortment of cooking programs. A lucky few attended Beard's own cooking school, operated out of his townhouse in Greenwich Village in New York City from 1955 through the mid-1980s; others studied *Theory and Practice of Good Cooking* (1977) by Beard, which breaks down each of the major cooking techniques into easily

Cooking School. Class at Institute of Culinary Education, New York. *Courtesy of the Institue of Culinary Education*

understandable lessons, a model that continues to be emulated by many amateur programs designed to turn their students into confident, recipeless cooks.

The exploding number of worldwide venues for cookery instruction is cataloged in *The Guide to Cooking Schools*, published annually by Shaw Associates since 1988. The Shaw guide covers both professional and hobbyist programs, describing class sizes, faculty credentials, kitchen facilities, tuition costs, and curricular offerings. Thousands of classes at hundreds of schools are available in the United States, including basic "how to boil water" instruction; specialty instruction in esoterica, such as sushi-rolling or sugar work for ambitious home cake decorators; special classes for children; and even shadow versions of professional curricula, in which aspiring chefs are outfitted in starched whites to master the arcane and difficult art of turning

vegetables. Recreational schools report that, at least in affluent urban areas, hobbyist classes seemed immune to the economic fluctuations of the late twentieth and early twenty-first centuries, with food-obsessed amateurs trying to develop skills to emulate celebrity chefs, either for the joy of cooking or as an alternative to steep restaurant checks.

Cooking as entertainment has led to a resurgence of the celebrity chef instruction pioneered by Pierre Blot. Some of the country's most prestigious chefs travel widely to lecture and demonstrate their signature dishes to packed audiences. A typical but by no means unique example is the teaching kitchen De Gustibus, located in Macy's Department Store in Manhattan, New York City. Since its founding in 1983, De Gustibus has hosted many of the prominent names in the food world, both American and foreign.

Another take on celebrity chef instruction is quite exclusive: the opportunity for amateurs to apprentice in preeminent restaurant kitchens, working at simpler stations and absorbing firsthand the balletic operations of the professional kitchen. Among the restaurants that have opened their doors (the students pay richly, albeit sometimes to charities, for the privilege) are Charlie Trotter's in Chicago and Le Bernardin in New York City.

Finally, culinary instruction can be the centerpiece of a vacation. Depending on their palates, tony Americans flock to the Napa Valley in California, quaint villages in Tuscany or the South of France, exotic Bangkok, or other pleasing destinations to absorb cookery and local culinary culture. The Disney Institute of Walt Disney World used to offer adult recreational cooking classes; these classes have morphed into a profitable, two-year career program in Orlando, Florida, under the aegis of Valencia Community College. Disney still teaches the Mickey Mouse set, however, with fruit kabobs assembled by four-year-old Escoffiers.

[See also Beard, James; Child, Julia; Cooking Techniques; French Influences on American Food.]

BIBLIOGRAPHY

"Focus on Culinary Education." *National Culinary Review* (June 1998): 21–28. A collection of essays.
The Guide to Cooking Schools. Coral Gables, FL: Shaw Associates, 1988. Published annually, covering vocational and avocational cooking schools.
Klein, Camille. *The Professional Cook: His Training, Duties, and Rewards.* New York: Helios Books, 1965.
Scotto, Charles. "What to Do about Apprentices for Our American Kitchens? Reviewing the Various Methods Followed to Assure Trained and Efficient Future Workers." *Hotel Bulletin and Nation's Chefs* 46 (June 1931): 543–544.
Trubek, Amy. *Haute Cuisine: How the French Invented the Culinary Profession.* Philadelphia: University of Pennsylvania Press, 2000.

CATHY K. KAUFMAN

Cooking Techniques

The ability to control fire may date to 500,000 B.C.E. No one knows exactly when, where, how, and why humans concluded that cooked foods were worth the effort of building a fire, waiting for the food to be done, and suffering the periodic losses when foods accidentally were burned beyond the point of being edible or a fire raged out of control. What seems probable is that fire discouraged predators and scavengers from competing for the kills and that humans learned that heating coarse foods, such as game, tubers, fibrous vegetables, and grains, made the foods easier to chew. People in prehistoric times most likely came to believe that cooked foods were tastier, and from this cultural conclusion, fine cookery evolved.

Despite the advantages, cooking was viewed warily. Mythology holds that Prometheus introduced cookery to the Greeks through theft and deception, and even the French word for cookery, *la cuisine*, has the idiomatic meaning "underhanded trick" or "subterfuge." Sages dispute whether virtuosic cookery civilizes or encourages barbaric overindulgence. America, with its Puritan heritage, has been particularly suspicious of cookery. According to the early-twentieth-century physician and advocate of raw food, Julian Thomas: "The principal good effect of cooking is to produce abnormal, stimulating flavors. Occasionally this principle may be used to good effect, although it is not desirable to eat for flavor in place of nutriment."

The Choice of Technique

Notwithstanding Thomas's cautionary advice about abnormal stimulation, most cookery has two simple goals: to control the temperature and to control the moisture content of foods to attain a desired result. Before considering the equipment and technique to be used, the cook must assess the characteristics of the raw ingredients. Only then can the cook decide, first, whether to use wet or dry heat and, second, whether to apply that heat directly (by submersion in a liquid or by contact with a heat-conducting metal) or indirectly (by contact with heated air). The answers dictate the cooking technique.

The basic wet-heat cooking methods are boiling—with its variations, stewing and poaching—and steaming. The basic dry techniques are roasting, baking, grilling (and its cousin, broiling), and panfrying or sautéing, the French term widely adopted in American cookbooks since the late nineteenth century for shallow frying. Although it may seem counterintuitive, deep-frying, in which food is submerged in fat, is a dry technique; wet techniques require a water-based liquid. Many dishes combine two or more techniques sequentially, such as sautéing meat before stewing it. Techniques occasionally are merged, such as cooking a custard in a water bath, which is a baking-poaching hybrid method.

In all wet-heat techniques and in the dry techniques of grilling, sautéing, and deep-frying, heat is directly transferred to the food through the cooking liquid or the pan in which the food is placed. Roasting, baking, and steaming entail indirect heat; that is, hot air circulating around the food is the cooking medium. The difference between direct and indirect (also called radiant) heat is the difference between reaching into a 425°F oven to remove a baked dish and reaching into a pot of 212°F water to check a strand of spaghetti. The brief exposure to the hot air in the oven does not cause a burn, although touching the heated baking dish does. The boiling water, however, although only half as hot as the air, burns immediately. The lesson is that air, especially dry air, transfers energy less efficiently than does water. When fuel is expensive or labor intensive to obtain, roasting and baking are comparatively luxurious techniques. Relative fuel costs influenced colonial diets: frugal homemakers most likely did not bake every day and sometimes used communal ovens, but each had a bubbling pottage.

The second pillar of cookery, controlling the moisture content of food, is manipulated by chemical catalysts, such as salt and sugar, or by what the Catharine E. Beecher and Harriet Beecher Stowe called, in *The American Woman's Home* (1869), "the philosophy of the application of heat." Salt and sugar extract moisture from foods. By altering the water content of foods, these hygroscopic agents traditionally have been used to preserve meat, fish, fruits, and vegetables and to transform the texture of foods. Depending on the amount and length of exposure to salt and sugar, and on the inherent characteristics of the foodstuff, the cook can break down tissue into a saucy mush (for example, sugaring and straining berries) or can dehydrate and firm the tissue (for example, salting and hanging a ham).

The philosophy of the application of heat concerns the intensity and rapidity with which the heat is applied and is the cook's single most powerful method for adjusting the finished texture of foods, especially animal proteins. When a cube of meat is dropped into water at a full boil, the meat fibers shorten visibly, forcing out juices. The resulting meat seems tough and dry, even though it is cooked in liquid. Placed in cool water and slowly brought up to a simmer (defined as lazy bubbles meandering to the surface), that same cube shrinks less and retains more moisture. The principle applies equally to dry heat: slow (that is, relatively cool) roasting or baking results in less shrinkage and greater juiciness.

For centuries cooks manipulated wet, dry, direct, and indirect heat using equipment that had changed little since the introduction of chimneys in medieval Europe. In the nineteenth and early twentieth centuries, changes in kitchen equipment eased much of the physical labor of hearth cookery, use of coal and wood stoves, and primitive

Sautéing. Sautéing at the Institute of Culinary Education, New York. *Courtesy of the Institue of Culinary Education*

refrigeration. The cooking techniques themselves, however, changed little, notwithstanding the addition of electric clocks, thermometers, calibrated ovens, and standardized measuring cups that took the place of years of cooking experience. What did change was the language of cookery. As the Inuits have dozens of words for snow, each identifying slightly different qualities, from the mid-nineteenth through the mid-twentieth centuries, increasingly specific terms came to identify minor variations in basic techniques. This linguistic evolution has been uneven at best, stymied by cooks who have the luxury of using language carelessly because they understand the result they are seeking. Moreover, eighteenth- and nineteenth-century cooks ascribed different meanings to certain terms. In the third edition of *Miss Beecher's Domestic Receipt Book* (1858), Catharine Beecher confounds contemporary readers with her recipes for "poached" eggs that are now called a "scramble," and "boiled" eggs that are now deemed a "poach." Even with later recipes, astute reading between the lines clarifies all but the most pedantic instructions. For historical recipes, interpretation is essential.

The Wet-Heat Techniques

In American cookbooks and manuscripts from the seventeenth century through much of the nineteenth century, the term used most frequently to describe any wet-heat method was "boiling." Whether in a cauldron suspended over a roaring fire, in a Dutch oven nestled in the hearth embers or an oven chamber, or in a pot set on top of a coal-fired stove, the resulting dish usually was categorized a boil. "Boil" did not have the contemporary cook's understanding of water volcanically erupting at 212°F. An illustration in Beecher's *Domestic Receipt Book* differentiates the degrees of "boiling":

> In boiling meats, it is important to keep the water constantly boiling, otherwise the meat will soak up the water. . . . Be sure not to let the fire get hot, so as to make a hard boiling, especially at first. The more gently meat boils the more tender it is, and the more perfectly the savory portion is developed and retained.

Beecher's instruction to keep the water boiling but not to make a "hard boiling" makes sense in light of the knowledge that cooks in Beecher's time used wood- or coal-fired stoves. These stoves needed regular stoking to produce heat, as opposed to the simple turn of a dial required for use of a gas or electric range. In *The Cook's Own Book* (1832), N. K. M. Lee differentiated fast and slow boils and debated the merits of starting foods in cold, tepid, or boiling water. In *The Kentucky Housewife* (1839), Lettice Bryan noted that "the precise length of time that is required to cook it [fish] tender depends greatly . . . on the quantity of heat that is applied to it." These and myriad other details hidden within recipes, such as placing sealed vessels in the hearth's embers, adjusting the distance of the vessel from the fire, varying the amount of liquid to be used, and even the instruction to cook slowly, indicate that boiling encompassed a range of techniques, from the gentlest poaching through moderate simmering to rapid boiling.

Stewed dishes were particularly prevalent. Simple pottages were a staple among working classes and on isolated farms, because these dishes were easy to execute and entailed efficient use of fuel. More affluent and urbane tables from the seventeenth through nineteenth centuries served more elaborate stewed dishes under the names "ragoo," "fricassee," and the ubiquitous "beef à la mode." Hannah Glasse's recipe Ragoo of Lamb in *The Art of Cookery* (1805) calls for stewing a browned and larded forequarter of lamb in broth; separately browning oysters; adding the cooking liquid from the lamb to the oysters; and then, after a few more adjustments, pouring the oyster mixture over the lamb as a sauce. In Bryan's typical recipe for beef à la mode, the beef was stuffed with forcemeat, surrounded by vegetables, simmered, skimmed, and then "baked" in the pot liquor with additional seasonings and served hot or cold with the jelled gravy. Fricassees, often made with fowl or rabbit, were popular, affordable variations on basic stews. Regional and ethnic preferences varied. The meats were sautéed after stewing and garnished with meatballs in the North. In the South meat was served with a cream sauce made from the cooking liquid and with dumplings. *The Boston Cooking-School Cook Book* (1896) by Fannie Farmer helped popularize a French cookery term for this long-established technique—braising—which Farmer defined as "stewing and baking (meat) . . . in an oven at low uniform temperature for a long time." Although the term had appeared sporadically in a few cookbooks in the mid-nineteenth century, Farmer brought it into common jargon. "Braising" evolved into a favored term on restaurant menus in the late twentieth century.

A significant difference between Farmer's braises and those of succeeding generations was that Farmer was

Chopping Vegetables. At work at the Institute of Culinary Education, New York. *Courtesy of the Institue of Culinary Education*

writing for housewives toiling with wood- or coal-fired stoves that required careful manipulation of dampers and regular stoking to maintain the recommended "low uniform temperature for a long time." With the introduction of thermostatically controlled electric and gas stoves in the early twentieth century, homemakers, increasing numbers of whom had no servants, could prepare stews simply by flicking a switch. In *Good Meals and How to Prepare Them* (1927) writers at the Good Housekeeping Institute streamlined the braising process by recommending braising in a casserole dish rather than a baking pan, a procedure that "saves washing an extra pan and is an attractive method of serving." This method required "little attention" of the cook. By the late twentieth century, braised dishes were praised for their simplicity and rustic, falling-off-the-bone tenderness. Although styles and effort have changed, both the elegant eighteenth-century ragoo and the twenty-first century stew are made by the same technique.

Steaming, cooking in trapped water vapor, was an identified technique by the 1850s, when a potato steamer was considered an essential tool. Tightly lidded baskets with perforated bottoms straddled saucepans and captured the rising steam from saucepans boiling atop the iron cookstoves that were rapidly dominating kitchens. By the early twentieth century, nutritionists and home economists were recommending steaming all vegetables to preserve the newly discovered vitamins, many of which are water soluble. The technique is regularly used by the health conscious, notwithstanding research findings that the nutritional differences between boiling and steaming are small.

Poaching, in which foods are completely submerged in relatively cool cooking liquid, largely has lost favor with home cooks except as a method for preparing eggs. There are two reasons for the fading popularity of poaching. First, poached items tend to be bland and require a separately made sauce to make them interesting. Second, although poaching is particularly well suited to fragile foods, especially whole fish, that require gentle handling, a special pan is needed. During the nineteenth century, every well-equipped kitchen had a "fish kettle," an oblong pan with a removable, perforated insert that cradled a side of salmon or whole carp and facilitated removal of the cooked fish. The whole fish was presented intact on middle- and upper-class tables. With changing service styles, such presentations declined and have been relegated to banquets.

The Dry-Heat Techniques

Contrary to their use of the generic term "boiling," which covered a spectrum of related techniques that could be accomplished with different equipment, the earliest colonists unambiguously differentiated roasting, baking, and broiling (what later cooks called "grilling"). This linguistic precision probably derived from the facts that each technique had specific equipment and that the techniques were not interchangeable. As kitchen technology changed, rather than abandon the vocabulary, Americans changed their definitions of these terms.

Most striking is roasting. Any animal roasted in 1650 most likely was cooked by a process very different from one roasted in 1950. The former was mounted on a turning spit in front of an open hearth, which often had a reflector oven to capture heat that would otherwise escape. These roasts developed a crackling crust encouraged by a last-minute dusting with flour, and a dripping pan was set beneath the meat to catch the juices for a light gravy. Later the roast is cooked inside a tightly closed oven, bathed in steam. Mary Randolph's famous complaint in *The Virginia Housewife* (1824) that "no meat can be well roasted, except on a spit turned by a jack, and before a steady, clear fire—other methods are no better than baking" was regularly paraphrased through the nineteenth century, while hearth roasting was a living memory. The anonymous author of *The American Home Cook Book* (1854) was even more vitriolic, complaining that, "*roasting*, in most families these days, has degenerated into baking." By the turn of the twentieth century, as the flavor of the hearth faded, fewer and fewer cooks bristled at the notion of "oven roasting." Twentieth-century idiom dictates that one "roast" a chicken but "bake" a cake, even though both dishes may be placed in the same oven, set at the same temperature, for the same amount of time.

The aesthetics of the roast changed as well. In the seventeenth, eighteenth, and early nineteenth centuries cooks such as Lettice Bryan preferred a "delicate brown" roast and offered instructions for preventing the meat from becoming "too brown." By the later nineteenth century, Americans had developed a taste for increasingly darker-crusted meats that has culminated in the late twentieth-century idolization of rich mahogany and even a bit of char. These browner roasts are more flavorful than their paler counterparts, as the result of the complicated chemical alteration of the proteins and carbohydrates in meats known as the Maillard reaction. This preference for darker-crusted meats may compensate for the presumed blandness of industrially produced meats.

Cooks immediately recognized the inferiority of oven roasting. "A lady," the author of *The Housekeeper's Book* (1837), complained that "the inventors of cast-iron kitchens seem to me to have every other object in view but that of promoting good cooking." Almost from the introduction of stoves, cooks searched for ways to simulate the dry, indirect heat of hearth roasting in moisture-trapping stoves that generally did not get as hot as an open hearth. By the 1920s, the Good Housekeeping Institute recommended setting calibrated ovens at 500°F to 550°F to begin the roasting process and then reducing the heat after the initial cooking. Although it remains popular in some quarters, the high-heat technique tends to spatter fat and generate smoke, reminiscent of poorly executed hearth cookery, and some chefs dispute the need for high heat. Cooks may begin oven roasting with preliminary searing of the meat or poultry in a frying pan, the intense, direct heat promoting fast browning, and then transfer the seared item to the oven to finish baking in gentler heat. Another technique used by oven roasters since the late nineteenth century is periodically turning the meat while it cooks in the oven. This procedure redistributes internal juices and promotes uniform browning, as if the meat were on a spit.

The final effort to re-create hearth roasting in technologically modern kitchens (apart from the few cookbooks that advocate fireplace cookery) came in the late 1980s with the introduction of convection ovens to upper-middle-class kitchens. The ovens contain a fan that circulates air, mimicking some of the air currents of hearth roasting, although steam does build up in the oven chamber. Convection ovens are spreading as the price of the technology has decreased. These ovens promote slightly faster cooking and deeper browning than conventional, radiant ovens.

Grilling and broiling were important parts of hearth cookery that have been modified only slightly with the introduction of modern stoves. Early cookbooks abound with descriptions for rubbing the gridiron with a bit of fat and heating it before the open fire before adding thin, naturally tender cuts of meat for a quick "broil." Grill pans thoroughly heated on a stovetop, regardless of the type of fuel, can attain similar results. Modern home ovens often contain "broilers," that is, open gas flames or infrared heating units designed for cooking meats placed immediately

Cooking Meat. Grilling meat at the Institute of Culinary Education, New York. *Courtesy of the Institue of Culinary Education*

beneath the heat source. These "broilers" rely on indirect heat for cooking the meat, unlike the direct heat of the gridiron or grill pan, and generally do not provide the intensity of heat needed for successful broiling.

The most important change in frying and sautéing since colonial times has been an increase in safety as equipment has evolved. Long-handled pans set on trivets or made with stubby legs to allow a pan to heat over coals were awkward to handle, especially by women in long dresses. (Much like the long-sleeved chefs' jackets worn in stifling kitchens to protect cooks' arms from spattering grease, heavy woolen skirts were essential because they were slower to catch fire with the precarious moving of frying pans around open hearths.) More compact saucepans set on sturdy cooktops minimize the risk of fat spills, and thermometers warn inattentive cooks when fat is dangerously overheating.

Lost Cookery Techniques

As modern conveniences have changed kitchens, a few techniques that once were common are no longer practiced at home except by the most nostalgic and dedicated cooks. These techniques include salting, corning (brining), smoking, canning, preserving, potting, and pickling, and all fell into disuse with widespread distribution of the refrigerator. Most of these techniques rely in part on the hygroscopic properties of salt and sugar: by pulling water from animal and plant products, the process retards bacterial growth and spoilage. Other techniques exclude air, an essential nutrient for most bacteria, or entail high temperatures or changes in the pH of foods for killing or immobilizing contaminants.

Changes in raw ingredients and dietary guidelines account for the loss of other techniques. Through the early twentieth century larding, whereby meat is pierced with strips of fat before roasting or braising, was relatively common for lean meats, particularly beef, and tough game birds. Larding added succulence. As techniques of animal husbandry changed, so that cattle received less exercise and developed more flab and quail was bred in captivity rather than captured in the wild, the use of larding declined. In the fat-phobic atmosphere of the late twentieth and early twenty-first centuries, animals, especially hogs, are deliberately bred for leanness, and it is almost impossible to find a butcher or cook conversant with larding. Barding is a related technique by which a piece of lean meat is covered with thin leaves of fat to add flavor and richness. Much of this fat melts in the roasting or baking process, and it, too, is disappearing, although rare dietary splurges of wrapping meat in bacon or pancetta still occur.

Indigenous Techniques

Most culinary techniques used in later-day America were imported with colonial and immigrant groups. One highly popular technique, barbecuing, is traceable to the earliest colonists' encounters with indigenous, pre-metallurgical cultures. The term derives from *barbacoa*, the word used by the Taino of Haiti to describe an apparatus of sticks straddling a pit fire used to roast, grill, and smoke foods. Early colonists found this basic dry, indirect-heat method sufficiently distinctive to adopt the term "barbecue," which appears in American sources by the mid-seventeenth century. Soon the term referred to outdoor social gatherings as well as to the specific cooking technique. Lettice Bryan's *The Kentucky Housewife* has an early barbecue recipe, distinguished from other slow-grilling techniques by a preparatory salt-and-molasses rub and finished with a squeeze of fresh lemon, melted butter, wine, and bread sauce. Barbecuing has cult status as America's culinary pastime. Cooks are aided by implements such as kettle smokers and outdoor gas grills that make "barbecuing" a catchall term for most outdoor cookery.

Another indigenous variation on roasting and baking is plank cookery, in which fish, frequently shad or salmon, shellfish, or fowl, is affixed to a hardwood board. The loaded board is then held before an open fire or placed in an oven for cooking, and the foodstuff absorbs a bit of the board's woody flavor. Cookery authors as disparate as Eliza Leslie, in her *New Cookery Book* (1857), and Fannie Farmer, in her *Boston Cooking-School Cook Book* (1896), enthusiastically recommended planking.

Another "American" technique is microwaving, which rapidly cooks foods by agitating a food's internal water molecules to create heat. Invented in Massachusetts during World War II, microwaving is cookery divorced from the cook's judgment. Pop food into the oven chamber, push a few buttons indicating the number of portions and whether the food is raw or merely a reheat, and the machine calculates the rest, turning itself off and beeping cheerfully when the task is done. Microwaves excellently mimic steaming and poaching in record time, and reheating prepared foods in the microwave seems almost indispensable for people eating alone, whether single householders or latchkey children.

Cooking without Heat

Some cookery requires no heat at all, such as certain cures and pickles. Other processes take advantage of climate variations, such as sun drying, or mechanical reactions, such as whipping cream or emulsifying eggs, oil, and vinegar into mayonnaise.

Health food advocates have periodically recommended a diet of raw foods, and no other culinary preparation in America has been so zealously promoted as the key to longevity and marital bliss, as it theoretically freed women from extended kitchen drudgery. Fruit and vegetable salads predominate, although raw meats such as steak tartare also appear. Unbaked breads and cakes are made from an amalgam of dried fruits, ground nuts, and cereal held together by oil or honey and then allowed to dry in the sun or dehydrate in a carefully moderated oven. Juicing, blending, marinating, and sprouting also are techniques of raw cuisine. In the early phase of the movement, advocates of raw food emphasized utter simplicity in eating, limiting the foods at any one meal to two or three main ingredients, and in eliminating dangerous ingredients, such as vinegar and alcohol, both considered poisons by the most extreme practitioners.

Unfired or living foods (the terms preferred to "raw" by adherents) have evolved considerably in both the scientific claims made and the sophistication and complexity of the cuisine. Although dehydration is permitted, temperatures are not supposed to exceed 118°F, the point at which the natural enzymes in the food are believed to be impaired and, thus, less digestible. Unlike their predecessors, twenty-first-century practitioners of a raw-food lifestyle welcome wine, because wine never exceeds 118°F during processing.

[*See also* Barbecue; Hearth Cookery; Kitchens; Meat; Microwave Ovens; Refrigerators; Stoves and Ovens; Turnspit Dogs.]

BIBLIOGRAPHY

American Home Cook Book. New York: Garrett, 1854. Facsimile, Whitstable, UK: Pryor Publications, 2000.

Beard, James. *James Beard's Theory and Practice of Good Cooking*. New York: Knopf, 1977.

Beecher, Catharine E. *Miss Beecher's Domestic Receipt Book*. 3rd ed. New York: Harper, 1858. Facsimile, New York: Dover, 2001.

Beecher, Catharine E., and Harriet Beecher Stowe. *The American Woman's Home*. New York: Ford, 1869.

Blot, Pierre. *Hand-Book of Practical Cookery*. New York: Appleton, 1869. Facsimile, New York: Arno, 1973.

Bryan, Lettice. *The Kentucky Housewife*. Bedford, MA: Applewood Books, 2000. The original edition was published in 1839.

Carson, Jane. *Colonial Virginia Cookery*. Charlottesville: University of Virginia, Colonial Research Studies, 1968.

Christian, Eugene, and Mollie Griswald Christian. *Uncooked Foods and How to Use Them: A Treatise on How to Get the Highest Form of Animal Energy from Food*. 5th ed. New York: Health-Culture, 1904.

Colicchio, Tom. *Think Like a Chef*. New York: Clarkson Potter, 2000.

Corriher, Shirley O. "Does Cooking Boost or Bust Nutrients in Vegetables?" *Fine Cooking*: 57 (April-May 2003) 26–27.

Culinary Institute of America. *The Professional Chef*. 7th ed. New York: Wiley, 2002.

Farmer, Fannie Merritt. *The Boston Cooking-School Cook Book*. Cambridge, MA: University Press, 1896.

Henderson, Mary F. *Practical Cooking and Dinner Giving*. New York: Harper, 1877.

Housekeeper's Book. Philadelphia: Marshall, 1837.

Kamman, Madeleine. *The New Making of a Cook: The Art, Techniques, and Science of Good Cooking*. New York: Morrow, 1997.

Lee, N. K. M. *The Cook's Own Book, Being a Complete Culinary Encyclopedia*. Boston: Munroe and Francis, 1832. Facsimile, New York: Arno, 1972.

McGee, Harold. *On Food and Cooking*. New York: Macmillan, 1984.

Perlès, Catherine. "Feeding Strategies in Prehistoric Times." In *Food: A Culinary History from Antiquity to the Present*, edited by Jean-Louis Flandrin and Massimo Montanari. English edition by Albert Sonnenfeld, translated by Clarissa Botsford et al. New York: Columbia University Press, 1999.

Plante, Ellen M. *The American Kitchen 1700 to the Present: From Hearth to Highrise*. New York: Facts on File, 1995.

Randolph, Mary. *The Virginia Housewife*. Washington, D.C.: Davis and Force, 1824. Facsimile with historical notes and commentaries by Karen Hess. Columbia: University of South Carolina Press, 1984).

Rombauer, Irma S., and Marion Rombauer. *The Joy of Cooking*. St. Louis, MO: Clayton, 1931.

Thomas, Julian P. *The Advantages of Raw Food*. New York: published by the author, 1905.

Trotter, Charlie, and Roxanne Klein. *Raw*. Berkeley: Ten Speed, 2003.

Verdon, Rene, and Mallorca, Jacqueline. *Convection Cuisine: Great Taste and Maximum Results from Your Convection Oven*. New York: Hearst, 1988.

CATHY K. KAUFMAN

Cookout, *see Historical Overview, subentry From World War II to the Early 1960s*

Cooperatives

Food cooperatives, or co-ops, have a long history of helping American consumers to improve the quality of their lives. They are nontraditionally structured businesses that are owned, democratically controlled, and operated to serve the needs of the consumers who use them. Members

Food Cooperative. Shoppers at Park Slope Food Coop, Brooklyn, New York. The cooperative was established in 1973. *Photograph by Joe Zarba*

invest limited capital in order to start or join the co-op. As members they share in the benefits or profits generated by the business. Co-ops differ from traditional corporations in that each shareholder has only one vote regardless of the number of shares owned. Although food co-ops in the United States differ widely in the philosophy, size, and services offered, they are generally socially and environmentally conscious organizations. More than 750 million people participate in cooperatives worldwide.

Cooperative buying groups or clubs, also known as pre-order co-ops, are usually informal nonprofit organizations made up of individuals and families who have come together to save money on groceries and gain greater control over the choice and quality of food available to them. Goods ranging from organic and natural foods to standard grocery items are purchased in bulk from wholesale suppliers or farmers and then are divided among co-op members. Members manage the ordering, buying, and distribution of goods. The number of buying clubs in the United States is large, far exceeding that of retail co-ops.

Retail consumer food cooperatives range from storefront natural food stores to multi-outlet supermarkets. Many storefront food co-ops began as buying clubs, which then expanded in response to membership growth and increased sales volumes.

Cooperative food warehouses or wholesales serve as the distribution component of the co-op system, supplying retail co-ops and buying clubs with goods and services, thus enabling them to combine their collective buying power. The warehouses generally offer a wide variety of natural and organic foods as well as other groceries.

Origins of the Cooperative Movement

The modern consumer cooperative originated in nineteenth-century Great Britain. It was a response to the depressed economic conditions brought about by the Industrial Revolution, which effectively did away with the prevailing rural agrarian way of life in England. The depression of the 1840s also caused widespread unemployment and crushing poverty, especially in many newly industrialized urban areas. Corrupt company stores controlled most of the food supply, selling contaminated food at inflated prices.

Cooperative businesses were seen as a solution to the desperate conditions of the time and many ventures were attempted. None, however, experienced any lasting success. In 1844, a group of twenty-eight unemployed craftspeople called the Rochdale Pioneers Equitable Society established a cooperative grocery store on Toad Lane in Rochdale, England. Influenced by the ideas of socioeconomic theorists such as Robert Owen and Dr. William King, the Pioneers codified a set of basic organizational principles for operating a cooperative business. Despite enormous odds, their enterprise proved extremely successful: by the 1860s, more than four hundred Rochdale-inspired cooperatives were operating across England. The Rochdale principles of cooperation spread rapidly to other industrial nations with similar success.

Food Cooperatives in the United States

Cooperative activity in America dates back to the days of the early colonists. In 1752, Benjamin Franklin organized the first successful cooperative in the United States, the Philadelphia Contributorship for the Insurance of Houses from Loss by Fire. During the nineteenth century, cooperative experiments such as the Grange were widespread, with the majority resulting in failure. Immigrants from Finland and Bohemia who were familiar with the Rochdale cooperative principles established the first successful American food cooperatives in the early twentieth century.

The economic hardships and food shortages of the Great Depression of the 1930s spurred a wave of food co-op organizing. Buying clubs provided a way for consumers to reduce high grocery costs by combining their money and buying food in bulk. The Federal Emergency Relief Administration also promoted buying clubs as a method of self-help. Consequently, food co-ops from this period are referred to as New Deal or old-wave co-ops. For the most part, the co-ops faded away as economic conditions improved. A small number of the Depression-era buying

Consumer Education. Notice board at Park Slope Food Coop, Brooklyn, New York. *Photograph by Joe Zarba*

clubs, however, expanded into large supermarkets, which were still operating successfully after more than fifty years.

The tumultuous political, social, and cultural forces of the late 1960s and 1970s brought renewed interest in food co-op experimentation. New-wave food co-ops assumed many forms, from buying clubs (also called food conspiracies) and storefronts to worker collectives and communes. Radically different in style and substance from its New Deal predecessor, the new-wave co-op provided an innovative forum for addressing many diverse countercultural issues such as alternative health and nutrition and political activism. Great value was placed on natural, organic, and unprocessed foods, many of which were sold in bulk—an unheard-of practice at the time. The co-ops also provided a vehicle to connect countercultural consumers with the producers of the locally or regionally produced foods they required. The ecology movement of the early 1970s further increased the market for the co-ops, as did the high food prices caused by inflation. Food co-ops also were established by government agencies such as Volunteers in Service to America to assist the urban poor. It is estimated that 5,000 to 10,000 food co-ops were established in the United States between 1969 and 1979. Poor business management caused the majority to fail eventually; however, approximately three hundred of the new-wave co-ops still live on with varying degrees of success.

Influence of the American Food Co-op Movement

The widespread practice of community support for sources of sustainably grown food and family farms and farmers' markets is firmly rooted in the co-op movement.

As such, the co-ops made a fundamental contribution to changing the American food system.

Further, by expanding Americans' awareness of the importance of unprocessed, whole, and organic food, the co-ops introduced a viable alternative to the products and experience of mainstream shopping. Food retailing also was changed as a result of the introduction of bulk foods made available for individual consumption. In addition, the food co-ops were pioneers in the areas of food labeling, consumer education, and environmentalism.

[*See also* Community-Supported Agriculture; Counterculture, Food; Farmers' Markets; Organic Food.]

BIBLIOGRAPHY

Belasco, Warren J. *Appetite for Change: How the Counterculture Took on the Food Industry.* Ithaca, NY: Cornell University Press, 1993.

The Co-op Handbook Collective. *The Food Co-op Handbook: How to Bypass Supermarkets to Control the Quality and Price of Your Food.* Boston: Houghton Mifflin, 1975.

Cox, Craig. *Storefront Revolution: Food Co-ops and the Counterculture.* New Brunswick, NJ: Rutgers University Press, 1994.

ELYSE FRIEDMAN

Coors Brewing Company

The Coors brewery was founded in 1873, just west of Denver, Colorado, by the twenty-six-year-old German immigrant Adolph Coors and his partner, Jacob Schueler. Coors invested $2,000 in the venture and Schueler added the remaining $18,000 needed to purchase the eleven acres where the brewery first was built. In 1880 Coors, the proud father of his first child, a daughter, bought out Schueler; brewing production had doubled by 1887, when Coors's children numbered six and the brewery was rolling out seven thousand barrels of beer a year.

When Coors had to borrow money in the late 1890s to cover debts and expenses, he vowed that once his debts were paid off, he would never borrow money again. This sense of self-reliance continued to permeate the organization long after his death. In the early 1900s Coors purchased a porcelain business, which kept the company afloat during Prohibition, when the brewery switched to malted milk and near beer. In 1959, while the company was still a regional brewery, Coors introduced the first all-aluminum two-piece beverage can. Reflecting the spirit of its founder, Coors launched a recycling program, offering a penny for every returned can.

Until the 1970s, Coors existed with just one product sold in eleven western states, but the company entered the twentieth-century marketing wars when it introduced Coors Light, "The Silver Bullet," in 1978. Three years later, in an attempt to take market share from the imported beer market segment, Coors introduced George Killian's line of products, which included Irish Red Lager, Irish Brown Ale, and Wilde' Honey Ale. This initiative was followed by the introduction of Coors Extra Gold (1985), Coors Arctic Ice, Coors Arctic Ice Light, and Coors Cutter (1991).

The growth of small breweries in the United States inspired Coors to introduce Winterfest, a specialty lager brewed in limited quantities for distribution during the holiday season. It became available nationally in 1987, after first being introduced in Colorado in 1986. In the mid-1990s Coors used its Sand Lot Brewery at Coors Field to produce the Blue Moon line to win over beer drinkers who had created a growing market for craft beers or microbrews. The Blue Moon products included Belgian White Ale, Honey Blonde Ale, Nut Brown Ale, Raspberry Cream Ale, and Harvest Pumpkin Ale. Coors's nationwide introduction in 1994 of Zima, a clear, carbonated alcoholic malt beverage, made news in the advertising industry, as it was one of the first of the nonbeer sparkling malt beverages to hit the U.S. market.

In 1990 Coors purchased its first brewery outside of Colorado, a Stroh Brewery Company plant in Memphis, Tennessee. In addition to its Denver headquarters and the Memphis brewery, Coors also has a brewery in Zaragoza, Spain, a packaging facility near Elkton, Virginia, and a Korean joint venture. It has about sixty-two hundred employees worldwide. The Coors family retains 100 percent of the company's voting stock, while 50 percent of the nonvoting stock is publicly traded.

[*See also* Beer; Brewing; Microbreweries.]

BIBLIOGRAPHY

Baron, Stanley. *Brewed in America: A History of Beer and Ale in the United States*. Boston: Little Brown, 1962.
Baum, Dan. *Citizen Coors: An American Dynasty*. New York: William Morrow, 2000.
LaFrance, Peter. *Beer Basics: A Quick and Easy Guide*. New York: J. Wiley, 1995.
Rhodes, Christine P., ed. *The Encyclopedia of Beer*. New York: Henry Holt, 1995.
Van Wieren, Dale P. *American Breweries II*. West Point, PA: Eastern Coast Breweriana Association, 1995.

PETER LaFRANCE

Cordials

Cordials, sometimes referred to as liqueurs or schnapps, are made from distilled spirits flavored with fruits, herbs, spices, or other botanicals; they are sweetened with sugar, honey, or other agents and diluted with wine, water, or other liquids bearing less alcohol than spirits. Cordials are one of the earliest forms of distilled beverages and frequently were used as medicines, since it was believed that the curative properties of certain herbs could be preserved in spirits. Benedictine, for example, is an herbal cordial that was developed in 1510 by the Benedictine monk Dom Bernardo Vincelli. Chartreuse, another herbal liqueur, was first made in 1737 by Carthusian monks, who still make this cordial. Early cordials were used both as potable medicines and as liquid ointments for bathing wounds.

Cordials can be made in many different ways. Sometimes the botanicals or flavoring agents are distilled into the spirit, sometimes they are added to the spirit and left to infuse, and sometimes less expensive bottlings are made merely by adding flavorings, such as citrus oil, to the base product. By law, effective in 1936, U.S. commercial cordials must contain a minimum of 2.5 percent sugar.

The use of cordials has changed drastically over the years. Although they have been used as an ingredient in mixed drinks since at least the mid-1700s, more often they were served neat as after-dinner drinks until the latter half of the twentieth century. Cream liqueurs, such as Baileys Irish Cream, were not created until the early 1970s when a way to stabilize cream in distilled products was discovered, and they contributed greatly to the world of mixed drinks as ingredients in cocktails such as the B52. Before this time, however, liqueurs were used to make brandy Alexanders, pink squirrels, sidecars, and golden dreams; curaçao, an orange-flavored cordial, was an ingredient in some of the first Manhattan recipes published in the late 1800s.

Triple sec, another orange-flavored cordial, is perhaps the most important liqueur in the world of American mixology, since it is used in popular drinks such as the margarita, sidecar, kamikaze, cosmopolitan, and metropolitan. Other cordials such as Amaretto, an almond-flavored liqueur; Chambord, flavored with black raspberries; crème de menthe; crème de cacao; Drambuie; Grand Marnier; and Kahlúa are also integral to the bartender's craft.

Jägermeister, an herbal cordial from Germany, became very popular in the 1990s when it was served ice-cold as a shooter, and many other cordials also became fashionable at that time and were consumed in a similar fashion. Produced in many different flavors such as root beer, butterscotch, ginger, and even bubble gum, these were favored by younger drinkers at bars and parties across the nation.

Although some cordials are made in the United States, they are mainly generic items such as triple sec, curaçao, crème de menthe, and crème de cacao. The more easily recognizable brand names such as Drambuie, Kahlúa, Disaronno, and Galliano are all imported.

More recently, new cordials such as green apple schnapps have been used by bartenders to create runaway hit cocktails such as the green apple martini—perhaps the most popular new drink of 2001. The craze for cocktails that started in the 1990s has done much to increase the popularity of cordials, and new flavors are being introduced on a regular basis.

[*See also* Cocktails; Cordials, Historical.]

GARY REGAN AND MARDEE HAIDIN REGAN

Cordials, Historical

Rummage through an American's liquor cabinet from the seventeenth through the nineteenth centuries and you likely would find an assortment of homemade cordials. Made from a mixture of distilled liquor, usually brandy but occasionally whiskey or rum, heavily sweetened, and distinctly flavored fruit juices or aromatics, the cordial was left to infuse, often for weeks or months, before being filtered for the most elegant translucence. The alcohol kick varied. Lettice Bryan's recipes in *The Kentucky Housewife* (1839) dilute the brandy with two or three parts fruit juice or herbal syrup, depending on the flavor. Mary Randolph's recipes in *The Virginia House-Wife* (1824) recommend diluting the brandy "to the strength of wine" or, in the case of her stronger lemon cordial, diluting the brandy by half. Most robust is Mrs. Harriott Pinckney Horry's 1770 recipe for Golden Cordial, which infuses lemon rind and flavorings into undiluted brandy.

Cordials historically played a dual role, as part of the medical arsenal and as a pleasant sociable nip. Recipes for physicians' "cordiall waters" and "cordiall powders,"

found in collections such as Martha Washington's *Booke of Cookery and Booke of Sweetmeats* (which dates to the mid-seventeenth century), were some of the few arrows in the housewife's quiver for treating diseases, especially those of the heart. Robert Roberts's *The House Servant's Directory; or, A Monitor for Private Families* (1827) offers a "strong anise-seed water" that is "a fine stomachic." Even those inclined to temperance, such as Sarah Josepha Hale in *The Good Housekeeper; or, The Way to Live Well, and to Be Well While We Live* (6th ed., 1841), reluctantly conceded that liquors might be "necessary, sometimes, as a medicine, but never, never consider them a necessary item in house-keeping."

Yet Americans in the eighteenth and nineteenth centuries did consider cordials necessary, drinking them neat with or following dessert. Sipped from small cordial cups and saucers or delicately proportioned stemmed glasses, each with a capacity of 1.5 ounces or less, cordials were savored digestives.

Americans began to consume cordials differently during the nineteenth century. With the development of cocktails, cordials became ingredients in more complicated drinks. Bartenders' guides inventoried the array of cordials needed for a full-service bar. Works such as Christian Schultz's *Manual for the Manufacture of Cordials, Liquors, Fancy Syrups, &c., &c.* (1862), appended to Jerry Thomas's *The Bon Vivant's Companion; or, How to Mix Drinks* (1862), gave professional formulas for manufacturing cordials. European imports such as kirsch, curaçao, and Chartreuse, many of which are still popular, flooded the American market. These standardized products could yield consistently flavored mixed drinks. Although still served after dinner, cordials increasingly were shaken into predinner libations.

Commercially manufactured cordials dominated the twentieth-century liquor cabinet. Recipes for homemade cordials, however, still could be found in books such as Magnus Bredenbek's *What Shall We Drink? Popular Drinks, Recipes, and Toasts* (1934), which evokes the old-fashioned tradition that "[c]ordials really take the place of sweets and should be sipped with exquisite relish, hardly more than moistening the lips at each raising of the glass."

[*See also* Cocktails; Cordials.]

BIBLIOGRAPHY

Belden, Louise Conway. *The Festive Tradition: Table Decoration and Desserts in America, 1650–1900.* New York: Norton, 1983.

A well-documented book with a small chapter on after-dinner drinks, including cordials.

Bredenbek, Magnus. *What Shall We Drink? Popular Drinks, Recipes, and Toasts.* New York: Carlyle House, 1934.

Johnson, Sharon Peregrine, and Byron A. Johnson. *The Authentic Guide to Drinks of the Civil War Era, 1853–1873.* Gettysburg, PA: Thomas Publications, 1992. A nicely done compilation of recipes with identified original sources, plus some useful introductory essays.

CATHY K. KAUFMAN

Corers, *see Apple Preparation Tools*

Corks

Cork was probably first used as a wine stopper by the ancient Romans, who, none the less more commonly closed their amphorae with clay or wood sealed with gypsum. The modern cork tradition reportedly dates to the seventeenth century, when Dom Perignon plugged one of his bottles of bubbly with a piece of bark. By the eighteenth century, corks had become the stopper of choice.

Corks are made from the bark of the cork oak tree (*Quercus suber*), which is harvested by hand every nine or ten years and is a renewable resource. These natural corks are well suited to their primary purpose of keeping wine in and air out, and traditionalists love the ritual and romance associated with them. But that tradition is threatened, as a number of prominent wineries turn to synthetic corks, which do not crumble, dry out, or run the risk of cork taint. This unwanted "corkiness," caused by the moldy-smelling compound 2,4,6-trichloro anisole (TCA), affects one in twelve bottles of wine and costs wine producers as much as $10 billion every year.

In some places, corks are being supplanted by the formerly déclassé screw cap. In the United States, consumer resistance is preventing broader adoption of corkless bottles, though environmentalists fear that it is only a matter of time before the centuries-old cork forests of such Mediterranean countries as Portugal (the origin of 85 percent of wine corks) succumb to lack of demand.

BIBLIOGRAPHY

Prial, Frank J. "Wine Talk: A Secret about Corks Is out of the Bottle." *New York Times*, 3 February 1999.

Prial, Frank J. "Wine Talk: Now in the Best Bottles—Plastic." *New York Times*, 8 August 2001.

MERYL S. ROSOFSKY

Corn

Corn is both one of the most familiar and one of the least understood of America's common plants. Although most Americans can identify corn as they see it growing between May and November from New England to Florida and westward to the Pacific, they consume corn unknowingly in hundreds of foods, most of them bearing no resemblance to the original grain. It is one of the most easily identifiable grain plants to the eye, but its story is complex and full of mystery and much debate.

The use of the word "corn," for what is termed "maize" by most other countries, is peculiar to the United States. Europeans who were accustomed to the names "wheat corn," "barley corn," and "rye corn" for other small-seeded cereal grains referred to the unique American grain maize as "Indian corn." The term was shortened to just "corn," which has become the American word for the plant of American genesis.

Basically, maize is an annual grass, of the Maydeae tribe in the family Gramineae, which includes such plants as wheat, rye, barley, rice, sorghum, and sugarcane. The Maydeae tribe has two genuses: *Tripsicum* and *Zea*. *Zea* consists of two major species: *Zea mays*, the maize Americans call "corn," and *Zea diploperennis*, a perennial type of *teosinte*. *Zea mays mexicana*, the annual variety of *teosinte*, is the closest botanical relative to maize and still grows as an annual in the wild in Mexico and Guatemala. These scientific names are important in the discussion of the mysteries of the origin of maize.

That maize is a New World plant from the Central American area is almost universally accepted. Archaeologists have found prehistoric traces of maize-like pollen in the Mexico City area dating from about seventy thousand years ago, and tiny cobs dating from about 5200 B.C.E. have also been identified in caves in the Tehuacan Valley of Central Mexico. But the precise ancestry of maize, the actual plant origin, remains a mystery. There are three recognized theories about the origins of corn: the ancestor of maize is annual *teosinte*, corn evolved from an actual form of wild corn that is now extinct, and corn derived from hybridization involving both *teosinte* and *tripsicum*.

Another mystery still shrouding the wild ancestry of corn is its inability to disperse seeds and hence its dependence upon the intervention of humans for its perpetuation. Corn plants bear seed heads (ears) that are

Corn People. Advertising card, nineteenth century. *Culinary Archives & Museum at Johnson & Wales University, Providence, R.I.*

Types of Corn

Mature corn seeds (kernels) consist of three main parts: the germ (embryo for a new plant), the endosperm (the storehouse of food energy as starch), and an outer hull, or pericarp. The many varieties of corn can be classified into six major types based predominantly on the different characteristics of the kernels: dent, flint, flour, sweet, pod, and popcorn. Dent corn gets its name from the dent (or depression) on the dried, mature kernel as a result of the shrinking of the soft, floury starch within the hard starch in the endosperm of the kernel. Most dent corn is yellow or white. Americans grow more dent corn than any other type, and it is important for livestock feed. Flint corn has a smooth kernel and either a complete absence of soft starch or a limited amount fully surrounded by hard endosperm. The kernels range in color from white to deep red. It grows well in cool climates, reaches maturity early, and resists insect pests and disease.

Flour corn is one of the oldest varieties of maize. The kernel resembles the kernel of flint corn in size and shape, but soft starch predominates, so the kernel can be easily crushed into flour. Flour corn is mostly white or blue and is cultivated primarily in the southwestern United States. Sweet corn has kernels that are easily recognized by their wrinkled exterior. Their sweetness is the result of a genetic defect in metabolism that prevents the sugars in the kernel from being completely transformed into starch. The kernels are typically white or yellow, with a soft, sugary endosperm. Sweet corn is grown mainly in the northern United States and is eaten chiefly as corn on the cob. Corn is eaten fresh in many parts of the world, but outside the United States relatively little corn is of the sweet type.

Pod corn is the most primitive and, together with popcorn, possibly one of the oldest types of maize. Each kernel of pod corn is enclosed in a glume, or husk. Pod corn is not of any commercial importance but is grown almost entirely for scientific research. There is archaeological evidence that the earliest maize was of a popcorn-pod variety. Popcorn has small, hard kernels with a high proportion of hard starch. The pericarps can be multicolored, but the most common colors are yellow and white. The characteristic trait of popcorn is its ability to explode and produce a white flake when the raw kernels are exposed to heat.

Dissemination of Corn

Most scientists believe that the earliest domesticated corn was of the pod-pop variety and was grown in the

larger than those of any other grass. The seeds (kernels) are set in an even number of rows on a solid central cob. The whole ear is covered by husks, a fact that created an interdependence of corn and humans that stretches back far before the time of European contact. All other grasses, wild or cultivated, can reseed themselves naturally, but corn cannot. Its seed-bearing ear, tightly encased in husks, is unique in the plant kingdom, preventing seed dispersal by wind, birds, or other means. If left unattended by humans, the corn ear would fall to the ground, and many seeds would germinate, but the resulting plants would grow so closely clustered that few, if any, would produce ears. For the perpetuation of corn the seeds must have the spaced planting that only humans can provide.

area of central Mexico, Guatemala, or Honduras about eight thousand years ago. But by the time of sixteenth-century European exploration, the Native Americans had developed the other four categories of corn: flint, dent, sweet, and flour. The dissemination of corn into what is geographically the United States was slow. Corn was cultivated in the American Southwest more than 2,500 years ago. But the vast, marginally populated, arid areas of New Mexico, Arizona, and Texas served as natural barriers, slowing the spread of corn northward or eastward. And the Rocky Mountains also provided a barrier for movement northward and westward.

Archaeological and modern historical evidence has shown convincingly that an eight-rowed type of flint corn first appeared in western Mexico about 700 C.E. and spread into the region of the southwestern United States and then proceeded northward and eastward. These flint varieties were found in the Eastern Woodlands region of the midAtlantic states and New England around A.D. 800. Dent corn was the predominant corn disseminated from the American Southwest to the southern states. More than likely, the only two races of corn that populated the Eastern Seaboard of America before European contact were the eight-rowed flint corn (*maiz de ocho*) of the north and the dent corn of the south.

The gradual spread of corn north and northeast from its native tropical America occurred over many centuries via the migration of the Native Americans. A second major movement of corn began in the late 1700s, as the European settlers migrated inland from the coastal colonies, crossing the Appalachians to the Ohio Valley and eventually to the mid-continent prairie. As the settlers migrated with their corn seed, the southern dent and the northern flint were brought into close proximity and hybridized naturally to form a new dent variety and give rise to what has become the world's most important agricultural region, the Corn Belt of the United States. The Corn Belt is an area of about 350,000 square miles extending from western Ohio to eastern Nebraska, including the states of Indiana, Illinois, and Iowa and parts of Missouri, Kansas, Nebraska, South Dakota, Ohio, and Minnesota. Just 10 percent of the United States now produces over 80 percent of the country's corn.

Corn has become the basic food plant of our modern American civilization. Corn feeds the nation or, more precisely, the nation's animals—the cattle, pigs, and poultry that are the basis of the American diet. As the country's population grew, it became important to increase the production of corn; corn's ability to hybridize made it possible to meet demand. Natural hybridization has been at play throughout corn's history, and all natural evolutional changes were produced through the centuries by corn's being fertilized by wind-borne pollen from the tassels of many other corn plants. All corn within the United States is genetically related; thus, when corn is allowed to cross-pollinate between types separated for long periods, either by distance or by diverse growing conditions, the yield increases. Controlled hybridization for higher yields, earlier maturity, and resistance to disease and drought began to be developed and utilized at the beginning of the twentieth century.

Corn as Food

Throughout American history there has been wide diversity in the methods of preparation and use of corn as food. Native Americans parched corn by roasting it in ashes until the kernels were brown and then pounded the kernels into flour or processed the kernels with lye water (prepared from ashes or lime) to remove the hulls for whole hominy, which is easier to grind. Parched corn would keep indefinitely and could be mixed with hot or cold water. In the Southwest the most common process was to boil the corn in lime solution before grinding the grain into a fine masa (corn flour).

The process of nixtamalization (alkaline processing of corn kernels) loosens the hulls or pericarps, increases the nutritional content of the grain by improving the amino acid balance of corn and making the niacin content more available, and ensures that a flexible flatbread (tortilla) can be made. A tortilla is a round, thin, unleavened bread

Grinding Corn. Hopi woman grinding corn, Arizona. *Culinary Archives & Museum at Johnson & Wales University, Providence, R.I.*

Corn on the Cob. Eating corn on the cob. From George Augustus Sala, *America Revisited*, 3rd edition (London, 1883), vol. 1, p. 174.

made from finely ground corn or masa. A commercial product called masa harina, a flour made from the alkaline-prepared kernels, can be mixed with water to make a tortilla. Fresh tortillas are eaten as bread, used as plate and spoon, or filled to make composite dishes, such as tacos and enchiladas.

Whole hominy or great hominy is the result of the alkaline (lye) process of removing the hull from the kernel. But the word "hominy" refers to dried and hulled corn kernels, coarsely ground and prepared for use in puddings and breads, in particular. The term "grits," or "hominy grits," especially in southern states, refers to finely ground hominy. Hominy grits, usually of white corn, have been called "the potatoes of the South," so heavily have they been relied upon for the starch in that region. Hot hominy is simmered over slow heat for hours with butter, perhaps cream, and salt or sugar to taste. Grits for breakfast, served with eggs and ham or as a side dish, is a long-established dish of the South. A specialty of Louisiana is "grillade and grits," which consists of beef or veal braised with seasonings and served with buttered grits.

Cornbread was the staff of life in America until wheat bread began to catch up in the middle of the nineteenth century. Early American cornbreads included corn pone, hoecakes, johnnycakes, ash cakes, bannocks, and dodgers. However, the whole complex of terms for such cornbreads is at best difficult, as the usage varied with place and time and the recipe for all was just cornmeal, water or milk, and perhaps a little salt, sugar, or fat. Later recipes for cornbread are more elaborate, mixing cornmeal with wheaten flour and sometimes raising agents to make a light bread. Spoon breads were soft, rich corn-

breads made with milk, butter, and beaten egg and best eaten with a spoon.

During the nineteenth century, food industries began the production of corn syrup, corn oil, and cornstarch from the basic corn kernel, and corn became less identifiable in the diet. Americans can avoid all visible corn products, fresh corn, canned or frozen corn, corn flours, and cornstarch and still be eating invisible corn products at almost every meal. The supermarket shopper trundles corn to the checkout counter with every purchase of baby foods, bread, crackers, doughnuts, cakes, pies, pie fillings, ketchup, chili sauce or other flavoring sauces, prepared dessert powders and puddings, candy and chewing gum, ice cream and sherbet, soft drinks, canned and frozen fruits and vegetables, fruit butters, fruit juices, jams, jellies, processed meats like frankfurters and sausages, salami and luncheon loafs, canned corned beef hash, pickles and condiments, vinegar, yeast, table syrups, and sweetened condensed milk. Indeed, a supermarket without the American grain corn would be little more than a fresh fruit and vegetable stand with a fish counter.

[*See also* Beer, Corn and Maple; Corn-Preparation Tools; Corn Syrup; Mexican American Food; Native American Foods; Popcorn; Southern Regional Cookery; Southwestern Regional Cookery.]

BIBLIOGRAPHY

Fussell, Betty. *The Story of Corn*. New York: Knopf, 1992.
Parker, A. C. *Iroquois Uses of Maize and Other Food Plants*. Ontario, Canada: Iroqrafts Ltd., 1994. A well-documented and finely illustrated book on Native American uses of corn.
Roberts, Jonathan. *Cabbages and Kings: The Origins of Fruit and Vegetables*. London: Collins, 2001. An excellent illustrated book on the origins of many fruits and vegetables, including corn.
Smith, Andrew F. *Popped Culture: A Social History of Popcorn in America*. Columbia: University of South Carolina Press, 1999.

SUSAN PLAISTED

Cornbread Baking Pans

Cornmeal recipes abounded in the nineteenth century, and cornbread in particular was very popular all over the country. It was baked in cast-iron skillets, some of which had divisions or partitions that formed wedge-shaped sections of cornbread. By about 1900 cast-iron stick pans that made long, thin sticks of cornbread were in use. By the 1920s several foundries were making mold pans with more or less realistic corncob cups. Some of these pans were called "corn-" or "wheat-stick" pans. The most interesting pans look as if the casting molds to make them were created with actual corncobs, each kernel is so individualistic.

[*See also* Corn.]

BIBLIOGRAPHY

Franklin, Linda Campbell. *300 Years of Kitchen Collectibles*. 5th ed. Iola, WI: Krause Publications, 2003.

Smith, David G., and Chuck Wafford. *The Book of Griswold and Wagner: Favorite Piqua, Sidney Hollow Ware, Wapak*. Atglen, PA: Schiffer, 1995.

Smith, David G., and Chuck Wafford. *The Book of Wagner & Griswold*. Atglen, PA: Schiffer, 2001.

LINDA CAMPBELL FRANKLIN

Corned Beef

All-American as beef in most forms may be, corned beef has never quite managed to shed its Old World image. Even the name sounds quaint—"corn" being a bygone English synonym for "granule," a reference to salt as the product's active ingredient. To complicate matters, the English themselves prefer the term "salt beef" (or "pickled beef") to distinguish the cured brisket (or other comparable cut) found in delicatessens from the canned loaf found on supermarket shelves; in the United States, however, "corned beef" is used for both items.

The history of corned beef is likewise confusing. Salting as a mode of food preservation is as ancient and widespread as civilization itself, such that the genesis of any one product is hard to pinpoint. For instance, the consensus is that salt meat was well and widely known in Europe by the Middle Ages, but opinions continue to differ as to whether the origins of corned beef per se lie in the British Isles and, more specifically Ireland, or in central and eastern Europe and, in particular, among the Ashkenazi Jews. It is clear, however, that Ireland created and led the market on exportation of corned beef until the nineteenth century, when the canning industry emerged in England and opened doors for the cattlemen of South America, who came to dominate production of canned corned beef—although its heyday passed with World War II, at least among civilians. (Consumption is still notable among British and U.S. armed forces).

Techniques for salting meat vary, from dry salting, a method based on topical application and absorption, to wet salting, whereby the meat is immersed in brine. These procedures, which can take days to complete, are also known as curing and pickling, respectively. For corned beef the latter process is key, although it is often preceded by the former; brines may contain sugar, saltpeter, and spices in varying amounts.

What does not vary much is the way in which corned beef brisket is traditionally prepared: it is simmered with a blend of seasonings that may include garlic, peppercorns, bay leaf, tarragon, mustard, parsley, thyme, marjoram, cloves, nutmeg, or allspice. It can then be served hot, accompanied by onions, potatoes, and the like, or cold, with copious condiments from horseradish to sweet relish. Corned beef and cabbage is the most famous version, one with Irish roots but American blossoms—especially on Saint Patrick's Day, where it forms the centerpiece for the proverbial New England boiled dinner.

Strangely, this peasant dish appeared regularly on the elaborate menus of America's grand hotels in the nineteenth century. Its even more humble relatives have taken different routes: from the hash houses of the period to modern-day greasy spoons, corned beef hash, frequently paired with eggs, remains a staple, while the Reuben, a classic deli sandwich of sliced corned beef piled high on rye with Swiss cheese, sauerkraut, and Thousand Island dressing, continues to inspire heated debate between Nebraskans and New Yorkers as to its birthplace.

[*See also* Jewish American Food; Reuben Sandwich; Saint Patrick's Day.]

BIBLIOGRAPHY

Allen, Darina. *The Complete Book of Irish Country Cooking: Traditional and Wholesome Recipes from Ireland*. Foreword by Regina Sexton. New York: Penguin Studio, 1996.

Froud, Nina. *The International Jewish Cook Book*. New York: Stein and Day, 1972.

Shephard, Sue. *Pickled, Potted, and Canned: How the Art and Science of Food Preserving Changed the World*. New York: Simon and Schuster, 2000. Comprehensive yet focused; thorough but not laborious.

RUTH TOBIAS

Corn Oil, *see Fats and Oils*

Corn-Preparation Tools

From the early days of the United States, corn was grown for livestock feed and human consumption. For livestock, husked ears of corn were usually dried and stored in corn cribs—ventilated structures that were open invitations to rats. Husking pegs or corn huskers were short metal or wooden rods, pointed on the end and often fitted to a leather strap that was worn around the hand so that the peg and sometimes a hook for pulling off the husks were in the palm of the hand. The first of dozens of U.S. corn hullers (huskers) was patented in 1836; previously they were homemade.

The first U.S. corn sheller, patented in 1815, was followed by many more from the 1830s to the 1920s. When dried ears were fed into the hopper, it knocked off the hard kernels—for seed or for grinding into meal. In the 1840s so-called unrefined folks ate corn on the cob with butter and salt. Others believed the kernels must be slit open, releasing the milky juices and making the corn digestible. Corn graters (colloquially called "gritters") "creamed" the corn by slitting the kernels and expressing the contents; these tools were made as early as the 1840s to 1850s. Some were small, flat tables with grating blades, something like cabbage cutters. Corn cutters dating from the 1870s were cylindrical metal devices with rows of sharp teeth, pulled over fresh ears of corn.

[*See also* Corn; Cornbread Baking Pans.]

BIBLIOGRAPHY

Franklin, Linda Campbell. *300 Years of Kitchen Collectibles*. 5th ed. Iola, WI: Krause Publications, 2003.
Moffet, Jim. *American Corn Huskers: A Patent History*. Sunnyvale, CA: Off Beat Books, 1996.

LINDA CAMPBELL FRANKLIN

Corn Syrup

Corn syrup is a clear, colorless sweetener made from cornstarch. In the refining of cornstarch, a chemical breakdown by heat, acid, enzymes, or any combination of the three results in dextrose or starch sugar. More complete conversion of the starch yields a sweeter syrup.

In the food industry, the beneficial properties of corn syrup are myriad. In ice cream, corn syrup improves body and texture and prevents ice crystal formation. With baked goods, it regulates the rate of fermentability in yeast doughs. Corn syrup lends a chewy texture to many candies and chewing gum. Its browning characteristics promote crust color in baked products. When used with other sugars, corn syrup controls crystallization. Naturally hygroscopic, it readily absorbs moisture and adds pliability to many foods. Above all, it has replaced cane sugar as a food sweetener.

The first attempts at converting corn into a sweetener resulted from the Molasses Act of 1733. Molasses was taxed heavily and the colonists sought a cheap substitute. War between France and Great Britain in 1806 led to the British blockade of France's West Indies cane producers. Napoléon I offered a monetary reward for a natural sugar replacement and the Russian chemist K. S. Kirchhof produced a sweet syrup from potato starch by adding sulfuric acid. Kirchhof's technique of acid hydrolysis of starch was applied to corn in the mid-1860s. At the same time, commercial production of corn syrup began in the United States with the Union Sugar Company in New York City and a decade later with the American Glucose Company of Buffalo, New York.

In the 1870s economic conditions made the production of dextrose from corn profitable and new markets for corn syrup opened up in the baking, candy, and brewing industries. During World War I sugar shortages led to an increased dependence on corn syrup, as confectioners, bakers, and jam and jelly producers replaced cane or beet sugar in their formulas. The development of a process for the purification and crystallization of dextrose in 1921 allowed corn sweeteners to compete more fully with sugar.

Using enzymes to hydrolyze cornstarch, the major corn refiner A. E. Staley Manufacturing Company marketed a product called Sweetose in 1938 that was 60 percent as sweet as sugar. Twice as sweet as regular corn syrup and three times more fluid, it was used in candies and fruit packing, then later in jams, jellies, preserves, and ketchup.

In 1967 new Japanese enzyme technology brought about a revolution in corn syrup development. High fructose corn syrup was made by a more complete hydrolysis of glucose to fructose. IsoSweet, a high fructose corn syrup developed by Staley, was approximately 92 percent as sweet as sugar.

In the early 1970s imported sugar made up almost 60 percent of U.S. sugar demand. Prices quadrupled and food processors increased their use of IsoSweet. In 1974 Coca-Cola used IsoSweet to replace 25 percent of the sugar in its minor flavors. Corn syrups in food processing took off after 1978, when Staley developed a 55 percent fructose syrup, which was essentially as sweet as sugar. By the mid-1980s corn syrups had replaced sugar as the sweetener of choice for the soft-drink industry. As of 2002 corn syrup sweeteners comprised more than 55 percent of the U.S. nutritive sweetener market.

By the early 2000s corn sweeteners were under attack by critics who claimed that the rise in American obesity was partly the result of an overuse of cheap sweeteners in fast foods. Soft-drink servings, for example, rose from a standard eight ounces to twenty ounces, and many other foods experienced the same kinds of expansion.

[*See also* Soda Drinks; Sweeteners.]

BIBLIOGRAPHY

Forrestal, Dan J. *The Kernel and the Bean: The 75-Year Story of the Staley Company*. New York: Simon and Schuster, 1982.
Fussell, Betty. *The Story of Corn*. New York: Knopf, 2004. Impact of corn on American diet, history of corn.

SALLY S. DEFAUW

Counterculture, Food

Great strides were made in American agriculture during the twentieth century, but with progress came protest. As farming and food processing became more centralized, mechanized, and chemically enhanced, some Americans voiced concerns about the quality, safety, and palatability of the food supply. The food counterculture, best described by Warren Belasco in his book *Appetite for Change: How the Counterculture Took on the Food Industry, 1966–1988*, included a broad cross section of individuals and groups opposed to corporate agriculture, corporate manufacturing of food, and perceived government protection and subsidy of corporate food producers. Many participants in the counterculture eschewed foods processed with additives. They also avoided fruits, vegetables, grains, and meats that had been grown or prepared for market with chemicals. The question became, What steps can be taken to produce and distribute a chemical-free food supply? The counterculture answers were communes, urban gardens, food cooperatives, greenmarkets, and organic farming.

During World War II, American farmers supported the war effort by maximizing production to feed the United States and hungry Allied nations. After the war, farmers were able to increase production with newly available pesticides, herbicides, petrochemical fertilizers, and hormones that were developed to prevent disease and maximize yield of both plants and animals. Farmers also increased mechanization and irrigation, and more of them specialized in growing a single crop or raising only one type of animal, abandoning the diversity characteristic of American family farms. Each of these changes required major financial investments, and once the improvements were made, the cost of food production declined. Many small farmers could not compete, were unable to make a living, and sold out to large corporate operations.

During the postwar years, food processors increased automation in their plants and vastly expanded the use of additives, which lengthened the shelf life of products and reduced losses from spoilage. Some additives (for example, the iron added to white bread) offered health benefits to consumers, but many (such as the substitution of cheap synthetic vanilla flavor for pure vanilla) simply saved money for processors. Food companies began consolidation during this period, and the result was the emergence of a few corporate food giants. By the mid-twentieth century, Americans spent less of their disposable income on food than did the people of any other nation. At the supermarket, Americans were confronted with an amazing array of new processed foods—boxed, frozen, and canned—in bright, eye-catching packages. To encourage Americans to buy these goods, food-processing companies engaged in a massive advertising blitz, which was particularly effective in the new medium of television.

Concerns

Despite increases in production and decreases in prices, concerns about food processing had been expressed since the 1930s, and they intensified during the postwar years. Arthur Kallet and Frederick Schlink, for example, wrote *100,000,000 Guinea Pigs: Dangers in Everyday Foods, Drugs, and Cosmetics* (1932), exposing practices of the nation's food manufacturers that the authors believed were dangerous to consumers.

The U.S. Food and Drug Administration (FDA) was responsible for guaranteeing the safety of the nation's food supply, but the understaffed agency was unable to keep up with the deluge of chemicals and additives entering the nation's food supply. In 1958, after eight years of discussion by the Delaney Committee, Congress passed the Food Additives Amendment, which required manufacturers of new food additives to establish their safety. Under this new law, however, manufacturers and the laboratories they hired conducted the testing—a system open to concerns about conflict of interest. The Delaney clause prohibited the approval of any food additive shown to cause cancer in humans or animals, regardless of dosage. But the new legislation grandfathered in existing chemicals, and without testing, the FDA published a list of almost two hundred additives "generally recognized as safe."

The dangers of pesticides, fertilizers, hormones, and additives became apparent and were made known to the public at large in the 1960s. William F. Longgood in *The Poisons in Your Food* (1960) dramatically reported how chemicals had invaded America's daily diet. Two years later, Rachel Carson in *Silent Spring* exposed the evils of DDT. James S. Turner in *Chemical Feast* (1970) concluded that the meager efforts of the FDA to regulate chemical additives in food had been neutralized by the powerful food industry.

One proposed solution to the use of pesticides and petrochemical fertilizers was organic gardening, championed by Jerome I. Rodale. Rodale purchased a farm in Emmaus, Pennsylvania, and in 1940 launched the magazine *Organic Gardening and Farming,* which emphasized composting, soil building, and biological control of pests. Organic farming was best practiced on a small scale and consequently threatened corporate agriculture and the food distribution system, which was increasingly centralized and dependent on long-distance transportation. Chemical-free, and thus more perishable, organic foods had to be distributed locally. In the ideal situation, farmers and customers would deal directly with each other in farmers' markets, and the middle level, including shippers, wholesalers, and supermarket owners, would be eliminated.

Rodale was also concerned with nutrition, and he launched *Prevention* magazine in 1950 to offer advice on healthy eating. This concern was shared by many others, including Adelle Davis. Trained in dietetics and nutrition and having a master's degree in biochemistry, Davis wrote *Let's Cook it Right* (1947), *Let's Eat Right to Keep Fit* (1954), and subsequent books that emphasized the role of diet in a healthy life, recommended specific food regimens for various ailments, and advised avoidance of most processed foods, artificial additives, and chemical fertilizers. Davis's beliefs were accepted by many nutritionists, but the American medical profession challenged her views on the therapeutic qualities of the diets she recommended. Despite the views of the medical profession, Davis's work helped launch the health food movement in America.

Counterculture Food Movement

The term "counterculture" was coined in 1968 to refer to a vast array of antiestablishment activities, including protests against the Vietnam War, the struggle for civil rights, advocacy of women's rights, and the rise of the hippie or new age movement. Many counterculture advocates were people who had lost faith in the government and the capitalist system. There were a number of culinary implications of this political foment. Quakers, for example, led fasts against the war; those fighting for civil rights held integrated sit-ins at segregated diners; and consumers boycotted lettuce and grapes in support of migrant workers who picked these foods. Along with its opposition to other parts of the establishment, the counterculture revolted against the domination of the American food industry with its factory farms and chemical-laced canned goods. Members of the counterculture looked elsewhere for their food supply, and one conclusion was that consuming locally grown food eliminated the need for the energy-wasting, pollution-spewing trucks used for transporting food from coast to coast.

Until the 1960s, the followers of Jerome Rodale were mainly small-town and suburban backyard gardeners, many of them first-generation immigrants. Rodale invoked the Jeffersonian ideals of small farmers and shopkeepers, and those who adopted organic methods ran communal operations based on a utopian agricultural model of simple, natural lifestyle. The DDT scare from 1962 to 1972 gave a boost to the popularity of organic gardening. Urban communes were launched in which participants lived together and shared work. Gardens were established in vacant city lots. Communes and community gardens followed the principles of organic gardening.

The counterculture established food cooperatives because commercial health food stores were plagued by charges of fraud and hucksterism. Food co-ops, self-run by members who each contributed a certain amount of time to the project, were initially no-frills sources for staples such as brown rice, whole-grain bread, herbal tea, nuts, seeds, beans, dried fruit, honey, and soy products. As they became more commercial, food co-ops began offering natural cheeses, yogurt, organically grown fruits and vegetables, pure juices, granolas, oils, and vitamin and mineral supplements. There were an estimated five to ten thousand food co-ops in America by the 1970s.

The counterculture was concerned about what foods should be eaten, less-processed products usually being preferred. Brown rice, tofu, granola, yogurt, and bean sputs became symbols of the culinary counterculture. Natural foods were touted as healthier and tastier than processed foods. Several cookbooks emerged that were based on communal and natural-foods cookery, including *The Commune Cookbook* (1972) by Crescent Dragonwagon and *Eat It: A Cookbook* (1974) by Dana Crumb and Sherry Cohen.

The counterculture discouraged the consumption of meat for a number of reasons. Some vegetarians based their diets on the teachings of Buddhism and Hinduism. Others pursued macrobiotics, a rigorous system of purification of the diet based on Taoist thought. Edward Espe Brown, a Buddhist in California and the author of *Tassajara Cooking* (1973), encouraged readers to enjoy the natural flavors of seasonal vegetables and fruits combined with rice or beans. Brown's sauces, often Asian-inspired, were simple and lightly seasoned, and Zen philosophy enlightened the text. Other vegetarian cookbooks from the 1970s were more lighthearted, among them *The Vegetarian Epicure* (1972) by Anna Thomas.

Some members of the counterculture saw a vegetarian diet as a way to improve one's health and help fight hunger in America and around the world. The popularity of this view can be attributed in part to Frances Moore Lappé. Discouraged by an unrewarding career in social work, Lappé turned to ecology in 1969. She read about the vast amount of acreage devoted to growing feed grain for livestock and encountered the theory of protein complementarity. According to this theory, one could creatively combine beans, seeds, grains, and dairy products to meet daily protein needs without resorting to ecologically wasteful meat. Lappé's book, *Diet for a Small Planet* (1971), sold more than 3 million copies. The book explained that by feeding vegetable protein to animals rather than directly to humans, Americans were wasting scarce protein resources at a time when much of the world was going hungry or suffering from serious nutritional deficiencies. This inefficient process required vast quantities of land, fertilizer, water, pesticides, and herbicides. If Americans were to eat their protein directly in grain and bean form, stated Lappé, they would free up large amounts of food for redistribution elsewhere. Lappé showed that a vegetarian diet could be nutritionally adequate if the right combinations of foods were consumed. She recommended "getting off the top of the food chain" as a way of transforming consciousness, reintegrating mind and body, and embracing social responsibility.

The countercultural food movement reached the mainstream by the mid-1970s. Food companies ridiculed food reformers, calling them lunatics, faddists, and quacks while couching their own views, publicized in product advertisements and corporate press releases, in a reassuring stream

Diet for a Small Planet. Cover of the landmark book by Frances Moore Lappé.

of words such as "knowledgeable," "scientific," "constructive," "generally recognized," "responsible," and "the best scientific judgment attainable." Many older, middle-class adults had become interested in the culinary issues raised by the counterculture, and as a response to market pressures, food companies began to change their labels and advertising slogans, which soon abounded with references to the foods' being "additive-free," and "all-natural." Large food companies began producing their own granolas and protein supplements and decreasing or eliminating the additives in many of their products. At times commercially produced foods changed in appearance, cost, and nutritive value, making it difficult for even an alert consumer to make an intelligent choice among them. The American public became confused. Wooed by representatives of the food industry and warned by advocates of health foods and repeatedly alarmed by gloomy stories of chemical-laden foods only to be reassured by industry-hired academicians, the public was driven into uncertainty.

Countercultural Legacies

The counterculture spurred interest in food and nutrition. Because many participants distrusted the establishment, which included food companies and the FDA, there was a clear need for improved research. The Center for Science in the Public Interest (CSPI) was founded in Washington, D.C., in 1971. One of the founders, Michael Jacobson, worked on food additives and nutrition. By 1977 CSPI was focused almost exclusively on food issues, publishing eye-opening nutritional analyses and critiques of fast food and convenience foods. Jacobson wrote *What Are We Feeding Our Kids?* (1994) and *Marketing Madness* (1995). CSPI publishes *Nutrition Action Healthletter*, a newsletter for consumers. CSPI publications have led to several congressional hearings and the passage of food safety legislation.

Some enterprises launched by those in the counterculture food movement have survived and thrived. Erewhon was founded as a cooperative in 1966 to supply Boston-area followers of the macrobiotics gurus Michio and Aveline Kushi. Erewhon opened retail shops in the Boston area and then on the West Coast. Celestial Seasonings, started in 1969 in Boulder, Colorado, offered herbal teas that were additive free and organically grown or gathered in the wild. Some of the teas were suggested as remedies for ailments such as sore throat and insomnia. Erewhon, after acquiring the venerable cereal company U.S. Mills in 1986, was one of the largest retailers, manufacturers, and distributors of natural foods in the United States in the early 2000s. Celestial Seasonings, which had been sold to Kraft Foods in 1984, became independent again in 1988 and as of 2004, was the largest purveyor of herbal teas in the United States.

From the counterculture emerged some of America's most famous restaurants. As a student at the University of California, Berkeley, Alice Waters had been involved in the Free Speech movement. Her groundbreaking restaurant Chez Panisse was launched in 1971 as an extension of home-cooked meals that she had been preparing for free-speech activists. Waters emphasized fresh, local, seasonal ingredients. Mollie Katzen's Moosewood Restaurant in Ithaca, New York, started out as a communal operation in which all decisions were made by the entire staff. Menus were improvisational and

Fiddlehead Ferns and Organic Eggplant. The Park Slope Food Co-op in Brooklyn, New York, offers a wide selection of organic produce. *Photograph by Joe Zarba*

were listed daily on blackboards. The menu was vegetarian with diverse ethnic dishes and plenty of whole grains, following the teachings of Lappé on how to live well without wasting the earth's protein resources. Both Waters and Katzen published cookbooks: Waters's initial effort was *The Chez Panisse Menu Cookbook* (1982) and Katzen's first was *The Moosewood Cookbook* (1977). The efforts of Waters, Katzen, and many others have led to a revolution in American cookery that emphasizes fresh ingredients and locally grown food.

The counterculture food movement greatly increased interest in vegetarianism. The North American Vegetarian Society was founded in 1974, and several vegetarian magazines, such as *Vegetarian Times*, have large numbers of subscribers. Lappé has continued her work through Food First/Institute for Food and Development Policy in San Francisco, and she and her daughter Anna have written a second book, *Hope's Edge: The Next Diet for a Small Planet* (2003).

Counterculture food concerns increased interest in organic gardening, which has blossomed since the 1970s. Associated with organic gardening has been a movement to preserve family farms by connecting people in cities with small farmers in surrounding areas. One such effort was the growth of greenmarkets in cities. In these urban markets, local farmers sell their produce directly to customers. One example is Greenmarkets in New York City, a program started in 1976 by Barry Benepe. There are twenty Greenmarket sites in the city, and Benepe's efforts have served as a model for other urban farmers' markets.

Another effort to connect farmers to consumers is community-supported agriculture, which originated in

Japan in the 1960s and first appeared in the United States in the mid-1980s. Community-supported agriculture was championed as a way for farmers and community members to work together to create a local food system whereby the farmers produce vegetables, fruits, meats, and related products and sell them directly to community members. At the start of the growing season, the community members must commit to purchasing the foods at a specific price, thus sharing the risks of production. Since the 1980s the number of community-supported agriculture programs in the United States had grown to an estimated six hundred in 2002, according to the BioDynamic Farming and Gardening Association.

Issues raised by the counterculture food movement persist in concerns about the globalization of food and the resistance to genetically modified foods. The slow food movement, which embodies many of the original concerns, was launched in 1986 by Carlo Petrini as a response to the opening of a McDonald's restaurant in Rome. The International Movement was founded in Paris three years later and has more than 65,000 members. Slow Food USA, which was launched in 1999, has ten thousand members. It is dedicated to saving America's food heritage and to supporting and celebrating the food traditions of North America. Slow Food USA encourages the organic movement and supports the raising of old livestock breeds and heirloom fruit and vegetable varieties, as well as the production of handcrafted wine and beer, farmhouse cheeses, and other artisanal foods that are at risk of succumbing to the effects of culinary industrialization and degradation of farmland.

[*See also* Biotechnology; Chemical Additives; Community-Supported Agriculture; Cooperatives; Farmers' Markets; Fast Food; Food and Drug Administration; Food and Nutrition Systems; Health Food; Organic Food; Organic Gardening; Politics of Food; Slow Food Movement; Transportation of Food; Vegetarianism.]

BIBLIOGRAPHY

Belasco, Warren J. *Appetite for Change: How the Counterculture Took on the Food Industry, 1966–1988*. New York: Pantheon, 1989.

Biodynamic Farming and Gardening Association. http://www.Biodynamics.com

Davis, Adelle. *Let's Eat Right to Keep Fit*. New York: Harcourt, 1954.

Dragonwagon, Crescent. *The Commune Cookbook*. New York: Simon and Schuster, 1972.

Lappé, Frances Moore. *Diet for a Small Planet*. New York: Ballantine, 1971.

Lappé, Frances Moore, and Anna Lappé. *Hope's Edge: The Next Diet for a Small Planet*. New York: Tarcher/Putnam, 2003.

Nestle, Marion. *Food Politics: How the Food Industry Influences Nutrition and Health*. Berkeley: University of California Press, 2002.

Wells, Betty, Shelly Gradwell, and Rhonda Yoder. "Growing Food, Growing Community: Community Supported Agriculture in Rural Iowa." In *Food in the USA: A Reader*, edited by Carole M. Counihan, 401–407. New York: Routledge, 2002.

ANDREW F. SMITH

Cowpeas

Cowpeas—also known in the United States as bird peas, black-eyed peas, cornfield peas, conch peas, Congo peas, crowder peas, pigeon peas, red peas, southern peas, whip-poor-will peas, zipper peas, *gandules* (Puerto Rico), and simply "peas"—are various warm-weather beans, descended from the wild African cowpeas *Vigna unguiculata*. Cultivated varieties were developed as early as 3000 B.C.E. in Africa and came to the Americas with the slave trade. They remained a popular slave food, as reported in a southern journal in 1850: "There is no vegetable of which negroes are more fond than of the common field pea" (quoted in Breedon, p. 98).

The best-known dish of cowpeas is South Carolina's hoppin' John, a pilaf of rice and beans and usually pork or bacon, probably of African or Afro-Caribbean origin. The dish is thought to bring good luck when eaten at New Year's. In West Africa, cowpeas are soaked to remove the skins and ground to make creamy-white fried or steamed cakes. There is some evidence of African-style cowpea preparations retained in Georgia through the nineteenth century. Neo-African cowpea cakes have entered the United States via Key West, Florida (where they have been known by an anglicized Cuban name, *bolos*, since at least 1948), and are found among the recent immigrant communities of Afro-Cubans, Haitians, Brazilians, and Nigerians.

[*See also* Peas.]

BIBLIOGRAPHY

Breedon, James O., ed. *Advice among Masters: The Ideal in Slave Management in the Old South*. Westport, CT: Greenwood Press, 1980. Chapter 7 collects twenty-four grisly pages of advice on the feeding of slaves.

Hess, Karen. *The Carolina Rice Kitchen: The African Connection*. Columbia: University of South Carolina Press, 1992. Extended discussion of hoppin' John.

Hill, Annabella P. *Mrs. Hill's Southern Practical Cookery and Receipt Book*. New York, Carlton Publisher, 1867. Facsimile with historical commentary by Damon L. Fowler. Columbia:

University of South Carolina Press, 1995. Recipe for pease pudding mentions cornfield peas.

Lumpkin, Mrs. Henry, ed. *The Atlanta Exposition Cookbook*. Athens: University of Georgia Press, 1984. Facsimile of 1895 *Tested Recipe Cook Book*.

Rutledge, Sarah. "A Lady of Charleston." In *The Carolina Housewife; or, House and Home*. Charleston, SC: W. R. Babcock, 1847. Facsimile with an introduction by Anna Wells Rutledge. Columbia: University of South Carolina Press, 1979. The first printed recipe for hoppin' John.

MARK H. ZANGER

Crab Boils

Blue crabs, *Callinectes sapidus*, are native to the western Atlantic, from New England to the Gulf coast of Florida—but nowhere are they more abundant or more abundantly enjoyed than in the vicinity of Chesapeake Bay. Half of all the blue crabs caught in the United States are captured by Chesapeake watermen along its four thousand miles of shoreline. Since the 1850s watermen have harvested oysters in the winter months. The oyster catch is declining, but each year up to 100 million pounds of crabs are caught between April and fall.

During crab season, crab houses flourish around the bay. At the beginning of the twenty-first century, at least seventy-five crab houses surrounded the bay and the Potomac estuary, serving all sorts of crab dishes—but none more popular than the traditional Maryland crab boil.

"Crab boil" is something of a misnomer because the crabs are not boiled but steamed over water, beer, vinegar, or some combination thereof. Crab boils' distinguishing features are their informality—cooked crabs are usually served without plates on paper-covered tables with no utensils other than small wooden mallets for cracking the shells—and their salty-spicy crust, which clings to diners' fingers and calls for lots of cold beer.

The spice blend is sprinkled on the crabs as they are placed in the steamer, and the lid is quickly replaced so that the crabs do not escape. Many places use their own spice blends, but Old Bay Seasoning is most often the choice. The seasoning was invented in Baltimore in 1939 by the German immigrant Gustav Brunn; its primary ingredient is celery salt, but the peppery mixture includes many other spices. Old Bay was sold to McCormick and Company in 1990.

[*See also* Seafood.]

BIBLIOGRAPHY

Blue Crab Archives. http://www.blue-crab.org.
Davidson, Alan. *North Atlantic Seafood*. London: Macmillan, 1979.
Warner, William W. *Beautiful Swimmers*. Boston: Little, Brown, 1976.

GARY ALLEN

Cracker Jack

During the 1870s the German immigrants Frederick and Louis Rueckheim sold popcorn on the streets of Chicago. They began to experiment with combining popcorn with several other products. When the Columbian Exposition opened in Chicago in 1893, they sold a confection composed of popcorn, molasses, and peanuts, which they prepared in a small factory. After the exposition, orders for the confection rose. The Ruckheims increased production, repackaged the product so that it would stay fresh, named it Cracker Jack, and promoted it nationwide. Conflicting stories as to how "Cracker Jack" acquired its name have surfaced. The most commonly told story goes as follows. While sampling and tasting the new confection, John Berg, a company salesman, purportedly exclaimed: "That's a crackerjack." Frederick Rueckheim looked at him and said, "Why not call it by that name?" Berg responded, "I see no objection." Rueckheim's decisive reply was "That settles it then." The story is probably apocryphal as, at that time, the term "cracker jack" was commonly used slang that meant "first-rate" or "excellent."

Cracker Jack was soon sold in snack bars at circuses, fairs, and sporting events. In 1908 the lyricist Jack Norworth and the composer Albert von Tilzer immortalized Cracker Jack in their song, "Take Me Out to the Ball Game" with the lyrics: "Buy me some peanuts and cracker-jack— / I don't care if I never get back." Unlike other fad foods, Cracker Jack survived. Throughout the early twentieth century the company expanded, opening operations in Canada and the United Kingdom. By 1913 Cracker Jack was the world's largest-selling commercial confection. A major reason for its longevity was extensive national advertising, specifically focused at children. In 1912 a small toy was included in every package. The little sailor boy and his dog were first used in advertisements in 1916, and three years later they appeared on the Cracker Jack box. They were based on a picture of Frederick Rueckheim's grandson with his dog, named Bingo. His grandson, Robert, died of pneumonia shortly after the package was introduced.

In 1970 Cracker Jack was enjoyed in 24,689,000 homes, or 41 percent of all American households. Then other companies began manufacturing Cracker Jack-like snacks, and Cracker Jack sales declined. By the 1990s Cracker Jack ranked behind its competitors in sales.

[*See also* Advertising; Popcorn.]

BIBLIOGRAPHY

Piña, Ravi. *Cracker Jack Collectibles with Price Guide*. Atglen, PA: Schiffer, 1995.
Smith, Andrew F. *Popped Culture: A Social History of Popcorn in America*. Columbia: University of South Carolina Press, 1999.

ANDREW F. SMITH

Crackers

Crackers started out as thin, crisp, nonsweet, bite-size flatbreads. The making of crackers was among the first food industries in America. During the eighteenth century, cheap, hard crackers called "ship's bread," "ship's biscuits," and later, "hardtack" were widely manufactured for use on ships and for those migrating westward. These large, sturdy crackers, made only of flour and water—no shortening—kept for a very long time. One of the earliest brand-name foods was Bent's water crackers, which were initially manufactured in 1801 by Josiah Bent, a ship's bread baker in Milton, Massachusetts. The Bent Company continues to manufacture these crackers.

Crackers were packed in barrels and sold to grocery stores and restaurants. Recipes for simple crackers appeared in early American cookbooks. These crackers were little more than baked flour and water and were not made with fermented dough. By the 1840s three major cracker varieties made with shortening had been introduced: the soda cracker, the butter cracker, and the round sugar biscuit. During the 1850s a new product, the graham cracker, was probably first manufactured by Russell Thacher Trall, a follower of Sylvester Graham and the author of *The New Hydropathic Cook-book* (1854). Graham crackers were made with graham flour—coarsely milled, unbolted whole wheat flour—and were intended for use by those following the dietary regimen advocated by Sylvester Graham. Graham crackers made commercially contain sugar and other ingredients that Sylvester Graham most likely would not condone.

During the Civil War, the Northern armies and navy were supplied with hardtack. To meet the greatly increased demand, cracker bakers constructed continuously fired, revolving-reel ovens, which greatly increased output. They also installed mixing machines, dough brakes, rolling machines, automatic dough cutters, and stamps for cutting the dough into various shapes. After the Civil War sales of hardtack declined, but crackers made with sugar became popular. Commercial production of crackers increased when compressed yeast became available in America in the late 1860s. In the nineteenth century, crackers were generic products, sold from open barrels, so the crackers were exposed to air, dust, moisture, odors, and the depredations of flies and mice. In the South the term "cracker" was used as a pejorative term for poor whites, particularly in Georgia.

The era of the generic crackers ended in 1898 with the formation of the National Biscuit Company, the forerunner of Nabisco. The company had been formed by a merger of several companies and at the time controlled approximately 70 percent of the American cracker industry. The new company introduced wrapping and packaging machines for their new brand-name product, Uneeda biscuits. To promote these crackers, National Biscuit launched the first major national advertising campaign for a food product, emphasizing a particular advantage: The crackers were sealed in a moisture-proof package that kept them dry, crisp, and unspoiled. In the first full year of the campaign, National Biscuit sold 120 million packages of Uneeda biscuits. Another cracker in the National Biscuit product line almost from the company's beginning was the Premium saltine, a square soda cracker. Salt-topped Ritz crackers, made with considerably more shortening than other crackers, were first manufactured in 1935.

After World War II, the cracker industry expanded along with the rest of the snack food field. As Americans broadened their tastes, new technology made possible a greater variety of flavors and shapes. Crackers are flavored with onion, herbs, and spices and topped with sesame or poppy seeds. No longer only rectangular or round, crackers may be triangular, oval, scalloped, and fish shaped. In response to market demand, some crackers, including saltines, are made in low-sodium versions, and a few manufacturers have reduced the amount of hydrogenated fat in their products. Crackers are eaten with soups and chowders, softened in milk, and served as a snack food and for dipping.

[*See also* Graham, Sylvester; Hardtack; Nabisco; Snack Food.]

BIBLIOGRAPHY

Cahn, William. *Out of the Cracker Barrel.* New York: Simon and Schuster, 1969.

Crackers. New York: Mintel, 2003.

Manley, Duncan J. R. *Technology of Biscuits, Crackers, and Cookies.* 3rd ed. Boca Raton, FL : CRC, 2000.

Panschar, William G. *Baking in America.* Evanston, IL: Northwestern University Press, 1956.

ANDREW F. SMITH

Cranberries

Cranberries (*Vaccinium macrocarpon*), native to bogs and swamps of the northeastern United States and adjacent parts of Canada, were cultivated by Native Americans long before white settlers arrived. Commercial farming, by management of native stands, began early in the nineteenth century on Cape Cod, Massachusetts. The plant enjoys cool summers and requires soils that are very acidic, sandy, moist, and rich in humus. Suitable sites, which have also been developed in Wisconsin and the Pacific Northwest, are furnished with dikes and drainage ditches for water management, important for periodically flooding fields for winter cold protection, harvest, and irrigation.

Although more than 150 cultivars exist, the market is dominated by four—Early Black, Howes, Searles, and McFarlin—which were all selected from the wild in the nineteenth century. The cultivars differ mostly in such characteristics as harvest date and yield. Flavor differences are insignificant, especially for a fruit that is consumed only after processing, so varieties are not marketed by name.

Cranberry plants are woody evergreens whose low stature, thin stems, half-inch leaves, and small blossoms give the plant a delicate appearance. So-called runner stems creep along the ground, forming roots wherever they contact moist soil. In lieu of pruning, cranberry bogs are covered every few years with a two-inch depth of sand, which rejuvenates plants by stimulating formation of new roots on covered portions of stems. The flowers, poised like white cranes on the stalks (the inspiration for the name "craneberry," which became "cranberry") are self-fruitful. Fruits ripen from 60 to 120 days after flowering, depending on the cultivar.

Cranberries are harvested either dry or wet. All the vines are trained in the same direction for dry harvest, and the berries are popped off the vines as they are combed with a rake. Fields are flooded for wet harvest,

---

CRANBERRIES IN HISTORY

Native Americans introduced cranberries to New England colonists, who quickly adopted them into their cookery. John Josselyn reported in *New England's Rarities Discovered* (1672) that "the *Indians* and *English* use them much, boyling them with Sugar for Sauce to eat with their Meat; and it is a delicate Sauce especially for roasted Mutton; Some make Tarts with them as with Goose Berries." In 1728 cranberries were identified as a food that children could eat between meals. America's first cookbook author, Amelia Simmons, recommended in *American Cookery* (1796) that turkey be served with cranberries, a connection most likely made since early colonial times. During the nineteenth century, cranberries were used extensively in pies, sauces, jellies, jams, preserves, puddings, dumplings, marmalades, and ketchup. Cranberries were also mashed and made into a beverage called "cranberryade."

ANDREW F. SMITH

---

and special machinery is used to beat the berries from the vine. The dislodged berries float and can then be gathered together for harvest. The bulk of the cranberry crop is sold processed. Fresh fruits keep well and will ripen and redden to some degree even off the vine. The fruit, which is high in vitamin C, is processed into sauces, juices, relishes, and, of course, jelly, the traditional accompaniment to the Thanksgiving turkey.

BIBLIOGRAPHY

Da, M. "Cranberry Management." In *Small Fruit Crop Management,* edited by Gene J. Galletta and David G. Himelrick, 334–362. Englewood Cliffs, NJ: Prentice-Hall, 1990.

Eastwood, B. *A Complete Manual for the Cultivation of the Cranberry, with a Description of the Best Varieties.* New York: C. M. Saxton & Co., 1856.

LEE REICH

Cream

Cream is a dairy product, rich in fat and skimmed from milk, usually cow's milk. Cream contains all the main constituents of milk but in different proportions, especially butterfat. The fat globules in cream are lighter than the rest of the milk so they naturally cluster and float, rising to the surface when whole milk is left to stand. Once skimmed by hand, commercial cream now is separated by centrifugal force in a mechanical separator that rotates at 5,400 revolutions per minute. Jersey cows yield more cream per gallon of milk than a Holstein and were popular in the nineteenth century. But the demand for milk eventually caused yield to be more important than butterfat, and thus the prevalence of the black-and-white-spotted Holstein, America's most popular and productive dairy cow.

The natural thickness of cream depends on the fat content. Single cream has a minimum butterfat content of 18 percent, but its thickness also can be manipulated by manufacturing processes to produce whipping cream (35 percent butterfat), clotted cream (55 percent butterfat), and half-and-half (10 percent butterfat). Sour cream, found in the grocery store's dairy case, is made from pasteurized, homogenized single cream, has a butterfat content of 18 percent, and is soured by the addition of a starter—a bacterial culture that grows in the cream and converts lactose, the natural milk sugar, into lactic acid. Cream also can be found bottled, canned, and preserved by ultra-high temperature (UHT) processing, but may have a slightly cooked flavor.

The preservation and availability of cream was a dilemma for early American housewives. The richness of the milk varied with the weather, and cream would spoil unless measures were taken to keep it fresh. The traditional English technique for preserving cream (pour milk into shallow pans until the cream has risen, then heat it to 82°F for half an hour and allow to cool overnight) was adopted in America with few modifications. Lettice Bryan's *The Kentucky Housewife* (1839) includes a technique for boiling sugar-sweetened cream, bottling it with corks dipped in melted rosin, and storing it in a cool place such as a root cellar. Pioneer women sometimes invoked myth and superstition to blame the cream for going sour (thunder and lightning) or butter for being slow to form (pixies in the churn). In North Carolina they called for someone with an ugly face to peer into a cream jar and clot the cream.

Cream is widely used in baking and confectionary, soups and sauces, and desserts, where it is an essential ingredient whether frothily whipped or frozen into ice cream. It is the basic component of butter and is important in cream cheese and acidulated creams, such as mascarpone and crème fraîche, which originated in Europe but later were manufactured in America as well.

Cream is integral to many beverages, from the Elizabethan syllabub, brought to America and popular through the nineteenth century, to cocktails such as the grasshopper. It is the epitome of coffee additives, memorialized by the singer Ruth Etting in the 1929 recording of the love song "You're the Cream in my Coffee." The famous egg cream soda fountain confection first produced in New York City contains neither eggs nor cream.

[*See also* Butter; Creams, Dessert; Dairy Foods; Milk; Syllabub.]

BIBLIOGRAPHY

Beeton, Mrs. Isabella Mary. *The Book of Household Management . . . also, Sanitary, Medical, and Legal Memoranda; with a History of the Origin, Properties, and Uses of All Things Connected with Home Life and Comfort.* London: S. O. Beeton, 1861.

Rath, Sara. *About Cows.* Minocqua, WI: NorthWord Press, 1987.

SARA RATH

Creams, Dessert

Dessert creams are sweet dishes incorporating cream or egg whites, usually whipped, into a flavorful base. Highly popular in America in the eighteenth and nineteenth centuries, creams were a ubiquitous treat on English and French tables no later than the seventeenth century and were transported to American shores as domestic dairying grew.

Creams were made easily at home, requiring only a pan set over a heat source, a fork or whip to create the volume, and a way of cooling the mix. Creams were originally and most typically flavored with fruits, nuts, coffee, or tea, although chocolate and vanilla debuted in the nineteenth century. Recipes fell into two basic categories, and the texture ranged from a spoonable, thick sauce to a billowy cloud.

The simplest recipes are essentially enriched medieval nut milks: cream was boiled with ground nuts until thickened and then strained into glasses for chilling. Much more common were cream recipes based either on whipped eggs, particularly whites, or whipped cream. Some recipes used both. These creams, decoratively tinted in pastels, could be spooned into glasses or elaborate jelly dishes and chilled, or frozen into ice cream. Highly perishable, creams were elite and effete, referred to as "the little end of nothing whittled down."

By the early twentieth century, readily available commercial gelatin added to the base created Bavarian creams, which are sturdy enough to unmold and slice. Even with the gelatin, however, creams, unless frozen, were never good candidates for commercial production and transportation. Requiring fresh whipped eggs or cream, they remained a homemade dessert, although the shrinking number of recipes in twentieth-century cookbooks attests to their declining popularity.

[*See also* Cream; Desserts; Eggs.]

BIBLIOGRAPHY

Belden, Louise Conway. *The Festive Tradition: Table Decoration and Desserts in America, 1650–1900.* New York: W. W. Norton, 1983.

CATHY K. KAUFMAN

Cream Soda

Cream soda is a carbonated soft drink whose main ingredients are water, sweetener, and vanilla. Although some bottlers use cane sugar for the creamiest texture, most varieties are made with high fructose corn syrup. Cream soda is naturally clear, but most are colored with caramelized sugar, which also adds a slight flavor. Red cream soda has been popular occasionally, and there has even been a vogue for blue cream soda.

There are a number of explanations for the name "cream soda." The most obvious is the soda's creamy feel in the mouth. Another possibility is that some recipes call for cream of tartar, which adds to the creaminess of the drink. And, last, some people believe that it was originally called "ice cream soda," because it tastes as though it were made from vanilla ice cream.

Carbonated vanilla drinks were known in the United States as cream soda by 1854. Gray's Brewing of Wisconsin has been selling its cream soda since 1856. Although cream soda has captured only a small piece of the soft-drink market and has sometimes been considered an older person's drink, bottlers have been going after a younger market with hand-crafted cream sodas using more expensive ingredients, such as Tahitian vanilla and exotic honeys.

[*See also* Soda Drinks.]

BIBLIOGRAPHY

Mariani, John F. *The Dictionary of American Food and Drink.* New York: Hearst Books, 1994. An entertaining and reliable source.

SYLVIA LOVEGREN

Creole Food, *see Cajun and Creole Food*

Crisco

In 1911 the Procter & Gamble Company of Cincinnati, Ohio—until then best known for Ivory soap—introduced "An Absolutely New Product. A Scientific Discovery Which [would] Affect Every Kitchen in America. Something that the American housewife had always wanted" (Krondl, p. 266). It was Crisco. P&G was well placed to manufacture hydrogenated vegetable shortening, because the technology to make soap is substantially the same. Moreover, the company had been in the shortening business since at least 1870, when lard was part of its line.

Crisco was launched with one of the most comprehensive and successful advertising campaigns of all time. The shortening was hailed as modern and pure, playing on the public's fears concerning the unhygienic practices found in the meatpacking plants where commercial lard was processed. Advertisements extolled the immaculate factory housed "in a specially designed building lined with tile and flooded with sunshine" (Krondl, p. 272). The fat was individually packaged to safeguard it from contamination. In addition, numerous premium recipe collections were produced, including a kosher cookbook in 1933. P&G's literature quoted Rabbi Margolies of New York stating that "the Hebrew Race has been waiting 4,000 years for Crisco" (Krondl, p. 267). However, the most important selling point to Jew and Gentile alike was that Crisco was considerably cheaper than butter or even lard.

Over the years the brand name has been used for vegetable oil (from 1960) as well as vegetable sprays

Crisco Advertisement. *Culinary Archives & Museum at Johnson & Wales University, Providence, R.I.*

(from 1995). Since 1991 Crisco has been sold in butter-sized sticks besides the original tubs. Perhaps more remarkable, though, was the introduction of butter-flavored shortening in 1981—this from a company that had once claimed that "upon thousands of pages, the words 'lard' and 'butter' [had] been crossed out and the word 'Crisco' written in their place" (Krondl, p. 267).

BIBLIOGRAPHY

Krondl, Michael. *Around the American Table: Treasured Recipes and Food Traditions from the American Cookery Collections of the New York Public Library*. Holbrook, MA: Adams Publishing, 1995.

MICHAEL KRONDL

Croly, Jane Cunningham, *see Jenny June*

Crullers

In essence, a cruller is a twisted piece of deep-fried sweet dough. It originated with the Dutch, who named it for its distinctive shape (the verb *krullen* means "to curl"). In practice, especially U.S. practice, exceptions and variations abound—not only among the Dutch Americans whose forebears are credited with introducing the cruller to New York, but also among bakers of Scandinavian, Austrian, and Polish descent, each with their own twist (if you will) on the recipe. No ingredient save flour is completely indispensable, not even butter, sugar, milk, or eggs. Flavorings run the gamut from cinnamon, nutmeg, cardamom, lemon, and vanilla to wine, whiskey, rum, and even rose water (a suggestion from the seminal nineteenth-century cookbook author Eliza Leslie). The namesake shape is only one of many crullers may take. Various recipes specify diamonds, braids, corkscrews, cigars, rectangles, and even rings (whereupon they are dead ringers for doughnuts). Some are plain, others are glazed, dusted with sugar, or topped with syrup or jam. Finally, crullers are known by a slew of alternative names, including twist cakes, love knots, matrimony knots, angel wings, and Henriettes. Leslie knew them additionally as wonders, and Louisiana Cajuns proffer *croquignoles*.

[*See also* Doughnuts; Dutch Influences on American Food; Pastries.]

BIBLIOGRAPHY

Leslie, Eliza. *Miss Leslie's Directions for Cookery: An Unabridged Reprint of the 1851 Classic*. Mineola, NY: Dover, 1999.
Rose, Peter G., trans. and ed. *The Sensible Cook: Dutch Foodways in the Old and the New World*. Syracuse, NY: Syracuse University Press, 1989.
Thomas, Gertrude I. *Foods of Our Forefathers*. Philadelphia: F. A. Davis, 1941.

RUTH TOBIAS

Cuba Libre

"Cuba Libre" was shouted over raised glasses in bars in the United States and Cuba during and after the Spanish American War. The combination of Cuban rum with the newly invented American Coca-Cola seemed natural for a drink. The Cuba Libre became Cuba's national cocktail and is widely consumed in South Florida. It is made with rum, Coca-Cola, and a dash of key lime juice; it is served over ice in a chilled highball glass with a lime wedge. Many bartenders naturally put a lime wedge in a rum and Coke even when the drink is not ordered by its original name.

[*See also* Coca-Cola; Cocktails; Rum.]

MARIAN BETANCOURT

Cuban American Food

Located barely ninety miles from Key West, Florida, Cuba is the largest island nation in the Caribbean. It is a slender, crocodile-shaped island with fertile soil and a moderate tropical climate. The cuisine of the island was created by the native Taino (Arawak) Indians and transplanted peoples from four continents: Caribbean Indians and some from Florida brought to work in the mines, Spanish colonists, African slaves, Chinese contract workers, French refugees from Haiti, and peasants from Jamaica and Haiti.

Two events have marked the history of Cuba and defined its cuisine: the Spanish conquest and settlement, which lasted more than four hundred years, and the socialist revolution that began in 1959. Cuban cuisine formed almost biologically through the cross-fertilization of successive waves of peoples and cultures under Spanish colonial rule. The cuisine has preserved more of a Mediterranean character than many other Latin American cuisines. There is little use of the hot peppers or cilantro as in Mexican and some Andean cooking and relatively little use of corn. The corn that is used is prepared simply: fresh in tamales and both fresh and dried in sweet and savory porridges (*harina de maiz* and *tamal en cazuela*). The basis of most Cuban dishes is a classic Spanish *sofrito* (sauce base) made of sautéed garlic, onion, and green pepper and often enriched with bacon or Spanish sausage (chorizo) and a touch of beer or wine. Cubans seldom cook meat, fish, or game before seasoning it with adobo, a paste made with a mixture of an acid medium, such as lime, sour orange, or vinegar, and crushed garlic, pepper, salt, cumin, and oregano. Permanent food shortages and the concurrent erosion of traditional foodways have been part of the fallout of the revolution and accompanying international tensions.

Cuba's proximity to the United States and the cultural and political ties that have joined the two countries since the Spanish American War in the 1890s turned the United States into the natural destination for Cubans seeking political asylum. José Martí and hundreds of Cuban exiles had relocated to Key West and Tampa, Florida, and New York City before the war. Cubans first came to the United States in large numbers after the 1959 revolution, arriving on chartered planes sponsored by the U.S. government. When the Cuban government stopped the legal exodus, immigrants swam across Guantánamo Bay to find refuge at the American naval base ("Gitmo") or risked their lives crossing the Straits of Florida by boat or on flimsy rafts. The first wave of post-1959 immigration was composed of affluent Cubans, mostly from Havana and the western provinces of the island. Exiles from all regions of the country and representing all social groups and occupations gradually began arriving in large numbers. The 2002 U.S. Census estimated that 1,241,685 Cubans, including exiles born in Cuba and their U.S.-born descendants, live in the United States. Although Cubans live all over the United States, most have settled in Dade County, Florida, particularly in Miami, and in Hudson County, New Jersey. The trend is for retired Cubans living in the Northeast to move to Florida. Immigration of Cubans in the early 1960s transformed Miami, which was once little more than a tropical vacation enclave, into a durable and cosmopolitan city. Most Cubans had left behind family, friends, and material possessions but clung strongly to their cultural identity. Unable to return to Cuba legally for more than a decade, Cubans were unique among Hispanics living in the United States for their speedy assimilation into mainstream society coupled with a strong attachment to Cuba, its music, and its cuisine.

The Cuban exodus to Florida had a historic precedent. During the war of independence at the turn of the nineteenth century, Cuban political dissidents, mostly cigar makers, sought refuge in Key West. This tiny island at the tip of Florida became a lively Cuban enclave with cultural centers and restaurants, cigar factories where novels were read to workers as was traditionally done in Cuba, and a distinct Cuban cuisine. After Cuba gained its independence from Spain, Key West became the gateway for citrus fruits and avocados ferried from Cuba. These foods were transported north by train by Martin Brooks, the founder of Brooks Tropicals, a prominent grower and distributor of tropical fruits and vegetables in the Redlands of Homestead, Florida. After 1935, Brooks began to grow avocados and tropical fruits from Cuban seed in the fertile fields of Homestead, just south of Miami. In the 1960s, newly arrived Cuban farmers, mostly from Las Villas, planted tropical tubers and fruits, such as yuca (cassava), sweet potato, malanga coco, and mamey, near those same fields, changing the landscape and providing the raw materials for a transplanted Cuban cuisine.

Cuban restaurants sprang up all over Miami and wherever Cubans settled. Small restaurants and cafeterias kept the home fires burning by serving traditional foods: black beans, roast pork seasoned with adobo marinade, tender yuca doused in the garlicky table sauce called *mojo*, twice-fried green plantain (*tostones*); tropical juices and milk shakes; pressed Cuban sandwiches with layers of ham, pork, swiss cheese, and a pickle; and creamy flan sweetened with condensed milk. There also are numerous bakeries where people gathered for their daily *cafecito cubano* (inky espresso served in tiny cups) and sweet guava pastries. In the bakeries, Cubans also buy their traditional flaky bread for sandwiches and order elaborate, towering cakes for a girl's *fiesta de quince* or "sweet fifteen" party. From Boston to Hialeah, from New Jersey to Las Vegas, Cuban restaurants and cafeterias have a sameness that Cubans find comforting. Two dishes from other Latin American nations have become firmly established on the menus of Cuban restaurants. Argentinean-style skirt steak, which is generically listed as *churrasco* is served with *chimichurri*, a mildly spicy Argentinean table sauce. *Tres leches*, a trifle cake made popular by Nicaraguans in Miami, consists of a simple sponge cake soaked in three milks: condensed, evaporated, and heavy cream.

Fritas Cubanas. Las Americas Restaurant in Hoboken, New Jersey, serves Cuban food. *Photograph by Joe Zarba*

The usual restaurant menus do not represent the original range of Cuban regional dishes. At home, Cubans continue to cook traditional foods, but like other immigrant groups, they have also embraced American convenience foods and fast food, diversifying their diets with other ethnic cuisines, particularly Chinese and Italian. Although Cubans constitute only 3.7 percent of the total Hispanic population in the United States, Cuban food is the second most influential Latin cuisine in this country after Mexican cooking. Cuban food and drinks, particularly the *mojito*, a lemony rum cocktail perfumed with crushed mint leaves, have begun to stir the imagination of Latino and American chefs. Cuban food has been represented in the United States for a very long time with no major consequences and little crossover, except for black bean soup, Cuban sandwiches, and some rum cocktails, such as the daiquiri. Havana's fabled reputation as the playground of the rich and the watering hole of the Americas has contributed to a revival of the Cuban cocktail tradition. One result of interest in Cuban culture is the emergence of restaurants that play on the mythology of Cuba's elusive and fun-filled past. Old cigar labels, Cuban paraphernalia, and decor reminiscent of sultry street corners in Havana become props for Cuban cuisine of the imagination—at best, American fusion with a thin tropical veneer. A more genuine revival must await freer communication between chefs in the United States and the Cuban culinary tradition back on the island.

[*See also* Caribbean Influences on American Food.]

BIBLIOGRAPHY

Lluria de O'Higgins, María Josefa. *A Taste of Old Cuba*. New York: HarperCollins, 1994.

Presilla, Maricel. "The Making of the Cuban Culinary Tradition." *Journal of Gastronomy* 3 (Winter 1987/1988): 44–53.

Presilla, Maricel. "Miami Cubans." In *The Food of Miami: Authentic Recipes from South Florida and the Keys*, edited by Caroline Stuart, 16–18. Boston: Periplus, 1999.

Presilla, Maricel. "My Eternal Cuba." *Saveur*, December 1999.

Rodriguez, Douglas. *Nuevo Latino*. Berkeley, CA: Ten Speed, 1995.

Urrutia Randelman, Mary, and Joan Schwartz. *Memories of a Cuban Kitchen*. New York: Macmillan, 1992.

MARICEL PRESILLA

Cucumbers

The cucumber, *Cucumis sativus*, is a subtropical annual originating in India. Domesticated by the seventh century B.C.E., the cucumber soon spread to China and the ancient Mediterranean world. Galen ascribed diuretic properties to cucumbers but cautioned that overindulgence produced a "wretched juice that is the cause of malignant fevers."

The Romans spread the cucumber through the empire; the plant thrived in Mediterranean areas. Seeds have been found at Roman sites in Britain, although archaeologists debate whether cucumbers were a luxury import or were grown at villas of the rich during classical times, as they would have required fancy cold frames or other agricultural techniques to flourish in the chilly British climate. By the sixteenth century, cucumbers were a fad foodstuff in England: aristocrats built cold frames and hothouses, developing what would become heirloom varieties from experiments in forcing stock.

Cucumbers first arrived in the New World with the Spanish, landing in Haiti in 1494. They spread quickly to Florida and then through Native American populations ranging as far west as the Great Plains. Cucumbers were introduced separately in the North. Sometimes called "cowcumber" in British and early American sources, allegedly because the cucumber's perceived indigestibility made it fit only for cows, both British and Dutch colonists boasted of the cucumber's success in sultry colonial summers. Related to but distinct from cucumbers are gherkins, *C. anguria*, which were introduced into America only in 1793 but which spread quickly as a reliable crop free from the insects that plagued *C. sativus*.

Cucumbers are most frequently pickled or used raw in salads with vinaigrettes or "high" seasonings. In the nineteenth century cucumbers were often stewed and flavored with gravy, fried, stuffed, or even added to cold soups as part of a Spanish gazpacho. Cucumbers are also sautéed, creamed, or served with rich butter sauces, and they are used decoratively in thin slices to simulate fish scales on large sides of cold, poached salmon.

Cucumbers have maintained a reputation for indigestibility, with different preparation tricks suggested to reduce the danger. In *The American Frugal Housewife* (1829), Lydia Maria Child recommends slicing cucumbers thinly and soaking them in cold water to take out "the slimy matter, so injurious to health." Thomas J. Murrey gives precisely the opposite advice in *Salads and Sauces* (1884), in which he blames digestive difficulties on removing the natural juices; he urges peeling the skins and dousing the juicy remains copiously with oil.

Early Americans appreciated the different varieties of cucumbers. In *American Cookery* (1796), Amelia

Simmons identifies preferred uses for the "many kinds": prickly (she is most likely referring to the gherkin, *C. anguria*); tender whites; and smooth, bright green ones. In 1806 Bernard M'Mahon identified eight varieties in his authoritative *The American Gardener's Calendar*. Modern American growers generally classify cucumbers by their culinary purposes: either pickling or slicing, with greenhouse (also known as European), Middle Eastern, and Oriental groupings further dividing the slicing category. Those subgroups include many cultivars that have been bred for different qualities: seedlessness and digestibility, flavor and smooth skin, and crispness. The Southeast, along with California, leads in growing slicing cucumbers, while Michigan and North Carolina lead in growing pickling cucumbers.

[*See also* Pickles; Salads and Salad Dressings; Vegetables.]

BIBLIOGRAPHY

Facciola, Stephen. *Cornucopia II: A Source Book of Edible Plants.* Vista, CA: Kampong Publications, 1998.

Hedrick, U. P. *A History of Horticulture in America to 1860.* New York: Oxford University Press, 1950.

Phipps, Frances. *Colonial Kitchens, Their Furnishings, and Their Gardens.* New York: Hawthorn Books, 1972.

Weaver, William Woys. *Heirloom Vegetable Gardening.* New York: Holt, 1997.

CATHY K. KAUFMAN

Culinary Historians of Boston

The Culinary Historians of Boston, founded by Barbara Ketchum Wheaton and Joyce Toomre, was the first group of its kind and, as of the early 2000s, has been meeting every month of the academic year since 1980. The first meeting took place on May 29 with a brown-bag lunch under a maple tree in Radcliffe Yard. Most of those who came to that first meeting did not know one another but had heard about the founding meeting by word of mouth. Wheaton recalls that it was a very informal but enthusiastic get-together. Those first members came from a variety of academic and work backgrounds, a pattern that has continued.

One common theme shared by the members of the group was the desire to expose the misinformation that had been published about food and to set a standard for excellence for doing food and culinary research.

Some of those early members included Barbara Haber, a bibliographer of women's history and a curator of printed books at the Schlesinger Library; Ann Robert, a French restaurateur; Joyce Toomre, a college professor and a specialist in Russian cookery; Ruth Palombo, a dietitian at Massachusetts General Hospital; David Miller, an expert on the history and manufacture of metalwork, especially molds; Tom Lam, a graduate student studying the life and work of Ellen Swallow Richards; and Nina Simonds, an expert on Chinese cookery.

Since the beginning, the final event for the year has been a period banquet. At the first banquet members prepared recipes from *Savoring the Past: The French Kitchen and Table from 1300 to 1789* by Barbara Wheaton. Other dinners have included a Roman banquet, an 1830s American picnic, a Civil War banquet, a Russian banquet, and an Indonesian feast.

After a quarter of a century some of the original members were still attending the monthly meetings. At the beginning of the twenty-first century the Culinary Historians of Boston was continuing as a nonprofit organization dedicated to the study of foodways. Members around the country receive a newsletter with announcements of meetings, accounts of previous meetings, notices of new books, and information on exhibits and food-related conferences.

[*See also* Culinary vs. History Food History.]

BIBLIOGRAPHY

Culinary Historians of Boston. http://www.culinary.org/chb/Newsletters/ns_2000.htm. Official website includes information about the organization and back issues of the newsletter.

JOSEPH M. CARLIN

Culinary History vs. Food History

American academics are relative newcomers to the study of food, a subject that in the past has been pursued almost exclusively by independent scholars whose interest in the historical dimensions of food grows out of a deep knowledge of the techniques of cooking and the equipment it requires. They work with recipes and think of themselves as "culinary historians." In contrast, academics see themselves as "food historians," studying food in all of its various meanings—except for cooking—including its symbolic meanings, and as an instrument of analysis that can throw light on such broad areas as immigration history, the history of science and technology, and the impact upon culture and society of specific foods.

Food Historians

Social, Political, and Economic Influences In *Sweetness and Power: The Place of Sugar in Modern History* (1985), the anthropologist Sidney Mintz created an influential interdisciplinary model for food historians by combining his field work with Caribbean sugarcane workers and a study of the social, economic, and political history of a major agricultural product. He argues that in England before 1800 sugar was a scarce food available only to the rich, but it later became available to everyone largely because plantation slaves in the Caribbean provided cheap labor while industrialists in England developed efficient manufacturing techniques for processing sugar.

Other major works by American academics soon followed. The historian Harvey Levenstein's *Revolution at the Table: The Transformation of the American Diet* (1988) gives academic weight to the study of food by relating changing eating habits in America between 1880 and 1930 to such major forces as immigration, urbanization, developing technologies, and the growth and power of the corporate food industry. In *Paradox of Plenty: A Social History of Eating in Modern America* (1993), he updates the story by looking at the ways in which the American diet has been shaped by cultural, political, and economic forces since the 1930s. Other American academics are bringing a range of disciplines to the study of food. In *Appetite for Change: How the Counterculture Took on the Food Industry* (1989), the American studies professor Warren Belasco analyzes the ways in which corporate America co-opted such counterculture foods as brown rice and whole wheat bread in order to profit from the very products that had symbolized radical opposition to capitalism in the 1960s.

The impact of immigration on American food is the focus of the geography professor Richard Pillsbury's *No Foreign Food: The American Diet in Time and Place* (1998), which explores dietary changes from colonial times to the present. In the same year, Donna Gabaccia, a historian specializing in immigration and women's history, published *We Are What We Eat: Ethnic Food and the Making of Americans*, which also looks at the impact of ethnicity on American eating habits, using insights from anthropology to examine the meanings people give to food, especially in maintaining their identities. The immigration story is picked up again by the historian Hasia Diner in *Hungering for America: Italian, Irish, and Jewish Foodways in the Age of Migration* (2001). In this volume, she contrasts the Old World food experiences of three immigrant groups—the Irish, Italians, and Jews—with what they found in America, and she explores the ways in which the preservation of ancestral foodways forged ethnic community and identity in the United States.

Women's and Ethnic Studies   By the end of the 1990s books on food written by academics focusing on women's history were contributing to the flow of scholarly work. Among these volumes were Amy Bentley's *Eating for Victory: Food Rationing and the Politics of Domesticity* (1998), which examines the importance of women's roles relative to food in supporting the nation during World War II and its aftermath. Sherrie Inness, an associate professor of English, has edited three collections of essays on women and food in addition to her own study, *Dinner Roles: American Women and Culinary Culture* (2001). In that book, Inness uses a wide range of sources to elaborate on the deep connections between women and food throughout the twentieth century.

Another literary scholar, Doris Witt, makes connections between African American studies, cultural studies, and food history in *Black Hunger: Food and the Politics of U.S. Identity* (1999), which explores the relationship between African American women and food and examines the representation of that connection in literature, art, and advertising. In *Eat My Words: Reading Women's Lives through the Cookbooks They Wrote* (2002), the folklorist Janet Theophano clarifies the value of cookbooks as a literary genre and, in so doing, dignifies food and its importance not only to women's history but also to human history.

No longer ignored or trivialized because of its connection to ordinary life and the domestic concerns of women, the subject of food has been given credibility by the work of college and university researchers of every discipline. Faculty and graduate students interested in pursuing food-related topics have been aided by the establishment of an annual joint meeting of two organizations: the Association for the Study of Food and Society and the Agriculture, Food, and Human Values Society. These conferences provide opportunities for students to report on their works in progress and to receive feedback from more seasoned scholars. As more young people take up the serious study of food, it is likely that such academic work will grow from the margins of the disciplines into the mainstream. As this occurs, more academics may understand the value of using cookbooks as essential texts and recognize the importance of knowing about the history of ingredients and the techniques of cooking, subjects that have always been starting points for culinary historians.

Culinary Historians

Working from a basic knowledge of how a dish is cooked, culinary historians have commonly been curious about the origins of different dishes and the people that produced them. At the same time, many of these largely independent scholars have gone on to investigate such related subjects as the specific foods people grow, which animals they domesticate, and the ways in which foods move from one culture to another. The scope of their work is without limit and often provides an informed analysis of how food reveals the nature of a culture in a particular time and place.

Cookbooks as Historical and Cultural Artifacts The methodology of the culinary historian is well illustrated in the work of Karen Hess, who is renowned for her facsimile editions of *Martha Washington's Booke of Cookery* (1981), *The Virginia House-wife* (1984), *What Mrs. Fisher Knows about Old Southern Cooking* (1995), and the *Carolina Rice Cook Book*, compiled by Mrs. Samuel G. Stoney, which is included in Hess's study *The Carolina Rice Kitchen: The African Connection* (1992). In all of these works, Hess provides thoroughly researched introductions or afterwords, annotations, and notes that offer historical contexts to the recipes she examines and lead readers to important conclusions about the people who wrote the cookbook texts. In *The Carolina Rice Kitchen*, for instance, she successfully establishes the connections between the South Carolina rice culture and the early African American cooks who introduced such dishes as rice and bean pilafs.

Like Hess, William Woys Weaver sees cookbooks as cultural artifacts, as demonstrated in his facsimile edition of *A Quaker Woman's Cookbook: The Domestic Cookery of Elizabeth Ellicott Lea* (1982). Originally published in 1845, the book was meant to serve as a handbook for inexperienced young wives who knew little about the art of cookery. To Weaver, it is a rich source of information about the role of Quaker women in the Middle Atlantic region of nineteenth-century America. Weaver also has written extensively on Pennsylvania Dutch cooking and Pennsylvania German foods in *Sauerkraut Yankees: Pennsylvania-German Foods and Foodways* (1983) and *Pennsylvania Dutch Cooking* (1993).

Another independent scholar, Sophie Coe, has contributed valuable early historic information to our understanding of pre-Columbian civilizations—Aztec, Maya, and Inca—in her book *America's First Cuisines* (1994). Trained in anthropology, Coe examines the fragmentary evidence about these cultures in the writings of early Spanish settlers, who, for instance, give descriptions of amazing varieties of tomatoes and potatoes. Through the examination of the remnants of cooking vessels, she concluded that frying was probably not a style of cooking used by these groups. Coe even suggests that the Spaniards, accustomed to olive oil and other fats, might have been drawn to the bitter chocolate drinks they were offered because of the fat content of the beverage.

Bringing Culinary History to Life Culinary historians know of one another's work through their publications and by attending the growing number of meetings and conferences that have been held since the early 1980s. The first such gathering, the Oxford Symposium on Food and Cookery, organized by the British food historian Alan Davidson, brought together an international group of mainly independent scholars that continues to meet on the campus of Oxford University. Since then, culinary history groups have sprung up across the United States, drawing like-minded members for whom the study of food history is a passion. These groups typically invite outside speakers who are recognized authorities in subjects that range from growing heirloom apples to interpreting classical cuisines. Often, they also create period meals as a hands-on way of understanding the past. Themes range from the favored foods of Native Americans, the efforts required to produce a particular historical meal, or the menu items served at Thomas Jefferson's table, illustrating the crops he grew and imported and the equipment he introduced.

These insights are also available through the demonstrations of authentic period meals produced in living-history museums throughout the United States. Plimoth Plantation reproduces life in seventeenth-century Massachusetts, while Sturbridge Village recreates an early nineteenth-century New England town. Colonial Williamsburg in the Southeast, Old World Wisconsin, and Fort Walla Walla in Washington State are just a few examples of the living-history, agricultural, and open-air museums that try to cultivate heirloom fruits and vegetables and demonstrate the preparation of meals appropriate to various historical periods. Culinary historians appreciate and make great use of these valuable resources.

Differences Bridged

Many academic food historians are apt to be dismissive of culinary historians, whose examination of recipes and concern with hands-on cooking often strikes academics as more "womanish" than scholarly. Yet, without a real sense of what is involved in the preparation of a dish—the labor, the techniques of cooking, and the knowledge of ingredients and their history—professional scholars run the risk of making serious errors of fact and interpretation. Ingredients that are familiar to cooks, such as nasturtiums in salads or candied violets in cake decorating, may strike scholars as unusual and exotic. Or they may not have a grasp of the amount of work that was involved in preparing meals in nineteenth-century American kitchens, knowledge that would provide a fuller understanding of why, for example, ordinary families employed servants. In time it may be universally recognized that an understanding of how food is cooked and eaten is indispensable to the proper study of food. When that happens, employing the terms "food historian" and "culinary historian" will seem like making a distinction without a difference, and research on food by academic and independent scholars will become even richer and deeper as well as more accurate.

[*See also* Culinary Historians of Boston; Historic Dining Reenactment; Historiography.]

BIBLIOGRAPHY

Davidson, Alan. *The Oxford Companion to Food.* Oxford: Oxford University Press, 1999.
Flandrin, Jean-Louis, and Massimo Montanari. *Food: A Culinary History from Antiquity to the Present.* English edition by Albert Sonnenfeld. New York: Columbia University Press, 1999.
Gastronomica: The Journal of Food and Culture. Journal series. Berkeley: University of California Press, 2001–.
Neuhaus, Jessamyn. *Manly Meals and Mom's Home Cooking: Cookbooks and Gender in Modern America.* Baltimore: The Johns Hopkins University Press, 2003.
Petits Propos Culinaires: Essays and Notes on Food, Cookery and Cookery Books. Journal series. London, Prospect Books, 1979–.
Zanger, Mark H. *The American History Cookbook.* Westport, CT: Greenwood Press, 2003.

BARBARA HABER

Culinary Institute of America

The Culinary Institute of America (CIA) is the only residential college in the world with a curriculum devoted entirely to the culinary profession. First known as the New Haven Restaurant Institute, it was founded in 1946 in New Haven, Connecticut, as a vocational training school for World War II veterans. Demand for food-service professionals in a burgeoning industry sparked rapid expansion, and in 1947 the cooking school moved to larger quarters and was renamed the Restaurant Institute of Connecticut. In 1951 the school became known as the Culinary Institute of America.

Continued growth in the food industry placed increased demand on facilities, and in 1970 the CIA moved to Hyde Park, New York. Saint Andrew-on-Hudson, a former Jesuit seminary, was purchased, and it served as the nucleus around which the campus was built. In 1995 the CIA expanded to the West Coast, purchasing the former Christian Brothers Winery–Greystone Cellars in the Napa Valley of California.

The CIA offers bachelor's and associate's degree programs in culinary arts and baking and pastry arts as well as continuing education for wine and food professionals. Research and study of nutritional cooking are centered at the CIA's General Foods Nutrition Center, and the culinary collection at the Conrad N. Hilton Library serves both students and food scholars. The CIA is the only school authorized to administer the American Culinary Federation's master chef certification program. The Learning Resources Center produces and maintains instructional videotapes for the culinary profession.

Students staff the CIA's five Hyde Park restaurants, gaining hands-on experience in all venues of food preparation and service. The restaurants, which are open to the public, have garnered several industry awards for outstanding cuisine. The Escoffier Restaurant, specializing in modern interpretations of classic French cuisine, is the recipient of *Restaurants and Institutions* magazine's coveted Ivy Award.

[*See also* Cooking Schools.]

BIBLIOGRAPHY

Culinary Institute of America. http://www.ciachef.edu/. The official website of the CIA, providing information on its history, admissions, degrees and curriculum, and restaurants.

BECKY MERCURI

Cupboards and Food Safes

Convenience for cooks and protection from pests are the driving forces in storing food. From the beginning of American kitchens, containers, bowls, and tools have been stored on shelves or in built-in or freestanding cupboards with shelves and drawers. Before refrigeration various foods were kept in food "safes."

Cupboards fixed to kitchen walls were often fitted with sliding shelf-boxes for storing such items as cleaning supplies and closed bins of meal and flour. Freestanding cupboards held preparation tools as well as tableware and serving pieces. Sometimes such cupboards were called "dressers." In 1869 Catharine Beecher and her sister, Harriet Beecher Stowe (author of the antislavery novel *Uncle Tom's Cabin*, 1852), published *The American Woman's Home*. It depicts a practical kitchen layout with fixed shelves, some below the work surfaces, laden with boxes and tins.

Meat and other food safes are wooden, furniture-like cases with one or more shelves, with or without legs, and with punctured tin or wood panels or screening for air circulation and insect protection. They could be fixed to joists or set where convenient in kitchen or pantry. An amusing household hint was to put each leg of a food safe in a container of water to deter ants. The most notable U.S. food safes are pie safes, sometimes decoratively painted and with ornamental patterns in the punctured tins.

From the late 1800s to the 1930s freestanding cabinets (generally known as "Hoosier" cabinets because so many brands came from Indiana) with shelves, storage bins, and enameled work surfaces were popular. Some had pullout dough boards, and even coffee grinders and flour sifters were built into them.

[*See also* Kitchens.]

BIBLIOGRAPHY

Franklin, Linda Campbell. *300 Years of Kitchen Collectibles*. 5th ed. Iola, WI: Krause Publications, 2003.
Kennedy, Phillip D. *Hoosier Cabinets*. Indianapolis, IN: privately published, 1989.

LINDA CAMPBELL FRANKLIN

Currants

Currants are making a comeback in America, after once having gone out of favor for being implicated as alternate hosts for a white pine disease. They are plants of northern regions, thriving where summers are cool.

Red and white currants are different-colored forms of hybrids of *Ribes rubrum*, *R. sativum*, and *R. petraeum*. They became popular in northern Europe in about the fifteenth century and were one of the first plants brought over by early colonists to America. Into the early part of the twentieth century, red currants were a significant crop and were grown, for example, between apple trees in New York's Hudson Valley for sale locally and for shipment to New York City. Red and white currants are generally concocted into a beautiful, translucent jelly, although some varieties are tasty when eaten fresh.

Black currants, mostly of the *Ribes nigrum species*, are susceptible to the pine disease, although resistant varieties have been bred. Black currants first came into favor in Europe in the sixteenth century, as a medicinal plant whose fruits are recognized as a potent source of vitamin C. The robust raw flavor does not appeal to everyone, but it makes a delectable jam and juice and is the fruit flavoring for cassis. The clove currant, *R. odoratum*, is a native American black currant that was once valued for the spicy fragrance of its yellow, trumpet-shaped blossoms; its aromatic, sweet-tart fruit is larger than that of the European black currant. "Dried currants" are not made from currants but from grapes.

BIBLIOGRAPHY

Hedrick, U. P. *The Small Fruits of New York*. Albany, NY: J. B. Lyon, 1925.
Reich, Lee. *Uncommon Fruits for Every Garden*. Portland, OR: Timber Press, 2004.

LEE REICH

Custards

Custards are a combination of eggs and milk or cream, with additional flavorings added, either sweet or savory, and gently cooked until thickened. Cooking techniques vary. Stirred custards, misleadingly called "boiled" (as boiling curdles the texture and is usually considered a fault), are made in a pan over a heat source and result in a rich but pourable sauce. Baked custards are gently cooked in an oven until they become a solid gel. Virtually all European cuisines have had some form of custard since the late medieval period; most—such as boiled pudding sauces (often called "crème anglaise") from England and flan from Spain—have found their way into American kitchens with successive waves of immigrants.

Historically custards were frequently baked in a crust, forming an important component of medieval meat pies. Recipes for such dishes came to America in colonial manuscripts and continue to appear under the name of "quiche." Quiche enjoyed a brief renaissance in the 1970s, one that was squelched by the assertion that "real men don't eat quiche."

Perhaps custard's most popular form is crème brûlée, which rocketed to cultlike status in restaurants in the 1980s and 1990s. Home cooks emulated, purchasing tiny torches for caramelizing the custard's crackling sugar lid. Had they read the "receipt" for burnt custard in *The Kentucky Housewife* (1839) by Lettice Bryan, they would have used a red-hot shovel or a salamander to singe the sugar.

[*See also* Cream; Desserts; Eggs.]

BIBLIOGRAPHY

Washington, Martha. *Martha Washington's Booke of Cookery*. Transcribed and edited by Karen Hess. New York: Columbia University Press, 1981. Highly informative notes accompany custard recipes.

CATHY K. KAUFMAN

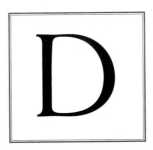

Dagwood Sandwich

The Dagwood sandwich was the creation of the Blondie cartoonist Murat "Chic" Young. In the late 1930s fans first witnessed its construction when Blondie's husband, Dagwood Bumstead, clad in his famous polka-dot pajamas, threw open the refrigerator and built a sandwich based on any and all ingredients that came to hand. In 1947 the recipe appeared in Young's *Blondie's Soups, Salads, Sandwiches Cook Book* as the "Skyscraper Special," and it included sardines and baked beans, along with suggestions for other somewhat incompatible foods. The term "Dagwood" is used for any large, multilayered sandwiches, like hoagies or submarines, consisting of various cold cuts, fillings, and condiments.

[*See also* Hoagie; Sandwiches.]

BIBLIOGRAPHY

Mercuri, Becky. *Sandwiches That You Will Like*. Pittsburgh, PA: WQED Pittsburgh, 2002.

BECKY MERCURI

Dairy

Dairy constitutes a large category of fresh and frozen foods that includes milk, butter, buttermilk, cream, sour cream, cheese, ice cream, milk sherbet, and yogurt. Each American consumes over five hundred pounds of these products a year, the largest food group by weight in the nation's diet. Consumption may be in the form of such all-American dishes as apple pie à la mode, cheeseburgers, bagels with cream cheese, pizza, American cheddar cheese, milkshakes, baked Alaska, macaroni and cheese, cheesecake, and ice cream sandwiches, sundaes, and cones.

Milk: America's "Perfect" Food

The United States each year produces 38 billion gallons of cow's milk, the raw material for almost all dairy foods, making it the largest milk-producing country in the world; California, Wisconsin, New York, Pennsylvania, and Minnesota are the leading dairy states. In 2001, 34 percent of milk production was sold as fresh milk or cream, while 36.7 percent went to make cheese, 13.3 percent for butter, 8.9 percent for frozen desserts, 6.2 percent for condensed or evaporated milk, and the remainder for other uses.

Milk is not, of course, produced only by cows. Increasingly, goats, buffalo, and sheep are being raised for milk, primarily for artisanal cheeses. Goat's milk is a common alternative to cow's milk for the 5–7 percent of the infant population that suffers from cow's milk allergy, a reaction of the immune system against the proteins in milk.

Milk is a symbol of the American national identity and, with its whiteness and presumed perfection, a reminder of mother's milk. This association lends some dairy products both a life-giving and an erotic quality. According to the food historian Margaret Visser, domelike scoops of ice cream suggest motherly breasts. Hot milk is used as a soporific and also forms the basis of custard, baby-food-like desserts, such as rice pudding. The substance has attained tremendous importance in our culture as "the perfect, essential food," and, until the 1960s, it was considered the pinnacle of human nutrition.

Dairy still provides 75 percent of the calcium in the American diet, especially important for pregnant, nursing, and menopausal women. Research in 2002 also reported the unexpected finding that increased calcium levels might lower high blood pressure and help people lose weight. On the basis of their high fat content, however, dairy foods have also been implicated in elevating HDL cholesterol, which contributes to heart disease in those at risk. Moreover, the use of recombinant bovine growth hormone (rBGH), a genetically engineered product that increases milk yield by 50 percent, as well as antibiotics to treat illness in cows has led to a strong antimilk consumer backlash and a dramatic decline in sales since the 1980s.

Cheese

The United States is the world's largest cheese producer, with 8.5 billion pounds in 2001, amounting to a per-person consumption of 29.37 pounds. The top five cheese-making states are Wisconsin, Minnesota, California, Idaho, and New York. In the last quarter of the twentieth century, cheese boosted overall dairy consumption significantly. The best known and most consumed of American original cheeses is American cheddar, originally called "English cheddar" but renamed after the Revolutionary War. In 2001 this cheese sold 12.7 pounds per person. The ranks of American cheeses include colby (named for the town in Wisconsin where it was invented in 1874), monterey jack (created in California after the gold rush of 1849), swiss (or, more precisely, swiss emmenthaler, developed by the Swiss farmer Adam Blumer in Wisconsin in about 1850), brick (also made in Wisconsin, in 1877), liederkranz (made first by the Swiss-born Émile Frey in Monroe, New York, in 1892), limburger (produced by German immigrants in upstate New York and a standard beer hall item), Tillamook (a highly esteemed yellow Oregon cheddar), and Vermont cheddar (a sharp, light-yellow cheese).

In the early 1980s a few small producers in California began making goat's milk cheese. The tangy flavor derives from a higher percentage of medium- and small-chain fatty acids than are found in cow's milk. It is also lower in levels of casein, which produces a smaller curd in the stomach and, therefore, has better digestibility but more calories, calcium, and vitamin A than cow's milk cheese. Goat, sheep, and buffalo milk are used to make artisanal cheeses, which in the last decade of the twentieth century began to rival European varieties for quality.

Cottage cheese, known in the early nineteenth century as "pot cheese," is made from whole, part-skimmed, or skimmed milk and is often used as a diet food. Perennial favorites, processed cheeses (combinations of cheese with emulsifers, acids, flavorings, and colorings) include Velveeta (introduced by Kraft in 1928) and Cheez Whiz (processed cheese sauce in a jar, introduced by Kraft in 1953), still top-selling brands.

History

Dairying was unknown in the New World until the settlers of Jamestown, Virginia, brought the first cows from England in 1611. The English, Dutch, and Germans who settled the Northeast brought their traditions of dairy farming and butter making and cheese making with

them. The colony was a "butter culture," meaning that the early settlers used the "ultimate fat" liberally both as their cooking fat and to slather on bread. The "family cow" became an indispensable feature of early American life. Milk itself was not consumed as a beverage but rather used in cooking, with any surplus fed to the hogs.

Milk drinking emerged as a food habit only in the mid-nineteenth century in urban areas, when cow's milk began to be substituted for breast milk. For different reasons, neither poor nor upper-class women consumed enough calories to produce sufficient breast milk, and upper-class women had little interest in breast-feeding. Still, feeding infants and children cow's milk was very risky, because of the likelihood of contamination. Lack of sanitation and pasteurization resulted in milk's accounting for a high infant mortality rate.

Pasteurization was introduced in 1895 but only mandated for the first time in 1912 by New York State. The process so changed the taste of milk that many consumers, especially those in the Northeast, refused at first to drink it. Pasteurization elsewhere was adopted slowly. People continued to mistrust the milk supply until the

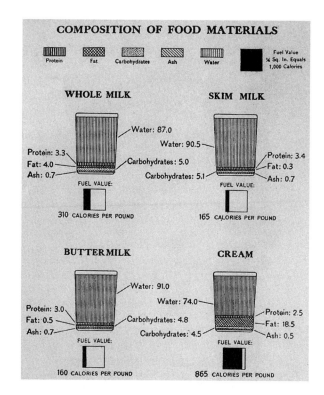

Dairy Foods. Composition of dairy food materials, from *Woman's Institute Library of Cookery: Essentials of Cookery, Cereals, Breads, Hot Breads* (Scranton, Pa., 1924), p. 15.

1920s. Eventually, milk would become and remain one of the most regulated commodities.

The dairy industry set about convincing the urban public that milk was clean by opening dairy lunch restaurants, where a limited menu of quick dishes, like milk toast, oatmeal and milk, and rice and milk, were served along with steaks and chops. The first of these lunch counters, Everett Dairy, opened in New York in 1875. Many other urban areas, including Chicago, Cleveland (Ohio), and Washington, D.C., soon had similar outlets. By the 1940s, the average American drank over a pint of milk a day, double the amount of the 1880s, and milk had become a staple of the nation's diet. For most of the twentieth century, children, adults, and older people drank milk in large quantities; a quart a day was considered the optimum for several decades.

Regional and Ethnic Influences on Dairy

Not surprisingly, the development of dairy cuisine emerged where the industry took root. New York State was the leading dairy state in 1839, producing almost one-third of the products for the entire nation. The first creamery was introduced in 1856 in Orange County, New York. Dairy dishes that were popular in the nineteenth century in the Northeast include New England clam chowder, bread puddings, ice cream, custard pies, chipped beef with milk gravy on toast, and milk-based soups, gravies, gratins, and scalloped dishes. These items continued to feature on menus into the twenty-first century.

The industry moved quickly to the Midwest, with Iowa surpassing New York in 1890 and Wisconsin becoming the most important dairy state a few years later. In the heartland, a new dairy cookery of German and Swiss German derivation developed. This white cuisine included cheese, milk, butter, and the white sauces that the French call "blanc," along with white meats (like milk-fed veal), white beer (*weisse bier*, made with sour milk), homemade cottage cheese, veal *paprikash* with sour cream, cooked caraway cheese, and Belgian cheese pie (actually a cheesecake), cream of beer soup, jellied veal, rhubarb bread (made with sour milk), white poppy seed soup (an uncooked milk soup), and German puffs (doughnuts).

During the immigration of the early industrial revolution (1785–1830), western and northern Europeans went to the Midwest: Swedes, Norwegians, and Finns moved to Illinois, Minnesota, and Wisconsin and later to the Dakotas, Iowa, and Nebraska. Scandinavians were not just big cheese eaters; they also introduced complicated butter-rich desserts made with a great deal of cream so that the cakes and cookies were light and fragile. The Norwegians made *lefse*—paper-thin potato pancakes bound together with a combination of milk, cream, and butter.

During the late Industrial Revolution migration (1875–1905), eastern and southern Europeans—Russians and Jews—moved mainly into industrial centers, such as New York and Chicago. Jewish immigrants who settled on the Lower East Side of New York introduced many popular dairy cuisine innovations. These dishes include New York cheesecake, with a cream cheese filling and graham cracker crust, sold in turn-of-the-century Jewish delis; kugel (noodle pudding), which often included dollops of sour cream or cottage cheese; and egg cream, a milk, seltzer, and chocolate syrup soda

Evaporated Cream. Advertisement for St. Charles Evaporated Cream, late nineteenth century.

fountain drink introduced in the 1930s. Although cream cheese was the 1872 innovation of a non-Jewish dairyman in France, the marketing opportunity as a complement to bagels was quickly perceived and exploited. The Breakstone brothers advertised their cream cheese specifically to the New York Jewish community.

Kosher dairy restaurants became popular in New York, to conform to Jewish dietary laws, which stipulate that meat and dairy dishes must not be served at the same meal and, in fact, must be prepared and eaten using separate sets of cooking utensils, pots, and dishes. These outlets served such items as hot and cold beet borscht soup with sour cream, cheese blintzes, macaroni and cheese, kosher milk, and cheeses made without animal rennet, including cottage (or farmer or pot) cheese and Muenster.

Italians, who settled mostly in New York and Philadelphia, particularly after World War II, introduced numerous cheeses, including Parmesan, Asiago, Romano, provolone, ricotta, and mozzarella, as well as Italian cheesecake made with ricotta, set on pastry crust, and containing bits of candied fruit. Pizza came with the second wave of immigration, and the first pizzeria opened in New York in 1905. The pie that today little resembles anything Italian did not become an American classic until after World War II.

Mexican migrant workers in the Southwest and California introduced *queso blanco* cheese and goat's milk *dulce de leche*, which rarely found their way into so-called Mexican restaurants. It was not until the 1950s and 1960s that Mexican foods began to enter the mainstream, where they were rendered unrecognizable under gobs of cheese and sour cream.

Changes in Dairy Consumption

Whole-milk consumption fell sharply from its 1950 peak of forty gallons per person to nineteen gallons in 1983, about a 50 percent decline. Until the 1950s, nutritionists believed that milk was an especially protective food. Then, however, the theory was propounded that saturated fat in dairy products (and also in meat) is responsible for raising the amount of "bad" cholesterol in the blood, which at high levels was said to put people at greater risk of coronary artery disease. The message was reinforced by private health organizations, such as the American Heart Association, and eventually, the government as well.

In the early 1960s, Americans began replacing whole-milk products with low-fat versions containing between 0.5 and 2 percent milk fat. The greatest change took place

between 1967 and 1994, when milk consumption dropped by more than 25 percent. In 1994 Americans drank only 19.1 gallons per person—less than the amount they ingested of soft drinks, tap water, coffee, or beer. Cutting back on butter began in the late 1960s. By 1991 consumers were buying more butter substitutes, such as margarine; volume sales of butter amounted to 15 percent of the total market, while margarine accounted for 85 percent.

Among other health factors contributing to this decline was the growing discussion of lactose intolerance, which affects 30 to 50 million Americans, most of them over age five; 75 percent of all African Americans and American Indians and 90 percent of Asian Americans are thought to be affected. Yogurt is a good source of calcium for people with lactose intolerance, even though yogurt itself is fairly high in lactose, because the bacterial cultures produce a lactase enzyme required for adequate digestion.

In short order, the disenchantment with dairy became marketing fodder for a deluge of dairy-free and reduced-fat cookbooks and a whole new product line of low-fat dairy products, including ice cream and cheese. Yogurt sales leaped by 500 percent between 1958 and 1968, when it was almost always sold in health food stores; the product went mainstream in 1975. By the early years of the twenty-first century Americans consumed about a billion cups of yogurt a year, increasingly sold as a frozen dessert.

In an interesting paradox, high-butterfat premium ice creams, such as Ben & Jerry's and Häagen-Dazs, and gold-foil-wrapped butters (containing more butterfat than the federal minimum of 80 percent) started to be marketed to the affluent, for whom risky dietary behavior is part of their privileged, invulnerable status. Ironically, they are the same class of people most dedicated to keeping fashionably slender.

As a final stroke against dairy foods, people became concerned about possible contamination with *Listeria monocytogenes*, a harmful microorganism that results in food-borne infections. It can occur in unpasteurized milk, cheese, and ice cream. Usual symptoms are nausea, vomiting, diarrhea, headache, and persistent fever. Although it is often relatively mild, listeriosis produces high fatality rates in unborn children, young children, older people, and anyone whose immune system is compromised. In 1985 an unaged and *Listeria*-infected cheese was responsible for twenty-nine fatalities, mostly stillbirths. People who are at risk are advised not to eat soft cheeses, including feta, Brie, Camembert, and mold-ripened blue cheese.

Move toward Organic Milk

In 1993 the Food and Drug Administration approved the first agricultural biotechnology product, recombinant bovine growth hormone (rBGH), created by a collaboration of dairy scientists at New York State's Cornell University and corporate farmers at Monsanto in St. Louis, Missouri. The substance, injected into cows, could induce them to produce a substantially greater amount of milk. The inventors foresaw small dairy farms being driven out of business and larger ones being absorbed into conglomerate agribusiness. The concept backfired. In 2001 less than one-third of all dairy farmers were using the substance. Many opted out because of strong consumer concern about the purity of the milk supply, even though there is no scientific consensus that the hormone has an adverse effect on humans.

The promotion of rBGH may actually have contributed to decreasing milk consumption. It also gave birth to a new dairy industry. While whole-milk sales declined precipitously, there was a dramatic increase in consumption of organic milk, defined as milk from cows that are not treated with either rBGH or antibiotics and that graze on grass. (By federal law, antibiotics may be used to treat sick cows but cannot be measurable or detectable in the milk itself.) The organic trade is growing at the rate of 50–80 percent annually from virtually nothing in the early 1990s. For the period from October 5, 2002 to October 4, 2003, organic milk accounted for 2.8 percent of all supermarket milk sales.

What distinguishes this new market segment is that it is composed of people who, for the most part, do not purchase other organic products, such as produce, and who are not members of a social movement, such as vegetarianism or anti–genetically modified food activists. Instead, the buyers are affluent professionals concerned with their health and interested in status foods. The irony is that 95 percent of the market is served by only three firms, two of which are multinationals that have purchased companies with strong local consumer preferences and have retained local brand names.

Politics of Dairy

In an effort to reverse the thirty-year decline in milk consumption, the $75-billion dairy industry has consistently pushed for greater quotas in government dietary publications. When the U.S. Department of Agriculture unveiled the *Food Guide Pyramid* in 1991, with milk included among those foods that should be consumed less often, dairy groups were influential in suppressing publication. In the final 1992 version, the *Food Guide Pyramid* recommends two to three daily servings of dairy foods.

The fifth edition of the USDA *Dietary Guidelines for Americans*, released in 2000, suggests that portions of dairy foods should be fat free or low fat. As a result of industry lobbying, dairy foods are not labeled as prime sources of fat, even though they, along with meat, account for more than half of dietary fat. High-fat cheeses are recommended as good sources of calcium. Industry promotion to the contrary, some nutritional scientists question whether dairy foods confer any special health benefits. Others suggest that hormones, growth factors, and allergenic proteins in dairy foods do more harm than good.

As a partial result of the industry's advertising campaign, milk consumption increased. In 2001 annual consumption among children reached twenty-eight gallons, the highest level in ten years; among teens between the ages of twelve and seventeen, it was up almost 3 percent, the first rise in consumption among this age group in five years.

Perfect Food?

For 150 years milk was considered the perfect food. The halo effect extended to all the dairy products that flowed from milk. One researcher has suggested that the American canonization of this food has much to do with the white Anglo-Saxon Protestant heritage of the first settlers. Milk symbolized a perfection of class, race, and religion. As the political voice shifted from rural dairy farmers to urban consumers, even more perfection was demanded of milk, which, it was thought, should be supplied on demand. In the 1960s, dairy products fell from grace for health reasons and because of fear of the unknown effects of biotechnological boosters. Recombinant bovine growth hormone, the first biotechnology product to be approved in this country, stimulated a strong and powerful consumer backlash that demanded once again that milk be perfect. In its organic version, directed toward the elite purchaser, its image and status have been restored in part for those who can afford it. Some people even receive deliveries to their homes in vintage 1950s glass bottles. Nostalgia for "pure" milk and the right to access seem to be enduring American food issues.

[*See also* Butter; Buttermilk; Cheese; Dairy Industry; Department of Agriculture, United States; Food and Drug Administration; Ice Creams and Ices; Jewish Dietary Laws; Milk; Milk Packaging; Politics of Food.]

BIBLIOGRAPHY

DuPuis, E. Melanie. *Nature's Perfect Food: How Milk Became America's Drink.* New York: New York University Press, 2002. A social history of America's preoccupation with milk, including information on the organic milk industry, the symbolism of milk, and dairy politics.

Floegel, Mark. "From Elsie to the Corporate Cow." *Eating Well Magazine* 1, no.2 (2002): 36, 37, 75, 77.

Nestle, Marion. *Food Politics: How the Food Industry Influences Nutrition and Health.* Berkeley: University of California Press, 2002. Includes information on the efforts of the dairy lobby to influence the *Dietary Guidelines* and *Food Guide Pyramid.*

Visser, Margaret. "Butter—and Something 'Just as Good'" and "Ice Cream: Cold Comfort." In her *Much Depends on Dinner: The Extraordinary History and Mythology, Allure and Obsessions, Perils and Taboos, of an Ordinary Meal,* 83–114 and 285–322. Toronto: McClelland and Stewart, 1986. Discussion of the symbolism and meaning of butter and ice cream, not exclusive to America.

Werlin, Laura. *The New American Cheese: Profiles of America's Greatest Cheesemakers and Recipes for Cooking with Cheese.* New York: Stewart, Tabori, and Chang, 2000.

Whitaker, Jan. "Dairy Lunches." *Newsletter of the Culinary Historians of Boston* 12, no. 1 (1991): 5–8. Historical piece on the dairy lunches that appeared in urban areas in the late 1800s.

Zukin, Jane. *Dairy-Free Cookbook: Over 250 Recipes for People with Lactose Intolerance or Milk Allergy.* 2nd ed. Rocklin, CA: Prima Health, 1998.

LINDA MURRAY BERZOK

Dairy Industry

The dairy industry is one of the highest-value agricultural sectors in the United States. Its story is highlighted by *increasing* organization, specialization, production, and industrialization and *decreasing* numbers of both dairy farms and cows. Surprisingly, given this situation, the United States did not have a true "dairy industry" until the mid-nineteenth century. Previously, most farms had one or more cows, and cheese and butter were manufactured and sold into cities, but there were few dairy "factories" until the nation was almost a century old. Once such factories appeared, industrialization and specialization proceeded at a relatively constant pace, punctuated by periods of particularly fast innovation. The geography of dairy production has also changed during this time, moving from production centers in the Northeast to the upper Midwest, and then to California.

American Dairy Industry to 1850

The first herd of one hundred cows arrived in Jamestown in 1611, on a relief ship that landed just four years after the first colonists. While dairy products were not eaten by Native Americans, they were an important source of food to the early colonists, primarily in the form of butter and cheese rather than fluid milk, although total consumption was much lower than in modern times. This was particularly true in the South, where fresh milk spoiled very quickly. In general, milking was done almost entirely in the warmer months, when pastures were high, so milk needed to be turned into longer-term storage products for the winter.

Following their first introduction in Virginia, cows were established up and down the East Coast. These cows were usually kept to produce milk for family consumption, but as herds multiplied, surpluses developed, and families began to sell excess products. A market in long-term storage products, such as cheese and butter, began to appear, as did direct selling of fluid milk. As the United States entered its infancy, rings of production formed around northeastern cities, with fluid-milk producers just outside the city, followed by butter and then cheese producers.

While most farmers were still generalists, there was some specialization. In the mid-nineteenth century, Orange County, New York, became famous for its high-quality butter. Farmers in Rhode Island, the Berkshires (Massachusetts), and northern Vermont also specialized in marketing to the city trade. Other Upstate New York areas, for instance, Herkimer County and the Mohawk and Saint Lawrence Valleys, focused more on cheese. Dairy women were generally saddled with the tasks of churning butter and making cheese, and despite small improvements in technology, production levels were limited. Farms were small, even in the most intensive dairying areas, and even the production of forty cows (a large farm at the time) could not support industrial dairying processes.

In the cities, citizens for a long time had kept cattle in common grazing areas and in backyard fields. Farmers from nearby areas would peddle their milk in the city for those without cows. In New York City the first truly intensive dairies in the United States appeared. These were "swill" farms operated by distilleries. At these farms, cows, often kept in horrible conditions, were fed the by-products of distilling. Swill farms could be huge, possessing more than one thousand cows. The cows rarely left the barns, and disease was rampant. While this practice soon came under fire, it provided the majority of New York's milk supply during the mid-1800s.

Early Industrialization: 1850–1900

The first spark in the industrial dairying movement came in 1851, when a cheese maker in Oneida County, New York, began contracting for his neighbors' milk in order to create a larger and more efficient cheese plant. The system took a few years to gain popularity. Farmers were apprehensive about combining their milk with that of neighboring farms. By the 1860s, however, the practice swept through New York, was adopted by the butter industry, and began to penetrate other areas of the country.

This growth was fostered by increased cheese and butter exports to Britain (which was undergoing a series of crop failures) and rising prices. Exports rose tenfold between 1860 and 1875. Prices doubled between 1860 and 1865. Pushed by these higher prices, the number of cheese factories in New York State grew from 38 to 402 between 1860 and 1864. The trend soon spread westward, particularly to Wisconsin, where the first factory opened in 1864. Land in Wisconsin was cheaper than in New York, as were feeding costs, since New York farmers fed their cattle western grain. Cheese factories multiplied in Wisconsin as troubles hit the wheat market following the Civil War. By 1880 Wisconsin had more than twelve hundred cheese factories, although it was still second in production to New York.

The industrialization of the butter and cheese manufacturing processes was slowed somewhat by two factors. First, to make cheese and butter, cream had to be separated from milk, a slow, gravity-based process. The waiting period associated with separation slowed the manufacturing process and limited factory size. In addition, factories that bought milk were most interested in milk fat, yet there was no way to measure the percentage of milk fat quickly and accurately in a sample of milk.

The solution to the cream-separation problem came with the mechanical separator, which allowed cream to be separated from milk in a matter of minutes. At first, these were large machines, not suited to on-farm use, but in 1885 the hand separator was introduced. This device could be used on the farm and allowed cheese and butter plants to collect cream from the surrounding farms, rather than guessing how much cream a gallon of milk would make and having a large amount of leftover milk. In 1890 Dr. Stephen Babcock of the University of Wisconsin

developed a simple test for measuring milk fat. The test, which was accurate, quick, and cheap, could be preformed on the farm or at the factory and allowed for accurate pricing of milk according to its fat content.

Sanitary Revolution: 1850–1917

At the same time that improvements were quickly occurring in dairy manufacturing, the fluid-milk industry was being transformed through the development of laws and processes that protected milk from contamination and consumers from disease. These changes eventually affected the entire industry. The movement began in the 1840s with an exposé on the evils of the New York swill milk industry. As objections to swill milk grew, the milk for large cities was increasingly brought in by rail, enhancing the potential for contamination. Breaking connections between producer and consumer also afforded the dealer more opportunities to adulterate the product. Farmers and dealers both attempted to sell skimmed milk (then considered almost worthless) as whole by adding chalk and other colorants. To retard souring, dealers sometimes added formaldehyde.

The first urban milk laws were thus to control swill milk production and adulteration. These laws often were difficult to enforce, but cities opened municipal laboratories to test their milk, and adulteration generally declined. Soon, however, concern with contamination became larger than concern about adulteration. Development of the germ theory of disease in the late 1800s led to the realization that fresh milk, which flowed daily from the country, was a great vector for epidemics. To stop the contamination, two separate methods were put into place: pasteurization, which heated milk to destroy germs, and certification, which carefully inspected leading dairy farms to "certify" their ability to produce milk for the city. Pasteurization was much cheaper and won out, but certification also affected the dairy industry, as cities adopted long lists of regulations to which farmers had to adhere to gain a license to send fluid milk to the city. By 1917 many cities required both pasteurization and inspection. The extra expense associated with pasteurization led many smaller dealers to leave the industry. In many cities two or three firms dominated milk distribution.

Dairy Farming: 1850–1917

Dairy farming in the seventy years before World War I was a picture of contrasts. On the one hand, areas of heavy concentration were being developed. Zones around

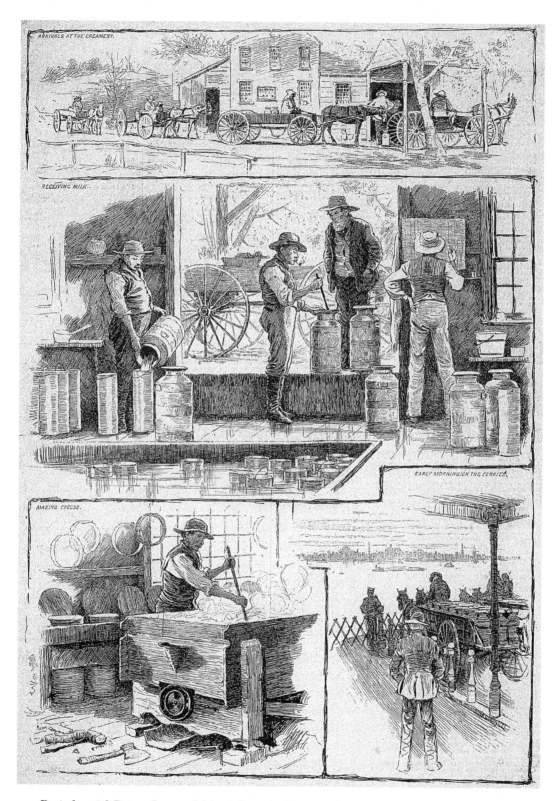

Preindustrial Dairy. Scenes of dairy industry by Howard Pyle, *Harper's Weekly*, 27 May 1882. As farmers deliver milk to the creamery (*top*), the milk is poured into the creamery's containers (*middle*). A worker makes cheese (*bottom left*). Dairy products are brought to the city by ferry (*bottom right*). *Collection of Alice Ross*

cities became devoted to fluid-milk production and underwent modernization prescribed by city milk ordinances. Other areas became devoted to butter production. In Wisconsin thousands of cheese factories opened, some specializing in "foreign" varieties, such as Swiss and Limburger. By 1919 Wisconsin had overtaken New York as the top dairy-production state, with the vast majority of its milk going into manufactured products, mostly cheese. In many states, progressive farmers banded together into state dairy associations, which promoted scientific dairying. This meant keeping records of production by particular cows, culling low-producing animals, being careful with cleanliness, and sometimes adopting breeds known for high-volume milk production, particularly Holsteins.

On the other hand, much remained the same. Dairying in 1900 was described by the census as "incidental," meaning that most dairy cows were on farms that did not specialize in dairying. Overall, 78.6 percent of farmers reported having dairy cows, but for only 6.2 percent was dairying their principal source of income. Most farms had at least one dairy cow, the milk from which was usually used on the farm. The average dairy farmer in the United States owned just 9.6 cows. Even dairy farmers serving the fluid market also relied on other crops and livestock to supplement their incomes. A very small percentage of the value of the average dairy farm was in machinery. Just 4.2 percent of the total value of dairy farms was taken up by farm implements in 1900. Available implements included scales, Babcock testers, and rudimentary milking machines. During the next twenty years, farmers adopted more of these devices, but for the most part "scientific dairying" was still focused on choosing the right cow rather than the right equipment.

Cooperation, Industrialization, and Government Programs: 1917–1980

The period 1917–1980 was, in a way, the apex of the American dairy complex. Industrialization and concentration increased, government programs protected both the milk and the dairy farmers, and cooperatives appeared, putting dairy farmers on an equal standing with dealers. The story of the early years of this period is the story of the rise of the modern American food system. During and after World War I, high prices led many dairy farmers, particularly in fluid-milk-production regions, to invest in improved technology, including milking machines, trucks, and tractors. Production began to rise, but farmers

also became more indebted. A fall in prices in 1921 led to the beginning of the agricultural depression.

This state of affairs was combated somewhat in 1922 by the passage of the Capper-Volstead Act, which gave agricultural cooperatives antitrust protection. Farmers, who previously had been price takers, were able to negotiate with dealers for higher prices. Larger cooperatives soon began manufacturing and marketing their own products. While depression conditions remained in agriculture in general, by 1929 many cooperatives were able to negotiate favorable contracts. At the same time, modernization continued to take place among processors, with milk plants growing larger and larger, truck pickup of milk replacing rail in all but the largest cities, and pasteurization and sanitary rules, such as testing for tuberculosis, becoming standard. Production levels of fluid milk, ice cream, cheese, and butter also continued to rise.

This situation came to a sudden halt when the economic downturn expanded from agriculture to the rest of the American economy in late 1929. Consumers refused to pay high prices for milk and began to go to alternative sources, in particular "cash and carry stores" that did not deliver and often worked outside the cooperatives. Some truly cut-rate dealers opened up just outside city boundaries, selling milk from noninspected herds. Dealers had to cut prices, but they were locked into contracts with cooperatives, which were loath to lower prices for their members. Often cooperatives struck, withholding their milk from the city. Sometimes groups even struck against the cooperatives themselves, demanding higher prices from the organization. These strikes were often violent. In many cases the National Guard was called out to protect milk entering the city.

The response of the federal government to this crisis was the milk marketing order system, which sets minimum prices to producers in fluid markets that ask to be regulated. The government also began buying stocks of cheese, butter, and dried milk when the overall milk price fell too low. In setting the prices in each district and in buying stocks of dairy products, the government worked closely with dairy cooperatives. This government involvement increased even more during World War II, when government purchases of manufactured dairy products helped right the industry. The Navy even built a floating ice cream parlor. Finally, working with the government, the dairy industry also put in place the "checkoff" program, which charged farmers a small amount for each gallon they sold for advertising their product. This

Dairy Case. Back to the Land Natural Foods, Brooklyn, New York. *Photograph by Joe Zarba*

money went mainly to the National Dairy Council's milk-promotion programs.

Following the war, the modernization of the American dairy industry truly took off. The milk-marketing program and government dairy purchases stabilized dairy prices. Strikes became almost nonexistent. Farmers and dealers were more able to invest in new equipment and concentrate their operations. Between 1945 and 1978 the number of commercial dairy farms dropped from 602,000 to 168,000. At the same time, total production per cow more than doubled, and the percentage of farms with more than fifty cows went from less than 1 percent in 1949 to more than 20 percent in 1981. Milking machines became ubiquitous. Bulls disappeared, replaced by artificial insemination. Bulk storage tanks allowed milk pickup to occur three times rather than six times weekly. The seasonality of milk production was also modified, as government incentives and more nonpasture feeding encouraged higher winter production. The location of production remained surprisingly stable. Wisconsin was still the top dairy state, and other longtime centers, such as New York, remained high producers. The one exception was California, which in 1980 surpassed New York as the second-highest-producing dairy state, focusing on providing fluid milk to its own rapidly growing population.

Great changes also took place off the farm. Pasteurization and bottling became almost entirely automated. The number of plants declined from more than eight thousand in 1945 to just over one thousand in 1981. In the same space of time, the amount of product per plant had increased more than twelve times. While national dairy firms had existed in earlier times, between 1957 and 1980 the number of local firms declined sharply, from almost five thousand to less than one thousand. Cooperatives merged. In 1957 there were 455 cooperatives, but in 1980 there were only 45. The products produced at these plants also changed. Fluid milk went from being packaged in glass bottles to paper containers to plastic containers.

Industrial and Craft Farms: 1980 to 2004

The dairy industry, in one sense, was larger at the end of the twentieth century than it ever had been in previous years. The value of products shipped annually by the fluid-milk industry alone (including fluid milk, yogurt, cream, and cottage cheese) was over 23 billion dollars. While the numbers of dairy employees, plants, farms, and cows were all declining rapidly, total production and production per cow were growing just as quickly. Total milk production in 2000 was 167 billion pounds, an increase of twenty billion pounds over 1990. In general, dairy farms were becoming larger and more industrial at an amazingly fast pace. In 1998 there were more than forty thousand fewer dairy farms than in 1993, but the total number of dairy farms with more than two hundred cows rose by 590. Smaller dairy farmers that wanted to survive had to choose either to grow or to develop alternative marketing and production strategies, such as organic production. Concentration was also occurring among dairy-processing companies. In 1997 there were 405 fluid-milk-industry companies in the United States, 120 less than just five years earlier.

While production increased, per-capita sales of most dairy products declined. This was particularly true of whole-milk consumption, which by 2000 was less than half of what it was in 1980. While drinking of lower-fat milks rose, overall per-capita milk consumption went down. Exceptions to the declining per-capita consumption rates included yogurt and cheese. Consumption of mozzarella, in particular, almost tripled between 1980 and 2000, as Americans ate more pizza.

The places of production shifted west. In 1993, California overtook Wisconsin as the nation's leading dairy state. By 2001 the competition was not even close, with California production surpassing Wisconsin's by 10 billion pounds. California processors began to concentrate more on producing manufactured products for export outside the state, taking advantage of lower milk costs. Production in California is much more industrialized than in the rest of the country. In 1997 average herd size in California was 530 compared with just 59 in

Wisconsin. Average production per cow in California in 1998 was two thousand pounds greater than anywhere in the rest of the country.

All small dairy farms have not disappeared. There remain some niches in which "craft" methods are profitable. Organic, hormone-free milk companies, such as Organic Valley and Horizon, have emerged. These companies tend to buy milk from smaller farms, although Horizon owns an intensive, California-style dairy of its own. Particularly in New England and New York, states and communities have attempted to protect their small-dairy-farm tradition. Such companies as Ben and Jerry's base their advertising on buying milk only from local sources. High-end local-milk-delivery systems have appeared in some communities. Finally, some farmers have decided to attempt to create a new production methodology, focusing on production per hour worked rather than total production. This method, termed "intensive rotational grazing," takes the cows out of the barns and focuses on low inputs. While concentration and industrialization will continue, the future of the dairy industry may also include growth of alternative producers.

[*See also* Butter; Buttermilk; Dairy Foods; Ice Cream and Ices; Milk; Milk Packaging.]

BIBLIOGRAPHY

Bailey, Kenneth W. *Marketing and Pricing of Milk and Dairy Products in the United States.* Ames: Iowa State University Press, 1997.

Beal, George Max, and Henry H. Bakken. *Fluid Milk Marketing.* Madison, WI: Mimir Publishers, 1956.

Black, John Donald. *The Dairy Industry and the AAA.* Washington, DC: Brookings Institution, 1935.

Butler, L. J., and Christopher A. Wolf. "California Dairy Production: Unique Policies and Natural Advantages." In *Dairy Industry Restructuring*, edited by Harry K. Schwarzweller and Andrew P. Davidson, 141–161. New York: Jai, 2000.

DuPuis, E. Melanie. *Nature's Perfect Food: How Milk Became America's Drink.* New York: New York University Press, 2002.

Hartley, Robert Milham. *An Historical, Scientific and Practical Essay on Milk as an Article of Human Sustenance.* New York: Arno Press, 1977. Reprint of the 1842 edition.

Hunziker, Otto Frederick. *The Butter Industry.* 3rd ed. LaGrange, IL: published privately, 1940.

International Dairy Foods Association. *Milk Facts.* Washington, DC: Milk Industry Foundation, 2002.

Jackson-Smith, Douglas, and Bradford Barham. "Dynamics of Dairy Industry Restructuring in Wisconsin." In *Dairy Industry Restructuring*, edited by Harry K. Schwarzweller and Andrew P. Davidson, 115–140. New York: Jai, 2000.

Lampard, Eric E. *The Rise of the Dairy Industry in Wisconsin: A Study in Agricultural Change, 1820–1920.* Madison: State Historical Society of Wisconsin, 1963.

Manchester, Alden C. *The Public Role in the Dairy Economy: Why and How Governments Intervene in the Milk Business.* Boulder, CO: Westview Press, 1983.

Selitzer, Ralph. *The Dairy Industry in America.* New York: Dairy and Ice Cream Field and Books for Industry, 1976.

Straus, Lina Gutherz, comp. *Disease in Milk: The Remedy Pasteurization—The Life Work of Nathan Straus.* New York: Arno Press, 1977. Reprint of 1917 edition.

Wiest, Edward. *The Butter Industry in the United States: An Economic Study of Butter and Oleomargarine.* New York: AMS Press, 1968. Reissue of the 1916 edition.

DANIEL R. BLOCK

Dates

The date is the fruit of a palm tree, *Phoenix dactylifera*, native to the deserts of North Africa and the Middle East. In the late nineteenth century, settlers in the American Southwest noted that parts of the area enjoyed similar conditions suitable for growing dates—fierce heat, access to water, and dry weather during harvest in late summer and autumn. They planted seeds from imported dates, but these seedling trees mostly bore inferior fruits; only after plant explorers from the U.S. Department of Agriculture and private nurseries brought back offshoots of superior varieties from the Middle East, in 1900 and over the next two decades, did commercial cultivation begin.

Most American date production comes from two California districts, the Coachella Valley, southeast of Palm Springs, and the Bard Valley, near Yuma, which together have 4,300 bearing acres (as of 2002); there are also several hundred producing acres in southwestern Arizona. The harvest takes place from August to December. The major varieties are Deglet Noor, typically picked fully dried and later rehydrated; Medjool, a large, luscious fruit that is increasing in popularity; and Barhi, sometimes marketed in the *khalal* stage, when it is yellow, crunchy, mildly astringent, and the fruit is at maximum size. Virtually all dates are sold in the dried *tamar* stage, in which the fruit has dried to a fairly firm consistency, but connoisseurs prefer fruits in the softer *rutab* stage (soft, moist, and delicious), available at local markets in California and by mail order. Very high in sugar content, dates have been consumed since the nineteenth century as dessert fruits and in cakes, cookies, and puddings.

[*See also* Fruit; Middle Eastern Influences on American Food.]

BIBLIOGRAPHY

Heetland, Rick I. *Date Recipes*. Phoenix, AZ: Golden West, 1993.
Popenoe, Paul B. *The Date Palm*. Coconut Grove, FL: Field
    Research Projects, 1973.

DAVID KARP

Delicatessens

"Delicatessen" is a German word meaning "to eat
delicacies"; in Germany it referred to a retail store selling
specialty food items. Nineteenth-century German delicatessens sold raw, pickled, roasted, spiced, and smoked
hams, sausages, fowl, fish, and venison, as well as the
heads and feet of calves, sheep, and swine. They also
offered prepared salads made from chicken, herring, or
potatoes, as well as raw and cooked sauerkraut and pickles of all descriptions. Frequently, a wild boar's head, the
quintessential symbol of the feast, was placed in the window of the shop to symbolize the abundance within.

German immigrants introduced the delicatessen to the
United States. According to Artemas Ward, a chronicler
of the nineteenth-century grocery trade, the first delicatessen in America opened on Grand Street in New York
City around 1868. At that time Manhattan's Lower East
Side had a substantial German immigrant population.
Delicatessens attracted not only German Americans but
also a wide variety of others who were enticed by foreign
and gourmet-type foods. During the late nineteenth century, delicatessens filled the gap between butcher shops,
which mainly sold uncooked meats, and general grocery
stores, which mainly sold generic and packaged goods.
Delicatessens quickly spread to other cities. By 1910
they were common throughout urban America and ubiquitous in New York City. Delicatessens have traditionally been family owned. They tended to be smaller and to
sell fewer items than grocery stores.

The first American delicatessens sold cooked, ready-
to-eat meats, poultry, and fish, as well as specialty products, such as cheeses, teas, mushrooms, caviar, olive oil,
pickled foods, and imported canned goods. Later, delicatessens sold tuna and chicken salad sandwiches and
salads, such as coleslaw and potato salad. Originally, the
prepared foods were taken out and consumed elsewhere,
but as delicatessens thrived and expanded, some made
a place for customers to sit down and eat in the store,
particularly at lunch. The German deli had largely disappeared by World War I.

During the 1880s, larger numbers of Jewish immigrants
began moving into New York and other eastern cities.

Delicatessen. Abe Lebewohl's 2nd Ave. Deli, located on Second Avenue at Tenth Street on the Lower
East Side of Manhattan, has been serving kosher delicacies since 1954. *Photograph by Joe Zarba*

In the Deli. Making a selection at Zabar's in New York City. *Photograph by Joe Zarba*

Some Jews opened delicatessens that paralleled German delicatessens. If the delicatessen was kosher, only meat and pareve (neutral) foods were served. These offerings eventually included chicken soup, corned beef, gefilte fish, lox, knishes, pastrami, chopped liver, tongue, and garlic pickles. If kosher laws were not followed, the menu expanded in the 1920s to include bagels, bialys, cream cheese, and Jewish-style cheesecake. Delis also popularized Jewish-style breads, notably rye and pumpernickel. Famous kosher or Jewish-style delicatessens include Katz's, the Carnegie Deli, and the Second Avenue Deli in New York City; Shapiro's Deli in Indianapolis, Indiana; Eli's Stage Deli in Chicago; and Langer's and Canter's in Los Angeles. During the mid-twentieth century some delicatessens became full-fledged restaurants and remained delicatessens in name only. Although Jewish delicatessens still survive and thrive in major cities, their heyday has passed.

Delicatessens were the birthplace of some prepared foods that reached national markets. Around the turn of the twentieth century, a delicatessen owner in Philadelphia produced large batches of mayonnaise in the back of his store. Sold under the name Mrs. Schlorer's, it was the first commercial mayonnaise brand. It was so successful that the owner began producing other products and created the Schlorer Delicatessen Company

to market and distribute them. Richard Hellmann, a German immigrant, opened a delicatessen in New York City in 1905. He began selling commercial mayonnaise in 1912 under his own name and later expanded his product line.

Still others created businesses that catered to delicatessens. Frank Brunckhorst, for instance, began supplying other New York delicatessens in 1905. At the time, competition was heavy. Brunckhorst opened a manufacturing plant in Brooklyn in 1933 and sold his products under the brand name Boar's Head. Boar's Head Provision Company has become one of the largest suppliers of prepared meats to delicatessens and supermarket deli counters.

During the mid-twentieth century, mainstream America adopted many traditional "deli" specialties. Supermarkets incorporated delis into their operations, and many foods sold in delicatessens—such as pastrami, corned beef, and lox—have become popular American foods. For those who want old-fashioned deli flavors and aromas in their homes, several cookbooks have preserved the recipes, such as *Deli: 101 New York–Style Deli Dishes, from Chopped Liver to Cheesecake* (1985) by Sue Kreitzman and *Second Ave Deli Cookbook: Recipes and Memories from Abe Lebewohl's Legendary New York Kitchen* (1999) by Sharon Lebewohl and Rena Bulkin.

The name "delicatessen" remains an important component of American cities, but the term is used loosely today. As new immigrants—Italians, Greeks, Puerto Ricans, West Indians, Asians, Russians, and Mexicans—moved into American cities, many found that deli proprietorship was one way to enter American economic life. Some delis serve foods similar to those of the past, and most have incorporated culinary treats from their different homelands. For instance, some Korean Americans frequently sell kimchi and other Asian delicacies. Other "delis" are small grocery stores that may or may not sell prepared food. There are more delicatessens than ever, and several chains franchise "New York" delis throughout America, although many are related to traditional delicatessens in name only.

[*See also* Corned Beef; German American Food; Jewish American Food; Mayonnaise; New York Food; Pastrami; Restaurants.]

BIBLIOGRAPHY

Finck, Henry T. *Food and Flavor*. New York: Century, 1913.

Kreitzman, Sue. *Deli: 101 New York–style Deli Dishes, from Chopped Liver to Cheesecake*. New York: Harmony Books, 1985.

Lebewohl, Sharon, and Rena Bulkin. *The 2nd Ave Deli Cookbook: Recipes and Memories from Abe Lebewohl's Legendary New York Kitchen*. New York: Villard, 1999.

Moon, Rosemary. *Delicatessen: A Celebration and Cookbook*. Newton Abbot, UK: David and Charles, 1989.

ANDREW F. SMITH

Delmonico's

For nearly a century, from the early 1830s until the 1920s, Delmonico's was the place for New York City's rich and famous to eat and be seen. Often credited with the introduction of French haute cuisine to Americans, it was founded by John Delmonico, a sea captain from Ticino in the Italian-speaking part of Switzerland who settled in New York in 1825 and opened a wine shop near the Battery. In 1828 he opened a café, Delmonico & Brother (John's brother Peter, a pastry cook, had emigrated to work with him) at 23 William Street; the menu offered pastries, confections, tea, coffee, chocolate, and liqueurs. In 1831 the Delmonicos hired a French chef, who prepared potages, ragoûts, and other hot dishes; thus, Delmonico's became one of the city's first "restaurants" in the true sense of the word—an eating house where one went to be "restored" with rich broth and other sustaining fare. A year later the Delmonicos' nephew

Lorenzo (destined to lead the family business into its golden age) joined them, followed by three more nephews brought over from Switzerland.

That first restaurant burned in the great fire of 1835, but the new Delmonico's, opened in 1837 at Beaver and South William Streets, became a true palace of haute cuisine, right down to the marble pillars that flanked its entrance. By 1838 a seven-page Carte du Restaurant Français offered a staggering selection of soups, hors d'oeuvres, salads, omelets, meats, seafood, and game; a choice of eighteen vegetables (including uncommon ones, such as eggplant and artichokes); the exotic Macaroni à l'Italienne (translated on the English side of the menu as "Macaroni with gravy"); a rich array of pastries, soufflés, cheese, and fruits; and no fewer than fifty-seven wines and two dozen liqueurs.

Moving uptown as the city grew northward, Delmonico's was variously located on Broad Street (hard by the stock exchange); Broadway at Chambers Street; Broadway and Pine Street; Fifth Avenue and Fourteenth Street; Fifth Avenue and Twenty-sixth Street; and, finally, at Fifth Avenue and Forty-fourth Street, where it opened in 1897 and closed for good in 1923.

From the time Lorenzo Delmonico assumed the helm in 1845, Delmonico's waxed ever more luxurious and exclusive. Food quality was paramount: Lorenzo's early-morning market purchases were complemented by fine fruits and vegetables grown on the family's 220-acre Brooklyn farm, established to supply the restaurant's needs. Charles Dickens was feted at Delmonico's in 1868; the first debutante to meet society in a public place (not a private home) made her debut there in 1870. During the 1880s and 1890s the Four Hundred—the cream of New York society—dined at Delmonico's on oysters by the dozen, terrapin soup, roast canvasback duck, and endless rivers of Champagne. The restaurant served parties of Vanderbilts, Astors, and Belmonts and frequently hosted the music-hall star Lillian Russell and her constant companion, "Diamond Jim" Brady, renowned for his insatiable appetite.

Delmonico's produced some memorable culinary celebrities and creations. The Swiss émigré Alessandro Filippini, having worked his way up through Delmonico's kitchens, published several cookbooks, including *The Table* (1889), a comprehensive manual of high-class home cooking. In 1894 Charles Ranhofer, another Delmonico's chef, published *The Epicurean*, a massive manual of restaurant cooking that enshrines the taste of those times. Some dishes associated with the restaurant are lobster Newberg, Delmonico steak, Delmonico potatoes, chicken à la King, and baked Alaska.

[*See also* Brady, Diamond Jim; Ranhofer, Charles; Restaurants.]

BIBLIOGRAPHY

Batterberry, Michael, and Ariane Batterberry. *On the Town in New York: The Landmark History of Eating, Drinking, and Entertainments from the American Revolution to the Food Revolution.* New York: Routledge, 1999.
Filippini, Alessandro. *The Table: How to Buy Food, How to Cook It and How to Serve It.* New York: C. L. Webster & Co., 1889.
Ranhofer, Charles. *The Epicurean.* 1893. Reprint, New York: Dover Publications, 1971.
Root, Waverly, and Richard de Rochemont. *Eating in America.* Hopewell, NJ: Ecco Press, 1981.
Thomas, Lately. *Delmonico's: A Century of Splendor.* Boston: Houghton Mifflin, 1967.

BONNIE J. SLOTNICK

Del Monte. Advertisement for Del Monte canned fruits and vegetables from the back cover of *The Del Monte Fruit Book* (1929). *Collection of Andrew F. Smith*

Del Monte

Eighteen California packers, representing about half of the fruit canners in California, formed the California Fruit Canners Association in 1899. Seventeen years later the association incorporated under the name California Packers Association (Calpak); its premier brand was Del Monte. It was not until 1967 that the Calpak name was phased out and the company used only "Del Monte."

From the beginning, the company expanded its operations and packed a vast array of products, including peaches, baked beans, olives, berries, squash, sweet potatoes, peppers, and cranberries, as well as dried fruit, jams, and jellies. It also aggressively marketed its products. In 1914 the company produced a silent film, *The Winning of a Peach*, which may have been the first industrial promotion film produced in the United States. In 1917 Calpak enlisted the culinary expert Marion Harris Neil to write an advertising cookbooklet, *Good Things to Eat*, featuring Del Monte products. The company has regularly published cookbooklets ever since. Early print advertisements announced that Del Monte was "not a label, but a guarantee." During the 1920s the company expanded its operations into an array of other canning businesses, including tuna and coffee.

Del Monte survived the Depression by belt-tightening and increased advertising. When the United States entered Word War II, Calpak sent 50 percent of its canned fruits and vegetables to the military. Because of the wartime shortage of metals for cans, some domestic products were sold in glass containers.

After the war Calpak launched a $50-million expansion program and initiated a national advertising campaign. One beneficiary of this campaign was Del Monte Catsup. Calpak had bottled ketchup since 1916, but it was not a particularly important product. After Del Monte acquired the Edgar H. Hurff Company of Swedesboro, New Jersey, its national ketchup production took off. In 1948 Del Monte first advertised its ketchup nationwide. An advertisement in *Collier's* asked, "Catsup? Now Try It Del Monte Style!" Later, Del Monte ketchup highlighted that it used pineapple vinegar, which gave its ketchup a special zesty flavor.

Del Monte established operations in Hawaii shortly after its founding. During the 1930s it created the Philippines Packing Corporation. After World War II, Calpak increased its sales to foreign countries, and by 1965 exports topped $96 million. Del Monte has continued to expand its operations and exports abroad.

In 1979 Del Monte merged with RJ Reynolds Industries. During the following two decades there were several ownership changes. In 1999 Del Monte Foods became a publicly traded company. The company added new products and acquired companies with other product lines. In 1998 Del Monte acquired Contadina, which sold foods of Italian heritage. It also began to manufacture Orchard Select and Sunfresh citrus and tropical fruit. In March 2001 it acquired the S&W brand of beans, condiments, fruits, and vegetables. At the beginning of the twenty-first century, Del Monte was one of the largest producers and distributors of processed fruit and vegetable products in the United States.

[*See also* Canning and Bottling; Ketchup.]

BIBLIOGRAPHY

Braznell, William. *California's Finest: The History of the Del Monte Corporation and the Del Monte Brand.* San Francisco: Del Monte Corporation, 1982.
Del Monte Foods. http://www.delmonte.com/.
Smith, Andrew F. *Pure Ketchup: The History of America's National Condiment.* Columbia: University of South Carolina Press, 1996.

ANDREW F. SMITH

Denver Sandwich

The Denver sandwich, also known as the Western sandwich, is composed of toasted white bread encasing an omelet filled with diced ham, onion, and green pepper. Several tales have been written as to the origin of the Denver sandwich, but as yet none has been confirmed. Some say that it was developed to disguise the tainted taste of no-longer-fresh eggs carried by pioneers or of eggs that were later hauled into settlements in the West. A second theory states that the sandwich was developed by chuck-wagon cooks as a snack to be carried in the saddlebags of cowboys. Finally, James Beard noted in James Beard's *American Cookery* (1972) that Chinese cooks working in logging camps and railroad gangs concocted it as an Americanized version of egg foo yong. The first identified print reference to date is from a 1918 restaurant industry publication. The Denver, known as a "cowboy" in diner lingo, is common on American menus throughout the country, and it may actually be America's oldest breakfast sandwich.

[*See also* Beard, James; Breakfast Food.]

BIBLIOGRAPHY

Mercuri, Becky. *Sandwiches That You Will Like.* Pittsburgh, PA: WQED Pittsburgh, 2002.

BECKY MERCURI

Department of Agriculture, United States

The United States Department of Agriculture (USDA) has grown over the past 150 years from a small government office with subcabinet status to a giant cabinet-level bureaucracy with over 100,000 employees. In addition to agriculture, the USDA has had an enormous impact on American cooking and nutrition, helping transform the American diet. The USDA is divided into seven large agencies: Farm and Foreign Agricultural Services; Food, Nutrition, and Consumer Services; Food Safety; Marketing and Regulatory Programs; Natural Resources and Environment; Research, Education, and Economics; and Rural Development. Under each large agency are many smaller services; together, these groups constitute the largest single agricultural organization in the world, devoted to agricultural research and aid and the dissemination of agricultural information. The USDA's specific functions are enormously broad, ranging from lending programs for farming cooperatives to forestry to home economics and human nutrition. Its impact on the American diet is both direct, through nutrition standards and the like, and indirect, for example, the effect of food price supports on the price and thus on the public demand for various foods. The focus here is on those areas with a direct influence on the American diet.

Early Years

The USDA had modest beginnings. In the 1700s George Washington suggested that the country needed a central board to promote sound agricultural practices and collect information about crop yields, livestock prices, and so on. It was not until the 1820s, however, that both houses of Congress established agriculture committees and 1840 that the first Census of Agriculture provided the first nationwide crop report.

On May 15, 1862, Abraham Lincoln signed a bill creating the Department of Agriculture. At the time, agriculture was the single most important U.S. economic activity; at $182 million it comprised 75 percent of total U.S. exports and employed 58 percent of all able-bodied workers. (In 2002 the value of agricultural exports rose to $57 billion, but as a percentage of total exports, agriculture shrank to 12 percent. Farmers now make up less than 3 percent of the workforce.) In 1889 the Department of Agriculture was made an executive agency, whose chief, the secretary of agriculture, was given cabinet status.

Early on, the USDA began to increase its functions in the area of food safety and nutrition. Its first success came indirectly. In 1889 the Land Grant Education Act was passed, offering public lands to each state for the establishment of colleges of agriculture. These schools provided a forum for scientific study and discussion not only of agriculture but eventually also for nutrition. Two years earlier the department had received funding to set up agricultural stations in each state. The original intent was to study ways of improving animal fodder, but under its first director, Wilbur O. Atwater, the federal Office of Experiment Stations (OES) also began researching human nutrition. This move was controversial; Atwater had to convince a skeptical Congress that the need for such study even existed.

The initial impetus had come from the private sector. A wealthy Democrat had prevailed upon his friend President Grover Cleveland to hire Atwater in the first place: he had been impressed with Atwater's writings on the need for a more scientific basis for standards of nutrition, especially for the working classes. Ironically, many of Atwater's advanced scientific findings were abysmally wrong. In the era before vitamins were known, Atwater denigrated vegetables as a source of empty carbohydrates; advocated eating the fattiest meats possible as a cheap, efficient source of energy; and was a believer in the benefits of white bread.

In 1894 the USDA developed the first tables of food composition and dietary standards for Americans. Even if somewhat misdirected, the idea of scientifically based nutrition was evident, and as the land grant colleges became established, they began relying on USDA publications for their scientific instruction. In this arena, too, the USDA was very influential. An academic battle was raging at the turn of the century among home economists, between advocates of a more traditional recipe-based approach and those who promoted "scientific" diets based on the latest research. By 1918, when Atwater's old OES was renamed the State Relations Office and a special Bureau of Home Economics Office was created under it to disseminate scientific research to home economics schools at public universities, it was clear which side had won.

Over the years, as nutritional science advanced, so did department nutritional guidelines; new guidance was issued in 1916, 1933, 1942, 1956, and 1992, in the form of the *Food Guide Pyramid* pamphlet. The department also made its food recommendations directly known to the public. For example, the USDA radio service broadcast a talk show in the 1920s. *Aunt Sammy's Daily House-keeper's Chat* was popular, and the associated cookbook became a byword in rural areas. In 1926–1927 alone more than forty thousand "Aunt Sammy's" cookbooks were distributed, further advancing the cause of scientific nutrition. The idea that food should be healthy is axiomatic, thanks in no small part to USDA efforts.

Food Safety

The USDA has also been active in food safety. As with nutrition, much of the initial impetus came from the private sector. Dr. Harvey Wiley, an outspoken chemist from Purdue University who, in 1883, was hired to head the Bureau of Chemistry at the USDA, agitated for general U.S. food-safety standards but was consistently rebuffed by Congress. Finally, after a series of food-poisoning scandals and the publication of Upton Sinclair's exposé of the meatpacking industry, *The Jungle*, which revealed its horrific conditions, the Pure Food and Drug Act of 1906 and the accompanying Meat Inspection Act were passed and food-labeling standards established. Inspection and regulation fell to the Bureau of Chemistry, renamed in 1930 the Food and Drug Administration; in 1940 it passed out from the USDA, eventually becoming a part of the Department of Health and Human Services.

The USDA has, of course, been active all along in helping farmers, by working to enhance agricultural yields and to decrease costs. This has led, however, to charges that the U.S. government and, by implication, the USDA have discouraged crop diversity, and thus a more diverse diet, by focusing the bulk of farm research—and government money—on a limited number of traditional crops. USDA farm aid for specific agricultural crops comes in many forms.

Government price supports, for example, guarantee certain prices for specified agricultural commodities through regulated purchases by the USDA Commodity Credit Corporation. Price supports prevent the laws of supply and demand from working normally; they artificially keep certain crops at high levels of production and certain types of farmers in business.

Of course, this has been justified as a way of smoothing out the business cycles and preventing farm bankruptcies. Nevertheless, price supports also artificially promote certain crops, farming practices, and farms at the expense of others and at the expense of crop and food diversity. In particular, price supports have been criticized as supporting large factory farms; these farms do not tend to grow unusual heirloom varieties or local and more perishable types of fruits and vegetables. USDA aid for specific crops at the expense of others can also be less direct: it can come through support of agricultural research to produce better-yielding plants, insecticide research, and fertilizer and soil studies, often geared to specific crops or farming practices.

All of this USDA aid has been extremely successful—especially for those few crops. Today, for example, almost 80 percent of annual row crops in the United States are wheat, corn, or soybeans. This type of concentration comes with a price: it increases U.S. agricultural vulnerability to commodity price swings or disease. All of this success has produced a paradoxical result: it has prompted the USDA to encourage more strongly greater crop diversity. Lack of crop diversity has had an unquantifiable effect on U.S. diets as well; popular and cheap government-supported agricultural commodities drive down production—and thus consumption—of less common foods. Of course, many of these results also come from the industrialization of agriculture. As mechanized farming and distribution entered U.S. agriculture, so, too, came standardization and fewer basic varieties.

Agricultural Diversity

In the early 2000s this situation began to change. Biodiversity and food diversity are becoming big business, and in this area, too, the USDA has had a role. Partly because it is a large bureaucracy with many diverging programs, the USDA has actually long had a positive role in promoting agricultural diversity at the same time as other of its programs may have discouraged it. Its agricultural research programs have developed new seeds and produced new foods throughout its history.

For example, over 70 percent of all citrus fruits grown in the United States are varieties developed by the USDA Agricultural Research Service; one favorite variety, the Washington navel, was introduced into California with trees from Brazil back in 1873. In another instance, in 1908 Franklin Colville of the USDA began collecting wild blueberries and began crossing varieties; a few years later the domesticated blueberry was created. The USDA also became involved in agricultural production techniques that have improved food delivery and presentation and so increased diversity on a broad scale—for example, USDA studies of precooling red raspberries led to precooling as a standard practice and helped bring more and fresher fruits and vegetables to the American

table. (However, skeptics may add that precooling also aided "factory farm" production and so hurt local farms with fresher produce.)

In another case, USDA scientists improved, or at least changed, a common taste, when they found that the oily flavor in butter could be eliminated by pasteurization. The USDA role in diversity has been indirect as well; early in this century USDA scientists produced an alfalfa variety that could survive harsh midwestern winters and so helped produce the green mainstay of a huge new dairy industry in this region, where formerly it would have been difficult to support. Here, too, interest in diversity has grown. For example, in the early years of the twenty-first century USDA scientists were at work on methods to diversify the very forage crops they helped develop in the first place.

Social Programs

Besides advising on food and aiding the production of crops, the USDA has a direct role in feeding many millions of Americans, particularly through the Food and Nutrition Service (FNS). One of six Americans in the early 2000s received some sort of food assistance from the FNS. Two forms of assistance, in particular, are noteworthy: the Food Stamp program and the School Lunch program. The School Lunch program was created in 1946 to provide nutritionally balanced and low-cost meals to children from low-income families in schools across the United States; the food is provided by the USDA from agricultural surpluses or via donation or through cash subsidies. Meals must meet federal nutritional guidelines, although one study by the USDA has found that many schools violate that standard and offer meals that contain more fats and fewer nutritious items than is required.

One problem may stem from the agricultural surpluses the USDA provides; according to at least one report, a large percentage consists of high-fat milk, ground beef, butter, and cheese; and canned vegetables and fruits are usually processed. Yet the program as a whole has been successful; it served 7 million children in 1946, a number that grew to 26.3 million fifty years later, and provides many children with their only hot meal of the day. The USDA itself has expressed concern about meeting federal guidelines; its own publications stress the need for fresh fruits and vegetables in children's diets and better overall nutrition.

The Food Stamp program is another cornerstone of the USDA. Eligible recipients are provided with coupons or Electronic Benefit Transfer (EBT) cards that can be used in lieu of cash for buying food. As may be expected, providing Food Stamps increases not only recipients' overall food consumption but also their consumption of certain foods, especially meat, milk, and chicken.

Organic Foods

The most noticeable impact of the USDA on the American diet has been in the "natural versus artificial" foods debate: with bioengineered and irradiated foods and the controversy over their safety as well as with chemicals in the food supply. The USDA role has not been monolithic. While in 1995 the agency approved irradiation of meat to enhance preservation, it also continued to ban irradiated meats in its own "commodity programs," like the school lunch programs; even after a congressional mandate in 2002 the USDA delayed and sought "public input." In 1985 USDA scientists warned that agricultural chemicals were seeping into groundwater more than previously thought, yet it was not until 2002 that the USDA began implementing national standards for organic agricultural products that seek to reduce the use of chemicals in agriculture. Interestingly, it was a USDA scientist, C. V. Riley of the Division of Entomology, who was one of the pioneers, in the 1880s, of modern biological controls that provide an alternative to chemicals and which organic farmers prefer. This early USDA role in organic farming is not really surprising, given the USDA's size, breadth, and energy: it is a huge bureaucracy with a wide-ranging mandate, and it has had an enormous impact, for better and sometimes for worse, in all areas of American agriculture and food.

[*See also* Farm Subsidies, Duties, Quotas, and Tariffs; Food and Drug Administration; Food and Nutrition Systems; Food Stamps; Law; Nutrition; Politics of Food; Pure Food and Drug Act; School Food.]

BIBLIOGRAPHY

The Food Timeline. http://www.gti.net/mocolib1/kid/food.html. A K–12 teacher resource for food history lessons.

Levenstein, Harvey. *Revolution at the Table*. New York: Oxford University Press, 1988. A comprehensive and fascinating look at the changing American diet.

United States Department of Agriculture. http://www.usda.gov. The USDA maintains a number of different sites, many of them difficult to navigate. Persistence pays off with a great deal of original historical materials.

Sylvia Lovegren and Ross Petras

Desserts

The final course served at meals, dessert is most often a prepared sweet, such as pudding, pie, or cake, although fresh fruit, nuts, or cheeses may be served. The word "dessert" derives from the French *desservir*, to remove what has been served or clear the table, and was popularized in England after the restoration of Charles II in 1660. The English also adopted fashionable French desserts and incorporated them with the traditional sweets that, by Tudor and Stuart times, were served in England as a final course at formal meals. Both traditions were transported to North America, where colonists, using native fruits and other ingredients as well as imported foods, replicated many of the familiar desserts of home.

Rich planters and merchants entertained lavishly during the colonial era, and dessert assumed great importance as the conclusion of an impressive meal or a late evening party. The easy availability of sugar, spices, exotic fruits, nuts, and wines from the extensive Atlantic shipping trade allowed for a wide range of desserts.

Sweetmeats of preserved fruit as well as cake and creams were very popular. Throughout the colonial era and the early years of the republic, icehouses provided year-round ice and cold storage, and creams of all sorts remained in fashion through the early twentieth century. Only ice cream, however, continued to be served regularly through the remainder of the century. Fresh fruit, when available, was presented at the dessert table through the early twentieth century. Almonds, walnuts, and other nuts were served as well.

While usually not served at parties in wealthier households, pie was regularly eaten as a family dessert,

Dessert. Lithograph, late nineteenth century.

and making "paste" was an important part of the housewife's activities. By the end of the nineteenth century, pie was consumed in many households on a daily basis and continued to be a popular dessert throughout the twentieth century.

Pudding moved from the forefront of the meal to the last course as grain and vegetable puddings gave way to sweeter dishes, such as Indian pudding, a variation on traditional English grain puddings made from ground corn and molasses. By the end of the nineteenth century, puddings were made with vanilla and chocolate as these flavorings became popular. Thrifty bread and rice puddings continued to be popular through the twentieth century.

Gingerbread was an old favorite commonly eaten in America through the nineteenth century, either as a cake in the American style or rolled flat and baked hard in the older English tradition. Other cakes were popular and most often were baked in deep bowls. Layered cakes did not appear until the nineteenth century.

Little sugar cakes and seedcakes came to be known as "cookies," a word derived from Dutch settlers in New York who had brought their fondness for *koekjes* from the Lowlands. Jumbles were twisted ropes of dough, either baked like cookies or deep-fried. As doughnuts, they now are more often eaten as breakfast food.

While the early desserts derived from the English colonists, many desserts came from the large German population, particularly in Pennsylvania. The Pennsylvania Dutch continue to be known for shoofly pie, special Christmas cookies, and pastries.

The English, French, German, and Dutch were significant in forming American dessert traditions, but other cultures also contributed to the richness of the American dessert table. Native Americans mixed ground corn with crushed strawberries to create a crude strawberry shortcake and also traditionally introduced early settlers to maple syrup as well as pumpkin. In the South, African slave cooks baked benne wafers made with sesame seeds brought from Africa. Sweet potato and bean pies substituted for the rich man's pecan pie, and southern cooks mixed fresh coconut and oranges to create ambrosia, a popular holiday dessert. Puffy, deep-fried sopaipillas have been eaten in the Southwest for over two hundred years. Cardamom and ginger of Southeast Asia are used in contemporary American desserts as well as in traditional favorites. Italian cannoli and Greek baklava are widely available, and Jewish rugalach is a bakery staple throughout urban America.

Until the beginning of the twentieth century, dessert-making was tedious work. Boiling calves feet for gelatin, purifying sugar, making butter, beating batters, and steaming puddings all required extensive time. Open hearths, primitive stoves, and the dangers of cooking fires made preparation of all meals, not just dessert, extremely hard work. Many desserts could not be stored for any length of time, thereby requiring daily preparation.

By the late nineteenth century, innovations in stoves and ovens led to widespread baking of cakes and cookies. The easy availability of commercial sugar, leavening agents, gelatin, and uniformly milled flour allowed housewives to create desserts in a few hours, a boon to servantless households. Affordable and available refrigeration allowed gelatins, puddings, and creams to be made ahead and stored at home.

The Great Depression of the 1930s and the shortages imposed by rationing during World War II made desserts

Dessert from a Box. Recipes using Junket Rennet Dessert Powder and Tablets issued by Chr. Hansen's Laboratory, 1936. *Collection of Andrew F. Smith*

luxuries for many, while others used ingenuity to create simple, inexpensive sweets for their families. By the 1950s cake mixes, instant puddings, and flavored gelatin powders had transformed the American dessert table. Ice cream was more popular than ever because of the prevalence of freezers in every home. Packaged cookies, given shelf life with preservatives, became readily available, as did commercially packaged cupcakes and doughnuts. Frozen pies and piecrusts meant that pie baking was a lost art, and fewer people made desserts from scratch.

The diet and health concerns of the late twentieth century led to the decline of desserts served at home, except for celebrations and special occasions. Recreational "gourmet" cooking inspired by Julia Child and other celebrity cooks called for elegant conclusions to dinner parties. Restaurant desserts came to be extravagant demonstrations of the pastry chef's art, dramatically presented on individual plates rather than served from traditional dessert carts or sliced from one cake or pie. At the same time, low-fat and low-calorie desserts dominated the freezer sections of supermarkets and recipe columns of popular magazines at the end of the twentieth century.

Intermarriage of ethnic and religious groups, mass marketing, and the fluid mobility of American society have produced increasing uniformity in American desserts, yet regional favorites are found still throughout the country. Cooks and pastry chefs continue to refine traditional desserts to suit contemporary tastes while increasing globalization and changing immigration patterns are introducing new flavors and traditions to the American dessert table.

[See also Cakes; Cookies; Dutch Influences on American Food; French Influences on American Food; German American Food; Ice Cream and Ices; Nuts; Pies and Tarts; Puddings; Sugar.]

BIBLIOGRAPHY

The American Heritage Cookbook and Illustrated History of American Eating and Drinking. New York: American Heritage, 1964.
Belden, Louise Conway. *The Festive Tradition: Table Decoration and Desserts in America, 1650–1900.* New York: Norton, 1983.
Weaver, William Woys. *The Christmas Cook: Three Centuries of American Yuletide Sweets.* New York: HarperPerennial, 1990.

MARY SANKER

Diets, Fad

A "fad diet" is a scheme of eating that enjoys temporary and sometimes enthusiastic popularity. Usually created by one person or the product of a religious movement, these diets are meant to improve the practitioners' health, vitality, and appearance. Such diets often either limit or emphasize one particular food or type of food. The origin of American food faddism is commonly attributed to the health movement of the 1830s. William Sylvester Graham, who championed the use of graham (whole wheat) flour, was a leading figure in the movement. Posed against professional medicine, the movement sought a more natural, less complicated lifestyle based on several key elements: a simple, vegetarian diet using whole grains and daily exercise to promote physiological and spiritual reform. Highly seasoned food, rich dishes, and meat were considered stimulating, sinful food. James C. Jackson, one of Graham's disciples, advocated hydropathy, also known as water-cure, as an addition to Graham's health reform. Jackson's invention of Granula, made of graham flour and water, was said to be the first cold breakfast cereal.

Like patent medicines, fad diet plans abounded in the nineteenth century, and some led to major food companies. John Harvey Kellogg was formally trained in medicine, performed surgical procedures, and wrote tracts about his healthreform ideas. Kellogg was a Seventh-day Adventist and a vegetarian, and, like his coreligionists, he believed that the body is a temple of the Holy Spirit. Adventists founded a religious colony and sanitarium at Battle Creek, Michigan, often called "the San," where Kellogg's wealthy clients "detoxified" with enemas and high-fiber diets, including corn flakes and granola, a baked and ground mixture of oatmeal and cornmeal. By 1899 the Kellogg Company's cornflakes had become a multimillion-dollar business. Their chief competitor, among many, was Charles W. Post, a former Kellogg patient. Post's wheat and barley Grape Nuts, a supposed cure for appendicitis, malaria, consumption, and loose teeth, also became a nationally sold product. Both Kellogg and Post came to dominate the breakfast food industry throughout the twentieth century.

Bernarr Macfadden took a slightly different road to wellness. Known as the "Father of Physical Culture," he was a lifelong advocate of physical fitness through natural food, outdoor exercise, and the natural treatment of disease. The core of his philosophy held that impurities in the blood from poor diet and lack of proper exercise were the real causes of ailments. Fruits, vegetables, and whole grains were the keys to good health, but white bread was one of the worst things a person could eat. Believing that almost all diseases could be cured by

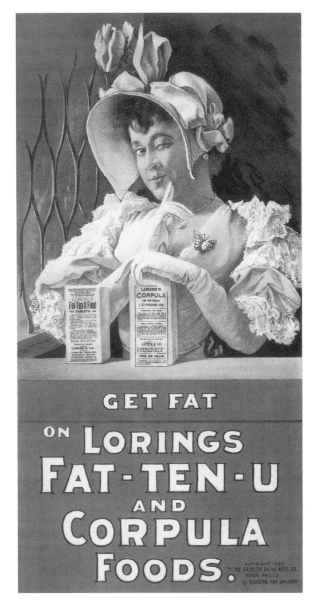

Diet Advice. Advertisement for Lorings weight-gain products, 1895. *Prints and Photographs Division, Library of Congress*

correct fasting, Macfadden advocated fasting both on a regular basis and during illness. Macfadden was a genius at self-promotion, and his influence is still present in the health food industry, literature, and clinical practice.

In the 1930s George Ohsawa, a Japanese philosopher, developed Zen macrobiotics. It is a belief based on the laws of yin and yang described in the ancient Buddhist philosophy. An extremely restrictive diet regimen, this diet consists of whole cereal grains; locally and organically grown vegetables; small amounts of soups; beans; sea vegetables; and meat, fish, and fruit in limited amounts. Popular from the 1960s into the 1980s, this dietary concept has been criticized as having been developed without the benefit of scientific evidence, but its principles have made their way into mainstream healthy-diet literature and practice.

Fruitarianism is a subcategory of the holistic health doctrine of Natural Hygiene and is related to an ascetic form of vegetarianism called "vegan." Fruitarians believe that eating only fruit is the highest moral concept of nutrition because less destruction of life is required to obtain fruits than other types of foods. Choice of foods for fruitarians is limited only to raw fruits. However, nuts, some fermented cereals, olive oil, and honey are allowed in less restricted regimens.

Weight-Loss Industry and Fad Diets

The numbers of overweight adults and obesity in the United States increased from 45 to 55 percent from 1960 to 1994, when the figure reached more than 97 million. From 1991 to 1998 obesity increased in every state, regardless of gender, race, age, or educational level. Total costs (medical costs and lost productivity) attributable to obesity amounted to an estimated $99 billion in 1995. By 2000 the national obesity rate was pegged at 28 percent. Serious health risks, such as cardiovascular disease and diabetes, together with social stigma, drove many Americans to seek fast-working weight-loss programs. As a result, a wide variety of fad reducing diets appeared on the market. By the turn of the millennium, Americans were spending more than $30 billion on diet products and diet plans each year. Weight-loss fad diets may work for a short period at first due to extremely low caloric intake, but their effectiveness may be difficult to maintain in the long run.

Fad diets can be categorized into five groups: food-specific diets; high-protein, low-carbohydrate diets; high-fiber, low-calorie diets; liquid diets; and fasting. An example of a food-specific diet is the popular cabbage soup diet. These diet plans rely heavily on a specific food or food group and thereby do not provide healthy eating habits and are not nutritionally balanced. High-protein, low-carbohydrate diets such as the Dr. Atkins' New Diet Revolution, the Zone Diet, the Scarsdale Medical Diet, and the Protein Power Diet, were on the market from the early 1970s and remained popular. These diets are based on the principle that eating excessive carbohydrates causes production of excessive amounts of insulin, leading to obesity and other health risks. Critics claim that high-protein foods are often high in saturated fat and cholesterol and thereby may increase risks of coronary heart disease and kidney problems. High-fiber, low-calorie diets promote eating vegetables for their low caloric content and the feeling of satisfaction. However, eating more than fifty to sixty grams a day can cause cramping, bloating, and diarrhea. Liquid diet products, such as Slim Fast and Sweet Success, were on the market as early as the 1930s. Although convenient, replacing regular meals with these products is not healthy and requires medical supervision. Fasting has been practiced historically by various religions as an accompaniment to religious reflection and meditation. However, fasting deprives the body of nutrients; weakness, lightheadedness, and medical problems may result.

Religion, health, fashion, and social and individual psychologies have all been important factors in the appearance of fad diets. Each diet scheme has its own internal logic that is related to external "facts," be they religious belief or scientific evidence, and therefore can appeal to general consumers. For all of these reasons, fad diets will likely continue to appeal to a wide body of Americans.

[*See also* Cereal, Cold; Health Food; Kellogg Company; Kellogg, John Harvey; Nutrition; Post Foods; Vegetarianism.]

BIBLIOGRAPHY

Herbert, Victor, and Stephen Barrett. *Vitamins and "Health" Foods: The Great American Hustle*. Philadelphia: Stickley, 1981.

Schwartz, Hillel. *Never Satisfied: A Cultural History of Diets, Fantasies, and Fat*. New York: Free Press, 1986.

American Dietetic Association. "Send Fad Diets Packing." American Dietetic Association home page Healthy Lifestyle feature [online]. Available at http: www.eatright.org/.

National Institute of Diabetes and Digestive Kidney Diseases. "Statistics Related to Overweight and Obesity." National Institute of Health home page [online]. Available at http: www.niddk.nih.gov/health/nutrit/pubs/statobes.htm#other.

Whorton, James C. *Crusaders for Fitness: The History of American Health Reformers*. Princeton, NJ: Princeton University Press, 1982.

HEA-RAN L. ASHRAF

Diners

In 1872 a street vendor from Providence, Rhode Island, named Walter Scott converted a horse-drawn freight wagon into a self-contained food-service facility. Noting that most restaurants closed in the early evening, Scott parked his wagon outside the offices of the *Providence Journal*, dispensing simple hot meals, sandwiches, pie, and hot coffee. The immediate success sparked a growing number of competitors and an industry of constructing such wagons for operation by others.

Observing Scott's operation on a rainy evening in 1880 inspired Samuel Messer Jones of Worcester, Massachusetts, to start his own business building larger wagons that provided indoor seating, thus also establishing that city as the birthplace of the diner-building industry. His new business constructed and operated a small fleet of wagons serving late-night shift workers, agricultural fairs, and other public events. Subsequent Worcester entrepreneurs, Charles H. Palmer and T. H. Buckley, Charlie Gemme, and others, constructed larger and increasingly ornate wagons for sale to others to operate.

With more cities banning mobile lunch wagons, citing concerns related to public safety, Patrick Tierney in New Rochelle, New York, established his own company in 1905 to build stationary lunch wagons for permanent locations. Jerry O'Mahony in Bayonne, New Jersey, followed suit in 1917, soon claiming the construction of a "diner a day." From the 1920s until World War II the industry grew, adding to its roster dozens of new companies—most in New Jersey—to serve a growing fast-food trade. During this time, construction quality hit its stride, incorporating all relevant technological and construction advances in a continual effort to trump the competition. For the enterprising operator willing to work very hard for long hours, the diner industry offered a turnkey restaurant operation on credit for a 10 percent down payment. If business outgrew the existing diner, operators could trade in old structures for newer, larger, and more capable units.

The iconic stainless-steel diner first hit the roadsides in the early 1940s, as builders used the material to advance both design and function of their product. Always stressing the cleanliness and efficiency of diners, builders used durable, smooth-surfaced materials, such as porcelain enamel, polished laminates, and ceramic tile, during a period regarded as the diner's golden age.

Designed to serve full meals in a short time, the diner's profitability demanded high turnover. Menus then consisted mainly of meat-and-potatoes fare, with roasts, soups, stews, and other meat dishes among the bestsellers. Larger operations also featured fresh-baked desserts. Diners located in ethnic neighborhoods offered specialties that reflected the local market.

Until World War II the diner remained primarily a male preserve, since men dominated the industrial workforce. Although dining out remained a relative rarity by modern-day standards, savvier operators attracted women customers seeking a break from cooking for their families, stressing their diner's cleanliness, comfort, and affordability. During World War II many women entering the workforce landed behind the counters of the neighborhood diner for the first time. Unlike their counterparts in the factories, however, the waitress became a permanent practitioner in the trade.

As diners left the cities and mill towns for more suburban locations after the war, the demand to make them ever larger led to the development of the first multisectioned, prefabricated restaurants. The industry could build and ship units that accommodated one hundred customers or more, in buildings transported by road or occasionally by rail, theoretically to any location in the country.

By the 1950s diners still had their counters, but they shed other Victorian vestiges, such as wood and tile, for a completely modernized appearance using stainless steel, Formica, and terrazzo. Menus in larger diners usually incorporated full breakfasts, lunches, and dinners. At the busier locations, these diners rarely closed. Customer

demographics often incorporated all walks of American society, with the industry systematically building the first restaurant type that catered to whole families based on modular, prefabricated construction. In this way, diners helped establish the American habit of dining out.

Diner owners traditionally consisted of families or individuals seeking relatively easy entry into the restaurant trade. A wave of Greek immigration in the 1950s established the dominance of their ethnicity in the industry. Although some units shipped to other parts of the country, the industry's northeastern locus meant that relatively few diners landed west of Cleveland, Ohio, or south of Baltimore, Maryland. By the late 1950s the introduction of national chains such as Howard Johnson's, franchising, and fast-food burger stands loomed as the industry's biggest threat, eventually displacing the diner from its role as family restaurant. As the industry squeezed profits through efficiency and scale, the family-run, full-service diner faced marginalization, thriving only in local niches and markets.

By 1964 diner design shed the transportation metaphor by adopting first early-American themes and then Mediterranean, colonial, rococo, or "modern" styling. Menus expanded with seating capacity to provide several aspects of American cuisine, including but not

Comfort Food in the City. The Cheyenne Diner at Thirty-third Street and Ninth Avenue in New York City. *Photograph by Joe Zarba*

limited to Greek, Italian, eastern European, southern, and other specialties. The larger operations strove to serve almost anything at anytime, while smaller, older diners in the struggling mill towns and on bypassed highways contracted into breakfast and lunch operations, owing to the decreased need for prep work and lack of demand.

The diner's revival began in the mid-1970s, with the almost simultaneous establishment of upscale diners, the publication of diner-related book titles, and the growing ubiquity of diner iconography in the mass media. This higher profile attracted people who were increasingly bored with homogeneous fast-food meals and nostalgic for basic meals in locally owned establishments. As people rejected the haute cuisine of the 1980s during the recession of the early 1990s, the American diner serving "comfort food" started a trend in the industry.

By the late 1990s larger restaurant chains made their own forays into the field. Denny's led the way with their brand-new, factory-built structures introduced in 1997, followed by a new McDonald's Diner in Kokomo, Indiana, which opened in 2001. Still, as it has for more than a century, the classic local diner continues to provide inexpensive home-cooked meals to the hungry patron.

[*See also* Fast Food; Luncheonettes; Restaurants; Roadside Food; Soda Fountains.]

BIBLIOGRAPHY

Baeder, John. *Diners*. New York: Abrams, 1995.

Butko, Brian, and Kevin Patrick. *Diners of Pennsylvania*. Mechanicsburg, PA: Stackpole Books, 1999.

Gutman, Richard J. S. *American Diner Then and Now*. 2nd ed. Baltimore: Johns Hopkins University Press, 2000.

Liebs, Chester H. *Main Street to Miracle Mile: American Roadside Architecture*. Baltimore: Johns Hopkins University Press, 1995.

Witzel, Michael Karl. *The American Diner*. Osceola, WI: MBI, 1999.

RANDY GARBIN

Dining Car

From their inception in 1831, American railroads wrestled with techniques for feeding passengers. Early passengers, plagued by long delays caused by derailments, faulty equipment, and the lack of signaling devices to control train movements, resorted to foraging for food, packing meals of varying quality and scent, or buying food of questionable quality from vendors at stations.

Eventually passengers could purchase food from an onboard "news butcher" who passed through the train selling all manner of sundries, or at scheduled stops at stations outfitted with eating houses established for the purpose. However, as the industry continued to consolidate, regional trunk lines formed between 1865 and 1900 to connect major cities, and competition among them for passengers and shippers intensified. With train speeds exceeding a mile a minute, it became inconvenient to stop a train every several hours so that passengers could eat.

In July 1866, the industrialist and inventor George M. Pullman introduced the first railroad car designed for preparing and serving food to passengers in transit. Named the President, the car was built in the Aurora, Illinois, shops of the Chicago, Burlington and Quincy Railroad. This "hotel car" consisted of the patented Pullman face-to-face sleeping-car seating and had mountings for a table that could be inserted between the seats at mealtimes. The car had a small (three feet by six feet) kitchen at one end. Two years later Pullman introduced the dining car Delmonico, which was outfitted with a fully equipped eight-foot by eight-foot kitchen. Meals were served as in a restaurant, usually with a waiter for each "section" consisting of two tables that seated either four and two or four and four passengers. A steward supervised.

Dining car kitchens evolved to measure approximately eight feet by fifteen feet, typically containing a range and a broiler with fire boxes beneath and warming shelves above. Other equipment included a coffeemaker with cup warmer, steam table, carving board, refrigerator, two sinks, and a pastry table. The kitchen had storage space for ingredients, pots and pans, cooking utensils, dishes, and ice, coal, and

A Dining Car. Engraving, nineteenth century. *Culinary Archives & Museum at Johnson & Wales University, Providence, R.I.*

charcoal. In this space three cooks and a chef prepared all portions for as many as two hundred people per meal for each of three meals a day. An adjoining pantry measuring approximately eight feet by twelve feet held the items needed for making salads, serving bread, and preparing drinks, as well as the dishes and tableware needed for completing setup and service. Compact and efficient, dining car kitchens inspired the architects and designers who first constructed apartment buildings.

Seen as a promotional necessity by the railroads, the dining car showcased a railroad's approach to service and offered some of the best cuisine available in America. Railroads attracted top chefs to create menu items, instruct in their preparation, and supervise their success. American tastes expanded because passengers from all walks of life and from throughout the land could experience culinary achievements only found otherwise in expensive restaurants and hotels in the big cities. Dining cars introduced regional ingredients to a national audience, from the Idaho potato (Union Pacific) to the Great Big Baked Apple (Great Northern). Railroad test kitchens found many uses for items transported by the respective company's freight department, such as cantaloupe pie (Texas and Pacific) and curried rice (Southern Pacific). Railroads pioneered the food service manual, standardization of preparation and portions, and the use of quality ingredients and fewer preparation steps to ensure quality and prompt service, all hallmarks of restaurant chains in the early twenty-first century. Common food products such as Bisquick baking mix (Southern Pacific) and square sandwich bread (Pullman) and preparation aids such as pressed sawdust logs (Union Pacific) originated in dining cars.

Amtrak, the National Railroad Passenger Corporation, operates all intercity passenger trains in the early 2000s. Amtrak's food service cars fall into three categories. Café or lounge cars, found in all trains, offer snack items, beverages, and packaged salads, sandwiches, and entrées, some warmed in microwave ovens. Full dining cars come in two configurations. Heritage and Viewliner cars, which are one level high, enable operation through tunnels in and out of New York and Washington, D.C., and resemble the floor plans of the earliest dining cars. Superliner, or bilevel, cars for western trains consist of a ten-foot by forty-foot kitchen on the lower level and a seventy-two-seat dining room on the upper level, which is serviced by dumbwaiters.

[See also Bread, Sliced; Harvey, Fred; Kitchens, *subentry on* 1800 to the Present; Pullman, George.]

BIBLIOGRAPHY

Menchen, August. *The Railroad Passenger Car: An Illustrated History of the First Hundred Years with Accounts by Contemporary Passengers.* Baltimore: Johns Hopkins University Press, 2000.
Porterfield, James D. *Dining by Rail: The History and the Recipes of the Golden Age of American Railroad Cuisine.* New York: St. Martin's Griffin, 1998.

JAMES D. PORTERFIELD

Dining Rooms, Table Settings, and Table Manners

> The dining-room ought to be the pleasantest place in the house; it is the meeting room where the family are expected to be always present at stated times, and where the events of the day are talked over while the pleasant business of eating is being discussed.

So writes Laura Holloway Langford in her household manual *The Hearthstone* (1883), capturing the Victorian sentiment of the dining room as domestic sanctuary. Icons such as Norman Rockwell's "Freedom from Want," in which three generations of smiling faces gather round the table, fuel the nostalgia for the dining room as the heart of middle-class family life.

This vision was new. In the eighteenth and early nineteenth centuries, dining rooms belonged to the elite, who uniquely possessed spacious houses, expensive silver, glassware, and dishware along with the table manners to use such implements politely. Before the mid-nineteenth century, it did not occur to many Americans that they should have a special room just for meals. But material and cultural changes were underway that would make the dining room the symbol of middle-class prosperity: increasingly affordable tablewares united with the democratically optimistic belief that learned etiquette could be a social equalizer. No physical space provided a better stage for the classless American dream of the family homestead than a dining room neatly outfitted with the props needed to serve a late-nineteenth-century dinner.

Ironically, no room did more to point out class distinctions within American society. Moreover, no sooner had the dining room come to symbolize idealized domesticity than its pull as the family's magnet started to weaken. During its first year of publication in 1885, *Good Housekeeping* tackled the challenge of luring the family to shared meals in the cloistered dining room when the tantalizing world beyond beckoned. By the 1920s anthropologists blamed the frenzy of modern life for the regrettable decline of the at-home family dinner even in conservative, small-town America. As the twentieth century progressed, traditionalists, who saw moral rigor in a separate dining room, with its carefully set table and whiff of formal ceremony, locked horns with modernists, for whom the dining room was an obsolete appendage from a romanticized past and a burden to housewives. The modernists have largely won, as even some mainstream furniture retailers urge consumers to abandon the notion of a dining room, with its imposing mahogany or black walnut table, and to utilize the space efficiently as a home office, turning the room to its traditional function only on occasion by "setting" a handsome desk for dinner.

Evolution of the Dining Room

To dedicate a room exclusively to eating is an unusual and luxurious allocation of space. Few cultures conceived of such single-purpose domestic spaces. Wealthy ancient Greeks and Romans had their *andrones* (men's rooms, a place where men gathered to eat and be entertained) and triclinia, sometimes with immovable stone tables and couches, but by the Middle Ages no abode, regardless of the socioeconomic standing of the owner, reserved a space solely for dining, with tables and seating permanently displayed. Whether one dined in the great hall of an aristocrat's castle, the main room of a comfortably middle-class home, or the only room of a peasant's shanty, the eating area was used for other functions once meals were finished. Crude, wooden trestle tables, disguised by silky damask or serviceable linen, were set up and broken down as needed. The affluent sat on chairs; those of more modest means pulled up a limited number of stools or benches, and the lowest in rank, such as children, stood. In the poorest households, there was frequently neither table nor seat for anyone, with a common cooking pot or a large trencher set on the floor or improvised surface for all the eaters to dip into. In the mid-seventeenth century, just as Europeans were colonizing America's eastern seaboard, dining rooms were beginning to emerge as distinct domestic spaces for the most affluent, although the process would not be complete even in these classes until the eighteenth century. Simultaneously, the middling classes were enjoying homes with multiple rooms, devoting some to more public and others to more private functions.

The journal of William Bradford, the second governor of Plymouth Colony, suggests that some early immigrants knew of this trend toward greater room specialization and increasing privacy and were disappointed when they could not immediately duplicate it in the wilds of Massachusetts. Shelters at Plymouth were mostly one or two rooms, plus a loft, for cooking, eating, sleeping, working, and keeping warm, sometimes shared with valuable livestock. Mealtimes followed European practice: a table was assembled in the "hall" and then broken down to make room for other activities. Similar extremely modest homes continued to be built throughout the eighteenth century in rural and frontier areas. However, by the early eighteenth century, typical floor plans of moderately prosperous town houses reflected a burgeoning classical sensibility that translated into less cluttered dining areas. A spacious entryway divided the ground floor into four rooms, including a "best room" or "parlor" (from the French *parler*, to speak), where the most stylish furniture would be used for entertaining guests, and a "back parlor" more simply fitted for family gatherings. Homes of successful farmers followed suit, sometimes on a grander scale. The probate records from 1720 for the German immigrant planter Charles Carroll show an eleven-room home in Maryland complete with silver plate and fine linens for the dining room and fed by a well-equipped, sophisticated kitchen.

Although the floor plans of these homes sometimes indicate a "dining room" or "dining parlor" (the earliest in America appears to be in highly fashionable Boston in 1681), the rooms were still used for functions other than eating. As late as 1794 George Hepplewhite, in *The Cabinet-Maker's and Upholsterer's Guide*, advised that a sofa was both "proper and necessary" in "a Drawing-room or Dining Parlour," with the substitution of a dining table for the more flexible pier tables only if the room was to be used exclusively for dining. French visitors of the time contrasted the American custom, borrowed from the English, of lingering to converse in the dining parlor with the French habit of adjourning promptly to another room after the meal. Americans also relocated their dining space to suit season and climate. Chilly northern households might close up the fancy ground-floor dining parlor and move to a cozy winter eating parlor situated over the kitchen. Tables on casters could be wheeled into the most comfortable room for eating, regardless of the other activities that might take place.

Dinner on Horseback. The industrialist and horse fancier C. K. G. Billings hosted a dinner in the ballroom of Sherry's restaurant in New York on 28 March 1903. Guests ate off dining trays attached to the saddles. At the end of the dinner, the horses were served oats. *Museum of the City of New York, The Byron Collection, 93.1.1.3940*

Decorating the dining areas was largely a masculine activity in the eighteenth and early nineteenth centuries. The furniture pattern books recommend a somber, serious, and substantial feel to the room. Blues, greens, and yellows were favored colors, particularly in wallpaper, for dining parlors in the late eighteenth century, while walls painted in muted earth tones came into fashion in the early nineteenth century. Fabrics were to match or harmonize, lending a tranquil sense of order and neatness to the room, devoid of the clutter that was endemic to many of the seventeenth century's crowded spaces. That men were responsible for the decorative schemes is hardly surprising given the frequent exclusion of women, other than the mistress of the house, from eighteenth- and early nineteenth-century dinners. When women were included in dinner parties, they often were seated at one end or side of the table, with the men at the other. It was not until the second quarter of the nineteenth century that mixed-gender seating became common, and the etiquette books are full of much-needed instructions on precisely how to escort ladies to the dinner table.

The multiple functions and locations of dining spaces continued until well into the nineteenth century, when rooms devoted solely to dining signaled middle-class success. Even the newfangled, space-saving apartments of Manhattan, built in the 1870s as the next step up from tenement life, gave middle-class New Yorkers both a parlor and a formal dining room. Whether in large cities, small towns, or isolated farmhouses, the vogue for a separate, dedicated dining room was fueled by the widespread distribution of etiquette books and household manuals that described both how to furnish such a room and how to behave therein. Paintings of the hunt and heavy wooden sideboards adorned with carvings of dead game were elite mid-century furnishings that telegraphed the paterfamilias's role as a hunter and a provider, reinforced by blood reds and crimsons that subtly communicated ruthless domination. By the 1870s, the most fashionable dining room furnishings were neo-Gothic in style, evoking churchly sanctuaries and underscoring the home as the bastion of moral values.

A separate dining room might pose additional housekeeping burdens for the housewife, but the growing ranks of domestic servants, stoked by immigration throughout most of the nineteenth century, helped to ease the load. Servants made up between 5 and 8 percent of the labor force in the nineteenth century, although housewives complained bitterly of the difficulty in finding good help. In major cities and their suburbs, there was roughly one live-in servant for every four families in the 1870s, with a national average of one servant for every eight. This relative labor glut supported the explosion of dining paraphernalia after the Civil War. Without help, comfortably situated housewives could not maintain the elaborate material culture necessary for stylish dining. With industrialization, the number of people engaged in domestic service plummeted. By 1920, there was only one servant for every twenty-one families in Detroit, and the national average had dropped to one for every sixteen. The first decades of the twentieth century witnessed a growing "servant problem" and the need to rethink the physical structure of middle-class homes to function in what was rapidly becoming a servantless society.

Those who wanted to maintain family dinners at home had two options: streamline the dining room or eliminate it altogether in a return to the multifunctional "hall" of the colonial period. Designers at the turn of the twentieth century proposed laborsaving designs to make the dining area beautiful and functional. *Craftsman*, Gustave Stickley's short-lived magazine, suggested building china cabinets in the wall between the dining room and the kitchen or pantry, with access on both sides, to allow dishes to be put away without the extra steps of carrying them into the dining room. Frank Lloyd Wright's "open plan" fused living and dining rooms (although kitchens remained distinct, enclosed spaces), allowing families to make use of the dining area for other purposes outside of mealtime. By the 1920s, these ideas had trickled into popular magazines such as *Better Homes and Gardens*, which offered floor plans for houses without dining rooms, expressly created in response to the servant problem. These promoted family dining in the kitchen, company dining in the living room (approximately equivalent in function to the nineteenth-century parlor), and outdoor dining in the summer.

Were people following these modern trends? The evidence suggests that while the lower maintenance approach was slowly gaining appeal, tradition had its adherents, especially among the working classes who had only recently acquired a few of the badges of gentility. One 1907 study glowingly lauded a New York City policeman's family that ate all of its meals in the dining room, set with white linens and wedding silver. But as the

Family Dinner. Lithography, late nineteenth century.

twentieth century progressed, the formal dining room slipped as the idealized place for daily family gatherings. In a 1944 *McCall's* magazine survey, 55.1 percent of respondents preferred, in theory, a combined living and dining area over a traditional dining room, frequently on grounds of housekeeping ease, even though only 10 percent had such spaces. The *McCall's* respondents used traditional dining rooms for company meals, but relatively few family meals were served therein. The survey elicited emotional and vehement comments, which the editors interpreted as proof of "two basic homemaking philosophies, a Modern and a Traditional one, which in their purest expression [in the dining room] are pitted squarely against each other."

In 1950, the industrial designers Mary and Russel Wright published their *Guide to Easier Living*. Chapters titled "The Vanishing Dining Room" and "The New Hospitality" advised postwar suburbanites of the easiest ways of setting, serving, and clearing meals, whether for family or for guests. Among the Wrights' self-consciously radical suggestions were eliminating tablecloths, place mats, and cloth napkins; limiting utensils to a maximum of one knife, one fork, and one spoon per diner (even fewer with a well-designed, one-dish menu); and getting the guests to wash the dishes by providing plastic aprons for both men and women. Easy-to-clean materials predominate, including plastic slipcovers encasing a sofa in the combination kitchen-dining-family-living room.

As more people require home offices, and fewer domestics are available to polish the silver, much less butler the dinner, the dedication of valuable floor space to an old-fashioned dining room fits fewer American lifestyles. The formal room dedicated to dining is once again becoming an emblem of the wealthier classes. For middle-class Americans, many contemporary architects design flexible "great room" plans that combine kitchen, living, and dining spaces into a communal area reminiscent of the colonial American home, albeit on a more spacious scale.

Setting the Table and Serving the Meal

How one sets a table and serves a meal depends, quite obviously, on the menu and cultural norms. A multicourse "soup to nuts" dinner requires different accoutrements than does a casserole supper. Compare the differences in even the simplest dinners over the past four hundred years. Early-seventeenth-century Dutch colonists ate a steaming pottage from the center of a dining board (some

were specially hollowed out with a shallow depression to restrain the runny mash) by scooping bites with a spoon, a bit of bread, or the last three fingers carefully arched. No plates formed an intermediate way station for food to rest on in the journey from common dish to mouth. The eating utensil (spoon or fingers) returned unwashed to the trough, although unwritten rules of etiquette sanctioned precisely how one would divide areas within the common dish for each diner. Drinks were drained from a communal cup, the lip wiped in a nod to delicacy before passing it on. The entire experience was based on sharing comestibles. A comparable stew dinner, even in a very modest household from the late nineteenth century forward, came to the table in a serving vessel with a serving spoon and individual plates, utensils, and drinking glasses for each diner. The diners helped themselves to portions, rather than mouthfuls, from the common dish, with each portion transferred to a personal plate before being eaten. Contemporary etiquette bans using the serving utensil for eating, and any diner (except those on the most intimate terms) who tries to sneak a fork into the common pot to grab a tempting morsel is slapped on the wrist. The entire dining experience stresses eating from the individual plate rather than the communal platter.

Many early immigrants dined with relative comfort, given the standards of the times. One young Plymouth colonist favorably compared the ware on her family's table, made from the top of an abandoned packing crate spread with a cloth, with what she had known in England. They had brought their English wooden cups, made other drinking vessels from gourds grown in the Massachusetts garden, molded new pewter spoons from worn pewter ware, and had a few "expensive" dishes (possibly pewter or earthenware), some wooden trencher bowls, and a larger wooden trencher for serving. Conspicuously absent is a dining fork, which was just becoming known, although not widely adopted, in the upper middle classes in England. In *Coryat's Curiosities* (1611), the Englishman Thomas Coryat fastidiously urges his compatriots to adopt forks because "all men's fingers are not alike cleane," yet some members of Plymouth Colony considered the fork a vain affectation, unnecessary if one had one's "own cleanly fingers, and napkins of linen on which to wipe them."

There were few indications of elegant dining for this first generation of colonists. Yet by the 1650s, dining apparatuses began to differentiate along socioeconomic lines. The wealthiest sported a few items of silverware and extensive collections of linens; one Plymouth matron's 1654 estate listed a phenomenal eighteen tablecloths and sixty-six napkins. Other New England inventories confirm increasing luxury, with fixed-leg tables, chairs with "wrought Cushions," and glassware. The stark contrast between the simple comforts found at Plymouth Colony in the 1620s and household inventories one hundred years later coincides with the start of a consumer revolution, a desire to acquire material goods that would trickle through society over the next 150 years. According to the historian Cary Carson, "by the 1730s & 40s people in the middle ranks of society were purchasing many newly imported 'elegancies' as well. By the Revolution even some of the poorer sort had made 'necessities' of goods that were their fathers' 'decencies,' their grandfathers' 'luxuries,' and before that simply unheard of." The Scottish physician Alexander Hamilton, traveling up the Hudson River in 1744, recorded a poor family's dining aspirations: although living in a scantily furnished cottage, the family had some stoneware tea dishes, a tea pot, and a dozen worn, but shiny, pewter plates and spoons. A generation earlier, simple wooden implements would have been expected. The same Dr. Hamilton noted that the affluent Dutch community in Albany, New York, "set out their cabinets and *buffets* much with china," some of which, with its pierced feet, was hung decoratively.

By the mid-eighteenth century, wealthy Americans could dine as elegantly as their English counterparts. In directing his London agent to purchase Chinese porcelain dinnerware for Mount Vernon in the late 1750s, the young George Washington was unequivocal about the need to be chic: "pray let them be neat and fashionable or send none." This sentiment was repeated by another wealthy Virginian, who wrote to England in 1762 seeking a dinner set "of the most fashionable sort . . . sufficient for 2 genteel Courses of Victuals." The passion for fashion linked colonial America to England more tightly than any political compact.

French Service vs. Russian Service

The demand for fashionable dishes to serve "2 genteel Courses of Victuals" is enormously telling. Through the eighteenth and much of the nineteenth centuries, prosperous diners aspired to eat in what is generally known as the French style, used by the affluent not only in France, where the style originated in the seventeenth century, but also throughout Europe, England, and America during the eighteenth century. By the late nineteenth century, a very different style of dining, called Russian service, dominated fashionable tables. While the foodstuffs offered could be similar, their mode of presentation varied. In a nutshell, a meal served *à la française*, or French style (sometimes called *à l'anglaise*, or English style), was divided into two main courses plus a separate dessert course. Each course consisted of many platters placed on the table simultaneously, much like contemporary groaning Thanksgiving boards, from which the diners would receive their portions. A meal served *à la russe*, or Russian style, did not place platters on the table but instead presented a succession of separate courses to each diner. Although fifteen- to twenty-course meals were most typical, some accounts describe a very few grandiose meals estimated at one hundred and fifty separate courses.

The shift from French to Russian service was gradual, starting in the 1830s in such cities as New York, Philadelphia, and Washington. Moreover, the services were mutable, adapting to the needs and capacities of different households. The following is a general guide to the services as practiced in America, although no one model embraces all meals served in either the French or Russian style.

French Service French service was a feast for the eye. Serving dishes were arrayed on the table in a symmetrical, artistic pattern, illustrated by charts in many elite English and French cookery books. A few American editions of these works, such as *The French Cook* (1828) by Louis Eustache Ude, include table charts, but most of the pictorial guidance came from imported sources. Diners did not enter the room until the first course of dishes was laid so that a gleaming, aromatic, and copiously decked table greeted the guests. Dishes were often covered by silver domes that sparkled in the candlelight or were placed over elegant hot water baths to keep the dishes warm. Once seated, diners selected their preferred viands (it was considered greedy to sample everything) and used their single fork, knife, and spoon to eat all of their choices within the course. In carefully choreographed hospitality, the host and hostess performed as manorial lord and lady (significantly, the word "lady" derives from the Old English for "bread-giver") by physically portioning the most important foods. The meal was highly interactive and communal as guests helped serve the dishes nearest them, often with the assistance of servants. Etiquette books throughout the nineteenth century teach hosts and guests how to serve, with such useful gems as placing only dainty portions on the plate, for fear of squelching appetite, or stirring the gravy before ladling a bit to the side of the meat, to avoid serving only grease.

A dinner served *à la française* usually started with soup, cradled in an impressive ceramic tureen or, at the highest tables, one of magnificent silver. An important meal would include two soups, one clear and one thick, placed at opposite ends of the table. The tureens were some of the most elaborately decorated service pieces, carefully anchoring positions of authority. The hostess would inquire as to the guest's preference and place a scant ladleful of soup (or summon assistance from the person nearest the requested dish) into a shallow, rimmed soup plate (the small, double-handled bouillon cups would emerge only later as part of sets designed for serving *à la russe*), to be delivered to the diner. Servants whisked away the tureens as soon as the soup was served, for etiquette forbade a second helping of soup; it suggested a crass concern that the rest of the dinner might be found wanting. It was, however, anathema to leave a space on the table; in the gap left by the tureens would be placed the "removes," that is, the dishes prepared and waiting on the sideboard to be substituted for the introductory soup. The removes might be imposing fish, such as salmon or turbot, although other savory dishes, such as a ham, could fill the voids. Carefully spread about the table would be less important meat or egg dishes (very frequently in a sauce) called the entrées, plus a number of small hors d'oeuvre plates holding piquantly seasoned tidbits, such as olives, the newly fashionable raw celery stalks, relishes, pickles, or other dainty bites. The dishes bearing the entrées and hors d'oeuvres could be fancifully curved or take organic shapes, such as the creamware shells and leaves that George Washington ordered for pickles.

Once the soup was cleared, the host and hostess asked each guest what he or she would like and prepared a plate, often with the assistance of a servant or the person seated closest to the desired dish, to be passed to the identified guest. One started eating as soon as one was served and did not pass the plate along if it contained one's expressed preferences. The host and hostess were served last. Attentive hosts noticed when a guest had finished what was on his or her plate and would inquire as to what the guest "would be helped." The words "next"

or "more" or "another" never were uttered in polite company; how much or what a person ate was beneath comment. The guest passed the plate to a servant or the person nearest the requested dish for his or her portion. One unresolved etiquette question was whether the fork and knife journeyed with the plate as it was passed or remained at one's place. It was poor form to hold utensils when one was not actively eating but equally rude to soil the cloth by laying them on the table while one's plate made its rounds. Some suggested leaning the utensils on bread (served at this time on the cloth, as bread plates had not yet been invented), but the most common solution was to slide one's knife and fork onto the plate at right angles, the cover traveling as a precarious trio. Eighteenth-century plates were a bit deeper than modern ones, helping to stabilize the utensils.

The first course concluded, all of the dishes were removed and the top tablecloth (always white) was carefully rolled up to reveal a fresh cloth underneath. For large tables, the cloth might come in segments to facilitate removal. Fresh plates and flatware were distributed, and the second course was brought in, consisting of the main roasts, the game, and the entremets (literally, the dishes between the main platters). The stimulating hors d'oeuvres were returned, to be nibbled during any lull in serving the more substantial foods. The entremets ranged from vegetable side dishes and salads to hot soufflés, sweet or savory pies, and sweetened custards. This mixing of sweet and savory foods within the second course lingered from late medieval meal structures. The roasts assumed the positions vacated by the tureens and first-course removes, and the entremets replaced the entrées. The diners remained at the table throughout this cumbersome resetting. As in the first course, many platters and dishes had lids to keep their contents warm; the lids were removed with careful ceremony to prevent dripping condensation only after the table regained its orchestrated symmetry. We still find lidded dishes keeping vegetables warm in contemporary china sets.

The host and hostess again portioned, this time the most important roasts, in symbolic hospitality. Skill in carving the roast marked a gentleman, although the craft was admired in ladies as well. Etiquette preferred that the carver (host, hostess, or accommodating guest) remained seated while deftly portioning the various birds and joints, and a guest should decline the honor of carving if lacking in skill. Guests were expected to express a preference for cut or degree of doneness, as it was deemed vulgar not to know one's mind about such trifles. The dishware matched from the first to the second course.

The final course was dessert, from the French *desservir*, meaning to clear away the cloth. The name comes from the late-medieval custom of adjourning from the hall where dinner was held to another room for the concluding sweet wafers and candied spices; the first step in breaking down the hall was to remove the tablecloth from the impermanent tables. This practice evolved into the custom that continued through the mid-nineteenth century of serving dessert on a bare tabletop, exposing the burnished wood, usually mahogany, to admiring eyes. In *The House Servant's Directory* (1827), the Bostonian butler Robert Roberts offers painstaking instructions for this intrusive manipulation. Servants carefully rolled up the heavy damask tablecloth and quickly laid the multiple desserts with their serving pieces as well as the diners' individual dessert plates, wineglasses, and water glasses, all without inconveniencing the diners or making any noise. Dessert itself might consist of fresh, candied, and preserved fruits; ice creams; nuts; cakes; and cheeses, often served on distinctive plates such as glass or striking polychrome porcelain. Again host and guest were pressed into service to portion from communal dishes. By the mid-nineteenth century, colored dessert napkins often replaced the classic white linen to camouflage the staining juices oozing from fruits. By the latter half of the nineteenth century, the cloth remained on the table through dessert, although it was carefully crumbed. Coffee was not necessarily part of the dining room fare but might be served in the drawing room or parlor after the ladies withdrew from the dining room, leaving the gentlemen to the often criticized interval of brandy and cigars. Guests left promptly after coffee.

These dizzying acrobatics of a dinner *à la française* explain Eliza Farrar's oft-quoted sentiment in *The Young Lady's Friend* (1837) that "a dinner, well performed by all the actors in it, is very fatiguing, and, as it generally occupies three hours or more, most persons are glad to go away when it is fairly done." In fact, at precisely this time, dining *à la russe* was making its first tentative forays onto the American dining scene. It would take the rest of the century for Russian service to infiltrate elite dining, in part because many Americans, accustomed to the heavily laden tables of French service, simply did not like what was perceived as a meagerly outfitted table.

Russian Service In dinners *à la russe*, rather than enter a room redolent of the delicious savors of dinner, one sat at a table laid with a plate, wineglasses, water glasses, and, as the century progressed, a thicket of forks, knives, and spoons, many of specialized shape and function, used serially to consume the successive courses. Etiquette writers struggled with how many forks, knives, and spoons properly could be laid on the table, as it was spatially impossible to have all the silverware needed for a fifteen-course meal set in advance. By the end of the nineteenth century, the consensus was that no more than three forks (excluding the tiny seafood fork), two knives, and a soupspoon were appropriate at the meal's start. The center of the table could be decorated with a mirrored plateau, porcelain figures, candelabra, condiment castors, or epergnes (all of which had appeared at extremely elite tables in eighteenth-century French service), plus dishes of hors d'oeuvres, bonbons, and desserts. Missing, however, were the substantial comestibles, leading some to worry whether their appetites would be sated. Philip Hone, the mayor of New York City in 1825, condemned his first dinner served in this modern style in January 1838:

> The table, covered with confectionery and gewgaws, looked like one of the shops down Broadway in the Christmas holidays, but not an eatable thing. The dishes were all handed round; in my opinion a most unsatisfactory mode of proceeding in relation to this important part of the business of a man's life. One does not know how to choose, because you are ignorant of what is coming next, or whether anything more is coming. Your conversation is interrupted every minute by greasy dishes thrust between your head and that of your neighbor, and

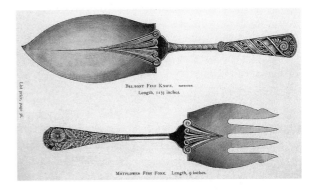

Specialized Silverware. Belmont fish knife and Mayflower fish fork. From C. Rogers & Bros. Catalog, 1890.

it is more expensive than the old mode of shewing a handsome dinner to your guests and leaving them free to choose. It will not do.

Russian service depended heavily on bevies of liveried servants to perform many of the host's prerogatives in French service. Butlers presented beautifully arrayed platters for each diner's approval, starting with the hostess; if the diner approved, the butler placed a portion on the diner's plate, with appropriate accompaniments and garnishes. In the most elite homes, the diner never saw a "broken" platter, that is, one from which portions had been removed. Plates were filled from duplicate platters on the sideboard or in the butler's pantry, served by waiters noiselessly shuttling after the display. One waiter to every four diners (outside help was hired for larger parties) was recommended to keep the meal proceeding apace. Waiters pulled dirty covers as soon as the guest had finished, substituting fresh utensils in anticipation of the next course. Thus, expert waiters had to distinguish among fish, meat, salad, pastry, and ice cream forks, even if fork-phobic guests could not. In *The Complete Handbook of Etiquette* (1884), M. C. Dunbar admires the ease and grace of a meal served *à la russe*: "Both host and guest are relieved of every kind of responsibility. Dish after dish comes round, as if by magic; and nothing remains but to eat and be happy."

Although nineteenth-century menus seem astonishingly large, the question of how much people ate varied with the individual. The pleasingly plump ladies and ample-bellied plutocrats show that many dined with uninhibited gusto. Nonetheless, French waiters were especially praised for knowing how to serve demure portions. Etiquette permitted a diner to decline any offered course other than the initial soup and the roast, so one did not necessarily eat every course, in much the same way in which one did not sample everything in French service. Until the 1930s, etiquette also required a diner to leave a bit on his plate "for manners" and mostly disapproved of the gaucherie of using bread to sop up a delicious sauce. Some courses were small, such as icy Roman punch (a slushy sorbet spiked with liquor), which cleansed the palate between roast and game; individually served vegetables, such as a plate of peas or asparagus; and the concluding coffee.

The transition from French to Russian service wrought radical changes in the dining experience. The meal became more tightly structured in time rather than in space. The same dishes that were displayed *à la française* were served seriatim *à la russe*; the four entrées that might be placed on the first course of the French table now might be four separate courses. The rhythm of the meal changed from two grand acts to a constant buzz of plates coming and going. In *The Epicurean* (1893), Charles Ranhofer recommends no more than eight or ten minutes per course. By his calculation, a fourteen-course meal could be served in a little under two hours; an eight-course meal took barely an hour. Most writers agreed that, while dinners might last five hours, anything extending beyond two was torture.

The introduction of Russian service marked a red-letter day for conspicuous consumption, with a dramatic increase in the number of objects needed to serve the meal elegantly. The most extravagant tables boasted different dishware for each course, the goal being to surprise and delight the diner with novel objects. Matching sets of dishes "sufficient for 2 genteel Courses" were inadequate and passé to the trendsetters of the Gilded Age, who displayed such new forms for personal place settings as majolica oyster plates, demure footed bouillon cups, or crescent-shaped side plates for a chilled salad that nestled against a warm plate holding game in a popular *chaud-froid* juxtaposition that was a rare exception to the one food per course rule. Each course demanded flatware ergonomically engineered to be the most subtly efficient way of consuming a particular food. Different wines were served every few courses, and glasses of varying shapes, colors, and sizes showcased the selections. Elaborate fresh floral arrangements became fashionable in the late nineteenth century (until that time, silk or porcelain flowers were used), always with the caveat that they should not obstruct anyone's view. Depictions of tall vases with arching cascades of blooms suggest that horticultural excess regularly trumped conversation. In *Etiquette: Good Manners for All People* (1906), Agnes Morton explains that "in arranging the modern dinner-table, when the service is to be *à la Russe*, floral decorations are almost indispensable. Without something attractive for the eye to rest upon, the desert stretch of linen looks like the white ghost of famine mocking the feast."

Dining for the Aspiring: Vernacular Emulation from 1830 to 1920

Many middle- and upper-middle-class Americans wanted to emulate the wealthy's "genteel" meals; the conundrum was how to dine elegantly when one was neither to the manner born nor possessed of a phalanx of European-trained servants. Imagine a young housewife's jitters in navigating the shoals of dinner *à la française* upon reading in *Recollections of a Housekeeper* (1834) by Clarissa Packard that "a lady may as excusably stand on her own head at her table, as have her turkey or goose in an unauthorized posture."

From the mid-nineteenth through the mid-twentieth centuries, cookery, etiquette, and housekeeping books comforted bourgeois, middle, and working classes with practical advice on how to behave politely at table, whether as host or guest. Added to the more bourgeois works was important guidance on training domestics, frequently immigrants or freed slaves untutored in the increasing frippery of middle-class tables. Most of the works were addressed to (and written by) women, who assumed an increasingly prominent role in running the home while men went to their offices. Many preached a reassuring modesty. Genteel dining could be frugal, but not mean, requiring only a simple, competently prepared menu, pristine linens, polished flatware and glasses, and unchipped dishes.

By the 1850s, a new style of service was penetrating the comfortably ensconced middle classes. It married some of the communality of French service with the increasing materiality of Russian. In her *Domestic Receipt*

NAPKINS

Napkins have been used since at least the classical Roman world, when guests brought cloths to dinner to wrap up leftovers—the original doggie bag. Seventeenth-century European elites were dazzled at table by damask napkins intricately folded into flora or fauna. Contemporaneous Plymouth colonists, who ate without dining forks, wiped their soiled fingers on more plebeian linen. Napkins were one of the first "luxuries" listed in the simplest colonial decedent's estate. Yet Americans by no means universally used napkins, and it was not simply a question of cost. As use of the dining fork spread, some assumed that the napkin was superfluous.

Mid-nineteenth-century etiquette books explained what to do if no napkin was provided: as finger licking was never acceptable, the gentleman unfortunately had to choose between smearing the tablecloth or gallantly whipping out his handkerchief. The disagreeable consequence of the latter action, of course, was that the gentleman then had to stuff the besmirched fabric back in his pocket. Many exasperated writers queried why the napkin had not been universally adopted, and a few tried to shame the recalcitrant by labeling napkins indispensable. The napkin question was sufficiently open in the 1850s that in *The Practical Housekeeper* (1857), Elizabeth Ellet gives detailed, illustrated instructions for seven decorative folds, telling the housekeeper to place the bread under the convoluted napkin on the dinner plate. She then blithely states that if dinner napkins are not used, the proper place for the bread is to the left of the plate.

Although napkins became ubiquitous after the Civil War, essayists could rely on them for a knowing laugh. An article published in *The Nation* in 1879 delights in fathers who liked to mortify "their aspiring daughters by remarks in peculiarly aggravating circumstances about the frivolousness of napkins." Issues still arose about their proper size and color. White or ivory, denoting purity and cleanliness, were the only acceptable hues for a dinner napkin through the nineteenth century, although colored napkins enlivened the fruit course, when the juicy fruits might leave indelible stains. Colored (read "potentially soiled") napkins otherwise were never permitted. This strict rule was relaxed first for ladies' "color" luncheons at the turn of the twentieth century, when pastel linens matching the meal's theme color were encouraged. Colors, especially tied to holidays, eventually filtered to dinner. Finally, in a complete inversion of tradition, the painfully chic have applauded the introduction of black napkins that leave no uncool lint on the laps of black-clad hipsters.

In addition to playing chameleon, napkins have shrunk. Thirty-inch squares (suitable for decorative folding) have given way to the standard twenty- to twenty-two-inch dinner square, impossibly small to contort into elaborate shapes. Luncheon napkins are even smaller, at about fourteen inches square. Cocktail napkins, developed to meet the needs of twentieth-century cocktail parties, are the tiniest of all, at about eight inches square.

Paper napkins appeared no later than 1915, when they were critiqued by Lucy Allen in *Table Service*. Although paper napkins were tolerated for family meals by the 1930s, fastidious hostesses still considered them insulting to guests, as they bespoke a lack of effort. Nonetheless, good-quality paper napkins, particularly with the host's monogram, gained acceptance at that time for informal entertaining. Paper is still shunned for formal meals.

CATHY KAUFMAN

Book (3rd ed. 1858), addressed to "young and inexperienced housekeepers" hosting a "plain, substantial" but emphatically not stylish dinner, Catharine Beecher explains this pragmatic model suitable for a bourgeois household with two cooks and an experienced waiter. The meal visually resembled a simplified French service: soup and fish awaited the guests entering the dining room and were served by the hostess and host, respectively. The remaining savory dishes were placed on the table in a single course after the soup and fish were removed, following Beecher's diagram. The host and hostess portioned at the table, and the waiter delivered filled plates. However, unlike French service, with its single plate for each of "2 genteel Courses of Victuals," each important food on the table was served on a fresh plate. Thus, as the waiter vigilantly removed dirty plates and replaced the silverware, the host, inquiring as to what the guest "would be helped," filled a fresh plate from stacks amassed on a convenient side table. For a dinner for twelve, Beecher recommends a minimum of three dozen dinner plates "to allow one plate for fish, and two for two changes of meat for each guest. Some would provide more." This generous supply of plates and flatware eliminated the traditional French service's question of what to do with one's knife and fork while getting seconds.

Once the meats were done, the waiter cleared the table, including the upper cloth, and set down the pudding, cheese, and pastry. Three dozen dessert plates, one dozen saucers, two dozen dessert forks and knives, and one dozen dessert spoons are recommended to serve twelve, as the guests sample the offerings. These levels of material goods would have been astounding to all but the wealthiest fifty years earlier; here, they are considered minimums for a merely respectable dinner.

By the last quarter of the nineteenth century, aspiring households attempted "course dinners" adapted mainly from the Russian model. In *Practical Cooking and Dinner Giving* (1877), Mary F. Henderson describes this "compromise" style, in which each course appears sequentially from the kitchen, to be carved and portioned at table by the host. If the host lacked this gentlemanly accomplishment, the meats would be carved in the kitchen and served "from the side," that is, by waiters or maids (note the use of less prestigious and cheaper female servers) holding platters from which guests could help themselves. Henderson applauds the commonsense American decision to reduce the number of courses by serving a vegetable with each substantial fish, meat, or game course. Her "stylish" dinner

for those of moderate means (elite dinners of the time could easily have twice as many courses) consists of a soup, a fish (always garnished with potatoes), and a roast (garnished with a vegetable), possibly followed by a game course and then a salad (simple greens, vegetables, or even a lobster mayonnaise), cheese, and dessert. Henderson reassures the budget-conscious that, with a little practice, one cook can easily prepare this dinner, aided by the clever purchase of desserts from the confectioner's shop.

Henderson sets the table with a floral centerpiece surrounded by the desserts, a dated convention abandoned in elite circles. Following the affordable fashions of the day, she recommends "fancy ware" ornaments over silver and is especially fond of majolica, cooing over "tripods of dolphins, with great pink mouths, to hold salt and pepper." She writes for an aspiring rather than an established audience, cautioning that one should have "chairs of equal height at table. Perhaps every one may know by experience the trial to his good humor in finding himself perched above or sunk below the general level." Yet even though matched chairs are not a given, the existence of a formal dining room is: one tasteful decorative scheme is to select china in colors matching the room. Most important, course service transcends any material shortcomings, even for the quotidian family repast: "If one has nothing for dinner but soup, hash, and lettuce, put them on the table in style: serve them in three courses, and one will imagine it a much better dinner than if carelessly served."

Such pretentiousness, teetering on the preposterous, led to predictable retrenchment. The *Etiquette for Americans* (1898), by a mysterious "woman of fashion," dissuades ambitious householders of limited means from attempting stiflingly formal course entertainments. The anonymous author puts pleasure over pomposity, finding it more enjoyable to "give supper-parties consisting of Welsh rarebits and beer, and Frankfurt sausages, and scrambled eggs, when you can all 'wait' and be jolly, than wear a worried, hunted air for days, overtax your establishment, and lie awake gnashing your teeth and bedewing your pillow through a bitter night." These ostensibly "etiquette-free" dinners would become the blueprint for twentieth-century entertaining.

Dining after 1920

The 1920s brought to a head major transitions. For the elites, the twenty-course Russian dinners were fading; already in the first decade of the twentieth century, "short" six- or seven-course dinners were touted as modern.

Changing notions of health and slimmer body ideals certainly contributed, but the shrinking servant population was key. Factory assembly lines offered more attractive employment than did live-in servitude. Moreover, the historian Daniel E. Sutherland points out that the radical dislocations engendered by World War I led many to question the propriety of the master-servant relationship. Although Congress declared one servant to be the "inalienable right of every American family" in defeating a 1918 proposed "Servant Tax," the debate was academic: the days of resident domestics butlering course dinners were largely over.

Etiquette: The Blue Book of Social Usage (1922) by Emily Post, although most famous for explicating special occasion formal dinners with cadres of servants and flatware, sympathetically and aptly captures the "Mrs. Three-in-One" dilemma of aspiring homemakers trying to perform as cook, maid, and hostess. Like the anonymous "woman of fashion," Post dismisses the formal dinner, proposing all sorts of little tricks, such as placing chafing dishes filled with hot foods on side tables the moment guests arrive so that they can be served without the interrupting dash to the kitchen, and placing cold dishes, such as salad and dessert, on the table throughout the entire meal, again eliminating the need to fetch while entertaining. Her only rules for servantless meals are courtesy and expediency.

Most etiquette books and lifestyle guides from the mid- through the late twentieth century assume servantless households, although a few retrograde works, such as *The Table Graces: Setting, Service and Manners for the American Home without Servants* (1941) by Beth Bailey McLean, belie their mission by pressing children or "Mother" into the harried role formerly played by liveried servers. McLean's litany of picayune instructions for everything from refilling glasses to serving dessert and coffee simultaneously in the "new American" style departed from nineteenth-century norms but still preached proper dining as formally structured course meals.

For much of the past century, most Americans have sought strategies for achieving casual conviviality in a changing domestic environment. Some have explored Mary and Russel Wright's iconoclastic suggestion that salad, bread, and butter share the same (preferably disposable paper) plate with the steaming stew. Most embrace Post's assessment that "in a small apartment or in a bungalow that everybody knows is normally run by

yourself alone, to acquire a staff of servants is likely to give an impression of pretentious effort." Indeed, in *Table Setting Guide* (1990), Sharon Dlugosch explains how to host a dinner party when both a dining area and even a dining table are lacking: fill the plates in the kitchen and invite guests to pick one up and convene round the coffee table or desk. Set the desk for dinner, anyone?

[*See also* Etiquette Books; Glassware; Plates; Silverware.]

BIBLIOGRAPHY

Alpern, Andrew. *Historic Manhattan Apartment Houses*. New York: Dover, 1996.

Ames, Kenneth L. *Death in the Dining Room and Other Tales of Victorian Culture*. Philadelphia: Temple University Press, 1992. Particularly interesting for the title essay, which contains an intriguing analysis of the symbolism inherent in Victorian furnishings.

Auchincloss, Louis, ed. *The Hone and Strong Diaries of Old Manhattan*. New York: Abbeville Press, 1989. Enjoyable primary sources for elite New York in the nineteenth century.

Becker, Hazel T. "Four Dining-room-less Houses." *Better Homes and Gardens*, June 1926.

Blaszczyk, Regina Lee. *Imagining Consumers: Design and Innovation from Wedgwood to Corning*. Baltimore: Johns Hopkins University Press, 2000. An important study of the diffusion of material culture from the elites to the masses through the prism of manufacturers' responses to market demands. Thoroughly documented.

Bushman, Richard L. *The Refinement of America: Persons, Houses, Cities*. New York: Knopf, 1992. A leading scholar on the relationship among etiquette, material culture, and changing behavior. Thoroughly documented.

Carson, Barbara G. *Ambitious Appetites: Dining, Behavior, and Patterns of Consumption in Federal Washington*. Washington, DC: American Institute of Architects Press, 1990. An extremely well-documented study of early- to mid-nineteenth-century dining in Washington.

Carson, Cary, Ronald Hoffman, and Peter J. Albert, eds. *Of Consuming Interests: The Style of Life in the Eighteenth Century*. Charlottesville: University Press of Virginia, 1994. A collection of scholarly essays with copious footnotes; see especially Carson's excellent article, "The Consumer Revolution in Colonial America: Why Demand?"

Garrett, Elisabeth Donaghy. *At Home: The American Family 1750–1870*. New York: Abrams, 1990. Very well-documented study of the home, relying on private papers and a deep knowledge of material objects.

Gillies, Mary Davis. *What Women Want in Their Dining Rooms of Tomorrow: A Report of the Dining Room of Tomorrow Contest*. New York: McCall Corporation, 1944. A survey of more than eleven thousand *McCall's* readers covering every aspect of the dining room, from architecture to preferred flatware patterns.

Gould, Mary Earle. *The Early American House: Household Life in America 1620–1850*. Rev. ed. Rutland, VT: Tuttle, 1965. A well-illustrated, very readable account describing artifacts and their use. No bibliography.

Grover, Kathryn, ed. *Dining in America, 1850–1900*. Amherst: University of Massachusetts Press, 1987.

Hamilton, Alexander. *Hamilton's Itinerarium, Being a Narrative of a Journey from Annapolis, Maryland, through Delaware, Pennsylvania, New York, New Jersey, Connecticut, Rhode Island, Massachusetts, and New Hampshire, from May to September, 1744.* Edited by Albert Bushnell Hart. New York: Arno Press, 1971.

Hamilton, Thomas. *Men and Manners in America.* New York: Kelly, 1968. An English visitor's travel diary describing many meals and entertainments; delightful reading.

Hechtlinger, Adelaide. *The Seasonal Hearth: The Woman at Home in Early America.* Woodstock, NY: Overlook Press, 1986. An informative collection of excerpts from contemporaneous materials that is marred by failing to give thorough documentation.

Kasson, John F. *Rudeness and Civility: Manners in Nineteenth-Century Urban America.* New York: Hill and Wang, 1990.

Leavitt, Sarah A. *From Catharine Beecher to Martha Stewart: A Cultural History of Domestic Advice.* Chapel Hill: University of North Carolina Press, 2002.

Lynd, Robert S., and Helen Merrell Lynd. *Middletown: A Study in Contemporary American Culture.* New York: Harcourt, 1929. Anthropologists' study of daily life in Muncie, Indiana, in the 1920s; limited but revealing references to dining.

Mayhew, Edgar de N., and Minor Myers Jr. *A Documentary History of American Interiors: From the Colonial Era to 1915.* New York: Scribners, 1980.

Morton, Agnes H. *Etiquette: Good Manners for All People.* Philadelphia: Penn Publishing, 1906.

Post, Emily Price. *Etiquette: "The Blue Book of Social Usage."* New York and London: Funk and Wagnalls, 1922.

Sarti, Raffaella. *Europe at Home: Family and Material Culture, 1500–1800.* Translated by Allan Cameron. New Haven, CT: Yale University Press, 2002. Highly instructive scholarly background for the material antecedents of the American dining room.

Shapiro, Lindsay Stamm. "A Man and His Manners: Resetting the American Table." In *Russel Wright: Creating America*, edited by Donald Albrecht, Robert Schonfeld, and Lindsay Stamm Shapiro, 22–81. New York: Abrams, 2001.

Sprackling, Helen. *Customs on the Table Top: How New England Housewives Set Out Their Tables.* Sturbridge, MA: Old Sturbridge Village, 1958.

Sutherland, Daniel E. *Americans and Their Servants: Domestic Service in the United States from 1800 to 1920.* Baton Rouge: Louisiana State University Press, 1981.

Venable, Charles L., Ellen P. Denker, Katherine C. Grier, and Stephen G. Harrison. *China and Glass in America, 1880–1980: From Tabletop to TV Stand.* Dallas, TX: Dallas Museum of Art, 2000. Lavish photographs of china and glass with documented essays on industrial and social history relating to the objects.

Williams, Susan. *Savory Suppers and Fashionable Feasts: Dining in Victorian America.* New York: Pantheon Books, 1985. Well-illustrated and thoroughly documented description of Victorian dining.

Wright, Mary, and Russel Wright. *Mary and Russel Wright's Guide to Easier Living.* New York: Simon and Schuster, 1951.

CATHY K. KAUFMAN

Dinner, *see Meal Patterns*

Dinner Pails, *see Lunch Boxes, Dinner Pails, and Picnic Kits*

Dips

Humankind has been dipping solid food into semiliquid complements for thousands of years, but it was not until the second half of the twentieth century that commercial dips emerged as an important category of food. Credit for this shift goes to the Thomas J. Lipton Company, which mounted a massive promotional campaign in the 1950s featuring dips made from its dried onion soup mix combined with sour cream or cream cheese. At that time Lipton sponsored Arthur Godfrey's popular *Talent Scouts* radio and television program, and these dips were advertised extensively on the weekly show. Lipton also distributed tens of thousands of hanging cards to retailers, promoting these dips, and provided dip recipes on millions of their packages.

While the Lipton dips could be served with many foods, such as carrots and celery, the major host foods were salty potato and corn chips, which were also extensively marketed during the 1950s. Within six months of its release in 1952, sales of Lipton soup mix skyrocketed. Lipton's success encouraged other manufacturers to enter the commercial dip world, and new product lines emerged. One was the fondue, which had originated in Switzerland as an egg-and-cheese casserole into which bread was often dipped. During the 1950s fondue morphed into a way of making dips, and fondue pots became a major selling item in America. In 1952 some fondue recipes replaced the cheese with oil, and chunks of skewered meats were cooked and dipped into sauces. By 1964 fruit was being dipped into heated chocolate. Fondue became the culinary hit for parties during the 1960s and 1970s.

Many successful commercial dips have been based on strong flavors. By far the most successful dips, for instance, were drawn from the Mexican culinary heritage, such as chili, guacamole, and salsa. Guacamole, a combination of mashed avocados, chili, garlic, and other ingredients, became popular in America during the late nineteenth century, consumed as a salad. During the 1930s Calavo, the California association of avocado growers, began publishing pamphlets that included directions for making guacamole. Subsequent recipes encouraged the use of pieces of tortilla to scoop up the dip. After World War II potato chips were recommended as guacamole dippers. Guacamole did not become a prominent dip until the commercial production of larger and thicker corn chips in the 1960s and the adoption of this combination in Mexican-style restaurants in the United States. In the 1960s Calavo produced the first commercial guacamole, which was subsequently sold to restaurants and grocery stores.

Another dip originating in Mexican culinary traditions is salsa, generally composed of chili peppers, tomatoes, vinegar, and flavorings. Salsas are diverse and traditionally were intended as condiments for other foods, such as tacos and enchiladas. Their use as a dip was championed by Mexican restaurants in the United States, which served salsa with tortilla chips. Soon the combination became an American staple. The first known manufacturer of salsa was Pace Foods of San Antonio. Its owner, Dave Pace, experimented with bottling salsa in 1947 and finally succeeded in perfecting the formula the following year. His success encouraged other manufacturers to produce salsa, including Old El Paso and Ortega. The salsa market exploded during the 1980s and continued to grow in the following decade. During the 1990s salsa briefly outsold ketchup, which shook up the condiment world.

By the end of the twentieth century, hundreds of commercial dips were sold, and by 2002 this category of foods had sales of $1.5 billion per year. In addition, thousands of dip recipes appear in cookbooks for fish, poultry, dairy, meat, fruits, and vegetables. Among the most famous dips are ones made from beans, clams, crabs, and cheese. Americans have also adopted and adapted dips from other cuisines, such as soy sauce from Japan and China, *quesa* from Mexico, *satay* sauce from Thailand, curry-based dips from India and Indonesia, seasoned olive oil from Italy and Spain, and fish sauces from Southeast Asia. The major host foods for dips remain chips, bread sticks, and vegetables, such as celery and carrots.

[*See also* Condiments; Fondue Pot; Salsa; Snack Food.]

BIBLIOGRAPHY

Costenbader, Carol W. *The Well-Stocked Pantry: Mustards, Ketchups and Vinegars; Dips and Dressing, Sauces and Oils.* Pownal, VT: Storey Communications, 1996.

Dunham, Judith, and Jane Horn. *Dips, Salsas, and Spreads.* San Francisco: Collins, 1996.

France, Christine. *The Complete Book of Sauces, Salsas, Dips, Relishes, Marinades, and Dressings.* New York: Lorenz Books, 2001.

Puckett, Susan. *Dips: Great Recipes for Spreads, Salsas, Fondues, and Other Party Fare.* Atlanta, GA: Longstreet Press, 1995.

Stock, Dawn. *The Encyclopedia of Homemade Dips.* Philadelphia: Courage Books, 1996.

ANDREW F. SMITH

Dishes, *see Plates*

Dishwashing and Cleaning Up

In cleaning up after cooking, sanitation is the major concern, but food that is stuck on pans also interferes with cooking. Useful patinas on cast-iron wares, deliberately and slowly built up from grease and carbonized food, act like a Teflon coating. For centuries, until the 1850s or so, most cooking fat and grease was saved to make soap. Farm wives scraped plates into slop jars to feed their pigs well into the twentieth century.

Along with dishpans, dish mops, and drainers, tools included scouring sands, brushes, scrapers, and chain cloth pot cleaners. In the eighteenth and nineteenth centuries, knives were placed on long scouring boards so that fine polishing grit could be rubbed on the blades. Cranked knife cleaners came in the 1860s. Clamshells were used as early pot scrapers; by the 1880s scrapers were made of metal in odd shapes so that corners fit the contours of different pans.

In the twenty-first century, just as scouring pads and powdered cleansers have early precedents, so do electric dishwashers: an early mechanical (though not electric) dishwasher was patented in 1891 by a Mrs. Stevens, shortly followed by a see-through glass dishwasher invented by Josephine Cochrane.

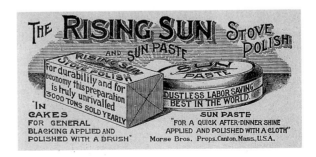

Cleaning Up. Rising Sun and Sun Paste advertisement, 1898.

[*See also* Kitchens.]

BIBLIOGRAPHY

Franklin, Linda Campbell. *300 Years of Housekeeping Collectibles.* Florence, AL: Books Americana, 1992.
Franklin, Linda Campbell. *300 Years of Kitchen Collectibles.* 5th ed. Iola, WI: Krause Publications, 2003.

LINDA CAMPBELL FRANKLIN

Distillation

Distillation is the process of controlled heating of a mixture to separate the more volatile from the less volatile parts, then cooling and condensing the vapor to make a purer substance. The word "distill" comes from the Latin *destillare*, meaning "to drip."

There are hints about oils and "essences" in books of the Ayurvedas from India ca. 3000 B.C.E., and distilled rice or barley liquor was consumed there as early as 800 B.C.E. Egyptians distilled oils for perfumes and medicines as early as 2500 B.C.E. Chinese alchemists used distillation in approximately the sixth century B.C.E. These peoples used distillation primarily for alchemy and transmutation of various substances. Arabs developed the technology that shaped European distillation until the Middle Ages. The basic piece of equipment for distillation was the alembic.

Until the Middle Ages, distillation was used for alchemical and medical purposes. Europeans began to distill alcohol in larger quantities for its health-giving properties. The name "water of life" appears in almost all European languages; related terms include aqua vitae, aquavit, eau-de-vie, and *uisquebeatha* or *uisce beatha*, the parent of the word "whiskey."

As a medicine, alcohol was amended with roots, berries, leaves, stems, and even animal components. The fifteenth century saw the change of distilled alcohol from a pharmaceutical product to a beverage. Wine was distilled to concentrate the alcohol and was called *brannten Wein*, "burned wine," in German. The Dutch variant of that name, *brandewijn*, provides us with the word "brandy." Grain beers were distilled in Celtic lands between 1100 and 1300 to create whiskey, or "whisky," depending on where it is from. Scotland alone spells the product without the "e."

American settlers made familiar beers and wines as well as some new ones based on new raw materials. Sugarcane was readily available to make rum. Barley and rye were used for whiskey in the North. Corn was common throughout the South and gave rise to the unique American whiskey called bourbon, either with a "sweet mash" of all-fresh ingredients or a "sour mash" in which some of a prior batch was added for a fuller flavor.

Whereas until the nineteenth century distillation of beers and wines (called the "wash") was accomplished in pot stills that required shutting down, emptying, and cleaning after each batch, modern distilling is most often accomplished in column stills that deliver a continuous stream of distillate from a continuous input of wash. The advantages of the column still are the quantity of distillate produced and the ease of operation. A disadvantage is that the distillate contains less of the flavor elements and so produces a relatively mild-tasting product. These grain-neutral spirits are used to make other infused or flavored liquors and blended whiskeys.

Americans consumed beer, wine, and distilled alcohol in the 1970s in the approximate volume ratios of 100 units of beer to 10 units of distilled spirits to about 7 units of wine. In the 1980s wine sales pushed ahead of distilled spirits. Approximate ratios in the late twentieth century were beer, 100 units; wine, 8.5 units; distilled spirits, 5.6 units. The decline is both in percentage consumed and in actual volume.

[*See also* Beer; Bourbon; Brandy; Whiskey.]

BIBLIOGRAPHY

McGee, Harold. *On Food and Cooking: The Science and Lore of the Kitchen.* New York: Scribner, 1984. The most authoritative book on the science and history of culinaria.
Barnes-Svarney, Patricia. *The New York Public Library Science Desk Reference.* New York: Macmillan, 1995. Good overview of important scientific information.
"Apparent Per Capita Ethanol Consumption for the United States, 1850–1996." About.com. http://alcoholism.about.com/library/nconsum01.htm. Statistical charts.

BOB PASTORIO

Dr. Brown's

Dr. Brown's is a line of sodas best known for Cel-Ray, a celery soda. A brand with distinct regional appeal, it can be found in New York City and major soft-drink markets where New Yorkers have relocated. The cans claim that Dr. Brown's has been sold since 1869. Whether there really was a Dr. Brown who founded the brand is obscured by time. The sodas were produced by Schoneberger & Noble, a New York-based drink company, which originated the brand.

By 1910 its labels advertised "Dr. Browns [sic] Celery Tonic," made with crushed celery seeds, as a "pure beverage for the nerves" that "strengthens the appetite and aids digestion." By 1928 the American Beverage Corporation had produced and bottled the brand. In the 1930s it was advertised in local Jewish newspapers and on the radio. In the 1950s Food and Drug Administration objections to the use of the word "tonic" led the company to change the name to Cel-Ray. Dr. Brown's is also known for its black cherry soda and vanilla-flavored cream soda.

The sodas enjoyed a wide Jewish following in New York delis in the early twentieth century. But in the early 1980s, as Jewish delis in New York vanished, the company expanded distribution to include delis, gourmet shops, and restaurants in major markets around the country, bringing a formerly "ethnic" drink into the mainstream. Canada Dry Bottling Company of New York acquired Dr. Brown's in 1982.

[*See also* Cream Soda; Food and Drug Administration; Soda Drinks.]

BIBLIOGRAPHY

Hillinger, Charles. "Drink of the Deli People: Dr. Brown's Cream Soda Making Its Mark Outside of New York." *Los Angeles Times*, July 4, 1986.

Lewis, Joel. "Today the Delicatessen, Tomorrow the World." *Forward*, July 28, 1995.

Turan, Kenneth. "Cel-Ray Is on the Way: Ethnic Tonic, or a Way of Life?" *Washington Post*, December 28, 1977.

SANDRA YIN

Dr Pepper

Dr Pepper is a soft drink created in 1885 by a pharmacist from Waco, Texas, named Charles Alderton. The American soft-drink industry, which began in the 1830s, had developed steadily as the result of antiliquor pressure from the temperance movement. Local pharmacies had become popular gathering spots for refreshments, and pharmacists naturally developed innumerable new soft-drink flavors. Alderton supplemented his pharmaceutical duties at Morrison's Old Corner Drug Store by serving its soda-fountain customers. Fascinated by the various carbonated beverages, he developed a successful new combination of flavors that patrons called "a Waco," in reference to its local affiliation. Wade B. Morrison,

owner of the drugstore, reportedly named it Dr Pepper after a former employer named Dr. Charles T. Pepper in Rural Retreat, Virginia.

By 1891 demand outstripped the amount of Dr Pepper that Morrison's drugstore could supply, and Morrison formed a partnership with Robert S. Lazenby, a Waco beverage chemist. They formed the Artesian Manufacturing and Bottling Company, and they also struck a deal with Sam Houston Prim, owner of a bottling plant in Dublin, Texas. Dr Pepper was introduced at the 1904 World's Fair Exposition in Saint Louis, but despite national exposure, the company remained a regional operation, selling primarily to the southern and southwestern markets. Not until 1963, when a United States District Court ruled that Dr Pepper was not a cola, was the firm able to circumvent franchise contract conflicts with Pepsi-Cola and Coca-Cola and sell Dr Pepper to independent bottlers nationwide.

In 1986 Dr Pepper merged with the Seven-Up Company. In 1995 Cadbury Schweppes of London, England, purchased the company. By the end of the twentieth century Dr Pepper/Seven-Up was the largest North American purveyor of noncola soft drinks, with about 16 percent market share. Dr Pepper's advertising slogans have ranged from "King of Beverages" (1910–1914) to "Old Doc" (1920s–1930s) and then to "the friendly Pepper-Upper" (1950s). In response to changing times, the 1970s marked the slogan "the most original soft drink ever in the whole wide world," followed by the famous 1977 campaign "Be a Pepper." In 2002, the company launched its promotional "Be You" campaign.

Two museums celebrate Dr Pepper. The Dr Pepper Museum and Free Enterprise Institute is located in the 1906 Artesian Manufacturing and Bottling Company building in downtown Waco. Donated by the Dr Pepper Company in 1988, it is listed in the National Register of Historic Places as the "Home of Dr Pepper." Exhibits teach the history of soft drinks and the free-enterprise economic system. Old Doc's Soda Shop, located in Sam Houston Prim's original Dr Pepper bottling plant in Dublin, Texas, also serves as a shrine to the product. This is the only facility licensed to manufacture Dr Pepper with the original formula calling for cane sugar, rather than the high fructose corn syrup adopted by the soft-drink industry in the 1970s. In the United States, Dr Pepper serves as a cocktail mixer as well as an ingredient in numerous home-cooked dishes, such as cakes, candies, jellies, desserts, molded salads, breads, and marinades.

[*See also* Advertising; Cola Wars; Soda Drinks.]

BIBLIOGRAPHY

Rodengen, Jeffrey L. *The Legend of Dr Pepper/Seven-Up.* Fort Lauderdale, FL: Write Stuff Syndicate, 1995.

BECKY MERCURI

Doughnut-Making Tools

The center holes in the deep-fried cakes known as doughnuts (also called *oliekoecken*, fried dough, or dough nuts in the 1800s) have been accomplished with gadgets since at least the 1850s. The first cake cutter patent, in 1857, shows a strap-handled, round cutter for cookies plus an insert piece to be snapped on to cut center holes. In 1867 a patent was issued for a rolling "confectionery" cutter that had rolling-pin-like handles and cut two with every revolution. An 1876 spring-activated cutter was placed on dough, the center knob was depressed to cut a hole quickly, and the cutter sprang back. In 1954 an almost identical ejection cutter was patented. Also in the 1870s cookie dough presses, consisting of a tube and a plunger, were widely used for making jumbles. Similar tools continued to be made through the 1930s but were finally called "doughnut presses." Such presses were filled with dough, and the doughnuts were expressed directly into the boiling fat.

[*See also* Cookie Cutters *and* Doughnuts.]

BIBLIOGRAPHY

Franklin, Linda Campbell. *300 Years of Kitchen Collectibles.* 5th ed. Iola, WI: Krause Publications, 2003.

LINDA CAMPBELL FRANKLIN

Doughnuts

Doughnuts are deep-fried cakes with a long European history and roots in still earlier Middle Eastern cuisine. They were introduced to America by the Dutch in New Netherland as *oliekoecken* (oil cakes or fried cakes). Made of yeast dough rich in eggs and butter, spices, and dried fruits, their sweetness came from the fruit and the final dusting of sugar. The dough was often somewhat sticky (additional flour toughened and masked the spicy and buttery flavors) and was dropped as blobs off the end of a spoon into hot rapeseed oil (canola). The resulting doughnuts took the form of irregular balls, at some point called *oliebollen*, or oil (fried) balls. They were eaten during the Dutch Christmas season, which extended through New Year's to Twelfth Night (6 January), and for special occasions throughout the year. Once in the New World, the Dutch replaced their frying oil with the preferred lard (far more available here), as it produced a tender and greaseless crust.

Other ethnic groups brought their own doughnut variations. The Pennsylvania Dutch and the Moravians who settled in North Carolina made *fastnachts* on Shrove Tuesday, and the French established beignets in New Orleans. Ultimately, the English American cooks adopted them as well. By 1845 doughnuts appeared in American cookbooks as staples, and the weekly Saturday baking (breads, cakes, and pies) included doughnut frying.

In this same antebellum period, two changes in technology contributed to a basic alteration in the doughnut. Chemical leavening (notably baking powder) was substituted for the yeast, producing a more cakelike and less breadlike product. In the same era inexpensive tin doughnut cutters with holes were manufactured commercially and sold widely. Before the end of the century they were distributed as commercial giveaways, a testament to continuing interest in doughnut making. Home cooks had adopted the form and textures dictated by the technology, but continued to fry both kinds.

Throughout the twentieth century doughnuts remained popular at home and in coffee shops. During World War II they were associated with mass-produced canteen snacks and USO hospitality for GIs. The familiar twentieth-century jelly doughnut, now the Israeli Hanukkah icon *sufganyot*, has made its way into Jewish American homes. Sustained doughnut popularity is reflected in such successful chains as Dunkin' Donuts and Krispy Kreme, although they are prepared only rarely in home kitchens.

[*See also* Breakfast Foods; Doughnut-Making Tools; Dutch Influences on American Food.]

BIBLIOGRAPHY

Rose, Peter G. *The Sensible Cook: Dutch Foodways in the Old and the New World.* Syracuse, NY: Syracuse University Press, 1989.

ALICE ROSS

Dressings and Stuffings

Important as it is to America's festive culinary traditions, "dressing" is a term that wants some pinning down. Above all, whether it is interchangeable with "stuffing" is a matter of continual debate. On the one hand, insofar as "dressing" came into use in the nineteenth century as a prim euphemism for the latter term, we can assume it is equivalent. On the other hand, the verbs "to dress" and "to stuff" have historically connoted distinct culinary procedures—the one having to do with the cleaning and preparing of the carcasses of fish or fowl and the other with the making of fillings of all sorts. In this light, dressing might be viewed as a subtype in the more general category of stuffing, namely, one related directly to meat cookery—whereby filling the animal cavity with various ingredients would simply constitute a later step in the dressing process. This verb-based distinction accords to some extent with the popular notion that, technically, stuffing is the mixture actually inserted into the animal to be consumed, while dressing is the same mixture cooked separately, "on the outside." At any rate, "stuffing" is the dominant term, while "dressing" inheres in regional vocabularies, particularly in the South and Southeast.

When it comes to recipes, however, dressing is all over the map. A central component of the Thanksgiving repast (among others), it ultimately reflects all manner of culinary considerations, from basic technique to ethnic background to regional and national custom. For instance, to the extent that there is such a thing as a classic American recipe for dressing, it is the one that draws upon our Anglo heritage to include white bread, sage, and sausage—a bland combination that nonetheless happens to pair especially well with turkey, the standard centerpiece of our holiday meal. That said, one of the very distinctions between British and U.S. culture that, for better or worse, Americans have chosen to emphasize is an "anything goes" attitude—such that we might as soon deem "classics" those recipes that must once have seemed boldly experimental: oyster dressing from the Gulf Coast of Louisiana, say, or Minnesotan wild rice stuffing. By the same token, we are quick to appropriate as "new" ideas that, to the immigrants who introduce them, are anything but novel; we may give our dressing an Italian makeover with ingredients like truffles, chestnuts, and pancetta or add dried fruits for Germanic flair. Thus, future classics may exist even among today's quirkiest-seeming dressings, from southwestern versions using blue cornbread, green chilies, and pine nuts to Caribbean-style mixtures of curried chickpeas and rice.

Of course, questions of taste aside, it is not exactly the case that anything goes in the preparation of dressing. After all, dressing serves a specific culinary function—it helps maintain, or even enhances, the moisture content of the meat containing it; its ingredients, then, must strike a balance between absorbent starch and absorbefacient fat. What is more, because it makes contact with potentially contaminating raw meat juices, care must be taken to ensure that the dressing is fully cooked before it is served. The unfortunate upshot is that fears of food-borne illness—instilled in part by an anxious United States Department of Agriculture via media that love a good scare—have led many to abandon the practice of stuffing meats altogether.

[*See also* Thanksgiving; Turkey.]

BIBLIOGRAPHY

Baker, James W., and Elizabeth Brabb. *Thanksgiving Cookery*. New York: Brick Tower Press, 1994. Includes a lengthy historical introduction.

Rodgers, Rick. *50 Best Stuffings and Dressings*. New York: Broadway Books, 1997. Handy for its display of the range of possibilities attending the art of stuffing.

Simmons, Amelia. *American Cookery; or, The Art of Dressing Viands, Fish, Poultry, and Vegetables, and the Best Modes of Making Puff-Pastes, Pies, Tarts, Puddings, Custards, and Preserves and All Kinds of Cakes, from the Imperial Plumb to Plain Cake.* 2nd ed. Bedford, MA: Silverleaf Press, 1996. Facsimile of the original 1796 edition.

RUTH TOBIAS

Drinking Songs

American drinking songs fall into two main categories, with much overlap: songs about drinking (with lines like "It's beer, beer, beer that makes me wanna cheer") and songs generally sung when one is drinking or drunk. They are almost always loud, boisterous, and long. ("Ninety-Nine Bottles of Beer on the Wall" is seldom sung from start to finish—an earlier version had only forty-nine bottles.) Often, they are sentimental or profane. These songs are usually sung slightly out of tune in large groups, with the understanding that sober people are too repressed to sing them, but, fortified with alcohol, singers can drape arms around one another's shoulders and let loose.

The earliest American drinking songs were mostly imported from Great Britain. Robert Burns's "Auld Lang

Syne," based on a seventeenth-century Scottish folk song, was still sung in 2004 by American New Year's revelers. Others were quintessential American folk songs, such as "Clementine" and "I've Been Working on the Railroad." Two drinking songs that appear regularly in published collections are "Little Brown Jug" ("My wife and I live all alone / In a little brown hut we call our own, / She loves gin and I love rum, / Tell you what, don't we have fun?") and "Frankie and Johnnie" ("He was her man, but he done her wrong"). Dean Henry Aldrich's seventeenth-century verse on drink is also a classic:

> If on my theme I rightly think,
> There are five reasons why I drink,—
> Good wine, a friend, because I'm dry,
> Or lest I should be by and by,
> Or any other reason why.

Drinking songs usually exist in several versions, each more ribald than the last. Published drinking songs tend to be toned down, with "dirty" words removed. Some songs even make a joke out of this, like "The Crayfish in the Chamber-Pot," which begins with obscene rhymes and then backs off ("Children, children, hear you mother grunt, / The crayfish in the chamber pot has got your mother's . . . nose").

Drinking songs are often familiar tunes with new lyrics, like "I want a beer just like the beer that pickled dear old dad" (sung to the tune of "I Want a Girl"). Some have become so well known that children sing them on the playground or at summer camp: "Be Kind to Your Web-Footed Friends" (to the tune of John Philip Sousa's "The Stars and Stripes Forever") or "Great Green Gobs of Greasy Grimy Gopher Guts" (to the tune of "The Old Gray Mare"). The most famous example, of course, is Francis Scott Key's "The Star-Spangled Banner," the national anthem of the United States, which is based on "To Anacreon in Heaven," an eighteenth-century drinking song from a London social club.

In the late nineteenth century the American temperance movement countered with songs of its own, like "Father, Come Home," from the temperance play *Ten Nights in a Bar-Room*, and "Touch Not the Cup" (to the tune of "Long, Long Ago"). Lord Charles Neaves responded, in turn, with "I'm Very Fond of Water: A New Temperance Song":

> I'm very fond of water,
> I drink it noon and night
> . . . But I forgot to mention—

> 'Tis best to be sincere—
> I use an old invention
> That makes it into Beer.

Many twentieth-century drinking songs are college- or club-specific, like "The Engineers' Drinking Song" from MIT ("We are, we are, we are, we are, we are the Engineers / We can, we can, we can, we can demolish forty beers") or "What Do We Do with a Drunken Alien" (to the tune of "What Shall We Do with a Drunken Sailor"), sung around the campfire at pagan festivals or at science fiction convention parties.

The twentieth century has yielded a few drinking songs with known composers and one official set of lyrics, like "Madeira, M'Dear" by Michael Flanders and Donald Swan, "An Irish Ballad" by Tom Lehrer, "Margaritaville" by Jimmy Buffett, and "Escape (The Pina Colada Song)" by Rupert Holmes. In the late twentieth century, American bars began purchasing Japanese karaoke machines, which allowed patrons to sing along to recorded music. Performing popular songs solo, and watching your friends do the same, became one more form of musical entertainment to accompany drinking.

[*See also* Beer; Temperance.]

BIBLIOGRAPHY

McClure, John Peebles, ed. *The Stag's Hornbook*. 2nd rev. ed. New York: Knopf, 1943.
Shay, Frank. *Barroom Ballads*. New York: Dover, 1961. Reprinting of *My Pious Friends and Drunken Companions* and *More Pious Friends and Drunken Companions*, first published in 1927 and 1928, respectively.

JESSY RANDALL

Drive-Ins

"People in their cars are so lazy that they don't want to get out of them to eat!" The proclamation still rang as true at the end of the twentieth century as it did when the candy and tobacco magnate Jessie G. Kirby first uttered the words in 1921. At the time, he was trying to interest Reuben W. Jackson, a physician from Dallas, Texas, in investing in a new idea for a roadside restaurant—a sort of fast-food stand, although he did not call it that.

Introducing America's New Motor Lunch

Kirby's idea was simple: patrons were to drive up in their automobiles and make their food requests from behind the wheel. At the curbside a young lad would take the orders directly through the window of the car and then deliver the food and beverages the very same way. It was a novel way to dine. Customers could remain in their cars and consume their meals while still sitting in the front seat.

Of course, the Roaring Twenties was an era ripe for such a brazen idea. Adventurous folk perched atop flagpoles, danced the Charleston at around-the-clock marathons, and consumed illegal bathtub gin at speakeasies. During Prohibition, freedom of travel emerged as the new thrill, fueled by automobile ownership that soared from 6 million to 27 million motorcars by the decade's end.

The automobile was America's newest fad, and people hit the highways for many reasons, including recreation, romance, adventure . . . and to get a bite to eat. When Kirby and Jackson's Texas "Pig Stand" beckoned cars to pull off the busy Dallas–Fort Worth Highway in the fall of 1921, hordes of Texas motorists tipped their ten-gallon hats to what the highway billboards called "America's New Motor Lunch." Here was the ultimate dining-in-your-car experience, positioned strategically between the cities of Dallas and Fort Worth, Texas.

Good Food and Innovative Service

The star of the show was the "Pig Sandwich," Kirby and Jackson's contribution to the emerging culinary category known as "fast food." Prepared with tender slices of roast pork loin, pickle relish, and barbecue sauce layered inside a bun, the entrée quickly gained a loyal following and became the soon-to-be chain's signature (and later trademarked) sandwich. A frosty bottle of Coca-Cola or Dr Pepper, another Texas original, washed down the savory motoring meal.

At the Pig Stand the dining arrangements followed the menu's simplicity. Unlike conventional sit-down restaurants of the era, the Pig Stand offered an atmosphere where patrons did not have to contend with stuffy waiters and formal table etiquette and the exorbitant prices that accompanied them. A simple board-and-batten shack housed a small galley for food preparations, and a detached barbecue pit was used to prepare the pork. With no need to dress for dinner, service workers, such as delivery men, taxi drivers, and tradesmen, could grab a meal on the go without being concerned about appearances. Whether a person arrived in a Model T Ford or a Duesenberg did not matter. Both the patron and the car were king.

But the casual atmosphere was not the only attraction. From the beginning, the fleet-footed lads who took the orders and delivered food became the focus of the drive-in's appeal. Donning white shirts, white hats, and black bow ties, the eager carboys were a sight to see, routinely jumping into action before arriving vehicles rolled to a complete stop. "As soon as they saw a Model T start to slow down and tires turn towards the curb, they'd race out to see who could jump up on the running board while the car was still moving," recalled Richard Hailey, successor to the pork sandwich dynasty and president of Pig Stands, Inc., with headquarters in San Antonio, Texas. Vying for tips, the nation's first automotive food servers became a phenomenon, and the term "carhop" was coined to describe the flashy combination of waiter, busboy, cashier, and daredevil.

America Embraces the Drive-In

As the carhop replaced the soda jerk as the new hero of recreational dining, the reputation of the Pig Stands spread. As the stands were propelled beyond the borders of Texas by one of the first franchise arrangements in the industry, the number of locations quickly multiplied. Between 1921 and 1934, more than one hundred Pig Stand drive-in restaurants were constructed in Alabama, Arkansas, California, Florida, Louisiana, Mississippi, New York, Oklahoma, and Texas.

Innovation followed growth. In 1931 California Pig Stand Number 21 achieved a milestone when it pioneered the concept of "drive-through" car service with the first drive-up window. The customers eased their cars up to the window, issued their food orders, grabbed their lunches from the cook, and returned to the roadway. With its year-round sunny climate and car-filled boulevards, California proved to be particularly well suited for dining with one's motor running. During the 1930s surface streets like Sepulveda Boulevard, Cahuenga, and the Sunset Strip emerged as a haven for restaurants that catered to the car crowd. By the time Pig Stand Number 27 opened in Los Angeles, savvy restaurateurs saw the opportunity to make big money with a proven format. Featuring multilayer ziggurats, rooftop pylons, and miles of neon, new drive-ins like Bob's Big Boy, Carpenter's, Dolores, Herbert's, Simon's, Stan's, McDonnell's, Mel's, Roberts Brothers, and Van de Kamp's trumped the Pig Stands with the architectural styling of art deco and streamlined modern.

In the decades to come, Pig Stands and their raft of imitators continued to fine-tune the basic format of drive-in service. When automobiles became more streamlined and lost their running boards, carhops strapped on roller skates in an effort to speed up service. Electronic intercom systems came into vogue during the 1960s and replaced the human element with vacuum tubes and wiring. Gradually, as automobiles became faster and highways wider, the novelty of carhop service wore off.

The motoring public grew increasingly impatient with carhop service, despite the best efforts by drive-in operators to enhance the customer experience. Even with a speaker box that was conveniently mounted to take one's order, customers still had to wait for someone to walk out and bring them their food, collect their money, and bring back the change (eyed by carhops as a potential tip).

By the 1970s it was clear that the drive-through window was superior in terms of its speed, simplicity, and practicality. Not surprisingly, many of the emerging burger chains embraced it as the best way to serve customers in their cars. While the number of drive-in restaurants that used carhop service dwindled, the clever service innovation originated by the Texas Pig Stands became integral to the new wave of American fast-food eateries. Although the format had evolved since those early days of the drive-in, Kirby's prophetic words stood the test of time. By the early years of the twenty-first century, the public's desire to order, pick up, and eat an affordable meal—while still seated in their automobile—was as strong as ever.

[*See also* Fast Food; Roadside Food.]

BIBLIOGRAPHY

Flink, James J. *The Automobile Age.* Cambridge, MA: MIT Press, 1988.
Hailey, Richard. Interview by author with president of Texas Pig Stands, Inc. Austin, TX, 1993.
Langdon, Philip. *Orange Roofs, Golden Arches: The Architecture of American Chain Restaurants.* New York: Knopf, 1986.
Liebs, Chester H. *Main Street to Miracle Mile: American Roadside Architecture.* Boston: Little, Brown, 1985.
Witzel, Michael K. *The American Drive-in: History and Folklore of the Drive-in Restaurant in American Car Culture.* Osceola, WI: Motorbooks International, 1994.
Witzel, Michael K. *Drive-in Deluxe.* Osceola, WI: Motorbooks International, 1997.

MICHAEL KARL WITZEL

Drying

The microorganisms that normally inhabit fresh foods require water in order to multiply. Removing that moisture prevents spoilage and prolongs the storage life of foodstuffs; dried foods also weigh less and occupy a smaller volume. An ancient technique, drying is very easy and cheap. Before canning and refrigeration, it was an important method of food preservation. Drying can be accomplished with direct sunlight or dry air. The chile *ristras* of the Southwest are an example of simple drying; whole chiles are strung into garlands and hung outdoors to dry.

Applying heat is an easier way to dry foods where sunlight or dry air is not plentiful. Foods can be dried at home in ovens, special dehydrators (bought or built at home), or even in the microwave. Commercial drying methods include freeze-drying (where water is removed from frozen foods under vacuum) and spray-drying (by spraying liquids into columns of hot air). Herbs and instant coffee and tea are often freeze-dried, and powdered milk is typically spray-dried.

Dried foods retain much of their nutritional value, although some vitamins are lost with heat or air exposure. Properly dried foods can be stored without refrigeration, provided that moisture and insects are kept out. Even with the availability of canning, refrigeration, and freezing, home production of dried foods is still common. The use of dried foods in traditional regional recipes, such as the Pennsylvania Dutch dish *schnitz und knepp* ("slices and buttons," made with dried apples, ham, and dumplings), can be done by choice rather than necessity.

[*See also* Coffee, Instant; Freeze-Drying; Milk, Powdered.]

BIBLIOGRAPHY

Hobson, Phyllis. *Making and Using Dried Foods.* Pownal, VT: Storey Communications, 1994. A general manual with recipes.
Solar Cooking Archive. Available at http://www.solarcooking.org/.
Kesselheim, Alan S. *Trail Food: Drying and Cooking Food for Backpacking and Paddling.* Camden, ME: Ragged Mountain Press, 1998.
McClure, Susan, ed. *Preserving Summer's Bounty.* Emmaus, PA: Rodale Press, 1998. A general manual with recipes.

ASTRID FERSZT

Duck

The word "duck" is a generic term for small, web-footed birds of the Anatidae family, especially the genera *Anas*, *Aythya*, and *Cairina*. Ducks are generally smaller than other members of this order, which includes geese and swans. Ducks are found throughout the world. They are good swimmers and flyers but are awkward on land.

Ducks in the Old World and the New World have been captured and used for food since prehistoric times.

The mallard (*Anas boschas*) was probably domesticated in China in approximately 1000 B.C.E. and spread throughout the Old World in ancient times. Ducks became an important food, served particularly on the tables of the wealthy and on special occasions by other classes. Europeans introduced domesticated ducks into the New World, where they have thrived since colonial times.

The New World also had many species of wild ducks, but only the Muscovy (*Cairina moschata*) was domesticated. By the time Europeans arrived, the Muscovy duck was widely distributed throughout the tropical regions of Central and South America. The Spanish probably introduced it into the Caribbean, and the Portuguese introduced it into West Africa, where it thrived. The slave trade introduced the Muscovy duck into British North America. Archaeological evidence has surfaced demonstrating that slaves raised and consumed these fowl and later introduced them to the rest of America. By the 1840s the Muscovy duck was widely distributed throughout America. It survived as a commercial poultry item in the United States until the late nineteenth century but then largely disappeared as chicken and turkey began to dominate the poultry market.

Domesticated ducks were raised on a small scale on farms and were herded to market, usually with the help of specially trained dogs. An advantage of raising ducks was that these birds foraged and consumed food not eaten by other poultry. In addition, duck feathers were used for clothing and bedding. Canvasback ducks were raised on the Potomac and Susquehanna Rivers in the early nine-

Ducks. Pair of Rouen ducks. From Simon M. Saunders, *Domestic Poultry* (New York, 1866), p. 101.

teenth century and later were shipped to all major East Coast cities and to Europe. Likewise, the Cayuga duck was bred in central New York and after the completion of the Erie Canal became available in East Coast cities. It was sandy and pond-filled Long Island, however, that became the center of early American duck raising. Long Island farms had easy access to the market in New York City, and Long Island green duckling became an important food in America.

In the mid-nineteenth century, duck breeding became an important business, and American efforts to improve the quality of ducks was greatly enhanced by the introduction of the Pekin duck (*Anas domesticus*) from China in 1873. Almost all commercial production uses strains of this variety. The small American duck industry is concentrated in the Midwest—Wisconsin, Indiana, and Illinois. The duck industry is small compared with the chicken and turkey industries. Commercial ducks are generally sold frozen. There is also a niche market for duck eggs.

Ducks were served for special occasions, such as Thanksgiving and Christmas. Most nineteenth-century American cookbooks contain recipes for preparing ducks for the table. N. K. M. Lee's *Cook's Own Book* (1832) lists twelve recipes, including instructions for roasting, stewing, hashing, and boiling ducks. Several recipes contain directions for duck stuffing, which is similar to that for other fowl. Duck cookery was especially important among French American chefs, and numerous duck recipes appeared in their cookbooks. For example, Felix Déliée's *Franco-American Cookery Book* (1884) included forty-four duck recipes, including dishes with peas, onions, turnips, jellies, cranberries, anchovies, and assorted sauces and stuffings. Likewise, *The Picayune Creole Cook Book* (1901) featured many duck recipes. These included recipes for specific types of ducks, such as the canvasback (*Aythya valsineria*), which acquired its name for the coloring on its back, teal (*Anas crecca*), and widgeon (*Anas americana*). Ducks were served with a variety of other foods, including peas, oranges, and carrots. Despite the diversity of recipes and the quality of preparation, duck never achieved the popularity in America that it had in Europe. Duck recipes largely disappeared from American cookbooks in the early twentieth century, and ducks are mainly sold in specialty shops and French restaurants.

With the introduction of *magret* (boneless breast of the Moulard duck) in the 1980s through small East Coast breeders, duck has made a comeback. This resurgence coincides with a culinary shift toward the use of rare duck meat by upscale restaurants and ambitious home cooks.

[*See also* Chicken; Christmas; Dressings and Stuffings; French Influences on American Food; Game; Goose; Thanksgiving; Turkey.]

BIBLIOGRAPHY

Batty, Joseph. *Domesticated Ducks and Geese*. Mildhurst, UK: Beech, 1996.

Dohner, Janet Vorwald. *The Encyclopedia of Endangered Livestock and Poultry Breeds*. New Haven, CT, and London: Yale University Press, 2001.

Wilcox, Leroy. "Ducks: An Industry Spawned on Long Island, N. Y. Has Spread Extensively to Middle West." In *American Poultry History 1823–1973*, edited by Oscar August Hanke et al. Lafayette, IN: American Poultry History Society, 1974.

ANDREW F. SMITH

Dumplings

Dumplings are plump, delicious, and unpretentious foods that defy precise definition. Even Maria Polushkin, in her *Dumpling Cookbook*, despairs that "no one seems to be very sure just what is and what is not a dumpling."

What is certain is that dumplings originated in Asia, and four regions of the world have contributed American adaptations: England invented the Norfolk dumpling, the archetypal and most authentic dumpling, according to the British; Central Europe contributed flavored and filled dumplings; and Italy is the home of ravioli and gnocchi. The American-Asian dumpling connection includes the multiplicity of dim sum, a Cantonese snack named for a phrase that means "to touch the heart."

Adding to the dumpling distress, no one seems to know the actual derivation of the word. Dictionaries offer the dismal "origin obscure." Early American usage included "dumperling," as in "a mess er turnip-greens an' dumperlin's" (1877). The actual word "dumpling" appeared in print in America for the first time at the beginning of the seventeenth century to denote a small ball of boiled or steamed dough. That kind of dumpling probably evolved when a bread-making farm wife dropped a walnut-sized piece of dough into a simmering liquid, where it fell to the bottom of the pot like a lump of lead, then rose, puffed and beautiful, light and savory, to the top. Polushkin divides dumplings into "dropped

dumpling" and "filled dumpling," with the seventeenth-century version unquestionably falling into the "dropped" category.

The dropped dumpling—usually a mixture of flour, eggs, and butter with herbs, spices, and other ingredients sometimes added to the basic dough—is simmered or boiled in liquid. Parsley dumplings (all-purpose, all-American, according to Polushkin) are prepared with stew, soup, chowder, fricassee, or ragout. Matzo balls (*knaydelach* is Yiddish for dumplings) are simmered in chicken broth or chicken stew and are traditionally served at the Passover Seder; they are also eaten year-round. Leftovers are incorporated in bread dumplings and mashed potato dumplings. Spaetzle—tiny, buttery German dumplings ("spaetzle" means "little sparrows")—are made with a spaetzle mill and can be eaten as a meal by themselves. *Kluski*, Polish dumplings, are served with pot roast or stewed chicken. Elegant French quenelles are dropped dumplings. So are gnocchi, straddling the fine line that divides pasta from dumplings.

The filled dumpling basically consists of flour and water, sometimes with egg and a little shortening, rolled out and cut into circles or squares. A small amount of the filling goes in the center, and the edges are tightly sealed before the dumpling is boiled, fried, or steamed. Kreplach—Jewish dumplings stuffed with meat, cheese, or kasha (buckwheat groats)—are in the filled dumpling category. So is the knish, a kind of potato and flour dumpling stuffed with mashed potato and onion, chopped liver, or cheese; "knish" comes from the Polish word for dumpling. Empanadas from Argentina, ravioli and tortellini from Italy, and even wonton and egg rolls from China are popular dumplings in this category.

Early Moravian records indicate that pork and dumplings was a common dish eaten at the main meal of the day in the Carolinas during the eighteenth century. Polish pierogi—filled dumplings containing cheese, butter, potato, spinach, or onion—were brought to central Canada by Ukranian immigrants in the late 1800s. Joe Booker stew, made of lean beef, vegetables, and parsley dumplings, was a favorite dish during Maine winters when men came in from cutting ice or chopping down trees—but just as with the dumpling, no one seems to know who Joe Booker was.

For dessert, sweet-pastry dumplings might consist of an apple, cored and baked inside a snug pocket of dough. A special favorite of early Carolina setters, the apple dumpling was made from cored apples filled with cinnamon and sugar, then snuggled in a jacket of puff pastry and boiled. Each apple dumpling was served with melted butter and sprinkled with sugar.

On Chinese New Year it is traditional to eat dumpling soup on the first day of the five-day celebration. Whoever bites into the dumpling with the surprise inside is sure to have good luck throughout the coming year.

A peculiar claim to dumpling diversity may be discovered in the frozen food section of American grocery stores; the pizza dumpling, a dumpling filled with Italian pizza ingredients, is manufactured by a Korean firm.

Closely related to dumplings are fritters, deep-fried batter that may include additional ingredients like vegetables, mushrooms, cheese, oysters, or shrimp. Calas, the traditional deep-fried yeasted fritters from New Orleans, Louisiana, are made with rice, eggs, vanilla, and nutmeg, and are served hot with thick coffee.

Doughboys (the nickname given to American soldiers in World War I) may or may not be related to a kind of flour-based dumpling that developed into the doughnut and was in use by the late eighteenth century.

[*See also* Chinese American Food; Doughnuts; German American Food; Italian American Food; Jewish American Food; Soups and Stews.]

BIBLIOGRAPHY

Moss, Kay, and Kathryn Hoffman. *The Backcountry Housewife.* Vol. 1, *A Study of Eighteenth-Century Foods.* Gastonia, NC: Schiele Museum, 1985.

Polushkin, Maria. *The Dumpling Cookbook.* New York: Workman, 1977.

Rombauer, Irma S. *The Joy of Cooking.* Indianapolis, IN: Bobbs-Merrill, 1967.

SARA RATH

Dutch Influences on American Food

The history of the Dutch colony New Netherland begins in 1609. In that year Henry Hudson explored the Hudson River, as it was later named, on behalf of the Dutch East India Company. His aim was to find a northern passage to Asia. Through his explorations the Dutch claim to a vast area between New England and Virginia was established. This claim reached from the Connecticut River to the Delaware Bay. In 1621 a charter with exclusive trading rights in the Western Hemisphere was given to the Dutch West India Company. In 1626 the island of Manhattan was purchased, and in 1664 the English took over New Netherland, and, with the exception of a brief interlude in 1673–1674, the area remained in British hands until the American Revolution. In only seven brief decades, those persistent settlers managed to entrench themselves in their new homeland.

The Dutch colonists brought with them seeds and tree stock as well as horses, cows, pigs, and other domesticated animals. The settlers contributed the foodstuffs we so readily associate with the Hudson River Valley: vegetables such as cabbage, carrots, peas, onions, parsnips, and turnips; herbs such as parsley, rosemary, and chives; and fruits such as apples, pears, and peaches. In his 1665 book, *A Description of the New Netherlands*, Adriaen van der Donck reports that they all "thrive well." By 1679 a traveler notes that he has never seen finer apples. He particularly enjoyed the Newtown Pippin, the Esopus (in the area of Kingston, New York), the Spitzenburgh, and the Poughkeepsie Swaar apples. Some of these old varieties are still grown in the orchards of the Hudson Valley. A century later the Swedish botanist Peter Kalm marveled in his diary at peach trees bearing such abundant fruit that roaming pigs gorged themselves.

Diaries and inventories show that the Dutch also brought with them the implements used for cooking those familiar foods cultivated in the New World. For example, Margareta van Slichtenhorst Schuyler (1630–1711) owned a brass "poffer" (silver-dollar pancake) pan as well as a waffle iron, according to the inventory of her estate. The twelve thousand assorted documents that remain from the Dutch period, partly translated by the New Netherland Project in Albany, make it clear that the settlers wanted to re-create their life in the Netherlands in New Netherland.

Dutch Contributions

Doughnuts, pretzels, coleslaw, pancakes, waffles, wafers, and, above all, cookies are all part of America's culinary heritage brought to New Netherland by the Dutch in the seventeenth century. The Dutch words *koolsla* and *koekje* were even adopted into American English with only slight transformations. *Kool* (pronounced like "cole") means "cabbage," and *sla* means "salad"; together they became our American "coleslaw." The Dutch *koekje* (the "oe" is pronounced like "oo"), which is the diminutive of *koek*, a flat, not highly risen baked good, forms the root of the American word "cookie." The British call cookies "little cakes" or "biscuits." The first American cookbook,

Amelia Simmons's *American Cookery*, published in 1796, features several cookie recipes, and Americans have loved cookies ever since.

Bread was the mainstay of the Dutch diet. It was consumed with butter or cheese for breakfast, paired with meat or a stew for the midday main meal, and served with the evening's dish of porridge. At holiday time, festive breads such as the *duivekater,* made with white flour and sugar, were given to the poor, as the deacon's accounts of the Reformed Church in Brooklyn show. Bread was even used in trade with Native Americans. Court records contain an account of a case in which a Beverwijck (Albany) baker was charged with selling a sugar bun to a Mohawk Indian in a period when, owing to grain scarcity, such sales were forbidden. To protect the population, government ordinances in the colony (or, as the Dutch called it, "the province"), as well as in the homeland, closely regulated the price, sale, and quality of bread. The same can be said of beer, the common drink before tea and coffee became fashionable at the end of the seventeenth century.

The typical meal pattern consisted of breakfast, along with midday, afternoon, and evening meals. Breakfast was mainly bread and butter or cheese. Beer was the usual drink for all meals. On the farms, buttermilk was drunk as well. The midday meal was the main meal of the day, made up of no more than two or three dishes. The first was often a *hutspot* (or hotchpotch), a one-pot dish of meat and vegetables; the second dish might be some sort of fish or a meat stewed with prunes and currants; and the third might be fruit, as well as cooked vegetables and cakes or savory pies. On the farm this midday meal was often simply a porridge, bread, and meat. A few hours after the midday meal, between two and three o'clock, some bread with butter or cheese was eaten. The last meal of the day, usually a porridge or leftovers of the noon meal and bread, was served just before bedtime.

For people used to eating porridge, it was easy to get used to the Native American cornmeal mush called *sapaen*, made from ground corn and water. The Dutch added milk to it, and it became an integral part of the Dutch-American diet. *Oliekoecken*, deep-fried dough balls filled with apples and raisins, were the edible symbols of the Dutch in America and the forerunners of the doughnut. They were always served at gatherings, church socials, or festive occasions. Descendants of the settlers continued the foodways of their ancestors. They might have forgotten the native tongue, but they did not forget the taste of the foods of their forebears and continued to enjoy the pastries and other items connected with feasts and holidays well into the nineteenth century and even up to the present day. Recipes for those familiar Dutch foods can be found in the handwritten manuscript cookbooks, spanning more than three centuries, that belonged to the descendants of families such as the Van Rensselaers of Albany, the Van Cortlandts of Croton-on-Hudson, or the Lefferts of Brooklyn. The Dutch touch left a lasting mark on the American kitchen.

[*See also* Beer; Bread; Breakfast Foods; Cookbooks and Manuscripts, *subentry* From the Beginnings to 1860; Doughnuts; Historical Overview, *subentry* The Colonial Period.]

BIBLIOGRAPHY

Danckaerts, Jasper. *Journal of Jasper Dankaerts, 1679–1680*, edited by Barlett Burleigh James and J. Franklin Jameson. New York: Scribners, 1913.

Kalm, Peter. *Peter Kalm's Travels in North America*, revised and edited by Adolph B. Benson. New York: Dover, 1987. Reprint of the English version of 1770.

Rose, Peter G. trans. and ed. *The Sensible Cook: Dutch Foodways in the Old and the New World*. 2nd ed. Syracuse, NY: Syracuse University Press, 1998. Includes a translation of a seventeenth-century Dutch cookbook.

Van der Donck, Adriaen. *A Description of the New Netherlands*, edited by Thomas F. O'Donnell. Syracuse, NY: Syracuse University Press, 1968. Reprint of the first English translation, published in 1841.

PETER G. ROSE

Dutch Ovens

The term "Dutch oven," as used here, refers to an American pot of European ancestry, a small, portable, cast-iron oven that has evolved to accommodate changing fuel sources since the eighteenth century. This is to distinguish it from the English use of the same term, which refers to what Americans call tin-reflecting ovens or side-wall fireplace brick ovens. The derivation of the term is similarly unclear, perhaps referring to legendary Dutch frugality (far less fuel required) or perhaps early Dutch expertise in casting iron, but it is probably an American designation. In any case, the American Dutch oven has been valued for its combination of steaming and baking, stewing, and braising.

Eighteenth-century American Dutch ovens were designed for the hearth, where they were heated with glowing embers. The high rims of their heavy lids held the glowing fuel on the top. Additional heat was provided by piles of coals underneath, and the oven's three legs held it at a good height above the heat source. Dutch ovens hung over the heat from swinging bail handles or were maneuvered by C-shaped handles on their sides. They were made in different sizes—the smallest was simultaneously pot and oven, while the larger ones could also contain pans of food.

American Dutch ovens can be traced to seventeenth-century Europe in such still-life paintings as Harmen Van Steenwyrk's *Skillet and Game* (1646). These examples were somewhat shallow and graceful and were often used as tart pans. Others, probably limited to wealthier families, were made of bronze or copper, exemplified by French *daubieres* (stew pans). An English version called the "bake kettle" varied, in that it was sometimes a round-bottomed, straight-sided kettle that hung covered over the heat and at other times was a flat-bottomed hanging kettle called a "yetling" in the West Country of England and a "bastable" in Ireland. These kettles were often found in remote European rural areas with little access to commercial bakeries or enough wood to fuel home brick ovens. Bats of smoldering peat or other fuel substitutes were placed above and below. Peat produced lower temperatures than wood; its use resulted in heavy and moist breads that required additional drying.

American Dutch ovens were manufactured in the colonies in the eighteenth century—the Pine Grove Furnace (Pennsylvania) produced three sizes. No longer limited to affluent kitchens, they were inevitably made of cast iron and figured in such dishes as overnight beans, stewed or potted meats, tea cakes, cornbreads, pies, and puddings.

By the mid- to late nineteenth century, early American manufacturers of cast-iron implements were producing

Dutch Oven. From the Duparquet, Huot, & Moneuse Co. catalog (Boston, 1915), p. 167.

variations of hearth Dutch ovens called "spiders" (frying pans) and ovens that retained their legs and high-rimmed heavy lids. At the same time, in response to the proliferation of the woodstove, new dome-lidded, flat-bottomed forms, sometimes porcelain lined, were offered by such noted manufacturers as Griswald (Pennsylvania), who added such innovations as self-basting lids. Legs and high-rimmed lids had become obsolete with the passing of the kitchen hearth, but twentieth-century ovens, also called casseroles, continued to be popular kitchen equipment and are still essential adjuncts to the pot roasts and stews we honor as slow food.

[*See also* Casseroles; Frying Pans, Skillets, and Spiders; Hearth Cookery; Slow Cookers; Soups and Stews.]

BIBLIOGRAPHY

Ragsdale, John G. *Dutch Ovens Chronicled: Their Use in the United States.* Fayetteville: University of Arkansas Press, 1991.

ALICE ROSS

Easter

Easter celebrates spring and the resurrection of Christ. It also ends Lent, the forty-day penitential period beginning on Ash Wednesday that, until the mid-twentieth century, greatly influenced the diet of Catholics worldwide. Beginning in the seventh century, Catholics were expected to abstain from eating all animals and animal products during Lent, except on Sundays. Over time, the Roman Catholic Church relaxed these strictures to permit eating fish (ninth century) and dairy products (fifteenth century), although meat and poultry remained forbidden. In 1966 all fasting obligations were removed except for those related to Ash Wednesday and Good Friday. The Eastern Orthodox Church continues Lenten fasts. Protestants traditionally do not fast, but there is a growing movement among some American Protestants, as well as Catholics, to relinquish a favored treat, frequently chocolate, caffeine, or pastry.

The history of Easter celebrations in America parallels the controversies surrounding Christmas. Puritan sects viewed Easter dimly, as a holiday that smacked of popery. Until the mid-nineteenth century, only certain Protestants and the relatively small handful of Catholics in America venerated Easter as a religious feast. American folk observations of Easter (the name derives from an Anglo-Saxon goddess of fertility or spring, Eostre, whose sign was the rabbit), however, date back to the eighteenth century and greatly influence contemporary celebrations. The Pennsylvania Dutch imported the *Oschter Haws*, or Easter Hare, who delivered colored eggs to good children (or rabbit pellets to the naughty) who put out their hats for a "nest." By the early nineteenth century, entire Pennsylvania Dutch villages would turn out with gaily decorated Easter eggs to play games, including egg-eating contests and "picking" eggs, in which young gladiators would butt eggs until one competitor's egg broke. For good health, the Pennsylvania Dutch ate wild greens, especially dandelion, on Maundy Thursday. They gathered eggs laid on Good Friday for consumption on Easter, for use in folk medicine, or as talismans against evil spirits. A favorite Pennsylvania Dutch Easter bread depicts a rabbit in the preposterous posture of laying an egg.

By the later nineteenth century, most Protestant groups had eased their opposition to Easter, and Sunday-dress Easter parades became a national pastime. The renamed Easter Bunny visited children, and confectioners began producing special sweets for the holiday, especially candy eggs to replace the dyed hens' eggs. Seasonal treats included marzipan, chocolate eggs, garishly colored jelly beans, and, more recently, "Peeps" (tinted marshmallow chicks and bunnies), all stuffed into the Easter baskets that replaced the hare's nest.

In the late nineteenth and early twentieth centuries, Catholic immigrants maintained Easter culinary rituals with overtly religious symbolism. Slovenian and Polish immigrants brought baskets of food to churches for blessings on Holy Saturday. The baskets contained hams and sausages (representing Christ incarnate), eggy breads (a Eucharistic allusion), vinegar (recalling the sponge soaked with the cheap sour wine, or posca, that was offered to Christ on the cross), a sugar or butter lamb (evoking Christ as the Lamb of God), and horseradish (denoting Christ's bitter sorrows).

Significantly, horseradish also plays an important role in the Jewish Passover feast, reinforcing the connection between Passover and Holy Week—considered by some the "Christian Passover." Another link is the Paschal Lamb, believed to have been eaten at the Last Supper, widely thought to have been a seder. Not only did the lamb become a Christian symbol, but also the Hebrew *Pesach* provides the common etymology for both Easter and Passover in many languages.

Special Easter breakfasts, popular from the early twentieth century, prominently feature egg dishes or foods shaped as eggs, such as delicately tinted blancmange

Easter Egg. Children dismantling a giant chocolate Easter egg, nineteenth-century print.

puddings molded in blown-out eggshells. Unlike the formulaic dinners touted as "traditional" for Thanksgiving and, to a lesser extent, Christmas, there is no archetypical American Easter dinner. Moreover, according to one 1959 survey, only 75 percent of respondents judged a family Easter dinner very or somewhat important, compared to 94 percent for Christmas and 97 percent for Thanksgiving. Relatively few cookbooks or magazines published before the mid-twentieth century suggest Easter menus; those that do favor ham, with lamb running a close second. Other meats and even salmon had muscled their way onto Easter menus by the late twentieth century. Eggs may appear as starters for Easter dinner, in rich hollandaise sauce enrobing asparagus, as hard-cooked eggs garnished with caviar, or even as *oeufs en gelée*.

With Americans' increasing interest in ethnic cuisines, mainstream magazines offer recipes for "traditional" Easter meals from such Roman Catholic and Eastern Orthodox strongholds as Italy, Poland, Ukraine, and Greece. Common to all of these menus are massive, yeasted enriched cakes and breads. Hot cross buns—currant-studded, sweetened rolls decorated with royal icing crosses—are a more diminutive Holy Week treat.

[*See also* Candy Bars and Candy; Christmas; Eggs; Passover.]

BIBLIOGRAPHY

Better Homes and Gardens Holiday Cook Book. Des Moines, IA: Meredith, 1959.

Cohen, Hennig, and Tristram Potter Coffin, eds. *The Folklore of American Holidays: A Compilation of More Than 600 Beliefs, Legends, Superstitions, Proverbs, Riddles, Poems, Songs, Dances, Games, Plays, Pageants, Fairs, Foods, and Processions Associated with over 140 American Calendar Customs and Festivals.* 3rd ed. Detroit: Gale, 1999.

"International Easter." *McCall's*, April 1979.

Shoemaker, Alfred L. *Eastertide in Pennsylvania: A Folk Cultural Study.* Kutztown, PA: Pennsylvania Folklife Society, 1960.

CATHY K. KAUFMAN

Eating Disorders

Eating disorders are, to be sure, a sign of the times. And yet, if the matrix of social values and pressures that attend them is especially dominant today, it has been taking shape within the framework of bourgeois culture since its beginning—and beyond, within that of Western culture itself. Broadly speaking, what is at stake in an eating disorder is a sense of control or, perhaps more accurately, possession, both of oneself and of one's surroundings—a vexed issue for females in a patriarchal capitalist setting (no less so, and in some ways even more so, after the advent of feminism). The notion of a fully realized identity, and of the expectations, rights, and responsibilities that come with it, becomes bound up with the image of a fully grown body and its needs; when psychological disposition or family dynamics render these bindings particularly uncomfortable, an eating disorder may develop. In the United States, in fact, at any given time, between 5 million and 10 million people are affected; typically, they are young women, although numbers are rising among females of all ages, including children, as well as among men. Eating disorders generally fall into one of the three following categories: anorexia, bulimia, or binge-eating disorder.

Anorexia

Anorexia nervosa is characterized not, as the name suggests, by a lack of appetite but, on the contrary, by a relentless fear of the insatiability thereof. Extreme restriction of food intake, drastic weight loss, and a host of obsessive-compulsive forms of behavior involving diet, elimination, and exercise—to the exclusion of many, if not all, other activities—are hallmarks of the disease. Aside from emaciation itself, the systemic complications it presents may include amenorrhea (cessation of menses), anemia (iron deficiency), edema (abdominal swelling due to abnormal water retention), early-onset osteoporosis (bone thinning), or hypotension (low blood pressure) leading, ultimately, to heart arrhythmia and heart failure.

The psychological profile of a typical person with anorexia might read as follows: She is a woman (for nine out of ten are female) in her teens or early twenties, with a middle- or upper-middle-class background. Her persona is that of the Good Little Girl, as she exhibits signs of perfectionism, social reserve, discomfort with sexuality (namely, her own), and so on—indications of low self-esteem. Theories as to why these esteem issues should translate into preoccupations with thinness abound, but many of them—rightly, it would seem—consider the extent to which size and power are conceptually linked.

For instance, feminist scholars have made much of the limestone figurine called Venus of Willendorf, the exaggeratedly full-figured fertility symbol of a Paleolithic people who lived in present-day Austria. The fact that it was a positive symbol, one that was revered, is important in context. It is a figure at odds with the heroines of Judeo-Christian civilization, from the Virgin Mary to the medieval-era martyrs and saints who, engaging in fasts as a rite of purification, may, in fact, have been suffering from anorexia, or "anorexia mirabilis," as it was known early on (that is, lack of appetite due to miraculous circumstances). That the struggle to fill the spirit by emptying the body would be waged by holy women far more than men seems to stem from the influence of the Bible, in which it is woman, after all, who opens the Pandora's box of appetite and the degrading bodily functions connected with it; so must woman, in atonement, commit to the impossible task of reclosing the box, to renouncing the appetite, such that these bodily functions—digestive, sexual, and other—cease, and a preexilic state of innocence returns.

Of course, gender-based penitence was only one of many motivations that saints such as Catherine of Siena may have had for fasting. It is worth noting, as does Caroline Walker Bynum, that these legendary women, like modern-day women with anorexia, often came from relatively wealthy households with a stake in maintaining the status quo; their rigidly prescribed roles thus involved obediently nurturing the family and all it stood for. To refuse instead to have anything to do with food— except, often, to donate the family's own store to the poor—was to choose a form of piety that was something like a rejection of materialism, in every sense of the word, as well as of the imposed limitations on female identity. Such rebellion, however cloaked in Christ's teachings, was naturally deemed suspect by the church, who discouraged women's fasting practices. In addition, with the coming of the Enlightenment, scientific skepticism about those who came to be known as "fasting girls" waxed, as popular superstition as to their holiness (or, in some cases, demonic possession) gradually waned. By the late nineteenth century, physicians (and, eventually, psychologists) began to treat self-starvation as a pathologic condition rather than a supernatural phenomenon.

In the modern secular world, meanwhile, preservation of the patriarchal status quo still obtains. That the rise of the feminist movement and the entry of women into the workplace would be simultaneous with a shift in the ideal of female beauty—from the voluptuous, indeed, the Venus-like, stature of the actress Marilyn Monroe to the slim, angular, prepubescent profile of the sixties fashion icon Twiggy—strikes few as coincidental, though interpretations vary. Did the new look emulate boyishness in an attempt to embody the workforce? Or did it cling to prepubescent girlishness as a conciliatory gesture, in order to lessen any perceived threat to male privilege and power that might provoke a backlash? Either way, the implication was that woman's place would always be in the home, at least insofar as her naturally curvaceous body was forced to remain there, out of sight.

Obviously, social factors are not in themselves sufficient to explain eating disorders like anorexia; if they were, every woman in industrialized society—and no man, for that matter—would be affected, not just an estimated 15 percent (of which women with anorexia make up about 1 percent and those with bulimia 2 percent). Rather, these factors have an impact upon psychological and psychiatric issues—developmental, biochemical, and so on. Treatment of anorexia, and of all eating disorders, to varying degrees, takes a multipronged approach, including individual or group psychotherapy, cognitive or behavioral therapy, nutrition counseling, and medication.

Bulimia

If "anorexia nervosa" is a misnomer, "bulimia nervosa" is an insult; it is even dehumanizing, in that it compares the binge-eating central to the disorder with the eating habits of oxen (according to Merriam-Webster, the word is New Latin by way of the Greek term *boulimia*, or "great hunger," combining the prefix *bous* or "head of cattle" with the root *limos* or "hunger"). As it happens, in many cases, anorexia and bulimia are not so much distinct illnesses as different phases of the same illness, whereby the sufferer's habits of restricting food intake eventually begin to alternate with episodes of what seems to be uncontrollable eating. By the standard definition, a binge entails the consumption of food far beyond the body's caloric requirements in a disproportionately brief time period, two hours being the duration usually named.

The person with bulimia—also most likely a young female—is all too aware of her actions, which are thus accompanied by feelings of guilt, shame, and self-loathing. To compensate for the behavior, she will restrict intake all the more (at least until the next binge); exercise compulsively, sometimes for hours at a session; or engage in acts of purgation—forced vomiting and the abuse of laxatives being especially common. Of course, the binge-purge cycle can have devastating effects on health. The havoc wreaked on the digestive system can lead, in turn, to complications as varied as tooth decay; facial swelling; kidney, liver, and esophagus damage; and electrolyte imbalances that can ultimately cause heart failure.

It seems fairly obvious that bulimia, whether or not it is preceded by anorexia, begins as a response to malnourishment of a psychological as much as a physical sort; bulimics, like all sufferers of eating disorders, tend to swallow their emotions quite literally. Less clear is the extent to which biochemistry plays a part and whether any imbalances are a matter of genetics or the product, and in turn the perpetuating cause, of disordered eating. Certain neurochemicals and hormones appear to effect a linkage between mood and appetite; serotonin, for instance, is believed to regulate feelings of well-being, including satiety, which is why a certain class of antidepressants known as "selective serotonin reuptake inhibitors," or SSRIs, is frequently prescribed to patients with eating disorders, who may underproduce the chemical. Meanwhile, irregularities involving amino acids such as tryptophan and hormones such as leptin, both of which determine the production and release of serotonin, are a topic of much related study.

Binge-Eating Disorder

The third major type of eating disorder is binge-eating disorder, otherwise known as compulsive overeating. Like bulimia, it involves episodes of abnormal food intake, and these episodes stem from and sustain low self-esteem; unlike bulimia, they do not induce purgation. Sufferers from this disorder—of whom there are believed to be millions—are thus likely to be overweight.

Of course, excess weight has itself become a problem of epidemic proportions among Americans; studies that came out in the early twenty-first century indicated that as many as two in three Americans were overweight, one in three being clinically obese. It should be noted that overeating, in and of itself, is not a mental illness; it is only when the practice exacts a heavy emotional as well as physical toll on the practitioner, who despises her behavior but feels compelled to repeat it, that consultation with a therapist first and foremost, and not simply a dietitian, may be in order. Between these categories, there can admittedly be much overlap. In that case, or in the case of patients who meet the criteria for a specific diagnosis only partially or imprecisely, a fourth classification exists: EDNOS, or eating disorders not otherwise specified.

[*See also* Obesity.]

BIBLIOGRAPHY

Abraham, Suzanne, and Derek Llewellyn-Jones. *Eating Disorders: The Facts*. 5th ed. New York: Oxford University Press, 2001. A useful reference guide with a medical slant.

Brumberg, Joan Jacobs. *Fasting Girls: The Emergence of Anorexia Nervosa as a Modern Disease*. Cambridge, MA: Harvard University Press, 1988. Makes the connection between the postmedieval phenomenon of fasting girls and the modern-day epidemic of anorexia.

Bynum, Caroline Walker. *Holy Feast and Holy Fast: The Religious Significance of Food to Medieval Women*. Berkeley: University of California Press, 1987. Fascinating study of the lives and motives of medieval women and their relationship to such food practices as fasting, communion, and feasting.

Chernin, Kim. *The Hungry Self: Women, Eating, and Identity*. New York: Times Books, 1985. A moving treatise on the relationship between women with eating disorders and their mothers, as it is colored by gender identity before and after the advent of feminism.

Chernin, Kim. *The Obsession: Reflections on the Tyranny of Slenderness*. New York: Harper and Row, 1981. Poignant essays on women's sense of self and agency within patriarchal culture and how this sense of self affects eating habits.

Eating Disorder Referral and Information Center. http.//www.edreferral.com. Comprehensive in scope, providing disorder profiles, resources and links for further study, and a guide to types of treatment.

Vandereycken, Walter, and Ron Van Deth. *From Fasting Saints to Anorexic Girls: The History of Self-Starvation*. New York:

New York University Press, 1994. Provides the missing historical link between Bynum's and Brumberg's accounts.

RUTH TOBIAS

Egg Cream

The egg cream, a seemingly simple beverage, is produced from only three ingredients—milk, seltzer, and chocolate syrup—and contains neither eggs nor cream. While folklore, more so than fact, defines the egg cream's history, the origin and popularity of the drink indisputably belong to New York City. The egg cream, originally a drink associated with Eastern European Jewish immigrants, quickly became a beverage so linked to New York that it serves as one of the city's most recognizable icons. Almost exclusive to soda fountains and ice cream parlors, this New York specialty has been around since the 1920s, with popularity surging from the 1930s to the 1950s and then waning during the 1960s and 1970s, as soda fountains and ice cream parlors disappeared.

Because the drink contains neither eggs nor cream, the manner in which it got its name is interesting. Perhaps the most widely accepted story is that Louis Auster, a Lower East Side candy shop owner, invented it during the 1890s and named it after the white foam layer on top, which moderately resembles beaten egg whites. The drink soon caught on, and its popularity swelled. Stanley Auster, the last known Auster family member, maintained that egg creams never contained either eggs or cream.

According to another piece of folklore, "soda jerks" (those who work in soda fountains) first created the egg cream, using syrup made from eggs and adding cream to give the drink a richer taste. Legend has it that sometime later, milk and sugar-based syrup replaced these ingredients, but the name remained. In a 1906 version of the historical text *The Standard Manual of Soda and Other Beverages,* an egg cream recipe includes a preparation with egg yolks, cream, syrup, seltzer, and vanilla, but few egg cream enthusiasts give much credence to this recipe.

A third legend is that the name "egg cream" was merely a marketing gimmick. Producers could now replace costly ice cream sodas and malteds, favored during the 1930s, with inexpensive egg creams. One final legend speculates that "egg cream" resulted from a poorly pronounced English translation of the French *chocolat et crème* by the Yiddish actor Boris Thomashevsky; because the correct pronunciation of *"et crème"* is "ay krem," the drink slowly evolved into "egg cream."

Disregarding the egg and cream controversy, most New Yorkers agree that customary egg creams call for a mixture of chocolate or vanilla syrup, chilled milk, and seltzer. There is much debate, however, over who originated—and therefore who owns—the egg cream. Legend states that Brooklyn soda jerks begin with syrup, follow with milk, and end with seltzer, ensuring a "milky white" foam. Their Bronx counterparts begin with syrup thoroughly mixed with seltzer and completed with milk, generating a brownish head.

Like many nostalgia foods, egg creams began enjoying a newfound surge in popularity and consumption in the 1990s and after. A proliferation of egg creams has appeared on restaurant and diner menus. No longer quintessentially Jewish, egg creams are consumed throughout the United States.

[*See also* Chocolate Drinks; Dairy Foods; Ice Cream Sodas; Jewish American Food; New York Food; Seltzer; Soda Drinks; Soda Fountains.]

BIBLIOGRAPHY

Bentley, Harold. W. "Linguistic Concoctions of the Soda Jerker." *American Speech* 11, no. 1 (1935): 11–24.
Hiss, A. Emil. *The Standard Manual of Soda and Other Beverages: A Treatise Especially Adapted to the Requirements of Druggists and Confectioners.* Chicago: G. P. Engelhard, 1897.
O'Neill, Molly. *New York Cookbook.* New York: Workman, 1992.

JENNIFER SCHIFF BERG

Eggnog

Rich and creamy dessert drinks, such as eggnog and syllabub, reflect the English heritage in America, especially in the South. In England posset was a hot drink in which the white and yolk of eggs were whipped with ale, cider, or wine. Americans adapted English recipes to produce a variety of milk-based drinks that combined rum, brandy, or whiskey with cream. The first written reference to eggnog was an account of a February 1796 breakfast at the City Tavern in Philadelphia. Beginning in 1839 American cookbooks included recipes for cold eggnogs of cream, sugar, and eggs combined with brandy, rum, bourbon, or sherry, sprinkled with nutmeg. Southerners enjoyed a mix of peach brandy, rum, and whiskey.

Eggnog has been served at holiday parties since the nineteenth century and is a tradition of Christmas and

New Year's celebrations throughout the United States. In the nineteenth century, eggnog was also a nourishing drink prepared for invalids, especially fever patients. A commercial nonalcoholic version is available in the dairy cases of grocery stores beginning in mid-October. Canned eggnog can be purchased year-round. During the winter holidays, eggnog is used to flavor ice cream, pancakes, french toast, cheesecake, breads, and cookies.

[*See also* Christmas; Hot Toddies; New Year's Celebrations; Syllabub.]

BIBLIOGRAPHY

Walter, Eugene. *American Cooking: Southern Style.* New York: Time-Life Books, 1971.

VIRGINIA SCOTT JENKINS

Eggplants

Few foods can lay claim to causing insanity, acting as an aphrodisiac, and serving as a dental cosmetic. Eggplant, *Solanum melongena*, lays claim to all of the above and much more. Although most often considered a vegetable, eggplant is actually a fruit. Technically it is a berry and a member of the nightshade family. It is possibly this botanical relationship to belladonna, the deadly nightshade, that prompted early Europeans to dub eggplant the "mad apple" on the premise that it could cause insanity. Quite a contrary view emerged, however, as the "apple of love" was sought after as an aphrodisiac in sixteenth-century Spain. Eggplant was also used as a cosmetic in the fifth century C.E. in China, where women used eggplant skins to make a black dye. As was the fashion of the day, women then used the dye to stain and polish their teeth until they took on a metallic sheen.

Eggplant, as it is known in America and was once known in Britain, is so named because the earliest variety to arrive in England in the sixteenth century was small and white, similar to a hen's egg. Eggplant is also widely known by its French name, aubergine. Today eggplant is available in countless shapes and colors. The migration of eggplant can be roughly traced through the name "aubergine," which derives from the Catalan *alberginera*, the Arabic *al-bājinjān*, and the Persian *badin-gan;* the Arabic and Persian terms derive from the Sanskrit *vatin-ganah*. *Vatin-ganah* translates to "wind-go." Food historians have debated whether the word means that it does or does not cause flatulence. The

Italian name, *petonciano*, may shed some light on this debate as *petonciano* translates to "fart."

It is virtually universally accepted that the eggplant was first cultivated in India some four to five thousand years ago and was likely cultivated for ornamental purposes because of its attractive leaves and flowers. It is also probable that eggplant was first consumed as food in India. From India, eggplant was most likely introduced to China and then to the Middle East by Arab traders in the seventh century C.E., and possibly as early as the fourth century C.E. The Moors then introduced eggplant to Spain in the early eighth century C.E. By the thirteenth century, eggplant had made its way to Italy and then to the rest of Europe, brought on trade ships carrying spices and other goods from the East.

How and when eggplant first arrived in America is a subject of dispute. Early Spanish conquerors of Mexico and the Caribbean may have been the first to introduce eggplant to the Americas in the sixteenth century. Eggplant may also have been introduced to America by African slaves. According to one story, the eggplant was introduced to America by Thomas Jefferson. With its striking violet flowers and gray leaves, eggplant was grown for its ornamental as well as food value.

Despite having arrived in the Americas with or soon after the first European settlers, eggplant is often considered an ethnic food. In *Heirloom Vegetable Gardening* (1997), William Woys Weaver notes that Americans have been slow to expand their taste for eggplant. Weaver speculates that this lack of popularity may be due to the eggplant's horticultural weaknesses, including a rather finicky need for hot summer nights in order to fruit as well as its susceptibility to the flea beetle and such fungi as fusarium and verticillium wilt.

The eggplant is most commonly associated with foods of the Far East, the Middle East, and the Mediterranean, although many of these foods have become commonplace in America. Eggplant parmesan is an Italian favorite in America. Moussaka is an import from Greece, and baba ghanoush is from the Middle East. Eggplant is also a key ingredient in the French classic ratatouille.

There are few preparations of eggplant considered distinctly American. One such preparation is fried eggplant, a southern specialty that appears in *The Virginia Housewife* (1824), in which Mary Randolph likens fried eggplant to soft-shell crabs. Rather than salting eggplant to extract the allegedly bitter juices, as is the standard contemporary practice, nineteenth-century American cookbooks recommend parboiling eggplant before the final cooking process. Another common American preparation is baked eggplant mashed with butter and topped with bread crumbs, served both at breakfast and at dinner.

[*See also* Heirloom Vegetables; Indian American Food; Middle Eastern Influences on American Food.]

BIBLIOGRAPHY

Weaver, William Woys. *Heirloom Vegetable Gardening: A Master Gardener's Guide to Planting, Growing, Seed Saving, and Cultural History.* New York: Holt, 1997.

MAURA CARLIN OFFICER

Egg-Preparation Tools

Eggs are used so many ways in cooking that all sorts of specialized utensils and gadgets have been developed to prepare them. In the earliest American colonies, the equipment was simple. For boiling, a pan with room for water to cover the egg was enough. For frying, a three-legged skillet or even a griddle was used, along with a wide, flat-bladed turner, which was also used for flatbreads and pancakes. For beating eggs, peeled twigs, forks, or even spread fingers were used.

In the 1870s, perhaps earlier, wire racks for more than one egg were manufactured and widely used. A center vertical handle meant that the rack, with six, eight, or even more eggs held in wire cups, could be lowered into boiling water and then safely extracted after boiling and used to serve eggs at the breakfast table.

Egg openers are scissor-action devices to cut the shell at the smaller end, so that a soft- or hard-boiled egg can be eaten directly out of the shell. Egg slicers and wedgers have been made since the 1870s. These items have a slotted space for a peeled hard-boiled egg and a hinged or sprung frame tightly strung with fine wires that is passed through the egg to slice it as desired. For poaching, low pans were made in the late 1800s; each had a rack pierced with holes to hold the raw eggs in boiling water. Lift-out, tab-handled inserts made it easy to slip the eggs onto a plate. Other free-standing egg-poaching cups could be used with any pan.

Wire whisks became available in the nineteenth century for every kind of culinary need, from making candy to whipping cream to beating eggs. They are essentially a bundle of looped wires secured to a handle. They may be flat, somewhat like a flat spoon with the bowl made of wire, or they may have wires held together to form a rounded or egg-shaped ball. When beating eggs for meringues, chefs prefer deep, round-bottomed bowls and whisks.

The most inventiveness is displayed in the mechanical eggbeater. The first ones were patented in the 1860s; these operate by rotary action, like many other devices that use a cranked gear to spin the useful end many times per revolution of the crank. Based on the way a whisk, with many wires, works by cutting through the egg, four to eight thin blades or "wings" were spun through the egg. Variations have included rotary turbine beaters that were designed scientifically, with small bent blades at the bottom that would constantly move the beaten egg up the sides of the container to go through the blades again and again. Many rotary eggbeaters came with their own bowls. There were also one-handed eggbeaters worked by a squeeze-action handle, and simple cheap beaters with a knob that was quickly slid up and down a twisted central rod, causing the rod and attached beater blades to revolve one way, then the other. Most of these drill-action devices date from the 1880s through the 1920s.

The cranked-gear, rotary type of eggbeater with whisklike blades has mostly won out, and is still made. Electric beaters, which came into use in the 1930s, had heavy motors and were set into their own fitted bowls, like small mixers. Later electric beaters were lightweight and portable, useful in any container or bowl.

[*See also* Eggs; Frying Pans, Skillets, and Spiders.]

BIBLIOGRAPHY

Franklin, Linda Campbell. *300 Years of Kitchen Collectibles.* 5th ed. Iola, WI: Krause Publications, 2003.
Thornton, Don. *The Eggbeater Chronicles: The Stirring Story of America's Greatest Invention.* 2nd, enlarged ed. Moss Beach, CA: Thornton House, 1999.

LINDA CAMPBELL FRANKLIN

Eggs

All birds reproduce by laying eggs, from the ostrich's speckled, iridescent, football-size specimens to the songbird's tiny ovals. But humans discovered another role for birds' eggs: they were a good source of food, which elevated the birds' status. Although the eggs of quail, duck, and other birds are prized, by far the majority of eggs consumed in America are chicken eggs.

Early Egg History

The naturalist Charles Darwin named the red jungle fowl (*Gallus gallus*) as the wild ancestor of today's modern chicken (*Gallus domesticus*), although there may have been as many as four species of similar birds that were domesticated in Asia three or four thousand years ago. Keeping chickens for divination and fighting was just as important as keeping them for food, but eventually humans realized that the chicken's habit of laying eggs in clutches allowed people to remove eggs from under the hens, motivating the hens to lay more and providing a continuous supply of eggs. Generally, wild birds lay eggs only in the spring, but with domestication chickens would lay on a more regular cycle. The eggs could then be eaten or hatched in special incubators. The Egyptians and the Chinese, who both needed to feed an able-bodied workforce to build their elaborate construction projects, devised ways of hatching eggs on a grand scale. The Egyptians constructed large heated clay buildings where they turned eggs by hand and were thus capable of hatching ten to fifteen thousand eggs at a time, a feat duplicated in modern times only since about 1925.

The early colonists probably brought their best egg layers with them to America, but even those birds molted in the fall and did not resume egg production for several months, depriving their keepers of an important source of food. In the middle 1800s China loosened its export restrictions, allowing the direct importation of Asian chicken breeds into the West. This, coupled with an increased interest in scientific breeding, paved the way for the development of chicken breeds suited to specific tasks, such as those possessing spectacular plumage to compete as show birds, those producing eggs, or those providing meat. The raising of chickens became so popular during the latter half of the nineteenth century in the United States that farms both big and small had flocks of chickens suited to each task.

Industrialization of the Egg

Industry had a profound effect on the way chickens were raised; it was the beginning of the chicken and egg as commodities. Although Christopher Nisson had started Pioneer Hatchery, the first commercial hatchery on the West Coast in 1898 (and Jacob Graves had started the first commercial hatchery in the country in Boston in 1873), it was a small town in California that mastered the industrial production of chickens and eggs. Petaluma ascended to world-class status as the home of the largest

egg ranch, Corliss, in 1918 and the largest hatchery, Must Hatch, in 1929.

Nestled in fertile farmland forty miles north of San Francisco, Petaluma had an ideal climate for raising chickens and was well situated to transport chickens and eggs to the big city. But nature's way of production was too slow. Hens laid eggs to replenish their flocks—they would lay enough eggs to make a clutch, sit on them for twenty-one days until they hatched, and then raise the young chicks. In 1879 Lyman Byce and Isaac Dias, two Petaluma residents with a penchant for tinkering, invented an incubator that took over the hens' hatching chore. Soon other enterprising locals began making commercial incubators.

The invention of the incubator was the first step in the commercialization of egg production, but several other discoveries contributed as well. During the last decade of the nineteenth century, the single-comb white leghorn was found to be the best egg layer. The invention of the trap nest, a device that held a hen in a compartment until her egg could be identified as belonging to her, further refined egg production: prolific egg layers were chosen as breeders. The introduction of artificial lighting in chicken coops (promoted in a bulletin put out by the U. S. Department of Agriculture in 1926) also increased egg production by simulating long hours of daylight, when hens lay the most eggs. Farmers added conveyor belts to dispense feed and collect the eggs.

These changes meant that the chickens were confined to coops; the days of pecking and scratching in the chicken yard ended, and the changes had their consequences. The chickens became more susceptible to disease because of the crowded conditions, leading to the development of vaccines and antibiotics. The large number of eggs also meant that machines replaced hands to wash, grade, and pack them. Defects in eggs were once noted by holding them to the light of a candle, which showed cracks in the shell, blood spots, and contamination and indicated the thickness of the white. Electronic eyes replaced human eyes, and artificial sources of light replaced candles. Gradually, larger operations began supplying most of the country's eggs; the small farmer could not compete. Even chicken farmers in Petaluma, once the egg capital of the world, realized that selling their land and retiring from the poultry business was more profitable than raising hens.

Present-day farmers raise hens with good laying records, but instead of hatching the eggs, they ship them to hatcheries that are often hundreds of miles away, where they are pampered at precise temperature and humidity levels in artificial incubators. Computers have replaced mother hens. Once hatched, the chicks, not needing food or drink for the first forty-eight hours of life, travel to farms, where they reach egg-laying age. Then they are moved again to the modern-day version of a hen house, where more than a million hens may live out their days. The hens' eggs might not be touched by human hands until the consumer lifts one from a carton in the kitchen.

Eggs are graded by diminishing quality as AA, A, or B, although only grades AA and A are sold in retail stores. (Grade B eggs go to large food service operations or to egg-breaking facilities for use in egg products.) The difference depends on the proportion and thickness of the white and the strength of the yolk membrane. Eggs are also sized by the weight of a dozen in the shell, and these sizes range from jumbo to peewee, with jumbo and extra large being the most popular.

In addition to being sold in the shell, eggs are pasteurized, either whole or separated, and sold for industrial use to ice cream manufacturers and large-scale bakeries. The customers can specify further treatment—added salt or sugar or whipping aids to help the whites froth. Eggs can also be frozen or dried and powdered. The call for dried eggs to feed the troops during both world wars of the twentieth century provided a major source of income for the egg industry.

Smaller farms still exist, where chickens have room to move, and some eat only organic feed, qualifying their eggs as organic. Some coops house both hens and roosters, so the eggs are fertile. And certain eggs have brown shells; the color is determined by the breed of chicken and has nothing to do with the taste—Rhode Island Reds lay brown eggs. Taking the organic feed one step further, various farmers give their chickens docosahexaenoic acid, an omega-3 fatty acid derived from marine algae. The ingested supplement transfers to the eggs. Because this compound contributes to cardiovascular health and because American diets are generally lacking in this substance, its addition boosts the nutritional content of the eggs.

Once thought of as an almost perfect source of food, eggs suffered a blow in the 1980s when the amount of cholesterol in eggs was implicated in the development of heart disease. By 1993 annual per capita consumption of eggs was 232, a drop from 321 in 1960, even though saturated fat was then seen as a bigger culprit in heart disease than cholesterol intake. In later years the disease-producing bacterium *Salmonella enteritidis*, found inside some eggs, prompted more caution. President Bill Clinton's solution—a call for in-shell pasteurization—was deemed too costly and aesthetically unacceptable, as it often clouds the whites. The egg industry stepped up controls to ensure good sanitation in all aspects of production. They also embarked on an education program that emphasizes refrigeration, cleanliness during preparation, and adequate cooking. Very few cases of salmonella infection are caused by eggs.

Eggs as Myths and Symbols

In addition to their use for food, eggs symbolize life and rebirth in Easter and Passover celebrations. In Catholicism's stricter past, eggs were forbidden during Lent, so people saved them to eat on Easter Sunday, sometimes incorporating them into rich breads. Often, these breads had hard-cooked eggs, which were sometimes dyed, nestled in the dough. These traditions are kept alive in America and are exemplified by various Easter sweet breads, like Greek *lambrópsomo*, Russian *kulich* and *choerek*, French *echauds aux œufs de Pâques*, and Italian *colomba* (also *colomba de Pasqua*), an Easter bread baked in the shape of a dove. In addition to eggs and butter, most of these special breads also contain fruits, nuts, and spices. A roasted egg is part of the Passover seder, celebrating rebirth and regrowth.

The Pennsylvania Dutch introduced the egg tree, a custom that had developed in France, Switzerland, and Germany. A few weeks before Easter, families decorated emptied shells with elaborate designs and hung them on trees or shrubs, either outside or in the house. The *Reading* [Pennsylvania] *Eagle* of April 1876 described such a tree set up by a druggist in his parlor; made of spruce boughs hung with decorated egg shells as well as paper ornaments, it resembled a Christmas tree, except for the prevalence of the eggs.

The Quintessential American Egg

American housewives prided themselves on their baking abilities; bake sales were (and still are) common fundraisers for church and school groups. The advent of agricultural fairs let women compete and win ribbons for the best cake, just as their husbands collected honors for livestock. The women knew that beating eggs, either whole or after separating the whites and yolks, produced loftier cakes. Beating causes a rearrangement of the albumin proteins in the whites, allowing them to trap air and increase dramatically in volume. This air expanded in the heat of the oven and allowed cakes and other baked goods to rise. Beating eggs with a spoon was slow going; whisks are better tools, which may account for the long beating times advised in early recipes. In addition, true baking powder, a combination of an acid and an alkali that produces bubbles of carbon dioxide when moistened, was not available until about 1850, so air beaten into batters was a typical, if labor intensive, means of achieving lightness.

Eliza Leslie gives a recipe for an omelet soufflé in her book, *Directions for Cookery*, first published in 1837. Eggs are the star in this recipe: they are beaten with sugar and orange flower water or lemon juice and then baked in a Dutch oven. As her suggested cooking time is only five minutes, she advised assembling and baking it at the last minute. For a foolproof omelet soufflé, she advocated hiring a French cook who could whip up the dessert while everyone else was at the table.

Recipes in early cookbooks often include a number of eggs that seems excessive when compared with modern recipes. The size of an egg that a hen lays is subject to various conditions—her breed, age (some hens do not lay large eggs until they are thirty-two weeks old), and feed. It was not until the development of chicken and egg as commodities that egg sizes became more uniform. Now practically all eggs on the market are large or extra large, which was not always the case. Miss Leslie advises that ten eggs in their shells generally weigh one pound: today's extra large eggs are considerably heavier, so the modern cook should approach old recipes with some caution, particularly those for baked goods, where the ratio of eggs to the other ingredients is more important for a good outcome. Exceptions are recipes based on weights, such as pound cakes, rather than number of eggs.

[*See also* Combat Food; Department of Agriculture, United States; Easter; Egg-Preparation Tools; Passover.]

BIBLIOGRAPHY

Bothwell, Don, and Patricia Bothwell. *Food in Antiquity*. New York: Praeger, 1969.

Jones, Evan. *American Food*. Woodstock, NY: Overlook Press, 1990. Covers the history of gastronomy of American food, with recipes.

Kiple, Kenneth F., and Kriemhild Coneè Ornelas. *The Cambridge World History of Food*. 2 vols. Cambridge, U.K.: Cambridge University Press, 2000. See the entry on "chicken eggs" in the first volume.

Lowry, Thea S. *Empty Shells: The Story of Petaluma, America's Chicken City*. Novato, CA: Manifold Press, 2000. A detailed history of chicken farming in Petaluma.

Lowry, Thea S. *Petaluma's Poultry Pioneers*. Novato, CA: Manifold Press, 1993.

McGee, Harold. *On Food and Cooking*. New York: Scribners, 1984.

Newall, Venetia. *An Egg at Easter*. London: Routledge and Kegan Paul, 1971. Extensive coverage of eggs as myths and symbols.

Pliny the Elder. *Natural History*. Loeb Classical Library. Cambridge, MA: Harvard University Press, 1979.

Root, Waverly, and Richard de Rochemont. *Eating in America*. Hopwell, NJ: Ecco Press, 1981.

Smith, Page, and Charles Daniel. *The Chicken Book*. Athens: University of Georgia Press, 2000. A book that evolved from a course given in 1972 at the University of California at Santa Cruz.

FRAN GAGE

Endive

Endives (*Cichorium endivia*) are foliage greens native to the Mediterranean (where they once grew wild). Cultivated first by the Egyptians, endives were later introduced to the United States from Europe, possibly by German or Dutch immigrants. There are two basic endive types. Curly leaf cultivars grow low to the ground and feature pretty, ruffled, prostrate leaves around a creamy yellow heart. Broadleaf cultivars grow larger and taller and have coarse, crumpled leaves with speared tips. Escarole is an example of a broadleaf endive. Among the few winter greens, endives are often used raw in salads, and many varieties may be cooked as side dishes. The coarse outer leaves of the broadleaf endives are generally used in soups or stews.

Endives are closely related to chicories (*C. intybus*)—a relationship made confusing by the fact that the English call the curly leaf endive "chicory" (the French call it *chicorée frisée*), while what is known as "Belgian endive" is actually a variety of chicory. Both endives and chicories have a strong, slightly bitter taste. To prevent them from bolting or becoming excessively bitter, the plants are blanched before harvest by covering their centers or by tying their leaves together to keep out the light.

Among the principal chicory types are heading, loose leaf, forced, and root. Some varieties of chicory—favored particularly in Italy—are grown for their roots, which are boiled and sliced. The coffee substitute known as chicory is made from dried, ground Magdeburg root chicory.

Through the late eighteenth century, endives tended to appear more often as a hobby of gentlemen farmers than as part of kitchen gardens or market crops. By the mid-nineteenth century, endives were commercially cultivated around urban areas for luxurious French restaurants and caterers. By the 1870s and 1880s recipes for endive salads begin to appear in American cookbooks. These vegetables still retain a slightly exotic mystique and, depending upon the variety, may be associated with Belgian, French, and especially Italian cuisines.

[*See also* Salads and Salad Dressings; Vegetables.]

BIBLIOGRAPHY

Bittman, Sam. *The Salad Lover's Garden*. New York: Doubleday, 1992.

Facciola, Stephen. *Cornucopia II: A Source Book of Edible Plants*. Vista, CA: Kampong Publications, 1998.

Hessayon, D. G. *The Vegetable and Herb Expert*. London: Expert Books, 1997.

Murrey, Thomas J. *Murrey's Salads and Sauces*. New York: Hewitt, 1884.

Rubatzky, Vincent E., and Mas Yamaguchi. *World Vegetables: Principles, Production, and Nutritive Values*. 2nd ed. New York: Chapman and Hall, 1997.

KAY RENTSCHLER

Ethnic Foods

Ethnicity and ethnic food in America predate Columbus but became more prominent as diverse European powers colonized what became the United States, often drawing on minorities and subject peoples to fill a need for labor. After the Revolutionary War, the United States increasingly became a nation of immigrants. The prevailing view has gone back and forth many times between accepting diversity in people and foods and requiring that individuals conform to a simplified national identity and a bland, nondiversified diet. The meaning of ethnicity and the nature of ethnic food in America have changed many times, but the overall direction has been toward increased acceptance of diversity and a wide menu across the United States.

Americans can claim identification with hundreds of ethnic groups and Native American nations, and can buy a multitude of ethnic foods in supermarkets and restaurants. Two categories of ethnic food can be distinguished: food that is cooked and served to express membership in one's own ethnic group, and food that is identified with an ethnic group different from one's own. The first category feeds a hunger for belonging, in particular the need for the minority identity to persist while the person joins in the wider American culture. The story of American ethnic food eaten among fellow group members—or served proudly to outsiders at a church supper or folk fair—is about the survival of group feelings. The second category feeds a hunger to know "the other," and reflects the pendulum swings of mainstream American culture and changing attitudes toward eating outside the home and toward foods and people that are "different." The rise of mass media and frequent American migrations have accelerated the processes by which ethnic foods change in America, how some become mainstream foods and how in-group foods continue to be transformed.

It is important to note that not all ethnic groups are immigrant groups. Some are Native American groups; some formed in North America from European or African or Asian groups; some arrived in North America as slaves; and some ethno-religious groups were founded in the United States or substantially changed there.

American food has always been affected by a relative surplus of resources and a relative shortage of labor. Immigrants to the United States almost always have adjusted to a new life in which foodstuffs are less expensive and kitchen time is shorter than what they knew elsewhere. Almost every group has increased its use of meat and intake of calories but also has limited complex traditional cooking and baking, perhaps to only Sunday or a few annual holidays. Most groups have selected dishes that are easily assembled or quickly cooked, especially one-pot casseroles and sandwiches, for more frequent use in the United State and sometimes for public sale. Ethnic foods are Americanized over time with increasing use of meat, sugar, baking powder, tomatoes, and potatoes. Such "modernization" of ethnic dishes is a global phenomenon, but has occurred especially rapidly in the United States.

Ethnic foods can be identified in the earliest American cookbooks. Cookbooks by and for ethnic minorities first appeared in the mid-nineteenth century. Multiethnic cookbooks for outsiders began to appear around the turn of the twentieth century and contained dishes from some forty ethnic groups.

Authenticity in Ethnic Cooking

Both foods associated with one's own ethnic group and foods associated with other ethnic groups can be described as "authentic," but the meaning of the term depends on a variety of contexts. If ethnic home cooking is understood as being about belonging, what is most authentic is what most promotes the feeling of belonging to the group, whether the food in question is culturally conservative or substantially Americanized and modernized. Outsiders who eat an ethnic food may consider authentic that which is most foreign to them, whether or not it is food that members of the ethnic group actually eat in the United States or that their ancestors ate on another continent. This collision of authenticities is perhaps most easily examined in regard to Native American foods. Many outsiders believe that the most authentic Indian foods are tribe-specific dishes that date from before contact with Europeans. Contemporary Indians, who often live and work outside Indian reservations, may well treasure opportunities to hunt and gather and cook wild foods in the way of their ancestors, but they may have stronger feelings about more recent family recipes with more Pan-Indian origins: corn and wild rice casseroles, fry bread, Ojibwa bread pudding, and Navajo mutton stew.

Ethnic home cooking may be viewed as "looking back," and ethnic restaurant cooking as "looking forward." Both expressions, however, fill a spectrum of cultural conservatism and innovation. A French restaurant may serve vichyssoise, invented at a New York hotel, or it may serve French regional dishes closer to contemporary home food in France than almost anything served in a French American home. A Norwegian American men's group may serve lutefisk (dried codfish rehydrated in lye water), an authentic Scandinavian winter dish that is no longer served in Norway, where fresh fish is flown in during the winter. At the same dinner, the women may gather to make *lefse*, a potato flatbread, using instant mashed potatoes—with no apparent loss of ethnic meaning.

Ethnic food served to mainstream American clients in restaurants has generally been pressed into Anglo-American meal patterns. Where the ethnic cuisine is relatively prestigious, as with French cuisine, restaurant food may be less Americanized than what the staff eats at home. Where the group has less status, as was the case with early Greek and Arab immigrants, there may be only a few ethnic dishes on a restaurant menu of American favorites. Or the menu may even be that of another ethnic group, as in Greek-owned pizzerias of the 1970s and 1980s, Afghan-owned "Cajun" chicken outlets in New York City in the 1990s, and Korean-owned sushi parlors in the early twenty-first century. At the extreme of both assimilation and nonassimilation, Chinese American restaurants invented entire menus of heavily Americanized food by the 1890s while offering a more authentic menu written in Chinese characters, sometimes posted on the wall as an apparent decoration, a practice that continues in urban Chinatowns.

The historic waves of discrimination and progress for ethnic groups of color and Native Americans have made for more complex and layered foodways. Ethnic groups of color have been often involved in the food industry as cooks, caterers, and restaurant workers and thus are more central than most other groups to the story of ethnic food served to outsiders, although they have been generally pressured to produce Anglo-American foods, with perhaps a bit of original seasoning. Members of British Isles groups whose ancestors spoke English may not regard themselves as ethnic but often do have certain dishes that are served and eaten to commemorate their common background.

Individual dishes pass in and out of ethnic use and may or may not lose ethnic meaning if they are accepted into mainstream diets. Some dishes pass from one ethnic group to another and may be dropped by the original group. Tea cakes were an Anglo-American symbol of gentility, especially in the antebellum southern states. After the Civil War, northerners began calling these treats "cookies," a Yankee term originally from Holland Dutch. Freed African American slaves, however, remembered tea cakes as a treat they might have sampled at Christmas. Especially after migration north, these cakes became a prestigious treat in African American homes. Thus tea cakes, or at least the name, passed out of mainstream Anglo-American use in the northern states but were added to the African American ethnic repertoire.

Although there is surprisingly little true fusion food, many American families have a multiethnic recipe list derived from multiple heritages, exchanges with neighbors, and selections from ethnic dishes encountered in restaurants.

Defining Ethnicity and Ethnic Food

An ethnic group is usually defined as a group that shares a common history and often a common national origin, culture, religion, and home language. Most recognizable American ethnic groups share three or more of these characteristics, but some ethno-religious groups with distinctive food may share only religion. For example, Moravians originally shared all the characteristics of an ethnic group in their homeland in what became the Czech Republic, but the religious wars of the seventeenth and eighteenth centuries reduced them to a small

Protestant sect in Germany. Most Moravians then came to the British colonies in North America and became part of the Pennsylvania Dutch ethnic group, but global missionary work has since broadened the ethnic base of the church to the point at which the largest group of Moravians lives in Tanzania. All Moravians, however, prepare love-feast buns and coffee as part of their religious services, and many continue to enjoy German American Moravian sugar cakes and Moravian cookies. Thus some Pennsylvania Moravians have a common history (generations of membership), national origin (Czech Moravia), culture (Pennsylvania Dutch), religion (Moravian Church), and home language (English and Pennsylvania dialect German), but some share only the religion and some of the foods.

The understanding of ethnicity in U.S. history has been skewed by American racial categories. White ethnic group membership can be casual or optional, as it often is among the descendants of European immigrants, especially those of mixed background. A Slovak American may eat a great deal of European-style food at home, only at Sunday dinner, only at Easter and Christmas, or not at all. In contrast, group membership can be seen as mandatory for people of color, and informed by a history of struggle. Some African Americans may choose not to eat stereotypical African American foods, such as fried chicken and watermelon (which was introduced to the United States from Africa), among outsiders.

Ethnic subgroups have tended to merge into larger categories throughout American history. German speakers in the British colonies came from many provincial and religious backgrounds but eventually developed a common Pennsylvania Dutch identity, cuisine, and even dialect distinguishing them from their countrymen in Germany, Austria, Alsace, and Switzerland. Immigrants to the United States from Germany and Italy in the nineteenth century often had never thought of themselves as Germans and Italians, because these countries were not unitary until the 1860s and 1870s. Within a few generations, the German American table included specialties from all regions, because this large group was organized by language rather than origin. The Italian American community retained regional dialects and foods at home, but restaurants were southern Italian (red sauce) or northern Italian (white sauce) by the 1960s. Soon after, pesto sauce from Bologna was being spread on pizza from Naples and sold as Italian food by families whose ancestors were from Sicily.

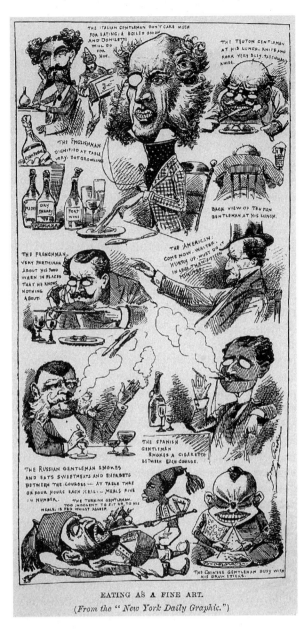

Ethnic Eating Habits. From George Augustus Sala, *America Revisited*, 3rd edition (London, 1883), vol. 1, p. 91. The cartoon originally appeared in the *New York Daily Graphic*.

Asian Indians, Indo-Caribbeans from Trinidad and Guyana, Pakistanis, Bangladeshis, and Sri Lankans all may be viewed by outsiders as Asian Indian Americans, but all may shop at the same ethnic groceries and offer similar menus in their restaurants. Igbo and Yoruba speakers who fought a bitter civil war in Nigeria in the late 1960s shop and eat together as Nigerian Americans in Houston, Texas, and Saint Louis, Missouri. The effect can be even stronger for groups who were national minorities elsewhere, such as Armenians, Basques, and Jews. Jewish Americans coming to New York from all over Eastern Europe combined Polish bagels, Romanian American pastrami, German American cream cheese, Baltic-style salt salmon, and Italian American salami into a Jewish delicatessen menu that mirrored their new and broader identity as Jewish Americans rather than Russian Jews, Polish Jews, German Jews, and so on. The enlargement of ethnic categories was partially voluntary but also was imposed by the larger society, most clearly in the cases of ethnic groups of color. Native tribes were deliberately resettled among former enemies. American slave owners worked to eradicate African culture (in contrast to more tolerance of African religious societies and culture in Cuba and Brazil).

Some ethnic groups have split in the United States, as when Jewish German Americans who had identified with German culture and food cut those ties during the Nazi period. And new ethnic groups have formed in North America, as early as the founding Pennsylvania Dutch and Acadians and as late as the Nation of Islam (Black Muslims) in the 1930s, which has unique dietary rules in addition to the traditional rules of Islam.

When ethnic choices have been available, they have been individual choices; however, there have been waves of ethnic revival and retreat. An ethnic revival in the 1980s was set off in part by the television series *Roots*. The U.S. Census ancestry survey, on which respondents volunteer up to two ancestries, showed large white ethnic groups expanding as much as 25 percent between 1980 and 1990. There was, however, a corresponding decrease in the 2000 survey. This trend reflected the ethnic revival of the 1980s and perhaps a swing back to generalized Americanism among native-born whites with the arrival of many new immigrants of color in the 1990s. In retrospect, many more ethnic recipes for home cooking were contributed to charity cookbooks published in the 1980s than in the 1990s.

Threats to Ethnicity

At many times in U.S. history, a melting pot ideology has reduced ethnic divisions by promoting a common culture, primarily Anglo-American culture. Anglo-Americans who accept this view therefore lose their sense of ethnic identity. A sizable minority of Americans do not consider themselves ethnic at all. Even the 1990 census ancestry survey resulted in the projection that almost 35 million persons would have refused to

respond or would have listed their ancestry as "American," "white," or "United States." Such people clearly do not subscribe to identity politics but may well enjoy Chinese or Mexican restaurants and prepare Italian dishes at home. Some foods are pointedly nonethnic, such as the vegetables in white sauce encouraged in cooking classes for immigrant girls at the turn of the twentieth century, and the gelatin salads of the cold war 1950s.

Increasing intermarriage and mobility change the nature of ethnic home cooking. Domestic partners may stick with the food they grew up with, take up some dishes from their spouse's side of the family, and even use their cooking skills to gain acceptance in a new ethnic group. Noncooking spouses may invade the kitchen for certain holiday specialties. The family may relocate—a feature of American life throughout U.S. history—to an area where different ethnic eating traditions are prominent. Thus, a Chicagoan may take up Hawaiian food or open the first Greek café in a town in Montana.

There have been periods of increased respect for diversity, including culinary diversity, as early as the Revolutionary War, when the Scotch-Irish and Pennsylvania Dutch minorities were communities relatively undivided by residual loyalties to Great Britain. The United States' centennial in 1876 and bicentennial in 1976 were both followed by national debates in which some Americanizers wanted to reform ethnic diets, whereas others were newly stimulated by the diversity in the kitchen and were curious to add regional and ethnic dishes to mainstream cookbooks.

Ethnic groups can disappear in the United States if the members assimilate into other ethnic groups or mainstream society. Assimilation seems to be the case with the Appalachian Melungeons, a mixed-race group that existed before the Revolutionary War. Melungeons fought to be registered as "white" under the racial segregation laws of southern states, migrated west to states with looser racial laws (especially about marriage), increasingly denied that they were Melungeon (which probably comes from the French word *mélange,* meaning "mixed"), and effectively vanished as racial segregation laws ended in the 1960s. In the early twenty-first century, Melungeons are people with Melungeon ancestors. They have organized conventions, scholarly studies, and Internet mailing lists to re-create the ethnic group. A Melungeon cookbook of remembered dishes includes obscure Appalachian dishes such as chocolate gravy, which may be considered ethnic dishes if Melungeons are revived as an ethnic group.

Ethnic Groupings in the United States

Ethnic membership is sometimes voluntary, and many people acknowledge multiple heritages. At many times in American history, people have denied their ethnicity or kept it secret. The U.S. Census has repeatedly changed categories and as a matter of law has not been allowed to record religious affiliation. For much of American history, African Americans were those with one great-grandparent of African descent. Full-blooded Native Americans were sometimes excluded from counts on the basis of tribal enrollment. Subethnic divisions were ignored among African Americans and emphasized among Native Americans.

The 2000 U.S. Census ancestry survey had almost six hundred ancestry codes, not counting those for the fifty states. Many codes overlapped, such as Mexican, Mexican American, Mexicano, Chicano, La Raza, Mexican American Indian, and Mexican State. The census does a separate estimate of approximately two hundred Native American groupings. As with ethno-religious groups, the 2000 census ignores multiracial groups, such as the Appalachian Melungeons, although the 1970 census enumerated two hundred such "tri-racial isolates," some of which are listed as Native American tribes in the 2000 census.

Three ethnic encyclopedias describe between two hundred and four hundred American ethnic groups and Indian nations, and the most extensive cookbook contains recipes for 122 groups. Because very small ethnic groups are increasingly aware of the importance of recipes to the preservation of identity, and because the Internet has become useful to dispersed memberships, it is likely possible to collect at least a few characteristic recipes for as many as two hundred to three hundred American ethnic groups. Several regional multiethnic cookbooks since the 1970s have forty to fifty groups represented.

Although foreign foods are more likely to follow nation of origin than sociological definitions of ethnicity, there are probably more than 191 cuisines (the number of countries represented in the United Nations) in American restaurants. What America may lack in lunch-eonettes specifically dedicated to the food of Iceland or Bhutan, for example, is made up in cuisines of peoples who have no national government, such as Basque restaurants in Idaho and Nevada, Native American restaurants in Florida, Arizona, and Rhode Island; Jewish delicatessens in New York; and regional specialties from multiethnic countries such as India, Mexico, and Italy.

Because of the popularity of Anglo-American foodways at Thanksgiving and other national observances, many people of Anglo-American extraction do not see themselves as eating ethnic food, although they may experience certain feelings about roast beef and Yorkshire pudding, Christmas fruitcake, and steak and kidney pie. This trait is less true of ethnic groups recognized as such in the British Isles, such as Welsh, Scottish, Manx, and Cornish Americans. It may be even truer for founding-stock groups such as the Scotch-Irish, who had migrated from Scotland to Northern Ireland in the early seventeenth century before removing to the backcountry of colonial America. Although some potato dishes, distilled liquors, sweets, and shortbreads survive among them, Scotch-Irish descendants may identify more with the wild foods and old-fashioned farm products of their Appalachian history than with their origins in present-day Scotland and Northern Ireland.

Food as Ethnic Symbol

Ethnic identification of food and people requires a combination of external pressure and internal solidarity, although no simple rule describes the persistence of either cuisines or peoples. "Authenticity" is used as a measure of foods both cooked for the group and partaken of by others, but perhaps it is more useful to describe dishes on a spectrum from culturally conservative to innovative or Americanized. One might view ethnic home cooking as naturally conservative and ethnic dining out as intrinsically innovative, but both experiences can be plotted on a full spectrum between conservatism and innovation. Some ethnic food that is authentic in terms of the intensity of group feeling and the degree of recognition provoked in outsiders can be foods that have changed extensively but remained powerful symbols for the group.

An example of a food that has become a symbol is Native American fry bread, which is made entirely of nonnative ingredients and is cooked in a postcontact iron pan. Fry bread may have its origins in the trade goods of French mountain men, in the sopaipillas of Spanish colonists in New Mexico, or in the preparation made by confined Navajos and Sioux in the nineteenth century from the subsistence allotments of low-protein flour and lard distributed by the U.S. government. Despite this possible history as the bread of affliction, fry bread spread to every native tribe through the Pan-Indian movement in the early twentieth century and early inter-tribal powwows. Tribes whose members were never confined to reservations, tribes whose traditional diet had no grains at all, tribes who were traditional enemies of the Navajo or the Sioux all consider fry bread the universal Native American dish. For them this dish may commemorate the turning point at which Native Americans began to revive their ethnicity on a Pan-Indian basis, or it may simply be a powwow treat from the past. Fry bread has become so identified with the Native American cause that it is a more compelling symbol of Indian identity than are uniquely Indian wild foods and game dishes and the revived dishes of individual tribes.

American ethnic food can include dishes that would be completely alien to past generations. Groups of Belgian American Walloons settled around Green Bay, Wisconsin, in the 1850s, bringing with them a dish of clear bouillon served with rice. The hen that had been boiled to obtain the bouillon made another meal the next day. Sometime in the 1930s, men took over the dish and turned it into a thick soup full of boned chicken meat and vegetables and often served with saltines at the annual Belgian American kermis harvest festival. The pots became larger, the men used a canoe paddle to stir the soup, and "booyah" became the name of an event as well as the central dish. Booyah is served at church fund-raisers, at a midsummer ethnic festival for visitors, and on Green Bay Packer football weekends. Secret recipes and booyah kings have been added to make booyah a male-bonding ritual like that surrounding barbecue, chili con carne, burgoo, and Brunswick stew—the latter two soup-stews being highly similar to booyah. It is possible that booyah has features of other Belgian soups, such as *hochepot*. It often happens that American ethnic dishes begin to accumulate features of several old-country dishes. It also may be that booyah is not descended from Belgian bouillon at all. Around Saint Cloud, Minnesota, Polish Americans believe that "bouja" is an old Polish soup, and men make it much as Belgian Americans do in Door County, Wisconsin, but flavored with pickling spices. The first recipe published, in 1940, describes "boolyaw" as a French Canadian dish from the hunting camps of Michigan. A more recent Wisconsin cookbook called it an old German recipe. The dish has gone from a thin soup made by women at home to a thick stew made by men for communal events. An Italian American might mistake booyah for minestrone, yet Belgian Americans in Wisconsin believe it is named for Godfrey of Bouillon, a leader of the First Crusade. The fruit tarts served for dessert at booyah feasts are made by women much as they were in Belgium in the early nineteenth century.

Ethnic restaurant food is not exactly like ethnic home cooking, but it can be as conservative as old-country dishes. Among third-generation Americans and later immigrant groups, ethnic restaurants are often a reserve of ethnic dishes that are no longer made at home, usually because they require too much labor. Ethnic restaurants provide more established immigrant groups a place in which to celebrate life-cycle events with ethnic feasts. In addition, seasonal and festival dishes modified to suit American meal patterns in public restaurants may come to signify group identity (more than their original seasonal meaning) at a later date. Thus a dish such as spaghetti and meatballs, featuring two items that were not combined on traditional, multiple-course, Italian festive tables, in Italian American restaurants suited the general American dinner pattern of starch, protein, and vegetables all on one plate (or including a side-dish salad) as well as the more rapid pace of American dining. But among third- and later-generation Italian Americans, spaghetti and meatballs can be a symbol of group membership and may be served at home as such.

Ethnic foods can enter mainstream American use and lose their original ethnic meaning. They also can move from group to group. Macaroni and cheese was introduced to the United States as French food by refugees from the French Revolution and became a mainstream dish in the southern states. The dish became creamier and richer and lost the French identification. Because they ate their macaroni less cooked and with less cheese (fettuccini Alfredo was invented in a Roman restaurant in the 1920s), Italian immigrants did not understand American macaroni and cheese as Italian food. If macaroni and cheese has any ethnic identification it would be as African American soul food. African Americans brought peanut soup recipes from Africa and eventually served simplified and enriched versions to early American planters. Peanut soup did not remain popular in the African American community, despite the efforts of George Washington Carver. Most twentieth-century recipes are in Anglo-American commemorative cookbooks, a suggestion that peanut soup signifies George

Washington and his guests more than it does the original cooks.

The succotash eaten at Thanksgiving is made from sweet corn and lima beans, which were alien foods to Pilgrims and seventeenth-century Native North Americans. The winter succotash eaten in Plymouth well into the nineteenth century was made from lye hominy and shell beans, usually with preserved meat. It was listed on the menu of the 1769 Forefathers Day dinner of the Old Colony Club in Plymouth, Massachusetts. At that dinner, Anglo-American men went to a local inn and dined on a number of Native American dishes that were, for them, symbols of their English forefathers and what the settlers had eaten in the early years of the Plymouth colony. On the symbolic level, the diners were expressing Anglo-American ethnicity by eating non-British foods, perhaps even symbolically consuming the Indians' food as they had taken over their village and cornfields.

Generations of immigrants have embraced Thanksgiving as a celebration of American abundance but have also yielded to it the additional symbolism of Anglo-American unity and displacement of the native peoples. Meanwhile, contemporary Native American cookbooks include recipes for succotash of the lima bean–sweet corn type. Thus succotash has become a mainstream food understood as an ethnic dish by some cooks and diners, as it was when Cherokee farm families made it with newly introduced lima beans in the eighteenth century.

The bagel can be considered the fry bread of Jewish Americans. Originally baked in Poland, though perhaps inspired by medieval soft pretzels from southern Germany, the bagel became the handy snack of millions of Jewish American immigrants around New York City, regardless of national origin. The bagel was a small, hand-rolled, boiled, rather tough breakfast roll. On Saturdays it may have been served spread with cream cheese and cheap salt salmon. Almost as soon as the bagel became universally Jewish American, such that it figured in many ethnic jokes, it began a long process of becoming larger and softer, easier to eat, and more like American bread. It also accumulated toppings from other Jewish baked goods, such as poppy seeds, sesame seeds, and onions. Bagels became popular outside the ethnic community, although not immediately outside the Northeast. As the Jewish American community advanced, salmon was used more frequently, sometimes as part of Sunday brunch, and the quality of the fish improved. The second wave of flavors compressed even more ethnic content into a single product: garlic, cheese, and the "everything" bagel, covered with many kinds of seeds. In the last thirty years of the twentieth century, the larger, softer bagels began to be made in nontraditional flavors, such as rye, raisin, garlic, and dill and then in postethnic flavors such as blueberry, honey-wheat, jalapeño, and sun-dried tomato. For St. Patrick's Day one can find green bagels. The question arises whether blueberry bagels are a "Jewish food." Some Jewish Americans of middle age complain about large, soft bagels, prefacing a possible revival of "real" bagels. Although bagels may become more closely associated with Jewish identity than matzo balls and chopped liver, it is likely that bagels, like pizza, spaghetti, hot dogs, and quesadillas, will lose their ethnic association and become a symbol of American prosperity. In 2002, the Bruegger's Bagel's chain introduced the Big Bagel Sandwich, described in the company's promotional literature as featuring "more ingredients on a BIGGER & SOFTER sandwich bagel." The accompanying picture shows turkey, lettuce, and tomato peeking out from the edges of a square bun with a small hole at the center and sesame seeds on top.

Evolution of Ethnic Foods

Ethnic food changes as the meaning of a group's ethnicity changes, not only for immigrant generations but also among groups that have been in America for millennia or that formed in the United States. Some Pueblo Indian tribes have lived in the same place for one thousand years but have altered their cuisine as their culture has changed. *Bizcochitos* (cookies) and fry bread are as much Indian food among Pueblo Indians as the most ancient corn and bean cuisine. New ethno-religious groups such as the Mormons and the Black Muslims were founded with dietary regulations that led to distinctive dishes (honey-wheat bread and bean pie, respectively) within a generation.

Restaurant ethnic food also undergoes changes. Crème vichyssoise glacée was invented at the New York Ritz-Carlton Hotel by the French chef Louis Diat, and the recipe was published in 1941. This soup was on the menu of every "authentic" French restaurant in the United States by the late 1950s and had virtually disappeared by the 1980s. Nachos were invented for a party of Anglo-American visitors by Ignacio "Nacho" Anaya in a Mexican border town in the 1940s. This dish consisted of neat canapés of tortilla chips, cheese, and jalapeño peppers. Nachos made their way onto every "authentic" Mexican restaurant menu in America by the 1960s, but by 1990, the appetizer had become unrecognizable from its original incarnation, with added ingredients such as refried beans, sour cream, onions, salsa, black beans, and kernels of corn piled on the chips in a messy heap. By 2000, "nacho" had become an adjective for the flavor of Mexican spices, as in nacho cheese and nacho popcorn. Because they were never Mexican American home food, nachos are unlikely to be revived in their original or "authentic" form, but they may take on new flavors and a new ethnic life in the future.

Hot tamales were a popular southern street snack of the late nineteenth and early twentieth centuries. These tamales were "hot" because the larded cornmeal of which they were made held the heat of steaming; they were seldom spicy. Tamales were sold by African American youths. Genuine tamales are one of the most revered ethnic foods of Mexican American and Central American immigrants. Groups of women make them in large quantities months ahead of Christmas, the Day of the Dead, and other events. But those tamales have yet to enter the American mainstream. Southern hot tamales have been replaced by sweeter, mass-produced snacks. Native American leaf breads, one of the universal treats in a corn cuisine, are remembered within native communities but are not part of the daily diet. These breads were noted by early English explorers of the East Coast and continue to be made as Cherokee broadswords, Navajo kneeldown bread, and other dishes.

Tamale pie is one of a group of American foods invented outside the ethnic communities that they refer to. It is a plausible combination of Mexican American flavors, but tamales-as-casserole is not understood by insiders as a Mexican American food. One such dish, Chinese chicken salad, has achieved some popularity in Chinese American homes, which are generally conservative with respect to traditional ethnic foods. Other foods of this type include ethnic-named foods that may or may not be used at home by ethnic Americans—such as Irish stew, Indian pudding, London broil, and Welsh rabbit—and some foods that are almost never in-group signifiers, such as french fries, tamale pie, caesar salad, American chop suey, chop suey sandwiches (eaten in southeastern Massachusetts), and egg foo yong sandwiches (eaten in Saint Louis).

Char siu bao (fluffy steamed bun with pork filling) served in a New York Chinese restaurant is an ethnic dish that can serve as an expression of group membership. It is authentic Cantonese food. Even when served in a Chinese American home or as part of a family or religious celebration, the message is not, "We eat these because we are Chinese Americans" but rather, "We eat these because we are Chinese." The same bun called *manapua* in Hawaii is still not an American ethnic dish, because it is regarded as local food rather than specifically Chinese Hawaiian or native Hawaiian. But when a Vietnamese family changes the filling to pork, egg, and bean-thread noodle and calls it "Vietnamese *manapua*," the dish becomes an American ethnic recipe that reinforces membership in the group. It is specific to the group, even though it is not authentic with respect to Chinese or Vietnamese cuisine.

Patterns of Americanization

Ethnicity in the United States has historically been problematic and remains controversial. At the turn of the twenty-first century there is no public agreement about immigration policy or how immigrants can best learn English. There is no general agreement on the role of ethnic food, delicious as it may be, in American culture, nor is there an accepted academic theory about how it evolves. Some phenomena, however, seem to repeat themselves over the centuries and across ethnic groups. The patterns in ethnic cuisine were first described in the so-called new immigration period of 1880–1924 but generally correspond to what is known about earlier immigrants, and can be observed—with help from the news media—among later immigrant groups. The apparent exceptions to these patterns are ethnic groups of color whose intermittent segregation and progress have produced either cultural conservatism (Chinese and Japanese Americans) or complex layers of meaningful foods (African Americans, Native Americans, and Mexican Americans).

Ethnic dishes in America are screened for adaptability to American lifestyles and are modified in parallel with mainstream American cooking developments. Dishes are selected for short and simple preparation in a country that has always been resource rich and labor poor. Dishes must be easy to eat and tend to become softer and whiter to conform to Anglo-American ideals. Ethnic flavors are combined into one-pot dishes, and dishes seem to accumulate flavors from several recipes as if to get the entire ethnic table and all four seasons onto one plate. Labor-saving machines are used. Baking powder is substituted for yeast because it is quicker and

Ethnic Melting Pot. "Uncle Sam's Thanksgiving Dinner," *Harper's Weekly*, November 20, 1869.

easier to use. The amount of meat, especially beef, is increased. Corn, chilies, beans, and squash are added or substituted. Tomatoes (and canned tomatoes) are increased in amount or substituted for other acidic ingredients, such as vinegar, lemons, and yogurt. Potatoes are used increasingly. Canned, frozen, premixed, and otherwise prepared foods are substituted for ingredients that are used in recipes made from scratch (for example, frozen, ready-made phyllo dough in baklava and strudel).

Ethnic dishes are subject to a process described by William and Yvonne Lockwood (describing the Cornish pasty of Upper Michigan) as

> diversification to standardization and, finally, to rediversification. In Cornwall as in U.P. [Upper Peninsula of Michigan], at the turn of the [twenty-first] century, it has many possible ingredients: rice and leeks, eggs and bacon, beef and potatoes, lamb and parsley, venison, fish, apple, and so on . . . The U.P. pasty became a standardization of but one of these forms. The range of variations narrowed to a basic mixture of meat, potatoes, onion, rutabagas and/or carrots . . . commercial competition has been very instrumental in this movement toward rediversification. Both health food stores and a few standard pasty shops have begun to offer a vegetarian version, often with whole wheat crust . . . in some restaurants pasty can be ordered with

cheese, bacon, or chili topping. Some pizza parlors offer "pizza pasty"—pasty ingredients enfolded by pizza dough, much like the Italian calzone.

The pasty was brought to the Upper Peninsula of Michigan by Cornish miners. Cornish cooks made many kinds of filling for pasties in England but narrowed them down to a single classic version. Later immigrants who worked in the mines adopted the Cornish pasty, which also became a regional food sold in bakeries and restaurants. As a result, the pasty developed many new fillings, much as bagels now come in numerous flavors. This process can be traced to earlier immigrant foods, such as Irish soda bread. In Ireland, soda bread is also made with a whole-wheat-flour recipe that was changed in the United States to concentrate on the sweeter form with raisins. Soda bread has not yet rediversified, however.

Later immigrants narrowed their cuisines and the diversity of particular dishes in the United States. A considerable regional variety of Korean kimchi has been narrowed to a few market brands as upwardly mobile Korean Americans have stopped making kimchi at home. Stuffed maize breads from Latin American, such as Colombian and Venezuelan *arepa* and Salvadoran *pupusa*, have been simplified to serve as American snacks and street foods. If any of these breads catches on, the form may become as diverse as Italian sandwiches or sushi. Sushi has come to incorporate smoked salmon and cream cheese, fried seafood, and unusual sauces while it continues to be understood as Japanese food.

Ethnic home cooking in America has adjusted to Anglo-American norms by substituting beef for pork, lamb, and other meats. It has adjusted to American prosperity by utilizing more meat. As noted, meatballs and spaghetti were separate courses in Italy; in the United States, the meatballs became all-beef, increased in size, and were consumed earlier in the meal as it was no longer necessary to fill up on pasta before partaking of a meager supply of meat. Even in the large Armenian American community around Watertown, Massachusetts, beef was substituted for the traditional lamb in *kofta*. French Canadian Americans substitute part or all beef in their Christmas Eve porkpies, as do Louisiana Cajuns, whose families may have been in Louisiana since the 1750s.

Immigrant Cuisines over Three Generations

The overall menu of an ethnic group goes through a three-generation process. The early arrivals, especially if they are working men who expect to return to their homelands, often eat almost entirely "American food," obtaining ethnic specialties only in packages from home and for special occasions. Attempts to cook for themselves produce traditional foreign foods with simple substitutions for ingredients that are not in American markets. Thus early Chinese immigrants substituted iceberg lettuce for bean sprouts. Ethiopian immigrants used buckwheat or a mixture of wheat and rye flour to make flatbread until they could obtain the African millet traditionally used (later grown in the Rocky Mountain states). This pattern was less pronounced for immigrant groups who arrived in families, such as Irish Americans, who quickly located potatoes, leeks, cabbage, and oatmeal but had to substitute corned beef for spiced beef and German American sausages for their own.

As import networks arise and wages accumulate, there is a reversion to authentic foreign food. However, the original meal patterns and repertoire are adapted to fit American lifestyles: Ethnic cuisine dishes that are quickly cooked (such as chicken cacciatore and Polish hunter's stew, or *bigos*) fit better into American weeknights. Foods that are easily transported to work sites and eaten out of hand, such as Italian panini and Cornish pasties, are likely to become more prominent in America. Elaborate dishes that take a long time to prepare are reserved for special occasions, or they may shift in usage,

as making lutefisk became a communal activity for Norwegian American men.

As a new American-born generation begins leaving home—an American family pattern that might not have been the norm in the old country—weekday cooking in ethnic homes becomes more Americanized. The old dishes become concentrated in weekly, often Sunday, dinners hosted by parents or grandparents. Although the dinner is a chance to work on the old dishes and transmit them, it also evolves its own favorites, including annual festival dishes, usually meat dishes, which can be weekly events in America. Because the first generation presides at weekend dinners, generational tensions are played out or reconciled at the table with the inclusion or exclusion of American dishes, adjustments to time spent at table, and participation or lack of participation in cooking. Outgroup daughters- and sons-in-law may or may not be trained as assistants or be permitted to contribute something of their own.

The third generation generally loses bilingualism but often seeks to revive ethnic cuisine. However, the cuisine revived by members of this generation may be broadened by the inclusion of other family members or simply by progress in food styles. What is revived in the third generation is often not the same ethnic group as the one rejected by the second generation. Southern Italians who immigrated to America in 1910 might have had grandchildren who in the 1960s made northern Italian food using a cookbook. The ethnic revival of the 1980s was led by the grandchildren of immigrants, as was some of the German American food revival of the period before World War I. Later immigrants (groups entering since the late 1960s) are in the first and second generations, speaking, for example, Korean on cell phones but unaccented English at school and frequenting both Korean and Pan-Asian restaurants.

Mainstreaming of Ethnic Dishes

Since the middle of the nineteenth century, immigrants have made substitutions with American commercialized foods, such as canned tomatoes for other acidic ingredients, baking powder in yeast breads, chilies for black pepper, potatoes for other starches, and cornmeal in some baked products. Groups often select a single dish that becomes emblematic of the ethnic group for outsiders. For Irish Americans, it is raisin soda bread. For Lithuanians, who have an elaborate cuisine but first came to the United States as male migrant laborers, it is

Knishes and Pizza. Ethnic fast food on Coney Island Ave. in Brooklyn, New York. *Photograph by Joe Zarba*

kugelis, a casserole of potatoes, onions, and bacon. Swedish meatballs, Jewish matzo balls, French Canadian pea soup, and Pennsylvania Dutch shoofly pie are intercultural shorthand for three ethnic cuisines.

For Armenian American members of Saint Vartan's Church in Oakland, California, the key to the annual church bazaar is *kofta,* a complicated dish of seasoned ground lamb stuffed into a shell of ground lamb and bulgur wheat. *Kofta* is a good signifier because it is too complicated to make often, can be made and frozen in advance, can be purchased frozen to take home for later private use, and requires the cooperation of many cooks. These characteristics make the dish a promoter of cultural continuity.

An ethnic home dish persists and crosses over to mainstream tables if it is suited to the American lifestyle by being easily and quickly eaten; if it carries cultural cachet (for example, Viennese pastry, French cuisine, and sushi in the 1980s and 1990s), if it can be prepared easily from storable ingredients (for example, pasta), and if it has wide flavor appeal (for example, pesto and cinnamon buns). To become a restaurant dish, the following additional conditions apply: The ethnic group has a community credit system for fostering small restaurants; the dish fits into Anglo-American meal plans and preferences for separate meat, starch, and vegetables (as does

the elaborate Irish breakfast or kebabs with rice and vegetables); the dish can be rapidly assembled or reheated from prepared components (pizza, for example); or the ingredients have the qualities of being expensive and exotic. Sushi, which has long been popular in Hawaii, where there are native traditions of raw fish dishes, was suddenly popular in the affluent 1980s and 1990s across the rest of America, in part because Japanese business success attached prestige to all things Japanese.

In communities that value diversity, it is possible for ethnic dishes to cross into regional mainstream use without modification. For example, according to Eleanor Ostman, the food editor of the *St. Paul Pioneer Press,* "It wouldn't be a wedding on the Iron Range without sarma (Croatian cabbage rolls), pasties (Cornish meat pies), porchetta (Italian pork roast), or pulla (Finish cardamom bread). We all grew up with them, no matter our ethnic heritage, because if our families didn't make them, our friends did" (quoted in Dooley and Watson).

In some cases, ethnic foods are in such general use that they are no longer meaningful to the original ethnic group. This case is increasingly true of bagels, pizza, spaghetti, tacos, kielbasa, and Cornish pasties. In a few cases, the original ethnic group has stopped eating these foods, either to reject stereotypes or because the original foods have been modified beyond recognition.

American Ethnic Food before Immigration

North America had ethnic foods of both categories long before Columbus. Native American tribes were differentiated and sometimes named by their foodways and met in trading networks to sample foreign foods. Plains Indians traded dried buffalo meat, skins, and fat for corn and beans at the pueblos or for wild rice in the Midwest. Pacific coastal Indians traded dried salmon for the acorns and berries of the interior tribes. Smoked fish and perhaps salt were traded up the Cherokee trail for venison. Christopher Columbus exchanged dinners with the Hispaniola Taino chief Guacanagari over Christmas in 1492. Columbus's log of his first American dinner is lost, but Guacanagari's review of Spanish shipboard food was eventually retrieved by Father Ramon Pané: "It is like human food. It is large and white, and it is not heavy. It is something like straw, but with the taste of a cornstalk, of the pith of a cornstalk. It is a little sweet, as if it were flavored with honey; it tastes of honey, it is a sweet-tasting food." Because Guacanagari's home food was a crispy cassava flatbread, it is speculation whether the cook on the *Nina* had devised wheat-flour bread, cake, or a hardtack pudding. New Yorkers in the twenty-first century who want to experience what Columbus experienced can pick up a package of cassava bread at any bodega catering to immigrants from the Dominican Republic.

Within a few decades of Columbus, hundreds of European fishing and whaling expeditions were heading for North America. Some of the ships may have come ashore in New England, trading metal pots and knives for furs and probably swapping foodstuffs as well. What became the United States was colonized by France, the Netherlands, Spain, and Sweden, as well as Great Britain, and most of the colonies had ethnic minorities within them. New Netherland had substantial Scandinavian and German minorities as well as some Portuguese and Spanish Jews. One of the largest ethnic settlements in colonial America was comprised of almost one thousand Catalan-speaking Minorcans, along with Italians, Greeks, and Turks, brought to British Florida in 1768. Descendants of this group in Saint Augustine retain Easter pastries and *pilau* and have acquired a taste for *datil* chilies, a variety of Caribbean hot pepper naturalized in Florida.

European colonists usually arrived with a supply of European food, such as wheat flour and ale, but when these supplies ran out, the settlers had to eat Native American food. Once colonies were more established, colonists maintained a clear distinction between Indian food and their own. Roger Williams wrote in 1644 about the ethnic differences in a food familiar to colonists as hasty pudding and to Indians as *nasaump*: "From this the English call their samp . . . and eaten hot or cold with milk or butter, which are mercies beyond the natives' plain water, and which is a dish exceedingly wholesome for English bodies." Thirty years later, John Josselyn knew of an Indian who kept a cow in Maine, so perhaps Anglo-American cooking and Native American cooking were already converging. The settlers, slaves, and Indians who later made up the founding stock of the United States began changing their traditional foods by the seventeenth century, and many of their first changes lasted. As colonies became more established, they were able to establish trade networks and restore to the table traditional European foods. This pattern of reversion continued with later immigrants, who might eat mostly "American food" for a few months until they are able to obtain proper Ethiopian bread or Nigerian cowpeas, for example. Among the poorer settlers and the nearest Indians and the African slaves doing kitchen work, local foodstuffs were being changed and exchanged.

By the time of the Revolutionary War, the British colonies were approximately 10 percent Scottish and Scotch-Irish and 8 to 10 percent German. Holland Dutch foodways remained in New York and parts of New Jersey, and there were smaller settlements of Austrians in Georgia, Moravians in North Carolina, Sephardic Jews and French Huguenots in South Carolina and New York, and scattered families from all over Europe and even the Middle East. The Pennsylvania Germans were already known for their dairy products and produce, and the Scotch-Irish had introduced the white potato to many areas and were beginning to develop American distilled spirits from rye and corn. The new nation quickly acquired former colonists of France and Spain, refugees from the Acadian diaspora and from the French and Haitian revolutions, and immigrants from the Caribbean.

Creole food of New Orleans, Louisiana, is poorly documented before the 1840s, but by the twentieth century its qualities were well known. Cajun food, with its Africanized use of hot spices and dark roux, may not have developed its characteristic palate until well after the Civil War. The food of the Acadians who remained in Canada is nothing like the Cajun food that became popular in the late twentieth century. Refugees from the French Revolution introduced pasta and French soups to

American food, and Haitian refugees are credited with peanut brittle and possibly the Philadelphia version of pepper pot.

The Irish immigrants of the 1840s were refugees from a famine and are thought to have arrived with little cuisine. However, the 1840s also were the period when the milk and potatoes typical of Irish soups began to thicken American chowders. Potato-crop failures also brought immigrants from across northern Europe, and the culinary contributions of the urban German Americans and Scandinavian pioneers are more widely documented. A significant immigrant group of the 1850s, Chinese Americans, was initially not known for its cooking. The men who came to pan gold and stayed to build the railroads were not skilled chefs or epicures, but they did create an import network for Chinese foodstuffs, soon were engaging in fishing and farming, and were pressed into service as cooks. Much culinary diversity in the early American period was acquired by the forcible relocation of Native Americans west of the Mississippi and the annexation of former Spanish colonies in the Mexican War of 1845. As with Chinese immigration, the annexation of Texas and the western territories was not initially seen as the culinary boon it was to become, although soldiers did get a taste of the spicy border cuisine later regarded as Mexican food.

Ethnic Foods in Early American Cookbooks

Ethnic groups brought cookbooks in various languages to the American colonies and began publishing foreign-language cookbooks early in the history of the United States. British cookbooks and manuscripts of the colonial period contained many dishes that were understood as "foreign" but were moving into the British mainstream, such as Irish stew, chutney, ketchup, soy sauce, the occasional curry, *caveached* fish (Iberian or West Indian), and many French recipes.

The first cookbook written by an American, *American Cookery* by Amelia Simmons, was substantially taken from British sources but contained a group of recipes that emphasized American ingredients such as Indian corn and cranberries. The cookbook also used the Dutch American culinary terms "cookie" and "slaw," suggesting that Simmons was influenced by the Dutch American minority, perhaps in upstate New York, where the second edition was published. By 1839, *The Kentucky Housewife,* by Lettice Bryan, had incorporated a Pennsylvania Dutch noodle recipe along with recipes

from France and elsewhere. Around the same time, German-language almanacs and a few cookbooks were being printed in the United States for that community. Catharine Esther Beecher's *Domestic-Receipt Book* added the recipe Bridget's Bread Cake, a recognizable variant of Irish soda bread, in the 1850s. African American recipes had been appearing uncredited in southern cookbooks such as *The Virginia House-wife* (1824) by Mary Randolph, and most apparently in *The Carolina Housewife* (1847). The latter contained recipes for an almost completely African peanut soup and sesame soup and for many uses of okra. It also contained the first Jewish recipe in a general American cookbook, Queen Esther's bread, a version of french toast served for Purim. The 1851 revision of *The Carolina Housewife* added Caribbean pepper pot, New Orleans gumbo, an Indian dish called *sofky* (probably the first explicitly Native American dish in a general cookbook), and another fried dough recipe that probably came from the Jewish community of Charleston.

In 1848, Tunis G. Campbell published the second book of recipes by an African American directed at other African Americans. This book was the first to include cornbread and a dish of stewed gizzards that might later be recognized as soul food. Eliza Leslie, the dean of antebellum cooking authors, was the first white author to state openly, at the beginning of *New Receipts for Cooking* (1854), "A large number [of recipes] have been obtained from the South, and from ladies noted for their skill in housewifery. Many were dictated by colored cooks of high reputation in the art, for which nature seems to have gifted that race with a peculiar capability." A number of Leslie's Philadelphia recipes may have been influenced by that city's popular and successful black caterers. *Home Cookery,* published in Boston and New York in 1853 and compiled by Mrs. J. Chadwick, contained an early reference to browned Cajun or Creole roux in Gumbo Soup— A Foreign Receipt, as well as genuinely foreign recipes from Brazil, Norway, and Denmark and recipes from the more familiar England, France, and Germany. These and other early American cookbooks contained recipes from English and French publications. Some continental recipes appeared in American print along with British Empire dishes from as far away as Malaysia and India. French restaurants, many with Italian-born chefs, were increasingly popular in large cities.

The period from the Civil War through the 1876 centennial marked a period of change in which Americans of all backgrounds were more open to ethnic diversity in food. For wealthy white southerners, the naval blockade during the war had reduced their access to imported delicacies and forced them to eat more of the locally grown food that their slaves were eating. The reputation of African American cooks and their food developed in this period, during which the mistresses of great houses had to rely on what their slave cooks could do with sweet potatoes, cowpeas, okra, and corn cakes. Interest in the food of non-Anglo Americans was represented by *Jennie June's American Cookery Book* (1866) by Mrs. J. C. Croly, an English immigrant. Croly included many French, German, and English recipes and an entire section of twenty-two "Jewish receipts." A few more Jewish recipes, including Matzoh Balls for Soup, appeared in 1873 in *The New Cyclopaedia of Domestic Economy, and Practical Housekeeper* by Mrs. E. F. Ellet. *The National Cook Book,* published in 1875 for the centennial exposition, included "seven receipts from an Oneida squaw," tropical and Spanish recipes from Florida, and a large selection of Jewish recipes.

Ethnicity and American Foodways

The massive immigration of 1880–1924 brought an entirely new level of diversity to American kitchens, along with renewed efforts at "Americanization through homemaking," to borrow the title of a 1929 pamphlet aimed at Mexican American students in California. In addition, the United States continued to add ethnic foods by conquest and migration, seizing multiethnic Hawaii and holding Puerto Rico and the Philippines after the Spanish-American War. At the beginning of the "new immigration," Scandinavians and Germans, some from eastern Europe, moved into rural areas in the prairie states. Where a group stayed together in a climate similar to their homeland, as did Germans from Russia in the Dakotas or Czechs in Texas, rural communities preserved many ethnic foodways. A small group like Luxembourger Americans tended to melt into Dutch and German American communities in Chicago or Dubuque, but retained distinctive peasant breakfasts and staples such as fried buckwheat dumplings (*sterchelen*) and scrambled pancakes (*durchaunder*) in Winona County, Minnesota.

As the wave of immigration continued, railroad camps, mining towns, and eastern cities absorbed an increasingly diverse group of Europeans. Ethnic boardinghouses gave working men a taste of home and provided income and status for women with ethnic cooking skills. In some cases, boardinghouses grew into small hotels or family restaurants. Ethnic dishes were exchanged in multicultural factory and mining towns. Often the first arrivals set up foodways that were adapted as mainstream American practices by the newer groups. For example, Cornish miners whose families knew how to make durable pasties were becoming foremen by the time Finnish and other miners were reaching the mining camps of northern Michigan, Minnesota, and Butte, Montana. The Finns had traditional meat pies of the same shape as pasties and picked up the most basic Cornish pasty and made it their own when later-generation Finns, especially in Michigan, opened bakeries and luncheonettes. In a few cases in the western states, Japanese American workers had learned the ropes from Chinese Americans and went on to open Chinese restaurants. In Hawaii, the larger group of Japanese contract workers set much of the cultural tone of the sugar plantations, and Chinese immigrants adopted the Japanese word shoyu as their working term for soy sauce.

The twentieth century saw a higher proportion of Italian and eastern European Jewish immigrants. They often lived in large cities and worked in industry and the garment trades. Cities allowed quicker assimilation than did rural areas and small towns, and urban areas also afforded many ethnic communities the opportunity to develop an import network for foreign foods and wines and a base of customers for restaurants. Thus even a small group such as Maltese Americans in Detroit, Michigan, and Astoria, Queens, New York, established noticeable communities where their descendants returned to find certain foods. Industrial cities had their own mixes of immigrants, and different cities became centers for different groups: Pittsburgh, Pennsylvania, for Slovaks and Carpatho-Rusyns; Detroit for Muslim Arab Americans and Albanians and for small Middle Eastern groups such as Assyrians (Iraqi Christians); and Cleveland, Ohio, for Romanians and Slovenians. Chicago and Milwaukee, Wisconsin, seemed to gather all ethnicities, as did the eastern ports of entry such as Boston, New York, and Baltimore. Large cities also provided markets for food vendors, from humble pushcarts through candy stores and cafés to diners and fine restaurants.

Ethnic foods made at home during the new immigration period progressed variously into the mainstream through factory and school lunch exchanges, church bazaars, and small restaurants, eventually becoming regional foods—such as pierogi in western Pennsylvania, pasties in Upper Michigan, Polish-style fish in Chicago, and pastrami in New York—and even becoming nationally loved foods. Among the latter are pizza, bagels, spaghetti with tomato sauce, hummus, pita, and yogurt, all of which were available only in urban ethnic markets or restaurants or private homes in 1920.

Periods of widespread immigration have often been difficult for African Americans and for other ethnic groups of color. The 1880–1924 period was full of setbacks for African Americans in many fields, but they were able to hold on to much culinary employment, including in all-black railroad dining cars. African Americans north and south gained prestige as cooks during this period, although the success was mixed with stereotypical views of alleged instinctive talents that blocked many African American cooks from executive chef positions. Commercial black cooks tended to cook in the style set by affluent white customers, although African American cooking as such was properly credited in the regional Creole styles of New Orleans and Mobile, Alabama, in some styles of barbecue, in the rice-based cuisine of the Carolina lowlands, and for the specialties of local caterers in most American cities.

The new immigration period also was the era of increasing mainstream patronage of Chinese American restaurants, both in Chinatowns and in elaborately decorated restaurants outside traditional Chinatowns. Written recipes for chop suey and chow mein date from the turn of the twentieth century. Many ethnic groups published their own cookbooks during this period—in foreign languages for the first generation and in English for the second generation and their spouses and for curious outsiders. Examples include the *Jewish Cookery Book* (1871) by Mrs. Esther Levy of Philadelphia; *What Mrs. Fisher Knows about Old Southern Cooking* (1881); the first New Orleans Creole cookbooks in the 1880s; *El Cocinero Español* (1898) by Encarnación Pinedo; a group of Pennsylvania Dutch cookbooks in English in the 1910s; and *The Art of German Cooking and Baking* (1909) by Lina Meier. By the 1920s, the Czech American (then known as Bohemian) community in Chicago had produced the *Lawndale Chapter Book of Recipes*. Several Chinese American cookbooks had been published by importers, and English-language cookbooks covered the restaurant and home food of Armenians, Holland Dutch, Norwegians, Scots, and Swedes. Foreign food was of increasing interest to cookbook buyers. *In Foreign Kitchens* (1893) by Helen

Campbell is mostly about the English, French, and German cuisines educated readers respected, but also includes dishes from northern Italy and Norway, Sweden, Poland, and Russia.

The new immigration period was also the time of the domestic science movement, which increasingly turned from educating would-be servants to training the poor in thrift and promoting a bland, late-Victorian menu of American foods for immigrants. The cookbook authors of this movement aspired to a national audience but varied in their interpretations of culinary Americanism. At one extreme was Mrs. F. L. Gillette, coauthor of *The White House Cookbook*, which was extremely popular with immigrant women; in a later work Gillette described her intention of "rejecting foreign recipes, which are not adaptable in most American homes." At the other extreme was Sara Tyson Rorer, herself of Pennsylvania Dutch extraction, who included sections of Jewish, Spanish, Creole, and Hawaiian recipes in *Mrs. Rorer's New Cook Book* (1902), although the authenticity of these recipes varied.

After World War I, fears about communism and the stagnation of workers' wages increased pressures to reduce immigration. For a period after the war, German food was considered suspect, and Italian restaurants were seen as meeting places for anarchists. Succeeding immigrant generations ate more "American food" while making selected ethnic dishes more visible. In a period marked by increasing urbanization and slow progress for immigrant groups, ethnic cookbooks continued to proliferate, and the first contributed multiethnic cookbooks drawing on the cooking knowledge of immigrant homemakers appeared. At the same time, "white-bread Americanism" continued to dominate general cookbooks.

The first series of multiethnic cookbooks was published by International Institutes of the YWCA, which had been established in the 1920s and 1930s as immigrant settlement houses in Providence, Rhode Island; Lowell and Lawrence, Massachusetts; and Saint Louis. In the same period, food manufacturers produced ethnic cooking pamphlets, including Yiddish-English bilingual pamphlets from makers of vegetable shortening and multiethnic pamphlets from the F. W. McNess baking powder company, which were bilingual in Spanish, Chinese, Danish, French, German, Greek, Hungarian, Italian, Norwegian, Polish, Russian, and Swedish. Some recipes in these multiethnic cookbooks were contributed by ethnic cooks; others were taken from foreign cookbooks or the recipe books of well-traveled supporters.

The widespread poverty of the Great Depression brought economical "old country" cooking to the fore, both at home and in family-run restaurants. At the same time, nonethnic treats outside the home, such as ice cream sundaes and invented sandwiches, provided escapist fun. The Depression was a great era for newspaper recipe contests, radio food programs with recipe exchanges, and magazine articles about foreign cuisines. But perusal of the winners, and even of the contributed cookbooks issued under these auspices, suggests that ethnic foods were not what Depression-era women would put forward publicly as the best of their repertoire. Another kind of contributed cookbook, those issued by elected officials, was also relatively free of ethnic foods. An exception was Fiorello LaGuardia's, at the time a Republican congressman, contributions of Italian American recipes to the 1927 and 1933 Congressional Club cookbooks.

Middle-class cooks who were curious about worldwide food could read *Recipes of All Nations* (1935), by Countess Morphy, although "all nations" were actually twenty-nine countries plus New Orleans Creole and general sections for Africa and South America. Pearl V. Metzelthin included seventy-five nations in her similar *World Wide Cook Book* (1939). The Great Depression and the New Deal revived interest in economical cooking of all kinds. A number of regional surveys showed interest in ethnic foods. The first was Sheila Hibben's *The National Cookbook* (1932), later *The American Regional Cookbook*, with recipes collected primarily from newspaper food editors. Later in the 1930s, the Works Progress Administration writers' project planned a survey of regional foods, edited volumes of which appeared in the 1990s. Home economists provided regional dishes for the *New York World's Fair Cook Book: The American Kitchen* (1939) by Cosby Gage, and the much larger *America Cooks: Favorite Recipes from the 48 States* (1940) by Cora, Rose, and Bob Brown. The Browns, who were interested in ethnic cooking, also wrote on European and South American food. In 1939, *The United States Regional Cookbook* by Ruth Berolzheimer included "Michigan [Holland] Dutch Cookery," "Wisconsin [German] Dutch," and "Minnesota Scandinavian" among ten regional cuisines and added an eleventh chapter of ethnic recipes of "Cosmopolitan America."

World War II accelerated the mainstream acceptance of ethnic cooking as the war effort required inclusion at all levels and servicemen and women became exposed to foods in foreign fields of battle. The long war for Italy made Naples a liberty port and pizza a postwar dish for all Americans. The postwar occupation of Japan resulted in an interest in Japanese food that began with sukiyaki in the 1950s and then accelerated with sushi. The cold war brought "captive-nation" ethnic groups to the fore and opened up immigration for Koreans, Cubans, and others.

Marian Tracy used recipes from newspaper food writers for *Favorite Regional Recipes of America* in 1952, selecting mostly European ethnic dishes but also Mexican food, a Chinese restaurant dish, and a gumbo. For most Americans in the 1950s, ethnic food meant dining out—pasta (not yet pizza in many areas) in Italian restaurants, chow mein and fried rice in Chinese restaurants, and elaborate dinners of dishes with French or German names. Travelers sought regional foods that were not nationally available, such as Mexican food west of the Mississippi, Creole food in New Orleans, Pennsylvania Dutch dishes in eastern Pennsylvania, Anglo-American chowders and Indian pudding in New England, and German food in Milwaukee, Chicago, and Saint Louis.

Ethnic Food since the 1960s

The success of the civil rights movement, the loosening of immigration restrictions, and the many cultural changes of the 1960s and 1970s set off an ethnic revival that peaked in the 1980s, probably around the time of the 1983 television presentation of Alex Haley's *Roots*. For many third-generation white ethnics, the 1980s also saw a revived interest in genealogy, European tourism, and old-country recipes. Home-style ethnic recipes were published in this period as never before. Ethnic foods were also revived in restaurants, and ethnic restaurants sometimes preceded actual immigrants. The Vietnam War was followed by the opening of numerous Thai restaurants serving spicy, vivid, exotic food and typically employing Thai cooks. Some Thai restaurants were owned by East Asian immigrants from Vietnam, Laos, Korea, China, and Malaysia. A wave of interest in spicy Chinese food from Szechwan and Taiwan followed the United States' formal recognition of the People's Republic of China in 1979.

Multiethnic food festivals and cookbooks proliferated in the 1980s, notably a series of contributed cookbooks published by state chapters of the American Cancer Society. Several of the chapters chose ethnicity as a theme and elicited recipes from dozens of backgrounds. Publication of cookbooks by politicians, both partisan efforts, such as the 1972 *National Republican Heritage Groups Council World Cookbook*, and nonpartisan and charitable collections suggested that many politicians across the ideological spectrum desired to present themselves as members of ethnic groups or at least as appreciating the ethnic dishes of their regional constituents. The 1960s and 1970s had opened the way for hobby cooks, with the Round the World Cooking Library series and the Time-Life Foods of the World series, the latter including many American ethnic dishes in its several volumes of U.S. regional cooking.

The *Roots* revival was followed by a swing back toward melting-pot nationalism, including populist campaigns against illegal immigration and bilingual education and heightened concerns about national security. However, as in the last quarter of the nineteenth century, culinary nationalism included an increased focus on regional and ethnic cuisines. With Americans eating almost as many meals outside the home as inside, ethnic restaurants have remained important. In many cities and towns, immigrants from Afghanistan, Egypt, Ethiopia, India, Iran, Korea, Thailand, Vietnam, and even Tibet have opened restaurants with mainstream appeal. Many contributed cookbooks include dishes of ten, fifteen, twenty, or more ethnic groups. For the Lutheran Brotherhood (*75 Years of Service and Still Cooking*, 1993), multiculturalism might be reflected in the inclusion of a section of heritage recipes from the various Scandinavian origins of members of this mutual-benefit insurance cooperative. For DuPont Pharmaceuticals (*There's Room at Our Table*, 1999), recipes from seventeen American ethnic groups combine with regional and international favorites to express the diversity of a multinational corporation. For St. Joseph Catholic Elementary School in Ogden, Utah (*We Are the World International Cookbook*, 1998), a mix of family and cookbook recipes from thirty-one countries provides a lesson in diversity. A small town in eastern Montana used 735 recipes to sum up seventy-five years as an incorporated town (*Wolf Point Montana 75th Jubilee Cookbook*, 1990). Most of the heritage recipes were German American or German from Russia, but the book also included recipes from Mexican, Danish, Swedish, Norwegian, Austrian, Czech, Dutch, French Canadian, Hungarian, Irish, Italian, Scottish, Ukrainian, and Yugoslavian Americans. Native American recipes, mostly from the nearby Fort Peck reservation, included Assiniboin, Meti, and Yakima dishes. This ethnic mix is not unusual for mining towns in the West, but Wolf Point is a wheat-farming area that was one of the last parts of the United States accessible for homesteading.

[*See also* African American Food; Cajun and Creole Food; Caribbean Influences on American Food; Central Asian Food; Chinese American Food; Cookbooks and Manuscripts, *subentry on* Community Cookbooks; Cuban American Food; Dutch Influences on American Food; German American Food; Iberian and South American Food; Indian American Food; Italian American Food; Japanese American Food; Jewish American Food; Korean American Food; Mexican American Food; Middle Eastern Influences on American Food; Native American Foods, *subentry* Before and after Contact; Polish American Food; Russian American Food; Southeast Asian Food.]

BIBLIOGRAPHY

Allen, Terese. *Home Cooked Culture: Wisconsin through Recipes.* Madison: Wisconsin Arts Board, 2001. Lengthy treatment of booyah with a story about Godfrey of Bouillon.

American Cancer Society, Minnesota Division, Inc. *Minnesota Heritage Cookbook: Hand-Me-Down Recipes.* Minneapolis: The Division, 1979. Early and completely ethnic book in this series. The recipes are contributed.

American Cancer Society, Wisconsin Division, Inc. *Ethnic Cooking Wisconsin Style.* Memphis, TN: Wimmer, 1982. The Michigan, Missouri, New York, and Massachusetts books in this series are also multiethnic.

Attaquin, Helen, Cynthia Akins, Amelia Bingham, et al. *Wampanoag Cookery.* Boston: American Science and Engineering, 1972. Dishes gathered primarily by Mashpee Wampanoags as part of their federal recognition and land case.

Baboian, Rose. *Rose Baboian's Armenian-American Cook Book: Simplified Armenian Near East Recipes.* Boston: Toumayan, 1966. An excellent demonstration of the Armenian American genius for ethnic survival. Baboian has preserved many delicacies of her childhood in Aintab and charts how to make up to 125 servings of important dishes for church suppers. She also anticipates Armenian American fusion dishes such as chocolate yogurt. When the book was published, home recipes for yogurt were needed because yogurt was not yet sold in supermarkets.

Cordova, Regina, with Emma Carrasco. *Celebración: Recipes and Traditions Celebrating Latino Family Life.* New York: Doubleday, 1996. Published for the Mexican American organization, National Council of La Raza. Many of the cooks are named and interviewed, and there is a brief introduction about Hispanic and Caribbean cultures and holidays.

Corum, Anna Kondo. *Ethnic Foods of Hawai'i.* Honolulu, HI: Bess, 1983. Recipes assembled by a school librarian represent the foods of nine ethnic groups.

Diner, Hasia. *Hungering for America: Italian, Irish and Jewish Foodways in the Age of Migration.* Cambridge, MA: Harvard University Press, 2001. Good data on all three groups around the periods of their major immigration to the United States and first generation of transition. No overall theory is presented in which to place the three groups. The author takes an extreme position that Irish Americans have no ethnic food.

Dooley, Beth, and Lucia Watson. *Savoring the Seasons of the Northern Heartland.* New York: Knopf, 1994.

Eberly, Carole. *Our Michigan: Ethnic Tales and Recipes.* East Lansing, MI: Shoestring, 1979. Twenty-one ethnic groups, including Cornish, Irish, Canadian, and Dutch.

Fitchburg Historical Society. *Folk Foods of Fitchburg: A Culinary Heritage in Recipes from Many Lands.* Fitchburg, MA: Fitchburg

Historical Society, 1961. More than fourteen ethnic groups are represented, including a prominent Finnish American community.

Gaines, Judy, Anna Sheets, and Robyn V. Young, eds. *The Gale Encyclopedia of Multicultural America.* New York: Gale, 1995. An update of the *Harvard Encyclopedia of American Ethnic Groups,* edited by Stephan Thernstrom. Contains articles on many immigrants, individual Indian Tribes, and subethnic groups from India. Most articles have a brief culinary section. The 1990 U.S. Census ancestry survey summary is an appendix, but the 1993 revised estimates of Native American membership by tribes and states are not included.

Hom, Ken. *Easy Family Recipes from a Chinese-American Childhood.* New York: Knopf, 1997.

International Institute of Metropolitan Detroit. *Cuisine International.* Detroit, MI: 1979. Includes hard-to-find recipes from Turkish, Bulgarian, and Rumanian immigrants.

Kaplan, Anne R., Marjorie A. Hoover, and Willard B. Moore. *The Minnesota Ethnic Food Book.* Minneapolis: Minnesota Historical Society Press, 1986. Fourteen ethnic groups in Minnesota from the Ojibwa and British to the Hmong.

Kirlin, Katherine S., and Thomas M. Kirlin. *Smithsonian Folklife Cookbook.* Washington, DC: Smithsonian Institution Press, 1991. Recipes drawn from summer festivals from 1968 to 1990. Organized regionally, but many ethnic recipes with very specific information are included.

Lackore, Mrs. A. G. (Lucille), ed. *Winona County American Bicentennial Recipes of the Past.* Winona, MN: Winona Printing, 1976. Very good sketches and recipes of a dozen ethnic groups, including Luxembourgers.

Laudan, Rachel. *The Food of Paradise: Exploring Hawaii's Culinary Heritage.* Honolulu: University of Hawaii Press, 1986. Recipe index by eleven ethnicities, including local and Kakaaina, a term that applies to longtime Anglo residents.

Leahy, Katie. "Feeding Nostalgia: Cookbooks and Armenian-American Identity." *Explorations: A Journal of Undergraduate Research* (University of California at Davis) 3 (2000).

Lockwood, William G., and Yvonne R. Lockwood. "The Cornish Pasty in Northern Michigan." In *Oxford Symposium 1983: Food in Motion—The Migration of Foodstuffs and Cookery Techniques; Proceedings,* edited by Alan Davidson. Leeds, UK: Prospect, 1983.

Nelsen, Peter J. T. *National Republican Heritage Groups Council World Cookbook.* Washington, DC: Atland, 1972. Recipes representing thirty-two groups organized to support the Republican national campaign and elected officials eager to show their ethnic roots. Contains a selection of foreign recipes.

Novas, Himilce, and Rosemary Silva. *Latin Cooking across the U.S.A.* New York: Knopf, 1997. The Cuban American authors collect food from named individuals of many later immigrant groups, including non-Hispanic Caribbean immigrants, and only sometimes make their own adaptations, which they describe with terms such as "Colombian-American."

Prudhomme, Paul. *The Prudhomme Family Cookbook: Old-Time Louisiana Recipes by the Eleven Prudhomme Brothers and Sisters and Chef Paul Prudhomme.* New York: Morrow, 1987. Cajun home cooking, including rare hard-times recipes from the 1930s.

Raichlin, Steven. *Miami Spice: Latin America, Cuba, and the Caribbean Meet in the Tropical Heart of America.* New York: Workman, 1993.

Stallworth, Lyn, and Rod Kennedy. *The Brooklyn Cookbook.* New York: Knopf, 1994.

Thernstrom, Stephen. *Harvard Encyclopedia of American Ethnic Groups.* Cambridge, MA: Harvard University Press, 1980. Groundbreaking and still definitive, although a work of its period in that it emphasizes European immigrant groups and passes quickly over African American subgroups and later immigrants from Latin America and the Caribbean.

West Kauai Community Development Corporation. *West Kauai's Plantation Heritage: Recipes and Stories for Life from the Legacy of Hawaii's Sugar Plantation Community.* Waimea, HI: West Kauai Community Development Corporation, 2002. Documents local history and contributions to the local food of twelve ethnic groups.

Williamson, Darcy, and Lisa Railsback. *Cooking with Spirit: North American Indian Food and Fact.* Bend, OR: Maverick, 1987. Includes traditional and contemporary reservation recipes.

Young, Carrie, with Felicia Young. *Prairie Cooks: Glorified Rice, Three-Day Buns, and Other Recipes and Reminiscences.* New York: HarperPerennial, 1997. Follows the path of Young's Norwegian-born mother as immigrant, homesteader, and matriarch.

Zanger, Mark H. *The American Ethnic Cookbook for Students.* Phoenix, AZ: Oryx, 2001.

Zanger, Mark H. *The American History Cookbook.* Westport, CT: Greenwood, 2003. Describes how ethnic foods were seen at different times in U.S. history.

MARK H. ZANGER

Etiquette Books

The dining room, perhaps even more than the parlor, has been the testing and proving ground of etiquette in America. Changing etiquette—which codifies the proper use of furniture and tableware, appropriate menus and recipes, and the specifics of table service and deportment—has been a guide to shifting social, economic, and cultural values and a means to understanding the various strata of the population at different times. During the earliest colonial decades, the wealthier classes set styles and fashions; later, the newly emerging middle classes, striving to become accepted into society, followed their lead. In the past this kind of idealized regimen was not as much a part of lower or working-class lives, presumably because the necessary leisure and resources were too scarce.

Social and Class Distinctions Codified

Regardless of period, codified etiquette was in part a statement of gentility and status and in part a way to avoid social confusion. Table manners were essentially a list of conventions devised to make dining an activity that people would be comfortable performing, often in a new, upwardly mobile environment. Every aspect of a dining event had a carefully prescribed ritual. For example, when everyone recognized that the water glass was placed above the knife to the right of the plate, no one would be reduced to walking around the table in search of a glass. And with a more complex table setting, comprising more than one set of knives, forks, and spoons, the guest who knew that the table was set according to menu began with the flatware placed on the outside and worked inward during the succession of courses. With such agreed-upon and generally understood conventions, diners were free to focus on conversational pleasantries and fine cooking, which were essentially the purpose and goal of the meal.

As in almost every other part of daily life, the requirements for proper behavior at the table began with the upper classes and worked downward to those aspiring to emulate them. Table manners emerged as the final test of refinement, character, and good breeding, and correct behavior at the table became an essential aspect of entry into proper society. As the social gaps narrowed, those at the top protected their place by devising more complex and expensive conditions, hoping to maintain class distinctions by keeping manners out of the reach of the lower classes. Manners became increasingly intricate and elaborate during the nineteenth century, and the details had to be thoroughly learned. Gentility at the table was painstakingly acquired, although it often had less to do with eating than with one's social aspirations. Many parents meticulously observed the rituals of the table on a daily basis and considered this a vital part of their children's preparation for advancement. To further this ambition, they consulted the burgeoning genre of style guides and etiquette books.

Manuals describing deportment and behavior at the table had existed in Europe before the settling of America and were brought to the American colonies by wealthy immigrants. George Washington, scion of an upper-class Virginia family, transcribed an influential French book of etiquette (1695) as a schoolboy's project. His *Rules of Civility & Decent Behaviour in Company and Conversation* (1774) was composed of a list of 110 rules, of which seventeen dealt with table manners.

By way of contrast, newcomers struggling in small towns or cities or establishing farms on the shifting frontiers lived on a far different scale. They rarely had individual plates, cups, or spoons, and they carried their own knives to the table and often used communal flatware or their fingers. Cleanliness was not essential at table; it was a luxury, and consequently there was little perceived need for the table manners and formality of the elite. This was the kind of behavior at table observed by the English traveler Frances Trollope in her *Domestic Manners of the Americans* (1832). She bemoaned what she saw as the crude and loathsome manners of Americans, a theme that was echoed by other journal-keeping visitors.

The Nouveaux Riche in the Victorian Period and Gilded Age

The growth of cities, the new cash economy, and the emerging middle class ushered in an entirely different mentality. The white Anglo-Saxon urban social ideal termed "the Doctrine of Separate Spheres" established a system that was soon to be embraced by a larger sector of the population. It directed that the mission of men was to become monetarily successful and that of their wives was to display the evidence of this wealth. Table manners took on a decidedly upwardly mobile cast, and etiquette books found a growing market.

Eliza Leslie, writing in *The House Book* (1840), described in intricate detail how to set the table and how to wait on it, as well as how to prepare for a dinner party from a domestic housekeeper's point of view. Such authors wrote for the upper classes. The American character of table etiquette did not truly begin to evolve until the onset of the American Industrial Revolution (ca. 1850). By the late nineteenth century, stylish manners were indispensable for the upwardly mobile middle classes and the new millionaire industrialists of the turn-of-the-century's Gilded Age. Style guides copied the manners of the landed gentry or Americans with long pedigrees for those eager to improve their social status.

When writers first saw the need to publish more egalitarian manuals or chapters on household management and cooking for the everyday housewife, such books as E. G. Storke's *The Family and Householder's Guide* (1859) appeared. Storke presented suggestions for a family keeping one, two, or even no domestics, complete with diagrams for setting the table properly. He recommended consistency in setting the table and achieving proper deportment. Other important authors of mid-nineteenth-century etiquette books were Eliza Farrar, Catherine Sedgwick, Lydia Maria Child, and Sarah Josepha Hale. Their etiquette books always contained chapters on behavior at table and covered every aspect of the dining event, such as pre-dinner etiquette, correct ways to enter the dining room; proper seating arrangements, handling of food and wine, and use of utensils; suitable dinner conversation; and the appropriate duties and behavior of servants (including serving protocols).

In the later years of the nineteenth century, an age of immigration, industrialization, and great social change, much time was given to maintaining the complex ceremonies of dining and deportment, manners of dress, the arrival ceremony, the duties of a hostess, after-dinner etiquette, and guests' departure. It was clearly important to own the right accoutrements and use them correctly. These standards were essential if one was to navigate the complicated social rituals set up by Victorian society.

America became the land of the hostess almost at once. Etiquette manuals, particularly those by Mrs. Mary Elizabeth Wilson Sherwood (who also published under her initials, M. E. W. S.) in the late nineteenth century, taught women how to dispense hospitality and manage in the society around them. Mrs. Sherwood wrote for *Harper's Bazaar*, and her columns were responsible in good part for the attention paid by the middle classes to polite society and the world of gracious living. Her *Manners and Social Usages* (1884) is a fine example of the kind of book that addressed the new audience of social achievers. She identified those who had recently made fortunes, exemplified them to excess, and described those who saw themselves as having native refinement and taste as the rightful arbiters of manners.

Egalitarian Etiquette

The place of formal and elegant dinners as models lasted into the early twentieth century. After World War I and the upheaval of the country's social structure, etiquette manuals dropped ceremonial sorts of rules in favor of more informal commentary and simpler manners. Emily Post's *Etiquette in Society, in Business, in Politics, and at Home* (1922) was readable and straightforward and did not assume that only the more prosperous would wish to know how to behave correctly. Her unique writing style provided guidance to the socially uncertain. She recognized that in America's dynamic society there were many people whose commercial success required the ability to deal with social situations for which their upbringing had not prepared them and that one might have a "pleasing dining room at limited cost" (Post, p. 193). Her book was publicized extensively, went through twelve editions, sold 12 million copies, and was used as a textbook in schools. Her name (which is trademarked) remains an authoritative voice for early-twentieth-century taste and manners.

After World War II, American women became house proud, and the acquisition of new appliances freed up their time to make preparations for entertaining that sometimes included elaborate dinner parties. Table items that were formerly part of a bride's dowry appeared on shop lists known as a bride's registry. This wish list of desired gifts was compiled for prestigious stores by couples about to marry. *The Joy of Cooking* (1953 edition), by Irma S. Rombauer and Marion Rombauer Becker, devoted a chapter to entertaining and table service for the "untried hostess" that included suggestions for setting and serving every type of meal. As the century progressed, a very new breed of arbiters of elegance was represented by the influential syndicated columnist "Miss Manners" (Judith Martin). Writing prolifically into the twenty-first century, she attempted to reintroduce fine manners into a society that had lost much of its civility. Her system of manners, expounded in columns and books, is demanding, unbending, and precise, and her writings are enthusiastically read and followed.

Entertaining at the turn of the twenty-first century became much more informal, but the trophy kitchen and dining room—the museum-like display of state-of-the-art equipment and accessories—still conferred high status, as did gourmet skills and savvy. The generation that had acquired money quickly needed ways to display it, and outfitting a proper table with the right expensive china, crystal, flatware, and linens, whether or not they were used often, became almost mandatory.

At the same time, most American families, limited by complicated schedules and time constraints, assembled around the dinner table only for special occasions and holiday feasts, hardly enough to impart rituals to youngsters. Dining etiquette became difficult to maintain and even pointless in the pervasive fast-food culture, although it was still recommended as a way of projecting success and savoir faire. Microwaved meals, take-out food, eating on the run, or "grazing" throughout the day made the dining ritual so casual so that it required very little in the way of good table manners. A guide to smooth social interaction soon became obsolete among those who eat alone or those who bought into the "me first" subculture of the time.

At the beginning of the twenty-first century there were still those who chose etiquette as a means to acquire and reflect standing and privilege. Subsequent generations probably will follow the same models and philosophies to determine manners and standards as were used for centuries. Our etiquette undoubtedly will continue to reflect the basic priorities of our society.

[*See also* Child, Lydia Maria; Dining Rooms, Table Settings, and Table Manners.]

BIBLIOGRAPHY

Aresty, Esther B. *The Best Behavior: The Course of Good Manners—from Antiquity to the Present—as Seen through Courtesy and Etiquette Books*. New York: Simon and Schuster, 1970.

Garrett, Elisabeth Donaghy. *At Home: The American Family 1750–1870*. New York: Harold N. Abrams, 1990.

Kasson, John F. *Rudeness and Civility: Manners in Nineteenth-Century Urban America*. New York: Hill and Wang, 1990.

Lynes, Russell. *The Domesticated Americans*. New York: Harper and Row, 1963.

Post, Emily. *Etiquette in Society, in Business, and at Home*. New York: Funk & Wagnalls, 1922.

Visser, Margaret. *The Rituals of Dinner: The Origins, Evolution, Eccentricities, and Meaning of Table Manners*. New York: Grove Weidenfeld, 1991.

CAROL A. GREENBERG

Farmer, Fannie

Fannie Merritt Farmer emerged from the domestic science movement to become the most famous cooking expert of her time, in part by harnessing the brisk, businesslike methods of "scientific cookery" to a cuisine of sweetness and affluence. She was born in Boston on March 23, 1857, to the bookish family of a struggling printer. A bout of childhood polio cut short her education and left her with a limp, making her an unlikely candidate for either marriage or a career. At age thirty-one she decided to attend the Boston Cooking School, whose graduates were busy across the country teaching in public schools, settlement houses, and other institutions dedicated to raising society's morals by improving women's domestic skills. She did so well that she became principal of the school in 1894.

A gifted and ambitious teacher, she brought the school to its height of success, especially after the publication of her landmark work, *The Boston Cooking-School Cook Book* (1896). Farmer borrowed liberally from an earlier text produced by the school's first principal, Mary Lincoln, in 1884, but the new book had an entirely different personality. It remained a comprehensive, science-based teaching manual, but unlike many of her colleagues, Farmer was interested chiefly in helping women serve appealing meals, not in turning the home kitchen into a chemistry lab. So she shortened the scientific explanations and added a decorative overlay to Lincoln's plainspoken recipes. Fashionable dishes inspired by New York restaurants were introduced, salads proliferated and became more fanciful, and a new section devoted to chafing-dish recipes appeared. Yet a pedagogical spirit reigned, notably on the subject of measuring. The school had introduced standardized measuring cups and spoons in the mid-1880s, but Lincoln's book still referred to "rounded" or "heaping" spoonfuls and cupfuls. Farmer wanted to make sure that even beginners could measure accurately. "A cupful is measured level," she instructed. "A tablespoonful is measured level. A teaspoonful is measured level." The regular deployment of a knife to level the surface of a cup or spoon was one of Farmer's lasting contributions to the American kitchen.

In 1902 Farmer left the Boston Cooking School and opened Miss Farmer's School of Cookery. Her lively, practical lessons in all aspects of home cooking drew so many students that the school soon had four kitchens and ten teachers. Classes in sickroom cookery were a specialty, as they had been at the Boston Cooking School. Farmer knew from experience the importance of feeding invalids properly and for years taught the subject herself at Harvard Medical School.

Fanny Farmer. *Culinary Archives & Museum at Johnson & Wales University, Providence, R.I.*

Farmer traveled and lectured widely and contributed a monthly column to the *Woman's Home Companion*. She also wrote five more books: *Chafing Dish Possibilities* (1898), *Food and Cookery for the Sick and Convalescent* (1904), *What to Have for Dinner* (1905), *Catering for Special Occasions, with Menus and Recipes* (1911) and *A New Book of Cookery* (1912). On January 15, 1915, she died in Boston of arteriosclerosis. Over the next six decades *The Boston Cooking-School Cook Book* went through eleven editions and sold nearly 4 million copies.

[*See also* Boston Cooking School; Cookbooks and Manuscripts, *subentry* From the Civil War to World War I; Measurement.]

BIBLIOGRAPHY

Shapiro, Laura. *Perfection Salad: Women and Cooking at the Turn of the Century.* New York: Farrar, Straus and Giroux, 1986.
Schlesinger, Elizabeth Bancroft. "Farmer, Fannie Merritt." In *Notable American Women 1607–1950: A Biographical Dictionary*, edited by Edward T. James. Cambridge, MA: Belknap Press, 1971.

LAURA SHAPIRO

Farmers' Markets

Since the 1970s, farmers' markets have blossomed across the United States. According to the U.S. Department of Agriculture, in the 1960s there were only about one hundred markets, while by 2002 more than 3,100 were in operation. These markets vary greatly in size and scope. Some, like the Dane County Market in Madison, Wisconsin, are beloved local institutions drawing thousands of shoppers each Saturday to browse among hundreds of stalls stocked with Asian greens, heirloom apples, and homemade pasta. Others consist of a handful of producers selling tomatoes, peppers, and sweet corn in church parking lots. Both kinds of markets offer to consumers a selection of fresh, local produce, typically far surpassing what can be found in supermarkets, in a cheery, social setting. For small farmers, this kind of direct marketing offers both an alternative to dealing with large-scale commodity markets and the possibility of receiving much higher returns on their products.

Although contemporary markets are a novelty for most Americans, they hark back to the colonial era, when farmers hauled their produce and meat into nearby urban centers to sell to city residents. As Hamilton (2002) recounts, the historic demise of direct marketing follows the development of the modern industrial food system. With the expansion of cities and transportation systems in the nineteenth century, growers were pushed farther away from their urban customers. These longer distances, and the ascendance of intermediary food handlers, increased the likelihood of spoilage. More and more, markets were viewed as unhygienic and old-fashioned, in contrast to the modernity associated with new processing technologies like canning and new forms of distribution such as grocery stores. While markets continued to play a role in urban commerce through the late nineteenth and early twentieth centuries, particularly in the West and in smaller towns, the dramatic rise of mass retailing, followed by the economic hardships of the Great Depression and the food shortages of World War II, contributed to their disappearance from the national landscape.

The resurgence of farmers' markets is linked to disenchantment with, and a search for alternatives to, the agro-industrial system that originally precipitated their decline. In the mid-1970s concerns about the environmental consequences of conventional agriculture, the quality and safety of food, and the future of family farmers spurred the markets' reappearance. Currently, markets not only have proliferated but are increasingly regarded as a means of "relocalization" of food production and distribution. Although the 67,000 producers who sell at markets represent only a sliver of the country's 2 million farmers, these markets, ideally, counter the dominance of agribusiness by promoting a series of linked environmental, economic, and social benefits. By supporting small farmers, including many organic growers, the markets encourage sustainable agricultural practices and permit a larger proportion of each food dollar to remain within the local area. In many instances, the higher returns of successful retailing enable family farmers to stay in operation, which contributes to the overall prosperity of rural and peri-urban communities. For city dwellers, purchasing fresh-picked produce directly from a favorite farmer not only presages culinary pleasures but also creates a new sense of personal connection with agriculture and the environment, especially when repeated weekly.

The prospect of finding a variety of fresh, local food draws people to markets. Farmers work hard to meet consumer expectations through close attention to customer preferences and innovation in their own production and marketing strategies. For example, with smaller, more

Farmer's Market. A vendor at the Greenmarket at Grand Army Plaza in Brooklyn, New York. *Photograph by Joe Zarba*

frequent plantings farmers can bring popular fruits and vegetables to market at their prime. Diversification is important as well, both in offering varieties of the same item and in introducing new ones. Farmers, on the lookout for the next hot product, have played a key role in acquainting consumers with "new" foods such as buffalo meat or hitherto unknown or forgotten varieties of hot peppers, radishes, tomatoes, and pears. Generous samples and preparation suggestions serve to educate shoppers and generate demand. Diversification extends to the elaboration of foods and nonfood crops in ways that add value to products and entice customers. Many vendors set out ready-to-eat foods—salsa, persimmon pudding, focaccia, and corn chowder—alongside their produce displays. Herb growers lengthen their selling season by packaging infusions and potpourris and preparing flavored vinegars. Others specialize in jams, fruit butters, honey, and baked goods (including vegetarian dog biscuits). The cumulative visual and olfactory panoply, often enhanced by the presence of flower producers selling bouquets and hanging plants, creates a festive atmosphere that, in itself, becomes one more reason for shoppers to abandon their local supermarket.

[*See also* Food Marketing; Organic Food.]

BIBLIOGRAPHY

Corum, Vance, Marcie Rosenzweig, and Eric Gibson. *The New Farmers' Market: Farm-Fresh Ideas for Producers, Managers, and Communities*. Auburn, CA: New World Publishing, 2001. This how-to manual provides a useful overview of the nuts, bolts, flowers, and berries of contemporary markets.

Hamilton, Lisa M. "The American Farmers Market." *Gastronomica* 2, no. 3 (2002): 73–77. Engaging synthesis of historical work on markets.

LISA B. MARKOWITZ

Farm Labor and Unions

Throughout American history there has been a constant effort made to increase the amount and improve the quality of farm products. To achieve these goals, farmers needed a predictable supply of workers, but the needs of growers and those of workers often conflicted. Agricultural workers have consistently faced similar problems in all sections of the country: low wages, unpredictable employment and a transient lifestyle, poor housing and medical care, exposure to chemicals and pesticides, onerous demands of employers, and the potential loss of jobs because of mechanization.

In their search for laborers, growers have imported workers and then isolated them, keeping them separate from society at large and the members of other ethnic groups so that they could not unite and organize. Farmers have also taken advantage of federal programs that allowed them to import temporary workers from poor areas like Mexico, Jamaica, and Puerto Rico.

The search for workers has forced growers to recruit people of many different ethnic groups, including Africans in the eighteenth century. After the Civil War, Chinese laborers in California were the first large group of farm workers, but in 1882 a law prohibited the importation of more Chinese labor. Japanese workers were next, but they were not easily subjugated, and many became independent farmers. Growers then turned to East Indians, Koreans, Middle Easterners, Filipinos, and Mexicans.

Unionization in agriculture resulted from the consolidation of smaller agriculture holdings into large farms. The owners and their supporters crushed early organizing efforts. Workers received little support from the American Federation of Labor (AFL) because they were unskilled laborers. The AFL was composed of skilled workers who were organized into unions based on their craft (such as carpentry, cigarmaking, plumbing). Because unskilled workers performed a variety of tasks, they could not be organized by individual craft, so the AFL was not interested in working with them. The unskilled workers often turned to more radical unions, like the Industrial Workers of the World (IWW), an affiliation that frequently led to violence. In 1913, for example, a violent dispute occurred near Wheatland, California. Owners of a ranch recruited more workers than they needed and forced them to live in squalid conditions, which prompted IWW leaders to organize. Police tried to break up a rally, leading to a riot that killed four people. IWW leaders were jailed, and the strike was broken. In the 1930s the Cannery and Agricultural Workers Industrial Union, an outgrowth of the Communist Party's Agricultural Workers Industrial League, led a series of strikes, but again there was violence. In 1933 a posse composed of police and growers fired on a crowd of workers in Pixley, California, killing two. There were other unsuccessful organizing efforts during the 1930s, such as those of the Southern Tenants Farmers' Union among workers in the southern cotton fields.

In 1935 the National Labor Relations Act guaranteed the right of employees to join unions, free from reprisals by employers. Farm workers were excluded from the act, however. In many areas, farm workers are also exempt from state regulations. During the 1930s a massive wave of poor whites migrated to California because the dust-

bowl conditions in the Midwest made it impossible for them to make a living on farms in that region. These workers vied for the same jobs as other farm workers, creating a glut of available labor and making it possible for employers to pay lower wages. Many of these individuals from the Midwest entered the military or took industrial jobs during World War II, so the growers again turned to Mexico. In 1942 the United States and Mexico created the bracero program, which allowed American growers to recruit large numbers of temporary Mexican workers.

One union achieved its goals during the 1930s. In 1937 the Congress of Industrial Organizations (CIO) chartered the International Longshoremen's and Warehousemen's Union (ILWU) in Hawaii. The ILWU led a successful dock strike and then turned to organizing agricultural workers. The union improved working conditions by forcing growers to mechanize their farms and created a powerful political alliance with the Democratic Party. Although many growers have moved their operations to the Philippines, Taiwan, South Korea, Thailand, Malaysia, and other countries where wages are lower, the union remains active in Hawaii, even though its membership has declined.

In 1963 Cesar Chavez formed the United Farm Workers (UFW) during an era of economic expansion that was more conducive to unionizing than the 1930s had been. The bracero program was ending, and Chavez received support from religious leaders, students, organized labor, and liberal activists. Chavez's tactics included a national boycott of California grapes and lettuce so effective that it persuaded growers finally to sign union contracts. Chavez worked to limit the use of pesticides on crops and negotiated agreements on the introduction of machinery in agriculture. The UFW also organized in Arizona, Texas, and Florida.

The Farm Labor Organizing Committee (FLOC) was created in 1979 to represent workers in the Midwest. The union adopted many UFW tactics and faced similar issues, such as mechanization, controlling pesticide use, and the elimination of child labor. In 1994 FLOC affiliated itself with the AFL-CIO. Unions continue to adapt to new developments in agriculture, such as genetically engineered crops, and, at the same time, work toward their traditional goals. Because they represent the labor force still needed to produce the nation's food, unions will continue to play a vital role in American life.

[See also Farm Subsidies, Duties, Quotas, and Tariffs.]

BIBLIOGRAPHY

Barger, W. K., and Ernesto M. Reza. *The Farm Labor Movement in the Midwest: Social Change and Adaptation among Migrant Farm Workers.* Austin: University of Texas Press, 1994.

Edid, Maralyn. *Farm Labor Organizing: Trends and Prospects.* Ithaca, NY: ILR Press, 1994.

Hall, Greg. *Harvest Wobblies: The Industrial Workers of the World and Agricultural Laborers in the American West, 1905–1930.* Corvallis: Oregon State University Press, 2001.

Meister, Dick, and Anne Loftus. *A Long Time Coming: The Struggle to Unionize America's Farm Workers.* New York: Macmillan, 1977.

Mooney, Patrick H., and Theo J. Majka. *Farmers' and Farm Workers' Movements: Social Protest in American Agriculture.* New York: Twayne, 1995.

RICHARD J. JENSEN

Farm Stands, *see Farmers' Markets*

Farm Subsidies, Duties, Quotas, and Tariffs

Farm subsidies, tariffs, and quotas are policy instruments used by the United States to support agricultural prices and to protect agriculture from foreign competition. Subsidies are payments made to farmers to support crop prices. Tariffs—or customs duties—are taxes levied on goods when they pass across national boundaries, usually made on imported goods and collected by the government of the importing country. Quotas are a government-imposed limit on the amount of a product that can be grown for the domestic market (production quotas) or, in international trade, on how much of a specific product can be imported or exported (quantitative restrictions).

Brief History

Subsidies became the cornerstone of American agricultural policy in the 1930s. Net farm incomes had fallen drastically in the Great Depression, and the solution, according to President Franklin D. Roosevelt, was to limit production as a way to boost prices. In 1933 he signed the Agricultural Adjustment Act, setting production quotas and authorizing subsidies for farmers in return for reducing crop acreage. Although they were originally intended as a crisis measure, subsidies became locked into American agricultural policy in the following decades and remain so today. Under commodity programs, farmers receive direct cash payments to make up the difference between the market price and a guaranteed price per bushel of commodity. Indirect subsidies also are provided, to limit production. While the Federal Agriculture Improvement and Reform Act of 1996 (the "farm bill") intended to change the direction of agricultural policy by reducing subsidies, direct payments increased once more in the 2002 Farm Bill.

Agricultural tariffs have an older history. The first tariff act was signed in 1789, with the purpose of raising revenues. Tariffs on imported agricultural goods were imposed in the 1920s and, to further protect domestic agriculture, raised to prohibitively high levels under the 1930 Smoot-Hawley Tariff Act. After a fierce trade war, the Reciprocal Trade Agreements Act of 1934 reversed the high-tariff policy. By the early years of the twenty-first century, the United States had relatively low tariffs on imported agricultural products—an average of 12 percent, compared with a global level of 62 percent. Along with subsidies, the United States tends to favor quotas as a means of protecting domestic agriculture, measures that are more restrictive than tariffs.

Farm subsidies, quotas, and tariffs are considered the enemy of free trade. For international institutions such as the World Trade Organization, they are anathema to the globalization of the world economy. In 1994 the General Agreement on Tariffs and Trade, originally signed in 1947, was renegotiated to include agricultural products for the first time. The resultant Agreement on Agriculture required the conversion of quotas to tariffs and the reduction of tariffs and defined the type and level of spending permitted on domestic subsidy programs. The United States also signed the North American Free Trade Agreement (NAFTA) with Canada and Mexico in 1994. Under NAFTA all nontariff barriers to agricultural trade between the United States and Mexico were eliminated, and many other tariffs were eliminated or phased out more gradually.

Effect on American Food

Farm subsidies, quotas, and tariffs have had profound impacts on agricultural production and trade in the United States. In turn, they also have influenced the American diet. Corn is one example. Federal subsidies of corn are among the highest of any commodity, amounting to $30 billion between 1996 and 2001. By the beginning of the twenty-first century, 80 million acres of land were being used for growing corn, 14 million more than in 1970. As a result, corn became cheap and plentiful. Corn is used to feed animals bred for meat. It is converted into high-fructose corn syrup and used as a substitute for sugar. It also is processed into starch, flour, and corn oil for use in prepared foods. The "cornification" of the American diet is palpable. The low cost of corn cheapened the meat supply and drove a threefold increase in the consumption of corn products between 1970 and the turn of the century. Corn is used in everything from cookies to soda.

Consider, in this respect, the Coca-Cola Company. As a cost-saving measure, the company switched to 100 percent corn sweeteners in the 1980s and so was able to sell larger bottles at no extra cost. For Coke, the problem with sugar was that it cost more than corn, a result, in part, of another measure intended to protect American farmers: quotas. Under the federal sugar program, only a certain quota of sugar can be imported. Above this quota, all sugar imports are subject to a prohibitively high tariff. The lack of real competition with other sugar producers boosts the price paid to producers—but costs domestic sweetener users $1.9 billion a year.

Tariffs have also affected the American food supply. After the implementation of NAFTA, Americans began to eat more imported food, especially fruits and vegetables. With lower tariffs affording a competitive advantage, Mexico became the largest supplier of fresh and frozen fruit in the United States, providing a steady supply of limes, melons, grapes, strawberries, mangos, and papayas year-round. Tariffs are also used as a weapon in "food wars." In 1996, for example, Florida tomato growers demanded that tariffs be placed on tomato and bell pepper imports from Mexico, claiming that they were losing $1 billion a year. In 1999 the United States retaliated against a European Union ban on hormone-treated U.S. beef, imposing $116.8 million worth of 100 percent tariffs on such gourmet foods as Roquefort cheese, Dijon mustard, and fresh truffles.

[See also Coca-Cola; Corn; North American Free Trade Agreement.]

BIBLIOGRAPHY

Watkins, Kevin, and Penny Fowler. *Rigged Rules and Double Standards: Trade, Globalization, and the Fights against Poverty.* Oxford: Oxfam, 2002.

CORINNA HAWKES

Fast Food

Fast food commonly consists of freshly prepared and wrapped food items sold across counters or through auto-mobile drive-up windows. Often referred to as "quick-service food" in the restaurant industry, fast food usually is served in a short amount of time, ranging from seconds to several minutes. Although many fast food restaurants offer customer seating, table service is rare. Varying widely in food type, fast food encompasses most meats, ethnic cooking styles, and cooking methods. Hamburgers dominate the industry, but other types of fast food include hot dogs, pizza, roast beef, pasta, chicken, and fish, in addition to a wide variety of ethnic specialties. Although the meal offerings and types of service vary, fast food commonly is inexpensive fare packaged for carry out and delivered quickly.

Vendors have sold foods to passersby on the roadside and city streets all around the world for thousands of years. Usually fast, inexpensive, and handheld, such foods were long popular for their convenience and cost. Fast food during the nineteenth century in the United States varied by region, ranging from fatty German sausage dominating northern cities to filled tortillas in the Southwest. By the early 1900s pushcart vendors sold sausages, stews, and meatballs to industrial workers outside factory gates. Although popular among urban workers, foods sold by these vendors never became mainstream fare.

Urban dining became a transitional phase between patronizing pushcart vendors and eating at fast food restaurants. Often constructed from old streetcars, diners served working-class customers inexpensive short-order meals usually cooked to order. The menu selection at diners varied, but fried foods predominated, and speed and quantity often were emphasized over taste.

The precise origin of modern fast food is in dispute, and competing theories are based on regional boosterism. Stories, usually lacking credible evidence, credit numerous individuals as the "inventors" of both the hot dog and the hamburger. Most verifiable is Walter Anderson's founding of a hamburger stand on a busy street in Wichita, Kansas. Five years later Anderson had a partner, Billy Ingram, an insurance broker, and the stand had grown into the White Castle System of Eating Houses. Quickly saturating the Wichita market, White Castle spread across the Midwest and ultimately defined itself as a "national institution" by the late 1920s. Setting a standard for fast food, Anderson and Ingram offered a streamlined menu of hamburgers, Coca-Cola, and coffee, emphasizing take-out, larger-quantity purchases "by the sack." White Castle succeeded by offering uniformly

Perils of Fast Food. Illustration from *Life*, 1907.

high-quality food, obsessive cleanliness, and courteous customer service in all stores.

The 1920s, an era of increasing prosperity and burgeoning technology, witnessed the rise of many large national companies, including grocery stores, processed food makers, and soft drink bottlers. At first cautious, consumers soon accepted these larger companies, eventually prizing "name brands" over locally produced items. White Castle succeeded in becoming both the leading nationally known chain and for a while even a synonym for fast food hamburgers. The success of White Castle spawned countless imitators, who closely copied White Castle's architecture, hamburgers, company name, and even its advertising slogan. For the next two decades, fast food hamburger outlets in the United States were largely in urban neighborhoods and usually resembled Anderson and Ingram's White Castle model. Formal recognition of the place of the fast food hamburger in society came in 1929, when the president of the American Restaurant Association proclaimed the hamburger and apple pie "America's foods."

Widespread poverty during the Depression caused stagnation in the growth of the fast food industry. Few new restaurants opened, and a shrinking customer base

forced fast food chains to contract or close. Notable exceptions were the openings in 1936 of the California-based Big Boy chain, which offered a popular double-decked, two-patty hamburger, and in 1939 of the original McDonald's restaurant. Even the growth of these chains was slow, first confronted by Depression-era hardships and then in the early 1940s by wartime food shortages and rationing of commodities. World War II further decimated the fast food industry by diverting the labor force to the military and to more lucrative jobs in the defense industry. Existing chains shrank to a fraction of their prewar size, many closing altogether. Prosperity after the war did not immediately revitalize fast food. Many chains were in shambles, and fears of food rationing continued. Rebuilding was a slow process. Regional chains of small, eat-in restaurants filled the void, especially in small towns and rural areas. Some urban fast food hamburger outlets survived, but postwar inflation dictated higher prices and decreased business.

The fast food industry rebounded in the 1950s with the development of modern suburbia. As veterans and their growing families fled traditional city neighborhoods, new fast food hamburger chains quickly followed. By the end of the decade, McDonald's and Burger King restaurants became fixtures at suburban crossroads, selling burgers, french-fried potatoes, and milkshakes to hungry customers. Both Ray Kroc, of McDonald's, and Jim McLamore, of Burger King, sought to build one of their franchised restaurants in every American town and actively worked toward that goal. They largely succeeded, opening hundreds of new outlets each year throughout the 1950s and 1960s. Consumers flocked to these restaurants, possibly viewing them as part of their modern, faster-paced lifestyle. While Burger King battled McDonald's for market share, Burger Chef restaurants joined the frantic competition, and Arby's, Kentucky Fried Chicken, and Taco Bell were not far behind. Introducing items such as roast beef, chicken, and tacos, these newest restaurants thrived, opening the door for countless other specialties. The term "fast food" was no longer synonymous with the hamburger alone. It became a generic term for describing many foods sold in a take-out style.

The fast food industry experienced turmoil in the late 1960s and early 1970s that caused even large chains to merge or fold, often edged out by the two industry leaders. As the field narrowed, McDonald's and Burger King gained even greater dominance, making it extremely difficult for new chains to compete. Some new companies, however, did successfully enter the market. Opening his Wendy's chain in defiance of the odds in 1969, Dave Thomas, a former KFC executive, offered consumers a bigger, more expensive burger, the popularity of which quickly earned Wendy's third place in the industry. Thomas's unexpected success and the continued prosperity of McDonald's and Burger King faced fresh challenges in the latter half of the 1970s. Environmentalists, health advocates, and unions attacked fast food companies about their products, trash, and labor practices. Some critics condemned the fried burgers, potatoes, fish, and chicken as health hazards, claiming these foods responsible for both obesity and poor nutrition. Others focused on how the fast food industry's packaging materials, such as plastic foam containers and aluminum or plastic wrap, were not biodegradable in garbage landfills. Labor activists criticized how the major chains maximized their profits by hiring teenage employees at very low wages. Despite these attacks, Americans continued to flock to fast food outlets in ever-increasing numbers.

Although conscious of health risks, by 2002 the average American consumer ate some type of fast food 16.4 times each month. Fast food remains popular because it tastes good and is inexpensive, predictable, and convenient. Americans may also eat fast food because it is a cultural norm, the American ethnic food. Fast food, especially the hamburger, is the most consumed type of food in the United States and is closely identified around the world as the centerpiece of distinctly American cuisine. In a nation composed of diverse ethnic backgrounds, the hamburger has emerged as the culinary common ground of a newly synthesized American ethnicity.

"Fast food" transcends the area of food, having become a broadly applied term describing other types of products and services. Meanings range from simple descriptions of speed and convenience of service to derogatory references of superficiality or low quality. Social critics often use "fast food" as a metaphor for deriding the homogeneity and commercialism of modern society. If the critics are correct, the usage signifies that good or bad, fast food is an important central factor in American culture.

[See also Burger King; Diners; Kentucky Fried Chicken; McDonald's; Roadside Food; Street Vendors; Taco Bell; Take-Out Foods; Wendy's; White Castle.]

BIBLIOGRAPHY

Emerson, Robert L. *Fast Food: The Endless Shakeout.* New York: Lebhar-Friedman, 1976.

Langdon, Philip. *Orange Roofs, Golden Arches: The Architecture of American Chain Restaurants.* New York: Knopf, 1986.
Mariani, John. *America Eats Out.* New York: Morrow, 1991.
Tennyson, Jeffrey. *Hamburger Heaven: The Illustrated History of the Hamburger.* New York: Hyperion, 1993.

DAVID GERARD HOGAN

Fats and Oils

Americans, like all members of the human race, crave and need fat. Fats and oils are indispensable cooking ingredients and are essential to good nutrition. Yet, for reasons both cultural and chemical, today's population is deeply ambivalent about the fats it consumes.

Native Americans

The first Americans had scant resources when it came to cooking fat because they had few, if any, domesticated animals that could be fattened up and, except for sunflowers, had no crops that could be easily processed for oil. Nevertheless, animals such as bear, beaver, and armadillo were hunted in large part for their high fat content. The fat, though, was seldom rendered. In much the way New Englanders would add salted pork back fat to their chowders, Native Americans included the fatty parts of animals in their long-simmered stews. To similar ends, pounded sunflower seeds might be added to enrich cornbread. Only among the Eskimos was animal fat a major component of the diet. In the far north aged whale blubber was a delicacy, and seal fat was used as both a food preservative and fuel for lamps.

Colonial Era and the Early Republic

When Europeans set up their stockades in North America, they brought with them pigs and cows, the four-legged factories that would produce virtually all of the cooking fat used in this country until the industrial revolution. Lard, rendered pork fat, was by far the most common shortening throughout the colonial era and well into the antebellum period. Lard was used for frying, breads, biscuits, cakes, and even as a dressing for vegetables. Before the advent of refrigeration, most of the nation's pork was salted, and the fattier parts were used for flavoring stuffings as well as stews. Bacon and the drippings that it would yield were prized ingredients. In this agrarian society lard was rendered at home and kept for many months in the cool confines of the aptly named larder. The crisp crust that lard produces in frying was particularly appreciated in the South, where, it has been suggested, black cooks adapted West African frying techniques to create regional specialties such as fried chicken and hush puppies. Certainly pork fat was much more available below the Mason-Dixon Line than in New England, where dairy and beef cattle were the more common forms of livestock. For many recipes, lard continues to retain favor in parts of the old Confederacy. More recently, Latin American cooks imported their penchant for the lard used in their native cuisines. Mexican-American cooks, for example, seek out pork fat for the texture and flavor it imparts to everything from tamales and flour tortillas to refried beans and mole.

Early recipes often called for butter or lard, or occasionally, as in pie pastry, for a combination of the two. Whether the cook used butter or lard was generally an issue of price and availability. In baking, dairy fat was preferred, but butter is much more perishable than lard and in many parts of the country was available only in the warmer milking months. Butter often was salted to extend shelf life.

In the colonial period most butter was produced and consumed on the farm. By the late eighteenth century butter began to be distributed commercially, especially around New York and Philadelphia. By 1812 New York butter wagons traveled as far south as Charleston, South Carolina. New York State remained the country's largest butter producer until displaced by Wisconsin in the early years of the twentieth century. Throughout the 1800s most butter was churned on the farm. Although the first commercial creamery opened in 1861 in Orange County, New York, large-scale butter production did not accelerate until the 1880s, when refrigerated railway cars became common. Many butter plants were run by cooperatives. The Land O' Lakes brand, for example, was founded by the Minnesota Cooperative Creameries Association in 1921. One of its innovations was to package butter in convenient quarter-pound sticks. Before the use of paper and cardboard packaging, butter had been packed in wooden tubs, wrapped in linen, and, at the crest of industrialization, sealed in cans.

Cows not only provided butter but also were a source for suet, deemed an essential ingredient in the many steamed, boiled, and baked puddings beloved by colonists from the British Isles. Nonetheless, despite the occasional recipe that begins "fry out suet" as a way of obtaining a shortening for sautéing, cow fat never enjoyed the popularity of lard.

The only oil regularly available to colonial Americans was olive oil. (Fats that remain liquid at room temperature are generally referred to as oils.) Only in the most elite enclaves within the Spanish colonies was this expensive import used for cooking. In the English and French settlements, olive oil was reserved almost exclusively for salad dressing.

Industrial Oils and Shortenings

As they moved from a self-sufficient rural setting to newly industrialized cities in the late nineteenth century, increasing numbers of Americans had to pay cash for the cooking fat that on the farm had been a substantially free by-product of livestock husbandry. An array of more economical ersatz butters, commercially processed lard, and newly perfected vegetable oils were developed and marketed. Giant food processors such as Armour used the by-products of meatpacking to sell industrially rendered lard for cooking and soap making. Soap makers such as Proctor and Gamble used their fat know-how to produce Crisco, a vegetable oil–based lard that was sufficiently cheaper than the real thing. Spry, a similar product, was explicitly marketed for its economy: "To the woman who must make ends meet!" ran the headline from a Spry advertisement as late as 1953.

Competition to butter came first from real butter that had been adulterated with other animal fats. Later came margarines that were produced from all manner of fats and oils. The powerful dairy lobbies in many states successfully pushed for legislation that protected butter to the detriment of its pretenders. The truly new products that were created as a result of scientific innovation are the many vegetable oils Americans find on grocery store shelves.

Among the first new oils to come to market was peanut oil. George Brownrigg developed a process for extracting "a well tasted" oil from peanuts in North Carolina around 1768, and the oil came to be used as a substitute for olive oil, at least in the South. Because of its low price the oil was often used as an adulterant in the much more expensive olive oil. By the 1840s peanut oil was used in the southern states as a cooking fat in its own right, but by the end of the Civil War production of peanut oil had ceased. Grocers had to turn to Europe to stock their shelves with peanut oil. It was not until World War I that government efforts lit a fire under the domestic peanut industry; the result was an improved oil used not only for cooking and the manufacture of other compound fats but also for numberless industrial purposes. In 1930 the

Cooking Oils. Cooking oils on sale at Sahadi's Middle Eastern market, Brooklyn, New York. *Photograph by Joe Zarba*

Planters peanut company harnessed its considerable marketing acumen to promote its own brand of oil.

After the Civil War, production of cottonseed oil largely replaced that of peanut oil in the cotton-growing states. Cottonseed processing on a commercial scale began in 1855 in New Orleans, Louisiana, and Providence, Rhode Island. Most processing plants were located wherever cotton was grown in quantity, and it was not until the railroads were expanded to many parts of the South around 1880 that the business took off. Demand increased further when cottonseed oil was sold under the Wesson brand as of 1900. Crisco shortening was also primarily composed of hydrogenated cottonseed oil. With the decline of American-grown cotton in the late twentieth century, cottonseed oil has largely been replaced by less expensive oils.

By the turn of the twentieth century food scientists had learned not only to add extra hydrogen atoms to make liquid oil solid at room temperature (thus the term "hydrogenated") but also to devise chemical techniques for extracting and refining oils from plants with a relatively low fat content. One of these new oils was first refined from corn at the Corn Products Refining Company in 1910 and marketed under the label Mazola. Increasingly, the new oil that came to dominate American and overseas production was processed from soybeans. The increase in output was particularly notable after World War II: between 1939 and 1986 world soybean oil production increased fifteenfold.

Fats and Health

Whereas throughout most of human history our ancestors had valued fats as a way of imbibing concentrated calo-

ries, in the post–World War II era, opinion, at least in the affluent corners of the world, began to look more critically at dietary fat in general and the composition of certain cooking fats in particular. In the 1950s and 1960s cholesterol was implicated as a risk factor for heart disease, leading many health professionals to advise against eating the highly saturated animal fats and tropical oils that appeared to boost the amount of cholesterol in the blood. This warning was a bonanza for margarine manufacturers, who until this point had only price to recommend their product over butter. Now margarine was the healthy alternative—but not for long. In the 1990s the trans-fatty acids produced in hydrogenation of vegetable oil for the manufacture of most margarines were found to be just as bad as saturated fat.

As science further refined its opinions about the composition of fats, oils high in monounsaturated and polyunsaturated fat became the new darlings of the mainstream press and marketers alike. Rapeseed, a relative of mustard, which in Europe had been pressed for industrial oil for hundreds years, was now lauded for its extremely low saturated fat content. Not until 1988, however, when the U.S. Food and Drug Administration allowed the product to shed its unsavory name in favor of "canola," did its sales hit the big time.

Olive oil was similarly promoted for its healthful qualities. The desirability of olive oil was buoyed after 1980 by the perennial popularity of foods from Italy and California. Although almost all olive oil was imported, a few small California producers began to press their own boutique oils at prices that rivaled those of fine wine. Americans used increasing quantities of olive oil in their cooking, yet many found that they did not actually like the flavor. Seeing a marketing opportunity, manufacturers concocted "light" olive oil, which had much of the flavor refined out of it.

Synthetic Fat

While rising health concerns led companies to reformulate their cooking oils and spreads (for example, McDonald's stopped using beef fat in its fryers, and Proctor and Gamble converted Puritan oil from a soybean blend to all canola oil), the holy grail of the American food industry was the creation of a fat that had all of its flavor and texture attributes but none of its calories. To this end, in 1991 A. E. Staley Manufacturing introduced Stellar, a corn-based product meant to replace oil in foods such as margarine and baked goods. The faux fat joined Simplesse, a dairy-derived product made by NutraSweet that had been developed to simulate high-fat flavor in frozen desserts.

The most notorious fat substitute, Olestra, was introduced in 1996 by Procter and Gamble under the brand name Olean. This "pseudofood" is chemically a fat, but it is formulated in such a way that it is indigestible and thus passes through the body without entering the bloodstream. Despite the mostly negative publicity the product received on its debut, it soon made its quiet way into potato and corn chips.

New Trends

While the food industry devoted its energies to its laboratories and to Madison Avenue, a food-focused minority created a market for more obscure fats and oils. In upscale grocery stores European and European-style butter joined tubs of duck fat, jars of avocado oil, and imported tins of walnut oil. Chefs in American restaurants experimented with French grapeseed oil, Moroccan *argan* oil, and Austrian pumpkin oil. An average grocery store stocks dozens of types of oil, butter, margarine, and even the lard that was so indispensable to America's founding mothers.

[*See also* African American Food; Butter; Butter-Making Tools and Churns; Corn; Dairy Industry; Obesity; Peanuts; Pig; Soybeans; Sunflowers.]

BIBLIOGRAPHY

Bock, Gordon. "Will Fake Fat Yield Plump Profits? The Race Is on to Develop a Low-Cholesterol Food Substitute." *Time*, May 25, 1987.

"Fake Fat of the Land: A. E. Staley Manufacturing Introduces Stellar, an Artificial Fat." *Time*, June 24, 1991.

Foster, Gaines M. "Cinderella of the New South: A History of the Cottonseed Industry, 1855–1955." *Agricultural History* (Fall 1996).

Horowitz, Janice M. Gordon. "A Card Game? No, Cooking Oil: Canola Is the Latest Love of the Cholesterol-free Set." *Time*, November 12, 1990.

Krondl, Michael. *Around the American Table: Treasured Recipes and Food Traditions from the American Cookery Collections of the New York Public Library*. Holbrook, MA: Adams, 1995.

Land O'Lakes. www.landolakes.com.

Procter and Gamble. www.pg.com.

Roach, Mary. "My Dinner with Nartok." *Health*, November/December 1994.

Roebbelen, Gerhard, R. Keith Downey, and Amram Ashri, eds. *Oil Crops of the World*. New York: McGraw-Hill, 1989.

"Wesson." ConAgra Foods. http://www.conagrafoods.com/brands/wesson.jsp.

Wrenn, Lynette Boney. "Cotton Gins and Cottonseed Oil Mills in the New South." *Agricultural History* (Spring 1994).

MICHAEL KRONDL

Fermentation

Fermentation is an ancient technique of food transformation and preservation. It is a natural part of metabolism and one way for microorganisms to derive energy from certain nutrients. Uncontrolled fermentation can render foods unpalatable or inedible. Encouraging the growth of benign bacteria and fungi inhibits spoilage—or disease-causing microorganisms, which must compete for nutrients. Fermentation generates various molecules, including alcohols and acids. These give fermented foods their complex flavors and odors. Altering conditions, such as salt or sugar content, temperature, humidity, or oxygen level, can alter those flavors. Most "natural" fermentations stop when the original food source has run out (the sugars in grape must, for example) or when conditions inhibit the fermenting organism (as acids accumulate in yogurt). Adding more nutrients or removing waste products can keep the process going if needed.

Some fermentations rely on a single microorganism: the carefully selected cultivated yeasts used in commercial production of alcohols. Others rely on a mixture, such as the wild yeasts and bacteria used to produce various sourdough breads. Sourdoughs (or sauerkrauts, cheeses, salamis, or pickles) made in different locations will have slightly different microorganisms, even though similar starting ingredients have been used. These differences contribute to the individuality of these products. Commercial producers control their domesticated organisms to avoid such variations.

Fermented foods contain many of the proteins and minerals, and some of the vitamins, of their starting materials. Some foods are felt to be more digestible after fermentation, as the offending polysaccharides have been

FERMENTED FOODS OTHER THAN ALCOHOLS

Product	Starting Materials	Microorganism(s)
Soy sauce	Soybeans and wheat	Fungi (Aspergillus spp) bacteria (Lactobacillus spp)
Poi	Taro	Yeast (Candida spp) bacteria (Lactobacillus spp)
Kimchi	Cabbage or other	Bacteria (lactic acid
Sauerkraut	Vegetables	Bacteria, different species)
Cured salami	Meat	Bacteria (Lactobacillus, Pediococcus spp) fungi (Penicillium spp) on the casing

processed. Fermented foods are not entirely immune to spoilage, although such contamination is often obvious prior to consumption.

[*See also* Beer; Cheese; Wineries; Yeast.]

BIBLIOGRAPHY

Most public libraries will have books on sourdoughs, brewing and wine making, pickling, and sausage making.

Campbell-Platt, G. *Fermented Foods of the World.* London and Boston: Butterworths, 1987. Covering a wide range of foods and the microorganisms and processes involved.

FSHN 420 Food Microbiology, a basic fermentation lecture available at the Iowa State University food science website http://www.ag.iastate.edu/departments/foodsci/classes/fshn420/ ferment.html.

Wood, Brian J. B., ed. *Microbiology of Fermented Foods.* 2nd ed. 2 vols. Dordrecht: Kluwer, 1997. A comprehensive reference work, available in larger libraries.

ASTRID FERSZT

Festivals and Fairs, *see Food Festivals*

Figs

Essentially Mediterranean fruits, figs (*Ficus carica*) prosper only in warm, dry climates. In the southeastern United States, fig plantings suffer from excessive humidity, exposure to rain, and occasional freezing injury. In the United States figs are grown commercially in large plantings only in California. The fig tree is the northernmost representative of the tropical banyans. The fruit develops inside-out: The stem forms the skin and encloses the sweet, edible pulp and seeds.

Fresh figs rarely appear in supermarkets. They are found more often in specialty fruit shops and also directly from the grower in areas of local production, including on the Delmarva Peninsula and southern seaboard (near Chesapeake Bay) and in Florida. The fruits are palatable only when fully ripe, when the interior pulp has softened to a jelly-like condition. Full ripeness is indicated by soft skin and limp stems. In such a state, the fruit is exceptionally perishable, and refrigeration is an absolute necessity. In poor seasons with little heat, even fully ripe fruit can be insipid.

The most widely grown cultivars in the United States are Brown Turkey and Brunswick (synonym in Texas, Magnolia), but the finest (Excel, White Adriatic, and Bourjassotte Noire) are found only in California. Dried figs, partially rehydrated in loose-filled plastic pouches, are produced in the Merced-Fresno district of that state in the Black Mission (dark skinned) and Calimyrna (light skinned) varieties. The former is common as a fresh fruit in California, although not of the highest quality; the latter is the Sari Lop of the Izmir district of Turkey and an outstanding, but rare, item as a fresh fruit. Tinned and, more often, bottled figs are a specialized commodity also in California and are made exclusively of the Italian Dottato variety (locally named Kadota).

[*See also* California; Fruit.]

BIBLIOGRAPHY

Condit, Ira J. *The Fig.* Waltham, MA: Chronica Botanica, 1947.

Ferguson, Louise, Themis Michailides, and Harry H. Shorey, "The California Fig Industry." *Horticultural Reviews* 12 (1990): 409–490.

C. T. KENNEDY

Filberts

Filberts (or hazelnuts) are native to both the New World and the Old World. The two species of hazel trees indigenous to the United States are *Corylus americana*, which grows primarily in the East, and *C. cornuta*, which ranges from the Atlantic to the Pacific. The nuts of both were consumed by Native Americans and early European colonists. However, filberts from the New World are small, with thick shells, and inferior in quality; the nuts have little commercial value. The European hazel (*C. avellana*) is the source of most commercial nuts. Hazelnuts have been an important human food since prehistoric times. The ancient Romans praised them, and hazelnuts were grown in Britain in Roman times. The seeds were sent to Massachusetts in 1629, and filberts were being sold in New York City by 1771. Oregon leads the nation in hazelnut production. Filberts are enjoyed as snacks, and their sweetness is used to advantage in baked goods and other desserts, often in combination with chocolate.

[*See also* Nuts.]

ANDREW F. SMITH

Film, Food in

Food has been appearing in film ever since the medium took shape. In one turn-of-the-century silent short film by the French Lumière Brothers, we watch a baby as she eats cereal and then, to her distress, makes a huge mess. In another by the duo, a thick wave of men exit and reenter a factory as they break and return from lunch—an image that defined the new industrial era. These everyday-life moments involving food have never faded from film; indeed, in American cinema, concern for realism has necessitated the regular appearance of food and eating. After all, if we are to relate to film characters, they must at least eat and drink like the rest of us.

But film in the United States has done more than present typical eating habits; over the history of cinema, food in American film has encompassed a wide range of meanings. From narrative to documentary, symbolism to structure, and obscure to obscene food displays, American film has presented food as a reflection of the culture's images and ideals. Attitudes and mores surrounding love, sex, gender, ethnicity, and social class are among the theoretical and historical issues that food in film regularly engages.

Interestingly, the largest body of written work on food in film derives from non-American films. *Lae Grande Bouffe* (1972), *Tampopo* (1986), *Babette's Feast* (1987), and *Like Water for Chocolate* (1992) are among the movies that have tended to get the most mouths watering and, apparently, the most pens to paper. However, American-made narrative cinema has started to catch on to the appeal of food-centric films: *Big Night* (1997) and *Soul Food* (1997) have both proved food to be a big box-office draw. Films featuring female chefs—*Chocolat* (2000) and *Woman on Top* (2000)—have also added to the "food film" catalog, even while reasserting the idea that a woman's power depends on her talents in the kitchen.

Aesthetics have played a major role in the drama and appeal of American "cuisine cinema." Improvements in cinematography have so enhanced the technical art of food styling that, increasingly, food on film looks good enough to eat. *The Godfather* (1972), with its lavish displays of Sicilian food, can be seen as a consequence of an Italian American director (Francis Ford Coppola) and writer (Mario Puzo) seeking not only visual splendor but also culinary authenticity. Up until that time, American-made films were fairly sparse in their food detail. Consequently, famous food stylists such as Rick Ellis, who styled Martin Scorsese's opulent *The Age of Innocence* (1993), have been put to work to meet directors' and audiences' demands for culinary accuracy and visual palatability.

Still, as effective as *The Godfather* was in giving filmed food audience appeal, the "food film" has been a relative newcomer to Hollywood's history. Comedies such as *Who Is Killing the Great Chefs of Europe?* (1978) and countless Italian Mafia film spoofs (from the ridiculous *Godson* [1998] to the sublime *Freshman* [1990]) have regularly delivered food as a recipe for laughs, especially when edibles are thrown, regurgitated, or ignited. The same is true of teen sex comedies, such as *American Pie* (1999), in which food is a recipe for sexual exploration and humiliation. Food as a comedic prop for social commentary can be traced back to Charlie Chaplin and the Keystone cop films. In Chaplin's *Modern Times* (1936), for example, an "eating machine" serves as a metaphor for the sterile perils of the Machine Age, and in the Keystone cop films, social oppression, as represented by the policemen, literally receives a pie in the face.

But not until the 1980s and 1990s did food begin to take center stage in major studio-supported American films. And then, screen eating ran to extremes: food was either voraciously consumed or vehemently despised, with consumption depicting deeply affectionate or severely impaired social relations. Two dominant types of films

Food in Film. Meryl Streep and Jack Nicholson in *Heartburn*, 1986.

developed: the ethnic-based food film and the weight-preoccupied one. In the first category came *Soul Food*, a tale of an African American family that coheres at Sunday dinners, and *Big Night*, a story of two Italian brothers whose failing restaurant embodies the struggle between the artist and society. Similarly, Terry Barr has categorized as "Jewish cinema" a large group of films—among them, *Avalon* (1987), *Crimes and Misdemeanors* (1989), and *Quiz Show* (1994)—that recapitulate stereotypes about Jewish food and eating traditions and reveal how food factored into the way immigrants assimilated into the dominant, Anglo-Saxon Protestant culture. Unfortunately, a common pitfall of such ethnically oriented food films is that, as in *Tortilla Soup* (2001)—a Mexican American version of the Taiwanese *Eat Drink Man Woman* (1994)—food becomes another way for Hollywood to reduce ethnic (or nonwhite) culture and differences to, in essence, a matter of "tastes." For example, the wildly successful *Moonstruck* (1987) tells of an Italian American woman in pursuit of love and passion, with her greatest revelations occurring while preparing or eating lusty Italian food.

Another category is film that presents the trials and traumas of overweight or obese characters, such as *Heavy* (1995) and *What's Eating Gilbert Grape?* (1993). *Eating* (1990) by Henry Jaglom deliberates on women's body insecurities and food obsessions during a birthday party, and in 2001, the famously thin actress Gwyneth Paltrow donned a fat suit in *Shallow Hal*. It seems no coincidence that in the later twentieth century, as diet and exercise fads appeared faster and more furiously, there was a significant increase in films that catered to the gastronomically tortured. No doubt *Chocolat* (which strongly echoes *Babette's Feast*) and its cinematic cuisine cousins tapped into their audiences' deep emotional and physical hunger, which only a zero-calorie film could satisfy.

Food taboos such as cannibalism have also been depicted in films, in particular in the horror and thriller film genres. *The Silence of the Lambs* (1991) and *Alive* (1993) exploit this particular repulsion, and science fiction films, from *Soylent Green* (1973) to *The Matrix* (1999), regularly compel us to probe deeper and to ask, What do we mean by "food," anyway? And when it comes to eating, how do we define what foods and behaviors are savage or civilized?

The inextricable relationship between food and sex often plays out in American films. Aside from pornography, in which the use of food in sexual acts is far from unusual, films often use food to allude to sex or even as a prop during sex. In popular language, food is often invoked to express affection or describe sexual organs: honeypot, buns, and cherry for her; beefcake, banana, and sausage for him. *Bonnie and Clyde* (1967), a gangster film in which the eponymous duo effectively eat their way across the country, also bears a number of references to peaches and pies, foods that carry heavy feminine connotations. Here they refer to Bonnie, who is aggressively sexual but, because of Clyde's impotence, repeatedly frustrated. More explicit was Adrian Lyne's *9½ Weeks* (1986), which took the country by storm with its kinky, food-based sex play that upped the ante first put up by the British release *Tom Jones* (1963) and matched by the lobster dinner in *Flashdance* (1983), the latter also by Lyne. Of course, even when relationships aren't consummated, food will still alert us to gender roles, especially regarding who provides, prepares, or serves the day's meals.

The attraction to food in film has proven considerable even in films that would never be heralded for their comestibles. Jack Nicholson's famous request for toast in *Five Easy Pieces* (1970) left us forever ready to challenge the phrase "no substitutions," and Sally's fake orgasm at a deli in *When Harry Met Sally* (1989) left everyone wanting "what she's having." Similarly, the grapefruit kiss James Cagney delivered to Mae Clark in *The Public Enemy* (1931) remains shocking for its brutality and barbarism. (It has also been countlessly reworked; in *Heartburn* [1986], the toss of a chiffon pie punctuates the same relationship disharmony.) Food is a common denominator, an element everyone can relate to and understand. When used or discussed in an unconventional way, the result is unforgettable.

In some cases, a film's food scenes enhance non-food ones and can serve as a key to its structure and themes. Take, for example, gangster films, in which scenes involving eating regularly precede ones of physical violence. Coppola's *Godfather* trilogy explicitly alternates between lavish ceremonies involving food and equally visceral killings. *Bonnie and Clyde* is similarly structured, although with fewer flourishes, so that following each meal comes a violent plot turn—as is the case with the food-laden, neo-noir *Pulp Fiction* (1993). As in life, dining scenes typically provide a time for characters to take a break from the action; perhaps this is why, despite their frequency, murders in restaurants always seem to take audiences (as well as characters) by surprise.

Food and Filmmakers

Narrative mechanics and symbolism aside, food and eating scenes can also be tempting, as a practical matter, for

Grapefruit Kiss. James Cagney and Mae Clark in *The Public Enemy*, 1931.

filmmakers. Dialogue scenes are easy to shoot at the table, and meals can bring out subtleties of character, especially if a meal that is meant to bond characters is shadowed by hostile conversation. Food, like cigarettes, also gives actors something to do with their hands. Of course, however casual or "throwaway" these images may seem, they still take considerable planning.

Documentaries offer another view of food in American film. As in narrative cinema, food in documentaries humanizes the characters and completes the picture. Here the filmmaker does not determine and place the food; rather, the food is organic to the events being filmed. The documentary filmmaker Les Blank is renowned for his loving attention to and focus on food. *Chulas Fronteras* (1976), *Garlic Is as Good as 10 Mothers* (1980), and *Yum Yum Yum! A Taste of Cajun and Creole Cooking* (1990) are among Blank's celebrations of diverse food types, rituals, and practices. Blank not only shows food preparation and consumption; he seems to relish conveying every noise and image associated with the food he presents: you swear that you can smell those ribs charring on the grill and that garlic stinking up the city.

Film, Food, and the Culture

At the end of the twentieth century, changing demographics were rapidly altering the culinary landscape. In addition, a mounting interest in food history and culture led to merchandise inspired by the food in film as well as television. The Mexican-made *Like Water for Chocolate* was, in fact, based on a novel that included recipes, but in the United States, it is successful films that have themselves inspired everything from cookbooks to copycat meals at restaurants. Although celebrity cookbooks have always been popular, the director Martin Scorsese, whose cinematic portraits of Italian Americans have included many a plate of pasta, helped his mother, Catherine, produce *Italianamerican: The Scorcese Family Cookbook*, a compendium of family memories and recipes, accompanied by film stills and stories from the sets where Catherine would regularly feed the cast and crew. In a wackier tribute, *The Star Wars Cookbook* (1998), released in tandem with *Star Wars, Episode 1: The Phantom Menace* (1999), offers concoctions that weren't in the films but were inspired by its characters and images. (Skywalker Smoothie or Wookiee Cookie, anyone?) Similarly, the television series *The Sopranos* has spawned a "family cookbook" in addition to food products, cooking

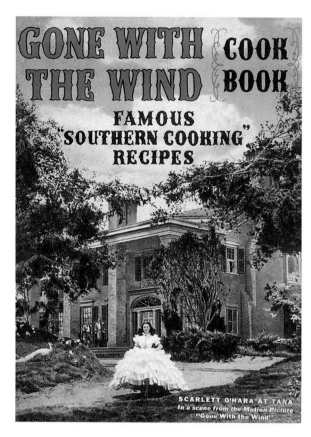

Movie Tie-in. Cookbooklet issued by the Pebeco Toothpaste Co. MGM's *Gone with the Wind*, directed by Victor Fleming, premiered in 1939. *Collection of Andrew F. Smith*

utensils, and apparel. Indeed, by 1999 television had caught the food wave in force, so that in addition to the creation of the Food Network (a cable channel devoted to food preparation, history, and lore), the film *Soul Food* became a TV series on Showtime, and another cable station offered "Dinner and a Movie," in which a chef prepares a dish during a film's commercial breaks.

Of course, Hollywood film and food have always gone together, especially the eating that took place off the screen. The documentary *Off the Menu: The Last Days of Chasen's* (1998) illuminates how Hollywood has always been a town where leisure activities, such as restaurant dining, have been an essential part of the filmmaking culture. From the industry's beginnings, gossip and allure circulated around establishments where stars ate, drank, and greeted their fans. Hollywood restaurants also became places for doing business—for "deals over meals." From Lucy Ricardo's embarrassing introduction to William Holden at the Brown Derby in an episode of *I Love Lucy* to Elizabeth Taylor's legendary demands for

Chasen's chili on the set of *Cleopatra* and post-Oscar parties at the famed eatery Morton's, the interconnectedness of Hollywood film and food has always existed for public consumption.

Aside from occasional newspaper and magazine articles, little has been written on the many roles food occupies in film. As of 2002, academic scholarship on the subject remained sparse, but there were stomach rumblings for more. Whether food is deliciously central to plot and motive or provides a subtle scent in the background, it has indeed fed the evolution of American film.

[*See also* Radio and Television.]

BIBLIOGRAPHY

Barr, Terry. "Eating Kosher, Staying Closer: Families and Meals in Contemporary Jewish American Cinema." *Journal of Popular Film and Television* 24, no. 3 (Fall 1996): 134–144. A close reading of several films that Barr has classified as "Jewish cinema," based on common character types and narrative concerns.

Davis, Robin. *The Star Wars Cookbook: Wookiee Cookies and Other Galactic Recipes.* San Francisco: Chronicle Books, 1998.

Goodwin, Betty. *Chasen's, Where Hollywood Dined: Recipes and Memories.* Santa Monica, CA: Angel City Press, 1996. A history of the restaurant, with anecdotes about celebrity patrons and recipes.

Lahue, Kalton C., and Terry Brewer. *Kops and Custards: The Legend of Keystone Films.* Norman: University of Oklahoma Press, 1968.

Loukides, Paul, and Linda K. Fuller, eds. *Beyond the Stars III: The Material World in American Popular Film.* Bowling Green, OH: Bowling Green University Popular Press, 1993. This anthology of essays includes several concerning food in film. See especially Parley Ann Boswell's discussion of culture as illustrated through film in "Hungry in the Land of Plenty."

Mast, Gerald. *The Comic Mind: Comedy and the Movies.* Indianapolis: Bobbs-Merrill, 1973. Includes discussion of food in silent comedies, especially the films of Charlie Chaplin.

O'Neill, Molly. "Eye Candy." *New York Times Magazine*, November 16, 1997. A brief discussion on "food films," plus related recipes.

Poole, Gaye. *Reel Meals, Set Meals: Food in Film and Theatre.* Sydney: Currency Press, 1999. The most comprehensive study of the topic at this writing.

Rowe, Claudia. "Cinematic Truth for Young Chefs." *New York Times*, August 16, 1998. An illuminating afternoon with Stanley Tucci, star, codirector, and cowriter of *Big Night*, at the Culinary Institute of America.

Scorsese, Catherine, and Georgia Downard. *Italianamerican: The Scorsese Family Cookbook.* New York: Random House, 1996. See especially the section "Movies: Cooking on the Set," pp. 101–150.

Steed, Tobias. *Hollywood Cocktails.* Minoqua, WI: Willow Creek Press, 1999. A gorgeous collection of film stills and cocktail recipes.

Stern, Michael. "I Like to Watch People Eat: A Life in Movies and Food." *Gourmet*, February 2000. Personal memoir, with many examples of food moments in film.

Westfahl, Gary, George Slusser, and Eric S. Rabkin, eds. *Foods of the Gods: Eating and the Eaten in Fantasy and Science Fiction.* Athens: University of Georgia Press, 1996. This anthology is composed of essays discussing film and literature in these genres, with arguments that significantly rely on social theory.

REBECCA L. EPSTEIN

Firehouse Cooking

Firehouse cooking has become entrenched in American popular culture. Firefighters conspicuously shop en masse, write cookbooks, and demonstrate their recipes on television. Excluding food-service professionals, perhaps no other occupation is so deeply and publicly involved in shopping, cooking, and eating as part of their work lives. Although each city has a slightly different story, New York City typifies and has influenced the evolution of firehouse cooking as a significant social fixture.

Historical Framework: New York as a Model

The Fire Department of New York was established in 1865 when funds were first allotted for standardizing the numerous community-supported volunteer companies in the New York area. Early professional firefighters worked and lived together in the firehouse, originally working nine twenty-four-hour days followed by a tenth day off. The firefighters were allotted three hours of breaks per day, which could be divided among one, two, or three meals, depending largely on the distance between the firehouse and the firefighter's home. These breaks would be suspended in the event of a major fire. Early professional firefighters walked or bicycled home or to local diners for meals and cooked in the firehouse only for festive occasions. The most common of these occasions was the Saturday night chowder, for which pots, utensils, and items of decor were collected from firefighters' homes, and the men chipped in for the food to have a firehouse-cooked meal open to family and friends.

Despite the existence of festive firehouse cooking in the nineteenth century, however, cooking did not begin to become a part of everyday firehouse life until the 1920s, a period of major change for the fire department. Many developments during this period dramatically changed the nature of firefighting and firehouse life. Perhaps most significant was the decision to change from a one-platoon system to a two-platoon system, whereby firefighters would work alternating twelve-hour shifts. This change eliminated meal breaks, prompting the firefighters to bring food from home or have it delivered by family, friends, or neighborhood children.

Along with these dramatic shifts came changes borne of practical considerations. A newly horseless engine house gave firefighters more space and a cleaner environment— they had been congregating and sleeping in a loft above the stable in most firehouses. In some houses firefighters installed rudimentary kitchens in the room where the stable had been, using equipment and utensils brought from home or purchased with pooled funds. The firefighters began pooling food as well and later appointed one man as cook on alternating days when things were calm.

Both the union and the city were impressed by firefighters' initiative in the kitchen. The union saw cooking as a way to regain the fraternal sentiment lost in the change from voluntarism to a tightly regulated paramilitary structure and to improve the quality of the working day. The department administrators saw the cooking as a way to keep the men together and away from alcohol, women, and other distractions of meal breaks. With such rare and powerful support of both the union and the department, firehouse cooking was becoming an institution in the United States.

Obstacles and Functions

Firehouse cooking has endured despite the presence of many obstacles. Most fire departments have never financially supported firehouse cooking. Firefighters negotiate the menu among themselves, ride the fire truck to shop together for food so that if they receive a call they are ready to abandon their carts at the market and respond to the emergency, and divide the cost of each meal among those present. Moreover, firefighters contribute to a commissary fund to provide staple ingredients and to fund necessary maintenance of the kitchen equipment.

Another obstacle to firehouse cooking is the unpredictable nature of firehouse life. Dennis Smith, a New York City firefighter, wrote, "I once kept a running account of how many meals I could eat in the firehouse without interruption. It went for three and a half months, and in that time I never ate one uninterrupted meal" (*Report from Engine Co. 82*). Furthermore, firefighters receive no training with regard to food and cooking, other than its nutritional aspects, which can produce some unsavory results among the new recruits.

Although the obstacles to firehouse cooking may be significant from a material standpoint, firehouse meals have important social functions that in a corporate environment might be called "acculturation," "diversity training," and "feedback sessions." One study of a firefighter training class and the students' placement in the field showed that housekeeping chores, especially cooking, served as "proving grounds" for new recruits (Chetkovich, *Real Heat*). In the urban fire department it is not sufficient to perform well at the fire ground or to master the book knowledge. One has to prove oneself competent and active in firehouse culture. This may include learning one another's cultural tastes and experiences, adapting to the meal system at each firehouse, and recovering from the day, most typically in the kitchen and at the table. Working together smoothly in the relaxed atmosphere of the firehouse kitchen is seen as insurance that the group will be able to work well in the stressful emergency environment.

Although it may endure as an icon of popular culture, firehouse cooking has value behind the closed doors of the firehouse. Firefighters never know which meal will be their last and may feel this more saliently than most people do. Firefighters tend to celebrate the everyday, and negotiating the intricacies of the meal, cooking elaborate meals together, and eating in a raucous and convivial atmosphere are important to this outlook.

[*See also* Kitchens; Material Culture and Technology, *subentry on* Social Aspects of Material Culture.]

BIBLIOGRAPHY

Cannon, Donald J., ed. *Heritage of Flames: The Illustrated History of Early American Firefighting*. Garden City, NY: Doubleday, 1977. Focuses on the preprofessional era of firefighting.

Chetkovich, Carol. *Real Heat: Gender and Race in the Urban Fire Service*. New Brunswick, NJ: Rutgers University Press, 1997. A scholarly and critical view of gender and race issues in the contemporary urban firehouse.

McCarl, Robert. *The District of Columbia Firefighters' Project: A Case Study in Occupational Folklife*. Washington, DC: Smithsonian Institution Press, 1985. A Smithsonian folklife study of firefighters.

Smith, Dennis. *Report from Engine Co. 82*. New York: McCall, 1972. A memoir by a New York City firefighter.

Zurrier, Rebecca. *The American Firehouse: An Architectural and Social History*. New York: Abbeville, 1982. Architecture is used as a lens for exploring the history of American firefighting.

JONATHAN DEUTSCH

Fireless Cookers

The principle of cooking with retained heat has been known for its usefulness in many times and many cultures. Peasants wrapped pots of partially cooked food in heavy feather beds. Well insulated, the food would continue to cook until the family returned from the fields to a hot meal. Native Americans used heated stones for clam bakes. Logging camps baked beans over hot stones in pits. Farmers carried fireless cookers into the fields so they could enjoy a hot meal at noon. Immigrants to America used their iceboxes as fireless cookers during the winter. Campers have used their sleeping bags to cook with retained heat.

Commercial fireless cookers were made with one to three wells in a tightly insulated covered box. A thick disk of preheated soapstone was placed under the pot in the cooker. Commercially made cookers were used at home, in institutions, and in the armed forces. Several cookers that crossed the plains in covered wagons can be seen in western museums. The advantage for westering cooks was that the food and pot could be made very hot over the fire after the breakfast foods had been removed. A fire did not have to be built to provide the family with a hot meal when they stopped at noon.

Fireless cookers were so popular in the early years of the twentieth century that a U.S. Department of Agriculture farmers' bulletin published in 1916 contained much information about fireless cookers. It presented directions for making a cooker at home as well as illustrations and recipes with suggestions on how to use the cooker. In that era there were numerous publications on fireless cookers. The U.S. Experiment Station Office in 1914 produced the *Illustrated Lecture on the Homemade Fireless Cooker*, which was accompanied by thirty-six lantern slides. State experiment stations also published booklets on this method of cooking.

A simple type of fireless cooker called the "hay box" was easily made at home. This device was used in England and the United States. A sturdy wooden box with a hinged top was lined with several inches of hay on the sides and bottom, allowing room for a pot and several inches on the top for a pillow or hay enclosed in a casing to completely cover the top of the box. Hot food was placed in a pot with a minimum of airspace and set in the box. When the lid was closed the hay box could be put aside to cook for hours. Pots with no handles or flip-down handles and tight fitting lids with recessed knobs were well suited for this type of cooker. Other insulating materials, such as newspaper or cork, also could be used. In later years plastic foam and packing "peanuts" could be adapted for use as insulating materials.

Many campers use hay boxes, which are particularly suited for cooking rice and other grains and cereals,

Fireless Cookbook. *Delicious Fireless Cooked Dishes,* issued by the Toledo Cooker Co., 1919. *Collection of Alice Ross*

stews, soups, and other foods cooked in liquid that adapt well to slow cooking. The cooker is made with a heavy cardboard box. The bottom and sides are lined with thick aluminum foil, and the box is filled with hay, into which a pot containing hot food is nestled. A pillows fits completely over the pot and hay, and when the lid is closed cooking proceeds without further attention.

There are many advantages to fireless cookers. They conserve fuel, because after the initial period of heating the pot and the food, no additional source of fuel is needed. Food can be safely left to cook while the family is away. Foods do not burn or "cook down" because there is no loss of moisture. Slow cooking is economical because less tender cuts of meat can be used.

As modern stoves and electrical cooking appliances came into use fewer and fewer cooks continued to use fireless cookers. Advertisements for commercial cookers disappeared from newspapers, and directions for using them disappeared from recipe books. Yet the idea was not entirely lost. In the late 1940s interest was revived by the

publication of *Fireless Cooking: A Traditional Energy-Efficient Method of Slow Cooking.* In a humorous article in *Ms.* magazine in 1982, titled "The Strangest Dinner Party I Ever Went To," Alice Walker related arriving for dinner but finding no odors of cooking food emanating from the kitchen. She was puzzled until the hostess uncovered the pot from the fireless cooker and served a delicious meal. Similar in many ways to the modern slow cooker and its many advantages for working people, the fireless cooker can still function in modern kitchens as a low-energy time-saver.

[*See also* Pioneers and Survival Food; Slow Cookers.]

BIBLIOGRAPHY

Homemade Fireless Cookers and Their Use. Farmers' Bulletin 771, prepared by the Office of Home Economics. Washington, DC: U.S. Department of Agriculture, 1916.

Huntington, Ellen Alden. *The Fireless Cooker.* Bulletin of the University Extension Series, Vol. 1, No. 1. Madison: University of Wisconsin, 1908.

Kirschner, Heidi. *Fireless Cookery: A Traditional Energy-Efficient Method of Slow Cooking.* Seattle, WA: Madrona, 1981.

Lovewell, Caroline B., Frances D. Whittemore, and Hannah W. Lyon. *The Fireless Cooker: How to Make it, How to Use It, What to Cook.* Topeka, KS: Home, 1908.

Rohde, Eleanour Sinclair. *Haybox Cookery.* London: Routledge, 1939.

MARY MOONEY-GETOFF

Fish

This entry includes three subentries:

Freshwater Fish
Saltwater Fish
Saltwater Shellfish

Freshwater Fish

Freshwater food-fish are the object of both fish farming and recreational fishing. Commercial freshwater fisheries and sportfishing often overlap, and both must deal with the effects of overfishing, pollution, and loss of spawning habitat to shoreline development. Freshwater fisheries occupy lakes, streams, and rivers above the fall line, where tidewater cannot go.

In North America, commercial fishing of any consequence for wild stocks of fish occurs mostly on the Great Lakes and in large rivers. The commercial advantage, which is considerable in some places, to fishing on smaller streams and lakes is derived from interest in sportfishing. Many states and small localities support the sport fishery through stocking as well as wildlife and environmental protections. Freshwater sportfishing enthusiasts have created a market for species-specific magazines, websites, and businesses that sell lures and other equipment and bait. Lodges and camps, boat rentals, and guides further serve freshwater-fishing enthusiasts.

The common names of freshwater fish, like those of saltwater fish, are highly regional and obscure a world of biological difference. Confusingly, the same name is applied to various fish and is sometimes applied to similar saltwater fish. For example, bass and perch both have saltwater counterparts.

Freshwater fish have appeared in cookbooks since the early days of America, but the recipes do not convey the natural variety and frequency of the fish. A small number of fish are named in the books; otherwise the general label "fish" is used. The size of the fish and nature of the bones and flesh determine its suitability for various culinary procedures. White flesh and bland-flavored fish are favored. Small fish are usually consumed as panfish, that is, fried or broiled, and larger fish are filleted. The catch of some freshwater fish prompts outdoor festivities such as crayfish boils, fish fries, and fish boils.

The Great Lakes Commercial Fishery

At one time the Great Lakes were an isolated environment. Because of the extraordinary fall line of the Niagara River, no species of fish that had not been in the Great Lakes at the retreat of the glaciers could enter the lakes from an ocean or river. The fish population included lake trout, whitefish, lake herring, seven species of lake chub, yellow perch, sturgeon, shiner, sucker, burbot, round whitefish, and sculpin. The French explorer Antoine Laumet de La Mothe, Sieur de Cadillac, observed Native Americans fishing for whitefish. The Native Americans used nets, weirs to trap migratory fish, and, particularly on rapids or falls entering the lakes, dip nets. They favored large trout, walleye (yellow pike), and sturgeon.

In the nineteenth century, cisco, also known as lake herring and chub, lake trout, whitefish, yellow perch, and sturgeon constituted the major commercial fisheries on the Great Lakes. George Brown Goode wrote in the 1880s that the pound net fishery was most important on Lake Superior and Lake Michigan and at the western end of Lake Erie,

delivering to market the most valuable fresh fish. The gill net fishery was next most important but required the strongest fishery and navigational skills on the lakes and was even conducted through ice in winter. In the upper lakes, the most important gill net catches were trout and whitefish. Elsewhere, lake herring, pike bass, sturgeon, trout, and whitefish were most important. Seine fishing was conducted in the summer for sturgeon, bass, herring, sucker, mullet, and whitefish. Not all fish were used as food; alewives, for example, were used for meal and oil. Ice fishing on Saginaw Bay in the later 1800s tended more to sport, utilizing hook and line or a spear. A small city of icehouses sprung up on the frozen lake, and in one instance, even a billiard table was hauled out. In summer there was much hand-line sportfishing on the lakes.

Great Lakes commercial fisheries peaked in 1899. Commercial fisheries inevitably were overfished despite artificial propagation of whitefish by the U.S. Fisheries Commission. But the main difficulty on the lakes was the introduction of exotic species, against which the native species had no protection from predation or competition for habitat. Invasions began as early as 1829 with the completion of the Welland Canal, which connected Lake Erie to Lake Ontario and the Saint Lawrence River. Sea lamprey, alewife, and white perch entered the lakes via canals. Other species, such as zebra mussels, came later in ballast water in vessels. Still others such as rainbow and brown trout, chinook and coho salmon, and carp were deliberately introduced.

The lamprey invasion proved to be disastrous to lake trout, destroying most of them by the 1950s and injuring many other fish populations. The alewives that entered the Great Lakes were food for trout. When the trout population collapsed, an alewife fishery developed but caused the elimination of six of seven chub species. Herring, yellow perch, and emerald shiner almost disappeared. Without a predator, the alewives overpopulated and the shores of the lakes were littered with dead fish. An alewife fishery supplying fish meal and oil has brought the population under control.

Freshwater Aquaculture

In America, farm raising of food fish is geared toward five basic species, three of which are freshwater: catfish, trout, and tilapia. Salmon and shrimp, the other two main food fishes, are largely saltwater raised, although there are freshwater salmon. Beyond fish for food, there is considerable farm raising of sport fish species, including trout, largemouth bass, catfish, red ear and bluegill sunfish, and striped bass. Crayfish, which is valued as food, and other small fish, such as minnows, are farm raised but are used more to supply the bait market than as food. The potential for raising some of the sport fish for food may increase as farm-raising technology improves.

Bass

The designation "bass" is applied to a great many fish, true bass being saltwater fish such as grouper and striped bass. The freshwater food fish most often called bass include largemouth or bigmouth, smallmouth, and spotted bass, which are members of the Centrarchidae family, which also includes sunfish. One traveler to America in 1800, John Maude, observed "Bass . . . is a favorite word with the Americans; they not only call trees by this name, but five or six distinct kinds of fish."

Like many favored fish, bass has been introduced beyond its usual range and is farm raised for stocking ponds and lakes. Largemouth bass (*Micropterus salmoides*) is a major warm water sport fish but is found in cooler northern waters as well. Largemouth bass, so called because the jaw line extends well past the eyes, averages approximately one to one and a half pounds in the north but is larger in southern waters, growing as large as five pounds. The subspecies Florida largemouth bass (*M. salmoides floridanus*) is the largest largemouth. Smallmouth bass (*Micropterus dolomieui*) is somewhat smaller than largemouth bass.

Bass is considered an excellent game fish and is fished in tournaments. Trophy bass weighing ten pounds are rare, although they were less unusual in the past, and are likely to be mounted rather than eaten. Bass meat is white, lean, and flaky and can be prepared many different ways, as most white-fleshed fish are. Bass is usually filleted and baked, stuffed, broiled, fried, or grilled. Largemouth bass may pick up flavor from its habitat, as do other wild fish. Some largemouth bass has what is described as a weedy or grassy flavor, which can be countered by skinning, seasoning, and deep-frying it. Bass from clean, clear water with woody cover usually has a milder flavor, and smallmouth bass is less likely to acquire off flavors.

Carp

Carp (*Cyprinius carpio*) was introduced to North America as a food fish in the late 1870s, although sources do not agree on whether the fish is native to Asia or to Europe. Because it is tolerant of relatively warm water, carp has been ideal for pond raising and can live as long as twenty years, quickly growing to a length as great as two feet in seven years. In North America, the largest reported carp caught was sixty pounds, although the common size is between one and two feet with a weight of eight to ten pounds.

Carp was once part of the commercial fishery of the Mississippi River basin. In other places where the fish are numerous, carp is an important food fish. Carp has become widely distributed in freshwater from Canada to the New Mexico border and from coast to coast. The English and Europeans find carp a fine sport fish because it is a strong fighter. In 1653 in *The Compleat Angler*, Izaak Walton described carp as "the Queen of Rivers: a stately, a good and a very subtle fish." But Americans have tended to disregard carp for sport or eating. Carp flesh is lean and white, somewhat coarse, and like catfish, it can assume the flavor of muddy water if raised in it. Carp is the fish most often used in making gefilte fish, the mixture of fish, matzo meal, and sometimes onion that is formed into balls and poached. Carp also can be baked, steamed, or battered and fried.

Catfish

A member of the family Ictaluridae, catfish is a warm water fish that has long been well regarded for food and sport. Catfish also is farm raised. Channel catfish (*Ictalurus punctatus*) is the most widely farm-raised fish in the United States. All wild catfish are descendants of catfish that originated east of the Continental Divide. The native western catfish is apparent only in the geologic record. Catfish has an odd appearance. Its barbels, which resemble whiskers, and sharp, spiny fins are venomous and capable of causing injury.

There once was a commercial trawl fishery for catfish on the Great Lakes, but sportfishing on the Great Lakes and in the Mississippi basin accounts for most of the wild catfish caught for food. Channel catfish is raised in ponds, mostly in the Mississippi delta. The catfish business sputtered in the delta in the 1960s but had a resurgence in the 1980s and 1990s. At that time an industry-wide effort was made to develop a freezing and transportation infrastructure for the product together with marketing efforts to promote farm-raised catfish. Fast-food franchises using large quantities of catfish helped support the industry.

Wild catfish can have a muddy flavor, but farm-raised catfish flesh can be flavorless, an attribute sought by catfish growers, who maintain laboratories for testing the flavor of sample fish from a pond full of the fish. When the right flavor is reached the pond is harvested. These fish are suitable for preparation as fish fillets, often breaded for deep-fat frying. Catfish fries and shrimp and crayfish boils are fish-based social events in the South, matching whitefish boils on the Great Lakes.

Cisco

Cisco (*Coregonus artedi*), like whitefish, with which it is sometimes confused, is found in northern waters, south to Ohio and Illinois. In the salmon family, cisco also is found in the Minnesota River because of introduction there, although it is not native to that river. Cisco is smaller than whitefish, a record catch in Minnesota being a four-pounder from Big Sandy Lake. Cisco is fished both for sport and commercially. There were at one time in the Great Lakes seven species of cisco, six of which disappeared when alewives invaded the lakes. Because the alewife population has declined in the Great Lakes, the one surviving species of cisco has recovered well enough to be fished commercially. Cisco is also called tullibee (a name given it by the fur traders), chub, and lake or freshwater herring. Cisco appears in markets in the round and smoked. It is suitable for steaming, frying, and broiling.

Crappie

Crappie is a small fish in the family Centrarchidae, which also includes bass and sunfish, and is a popular sport and food fish. Among sport fishers who call themselves "panfish anglers," black crappie (*Pomoxis nigromaculatus*) and white crappie (*Pomoxis annularis*) are favorites.

Crappie is found all over the United States, but black crappie originated in eastern America. It has been introduced to the western states, as has white crappie, which used to inhabit a range from New York to the Dakotas and south toward Texas. Black crappie prefers cold water but tolerates warmer, more saline water. Although it is found along the Gulf of Mexico and some East Coast areas, black crappie is more populous in northern lakes. White crappie is found more commonly in the South in freshwater rivers, lakes, and bayous.

Crappie eat other small fish, freshwater shellfish, and plankton. The fish seldom grow larger than half a pound to one pound. Record sizes for crappie are four or five pounds. The small size makes crappie ideal for panfrying, although the fish usually is dressed to remove tail, head, and fins before cooking.

Crayfish

Crayfish also are known as crawfish, crawdads, mudbugs, and, in France, *écrevisses*. In 1887 George Brown Goode wrote about this freshwater crustacean as follows: "Although fresh water crayfish are very abundant in any portions of the United States, they are seldom used as food, and, in fact, there appear to be only two regular markets for their sale, New York and New Orleans. One of the principal uses to which they are put is for garnishing fish dishes in hotels and restaurants." Goode reported that crayfish was such an inconsequential fishery that one could not collect statistics on it. It was known, however, that the crayfish appearing in New York came from Washington, D.C., and the Potomac River as soon as the ice was out and from Milwaukee, Wisconsin. Crayfish, a close relative of the lobster, were similarly shipped and sold live. "Crayfish are probably more commonly eaten in New Orleans than in any other American city," Goode observed, "and yet they are seldom seen in the markets there in large quantities."

Crayfish grow to be as long as six inches. There are many species, not any one of which in the United States can support a commercial fishery except along the Atchafalaya River in Louisiana, where red swamp and white river crayfish are harvested. Crayfish farming is gradually providing more and more product, and the United States and China are the major producers. Red swamp crayfish (*Procambarus clarkii*) is the major farmed species, and Louisiana and Minnesota are centers for producing it, often in rotation with rice.

For the Cajuns of Louisiana crayfish are a prime identity marker. Crayfish cookery was well developed in France, where the European crayfish is raised and harvested. In the Mississippi basin, crayfish are indispensable for use in gumbo, étouffée, and crayfish bisque. Boiled in seasoned water, crayfish are eaten straight from the shell, sometimes during social events called crayfish boils.

Eel

Eels (*Anguilla rostrata*) have an amazing life cycle, called catadromous, which begins with birth in the Sargasso Sea in the Atlantic Ocean. They drift on the Gulf Stream as transparent or "glass" eels to freshwater rivers and lakes, where they grow to be elvers and adults. Adult eels migrate back to the Sargasso Sea to spawn and die.

As food, eel is not much appreciated in America, although historically it was speared and trapped by Native Americans and English colonists. The Indian nation name "Algonquin" means "at the place of spearing fishes and eels." In the nineteenth century eel was caught to add variety to the diet and was most esteemed by European immigrants, particularly those from Germany, France, Italy, and the Netherlands. Asians value eel very highly. Since the 1970s, a market for elvers in Japan, China, Taiwan, and Korea has supplied eel for pond raising to adult size. The demand collapsed in the 1980s but returned in the 1990s, making elvers one of the most valuable per pound catches. In some parts of the United States, there is a concern that the elver harvest is too great and that not enough eels find their way to the streams and lakes. The season for elvers usually is limited to three months in the spring, and hand dip nets, or fykes, must be used.

Most modern fishers regard eels as a nuisance, although there is a small sport fishery for these fish. Eel flesh is oily, like that of mackerel, and it is good smoked, fried, and prepared in spicy stews. Earlier in American history, eel was roasted on spits, made into pies, and pickled.

Perch

The best-known food and sport perch in America is yellow perch (*Perca flavescens*). Perch is found mainly in the eastern and midwestern parts of the United States, the range extending south to Florida and Georgia and north to the Great Lakes and into Canada. Perch has been successfully introduced into western lakes. Perch prefers cool water, most often inhabiting lakes, but it also is caught in ponds and slow streams. Perch are small, averaging seven to ten inches, although a historic catch of a four-pound-three-ounce perch was recorded in 1865 at Cross Wicks Creek, New Jersey. Perch are predators, eating minnows, juvenile fish, insects, small crayfish, and snails. Yellow perch has supported a commercial fishery in the lower Great Lakes, although its value comes mainly from sportfishing. Although it is not a fighter, perch is known for feeding frenzies, which make it possible for an angler to catch a large number in a short time. The small size makes perch a panfish. It has firm, mild, lean flesh.

Pickerel

Pickerel, a member of the family Esocidae, is an elongated fish usually weighing between two and three pounds. The flesh is firm and lean but bony. Most popular with sport anglers are redfin pickerel (*Esox americanus*), also called little pickerel, mud pickerel, grass pickerel, banded pickerel, and red-finned pike, and chain pickerel (*Esox niger*). Pickerel grows less quickly than other pikes. Redfin pickerel, averaging one foot long, is smaller than chain pickerel, which can grow to two feet but usually is smaller. Pickerel seldom weigh more than two pounds, but one record catch was four pounds. The flesh is white, flaky, bony, and sweet, but eaten primarily as a sportfishing catch. Small fillets can be steamed or fried.

Pike

In the family Esocidae are three popular American sport and food fish—pike, pickerel, and muskellunge. Also in this group are walleye and sauger. Pike is the most widely distributed freshwater fish in the world, found in North America, Europe, and northern Asia, usually in lakes and slowly moving streams. Pike have elongated, even serpentine, bodies and flattened heads with duck-billed jaws and sharp back-slanting teeth. Muskellunge (*Esox masquinongy*), nicknamed "muskie" by sport anglers, is the largest of the pikes, averaging between ten and thirty pounds, some trophy fish weighing sixty pounds. Muskellunge occurs naturally in the Great Lakes but has been introduced elsewhere.

Northern pike (*Esox lucius*), also called common pike or American pike, jackfish, northern, and other names, averages eighteen to thirty inches in length and weighs slightly more than one pound to eight pounds, although the largest can measure more than four feet and weigh forty pounds. The Latin species name *lucius* is derived from the Greek *lukos* ("wolf") and describes the fish's fierce predatory habit and capacity for fight when caught.

Pike, a favorite with ice fishers, once was part of the Great Lakes commercial fishery and is considered good for eating. Another of the fish mentioned by Izaak Walton, pike was recognized by settlers coming to North America as a good food fish, although there is scant mention of pike by name in cookery literature. Depending on size, pike was traditionally baked, poached, or roasted. More recent recipes call for panfrying, stuffing and baking, grilling, or steaming. The mild-flavored fish requires saucing or vegetable accompaniments for flavor interest.

Salmon

Landlocked salmon is generally indistinguishable from its saltwater counterparts. Freshwater salmon are mostly harvested for sport. On the Great Lakes, however, where coho and chinook salmon were introduced in the 1960s, there is a valuable commercial fishery as well as a sport fishery. Salmon is a fine food fish.

Sauger

Sauger (*Stizostedion canadense*) is similar to walleye and walleye pike and has some of the same nicknames, such as jackfish, jack salmon, pike perch, and gray pike. Sauger is smaller than walleye and does not usually grow beyond two to four pounds. Sauger occupies most of the same waters as walleye. Sauger is a game fish and supports a commercial fishery in Canada.

Smelt

A member of the family Osmeridae, silvery, small true smelt is both freshwater and anadromous (spends part of its life in saltwater). Often abundant, smelt is harvested commercially both for human food and for fertilizer. Smelt also is used by sportfishers as bait for larger fish. Mostly carnivorous, smelt feeds on zooplankton, other small fish, and invertebrates. Schooling smelt can be harvested thousands at a time in nets. Smelt is a popular ice-fishing catch—shacks are erected close to the freshwater or brackish end of estuaries and rivers. Their small size and somewhat oily flesh make smelt ideal for frying. The heads and sometimes the tails are removed, and the fish are dipped in batter, fried quickly, and eaten whole.

Sturgeon

Lake sturgeon (*Acipsenser fulvescens*, family Acipenseridae) are found in North American lakes. By the turn of the twentieth century sturgeon had been almost entirely eliminated from the Great Lakes because it was believed that sturgeon were eating the eggs of favored species, particularly walleye. Sturgeon has been fished commercially, mostly in Canadian waters. The fish can live to be 150 years old and grow to great size. In 1968 a 162-pound fish was caught in the Rainy River in Minnesota. At one time, fish weighing more than 250 pounds were pulled from the Great Lakes. Sturgeon ranges from most waters that empty into Hudson Bay to Louisiana. Sturgeon flesh and roe are valuable and bring a higher price than do those of any other freshwater species. The flesh is richly flavored, white, and firm. Smoking is the most common method of preparation. The eggs are prized as caviar.

Sunfish

The sunfish family (Centrarchidae) is large and includes crappie and bass, but the word "sunfish" generally refers to bluegill (*Lepomis macrochirus*) and red ear or shell-cracker (*Lepomis microlophus*). Both bluegill and red ear are popular sport fishes, and both are farm raised to stock recreational fisheries. There are many regional and colloquial names for sunfish, including papermouth, silversides, calico bass, white perch, speck, speckled perch, slab, and among Cajuns *sac-a-lait* ("bag of milk"), which describes the white flesh. Sunfish also include pumpkinseeds (*Lepomis gibbosus*) and long-eared sunfish (*Lepomis megalotis*). Sunfish is widely distributed, being found in lakes all over America. Bluegill is a favorite for sport fishers and is a good panfish. Pumpkinseed also is regarded as a good sport fish, but it is generally too small for use as food. To be useful as panfish, sunfish have to weigh two pounds or less. The meat can be fried, baked, or broiled.

Terrapin

While the terrapin is a reptile, cookbooks traditionally categorize it as seafood. Like its seagoing relatives, the freshwater or brackish-water turtle, particularly the diamondback terrapin (*Malaclemys terrapin*) and its eggs, have long been esteemed as food. Terrapin is found in salt marshes and in waters along the East Coast from Massachusetts to the Gulf of Mexico. In 1918 Fannie Farmer's *Boston Cooking-School Cook Book* specifically mentioned that the terrapin of the Chesapeake Bay is the best, fetching the highest prices, but that terrapin from Florida and Texas was what Northeasterners could expect to find in the market from November to April. Female terrapins are larger than males and average six to nine inches long. The meat of females is generally considered more tender and thus better for cooking.

A nineteenth-century fad for turtle dishes, particularly soup, considerably reduced turtle populations. The fact that turtle dishes have fallen out of favor has protected turtle species. Loss of habitat has become the most serious threat, although conservation efforts are being made to protect the habitat. Some cookbooks in the early twentieth century described ways of preparing chicken and veal in terrapin style. Turtle meat can be found frozen and canned in specialty stores, sparing cooks from having to follow Farmer's advice to cook terrapin live.

Tilapia

Tilapia (*Oreochromis niloticus*) is a member of the family Cichlidae, which includes many species kept as pets in aquariums. Tilapia is a native of Africa but has become an important farm-raised, freshwater food fish in

America. Like perch, tilapia grows rapidly, requiring less feed than many other fish; spawns frequently; and tolerates high population density. Most tilapia farms, many of which are in the southwestern United States, use enclosed systems and so have less environmental impact than other forms of fish farming, because there is almost no water pollution or fish escape. Tilapia has firm, white, and relatively bland flesh, which can be broiled, fried, or baked and then sauced for flavor. Tilapia is a key fish for prepared battered fish products, such as fillets, fingers, and nuggets.

Trout

Trout is a legendary freshwater fish, both as a sport fish and as food. Trout has long been highly valued in lore and literature. Fly-fishing for trout has been richly described in terms of technique, equipment, and stories of memorable fishing experiences. As happens with other favored fishes, many names are applied to the same fish, causing much confusion. Most species of trout are in the genus *Salmo*, which also includes some species of salmon. Trout is found nearly everywhere in the world, occurring either naturally or because of introduction. Trout was among the earliest fish to be farm raised. It is widely raised both for food and for stocking lakes and ponds for sport. Trout is a good sport fish, prefers cool water, and has flavorful flesh. Each type of trout has its adherents among anglers, who equip themselves for catching their favorite type and travel to spots where they are likely to yield a catch.

Rainbow trout (*Salmo gairdneri*) is native to the mountains of the western United States but, beginning in the 1870s, has been introduced nationwide. Where the water is clear and cold, rainbow trout reproduce naturally after introduction. A good fighter, rainbow trout prefers streams but also lives in lakes if there are streams to which the fish can migrate to spawn. Rainbow trout is the most widely grown trout for stocking and food, because the fish grow quickly and seem able to adapt to nonnatural feed. Because of its abundant cold water, Idaho is a center for farm-raised rainbow trout, which needs temperatures less than 70°F. In the Great Lakes, rainbow trout can grow to two to almost three feet in length, sometimes being mistaken for coho or chinook salmon. Smaller fish are more usual outside the Great Lakes. Pond-raised rainbow trout usually reaches two to five pounds.

Brown trout (*Salmo trutta*) is an introduced fish. It is native to Germany and was brought to America in the 1880s. The U.S. Fish Commission first stocked the Pere Marquette River, in Michigan, with brown trout, and the fish spread to almost every other state. Because brown trout does not naturally reproduce in most places where it has been introduced, the best way to maintain populations is restocking. Brown trout has become established in the upper Great Lakes. Like rainbow trout, brown trout prefers cooler water but can tolerate temperature up to 75°F. Lake-caught brown trout can weigh as much as eight pounds and is predominantly silver, whereas stream-dwelling brown trout are spotted.

The cutthroat trout (*Oncorhynchus clarki clarii*) is native to America. The Latin name honors William Clark, of the Lewis and Clark expedition, during which, on June 13, 1805, the fish was found and identified, near the Great Falls of the Missouri River, Montana. Montana has named the cutthroat trout its state fish, partly to draw attention to the scarcity of this fish. Clark's cutthroat trout were sixteen to twenty-three inches in length and were described as being similar to speckled trout in the East. Cutthroat trout hybridizes with rainbow trout.

Lake trout (*Salvelinus namaycush*) and brook trout (*Salvelinus fontinalis*) are popular sport and food fishes, both have many regional names and nicknames, and both are char. Lake trout, called togue, salmon trout, forktail trout, and mackinaw, usually is one and one-half to two feet long and weighs three to nine pounds. This trout is a native of the Great Lakes, where it was part of the gill net fishery, but has been introduced elsewhere in America. Lake trout thrives in cool, deep water. Brook trout, also called brookie, speckled trout, square tail, and common or eastern brook trout, among other names, often is ten to twelve inches long when caught and weighs less than one to two pounds. Brook trout is native to eastern North America and has been widely introduced nationwide. Brook trout prefers cold water and can be found in small, cold streams and lakes at high altitudes. Brook trout is smaller than other species and so is not as popular with sport fishers, although the flesh rivals that of other trout for flavor. Also called trout is steelhead (*Oncorhynchus mykiss*, formerly *Salmo gairdneri Richardson*), an anadromous form of rainbow trout. Steelhead is large, often averaging five to ten pounds, and is a very good sport fish. Steelhead, like many freshwater sport fish, has a large following of enthusiasts. Trout meat is generally oilier and more flavorful than meat of other fish, making small trout excellent panfish. Trout also is good filleted and prepared in any number of ways. It is excellent smoked.

Walleye

Walleye (*Stizostedion vitreum*) has many alternative names that can lead to misidentification. Not to be confused with saltwater walleye of the Pacific coast, walleye, or walleyed pike, is a freshwater fish of the Great Lakes and central Canada. It is sometimes called green, blue, gray, or yellow pike. Other names include dory (from the French *doré*), jack salmon, jackfish, white eye, glass eye, and sauger, even though there is another fish properly called sauger. Walleye sometimes is called perch—pike perch, wall-eyed perch, yellow pike perch—and in fact it is the largest in the Percidae (perch) family.

Walleye, so-called because of its odd, large eyes, which help the fish locate their food, is a game fish, favored only over largemouth bass. A sport fishery for walleye has existed since the late nineteenth century. Because it is so important, walleye has been introduced to lakes and streams around the Great Lakes and even in southern and western lakes. There is a limited farm-raising effort for walleye, mostly for stocking, because even though it is a favored food fish, walleye is a carnivore, and once it approaches adult size is prone to cannibalism when confined. Most walleyes caught weigh between one and three pounds and are filleted. The firm, white flesh is used in many recipes for baking, broiling, poaching, or frying. The fish often is stuffed and prepared with other, more flavorful ingredients.

Whitefish

Whitefish (*Coregonus clupeaformis*), which is related to the salmon family, is found in cold lakes and streams across the northern states and Canada and is fished commercially in the Great Lakes. Whitefish is plentiful in Lake Superior and in northern Huron and Michigan. The flesh is firm and white, which makes whitefish popular for eating, and is available year-round. Whitefish is often caught in gill nets in summer and through ice in winter, although it is not considered a great sport fish. The roe is salted and sold as golden caviar. The flesh can be cooked in almost any way—broiled, grilled, baked, steamed, fried, or poached.

Around Lake Michigan, outdoor whitefish boils are popular traditional events, likely derived from the practice of boiling the fish on board the gill netters that caught them. The fish, cut in chunks, is put into a pot with small potatoes and onions and allowed to boil. Kerosene is added to the fire at the end of cooking, and the resulting flare-up causes the pot to boil over, a process that drives off the accumulated fish oil. The fish

and potatoes are served with butter and, often, coleslaw. Pie is served for dessert. Civic organizations host fish boils in the summer and early fall, and the region's restaurants and lodges offer whitefish boil on their menus. Whitefish is also called chub, cisco, lake herring, and tullibee, although these are different fish.

[*See also* Mid-Atlantic Region; Midwestern Regional Cookery; Pacific Northwestern Regional Cookery.]

BIBLIOGRAPHY

Active Angler. http://www.activeangler.com. Sportfishing website for salt and freshwater fishing. Articles on fishing techniques, places, equipment, and recipes.

Behnke, Robert J. *Trout and Salmon of North America.* New York: Free Press, 2002. A guide to fish and fishing.

Froese, R., and D. Pauly, eds. *FishBase.* 2003. World Wide Web electronic publication. http://www.fishbase.org/search.cfm. An extraordinarily comprehensive listing of world fishes with taxonomic cross-references and individual fish descriptions and photographs.

Gierach, John. *Death, Taxes, and Leaky Waders: A John Gierach Fly-Fishing Treasury.* New York: Simon and Schuster, 2001. Collection of essays about angling by a longtime fly-fishing author.

Goode, George Brown. *The Fisheries and Fishery Industries of the United States.* Section V: *The History and Methods of the Fisheries.* Vol. 1. United States Commission of Fish and Fisheries. Washington, DC: U.S. Government Printing Office, 1887.

Hemingway, Ernest, Jack Hemingway, and Nick Lyons, eds. *Hemingway on Fishing.* Guilford, CT: Lyons, 2000.

Mann, Tom, and Tom Carter. *Think Like a Fish: The Lure ad Lore of America's Legendary Bass Fisherman.* New York: Broadway, 2002.

Schweid, Richard. *Catfish and the Delta: Confederate Fish Farming in the Mississippi Delta.* Berkeley, CA: Ten Speed Press, 1992. A journalist's account of the social history of catfish farming in the Mississippi Delta.

Sorenson, Eric. *The Angler's Guide to Freshwater Fish of North America.* Stillwater, MN: Voyageur, 2000.

Waszczuk, Henry. *The Complete Guide to North American Freshwater Game Fishing.* Toronto: Fenn, 1992.

SANDRA L. OLIVER

Saltwater Fish

Until the second half of the twentieth century, the size, texture, bone structure, and oiliness of a fish determined its use in the American kitchen, a practice predicated on how various North American settlers used the fish or shellfish in their native countries. Wherever settlers landed they viewed any unfamiliar fish and shellfish with an eye toward what familiar seafood it resembled. They then would cook it in a comparable manner, merely adopting the new fish and adapting its preparation to what they already knew. The view of fish and shellfish from the kitchen broke into several categories of use that did not change much from the earliest settlement through the middle of the twentieth century.

Most fish were poached, fried, or baked. (Early cookbooks that recommend "boiling" fish usually caution the cook not to let the fish boil hard; since the fish were simmered more than boiled, most modern cooks would call the process poaching.) In the hearth cooking era, large fish were sometimes tied to a board and roasted before the fire in a process sometimes called planking, but when stove cookery superceded open fires, most cookbooks acknowledged that baking tended to dry out fish, and cooks who chose to bake were obliged to baste, serve with a sauce, or otherwise ensure moisture. Leftover fish was flaked up, the bones were carefully removed, and the meat was rewarmed in a sauce or made into fish cakes.

Small fish were usually fried, broiled, or grilled. Chowders called most often for white, firm-fleshed fish, and soups often used shellfish. During the mid- and later nineteenth century, certain fish and shellfish were favored for salads, and some shellfish were cooked and stuffed back into shells for presentation.

The average size of saltwater fish caught has changed over time. As a species is heavily fished, the older, larger fish are thinned out and the younger, smaller fish are left and may never achieve the size of the earlier catch. Because so many culinary decisions are based on fish size, the way some fish were prepared in earlier times is different from the present methods for some species.

Large, Solid Fish with Few Bones

Americans who liked a centerpiece entrée used meaty, large fish with bones that were easy to find and remove. Salmon, sturgeon, halibut, and, later, swordfish and tuna were poached or roasted, either whole or in large steak or roastlike pieces weighing several pounds. Codfish heads and shoulders, in the days when the cod was landed weighing upwards of thirty pounds, were also cooked and presented whole. These fish were usually served with a sauce, often containing anchovies or shellfish, such as lobster, oyster, crab, or shrimp.

Medium-to-Large White, Firm-Fleshed Fish

Some fish that once fit this category no longer do because overfishing has left mostly smaller fish of the species. Cod, both salt and fresh; cusk; striped bass, known as rockfish in the South; haddock; pollock; tautog, or blackfish; mullet;

Fish Market. Fulton Fish Market, New York City, spring 1943. *Prints and Photographs Division, Library of Congress/Gordon Parks*

drum; sheepshead; bream; red snapper; and recently, John Dory; Pacific cod; orange roughy; and Chilean sea bass have all shared this category. They have been baked, boiled, and stewed whole as well as put into chowders, and their fillets have been baked and broiled. Leftovers have been warmed up in cream sauces, scalloped, or mixed with potatoes and made into fish cakes or croquettes.

Many early cookbooks advise cooks to use fish without specifying which type, which shows this category to possess fairly elastic culinary interpretations. Fish migrate, so most fish would have appeared in market or at the end of a fishing pole only seasonally. A cook had to be flexible.

Medium-to-Large Oily-Fleshed Fish

Many of the fish in this category—shad, mackerel, bluefish, salmon trout, small salmon, eels, and others—were less popular table fish. Most Americans, historically and to the present, prefer bland, white-fleshed fish to the oilier, dark-fleshed fish. This group, however, contained sport fish and the famous anadromous fishes that Americans fished for family as well as commercial use.

Anadromous fish include alewives, salmon, and shad, which spawn in freshwater but live their adult lives in the sea. They appeared in springtime in great abundance in the seventeenth and eighteenth centuries as well as in the nineteenth century until many large rivers and streams were dammed for power. They were relatively easy to harvest as they surged upstream. Whether early New Englanders netting alewives, Philadelphians scooping up shad, or Native Americans in the Northwest harvesting salmon, the annual appearance of the fish caused tremendous excitement as fishermen took advantage of the opportunity. In the case of shad, the roe was often as much the object of the fishery as the flesh, which was famous for its boniness.

Many fish in this category were salted; some were subsequently smoked. The oily flesh took up salt well, and when the fish were smoked, they did not dry out unpleasantly. For the same reason, these fish were good for baking, roasting, or planking; they were also suitable for broiling. Eels could even be spitted to cook before a hearth fire.

Small White- or Oily-Fleshed Fish

This category included many fish, all of which could have been described as "panfish" because their small size allowed them conveniently to fit into a frying pan. Small and tinker (juvenile) mackerel, perch, herring, flounder, alewife, sole, smelt, and several freshwater fish fit this category of quickly cooked fish, though some were also filleted and are suitable for baking. Usually these fish were too thin or bony for convenient use in soups and stews. Some could be grilled. Some, like alewives, herring, and mackerel, were caught commercially and salted or smoked, which accounts for their appearance inland in cookbooks published in places far from the sea.

Anchovies

Anchovies (*Engraulis encrasicolus, E. ringens,* and *Anchoa hepsetus*) are small but important food fish that are found in the Atlantic Ocean, the Pacific Ocean, the Mediterranean Sea, and the English Channel. The primary anchovy for cookery is the Mediterranean variety. These anchovies are almost always preserved and used as a flavoring agent in cookery, with even very early cookbooks calling for them. Filleted, salted, and packed in cans with oil, they are also made into a paste sold in tubes. Modern recipes call for anchovies on pizza, in Caesar salad, in salad dressings, and in a variety of sauces often used on blander fish.

Bass

Bass (family Perichthydae) are typically medium-to-large, white-fleshed, mild-flavored fish. Some bass are freshwater fish, and some are saltwater fish; some are commercially fished, and others make good sport fish. In early cookery

Cooked Fish. Fish at Institute of Culinary Education, New York.

books, recipes for bass often do not specify which of many possible basslike fish might have been available in different regions of the country. For example, New Englanders liked striped bass, which in the South is called rockfish. Some fish in the family Serranidae that are usually called groupers also end up with "bass" in the common name. Stripers were introduced to the West Coast in the 1800s, and a hybrid of wild striped bass and white bass are farm raised.

Bass generally were prepared in the same manner as cod, pollock, and haddock. They can be baked or stewed; they are also used in chowders and as fillets for all sorts of fish dishes. Smaller bass and groupers can be cooked whole.

Blackfish

The blackfish (*Tautoga onitis*), which feeds on shellfish and crabs, is known by the names black trout, black ruff, tautog, black porgy, oysterfish, and chowderfish. It is most plentiful between Chesapeake Bay north to Cape Cod, but it has a range from Nova Scotia to South Carolina. Native Americans used the fish, and it was the object of inshore fisheries in earlier times. Amelia Simmons mentions blackfish in the first American cookbook, *American Cookery* (1796), though she does not comment on an ideal way of preparing the fish. The name chowderfish, however, is consistent with the tautog's reputation for firm flesh, though the fish can also be grilled and baked.

Flounder and Sole

Flounder and sole are part of a large category of flatfish, to which even halibut belong, that have been caught commercially in American inshore fisheries probably since the eighteenth century and sold in urban markets.

These fish did not reach large-scale commercial importance until the later nineteenth century. Many of these fish, especially the summer flounder, are becoming scarce, and conservationists seek to protect them.

There are many common names for this group of fish, Pleuronectiformes, which around the world includes over five hundred species caught in every ocean. Called flounder, sole, turbot, sand dab, fluke, and plaice, many of these fish move into estuaries in summer and are caught recreationally by hook and line. Among the most desirable as food fish are winter, summer, and yellowtail flounder.

Most of these are filleted and are good for baking or broiling; they are also used as panfish or are stuffed and rolled. In nineteenth-century cookbooks, the words "sole" and "turbot" often seem to describe a method of preparing a white-fleshed fillet rather than to specify preparation of a particular species. For example, there is no true American sole, in the family Soleidae, but the word "sole" is used to describe a way of preparing flounder.

Haddock

A handsome ground fish in the family Gadidae with cod and pollock, haddock (*Melanogrammus aeglefinus*) was valued for its firm, white flesh with its capacity for being salted and smoked to make finnan haddie. Old-time New England fishermen used to recall a day before haddock was appreciated, but it was fished in the late eighteenth century and more widely caught in the nineteenth and twentieth centuries. In *History and Methods of the Fisheries* (1887), George Brown Goode reports that in the mid-1800s salted and dried haddock was nicknamed "skulljoe" on Cape Cod. Finnan haddie was named for the town of Findon, Scotland, where haddock was early salted and smoked commercially, though the process caught on in New England and was widely prosecuted in Portland, Maine.

By the end of the nineteenth century, haddock was regarded as the ideal chowder fish, but it was useful for all purposes. In the twentieth century haddock was caught for fillets, as was cod, and in the 1920s haddock actually exceeded cod in tons caught. It is as stressed a fishery as cod, flounders, and other white-fleshed fish.

Halibut

The halibut (*Hippoglossus hippoglossus* and *H. stenolepis*), in the same Pleuronectidae family as other flatfish like flounder, reached popularity in the nineteenth century, when the size of the individuals sometimes reached heroic proportions of six hundred pounds.

Caught in northern Atlantic waters, inshore for many years but eventually on the Georges Bank as a commercial fishery in the mid-1800s, halibut was iced and shipped coastwise to the South and even inland by rail, which helps to account for cookbook writers across the country including halibut cooking directions. On the West Coast, the Pacific halibut is today an important fishery both commercially and recreationally, while the East Coast halibut fishery is mostly depleted.

Halibut has a firm, sometimes dark flesh, large, easy-to-find bones, and a meaty texture when cooked. Because the individual fish were so large, halibut was almost always sold as steaks, which can be fried or baked. Some halibut was salted and smoked, and when halibut became hard to find, salted and smoked sturgeon was substituted for it.

Like many fish, the halibut caught are smaller than they were at one time. For example, the average Pacific halibut weighs between thirty and forty pounds, whereas three hundred pounds was once a common size.

Herring and Sardines

Herring (*Culpea harengus*) belong to the same family of fish that includes shad, alewives, and sardines, though they do not spawn in freshwater. They school in huge numbers and were fished for commercially in Europe and off the New England and Middle Atlantic coasts. Their oily flesh made them ideal for salting and smoking, which meant that they were shipped inland for sale.

Some plantation owners arranged for catches of herring, which were salted to be food for slaves, but herring consumption was relatively low in America until more immigrants arrived, especially from the British Isles, Germany, and Scandinavia. Several products made from

Fish Market. Interior of Ocean Fish Market, Brooklyn, New York. *Photograph by Joe Zarba*

herring included hard or red herring, bloaters, kippers, and bucklings. Immature herring were canned in the same manner as true sardines (*Sardinia pilchardus*), when imported sardines from France became fashionable in the later 1800s. Although sardines were a favorite in saloons and bars in the twentieth century, sardine consumption took a nosedive during Prohibition. Sardine packing hung on through the end of the twentieth century in Maine, but most sardines eaten in America come from herring canned in Canada and Scandinavia.

Grunion

The grunion is a small fish that is found on the California coast between around Morro Bay to partway down the Baja peninsula. Its spawning habits, like those of anadromous fishes, have made it prey to humans. The grunion comes ashore at high tide, in Southern California always at night, in schools of males and females during the full and new moons. The females open a place in soft, watery sand and lay eggs. The males, finding a female doing so, wind themselves around the female and supply milt to fertilize the eggs. When they are done, the fish flop themselves back into the water, leaving the eggs to hatch and wash out to sea in a high tide about ten days later.

The grunion may be caught only by hand. Rolled in cornmeal and fried, it is considered a panfish. The grunion is protected, and conservation steps taken include a "no-take" season from March to May as well as efforts to discourage beach grooming with rakes, which disturbs the grunion eggs.

Mackerel

Because they are an oily-fleshed fished, mackerel (*Scomber scombrus* and *S. japonicus*) do not meet with as much favor as other fish, and seafood sections of large supermarkets do not often display fresh mackerel. In the nineteenth and twentieth centuries, mackerel were served, as were herring, as a "relish" at breakfast, supper, or tea, and they are often smoked and used as hors d'oeuvres. Mackerel flesh is tender, blue-gray, and rich in omega-3 fatty acids. These fish are very good grilled or fried as panfish.

Mackerel was an important East Coast fishery in the eighteenth and nineteenth centuries but declined considerably in the twentieth century. Beginning as a hook-and-line fishery, it progressed to jigging, and by the mid-1800s, mackerel were purse seined, which dramatically increased the catch. Dressed aboard the fishing vessel, mackerel were split, salted, and sold even inland in the United States. Among saltwater fish, mackerel appears nearly as frequently in early cookbooks as salt codfish.

Along the East and West coasts, where mackerel school in summer, they are popular among recreational fishermen and are relatively easy to catch because they will bite at almost anything, even bare hooks. They have great ranges, from the Mediterranean to the North Sea, all along the Atlantic, and from Mexico to Alaska. On the Pacific Coast they are called chub mackerel.

Jack mackerel, *Trachurus symmetricus*, are important commercial fish, often canned and distributed widely as inexpensive protein. In the earlier twentieth century commercial fishermen made relatively little distinction between chub and jack mackerel.

Sea Mammals

Seals, dolphins, and porpoises do not figure largely in the diet of most modern Americans, though among the Inuit, seals and whales are harvested for food and ceremonial purposes as part of the preservation of Inuit culture. In the Canadian maritime provinces, seal is captured and eaten, particularly in Newfoundland and Labrador. Historically, seal meat sustained explorers and adventurers in the Arctic and Antarctica.

At sea, American sailing ships caught dolphins and porpoises, and sailors cooked them for all the crew to eat, often in a dish called sea pie. The liver, often described as being very much like beef liver, was apportioned to the captain's cabin. Porpoise is sometimes caught and marketed in Japan, though America regards this trade as illegal.

Monkfish

Monkfish (*Lophius americanus*), nicknamed goosefish and anglerfish, is among the homeliest of edible species caught. It has a huge head and mouth, with lots of sharp teeth, and it feeds on almost anything. Another of the fish eaten by Europeans but not by Americans, it was of virtually no commercial value until after the 1960s; neither was it a common recreational fish. Monkfish was once a bycatch of the ground fisheries but was later caught for its own sake. Since the 1970s, because of the pressure on more favored fish like cod and haddock, monkfish has appeared in seafood markets, and the liver is prized in Asia. Most of the catch is landed on the East Coast from the Middle Atlantic states up through the Canadian maritime provinces.

It is mostly the monkfish's tail with its smooth, solid flesh that is sold for food. When cooked, the flesh hardly flakes apart, and because it resembles lobster meat, it is sometimes called poor man's lobster. It is best used in chowders or other moist heat cookery, such as fish stews or soups. It is not at all suitable for baking or grilling.

Mullet

The term "mullet" (*Mugil cephalus* and *Chaenomugil proboscidens*) applies to both saltwater and freshwater fishes. The saltwater gray, or striped, mullet is found in warm to temperate waters on both the East and West coasts of America and is regarded as a good food fish. Herbivorous, the mullet eats by grazing through mud. The flesh is firm and sweet; however, since it is more perishable than other fish, mullet is best eaten within a day or two of being caught and is found fresh in markets nearest its source, most often in the South. It is not usually frozen but is sometimes smoked or filleted; it can be cooked with almost any dry or wet heat methods.

Perch

There are several freshwater and saltwater fish called perch. Of the sorts called ocean perch, *Sebastes alutus* comes from the Pacific and *Sebastes marinus* from the Atlantic; the latter is also sometimes called redfish. Perch bones are among the most commonly found fish bones in colonial-era archaeological sites around the Chesapeake.

Because in historical culinary sources the fish is usually called merely perch, it is hard to determine which fish is meant. Most perch seem to have been of medium size and so were poached, baked, or broiled. Ocean perch are often filleted to be broiled, sautéed, or pan-fried. They are available both fresh and frozen; when frozen they can be marketed simply as "ocean fillets" or under some similar indistinguishable name.

Pollock

A member of the same Gadidae family to which cod, haddock, hake, cusk, tomcod, and ling belong, pollock (*Pollachius virens*) was caught and used as were the others—all mostly medium-to-large white-fleshed fish. Pollock could be salted and dried as cod were, but pollock was never considered to be as valuable and was among the salted fish sent to the South for slave food. A blue-gray cast to the flesh earned it the grand name of Boston bluefish in the late nineteenth and early twentieth centuries.

Pollock has become a candidate for sale as a breaded fillet. Many pollock come from Pacific waters around Alaska. The pollock is caught commercially in the Atlantic and as a sport fish.

Fish for Sale. Loup de mer and red snapper at Citarella's on the Upper West Side of Manhattan. *Photograph by Joe Zarba*

Red Snapper

There are quite a number of fish called red snapper. Generally of the family Lutjanidae, snappers are so called because of their tendency to snap at prey with their sharp upper teeth. In America, red snappers, *Lutjanus campechanus*, are found on the southeastern coast, particularly off of Florida and in the Gulf of Mexico, where other snappers like mutton, vermilion, mangrove, and yellowtail are also found. The red snapper has firm, white flesh. The smaller fish are panfried; the larger ones are filleted with the skin left on for broiling, grilling, and braising. The red snapper did not achieve important commercial value until the twentieth century.

Salmon

Salmon consumed in America comes from both the Atlantic and the Pacific and is caught wild as well as farm raised. The Atlantic salmon (*Salmo salar*) and its Pacific counterparts—sockeye (*Oncorhynchus nerka*); chinook (*O. tshawytscha*); chum (*O. keta*); coho, or silver, salmon (*O. kisutch*); and pink, or humpback, salmon (*O. gorbuscha*)—are all anadromous. Salmon ranks among the most favored of finfishes of the past and present. Salmon are eaten fresh and are available as fillets, as steaks, and in the round. They are poached, baked, and grilled. The rich flesh accepts salt and smoke; can be made into uncooked but cured products, such as gravlax and lomi salmon; and is used in sushi and sashimi. Tlingit people caught salmon on its way to spawning and dried the flesh.

In past times, the reddish flesh of salmon and its rich flavor meant that the fish was sometimes regarded as "red blooded" and was included on the list of "royal" fish, those presented to royalty. A version of this tradition continued in the United States until 1992 as the first salmon caught each year on the Penobscot River in Maine was traditionally sent to the president.

For centuries there have been both commercial and recreational salmon fisheries. Salmon have been caught by weirs along the shores of bays and inlets that the fish must pass to reach their spawning sites, with dip nets at the fall line where the fish must jump upstream, and by hook and line. Trollers use baited hooks in open seas to catch particular species of salmon, while seiners select individual schools of sockeye, pink, and chum salmon; gillnetters fish for sockeye and chum. Native American fishing employs nearly all of these methods, plus hooks and spears, sometimes by special governmental arrangements for tribal food and ceremonial salmon use.

Salmon were plentiful for Native Americans and colonists and were taken in large numbers. When those streams had been heavily fished, dammed for power in the 1800s, or polluted by industry, subsequent catches were greatly limited, especially on the East Coast. By the start of the twentieth century, West Coast salmon fisheries had greatly exceeded the East Coast catches, with most of the western fish canned and shipped all across the country. Evidence of the nationwide availability of salmon is apparent in early twentieth-century inland cookbooks with their recipes for salmon loaf and salmon salad.

Salmon are at the center of much controversy. On the West Coast, migratory salmon are caught by both U.S. and Canadian fishermen, but managing the stocks and developing workable treaties have become extremely difficult because once the fish are at sea, it is impossible to discern whether they originated in Canadian or American territorial waters. On both coasts, there is considerable discussion as to whether there are any truly genetically pure, indigenous salmon stocks left. For years hatchery-raised salmon were released into streams to replenish lost wild stocks, and farmed salmon are escaping and intermixing with the wild stocks. Salmon farming's intensive growing promotes disease among the fish, and fish farms are not always welcome neighbors as they upset local ecological balances and obstruct scenery.

Still, farmed salmon as a globally traded product is among the least expensive fish in markets. Organizations seeking to protect various fish caution against consuming farm-raised salmon from the Pacific Northwest, Chile, and Great Britain, and they advise that the Alaskan wild stocks are the strongest and most sustainable. However, alternative points of view are equally easy to find.

Seaweed

Historically, few seaweeds in American waters had much commercial culinary value, though to make a blancmange, some people in the nineteenth century gathered Irish moss, which they steeped in hot milk to obtain the carrageenan, a gelatin-like substance.

In the late twentieth century, as Americans learned about Asian, particularly Japanese, foods, they were introduced to the use of a wider variety of edible seaweeds. Among the seaweeds that are gathered and sold in the United States are alaria, kelp, dulse, laver, and red and green algae.

Some seaweeds are dried and pulverized to create seasonings or are added to other ingredients to make crackers or chips. Commercially, much seaweed is used in food production, particularly the products carrageenan, agar, and algin; these products probably account for the average American's seaweed consumption.

Sea Turtle

The green sea turtle is not the only edible turtle, but for the purposes of describing American seafood, this is the most exploited species. The taste and fashion for turtle soup probably traveled from the Caribbean to England and thence to North America. For much of the last half of the eighteenth century and into the early nineteenth century, turtle soup was so stylish that a mock version was developed to replace it. Some American sailing ships captured turtles for fresh meat, but sailors did not often welcome it.

Sea turtle was said to resemble veal and lobster. The edible portions—the flipper meat, called calipee, and the meat from the lower shell, called calipash—have a gelatinous characteristic, largely out of favor with modern people. There was a small commercial fishery of green turtles for canning in the later nineteenth century. Turtle eggs were also harvested. Sea turtles are now largely protected.

Shad

Like alewives, the anadromous shad are found running up freshwater rivers in the spring, originally along the East Coast from the South to the North and, after their introduction in 1871, along the West Coast as well. Although shad are very bony and oily, their great plenty in colonial times and the relative ease of catching them during their upstream migration made them welcome. Particularly prized was the roe from the females, and cookbooks from the 1800s provide many recipes for preparing roe. Some early sources say that buck (male) shad were thrown back as unmarketable.

There were commercial shad fisheries in the South and in the North, with southern-caught shad sent north by rail early in the spring until the fish appeared in northern rivers later in the season. A combination of overfishing, industrial damming, and pollution caused a great decline to near disappearance of shad in many East Coast rivers. Conservation efforts in the second half of the twentieth century were rewarded by the fish reappearing in greater numbers, though still not enough to support a commercial fishery.

Shad, introduced to California waters in 1871, have grown in numbers and spread from Monterey Bay to the Columbia River and Alaska. Mostly a sport fish on the West Coast, shad have not been a substantial commercial fishery there, except for a small fishery on the Columbia River, because there is a small market for them as well as a desire to avoid bycatch of protected salmon.

Shad were eaten fresh (often planked) and salted or sometimes smoked for later use. In the nineteenth century, outdoor bakes accounted for recreational shad consumption mostly in the South and Middle Atlantic regions. As with all fish, shad cooked with bone in are tastier, but by the late twentieth century, a filleting method nicknamed the "x, y, z cut" was being used. This method calls for removing most of the bones, but it shreds the flesh, obliging the fish sellers to wrap the fish in plastic wrap to hold the fillet together.

Shark

Several sorts of sharks have been regarded as edible, and their cartilaginous skeletons have made them desirable, though they were not an important commercial fishery in the United States until the twentieth century. The flesh is meaty. Shark have been overfished, however, and conservationists recommend that they not be caught for food.

Squid

A mollusk, squid (families Ommastrephidae and Loliginidae) more often appears on menus and in the market by its Italian name, calamari. The ommastrephids are the major commercial species around the world, but the American market depends mostly on squid caught off the New England and California coasts. That modern Americans know calamari at all is owing to immigrants from the Mediterranean who introduced its use in the twentieth century and provided recipes for its preparation. Battered and deep-fried calamari rings cut from the tube-shaped body are common fare in seafood restaurants, and prepared and frozen calamari is available for salads, stews, and stir-fries. The fishery for wild calamari is still abundant.

Sturgeon

Strange and rare, sturgeon (family Acipenseridae) were highly esteemed in the past for their reddish flesh; their cartilaginous external plates that meant fewer internal bones; their large size, with some individuals growing to six hundred or more pounds; and the sturgeon caviar, which was favored over other sorts. Sturgeon are found in the northern hemisphere, with seven species in North America, caught in both lakes and saltwater.

Few modern people will have eaten sturgeon, whose flesh is said to resemble veal in flavor; in most places the fish is a protected, endangered species. It was plentiful in America into the nineteenth century, heavily fished in the Hudson and Delaware Rivers and even nicknamed "Albany beef." It was mentioned slightly more often in southern cookbooks than in Northern ones, and toward the end of the nineteenth century, much of the commercial catch was smoked and sold wherever there was a large German population.

Since Atlantic sturgeon is anadromous, the fishery is now mostly conducted on the Hudson River. On the West Coast, there are two species of sturgeon, the green and the white, but the green is not considered to be good for eating. There is a small commercial fishery of sturgeon on the Columbia River. Some efforts are being made to farm raise sturgeon. The main object of sturgeon fishery worldwide is the caviar, but the beluga sturgeon is so overfished and poorly managed that conservationists list beluga caviar among seafood to avoid.

Swordfish

Swordfish (family Xiphiidae) were not a significant food fish until the late nineteenth century, though they were apparently harpooned and consumed by people on Nantucket and Martha's Vineyard in the early 1800s; these people also salted the swordfish for trade to the West Indies. In American cookbooks, swordfish were virtually ignored until the later 1800s, though the fish appeared in the market. Swordfish has meaty flesh and large bones, which helped it gain popularity, and it is enjoyed grilled and baked.

There is a substantial sport fishery around swordfish and marlin as well, which also has a swordlike bill. Swordfish were killed by harpoon in the early days of the fishery on the East Coast as well as on the West Coast in the early 1900s. Where the swordfish is still pursued, longlines are usually used. The Atlantic sword fishery is managed but is still considered stressed, and many restaurants will not offer swordfish on menus; it also appears on many lists of species to avoid eating. The Pacific sword fishery is considered by some to be stable and healthy, but it is not managed.

Whale Meat and Whale Oil

Whale meat and whale oil are significant foods for the Inuit people of Alaska. The Inuits have hunted whales for hundreds of years, and whale meat may account for up to 60 percent of the Inuit diet. Whale hunting, with its attendant ceremonies, helps to perpetuate the culture and ethnic identity of Inuits, who are permitted by the International Whaling Commission to harvest a limited number of bowheads annually. Still, the practice is controversial and is under fire from those interested in whale conservation.

The Inuit hunt for bowhead from the middle of April through the middle of June. The mammal grows to about sixty feet long and can weigh up to sixty tons. A whaling crew who catches a whale hosts a thanksgiving celebration, named *Naluqatak,* usually held in mid-June, and the meat is shared among members of their community. The daylong celebration is observed with a feast that includes a dish called *mikigaq,* or fermented whale meat, as well as other wild foods.

Among non-Inuit Americans, however, whale meat and oil as food products have had a very limited use and no appreciable commercial fishery. Whale oil was used for lighting and as an industrial lubricant in the late eighteenth and nineteenth centuries, when a substantial fishery was established for it. Some nineteenth-century whale men were known to eat portions of the flesh, but it was uncommon, and whale oil was used to fry doughnuts for the crew in an observance of the one-thousandth barrel of whale oil filled on any given voyage.

[*See also* Alaska; Pacific Northwestern Regional Cookery; Soups and Stews.]

BIBLIOGRAPHY.

Davidson, Alan. *North Atlantic Seafood: A Comprehensive Guide with Recipes.* 3rd ed. Berkeley, CA: Ten Speed Press, 2003.

Davidson, Alan, ed. *The Oxford Companion to Food.* Oxford: Oxford University Press, 1999.

De Voe, Thomas F. *The Market Assistant, Containing a Brief Description of Every Article of Human Food Sold in the Public Markets of New York, Boston, Philadelphia, and Brooklyn.* New York: Hurd and Houghton, 1867. Reprint, Detroit: Gale, 1975.

Goode, George Brown, ed. *The Fisheries and Fishery Industries of the United States.* 8 vols. Washington, DC: Government Printing Office, 1884–1887.

Kurlansky, Mark. *Cod: A Biography of the Fish That Changed the World.* New York: Walker, 1997.

McPhee, John. *The Founding Fish.* New York: Farrar, Straus and Giroux, 2002.

National Marine Fisheries. National Oceanic and Atmospheric Administration's National Marine Fisheries. http://www.nmfs.noaa.gov. Has many sections with current information on the state of American fisheries, including aquaculture, bycatch, trade, habitat, and endangered species information.

Oliver, Sandra L. *Saltwater Foodways: New Englanders and Their Food at Sea and Ashore, in the Nineteenth Century.* Mystic, CT: Mystic Seaport Museum, 1995.

Oregon Department of Fish and Wildlife Marine Resources Program. http://hmsc.oregonstate.edu/odfw/finfish/sp/fish_list.html.

Pierce, George Wesley. *Goin' Fishin': The Story of the Deep-Sea Fishermen of New England.* Salem, MA: Marine Research Society, 1934. Reprint, Camden, ME: International Marine Publishing Company, 1989.

"What's a Fish Lover to Eat?" *The Audubon Guide to Seafood.* http://magazine.audubon.org/seafood/guide/.

SANDRA L. OLIVER

Saltwater Shellfish

Oysters, relished by the aboriginal Americans, were joined by lobster and crab to find favor in America from the time of the first settlers and are the most frequently mentioned shellfish in cookbooks. Early on, commercial fisheries existed to harvest them, but these shellfish also were a subsistence food for those who could gather them. Thus these creatures were simultaneously of high and of low value. Of these three shellfish, oysters are the only one commonly eaten raw.

A disadvantage in eating any shellfish is that once the hard exterior is opened, only small pieces of meat are found. For this reason, the value of shellfish often lay in their use in sauces, soups, and, mixed with a binding ingredient, cakes and croquettes. Cooked lobster and crab became popular for salads in the mid-nineteenth century, and they became marketable as canned products. The larger the shellfish, the greater the meat reward for the effort required to pick it out of the shell. Thus the large Pacific Coast crabs are extremely popular.

For much of American culinary history, shrimps or prawns, crayfish, scallops, mussels, and clams have had a minor role. Not mentioned nearly as consistently in cookbooks as oysters, lobster, and crab, and with smaller fisheries attached to them, some of these shellfish did not become important or widely popular until the twentieth century. Like oysters, lobster, and crab, the other shellfish were used in stews, soups, and sauces and later in salads. Once harvested in New England to be used as bait, some species of clams are eaten raw; others, however, are good only after being chopped for soup or chowder. Some shellfish are popular for outdoor recreational cookery, such as crab, shrimp, and crayfish boils and clambakes. Many shellfish are farm raised and hold a more important place in cuisine, especially in ethnic cookery, than they once did. Abalone and sea urchins go almost unmentioned in early cookery sources.

Abalone

Now considered a luxury shellfish, abalone is found on the Pacific Rim and along the coast of California. The commercial abalone fishery was closed in 1997, although some abalone is taken in a sport fishery north of San Francisco, and it is being farm raised. In earlier times, abalone was taken by Native Americans. In the mid-nineteenth century the Chinese in California fished for abalone, drying and salting the meat for export to China and selling the shells, which were the chief object of the few Anglo-Americans involved in the fishery. The shells were polished and used for inlay, jewelry, mantle ornaments, and soap dishes. When the shallow-water abalone fishery was closed in approximately 1900, Japanese American divers fished for abalone in the subtidal zone.

The Latin species name for abalone, *haliotis,* means "sea ear" and refers to the shape of the creature. The name "abalone" comes from the Spanish word *aulon* or *aulone.* There are nine species of abalone, but the primary food species are the red and pink, or pinto, abalone, the red being harvested commercially in California, and the pinto being harvested in British Columbia, Canada, and Alaska. Red, pink, and green abalone are farm raised. Most abalone are considered suitable for harvest when the shells are approximately four inches long. The shellfish must be cooked very quickly, usually panfried, or else it toughens.

Crab

Valuable fisheries have formed around several species of American crab. The early history of crab consumption reflects highly regional tastes, although in more recent times many crabs are caught, packed, and shipped to all parts of the United States. Because of the labor-intensive effort of harvesting crabs, in colonial times the meat was used in small amounts (as was most shellfish) in soups, stews, sauces, and, like other flaked fish, in small fried cakes. Some recipes suggested that other shellfish could be substituted for crab.

Blue crab ranges from Delaware to Florida but that from Chesapeake Bay is most famous. The most popular way to prepare blue crabs is to boil them in seasoned water. Eating blue crab in the rough is a favorite recreational pastime. Soft-shell crabs are those that have shed their shells. They are cooked to be eaten whole, often in a sandwich. Blue crabs have long been a commercial fishery. The meat, and the famous she-crab soup of the Chesapeake region, is canned and distributed across the United States. The principal blue crab fisheries are in Maryland and Louisiana.

Snow crab, sometimes called queen crab (as opposed to king crab), from the colder waters of the North Atlantic and North Pacific oceans, appeared on the market in the 1960s. Snow crabs are caught in pots and with tangle nets, which are set by multiple-boat operations that obstruct the crabs' migration across the seabed. Snow crabs vary in size from one and one-half to five pounds and sometimes measure two feet from pincer tip to pincer tip. The crabs have worthwhile body meat, although the main object is the leg meat. The fishery is managed with quotas for the annual catch. Atlantic Canada is the center of the fishery, but a large fishery exists in Alaska, the crabs being sold cooked and frozen across the United States.

Alaska king crab is highly prized for its large meaty claws and legs, which can have a span of up to ten feet. In this fishery, which poses dangers to fishermen, six- to seven-hundred-pound pots set with herring bait are attached to long buoy lines. The pots are hauled in sometimes heavy seas in late fall and early winter around the Aleutian Islands and in the Bering Sea. The crabs, usually only male red, blue, or golden king crabs, are usually taken ashore alive but are processed soon after, the legs, called "sections," being cooked and frozen. These large crabs are highly desirable because of the ratio of meat to time spent picking it and because the large, well-flavored chunks of meat are good in salads, sandwiches, pasta, and Asian dishes. A great deal of king crab is sold to Japan. Although the fishery is managed, king crabs are nearly overfished, and seafood conservationists caution against overconsumption.

Dungeness crab is found on the Pacific coast from Mexico to Alaska in a fishery that usually opens in December, putting the fishers at risk of bad weather to get the earliest crab to market. The fishery, which is well managed, extends roughly from the central California coast to the Gulf of Alaska, centered between northern Washington State and northern Oregon. Only male Dungeness crabs may be legally caught, and the species is considered abundant. This crab averages approximately two pounds at commercial size and yields one-fourth of its weight in meat, approximately twice the yield of a blue crab.

Rock crab ranges from Labrador, Canada, to Florida. Although the crabs have good-tasting meat, extremely hard shells make rock crab an unattractive fishery. The crabs sometimes are a by-catch of lobstering along the New England coast. The meat is picked out of legs and claws for sale in traditional crab dishes such as salads, crab rolls, and crab cakes.

Crab Recipes. Pamphlet issued by the Madam Brand Crab Co. *Collection of Andrew F. Smith*

Lobster

Considered a luxury item in most seafood restaurants, cold-water lobster trapped in Maine and Canadian waters is shipped around the United States for consumption. There have been attempts to farm-raise lobsters in Hawaii and elsewhere. Some lobster trappers claim that even wild lobsters are accidentally farmed because they feed on bait from the bags placed in traps. Gradually rotting bait floats out into the surrounding waters, where the lobsters eat it. The lobsters creep into and out of the traps to feed there as well. Eventually the lobsters grow so large they cannot leave the traps, which have net openings as a conservation feature. Even so, American lobster trappers are required to measure the lobsters and throw back both undersize and oversize ones.

For more than one hundred years, New England lobster trappers have managed to follow various practices that have conserved lobster populations. Yet from the settlement of America to the present, average lobster size has declined. Lobsters had commercial value early. They were trapped and brought ashore in New England cities, where they were often cooked immediately to prevent spoilage and sold door to door. As early as the mid-eighteenth century, as reported by the Swedish naturalist Peter Kalm in 1749, lobsters were transported alive to Boston and New York in well vessels—boats with seawater flowing through portions of the hull, which contained the shellfish. That practice continued into the nineteenth century.

The establishment of lobster canneries along the New England coast in the mid-nineteenth century made the product available inland for salads, sauces, and bisques. Cannery refuse, sold to farmers as compost, may account for the oft-repeated claim that lobsters were so plentiful they were plowed into fields. The fishery was active along the New England coast for two hundred years but declined in the twentieth century along the southern New England coast. In the early twenty-first century, Penobscot Bay, on the coast of Maine, and adjacent areas report the greatest catches. Canadian and Maine trappers vie over the lobster populations in the eastern Gulf of Maine and argue about the appropriate and sustainable harvest size. Some seafood conservation groups have put American lobster on the list of species that need protection.

Mussels

In most of North America, mussels were almost ignored as a food source until the last half of the twentieth century. Mussels were known in Europe and Great Britain as edible, although some cookery literature pointed out that people sometimes became sick after eating them. As filter feeders, mussels are susceptible to the toxic algae blooms commonly called red tide, and the threat of food poisoning may have discouraged consumers. There was very minor commercial gathering of mussels for the New York market, and an effort was made around the turn of the twentieth century to persuade consumers to use them. In the last few decades of the twentieth century, with clams becoming scarce and expensive and with the public becoming more aware of various ethnic mussel dishes, the shellfish grew in popularity. Mussels are fairly

abundant in the wild but are being water-farmed from rafts where cables seeded with juvenile mussels hang, allowing the mussels to feed off naturally occurring plankton until they are a harvestable size.

Oysters

Oysters are difficult-to-open, rough-shelled bivalves, and once were the most popular of all seafood in America. Since ancient times Native Americans along the East Coast feasted on oysters, leaving behind large shell heaps. Colonists brought with them a long history of passion for oysters and took to them readily in the New World. Oysters were so popular that they were overharvested along many parts of the New England coast in the eighteenth century. By the mid-nineteenth century oysters were cultivated with seed oysters brought from the Chesapeake region, where these shellfish abounded.

Oysters were packed and shipped inland all through the eighteenth and nineteenth centuries, each era taking advantage of advances in transportation and packing technology. At home, oysters were used as side dishes, in sauces, and in soups or stews. In inns and taverns oysters were sold as "fast food" to accompany drink. In the nineteenth century, so-called oyster saloons were found in nearly all cities and towns of any size. At these establishments a bowl of oyster stew could be cooked up quickly or a plate of roasted or raw oysters could be quickly consumed.

Sea Urchins

Sea urchins were of no historical interest as a food fishery in America until the last decades of the twentieth century, when they were fished commercially for a high-value, global market, most going to Japanese buyers for use in sushi. Urchins are gathered by diving. Because there is no regulation over the numbers taken, the sea urchin population has been seriously depleted.

Scallops

In early times scallops were not favored the way other shellfish were. In more recent times a substantial commercial fishery for scallops has developed on the East Coast and in the Pacific Northwest. Scallops are increasingly the object of aquaculture. The fishery usually is conducted in winter, and scallopers refit their boats for that purpose. Two types of scallop, the large sea scallop and the smaller bay scallop, are preferred for eating. Although the whole scallop is edible, the American market prefers only the muscle that enables the scallop to scoot around the seabed. This preference dates to the nineteenth century, when scallops were cleaned and sold shelled. Scallops are cleaned at sea, and most are sautéed quickly for entrées, incorporated into fish stews and chowder, or skewered and grilled. Scallops also can be eaten raw.

Shrimp and Prawns

The terms "shrimp" and "prawn" are used almost interchangeably. Americans primarily use the word "shrimp" for large and small crustaceans in the Penaeidae and Pandalidae families. Elsewhere in the world "prawn" usually describes a smaller creature. In America, shrimp were harvested mostly in the South, where they were more abundant than in the North, and so appear with greater frequency in older southern cookbooks. In the North, canned shrimp from states on the Gulf of Mexico became available after the 1870s.

Mostly used in earlier times in sauces, soups, and stews, shrimp seemed to be interchangeable with other crustaceans and shellfish. Toward the end of the nineteenth century shrimp became popular in salads and sandwiches. In the twentieth century shrimp, often served alone with a cocktail sauce, became an important item on appetizer menus. In the early twenty-first century shrimp is used in Asian and fusion cookery. Shrimp also is a staple of the fast-food industry. It is battered and deep-fried and served as one of several shellfish on seafood platters, in baskets with french fries, or as so-called popcorn shrimp, small shrimp eaten like popcorn, with the fingers.

Until the 1940s shrimp were harvested along the Gulf of Mexico with seines set close to shore and hauled by men and horses. Shrimpers used trawlers thereafter, fishing in deeper waters of the Gulf. Use of bottom-trawling gear helped create a commercial shrimp fishery on the Pacific coast of Canada after the 1960s.

Many species of shrimp are eaten in America—from small cold-water shrimp harvested in winter in the Gulf of Maine, to the larger shrimp of the Gulf of Mexico variously called pink, white, gray, and green tailed, to large, imported tiger shrimp of the Indo-Pacific, which are common on restaurant menus. The United States is a shrimp-catching country, but it imports much more than it catches. Pink shrimp are considered abundant in the United States. The shrimp fishery by-catch includes sea turtles and juvenile populations of many other favored food fishes, such as red snapper and red drum, and trawling damages the seabed. Although shrimp can be farm raised, that business is underdeveloped in America, because shrimp can be imported inexpensively from South American and Asian countries willing to exploit their mangrove forests for shrimp aquaculture.

[See also California; Clambake; Clams; Crab Boils; New England Regional Cookery; Oyster Bars; Oyster Loaf Sandwich; Oysters; Pacific Northwest Regional Cookery; Seafood; Southern Regional Cookery.]

BIBLIOGRAPHY

Davidson, Alan. *North Atlantic Seafood.* New York: Viking, 1980.
Davidson, Alan, ed. *The Oxford Companion to Food.* Oxford: Oxford University Press, 1999.
DeVoe, Thomas F. *The Market Assistant.* New York: Hurd and Houghton, 1867. Reprint, Detroit: Gale, 1975.
Goode, George Brown, ed. *The Fisheries and Fishery Industries of the United States.* Washington, DC: U.S. Government Printing Office, 1887.
Lipfert, Nathan, and Kenneth R. Martin. *Lobstering and the Maine Coast.* Bath: Maine Maritime Museum, 1985.
Warner, William. *Beautiful Swimmers: Watermen, Crabs, and the Chesapeake Bay.* New York: Penguin, 1987.

SANDRA L. OLIVER

Fisher, M. F. K.

For more than fifty-five years, Mary Frances Kennedy Fisher, a self-styled third-generation journalist and widely acclaimed "poet of the appetites," crafted essays, stories, and articles that changed the character of culinary writing across America. Born on July 3, 1908, in Albion, Michigan, Fisher was the daughter of Rex Brenton Kennedy and Edith Oliver Holbrook, who in 1912 settled in Whittier, California, when Rex Kennedy became part owner and editor of *The Whittier News.*

Fisher attended private boarding schools, Illinois College, Whittier College, and Occidental College before continuing her education in 1929 at the University of Dijon, France, as the newly married Mrs. Alfred Fisher. The Fishers returned to California in 1932 and lived in Laguna Beach, doing odd jobs and writing. M. F. K. Fisher's first published article, "Pacific Village," appeared in *Westways* in 1934.

The pleasures of the table as well as the legends and lore of culinary history in cookbooks as old as *Apicius de re Coquinaria* and as influential as *Mrs. Beeton's Book of Household Management* were the subjects of Fisher's first book, *Serve It Forth* (1937). In *Consider the Oyster* (1941), Fisher distracted her second husband, Dillwyn Parrish, from the pain of Buerger's disease by writing about the legendary bivalve. Survival and dining well in wartime were Fisher's preoccupation in *How to Cook a Wolf* (1942). A year later in *The Gastronomical Me* she took the measure of her powers when she re-created her gastronomically satisfying moments at home and abroad and used food as a surrogate for easing basic human longings. A series of articles for *Gourmet* magazine about Fisher's experiences living in Hollywood and her third marriage, to Donald Friede, became *The Alphabet for Gourmets* (1948).

By the time these quintessential Fisher books were collected in *The Art of Eating* in 1954, M. F. K. Fisher had distinguished herself as a solo voice in gastronomical writing, distancing herself from the early twentieth century American gastronomers—George Wechsberg, Alexis Licine, Lucius Beebe, and A. J. Liebling—and from the pattern of food writing that concentrated on nutritional information, balanced meals, and entertaining tips. Innovative, autobiographical, and nostalgic, Fisher defined gastronomy as the art of eating and drinking with intelligence and grace, and she wrote about it in her own inimitable style. Extensively published in *House Beautiful* and *Gourmet* in the 1940s and in the *New Yorker* in the 1960s and 1970s, Fisher also contributed to *Vogue*, *Westways*, *Ladies Home Journal*, *The Atlantic Monthly*, *Esquire*, *Coronet*, and *Holiday*.

In the late 1940s, Fisher's literary reputation grew with an anthology of culinary selections from great literature, called *Here Let Us Feast: A Book of Banquets* (1946), the novel *Not Now But Now* (1947), and a translation of Brillat-Savarin's *Physiology of Taste* (1949). After periods of residency in France, Fisher added other places to her repertoire and published books on Aix-en-Provence, Marseille, and Dijon. By the late 1960s, she revisited the foods of her growing-up years as well as the accumulated recipes that had served her well and published the cookbook *With Bold Knife and Fork* (1969) and a memoir of her childhood, *Among Friends* (1970). It was with the publication of Time-Life's *The Cooking of Provincial France* (1968), however, that Fisher became more actively associated with the rising stars of America's culinary community—James Beard, Julia Child, and Craig Claiborne.

When North Point Press reissued many of Fisher's books in the 1980s, recognition and honors, including election to the American Academy of Arts and Letters in 1991, came her way, and Last House, Fisher's unique home in the Sonoma Valley, attracted both established and aspiring members of the culinary establishment.

After a ten-year struggle with Parkinson's disease, M. F. K. Fisher died on June 22, 1992, her literary reputation secured and her contribution to the art of eating recognized.

[*See also* California; Cookbooks and Manuscripts, *subentry on* From World War II to the 1960s; Myths and Folklore; Periodicals; Restaurant Critics and Food Columnists.]

BIBLIOGRAPHY

Ferrary, Jeannette. *Between Friends: M. F. K. Fisher and Me.* New York: Atlantic Monthly Press, 1991.

Fisher, Mary Frances Kennedy. Mary Frances Kennedy Fisher papers, 1029–1985. Unprocessed collection 71, 58–87, M68. Cambridge, MA: The Arthur and Elizabeth Schlesinger Library, Radcliffe College.

Fisher, Mary Frances Kennedy. Private journals and papers. Private Collection of Kennedy Friede Golden, Hayward, CA.

Fussell, Betty. *Masters of American Cookery.* New York: Times, 1983.

Reardon, Joan. *M. F. K. Fisher, Julia Child, and Alice Waters: Celebrating the Pleasures of the Table.* New York: Harmony, 1994.

JOAN REARDON

Flavorings

The term "flavoring" encompasses a range of definitions. General dictionaries define "flavoring" as "a particular sensation as perceived after placing a substance in the oral cavity," while the U.S. Food and Drug Administration provides the detailed explanation, "Flavoring means any substance, the function of which is to import flavor, which is derived from spice, fruit or fruit juice, vegetable or vegetable juice, edible yeast, herb, bark, bud, root, leaf or similar plant material, meat, fish, poultry, eggs, dairy products, or fermentation products thereof." Flavor has olfactory (smell) and gustatory (taste) components. The Monell Chemical Senses Center indicates, "It has long been established that our sense of taste detects four basic sensations—sweet, salty, sour and bitter. More recently, increasing consensus has developed for the addition of a fifth class of taste sensation: umami, sometimes described as brothy."

The term "flavor" is used ambiguously by consumers. For example, a stew may be perceived as having a good flavor because it contains spice, while strawberry Jell-O may be thought to have a good flavor even though it does not contain any spice. Flavors occur in foods in several different ways: they may be present already in a food, such as the banana flavor of a banana; a cook may add ingredients to flavor a food, such as using Bing cherries with duck, or white wine with fish; a cook may use a commercial, store-bought flavoring extract to flavor a food, such as adding vanilla extract to whipped cream; a food already may contain a flavor that has been added by a food manufacturer. Food manufacturers use commercial flavors purchased from flavor manufacturers, such as International Flavors and Fragrances, Givaudan, and Firmenich.

Flavors can be categorized as natural, artificial, natural and artificial, and natural with other natural flavors (WONF). Flavor chemists usually attempt to recreate flavors of foods found in nature. Natural flavors can only contain flavoring components derived from the named flavor. For example, natural lemon flavor contains components from lemons such as lemon juice and lemon oil. Artificial flavors usually contain a chemical that is the main characteristic flavor of the natural materials. Vanillin, characteristic of the flavor of vanilla, and benzaldehyde, characteristic of the flavor of cherries, both can be produced chemically. Using these flavor chemicals causes a flavor to be labeled artificial.

The U.S. Food and Drug Administration has the ultimate responsibility for the safety of foods and flavors. The 1958 Food Additive Amendment to the Pure Food Act established a law requiring that all ingredients added to food must be safe. An independent expert panel reviews the safety of flavor ingredients and establishes the ingredients' status as generally recognized as safe (GRAS). Flavors are used at very low levels in foods, usually at one to ten parts per million.

Use of Flavorings in the Home

Prior to 1850, Americans flavored their own foods and beverages using local and foreign sources of flavorings such as rum, fruit juice, and spices. By the mid-nineteenth century, food and beverage products containing commercial flavors started to appear in the United States. The addition of flavorings to whiskey, to simulate aging, was one of the first uses of a flavored product. Flavored ice cream was first produced commercially in 1841 in Baltimore. Coca-Cola was first sold in 1886. McCormick started selling flavor extracts directly to the consumer in 1900, and Jell-O became available in 1901.

The American consumer experienced a proliferation of flavored products throughout the twentieth century; in 2004, the U.S. flavor industry sold more than $2 billion of flavors. Coca-Cola and Pepsi added new flavors to their traditional cola lines. Formerly exotic flavors such as mango, kiwi, and Irish coffee became commonplace. Flavor companies continued to attempt to duplicate the flavor and aroma of fresh-brewed coffee for instant coffee, improve the fresh-squeezed flavor of orange juice, and capture the flavor of fruit on the vine.

History of the U.S. Flavor Industry

The U.S. flavor industry has its roots in the United Kingdom and Europe. Beginning in the early 1700s, natural plant and fruit extracts, essential oils, and distillates were prepared and sold. U.S. companies started using and manufacturing commercial flavors around 1850. Early flavors contained components derived from natural materials such as fruits and spices. One of the first synthetic aroma chemicals to be used in flavorings was citral, a chemical found in lemon that is characteristic of lemon flavor. The isolation, synthesis, and production of citral in the United States first occurred around 1900. Vanillin (vanilla) and cinnamic aldehyde (cinnamon) also became commercially available in the United States in the early 1900s.

It was common to ship European flavors to New York City as early as 1797. Most U.S. flavor companies started in a four-square-block area near the South Seaport (East River) in lower Manhattan. There were seventy-two flavor and essential flavor oil companies in New York City in 1927; only eighteen of these companies were in existence under same name in 1977. Four companies from that 1927 list (Givaudan, A. M. Todd, Ungerer and Company, and Manheimer) were in existence at the beginning of the twenty-first century.

There are now more than two hundred U.S. flavor suppliers. Most flavor companies moved from New York City to New Jersey by 1950. Givaudan purchased a number of companies through the years and ranks as the number-one U.S. flavor company. International Flavors and Fragrances is second. New Jersey is the leading state for flavor sales. Cincinnati, Ohio, the site of Givaudan's headquarters, is the leading city.

Development of New Commercial Flavors

The advent of the use of gas liquid chromatography (GLC) in 1960 to 1970 greatly expanded the flavor chemist's ability to identify new volatile chemicals in food. This led to a significant increase in the number of new flavors created by flavor companies. Research into flavor chemistry earned Nobel Prizes in 1910, 1939, and 2001.

Food and beverage companies develop new products to meet a real or perceived consumer need or want and drive the flavor companies to develop flavors for new products and to improve the flavors of existing products. Flavor salespeople identify flavor needs for food and beverage companies. Flavor application chemists determine which existing flavors meet the needs of the food or beverage manufacturer. If necessary, flavor chemists create a new flavor. The food or beverage company requests flavor samples from two or more flavor suppliers, and then it conducts consumer tests to determine the acceptability of the product or flavor. Once the product is marketed, the process of improving the flavor or reducing its cost begins.

More than six thousand new food and beverage products were introduced in 2003, and many of those products contained flavors. The trend is for the consumer to purchase more and more different types of flavored products, which bodes well for the creative and highly competitive U.S. flavor industry.

[*See also* Chemical Additives; Herbs and Spices.]

BIBLIOGRAPHY

Batterberry, Michael, and Ariane Batterberry. *On the Town in New York: The Landmark History of Eating, Drinking, and Entertainments from the American Revolution to the Food Revolution.* New York: Routledge, 1999.

Carlin, J. M. "Eating and Drinking in the Early Republic." *Nutrition Today* 33, no. 2 (March/April 1968): 71–76.

Dorland, Wayne E., and James A. Rogers, Jr. *The Fragrance and Flavor Industry.* Mendham, NJ: W. E. Dorland Company, 1977.

JOHN F. CASSENS

Floats, *see Milkshakes*

Flowers, Edible

Edible flowers, the most popular being nasturtiums, pansies, marigolds, violets, and roses, have enjoyed a renaissance that began in the 1980s. Far from being only an ornamental conceit of nouvelle cuisine, edible flowers were being used in American kitchens by the mid-seventeenth century for both culinary and medicinal purposes. English colonists were primarily responsible for introducing flowers into American cooking; cookery manuscripts and colonial-era cookbooks contain a wide range of recipes. Traditionally flowers have been pickled or used fresh, like herbs, to add color, texture, and very subtle flavor to salads; infused into wines, cordials, syrups, and teas; made into conserves and jellies; or candied and added to desserts and confections. More recently, Italian Americans have popularized zucchini blossoms stuffed with anchovy and mozzarella and deep-fried in a light batter.

Flowers are especially difficult to transport in peak condition, and with the decline in kitchen gardens as a ready supplier of produce, flower cookery also declined in the twentieth century, if not earlier in urban areas. The resurgence of urban farmers' markets and the increasing popularity of gourmet stores in the last quarter of the twentieth century reintroduced edible flowers as an ingredient.

Not all flowers are edible, most notably the beautiful but poisonous lily of the valley. Because of the fragility, potential danger, and sheer inconvenience of using fresh or candied flowers to decorate ceremonial cakes, an entire confectionery subspecialty has spawned legions of skilled artisans who fashion realistic-looking flowers from sugar-based pastes such as *pastillage*, fondant, or marzipan, delicately tinted to mimic or even better Mother Nature.

[*See also* Orange Flower Water; Rose Water.]

Nasturtiums. Burpee Seed catalog, 1914

BIBLIOGRAPHY

Brown, Cora, Rose Brown, and Bob Brown. *Salads and Herbs.* Philadelphia and New York: Lippincott, 1938.

Phipps, Frances. *Colonial Kitchens, Their Furnishings, and Their Gardens.* New York: Hawthorn Books, 1972.

CATHY K. KAUFMAN

Flytraps and Fly Screens

Woven wire screening was manufactured as early as the 1830s in the United States, in Connecticut, and was used to screen the sides and doors of food safes and to make sieves. Cheesecloth was used to cover serving dishes on the table until woven wire dish covers—round and oval domes of screening with metal rims, in many sizes—became available in the 1850s. In the early twenty-first century similar covers of flexible cloth are marketed for outdoor dining. After the 1890s window screens became fairly common, but most houses were not screened until the late 1920s. Window screens reduced the need to protect containers and dishes from flies. Other nineteenth-century tools in the battle against fly-borne diseases were flyswatters; wind-up fly fans with long-reaching gauzy wings, which were set on dining or worktables; baited flytraps of glass or wire mesh with funneled openings from which flies could not escape; and sticky coils of paper.

[*See also* Insects.]

BIBLIOGRAPHY

Franklin, Linda Campbell. *300 Years of Housekeeping Collectibles.* 5th ed. Iola, WI: Krause Publications, 2003.

LINDA CAMPBELL FRANKLIN

Folgers

Folgers, one of the two dominant mass-market American coffees, originated in San Francisco in 1850, when fourteen-year-old James Folger arrived with his two older brothers. The Folger boys, from a long line of Nantucket whalers, sought their fortune in the California Gold Rush, but James, the youngest, went to work for Pioneer Steam Coffee and Spice Mills. By the age of twenty-four, Folger was a full partner. He survived bankruptcy in 1865, paid off all his debts, and thrived with J. A. Folger and Company. After Folger died in 1889, his son carried

on. The salesman Frank Atha opened a Folger's outlet in Texas, while the main plant supplied the West. In 1906 Folger's was the only coffee roaster to remain standing through the San Francisco earthquake. During the Depression, Folger's sponsored *Judy and Jane*, a daytime radio soap opera, and in World War II, James Folger III was appointed to the War Production Board. The war swelled California's coffee-drinking population because many who had migrated to work in the war plants stayed, as did disembarking veterans.

Looking for a brand to compete with Maxwell House, Procter & Gamble purchased Folger's in 1964, taking over one of the last family-owned coffee companies and dropping the possessive apostrophe. The relaxed, personal style of the firm gave way to marketers with fat briefcases. With a major cash infusion, Folgers television advertisements, featuring Mrs. Olson, an omniscient Swedish busybody, saved marriages by showing up with a can of Folgers coffee. In a later campaign, Procter & Gamble produced effective commercials with the tag line, "The best part of waking up is Folgers in your cup," but the coffee in the can left a great deal to be desired, containing an unspecified amount of cheap robusta beans.

A boycott mounted against Folgers in 1990 because of its purchase of El Salvadoran beans during a time of death squad activity helped lead to a peaceful settlement of that country's civil war. In 1995 Procter & Gamble purchased the specialty roaster Millstone, which sells all-arabica whole beans.

[*See also* Advertising; Coffee; Politics of Food.]

BIBLIOGRAPHY

Pendergrast, Mark. *Uncommon Grounds: The History of Coffee and How It Transformed Our World.* New York: Basic, 1999. Comprehensive business and social history.

Swasy, Alecia. *Soap Opera: The Inside Story of Procter & Gamble.* New York: Times, 1993.

MARK PENDERGRAST

Fondue Pot

A fondue pot is a pot that goes over a small portable heating element, such as an alcohol burner or candle. Fondue pots may come with accessories such as a stand for the pot, a diffuser for the heating element, a tray, and fondue forks for dipping. The pots also may be electrified. The oldest and most traditional fondue pot is the *caquelon,* which is made of earthenware. As are most glazed ceramic and enameled iron pots, the *caquelon* is heavy and has a wide bottom, which ensures the steady, even heat ideal for temperamental cheese fondues and chocolate fondues. Heavy stainless steel or enameled iron pots are used for hot oil and broth fondues.

During the 1950s and 1960s, when fondue first became widely popular in the United States, stainless steel pots in Scandinavian modern designs were fashionable. These gave way to enameled pots in decorator colors such as harvest gold and avocado green and finally to wildly patterned pots by artists such as Peter Max. In the 1970s fondue pots were a popular wedding gift. Out of fashion for twenty years, fondue and its pots made a comeback in the late 1990s. Sales of Le Creuset brand cast-iron pots surged 20 percent, Williams-Sonoma reintroduced fondue pots in its holiday catalog, and West Bend added an extra large Entertainer pot to its line.

Fondue Cookery. *Fondue and Table Top Cookery,* cookbooklet. *Culinary Archives & Museum at Johnson & Wales University, Providence, R.I.*

[*See also* Cheese; Chocolate; Pots and Pans.]

BIBLIOGRAPHY

"Fondue." gourmetsleuth.com. http://www.gourmetsleuth.com/fondue.htm.
Lovegren, Sylvia. *Fashionable Food.* New York: Macmillan, 1995.
Rhule, Patty. "The Hottest Old Trend in Cooking: Fondue." *USA Weekend,* December 11–13, 1998.

SYLVIA LOVEGREN

Food and Drug Administration

The Food and Drug Administration (FDA) is an agency of the Department of Health and Human Services of the executive branch of the U.S. government. The FDA is authorized to enforce federal laws and make regulations pertaining to food production and food safety. With the exception of meat, poultry, and some egg products, which are under the jurisdiction of the U.S. Department of Agriculture (USDA), the FDA regulates the production, manufacture, processing, packaging, labeling, and distribution of all U.S. food shipped in interstate commerce and all food imported to or exported from the United States.

Although the FDA has been an agency within Health and Human Services since 1979, the beginnings of the FDA can be traced to 1862, when Congress passed a law establishing the Department of Agriculture and an 1863 appropriation authorizing funds "for the purpose of establishing a laboratory, with the necessary apparatus for practical and scientific experiments in agricultural chemistry." First called the Division of Chemistry and in 1901 renamed the Bureau of Chemistry, the laboratory focused its work on the identification of food products that were adulterated or were fraudulent substitutes. For example, in 1879 the bureau reported the fraudulent substitution and sale of yellow-dyed oleomargarine for true butter.

In 1883, Dr. Harvey Washington Wiley (1844–1930) became the sixth chief chemist of the Bureau of Chemistry. For more than twenty years, Wiley fought for congressional passage of a federal pure food law. When the Pure Food and Drug Act was finally passed by Congress and signed into law in 1906, Wiley's Bureau of Chemistry was chosen as the federal agency to examine all foods to determine whether they were adulterated or contaminated or were misbranded fraudulent substitutes. To accomplish this assignment, the first federal food and drug inspectors were selected and appointed in

1907. Thus the Bureau of Chemistry added a law enforcement function to its role as a scientific and research institution.

Although the 1906 law had criminal penalties, the primary enforcement mechanism was confiscation. Adulterated, contaminated, and substitute foods were seized by the inspectors and removed from the marketplace. Initial enforcement of the law by the Bureau of Chemistry led to successful prosecutions involving many adulterated or substitute foods: watered milk, short-weight cheese, cheese labeled "full cream" made from skim milk, decomposed and putrid eggs, artificially colored and chemically preserved jams and jellies, "pure" olive oil mixed with cottonseed oil, artificially colored imitation vinegars labeled "pure," contaminated ketchup, artificially colored and flavored "pure" lemon and vanilla extracts, and ground pepper made solely from other ingredients. However, the failure of Congress to authorize the USDA to adopt standards of identity or standards of purity for many foods seriously weakened the law. Without a standard of identity or purity, it was difficult to prove in court that a food was adulterated or a substitute.

Internal agency disputes about the legality of certain chemical preservatives led to Wiley's resignation from the Bureau of Chemistry in March 1912. He joined the Good Housekeeping Institute as director of its Bureau of Food, Sanitation and Health. At the Good Housekeeping Institute, Wiley continued his crusade for pure food, periodically reporting in *Good Housekeeping* magazine on the status of the government's efforts to regulate the food supply.

The Bureau of Chemistry was reorganized in 1927 to separate its scientific agricultural research function from food law enforcement. As part of the reorganization, the Food, Drug, and Insecticide Administration was established as the law enforcement agency within the USDA. Renamed the Food and Drug Administration in 1930, the agency continued to enforce the Pure Food Act of 1906. The passage of the Federal Food, Drug, and Cosmetic Act of 1938 significantly expanded the enforcement powers of the FDA. Under the 1938 law, the FDA was authorized to go to court to obtain injunctions to prevent illegal foods from reaching the marketplace. In addition, the 1938 law gave the FDA the authority to promulgate food standards. By 1960, FDA food standards were applied to half the food sold in the United States. In 1940, to promote consumer confidence, the FDA was transferred from the Department of Agriculture to the Federal Security Agency. In 1953, the FDA became part of the Department of Health, Education, and Welfare, which in 1979 was renamed the Department of Health and Human Services.

The FDA makes its own regulations for the efficient enforcement of federal food laws. In addition to regulations, the FDA may also make general statements of policy, guidelines, advisory opinions, and recommendations. As a result of this comprehensive regulatory power, the FDA has a wide-ranging influence on American food. The FDA has the power and responsibility to ensure that all imported food (except meat and poultry, which are regulated by the USDA) meets federal standards. After receiving notice of the arrival of an imported food from the U.S. Customs Service, the FDA inspects and obtains samples of the product for laboratory evaluation. The food product is detained at the border pending the FDA's determination of compliance. If it does not comply with all federal laws and regulations, the product must be removed or destroyed.

The FDA has found that pure food is not necessarily safe food. In 2001, the Centers for Disease Control and Prevention reported that each year 76 million Americans become ill from eating unsafe food. Of those, 325,000 are hospitalized, and five thousand die. To address the problem of food-borne illness in the United States, the FDA has instituted a number of programs designed to ensure the safety of the entire food production chain, often called "farm to table." Prevention-oriented programs such as the Hazard Analysis and Critical Control Point (HACCP) system have been established for seafood, fresh fruits and vegetables, sprouts, unprocessed juice, and eggs. Surveillance and outbreak response programs include mandatory recalls of contaminated food products to prevent further exposure and scientific investigations to identify causation so that the problem does not reoccur. The FDA in collaboration with other governmental entities, industry representatives, and consumer advocates conducts educational programs to inform consumers about the importance of proper sanitation, cooking, and storage to decrease the number of deaths and cases of illness caused by food-borne pathogens.

[*See also* Adulterations; Department of Agriculture, United States; Food and Nutrition Systems; Good Housekeeping Institute; Law; Nutrition; Organic Food; Pure Food and Drug Act; Transportation of Food; Wiley, Harvey.]

BIBLIOGRAPHY

Anderson, Oscar E., Jr. *The Health of a Nation: Harvey W. Wiley and the Fight for Pure Food.* Chicago: University of Chicago Press, 1958.

Hilts, Peter J. *Protecting America's Health: The FDA, Business, and One Hundred Years of Regulation.* New York: Knopf, 2003.

Wiley, Harvey W. *The History of a Crime against the Food Law: The Amazing Story of the National Food and Drug Law Intended to Protect the Health of the People, Perverted to Protect Adulteration of Foods and Drugs.* Washington, DC: H. W. Wiley, 1929. Available at http://cdl.library.cornell.edu/cgi-bin/chla/chla-cgi?/notisid=AGT3895.

ROBERT W. BROWER

Food and Nutrition Systems

The American food and nutrition system is a complex network of processes that link agriculture to health. The food and nutrition system transforms raw materials into foods and beverages, which are then consumed, the nutrients in the food and drink producing health and preventing illness. Considering the system as a whole provides a broad perspective for examining all aspects of food and drink. The food and nutrition system can be viewed as a food chain and a food web, each operating within food contexts.

Food Chain

A food and nutrition chain involves an ordered sequence of stages, each stage flowing into the subsequent one. A diagram of the American food and nutrition chain is presented in Figure 1, which includes resource inputs, three major subsystems, each containing three stages, and health outputs. This way of thinking about the food and nutrition system encourages consideration of what happens upstream and downstream in the system while examining the entire life cycle of any particular food or drink.

Resource Inputs Many types of resources are needed to produce foods, including biological and physical resources, such as seeds, animals, water, soil, sunlight, energy, and feed, and often other inputs, such as fertilizer, herbicides, pesticides, and drugs. In addition, human and social resources are required, including knowledge, money, effort, and skills. Without the appropriate balance of resources at the right time and place,

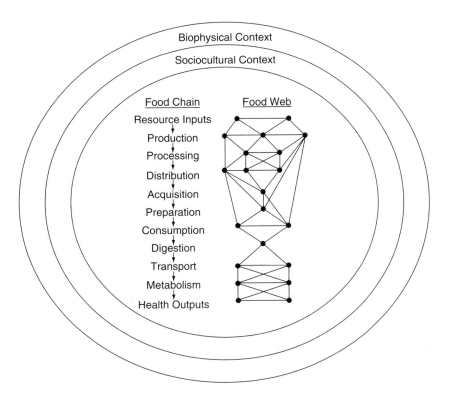

Figure 1. The food and nutrition system: food chains, food webs, and food contexts. *Adapted from Sobal et al. (1998) and Sobal (1999)*

the food system cannot successfully produce food and beverages. For example, drought, soil erosion, economic depression, and disease epidemics deprive food systems of essential resources needed to operate.

Food Production Production uses resources to propagate plants and engage in husbandry for animals. Until the development of agriculture more than ten thousand years ago, all foods in America were acquired by hunting and gathering. Since then, production of most American food and drink has shifted to agriculture, whereby many types of animals and plants are grown in or extracted from fields, pastures, forests, gardens, and waters. A result of the industrialization of U.S. agriculture is that most staple crops such as corn, wheat, soybeans, cattle, and poultry are produced by large agricultural corporations, although small private family farms continue to produce many vegetables, fruits, specialty crops, and animal foods.

Food Processing Processing occurs as crops and animals from farms are transformed into foodstuffs and foods that can then be distributed. The first step is crude processing, often on the farm, where cleaning, sorting, and other basic modifications occur. Although some American foods, such as apples, are only slightly processed and are eaten in much the same form as when they left the farm, most foods are highly processed by the food industry. Food manufacturing enterprises mill, butcher, combine, heat, cool, preserve, and package most U.S. food into forms that often bear little resemblance to the original form on the farm. Technological changes in food processing developed by food scientists have shifted the ingredients and types of foods available in the United States.

Food Distribution In distribution, foodstuffs and foods are channeled to particular sites where they are available to be purchased by consumers. Most U.S. food is distributed through supermarkets and related types of markets, such as farmers' markets and consumer food cooperatives. Some people gather, produce, and exchange their own foods. Individuals who cannot afford adequate food may use emergency food distribution sources such as food pantries and soup kitchens. Nearly one-half of the food distributed in the United States is prepared and served to consumers through the food-service industry, in which restaurants, cafeterias, vending machines, caterers, and other channels disseminate food to customers.

Food Acquisition Acquisition occurs as consumers procure foods at various distribution outlets. The acquisition process is the point of transfer between the food industry and individual food consumers and the households they represent. Acquisition may involve shopping for groceries, selecting a restaurant and particular items on a menu, being served or given foods by family or friends, or a wide variety of other ways by which people acquire food. Although most foods are acquired to be prepared and eaten later, some is ready to eat and consumed immediately.

Food Preparation Preparation involves the variety of activities broadly termed "cooking" that includes cleaning and preparing foodstuffs, combining ingredients, exposure to various forms and levels of heating or cooling, and serving foods. Preparation follows the rules of cuisines, which combine ingredients, spices and flavorings, cooking techniques, and serving and eating behaviors appropriate to a particular food culture.

Food Consumption Consumption occurs as individuals and families select and eat foods. Most people in the United States traditionally eat three multiple-course meals per day (breakfast, lunch, and dinner) plus snacks, although the conventional meal system is eroding as people skip meals, combine meals (for example, merging breakfast and lunch into brunch), or graze on snacks throughout the day. The ingestion of food begins the processes of incorporation and use of nutrients in the body.

Digestion Nutrient digestion begins in the mouth as food is chewed to reduce it into small pieces and to mix it with saliva; proceeds with swallowing to move food into the churning stomach, where digestive fluids chemically break down the food into individual components; and is completed as nutrients selectively diffuse through the walls of the small intestine into the body. Undigested elements of food continue into the large intestine, where they are fermented by bacteria, and water is extracted. What remains of food and drink is excreted as feces and urine, completing the passage of food from the farm to the waste disposal system.

Transport Nutrient transport occurs after foods are absorbed into the body across the walls of the intestines. Macronutrients such as proteins, carbohydrates, fats, and alcohol and micronutrients such as vitamins and minerals are either transported in the form in which they were absorbed or converted into other chemical forms to be moved by the circulatory system to sites in the body where they will be used or stored.

Metabolism Nutrient metabolism is the final stage of the food and nutrition system in the body, where each nutrient is used in particular biological processes. Nutrients are required for fundamental bodily functions such as producing energy in metabolic processes, growth of body tissues, repair of injuries, and preventing nutrition-related diseases. Deficiencies and excesses of nutrient supplies and stores disrupt body functioning, leading to various diseases.

Health Outputs Health outcomes occur as one of the ultimate consequences of the food and nutrition system. Adequate nutrition is necessary for growth and development, energy and materials to perform daily tasks, and maintaining and repairing the body. Many of the major causes of death in the United States, including heart disease, stroke, diabetes, cancer, and liver disease, are at least partly based on intake of foods containing adequate but not excessive levels of nutrients. The health of the U.S. population is shaped by the foods produced, processed, distributed, acquired, prepared, and consumed in the food system.

Food Web

Food webs provide a way of thinking about the food and nutrition system that focuses on interrelationships between individuals and groups involved with food and nutrition. A wide range of roles exist in the system, including farmers, butchers, grocers, cooks, food servers, dietitians, and many others.

The food web is experiencing increasing consolidation and concentration in the scale and scope of agriculture, food processing, food retailing, and food service. Many diverse small farms have been combined into large corporate farms. Only a small percentage of the U.S. population is engaged in farming, but it produces enough to supply food and drink to the rest of the more than 290 million food consumers in American society and to send exports to other parts of the global food system. Food production and processing are increasingly mechanized and employ an increasing proportion of unskilled workers. Small, local food processors have become centralized and integrated into global food corporations. Specialized community food distributors, such as butchers, bakers, and other food vendors, have declined, and large grocery chains have developed networks of supermarkets and even larger-scale hypermarkets. Independent restaurants have declined as restaurant chains and fast food franchises have standardized the food-service industry. Food distribution has become the largest employment sector in the food web.

Because of the size and complexity of the current U.S. food and nutrition system, workers in the system have tended to become specialized and isolated from each other. This increased de-linking has led to distancing of producers and consumers and of other forms of separation of people and processes in the system. Specific terms used in different parts of the system reflect the different interests of particular parts of the web, farmers producing crops, processors purchasing commodities as raw materials, grocers buying and selling food products, shoppers seeking to purchase foodstuffs, cooks gathering ingredients to prepare dishes, consumers eating foods in meals, dietitians examining nutrient levels, and health professionals treating diseases.

Food Contexts

Food contexts provide a way of thinking about the food and nutrition system that emphasizes the environments and settings within which the system operates. Contexts influence the inputs that enter into the system and also receive the outputs that exit from the system, which often operate in the form of food cycles. The U.S. food and nutrition system has moved from operating primarily as local "foodsheds" relying on seasonal foods to becoming highly globalized, the entire world providing a context that shapes American food, eating, and nutrition. For example, the international, national, and local policy environment offers laws and regulations that influence which foods are grown, how they are handled, where they are served, and how they are eaten. Similarly, the food system has waste material outputs at every stage that must be disposed of, recycled, or reused as agricultural refuse, food processing by-products, food products that cannot be distributed, kitchen scraps, and human waste. Two major types of contexts exist: sociocultural and biophysical.

The sociocultural contexts of the food and nutrition system include cultural, economic, political, and other social components of society that interact with the system. Other societal systems, such as governmental systems, economic systems, and cultural systems, interact with the food and nutrition system. For example, the economic system offers markets for food products, establishes prices for energy and other commodities needed to keep the system operating, and establishes interest rates for financing activities in the system.

The biophysical contexts of the food and nutrition system include physical, biological, geographical, and other material components of the world that interact with the system. Concern exists about the ecological sustainability of the current energy-intensive food and nutrition system because it relies on nonrenewable resources and produces a variety of wastes and by-products. Other biophysical systems, such as health systems, transportation systems, climate systems, and hydrological systems, interact with the food and nutrition system. For example, the transportation system is a component of the built environment and offers railroads, ships, trucks, airplanes, roads, and paths for farmers, food processors, grocers, consumers, cooks, and health professionals to interact and exchange materials within the food and nutrition system and those outside the system.

Conclusion

The food and nutrition system includes a broad scope of interrelated and integrated processes that link stages in the food chain from agriculture to health outcomes, relate components of the food web ranging across many food sectors, and relate the food and nutrition system to other systems such as the economy and the environment. The U.S. food and nutrition system involves highly industrialized agricultural production that is integrated with an extensive food processing and distribution network that serves consumers who often do not cook for themselves and frequently eat away from home. This practice has led to high-fat and low-fiber nutrient intake that promotes chronic diseases such as heart disease and cancer. Considering the American food and nutrition system as a whole offers a broad perspective about food and health, identifies pathways of specific foods and beverages, and reveals links between different aspects of agriculture, food, eating, nutrition, and medicine.

[See also Community-Supported Agriculture; ConAgra; Cooperatives; Department of Agriculture, United States; Food and Drug Administration; Grocery Stores; Hunger Programs; Material Culture and Technology; North American Free Trade Agreement; Organic Food; Politics of Food; Pure Food and Drug Act; Restaurants; Transportation of Food.]

BIBLIOGRAPHY

Atkins, Peter, and Ian Bowler. *Food in Society: Economy, Culture, Geography*. New York: Oxford University Press, 2001.

Heywood, P., and Lund-Adams, M. "The Australian Food and Nutrition System: A Basis for Policy Formulation and Analysis." *Australian Journal of Public Health* 15 (1991): 258–270.

Kneen, Brewster. *From Land to Mouth: Understanding the Food System*. Toronto: NC Press, 1989.

McMichael, Philip, ed. *The Global Restructuring of Agro-food Systems*. Ithaca, NY: Cornell University Press, 1994.

Royer, Jeffrey S., and Richard T. Rogers, eds. *The Industrialization of Agriculture: Vertical Coordination in the U.S. Food System*. Brookfield, VT: Ashgate, 1998.

Sobal, Jeffery. "Food System Globalization, Eating Transformations, and Nutrition Transitions." In *Food in Global History*, edited by R. Grew, 171–193. Boulder, CO: Westview, 1999.

Sobal, Jeffery, Laura K. Khan, and Carole Bisogni. "A Conceptual Model of the Food and Nutrition System." *Social Science and Medicine* 47 (1998): 853–863.

Tansey, Geoff, and Anthony Worsley. *The Food System: A Guide*. London: Earthscan, 1996.

JEFFERY SOBAL

Food Festivals

Millions of Americans attend thousands of annual food festivals throughout the United States. On the surface these festivals are family affairs, offering entertainment and something of interest to those of all ages. But they are much more than that. Through the celebration of food, Americans also celebrate history, heritage, culture, and economic opportunity.

Early immigrants from Europe continued the tradition of ceremonial harvest festivals, marking America's primarily agrarian economy and the staple food production that served to sustain life. The Industrial Revolution, however, brought sweeping changes that would have a lasting effect. America's rapidly developing industries created an enormous demand for workers, and large numbers of people abandoned farm life, resulting in an ever-growing urban population. Improved transportation, the introduction of commercial food preservation, and the mechanization of agriculture resulted in regional crop specialization, and fewer farmers fed increasing numbers of city dwellers.

Around the turn of the twentieth century, many of America's early harvest festivals were transformed into food festivals that celebrated pride in regional commercial crop production. Combined with an increase in commercial preservation and packaging and the growth of competitive marketing strategies, festivals celebrating local foods, grown or manufactured, evolved into promotional venues. Many such festivals are formally sponsored by trade organizations or manufacturers and thus serve as powerful advertising and marketing tools in an increasingly competitive global economy. Some food festivals are an outgrowth of political and religious gatherings of yesteryear, when barbecues and church picnics or suppers were an important part of such events; other food festivals serve to celebrate holidays or culinary traditions of the past, paying tribute to ethnic cultures and special dishes or to foodways, such as the collection of maple syrup in the spring or the making of apple butter in the fall, that are rapidly vanishing from modern America. In many cases these events also serve as marketing opportunities, attracting visitors and tourists whose business is critical to the local economy or fund-raising requirements. Despite the commercial aspect of food festivals, a single strong link to the past is prevalent. Food plays a central role from a societal perspective: food is the common denominator that draws people together, providing a sense of community, fellowship, and identity.

Every state in America hosts food festivals. The greatest number of such events is staged in California, followed by Texas and the midwestern states, a pattern that mirrors demographics related to food production and harvesting. Local community groups, clubs, and religious organizations often oversee these events, and primarily volunteers staff them. Other food-related festivals are held through the efforts of museums and historical societies. As they have grown and increased in popularity, food festivals are increasingly managed by professionals in concert with corporate sponsorship.

Festivals commonly feature food in several ways. Displays provide both education and promotional opportunities. Cooking competitions and demonstrations illustrate the diverse uses of various foods and ingredients. Tastings, formal meals, and snack vendors provide the opportunity for festival visitors to become familiar with new foods and dishes. Attendees can purchase food items from associated farmers' markets, auctions, and vendors. The eating contests that are often part of the festivities provide amusement. At the Feast of San Gennaro in New York City, contestants dive into Italian pastries called cannoli. At the Nebraska Czech Festival the entrant who can most quickly consume a traditional pastry called *kolache* and then whistle is the winner.

Harvest and Promotional Festivals

A large percentage of American food festivals celebrate local crops or industries, and they serve as promotional opportunities with attendant economic benefits. Nearly every fruit and vegetable produced in the United States is showcased in at least one festival. In the Salinas valley of California, where 75 percent of the state's artichokes are produced, Castroville hosts an annual Artichoke Festival. Hatch, New Mexico, also known as the "chili capital of the world," celebrates its important crop, as well as the unique culture of New Mexico, every Labor Day weekend. The National Apple Harvest Festival in Arendtsville, Pennsylvania, promotes apples with heritage demonstrations of cider pressing and apple butter cooking. Cherry production in Traverse City, Michigan, is so important to the local economy that it is celebrated in an eight-day extravaganza called the National Cherry Festival. Alexander W. Livingston, a resident of Reynoldsburg, Ohio, is honored for commercial development of the tomato at the town's annual festival, which features tomato exhibits and tomato cookery.

Americans pay tribute to the meat and poultry industries at annual festivals dedicated to beef, turkey, and chicken. Kansas is the nation's leading producer of beef; with beef consumption on the rise in the early 2000s, Beef Empire Days not only played a pivotal role in promotional activities but also garnered consumer interest in Chuck Wagons in the Park, which featured prize-winning beef dishes. North Carolina pays tribute to one of its largest commodities with a turkey festival held every year in Raeford. Chicken, at one time so expensive that it was reserved for special occasions, is an affordable, versatile, and popular American food. The World Chicken Festival in London, Kentucky, celebrates a favorite southern dish as well as Colonel Harlan Sanders, the promotional master behind Kentucky Fried Chicken.

From coast to coast, American festivals celebrate the country's maritime heritage and the bounty of the oceans. Rockland hosts the Maine Lobster Festival, where visitors feast on lobster steamed in the world's largest lobster cooker. The California seafood industry is celebrated at the Morro Bay Harbor Festival, at the beginning of National Seafood Month in October. The oyster is honored at St. Mary's County Oyster Festival in Leonardtown, Maryland. While visitors consume their fill of oysters prepared in every way imaginable, competitors vie for bragging rights in the National Oyster Cook-off and in the National Oyster Shucking Championship.

Traditions surrounding the gathering of nature's bounty are honored on the festival circuit. Among numerous maple syrup events is the Parke County Maple Syrup Festival in Rockville, Indiana. The concentrated growth of maple trees in the region represents their westernmost extent, and group tours of sugar shacks and the many covered bridges in the area provide entertainment.

Visitors partake of sausage and pancakes drenched in maple syrup, and they can purchase syrup and other maple products. In West Virginia the wild ramp, a form of leek, is a harbinger of spring. At the International Ramp Cook-off and Festival in Elkins, visitors enjoy a traditional ramp dinner that includes fried potatoes, ham, beans, and cornbread. Others enter the cook-off, a venue featuring creative uses for the pungent, odiferous ramp.

Commercially manufactured foods are often celebrated at food festivals. Wisconsin is known for cheese and for bratwurst, a spicy pork sausage of German origin. In Little Chute the Great Wisconsin Cheese Festival showcases the huge variety of quality cheeses produced in the state, and dedicated fans of cheesecake enjoy winning delicacies entered in the homemade cheesecake contest. Sheboygan, jokingly billed as the "wurst city of the world," hosts Bratwurst Days, during which visitors consume thousands of pounds of the sausage in traditional sandwiches made with hard rolls or in dishes such as tacos and pizza. The world's largest production of marshmallows is celebrated in Ligonier, Indiana, where visitors enjoy the traditional campfire treat s'mores, made from roasted marshmallows sandwiched between graham crackers and chocolate.

Heritage and Regional Celebrations

Food plays a starring role in the enormous number of ethnic festivals held throughout the United States. Established to celebrate heritage and preserve ethnic identity, traditions, and customs, these festivals commonly feature foods and recipes that have been handed down from generation to generation. In Staunton, Virginia, the annual African American Heritage Festival celebrates the heritage of the Shenandoah Valley. African American cuisine is represented by fried plantains, homemade biscuits, and chitterlings, small pieces of hog intestine that are coated and deep-fried. Also popular is Brunswick stew, which is said to have originated at an 1828 political rally in Brunswick County, Virginia. Bismarck, North Dakota, hosts the United Tribes International Powwow, where Native American culture is celebrated with song and dance competitions. An abundance of Native American foods is served, including Chippewa bannock bread, tripe and corn soups, fry bread, and beef and buffalo jerky. At the Hungarian Festival in New Brunswick, New Jersey, Hungarian heritage is honored, and an eight-block stretch of food vendors featuring traditional Hungarian dishes draws visitors by the thousands. Among the dozens of offerings are *kolbasz* sausage, chicken paprika, *palacsinta*

(crepes filled with cottage cheese or jelly), *kifli* (small pastries filled with apricots, prunes, or nuts), strudel, and nut or poppy seed rolls called *kalac*. Asian Americans celebrate their cultures at the Asian Moon Festival in Milwaukee, Wisconsin. Against a backdrop of sporting events, music, and artwork, Asian cuisine is served. Well-known items such as Japanese sushi and Thai spring rolls are presented along with more unfamiliar dishes, such as Philippine pork and chicken adobo and Vietnamese *bun thit nuong*, a dish made from grilled pork, rice, noodles, vegetables, and fish sauce.

America's regional food specialties are showcased at food festivals throughout the country. The South, for example, is noted for corn production, which goes hand in hand with hog raising. The National Cornbread Festival in South Pittsburg, Tennessee, pays homage to "the bread of the South." Cornbread is popular not only because it is a local product but also because it can be baked quickly during the heat of summer. Turnip greens and barbecue, other southern favorites, are served as typical accompaniments to the cornbread. Grits, another corn product favored in the South, are celebrated at the World Grits Festival in St. George, South Carolina. Both commercially ground and stone-ground grits are served as side dishes with regional breakfast and lunch specialties. Hispanic heritage and cultural pride are the focus of events surrounding the International Tamale Festival in Indio, California. Nearly a half million tamales, a beloved part of Hispanic Christmas celebrations, are consumed by visitors. Vendors offer creations ranging from traditional tamales based on meat and savory blends of chilies to vegetarian and sweet dessert tamales. Perhaps the most famous dish of southern Louisiana is gumbo, created by Creole and Cajun cooks. At the annual Bridge City Gumbo Festival, both devotees and initiates enjoy more than two thousand gallons of the stewlike dish. Gumbo, based on a fat and flour mixture called a roux, contains celery, green pepper, onions, and various spices. It is enhanced with shellfish, sausage, fish, game, or poultry and thickened with okra or filé powder.

Fund-raising, Communal Identity, and Holiday Festivals

Food festivals are often held for fund-raising designed to benefit various charitable organizations. Rhode Island's May breakfasts provide an interesting example of this type of festival. The May breakfast dates to 1867, when the Oak Lawn Baptist Church in Cranston initiated it. Held throughout the state during May, which is heritage month, the breakfasts are sponsored by religious and community groups, who serve traditional repasts that include Rhode Island's traditional johnnycake (always spelled "jonnycake" in South County), made from a variety of hard corn grown only in the region.

An interesting phenomenon surrounding some food festivals is that they are based on food products that no longer exist. These festivals essentially honor events of the past and create a sense of tradition and communal identity. The Peanut Butter Festival held in Brundidge, Alabama, is an example. During the 1930s citizens of the town pioneered the commercial manufacture of peanut butter, and the town benefited economically from employment in the mills. As manufacturing was consolidated, Brundidge retained its peanut cash crop, but the peanut butter mills closed. The town continues to pay homage to its peanut butter heritage with a celebration typical of the Deep South. Peanut butter appears in every imaginable dish, including the South's largest peanut butter and jelly sandwich, which measures fifty feet in length. The fifty-year-old jar of peanut butter on display serves as a reminder of boom days in Brundidge.

Many food festivals are held in conjunction with the observance of holidays. In Holland, Michigan, Christmas provides the inspiration for the Holland Dutch Winterfest, a celebration that encompasses both the Christmas Days of the Low Countries and the feast of *Sinterklaas* on December 6. Visitors shop for unique gifts and holiday food in the open-air *kerstmarkt*. Festival foods, ranging from hot pea soup to *oliebollen* (doughnuts), provide a true taste of the Netherlands. Chocolate *letterbanket* (also called "Dutch letters"), pastry filled with almond paste and formed into initials, are a popular holiday treat.

America's food festivals continue to grow in popularity. Like the National Buffalo Wing Festival in New York State, which commemorates the chicken wings that originated at the city's Anchor Bar, there is always something new to celebrate when it comes to food and fun. Each festival provides a sense of heritage and community in an increasingly fractured world.

[*See also* Ethnic Foods; Food Marketing; Fund-Raisers.]

BIBLIOGRAPHY

Camp, Charles. *American Foodways: What, When, Why, and How We Eat in America.* Little Rock, AR: August House, 1989.
Mercuri, Becky. *Food Festival U.S.A.: Red, White, and Blue Ribbon Recipes from All 50 States.* San Diego, CA: Laurel Glen, 2002.

BECKY MERCURI

Food Marketing

Food marketing brings together the producer and the consumer. It is the chain of activities that brings food from "farm gate to plate." Farmers' markets are a simple method of marketing whereby a farmer grows food and sells it directly to consumers. More highly processed foods, however, such as breakfast cereal, are marketed with a more sophisticated system: A farmer grows wheat and sells it to a miller, who processes the grain and sells it to a cereal company. The cereal company adds various ingredients and bakes, packages, and ships the product to warehouses, which distribute the cereal to grocery stores and food services.

The marketing of even a single food product can be a complicated process involving many producers and companies. For example, fifty-six companies are involved in making one can of chicken noodle soup. These businesses include not only chicken and vegetable processors but also the companies that transport the ingredients and those that print labels and manufacture cans. The food marketing system is the largest direct and indirect employer in the United States.

The Three Historical Phases of Food Marketing

There are three historical phases of food marketing: the fragmentation phase (before 1870–1880), the unification phase (1880–1950), and the segmentation phase (1950 and later). In the fragmentation phase, the United States was divided into numerous geographic fragments because transporting food was expensive, leaving most production, distribution, and selling locally based. In the unification phase, distribution was made possible by railroads, coordination of sales forces was made possible by the telegraph and telephone, and product consistency was made possible by advances in manufacturing. This new distribution system was led by meat processors such as Armour and Swift in midwestern cities and by companies such as Heinz, Quaker Oats, Campbell Soup, and Coca-Cola, which sold their brands nationally. Advertising in print media and direct marketing through demonstrations at stores and public venues were among the prime marketing tools. The initial Crisco campaign, in 1911, was an example. In the segmentation phase (1950 and later) radio and television advertising made it possible for a wider range of competing products to focus on different benefits and images and thus appeal to different demographic and psychographic markets. Distribution via the new national road system strengthened national brands.

Two Views of Food Marketing: The Production Focus and the Consumer Focus

There are two basic views of food marketing: production focus and consumer focus. The production-focused view is an institutional one that is primarily concerned with producers and institutions that work with producers. This view embraces the traditional agricultural view of food. People who work in the areas of production usually focus on producing a food as efficiently as possible and moving it on so it can be sold. In this perspective, "marketing" is essentially a distribution activity whereby food is distributed to the next institution in the process.

One key in determining which food will be produced is to understand what consumers demand. The farther from a consumer that a producer is, the more difficult this process becomes. Producers may not directly understand the needs of the consumer, and their product is likely to lose its identity as it is being processed. The more of a commodity a product is, the less control a producer has over pricing that product because it is undifferentiated from others.

At this level, producer commodity boards (such as the American Beef Council or the United Soy Board) can try to promote their products through advertising, recipe books, and cross-promotions. These efforts are focused on encouraging consumers to substitute one food for another, for example, eating more beef and less chicken. If the campaign is successful, all beef producers, for example, are likely to benefit if the price of beef rises.

Instead of focusing on institutions, the consumer-focused view is concerned with understanding what exactly consumers want and providing it to them in a form, in a manner, and at a price that is desired by consumers and is profitable for the institutions in the chain. Whereas a production focus is typically not flexible enough to anticipate consumer demands and interests, a consumer focus does promote this ability.

Once it is determined what certain segments of consumers want (for example, organic beef or high-iron spinach), it is necessary to produce the commodity in a way that meets these objectives. Although developing a consumer focus has long been the goal of companies that sell packaged goods to consumers, this focus is becoming important for producers of more traditional commodities. For example, packaging and production techniques make it possible to provide milk in single-serving bottles and to provide soybeans that are not genetically modified.

The Food Marketing Mix and the Four Ps of Marketing

The four components of food marketing are often called the marketing mix. They are also called the four Ps of marketing because they relate to product, price, promotion, and place. One reason food manufacturers receive the largest percentage of the retail food dollar is that they provide the most differentiating, value-added service. The money that manufacturers invest in developing, pricing, promotion, and placing their products helps differentiate a food product on the basis of both quality and brand-name recognition. In the case of products sold at a weekend farmers' market, for example, the four Ps are fairly straightforward. Farmers drive their freshly grown vegetables (product) to the market (place), where they put a price on them (pricing) and display them where they will attract the attention of shoppers (promotion). In the case of a highly processed product such as a frozen microwave dinner, the process of producing, placing, pricing, and promoting the product is much more complicated.

Product In deciding what type of new food products a consumer would most prefer, a manufacturer can either try to develop a new food product or try to extend or modify an existing food. For example, a sweet, flavored yogurt drink would be a new product, but milk in a new flavor (such as chocolate strawberry) would be an extension of an existing product. There are three steps to both developing and extending: generate ideas, screen ideas for feasibility, and test ideas for appeal. Only after these steps will a food product make it to national market. Of one hundred new food product ideas that are considered, only six make it to a supermarket shelf.

Price Unlike the producer, the manufacturer has a great deal of flexibility in how to price a product. This is because the product being sold is likely to be differentiated from other products available at retail. In trying to price food profitably, the manufacturer must keep in mind that the retailer takes approximately 50 percent of the price of a product. A frozen food sold in a retail store for $4.50 generates an income of $2.25 for the manufacturer. This money has to pay for the cost of producing, packaging, shipping, storing, and selling the product.

Promotion Promoting a food to consumers is done out of store, in store, and on package. Advertisements on television and in magazines are attempts to persuade consumers to think favorably about a product, so that they either go to the store to purchase the product or recall it favorably while in the store and then purchase it. Advertising also can be used to reinforce positive thoughts about the product for shoppers who have already purchased it. These promotions include Sunday newspaper ads that offer coupons such as cents-off and buy-one-get-one-free offers.

It is estimated that 70 percent of all food purchases made in stores are for brands that shoppers did not consider until they reached the point of purchase. That is, shoppers may know they want to buy cake mix but do not know what brand they will choose until they are in the store. Only a small percentage of food purchases are of specific brands that shoppers intend to buy before coming to the store. As a result, shoppers are susceptible to in-store promotions, such as coupons, displays and in-store signs, and attractive and compelling packaging.

Place Place refers to the distribution and warehousing efforts necessary to move a food from the manufacturer to a location where a consumer can buy it.

Segmenting Consumers on the Basis of Taste and Preference

The third historical phase of food marketing was built on the notion of market segmentation. This means that consumers have different tastes and different preferences. Many groups of people have different views and different preferences for any given food—lamb, for example. The vegetarian segment does not eat lamb, nor does the segment of meat eaters who do not like the odor of lamb. Certain ethnic segments eat lamb only in stews and in combination with other foods; other segments eat it only on special holidays. Another segment is those who enjoy fine dining and eat only young lamb that is tender and served in restaurants.

To believe that all lamb is the same and should be marketed in a generic or one-size-fits-all manner would miss many of the marketing opportunities within these segments. That is, different efforts should be made to target different segments. The ethnic segment could be targeted through in-store promotions in ethnic butcher shops where they might purchase meat. Those preparing holiday dinners could be reminded of lamb through in-store ads, and those who do not eat lamb might be reintroduced to it with a new version that has been produced in a manner

that reduces the characteristic smell. Aficionados of fine dining would be targeted by efforts in the distribution chain to promote lamb to finer restaurants.

The food marketing system in the United States is an amazingly flexible one. Consumer focus helps marketers anticipate the demands of consumers, and production focus helps them respond to changes in the market. The result is a system that meets the ever-changing demands of consumers.

[*See also* Advertising; Advertising Cookbooklets and Recipes; Community-Supported Agriculture; Dairy Industry; Farmers' Markets; Grocery Stores; Material Culture and Technology; Milk Packaging; Packaging; Radio and Television; Transportation of Food.]

BIBLIOGRAPHY

Belonax, Joseph J. *Food Marketing*. Boston: Pearson Custom, 1999.
Hampe, E. C., and M. Wittenbery. *The Food Industry: Lifeline of America*. 2nd ed. New York: McGraw-Hill, 1990.
Sudman, Seymour, and Brian Wansink. *Consumer Panels*. 2nd ed. Chicago: American Marketing Association, 2002.
Tedlow, Richard S. *New and Improved: The Story of Mass Marketing in America*. New York: Basic Books, 1990.
Wansink, Brian. *Marketing Nutrition*. Champaign: University of Illinois Press, 2004.

BRIAN WANSINK

Food Processors

When America's first food processor was unveiled at the national housewares exposition in Chicago in January 1973, it barely caused a ripple. With a blocky base about half the size of a shoe box, a broad clear plastic work bowl, and a fierce S-shaped blade some six inches across, the appliance was dismissed as an oversized, overpriced electric blender, even though it came with slicing and shredding disks. But Carl G. Sontheimer, the man behind the machine, was undaunted. A retired electronics engineer from Greenwich, Connecticut, and an accomplished hobby cook, Sontheimer knew that his food processor could revolutionize the way America cooked.

In 1971 Sontheimer and his wife, Shirley, had seen a small, powerful multipurpose machine put through its paces at a housewares show in Paris. Called Le Magimix, this was a home version of Le Robot-Coupe, the heavy-duty food processor that French chefs found indispensable for chopping, slicing, shredding, and puréeing—for making everything from flaky puff pastry to feathery fish dumplings. The Sontheimers were so impressed with Le Magimix that Carl tracked down its inventor, Pierre Verdun, who had also created Le Robot-Coupe. Obtaining distribution rights for Le Magimix, Sontheimer bought a dozen of the machines and shipped them home. In his garage workshop, Sontheimer took the machines apart, analyzed them, and put them back together. Then he and his wife kitchen-tested them. Sontheimer reconfigured the slicing and shredding disks, improved the torque, added safety features, streamlined the overall design, and gave it a new name: Cuisinart.

After the disappointing Chicago debut of the Cuisinart, Sontheimer contacted American's principal food writers and cookbook authors, gave each of them a personal demonstration, and quickly proved his point: The food processor was a supremely versatile machine that could spare the home cook endless tedium. It could shortcut the preparation of complicated classics and even speed the making of coleslaw and hash browns.

Soon the Cuisinart was being praised on television and in print. It was the miracle worker every cook had to have. In no time, nearly every appliance manufacturer introduced its own food processor. The exception was KitchenAid, whose standing electric mixers had long been the standard by which all others were judged. The company's attitude was wait and see. And what it saw was that few of the processors rushed to market could match the Cuisinart for stamina, dependability, and versatility. Within a few years, most of them had disappeared.

Sontheimer continued to improve the Cuisinart throughout the 1970s and 1980s. Pulse buttons were added, and work bowls grew larger as did their feed tubes, making it possible to slice entire oranges and tomatoes. Accessories proliferated, including thick and thin slicing disks, coarse and fine shredding disks, french fry cutters, citrus reamers, egg whips, and pasta makers.

In 1988, Sontheimer sold Cuisinart to a group of investors who the next year sold it to the Conair Corporation, of Stamford, Connecticut, a major manufacturer of household appliances. In 1994 KitchenAid at long last launched its own line of food processors—sleek machines in a range of sizes that had touch-pad controls and plenty of prowess; some models had miniature bowl and blade inserts, most in designer colors. In response to the competition from KitchenAid, Cuisinart introduced a new generation of food processors—streamlined machines with quick-to-clean keypad switches and gentle dough modes for kneading yeast breads. Carl Sontheimer

did not live to see the new Cuisinarts. He died in 1998 at the age of eighty-three, but by then the "white elephant" he had introduced at the Chicago housewares show in 1973 had revolutionized the way America cooked.

[*See also* Blenders; Chopping Knives and Food Choppers; Graters; Kitchens.]

BIBLIOGRAPHY

Anderson, Jean. *Jean Anderson's New Processor Cooking.* New York: William Morrow, 1983.
Anderson, Jean. *Process This! New Recipes for the New Generation of Food Processors plus Dozens of Time-Saving Tips.* New York: William Morrow, 2002.

JEAN ANDERSON

Food Safes, *see Cupboards and Food Safes*

Food Safety, *see Chemical Additives; Department of Agriculture, United States*

Food Stamps

The food stamp program is a federal initiative aimed at alleviating hunger and food insecurity in the United States. A version of the program first operated between 1939 and 1943, when the U.S. Secretary of Agriculture was authorized to promote domestic consumption of foods as a way to reduce surplus agricultural commodities. The current program was authorized in 1959 and begun as a pilot project in 1961 under the administration of President John F. Kennedy. At the urging of President Lyndon Johnson, Congress made food stamps a permanent federal program in 1964, though states and counties were permitted to decide how they would participate. By the early 1970s Congress established uniform eligibility requirements, and by 1975 all states and counties took part in the program.

Food stamps provide direct support to low-income people for the purchase of foods in a low-cost diet developed by the U.S. Department of Agriculture (USDA). Recipients may purchase breads, cereals, dairy products, meat, fish, poultry, fruits, and vegetables, among other foods, but are prohibited from using the stamps to purchase such items as alcohol, tobacco products, nonfood goods, and ready-to-eat foods intended to be consumed in a store. Food stamps traditionally were issued as denominated paper coupons; the program has added electronic benefit transfers, which move funds from the recipient's federal account to that of the retailer. At present, 85 percent of food stamp benefits are issued by this means.

Participation in the food stamp program peaked in March 1994 at nearly 28 million people, approximately 10 percent of the U.S. population. Since then, it has declined significantly, owing to welfare reform efforts of 1996, which limited the number of eligible people; placed time limits on benefits for unemployed, able-bodied, childless adults; and required all healthy, fit adults to meet certain work requirements. Eligibility for most legal immigrants also was eliminated, but then the Farm Bill of 2002 restored many of those benefits.

An enduring criticism of the program is that many eligible low-income people do not participate for a variety of reasons, such as stigma and shame associated with participation, lack of knowledge about eligibility, and difficulty in meeting state administrative requirements for signing up for the program. Research suggests that while the food stamp program has not eliminated hunger in America, it has, on the whole, benefited low-income households by increasing the availability of nutritional foods and raising the level of intake of certain nutrients within household diets. Critics of this research, however, have pointed out that distribution patterns among households and differential food-purchasing power based on geography contribute to varied results. Other critics have asserted that food stamps are to blame, in part, for the growing obesity epidemic among the poor because individual food purchases are not regulated by nutritional content.

The program has been the subject of long-standing complaints about fraud and abuse. The Government Accounting Office, for example, determined that recipient fraud between 1988 and 1993 totaled nearly $2 billion. Such fraud has undercut public support for the food stamp program and left it politically vulnerable to numerous efforts throughout its history to tighten eligibility, cut back the number of participants, and decrease the size of the program's budget.

[*See also* Department of Agriculture, United States; Hunger Programs.]

BIBLIOGRAPHY

Berry, Jeffrey M. *Feeding Hungry People: Rulemaking in the Food Stamp Program*. New Brunswick, NJ: Rutgers University Press, 1984.

Eisinger, Peter K. *Toward an End to Hunger in America*. Washington, DC: Brookings Institution Press, 1998.

Food and Nutrition Service. *Food Stamp Program: Frequently Asked Questions*. http://www.fns.usda.gov/fsp/faqs.htm#2. Run by the USDA, the site describes the food stamp program, eligibility criteria, the level of benefits, aggregate demographics of participants, and the ways in which to apply for food stamps.

Ohls, James C., and Harold Beebout. *The Food Stamp Program: Design Tradeoffs, Policy, and Impacts*. Washington, DC: Urban Institute Press, 1993.

BARRETT P. BRENTON AND KEVIN T. MCINTYRE

Forks, *see Silverware*

Fourth of July

The Continental Congress of the United States declared independence from England in its convention in Philadelphia on July 4, 1776. At first, celebrations were scattered and sporadic, but as years passed, the tradition of parades, picnics, and pyrotechnics was born and thrived.

There are no official national holidays that have any legal bearing on any entities but government employees, agencies, and Washington, D.C. They are "official" holidays only in the sense that they are days off for federal government operations. Holidays are left to the states and municipalities to decree and observe, and many have become essentially unanimous by this process. There is, therefore, no federally designated or mandated Fourth of July holiday for all Americans but only many, many local events. In 1870, Congress, which can only decree the days that its offices close, established the Fourth of July as a holiday, but without pay, for federal employees and the District of Columbia. In 1938, Congress amended it to be a holiday with pay. Congress has since modified the law further in consideration of changing times.

The First Fourths

Picnics or, at least, outdoor activities were natural events, given the midsummer weather, although the grand public displays with lengthy parades and large celebrations had to wait for the war with the British to be over and the country to grow. Some of the first few organized celebrations occurred at the public readings of the Declaration of Independence. The earliest of these were held in Philadelphia, followed shortly by Williamsburg, Virginia; Trenton, New Jersey; and New York, where a statue of King

George III of England (1738–1820) was torn down to be recast into bullets. In places across the nation where the Declaration was publicly read, people shouted their huzzas, fired their muskets, and pulled down British flags and other emblems.

As early as 1777, celebrations were occasionally raucous events. It became customary within a few years to fire thirteen cannonades to commemorate the number of colonies and drink thirteen toasts. In Philadelphia, leaders put together an extravagant event for Congress and guests to mark the first year. A newspaper reported that in attendance were, "President and Supreme Executive Council, and Speaker of the Assembly of this State, the General Officers and Colonels of the army, and strangers of eminence, and the members of the several Continental Boards in town." The day included the ringing of bells, crowds that cheered the parades, music, and fireworks, and a dinner accompanied by more music and the drinking of many toasts, all while the new nation's colors dressed up armed ships and galleys in the harbor.

Food was always an integral part of the celebration. Early dinners were held in taverns, coffeehouses, public buildings, schools, and homes, and the meals provided opportunities for socializing and neighborliness in the largely rural nation. These festivities became rather large-scale events in just a few years, and many were held outdoors in parks and other areas where there were trees for shelter and springs for water. They often drew hundreds of people and became increasingly more sumptuous as the eighteenth century ended and the nineteenth began. Menus might include several meats (usually beef, pork, mutton, and game), poultry (including chicken, turkey, pheasant, and other birds), vegetables and fruit in season, and a wide selection of desserts, including cakes, pies, cobblers, and other baked goods. The events grew so large that tickets were frequently necessary so the providers would know how much food to prepare and so that the size of the venue could be established and controlled.

As urban environments grew and became more settled, parks were created and were often the places where the people could assemble for the day's observances. Vendors set up booths and sitting areas in which they sold food and drink. According to newspaper accounts, in 1824 in what would later become New York's Central Park some of the booths sold "baked beans, roast pig and punch, custards and clam soup" (*New York Daily Advertiser*, July 5, 1824, p. 2).

In Smithfield, Virginia, in 1855, the *Daily Southern Argus* reported the city's efforts, beginning the day before, to prepare all that was necessary for a large celebratory feast:

> Tuesday was a great "preparation day" in Smithfield, for the Democratic jubilee and banner presentation was to take place on Wednesday. Chickens and ducks were decapitated by the hundred; fat pigs, lambs and calves, were slaughtered by the dozen, [sic] and a number of busy cooks were engaged in preparing immense bacon hams, and large joints and sides of fresh meat, as well as untold quantities of pies, puddings and cakes for the long tables that were spread for the numerous guests expected from Norfolk, Portsmouth, and elsewhere on the glorious Fourth.

As the nation expanded and moved westward, the celebrations continued with local, seasonal foods and celebrations suited to the setting. In Sacramento, California, the first Fourth of July celebration was held in 1849. During the Civil War and its aftermath celebrations were more subdued, generally, but that changed with the centennial in 1876, when there were many very large events with strong political elements. For the bicentennial, in 1976, the celebration featured the usual sorts of public events with an added layer of spectacular extras like a 69,000-pound birthday cake in Baltimore, while in Florida, 7,241 people became naturalized American citizens simultaneously, the largest single group in American history to that date to do so.

The Fourth of July. Shelburne (Vermont) rug commemorating Independence Day.

The celebrations have remained the midsummer holiday for all Americans, with picnics, barbecues, and fireworks as the essential ingredients. Gatherings in parks with parades, entertainment, fairground amusements, and kiddie rides, which are matched with a large selection of foods to choose from, remain part of the culture of most small towns across the United States.

Because of the shift toward urban and suburban growth, family and neighborhood gatherings are more frequent than in the past. People live in denser settlements than when the United States was a farming nation, and it has become easier to socialize with neighbors. The greater ethnic diversity of the American public ensures that new foods continue to arrive on the holiday table. Colonial Americans were largely limited to fresh, seasonal foods, but food choices have evolved with technology, and options have increased greatly. Well over two centuries have passed since the first Fourth of July and although some of the ingredients have changed, the tradition of celebrating remains.

[*See also* Barbecue; Ice Cream and Ices; Picnics; Watermelon.]

BIBLIOGRAPHY

American Memory: Historical Collections for the National Digital Library. http://lcweb2.loc.gov/amhome.html. American Memory features primary historical and cultural source materials with more than 7 million digital items from more than one hundred historical collections. It is part of the Library of Congress.

Heintze, James R., ed. and comp. *Fourth of July Celebrations Database.* http://gurukul.american.edu/heintze/fourth.htm. American University. Washington, DC. Very broad collection of information about the Fourth of July from 1776 to the present.

*Library of Congress of the United States.*http://www.loc.gov. An extraordinary source for research, including printed materials, video and sound recordings, and links to many collections of information.

Travers, Len. *Celebrating the Fourth: Independence Day and the Rites of Nationalism in the Early Republic.* Amherst: University of Massachusetts Press, 1997.

BOB PASTORIO

Fowl, *see Poultry and Fowl*

Frappes

A frappe is what Bostonians call a thick blend of ice cream, milk, and flavorings—known more commonly as a milkshake. The word comes from the French verb *frapper*, which means "to shake." A frosted is another name for a milkshake, as is a velvet. Around the turn of the twentieth century, when ice was a new commodity, a frosted was soda with ice in it, according to Ed Marks of Lititz, Pennsylvania, founder of the Ice Screamers, a national group devoted to ice cream memorabilia. Rhode Islanders call their version of the milkshake a cabinet. Some other New Englanders use "frappe," but the word seems to be primarily a Boston locution. In Boston, "milkshake" means a glass of milk with flavorings, shaken until frothy and containing no ice cream. This was the original definition of a milkshake. In the 1880s and 1890s, ice cream was added only occasionally. Milkshakes containing ice cream became more common around 1915.

To make things extra confusing, the term "frappé," with the accent mark, refers to a frozen slush made without dairy products. Fannie Farmer's 1896 *Boston Cooking-School Cookbook* defined a frappé as "water ice frozen to a consistency of mush." A recipe for clam frappé called for twenty clams to be steamed open, then the pot liquor cooled and frozen to a mush. Farmer's recipe for café frappé called for a beaten egg white, coffee, water, and sugar. It was frozen and served with whipped cream in special frappé glasses. Even though Farmer was based in Boston, the glossary of frozen desserts in her cookbook did not define the frappe as a milkshake. Soda fountain guides from the 1910s described frappes as half-frozen sherbets or well-shaken ice cream sodas. Some frappes from this era had nicknames, including ping-pong, buffalo, flinch, and delmonico. It is unclear when the concept of a frappe as a milkshake came into popular use, but this information suggests it was after 1920.

In the Boston area in the early twenty-first century, ice cream parlor frappes usually contained at least equal proportions of milk and ice cream, plus flavorings such as chocolate or coffee syrup. They were sometimes ordered extra thick. When ice cream parlors were most popular, frappes were prepared in stainless steel containers in commercial mixers. Anything that could not fit into one tall glass was poured into a second glass or left on the side for the customer to use for a refill. In the early twenty-first century a frappe was often served in a paper cup with a straw, although the thick consistency sometimes made a spoon more suitable.

Milkshakes originated nationally in the soda fountains of the 1880s and 1890s. One early recipe called for sweetened and flavored milk, carbonated water, and a raw egg, shaken by a special machine. In the early twentieth century, milkshakes became standard soda fountain fare, along with sundaes and ice cream sodas.

[*See also* Egg Cream; Ice Cream Sodas; Ice Cream and Ices; Milkshakes, Malts, and Floats; Soda Fountains.]

BIBLIOGRAPHY

California Culinary Academy. *Ice Cream and Frozen Desserts*, p. 36. San Ramon, CA: Ortho, 1988.
Damerow, Gail. *Ice Cream! The Whole Scoop.* Lakewood, CO: Glenbridge, 1996.
Farmer, Fannie Merritt. *The Original Boston Cooking-School Cook Book, 1896.* New York: New American Library, 1997.
Funderburg, Anne Cooper. *Chocolate, Strawberry, and Vanilla.* Bowling Green, OH: Bowling Green State University Popular Press, 1995.
Marks, Ed. "Don't Shake the Cabinet or You'll Spill the Frappe." *The Scoop,* Winter 1998.

CLARA SILVERSTEIN

Freeze-Drying

Freeze-drying, also known as lyophilization, is a method of food preservation by which frozen items are dehydrated in a vacuum. During this process, foods are placed in a pressure chamber and undergo sublimation, whereby ice converts directly from a solid to a gaseous state. Moisture quickly escapes as vapor, and the dried items are left with a porous texture. Unlike many other drying approaches, freeze-drying allows the final product to largely retain its shape, size, flavor, and nutritional makeup.

The principles behind freeze-drying have been applied for centuries. The ancient Incas used a form of this preservation technique by storing their food in the heights of the Andes mountains. There the temperature, low pressure, and high altitude effectively freeze-dried the food supplies. It was not until World War II that the process became industrialized, when it was developed to preserve blood plasma for the war effort. In the 1950s through 1970s, the Army Natick Labs, in Natick, Massachusetts (now called the U.S. Army Natick Soldier Center), was instrumental in developing and refining the process of freeze-drying food products.

Because they rehydrate easily and have an extended shelf life, freeze-dried products are well-suited for packaged goods, from liquids such as coffee and juices to dried fruit in cereals and components of soup mixes. The National Aeronautics and Space Administration has used freeze-drying in the development of foods for the U.S. space program.

[*See also* Space Food.]

BIBLIOGRAPHY

Francis, F. J. *Encyclopedia of Food Science and Technology.* New York: Wiley, 2000.
Potter, Norman N. *Food Science.* Westport, CT: AVI, 1986.

REBECCA FREEDMAN

Freezers and Freezing

By lowering the temperature of food, freezing slows bacterial growth and reduces spoilage. Humankind has understood for millennia that freezing preserves food, but only in the past few centuries has this process come under human control.

American colonists attempted to keep food cool by storing it in underground cellars. By the late eighteenth century, where local conditions permitted, ice was used to cool cellars. Ice became increasingly in demand, and the ice trade began during the early nineteenth century. By 1830 blocks of ice were harvested in New England during the winter and spring and shipped to insulated ice houses along the nation's coasts and navigable rivers. In this way ice was obtainable in large cities year round.

In addition to its use as a means of cold storage, ice was used for making frozen drinks and ice cream, which were fashionable in the early nineteenth century. Frozen poultry was sometimes shipped to eastern cities during winter months, and ice was occasionally used to freeze fish on ships at sea. After the Civil War, the ice trade expanded. In 1876 frozen meat was first shipped from the United States to the United Kingdom, but it was not until 1880 that the first Chicago meatpacking plant was refrigerated.

Directions for freezing food appeared in American cookbooks as early as the 1820s, and ice cream freezers were manufactured by 1846. By the 1880s ice cream freezers were constructed by several companies, including the White Mountain Freezer Company of Nashua, New Hampshire, and the Alaska Freezer Company of Winchester, Massachusetts. Many companies printed advertising cooking booklets that demonstrated how to use their freezers to make frozen desserts, such as ice cream, ices, sorbets, and frozen custards, as well as puddings, mousses, soufflés, frozen beverages, and salads.

Ice cooling, however, had many limitations. Ice was bulky and required expensive transportation, large insulated storage facilities, and a massive distribution system consisting of ships and ice wagons. Natural ice taken from lakes contained impurities. Even when machines were developed to manufacture pure ice, problems persisted. When the ice melted, the moisture frequently promoted the growth of mold and bacteria, creating unhealthy conditions within the icebox or room. Equally important was that ice was effective only when it was in direct contact with food. In rooms or small enclosures, ice, even combined with salt, had great difficulty lowering the temperature of food below freezing.

By the 1880s the ice trade was in rapid decline owing to the success of cooling systems based on absorption and condensation. These processes could lower the temperature of food well below freezing. The new technology encouraged the vast expansion of trade in frozen food. On land it allowed slaughtering and butchering of livestock close to where it was raised. The frozen meat then was shipped to cities hundreds or thousands of miles away. Because this system required large amounts of capital, the livestock industry became centralized, and major meatpackers, such as Swift and Armour, emerged during this period.

Advantages and Disadvantages

The development of frozen foods offered a variety of advantages. It encouraged regional specialization. Fruits and vegetables could be grown in the best climate and soil and then frozen and shipped great distances. Because frozen foods were stored, farmers and distributors could sell their products when they could obtain the highest prices. For consumers, freezing expanded year-round food choices because the availability of produce was no longer limited to its growing season. Freezing of food tended to stabilize prices. Because waste at the point of origin was eliminated, use of frozen food saved on transportation and storage. Frozen foods were particularly useful for restaurants. A small kitchen could supply a diverse demand, and restaurant chains could centralize their cooking, thereby lowering costs.

The limitations of frozen foods were that they required expensive freezing plants, special packaging, transportation, warehouses, and retail stores. Frozen food companies also had to educate the public about their products, because there was extensive opposition to frozen food. Many people believed that frozen foods were unhealthful;

others did not like the taste or smell of thawed food; and still others complained about the expense. There was some justification for these complaints during the years when the process of freezing was in its infancy. Some companies froze inferior-quality food because it was impossible for consumers to tell the difference between good and bad food at the point of sale. Some retailers thawed or refroze foods before sale, thus speeding deterioration. Corporate laboratories and the U.S. Department of Agriculture began experimentation on frozen food and made recommendations on matters such as the rapidity with which foods needed to be frozen, methods of freezing, storage temperature, dehydration, and the length of time that frozen foods could be held without spoilage. Hostility did not disappear entirely, however, and the industry engaged in mass promotional efforts to win over skeptical consumers. Package design was important both to prevent dehydration during storage and to attract consumers. The problems with frozen foods declined after 1911 and greatly decreased in the 1920s, when the cost of frozen foods was lowered and the use of the home refrigerator became more common.

Clarence Birdseye—perhaps the best-known name in the industry—began quick-freezing food in 1923. His major contribution was not the process of freezing but the invention of moisture-proof packaging, which allowed foods to be frozen faster and kept them from disintegrating when thawed. Birdseye also championed the use of the freshest food possible. Birdseye sold his company to General Foods. Under the brand name Birds Eye, General Foods invested the capital necessary to promote and market frozen food. Other companies began to compete, but sales were insignificant until the late 1930s, largely because of the Depression and the unwillingness of grocery stores to invest one thousand dollars for a freezer that held relatively little product.

Electric Refrigerators and Freezers

Electric refrigerators had been marketed since the 1890s, but none was successful until the Guardian Frigerator Company manufactured the Frigidaire in 1916. The company was purchased by General Motors Corporation, which began to mass-produce refrigerators, promoting them through national advertising and wide distribution. The small freezer section of the Frigidaire held ice trays and had room for little else. Only five thousand electric refrigerators were sold in America in 1921. It was not until 1930 that refrigerators outsold iceboxes.

In 1940 more than 4 million refrigerators were sold. The size of the freezer section of refrigerators steadily increased as commercial frozen foods became common.

Stand-alone freezers were marketed during the 1920s, but they were beyond the reach of most Americans. After World War II, home freezers became more common as the price declined and the number of frozen foods available in grocery stores grew. During the 1950s, freezers became common in American homes. At the same time, most grocery stores had large self-service freezers, which offered consumers convenient access to everything from frozen peas to ice cream.

Frozen Food

Before World War II, the main frozen foods were peas, beans, corn, spinach, berries, cherries, apples, and peaches. During the war, frozen foods and canned goods were rationed. When the war ended, frozen foods were de-rationed several months before canned goods, so many Americans tried frozen foods for the first time. This phenomenon encouraged the frozen food industry to invest in a major expansion.

Frozen prepared foods, such as chicken à la king, came on the market in 1939 but did not become popular until after the war. Breyers Ice Cream manufactured frozen chow mein and chop suey under the brand name Golden Pagoda. After the war an avalanche of new frozen foods hit the market, including Sara Lee cakes, Quaker Oats waffles, Swanson chicken potpies, and Birds Eye fish sticks. The first successful frozen meal, consisting of meat, potatoes, and vegetables, was marketed by the W. L. Maxson Company of New York. The meals were sold to Pan American World Airways.

The most successful of all postwar frozen foods was orange juice, which had first been marketed unsuccessfully during the 1930s. Experiments demonstrated that removing water from the orange juice before freezing improved the taste. Orange juice concentrate was sold after the war. By the early 1950s orange juice accounted for 20 percent of the frozen food market.

As the volume of sales of frozen foods increased, the price declined. A landmark in frozen food history was the TV dinner, first produced by Swanson in 1953. These meals were packaged in a covered foil tray with meat, vegetables, and potatoes in separate compartments. Because television was just becoming popular in America, many thought that this dinner was supposed to be consumed in front of the television set.

The success of frozen food manufacturers encouraged centralization: Coca-Cola purchased Minute Maid, and H. J. Heinz purchased Ore-Ida, a maker of frozen potatoes. In 1955 Campbell Soup Company purchased Swanson and expanded its line of frozen foods to sixty-five items. By 1965 the total sales of frozen food had reached $5.2 billion.

Microwaves and Frozen Food

The wedding of microwaves and frozen food was the next major leap forward. The microwave oven made it possible for frozen foods to be cooked in minutes, a particularly useful feature in restaurants. Food-processing companies needed to change their products for microwave use by reducing the moisture content of food and replacing metal foil, which blocked microwaves and damaged ovens, with other materials. At first the market was not big enough to encourage food processors to cater to the needs of microwave oven users. This situation had changed by the 1970s, when more than 10 percent of all American homes had microwave ovens.

The frozen food industry has continued to grow. As of 2001, 26.6 billion dollars worth of frozen food products were sold to consumers, and an additional $40 billion were sold to restaurants, cafeterias, hospitals, schools, and other outlets.

[See also Advertising Cookbooklets and Recipes; Airplane Food; Birdseye, Clarence; Birds Eye Foods; Campbell Soup Company; Coca-Cola; Fish, subentry on Saltwater Fish; Frozen Food; Fruit; Grocery Stores; Heinz Foods; Ice; Iceboxes; Ice Creams and Ices; Meat; Microwave Ovens; Refrigerators; Restaurants; Swanson; Transportation of Food.]

BIBLIOGRAPHY

American Frozen Food Institute. http://www.foodinfonet.com/outside.asp?path=http://www.affi.com/factstat-glance.asp.

Anderson, Oscar Edward. *Refrigeration in America; a History of a New Technology and its Impact.* Princeton, NJ: University of Cincinnati by Princeton University Press, 1953.

Bradley, Alice. *Electric Refrigerator Recipes and Menus: Recipes Prepared Especially for the General Electric Refrigerator.* Cleveland, OH: General Electric Company, 1927.

Cummings, Richard O. *The American Ice Harvests: a Historical Study in Technology, 1800–1918.* Berkeley: University of California Press, 1949.

Miller, Verna L. *Frigidaire Frozen Delights; Especially Prepared for Apartments with Frigidaire.* Dayton, OH: Frigidaire, 1929.

Williams E. W. *Frozen Food: Biography of an Industry.* Boston: Cahners, 1963.

ANDREW F. SMITH

French Dip

The french dip sandwich is composed of a french roll dipped in meat juices and filled with slices of roast beef, pork, ham, turkey, or lamb. Philippe Mathieu, a French immigrant, created the "french dipped sandwich" in 1918. The proprietor of a Los Angeles sandwich shop, Philippe the Original, Mathieu accidentally dropped a roll into the roast drippings as he prepared a beef sandwich for a hungry policeman. The policeman later returned with several friends, all requesting "dipped" sandwiches. It is not known whether the sandwich was named for the french roll on which it was made, for the Frenchman who created it, or for the police officer, whose last name was "French," but its popularity quickly spread. The french dip sandwich continues to be served at Philippe the Original and at restaurants nationwide.

[*See also* Sandwiches.]

BIBLIOGRAPHY

Mercuri, Becky. *Sandwiches That You Will Like*. Pittsburgh, PA: WQED, 2002.

BECKY MERCURI

French Fries

This entry contains two subentries, a historical overview and a survey of french fries in the twentieth century.

Historical Overview

Whether crispy strips or crackling, paper-thin chips, French fries came to the United States from France. American legend suggests that they were "invented" in Saratoga Springs, New York, in the early 1850s, but recipes for deep-frying exceedingly thin slices of raw potato had long been appearing in published French works, at least as early as 1795–1796 with the anonymous, revolutionary *La Cuisinière Républicaine*. In 1824 Mary Randolph gave a recipe "To Fry Sliced Potatoes," in which she directs that raw potatoes should be "cut in shavings" before frying them in lard "over a quick fire . . . till they are crisp," so it would seem that even in the United States, paper-thin, deep-fried potatoes were known decades before they were introduced as "Saratoga chips." Indeed, directions for deep-frying sliced raw potatoes appear in a

document in Thomas Jefferson's hand that clearly dates from the years 1801–1809, his years in the President's House when he had a French chef and *maître d'hôtel* in attendance; there can be little question that Randolph got her recipe from the Jefferson family, one that was plagiarized throughout the century. In both France and America, early published recipes call for very thin slices of raw potato to be deep-fried until crackling crisp, but some authorities believe that deep-fried strips of potatoes had been sold by vendors on the bridges of *vieux Paris* well before the appearance of the recipe of 1795–1796, citing *pommes de terre Pont-Neuf*, the crispy, thin strips found in any Paris bistro today; apparently they were regarded as plebeian, as indeed they still are.

[*See also* French Influences on American Food; Potatoes.]

BIBLIOGRAPHY

A[udot], L[ouis]-E[ustace]. *La Cuisinière de la Campagne et de la Ville*. Paris: Audot, 1823.
Carême, M. Antonin. *L'Art de la Cuisine Française au Dix-Neuvième Siècle*. Vol. 5. Paris: Renouard, 1844.
The Cook's Own Book. Being A Complete Culinary Encyclopedia . . . . By a Boston Housekeeper [Lee, Mrs. N.K.M.]. Boston, 1832. In facsimile, New York: Arno, 1972.
La Cuisinière Républicaine, Qui enseigne la manière simple d'accomoder . . . . les Pommes de terre; avec quelques avis sur les soins nécessaires pous les conserver. Cover title: *Paix au Chaumières*. Paris: Mérigot Jeune, 1795–1796. In facsimile, Luzarches: Daniel Morcrette, 1976.
Hess, Karen. "The Origin of French Fries." In *Petits Propos Culinaires* 68 (November 2001): 39–48.
[Randolph, Mrs. Mary]. *The Virginia House-wife. Method Is the Soul of Management*. Washington, DC: Davis and Force, 1824. Also, in facsimile, edited by Karen Hess, Columbia: University of South Carolina Press, 1984.
Soyer, Alexis. *A Shilling Cookery for the People*. London: Routledge, 1854. In facsimile as *Soyer's Cookery Book*. New York: David McKay Company, Inc., 1959.
Ude, Louis Eustache. *The French Cook*. Philadelphia: Carey, Lea and Carey, 1828.

KAREN HESS

The Twentieth Century

Throughout the nineteenth century, potatoes were fried in a variety of shapes and sizes. During the 1870s some types of fried potatoes were standardized into particular shapes and sizes. Those that were round and extremely thin became potato chips. Those that were long, rectangular, and approximately one-fourth of an inch thick, became "french fried potatoes," a name that had been shortened to "french fries" by 1918.

By the early twentieth century french fries were served in cafes, diners, and roadside eateries. Although franchised fast food establishments had been around since the 1920s, french fries did not become an important part of their menu until World War II, when rationed meat became scarce and fast food hamburger stands sought alternatives. When the war ended, french fries were well established on the fast food menu along with hot dogs, hamburgers, and sodas.

When it began to grow in the 1960s, the McDonald's restaurant chain needed a way to distribute its already famous french fries. Working with the Simplot potato company in Idaho, McDonald's devised new methods of freezing raw potatoes while keeping their flavor and texture. Other chains emulated this method, and french fries became the single most popular fast food in America. Similar methods were used for the home market; annual sales had grown to more than 1 billion dollars by 2000.

[*See also* Fast Food; Freezers and Freezing; Frozen Food; McDonald's; Potatoes; Restaurants.]

BIBLIOGRAPHY

Luxenberg, Stan. *Roadside Empires: How the Chains Franchised America.* New York: Viking Penguin, 1985.
Rozin, Elizabeth. *The Primal Cheeseburger: A Generous Helping of Food History Served Up on a Bun.* New York: Penguin, 1994.

ANDREW F. SMITH

French Influences on American Food

By the time America was settled in the seventeenth century, the French dominated professional cookery in Western Europe. They created cooking implements, defined food terms, and systematically ordered cooking processes. To foster their culinary empire, they established an apprentice system intended to prepare young men to become chefs. The English aristocracy hired French chefs, or English chefs trained in France, such as Robert May, author of *The Accomplished Cook* (1685). However, most of the English were suspicious of French cookery. Specifically, French food was "dishonest," the British believed, as its sauces, gravies, and other "made dishes" were designed to disguise the poor quality of French meat, poultry, and fish. Also, the French ate unusual and even repugnant foods, such as snails and frogs legs, which horrified English sensibilities.

Authors of many eighteenth-century British cookbooks expressed strong anti-French views. E. Smith's *The Compleat Housewife* (1728), for instance, reproached the reader with, "To our disgrace, we have admired the French tongue and French messes." Copies of *The Compleat Housewife* were regularly imported into the colonies, and in 1742 it became the first cookbook published in America. English author Hannah Glasse also railed against French cooks in *The Art of Cookery Made Plain and Easy* (1747): "the blind folly of this age, that would rather be imposed on by a French booby, than give encouragement to a good English cook!" Glasse does include some French recipes in her work. On one she comments: "This dish I do not recommend; for I think it an odd jumble of trash." Copies of Glasse's *Art of Cookery* were commonly imported into America, and it was one of the most popular cookbooks during the colonial period.

The English were by far the largest group to settle the American colonies, and their cooking traditions and culinary prejudices dominated early America. Initially, many Americans held the same anti-French view as did the English, even though a large number of French immigrants, such as the Huguenots in South Carolina and French Canadians in New England, settled in America. The French controlled Canada and claimed the entire Old Northwest and the Mississippi Valley. Protestant American colonists had fought French Catholics in several wars, of which the French and Indian War (1754–1764) was the most important. Thanks to this war, the English gained control of all French territories east of the Mississippi River and all of Canada. A number of French Canadians, called Acadians or Cajuns, chose to migrate to Louisiana; others were deported by the British.

When Glasse's *Art of Cookery* (1805) was finally published in the United States, the negative comments regarding French cookery were omitted. American views toward the French and their food had changed dramatically during the previous two decades. During the Revolutionary War, the French had become allies of the American colonies. French troops introduced some Americans to French cookery. American exposure to French cookery expanded further after the French Revolution of 1789, when many nobles and their chefs fled France. Some moved to England; others came to the United States. One of these was the epicure and author Jean-Anthelme Brillat-Savarin. While in America, he visited Jean Baptiste Gilbert Payplat dis Julien, another French refugee, who had opened a public eating house in Boston in 1794. Other French restaurants opened in New York, Philadelphia, Baltimore, and Charleston.

Almost simultaneous with the French Revolution was the slave uprising in Haiti. Many French and Creoles, along with their slaves and servants, immigrated to New York, Boston, Charleston, Philadelphia, and New Orleans. They brought their culinary traditions with them, and some opened restaurants. The result of the French and Creole immigration to America was that some French culinary traditions were adopted by many upper-class Americans, and French food was often served at fashionable dinner parties.

The French Influence from Louisiana

Thomas Jefferson, who had served as American ambassador to France (1785–1789) before becoming president (1801–1809), had a great interest in French cooking. When he lived in France, he took advantage of this opportunity to explore French cookery. When he moved into the White House, he brought along a French chef. Jefferson's acquisition of Louisiana in 1803 gave further impetus to the increasing popularity of French food. Louisiana was home to French and Haitian immigrants, Creoles, Cajuns, African Americans, and Native Americans; they combined to create a culinary cauldron that influenced early American cookery and has continued to do so ever since. Creole cuisine shows the French influence in its use of roux, stocks, and adaptations of classic sauces; traditional French seafood soups evolved into gumbo, made with local shrimp, crawfish, and oysters.

French Cookbooks in America

The French influence also filtered into America through cookbooks. Louis Eustache Ude, the cook of Louis XVI, who had fled to England during the French Revolution, published *The French Cook* (London, 1813); this book demonstrated the elegant cooking that was the mark of a fashionable household. It was published in Philadelphia fifteen years later, the first of many French cookbooks in America. Other nineteenth-century books of French cookery published in the United States include Eliza Leslie's translation of *Domestic French Cookery* (1832), Mme. Utrecht-Friedel's *La petite cuisinière habile* (1840), the first French language cookbook published in America, and Louis Eustache Audot's *La cuisinière de la campagne et de la ville*, which was translated into English and

published in America as *French Domestic Cookery* (1846). Charles Elmé Francatelli, Queen Victoria's maître d'hôtel, was born in London of Italian heritage, but he studied under the legendary French chef Marie-Antoine Carême. Francatelli's *French Cookery* was first published in the United States in 1846.

French Restaurants

By the early nineteenth century, the French influence was clearly visible on the menus of America's restaurants. Most Americans ate at home during the late eighteenth and early nineteenth centuries. Taverns, saloons, public houses, and inns served mainly travelers. Restaurants were opened toward the end of the eighteenth century, mostly by French refugees. Their clientele consisted of businessmen and an increasingly affluent upper class. In 1827 Joseph Collet opened a French restaurant on the lower floor of his Commercial Hotel on Broad Street in New York. Eight years later Collet sold his hotel and

French Cookbook. Cover of François Tanty's *La Cuisine Française: French Cooking for Every Home, Adapted to American Requirements* (Chicago, 1893).

restaurant to the Swiss emigrés John, Peter, and Lorenzo Delmonico. The Delmonico brothers had established a café and pastry shop in New York in 1827, and ten years later they opened what became known as Delmonico's Restaurant. From its inception it offered a variety of French dishes. Delmonico's was only one among many of the restaurants in American cities that served French food during the nineteenth century.

So prestigious was French cooking in nineteenth-century America that many American chefs claimed to have been born in France, although most were not even trained in French cookery. For the same reason, French culinary terms, such as "café," "filet," "fricassee," "meringue," and "entrée," commonly appeared on restaurant menus. Some words changed in meaning when used in America— the word "entrée," for instance, came to mean a main course, while in France it means a small dish served between main courses. French food words were further popularized in the United States during the 1850s, when some wealthy American families employed French chefs.

After the Civil War, the chefs in America's most prestigious restaurants were French or French-trained. Several of them published cookbooks during the late nineteenth century. Felix Déliée, who cooked at the New York Club and the Union and Manhattan Clubs, published *The Franco-American Cookery Book* in 1884. Charles Ranhofer, chef at Delmonico's, wrote *The Epicurean* (1896); Oscar Tschirky, maître d'hôtel at the Waldorf, wrote *The Cook Book of Oscar of the Waldorf* (1896). Another influential Frenchman was Auguste Escoffier (1846–1935), who connected with César Ritz to create Ritz hotels beginning in 1890. Escoffier's *Guide culinaire*, translated as *A Guide to Modern Cookery* (1907) was regularly published in the United States.

The French influence in American cooking schools and professional culinary organizations is also apparent. Elizabeth Goodfellow opened a cooking school in Philadelphia during the early nineteenth century and included French cookery in the course of studies. One of her star pupils, Eliza Leslie, translated and published *Domestic French Cookery*, which was based on a French cookbook published in Belgium by Sulpice Barué. Pierre Blot (1818–1874) immigrated to the United States about 1855, where he wrote articles and two cookbooks, *What to Eat, and How to Cook It* (1863), and *Hand-Book of Practical Cookery* (1867), which went through several editions. He also founded the New York Cooking Academy, which was America's first French cooking

school. French cookery in some form has been a part of the course of studies of most American cooking schools.

French Influences in the Twentieth Century

During the twentieth century, French cuisine continued to influence American cookery. Elizabeth Pennell, M. F. K. Fisher, and Julia Child spent time in France and brought their discoveries back to the United States. Julia Child, along with Simone Beck and Louisette Bertholle, published *Mastering the Art of French Cooking* (1961) and two years later Child began her stint on the WGBH television program *The French Chef*, which ran on Public Television for two hundred episodes, with reruns that were being broadcast in the early 2000s. This program introduced her version of French cooking into American homes and clearly sparked an interest in French cooking in America. Her sign-off, "bon appétit," has become a part of America's vocabulary. Simultaneously, French chefs and French-trained chefs, such as Jacques Pépin and Emeril Lagasse, have flooded into the United States to dazzle

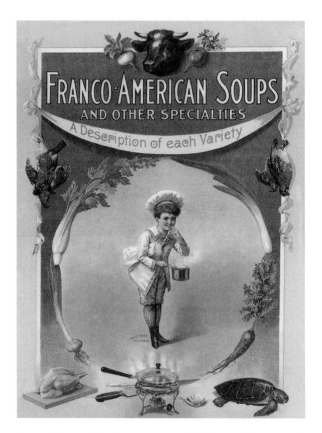

Soup. Franco-American soup cookbooklet, early twentieth century. *Collection of Andrew F. Smith*

Paris in Brooklyn. Café Moutarde in Brooklyn, New York. *Photograph by Joe Zarba*

Americans with French cooking on other television series. Other Americans used their experience in France to criticize American cooking rather than convince Americans that they should learn how to cook a bastardized form of French cookery.

As the twenty-first century began, most American cooking schools used classic French cookery as the basis for their training. In addition, Americans continued to go to France to study the culinary arts. An association, Les dames d'Escoffier International, was launched in 1978 to honor women who have achieved excellence in the food, beverage, and hospitality professions. In 1984, the French Culinary Institute was founded in New York with the expressed purpose of combining classic French techniques with American inventiveness.

Nouvelle cuisine, a term coined in 1973 by the French restaurant critics Christian Millau and Henri Gault, stressed use of the best local ingredients rather than elaborate preparations. It rejected unnecessarily complicated and pretentious dishes and encouraged seasonal and available ingredients. It encouraged creativity and experimentation. Nouvelle cuisine was introduced into the United States by a number of chefs and restaurateurs. One was Alice Waters, who in 1971 opened Chez Panisse in Berkeley, California. At first Waters served simple French food with a particular emphasis on the traditions of Provence. As time went on, she began experimenting with local ingredients. While a chef at Chez Panisse, Jeremiah Tower began adopting the principles of nouvelle cuisine into his cookery. Another apostle of nouvelle cuisine was Wolfgang Puck, the Austrian-born chef at Ma Maison in Los Angeles. His *Modern French Cooking for the American Kitchen* (1981) was among America's best-selling "French" cookbooks. The efforts of Waters, Tower, Puck, and many other chefs have helped create a culinary renaissance in America.

[See also Cajun and Creole Food; Celebrity Chefs; Child, Julia; Child, Lydia Maria; Delmonico's; Fisher, M. F. K.; Jefferson, Thomas; Lagasse, Emeril; Leslie, Eliza; Nouvelle Cuisine; Prudhomme, Paul; Puck, Wolfgang; Ranhofer, Charles; Simmons, Amelia; Tschirky, Oscar; Waters, Alice.]

BIBLIOGRAPHY

Gabaccia, Donna R. *We Are What We Eat: Ethnic Food and the Making of Americans.* Cambridge, MA: Harvard University Press, 1998.

Hess, John, and Karen Hess. *The Taste of America.* Urbana: University of Illinois, 2000.

Trubek, Amy B. *Haute Cuisine: How the French Invented the Culinary Profession.* Philadelphia: University of Pennsylvania Press, 2000.

Zanger, Mark H. *The American Ethnic Cookbook for Students.* Phoenix, AZ: Oryx Press, 2001.

ANDREW F. SMITH

Frito-Lay

Herman W. Lay was a salesman for Sunshine Biscuit Company, but during the Depression he lost his job. In 1932, Lay was hired by Barrett Foods, a snack-food firm in Atlanta, Georgia, and began selling peanut butter sandwiches in southern Kentucky and Tennessee. Lay was an aggressive businessman and began acquiring distributorships. When Barrett's founder died in 1937, Lay bought the company, which included plants in Atlanta and Memphis, Tennessee. Popcorn, manufactured in Nashville, Tennessee, was the first product to have the "Lay's" brand name. Lay also manufactured potato chips.

Lay's potato chip sales increased during World War II, mainly because snack foods that contained sugar and chocolate were unavailable due to rationing. After the war, Lay fully automated his potato chip manufacturing business and diversified its products. The firm had become a major regional snack food company by the end of World War II. In 1945, Lay met Elmer Doolin, who manufactured Fritos corn chips in San Antonio, Texas. Doolin granted Herman Lay a license to distribute Fritos. The two companies also cooperated on other products. For example, Chee-tos cheese-flavored snacks were invented by the Frito company and were marketed by Lay in 1948.

When Doolin died in 1959, his Frito company merged with Lay's company, creating Frito-Lay Inc., headquartered in Dallas, Texas. The merged company continued to grow. By the end of the 1960s, Frito-Lay was the dominant company in the snack world. In 1965, Frito-Lay merged with Pepsi-Cola Company, creating PepsiCo. The newly merged company launched many products. In 1966, Frito-Lay introduced Doritos corn chips, which the company claimed tasted like authentic tostadas. Doritos became popular nationwide as the era of the Anglo corn chip dawned. By the early twenty-first century, Doritos had become the largest-selling snack food in the world.

The main target of Fritos advertising was children. A cartoon character, the Frito Kid, was launched in 1953. In 1958, the company launched a campaign featuring "Munch a bunch of Fritos corn chips" as its slogan. In 1963, with growing awareness of niche markets, Frito-Lay introduced the Frito Bandito, a move that appalled the Mexican American community. The Frito Bandito soon disappeared.

Frito-Lay continued to innovate and develop new products. For example, in 1983 the company produced Ruffles potato chips, a thick chip with ridges made especially for dipping. In 1988, Frito-Lay introduced Chee-tos cheddar cheese flavored popcorn and launched a major promotion campaign starring Chester Cheetah, a cartoon character aimed at children and young adults. Rold Gold brand pretzels were introduced in 1989 and were subsequently promoted by "Pretzel Boy," portrayed by the actor Jason Alexander of the *Seinfeld* television series. In 1993, Doritos Thins brand tortilla chips were introduced nationally with Chevy Chase as the celebrity spokesman.

Frito-Lay has acquired other food companies, such as Cracker-Jack in 1997. By 2000, Frito-Lay had become the largest snack food conglomerate in the world.

[*See also* Mexican American Food; Popcorn; Potatoes; Snack Food.]

BIBLIOGRAPHY

Guenther, Keith J. "The Development of the Mexican-American Cuisine." In *Oxford Symposium 1981: National and Regional Styles of Cookery; Proceedings*, edited by Alan Davidson. London: Prospect, 1981.

Smith, Andrew F. "Tacos, Enchiladas and Refried Beans: The Invention of Mexican-American Cookery." In *Cultural and Historical Aspects of Foods*, edited by Mary Wallace Kelsey and ZoeAnn Holmes, 183–203. Corvallis: Oregon State University, 1999.

ANDREW F. SMITH

FRITO PIE

Frito Pie consists of beef or bean chili, cheese, onions, and jalapeños layered over Frito corn chips. The dish traditionally was served directly inside the corn chip bag, but because the bag has become thinner, the dish is usually served on a plate. Although, or perhaps because, Frito pie is a quintessential road food from the southwestern United States, its origins are undetermined. Both Texas and New Mexico claim to have created Frito pie. The dish gained renown at the Woolworth lunch counter in Santa Fe, New Mexico. According to the Dallas-based Frito-Lay company, the mother of Elmer Doolin, the founder of Frito-Lay, invented the dish in 1932. The latter is the most likely answer, because snack food companies have a history of creating recipes with their products to increase sales. Frito pie is essentially an Americanized version of the Mexican tostada—corn tortillas topped with ingredients similar to those used in Frito pie.

[*See also* Mexican American Food; Roadside Food; Snack Food; Southwestern Regional Cookery.]

JEAN RAILLA

Frontier Cooking of the Far West

America's westward push created a series of new frontiers, ranging through the plains of the Mississippi, across the Rockies, to the far reaches of the Pacific coast and the Southwest. New frontiers quickly turned "old," to be replaced again by new, but the designation of Far West, for the purposes of frontier cooking, extends from 1820 to 1880 and includes five major westward population thrusts: the trading frontier of the mountain men, the trans-Mississippi West of the overland migration, homesteading on the Great Plains, the gold boom, and the great cattle drives. The range of such movements is vast, with countless foods and culinary styles that were brought, exchanged, enjoyed, and discovered along the way.

Traders, Trappers, and Mountain Men

Earliest to explore the Rocky Mountains were the trappers, traders, and mountain men of the French trading companies, the Indian forts, and the U.S. Army; their presence began as early as 1803, and they were well established west of the Rockies by 1820. Shaggy, recondite men, clad in buckskin and isolated for months at a time, these "old mountain hands" had long abandoned the ways of civilization, bringing along only the barest of implements—matches, a butcher knife for quartering buffalo, a small knife for sharpening roasting sticks, a skin hat used to wear or to melt snow, and a pouch of beaver castor that, when mixed with spicebush roots, could be used as elixir, tea, or medicine. Outfitted with tobacco, well-greased leather clothes, and an occasional tin pot, if they were lucky, they had salt and little else by way of supplies.

Mountain men avoided the toil of agriculture to spend summers drying elk meat; basting venison in its own fat to sustain the dark, gamy flavor; or trading with the Blackfeet or Sioux for dried salmon. For sweetening, they plucked succulent berries from vast quantities of cherries, plums, and wild fruits growing abundant and wild in the Rockies. Freedom, for the mountain man, was in the splash of crystal water or the tang of sweet mountain berries. Bear, elk, buffalo, or deer were hunted at will, and vast numbers of buffalo—sixty million had once roamed the plains—were killed, their tongues considered the most savory part.

Armed with one-shot flintlock rifles, trappers and mountain men felled "white bears," or grizzlies, with a single shot and sold the rendered fat to the nearest trading company, packing the product in sewn skin pouches.

An adult grizzly would yield ten gallons of pure white bear oil when processed. The meat would last an entire year when jerked or turned into pemmican—a compressed "packet" of meat flakes and berries, dried over a slow fire, pounded to powder between two stones, sewn into an animal-hide bag, and smothered in a thick coat of melted grease. To this savory staple might be added the Native American overland staple of "cold flour," a roasted and dried corn, pounded and spiced with sugar—a hungry male adult required 2.35 pounds of food daily to traverse the mountains without ill effects. Jerked meat, particularly useful on the long trail, was sun dried on strings, then packed away in saddlebags, where it would stay without putrefying for months on a long journey.

When large game was scarce, the mountain man might savor a favorite backwoods mainstay—raccoon—eating coon for breakfast, midday meal, and dinner, with no relief in vegetables or sauce. One trapper's favorite savory was coon cake, made by taking what flour he had, mixing it with water, shortening it with coon oil, and frying it in coon fat. During winter's heavy snows, scanty game forced the mountain men to find leaner fare, usually pine bark boiled as tea, dried juniper berries still on the bush, and dried salmon. In the wet Pacific Northwest, they dug camas root and pounded it into a flat mound of dough. If dried, it turned into a thin, slightly sweet cookie. Otherwise, it was simply damp dough. Irish moss, the common term for seaweed, was boiled as a tea.

In the trapper's West, the social impact of food and drink far outweighed the nutritive value, becoming a vital aspect of the unwritten "code of the West," one tenant being that temporary property rights began within fifty feet of a person's cook pot—moving any closer required an invitation. Generosity was integral to the code, revolving around the sharing of food. Mountain men quickly learned what the Indians had long understood—to thank a fellow hunter for food freely given was an insult, implying that generosity was episodic, not ongoing.

Soldiers and Settlers

A crucial influx into western territories came with the military—by 1850 nearly all of the U.S. Army was deployed to seventy-nine military posts below St. Joseph, Missouri, assisting the overland immigrants with a network of armed forces, Indian agents, surveyors, road builders, and mail carriers. Many soldiers were Civil War veterans who had primed their muzzle loaders with the same gunpowder that "salted" their stew—potassium nitrate, or saltpeter, had the same zing as salt, and they found slight improvement in the military fare served in the West, where they were sustained at mealtime by paltry portions of coffee, hardtack, raw salt pork, and the interminable soaked beans. Nutritional shortcuts meant that military food was of poor quality and often spoiled. Soldiers' provisions were bland and monotonous; meats arrived in camp worm ridden, beans and potatoes were tainted with mold, and the hardtack had been nibbled by mice. By the 1870s the increased use of canned goods, transported by railroad, offered a more varied selection. Included were the ubiquitous tinned oysters—one of the most popular canned foods in the West. During long campaigns, soldiers hungered for a taste of potato. In winter they shot prairie chickens or woodcocks, or they waited patiently for shipments of government beef to catch up so that the cook could make oxtail soup, often from salted beef—a welcome change from a larder stocked only with bacon, flour, beans, coffee, tea, rice, sugar, and dried apples.

Military life influenced American culinary practices in that monotonous and predictable food, served to officers and enlisted men alike, reinforced a kind of egalitarian outlook in keeping with democratic principles—at least up to a point. The army's organized supply network prompted a quicker distribution of canned goods and out-of-area specialties, broadening the food pool. Thanks to military life, men who had never tasted coffee became avid coffee drinkers. As the military crisscrossed the country, it brought new foods to new areas, joining together tastes and styles, at least temporarily.

Another new group to head west was the overland emigrants, settlers leaving the eastern seaboard, the South, and the Midwest to travel beyond the 98th meridian, which cut through the Dakotas, Nebraska, Kansas, and Indian territory. They traveled in the greatest numbers from 1840 to 1860—although wagons continued along the overland routes as late as 1900—with a general terminus of California. Along the way, they found much that was new; even the food prepared and eaten around an open fire was extraordinarily different from the familiar foods of home. Amazed at the luxurious foliage and tall grasses, emigrants could scoop up sprouting potherbs and flowers for salads and tea, including portulaca, or purslane—refreshingly green and tart—and Indian lettuce, of the genus *Montia*, with bunches of edible, pleasant-tasting leaves. Women gathered wild grapes or harvested fruits in abundance, including delicious strawberries; seedy, pink gooseberries tasting of grapes; cranberries; amber yellow salal berries

or salmonberries, too tart to eat without cooking, related to the raspberry; and sarvis berries, red and purple fruits plucked from the vine and eaten either as a medicinal cure for nausea and headache or for their rich content of vitamin C. "Sarvis" is shortened from "service," another name for the white-blossomed Juneberry tree. Thick clusters of mesquite beans from the small, lime-green mesquite bush were ground into flour and eaten as "bread fruit." The twisted black pods were used as fodder.

White beans were an overland traveler's mainstay, simmered through the night or buried in a "bean pit" to cook in a tightly covered kettle, perhaps a Dutch oven, surrounded by layers of glowing coals. Laced with bones, vegetables, and savory meat scraps, such as salt pork, the beans were ready for breakfast or dinner the following day. Pocket soup was made of bones or meat—usually veal, beef, or pig's trotters—cooked into a broth and strained, with the remaining broth cooked again to the consistency of a thick, often bland, glue. Even years later, it could easily be dissolved in hot water to create stock. Emigrants knew that a pound of bacon went as far as three pounds of beefsteak and that pork was popular because it kept well as smoked ham or bacon or salt pork, its flavor actually improving as part of the preserving process. The summer season kindly offered wild berries, while winter offered greater ease in hunting and preserving game. Small game abounded year-round—woodchucks, prairie chickens, myriad birds, rabbits, squirrels, raccoons, and opossums. Southwestern mesquite roots and dried cow manure, or cow chips, were ready fuel. Crossing the plains, travelers cooked their food nightly over little fires of dried buffalo dung.

Despite occasional festivities, monotony prevailed. Culinary relief might come from a hidden supply of "ardent spirits" or tinned "substitute foods," perhaps sardines or oysters, or Borden's canned condensed milk, the first canned food product to become popular during the Civil War. In the Great Plains, canned goods such as peaches or tomatoes could be purchased at trading posts, bringing the impact of technology to bear in the most remote reaches of the country. Bread was baked in a Dutch oven, often using the rank-tasting saleratus, or baking soda. Although saleratus was quicker rising than yeast, its telltale alkali flavor was detested by travelers, who tried to kill the taste with onions. Baking powder, or "Sally Ann," also bore a metallic aftertaste if used in large amounts. Bread starters, or a "sponge" of sourdough, salt, and yeast, were a treasured brew of secret

Pioneer Camp. From George Augustus Sala, *America Revisited*, 3rd edition (London, 1883), vol. 2, p. 139.

ingredients, nurtured and tended like a child. Yeast often fermented and turned sour in the heat. Cooks crossing the Continental Divide would take their "sponge" to bed at night in order to keep it active—ready to bake biscuits or bread quickly in the morning.

A legacy of the frontier crossing was a subtle shift in the pioneer diet. Meat preference changed from beef to pork in some areas, as pork was cheaper and easier to preserve. The European taste for tea had declined before the American Revolution for political reasons, leading to increased use of coffee.

Miners and Prospectors

During the gold rush, 1849–1860, a major segment of the overland emigration rushed toward the gold and silver regions of California and Nevada, forming a mining population isolated in the remote reaches of the Sierra Nevada, in the Comstock Lode, and in the gold-mining regions of Idaho and Colorado. Drawn from every nationality—including Chileans, French, Australians, Chinese, Hawaiians, and more—and from every region of the country, the gold rush population veered from privation to plenty, with foods to accommodate every pocket.

Early mining camps served monotonous fare, usually hardtack biscuits washed down with coffee. The camps were so remote that when limited supplies did arrive, the fresh meat was often decayed, flour supplies were weevil ridden, and tinned butter, packed in a light salt brine in metal containers, was brown and spoiled. In the early camps, scurvy was rampant and could be countered only by the antiscorbutic effects of lime juice, wild lettuce, potatoes with vinegar, or even, in desperation for what little citrus might be found, orange marmalade.

As the mines prospered, the number of western hotels grew—many serving luxurious helpings of elk steak, codfish balls, roast grizzly (special, one dollar a plate), and fish chowder stewed in claret. The Mammoth Caves Hotel in California offered "venison steak, bass fried in corn meal, bacon cured over a hickory wood fire, snap beans cooked with green corn, pone bread from the skillet, cider, rum, French brandy and home made wines." California forty-niners often feasted upon salmon, easily caught in the Sacramento River, while others sampled German sausage and Italian confections. Coffees, chocolates, and cakes were common, while cash-poor miners dined upon Chinese chop suey. A square meal cost three dollars—nearly thirty dollars by today's standards—yet often fell within a miner's budget, making restaurant dining on the mother lode more common in the gold regions at a time when comparatively few Americans ate out. The transient nature of the mining regions, attracting young, footloose adventurers without families, contributed to the surge of restaurants, boarding houses, and hotels.

Gold boom cooking took on a cosmopolitan appeal with another boomtown enticement, the free saloon lunch, where the most ordinary deep rock miner turned bon vivant as he dug into lavish helpings of seafood, deviled crabs, kippered fish, anchovies, liverwurst, and platters of meat, fried or barbecued. Buffalo and bear entrées were advertised by the corresponding hide hung from the saloon door. Gaming tables vied with loaded luncheon tables, and in one hotel, a cooked bear loomed straight up from a table—men would simply slice off a steak as they passed by. Rambunctious California miners invented the Hangtown fry, an egg and oyster dish, as well as the oyster cocktail—the result of a miner awaiting his main dish idly mixing oysters with tomato catsup. During the gold rush, culinary qualifications went to those who claimed them—women were able to claim work as boardinghouse cooks, although men generally presided over the pots and pans in restaurants.

Cowboys

The most colorful arrival on the far frontier was the cowboy, whose heyday lasted from the end of the Civil War until the mid-1880s but whose influence, even decades later, seemed near mythical. Hardworking trail hands, their main occupation was transporting cattle from the range to the slaughterhouses or tending the vast cattle herds that grazed the grasslands on ranches from Canada to the Rio Grande. Longhorns from Texas, descended from cattle brought to Mexico by Spaniards, proliferated, as did the mounted men who herded them.

Cowboy cooking seldom lived up to the romance of the open range, as the trail hands herded the great remudas—a band of saddle horses pushing the cattle along—along the Chisholm or the Goodnight-Loving trails. Cowboy fare varied according to the whims of the cook; often dubbed with a female name, such as "Miss Sally," the cook was usually an ornery single man known for temperamental displays of anger whose skill ranked him near the top of the cattle drive hierarchy. The cook dished up chuck for hard-worked men with peckish food tastes—those from the border states hated mutton, raw greens, and rare meat. Any cook unable to whip up the trailside favorites—hot breads; mallet-softened meat dredged in flour, called chicken-fried steak; beans; and succulent, syrup-drenched, straight-from-the-can yellow cling peaches—became an unpopular "cookie" and did not last long. Few chuckwagon cooks were Chinese, and none were women.

Cooking from an echelon of sizzling hot Dutch ovens, cast-iron skillets, and lidded pots supported on a tripod over a wood fire by fire hooks, with a metal pothook for unlidding, the trail cook satisfied the appetites of eighteen to twenty-five cowpunchers with everything from beans to barbecue, with dishes concocted from such bulk staples as flour, sugar, dried fruit, onions, potatoes, and pinto beans and such essentials as vinegar, a keg of sourdough starter,

lard, molasses, and whiskey. A well-funded outfit enjoyed luxury items, such as pickles and spices, while an imaginative chef might add green purslane, a succulent green potherb, or cactus buds, fried up like green beans and used to deter scurvy. A savory buffalo hump stew would be laced with onions or "cracklin'" cornbread with pork skin flavoring. One chef produced a trailside banquet with fried catfish and an impromptu "plum duff"—boiled dried fruit and suet pudding, with raisins, brandy, flour, and bread crumbs tied in cloth and boiled in a pot for eight hours or more. The word "duff" comes from an old English pronunciation of "dough."

Less inspired cooks relied solely on pinto beans or potatoes and bacon spiced with chili, flour, saleratus, and grease. An occasional dessert might be molasses or, as a treat, Karo syrup, called "lick," dripped over canned tomatoes and leftover biscuits. A more stylish chef would offer the popular "moonshine"—not the southern corn whiskey, but a concoction of rice and raisins simmered in a Dutch oven. Butchered yearling calf, a trailside favorite, was simmered in a pot with its cut-up tongue, kidneys, and heart along with potatoes, onions, pepper, and salt. Son-of-a-bitch stew—hardly as lively as its name—consisted of boiled bone marrow sautéed in hot grease with peppers and potatoes. To tenderize beef, the

Old West Cuisine. Cowboys eating near a chuck wagon, Arizona, 1907. *Prints and Photographs Division, Library of Congress/Russell Lee*

cook would roll a section of meat into a bedroll and hang it from a tree for days, where men would take turns hitting it with a stick to soften it up so that they could slice off steaks for cooking. Coffee was the cowboy's mainstay, brewed with eggshells in order to keep down the grounds and sweetened with coarse, brown, granulated sugar.

Homesteaders

The overland emigrants bound for homestead lands were another significant group to travel west, from 1840 to 1860. Shopkeepers, traders, schoolteachers, and small farmers, they moved west to claim free land and settle in growing communities. The early years of settlement on farms differed according to time, location, and settlers' backgrounds. Emigrants arriving west from the Mississippi often arrived at their destinations with little capital to begin homesteading. Those emigrating from the cities left behind a cash economy to rely on hunting, growing, and bartering. They also had to learn to farm; some were successful, but others abandoned farming for more familiar pursuits in the growing towns and cities. Despite habit and homesickness, the emigrants found that, no matter how hard they tried to replicate the foods of home, differences abounded in the West.

At first rural communities were far distant from one another, with little exchange of goods, foods, or recipes. As time passed, the growth of rural communities brought neighbors closer, with trading, social events, schools, shared religious activities, and food exchanges, as they attempted to recreate the community life they had left behind. In the East, to leave a farm generally meant failure, while in the West, one of the striking features of the farm, ranch, or homestead was the constant uprooting, as settlers sought better land and greater opportunities.

Such uprooting resulted in fewer crop foods. However, on farms, ranches, and western homesteads in the late 1800s there was an abundance of game to augment the usual mealtime portions. Huge helpings became the hallmark of hospitality, with farm wives—when possible—serving up fish for breakfast, antelope at the noon meal, and fried bread, a luxury, for evening dinner. A typical breakfast might include skinned and salted deer, juicy ham steaks, hot buttermilk biscuits, fruit preserves, cooked porridge (particularly corn mush), cornbread, cream gravy, and potatoes.

As rural communities stabilized, so did the food supplies, including cattle and poultry. So bountiful were some areas—particularly in Oregon—that a dozen eggs sold for a dime and butter was often given away. Many farms kept cattle, adding milk, curds, and cheese to the daily menu, while truck gardens, established usually after the farm had been settled for several years, offered a seasonal bounty—tomatoes, snap beans, melons, and squash. Wheat flour might be milled locally or trundled by horse from the nearest general store.

Some habits of home prevailed, no matter how many times a family might move. Eastern emigrants had a penchant for fruit pies, served daily, and many preferred not to eat varmints, such as opossum and raccoon, or the deep-fried meat of a skinned, cleaned rattlesnake. Vegetables were unpopular with many. "Eat a raw turnip? We would not have dared!" wrote one Texas settler, although diaries reveal that cucumbers, chards, sweet corn, beans, and collards were often eaten and enjoyed.

Adaptation and Adjustment

Others adapted to the new foods of the new terrain, and regional preferences held sway. Southwestern settlers used the ubiquitous jalapeño to spice barbecued meat, red beans, and agarita jam, pressed from the pungent berry of the sharp-tipped agarita bush. They embraced the Spanish legacy of savory carne seca, spicy jerked beef, a form of preserving meat that originated in South America and was quickly adopted by the new Anglo-Californians. Barbecued meat, spit-roasted over an open fire, was popular, as was colache, or vegetable succotash, spiced with garlic, olive oil, and green chilies. Favorite of all were tortillas, tamales, and *chile con carne*.

Southerners washed down a typical dinner of wild greens, boiled pork, and cold cornbread with "beverage" made of vinegar, brown sugar, and warm creek water—some might add ginger to make this poor man's lemonade, often drunk in the fields to quench thirst on hot days. Buttermilk was also a drink of hot climates; the liquid left over after making butter from cream, then thickened, was often drunk, as milk might spoil in sultry weather without a cool root cellar. Soured milk, however, leant a special flavor to quick breads such as biscuits

When supplies ran low, substitutions were made: wild plum syrup, tart and flavorful, instead of sugar; stump tree pods in place of coffee beans; grape leaves instead of tobacco; and white wood ashes instead of salt. Economy presided in the pioneer homestead, and on the occasion of a cake, the leftover scraps and crumbs, added to water, made sponge starter for bread. Crumbs pounded flat and cooked in a cloth made a thick, roly-poly crust.

Cornbread, cracker, and bread crumbs moistened with water, spiced with sage, and usually baked in a cast-iron oven created a common dish called gosh, as in "Gosh, do we have to eat *that again?*"

Meanwhile, urbanites found that life in the western towns and cities eventually offered as varied a diet as that of the East. They could pick and choose from a wealth of supplies, from fresh green peas to imported pâté, supplied by a growing railway network that linked small, localized markets to city shoppers. Fashionable magazines instructed women in the newest dessert developments, such as bananas that were cut lengthwise and heaped with whipped cream or lavish main course dishes, such as saddle of mutton covered in an "iced" topping of cooled meat drippings with the white top fat skimmed off, remelted, and spread over the meat in a smooth, white coat. For urbanites, Continental dining arrived with delicious little side offerings of French foods—hors d'oeuvres, sauced vegetables, dense meat stocks, scalded calves feet for jelly, and desserts such as constructed gilt cakes, bonbons, and fondue, often savored at popular outdoor cafés.

Many Asians flooded into the West after the gold boom, bringing with them foods and cooking styles based on their culinary roots. Using inexpensive vegetables, Asian immigrants added a savory cooking style that was healthy and cheap. Chop suey houses served rice and hot, brewed tea, as well as two distinct cooking styles: stir-frying and steaming. Both methods preserved the nutrients and were seen as healthy. Boiled tea protected the Chinese from waterborne diseases, and, armed with herbs and talismans, many Chinese also brewed up local roots and barks for medicine, flavorings, and spices. The Chinese also enjoyed dried herring. Westerners were mixed about Chinese food—they enjoyed its exotic appeal and healthful results, and the economy of Chinese chop suey and chow mein were understood by frugal chefs of all cultures. In the West, the Chinese discovered an abundance of meat, so different from China, and began to use more beef and lamb.

Other immigrants to America brought their favorite foods: Italians settled in Northern California and Nevada, introducing pasta and meat dishes and enjoying lentils. Texas Germans made wurst from fatty venison or pork mixed with coarse salt, pepper, and saltpeter. Jewish immigrants, some of whom traveled as salesmen, some of whom farmed, brought garlic-flavored pickles and gunnysacks filled with kasha, in case they ran out. African Americans migrated into Iowa after emancipation, and many came to California, bringing traditional southern cooking practices, such as rice and black-eyed pea concoctions. Black sharecroppers wrapped meat in cabbage leaves and baked it in the ashes or smoked meat over apple wood or sassafras. Women ground corn husks into meal to make bread—anything to keep from starving. Black cooking introduced peanuts, molasses, and sesame seeds as well as salads made of wild greens.

Culinary crossovers abounded. The culinary pluralism of the Old West included foods from Native Americans—cornbread, clam chowder, succotash, sweet potato pie, beans, and black-eyed peas—as well as others.

One of the West's most important contributions from 1840 to 1890 was to provide a meeting ground in which groups cooperated to share skills, information, and resources. The unwritten code of the plains was the ethic of hospitality—particularly on the Great Plains of the American West. Good food was both cause and means of celebration, and the lexicon of "plain cookin'" on the frontier encompassed savory or plain, salted or sweet. Food also subtly revealed class and education as well as culinary preference, as those sitting "below the salt" might attest. The pioneering process turned cooking, American-style, into a savory blend of spices, herbs, flavors, and techniques that combined the Old World and the New World. Foods mirrored not only the land and the region but also the outlook, status, and tastes of frontier cooks.

[*See also* Barbecue; Buffalo; Buttermilk; California; Chinese American Food; Coffee; Pacific Northwestern Regional Cookery; Restaurants.]

BIBLIOGRAPHY

Armitage, Susan, and Elizabeth Jameson, eds. *The Women's West.* Norman: University of Oklahoma Press, 1987.

Conlin, Joseph R. *Bacon, Beans, and Galantines: Food and Foodways of the Western Mining Frontier.* Reno: University of Nevada Press, 1986.

Faragher, John Mack. *Women and Men on the Overland Trail.* New Haven: Yale University Press, 1979.

Jeffrey, Julie Roy. *Frontier Women.* New York: Hill and Wang, 1979.

Luchetti, Cathy Lee. *Home on the Range: A Culinary History of the American West.* New York: Villard, 1993.

Packman, Ana Bégué de. *Early California Hospitality: The Cookery Customs of Spanish California.* Glendale, CA: Clark, 1938.

Robson, J. R. K. *Food, Ecology, and Culture: Readings in the Anthropology of Dietary Practices.* New York: Gordon and Breach, 1980.

Ross, Nancy Wilson. *Westward the Women.* New York: Knopf, 1944.

Stratton, Joanna L. *Pioneer Women: Voices from the Kansas Frontier.* New York: Simon and Schuster, 1981.

Unruh, John D. *The Plains Across: The Overland Emigrants and the Trans-Mississippi West, 1840–60.* Urbana, IL: University of Illinois Press, 1979.

CATHY LEE LUCHETTI

Frosting, *see Cakes*

Frozen Food

After more than thirty years as publisher of the trade journal *Quick Frozen Foods*, E. W. Williams, always the optimist and often the hyperbolist, described an American utopia of frozen dinners: "Where can a consumer buy its equivalent in a restaurant? It is economical, saves dishes and cooking. It is the perfect answer to modern living. Of course, not every one wants a frozen meal but I believe there are *enough* Americans who will sacrifice home cooking for convenience." He added, however, "I also think there is room for a somewhat fancier meal in a slightly higher [price] bracket." These comments appeared in 1970 in Williams's book *Frozen Foods*. By that time, frozen foods had become a staple in the American diet. During his tenure as publisher of the journal, Williams saw sales of frozen foods climb from 150 million dollars in 1940 to 7 billion dollars three decades later. Retail sellers of frozen foods numbered in the hundreds in the mid-1930s. Fifteen years later, 200,000 stores were equipped with freezer cabinets. In 1928, during the infancy of the frozen food industry, 1 million pounds of fruits and vegetables were frozen. In 1946, a year during which supply exceeded demand, 860 million pounds of fruits and vegetables were in cold storage.

The commercial freezing of food was not new in the 1920s. Frozen meat, packed in ice and salt, was shipped from the United States to England in 1876. In the Pacific Northwest strawberries were being frozen as early as 1909. It is generally acknowledged, however, that one man was responsible for the mass production of frozen foods: Clarence Birdseye.

Birdseye was born in Brooklyn, New York, in 1886. After failing to pay his college expenses from the money he had earned as an amateur trapper and taxidermist, Birdseye took a job with the U.S. Department of Agriculture in Washington, D.C. That job did not last long. Birdseye moved with his wife and son to Labrador, in northeastern Canada, where he traded furs. The family lived remotely and survived on fish and game that they caught themselves. In the subzero temperatures of the region, food storage was not a problem—the Birdseyes simply left meat and fish outside, where it promptly froze. The thawed food, Birdseye noticed, tasted freshly caught. An entrepreneur as well as an avid experimenter, Birdseye saw great market potential for the quick freezing of all kinds of food. In 1917 the family moved back to the United States. There Birdseye began developing equipment for freezing foods mechanically as quickly as the Labrador winters had naturally. Years passed before Birdseye could muster the backers he needed to adequately fund his project, but in 1924, on a shoestring budget, he founded General Seafoods. Birdseye began to market frozen fish fillets the following year, but his business remained small. Then, in 1926, an order for frozen goose filled by Birdseye's company proved serendipitous. Marjorie Merriweather Post, whose family owned the company that made Postum cereal, tasted the goose and immediately saw the potential for Birdseye's freezing process. Three years later, just before the crash of the stock market ushered in the Great Depression, the Postum Company and the Goldman Sachs Trading Company together acquired General Seafoods and Birdseye's patents for $22 million. They called the newly formed company General Foods.

Growth of an Industry

After the development of commercial methods of freezing food quickly, there remained the problem of convincing the American public to buy frozen foods. Before Birdseye,

---

TV DINNERS

Swanson introduced the frozen TV dinner in 1954 in a package designed to resemble a television set. The three-section aluminum tray containing turkey and gravy, peas, and sweet potatoes required only reheating—a hallmark of convenience. It was also a hallmark of changing American cooking and eating habits. Critics judged TV dinners and their imitators guilty of promoting bland uniformity on a grand scale, the same judgment they leveled against television. A potent symbol of social change, the original aluminum tray, replaced by a plastic one with the advent of the microwave oven, is housed in the Smithsonian Institution.

MATT McMILLEN

TV DINNERS: A FIRSTHAND ACCOUNT

C. A. Swanson and Sons' signature product was turkey, and in 1951 the company possessed a record crop of Ute turkeys that had been produced from California to Minnesota. Credit for this plenitude could be attributed to the system established by Carl Swanson of Omaha, Nebraska, founder of the company, who had been dubbed the "Turkey King of America" by *Fortune* magazine. In order to stabilize the production of turkeys, each year he guaranteed a purchase price for turkeys grown for Swanson and delivered in prime condition. This generous contractual arrangement assured Swanson of an abundance of birds each year, but they had to be sold prior to Thanksgiving, since in those years 90 percent of all turkeys were sold for that holiday. The unsold inventory was so great in February 1952 that an emergency meeting was convened to discuss the matter. Thanksgiving had long since passed, and the next "season" was nine months away. At the meeting we learned that we had over twenty refrigerated train carloads of turkeys—52,000 pounds in each car—going back and forth across the country because there was no market. There wasn't enough static cold storage space, so they had to remain in the refrigerated cars, on the track and moving.

Driving my Plymouth home from the meeting, slowly, on those snow-rutted Omaha streets, I remember thinking that I'd been passionately involved in the frozen food business ever since being hired by Swanson in 1948. Every day anticipated some kind of discovery. World War II was just concluded, and it was a time of great optimism and adventure. Hell, I nearly tap-danced to work every day, I was that eager to get on the job.

There are similarities, I think, between the frozen food technology of the 1940s and 1950s and the digital technology of the 1980s and 1990s. The technology is far different, of course, but both industries offered rewards for creativity featuring value-added products. We received the same siren call then that men and women in the digital age heard in the 1980s and 1990s. It was seductive, compelling, and exciting.

The Monday after the February 1952 meeting, I inspected a frozen food warehouse with one of our distributors in Pittsburgh. I noticed some shipping cartons holding foil-wrapped products. The distributor said the cartons belonged to Pan Am Airlines. They had just ordered new jet passenger planes for overseas flights, featuring, for the first time, hot meals prepared on board in convection ovens. With a mental "flicker of a light bulb," I slipped a product into my overcoat pocket for the flight back to Omaha. At a follow-up meeting the fol-

lowing Saturday morning, ideas for turkey sales were conventional commodity oriented, then I showed the group the experimental consumer product I'd discovered. It was a single-compartment aluminum tray holding mashed potatoes, a slice of beef, and gravy. I had noodled with an idea on the DC-3 returning from Pittsburgh via Chicago to Omaha, drawing diagrams of three-compartmented trays, suggested to me by my negative experience in World War II with single-compartment mess gear, which resulted in stew for every meal. I suggested that we might consider a prepared "meal," because our success in 1950 with frozen chicken pies had generated public expression of wanting everything faster with more convenience.

We reviewed the pros and cons of such an undertaking. Clarke and Gilbert Swanson had been raised in the price-driven commodity business by their father and were born gamblers. They were more than willing to take risks. They also, at the time, happened to be up to their eyeballs in turkeys.

Without blinking, Clarke said, "Hell, Gil, let's do it."

Once the idea had been mutually embraced by the Swanson brothers, everyone on the small staff proceeded to move with haste—each in their own field of expertise—to create an environment for success.

Marketing was my field of expertise. When I joined Swanson in 1948 the company had scant interest and no education in product names or branded consumer packaging. In fact, except for annual calendars sent to suppliers, there had been no expenditures for advertising. I was hired by Clarke and Gilbert, with my freshly earned University of Nebraska B.S. degree in Marketing, to fill that void in management.

A brainstorming session of key management players generated significant decisions on packaging and finalized the side dishes for a turkey and gravy entrée—corn bread dressing, mashed sweet potatoes, and petite peas. Both the potatoes and petite peas would be topped with a pat of 92 score Swanson butter. At the session's conclusion, Clarke fixed cool blue eyes on me and in his warm but husky voice added, "One more thing, Gerry, this is your baby, what are you going to call it?"

I'd given the subject a lot of thought. The juxtaposition of letters, the forming of words and acronyms, had been my preoccupation since childhood. In the army in World War II my specialty had been cryptography and cryptanalysis. This revolutionary new product demanded a unique personality. My thoughts went to the most popular entertainment attraction happening in America—television. By marrying the word "television" to a frozen

Continued

TV DINNERS: A FIRSTHAND ACCOUNT (Continued)

meal, the "issue" would automatically become contemporary. The name would be easy to say and remember . . . and it was "cool."

The name I coined was "TV dinner."

In society, a perverse dichotomy was at work. Women, fresh from the liberation of working outside the home during World War II, were eager to embrace a product that permitted them to provide satisfying meals for their family and still work part-time. On the negative side, there were few home freezers, limited equipment in stores for display and storage, no equipped delivery

trucks, and little knowledge of frozen food preparation. In this environment success was questionable.

Within two years we had a line of products that included fried chicken, roast beef, and filet of haddock, each variety with appropriate side dish components. We were selling turkey dinners at a rate of 13 million a year by 1954. Then in April of 1955, Campbell Soup Company, recognizing the leading edge of a dynamic new industry, frozen heat-n-serve dinners, acquired C. A. Swanson and Sons . . . and the "TV dinner."

GERRY THOMAS

freezing was primarily used as a means of preventing food that had already begun to deteriorate from getting any worse. In the public consciousness, therefore, frozen foods were associated with poor quality and spoilage. To counter this perception, marketers had to create new perceptions. The first step was dissociation. General Foods dubbed the new products "frosted" foods and sold them under the brand name Birds Eye, claiming only the freshest of foods were frozen and then offered for sale.

Quick freezing, however, was more than a marketing gimmick. It was a revolutionary method for extending the shelf life of any number of foods. Bacteria, which multiply exponentially and hasten the spoilage of meat stored at 40°F and warmer, are slowed in lower temperatures, especially those below freezing. However, freezing as it had been practiced before Birdseye was too slow to prevent the loss of nutritious proteins, vitamins, and salts. Ice crystals that formed during slow freezing caused a chemical reaction that resulted in drier and tougher meat. Slow freezing also led to oxidation of fats, which turns meat rancid. The degree to which each of these negative effects could be reduced, as Birdseye discovered and then demonstrated, was determined by the rate at which a given food was frozen: the quicker the freezing, the less damage was done.

On March 6, 1930, in Springfield, Massachusetts, at a market owned by Joshua Davidson, Birds Eye frosted foods went on sale for the first time. Quick-frozen peas and spinach were offered along with quick-frozen raspberries, loganberries, and Oregon Bing cherries. Although the Depression precluded the immediate success of the new industry, in the coming years American food and eating habits were transformed.

The nascent frozen foods industry faced an obstacle that was exacerbated by the sour economic climate of the

1930s: how to convince retailers that frozen foods were not simply a fad and that investing in expensive freezer cabinets was a wise outlay of closely guarded funds. Davidson was one of a only a small number of grocers willing to take the risk. Birds Eye, in an effort to educate shoppers, most of whom were women, sent "lady demonstrators" to Davidson's store to explain both how the products were made and how they were to be cooked. Even those who were relieved of their skepticism about frozen foods, however, often found the foods too expensive. If they found them at all: placed in ice cream cabinets, the new products were hardly given the visibility they needed to become a familiar part of the grocery landscape.

General Foods, with a huge investment riding on the success of frozen foods, contracted with the American Radiator Company to manufacture freezer boxes that were then offered to grocers on a payment plan. Those first freezers, or "cabinets" as they are known in the industry, were derided by industry boosters and dubbed "coffin cabinets"—products were buried out of sight in their interiors. Customers chose items from an illustrated list, and then a clerk dug through the cabinet in a search for the foods. Williams, the publisher of the industry's first trade journal, pushed for self-service cabinets. His dissatisfaction with the early cabinet models, however, did not stop him from equating them with a very American symbol of progress: "What the modern highway was to the automobile . . . the cabinet would be to frozen foods" (*Frozen Foods*).

In 1939 the first precooked frozen meals appeared on the market: Birds Eye chicken fricassee and criss-cross steak. These were soon followed by beef stew, roast turkey, and creamed chicken. By 1940 the number of retail stores equipped to sell frozen foods had increased to fifteen thousand, a thirty-fold increase over seven years. But the industry had yet to enter a boom stage. Despite the rising numbers of stores outfitted with freezer cabinets, retail sales of frozen foods accounted for only approximately 10 percent of the total amount of frozen food sales. Sales were limited to urban centers, primarily on the East Coast, New York, Washington, D.C., and Philadelphia being the largest markets.

Frozen Food Comes Home

Frozen foods were marketed from the beginning as equal in flavor to and superior in convenience to fresh foods. With the new technology, seasonal foods such as strawberries, once available only during a short growing season, could be purchased anywhere and at any time during the year. A major problem for consumers, and therefore the industry, was where to put the foods once they were brought home. Freezers for the home were still considered luxuries. Refrigerators of the period generally offered enough freezing space to hold only a few trays of ice. Ice boxes, another American invention, were still quite common, as was residential ice delivery. It was not until after World War II that this situation changed.

On December 9, 1941, two days after the Japanese attacked Pearl Harbor, meatpackers in Chicago boned and froze 1 million pounds of meat and shipped it to the Pacific. In 1942 the industry was asked to set aside 35 to 60 million pounds of frozen food for the war effort. The next year, that number climbed to 70 million pounds. Throughout the war, frozen foods also made advances on the home front. According to Wilson, "Tin went to war; frozen foods stayed at home" (*Frozen Foods*). Tin quickly became in demand for use by the American military and for lend-lease programs that benefited Allied forces. Frozen foods, on the other hand, were packaged in a variety of materials, including parchment, cellophane, paper bags, cardboard, and waxed paper bags.

When rationing became necessary, the wartime Office of Price Administration (OPA) assigned point values to all foods in order to regulate prices and prevent inflation due to war-related shortages. Frozen foods were pictured along with other foods on OPA-distributed posters—free advertising, in effect, for an industry still trying to find its footing in the market. That frozen foods were taken off the rationing list a year and a half before canned goods helped encourage sales. Prepared frozen foods were not rationed at all. Dishes such as seafood à la king, flaked shrimp, and lobster and fish in milk sauce came on the market and were advertised as "heat and serve" items.

Frozen dog food was introduced as well. Department stores such as Macy's in New York installed frozen food cabinets. Specialty stores that traded only in frozen foods opened in White Plains, New York, Chicago, and the Washington, D.C., area.

Storage space increased during the war, although not in the home. The building of frozen locker plants, which housed freezer cabinets for individual family use, was facilitated by the Farm Credit Administration. The number of plants increased to approximately twelve thousand over the course of the war and in the period immediately following. Steel and other materials necessary for the construction of home freezers remained in reserve to aid the war effort. The increasing presence of frozen foods on the market, however, as well as the more relaxed rationing applied to them, helped build anticipation for a postwar period in which freezers would be available and affordable.

In September 1945, one month after the bombing of Hiroshima and Nagasaki ushered in the atomic age, the first television program featuring frozen foods was produced. Representatives of Marshall Field's, the Chicago department store that sponsored the program, demonstrated how to prepare frozen foods. American housewives, the target audience, were told that frozen foods would give them more time away from the stove. Frozen food producers were eager to give them that time; in fact, they were overeager. In 1946, 1.3 billion pounds of frozen foods were packed in an effort to meet growing demand—an almost 100 percent increase from the previous year. In their rush to market, though, many producers skimped on quality. This practice created a backlash from shoppers, who wanted to avoid inferior products. The resulting surplus of frozen food caused a drop in price as well as a drop in consumer confidence.

Despite the setback, the number of frozen foods on the market continued to grow. In the decade after World War II, items such as french fries, fish sticks, waffles, and baked goods appeared. Frozen orange juice concentrate, which had been in development for several years, commanded 25 percent of the Florida orange crop. Supermarket chains such as Safeway greatly expanded the space they devoted to freezer cabinets. By the middle of the1950s, a quarter million retail stores were selling one thousand frozen food products. Ten years later, that number had grown to nearly 2,500. The selection was not restricted to meat and potatoes. Companies such as Patio Foods in Texas marketed hot tamales, chili con carne, and enchiladas; Milady's Food Products froze and sold blintzes and potato pancakes;

Frozen Food Dispenser. *Culinary Archives & Museum at Johnson & Wales University, Providence, R.I.*

Breyers Ice Cream created the Golden Pagoda label, which offered frozen chow mein and chop suey with vegetables.

Here to Stay

Frozen food became a market mainstay. The industry experimented with package sizes and design, Eskimos and huskies giving way to pictures of the vegetables themselves. Pour and store bags were introduced to the market in 1959, allowing consumers to cook only the amount they wanted. One packaging innovation and catchy design caught the market in 1954: the Swanson TV dinner. Although complete dinners had been introduced ten years previously, sales had been sluggish. The all-American dinner made by Swanson—in a three-section aluminum tray containing turkey with gravy and dressing, peas, and sweet potatoes—radically changed the way Americans eat. The box pictured the dinner on a television screen, not only as encouragement to eat while viewing but also to tie the product to the rising star, television. The concept worked. By 1960 annual sales of frozen dinners, TV and otherwise, surpassed 200 million dollars. Williams had

been right: There were enough Americans willing to sacrifice home cooking for convenience.

The next several decades saw many emerging trends. Frozen ethnic cuisines became big business as companies such as Deep Foods in New Jersey began to offer the growing immigrant community a taste of home. Meals for weight-conscious consumers, such as Weight Watchers, Lean Cuisine, and Healthy Choice, entered the market over the years. Frozen pizza became a constant, as did rising annual sales figures. After surpassing $5 billion in 1965, sales increased tenfold over the next three decades.

In 1967 the introduction of the compact home microwave oven confirmed the future of frozen foods in the market. Frozen foods, which had always been marketed as convenience foods, were finally matched with a technology that made that claim indisputable. Williams apparently had been correct when he claimed that the frozen meal "is the perfect answer to modern living." Sales in 2001 exceeded 50 billion dollars. Even the federal government supported frozen foods. On March 6, 1984, the fifty-fourth anniversary of the first retail sales of frozen foods, President Ronald Reagan declared National Frozen Food Day, "in recognition of the significant contribution which the frozen food industry has made to the nutritional well-being of the American people."

[*See also* Birdseye, Clarence; Birds Eye Foods; Freezers and Freezing; General Foods; Grocery Stores; Historical Overview, *subentry on* World War II; Iceboxes; Meat; Microwave Ovens; Packaging; Refrigerators; Swanson.]

BIBLIOGRAPHY

Gabaccia, Donna R. *We Are What We Eat: Ethnic Food and the Making of Americans.* Cambridge, MA: Harvard University Press, 1998.

Hess, John L., and Karen Hess. *The Taste of America.* Urbana, IL, and Chicago: University of Illinois Press, 2000. Reprint of a classic critique of American cookery; contains some choice attacks on frozen foods.

Inness, Sherrie A. *Kitchen Culture in America: Popular Representations of Food, Gender, and Race.* Philadelphia: University of Pennsylvania Press, 2001. Features an excellent essay on frozen foods in postwar America.

Levenstein, Harvey. *Paradox of Plenty: A Social History of Eating in America.* Berkeley: University of California Press, 2003.

McGee, Harold. *On Food and Cooking: The Science and Lore of the Kitchen.* New York: Scribners, 1984. A concise look at the science of freezing and food preservation in general.

Shephard, Sue. *Pickled, Potted, and Canned: How the Art and Science of Food Preserving Changed the World.* New York: Simon and Schuster, 2000.

Williams, E. W. *Frozen Foods: Biography of an Industry.* Boston: Cahners, 1970.

MATT MCMILLEN

Fruit

The botanical definition of the word "fruit" is the "ripened ovary of a seed plant and its contents, including such adjacent tissues as may be inseparably connected with it" (*Merriam-Webster's New International Dictionary of the English Language*, second edition, 1934). This definition includes such forms as pea pods, maize ears, and cucumbers, as well as items generally regarded as fruits, such as apples, oranges, and strawberries. In the latter, everyday sense, "fruit" refers to fleshy, typically sweet or sour forms that are likely to be eaten raw, for dessert, or in sweet preserves. Vegetables, in contrast, are usually eaten during the principal part of a meal or in salads. However, no rigid binary taxonomy differentiates fruits from vegetables. For example, mangoes and papayas are used as vegetables when immature and as fruits when ripe. Similarly, although bananas are used as fruits, and their starchier relatives, plantains, as vegetables, there exist forms intermediate between the two. Avocados and olives are used chiefly as vegetables but often are considered, because of their form, fruits, whereas rhubarb grows as a leafy vegetable but is used and regarded as a fruit.

Statistical Overview

In 2002 there were approximately 3.4 million bearing commercial acres of major fruit crops in the United States. These plantings produced 36.6 million tons (using the fresh equivalent for processed fruits), worth $11.7 billion to farmers. Per capita consumption of fruits in 2001 (including imports) amounted to 304.8 pounds, including 125.7 pounds consumed fresh; 119 pounds (fresh equivalent) in juice form; 27.3 pounds (fresh equivalent) as wine; 17.9 pounds canned; 10.3 pounds dried; and 4.3 pounds frozen. (U.S. Department of Agriculture statistics include reported commercial plantings but exclude some minor crops, crops in states with small plantings, home gardens, and some small-scale producers, such as farm stands and farmers' markets. The figures include melons, avocados, and olives.)

Types of Fruit

Of the thousands of species of edible fruits growing wild and cultivated throughout the world, more than seventy are grown commercially or in home gardens in the United States. Fruits are generally classified by growing region as follows:

- Temperate fruits: pome fruits, such as apple, pear, and quince; stone fruits, such as apricot, cherry, peach and nectarine, and plum; small fruits and berries, such as blackberry, blueberry, currant, grape, raspberry, and strawberry; melons, such as cantaloupe and watermelon; and rhubarb
- Subtropical fruits: citrus fruits, such as grapefruit, lemon, lime, mandarin, and orange, and others, such as avocado, cactus fruit, date, fig, kiwifruit, mulberry, olive, persimmon, and pomegranate
- Tropical fruits, such as banana and pineapple

Native Fruits

Few fruits of commercial importance, including blueberries, cranberries, strawberries, and cactus pears, are indigenous to the United States. Before the arrival of European settlers, Native Americans commonly gathered raspberries, blackberries, and strawberries that grew wild in openings in the forest. They also ate many species of wild grapes, blueberries, cranberries, native persimmons, and mulberries. Native species of plums, typically smaller and more astringent than cultivated imported species, as well as crabapples and choke cherries, grew from coast to coast. Native Americans mostly gathered berries and small fruits that grew wild but did plant tree fruits around their villages. They ate fruits fresh and cooked, and added them to pemmican, which otherwise consisted of dried meat and melted fat. The Spanish brought peaches and watermelons to Mexico and Florida, and well before Jamestown was settled, Native Americans commonly planted these fruits.

Fruits in Colonial America

European settlers brought with them the fruits familiar in their homelands, including apples, pears, quinces, peaches, nectarines, apricots, cherries, and plums. There were some grafted trees in seventeenth-century American plantings, but for the most part the numerous small orchards planted in the colonies consisted of seedlings. (For most species, seedlings bear inferior fruits that are not true to the type of the parent tree.) In the beginning most of the named varieties that were grown were imported from Europe, but over time more and more varieties of native origin, such as Roxbury Russet, Rhode Island Greening, and Newtown Pippin apples, were propagated from the few superior seedlings. It is not clear exactly

Blueberries. Picking blueberries in Lehigh County, Pennsylvania, in the 1920s. *Collection of Georgia Maas*

when grafting became common, but by the early eighteenth century varieties were transported from place to place, an indication that grafting and budding were practiced. The southern colonies made more use of grafted varieties than the northern colonies. In the eighteenth century some fruits were shipped to cities such as Boston, Philadelphia, and New York, although to a limited extent. At the same time, the first nurseries for the propagation and sale of named varieties started operating.

Apples and peaches were the fruits most commonly grown in the colonies. Apples were grown chiefly for cider, which was a common drink of rich and poor, used for farmers' own consumption and for sale, trade, and export. Both apples and peaches were commonly used for distilling brandy and as fodder for livestock. Diseases specific to fruit crops followed the plants and made some fruits, such as pears, difficult to grow in the humid eastern climate. Better-adapted seedlings were then selected, and one small but exquisite pear variety, Seckel, originated in Pennsylvania. Some farmers used ovens to dry tree fruits and berries, which stored and shipped well. Settlers in the southern colonies grew oranges, lemons, and figs and used native persimmons for beer and brandy.

Expansion of Fruit Culture in the Nineteenth and Twentieth Centuries

Over the course of the nineteenth century fruit cultivation spread westward, and the number and extent of orchards and nurseries increased dramatically. By the middle of the century commercial fruit culture had become well established as cities grew and transportation facilities improved. Fresh fruit became more readily available in urban areas. Many people had previously believed that the consumption of fresh fruits led to disease, but in the nineteenth century, diet reformers preached the virtues of simple, natural, plain foods. Men of wealth and culture took a great interest in growing and appreciating fruit.

In the nineteenth century apples and peaches continued to be the leading fruits and came to be grown more commonly as grafted varieties. In several areas from the Delmarva Peninsula to the eastern shore of Lake Michigan, peach growing boomed. But crops declined as a disease called "peach yellows" devastated orchards. Commercial cultivation of native grape varieties, centered in western New York state and nearby areas, surged after the introduction of the Concord variety in the 1850s. At this time, too, cultivation of strawberry and bush fruits became more popular. In northern climates, wealthy gentlemen and a few entrepreneurial farmers built special glasshouses to grow grapes, oranges, lemons, and pineapples, which fetched fancy prices.

The great interest in fruit resulted in many books. The first devoted entirely to fruit to appear in America was William Forsyth's *A Treatise on the Culture and Management of Fruit Trees*, an English work that was published in 1802 in an edition adapted to American readers. William Coxe's *A View of the Cultivation of Fruit Trees* (1817), was the first fully American pomological book. The greatest American fruit treatise, A. J. Downing's *The Fruits and Fruit Trees of America*, first appeared in 1845 and lasted through twenty editions, the last in 1900. Charles Mason Hovey's *The Fruits of America*, issued in parts from 1852 to 1856, was a lavish work illustrated with 110 richly colored lithographs.

From the mid-nineteenth century on, American writers produced many in depth studies of single fruits, such as R. G. Pardee's *A Complete Manual for the Cultivation of the Strawberry* (1854), Thomas Field's *Pear Culture* (1859), and John Warder's *American Pomology* (1867), on apples. Works adapted for regional audiences, such as Chaucey Goodrich's *The Northern Fruit Culturist* (1849), also were popular.

Several waves of fruit mania swept farmers and amateurs. In the "multicaulis craze" that started in 1825 on the basis of cultivation of mulberry leaves as fodder for silkworms, wild speculation led many nurserymen to give up other business to grow millions of mulberry trees. At one point a single tree brought more than one hundred dollars at auction, but the market collapsed in 1839, ruining thousands of speculators and growers.

From approximately 1820 to 1870 a mania for pears raged in New England, particularly in eastern Massachusetts. Gentlemen farmers vied to produce the most luscious specimens of fine European pears and in the selection of seedling varieties. They savored the fruits in the library as an occasion for male bonding and connoisseurship, much as they played golf and smoked cigars together in later periods. Once California started shipping tons of fruit by rail car to the east, interest in the pear as a status symbol diminished.

Starting in the mid-nineteenth century, the expansion of railways and the development of the compound steamship engine made bulk cargo economical. Orange cultivation in Florida and California expanded rapidly in the decades after 1870. Lemon and grapefruit plantings followed after 1880. Setbacks such as Florida's "big freeze" of 1894–1895 taught growers where not to plant. In the last decades of the nineteenth century, stone fruit production surged in California. After 1890 apple and pear growing became an important business in Washington State.

In the late nineteenth and early twentieth centuries, the deliberate, systematic breeding of new fruit varieties became more common. The most celebrated inventor, Luther Burbank of Santa Rosa, California, developed the modern market plum. Particularly after the establishment of the Foreign Seed and Plant Introduction Section of the U.S. Department of Agriculture in 1898, plant explorers

Fruit Drier. Pneumatic fruit drier. From the Vermont Farm Machine Co. catalog, 1900.

such as David Fairchild, Walter Swingle, and Frank Meyer combed the world and brought back plants and seeds of new fruits and varieties. Some of these, such as the Fuerte avocado, Deglet Noor date, and Meyer lemon, became important commercially and in home gardens.

The early twentieth century witnessed many remarkable booms in the production of subtropical fruits, such as avocados, dates, figs, persimmons, and pomegranates, in California. Real estate promoters fueled the great date boom of 1910 to 1920, enticing settlers to buy plots of Southern Pacific Railroad lands in the Coachella desert. A 1912 pamphlet trumpeted: "Someone is going to make a lot of money during the next few years out of dates. Why not secure your share?"

The organizational, economic, and scientific bases of fruit growing evolved as it became big business. Instead of diversified plantings, farmers more often cultivated large blocks of single fruit crops. Traditional districts surrounding metropolitan markets yielded to distant growing areas with lower costs of production. Growers organized marketing cooperatives to secure better prices for their crops and negotiate railroad rates. One of the most notable cooperatives was the Southern California Fruit Exchange, founded in 1893 to market citrus, and later renamed Sunkist. Researchers at state universities and those employed by the government determined the best practices for irrigation, fertilization, pruning, and combating insect pests. Farmers joined state pomological societies to share their experiences and concerns.

To ship fruit long distances, large growers and cooperatives established special fruit packing houses. Specialized machinery and improved techniques were developed to wash, sort, and package fruit crops. Many fruits were packed in wooden lug boxes in standard sizes. Often some or all of the fruits were wrapped in tissue paper to protect them and to keep mold from spreading from a few infected fruits to the entire lot. In the 1880s growers started affixing brightly colored printed paper labels to the ends of the rectangular wooden crates to identify and to advertise a perishable product for customers who lived thousands of miles away.

Over the course of the nineteenth century, as the cost of containers dropped, fruit canning became common in American homes. Commercial canning for urban populations surged when California became a great fruit-growing state in the late nineteenth and early twentieth centuries, because a canned harvest could be easily shipped and marketed year-round. For similar reasons, consumption of dried fruits such as prunes, peaches, and apricots increased dramatically. The commercial sale of frozen fruit, including frozen juice concentrate, however, became popular only in the mid-twentieth century, as processing techniques advanced and consumers bought freezers. As a result of the many innovations, fruit had shifted from being a relative rarity and luxury in the mid-nineteenth-century to being a staple of the American diet in the mid-twentieth century.

Trends in Modern Fruit Production and Marketing

In the twentieth century, several factors combined to greatly extend the season of fresh fruits, so that many came to be available year-round. For example, fresh peaches once were sold in the northeast from late July to October, but the harvest from California and the southeast arrives starting in April or early May, whereas imports from the southern hemisphere fill the market from November to April. Fruit breeders have devised early- and late-maturing varieties that avoid the seasonal peak in volume usually accompanied by low prices and thus bring better returns for farmers. Growers have planted in the earliest- and latest-maturing districts and used farming practices such as girdling grapevines to manipulate maturity. In addition, handlers have perfected techniques of storing fruit under modified atmospheric conditions (low oxygen and high carbon dioxide), which slows respiratory metabolism, allowing some fruits, such as apples, to be held for a year or more.

Since the mid-1970s, while overall per capita consumption of fruit held steady, fresh fruit consumption increased 23 percent, from 102 pounds annually in 1976 to 125.7 pounds in 2001. During the same period, consumption of both canned and dried fruits declined 23 percent. Educated and affluent consumers especially became more interested in a healthful, varied diet, and producers responded by supplying larger quantities and a greater diversity of fresh fruits. Supermarket produce sections, which once typically carried a few varieties of apples, offer a dozen choices or more. Immigration from non-European countries, such as China, India, and Mexico, spurred production and import of exotic fruits such as lychee, pummelo and mamey sapote.

In the 1980s and 1990s technology played an increasing role in fruit distribution and marketing. "Product look up" (PLU) stickers, affixed at the packing house to many fruits, enabled checkout clerks to speedily and accurately identify fruits and varieties. Produce marketers responded to consumers' demand for convenience by offering "ready-to-eat" fresh-cut fruits, such as sliced melon and pineapple, and by packaging fruits such as berries and plums in plastic containers.

In the 1990s and early 2000s, genetically engineered crops such as cotton and soybeans claimed an increasing share of world production, generating considerable controversy over their safety. Few genetically engineered fruits have been introduced or grown in the United States, the most significant being Rainbow papaya, devised for protection against the ringspot virus, which had devastated the Hawaiian papaya industry.

Since 2000 several facilities using electron-beam radiation to treat produce have started operating in the United States, and more are being constructed abroad. This process kills insect pests that would otherwise disallow the distribution of fruits such as rambutan from Hawaii and citrus from quarantined areas of California. Although scientists in favor of irradiation maintain that it does not harm fruit quality or human health, some advocates of organic agriculture claim that the process produces molecules with health-damaging free radicals.

Some farmers and consumers have responded to the industrialization of fruit production by circumventing conventional commercial pathways. Small farmers, who often cannot compete economically with large-scale growers, have sought to market their fruit directly to consumers through farm stands and farmers' markets, which have multiplied in recent decades. Production of organically grown fruit, driven by consumer concern about pesticide use and the sustainability of agricultural practices, has surged to the point that many commercial produce companies have established large organic plantings.

Factors Affecting Fruit Quality

From the standpoint of the consumer, the primary elements of fruit quality are flavor and texture. Flavor, the most complex trait, is composed of sweetness, sourness, astringency, and aroma. The factors that affect fruit quality may be considered in five categories: genetics, environment, farming practices, harvest maturity, and postharvest handling. These factors have changed markedly over the last century.

The genetic heritage of a fruit, including its variety and the rootstock on which it is grown, strongly influences its eating quality. Through the nineteenth century, most new varieties discovered by growers were the results of chance pollination and mutation. Later, as fruit breeders deliberately produced thousands of crosses and systematically selected for considerations such as size, color, yield, season, resistance to disease, and other horticultural characteristics, they inadvertently bred out flavor by not selecting for it. For example, fruit breeders have selected peach and nectarine varieties for full red skin coloration, considered an attractive commercial characteristic, although this trait appears to be genetically linked to mediocre flavor. Moreover, when a fruit is intensely flavored, such as a Muscat grape, it risks offending a portion of potential buyers, a deadly offense in the modern fruit market, which seeks to appeal to the lowest common denominator by favoring bland, neutral-flavored seedless grapes. It is by no means the case, however, that heirloom varieties (types more than fifty or seventy-five years old) are invariably superior. In some instances the old varieties were good for their day, but better varieties have been developed. In other cases old varieties may have become infected by viruses, or the authentic variety may have been lost or confused over the years with mediocre seedling progeny.

The influence of environment includes the growing area, soil, water, climate, and weather for individual seasons and can be quite pronounced. For example, navel oranges thrive in the Mediterranean climate of the interior valleys of southern and central California, where hot, dry summers add sweetness, and cool winters deepen color and retain adequate acidity. By comparison, Florida-grown navel oranges are larger, paler, and thinner skinned and have juicier but relatively insipid pulp.

Many fruits flourish in areas that humans also enjoy. Urbanization has pushed commercial prune, apricot, and cherry orchards out of the Santa Clara valley in California (also known as Silicon Valley)—where warm summer days and cool nights help many stone fruit varieties to mature slowly and develop rich, balanced flavor—and into a less ideal district, the Central Valley, which is farther inland, where land is cheaper.

Farming practices include irrigation, pruning, and fertilization. In arid climates, dry-farmed fruits, grown without irrigation, are smaller but have richer, more concentrated flavor than those from irrigated orchards. Because irrigated farms more dependably bear larger quantities of larger fruits, they are more profitable. Since the mid-twentieth century farms that are not irrigated have faded from commercial production in the West.

Most tree fruits such as apples and cherries traditionally were grown as standard-sized trees, reaching forty feet or more in height. Using dwarfing rootstock and pruning, farmers increasingly have established higher density plantings of smaller trees to increase production and lower picking costs. Proper pruning maximizes exposure to sunlight, which in general leads to a higher content of soluble solids, a measure of sweetness in fruits. In addition to pruning, thinning of fruit trees determines crop load and fruit size, which can influence flavor.

Proper fertilization is essential for optimal fruit production and quality. For some crops, such as apples and pears, too much nitrogen causes trees to become overly vigorous and put all their energy into foliage, lowering the amount of soluble solids in the fruits. Proponents of organic growing practices maintain that soil rich in organic matter and nutrients (achieved by using natural ground cover, compost, and manure) results in fruit with superior flavor.

Fruits are classified according to respiratory and ripening patterns. Climacteric fruits, such as bananas and avocados, can ripen off the tree if picked when they are mature. Nonclimacteric fruits, such as berries and citrus, must be picked ripe, because they do not ripen after harvest. Fruits from both categories taste best when picked at the optimal stage of maturity, but farmers often harvest early to earn the highest prices—when their crops are hard, look good, and ship and store well. What makes sense for individual farmers in the short run, however, can erode consumer interest in the long term as buyers avoid repeat purchases of mediocre fruit. Only some fruits (such as Honey tangerines from Florida) are subject to regulations that enforce meaningful maturity standards. Grades of fruit, such as fancy and choice, typically reflect mostly cosmetic standards, which have little relation to internal fruit quality. From a structural perspective, the modern fruit market inadequately rewards growers who take the trouble to produce superior fruit. Marketers of stone fruit have attempted to address this issue by offering a tree-ripe grade, but in general most growers harvest fruit only as good as it has to be to meet commercial acceptance.

In the United States, where most fruits are shipped long distances to market and stored for prolonged periods, methods developed through decades of research and experience have enabled handlers to greatly extend the season and shelf life of fruits. Many fruits are cooled by cold water or air immediately after harvest to remove field heat; are washed, waxed, and sprayed with fungicides; are packed in cartons that protect them from injury during transport; and are kept in cold storage or controlled atmospheric conditions. Each of these steps reduces spoilage and helps ensure a marketable product. These processes, although necessary in produce commerce, sometimes have negative effects. An orange at the end of the packing line loses some of its flavor compared with fruit fresh off the tree, although it is difficult to pinpoint the factor responsible. Retailers often store peaches and nectarines at the wrong temperature, and the result is a mealy, woolly texture. Year-old apples lose their crunch, and they taste of storage. The compromises of commerce that make fruit readily available often degrade its quality.

[See also Apples; Apricots; Avocados; Bananas; Batidos; Biotechnology; Blackberries; Blueberries; Cactus; California; Canning and Bottling; Cherries; Cider; Citrus; Coconuts; Cooperatives; Cranberries; Currants; Dates; Farmers' Markets; Figs; Food Safety; Fruit Juices; Fruit Wines; Grapes; Irradiation; Kiwis; Melons; Mulberries; Nuts; Olives; Organic Food; Organic Gardening; Peaches and Nectarines; Pears; Persimmons; Pineapples; Plums; Pomegranates; Pummelo; Quince; Raspberries; Rhubarb; Strawberries; Tomatoes; Transportation of Food; Vegetables; Watermelons.]

BIBLIOGRAPHY

Bailey, Liberty Hyde. *Sketch of the Evolution of Our Native Fruits.* 2nd ed. New York: Macmillan, 1906.

Coxe, William. *A View of the Cultivation of Fruit Trees, and the Management of Orchards and Cider.* Philadelphia: Carey, 1817.

Downing, Andrew Jackson. *The Fruits and Fruit-Trees of America.* 2nd ed., revised and corrected by Charles Downing. New York: Wiley, 1869.

Hatch, Peter J. *The Fruits and Fruit Trees of Monticello.* Charlottesville: University Press of Virginia, 1998.

Hedrick, Ulysses Prentiss. *Cyclopedia of Hardy Fruits.* New York: Macmillan, 1922.

Hedrick, Ulysses Prentiss. *A History of Horticulture in America to 1860, with an Addendum of Books Published from 1861–1920.* Portland, OR: Timber, 1988.

Knee, Michael, ed. *Fruit Quality and Its Biological Basis.* Boca Raton, FL: CRC, 2002.

Poole, Hester M. *Fruits, and How to Use Them.* New York: Fowler and Wells, 1890.

Stoll, Steven. *The Fruits of Natural Advantage.* Berkeley: University of California Press, 1998.

Upshall, W. H., ed. *History of Fruit Growing and Handling in United States of America and Canada 1860–1972.* University Park, PA: American Pomological Society, 1976.

Waters, Alice. *Chez Panisse Fruit.* New York: HarperCollins, 2002.

Wickson, Edward J. *The California Fruits and How to Grow Them.* 10th ed. San Francisco: Pacific Rural, 1926.

DAVID KARP

Fruit Juices

Old World fruits were introduced in America by European settlers in the sixteenth and seventeenth centuries. The Spanish introduced citrus trees, such as lemons, limes, and oranges, into Florida and the Caribbean, and the fruits were regularly exported to British North America. The English, French, and German colonists introduced other fruits, including apples, cherries, plums, and pears. Native fruits, such as elderberries, cranberries, and huckleberries, rounded out the early American fruit basket. In addition to being eaten fresh, these fruits were pressed or squeezed into juice. Apples, lemons, and oranges were the main juice fruits, but currants, grapes, peaches, pineapples, plums, raspberries, and strawberries also were used for juice. Beginning in the nineteenth century, the most common way of serving fruit juice was with added sugar and water in the form of "ades," such as appleade, lemonade, orangeade, and strawberryade. These juices were sometimes served ice-cold and called "sherbet." For a lighter drink, a few spoonfuls of these sweetened juices were stirred into cold water. By the nineteenth century, a wide range of fruit juices was used to flavor ice cream and soda fountain drinks.

Fruit juices also were cooked with a large quantity of sugar and preserved for future use, mainly for use in cooking and baking. In addition, juices were fermented into flavorful vinegars, and they were used in alcoholic and temperance beverages, including shrubs, which were composed of fruit juice plus spirits or vinegar. Most fruit juices were fermented to produce alcoholic beverages such as hard cider, perry (made from pears), wine, brandy, including applejack, and cordials.

In the home, fruit was juiced by hand until 1930, when the first commercial juicing machine was marketed by Norman Walker, who encouraged a diet of raw food and juices. Juicing became popular in America during the 1970s. Smoothies, thick drinks consisting of fresh fruit blended with milk, yogurt, or ice cream, became popular in the 1980s. Juice bars, which frequently serve smoothies, were launched in the early 1990s in health food stores and quickly evolved into major independent businesses.

The first nonalcoholic fruit juice sold commercially was made from grapes. In 1869 Thomas Bramwell Welch of Vineland, New Jersey, a Methodist minister who strongly favored temperance, manufactured what he called "unfermented wine" intended for sacramental use. Welch was unsuccessful in his attempt to replace wine in church services, and he stopped making the juice in

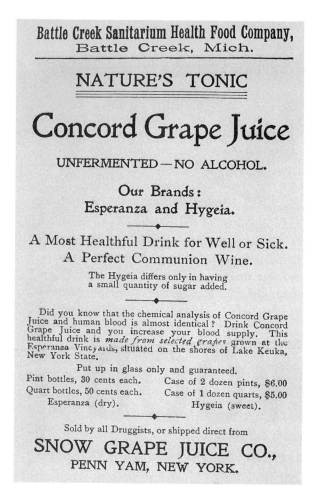

Juice Advertisment. From *American Kitchen.*

1873. His son Charles Welch revived the idea two years later, marketing Welch's Grape Juice as a temperance beverage with the slogan "The lips that touch Welch's are all that touch mine." It was the beginning of the pasteurized fruit juice industry in America. Welch Foods has been bottling, canning, and freezing juice and selling jelly and other related products ever since.

When the citrus industry was launched in Florida and California in the 1880s, growers canned and bottled fruit juice in addition to selling the fresh fruit, but sales of juice were limited. In 1907 California citrus growers banded together in a cooperative called the California Fruit Growers Exchange, which later sold its products under the brand name Sunkist. In 1920 the cooperative began to advertise that its products contained vitamins (first identified in the previous decade), particularly emphasizing vitamin C. Three years later, the co-op distributed 100 million promotional brochures. Florida growers followed Sunkist's lead, emphasizing the therapeutic

CONCENTRATED ORANGE JUICE

Oranges must ripen on the tree, between December and June, before they can be picked. In Florida, 98 percent of all oranges are harvested by hand after testing determines that the ratio of Brix (soluble sugar content) to acidity is just right. The ripe oranges are transported to a processing plant, washed, and graded and the juice is extracted. Next the peel, pulp, and seeds are removed. The juice can be pasteurized for "not from concentrate" products or it can go into vacuum evaporators, where most of the water is removed. The concentrated orange juice is then chilled and frozen. It is packaged into cans for sale in supermarkets or shipped by tanker truck to dairies, to be reconstituted with fresh water and packaged into cardboard cartons, glass bottles, or plastic jugs.

John M. Fox, the founder and president of the Minute Maid Company, is credited with developing frozen orange juice concentrate in the 1940s. He used a technique he had seen demonstrated during World War II to dehydrate penicillin and blood plasma. Fox intended to make a soluble orange juice powder but it had a bad taste. However, by adding water to the reduced concentrate, the juice had a fresh-squeezed taste. An advertising agency in Boston, the city famous for its minutemen, created the name "Minute Maid," to emphasize the product's convenience and ease of preparation. The company was sold to Coca-Cola in 1960.

BIBLIOGRAPHY

Encyclopedia of Consumer Brands. Vol. 1, *Consumable Products.* Detroit: St. James Press, 1994.

JOSEPH M. CARLIN

qualities of lemons and oranges. The sales of fruit juice increased threefold within two decades, and fruit juice became a breakfast mainstay. In addition, fruit juices, especially apple juice, became an important component of babies' diets and children's lunches.

Frozen juices were a new addition to the fruit juice market, first marketed during the 1930s. During World War II scientists developed a process for making powdered orange juice. After the war, the powdered juice concentrate was marketed by Florida Foods Corporation. It was not greatly successful, but then the company launched a new line of frozen juice under the brand name Minute Maid, and sales skyrocketed. The company changed its name to the Minute Maid Company. Minute Maid was acquired by the Coca-Cola Company in 1960. Canned fruit juices are sold in vending machines and stores along with soda pop.

[*See also* Applejack; Brandy; Cider; Citrus; Fruit; Fruit Wines; Juice Bars; Juicers.]

BIBLIOGRAPHY

Bitting, A. W. *Appertizing or the Art of Canning.* San Francisco: Trade Pressroom, 1937.
Chazanof, William. *Welch's Grape Juice: From Corporation to Co-Operative.* Syracuse, NY: Syracuse University Press, 1977.
Merlo, Catherine. *Heritage of Gold: The First 100 Years of the Sunkist Growers, Inc., 1893–1993.* Los Angeles: Sunkist Growers, n.d.

ANDREW F. SMITH

Fruit Wines

Wines made from the fermented juice of any fruit except grapes are known as fruit wines. Berry, citrus, melon, tree fruits (apple, cherry, peach, pear, and plum), and dried fruit such as raisins are used in home recipes and at commercial wineries throughout America to make wine. Most fruit requires the addition of sugar, water, acid, and yeast nutrients to trigger the fermentation process and achieve the alcohol level of wine, between 7 percent and 15 percent by volume. Yeast converts sugar to alcohol, and more sugar may be added for sweetness.

Grapes do not generally require these additions as they are naturally high in sugar, water, bacteria-resistant tartaric acids and yeast. Some producers of grape wine add sweeteners, fruit flavoring, and sometimes carbonation to make what are commonly called pop wines. Such products, designed to appeal to young, casual wine drinkers or those seeking sweeter tastes, are not true fruit wines in the strictest sense.

Since most edible fruits have the potential to ferment without human intervention, winelike fruit beverages have a global history dating back to humanity's earliest origins. Peoples throughout Africa, Asia, Europe, the Americas and the world's archipelagoes are all known to have made wines from indigenous fruits historically, and many still do so. Ancient Egyptian pomegranate wines and Mesopotamian date wines are among the earliest documented examples. Many European colonists and pioneers who settled what is today the United States had come from northern regions where grapes were not primary crops, so they were accustomed to making fermented concoctions from apples, wild berries, and grains.

Prior to mass production of American consumer goods, homemade fruit wine was an integral part of American cookery, like canning and preserving foodstuffs to last beyond a harvest. As in cooking, recipes and techniques varied greatly, but there were key requirements: crushed fruit, sugar, gallons of water (usually boiled), active yeast components, clean utensils to avoid contamination, good ventilation, large, airtight storage vessels, and space to store them at appropriate temperatures. In addition, time and diligence were needed to carry out the multistep winemaking process: several days for flavor extraction, fermentation and storage transfer; siphoning, over the course of a few weeks; and weeks or months after bottling and corking for the wine to develop.

Before Prohibition and after its repeal, fruit wines were sold at general stores in small towns throughout America, notably in rural areas and in the South. During Prohibition, much fruit wine was made in American homes, due in large part to clauses in federal law that allowed families to make up to two hundred gallons per year of fruit "juice" (that sometimes fermented) for personal use. As efficient winemaking equipment was often unavailable or expensive, this practice continued on many American farms and fruit orchids, further underlining the strong association of fruit wines with country living.

By the end of the twentieth century, the making of fruit wines had become an American hobby supported by numerous societies and websites linking enthusiasts to information and technological advances that foster quality winemaking. Nevertheless, most fruit wine in the United States is produced and sold at wineries, generally using locally grown fruit. Many wineries cooperate with local tourist enterprises to promote seasonal fruit wines at county harvest festivals. Outside of this context, one of the most popular fruit wines consumed in the United States is plum wine, available at many Japanese restaurants and some retail liquor stores.

[*See also* Fermentation; Fruit; Fruit Juices; Wine, *subentry* Historical Survey; Wineries; Yeast.]

BIBLIOGRAPHY

Behind the Label: Introducing Wines and Spirits and Associated Beverages. 2nd ed. London: Wine and Spirit Education Trust, 2002.

Darden, Norma Jean, and Carole Darden. *Spoonbread and Strawberry Wine: Recipes and Reminiscences of a Family.* New York: Doubleday, 1994.

McGovern, Patrick E. *Ancient Wine: The Search for the Origins of Viniculture.* Princeton, NJ: Princeton University Press, 2003.

Vargas, Patty, and Rich Gulling. *Country Wines: Making and Using Wines from Herbs, Fruits, Flowers and More.* Pownal, VT: Storey Communications, 1992.

TONYA HOPKINS

Frying Baskets

While deep-frying foods, cooks need a safe way to remove cooked food from dangerously hot fat. With a frying basket, a cook lowers cut-up food into the fat all at once and then removes it as soon as cooking is complete. In the late 1800s paired, close-fitting baskets—called bird's-nest baskets—were used for frying various sizes of "nests" of cooked noodles or rice that were filled with other foods before being served. Large deep-fryer sets comprised a stamped-iron kettle and a high, fixed hoop from which was hung a removable wire or perforated basket. These devices were commonly used for frying large batches of foods such as crullers, doughnuts, and potatoes.

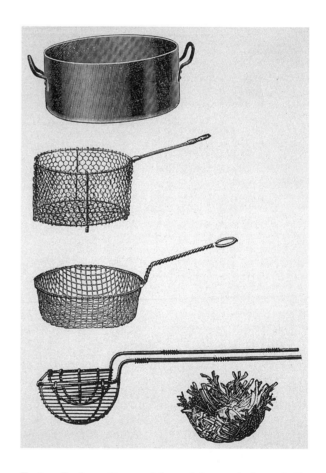

Frying Baskets. Imported (*second from top*), domestically produced (*middle*), and birds' nest frying baskets. From the Duparquet, Huot, & Moneuse Co. catalog (Boston, 1915), p. 181.

[*See also* Crullers; Doughnut-Making Tools; Doughnuts; Frying Pans, Skillets, and Spiders; Potato-Cooking Tools.]

BIBLIOGRAPHY

Franklin, Linda Campbell. *300 Years of Kitchen Collectibles*. 5th. ed. Iola, WI: Krause, 2003.

LINDA CAMPBELL FRANKLIN

Frying Pans, Skillets, and Spiders

The first colonists in America brought with them and used frying pans and skillets developed over centuries of forging and casting in Europe. Early American foundries, beginning in 1646 with the Saugus Mill in Massachusetts, produced similar designs—a shallow pan with a long handle and three legs, designed for perching above fireplace embers. Some, lacking legs, worked on high cooking trivets. The variant term "spider," whimsically derived from the pan's long handle, body, and legs, originated in early New England and spread regionally after 1800. The related term "skillet" seems to have been less precise—sometimes referring to a deeper, three-legged, long-handled saucepan called, at the time, a "posnet," and sometimes to the frying pan.

By the middle of the nineteenth century, industry had adapted to the stovetop, manufacturing legless frying pans with shorter handles of wood or metal. By the late 1800s sheet-iron and cast-iron pans, called "skillets," "fry pans," "frying pans," "spiders," and "deep fryers,"

Spider. The spider was a basic hearth-cooking tool in the eighteenth century. *Collection of Alice Ross*

were being made with new finishes; some pans were manufactured of cast aluminum to reduce weight. Many incorporated pouring lips and secondary tab handles, heat rings, grease moats, and self-basting domed lids, often available in diameters from 4½ inches to more than 16 inches. Cheaply made thin skillets, in use by the 1900s, were popular despite poor quality. Twentieth century advances included electric frying pans in the 1950s and coatings of Teflon, to prevent food from sticking to the pan, in the 1960s.

[*See also* Cooking Techniques; Kettles; Pots and Pans.]

BIBLIOGRAPHY

Franklin, Linda Campbell. *Three Hundred Years of Kitchen Collectibles*. 5th ed. Iola, WI: Krause, 2003.
Smith, David G., and Chuck Wafford. *The Book of Griswold and Wagner*. 2nd ed. Atglen, PA: Schiffer, 2000.

ALICE ROSS AND LINDA CAMPBELL FRANKLIN

Fudge

Fudge, typically chocolate but commonly marketed in dozens of flavors, is a candy made by boiling a sugar mixture until it makes a soft ball when dropped into ice water (or reaches 234°F to 238°F at sea level), then stirring to make a soft candy. Soft candy was known as fondant in classical French confectionery, but fondant is mostly used as a soft center for candies dipped in chocolate or a harder candy mixture. In America, early fudge was strongly associated with the "seven sisters" women's colleges of the 1890s. Students at the colleges spread the popularity of fudge by bringing it to their homes. The name probably developed in 1888 at Vassar College, in Poughkeepsie, New York, and refers to an expression young women might have used instead of swearing. Fudge was something that homesick girls at school could make in their dormitories late at night using a spirit lamp borrowed from the chemistry laboratory, a gaslight, or a chafing dish—a popular gadget at the time. When Fannie Farmer recorded a fudge recipe in 1906, it was not in her practical *Boston Cooking-School Cook Book* but in her more casual book, *Chafing Dish Possibilities*.

The first published recipe for "fudges" (for approximately ten years, one square was "a fudge" and a plateful were "fudges") may have been that in the 1893 cookbook produced by the women's building at the Columbian Exposition in Chicago. A 1908 pamphlet published by

Walter Baker and Company, the chocolate maker, contained recipes for eight kinds of fudge, including Vassar fudge, Smith College fudge, and Wellesley marshmallow fudge, contributed by Janet McKenzie Hill.

Soft candies in general have a documented existence well before 1888, and brown-sugar fudge in particular has a clear line of descent from Mexican sweets perhaps a century older or more. By the 1890s, brown-sugar fudge was known to American college women as penuchi, penuche, ponouche, penucio, and panocha. The term "panocha" was used as early as 1870 in a federal report describing a sweet distributed on Indian reservations to the detriment of the health of the Indians. *Panocha* (or *panucho*) was Mexican-border Spanish for a round corn pancake or johnnycake, and by analogy the name was applied to a round cake of soft sugar candy with nuts. Such candy is still made in Mexico and is known as *cajeta* (because it is packed in small boxes) or *palenqueta* (because it naturally spreads out like a plaque). The same candy is called a praline in New Orleans, which was under Spanish government for most of the late eighteenth century. (The original French pralines are nuts with a sugar coating.) Any recipe for New Orleans pralines can be used to make fudge, and vice versa. The main difference is that brown-sugar fudge is poured into pans and cut into squares, whereas New Orleans pralines are poured onto marble slabs and are more or less round.

Many nineteenth-century recipes for caramels can be used to make fudge, because instructions are unclear about how long to boil the candy. By the 1870s, there were American recipes for "soft candy" that specified cooking to the soft-ball stage, stirring the candy as it cooled to make it smoother, or using a combination of the two techniques. A recipe for "soft candy" that can be made by children appeared in the 1878 cookbook *Six Little Cooks*.

Early fudge was thought to be an easy candy to make, because it required relatively less boiling than hard candies and toffee. Being softer than caramels, fudge was easier to eat. But preparation of fudge can be tricky, especially without an accurate thermometer. Results are affected by both weather and altitude. (Boiling temperature also varies by altitude.) Sometimes fudge does not stiffen, and sometimes it is granular.

By the 1900s, fudge was a staple in candy stores across America, especially at summer resorts in New England and on Mackinac Island, Michigan, where it became a celebrated local specialty. Divinity, which is made by a technique that combines those for nougat,

fudge, and Italian meringue (marshmallows), became popular around the same time. There was a recipe for divinity in the *New York Times* by 1907, and this confection became more popular in the southern states. A number of nontraditional soft candies not based on boiling sugar are sometimes called fudge. Among them are the quick or no-cook fudges that were developed in the 1950s (including the recipe widely attributed to Mamie Eisenhower), mashed-potato candy, peanut butter candy, and freezer frosting fudge. Early flavors other than chocolate and brown sugar were maple sugar, vanilla, butterscotch, candied fruit, coconut, and fudge layered in two flavors and colors. More recent additions are coffee, peanuts, various fruits such as strawberries, and liquor flavorings.

[*See also* Candy Bars and Candy; Chafing Dish; Chocolate; Farmer, Fannie; Mexican American Food; Sugar.]

BIBLIOGRAPHY

Bening, Lee Edwards. *Oh, Fudge: A Celebration of America's Favorite Candy*. New York: Henry Holt, 1990. A book-length study with three hundred careful recipes, a total reached by including nonfudge candies such as nougat, fondant, taffy, and marshmallows.

Theophano, Janet. *Eat My Words: Reading Women's Lives through the Cookbooks They Wrote*. New York: Palgrave, 2002. Contains an 1892 letter between the Philadelphia suffragists Anna Shaw and Jane Campbell that describes a recipe for "penucio."

MARK H. ZANGER

Fund-Raisers

At the time of European settlement in the New World, the male-driven church and state together managed the governmental, economic, and social aspects of life. Church funds were gathered by a system of levies and donations. People in need, lacking other resources, became the responsibility of the community. The nineteenth century generally disrupted this tradition. As part of the shift to a more secular, mercantile, and urban culture in the north, male involvement was replaced by the fund-raising of urban, middle-class, home-centered women. With discretionary time available for local church, charitable, and reform work, women used traditional cookery skills to raise funds for the church—missionary support and building maintenance—and for addressing such community concerns as education, clean water, prison, housing reform, and the needs of the poor. Although the century idealized and emphasized women's private role, the public, philanthropic contributions of women were usually applauded as well. Many women's projects eventually evolved into national charities such as the Red Cross.

A community would sometimes raise a minister's salary by means of the quarterly donation party. The entire congregation gathered in the large home of one of its wealthier members to enjoy an evening of conviviality. Women prepared and donated their best dishes, counting on the resulting good spirits to loosen purse strings and produce a significant sum. During the Civil War various social gatherings, among them "oyster suppers," raised large sums for soldiers and hospitals. Such efforts inspired the United States Sanitary Commission, which started in New York in 1861. This large organization, with its many branches, ran hospitals and soup kitchens with funds raised at ambitious fairs where the donated items on sale included food.

The late nineteenth century was a time of ice cream socials, festivals, fairs, and complex church suppers. At first donated foods were brought from home, but, as churches built their own kitchens, menus expanded. Some churchwomen raised funds by preparing conference banquets. As these events became increasingly successful financially and socially, they were undertaken by secular groups such as the Grange, an organization of farm families. These food-based fund-raisers are still important social events in local communities nationwide, offering fine traditional ethnic and regional cuisines.

Charity cookbooks served a similar function. Instituted at Sanitary Fairs to raise funds for the victims of the Civil War, they became one of the more common philanthropic strategies across the country. Although most of them were compiled by church groups, they were published also for secular charitable causes such as the temperance movement, suffrage, hospitals, and schools. They are still going strong.

The Woman's Exchange movement provided another way of using food to raise money, this one through a self-help system for middle-class women in need of support. Begun in 1832, the exchanges sold their handmade products anonymously (protecting their donors from embarrassment), keeping only a small percentage to cover their overhead. Some exchanges developed restaurants and raised funds with fashionable and popular meals; others distributed catalogs of nonperishable foods nationwide, and they, too, compiled cookbooks. They remained viable well into the twentieth century.

At the turn of the twenty-first century the gender lines had blurred and the practice of fund-raising with food had become a useful tool universally. Community fund-raisers, cookbooks, and even some exchanges survived. The most common examples of the practice were Girl Scout Cookies, pancake breakfasts, clambakes, bake sales, raffled cooking lessons and dinners, restaurant donations, and political banquets.

[*See also* Cookbooks and Manuscripts, *subentry on* Community Cookbooks; Gender Roles; Settlement Houses.]

BIBLIOGRAPHY

Burdett-Coutts, Baroness Angela Georgina, ed. *Woman's Mission: a Series of Congress Papers on the Philanthropic Work of Women, by Eminent Writers.* Chicago International Exhibition of Women's Work. London: Low Marston, 1893. Facsimile edition, Cheshire, UK: Portrayer, 2002.

Ross, Alice. "Ella Smith's Unfinished Community Cookbook: A Social History of Women and Work in Smithtown, New York 1884–1922." In *Recipes for Reading: Community Cookbooks, Stories, Histories,* edited by Anne L Bower. Amherst: University of Massachusetts Press, 1997.

Sander, Kathleen Waters. *The Business of Charity: The Woman's Exchange Movement, 1832–1900.* Chicago: University of Illinois Press, 1998.

ALICE ROSS

Funeral Food

In the American South, people used to say that a man's standing in the community could be judged by the number of plates his widow had to return after his funeral. The bounty of foods spread out for mourners in the South is legendary, fondly chronicled in novels and short stories. As the folk artist Kate Campbell sang in "Funeral Food," in 1998, "We sure eat good when someone dies." Fried chicken, baked ham, potato salad, deviled eggs, rolls, pound cake, and endless pies filled the home, brought by friends, family, and neighbors.

Funeral food is more than a southern ritual. All over America, funeral food is both comforting and practical, giving mourners something to do, surrounding the bereaved with proof that life goes on, and relieving the family of the burden of feeding guests. In many regions, the best-known funeral foods are casseroles—familiar, practical, and transportable. Utah is known for "funeral potatoes," a mixture of hash browns, sour cream, and cream soup that is topped with a cornflake crust. The dish is so common that it was one of the images used on pins for the 2002 Winter Olympics in Salt Lake City.

In the early twenty-first century, the fried chicken may be takeout and the ham is spiral cut, but the impulse to accompany mourning with food is the same as it always has been. That funeral food is less likely to come from busy neighbors and more often from restaurants and caterers is, in a sense, a return to old ways. Providing food and edible mementos at funerals has always been a business. In the eighteenth and nineteenth centuries, funeral tokens, particularly funeral biscuits, were used in many communities. Like the cake slices given to departing wedding guests, funeral biscuits stamped with symbolic images were given as tokens or were served after the funeral, often with wine. William Woys Weaver, in his book *America Eats: Edible Forms of Folk Arts* (1989), records many designs, including hearts, cherubs, and hourglasses. Providing food for mourners who traveled long distances was such a burden that it was sometimes accounted for in eighteenth- and nineteenth-century estate inventories. In the North Carolina Archives in Raleigh, the historian James Jordan III found the following in the 1779 inventory of the estate of Timothy Clear, a New Bern merchant: "(In the trunks) No. 3 a case with 10 bottles three of them full of wine—expended at his funeral . . . No. 6 one iron-bound case, key found, contains 11 bottles, 6 full wine . . . used at his funeral . . . one half of one keg used . . . ditto."

Not all funeral foods have disappeared. Funeral pie is still found in Amish and Pennsylvania Dutch communities. According to some sources, the simple filling of raisins and sugar is made from inexpensive staples a homemaker would have had available at any time of the year. However, some historians note that before the twentieth century, raisins had to be seeded. Going to the trouble to make a raisin-baked pie showed how much the cook valued the deceased. The following are examples of rituals that continue in some form among ethnic groups in the United States.

Jewish

Se'udat havra'ah (there are various spellings), the Jewish meal of condolence, is loving and practical. The first meal served to the bereaved after the burial, *se'udat havra'ah* is prepared by friends or relatives from their own food. This practice can be seen as life-giving: Because the foods are prepared by others, mourners are obligated to eat. Many of the foods served are symbolic. Round foods are often used, to signify the continuance of life. Commonly used foods are round breads, such as challah, and lentils, used both for their round shape and because of a tradition that lentils were prepared by Isaac after he heard of the death of his father, Abraham. Hard-boiled eggs are served without salt. The eggs symbolize the cycle of life, and the lack of salt may symbolize the end of tears. Salt on the Passover seder table represents the tears of Hebrew slaves.

Mexican

Mexican funerals may include treasured foods, such as mole and tamales, but it is the annual commemoration of those who have died that is best known. In Mexico *Dias de las Muertos* (Days of the Dead) is a week-long community event leading up to All Souls Day, November 2. Because the dead are often returned to Mexico for burial, it is a much smaller observance in the United States. In communities with small or developing Mexican communities, Day of the Dead may be noted only as a folk festival. The traditional bread, *pan de muertos*, can be found in cities with large enough Mexican populations to support traditional bakeries. Lightly sweet and covered with sugar, the bread is made in various shapes, including bodies decorated with lumps of dough that represent the skeleton and round shapes that represent the soul.

Italian

Italians mark All Souls Day with special cookies. Called *fave dei morti* (beans of the dead) and *osso dei morti* (bones of the dead), these are very hard, dry cookies, often containing chunks of almonds and shaped to resemble beans or bones. The beans have various meanings. Some stories connect them to immortality and the underworld. In other explanations, fava beans were used to weight the eyes of the dead. *Osso dei morti*, with a dry texture resembling chunks of bone, are more common in Italian-American bakeries and are sold all year despite their macabre name.

Chinese

In Chinese communities ancestors are honored participants in the lives of the living. At funerals symbolic foods are taken to the grave as a last offering—piles of oranges to symbolize good luck and roasted chickens or ducks to represent a whole life. After being offered to the deceased, these dishes or duplicates may be served to mourners as a way of sharing a last meal with the loved one. On the first anniversary of the death, on the person's birthday, or during the spring festival of Ching Ming, the food offerings may be repeated.

Greek

Rather than food brought by others, a unique food served at Greek funerals is made by the family of the deceased and given to mourners. *Koliva* (or *kolyva*) is a sprouted wheat salad, taken from Jesus's words in John 12:24: "Unless a wheat grain falls in the earth and dies, it remains alone; but if it dies, it bears much fruit." Preparation of *koliva* is a two-day process that ideally involves the family. Wheat is soaked overnight and then boiled and mixed with toasted sesame seeds, raisins, nuts, parsley, and sometimes pomegranate seeds. Sometimes sweetened, the mixture is dried, shaped in a mound, covered with bread crumbs, and topped with confectioners' sugar. The top is decorated with icing or Jordan almonds in the sign of the cross and the deceased's initials. The *koliva* is taken to the church and distributed after the funeral as a symbol of immortality and resurrection.

[See also Cakes; Casseroles; Chinese American Food; Ethnic Foods; Italian American Food; Jewish American Food; Mexican American Food.]

BIBLIOGRAPHY

Food for the Ancestors [documentary]. Chicago: Food for Thought Productions, 1999.
Kolatch, Alfred. *The Jewish Mourner's Book of Why*. Middle Village, NY: David, 1993.
Koliva Program of Ascension of Our Lord Greek Orthodox Church, Lincolnshire, Ill. "Index of Philoptochos." http://www.ascensiongoc.com/philoptochos.
Levine, Rabbi Aaron. *To Comfort the Bereaved*. Northvale, NJ: Aronson, 1996.
Nathan, Joan. *The Jewish Holiday Kitchen*. New York: Schocken, 1998.

KATHLEEN PURVIS

Fusion Food

"Fusion cuisine," an American term, was coined in the 1970s to describe the combining of ingredients, flavors, and culinary techniques from two or more cultures (for example, French techniques with American Southwest ingredients) to create totally new dishes. The Florida chef Norman Van Aken takes credit for inventing the phrase, borrowed from jazz vernacular, in which "fusion" means a blending of jazz with other musical elements, such as rock. Continuing this musical analogy, the *New York Times* food critic William Grimes described fusion at its best as "the culinary version of counterpoint, in which precisely defined flavors talk back and forth to each other rather than blending into a single smooth harmonic effect; it keeps 'your palate on edge'."

Fusion is distinct from "crossroads cooking," which results from the accidental meeting and mating of culinary traditions of different cultures that may occur as a consequence of migration, commerce, or war, for example, Creole cooking in New Orleans, which came about as a melding of the foods of African slaves and French colonizers and Tex-Mex traditions of the Southwest that occurred because of the Mexican settlement of Texas. Fusion, on the other hand, implies the deliberate manipulation by a chef of the cuisines of two cultures. It is an artificial blending of flavors and techniques.

Fusion is both a chef- and a restaurant-driven phenomenon. Since the style of cuisine was introduced in the 1970s, fusion has progressed from confusing and even offending diners to becoming mainstream, especially in metropolitan areas and among people younger than age thirty, who seem to be more receptive to the breaking down of culinary cultural barriers than older people. Menu descriptions of fusion dishes can sound jarring: rare duck breast with hot and sweet pineapple fried rice and white pepper ice cream (Jean-Georges Vongerichten, Vong, New York City); seared Maine scallops nestled in a shell served with potato cabbage purée and red wine black bean sauce (Wolfgang Puck, Chinois on Main, Santa Monica, California); *mofongo*-stuffed roasted breast of chicken with very black beans and homestead mango chutney (Norman Van Aken, Norman's, Coral Gables, Florida); lobster roll wrapped in slivers of pear with a drizzling of sevruga caviar, potato foam, and a shot glass of ginger ale granité (Marcus Samuelsson, Aquavit, New York City and Minneapolis, Minnesota); roast *poussin* and blue corn stuffing and blue corn muffins (Janos Wilder, Janos, Tucson, Arizona); and warm foie gras with caramelized jicama and cinnamon star anise sauce (Claude Troigros, C.T., New York City).

Some home cooks try their hands at fusion. Glossy cookbooks, food magazines, and television cooking shows, specifically *East Meets West with Ming Tsai* with the Chinese American chef Ming Tsai (first aired on the Food Network in 1998) have introduced home chefs to the concept. Tsai, who takes credit for introducing the term "East-West cuisine" in 1980, combines traditional Chinese flavors and techniques with contemporary American foods. For Thanksgiving 2002 on his new show, *Adventures with Ming Tsai*, Tsai devised a recipe for brining cut-up turkey, deep frying it in a wok, and serving the dish with a cranberry dipping sauce containing rice wine vinegar and ginger.

Origins

Although "fusion" is an American term, the trend has antecedents in French nouvelle cuisine of the 1970s, in which Gallic chefs rejected traditional rich sauces in favor of lighter dishes and fresh ingredients. Undercooked, crisp vegetables were served with fruit-based as well as wine-reduction sauces. French master chefs such as Paul Bocuse visited the Orient for inspiration. The French were already well versed in the East-West concept because of their colonization of Indochina (Vietnam, Cambodia, and Laos). The blending of compatible ingredients and techniques formerly isolated in Asian or European kitchens paved the way for experimentation by future chefs.

The challenge was taken up in California in the 1970s and 1980s when the chef Alice Waters of Chez Panisse restaurant began fashioning her groundbreaking combinations of elements, creating the best and seminal interpretation of California cuisine. Among her signature dishes were duck confit pizza with sun-dried tomatoes and calzone stuffed with goat cheese, fresh herbs, and prosciutto.

The development of fusion, the major culinary trend of the twentieth century, owes much to changes in the larger culture that chefs reflect in their cooking. In the late 1960s in America, people began eating less fat and cholesterol in response to health warnings. Since about 1970 citizens around the globe have experienced an increasingly compressed economic, political, and cultural environment—the shrinking-world phenomenon. Under the stimulus of tourism in the 1960s and 1970s, Americans were exposed to culinary cultures in other parts of the world. This phenomenon helped foster an intense interest in ethnic food in the 1980s. At the same time, new immigration patterns brought an influx of people, particularly from parts of Asia, to the United States. They brought along their culinary customs and habits, opened restaurants, and began to sell the exotic ingredients of their native cuisines. Trade expansion lead to year-round availability of food resources, including produce and other foodstuffs, not limited to particular geographic regions. Culinary globalization produced an international melting pot in which various culinary cultures blended and became constituents of one another, not neatly bounded but bleeding into and mutually constituting

each other. High-end chefs and restaurant owners quickly discovered that cultural diversity sells, allowing diners to participate in culinary tourism without leaving home. Fusion has moved beyond East-West cuisine to include Central and South American, Moroccan, and other national culinary identities.

As a result of these social developments, the evolution of fusion food may have been inevitable. The Japanese American poet David Mura pointed out that multiculturalism is a fact in the modern world ("A Shift in Power, A Sea Change in the Arts"). Just as the sphere of innovation in the arts has shifted to the "margins," these tangential areas have become the point of departure for the cutting edge in cuisine as well.

Fusion vs. Confusion

Fusion is not without controversy among food critics, historians, and culinary luminaries. Not surprisingly, the strongest proponents are fusion chefs: once ethnic food became acceptable for fine dining, the way was opened to combine elements of various cuisines in one dish. Simply focusing on one culture was too restrictive to creativity. Cross-fertilization allows for a highly personal style based on the "chef's odyssey." Multicultural chefs create food for multicultural diners. For example, the chef Marcus Samuelsson of the Aquavit restaurants in New York and Minneapolis was born in Ethiopia, was orphaned at age three, and then was adopted by a Swedish family who taught him traditional Scandinavian cooking techniques and sent him to culinary school in Sweden. Samuelsson later studied pastry cooking in Switzerland, worked at a three-star restaurant in France, and traveled widely. At Aquavit Samuelsson combines Swedish cuisine with flavors from Asia and Africa. Chef Jean-Georges Vongerichten, who has six restaurants in New York alone, was born in Alsace, France, and attended culinary school there. He then worked his way through the ranks at a series of three-star restaurants before cooking French food at a hotel in New York City. Vongerichten's turning point came when he opened a French restaurant in Bangkok, Thailand. In Thailand Vongerichten became fascinated with local flavors such as lemongrass, fish sauce, ginger, curry pastes, and coconut milk. This experience changed his food forever. When he opened Vong in New York, Vongerichten served his signature "Thailoise" Franco-Asian cuisine.

The products of fusion cuisine are not always harmonious on the palate or universally appreciated. Many detractors discredit this style of cooking for having more to do with sensation and novelty than with integrity. These purists argue that individual ethnic flavors become diluted and that fusion undermines generations of culinary traditions that have culminated in the signature flavors, spices, and herbs that make each cuisine distinctive. Another criticism is that fusion is often carelessly practiced—that chefs combine too many elements and have only superficial knowledge of the individual cuisines involved. Albert Sonnenfeld, Ph.D., the English language editor of *Food: A Culinary History* (1999), wrote that he is not opposed to fusion per se, just the way it is manifested in America, where the use of too many ingredients leads to "clashing flavors." In Europe, on the other hand, Sonnenfeld found that chefs understand the principle that less is more. He maintained that confusion of ingredients with flavor caused much of the "confusion" in 1990s America.

Additional negative criticism came from Felipe Fernandez-Armesto, Ph.D., a historian and professor at Oxford University, England, and the author of *Near a Thousand Tables: A History of Food* (2002). Fernandez-Armesto called fusion cuisine "Lego cookery" and wrote that only the availability of worldwide produce and culinary resources has made this trend possible with mix-and-match elements that arrive in kitchens in processed form. Fernandez-Armesto claimed that far from being inventive, fusion kitchens are really nothing more than factories.

Mura argued that the new multicultural approach in the arts cannot be judged by the old European assumptions. This is not to say there are not standards. Most fusion chefs agree that the it is essential to have a deep understanding of the individual culinary traditions before fusing. Many culinary educators maintain that it is only after a solid grounding in French techniques at the undergraduate level that a chef is ready to take on the study of the cooking methods of Asia or Mexico, for example. Finally, good fusion cuisine must "work" on the palate with flavors, textures, and techniques that complement each other. Fusion cuisine has been called daring, innovative, and cutting edge. It does emanate from a certain irreverence and iconoclasm. Perhaps it truly is modern American cooking.

[*See also* California; Celebrity Chefs; Chinese American Food; Ethnic Foods; French Influences on American Food; Nouvelle Cuisine; Restaurants; Scandinavian and Finnish American Food; Southeast Asian American Food; Southwestern Regional Cookery.]

BIBLIOGRAPHY

Carpenter, Hugh, and Teri Sandison. *Fusion Food Cookbook*. New York: Artisan, 1994. Fusion food made simple for home cooks.

Fernandez-Armesto, Felipe. *Near a Thousand Tables: A History of Food*. New York: Free Press, 2002.

Grimes, William. "A Fearless Chef with an Artistic Streak." *New York Times*, May 23, 2001.

Mura, David. "A Shift in Power, A Sea Change in the Arts: Asian American Constructions." In *The State of Asian America: Activism and Resistance in the 1990s*, edited by Karin Aguilar-San Juan. Boston: South End, 1993.

Sonnenfeld, Albert. "Complex and Simple Gifts." *Bulletin La Varenne*, Fall 2001. http://www.lavarenne.com/newsletter/pdf/newsletter-fall2001.pdf.

Tsai, Ming, and Arthur Boehm. *Blue Ginger: East Meets West Cooking with Ming Tsai*. New York: Clarkson Potter, 1999.

LINDA MURRAY BERZOK

G

Gallo, Ernest and Julio

Ernest (1909–) and Julio Gallo (1910–1993), although brought up in a grape-growing and wine-making family, did not start what is America's largest wine empire until after the mysterious deaths of their parents in 1933. The Gallo family had continued to grow grapes throughout Prohibition for "home wine making" and the murder-suicide—the official verdict of the deaths on June 21, 1933—has been shrouded with questions. The Prohibition era was a time of widespread lawlessness, and it would have been very difficult for a significant grape grower to have avoided contact with unsavory elements. This was especially true in California, where organized crime from the East Coast and Midwest was establishing itself in everything from film unions to clandestine alcohol production. The "accidental death" of the film star Thelma Todd in 1935 led to a great deal of unwanted publicity on this issue and on the corruption of many California institutions and industries.

Soon after their parents' deaths, the Gallo brothers obtained a permit to produce 50,000 gallons of wine. When Prohibition ended several months later, the brothers, unlike most of their neighbors, had a large inventory to sell legally. In 1935, production was 350,000 gallons, and by 1936 the Gallos had built a storage facility with a capacity of 1.5 million gallons. This huge growth was the result of strong management. Ernest did the front-office work of marketing and planning, and Julio was in charge of wine crafting and land management. Their philosophy was to establish control over as many aspects of production as possible, so the Gallos began acquisition of transportation, bottling, printing, and marketing companies. The business plan was so successful that by 1950 the Gallos had the largest wine production capacity in the United States. Production increased to the extent that in 1992, storage capacity in the four primary Gallo facilities was estimated to be 330 million gallons, or 660 times the capacity in 1933. Gallo has remained a private family business. One out of every four bottles of wine purchased in the U.S. market is a Gallo brand.

Despite its success, the Gallo family was not immune to tragedy and family acrimony. One of Julio's sons committed suicide. Ernest and Julio were estranged from their younger brother, Joseph Jr. In addition, they sued Joseph Jr., and won, in a trademark infringement case over Joseph's use of the Gallo name for his cheese business. Julio Gallo was killed in a jeep accident in 1993 at the age of 83. To give the family's point of view of these events, the Gallo family released *Ernest and Julio: Our Story* (1994) in response to an exposé, *Blood and Wine: The Unauthorized Story of the Gallo Wine Empire* (1993), by Ellen Hawkes.

Until 1974, core wine production at Gallo was either generic, mass-produced wines or sweet, fortified wines, such as the lemon-flavored white port marketed as Thunderbird. These sweet wines sold in pint bottles were controversial because many of those who bought them did so to become quickly and inexpensively intoxicated. In the early days, Gallo marketers had secured the most favorable shelf space in the urban package stores that catered to this market, and Gallo came to dominate the market. The change in direction to premium varietal wines was an important change in marketing strategy.

As a result of Gallo's change in focus to varietal wines, thousands of acres were turned to production of premium grapes and development of brands such as Dry Creek, Anapuma, Zabaco, Indigo Hills, Marcelina, and Frei Brothers, new brands seemingly being added monthly. A large portion of the shelf space of local wine stores is devoted to Gallo, albeit under many brand names. The economy of scale allows Gallo to buy high-quality products, pay good wages, and not use grapes it believes are inferior to its standard. The prevalence of Gallo products, however, makes it difficult for other companies to compete for shelf space and can lead to creation of many labels without meaningful difference in the product inside the bottles—much as generic products established the family fortune. The wines have met with critical acclaim and in terms of price to quality ratio are among the best values on the market. In 1993 Ernest Gallo told the *Wine Spectator* that his firm's historic entry into the premium wine market was an attempt to make the best possible wine in America and that the venture was driven by "largely a matter of personal satisfaction" and "certainly it's not for the profit."

Because the United States is a market where, as of the early 2000s, 11 percent of wine buyers buy most of the wine and because of competition from producers in countries where land and production costs are considerably less expensive than in the United States, Gallo is seeking to boost its sales abroad. Because U.S. wine exports are less than 4 percent of production, the venture represents a vast new market for the dominant American wine maker. The success of two of Julio's grandchildren, Gina and Matt Gallo, at the Dry Creek and Marcelina vineyards seems to indicate that the company will remain "in the family."

[*See also* Wine, *subentries* Historical Survey, Later Developments, California Wines; Wineries.]

BIBLIOGRAPHY

Gallo, Ernest and Julio, with Bruce B. Henderson. *Ernest and Julio: Our Story.* New York: Times Books, Random House, 1994.
Hawkes, Ellen. *Blood and Wine: The Unauthorized Story of the Gallo Wine Empire.* New York: Simon and Schuster, 1993.
Laub, James, and P. H. M. *The Wine Spectator.* November 30, 1995, 72–73.

STEVEN M. CRAIG

Game

From the beginning of human habitation of North America in prehistoric times, game has been an important food source. Before 12,000 B.C.E., small groups of hunters began migrating from Asia to North America via a land bridge connecting the two continents. These first Americans hunted big game, such as New World mammoths, mastodons, giant bison, and giant ground sloths. The hunters were so proficient that most of these animals disappeared from North America approximately nine thousand years ago. The early hunters were followed by successive waves of hunters who moved farther into the continent, where they found a land plentiful with smaller game. Almost all animals were hunted, including beaver, birds, buffalo, deer, elk, mountain sheep, prairie dogs, rabbits, raccoons, reindeer, and seals. In addition to meat, animals provided fur and skin for clothing, shelter, bedding, and shoes. Animal stomachs were used for storage containers, and other animal parts were used for ceremonial and religious purposes.

The New World was particularly well endowed with edible fowl. Native Americans prized ducks, geese, partridges, pheasants, pigeons, and seabirds. Nonmigrating land birds, such as ruffed grouse and wild turkey, were plentiful in New England, the Midwest, and the Great Lakes region. These birds were particularly important during the winter, when other food sources were scarce. Native Americans captured wildfowl with nets and snares and occasionally shot them with arrows. Although wild turkeys were easy to capture and supplied generous amounts of badly needed protein, Native American groups were widely divergent in their esteem for the bird. Some ate turkey with gusto, whereas others would not eat it even when faced with starvation, although they may have used turkey feathers for arrows, clothing, decoration, and religious ceremonies.

The hunting lifestyle, supplemented with gathering of edible plant foods, survived for thousands of years. It was modified with the introduction of agriculture, which was adopted by some Native Americans, but even those engaged in farming continued to hunt game where possible. The arrival of Europeans in the sixteenth century drastically changed Native American diets. The introduction of the horse by the Spanish in the sixteenth century, for example, greatly improved the Native Americans' ability to hunt game. The Plains Indians became highly proficient at tracking and hunting buffalo on horseback. Likewise, the introduction of firearms greatly improved Native Americans' ability to acquire game. Intensive European-style agriculture, however, led to the destruction of forests and other game habitats.

European Colonists

At the beginning of the colonial era, North America teemed with game and wildfowl. However, early English colonists were ill prepared to take advantage of this abundance, and many survived only because Native Americans supplied food and taught them how to hunt. After the first few years, colonists became proficient at trapping and hunting, and game became an extremely important food source for early Americans. The main advantage of wild game and fowl was that, unlike domesticated animals, they cost nothing to maintain. In addition, many birds and wild animals were crop pests, and killing them increased farm yields.

Game was particularly important in the settling of the West. When families first made their homes in a wilderness area, they had just the food they brought with them. Hunting provided the protein needed to survive while fields were being prepared and crops planted, and hogs, chickens, and other livestock were obtained. Had it not been for the vast population of deer and wild turkeys, the westward expansion of America would have been long delayed.

The four most important game animals in colonial and early America were the deer, bear, buffalo, and wild turkey. Deer was by far the most important. It was plentiful throughout the colonies and was relatively easy to hunt. Because deer hunting was restricted in many parts of England, the abundance of deer in America was a most welcome boon to the colonists. For Americans migrating west, deer was a major food source, particularly while settlers built homes and prepared land for farming. Venison was a mainstay in almost all European settlements in eastern America. The haunch, the largest muscle and hence the meatiest portion, was roasted, broiled, fried, or cut into slices (collops). Currant sauce was a popular accompaniment. Other parts, such as the neck, shoulder, and saddle (the ribs and loin), were hashed and used in soup, stew, sausage, pie, and pasties. Deer tripe was considered a delicacy in some circles. Venison was also potted and jerked for future use. Most nineteenth-century cookbooks included at least a few recipes for venison; some offered a dozen or more. In addition to home consumption, venison was served as a luxury in fashionable restaurants throughout the nineteenth century. Venison was also associated with Thanksgiving, and throughout the nineteenth century it was served at dinner along with turkey and savory pies.

In early colonial America, brown and black bears (*Ursus americanus*) were numerous, and their meat was an important food source in the eastern colonies. Although bear meat had a strong flavor and was often stringy, many Americans considered leg of bear a delicacy. Rendered bear fat was used for shortening, and most frontier homes contained a deerskin bag of bear oil. Bear meat was also jerked for later use. Black bear meat was occasionally sold in eastern markets during the early nineteenth century but largely disappeared by the middle of the century. Few recipes for bear meat appeared in American cookbooks, but bear remained a special treat served in restaurants until the end of the nineteenth century.

In the early colonial era, buffalo (*Bison bison*) roamed throughout much of eastern North America. The buffalo was an extremely important food source simply because of its size. An adult animal supplied seven to twelve hundred pounds of meat. Colonists prepared buffalo in the same manner as did Native Americans: broiled on wood cinders or buffalo chips with wood ash rather than salt used as a flavoring. Buffalo were hunted with such skill that by 1770 they had disappeared from America east of the Mississippi River, but they remained an important food source on the Great Plains. Particularly prized were the lean buffalo steaks and the fatty hump. Also consumed were buffalo liver, udder, and brain. The bone marrow was used as butter, and the rendered fat as a substitute for lard. Hunters frequently roasted the haunch. Dried buffalo tongues were sold to eastern markets for fifty cents each. In the West, frontiersmen considered boiled buffalo fetus a treat. During the late 1860s, William F. Cody was hired to supply buffalo meat to work crews constructing the eastern part of the transcontinental railroad, which was completed in 1869. Cody was so successful at hunting buffalo that he acquired the moniker "Buffalo Bill." The arrival of the railroads and increased European settlement on the Great Plains diminished the buffalo population as many of the animals were killed for sport. The Plains Indians, unable to hunt buffalo or other game, were herded onto reservations. Even in restaurants, buffalo was rarely served by the end of the nineteenth century.

Wild turkeys were initially an important food source for early European colonists. At the beginning of European settlement, an estimated 10 million wild turkeys roamed eastern America. In the Ohio River valley, flocks of more than five thousand birds were recorded. Wild turkeys were fast runners and were known to fly as far as a mile. Turkeys were hunted at night, when they perched in low branches, and were also herded into corrals. Wild turkey was eaten from the beginning of colonization, and it was a mainstay throughout the colonial period. The French gastronome Anthelme Brillat-Savarin, in *Physiologie du goût* (1826), described the wild turkey he ate in New York in the 1790s as "charming to the sight, flattering to the sense of smell, and delicious to taste." Wild turkeys were sought after throughout the nineteenth century. Many cookbooks included recipes for preparing wild turkey. Even as turkeys were being domesticated and "improved," many people believed wild turkey tasted better than meat from farm-raised birds. Brillat-Savarin wrote, "The flesh of the wild turkey is more highly colored and more perfumed than the domestic fowl." As wild turkeys became rarer during the nineteenth century, they also became more highly valued. Hunters in western Pennsylvania, for example, found it profitable to hunt wild turkeys and ship them to East Coast markets, where the finer city restaurants served roast wild turkey stuffed with truffles. By the nation's centennial, wild turkey was seldom served in the cities of the Atlantic coast.

Small Game and Wildfowl

Over the centuries, Americans have eaten an astonishing array of game animals and birds. Large birds, such as cranes and swans, were so prized that they had largely disappeared from the East Coast by 1750. Wild ducks were plentiful, and early colonists ate them often. Canvasback ducks, for example, wintered along the shores of Chesapeake Bay, where the wild celery they fed on flavored their flesh. Canvasbacks commanded high prices. Not far behind as delicacies were redhead and blackhead ducks, followed by teal and mallard.

Smaller birds caught or shot for food included blackbirds, blue jays, crows, herons, larks, orioles, plovers, quail, reedbirds, robins, sandpipers, snipes, turtledoves, and woodcocks. An excellent source of dietary protein, wild birds were sometimes kept in cages to be fattened for later slaughter. The birds were stewed, roasted, broiled, baked into pies, and simmered in soup. Their eggs were considered a delicacy.

One of the most important small birds on nineteenth-century tables was the pigeon. Most cookbooks contained directions for trussing and cooking these birds. Pigeon was eaten in every conceivable way—roasted, boiled, braised, broiled, stewed, and fricasseed. Pigeons were often stuffed before roasting and served with special sauces. Pigeons were also potted, dried, and pickled for future use. During some times of the year, pigeon was the most common food in many midwestern and southeastern areas of America. The most colorful and common of these birds was the passenger pigeon, which numbered an estimated 5 billion before European colonization. Passenger pigeons wintered along the southern coasts, where they were easily caught. Throughout the nineteenth century, these birds were caught in rural areas and shipped by the millions to Pennsylvania and upper New York. Because the supply was abundant, passenger pigeons made inexpensive food for the poor; leftovers were given to hogs.

Frontiersmen and trappers killed and ate a wide variety of animals, some of which became important culinary items. Beaver, for example, was trapped mainly for its fur, but frontiersmen also considered it tasty. A particular delicacy was beaver tail, which was frequently dried and shipped to market along with the pelt.

Small game was particularly important for slaves and the rural poor. Because they were forbidden firearms, slaves focused on what they could acquire by trapping, snaring, and hunting with dogs. Slaves, poor whites, and frontiersmen commonly ate opossum, raccoon, porcupine, rattlesnake, squirrel, and occasionally skunk. In Kentucky and Tennessee, game meats were combined with vegetables to make burgoo, a soup or stew traditionally based on squirrel or opossum. In Oregon, jackrabbit stew was common. In Virginia and North Carolina, Brunswick stew, which frequently included squirrel meat, was a favorite. Throughout the nineteenth century, American cookbooks included recipes for frying, stewing, broiling, and barbecuing hare, rabbit, squirrel, and other small animals. Even smaller animals found their way onto America's tables. On the frontier, frogs' legs were eaten when nothing else was available, but beginning in the mid-nineteenth century, frogs' legs were fashionable. Recipes appeared in American cookbooks, and the dishes were regularly served in the finest restaurants. Likewise, snails were enjoyed by those familiar with French cookery. Grasshoppers were occasionally consumed in the West, but only when there was nothing else to eat. In the late nineteenth century, specialty cookbooks focusing on outdoor cookery included extensive selections of game recipes. Examples included *Camp Cookery: How to Live in Camp* (1878) by Maria Parloa, *Canoe and Camp Cookery* (1885) by H. H. Soulé, and *The Hunter's Handbook* (1885) by Barry Stratton.

Demise of Game

By the early nineteenth century, game and fowl were dwindling east of the Mississippi. The buffalo were already gone, and bears disappeared from New England in the eighteenth century. By the nineteenth century, bear survived only in the southern and western areas of the United States, where the human population was small. Vast herds of buffalo continued to roam the Great Plains, but during the nineteenth century hunters and sportsmen

England. By 1900 wild turkeys had vanished completely from twelve states and were fast disappearing elsewhere. By the Great Depression, there were only approximately thirty thousand wild turkeys in America. Other wildfowl also disappeared from America. The brant, which was still seen in the 1870s along the East Coast, had almost disappeared by the 1880s. The canvasback duck became nearly extinct. Passenger pigeons had been killed in such profusion that by the 1870s public anger led individual states to ban their slaughter. These laws were not effective, and by 1909 only two passenger pigeons remained alive. By 1914 the species was extinct. In parts of Appalachia and the rural South, venison, bear, wild turkey, and squirrel remained staple foods for decades, but generally game faded from the American culinary scene in the early twentieth century. Although game occasionally appeared on the menu at swank restaurants, few ordinary cookbooks included recipes for it.

Return of Game

The 1937 passage of the Federal Aid in Wildlife Restoration Act placed an excise tax on hunting equipment. The proceeds were designated for the management and restoration of wildlife and their habitats. The program has been largely responsible for the recovery of deer, elk, antelope, beaver, black bear, duck, giant Canada goose, elk, bighorn sheep, and other species. Three exemplary success stories are those of the wild turkey, white-tailed deer, and buffalo. The first efforts to reintroduce wild turkeys took place in the late 1930s. By the 1950s, the wild turkey population in New England had begun to increase. There are an estimated 5.6 million wild turkeys in America. Likewise, the white-tailed deer population is estimated at approximately 18 million. In the early twentieth century, conservationists and ranchers began taking steps to save the buffalo. Buffalo is no longer an endangered species and has become a sought-after food because it is leaner than beef. A number of ranchers raise buffalo for meat, and the numbers in public and private herds combined are more than 350,000 head.

The change in circumstances for some wild animals increased culinary interest in game. Although game generally disappeared from mainstream cookbooks in the latter part of the twentieth century, specialty game cookbooks have become a major genre since the 1930s. Among the more important game cookbooks are *The Derrydale Cook Book of Fish and Game* (1937) by Louis

Shopping for Game. Scene in Washington Market, New York City. From George Augustus Sala, *America Revisited*, 3rd edition (London, 1883), vol. 1, p. 98.

slaughtered them in huge numbers. By 1891 only 540 buffalo were known to have survived.

The common deer had become scarce in some colonies even before the American Revolution. Thomas F. De Voe, in *The Market Assistant* (1867), reported that "a gradual extermination has been going on for several years past," and venison became rare in eastern markets. By the 1860s New York and other states had begun to pass laws prohibiting hunting and selling deer during certain months. But these laws were difficult to enforce, and by the end of the nineteenth century, deer had largely disappeared from New England. Deer remained an important food source in rural areas and in the South and West. Western hunters brought deer to market in eastern cities, although in an era before refrigeration and rapid transportation, many venison lovers complained about the condition of the meat when it arrived at market. By 1900 deer had become rare even in many western states, and state game laws had largely forbidden deer hunting. The result was the virtual elimination of venison from the American diet.

Wild turkeys were hunted to such an extent that by the time of the American Revolution they were scarce in New

De Gouy, *Fish and Game Cook Book* (1947) by Harry T. Botsford, *A Taste of the Wild: A Compendium of Modern American Game Cookery* (1991) by A. J. McClane, *The Complete Venison Cookbook* (1996) by Harold Webster, and *Wild Turkey Cookbook* (1995) by A. D. Livingston. Game has returned to the table. Wild turkey, venison, and farm-raised buffalo are sold in specialty stores throughout the United States.

[*See also* Buffalo; Native American Foods; Passenger Pigeon; Poultry and Fowl; Turkey.]

BIBLIOGRAPHY

Arnold, Samuel P. *The Fort Cookbook: New Foods of the Old West from the Famous Denver Restaurant; 190 Recipes for Game, Buffalo, Elk, and Much Standard Fare.* New York: HarperCollins, 1997.

Botsford, Harry T. *Fish and Game Cook Book.* New York: Cornell Maritime Press, 1947.

Canoe and Camp Cookery: A Practical Cook Book for Canoeists, Corinthian Sailors and Outers. New York: Forest and Stream, 1885.

De Gouy, Louis, *The Derrydale Cook Book of Fish and Game.* New York: Derrydale Press, 1937.

De Voe, Thomas F. *The Market Assistant.* New York: Hurd and Houghton, 1867. Reprint, Detroit: Gale Research Company, 1975.

Haines, Francis. *The Buffalo: The Story of American Bison and their Hunters from Prehistoric Times to the Present.* Norman and London: University of Oklahoma Press, 1995.

Hooker, Richard J. *A History of Food and Drink in America.* Indianapolis and New York: Bobbs-Merrill, 1981.

Livingston, A. D. *Wild Turkey Cookbook.* Mechanicsburg, PA: Stackpole, 1995.

National Buffalo Association. *Buffalo Meat Recipes/Cookbook.* Ft. Pierre, SD: National Buffalo Association, 1989.

Parloa, Maria. *Camp Cookery: How to Live in Camp.* Boston: Graves, Locke and Company, 1878.

Stratton, Barry. *The Hunter's Handbook.* Boston: Lee and Shepard; New York: Dillingham, 1885.

Webster, Harold. *The Complete Venison Cookbook.* Brandon, MS: Quail Ridge, 1996.

ANDREW F. SMITH

Garlic

For centuries people have attributed medicinal qualities to garlic. And in more recent years scientists have studied garlic's potential for healing. No one can say with certainty that the risk of heart disease or cancer is reduced by eating garlic, but it is certain that garlic improves the flavor of food.

Garlic has long had a bad image. Garlic, like all alliums, contains sulfurous compounds that can burn the mouth and eyes and leave a powerful smell on the breath. (Many believed that garlic was strong enough to repel a vampire.) The English writer John Ruskin called garlic a "strong class barrier," good for laborers, perhaps, but nothing that would be brought into a decent kitchen. Amelia Simmons, in the first American cookbook, wrote, "Garlicks, tho' used by the French, are better adapted to the uses of medicine than cookery." In 1896 Oscar Tschirky, better known as Oscar of the Waldorf, put 3,455 recipes in his famous cookbook, but only one featured garlic. Sixty-five years later, when Craig Claiborne's *New York Times Cookbook* appeared, things were starting to change. Although only two of the fifteen hundred recipes in the book contained the word "garlic" in the title, there were dozens of others in which a clove or two had made its way onto the page (sometimes qualified as optional).

The food writer James Beard made a major contribution to getting garlic on the map. In 1954 Beard wrote about an old Provençal recipe that called for cooking a chicken with forty cloves of garlic. Thousands of his readers tried it and liked it. At about the same time, the social critic Russell Lynes, in his famous discourse on high-brow and low-brow phenomena, wrote about how the upscale cook might rub a wooden salad bowl with a clove of garlic to make the lettuce taste better. Whether for health or culinary reasons, the use of garlic in the United States has quadrupled since the early 1970s.

Most of America's garlic is grown in the Central Valley of California. More than 90 percent of the garlic used in the United States is the California Early or the California Late variety. These are solid, long-lasting softneck varieties that lend themselves to braiding. Most California garlic is processed in Gilroy in a huge plant, packaged as dried garlic powder or flakes, and shipped in huge cartons to major food processors. In most other places, hardneck varieties of garlic rule. They grow a tough stem that comes up from the middle of the head. As the plant matures, the stem circles around and forms a small bulb called a "scape." The scape is removed so that it will not use resources that should go to the bulb. Often the tender scapes are marketed to Asian restaurants and cooked as a delicacy. Sometimes hardneck garlic is harvested early, before the cloves form in the heads, and it is coveted as green garlic.

Although they have developed thousands of onion cultivars, plant breeders have not been able to do the same with garlic, which does not produce seed. Garlic growers must put aside at least 10 percent of their crop to be broken into cloves for October planting. Strains of garlic that grow in one place for a long time develop particular characteristics. The garlic may be red or purple or blue. There may be a lot of cloves or just a few. The heads may be big or small. Some are hotter than others. But there is consistency in the strain. If that same garlic were grown in a new place, a new set of characteristics might evolve. The garlic responds to different soil conditions, different day lengths, different climates, and different altitudes. Although hundreds of garlic varieties are grown around the world, local growing conditions make each variety unique. Scientists in the early 2000s are conducting research on shaping the garlic of the future and on getting garlic to produce true seed.

Like many of the alliums, garlic originally grew in south central Asia in what some call the "garlic crescent." The original genetic material has disappeared. Garlic was carried by migrating populations all around the Mediterranean. Early Egyptians, Greeks, and Romans used garlic as both medicine and food. Not a truly nutritious food, garlic is made up of approximately 60 percent moisture, 30 percent carbohydrate, a small amount of protein, and traces of vitamins and minerals. Whether garlic is food or medicine continues to be debated.

[*See also* California; Herbs and Spices; Homemade Remedies; Simmons, Amelia; Tschirky, Oscar.]

BIBLIOGRAPHY

Aaron, Chester. *Garlic Is Life*. Berkeley, CA: Ten Speed, 1996.
Beard, James, and Sam Aaron. *How to Eat Better for Less Money*. New York: Simon and Schuster, 1954.
Bergner, Paul. *The Healing Power of Garlic*. Rocklin, CA: Prima, 1996.
Crawford, Stanley. *A Garlic Testament*. Albuquerque: University of New Mexico Press, 1998.
Engeland, Ron L. *Growing Great Garlic*. Okanogan, WA: Filaree, 1991.
Griffith, Linda and Fred. *Garlic Garlic Garlic; Exceptional Recipes from the World's Most Indispensable Ingredient*. Boston: Houghton Mifflin, 1998.
Harris, Lloyd J. *The Book of Garlic*. Reading, MA: Addison-Wesley, 1998.
"High-Brow, Low-Brow." *Life*, April 11, 1949, 100. An illustrated essay on the writings of Russell Lynes.
Lynes, Russell. *The Tastemakers*. New York: Harper and Bros., 1954.

LINDA GRIFFITH AND FRED GRIFFITH

Gas Grill

Modern Home Products (MHP), founded by Walter Koziol in the 1950s, invented the first outdoor gas grill and brought it to market in 1960. MHP was the first company to offer affordable residential outdoor gas lighting to the homeowner. This business grew and inspired Koziol to explore other ways to use gas outdoors. MHP produced the first outdoor gas barbecue grill, called Perfect Host, a twenty-two and one-half–inch round steel grill on a portable cart supplied with either natural or liquid propane gas. By 1964 the first rectangular grills with rust-free solid aluminum construction were produced, and this design continues to be the industry's most popular.

By 1989 sales of gas grills had more than doubled, surpassing sales of charcoal grills almost two to one, according to the Barbecue Industry Association. Unlike briquette-fired grills, gas grills emulate indoor cooking ranges with more precise control of cooking conditions, which makes them very popular. According to the Hearth, Patio and Barbecue Association, because of the great taste of food cooked outdoors, easy cleanup, and informal mode of entertainment, 69 percent of gas grill owners cook out year-round. Although hamburgers, steak, hot dogs, and chicken breasts remain popular nationally, outdoor cooking styles vary regionally—from pork in the Carolinas to Cajun spices in the Deep South to lighter fare such as vegetables and fish on the West Coast.

[*See also* Stoves and Ovens.]

BIBLIOGRAPHY

Bennett Clark, Jane, and James Ramage. "Cooking With Gas." *Kiplinger's Personal Finance*, June 2000.
Modern Home Products. http://www.modernhomeproducts.com. Home page for the company that invented the first gas grill. See "About Us" for a history of production.
Hearth, Patio and Barbecue Association. http://hpba.org. International trade association that supplies consumer research, trivia, and safety information for barbecues, grills, and accessories.

COLLEEN JOYCE PONTES

Gender Roles

Ancient Background

In early hunter-gatherer societies, the limitations and responsibilities imposed by child care kept women nearer to the home fires, at least for certain periods of time, and made them the more logical choice to be cooks. Even then the lines were not strictly drawn because women without dependent children participated in community hunts and trapped smaller animals. Later agricultural and pastoral societies maintained gender divisions in which men managed herds and women were the agriculturists. Such early dichotomies have survived in the ancient mythological tales about the Greek goddess Demeter (the Roman Ceres, source of the word "cereal"), who nurtured the crops and wild plants, or Pan, a lesser god who tended the herds. The responsibilities for cookery were similarly divided: the food that women prepared nurtured the family while the food that men prepared strengthened the public polity and community prosperity. Women prepared porridges, stews, and soups of staple grains, breads, vegetables from their own gardens, and small game by stewing, boiling, and simmering them in earthenware vessels over small fires (often indoors or just outside the doorway). Men, on the other hand, roasted meats with iron tools over large beds of embers out of doors.

The growth of civilizations and wealth produced both complex cuisines and businesses. Men conducted vast trades in foodstuffs. At the simplest level, they obtained the products of the surrounding countryside and sold raw foodstuffs and prepared foods in the public marketplace. On an international scale, Romans imported exotic foods from their outposts in other countries, among them luxurious Asian spices from Arab traders, and much-needed wheat from Egyptian granaries. Men also constituted a new class of professionally trained chefs who cooked expensive ingredients in elaborate recipes, preparing legendary banquets for the male Roman aristocracy. Some men of higher status formed gourmet dining clubs. Some developed their own notable cooking skills as a mark of culture and cooked to impress their peers. A substantial part of the Roman diet was cooked, bought, and eaten at the public stalls of marketplaces. Male proprietors cooked snacks and simple dishes for tradesmen, shoppers, and those with public business.

Women were limited to the domestic sphere and cooked for the family. Depending on the family's wealth or station, the cook might be the mistress of the house, a servant, or a slave. Among the very wealthiest, the family cook might have been a professional male chef.

Throughout subsequent European history this kind of separation continued and became especially strict during the centuries following the medieval period. Role limitations were incorporated into law throughout Europe, where food preparation was very much tied to class. Aristocratic women did not generally cook (apart from

specialties on important occasions). They maintained supervisory contact with the kitchen and enjoyed the high standards of hired professional chefs. Working women (unskilled laborers on farms or in large households) did not often cook, although they performed menial kitchen jobs, and survived either on nourishment they were given at work or on inexpensive street food. As always, families of average means on farms or in towns ate the simple cookery of their women. These patterns were carried to the New World settlements, where they were reestablished with relatively few changes.

American Colonial Cookery

The colonies of the New World followed European gender traditions. English custom prevailed, since the English dominated the young colonies legally and by virtue of their considerable numbers. For example, under English common law, the economic and social unit of the family was recognized through the male head of household, and only men could own and run a business, trade, or profession. Married women, theoretically represented by their husbands, were not allowed to pursue their own businesses in the public workplace and could not own property or sign contracts (although there was some variation among the colonies). At first the communities populated by different national groups were able to maintain their own gender systems. The French Napoleonic code permitted married women to own property in their own right, making possible their establishment of such food-related businesses as taverns in French communities. Among the Dutch colonists, women also had more rights in business. However, the English gained control over these other colonies, instituting their own system.

Regardless of ethnicity, the gender rules surrounding food were applied, for the most part, to the middle or yeoman class. Married women of the more privileged families usually performed in a supervisory capacity, cooking only for special occasions and then preparing special dishes. The poor, for whom entrepreneurial business was generally beyond reach, were limited to the menial, unskilled work of the scullery, barnyard, or garden. Some women with clear talent managed to rise above their station—in particular the African American slave women, who often proved to be gifted cooks, were rewarded with the special conditions and privileges (and sometimes drawbacks) of working in the big house. These southern women have been credited with the creation of a fine regional cuisine, comparable to the female development of bistro cooking of France.

Married Women In the realm of food production and food preparation, farm women bore a substantial weight of the work and responsibility, albeit without legal ownership of their hearths or pots and with heavy dependence on their husbands' goodwill. This was not always forthcoming; in one legal case, an unfortunate woman who had run afoul of her husband was forced to seek the goodwill of the courts in order to have access to the kitchen equipment she needed to perform her duties. Most settlers were farmers. Men and women worked together at home, dividing the work according to the traditional view of gender patterns for the common good of the family. A farmwife who produced eggs or butter for the marketplace would do so under her husband's authority, and he was entitled to the profits.

The vast percentage of American colonists were engaged in farming (some 95 percent in 1781, according to George Washington's census), and subsistence farming was the rule: Families raised most of what they needed for survival and bartered for the rest. If they had a surplus they could barter for or buy luxuries. Work was clearly divided by gender. Women managed their home kitchens, kitchen gardens, and barnyards. There was a good deal of highly seasonal work; such major projects as preserving the autumn harvest were added to the year-round work of daily meals. And women were the cooks, putting forth sustenance each day while at the same time training their young daughters to prepare meals for their eventual days as wives and householders. Their skills were basic and broad, and they were generalists, if anything. They not only raised their barnyard animals (pigs, goats, dairy cows and calves, chickens, ducks, geese, turkeys) and collected eggs, but they also killed and dressed the poultry and small game they ate. In addition to managing the care and breeding of their dairy cows, they made butter and cheese. They planted, maintained, and harvested kitchen gardens, while also utilizing wild berries and orchard fruit, to provide for the table in warm months and to stock the root cellars with dried food preserves for winter. They made beers from almost anything at hand that they could get to ferment, from the usual barley to pumpkin. This kind of work on a daily basis, done from childhood on, made their bodies strong; women had both the physical capacity and the skills for this work.

In addition, the sale of women's products (butter, cream, eggs, baked goods) often brought in needed cash that ordinarily was, in the main, available only from the autumn and winter sale of the men's products (grain, livestock). If the season had been good, men realized a profit in cash and used it to improve the farm or to pay off things bought on credit. The "pin money" that women earned helped to provide the family with the manufactured goods that were often beyond reach. A competent food producer, male or female, was more likely to earn higher status within the family; capable women were also more likely to be rewarded with otherwise-rare rights of decision making.

In contrast, a woman married to someone in trade was limited by the same constraints, but to assist her husband she might have learned at least some of the male-designated skills. For example, a woman cooking for her husband's tavern, inn, or ordinary would be quite likely to know how to obtain foodstuffs with an eye to quality and expense, to supervise kitchen help, to tend bar, and to keep books. Such gathering places, the precursors of bars, hotels, and restaurants, filled an important social function both for the men of local communities and for travelers. In addition to selling spirits, the taverns provided meals—often in a competitive environment—and offered necessary accommodations for those in transit. The quality of food and the circumstances of service varied considerably according to clientele and location. In most cases the food prepared by women in these establishments was the same as the food the women prepared for their own families, required the same domestic skills, and reflected the ethnicity of their region and the prosperity of their customers.

Single Women Single women of the middle class were afforded more rights and operated under a more lenient set of rules that permitted them to work publicly and to support themselves, so that they would not burden the community. Some worked as cooks, some ran their own specialty food shops, and some ran taverns.

For example, the daughter of an innkeeper who had learned her father's trade (particularly if there was no son to do so) might inherit and continue his business until she married, at which time her property became her husband's and she lost control of it. In a few cases, women resisted the public pressure to marry and remained single, retaining proprietorship and a more independent life. Widows were permitted a semipublic role (they still had no vote, and in some colonies had limited ownership rights), but in business they functioned as men. Without the rights of ownership, they were given the use of their husband's legacies, which at their deaths reverted to their eldest sons. A widow who had thus inherited the use of her husband's tavern might prefer to maintain her role as a single entrepreneur rather than remarrying and having her tavern pass to the control of a new husband.

The kind of cookery women did in such taverns varied according to location. For example, a tavern situated near the government buildings of a prominent city, or on a major post road, attracted more people of means and required more attention to complex foods, exotic ingredients, and fashion. Such establishments sometimes belonged to chef-owners of great renown, among them Samuel Fraunces, but sometimes a widowed tavern keeper, accustomed by background to fine food, achieved the necessary cooking skills herself or hired appropriate help. Just such a woman was the Widow Blydenburgh, of Smithtown, New York. On George Washington's tour of Long Island, her tavern served him a meal he deemed comparable to anything he had eaten in New York City.

Although the names of male professional chefs working in aristocratic kitchens and high-quality inns abound, historical records rarely contain the names of women so employed. However, there is evidence to suggest that they sometimes did work professionally as chefs. For example, when the male chef of Virginia's Governor Botetourt (ca. 1770) retired and returned to England, he was replaced by a woman of unknown identity, background, or credentials. That she was professional and competent enough to meet the many demands of the governor's palace is not in question, and she was probably not unique. Thomas Jefferson, served by a series of trained French chefs, also hired women, who must have been professional enough to meet his high culinary standards. And similar mystery surrounds the identity of the woman who cooked for Rufus King, wealthy framer of the Constitution.

Other single women in the food workplace were caterers or confectioners of a sort. They sometimes ran small shops that specialized in their own preserves, candies, or baked delicacies. They were more likely to be situated in affluent and bustling towns in which people followed fashion and made their purchases with cash (rather than by bartering). Similarly, they often depended on imported ingredients (spices, special English preserves, or isinglass for firming jellies, for example) more easily available in port cities. Some women baked to order and undertook simple catering from their own homes. Their

Separate Spheres. At left, the wife cooks while the husband prepares for dinner. Lithograph, 1890s. *Collection of Kit Barry*

advertisements appeared regularly in eighteenth-century newspapers.

The Men Colonial American men did the heaviest physical work in general, particularly in agriculture, herding, hunting, hauling, professional butchering, and baking. For example, European traditions in America assigned men to the hunt and to the most strenuous tasks of butchering, expecting women to take over the somewhat lighter (but no less arduous and lengthy) work of cutting meat and processing lard and sausage.

Their strong and unyielding commitment to division of work by gender colored male interpretations of Native American life. The first explorers of the New World found women doing not only the cooking but also the heaviest physical work (agriculture, butchering, hauling) without the help of men, and they came to the ethnocentric conclusion that women were kept in a position subordinate to men. Early travelers commented on the "laziness" of men, clearly unaware of the more equitable work divisions in effect. They had little understanding, for example, of the time-consuming coordination and planning needed for lengthy communal fishing and hunting trips, often of months' duration.

European men in the colonies came prepared to continue the historical gender divisions in which men worked in the food world in many different capacities. As farmers they produced staple grains and beef cattle, for which they needed knowledge and physical strength, as well as financial investments in land, buildings, draft animals, and equipment. In addition, they owned and ran food shops. The European method of training skilled artisans through the apprentice-journeyman-master system produced proficient bakers and butchers, and they prospered in expanding colonial cities. Professional cooks, sometimes of the highest quality, worked privately for the wealthy, and sometimes opened taverns or inns, the precursors of restaurants. Perhaps the most famous of these was Samuel Fraunces, tavern keeper of New York City, who cooked gourmet meals for George Washington during the War of Independence and continued to cook for him through his presidency and his years at Mount Vernon. Thomas Jefferson, another aristocratic Virginian with a strong interest in fine food, hired French-trained male chefs. These fine chefs were deeply influenced by French cuisine and its historical contributions, as well as the European cookbook legacy written by and for professionals.

The Nineteenth Century

The nineteenth century began with changes that would eventually revolutionize the food roles of American men and women. A series of innovations—steam engines, railroads, canals, and the first steps toward heavy manufacturing—pushed many small towns into becoming cities. Rural people came to the new cities for jobs, giving further impetus to their growth. Urban families adapted to a different kind of social and economic culture in which some earlier gender divisions were maintained and some were weakened.

Men, no longer farm-based, took jobs in construction, shops, and in the new factories and offices. Their work often took them some distance from home, weakening minute-by-minute involvement with family, but allowing them greater economic opportunities. Public education now took children from the home also, and women found themselves with discretionary time previously used in food production. New idealizations of middle-class gender differences, especially among urban, white, Anglo-Saxon, Protestant populations, strengthened the physical and social gaps between men and women.

Men were now redefined in terms of their "constitutional" talents for business, decision making and problem solving, forcefulness, logic, and organization. For the first time in Western culture, women were considered "innately" superior to men in the areas of nurture, emotion, religion, and art, but physically and mentally frail. Men aspired to be "self-made" successes and women to demonstrate the successes of their men. Men adjusted to the demands of their new work environments and the anxiety-producing pace and relative lawlessness of the new city; ideally, women were to balance these demands by creating a beautiful, serene, and fashionable oasis, efficiently run and free of tension or disorder, ruled by saintly example and perpetual cheerfulness. Both genders were now immersed in the cash economy—as men made money, women learned to spend it wisely, budgeting and seeking good value through comparison shopping.

Among the large numbers of families remaining on farms, the social ideal of separate spheres appears to have found less acceptance. These women continued in earlier roles, producing and preparing foods, and sharing in the decision making.

The end of the century saw changes in the separate food worlds of men and women, as the domestic and business worlds moved further apart. At the same time, the first steps were being taken toward decreasing the gap.

The Men   In the first half of the nineteenth century, men were integral to the progress leading to the American Industrial Revolution (ca. 1850), jump-starting the commercial world with ingenuity and ambition, creating the structures of what would eventually develop into the modern corporate world. Evolving city culture included a great many new opportunities for work with food. By midcentury, men had already invented, improved, patented, and manufactured revolutionary kitchen technologies, foremost among them the cast-iron cookstove. By the end of the century, men had taken control of the market, creating monopolies in the production and distribution of such basic products as sugar, flour, beef, pork, and wheat and instituting sophisticated advertising and brand names.

On a smaller scale, men permeated the commercial food world with urban retail shops, among them the conglomerate general store that sold staples and a far greater range of foodstuffs than was to be found in earlier markets. They also owned and ran markets specializing in dairy products, meats, fish, or fruits and vegetables. By the late 1800s the shelves of these markets were filled with commercially prepared, mass-produced prepackaged foods and out-of-season tinned products.

Men also created the restaurant. A number of expatriate French chefs, disenfranchised by the French Revolution, found their way to America, where they stimulated the development of public eating houses. These new, sophisticated, and exclusive dining halls, which were extensions of the tavern tradition, catered to wealthier men (women continued to socialize at home in family groups). New York City's Delmonico's and Niblo's were among the most famous, and they were indeed pleasure palaces, offering haute cuisine in an extravagant decor.

As cities grew, public eating facilities for men of other economic levels were required. Work schedules did not always provide enough time for men to take their noon dinner at home, and a wide range of expanded taverns and restaurants served them. By the late 1800s, large department stores developed their own restaurants with appropriate menus for women on downtown shopping jaunts. And snack food became entertainment for the masses through male-generated street food, soda fountains, and ice cream parlors.

The Women   Evolving technologies and urban living entrenched the woman's traditional food role in many ways, while, in a seemingly contradictory way, permitting the first steps toward participation in the public world.

Domestic cooking   Women embraced their new profession as "homemakers" and hoped it would be an opportunity, parallel to that of their husbands, to achieve a more professional status. Their most common food involvement remained that of domestic cooking. During the course of the century, a number of factors brought about significant change in both the work and the cuisine. Most notable among these factors were technology as exemplified in new cookstoves, broadened availability of ingredients, more discretionary time, immigrant unskilled kitchen help, and fashion. Women expanded their cooking skills, serving more complex and ambitious foods to family and friends. As they became increasingly literate, they culled recipes from women's magazines and cookbooks. Over the course of the century, women spent more time in the kitchen, turning out more complicated meals, canning foods (in glass jars), and creating myriad entertainment foods—preserves, pickles, cakes, pies, cookies, snack foods, beverages, and candies. (In fact, candy making, especially taffy-pulls, became a popular social activity for young people in the century's later decades.)

By the end of the century, these entertainment foods had become the nucleus of a female-oriented subcuisine known for its daintiness. Significant items included consommé, dainty salads and finger sandwiches, white sauce on white vegetables on a white plate, and cunningly shaped rolls. Perhaps its most esteemed icon was the filled and iced coconut layer cake. Served by women to other women at luncheons and teas, these foods were to be the culinary basis of twentieth-century women's tearooms. Perhaps it goes without saying that this style of eating was not expected to please men, who continued to prefer substantial meals of meat and potatoes.

Household cuisine changes were also accomplished by means of inventive technology. In particular, the new cookstove was faster and more convenient to cook and bake with than the hearth and the brick oven were. The cookstove was in common use in urban middle-class kitchens by 1850. The development of the glass jar for putting up preserves (ca. 1850) expanded women's range of cooking responsibilities, while a flood of labor-saving, geared gadgetry saved time and muscle. Although most of the new inventions were male-generated, some were female. Among these were Nancy Johnson's hand-crank ice cream maker (1864) and Josephine Cochran's dishwasher (ca. 1893). Some women, among them Cochran, navigated the male world and successfully patented, manufactured, and sold their products, but they were anachronistic in their world.

Cookbooks and cooking schools This area of women's work saw the early blurring of gender lines, as women turned to work in the public sphere. In accordance with middle-class dictates, women in need preferred work that could be done at home. Selling cookery expertise as authors and cooking-school proprietors was an obvious means of both entering the marketplace and staying close to home. Following the example of the female cookbook authors of eighteenth-century England, who largely wrote for economic reasons, American women supported themselves by publishing cookbooks intended for women at home. Amelia Simmons, the first to do so with her *American Cookery* published in 1796, was unmarried; Mrs. Mary Randolph's 1824 *Virginia Housewife* was written only after her husband had lost his income. Women announced their marital situation (and credentialing) in their book titles as Miss Parloa or Mrs. Rorer, for example; some remained anonymous, perhaps to avoid the implied social embarrassment. By the end of the 1800s there was a large roster of famous food writers, many of whom wrote testimonials for name-brand food products. Some produced ephemera—the small promotional pamphlet cookbooks distributed by male-controlled food companies. Their inclusion in these male industries may have appeared as a mark of success.

Other women used their food expertise at home by running boardinghouses and were sometimes famous for their fine noon dinners, which might also be available for purchase by nonboarders. Such women provided an intermediary link between home kitchens and the development of restaurants in the male world. In the early 2000s there was little data on the extent to which women moved into the public sector by selling meals.

Another group of women stepped out of the home to forge respectable careers in the public work world. Catherine Beecher introduced her views on women, education, and domesticity, influencing the development of female careers before marriage. Others organized cooking schools, at first modest. These were exemplified by the classes of Mrs. Goodfellow of Philadelphia, where the soon-to-be-famous writer Eliza Leslie studied. During the century these schools expanded and by the late 1800s had reached the professional heights of the Boston Cooking School, which offered classes in cookery, contemporary theories of nutrition, and kitchen management. Students in these cooking schools earned respected credentials that would take them into professional careers as nutritionists and educators. The institution of land grant colleges (ca. 1861) and their innovative home economics departments, schools, and colleges further professionalized home and career involvements with food. The gap between men's and women's worlds was again decreasing.

Women of the nineteenth century also found a public forum through food and sometimes used it to further their efforts at philanthropy and reform. For example, many women used cookbooks to underscore their concern with temperance issues by substituting nonalcoholic components for otherwise spirit-laced homemade punch and the sacramental wine of religious rituals. Massive problems

Special for Ladies. Bill of fare, Dunn's restaurant, Boston, late nineteenth or early twentieth century.

created by the Civil War became the focus of women's fund-raising, often accomplished by selling their food (and other articles) at such mammoth fairs as those staged by the Sanitary Commissions. On a smaller level, women organized fund-raising suppers, festivals, bake sales, sales of community cookbooks, and women's exchanges. Many of these techniques, which were new in the nineteenth century, continued to be used well into the next century, as women gathered money for their causes.

The Twentieth Century

The new century saw gender roles associated with food continuing in the directions already established. Male-run chain stores, begun in the nineteenth century by A&P, expanded during the 1920s, facing competition from Grand Union, Piggly Wiggly, and Krogers. Large food corporations merged and remerged, forming international networks of male trade and production.

Waves of immigration provided a labor force of women with their own domestic experience, and many of them hired out as cooks to middle-class households. When it was financially possible, women stayed home and cooked, providing both nutrition and culture. Generally immigrant women arrived versed in the gender divisions found in the United States. Many were able to support their families upon arrival, as their food skills were easily marketable and they quickly found work as cooks or workers in canning factories, for example. In many cases the men were slower to find their way into the male job market and found themselves cooking at home, if only temporarily. Consequent reversals of acceptable gender roles were, in the main, unsettling to the family and often disrupted family status hierarchies. Acculturation was accomplished with a certain urgency. The women of immigrant families were sometimes targeted by social workers, who tried to expedite the process of acculturation and assimilation by teaching them American cookery.

Italian women were particularly dedicated to home cooking, as the family was the most important unit of their culture and food was the glue that held it together. These women were unlikely to seek work outside the house. Men also maintained the strong gender lines, participating at home by gardening and earning their living as greengrocers, importers, and retailers of essential ethnic specialties for their communities. However, upon retirement, some Italian men reversed roles and did home cooking for the pleasure of it, suggesting that the family connection to food was more important than gender roles. General commitment to women's home cookery also helps to explain Italian lack of interest in restaurant food before World War II and the concomitant absence of Italian male chefs and restaurateurs.

Men in other ethnic groups found economic opportunity in food. In patterns similar to those of the Italian foodways, they followed their own cultural and social traditions and experiences. In addition to importing and retailing food, many opened restaurants and taverns comparable to those at home. The Germans, arriving with a tradition of restaurant food, had already become famous for restaurants and beer halls. Greek male coffeehouses reflected the strongly separated Middle Eastern gender customs. Chinese men, who had been separated from their wives by immigration laws and exploitation, became cooks as a survival tactic and opened restaurants intended, at first, for their own male communities.

Women's professional work in cookbook writing and education intensified in the twentieth century. College programs were enlarged, offering both positions for faculty and classes for students. Public schools hired licensed home economics teachers to instruct students, kindergarten to twelfth grade, in cookery and nutrition. Nutritionists worked in the health industries, researching and prescribing diets.

Major events of the twentieth century continued to jar the nineteenth-century relegation of women to the household. The most important food issue of World War I (1918–1919) was the shortage of staples, such as wheat, sugar, and meat. Women referred to government publications that suggested substitutions. And, as they had during the Civil War, they raised money with their cooking skills, as best they could given the food shortages. After the war, the increasing popularization of the car afforded women the opportunity to open tearooms along popular auto routes. These tearooms, sometimes in women's own homes, would lead to the development of such popular urban women's restaurants as Schraffts.

The Great Depression that cost so many men their jobs put many women to work, since once again their food skills were more marketable. World War II required adjustments to food rationing and scarcities that led to cultivation of home victory gardens and a renewed interest in canning. Women went out to work in jobs that traditionally had been considered men's. After the war, Americans "returned to normalcy," and women returned to domesticity. A long period of economic prosperity enabled more restaurant eating, but home cookery continued in its largely traditional patterns.

In the 1960s, a series of forces began to produce what would eventually become major changes. The women's movement gradually undermined the distinction between male and female spheres with a new vision of equality in the home and workplace. Some women proclaimed their new status with the phrase "I do not cook." Others in the job market, but short of time, found help with family cooking in the growing frozen food industry, in convenience foods, fast foods, and takeout, all of which were male-generated food innovations that helped to restructure the cuisine and the ritual of the family meal.

Some men helped their wives by cooking. As divorce statistics escalated, more men learned to run kitchens for themselves and their children. Men sometimes responded to the changes with new interest in cookery as a viable hobby. Home barbecuers (often affluent and educated) cooked for friends and family and experimented with new techniques, equipment, and home smoking. At the other end of the spectrum were male immigrant vendors of street food and Mexican men working in restaurants.

The same period saw women changing the cuisine. Julia Child's pioneering cookbooks and television programs of the 1960s woke American women to more challenging and rewarding home cookery, creating a bridge between men's professional food and female home cooking. Women sought and slowly gained access to professional cooking and baking spheres, one of the last male bastions, eventually earning positions of authority and economic reward. Business-oriented women earned national reputations with fine, innovative restaurants; among them were Alice Waters, owner of Chez Panisse (featuring natural foods), Mollie Katzen, an owner of the cooperative vegetarian Moosewood, and Lidia Bastianovich, owner of Felidia.

Recent laws legislating equal employment and education opportunities have specified that coeducational classes in cookery and nutrition be required of secondary school students. Gender has also become less of an issue in the food industries. Home cooking and professional cooking have lost some of their gender distinctions, just as male and female roles have lost some of theirs. Professional cooking schools are flourishing, and both men and women train to be chefs and bakers. In short, what began as a strict gender dichotomy has blurred and is moving closer, at the opening of the twenty-first century, to a situation without male and female limitations.

[*See also* Beecher, Catherine; Boardinghouses; Boston Cooking School; Child, Julia; Child, Lydia Maria; Cooking Schools; Delmonico's; Fund-Raisers; Home Economics; Leslie, Eliza; Lincoln, Mrs.; Parloa, Maria; Randolph, Mary; Restaurants; Roadhouses; Rorer, Sarah Tyson; Settlement Houses; Simmons, Amelia; Street Vendors; Taverns; Temperance.]

BIBLIOGRAPHY

Beecher, Catharine E. *A Treatise on Domestic Economy.* Boston: 1841. Reprint, New York: Source Book, 1970.

Counihan, Carole M., and Steven Kaplan. *Food and Gender: Identity and Power.* New York: Routledge, 1998.

Inness, Sherrie A., ed. *Cooking Lessons: The Politics of Gender and Food.* Lanham, MD: Rowman and Littlefield, 2001.

Matthews, Glenna. *"Just a Housewife": The Rise and Fall of Domesticity in America.* New York: Oxford University Press, 1987.

Spang, Rebecca L. *The Invention of the Restaurant: Paris and Modern Gastronomic Culture.* Cambridge, MA: Harvard University Press, 2000.

Strasser, Susan. *Never Done: A History of American Housework.* New York: Pantheon, 1982.

Ulrich, Laurel. *Good Wives: Image and Reality in the Lives of Women in Northern New England, 1650–1750.* New York: Knopf, 1982.

Willan, Anne. *Great Cooks and Their Recipes from Taillevent to Escoffier.* New York: McGraw-Hill, 1977.

ALICE ROSS

General Foods

The General Foods Company can date its beginning to 1895 when C. W. Post created the Postum Cereal Company to market Postum, a coffee substitute made out of wheat bran and molasses. He got the idea for the substitute while a patient at the Battle Creek Sanitarium operated by the Kellogg brothers.

In 1897 Post introduced a cereal that he called Grape-Nuts. This was followed in 1904 by Elijah's Manna, a corn flake cereal that would not be a hit with consumers until it was renamed Post Toasties. Upon Post's death in 1914 Marjorie Merriwether Post, his daughter, took over the company and began to create what would be General Foods. Ms. Post married Edward F. Hutton, an investment broker, in 1920. By 1923 he was chairman of the Postum Cereal Company.

In 1925 the company acquired the Jell-O Company and in quick order added Swans Down cake flour, Minute tapioca, Baker's coconut, Baker's chocolate, and Log Cabin syrup to an expanding list of consumer products. Maxwell House coffee was added in 1928, and the following year

Postum purchased the General Foods Company from Clarence Birdseye, the man who had perfected a successful method for quick freezing food. To reflect the diverse product mix under the control of the company, the name was changed to the General Foods Company. Over the next thirty years more brand names were added, including Gaines Dog Food and Yuban coffee. Shortly after World War II ended, Maxwell House instant coffee was introduced. Other successful products included Kool-Aid, Tang, Crystal Light, 4 Seasons salad dressing, Oscar Mayer meat products, and Open Pit barbecue sauce.

General Foods is a case study in how large companies acquire and assimilate smaller food companies. General Foods has been called the "prototypical American food processor." It was acquired and assimilated itself in 1985 when the tobacco giant Philip Morris bought General Foods. In 1989 General Foods and Kraft, which Philip Morris had bought the year before, were combined to form a food products division called Kraft General Foods. In 1995 the name was shortened to Kraft Foods Inc.

[*See also* Birdseye Corporation; Cereal, Cold; Coffee; Coffee, Instant; Coffee Substitutes; Jell-O; Kellogg Company; Kraft Foods; Maxwell House; Post Foods.]

BIBLIOGRAPHY

Paulakepos, Paula, ed. *International Directory of Company Histories*. Vol. 7. Detroit: St. James Press, 1993, p. 272.

JOSEPH M. CARLIN

General Mills

In 1866 Cadwallader Washburn opened a flour mill in Minneapolis, Minnesota, calling it the Minneapolis Milling Company. In 1869 Charles A. Pillsbury, another Minneapolis miller, established his flour mill across the Mississippi River from Washburn's. A century and a half later, these two competing firms would become one company. When John Crosby joined Washburn's business in 1877 the company changed its name to the Washburn Crosby Company. In 1880, after winning the gold, silver, and bronze medals at the first International Miller's Exhibition, the Washburn Crosby Company changed the brand name of its best flour to Gold Medal. After acquiring twenty-seven other milling operations, the company incorporated as General Mills in 1928. At the time, it was the largest flour-milling company in the world.

In 1921 General Mills introduced Betty Crocker to the world, a fictional spokeswoman originally created as a persona and a pen name to answer consumer letters. Betty Crocker was to become one of the most successful brand names ever introduced by an American food company. It was more than a name; it was a face, a signature, and a radio voice. For many people Betty Crocker really existed.

In 1933 the company scored another advertising success with the slogan "Wheaties—The Breakfast of Champions." However, the company's flagship cereal has always been Cheerios, created in 1941 as "Cheerioats" but renamed several years later. In 1995 the successful formula was supplemented with sugar-frosted Cheerios. Pursuing strength in the breakfast-food market, General Mills purchased the Chex and Cookie Crisp cereal brands, along with Chex Mix snacks, making it the second-largest ready-to-eat cereal company in America, just behind Kellogg.

After World War II, consumers demanded products that required less time to prepare. In response, General Mills introduced Betty Crocker cake mixes in 1947 and presweetened cereals in 1954. Building on its strong base of brand-name cereals and convenience foods, such as Cheerios, Chex, Cocoa Puffs, Kix, Total, Trix, Yoplait yogurt, and Hamburger Helper, the company expanded by acquiring Lloyd's Barbeque Company, a maker of refrigerated, microwave-ready entrees.

The company acquired the Red Lobster seafood chain in 1970 and in 1983 created the Olive Garden Italian restaurant chain, but in 1995 it sold the restaurant division to its shareholders to create Darden Restaurants, Inc. In 2001 General Mills acquired Pillsbury, which had begun as the mill across the river more than one hundred years earlier, to create one of the world's largest food companies.

[*See also* Betty Crocker; Cakes; Cereal, Cold; Pillsbury; Wheat.]

BIBLIOGRAPHY

"General Mills." In *International Directory of Company Histories*, edited by Jay P. Pederson. Vol. 36. Chicago: St. James Press, 2001.
General Mills Corporate website. http://www.generalmills.com.

JOSEPH M. CARLIN

Genetically Modified Food, *see* *Biotechnology*

German American Food

According to U.S. census data, German Americans are the largest American ethnic group. Because Germany was not a unitary country until the 1870s, German American identity was defined by language rather than by national origin. German speakers immigrating from many different countries have been counted as German Americans, whereas English-, French-, and Spanish-speaking immigrants have been divided and subdivided by national origin, religion, and even regional identity. Since the early eighteenth century, German Americans have been the largest non-British group in America. Between 1790 and 1910, more than 10 percent of all Americans spoke German.

Because the German presence has been so large and continuous, German Americans do not always receive credit for such all-American foods as casseroles, cheesecake, cream cheese, cream soups, hot dogs, jelly doughnuts, meatballs, meat loaf, milk gravy, potato salad, pretzels, sauerkraut, sticky buns, whoopie pies, and numerous types of pickles, cakes, and cookies. American beer is lager—like German beer and unlike British ale. On the other hand, German Americans are often falsely credited for hamburgers. The German American ethnic group is so large that it has become involved in almost every other kind of American food, from the cuisine of the German Cajuns who settled in Louisiana during Spanish colonial times to the many uses of Spam on Hawaiian tables. Especially among the immigrants of the 1840s and 1850s, German Americans included many professional bakers, brewers, butchers, chefs, grocers, restaurateurs, and wine merchants who dispersed to farm and frontier as well as major cities. German Americans started the well-known midwestern breweries as well as wineries in New York and Missouri.

The major founding stock German American population was the Pennsylvania Dutch, who were distinguished from later immigrants by a uniquely American dialect of Low German and by their prominent Protestant sects. Another distinctive subgroup was Germans from Russia, who in the 1870s began homesteading the prairie states in groups. Smaller groups of German Jews, Transylvanian Saxons, Danube Swabians, and German-speaking populations from Eastern Europe have maintained ethnic customs in food and culture distinct from the German American mainstream. The major story of German

American food and drink has been how so much of it has become assimilated as characteristically American mainstream while many dishes have stayed recognizably German American.

German-owned restaurants outside Pennsylvania arose first to feed the immigrants of the 1840s and 1850s and were regarded as cheap, unreliable, and somewhat exotic. After the Civil War, there appeared more elaborate saloons, beer halls, *Weinstuben*, and function rooms that appealed to the general American public. These establishments popularized not only Rhine wines and lager beer but also a variety of sausages, breads, and cakes. German American saloons offered an extensive free lunch, with emphasis on salty hams and pickles, which were thought to increase beer sales. Some of these places survived Prohibition by becoming sit-down restaurants and serving near-beer. German restaurants were popular in most American cities, even those without large German American communities.

German American identity has been greatly muted since World War I, when more than twenty states passed laws against using the German language in public meetings or schools. Prohibition meant the end of many more German American saloons and restaurants. Many German Americans changed their names or otherwise accelerated assimilation to Anglo-American norms. At the same time, the Pennsylvania Dutch and Germans from Russia began emphasizing their separation from German roots. (It is not true, however, that sauerkraut was renamed "liberty cabbage." According to the *The American Language* (1919) by H. L. Mencken, a rare contemporary source, this name was a short-lived local experiment.) When Germany was again an enemy country in World War II, the development of separate identities accelerated for Austrian Americans, German-speaking Bohemians (from what became the Czech Republic), German-speaking Alsatians, German Jews, Swiss Americans, and smaller groups of German-speaking persons from eastern Europe, from Latvia to Romania.

The ancestry survey of the 1990 U.S. census showed a dramatic increase in the number of citizens claiming German ancestry and corresponding decreases in the projections for other German-speaking immigrant groups. Thus German American identity is being revived, but German food has yet to regain its position among the leading ethnic cuisines in restaurants and cookbooks. Even so, although many German American foods have been assimilated into the American mainstream, many

German Caricature. The new immigrant Hans Schloppenberg finds work as a waiter in a tavern. Cartoon by Geo. Topp, 1882, in a series of four trade cards for Fiske's House Goods.

distinctively German American dishes have persisted. In some cases, such as the Salzburger raisin bread of Savannah, Georgia, the ethnic identity of a dish has outlived the group that produced it, in this case, an eighteenth-century Austrian settlement. Many Pennsylvania Dutch dishes developed in the United States, such as shoofly pie, continue to be recognized as ethnic rather than general American food, and the list of typically Pennsylvania Dutch foods includes many pickles and pies that were at one time mainstream American dishes but have been dropped by other populations.

Sauerbraten and *Rouladen*, among the most common German American dishes in contributed cookbooks, have been popular on German American tables since the 1840s, yet continue to be viewed as German American food. The sustained ability to maintain separate German American, especially Pennsylvania Dutch, foodways is in considerable contrast to the situation of other "founding stock" ethnic groups, such as the Scotch-Irish, Welsh Quakers, Huguenots, and Holland Dutch, and is rivaled only by the Cajuns and New Mexico Hispanics. The language barrier has been a factor, as have continuous reinforcement of German immigration through the 1990s and the presence of culturally conservative religious sects that live apart from the mainstream. More than a century of English-language cookbooks, media coverage, and Lancaster farmers' markets have failed to break down the idea that potato salad and perhaps pretzels are German American foods "on loan" to the wider culture.

The Formation of Pennsylvania Dutch Food

Germans were the largest minority in the New Netherland colony after 1650, but the group is usually dated from the arrival in 1681 of fourteen Mennonite families to found Germantown, Pennsylvania. The Pennsylvania Dutch came from many parts of the German-speaking world and belonged to many Protestant sects as well as mainstream Lutheran and Reformed churches. They moved into inland valley farms up and down the Appalachians and across the mountains to Ohio and Indiana. They were joined by Moravians settling around Winston-Salem, North Carolina, and Bethlehem, Pennsylvania, and by ten thousand Hessian deserters during the American Revolution. The Germans were regarded by other colonists and early Americans as thrifty and wise farmers and sometimes were caricatured for stinginess, backwardness, and their mixture of Low German and accented English speech. German food was noted for the quality of the farm produce, dairy products, and baked goods before the American Revolution and continues to be so noted in the early twenty-first century.

Although most Americans have an image of the old-fashioned lifestyles of the culturally conservative Amish and old-order Mennonites, Pennsylvania Dutch cooking has always been innovative. Thus it was possible for Alma Kauffman, who grew up Amish, to write in the 1970s:

> Traditional Amish cooking has not disappeared, it is just a bit overshadowed by new food fashions. To a student like [the Ohio radio broadcaster] Bill Randle the change is an interesting sign because it shows the Amish are a flexible, changing society. To a former Amish girl like me it's regrettable. In *my* cookbook Yumazetti (all sixty dozen variations) will never replace fried ham—or even bean soup.

The bean soup was served at Sunday collective meals from at least the mid-nineteenth century. Yumazetti, a pasta casserole, may have entered Amish life as late as the 1960s.

Pennsylvania Dutch farming evolved from a system centered on hogs to one that included dairy and beef cattle, and the smoked Lebanon bologna was developed. Many characteristic pies were taken from Anglo-American models. Pretzels were brought to Pennsylvania from Bavaria in the 1840s, and the first commercial pretzel bakery was established in 1861.

Among the best-known Pennsylvania Dutch dishes are *rivvel* (noodle) soup, chicken soup with sweet corn, *shnitz und knep* (dried apples and dumplings stewed with ham or smoked pork), *bouva shenkel* (beef-stuffed dumplings called "boys legs"), Philadelphia scrapple (known as *panhas*, or "pan rabbit," in farm country), hash dishes known locally as "hexel" and "mornix," red-beet pickled eggs, raisin pie, *schnitz* pie, shoofly pie, Moravian sugar cake, funnel cake, and *fastnacht*

doughnuts. Although the proverbial seven sweets and seven sours are not actually represented in fourteen condiment dishes on every Pennsylvania Dutch table, the medieval German palate of sweet and sour continues to run through much Pennsylvania Dutch cooking. Home pickling, preserving, and canning have continued long after they were a practical necessity.

German-language cookbooks were published in Pennsylvania and Ohio in the 1840s, joining an already active press of almanacs and periodicals. There are references to Pennsylvania Dutch dishes in *The Kentucky Housewife* (1839), the most explicit being a recipe for vermicelli and noodles: "These are German cookeries, principally used for thickening soups and sauces." By 1866, a recipe titled Snitz and Knep was published in *Godey's Lady's Book*. The first Pennsylvania Dutch cookbooks in English were published at the turn of the twentieth century. *The Inglenook Cook Book* gathered Brethren recipes. *Mary at the Farm and Book of Recipes* (1915) by Edith M. Thomas is organized around a running situation comedy

---

SHOOFLY PIE

SHOOFLY PIE, a brown-sugar pie filling topped with streusel, is the canonical dessert of Pennsylvania Dutch cuisine, but both the form of the pie and the name "shoofly" are relatively recent developments. The dessert is a combination of the thrifty molasses pies that hark back to English treacle tarts, and a German *Streuselkuchen*, translated as "crumb cake" in Pennsylvania manuscripts since the 1860s. The name is not likely older than the 1870s, when "shoo fly" was what (English-speaking) baseball players said instead of swearing when they missed a play. The phrase might have become attached to the easy cake and pie in much the same way that "fudge"—another euphemism—became the name of an easily made soft candy in the late 1880s. (There has been a fanciful suggestion that an Alsatian among the Pennsylvania Dutch might have compared the crumbs atop the pie to a cauliflower, or *chou-fleur* in French.) The American cake is especially casual because the same pastry crumbs are used for the cake and for the topping, while the German original uses a separate nut-based topping.

William Woys Weaver believes the dish first appeared as Centennial Cake in 1876 in Philadelphia, but his recipe dates only from the 1930s. The name spelled "shoe fly cake" appeared in a Pennsylvania manuscript of the 1890s. A Mount Carmel church cookbook of about the same era contained a recipe for "shoo

fly cake" made in pie pans and a "shoo-fly cake" made in a pie crust. The 1904 *Inglenook Cook Book* has the first printed recipe for a crumb pie, as well the cake. The 1915 *Mary at the Farm* suggests "pebble dash" as an alternate name. "Dash" is Pennsylvania German for "pie" or "sweet dumpling." A 1915 collection from Reading, Pennsylvania, had a recipe for "shoo-fly pie," but another from Reading a year later has "German shoo-fly." *Rivel kuche* was another early name for an all-streusel shoofly pie, or what Edna Eby Heller described in the mid-twentieth century as "shoe-fly cake"—the crumbs baked in a pie plate or cake pan without the wet layer. Heller also differentiated between "wet" and "dry" versions of shoofly pie, the latter for dunking in breakfast coffee. Coffee might be poured over the wet kind.

In Pennsylvania Dutch country today, one is as likely to find apple, cherry, or blueberry crumb pies as the original sugar base. A similar Pennsylvania Dutch pie with lemon flavoring was known as "Montgomery pie." Because brown sugar and molasses pies have always been important in Anglo-American cooking, from English treacle tarts to pecan pie, the increasing heaps of streusel on top may be the crucial Pennsylvania Dutch spin on an Anglo-American food.

MARK H. ZANGER

---

about Mary-from-the-City and her Pennsylvania German relatives, who had recipes for "schnitz and knopf" and an early version of shoofly pie. In the 1930s, a bewildering variety of recipe pamphlets were sold to tourists in the Pennsylvania Dutch country. The cuisine has been re-explored in popular cookbooks by Marcia Adams, Phyllis Pellman Good, Betty Groff, Edna Eby Heller, and William Woys Weaver, and a number of Amish and Mennonite women have been culinary missionaries through local publication and contribution. In an old Pennsylvania Dutch colony in Ontario, Canada, Edna Staebler popularized Mennonite food in books beginning with *Food That Really Schmecks* (1968).

The Forty-Eighters and Other Early Immigrants

Great numbers of German Americans arrived in the United States during the 1840s and 1850s, with a peak in 1854. Those fleeing the failure of the 1848 uprisings were known as "forty-eighters." This group, consisting mostly of speakers of High German, did not connect with the Pennsylvania Dutch farmers and more often settled in eastern and midwestern cities. A contingent of German Jews was included in this group, and they were joined by continuing waves of immigrants. Another peak occurred in the 1870s, motivated by Bismarck's laws against socialists and Catholics. These "new immigrant" German Americans settled heavily in Mid-Atlantic and midwestern cities, including Baltimore, Philadelphia, Cincinnati, Pittsburgh, St. Louis, and above all, Chicago and Milwaukee. In these cities, German-speaking communities were so large that they retained a sense of regional foods from Bavaria, Prussia, and Bohemia.

The forty-eighters brought German dishes not only for their own tables but also for popular restaurants and beer halls. Specialties included large breakfasts, lentil soup, liver dumplings, Wiener schnitzel, steak tartare, sauerbraten with potato pancakes and red cabbage, *Rouladen*, knockwurst, bratwurst, liverwurst, hasenpfeffer, Black Forest cake, *Lebkuchen*, *Schnecken*, strudel, and many cookies. Baked goods especially have been welcomed into the American mainstream, sometimes with translated names such as "cinnamon stars," "sand tarts," "cinnamon buns," "sticky buns," and "pepper nuts." Some of these cookies are also Scandinavian treats, and *Pfeffernussen* may be known as *Pepperkakkor*, if not "spice cookies." Despite their contributions, German Americans in the Midwest were subject to some of the most extreme wartime rhetoric

and were stigmatized into the 1960s for eating brains and blood sausage.

Although German-language cookbooks were written and published in the United States as early as the 1840s, Milwaukee editions of German cookbooks, such as that of Henriette Davidis, were popular in German American homes of the late nineteenth century. Many German Americans were eager to embrace American foods, so later and posthumous editions of Davidis have translated recipe titles. One frequently finds recipes handwritten in German script in English-language cookbooks of the late nineteenth century. A number of American cookbooks were translated into German, including *Dr. Chase's Recipes* (1865), the *Buckeye Cook Book* (1880), and *The "Home Queen" World's Fair Souvenir Cook Book* (1893). Many cookbooks by German Americans appeared in the twentieth century. Titles ranged from the barely adapted German recipes of the frequently reprinted *The Art of German Cooking and Baking* (1909) by Lina Meier to the deliberate Americanization of the first *The Way to a Man's Heart* (1901), later known as *The Settlement Cookbook*. A number of German American recipes were included in *The Joy of Cooking* by Irma Rombauer.

Germans from Russia

Although German immigration has been continuous, a third distinctive group began coming to the United States in the 1870s. These immigrants were Germans who had relocated to Russia in the eighteenth century. Many had left the same parts of Germany for some of the same reasons as the Pennsylvania Dutch but had acquired different dialects and foods over their 120 years in various parts of Russia. These Germans were invited by Catherine the Great in the 1750s and were encouraged to form distinctive German-speaking colonies along the Volga River and around the Black Sea. In the 1870s, however, Russian reform governments began repressing these Germans, and the process accelerated with the Russian Revolution in 1917. In the United States, Germans from Russia did not initially connect closely with either of the previous German American populations but set up their own settlements in the prairie states, becoming the largest ethnic minority in North Dakota. They kept to their religious and Russian regional identities, thus Black Sea Mennonites had a concentration in central Kansas. The most typical dish of Germans from Russia has been stuffed breads, known as either *bierocks* (a Germanized version of "pierogi") or *kraut runza* (German for "cabbage bun"). Their cookbooks include a number of recipes for *stirrum*, a scrambled pancake known as *schman* or *shmorran* in other German American communities but served with greens among Germans from Russia. The Mennonite church groups were among the channels of connection with other German Americans.

German American Foods in the Mainstream

German Americans have always been a diverse community, and their foods and foodways are diverse as well. Probably the largest subgroup is German American families who are assimilated Americans and eat no more German American food than did Presidents Hoover and Eisenhower. At the other extreme are German-speaking communalists, from the Rappites of the 1840s through the Amana colonies in Iowa to the ongoing Hutterites, who copy out nineteenth-century recipes and eighteenth-century German-language sermons whenever they launch a new collective farm.

Many of the mainstream American foods influenced by German Americans date to colonial and early American times. These dishes are poorly documented because the influence began at the fringes of Pennsylvania Dutch farm country and worked toward cities. Prominence in dairy farming suggests German American influence on the American love of cream soup and the preference for milk gravy in the farm country of Pennsylvania, Indiana, and upstate New York. Although there are medieval references in England to cream cheese, the modern American form was developed by German Americans in Philadelphia. Much the same can be said about modern American cheesecake, developed by German Jews in New York City.

The case of sauerkraut is much clearer because fermented cabbage was not a part of British or French foodways. The British army made a point of acquiring sauerkraut in Pennsylvania during the American Revolution because British scientists believed it might cure scurvy. Three-bean salad, popular since the 1950s, is a direct transcription of German *Bohnensalat*. Casseroles were not unknown in British and French cooking and may have been described in ancient Rome, but the American love of casseroles seems to emanate from Pennsylvania Dutch ovens and is strongest in the heavily German American Midwest.

Like casseroles, cookies and doughnuts are an area of overlap between German and Scandinavian cuisines.

Therefore, it is difficult to trace whose spice cookie or jelly doughnut (*Berliner kransen* in Swedish) is the original. Tracing origins is not a problem with explicitly German inventions, such as pretzels and lager beer, or explicitly German American inventions, such as whoopie pie and gob sandwich cookies. When potato salad becomes "German potato salad" is not clear. One theory is that the dish is "German" only when a clear dressing is applied to hot potatoes.

Philadelphia scrapple is generally thought to have been developed by German American butchers; however, the name is closest to Holland Dutch, and the Pennsylvania Dutch term is not scrapple but *panhas* (pan rabbit). There are similar pan sausages of oatmeal and pork parts across northern Europe, including England, but it seems to have been German American butchers in Philadelphia who adapted the recipe to include local buckwheat. German American butchers also receive the credit for marketing *goetta* (pork-oatmeal loaf) and "city chicken" (a ground pork roast) in Cincinnati. These butchers likely played an important role in the switch from veal loaf to American, beef-based meat loaf in the 1880s. German "false hare" is an old version of beef loaf. German-style chopped raw steak was the first popular form of steak tartare in the United States, and a German-language cookbook from Milwaukee contained a recipe for a steak tartare sandwich, although the popular name "cannibal sandwiches" did not appear until later. To complete the ground meat dishes, there are widely remembered Swedish, Danish, and Norwegian meatballs, but *Königsberger Klopse* appeared first and in greater numbers than the other forms. Probably the only kind of chopped meat German Americans did not help originate is hamburger, which first came to America in a British cookbook as "Hamburgh Sausage" and then appeared on a Delmonico's menu. In calling the dish "Hamburgh Sausage," the London publisher of Hannah Glasse's cookbook apparently considered chopped beef a German food. The hot dog is evidently a German-style cooked wurst, although not authentically a frankfurter (from Frankfurt) or a wiener (from Vienna). The bun, added for American convenience but not unprecedented in Germany, makes the sandwich an American hot dog.

Sticky buns, associated with Philadelphia, are fluffy versions of *Schnecken*. The significant and early German settlement in southern Texas suggests a strong association between wiener schnitzel and chicken-fried steak, as well as a possible influence of goulash soup on the addition of cumin to San Antonio chili.

The ancestry survey of the 2000 U.S. census suggested a decrease in the number of respondents claiming German descent, as it did in a number of white immigrant groups. This swing away from the ethnic revival of the 1980s may clear a space for a revival of German dishes in American restaurants.

[*See also* Beer; Beer Halls; Ethnic Foods; Goetta; Mid-Atlantic Region; Saloons; Scrapple.]

BIBLIOGRAPHY

Adams, Marcia. *Cooking from Quilt Country: Hearty Recipes from Amish and Mennonite Kitchens.* New York: Potter, 1989. Northern Indiana recipes are the basis of these somewhat different Pennsylvania Dutch dishes from a Public Broadcasting Service series.

Aurand, A. Monroe, Jr., ed. *Cooking with the Pennsylvania "Dutch."* Harrisburg, PA: Aurand, 1946. In this pamphlet, shoofly pie is also called "pebble dash" and "rivel kuchen."

Bryan, Mrs. Lettice. *The Kentucky Housewife.* Cincinnati: Shepard and Stearns, 1839. A facsimile by Image Graphics, Paducah, Kentucky, no date and apparently out of print. In her recipe for vermicelli and noodles, Bryan noted, "These are German cookeries, principally for thickening soups and noodles."

Davidis, Henriette. *Koch-Buch für die Deutschen in Amerika.* Milwaukee, WI: George Brumder, 1897. The original edition was published in 1877. A popular German cookbook posthumously published in Milwaukee with more and more American recipes and English translations, reaching even Pennsylvania Dutch country. Lists "Hamburg steaks" as the English translation of *Gute Beefstakes von gehacktem Fleisch.*

Gardner, Margaret Knoll. *Best-Loved Pennsylvania Dutch Recipes, Including Many of the Amish.* Mannheim, PA: Photo Arts, 1987. Shoofly pie topped with whipped cream.

Frederick, J. George. *The Pennsylvania Dutch and Their Cookery.* New York: Business Bourse, 1935. Reprint, *Pennsylvania Dutch Cook Book,* New York: Dover 1971.

Good, Phyllis Pellman, and Stoltzfus, Louise. *The Best of Mennonite Fellowship Meals: More Than 900 Recipes to Share with Friends at Home or at Church.* Intercourse, PA: Good Books, 1991. Two authors on Pennsylvania Dutch cooking collaborated on a book of contributed recipes, some from Germans from Russia and some from far afield, showing the effects of Mennonite missionary activity.

Groff, Betty, and Wilson, José. *Good Earth and Country Cooking.* Harrisburg, PA: Stackpole, 1974. Modern Mennonite Pennsylvania farm cooking from Groff's celebrated family farm restaurant.

Gueldner, R. M. H. *German Food and Folkways: Heirloom Memories from Europe, South Russia, and the Great Plains.* Bismarck, ND: Germans from Russia Heritage Society, 2002. Latest in a series of cookbooks preserving bierocks, stirrum, pickles, and other delights that kept Germans going through the hard years in Russia and the Dakotas.

"HLM's Plain Cakes and Cooking Receipts." 1869. Historical archives, Moravian Museum, Bethlehem, PA. Unpublished Pennsylvania Moravian English-language manuscript recipe book. "Crumb cake E. M. K." was written immediately after a soup dated July 4, 1869.

Heller, Edna Eby. *Edna Eby Heller's Dutch Cookbook.* Lancaster, PA: Vernon Martin, 1963. The original edition was published in 1953. The long-time food editor of *Pennsylvania Folk Life* magazine was the first writer to differentiate in print the wet and dry styles of shoofly pie.

Hershberger, Alma T. *Amish Taste Cookbook: More Than 500 Favorite Recipes from Amish Homes in the United States, Canada, and Africa.* Lenexa, KS: Cookbook, 1977. Discusses "jon-setti," "youmesetti," "yamisetta," and "yum zhetti."

Hoppe, Emilie. *Seasons of Plenty: Amana Communal Cooking.* Ames: Iowa State University Press, 1994. Detailed memories and recipes from religious communes in Iowa from 1855 to 1932 and local tradition since. The Amana Church Society was founded somewhat later than the sects that settled Pennsylvania and arrived in the United States in 1842 in upstate New York.

Kander, Mrs. Simon. *The Way to a Man's Heart: Under the Auspices of "The Settlement," 499 Fifth Street.* Bedford, MA: Applewood, 1996. The original edition was published in 1903. A German Jewish American fund-raising cookbook that expanded into a popular success. The first edition has recipes for German cakes and cookies alongside dull, Fannie Farmer–like recipes that were taught to immigrants at the settlement house.

Kant, Jonita. *The Hutterite Community Cookbook.* Intercourse, PA: Good Books, 1990. Recipes written by conservative Anabaptist communards from Russia and eastern Europe who settled the prairie states in 1871.

Kaufman, Edna, com. *Melting Pot of Mennonite Cookery.* North Newton, KS: Mennonite, 1964. Attempts to differentiate recipes of ten subgroups of Mennonites. Thus *bierogi* are called "Swiss volhenian," "Swiss galician," and "Polish."

Lancaster County Farm Cook Book. Lebanon, PA: Applied Arts, 1967. Uncredited recipes said to be gathered from farm families plain and "gay." Contains photographs of Lewis B. Sturges, age eighty-four, making pretzels in his father's bakery, built in 1861.

Lestz, Gerlad S. *The Pennsylvania Dutch Cookbook.* New York: Grossett and Dunlap, 1970. A contributed cookbook, mostly from Amish sources, with four recipes for shoofly pie.

Longacre, Doris Janzen. *More-with-Less Cookbook.* Scottsdale, PA: Herald, 1976. Popular and influential cookbook commissioned by the Mennonite Central Committee to incorporate ecological consciousness, health food, and international cooking in this theologically conservative but politically liberal denomination.

O'Brien, Marian Maeve, ed. *The Shaw House Cook Book.* St. Louis, MO: Historical Committee and Women's Association of Missouri Botanical Garden, 1963. Victorian recipes, some from German American and German Hungarian families in a German American city.

Pennsylvania Dutch Cook Book of Fine Old Recipes. Reading, PA: Culinary Arts, 1936. Constantly in print.

Pennsylvania Dutch Cooking: Traditional Dutch Dishes. Gettysburg, PA: Dutchcraft, n.d. A pamphlet with "rivel pie" instead of shoofly pie.

Randle, Bill. *Plain Cooking: Low-Cost, Good-Tasting Amish Recipes.* New York: Quadrangle, 1974. Amish and Mennonite recipes compiled by Randle, the popular radio announcer from Cleveland, Ohio, with an introduction by Alma Kauffman. Randle also compiled a multiethnic collection and three *Ask Your Neighbor Cookbook* collections.

Ruch, Louise A., ed. *Moravian Recipes from Past to Present.* Bethlehem, PA: Central Moravian Church, n.d. Six recipes for

Moravian sugar cake show the persistence of this ethnic treat among Moravian church members.

Sisters of the Church of the Brethren, subscribers, and friends of the *Inglenook* magazine. *The Inglenook Cook Book: Choice Recipes.* 12th ed. Elgin, IL: Brethren, 1974. The original edition was published in 1901. The Moravian Brethren have broadened the ethnic base of their church. They have already anglicized Pennsylvania Dutch dishes and included early Chinese American recipes from Brother Moy Wing of Chicago. This book contains recipes for *rivvel* soup, raisin cream pie, and *fastnacht* cakes, six recipes for *shnitz und knep,* and recipes crumb pies that are almost shoofly pie.

Snyder, Annie Iaegar. *Club House Cook Book.* Reading, PA: Women's Club of Reading. 1916. The members of an Anglo-American club in Pennsylvania Dutch country contributed recipes for several characteristic pickles, sand tarts, *fastnachts,* cinnamon flop, and German shoofly.

Talent Cook Book. Mt. Carmel, PA: Grace Evangelical Lutheran Church, n.d. Likely published in 1890–1905, because the book contains advertisements with no telephone numbers. The recipes for shoofly cake may be the first printed recipes for shoofly baked in pie crust.

Thomas, Edith M. *Mary at the Farm and Book of Recipes.* Harrisburg, PA: Evangelical, 1928. The original edition was published in 1915. The first thorough description of Pennsylvania Dutch cooking and recipes in English are from a running situation comedy about Mary-from-the-City and her Pennsylvania German relatives. The book contains recipes for schnitz and knopf, mouldashas, snitz pie, shoofly pie or pebble dash, and bean salad.

Weaver, Nevilee Maass. *Rezepte: German-Texan Culinary Art.* Austin, TX: Eakin, 1999. Nineteenth-century recipes translated by a third-generation descendant of an immigrant.

Weaver, William Woys. *Pennsylvania Dutch Country Cooking.* New York: Abbeville, 1993. This beautifully illustrated book brings together many of Weaver's strengths: his command of German dialects, his sense of history, and his knowledge of antique implements and heirloom gardening. Weaver's weaknesses are for the esoteric and for speculation, although he does include spins on shoofly pie, Moravian sugar cake, *shnitz und knepp,* and chicken corn soup.

Weaver, William Woys. *Sauerkraut Yankees: Pennsylvania German Foods and Foodways.* Philadelphia: University of Pennsylvania Press, 1983. A translation of the 1851 Pennsylvania Dutch cookbook, *Die Geschickte Hausfrau.* Contains recipes from other early sources and historical commentary, some fanciful. Shoofly pie, whoopie pie, and *rivvel* soup are not represented.

Yoder, Joseph W. *Rosanna of the Amish.* Scottdale, PA: Herald, 1995. Centennial edition. Autobiographical novel of nineteenth-century Amish life places bean soup at the center of Sunday dining.

MARK H. ZANGER

Gibbons, Euell

Euell Gibbons held a number of arbitrary occupations in the course of his life. He was at different times a hobo, a cowboy, a beachcomber, a surveyor, a boat builder, a newspaperman, a schoolteacher, a farmer, an educator, an author, and a spokesperson for Grape-Nuts cereal. But he is best known for being the man who taught America to forage for food in the wild.

Many European cuisines still rely heavily on foraging. For example, the French and Italians are infatuated with mushroom hunting, but modern Americans have not had a deep interest in gathering wild foods. Since Gibbons, great American chefs like Alice Waters and organizations like the Slow Food Movement are beginning to revive the concepts of, respect for, and exchange with nature and the environment. Early American Indians relied wholly on foraging and hunting for their sustenance. They believed in life lived in harmony with nature. Gibbons imparted this credo to the American public and was awarded an honorary degree by Susquehanna University in 1972.

Gibbons was born in 1911 and raised in Clarksville, Texas, until the family moved to New Mexico when he was eleven. Legend tells us that by the time he was a teenager he supplemented the family's food supply by hunting, trapping, and foraging, which he had learned to do from his mother. He would leave for the forest with a knapsack in the morning and return in the evening to feed his family from a bag full of wild, edible items.

He left home at the age of fifteen for the Northwest. Once there, Gibbons wandered, supporting himself by working at odd jobs and foraging. He served in the army for two years, from 1934 to 1936. While he was in the army he married his first wife, Anna Swanson; they had two boys and had divorced by 1945. Although he had joined the Communist Party in the 1930s, he later renounced his membership. Gibbons moved to Hawaii after his stint in the army, where he worked in a shipyard. After the war he became a beachcomber, finishing his high school degree, attending the University of Hawaii, and marrying his second wife, Freda Fryer. The couple taught on Maui until 1953 when they joined the Religious Society of Friends (Quakers) and moved back to the East Coast to teach in Quaker schools. It was there that Gibbons began to write what he thought was going to be a novel. However, when he handed in his manuscript, his publisher told him: "Take the novel out. Leave the wild food in." The result was *Stalking the Wild Asparagus,* published in 1962. It was immensely popular, taken up by those drawn to the back-to-nature movement, and it established Euell Gibbons as the authority in the area of wild food.

In 1963 the Gibbons family moved to a farm in Troxelville, Pennsylvania, where Gibbons wrote six other books: *Stalking the Healthful Herbs, Stalking the Blue-Eyed Scallop, Beachcombers Handbook, Stalking the Good Life, Stalking the Far Away Places,* and *Euell Gibbons' Handbook of Edible Wild Plants.* Gibbons wrote articles for magazines including *National Geographic* and *Organic Gardening and Farming.* He made television appearances in Grape-Nuts cereal commercials, on *The Tonight Show Starring Johnny Carson,* and *The Sonny and Cher Show.* Gibbons died in 1975 of a heart attack at the age of sixty-four.

[*See also* Cookbooks and Manuscripts, *subentry* From World War II to the 1960s; Slow Food Movement; Waters, Alice.]

LIZA JERNOW

Gin

Gin, a juniper-flavored distilled spirit (though many other botanical ingredients are now used in its production), takes its name from *genièvre,* the French word for "juniper." It is often said that gin was first created in the mid-seventeenth century by Franz Deleboe (1614–1672), also known as Dr. Sylvius, a professor at the University of Leiden in the Netherlands; however, some sources claim that similar juniper-based spirits were first made by Italian monks and used in attempts to combat the bubonic plague (1347–1350), since juniper was known to be a diuretic and one of the symptoms of the plague was enlarged glands in the groin. It is clear that the spirit was being made before Deleboe is said to have created it, because English mercenaries helping the Dutch in their war with Spain introduced gin to England in the late 1500s. It is possible that Deleboe's recipe was the first to use grain rather than fruit as a base. Grain is the base of all gins made in the twenty-first century.

Two styles of gin—Old Tom, a sweetened spirit, and dry gin—were both popular as cocktail ingredients in the United States by 1862, when Jerry Thomas, a celebrated bartender of the time, published the world's first cocktail recipe book, *How to Mix Drinks; or, The Bon-Vivant's Companion.* Whiskey, though, was the spirit of choice among Americans until Prohibition was enacted in January 1920. Using industrial alcohol and oil of juniper, bootleggers during Prohibition found it relatively simple to make a crude form of gin. Whiskey was much more difficult to replicate. So scofflaws during the so-called Noble Experiment, including many women who had been banned from most bars prior to Prohibition, preferred to drink gin when they visited speakeasies or threw cocktail parties at home. Even after Prohibition was repealed in December 1933, gin retained its popularity, especially as the main ingredient in the dry martini cocktail.

In the 1940s, when vodka was first widely marketed in the United States, gin began a very slow decline in popularity. Advertisers told Americans that vodka would leave them "breathless," while gin was fairly easy to detect on the breath. Some martini drinkers began switching to the less-aromatic spirit, especially when it was still acceptable to partake of three-martini lunches and return to work in the afternoon. Not until the 1980s, after Absolut vodka introduced a very seductive advertising campaign, did gin really fall from favor in this country. Meanwhile Bombay, a gin introduced to America in the 1950s, was lurking in the background.

Most gins have a highly perfumed taste with juniper flavors predominating, but Bombay is far subtler, and this style of gin started to gain in popularity in the mid- to late 1990s. Gin producers targeted vodka drinkers by wooing them with a softer style of gin that was easier to acquire a taste for than the bolder bottlings on the market, and this tactic appeared to have been relatively successful by the early 2000s. Many more gins have been introduced—some touting ingredients never before known as gin flavorings, such as cucumbers—to attract people who were not enamored of the bolder styles of regular gin. Many gins are available in the United States; the most popular brands at the beginning of the twenty-first century included Beefeater, Bombay, Bombay Sapphire, Boodles, Gordon's, Hendrick's, Plymouth, Tanqueray, and Tanqueray No. 10.

[*See also* Cocktails; Martini.]

BIBLIOGRAPHY

Brown, Gordon. *Classic Spirits of the World.* New York: Abbeville Press, 1996.
Kinross, Lord. *The Kindred Spirit: A History of Gin and the House of Booth.* London: Newman Neame, 1959.
Lord, Tony. *The World Guide to Spirits, Aperitifs and Cocktails.* New York: Sovereign Books, 1979.

GARY AND MARDEE HAIDIN REGAN

Ginger Ale

Ginger ale—a carbonated beverage sweetened and flavored with extract of ginger root (or imitations thereof)—serves as the transitional link between the home-brewed alcoholic small beers and small ales of old and modern-day mass-produced soft drinks. Small beers had been prevalent for centuries as affordable, if far less potent, alternatives to commercial alcoholic brews. Derived from almost any part of almost any plant available in England and colonial America, small beers and ales were generally presumed to be tonic in contrast to civic water supplies, which were believed to be potentially toxic. Ginger beer, which peaked in popularity in the early nineteenth century, was certainly considered to be healthy: Ginger's reputation as a counterirritant and digestive aid, among other things, was firmly entrenched in folk medicine.

At the same time, the rage for natural mineral spring-water fueled the development of artificially carbonated water or soda water. The first name in soda water manufacture was Jacob Schweppe, who set up shop in Geneva and London in the late eighteenth century. His ingenuity inspired chemists for decades to come, who added to his achievement by adding flavor, including, by the mid-nineteenth century, ginger. The company Schweppe founded—a multinational corporation in the twenty-first century—went on to become the foremost producer of ginger ale.

Though the precise circumstances of its invention remain unknown, ginger ale, also called ginger champagne or gingerade, achieved immediate fame throughout the British Isles and overseas as a product of Belfast. There may have been a few American antecedents. Kenneth F. Kiple and Kriemhild Coneè-Ornelas cite a sixteenth-century source that refers to a Native American concoction containing ginger boiled with cinnamon; however, the early date is suspect, since ginger is not indigenous to the New World. The same authors and others also allude to switchell, a curious-sounding colonial American beverage made by combining ginger with molasses and vinegar.

The role Americans played in the soda revolution is better known. Stateside pharmacists invented the soda fountain itself, the popularity of which surged throughout the nineteenth century. Over the course of the century, the health benefits of soda water were eclipsed by its refreshing qualities, just as had happened in the case of small beer. As the soda fountain became a form of entertainment, a destination in itself, the beverages it dispensed were increasingly drunk for pleasure rather than health.

And so it was with ginger ale, which occupied the top of the flavor-popularity charts from the moment of its introduction until the 1940s, with home consumption increasing as the bottling and, eventually, canning industries grew. Vernor's was the first American manufacturer of note. Ginger ale was also employed as a mixer in such classic cocktails as the buck and the highball, Prohibition notwithstanding, as well as the Shirley Temple, a nonalcoholic favorite of children. (The rum-based dark and stormy, meanwhile, is traditionally made with alcoholic ginger beer.)

Around the mid-twentieth century, however, colas began to dominate the market through the promotion of a youthful, all-American image. Ginger ale, by contrast, came to be associated with an old-school if not Old World quaintness, and at the beginning of the twenty-first century its share of soft-drink sales was all but negligible, despite modestly successful attempts to innovate with new flavors, such as raspberry and grape.

[*See also* Beer; Cocktails; Soda Drinks; Soda Fountains; Switchel; Water, Bottled.]

BIBLIOGRAPHY

Funderburg, Anne Cooper. *Sundae Best: A History of Soda Fountains*. Bowling Green, OH: Bowling Green State University Popular Press, 2002. An exhaustively researched and minutely detailed pop-culture analysis that is unusually scholarly.

Kiple, Kenneth F., and Kriemhild Coneè-Ornelas, eds. In *The Cambridge World History of Food*. Vols. 1 and 2. Cambridge, UK: Cambridge University Press, 2000. The subsection under "Dietary Liquids" titled "Soft Drinks" (702–708) provides a thorough yet succinct historical overview of the subject, while the section "History, Nutrition, and Health" (1540–1546) supplies useful data on the medical uses of roots.

RUTH TOBIAS

Glassware

Glassmaking is an ancient process of melting silica, usually from sand, with an alkali to form a malleable compound that hardens on cooling. Whether discovered in one location or several, by the fifteenth century B.C.E. glass was known in Egypt and Mesopotamia and thereafter spread to the Mediterranean region and China. Various metals were often added to mimic precious stones because it was technologically impossible to make colorless glass. Drinking glasses were a luxury, made by the arduous process of dipping a core mold into molten glass. With the invention of glassblowing in Rome in the first century B.C.E., glass vessels became more affordable and common. European glassblowing declined with the fall of Rome but was revived, most impressively, in medieval Venice.

By the seventeenth century, glassmaking was an active, competitive industry with many centers. Even the American colonies, which were rich in the raw materials needed to make glass, briefly engaged in the manufacture of glass. The purpose of the colonial glass factories, which were funded by entities such as the English Board of Trade, was to manufacture glass for the European market. Jamestown (1608 and 1621), Salem, Massachusetts (ca. 1639–1643), New Amsterdam (ca. 1650–1674), and Philadelphia (ca. 1683) had small glassworks. All failed, largely because of undercapitalization and the perils of transatlantic shipping.

Most early colonists drank their beverages from sturdy woodenware or pewter, but wealthy colonists imported luxury glassware for wine and spirits. Glass purchases tended to follow colonial trade patterns. English colonists bought British glass, and those in New Amsterdam bought Holland glass. An occasional bit of Venetian glass appeared in the richest homes. Glass sales were tied to liquor consumption: One Albany merchant bemoaned poor glass sales in 1657, blaming the slow market on that year's shortage of wine.

In 1739 Caspar Wistar rekindled the American glass industry with a glasshouse in Salem County, New Jersey, that was devoted to utilitarian windows, colored bottles, and a few items of tableware. Other early glassworks, founded by Henry William "Baron" Stiegel (active in Pennsylvania, 1763–1774) and John Frederick Amelung (active in Maryland, 1784–1794), produced blown and molded drinking vessels (mugs, goblets, tumblers, flips, and wine glasses), cruets, decanters, and other table glass. These manufacturers relied on highly skilled British and European glassworkers, who made items in different styles to satisfy the different tastes of Dutch, German, and English colonists. Although these businesses all succumbed to better-priced British competition, the economics changed after the War of 1812. Manufactories followed settlers west, supplying local markets with basic glass needs. Manufacturers near eastern cities produced luxurious tableware.

Most early wine glasses were quite small by later standards owing to the way wine was served at elegant dinners. Before the 1830s wine glasses and water glasses were typically kept on a sideboard and delivered by a servant to each diner upon request. The diner would drain the glass and return it to the servant, who would wash the glass and await the next beverage request. With changing service styles, diners started to leave their glasses on the table. By 1840 etiquette books were suggesting several glasses for each diner, including individual water tumblers, one or more wine glasses of different shapes for different wines, and small water bottles at each place so that diners could independently replenish their water glasses. Decanters, cruets, and casters continued to be placed on the table for communal use.

The forests of glasses on dining tables were made possible, in part, by one of America's most important contributions to glass technology: the perfection of machine-pressed glass. In the late 1820s and early 1830s, various American factories improved the existing mechanical processes so that good-quality glass could be produced with comparatively little skill. Semiskilled American workers supplanted trained European craftsmen in manufacturing all but luxury glass. Output tripled and costs fell, quickly making pressed glass an affordable refinement. The pressing technology opened a new design vocabulary that included intricate, lacy patterns, bull's-eye borders, and figurative motifs. Pressed glass was quickly adapted for propaganda: Presidential candidates distributed appropriately embossed plates, flasks, and other items as campaign mementos, and Manifest Destiny found expression in the popular "Westward Ho" pattern, which incorporated stylized animals and images of Native Americans.

Modestly priced pressed glass thoroughly penetrated the middle classes by the 1850s and the working classes by the 1880s, so that the affluent needed a distinguishing product. It came in the 1880s in the form of brilliant cut glass. Combining high-silica sand, which had been discovered in western Massachusetts, with lead oxide produced glass of extraordinary brilliance that could imitate the finest eighteenth-century English leaded glass. Having been wildly popular in upper-middle-class markets, particularly among men, brilliant cut glass lost its cachet after World War I.

With the successful complete automation of pressed-glass factories in the 1920s, attractive table glass became affordable for all. Glassmakers needed to invent new glass products to capture the public's purse. Adapting technology used in railroad signal lights, the Corning Glass Works pioneered thermal shock-resistant glass that could go from refrigerator to oven to table. First offered in 1915 through its Pyrex ovenware line, this multifunctional glassware capitalized on the efficiency espoused by the home economics movement. Pyrex was expensive and marketed to well-heeled women who were up-to-date in domestic science. Changes in the design, manufacture, and marketing of Pyrex brought it to the masses by the late 1930s, and it remains a staple item.

After World War II, competition from modernized European and Asian factories forced many of the remaining American luxury glass manufacturers out of business. With the trend toward increasingly casual entertaining, postwar consumers purchased a large numbers of glasses, but they were often inexpensive novelty items or made of plastic or paper. "Good crystal" decreased in importance as a status symbol. The final twentieth-century development was an extraordinary increase in the size and capacity of glasses, especially for wine. Modern oenophiles can opt for gargantuan twenty-eight-ounce bowls that permit lusty swirling of Bacchus's gift.

Although most American glass follows long-established forms, there were a few distinctly American innovations. One was the glass cup plate, which was designed to protect the table from trickles of tea when the hot drink was poured from a handleless cup into a deep saucer for cooling. Tea drinkers needed a place to rest their cups as they sipped delicately from their saucers. Other American creations are specially shaped glasses for martinis and for ice cream sundaes and sodas.

[*See also* Dining Rooms, Table Settings, and Table Manners; Wine Glasses.]

BIBLIOGRAPHY

Blaszczyk, Regina Lee. *Imagining Consumers: Design and Innovation from Wedgwood to Corning.* Baltimore and London: Johns Hopkins University Press, 2000.

Gardner, Paul Vickers. *Glass.* Washington, DC: Cooper-Hewitt/Smithsonian Institution, 1979.

McKearin, George S., and Helen McKearin. *American Glass.* New York: Bonanza, 1989.

Palmer, Arlene. *Glass in Early America.* Winterthur, DE: Winterthur Museum, 1993.

Spillman, Jane Shadel. *Glassmaking: America's First Industry.* Corning, NY: Corning Museum, 1976.

CATHY K. KAUFMAN

Goetta

A seasoned mixture of oatmeal and meat, usually pork, goetta (rhymes with "meta") is traditional breakfast fare of southwestern Ohio and northern Kentucky. The origin of the word "goetta" is unknown. It was used at the end of the nineteenth century in Cincinnati, Ohio, and nearby Covington, Kentucky, where goetta was popularized by German immigrants, although the local Irish population supposedly also ate it. Goetta probably began as a way to extend pork scraps by frugal German workers in Cincinnati's extensive pork-packing industry. Goetta is very similar to the Pennsylvania Dutch dish scrapple, which uses cornmeal rather than oatmeal, and is derived from the German tradition of meat puddings prepared at butchering time from meat remnants bound together with grains.

Goetta is prepared by first slowly cooking it in a pot to a thick, gluey consistency, then pouring it into a pan and chilling it. When served, goetta is unmolded from the pan, sliced, and fried. As breakfast food, it replaces bacon or sausage and often appears with eggs. It is sometimes used as a stuffing and modern cooks seek new applications, such as pizza toppings.

Area butchers began producing goetta and selling it as a winter specialty. A few commercial firms currently provide most of the goetta in the Cincinnati region, which is available fresh and frozen at local supermarkets. Renewed interest in regional foods has sparked an appreciation of this humble food and an annual goetta festival in Covington, Kentucky, celebrates the enduring popularity of goetta.

[*See also* Breakfast Foods; Dressings and Stuffings; Food Festivals; Midwestern Regional Cookery; Scrapple.]

BIBLIOGRAPHY

DuSablon, Mary Anna. *Cincinnati Recipe Treasury: The Queen City's Culinary Heritage.* Athens, OH: Ohio University Press, 1989.

Glier's Goetta on the Web. http://www.goetta.com. The home page of the primary producer of goetta in the Cincinnati region. Describes history, cooking methods, and U.S. government regulation of goetta production.

MARY SANKER

Good Housekeeping Institute

Founded in 1900 in Springfield, Massachusetts, as the Good Housekeeping Institute Experiment Station, for the evaluation of food products and, a few years later, of household appliances, the Good Housekeeping Institute is one of America's premier consumer-protection and quality-assurance facilities. Products that do not satisfy the requirements of the institute's product testing and approval programs are not allowed to advertise in *Good Housekeeping* magazine.

The institute's work supplies the essential foundation for the Good Housekeeping Consumers' Refund Replacement Policy, which in every issue of the magazine warrants that "if any product that bears our Seal or is advertised in this issue [of our magazine] . . . proves to be defective within two years from the date it was first sold to a consumer, we, Good Housekeeping, will replace the product or refund the purchase price." After *Good Housekeeping* magazine was purchased by William Randolph Hearst in 1912, the institute moved to New York City, where it was still located at the beginning of the twenty-first century.

The Good Housekeeping Institute played a significant role in twentieth-century American food history. Prior to the passage of the Pure Food and Drug Act in June 1906, the institute tested food products to determine their purity. Every month *Good Housekeeping* printed a "Roll of Honor for Pure Food Products," listing foods that were unadulterated. In 1910, in response to the spread of electricity, the electrification of the American home, and the development of electric appliances, the institute established test kitchens to determine which electric appliances were safe and effective. The names of reliable products were published in the magazine along with a seal that stated, in part, "Tested and Approved by the Good Housekeeping Institute."

After Dr. Harvey W. Wiley was hired as head of the institute's Bureau of Food, Sanitation, and Health in 1912, the institute broadened its scope to study all aspects of food and health; the results of these studies were also published in the magazine. Between 1912 and his death in 1930 Dr. Wiley authored or coauthored more than 175 articles on pure food and health that were published in *Good Housekeeping*. Many of these articles discussed proper nutrition with a special focus on babies and children. American women trusted Dr. Wiley, and this trust, in part, accounted for the popularity and success of the institute and the magazine. During the Great Depression, the institute developed recipes and menus designed to maximize the nutritional value of meals while keeping the cost of food low, and in World War II the institute helped Americans by providing strategies to deal with food shortages. Finally, with the advent of the Internet, the institute placed its Buyer's Guide on the Web at www.goodhousekeeping.com, allowing free access to anyone interested in consumer information about general cookware, flatware and tools, and kitchen appliances, among other things.

In the early 2000s the Good Housekeeping Institute had separate departments for food, nutrition, home care, chemistry, consumer and reader services, engineering, food appliances, and textiles. The institute continued to evaluate a wide variety of food and household products, publishing the results of those evaluations in the magazine as "Taste Tests" and "Institute Reports."

[*See also* Food and Drug Administration; Pure Food and Drug Act; Wiley, Harvey.]

BIBLIOGRAPHY

Good Housekeeping. *Good Housekeeping's Book of Menus, Recipes, and Household Discoveries.* New York: Good Housekeeping, 1922.

Wiley, Harvey W. *1001 Tests of Foods, Beverages, and Toilet Accessories, Good and Otherwise: Why They Are So.* Rev. ed. New York: Hearst, 1916.

ROBERT W. BROWER

Goose

Geese are large, web-footed birds of the family Anatidae, including the genera *Anser* and *Branta*. Geese have heavier bodies and longer necks than ducks but are smaller than swans. There are two dozen species worldwide, but the domesticated gray goose (*Anser domesticus*) derives from only two species, the wild gray goose and the greylag goose (*Anser ferus* and *Anser anser*). By 3000 B.C.E., geese were common in China and the Middle East. They were raised in ancient Egypt and have been part of everyday life in western Europe since prehistoric times. Geese are easily raised, and they consume foods, including many weeds, not eaten by other animals. In Europe geese were highly valued for their eggs, meat, grease, and feathers. In England geese were usually eaten on special occasions, such as Michaelmas and Christmas.

European settlers brought domesticated geese (*Anser domesticus*) to the New World. The Pilgrim goose was brought from England by early colonists. Embden geese were imported in 1821, followed shortly thereafter by Bremen geese. Chinese geese were imported by the 1840s, as was the African or Guinea goose, which was the largest breed in mid-nineteenth-century America.

Geese. Bremen or Emden geese. From Simon M. Saunders, *Domestic Poultry* (New York, 1866), p. 91.

These imported birds contributed to extensive breeding efforts to produce larger and meatier geese.

Geese were generally prepared for the table in the same manner that turkeys and ducks were. They were roasted, boiled, or used as ingredients in savory pies. Like other poultry, geese were stuffed with almost every conceivable concoction, from traditional chestnut fillings to those composed of onions, potatoes, and sauerkraut. Geese were usually served on special occasions, such as Thanksgiving and Christmas. Recipes for preparing geese were published in American cookbooks, ranging from Amelia Simmons's recipe in her *American Cookery* (1796) entitled "To boil a Turkey, Fowl or Goose" to Felix Délée's eight complex recipes in his *Franco-American Cookery Book* (1884).

Domesticated geese never achieved the culinary popularity in America that they did in Europe, however, perhaps because of the plentiful supply of wildfowl in America and the availability of low-cost and less greasy turkey. Since 1890 the consumption of geese in America has steadily declined, and recipes for preparing geese have generally disappeared from American cookbooks. Wild geese do remain a highly favored menu item among hunters, and recipes for their preparation appear in specialty cookbooks.

Geese were generally raised in small flocks on farms, but some commercial raising of geese did go on in Rhode Island in colonial times. These birds were usually driven to markets in towns during the fall. In the nineteenth century, geese were raised in the South and the Midwest mainly for their feathers, which were used for down comforters and featherbeds. Wing feathers were used for quill pens. Live geese were plucked several times during the summer. This practice, considered cruel and inhumane, did not stop until the early twentieth century, when demand for the feathers declined.

[*See also* Christmas; Dressings and Stuffings; Duck; Poultry and Fowl; Thanksgiving; Turkey.]

BIBLIOGRAPHY

Batty, Joseph. *Domesticated Ducks and Geese.* Mildhurst, U.K.: Beech Publishing House, 1996.

Dohner, Janet Vorwald. *The Encyclopedia of Endangered Livestock and Poultry Breeds.* New Haven, CT, and London: Yale University Press, 2001.

Merritt, E. S. "Geese." In *American Poultry History, 1823–1973.* Madison, WI: American Poultry History Society, 1974.

Owen, Myrfyn. *Wild Geese of the World.* Fakenham, U.K.: Fakenham Press, 1980.

ANDREW F. SMITH

Graham, Sylvester

His name lives on in a nursery cookie, but Sylvester Graham (1794–1851), one of America's earliest and most vocal advocates of dietary reform, left a far larger legacy: the concept that a vegetarian diet of natural and largely raw foods—whole grains, vegetables, fruits, and nuts—can restore and maintain health. Graham campaigned for pure, unadulterated food at a time when baker's bread might contain copper sulfate, plaster, or alum. And in an era predating scientific knowledge of carbohydrates, protein, fat, and fiber, he insisted that processing, milling, sifting, and overcooking stripped food of its most important components. Although mocked in his day, Graham's theories foreshadowed much modern nutritional knowledge.

The Connecticut-born Graham was ordained a Presbyterian minister in New Jersey; his first congregation was in Philadelphia, where he mingled with and learned from Quakers, temperance advocates, and vegetarians—notably, members of the Bible Christian Church, an English sect that had established a church in Philadelphia. As a traveling temperance lecturer, Graham studied the physiological effects of alcohol. He also researched the effects of foods on the human body, leading to his espousal

Sylvester Graham. *Culinary Archives & Museum at Johnson & Wales University, Providence, R.I.*

of a vegetarian diet with particular emphasis on firm, crusty bread—home-baked from coarsely ground, unbolted (not sifted) whole-wheat flour—and raw fruits and vegetables. Unadulterated, unprocessed, uncooked foods were preferable: "The simpler, plainer and more natural the food . . . the more healthy, vigorous and long lived will be the body," Graham wrote.

Increasing urbanization in early-nineteenth-century America promoted emotional and mental stress among city-dwellers, who suffered a virtual epidemic of dyspepsia, or indigestion, as they bolted down the era's fast food (meat and potatoes doused with greasy gravy and spicy condiments and washed down with whiskey or beer) in ever more bustling surroundings. Graham believed that such a diet was overstimulating, irritating to the digestive organs, and responsible for kindling unhealthy passions and desires. He developed an Edenic diet: what Adam and Eve ate was good enough for modern man. Foods forbidden as highly stimulating included meat (especially pork), shellfish, fatty sauces, salt, spices, sugar, coffee, tea, highly flavored condiments, and alcohol. Advocating

a regimen of fresh air, exercise, and personal cleanliness and inveighing against corsets and featherbeds, Graham pronounced that proper food calmed the senses while providing the jaws, teeth, and digestive organs with healthy exercise.

As a wave of cholera swept American cities in the early 1830s, Graham lectured to audiences desperate to learn how diet could help prevent disease. The mid-1830s saw the founding of Graham societies (promoting his brand of dietary reform) and Graham hotels (serving his recommended fare), which flourished in American cities. Graham flour, bread, and crackers—some of the first health foods—hit the market. Newspapers and magazines, including the *Graham Journal of Health and Longevity*, popularized Graham's theories. The Shakers adopted Graham's diet for a time, hoping that it would help their members adhere to their vows of celibacy. Other Graham followers were Bronson Alcott, cofounder of the utopian (and vegan) Fruitlands community in Massachusetts; Horace Greeley; and John Harvey Kellogg and Will K. Kellogg of Battle Creek sanatorium fame. Although Graham's unrelenting dogmatism and his sometimes excessive zeal on the lecture platform made him subject to scorn and ridicule by some members of the press and the public, from a modern perspective it is obvious that he was many, many decades ahead of his time.

[*See also* Alcohol and Teetotalism; Health Food; Kellog, John Harvey; Vegetarianism.]

BIBLIOGRAPHY

Giedion, Siegfried. *Mechanization Takes Command*. New York: Norton, 1969.

Graham, Sylvester. *Treatise on Bread and Breadmaking*. Boston: Light and Sterns, 1837.

Nissenbaum, Stephen. *Sex, Diet, and Debility in Jacksonian America: Sylvester Graham and Health Reform*. Westport, CT: Greenwood, 1980.

Whelan, Elizabeth M., and Fredrick J. Stare. *Panic in the Pantry*. New York: Atheneum, 1975.

BONNIE J. SLOTNICK

Grapes

Although the Old World was the first to exploit it, the grape vine is a particularly American plant. Only one species of grape is to be found wild in Europe, while there are few places in temperate North America, from

Canada to Mexico, without a native grape species. North America is the center of diversity for the grape. Twenty grape species are found there, and nowhere else.

American grapes found their first culinary use in the Native Americans' pemmican, a confection of animal fats, fruits, and shredded meats. No doubt grapes were also consumed fresh, although very few vines produced tasty fruits. Viking explorers named their Newfoundland landfall Vinland, for the vines there; early colonists from England remarked on the bounty of grapes in their new home—and also their acrid flavor. These grapes, *Vitus labrusca*, have two outstanding characteristics: a thick skin that separates readily from the berry and a highly pungent aroma, described as "foxy."

Introducing the wine grape of Europe (*Vitis vinifera*) to America was a matter of policy in the colonies, along with other commodities for export, such as rice, sugar, and olives. That attempts at introduction were not successful is evidenced by Thomas Jefferson's correspondence with Europe, seeking more robust as well as finer varieties of grape. Lack of success is explained not only by the occasionally harsh winters of the Atlantic seaboard but also by the numerous pathogens specific to the vine, such as the phylloxera root aphid, mildew, black rot, and above all Pierce's disease, a lethal viroid, to all of which most native American species had developed resistance or immunity, but to which the European grape had none at all.

American Hybrids

Until the 1850s, grapes of dessert quality remained a luxury for those few who maintained a greenhouse to grow varieties of European origin. At about that time, certain experimenters started to hybridize the few European grapes then known with wildlings selected from the American forests. These hybrids, although still far from perfect in hardiness and productivity, were a revelation that the future of American grape culture lay in seedlings of European and American species combined by hybridization. The first generations of American hybrid grapes were the basis of a wine industry founded on the Ohio River near Cincinnati, and later on Lake Erie and in upstate New York, which survived until national Prohibition.

Concord, considered the type for all labrusca grapes, is probably a native *V. aestivalis*. It is dark skinned, adaptable to most of the East and Midwest, and still accounts for nearly half the Eastern grape production, notwithstanding its very modest eating quality. Niagara is a yellow-skinned counterpart, of higher value for dessert. Catawba is the most-grown red-skinned type, though it ripens very late in the season, too late for most of America. All three are used in the making of bottled juice, and the tonnage of Concord devoted to manufacture of jellies is formidable indeed. Hybrid varieties are preferred for dessert use by knowledgeable grape fanciers. Delaware grapes are first among these, forming small clusters of small berries. Jefferson and Iona grapes

Grapes. From left to right, Brighton, Moore's Diamond, and Eaton grapes. From the 1894 catalog of Peter Henderson & Co., New York.

are also fine red grapes. Brilliant and Steuben are fine varieties of black and Seneca of white.

For a brief period from 1900 to 1940, French nurserymen believed hybrids between American species and local grapes would prove the salvation of French vineyards from phylloxera. During these years, very many such hybrids were created and proved competent producers of fair wines, but not wines of the accustomed standard. These hybrids were later introduced to New York, Virginia, and elsewhere. In those areas, dessert grapes of these French hybrids, although small, are sometimes available for the fresh market and are highly prized over American hybrid grapes, whose slipping skins and foxiness they lack.

The market prevalence of California table grapes that lack seeds has led some state experiment stations, notably in Arkansas and New York, to begin breeding programs featuring crosses between American hybrids and the seedless grapes of California. The resulting progeny—Interlaken, Himrod, Remailly, Reliance, Venus—derive either from the sultana type and share their very neutral flavor or from Black Monukka and are likewise imperfectly seedless. They are rapidly driving older seeded varieties of greater character from the marketplace.

California Grapes

The *V. vinifera* of Europe was introduced to California in 1769 to produce altar wines for the missions. The easy growth of this species under California conditions impressed later immigrants from the Eastern states and a wine industry soon developed. The market was limited for dessert fruit until the advent of the refrigerated railway car in the 1880s. At that point, grape plantings in the Modesto and Fresno districts expanded, chiefly in varieties of character and flavor: White Malaga, Ahmeur bou Ahmeur (as Flame Tokay), Alphonse Lavallee (as Ribier), Olivette Blanche, and Muscat of Alexandria.

At the same time, the sultana type of *V. vinifera*, which has no seeds, was planted for sun-drying, especially in the southern San Joaquin valley. There the grape experiences extremely low humidity and no rains before October. It was discovered by the 1930s that the popular Sultanina Bianca (grown as Thompson Seedless) was a versatile fruit. If picked immature, before turning fully yellow in color, it has sufficient acid to make a pleasant dessert fruit, and one without seeds. When fully ripe, it is of high sugar content and useful for making the cheapest

of wines, as well as for drying. By the 1980s, it and the many progeny of the sultana type, such as Perlette, Flame Seedless, Fantasy Seedless, Ruby Seedless, and certain varieties proprietary to large industrial growers, had displaced nearly all the seeded true table grapes in American commerce.

For drying purposes, the Black Corinth type of *V. vinifera*, a quite distinct small seedless grape, is grown for production of the so-called currants of commerce. At the turn of the twenty-first century, fresh fruit of this variety was sold as a novelty under the false name champagne grape. The traditional dried Muscat of Alexandria had vanished from nearly all American supermarkets. Typically these were processed to remove the seeds, and the resulting product was lubricated with grapeseed oil to prevent consolidation in the package. Black Monukka produces a tough raisin of high acidity and character, with occasional seeds. An innovation has been the breeding of sultanas named DOV (dried on vine) that can dry while attached to the severed vine and then be mechanically gathered. A very small secondary industry evolved in the Fresno area for production of grape derivatives, such as verjus and grape syrup, or so-called molasses. These products rarely leave California.

The Muscadine

In the southern states, where the conventional American hybrid and European grapes cannot be grown, the Muscadine grape (*V. rotundifolia*) is at least as important in the market and in local culture. Muscadines have a tan, green, or purple-black slipping skin that is tough and papery and never eaten; the berry is pulpy and cohesive and must be chewed. The aroma is higher than in the American hybrid grapes. Scuppernong is the best-known variety and indeed is the oldest American grape variety on record, dating from the early eighteenth century. Other varieties have had far shorter lives, as private individuals are still engaged in breeding superior fruit and wine varieties of Muscadines.

[*See also* California; Champagne; Currants; Fruit; Fruit Wines; Insects; Wine, *subentries on* California Wines, Eastern U.S. Wines.]

BIBLIOGRAPHY

Hedrick, U. P. *The Grapes of New York*. Albany, NY: New York Agricultural Experiment Station, 1908.

Munson, T. V. *Foundations of American Grape Culture*. Denison, TX, 1909.

Winkler, A. J., James A. Cook, W. M. Kliewer, and Lloyd A. Lider. *General Viticulture*. Berkeley, CA: University of California Press, 1962.

C. T. KENNEDY

Grasshopper

In the 1930s the grasshopper, supposedly named for the jumpy effect it produced, was a temperance drink made of lemon juice, orange juice, a raw egg, sugar, and ice. The alcoholic version, probably invented in the 1960s, was an after-dinner drink of crème de menthe, crème de cacao, and heavy cream, shaken with ice and strained into a cocktail glass. It became a sweet and minty "girl drink," named for its color. The grasshopper had fallen out of favor by the early twenty-first century but was still available in a frozen, ice cream version, the "Flying Grasshopper," at the international T. G. I. Friday's chain.

"Grasshopper" has since become a descriptor for mint-flavored or green-colored desserts, such as grasshopper pie, which appeared soon after the drink. It is a frothy, mint-green dessert of crème de menthe, crème de cacao, whipped cream, and beaten egg whites in a graham-cracker or cookie-crumb crust, served chilled. Variations on grasshopper pie include versions made with lime gelatin, pistachio pudding, Oreo cookies, cream cheese, or marshmallows. One can also find recipes for grasshopper brownies, grasshopper bars, grasshopper milkshakes, and the like, usually incorporating crème de menthe. In 2002 the menu of the chain restaurant Denny's listed a "Grasshopper Sundae" and a "Grasshopper Blender Blaster," both nonalcoholic mint desserts.

[*See also* Cocktails; Desserts.]

JESSY RANDALL

Graters

Foods such as raw root vegetables, hard cheese, and baking chocolate can be reduced to shreds by hand with a grater. Grating reduces food to a more easily chewed, cooked, or melted state, and produces flavorful tidbits to mix thoroughly through a dish. Small bits of food are removed with each rubbing across a surface made rough with punctures—holes with sharp, raised edges.

Graters have existed for centuries. Most are metal (wrought iron, sheet iron, tin, sometimes brass). Some

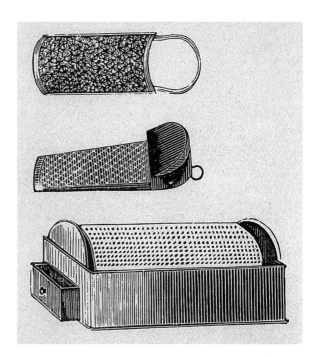

Graters. From top to bottom, tin grater, heavy nutmeg grater, and box grater. From the Duparquet, Huot, & Moneuse Co. catalog (Boston, 1915), p. 228.

have a flat or curved surface fixed to a wire frame that forms a grip or a prop to position it over a mixing bowl or other receptacle. Others are half-rounds fixed to a small board. Box graters are built into the top of a wooden box so that the gratings fall within. Some graters are free-standing cylinders or open-ended boxes, with various size grating holes on different sides. Graters with tiny burrs are called zesters and are used for grating the rind, or zest, of citrus fruits. Mechanical graters with cranks and revolving grating drums were patented in the 1850s for corn, vegetables, and nutmeg.

[*See also* Corn-Preparation Tools; Nutmeg Graters.]

BIBLIOGRAPHY

Franklin, Linda Campbell. *300 Years of Kitchen Collectibles*. 5th ed. Iola, WI: Krause, 2003.

LINDA CAMPBELL FRANKLIN

Grinders

Mechanical grinders saved time and required relatively little physical strength and thus were a vast improvement over women's age-old chore of pounding and chopping foodstuffs by hand. Among the first grinders to be developed to deal with new food imports into Europe were those for spice and coffee. By the late seventeenth century, small, geared, forged-iron grinders were designed with an upper holding hopper, hand-cranked grinding surfaces, and a lower collecting chamber. This basic design continued to be used during the next centuries. As costs of spice and coffee dropped, inexpensive casings of wood or tin replaced the iron grinders. Electric versions appeared in the last decades of the twentieth century in response to gourmet interest in the freshest flavors.

By the early 1800s a second form of grinder was developed for making sausages. Strong wooden cases fitted with screwlike bores coarsely chopped the meats. Still cranked by hand, the core's rows of iron pegs pushed the meat against arrays of small sharp knives embedded in the box walls. By the middle 1800s the design was re-created in cast iron for small tabletop grinders. The late 1800s saw the household cast-iron meat grinder, fitted with a choice of nozzle plates for different grades of coarseness, clamped to the kitchen table. Made by many different companies, the Enterprise models were probably the most famous and survived well into the twentieth century.

[See also Nutcrackers and Grinders.]

ALICE ROSS

Grits, see Corn

Grocery Stores

For almost three hundred years, public markets were the primary retail and wholesale food source for urban Americans. Financed and regulated by municipalities, public markets originally were scheduled events held in the street one or two days a week. During the eighteenth century, street markets gave way to permanent markets constructed in a town's center. For those towns on the ocean or on navigable rivers, markets were built near the wharves so that goods could easily be unloaded and transported from ships. These markets were frequently grand structures, such as Faneuil Hall and Quincy Market in Boston. Within these spaces, civic authorities leased stalls to butchers, fruiterers, vegetable farmers, and other merchants.

In rural areas, even self-sufficient farmers needed to buy some food products, such as salt and sugar. All-purpose country stores sold necessities and, occasionally, luxury items. Proprietors of country stores sometimes bartered with local farmers for produce and other perishables, which they then sold to town- and city-dwellers

As American towns grew into cities, small grocery stores emerged to accommodate residents who lived too far from the city center to shop conveniently at the public markets. At first these small, family-owned stores sold imported specialty items such as tea, wine, and spices, as well as domestic homemade syrups and jellies. The stores themselves, as well as the range of goods they stocked, expanded during the early nineteenth century, selling mainly nonperishable packaged foods, which were stacked along the walls. Staple foods, such as flour, grains, and sugar, were sold from barrels or sacks. Counters separated clerks from customers, and a wide aisle in the middle of the store permitted customers to view the food displays. Customers requested what they wanted, and the clerks then retrieved the items, wrote up the order, and recorded it on the customer's account—which frequently was not paid until much later. The rapid growth of cities accelerated the trend away from the crowded public markets—many of which had become dingy and unsanitary—to grocery stores, which were larger than market stalls and therefore able to sell more goods from larger inventories. By the early twentieth century, public markets had been almost entirely replaced by grocery stores.

Grocery Chain Stores

In 1859 George F. Gilman, a prosperous New York businessman, and George H. Hartford started selling tea in New York City. Three years later they named their business the Great American Tea Company. At the time, most grocers bought their stock from middlemen. Gilman and Hartford decided to buy tea in bulk directly from the source in China and sell directly to the customer, thereby eliminating the middleman, dramatically lowering the retail price and underselling their competition. Their system was so successful that by 1865 Hartford and Gilman had five small stores in New York City, thus creating what would become America's first grocery chain. When the transcontinental railroad was completed in 1869, Gilman and Hartford changed the name of their company to the Great Atlantic and Pacific Tea Company, subsequently called A&P.

Independent grocers protested the early success of A&P. The *American Grocer,* a national trade publication, was launched in 1869, and it attacked A&P almost from its first issue. Specifically, it charged that A&P tea was priced so low because it was substandard, damaged, or reused tea from restaurants. Independent grocers also criticized A&P and other chain stores for predatory pricing and destroying local businesses. Despite this continuous opposition, A&P expanded the chain and entered the general grocery business by increasing the number of products sold. Coffee was added in the 1870s, and sugar, spices, and canned milks were carried during the following decade.

By 1900 the A&P had 198 stores, and the number continued to increase slowly until 1912, when A&P created the Economy Store, a small, self-contained module designed to fit into similar buildings. At about the same time, the A&P stopped extending credit and stopped making home deliveries. The Economy Stores looked like independent grocery stores and were about the same size—five hundred to six hundred square feet—but because A&P bought in volume for all its stores, they were able to undersell their competition. The new model worked: there were 14,034 Economy Stores by 1925.

Other entrepreneurs saw the success of A&P and emulated its operation. In 1872 the Grand Union Company was founded in New York, and by the early twentieth century it had become the nation's second-largest food retailer. Bernard H. Kroger began a Cincinnati-based chain store operation in 1883 and had expanded to almost thirty stores by 1900. In 1916 in Memphis, Tennessee, Clarence Saunders launched the Piggly Wiggly grocery store and with it the revolutionary concept of self-service. Customers collected their own groceries, placed them in small hand baskets, and took them to a cashier. The main advantage of self-service was reduced labor costs, as fewer clerks were needed to serve customers.

Even without self-service, chain stores had many advantages over the independents. They were able to promote themselves through premiums, such as the Green Stamps issued by the Sperry and Hutchinson Company Inc. which were widely used after 1900. The chains usually had better insurance, so when struck by a fire or other catastrophe they could still reap profits from their other stores while reconstruction was in progress. Chain stores were also able to survive economic hard times by closing financially troubled stores while keeping the more successful locations open. Furthermore they

Grocery Store. Meat counter, Greendale, Wisconsin, 1939. *Prints and Photographs Division, Library of Congress*

had the wherewithal to analyze and select the best sites for stores and to establish new outlets when the opportunity arose. Chain stores could hire buyers who specialized in certain product lines; their job was to maximize volume purchases and thereby reduce unit costs. To capture control of wholesale prices, some grocery chains launched their own store brands, which eliminated the middleman and further reduced overhead costs. The chains could afford advertising, and when radio became available, they were able to advertise regionally and then nationally. The independent grocer hardly stood a chance against the chain stores.

Independent grocers made numerous legal attempts to halt or limit the growth of the chain stores. These efforts succeeded to some extent on the state level, but national efforts to impose a tax on chain stores did not. Eventually independent grocers banded together to form associations that gave them many of the strengths of the chains. By the 1930s the overwhelming majority of American grocery stores either belonged to a corporate chain or were affiliated with an association of independents.

Supermarkets

The chain-store system and the self-service concept shaped the supermarket. In many ways, the supermarket was an application of a business approach previously developed in the super-size department stores of John Wanamaker in Philadelphia and Marshall Field in Chicago early in the twentieth century. Department stores had discovered how retail prices could be reduced by bulk buying and how the subsequent increased volume of sales could raise the profit rate. Although the term "super market" was first used in the grocery trade by William Albers, who opened the Albers Super Market in Cincinnati in November 1933, the concept had originated in Southern California during the previous decade. In the 1920s Los Angeles was sprawling in area and highly dependent on the automobile. Land was relatively inexpensive, and two chains—Ralph's Grocery Company and Alpha Beta Food Markets—constructed large stores that were laid out in sections according to categories of food. The major innovation of these stores was size: some of them covered five thousand square feet—ten times the size of A&P Economy Stores.

The success of the early supermarkets in southern California was at first ignored as a passing phase by other corporate chains and affiliated independents. Two developments changed their minds. The first was engineered by Michael Cullen, who had been an employee of Kroger Grocery and Baking Company. In 1930 Cullen launched his own chain, called King Kullen, in Jamaica, New York. Cullen cut prices by increasing volume. To accomplish this, he built larger stores, with 5,200 to 6,400 square feet of floor space, and provided parking, making

the stores more convenient for suburban customers. Cullen also advertised in newspapers and radio, positioning his stores as "price wreckers" with prices that could not be beaten. The second development that encouraged large chains to develop their own supermarkets was launched by Robert M. Otis and Roy A. Dawson. In 1932 they opened the first Big Bear store on the first floor of a factory building in Elizabeth, New Jersey. With fifteen thousand square feet devoted to selling groceries, it proved an enormous economic success. By the mid-1930s supermarkets were overtaking both chains and independent grocers. The A&P and other chains responded by closing their smaller stores and opening supermarkets. Independent grocers were unable to make the switch, and tens of thousands went out of business during the late 1930s and early 1940s.

The conversion from small stores to large supermarkets was hastened by the Depression. Customers saw supermarkets as a practical means of saving money. They were willing to forgo the pleasant atmosphere of the neighborhood grocery for the lower prices they found in the crude warehouse stores. World War II slowed the growth of supermarkets as wartime restrictions halted

Small Grocery. Proprietor of small grocery store weighing beans, near New Iberia, Louisiana, October 1938. *Prints and Photographs Division, Library of Congress/Russell Lee*

Technological Advances

Several advances in technology greatly enhanced supermarket shopping. The grocery shopping cart was invented by Sylvan Goldman in 1937 for his Standard Food Stores in Oklahoma City. The cart made it easy for customers to move their purchases from the cash register to their automobiles in the store's parking lot. A larger cart was an enticement to buy more. In 1947 "telescoping" shopping carts, which could be fitted into other empty carts, thus creating a more compact way of storing them, were first used. In 1940 Publix Supermarkets, launched by George Jenkins of Winter Haven, Florida, introduced the electric-eye door that opened automatically for customers as they entered and exited. Jenkins also equipped his stores with air-conditioning, fluorescent lighting, and music. By 1956, 80 percent of all new supermarkets had piped-in music and air-conditioning and many supermarkets provided special areas and rides for small children. Prices were stamped on items to reduce the time clerks spent writing down prices on each item, and price tags were installed on shelves so that consumers could easily see the cost of each product. Cash registers were redesigned to itemize purchases on the customer's receipt. To increase checkout speed, cashiers were trained to keep their eyes on the product price stamps, not the cash register keyboard. In 1967 the first bar code scanner was installed in a Kroger's supermarket in Cincinnati. Although not commonly used until the 1980s, bar codes combined with computer analysis revolutionized supermarket inventories and increased the ability to track and analyze customers' purchases.

Modern supermarket chains are challenged from three separate directions. The first is the return of the public market. Starting in the 1970s, green or farmers' markets sprang up in many urban areas selling produce and other food products. Many consumers prefer the fresh products from local farmers to the produce available at supermarkets. The second challenge is the rise of small stores. Delis, bodegas, mom-and-pop shops, fruit stands, and convenience stores such as those run by 7-Eleven Inc. rapidly increased at the end of the twentieth century. These stores typically sell commonly purchased foods at prices substantially higher than those of supermarkets, but many customers value their convenient locations and late hours. The third challenge is at the opposite end of the grocery spectrum. Sam Walton opened his first variety store in 1945. When he died in 1992, Walton was the richest man in America, and his

Supermarket. Entrance to supermarket at Corpus Christi, Texas, December 1940. *Prints and Photographs Division, Library of Congress/Russell Lee*

construction. Prior to the war, almost all the store clerks had been young men; as they went off to fight, women filled their jobs.

Wartime rationing of meat, sugar, chocolate, canned goods, and other products necessitated changes in supermarkets. For instance, as the war effort required metal that would otherwise have gone to make food cans, stores with freezers stocked more frozen foods. As many of the traditional grocery store products were rationed, supermarkets expanded into non-food products to fill the empty shelves. After the war, management significantly expanded floor space for non-food goods, including health products, cosmetics, children's books, magazines, records, glassware, hardware, toys, hosiery, and even children's wear.

The postwar growth of supermarkets was tremendous. Chain stores abandoned small inner-city stores and expanded into the suburbs with supermarkets. Again, the variety of inventory grew with the number of stores: in the 1940s, an average supermarket carried 3,000 different items; by the late 1950s this had increased to 5,800. By the 1970s supermarkets stocked more than 10,000 items.

company, Wal-Mart Stores Inc., was the biggest retailer in the world. After Walton's death, his heirs moved Wal-Mart into food and by 2002 Wal-Mart's food sales reached $75 billion annually. Wal-Mart applied its same cost-cutting principles to food. Wal-Mart was highly efficient in carrying out these practices, and early in the twenty-first century it was America's largest seller of grocery food. Other large chains, such as Costco Wholesale Corporation, have used a similar approach with similar success.

Supermarkets scrambled to meet these challenges. Many added delis of their own and started selling more prepared foods. Supermarkets diversified their product lines as organic, vegetarian, and ethnic foods became popular. As food became a global business, with foods shipped from thousands of miles from producer to consumer, United States supermarkets set the world standards. American food corporations have rapidly expanded abroad. With the implementation of trade agreements, it is likely that globalization will influence American grocery stores in the future.

[*See also* Delicatessens; Farmers' Markets; Food Marketing; Piggly Wiggly; Tea; Transportation of Food.]

BIBLIOGRAPHY

Brady, William W. *Supermarket Routes: Autobiographic Tale of the Retail Grocery Business 1924 to Present*. Miami Springs, FL: Pyramid, 1978.

Humphrey, Kim. *Shelf Life: Supermarkets and the Changing Culture of Consumption*. Cambridge, U.K.: Cambridge University Press, 1998.

Kahn, Barbara E., and Leigh McAlister. *Grocery Revolution: The New Focus on the Consumer*. Reading, MA: Addison Wesley Longman, 1997.

Marnell, William H. *Once Upon a Store: A Biography of the World's First Supermarket*. New York: Herder, 1971.

Mayo, James M. *The American Grocery Store: The Business Evolution of an Architectural Space*. Westport, CT: Greenwood, 1993.

Seth, Andrew, and Geoffrey Randall. *The Grocers: The Rise and Rise of the Supermarket Chains*. 2nd ed. Dover, NH: Kogan Page, 2001.

Walsh, William I. *The Rise and Decline of the Great Atlantic and Pacific Tea Company*. Secaucus, NJ: Lyle Stuart, 1986.

Ward, Artemas. *The Grocers' Handbook and Directory for 1886*. Bedford, MA: Applewood, 2001.

Ward, Barbara McLean, ed. *Produce and Conserve, Share and Play Square: The Grocer and the Consumer on the Home-Front Battlefield during World War II*. Portsmouth, NH: Strawbery Banke Museum, 1994.

Zimmerman, M. M. *The Super Market: A Revolution in Distribution*. New York: McGraw-Hill, 1955.

ANDREW F. SMITH

Grog

Rum had become a staple ration in the British navy by the late seventeenth century. On August 21, 1740, the British Vice Admiral Edward Vernon ordered that the rum ration be mixed with water to reduce drunkenness. English sailors named this mixture "grog" in honor of Vernon, who was called "Old Grog" because of the cloak he wore, which was made of grogram, a thick blend of silk, wool, and mohair. In 1756 the dilution of rum with water was institutionalized in British naval regulations. George Washington's home, Mount Vernon in Virginia, was named by Washington's elder half-brother, Lawrence, who had served under Admiral Vernon in 1740.

The American navy adopted grog, which was a part of a seaman's ration until it was discontinued in 1862. Over the years, the quantity of rum and water varied, producing "two-water grog" or "three-water grog," depending on the dilution. Other alcoholic beverages, such as arrack, were frequently substituted for the rum in grog, and sometimes other ingredients, such as sugar and lime, were added.

Grogshops had sprung up in American ports before the Revolutionary War. They were frequented by sailors and were considered among the most unsavory establishments in American cities. As the price of whiskey declined during the nineteenth century, it was often substituted for rum. Grogshop owners sometimes adulterated the whiskey in the grog with logwood (a dye), berries, tobacco, and strychnine. Raw eggs were also occasionally added to grog, and this may have been the origin of the American drink, egg 'n' grog or eggnog, which emerged in the United States during the nineteenth century and remains a favorite at Christmastime and on New Year's Day.

[*See also* Eggnog; Rum; Ship Food.]

BIBLIOGRAPHY

Brown, John Hull. *Early American Beverages*. Rutland, VT: Charles E. Tuttle, 1966.

Hooker, Richard J. *A History of Food and Drink in America*. Indianapolis and New York: Bobbs-Merrill, 1981.

Pack, James. *Nelson's Blood: The Story of Naval Rum*. 3rd ed. Annapolis, MD: Naval Institute Press, 1995.

ANDREW F. SMITH

Guacamole, *see Dips and Spreads*

Gyro

The gyro sandwich is most likely the invention of Greek immigrants who, sometime around the 1970s, adapted the cooking of their homeland as a way to earn a living by providing ground meat in a new manner, one that would tempt the sandwich-loving American public. Ground lamb or beef, or a mixture of both, is seasoned with herbs and spices and molded around a vertical spit that rotates before a flame. The word "gyro" means ring or circle, and the sandwich was thus named for the spinning spit on which it is prepared. As the meat cooks and forms a crust on the outside, it is shaved off, placed in pita bread, and served with lettuce, onion, tomato, and *tzatziki*, a yogurt sauce flavored with garlic and cucumber. Gyros have become so popular since their introduction that they can be found in major cities throughout most of the United States.

[*See also* Sandwiches; Street Vendors.]

BIBLIOGRAPHY

Mercuri, Becky. *Sandwiches That You Will Like*. Pittsburgh, PA: WQED, 2002.

BECKY MERCURI

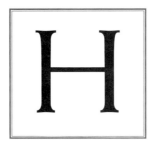

Halloween

Halloween may be the only American holiday that is not associated with a particular feast or recipe. Nineteenth-century Irish immigrants brought the October 31 celebration to the United States. On that night it was traditional to give soul cakes to visitors to their households in return for promises to say prayers on behalf of dead relatives. They also put lanterns made from vegetables in the windows to welcome ghosts and wandering souls. In Ireland and Scotland, these candlelit lanterns were carved from large turnips or potatoes, and in England from beets, but in the United States immigrants used the larger native pumpkins.

Carved pumpkin jack-o'-lanterns are an integral part of Halloween festivities, but they are seldom eaten. The specially bred pumpkins, which can range in size from one to over one thousand pounds, are hollowed out and carved with holes to represent eyes, nose, and mouth. When a lighted candle or flashlight is placed inside, the pumpkin's face glows in the dark. Smaller species of cheese pumpkin, pie pumpkin, or sweet pumpkin, which have sweeter, less watery flesh, are used for making pies, soups, and breads. Some people save the seeds to dry, roast, and salt as a snack. Roasted, salted pumpkin seeds can be purchased commercially as well.

American harvest festivals called play parties were a precursor to the modern Halloween. In the mid-nineteenth century, Snap Apple Nights or Nut Crack Night parties were celebrated in some regions of the United States with games, such as dunking for apples or fortune-telling with nuts, that symbolized the end of the harvest season. Bobbing for apples was a British folk tradition in which young, unmarried people tried to bite an apple that was floating in water or hanging from a string without using their hands. The first person to bite into one would be the next to marry. For a Nut Crack Night party, pairs of walnuts were set on the hearth near the fire by courting couples. If the heated nuts bounced around and cracked open, they foretold a troubled relationship, but if the nuts roasted quietly, the relationship would be smooth.

In the late nineteenth century, middle-class Americans looking toward their Celtic heritage rediscovered (and reinvented) Halloween customs and made them respectable. Beginning in the 1870s, articles on Halloween appeared in periodicals that encouraged a new, more uniformly celebrated Victorian fete. By the twentieth century, Halloween parties for both children

Halloween. Embossed postcard, early twentieth century. *Collection of Alice Ross*

and adults had become a common way to mark the day, with games like bobbing for apples, festive costumes, and refreshments that included cider, doughnuts, candy corn, popcorn balls, and apples.

Candies made in the shape of corn kernels and pumpkins commemorated the harvest season. The Wunderle Candy Company of Philadelphia was the first to commercially produce candy corn in the 1880s. The sons of German immigrant Gustav Goelitz, founder of Goelitz Confectionery Co., began commercial production in 1898 in Cincinnati, Ohio. The company he founded claims to be the oldest manufacturer of the holiday icon. Brach's in Chicago began manufacturing the small, soft, triangular and tricolor (orange, yellow, and white) candies in the late 1920s. By the 1990s, the company was turning out 30 million kernels a day. In 2001, candy corn manufacturers sold more than 20 million pounds, or approximately 8.3 billion kernels.

Before World War II, Halloween pranks were the norm, while families hosted small parties at home for young children. During the war years, little candy was available because of sugar rationing. In the 1950s, Halloween evolved into a family- and neighborhood-centered holiday directed mainly at the young, in an attempt to discourage teenage pranksters. Home bakers produced pumpkin or witch cookies, shaped with newly available cookie cutters, and devil's food cupcakes frosted with orange and black icing.

The ancient Halloween ritual of trick or treat was revived as a relatively inexpensive way for the new postwar suburban communities to share the Halloween celebration. It became a child's right and privilege to go from house to house filling a pillowcase with apples, popcorn balls, and candy. The tradition of Trick-or-Treat for UNICEF began in 1950 when Philadelphia schoolchildren collected money in decorated milk cartons to help the world's children through the United Nations Children's Fund. Trick-or-Treat for UNICEF spread across the country, and as the twenty-first century opened millions of children participated each year in Halloween-related fund-raising campaigns in the United States, Canada, Ireland, Mexico, and Hong Kong.

Door-to-door trick-or-treating became less popular at the end of the twentieth century when fabricated urban legends grew up about poisoned candy and neighbors who gave children apples containing razor blades or needles. Many communities and churches tried to redirect the holiday to well-chaperoned indoor parties and some children were not allowed to eat noncommercial, unpackaged treats.

In addition to holiday candy and games, Americans play with their food at Halloween by creating party foods in the shape of pumpkins, black cats, ghosts, and witches. Jack-o'-lantern cheese balls are consumed, along with quantities of candy. Many enjoy foods that are frightening or disgusting, such as candy worms in chocolate pudding dusted on top with crushed chocolate-cookie crumbs to look like dirt, licorice spiders, pretzel witch fingers with almond fingernails, or ice cubes containing stuffed olives that simulate eyes. Food is used as a substitute for human body parts in haunted houses, a popular party game or community fund-raiser. Visitors to the haunted house are blindfolded and told to put their hands in bowls of cooked pasta representing intestines, dried apricots representing ears, or peeled grapes representing eyeballs. Gourmets experiment with pumpkin soups, seasonal vegetables, and unusual sauces.

Halloween Goblin. Postcard, c. 1909. *Collection of Alice Ross*

In the 1990s, Americans spent an estimated $6.9 billion annually on Halloween, making it the country's second-largest commercial holiday next to Christmas. By the late twentieth century, the holiday had changed again from a children's festival to an all-ages extravaganza. By the early 2000s, Halloween had become a bigger holiday for candy consumption than Valentine's Day, Christmas, or Easter. Miniature candy bars, produced especially for Halloween, were popular with trick-or-treaters, and candy corn continued to outsell all other nonchocolate Halloween candy.

[*See also* Candy Bars and Candy.]

BIBLIOGRAPHY

Bannatyne, Lesley Pratt. *Halloween: An American Holiday, An American History*. New York: Facts On File, 1990.

Cahill, Thomas. *How the Irish Saved Civilization*. New York: Doubleday, 1995.

Halloween: Bewitching Treats, Eats, Costumes and Decorations. New York: Lorenz Books, Anness Publishing, 1999.

VIRGINIA SCOTT JENKINS

Ham, *see Pig*

Hamburger

The hamburger is the single most popular food item consumed in the United States, with Americans eating billions of them each year. Originally known as the hamburger sandwich, hamburgers commonly consist of a flattened patty of ground beef placed between two halves of a white flour bun. To enhance the flavor, hamburger eaters routinely adorn their grilled or fried ground beef patties with a variety of possible cheeses, vegetables, and sauces, creating a seemingly endless combination of tastes. French-fried potatoes and carbonated soft drinks traditionally accompany the burger, creating America's favorite fast-food meal. In fact, this burger-and-fries feast is viewed worldwide as American food.

The hamburger's exact origins are vague. Explanations of its roots are based more on myth than on verifiable fact. Chopping or grinding up meat before eating it is possibly as old as our species, dating far back into prehistory. Food historians offer numerous, often contradictory, accounts of where the hamburger originated, but most trace it to northern Germany, which had a similar beef sausage. The hamburger, in turn, accompanied the massive wave of German immigrants coming to America during the early- to mid-nineteenth century. Their ethnic dish of seasoned ground beef appeared on the menu of New York City's elite Delmonico's restaurant in 1834, featured as the Hamburg Steak. By the latter half of the century, American cookbooks included recipes for Beefsteak a la Hamburg and for the identical, yet Americanized, Salisbury steak.

How the hamburger became a popular part of the mainstream American diet is also in question, as competing tales credit its introduction to several different entrepreneurs. Residents of New Haven, Connecticut, insist that the immigrant Louis Lassen began selling hamburgers from his lunch wagon by 1900. Another hamburger legend has Charlie Nagreen serving the first true hamburger at a fair in Seymour, Wisconsin, in 1885. The Akron, Ohio, native Frank Menches is locally acclaimed for serving the world's first hamburger at his local Summit County Fair. Menches, however, also claims credit for inventing the ice cream cone. Seemingly more verifiable was the work of the Texan Fletcher Davis, who probably sold what he termed hamburgers to fairgoers at St. Louis's 1904 Louisiana Purchase Exposition. Regardless of who was first, the early hamburger did not immediately gain a popular following, remaining either somewhat of a "fair food," or an inexpensive snack sold to workers from food carts at factory gates.

One factor that may have hindered the hamburger's popularity was the common distrust of the meat industry in the early twentieth century, prompted by the 1906 publication of Upton Sinclair's *The Jungle*. Sinclair's book exposed the unsanitary and dangerous conditions in meat-processing plants, discouraging meat consumption. Ground meat was even more suspect, since at that time most meat was only ground up after it had begun to spoil. Butchers regularly ground their unsold meat, keeping it salable longer by adding chemical preservatives to the mix. The ground meat also commonly included a high percentage of animal fat and undesirable organ tissue. With such a dismal reputation, only the most impoverished consumers resorted to purchasing and consuming ground meat. Though inexpensive, ground beef patties long remained on the margin of the American diet.

The hamburger finally became popular in the 1920s because of the intensive marketing campaign by an upstart restaurant chain in Wichita, Kansas. In 1921, Billy Ingram and Walter Anderson opened the White Castle System of Eating Houses, featuring a five-cent hamburger as their primary offering. (In fact, another midwestern legend credits the White Castle cofounder and fry cook Walter Anderson with actually creating the first flattened hamburger patty on a bun.) Ingram realized the great profit potential from selling hamburger sandwiches. To persuade customers that the hamburger was safe to eat, Ingram aggressively marketed the concepts of cleanliness and purity by whitewashing his buildings' exteriors, using only gleaming stainless steel counters and fixtures, and constantly grinding good, fresh cuts of beef within customers' sight. Ingram later even commissioned a medical school study that indicated that hamburgers were a highly nutritious food. He succeeded in popularizing his hamburgers, both by stressing their purity and nutritional value and by offering them at an inexpensive price. Ingram also encouraged customers to purchase numerous burgers at one time, and to take them home "by the sack." This take-out format became the norm for most of their transactions and the precedent for modern fast food. White Castle quickly spread eastward across the Midwest in the early 1920s and was already firmly established in New York City by 1929.

Countless imitators of White Castle's buildings, products, name, and even slogan soon sprang up throughout the United States, extending the sudden popularity of the hamburger sandwich from coast to coast. White Tower overlapped White Castle's territory in the Midwest and East, and Crystal's and Little Tavern became the dominant hamburger chains in the South. By the end of the 1920s, the hamburger craze had completely saturated the restaurant market, so much so that the president of the American Restaurant Association announced in 1929 that the hamburger and apple pie had become America's favorite foods. The rate of hamburger consumption continued to grow, even during the Depression-era economic hardships of the 1930s. In fact, innovators even expanded beyond the White Castle–style burger, offering customers new and different variations. Most significant was the introduction in California of Bob Wian's Big Boy, a double-stacked, two-patty burger sandwich, including cheese, an extra layer of bread, lettuce, mayonnaise, and relish. The hamburger boom continued up until the beginning of World War II, when the restaurant industry was suddenly crippled by labor and food shortages. Workers either joined the military or took higher-paying war production jobs, leaving hamburger restaurants without employees. Compounding this labor void was a program of national food rationing that severely limited the availability of meat, coffee, and sugar. The

hamburger industry began to rebound after the war ended, making a slow recovery in the late 1940s.

In the 1950s the hamburger gained a new following, becoming the most popular food of burgeoning suburbia. Shedding their ethnic identities along with their urban neighborhoods, new suburbanites stressing conformity embraced the hamburger as their common food. Hamburger stands appeared soon after suburban housing tracts, making their products readily available to the young families of the baby boom. Nationally franchised chains, such as McDonald's and (Insta-) Burger King, began to edge out local and regional chains by the late 1950s, becoming the dominant force in suburban hamburger sales. By the mid-1960s, McDonald's emerged as the industry leader, dominating most market areas and introducing most of the industry's product innovations. Serving many millions of its inexpensive round, one-ounce burgers, with the already popular combination of ketchup, mustard, onion, and pickle condiments, McDonald's set the standard for what consumers expected from a hamburger. Its only variation on the hamburger was the cheeseburger, created by adding a slice of American cheese to the top during cooking.

By the 1970s, however, both McDonald's and the other leading chains offered a wide variety of oversized burgers. Most popular among this new generation of hamburgers was McDonald's two-tiered Big Mac—essentially a modified Big Boy burger—and Burger King's Whopper, featuring a larger beef patty topped by a gooey salad mix of lettuce, onion, pickles, mayonnaise-based sauce, and tomato slice. Dave Thomas's Wendy's chain first appeared in 1969, selling only bigger hamburgers, all made-to-order for each customer from a long list of possible condiments. Eventually, other companies sold burgers topped with everything from chili to bacon to bean sprouts, customizing their sandwiches to suit regional, ethnic, and trendy preferences.

The hamburger went from the margin of society to the mainstream during the twentieth century, becoming America's undisputed culinary favorite. More than simply a popular food, the hamburger emerged as a symbol of American culture, and even as a key aspect of American ethnicity. Hailed as "the" American food, ever-expanding multinational restaurant chains efficiently market the hamburger all around the globe.

[*See also* Burger King; Fast Food; French Fries; McDonald's; Meat; Roadside Food; Sandwiches; Wendy's; White Castle.]

BIBLIOGRAPHY

Hogan, David Gerard. *Selling 'em by the Sack: White Castle and the Creation of American Food*. New York: New York University Press, 1997.

Jakle, John A., and Keith A. Sculle. *Fast Food: Roadside Restaurants in the Automobile Age*. Baltimore: Johns Hopkins University Press, 1999.

Kroc, Ray, with Robert Anderson. *Grinding It Out: The Making of McDonald's*. Chicago: Contemporary Books, 1977.

Levenstein, Harvey. *Paradox of Plenty: A Social History of Eating in Modern America*. New York: Oxford University Press, 1993.

DAVID GERARD HOGAN

Hardtack

For centuries, hard breads made of flour and water and baked into round, oval, or square shapes have accompanied travelers on long treks, soldiers in military campaigns, and sailors at sea. Hardtack's first important North American role was in sustaining crews and passengers of European vessels en route to the New World and as a ration in the ensuing sea-borne trade. Ship's bread continued to feed seamen well into the twentieth century. Hardtack, was also known as biscuit, crackers, ship's bread or biscuit, hard bread or biscuit or crackers; soft tack was fresh bread.

Military biscuit predated the independent United States, serving armies in both Europe and North America and was an important ration for the Continental Army in the Revolutionary War (1775–1783). General George Washington constantly asked the baking superintendent Christopher Ludwick for large quantities to feed his campaigning soldiers, while the Revolutionary private Joseph Martin was served biscuit "hard enough to break the teeth of a rat."

This durable foodstuff achieved iconic status during the American Civil War (1861–1865). The three-inch square hardtack symbolized the hardship and singularity of a soldier's life, providing a tangible wartime and postwar link among veterans. Nicknames abounded: angle cake, cast-iron biscuits, teeth dullers, McClellan pies, Lincoln pies. Soldiers' correspondence, diaries, and postwar literature, evincing both fondness and antipathy, show that hardtack held a special place in the soldiers' collective consciousness. Capt. Francis Donaldson, of the 118th Pennsylvania, expressed this mixed attitude, writing in April 1862 of "the despised sheet iron cracker." Only six months later Donaldson noted, "I can make as enjoyable a meal on [hard] crackers as others can on roast chicken

Hardtack. Hardtack from the Spanish American War. The diameter is 4.5 inches. The hardtack was autographed by soldiers from Pennsylvania and mailed home to Pine Grove, Pa., by one of them, George Heiser. *Courtesy of Steven Heller, Heller's Antiques*

and trimmings." Hardtack appeared in verse too. "Short allowance prevailed throughout the brigade. The men changed the words of a song which goes 'Hard times! Come again no more,' [Stephen Foster, 1854] into the following, and sang it with much vigor and vim:

'Tis the voice of the hungry,
Hardtack, hardtack,
Come again once more!
Many days I've wandered,
from my little tent door
Crying hardtack, hardtack
Come again once more!"

Hardtack's special connotation both preceded and postdated the American Civil War. Soldiers sent or took samples home, and many are now in museum collections across the country. Other souvenir examples exist, such as an inscribed 1784 British ship's biscuit in the National Maritime Museum collections, Greenwich, England, and a Spanish-American War hardtack sent to Pine Grove, Pennsylvania, bearing the date "May 7 1898" along with the names of the correspondent and his four messmates. Hardtack remained an important part of

World War I army campaign rations (1917–1918) and continued to feed American soldiers on field maneuvers into the 1930s.

[*See also* Combat Food; Ship Food.]

BIBLIOGRAPHY

Acken, J. Gregory. *Inside the Army of the Potomac: The Civil War Experience of Captain Francis Adams Donaldson.* Mechanicsburg, PA: Stackpole Books, 1998.

Billings, John D. *Hardtack and Coffee.* New York: Time-Life Books, 1982, 112–120. Originally published 1887.

Heller's Civil War Antique Shop. http://www.civilwarantiqueshop.com/m12.htm. Photographs of a piece of Spanish-American War hardtack, George Heiser, Pine Grove, PA., 1898 (private collection), 2003.

Oliver, Sandra L. *Saltwater Foodways: New Englanders and Their Food, at Sea and Ashore, in the Nineteenth Century.* Mystic, CT: Mystic Seaport Museum, Inc., 1995.

Rees, John U. "Cooking with Biscuit and Hard Tack in Camp." *Food History News* 8, no. 4 (Spring 1997): 4–5.

Rees, John U. "'Hard Enough to Break the Teeth of a Rat.': Biscuit and Hard Bread in the Armies of the Revolution." *Food History News* 8, no. 4 (Spring 1997): 2–6.

Ship's biscuit, 1784 (British), Artifact AAB0003, National Maritime Museum, Greenwich, England. Pictured in *The National Maritime Museum: The Story of Britain and the Sea.* London: Centurion Press, Ltd.

JOHN U. REES

Harvey, Fred

Frederick Henry Harvey (1835–1901), a restaurant entrepreneur, immigrated to New York City from England at age fifteen in 1850. He found work in restaurants there and in New Orleans, before moving to St. Louis, where he and a partner opened a restaurant in 1857. The outbreak of the Civil War in 1861, combined with the dishonest behavior of Harvey's partner, left his business in ruins and him unemployed. He eventually found work as a railway mail clerk on the Hannibal & St. Joseph Railroad (1862), which later became part of the Chicago, Burlington, & Quincy Railroad (CB&Q). There he experienced firsthand the often-squalid conditions and chicanery that greeted passengers on trains scheduled to stop "twenty minutes for refreshments" at designated stations, which was at that time the primary means of feeding people traveling long distances by rail.

His sensibilities as a gourmand were outraged at what he saw and what he had to consume, so Harvey drew on his experience as a restaurateur to come up with a better idea. He proposed building eating houses at intervals that would allow trains to stop at times appropriate for dining. At each stop, passengers would be offered a clean and handsomely furnished dining room, with Irish linen and English silver at table, ample portions of well-prepared food, and efficient and courteous service. His plan to carry this out included preferred shipping arrangements for foodstuffs over the host railroad, offering attractive salaries to noted chefs of the day who joined his firm, and, eventually, hiring young women to serve as waitresses.

Harvey's employer, the CB&Q, turned this proposal down. Harvey next approached the Atchison, Topeka, & Santa Fe Railway (AT&SF), then building a line between Kansas and southern California. Through negotiations with that railroad and its existing food vendor, Harvey acquired the food concession at the depot in Topeka, Kansas, in 1876. From there he and his heirs and successors went on to establish fifty-two lunch and dining rooms, the Harvey Houses, twenty-three hotels, and thirty newsstands, a majority of them in association with the AT&SF. Meanwhile, when the AT&SF began running dining cars on their long distance trains in 1888, Harvey negotiated to staff and provision those eating establishments as well. When the AT&SF acquired rail access to the rim of the Grand Canyon, Harvey created, in 1903, the recreational and boarding accommodations there. His firm eventually also established corporate and public eating establishments that stretched from Cleveland, Ohio, to Los Angeles, California.

Harvey's contributions to American culinary history are of a pioneering nature. His establishments and his reputation for quality played a critical role in attracting riders to the Santa Fe system. He created centralized menu planning, which assured that passengers on the AT&SF would never encounter identical selections when traveling. He established standards for excellence in food and service that applied to an extensive chain of restaurants, with the result that patrons could be assured of a certain high-quality meal experience wherever they encountered a Harvey operation. Perhaps his most unique contribution is an outgrowth of his desire to offer exceptional service. He is credited with populating the American Southwest with thousands of educated, adventuresome, attractive, and single young women—the Harvey Girls waitresses—early in the region's settlement history, earning him the title "civilizer of the West."

[*See also* Dining Car; Johnson, Howard; Pullman, George.]

BIBLIOGRAPHY

Haber, Barbara. "The Harvey Girls: Good Women and Good Food." In *From Hardtack to Home Fries: An Uncommon History of American Cooks and Meals*, 87–106. New York: Free Press, 2002.

Henderson, James David. *Meals by Fred Harvey*. Hawthorne, CA, 1985.

Poling-Kempes, Lesley. *The Harvey Girls: Women Who Opened the West*. New York, 1991.

JAMES D. PORTERFIELD

Hawaiian Food

Food of Hawaii can be separated into two categories: Hawaiian food, the food of the native islanders, and local food, the eclectic blend of the cuisines of later settlers. Before explorers, missionaries, and immigrants arrived, Hawaiian food consisted of fresh ingredients that were prepared raw or cooked simply, using broiling, boiling, and roasting techniques. Protein sources included poultry, pig, and dog. Fish and other seafood, such as turtles, sea urchins, limpets, and shellfish, were also consumed but in modest quantities.

Bananas, coconuts, breadfruits, and mountain apples are native to the islands and were a big part of the Hawaiians' diet. Other tropical fruits, like pineapples, mangoes, gooseberries, passion fruits, guavas, and avocados, were introduced to the islands in the 1800s. Although there were few vegetables available, most of the daily calories came from the starchy tuber *kalo* or taro, which was usually boiled and then pounded into a paste

Poi. A couple making poi, Hawaiian Islands, early 1920s. *Frank and Frances Carpenter Collection, Prints and Photographs Division, Library of Congress*

called poi. Sweet potatoes might also be pounded, but were more often roasted like yams.

Poi is something of miracle food because of its long shelf life and nutritional content. When freshly pounded, poi is at its sweetest. If a more sour poi is desired, it needs to ferment a few days. *Kalo*'s heart-shaped pliable leaves, *lu'au*, are also edible. The *lu'au* can be wrapped around morsels of meat and then roasted, or they can be boiled plain as a spinachlike side dish. (The word *lu'au* became the name of the great feast because of the Hawaiians' favorite stew-like dish consisting of tender *lu'au* leaves and coconut milk baked with chicken or squid.) Because sweet potato greens were the only other green vegetable available, a large variety of seaweeds supplied essential vitamins and minerals to the Hawaiians' diet.

Local food was a product of the cultural melting pot in Hawaii. In the early 1800s, missionaries from New England were the first large group of immigrants to settle in the islands. They brought salted meat and salted salmon. When the pineapple and sugar industries exploded, more human labor was needed. Since the Hawaiian population had declined so rapidly because of diseases contracted from the missionaries, immigrants from Japan, China, Korea, Okinawa, the Philippines, Puerto Rico, and a large number of Portuguese from the Atlantic islands flocked to Hawaii seeking to fill the jobs. Smaller groups of immigrants from Samoa, Tonga, Vietnam, and Thailand soon followed.

As each ethnicity adapted their cuisine to the readily available ingredients and as dishes were borrowed and exchanged between groups, local food was born. The Chinese brought their leafy vegetables, rice, ginger, and chopsticks. The Japanese introduced charcoal grilling or hibachi, as well as stewed meat and fish dishes, tofu, and the ubiquitous teriyaki sauce. Yeast cakes and breads like *pao doce* (sweet bread) and *malasadas* (doughnuts) from the Portuguese became favorite island treats. The Portuguese also shared their love for rich bean soups and spicy linguica, or sausage. With the Koreans came pungent ingredients like garlic, onions, and red pepper. And the Filipinos shared dishes that were braised in vinegar, like pork adobo.

As these cultures worked side by side, a cuisine and a language were born: local food and pidgin. Through the decades, certain dishes from each ethnicity became staples and are prepared and loved in most homes in the twenty-first century. Cooking techniques and ingredients were exchanged and adapted to reflect the melding of so many ethnicities. A typical island gathering might include a hodgepodge of dishes: *shōyu* chicken (a Chinese-style

Hawaiian Food. *The Hawaiian Islands and the Story of Pineapple,* cookbooklet by Isabel N. Young issued by the American Can Company, 1935. *Collection of Andrew F. Smith*

braised dish named for its essential ingredient—Japanese soy sauce), Korean-style barbecued meat, Spam *musubi* (slices of fried Spam sandwiched between layers of short-grained rice and wrapped with nori or dried laver sheets), chicken chow mein, *manapua,* or *char siu bao* to the Chinese (sweet buns stuffed with minced roast pork), *kalua* pig (Hawaiian smoked roast pork), *lomi lomi* salmon (salted salmon with diced onions and tomatoes), and potato and macaroni salad dressed with a liberal amount of mayonnaise.

Desserts and sweets are equally diverse. The island favorites include a Hawaiian coconut pudding called *haupia,* which is present at every *lu'au,* and shaved ice with syrup, which is generally consumed after a long day at the beach. There are about fifty different flavored syrups to choose from. Locals also like to eat shaved ice stuffed with vanilla ice cream and adzuki beans (sweet red beans usually stuffed in Japanese sweet rice cakes called *mochi*).

[*See also* Chinese American Food; Japanese American Food; Korean American Food; Pineapple; Soy Sauce; Sweet Potatoes.]

BIBLIOGRAPHY

Corum, Ann Kondo. *Ethnic Foods of Hawaii.* Honolulu: Bess Press, 2000.
Laudan, Rachel. *The Food of Paradise: Exploring Hawaii's Culinary Heritage.* Honolulu: University of Hawaii Press, 1996.

ROBYNNE L. MAII

Hazelnuts, *see Filberts*

Health Food

The history of health foods in the United States is often intertwined with food faddism, defined as a prescription of foods with exaggerated and scientifically unproven health claims. Justifications for making statements about the health effects of specific foods or dietary regimes include divine inspiration, promoting public health, and capitalist profit. It is difficult for most consumers to separate the claims of the food faddist from the constantly changing and often contradictory nutritional and health information coming from the scientific community. The United States has had a colorful history of health reformers and food faddists, some of whom, such as herbalists and chiropractors, object to being labeled as faddist. They argue that the mainstream scientific and medical community is often too quick to pass judgment on health food claims and should reserve its opinions until more research has been done on holistic and alternative approaches to dietary therapy that may not conform to current scientific thinking.

It is difficult to separate the history of various health food movements in America from that of vegetarianism. Perhaps the individual most noted for ushering in a modern age of healthy-eating food reform in America was Sylvester Graham (1794–1851). Ordained as a Presbyterian minister, Graham in time shifted his activities to become a crusader for proper eating and temperance throughout the northeastern states. He believed that a vegetarian diet was the one that God had intended for mankind and went on to promote whole wheat bread that did not have the bran removed. His name is perhaps best known for his development of a high bran flour, graham flour, which was baked into a thin flat bread, the graham cracker.

By the mid-nineteenth century the influence of Graham and other food reformers, such as the newspaper editor Horace Greeley, as well as the interest of such literary figures as Bronson Alcott, Ralph Waldo Emerson, and Henry David Thoreau, led to the establishment of the American Vegetarian Society. The agenda of these health reformers was not just the promotion of a vegetable diet; they also criticized the newly emerging industrialized diet, which assaulted proper digestion by promoting increasingly refined carbohydrates, fatty beef, and salted pork. The industrialized food-processing complex that emerged after the Civil War had begun targeting a growing middle class with increased nationwide advertising and distribution of many of the packaged food brands that survived through the twentieth century. These processed foods have become a focal point of criticism by health food proponents who believe in fresh products produced locally.

Following Graham, a series of utopian communities and health reformers continued a tradition of Christian vegetarianism and temperance. Most notable was Ellen G. White (1827–1915), who helped to establish through her spiritual visions and guidance the Seventh-Day Adventist Church, which continued to promote spiritual vegetarianism into the twenty-first century. Her visions included the founding of both the magazine the *Health Reformer* in 1865 and in the following year the Western Health Reform Institute in Battle Creek, Michigan. One of the church's members, John Harvey Kellogg (1852–1943), went on to earn a medical degree and in 1876 took over the administration of the institute and renamed it the Battle Creek Sanitarium. Dr. Kellogg promoted not just a spiritual diet but a scientific one that sought to rid the body of toxins produced in the intestines from the putrefaction of meat. A vegetarian regimen in concert with enemas, water baths, and open-air exercise were the cures that lured thousands of Americans to the Sanitarium.

Cornflake Crusaders

In time Kellogg created a health-food marketing empire based on "biological living," a theory that extolled the virtues of his inventions, cornflakes and granola. By the early twentieth century however, his business ideals and concern about the commercialization of an originally spiritual enterprise led to his being cut off from the church. In 1906 the Battle Creek Toasted Corn Flake Company was incorporated under the management of John Harvey Kellogg's younger brother, William Keith Kellogg (1860–1951), who developed the cornflake that became a breakfast staple. In a short period the company would bear his name alone, much to the chagrin of his brother. The era of the cornflake crusaders also witnessed the start of companies founded by Charles William Post (1854–1914), who is known for Postum, a coffee substitute; Post Toasties, a competitor of the Kellogg cornflake; and Grape Nuts (essentially graham flour bread broken into bits). More than forty other cereal companies were also in operation in Battle Creek during that time.

One contemporary of Kellogg was Horace Fletcher (1849–1919), a portly entrepreneur who in an attempt to lose weight created a system of mastication that he believed was the pathway to health. Fletcherism, as it became known, required that food be liquefied before being swallowed. Each mouthful had to be chewed minimally thirty-two times, once for each tooth in the mouth, with many foods requiring fifty to sixty chews. Even the Battle Creek Sanitarium took up his method but in time abandoned it when faced with Fletcher's more radical beliefs, among them the notion that bowel movements would be essentially unnecessary if perfect digestion were achieved.

By the early twentieth century, the influence of health reformers was challenged by the development of nutritional science, especially the discovery of vitamins and other essential nutrients. Also, the passage of the 1906 Pure Food and Drug Act created a climate in which consumers could be protected from fraudulent health claims. Lobbying efforts for the bill, led by President Theodore Roosevelt, were influenced in no small way by the 1906 publication of *The Jungle* by Upton Sinclair, a book that depicted the horrific conditions of America's meat-packing industry. The 1906 Act also led to the creation of the Food and Drug Administration (FDA) which oversees the U.S. food and drug industry. Over the years new legislation filled in many loopholes. In the 1990s, however, the loosening of FDA labeling regulations regarding nutritional supplements and health claims has supported a growing billion-dollar industry in the United States.

Throughout the first half of the twentieth century numerous dietary plans for health and for weight loss were popularized. In short they called for a dietary combination or balance that restricted the use of some foods as being unhealthy and prescribed others as promoting health. Dr. William Howard Hay (1866–1940) believed that the underlying cause of many diseases (for example, diabetes, kidney and digestive disorders, and rheumatism) was an acid/alkaline imbalance in the body. He promoted a low-acid dietary regime, known as the Hay Diet, or Hayism, which held that restricting the consumption of acid foods (meat) and increasing the consumption of alkaline foods (starches) would restore health and prevent disease. Approaches to balanced eating were nothing new. Centuries-old folk systems of dietary balance, from the hot/cold humoral system of the ancient Greeks to the Asian yin/yang blending of foods, continue to be practiced throughout the world. From the 1960s onward macrobiotic diets became especially popular as a means of putting the "whole" body back in balance by proper eating. The ultimate goal of this approach is to become a complete vegan, eating a diet devoid of any animal products.

Vitamin Pushers

In the mid-twentieth century, Adelle Davis (1904–1974) emerged as one of the first multimedia spokespersons for "popular nutrition" via the radio, television, and the printed page. In books such as *Let's Eat Right to Keep Fit* (1954) she extolled the virtues of natural foods with an emphasis on dietary supplementation, especially vitamins, that could cure just about any ailment. Although she did have an academic background in nutrition, her ideas were criticized as lacking scientific proof and accuracy. Nevertheless, Davis sold over 10 million copies of her various books and still had supporters nearly thirty years after her death. The so-called vitamin pushers continue to promote high doses of various vitamins to restore and maintain health. One of the best known advocates for vitamins was the Nobel Laureate Linus Pauling (1901–1994) who believed that megadoses of vitamin C could even cure the common cold.

As other social movements captured America in the 1960s and 1970s so did a litany of ideas on alternative eating with a concomitant growth of vegetarianism and organic foods. Jerome Rodale (1898–1971), a pioneer of the organic food movement, began in the 1940s to promote the growing of fruits and vegetables without the use of pesticides and artificial fertilizers. He also founded *Prevention* magazine, an influential, mainstream outlet for extolling the virtues of health foods in America. While Rodale's message declared that the only healthy foods were those things produced from the good, green earth, other leaders were promoting weight-loss programs that restricted what someone could eat.

The late twentieth century saw the re-emergence of the physician as spokesperson for novelty diets and health-food cures. Perhaps the best-known is Dr. Robert C. Atkins (1930–2003) whose 1972 book *Dr. Atkins' Diet Revolution* was a million-copy best seller. His high protein/low carbohydrate approach to weight loss and healthy living, however, waned by the 1980s as the evils of saturated fat and cholesterol became known. But cycles come and go, and as the public's fear of cholesterol subsided in the 1990s, *Dr. Atkins' New Diet Revolution* (1992) also became a best-selling book. Although Atkins was criticized for his theories on ketosis and fat metabolism, most of his followers selectively hear that they can eat all the meat, eggs, and butter they like, while avoiding sweets, bread, pasta, rice, most fruits, and many vegetables.

A host of other low-calorie, low-carbohydrate, and food-combining diet plans followed Atkins, including *The Scarsdale Diet* (Tarnower), *The Zone* (Sears), *Protein Power* (Eades and Eades), and, nodding to our "caveman" ancestors, *The Origin Diet* (Somers) and *The Paleolithic Prescription* (Eaton, Shostak, and Konner). The frequent appearance of new weight-loss diets is a testament to their frequent failure. Their mere novelty may explain why dieters tend to ignore the mundane message promoted by most health professionals who simply advise people to eat smaller portions of a well-balanced diet.

Specific labeling of foods as medicine has come full circle in the form of nutraceuticals and functional foods that target specific ailments, often with the claim that they are working with an individual's own genetic make-up. Health foods are a growing multi-billion-dollar industry in the United States but still cater in most part to those who can afford the premium cost of the products. While the mainstream food-processing industry keeps reducing the prices of "supersized" food products with empty calories, the cost of healthy eating rises. At any nutritional supplement store or full-service organic food and health store, products that represent the entire history of health foods and fads are on sale: tablets, powders, and extracts of royal jelly; bee pollen; spirulina; kelp; garlic; ginseng; unprocessed, unbleached, organically grown granola; and a host of other food products that can be cooked from scratch or popped into the microwave.

[*See also* Food and Drug Administration; Graham, Sylvester; Kellogg Company; Kellogg, John Harvey; Nutrition; Organic Food; Post Foods; Pure Food and Drug Act; Sinclair, Upton; Vegetarianism.]

BIBLIOGRAPHY

Barrett, Stephen, and Victor Herbert. *The Vitamin Pushers: How the "Health Food" Industry Is Selling America a Bill of Goods.* Amherst, NY: Prometheus Books, 1994.

Deutsch, Ronald M. *The New Nuts among the Berries.* Palo Alto, CA: Bull Publishing, 1977.

FDA Consumer Magazine. http://fda.org.gov/fdac. This publication by the Food and Drug Administration (FDA) is available online and provides insights on current scientific knowledge concerning health and nutrition.

Quackwatch: Your Guide to Health Fraud, Quackery, and Intelligent Design. Available at http://www.quackwatch.org. Operated by Stephen Barrett, a crusader against food faddism and health quackery, this site provides current updates on events that shape public opinion concerning food and health.

Whelan, Elizabeth M., and Frederick J. Stare. *Panic in the Pantry: Facts and Fallacies About the Food You Buy.* Amherst, NY: Prometheus Books, 1992.

BARRETT P. BRENTON *AND* KEVIN T. MCINTYRE

Hearn, Lafcadio

In writing *La cuisine créole* (Creole cookery), Patricio Lafcadio Tessima Carlos Hearn—journalist, sometime novelist, and unsuccessful restaurateur—tapped into and celebrated New Orleans' heterogeneous culture. The landmark 1885 cookery book was the first to describe the cosmopolitan Creole cuisine, which blends the characteristics of the American, French, Spanish, Italian, West Indian, and Mexican traditions.

At first glance Lafcadio Hearn seemed an unlikely cookbook author. Born on a Greek island in 1850, the son of a minor British bureaucrat, he was reared by a rigidly religious aunt in Dublin, Ireland. Small in stature (five feet three), extremely nearsighted, one eye virtually blind and the other bulged to double normal size, he was frail, often ill, and almost constantly in pain. His extreme shyness and often irritable personality are thought to have influenced his morbid, gothic interests and writings. But Hearn's timidity also made him a keen and unobtrusive observer.

Coming to America, Hearn took a job as a reporter for the *Cincinnati Enquirer* in 1871. He wrote what have been described as "weird romantic stories" and eventually became a star crime reporter after writing about a murder case in "horripilating" detail. In 1876 he was sent to New Orleans to report on the disputed presidential election results in Louisiana. Immediately taken with the exotic city he described it as "fading, moldering, crumbling . . . a dead bride crowned with orange flowers." He would remain there for a decade working for low wages as a newspaperman and becoming a seminal figure in establishing New Orleans as a unique cultural center.

Hearn found the French market, with its colorful denizens, market cries, and foods exactly to his liking. He came to know the people of the city, from intellectuals to the common folk, and wrote about them voluminously, including a large number of sayings in the Creole dialect, which he called "gumbo French." Hearn got a friendly publisher to print them for the Cotton States Exposition of 1884 (in a volume he named after *gumbo z'herbes*, the traditional New Orleans dish), along with a historical guide and a cookbook. The books were not printed in time for the exposition, and they failed, save for one: *La cuisine créole.*

The recipes in the book came from the wives of two friends and were perhaps influenced by the cuisine of the African Creoles who fascinated him. Most of the recipes are American—pies and pastries, for example—and made plain for use in ordinary households. However, the collection includes key ingredients and dishes that distinguish this sophisticated cookery: jambalaya, crayfish, courtbouillon (a fish dish in a rich, roux-based sauce), and gumbos, many with okra. In *La cuisine créole* Hearn located food at the core of a people's culture. Its publication marked the beginning of a wave of nineteenth-century cookery books that preserved and popularized singular cuisines in their historical place.

Two years after publishing *La Cuisine Créole* and its sister volumes, Hearn left New Orleans forever. By 1890 he had found his way to Japan where he became world famous for his writings about that country, especially collections of ghost tales and folklore. He died there in 1905.

[*See also* African American Food, *subentry* Since Emancipation; Cajun and Creole Food; French Influences on American Food; Southern Regional Cookery.]

BIBLIOGRAPHY

Hearn, Lafcadio. *La cuisine créole*. New York: W. H. Coleman, 1885. Reprinted, with a foreword by Hodding Carter, as *Lafcadio Hearn's Creole Cook Book. With the Addition of Drawings and Writings by Lafcadio Hearn During His Sojourn in New Orleans from 1877 to 1887: A Literary and Culinary Adventure*. Gretna, LA: Pelican, 1990.

Tinker, Edward Larocque. *Lafcadio Hearn's American Days*. New York: Dodd, Mead, 1924.

Starr, S. Frederick, ed. *Inventing New Orleans: Writings of Lafcadio Hearn*. Jackson, MS: University Press of Mississippi, 2001.

Stevenson, Elizabeth. *Lafcadio Hearn*. New York: Macmillan, 1961.

BRUCE KRAIG

Hearth Cookery

Hearth cookery refers to the cooking and baking performed directly over or adjacent to a kitchen fire. It has played a major role in human existence for millennia. Early people developed the skills for managing the heat of fire, embers, and ash and thereby widened their scope of edible foods. Simple mastering of the uses of clay, stone, wood, and bone expanded the repertoire—improved the *batterie de cuisine*—and subsequent growth of civilizations and cultures diversified hearth cookery further still. During this long span of years the basic processes of boiling, frying, grilling, roasting, toasting, and baking changed surprisingly little.

The hearth continued to be the site of cooking in the early American colonies, where fireplaces were constructed in every dwelling. Europeans immigrating to the New World brought their own styles of hearths and cuisines, but basic cooking at the fire remained universal in America for roughly two hundred fifty years. Despite the varying ethnic, geographic, and economic factors, almost every kitchen incorporated a basic stone,

brick, or hardened mud or clay fireplace with a paved floor and apron jutting out into the room. Brick ovens built behind the fireplace had their doors in the back wall, sharing the chimney and hearth.

Everyone cooked and baked under conditions the contemporary eye would see as primitive. There were few laborsaving devices, and people characteristically worked hard physically and endured a good measure of physical drudgery. However, the results were often fine and to some minds frequently better than those achieved in the twenty-first century.

The Fire

Of first importance in hearth cookery was the matter of the fire. New World firewood was usually abundant, and it was possible to lay in a year's supply. This was generally a wintertime job when the heavy work of farming was quiescent. Moreover, the leaves were down in winter and there was greater visibility in the woods. In the North, it was easier to haul heavy loads over snow. Once felled the wood was sawed into lengths, split, and stacked for the necessary year of drying out and aging. Green wood simply did not work. It produced smoky and erratic fires and insufficient heat. Different woods were used, based on the knowledge of which woods burned hottest and produced the longest-lasting coals, and the cooks, well aware of the amount of heat they would need for each dish, chose appropriately. Experience taught, for example, that the wood of the Osage orange tree often burned far too hot for cooking and that pine deposited pitch in the chimney, which caused dangerous fires.

Hearth fires were started by means of a steel striker and a sharp piece of flint. One of the basic skills of the age was the ability to strike the iron tool against the flint's edge and produce streams of sparks. These were aimed into the tinder, which was made up of any material that would ignite quickly at a low temperature. Tinder was sometimes tow, the fine hairlike strands that remained after carding the fibers from linen plant stems for spinning. Once the sparks had set the tinder to smoldering, its heat would light a candle kept at hand (usually in a tinderbox that held all the necessities for making fires), and this became the match that started the actual cooking fire. It was important that a supply of twigs graded by size be ready to add to the fire, from smallest to largest, until the fire grew big enough to ignite substantial pieces of wood. Assuming that all the equipment was organized and ready, the process of starting a fire took seconds in the hands of the average colonist.

Cooking Hearth. Note the firebacks, heavy plates of cast iron, propped against the brick to reflect heat efficiently and protect the brick from heat damage. *Alice Ross Hearth Studio*

Controlling and regulating the flames were the next tasks. Uneven cooking resulted if the heat source constantly varied from one extreme to the other. Untended fires changed continually. A piece of newly added wood might block the heat from reaching the pot and then ignite suddenly, producing a lot of heat before burning out. Ongoing management of the heat of the fire, accomplished by adding the right wood judiciously, kicking the fire apart or together, controlling the air flow (more air caused hotter fires), and adjusting the pots' positions, was required for good cooking. The temperature of the fire, the coals, or the food in the pot was judged by feel. Cooks learned by the sensation on their hands whether the heat would do. Constantly checking the progress of both the fire and the food became habitual, almost automatic, because there was no certainty in predicting how the heat might be in even a few moments.

Cooking directly over the flames was limited to only a few processes, usually those involving moist preparations. Boiling water, gentle simmering, and stewing were easily accomplished, provided one had the paraphernalia to raise and lower pots as heat levels shifted. At first this was accomplished by securing pots with swinging bail handles to trammels, or hanging adjustable hooks, attached to a horizontal lug pole high in the chimney. If the fire was too hot, the pot was removed and the trammel hook adjusted to a higher position by means of its special hooks, ratchets, or toothed settings. Forged iron tongs, and later pokers, were requisite and were used at every hearth to adjust fires. Many fireplaces held firebacks, which were decorated cast-iron plates propped against the back wall to reflect heat and to protect the brick from extremes of heat. With the introduction in the early eighteenth century of

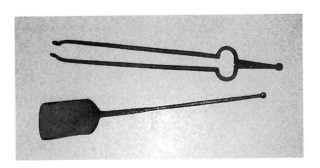

Shovel and Tongs. Essential tools at every fireplace. *Collection of Alice Ross*

swinging cranes and their attendant crane trammels and S-hooks, hanging pots could be moved in and out of the fire both horizontally and vertically, improving on heat control, comfort, and safety.

Ash Cooking

The simplest hearth cooking was done directly in the heated ashes, often in combination with glowing embers. This was not only necessary when the family had only a few pots but it also used the total space of the hearth more efficiently. Fireplaces were deliberately allowed to amass large amounts of spent ash because it reflected the heat, insulated the hearth floor, and provided another cooking site. Sometimes food was buried in hot coals between layers of ash to protect it from overcooking or burning in the extreme heat, and sometimes food was wrapped first in leaves. Although it might seem to be in danger of picking up unpalatable grit, when coated with cornmeal, handled properly, or rinsed, the food was often delicious and free of contamination. Many baked corncakes, vegetables, and meats required no technology other than a deep bed of insulating ash, hot embers, and experience.

Ember Cooking at the Hearth

Because of the problems inherent in cooking over open flames, a good deal of the work was done in front of the fire, at the hearth. Every fireplace was equipped with a small, long-handled shovel used to move coals from the hottest parts of the fire to the outer hearth or apron itself. When the cook knew that she would need these small piles of coals for a dish requiring gentle heat, she added additional logs some thirty or forty minutes in advance. It was the time needed to burn larger pieces of wood into usable embers. Another technique was to use finer-split wood that was quicker to catch and burn hot, but which produced fewer coals and did not last as long.

The pots used to cook over these small piles of coals were designed to take advantage of heat coming from underneath and from the front of the fire. Ember cooking required pots with protruding strap handles and high legs. Sometimes the legs were built into the pots and sometimes the same effect was created with portable cooking trivets, the point being to straddle the coals. Straddling was necessary to allow sustained airflow, since a pot set directly on coals would smother them. Embers on the hearth produced a range of moderate heats, appropriate to cooking on griddles or in posnets (saucepans), to low-temperature frying or sautéing, or to Dutch-oven baking.

Roasting in front of the fire produced superior meat dishes. The simplest way to roast was to use a plank, made from a board or split log, to which food was secured and then propped in front of the fire. In addition, an assortment of mechanically driven spits, tin reflecting ovens, standing roasters, drop trammels, or twisted string roasting (a method by which the meat is hung by a string and roasted evenly as the twisted string unwinds back and forth) worked effectively.

Skillets that stood on very high legs, which accommodated small flames underneath them, were good for frying and gridirons placed over hot coals broiled well. Iron and ceramic pots that required moderately high heats were pushed close to or directly into the fire's coals. Long-handled salamanders, wafer irons, and waffle irons were often propped into the fire's hottest embers.

One of the most versatile and ingenious pots was the American Dutch oven, so called by the English to distinguish it from their own hanging bake kettle. This cast-iron pot had three legs and could stand over a pile of coals, but at the same time its heavy lid, made with a high rim, could hold additional coals on top of it. It was made in several sizes and served as an all-purpose portable oven, a stewpan, and a baking dish. Cooking in it was the equivalent of baking in the embers but without the ash.

All in all, the hearth offered the cook great flexibility. One fireplace could, depending on its size, accommodate almost every cookery process and type of equipment at the same time. By the late eighteenth century, as English

Dutch Oven. The heavy rimmed lid held coals above, while the legs suspended the oven above piles of coals, producing a portable baking or stewing over. Dutch ovens were common in American kitchens and had myriad uses. *Collection of John C. Campbell.*

imports and domestic manufactures flooded markets and kitchens, hearth cooking in average homes reached its zenith and was capable of turning out complex meals consisting of several dishes. More affluent kitchens used more elaborate mechanical roasters, fauceted hot-water kettles, or iron-sided ovens installed in the fireplace wall.

Women, Work, and Safety

Women raised and trained at the hearth from childhood developed the strength and coordination for heavy lifting. Every day they maneuvered large pots of food and wooden buckets filled with water, which were heavy enough when empty. The typical household often had hired girls, teenage daughters, and unmarried relatives, in addition to the female head of the house, and when needed they worked together. Long years of experience also taught skills and intuitions. Even an uninspired cook could feed her family efficiently, serving large dinners by noon and accommodating both the variety of changing seasonal ingredients and the constancy of year-round staples. A good cook could produce superlative meals.

Women cooking at the hearth wore the long skirts and aprons, long-sleeved shirts, and bodices common in the colonial era. Although it might be expected that they died in flames in great numbers, in fact the wool and linen fibers their clothes were made of did not flame but instead smoldered, leaving small holes, usually near the hem. In an age of very little new clothing, the lower edges of skirts and aprons were constructed with a series of lengthwise tucks, parallel to each other and to the bottom hem. When the garment had accumulated too many charred spots, the bottom few inches were cut off and discarded, a tuck or two was let out to drop the hem, and a new hem was stitched.

The hearth was often blisteringly hot, and the long skirts and sleeves, aprons, and heavy boots that cooks wore offered them necessary protection. Hair was completely encased in a mobcap to prevent its scorching. Sometimes women tucked their skirts up into their apron bands when working at the fire. They avoided long and frilly ruffles while cooking. Many cooks shortened their work skirts by several inches to keep them safely out of the way. The real danger at the hearth was from scalding with liquids from overturned pots and from the associated infections of burns.

Cuisine

Despite its so-called primitive qualities, the hearth actually turned out diverse and delicious foods, depending on the skill of the cook, her access to ingredients of good quality, the amount of time she could put to the task, the help she had, and her ability to control the temperatures. Cuisine expanded as levels of colonial American material culture rose. Cookbooks of the time described a wide range of dishes from simple to complex, considered traditional, that remain delicious.

Professional chefs, such as Samuel Fraunces, the Philadelphia chef of George Washington, and Adrien Petit and his successors, who cooked for Thomas Jefferson, served up banquets and feasts of period haute cuisine, unconstrained by the hearth. Indeed, the fine results of their kitchens may have been in some part due to the beneficial effects of their hearths' smoke on flavors and the heat transmission of the hearth's utensils.

The End of Hearth Cooking

The nineteenth-century cookstove signaled the gradual demise of the American hearth. By 1850 most middle-class urban families had made the change, usually installing their new stove in the fireplace opening for easy access to the chimney, but effectively curtailing fine hearth roasting and baking. However, poorer and more remote areas of rural America, such as Appalachia, continued to depend on hearths. Well into the nineteenth century people reminisced sentimentally about the lost hearth. The American essayist Henry David Thoreau wrote in *Walden* (1846): "I used a small cooking-stove for economy . . . but it did not keep fire so well as the open fireplace. Cooking was then, for the most part, no longer a poetic, but merely a chemic process. . . . The stove not only took up room and scented the house, but it concealed the fire, and I felt as if I had lost a companion. You can always see a face in the fire."

In the last few decades, the study of hearth cookery has opened an important avenue of inquiry in American social and cultural history and has become a valuable tool for social scientists, educators, reenactors, living-history museum curators, chefs, and those who simply want to enjoy their fireplaces. The benefits of the hearth have also intrigued restaurateurs, who had begun in the early twenty-first century to feature fireplaces and hearth-cooked meals for the public.

[*See also* Dutch Ovens; Frying Pans, Skillets, and Spiders; Historic Dining Reenactment; Kitchens; Material Culture and Technology.]

BIBLIOGRAPHY

Barons, Richard I. *The American Hearth.* Binghamton, NY: Broome County Historical Society, 1976.

Franklin, Linda Campbell. *Three Hundred Years of Kitchen Collectibles*. 5th enlarged ed. Iola, WI: Kraus Publications, 2003.

Glasse, Hannah. *The Art of Cookery*. London: 1747; facs. ed. London: Prospect Books, 1983.

Harrison, Molly. *The Kitchen in History*. New York: Scribners, 1972.

Hess, John L., and Karen Hess. *The Taste of America*. New York: Grossman, 1977.

Phipps, Frances. *Colonial Kitchens, Their Furnishings and Their Gardens*. New York: Hawthorn Books, 1972.

Plante, Ellen M. *The American Kitchen: 1700 to the Present*. New York: Facts on File, 1996.

Rubel, William. *The Magic of Fire*. Berkeley, CA: Ten Speed Press, 2002.

ALICE ROSS

Hearts of Palm

Hearts of palm, an expensive delicacy, were served at fancy hotel restaurants early in the 1900s. But in Florida, where this luxury item was known as swamp cabbage, hearts of palm were so widely consumed during the Great Depression that the state of Florida had to enact laws to protect the palmetto tree, the source of these tender hearts. The Pulitzer Prize–winning author and Florida resident Marjorie Kinnan Rawlings loved this indigenous plant but seldom served it because she loved the environment more. "You cannot have your palm and eat it, too," she said. According to Rawlings only an expert knew how to cut down the cabbage palm and strip the bark to get to the crisp, white, tender core. The Florida bear, she claimed, was one of those experts, because she had found palms slashed by sharp claws "and the hearts torn out as though by giant forks." Rawlings, who named cooking as her only vanity, wrote about swamp cabbage in her memoir and her cookbook, *Cross Creek Cookery*, which was still in print in the early 2000s.

The palmetto, or cabbage palm (*Sabal palmetto*), is tall, tough barked, and graceful. It flourished for thousands of years throughout Central and South America. Columbus discovered the Carib Indians using the bark and leaves for houses. They ate the core of the young plants and the nuts of the mature tree. Today, this tree is grown as a cash crop harvested after one year, when it reaches a height of five feet.

Hearts of palm are slender, ivory colored, and delicately flavored and resemble white asparagus without tips. Their texture is firm and smooth, and they taste a bit like artichoke. Each stalk is about four inches long and can range in diameter from pencil-thin to one and a half inches. In the United States, they are available fresh only in Florida. Canned hearts of palm are packed in water and are sold in gourmet markets and many large supermarkets. They can be refrigerated in their own liquid for up to a week in a nonmetallic container.

Hearts of palm can be deep-fried or used in salads and in main dishes. Rawlings also loved them sliced thinly and soaked for an hour in ice water, then drained and served with french dressing or tart mayonnaise. "The flavor is much like chestnuts," she said. In *Cross Creek Cookery*, Rawlings based her recipes on fresh hearts of palm. She made swamp cabbage camp-style by simply boiling the palm hearts slowly in as little water as possible, with several slices of white bacon. She also simmered them tightly covered, for forty-five minutes or "until meltingly tender, and until most of the moisture has been absorbed." She liked to heat them to simmering in the cream from her cow, Dora. "Prepared this way, heart of palm is fit for a king," she said.

[*See also* Gibbons, Euell; Salads and Salad Dressings.]

BIBLIOGRAPHY

Rawlings, Majorie Kinnan. *Cross Creek Cookery*. 1942. Reprint, New York: Simon and Schuster, 1996.

MARIAN BETANCOURT

Heinz Foods

In 1869, at the age of twenty-five, Henry J. Heinz helped launch a pickle and horseradish preserving company in Sharpsburg, Pennsylvania. The business expanded quickly, but when the depression hit in 1875, the company went into bankruptcy. Two months later the company emerged from the ashes under the nominal control of Henry's brother and cousin. Under Henry's direction, the business thrived. By 1888 Heinz had paid off the debts incurred during the bankruptcy, bought out his brother and cousin, and named the firm H. J. Heinz Company. The company rapidly expanded operations and distribution facilities throughout the United States.

Heinz expanded its product line to include sauerkraut, vinegar, pepper sauce, chili sauce, apple butter, baked beans, tomato soup, sweet pickles, pickled onions, and pickled cauliflower. Around the turn of the twentieth century, H. J. Heinz selected the slogan "57 Varieties," because he liked the number fifty-seven. The slogan was

Commemoration. *57 Years of the 57,* commemorative booklet issued by H. J. Heinz Company, 1926. *Collection of Andrew F. Smith*

similar to those selected by other companies at the time, although it did not reflect the firm's product line—Heinz produced more than fifty-seven products.

Although Heinz had made the condiment since 1873, ketchup was initially not among the company's more important product lines. This status changed during the 1880s. Heinz began patenting ketchup bottles in 1882. By 1890 Heinz had hit upon what became the world-famous combination of keystone label, neckband, screw cap, and octagonal bottle, although he continued to explore other shapes and labels. Soon after the turn of the twentieth century, Heinz had become the largest tomato ketchup producer in America, by 1905 producing more than five million bottles of ketchup. By 1908 Heinz ketchup sales had reached $2.5 million, a phenomenal amount by the standards of the day.

Before 1903 Heinz ketchup was medium bodied with average acidity. Like most other manufacturers, Heinz added coal-tar coloring as well as benzoic and salicylic acids to ketchup. Also like most of its competitors, Heinz used non-tomato ingredients in ketchup. To meet new state pure-food laws, Heinz began experimenting with canning techniques that did not include preservatives. When the Pure Food and Drugs Act passed in June 1906, Heinz decided to produce all its foods without preservatives.

Advertising

A major reason for Heinz's success was advertising. As early as 1888 the company was printing small cards promoting its products. Heinz also displayed products at fairs all over the United States, setting up large booths. In 1899 in Atlantic City, New Jersey, Heinz built an ocean pier that featured cooking demonstrations, free samples, and lectures. Heinz placed advertisements on streetcars and billboards and soon became one of the largest outdoor advertisers in the United States. Heinz began advertising in magazines and newspapers during the early twentieth century and later advertised on radio. Advertisements and cookery pamphlets contained recipes for the use of Heinz ketchup that were supplied by the Heinz home-economics department.

With the launch of aggressive advertising campaigns by Hunt's and Del Monte after World War II, Heinz's market share for ketchup began to fade, and Heinz's U.S. profits fell to an all-time low, leading Heinz executives to greatly increase their advertising budget. Billboards, prevalent during the preceding decades, were abandoned. Half-minute color television commercials became the company's primary advertising vehicle. One of the most innovative commercials featured a ketchup-pouring race, which highlighted the phrase "thick and rich," the narrator commenting, "Heinz loses, Heinz always loses." The second commercial was "the plate test" in which no fluid ran out of the bottle because Heinz ketchup was thicker and richer than the other brand. These commercials were successful. By 1971 the Heinz market share had rebounded to 34 percent. It continued to increase, and in the first few years of the twenty-first century, the Heinz market share exceeded 50 percent.

Globalization and Diversification

Almost from its inception, Heinz was extremely interested in making sales outside the United States. Heinz regularly displayed its products at international food exhibitions.

Before the end of the nineteenth century Heinz sold ketchup extensively in Canada and the United Kingdom and had established agencies in Antwerp, Belgium, Sydney, Australia, and Bermuda. By 1899 new agencies had been established in Mexico City, Mexico, Liverpool, England, and the Canadian cities of Toronto and Montreal. By 1907 Heinz was shipping products in five-gallon cans and forty-six-gallon wooden casks to England, Australia, New Zealand, South Africa, South America, Europe, Japan, and China. In 1910 Heinz built its first factory outside the United States in Leamington, Ontario, Canada. Heinz has continued to expand abroad. Headquartered in Pittsburgh, Pennsylvania, in 2004 Heinz had two hundred major operations worldwide.

Like other food companies, Heinz has diversified. It is one of the world's leading marketers of branded foods. In addition to the Heinz brand, the company operates twenty other brand names. In 1963 Heinz acquired StarKist , which controls 50 percent of the tuna market. Ore-Ida was acquired in 1965 and commands 45 percent of the packaged potato market. Other major Heinz brands include Weight Watchers Foods and Boston Market. The 9 Lives and Kibbles 'n Bits operations make Heinz one of the largest pet food manufacturers. Heinz is also a major manufacturer of baby food. In 2002 Heinz spun off StarKist, 9 Lives, and other subsidiaries to Del Monte Foods Company. Heinz produces more than five thousand different products annually. Its 2001 revenue was $9.43 billion, making Heinz one of the world's largest food companies.

Heinz's flagship product continues to be ketchup. Heinz is the largest ketchup manufacturer, producing more than 1 billion ounces per year. Heinz has continued innovations of its ketchup, including the development of a plastic squeeze bottle for home use and a single-serve container for commercial use. During the late 1990s, Heinz introduced alternative-color varieties of its popular condiment, bringing out EZ Squirt green ketchup, which was followed by purple ketchup. These products made headlines around the world, and they captured the imagination of children, who are the main users of ketchup.

[See also Advertising; Advertising Cookbooklets and Recipes; Canning and Bottling; Condiments; Del Monte; Food Marketing; Ketchup; Pickles; Pickling; Pure Food and Drug Act; Tuna.]

BIBLIOGRAPHY

Alberts, Robert C. *The Good Provider: H. J. Heinz and His 57 Varieties.* Boston: Houghton Mifflin, 1973.

Dienstag, Eleanor Foa. *In Good Company: 125 Years at the Heinz Table (1869–1994).* New York: Warner, 1994.

Smith, Andrew F. *Pure Ketchup: The History of America's National Condiment.* Columbia: University of South Carolina Press, 1996.

ANDREW F. SMITH

Heirloom Vegetables

Heirloom vegetables are the produce of plants grown from original seeds. In the last decades of the twentieth century and into the next millennium, old and often forgotten varieties of food plants garnered renewed interest among gardeners and the grocery-shopping public. Although they are called heirlooms, no regulated nationwide standard has ever existed for them, though most experts agree on a general definition: The plant variety must have been introduced before 1951, which was when plant breeders began to hybridize inbred plant lines, and it must have been grown from a variety at least one hundred years old. The plant also must have been open-pollinated by natural means, such as wind, dew, insects, or birds.

Before seeds were bought from catalogs or from seed merchants, they were saved from one crop in order to plant the next and shared with neighbors and family. Prior to European colonization, North America had few varieties of indigenous domesticated food plants, but had a fair amount of wild or semidomesticated species. People emigrating from the Old World, including Africa, as far back as the sixteenth century, brought seeds with them to America. When the seeds were planted, many of them were able to adapt to the new weather and soil conditions. These hardy species brought considerable genetic diversity to the New World. As a result of centuries of natural adaptation, many heirlooms are resistant to different forms of blight and can survive bad soil and climate extremes.

Americans' interest in cultivating, developing, and preserving numerous varieties of native and newly acclimated imported food and ornamental plants goes back to the seventeenth and eighteenth centuries. Scientists, such as John Bartram of Philadelphia and Thomas Jefferson, experimented with new varieties, while farmers, such as the Pennsylvania Dutch, were more practically minded and focused on their kitchen gardens. The post–Civil War period saw the rise of commercial seed-growing. Most heirloom vegetables and their quirky names, as announced in colorful catalogs, for example, Esopus Spitzenburg apples, Kentucky Wonderbowl beans, and Boothby's Blonde cucumbers, date from the years after 1865 when American industrialization and urbanization were on the rise.

Truck farms, supplied by seed companies, proliferated and remained a major source of food for urban populations until after World War II. Some heirloom vegetables remained on these farms, but streamlined production methods led to modern single-variety and genetically manipulated vegetables and fruits. Fully industrialized farms that raised single crops, which were shipped hundreds or thousands of miles across the country, took over the market. Efforts at genetic modification concentrated on adapting plants for shipping and on streamlining production values, not on developing flavor; therefore modern industrialized farm products cannot match the flavors of heirlooms. In addition, commercial farms strive for uniformity in their plants. For example, all the tomatoes on a factory farm must be picked at the same time because it limits production overhead, so ideally they should all ripen at the same time. Genetic engineers have induced this process. Genetic engineers have also produced modified plant varieties (genetically modified organisms, or GMOs) to ship well, maintain certain uniform appearances, and have longer shelf lives. Modifying vegetables to yield a higher profit margin produces vegetables that may look bright and ripe on store shelves but which lack flavor. Winter-grown tomatoes shipped to northern cities provide a classic and reviled example. The flavor of summer once found in perfectly ripened August fruits has been lost.

American heirloom enthusiasts' concern with GMOs goes beyond a lack of flavor, however. Environmental awareness and activism has led to interest in heirloom produce. Concerns about the planet's biological sustainability and possible dangers inherent in gene modification technology became widespread, especially among younger Americans, in the early twenty-first century. Activists were concerned with biodiversity and with perpetuating the small farms and gardens that they favored. They noted that most commercial farms that supplied the nation's food practiced monoculture, that is, they planted only one or two species that had been genetically modified at a time. Based on such historical precedents as the Irish potato famine of the 1840s, when Irish potatoes, of Peruvian origin, were not resistant to a blight unintentionally brought from Mexico, activists argued that some common GMOs were resistant to only one form of blight rather than many different kinds.

Further, critics claimed, agribusinesses created so-called terminator seeds that produce plants that do not produce their own seeds. This not only limits biodiversity but also controls or halts natural food crop reproduction. Activists are concerned that farmers may become completely reliant on seed companies for crop reproduction. In reply, corporations, such as Monsanto, argued that all food plants throughout history have been genetically manipulated, that their genetically modified seeds had been extensively tested, were safe, and were the only means by which burgeoning world populations could be fed. If plant species had been lost, it was because of human population rise, not because of the planting of manipulated crops. The vigorous debate was going on worldwide without resolution at the beginning of the twenty-first century.

The reduction of the genetic-plant repository inspired the formation of historical farms and open-air museums to maintain heirloom varieties. For instance, a historical farm or an open-air museum might grow a kitchen garden of the same heirloom plants (from heirloom seeds) that had been planted in that same spot in colonial times. Seed-saving organizations, the earliest founded in 1895 in Russia, preserved diverse genetic-heritage seeds, focusing on heirloom plant varieties headed for extinction. The Seed Savers Exchange and Seeds of Change were among the best-known genetic repositories in the early 2000s. Seeds were either kept in suspended animation or planted to perpetuate the genetic stock. While seed savers worked with government agencies, open-air museums, and living history farms, their main focus was to maintain an ongoing genetic repository. Heirloom enthusiasts tended to support smaller farmers as well.

People who love heirloom vegetables do so for many reasons including taste, curiosity, and environmental consciousness. Beginning in the late 1970s, Americans renewed their romance with gourmet food and cooking; chefs and epicureans were constantly seeking out unusual ingredients and flavors, and heirlooms suited these new cooks' fancies. Alice Waters's restaurant Chez Panisse in Berkeley, California, and her cookbooks became a touchstone for the culinary aspects of a new heirloom movement.

For the weekend gardener, there are many seed companies that boast "antique" or "heirloom" on the labels of their products. True heirloom seeds are also always labeled "open pollinated." These seeds produce plants from an older seed stock with an unaltered, high-quality gene line that will grow the flavorful tomato, squash, or corn of yore. Unlike their commercial counterparts, heirloom vegetables are patchy in color and differ in taste. Some are oddly shaped and sized. Heirloom fans choose some squash for their sweet flesh, beans for their decorative flowers, or beets for their stripes. The rich, sweet flavor of a Brandywine tomato or the peppery crunch of a rocket leaf or a Persia Broadleaf Cress is unrivaled.

[See also Biotechnology; Vegetables; Waters, Alice.]

BIBLIOGRAPHY

Home and Garden Information Center, Clemson University. http://hgic.clemson.edu.

Michalak, Patricia. *Rodale's Successful Organic Gardening: Vegetables.* Emmaus, PA: Rodale Press, 1993.

Thomas Jefferson Center for Historic Plants. http://www.monticello.org/chp/.

Seed Savers Exchange. http://www.seedsavers.org/.

Weaver, William Woys. *Heirloom Vegetable Gardening.* New York: Henry Holt, 1997.

LIZA JERNOW

Herbs and Spices

The distinction between "herbs" and "spices" is problematic. Botanically, herbs are nonwoody vascular plants that die, or at least waste away, after flowering. That definition is useless for describing culinary herbs, since rosemary, bay, and even thyme can be quite woody, and do not "waste away" in winter. The traditional culinary distinction between herbs and spices is based upon the parts of the plant used: herbs usually consist of foliage or flowers, while spices more often consist of seeds, bark, and roots. In most cases spices are more potent, containing more of the essential oils and other flavoring compounds than herbs. The problem with these distinctions is that there are more exceptions to the rules than typical examples.

In practice, herbs are collected from plants that are traditionally grown in domestic gardens, while spices are almost always imported. Unfortunately, even that distinction has exceptions: mustard seed and coriander seed, both of which should be considered spices, grow in domestic gardens quite readily and both produce foliage that is used in ways more consistent with what are called herbs. The only practical definition for "herbs and spices" is collective: products from edible plants that are used to enhance other foods.

Some of the More Common Herbs and Spices

Allspice, *Pimenta dioica*, is also known as Jamaica pepper, myrtle pepper, piment, pimenta, tail pepper, and West Indian bay leaf. Among Caribbean immigrants it is called pimento, although there is no botanical connection with either true pepper (*Piper nigrum*) or any of the chilies (*capsicum* species). The name may reflect early confusion on the part of Columbus and his crews; on the other hand, "pimento" is used as a generic term for almost any spice in the islands. Allspice grows on a tropical tree that is indigenous to the Caribbean, Central America, and Mexico, but it can be grown in Southern Florida. Allspice is closely related to the bay rum tree, *Pimenta racemosa*. The dried berries smell of cinnamon, cloves, nutmeg, and black pepper, hence the name. Allspice is used in baked goods, condiments, such as ketchup, steak sauce, and jerk seasoning, pickles, sauces, soups, stews, and sausages, such as bologna, headcheese, and hot dogs.

Annatto, *Bixa orellana*, is also known as achiote, bija, bilol, and lipstick tree. It is a small tropical tree or shrub, native to the Old World tropics but naturalized in the New World tropics and grown in the southern United States. Dendê oil (made from the seeds of the African oil palm, *Elaesis guineensis*) was essential to the cooking of West Africa. In South America and the Caribbean, African slaves, long accustomed to palm oil, used annatto to color and subtly flavor local cooking oils.

In this country, the whole seeds—used in Latin American kitchens to add the traditional yellow-orange color to cooked foods—can usually be found in Hispanic markets or in the Caribbean or Hispanic section of large grocery stores. Achiote is also a name for a Mexican paste containing ground annatto seeds, black pepper, garlic, and the juice of Seville oranges. Bijol, a paste of corn, flour, cumin, artificial yellow and red dyes, and annatto is used to make yellow rice in the Caribbean and in the Yucatán. Annatto-colored lard can be found in markets catering to Latin American customers, especially those from Guatemala and Puerto Rico.

Other than the uses by ethnic groups, annatto's primary use in the United States is as a coloring agent for butter and cheeses, especially cheddar. Our American colby and longhorn, not to mention yellow American cheese, are pale—albeit colorful, thanks to annatto—imitations of British cheddars.

Basil, *Ocimum basilicum*. There are many species in the *Ocimum* genus and many cultivars of the species itself, some with decriptive names like anise, citriodorum, crispum or lettuce leaf, licorice, purple ruffles. Genovese is the most commonly grown cultivar. Basil is an annual, indigenous to the tropical Old World, but now grown everywhere, from temperate regions to tropics. Fresh basil

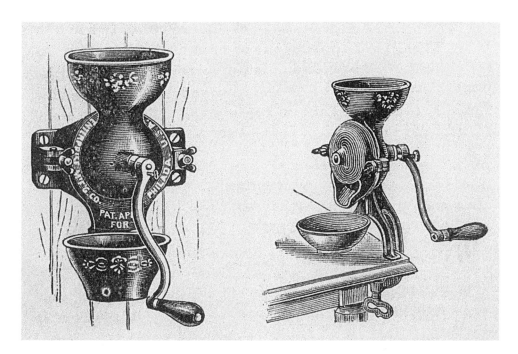

Spice Mills. *Culinary Archives & Museum at Johnson & Wales University, Providence, R.I.*

is probably best known in the form of the aromatic green pesto Genovese or as a garnish for tomatoes. Dried, it is used in tomato sauces, in sausages, and in commercial blends marketed as Italian seasoning.

Bay leaf, *Laurus nobilis*, is also known as laurel, noble bay, noble laurel, roman laurel, sweet bay, sweet bay leaf, sweet laurel, and true laurel. The broad-leafed evergreen shrubs, or small trees, are indigenous to the Mediterranean region but can be grown anywhere that they can be protected from frost. Bay leaves, and sometimes the stronger-tasting berries, are added to sauces (especially tomato sauces), vegetable soups, and stocks. They are cooked with poultry, beef, lamb, and veal, either whole or ground and used as a rub. Bay leaves, like basil, are often a component of grocery-store jars of "Italian Seasoning." While there are many so-called laurels found in North America, only *Laurus nobilis* and California laurel, *Umbellularia californica*, are nonpoisonous. Mountain laurel, *Kalmia latifolia* (named for Peter Kalm, a botanist sent to the New World by Linnaeus to discover new species), is one of the toxic so-called laurels. It is not related to laurel; its leaves only look like laurel.

Caper, *Capparis spinosa*, is also known as caper bush. The flowers and berries grow on a spiny shrub that is indigenous to the Mediterranean region. While the shrubs can be grown in frost-free regions of the United States, almost all caper products are imported from Italy and Spain—most commonly pickled in brine, although they are sometimes salted. The unopened flower buds are used as garnishes and add their tart, sour flavor to soups, vinaigrettes, and sauces, especially in combination with tomatoes and olives. Caper berries, somewhat larger, became something of a food fad in the 1990s.

Cardamom, *Elettaria cardamomum*. The pods are harvested from perennial plants indigenous to India and Sri Lanka. Cardamom is also commercially grown in Indonesia, Java, and Thailand. Sweetly aromatic cardamom seeds are used with meats, poultry, sausages, and in pickling, soups, and stews—especially in curried dishes, or those influenced by Arabic cuisines. They also appear in pastries, breads, and cookies, notably in the baking of Scandinavian and Dutch immigrants.

Chili, various *capsicum* species, but especially *Capsicum annuum*, is also known as chile pepper, chilli, chilly pepper, green pepper, pod pepper, red pepper, and countless regional and varietal names. "Chile" is the only spelling accepted by New Mexicans, who take their "chiles" very seriously. ("Chili" usually refers to a dish made with chilies.) In frost-free tropical America, where *C. annuum* originated, it is a perennial but it is grown as an annual in the United States. The "heat" of chilies is mainly due to an alkaloid, capsaicin, augmented by a number of minor capsaicinoids that create differences in the location, duration, and kind of burning sensations.

Columbus, the first European to experience this New World phenomenon, wrote in his journal on January 15, 1493, "There is much *Axí*—their pepper, much stronger than [our] pepper, and everyone refuses to eat without it, for they find it very healthful; in Hispaniola, it's possible to fill fifty caravels each year with it."

The chili powder commonly sold in supermarkets is practically never pure, ground chili. It is usually a mixture of chili, cumin, garlic powder, oregano, and sometimes ground coriander seed, along with some silicon dioxide (fine sand) to prevent caking. Serious chili afficionados prefer ground single-variety powders, whole dried pods, or fresh chilies.

Paprika is used primarily in the United States as a reddish garnish, because, unlike Spanish and Hungarian paprikas, it has little flavor.

Cassia, *Cinnamomum aromaticum*, is also known as bastard cinnamon, Canton cassia, cassia-bark tree, China hunk cassia, Chinese cassia, Chinese cinnamon, Hunan cassia, Kwangsi cassia, Kwantung cassia, and Yunnan cassia. Closely related to true cinnamon, *Cinnamomum zeylanicum*, it is the inner bark of an evergreen tropical tree that is indigenous to China. It is imported from Myanmar, Malaysia, southern China, and Vietnam. Cassia, a cinnamon-like spice, is stronger and less delicate than true cinnamon. In fact much commercial "cinnamon," especially in the United States, is actually cassia. Cassia is used in baked goods, candies, and condiments, such as ketchup, chili sauce, chutneys, and preserves.

Celery, *Apium graveolens*, is also known as celeriac, garden celery, smallage, and wild celery. Celeriac is actually a cultivar of the species *A. g. rapaceum*, grown for its enlarged root. Celery is a biennial, native to Eurasia, but commonly grown in all temperate regions. It is best known as a vegetable, but its seeds, which are actually the fruits of the plant, are used as a spice in breads, casseroles, curries, pickles, sauces, and soups. The leaves are used as an herb with fish, shellfish, poultry, and veal. A mixture of dried celery ground together with salt is sold commercially as celery salt.

Chives, *Allium schoenoprasum* (sometimes *Allium angustoprasum*), are also known as grass onions. These perennials originated in Europe and Asia but are grown in temperate regions everywhere. Chives are available fresh, freeze-dried, and as chive-flavored salt. While distinctly onion in flavor and aroma, chives are decidedly more civilized. They are used in sauces and stocks, as a garnish, or in salads, in compound butters, with fish, meat, and poultry dressings, and in soups, stews, omelets, and vinaigrettes.

Cilantro or **Coriander**, *Coriandrum sativum*, is also known as Arab parsley, Chinese parsley, cilantrillo, culantro, Indian parsley, and Mexican parsley. "Cilantro" refers to the foliage, and "coriander" to the seeds of an annual plant indigenous to the Mediterranean region but grown in temperate (and warmer) locations throughout the world. It is available as a fresh or dried herb, or as whole or ground seeds. Coriander seeds are used in baked goods, sugar-coated candies, poultry dressings, pork and pork sausages (such as bologna and hot dogs), pickles, and in salads, especially those containing beets. The fresh leaves of cilantro, long ignored in U. S. and European cooking, since the early 1970s have become a household staple in many homes. Cilantro appears in salads, sauces, and stews. It is essential in southwestern or Tex-Mex cooking, as well as the cuisines of Thailand, Laos, Vietnam, India, and parts of China.

Cinnamon, *Cinnamomum zeylanicum*, is also known as canella, Ceylon cinnamon, Seychelles cinnamon, Sri Lanka cinnamon, and true cinnamon. The dried inner bark of an evergreen tropical tree indigenous to Sri Lanka is imported from many tropical areas of south and Southeast Asia. Cinnamon is used in baking, especially in conjunction with fruits like apples, peaches, and pumpkin, of course, but also in cherry pies, pickling, desserts, and sauces (especially Greek and Balkan meat sauces), and is characteristic of Cinncinnati-style chili. Cinnamon sticks are the ideal stirrers, adding their flavor to already-warm winter drinks, such as grog, mulled wine, hot cider, toddies, or even coffee. Cinnamon appears in some herbal and black tea blends, but the hotter and less expensive cassia is more common.

Cloves, *Syzygium aromaticum*, are the dried unopened flower buds of an evergreen tropical tree indigenous to the Moluccas (Indonesia) but cultivated in tropical areas around the world. Cloves are commonly available in this country in powdered form or as whole cloves. Cloves lend their fragrant warmth to candies, cakes, mulled wine, and meats, such as hams, sausages made of blood or liver, headcheese, and bologna. Oil of clove, a penetratingly hot and oddly numbing substance, is sometimes used in over-the-counter toothache remedies and in the dentist's temporary fillings.

CINNAMON
Laurus cinnamomum.

Fig 1. Cinnamon tree.
" 2. Complete flower.

Fig 3. Vertical section of flower enlarged
" 4. Fruit of cinnamon tree.

Cinnamon. Cinnamon tree with its flower and fruit. From an advertisement for Davis, Sacker & Perkins Importers, Boston, 1878 *Collection of Alice Ross*

Dill, *Anethum graveolens*, is also known as Chinese adas or sweet adas. Dill is an annual plant that originated in Europe but can be grown in any temperate climate. Its foliage (dill weed) is available fresh as "salad dill" or dried, and whole seeds can be found in most supermarkets. Occasionally, whole dried stalks including the seed heads can be found. Dill is most commonly associated with pickles, vinegars, and both cooked and raw cucumbers. Dried dill leaves and seeds have a warm, aromatic scent, but fresh leaves and seeds have a stronger, somewhat hotter flavor that is similar to the warmth of caraway seeds. Dill is used with poultry and fish and to a lesser extent with asparagus, beets, cabbage, green beans, or mushrooms. The leaves are a delicious addition to emul-

sion-type sauces, such as mayonnaise served with cold poached fish or chicken, or in soft cheeses, compound butters, and salad dressings.

Epazote, *Chenopodium ambrosioides*, is also known as American wormseed, epazolte, hedge mustard, herba sanctae Mariae, Jerusalem oak, Jerusalem parsley, Jesuit's tea, Mexican tea, sweet pigweed, West Indian goosefoot, and wormseed. It is an annual, native to the tropical Americas, but has become a cosmopolitan weed found everywhere. Epazote is used in the southwestern United States and Mexico in both dried and fresh forms, usually with beans. Epazote is closely related to the milder-tasting lamb's-quarters (*Chenopodium album*) and Good King Henry (*Chenopodium bonus-henricus*), which are eaten as cooked greens, or in stuffings, salads, and soups. It is also related to *Chenopodium quinoa*, the source of the grain quinoa. Epazote's flavor is an acquired taste, which some people compare to kerosene. Like cilantro, it is either loved or hated.

Fennel, *Foeniculum vulgare*, is also known as anise, bitter fennel, Florence fennel, red-leaved fennel, sweet cumin, sweet fennel, and wild fennel. This weedy perennial is native to Europe but will thrive in any temperate region. It is available as fresh leaves and stalks, which are misleadingly called bulbs, and as dried seed. All parts of the fennel plant taste and smell of licorice or anise, however the flavor of the seeds is strongest. Leaves and stalks are used raw in salads or cooked in combination with beans, tomatoes, or chicken, and in salads, soups, stews, vegetables, and with oily fishes. Dried seeds season breads, fish, tomato sauces, and so-called Italian sausage.

Fenugreek, *Trigonella foenum-graecum*, is also called bird's foot, Greek hay, and Greek hayseed. Fenugreek is an annual that is native to southern Europe and eastern Asia and cultivated in India and North Africa. Fenugreek is available in the United States as ground or whole seeds, and as an extract. Fenugreek leaves are often used in Indian cooking. Fenugreek provides the characteristic sweet maplelike aroma to curry powders and is commonly used to flavor pickles. The sprouted seeds are sometimes used on sandwiches or in salads. Extracts from the seeds are used to make imitation maple and rum flavorings.

Filé, *Sassafras albidum*, is also known as ague-tree, cinnamon wood, fennel wood, gumbo-filé, gumbo-zab, hackmatack, mitten tree, saloop, saxifrax, and tea tree. Filé can be either the ground inner bark or leaves of sassafras, a shrub or small tree indigenous to the eastern United States. Filé is used for flavoring. It is also added to gumbos as a thickener, usually at the table, since it tends to become unpleasantly ropy if allowed to boil. The mildly spicy perfume of sassafras is a key flavoring in root beer and sarsaparilla. Herbal teas have been made from sassafras roots and bark. In fact, during World War II, a sassafras tea called grub hyson was used as a coffee substitute.

Garlic, *Allium sativum*. This perennial is native to Mongolia but is grown almost everywhere outside of the arctic and antarctic regions. Garlic is available in many forms: fresh, as fried flakes in Asian markets, as dried flakes, as garlic salt or powder, as a flavored oil, pickled, and peeled or chopped (and labeled fresh) in jars.

Everyone knows the flavor and scent of garlic. For a long time, the scent of the so-called stinking rose was regarded by Anglo-Americans as lower class, because it was associated with poor immigrants. Elizabeth David, speaking of England's aversion to this onion-cousin, wrote, "The grotesque prudishness and archness with which garlic is treated . . . has led to the superstition that rubbing the bowl with it before putting the salad in gives sufficient flavor. It rather depends whether you are going to eat the bowl or the salad." Her reference, of course, is to the start of the classic caesar salad, invented in Tijuana in 1924 for American diners and wholeheartedly accepted as "American" food.

The flavor of garlic goes with so many foods that it may be simpler to list the few things it does not pair well with. One might be tempted to say "ice cream," but garlic-laced ice cream is one of the biggest sellers at Gilroy, California's, annual garlic festival. San Francisco's fish and tomato soup, cioppino, reveals its Italian heritage and the natural affinity of garlic with tomatoes. Until relatively recently, many Americans thought that all Italian food reeked of garlic. The omnipresence of garlic bread in Italian restaurants certainly helped create that impression. Many of the first immigrants from Italy came from Sicily, where tomato sauces do use a lot of garlic, but most Italian cooking uses it more subtly. Garlic is used in sausages consisting of beef, chicken, duck, goose, lamb, pork, and venison, as well as with the same varieties of roasted meats. Combined with scallions and ginger, garlic provides the background flavor for most Chinese American food.

Ginger, *Zingiber officinale*, is also known as common ginger, Canton ginger, and true ginger. Ginger is made from the rhizomes of a perennial that is native to tropical Southeast Asia but grown commercially in China, Fiji and Tonga, Jamaica, northern Australia, and West Africa. In the United States, most fresh ginger comes from Hawaii, although it is also raised in southern Florida. It is available in a number of forms: candied, dried, green (fresh), powdered, in syrup, and pickled or preserved.

Ginger loses much of its fire when dried but becomes deeper, rounder, and more comforting in its warmth. Ground dried ginger is used in baked goods, candies, and condiments. Green, or fresh, ginger is an essential ingredient in most tropical cuisines. Thai, Caribbean, Chinese, Indian, and Indonesian food would be unthinkable without ginger's distinctive bite. Closer to home, its warmth is essential to ginger ale, ginger beer, and root beer.

Horseradish, *Armoracia rusticana*, is also known as great raifort, mountain radish, and red cole. It is the taproot of a Eurasian perennial, which is related to mustards, watercress, and the Japanese wasabi, *Wasabia japonica*, that grows in temperate zones around the world. Most commonly available, grated with a little vinegar and sometimes colored with beet juice, as bottled horseradish it is found in the refrigerated section of grocery stores. If mixed with an egg-based emulsion it is marketed as horseradish sauce. In late winter and early spring, the fresh roots are sometimes available. No bottled horseradish can rival the intensity of homemade sauce grated from the ugly brownish roots.

Mace and **Nutmeg**, *Myristica fragrans*, are two different parts of the fruit of a tropical evergreen tree native to the Moluccas (Indonesia), but cultivated in Brazil, Costa Rica, India, Indonesia, Sri Lanka, and the West Indies (Grenada). Nutmeg is the hard nut or seed. Mace is the red covering, or aril, that surrounds the nutmeg. This aril is peeled off the hard nut before its long drying process begins. Nutmeg is available ground or whole. Freshly grated nutmeg is vastly preferable to the canned ground spice, which fades rapidly on the shelf. Mace is commonly available in ground form, less frequently as whole so-called blades.

The flavors of the two spices are similar, characterized by a heady perfume with an underlying warmth. Nutmeg has the stronger flavor of the two. Nutmeg is used in baking and puddings. It is also used with meats: pâtés, poultry, sausages (such as bologna, headcheese, hot dogs, and liverwurst), lamb, and stews. Nutmeg is often added to dairy-based sauces, such as béchamel. Nutmeg adds a warm sweetness to balance the acerbic bitterness of spinach dishes. Mace is often used when a golden color is desired in the finished product, especially in baked goods, such as cookies or pumpkin breads.

Mint (various *Mentha* species) is also known as peppermint and spearmint, but there are many other species

NUTMEG
Myristica moschata.

Fig. 1.
Nutmeg tree.
Fig. 2.
Open flower enlarged.
Fig. 3.
Fruit in the shell.
Fig. 4.
Nutmeg natural size.

Nutmeg. Nutmeg tree with its flower and fruit. From an advertisement for Davis, Sacker & Perkins Importers, Boston, 1878. *Collection of Alice Ross*

and varietal names. It is a prolific perennial, native to the Old World, but found almost everywhere else. Once planted, it is almost impossible to eradicate. Its refreshing cool and hot taste is unmistakable. Mint is available fresh, dried, or as mint jelly.

Most familiar as the garnish for a glass of iced tea, lemonade, or a classic Kentucky mint julep, this familiar sweet herb can be minced and added to cream cheese, ice cream, sorbets, fruit salads (especially those containing pineapple), baked fish, and roast lamb. So strong is the association of roast lamb with mint jelly that many people cannot even imagine another way of serving ovine meats.

Mustard (several *Brassica* species) is also known as brown mustard, black mustard, cress, and white mustard. Mustards are annuals, indigenous to Europe and Asia,

but cultivated in Austria, England, France, Germany, Holland, Italy, India, North Africa, and the western United States. Pungent mustards are available as whole seeds, ground spices, prepared condiments, as flavored oil (in Indian markets), or as foliage to be used in salads or as potherbs.

Prepared mustards have been made in Europe for centuries, but the most common form seen in America is a relatively mild condiment, rendered bright yellow by the addition of turmeric. Brown mustards, more like their European counterparts, tend to be more popular in urban areas, especially on the east coast of the United States.

Oregano, *Origanum vulgare*, is also known as Italian oregano, French marjoram, marjoram, Mexican sage, pot marjoram, oregan, organy, origanum, and wild marjoram. Oregano is a perennial, native to Europe and to the area from the eastern Mediterranean to Central Asia. It is occasionally found fresh in the supermarkets but is most commonly seen dried, often in large jars. Very often, the so-called oregano sold in the grocery store is actually a form of marjoram (*O. majoran*).

Oregano is most associated with Italian and other Mediterranean-influenced foods, but it is also used in Tex-Mex cooking. This last use is of so-called oregano, not the actual herb, since in Mexico, "oregano" refers to several species of the *Lippia* genus—never *Origanum*. Any combination with tomatoes is a natural, but it is also good with beans, onions, and potatoes. Oregano is used not only with vegetables but also with beef, game, lamb, pork, and chicken.

Parsley, *Petroselinum crispum*, is also known as garden parsley, parsley breakstone, persele, persely, and rock parsley. Parsley is a biennial, native from Europe to Central Asia, but grown in temperate regions worldwide. It is available fresh in two forms: flat-leaf, or Italian, and curly. It is also available dried, which has virtually no flavor, and as parsley-flavored salt. So-called parsley root is sometimes seen, but it used as a vegetable and is therefore not discussed here. At one time curly parsley garnished nearly every plate in America. As the twenty-first century began, the flat-leaved (or Neapolitan) varieties, which have more flavor than curly parsley, had grown in popularity.

Rosemary, *Rosmarinus officinalis*, is also known as compass plant, compass weed, old man, and polar weed. It is an evergreen shrub that is indigenous around the Mediterranean and grows in frost-free herb gardens everywhere. Always available dried, either as whole leaves or powdered, it can also be found as fresh stalks or as potted plants, which are often trained in topiary shapes.

Rosemary's aromatic resin–flavor makes a perfect counterpoint to the unctuous sweetness of fresh pork. When combined with garlic, it is also used with roast chicken and lamb. It is also good with beans.

Cumberland Rosemary, *Conradina verticillata*, is an unrelated endangered plant native to the southern Appalachians that has been used as a substitute for true rosemary.

Saffron, *Crocus sativus*, is also known as saffron crocus. The autumn-flowering perennial bulb is native to the western Mediterranean region but is cultivated commercially in France, Iran, Italy, Kashmir, Sicily, and Spain. It is expensive and is usually sold in tiny packages of threads, which are the dried stamens of the flower. Powdered versions can be found, but they should be avoided, since they are easily adulterated by cheaper ingredients, such as safflower

Saffron's golden color and glorious scent blends well with chicken, lamb, rice, shellfish, and tomatoes, so it is natural to think of it in the context of Mediterranean-influenced dishes. But it is also a traditional ingredient in Scandinavian breads, cookies, and cakes and in Pennsylvania Dutch cooking as well.

Safflower, *Carthamus tinctoris*, also known as American saffron, bastard saffron, false saffron, and Mexican saffron, is an unrelated member of the Asteraceae, or aster, family. It has been used to dye foods yellow but cannot provide the scent and faint bitterness of the real thing. Safflower's primary value is as a source of cooking oil.

Sage, *Salvia officinalis*, is also known as common sage, garden sage, ramona, and sawge. There are dozens of cultivars and other species of *Salvia*—not all of which have culinary value. Most are perennials, native to the north coast of the Mediterranean, but popular in gardens in temperate climates everywhere. Salvia is usually found in powdered form (called rubbed) but is sometimes available as small fresh sprigs.

Sage is used in poultry stuffings and breakfast sausages and combines well with onions and tomatoes. The sagebrush (big sagebrush, common sagebrush, basin sagebrush) of the American West is not sage at all, but *Artemisia tridentata*, an unrelated member of the Asteraceae family. It smells only a little like sage.

Summer Savory, *Satureja hortensis*, and **Winter Savory**, *Satureja montana*, are closely related. Summer savory (calamint, satureja leaf, or savory) is an annual, while win-

ter savory (bean herb) is a perennial. Both originate in the Mediterannean region. The dried savory found on supermarket shelves is usually made of summer savory leaves.

Both savories have a warm aromatic flavor, somewhere between thyme and oregano, and can be used interchangeably, although winter savory is a bit stronger. They work well with strong-tasting meats, like mutton or goat, but also with poultry. Savory is especially good with dried beans, lentils, and limas. In fact *Bohnenkraut*, the German name for savory, means bean-herb.

Tarragon, *Artemisia dracunculus sativa*, is also known as French tarragon, German tarragon, little dragon, and mugwort (but this last more commonly refers to another plant of the same genus). Tarragon is a tender perennial indigenous to the Mediterranean region but cultivated in temperate regions everywhere.

When it is fresh, tarragon has a delicate, sweet taste, reminiscent of anise and fresh-cut grass. When dried, the sweetness persists, but the dried hay quality is enhanced, while the delicate licorice notes are lost. Tarragon is quintessentially French, but it makes an unexpected appearance in Mexican cooking as well. It is especially good with fresh tomatoes.

Russian Tarragon, which is the same species, but not the varietal, *sativa*, has little of the flavor or taste of French tarragon. It is more winter hardy, but it has little culinary use.

Thyme, *Thymus vulgaris* and *Thymus serpyllum*, are two of many species that are closely related. *T. vulgaris* is also known as common thyme, garden thyme, and narrowleaf French thyme; *T. serpyllum* is also known as continental wild thyme, creeping thyme, lemon thyme, mother of thyme, and wild thyme. There are also hundreds of cultivars and hybrids. Thyme is a perennial that is native to Europe and Asia but grows in temperate climates everywhere. In supermarkets it is commonly found in dried form, either as whole leaves or ground. Fresh thyme can be bought occasionally, but it is easily grown at home in pots on a windowsill or in the garden.

Because thyme has a natural affinity for chicken and turkey, it is a key ingredient in Bell's Poultry Seasoning. It also complements many other meats and fish and is commonly used in marinades, sauces, sausages, and soups.

Turmeric, *Curcuma domestica*, is also known as Indian saffron, misleadingly and confusingly as saffron, tumeric, and yellow ginger. It is the rhizome of a tropical perennial from south Asia. It is imported from China, India, and Southeast Asia. While generally sold as a powdered spice, it also can be found in Asian markets as either dried or fresh so-called roots.

Like saffron and annatto, turmeric is used primarily for its intense yellow color. It has a slightly musky and citric scent and a bitter taste. In the United States, turmeric is most commonly seen in the brightest yellow varieties of prepared mustard and in curry powder. Curry powders, which are rarely used in India, are made for export to Europe and the United States. They are spice blends containing turmeric along with cardamom, cinnamon, cloves, cumin, fenugreek, ginger, nutmeg, red pepper, and other spices. Madras curry powder is similar but hotter because it contains more red chili. Curry powder has been used in the United States and Great Britain to make food taste "Indian," the way soy sauce is used to make dishes taste "Oriental." Such gross oversimplifications were the result of ignorance and—fortunately for all of us—are rapidly disappearing.

Vanilla, *Vanilla planifolia*, is also known as bourbon vanilla and Mexican vanilla. It is the pod of a perennial vine from tropical America, cultivated in Mexico, Madagascar, Southeast Asia, Micronesia, and Polynesia. Tahiti vanilla, *V. tahitensis*, and West Indian vanilla, *V. pompona*, are not as flavorful as bourbon vanilla. Sold as an extract with the flavor and aroma dissolved in alcohol. Artificial vanilla extract contains the main component of vanilla, vanillin, which was first synthesized in 1925. More expensive, but much more flavorful, are whole dried vanilla beans, which are actually the pods.

Vanilla, once the rarest of ingredients, had by the mid-twentieth century become synonymous with ordinary, as in "plain vanilla"—a wholly undeserved reputation. Long relegated to baked desserts, ice cream, and cream soda, vanilla began to be used in nouvelle cuisine in the 1970s in savory sauces for delicately flavored foods, such as lobster.

Potherbs and Salad Herbs

If the confusion over the distinction between herbs and spices were not enough, consider the terms "potherb" and "salad herb." They refer to leafy parts of plants used more like vegetables than as seasonings—which would seem to contradict the collective definition, "edible plants that are used to enhance other foods." The confusion is not restricted to English. The German word *Kraut* is similarly used for herb, potherb, and salad herb. Some of these species, both native and imported, are well known in American kitchens and their culinary uses include, and go beyond, the traditional notion of herbs.

Common Dandelion, *Taraxacum officinale*, is also known as blow ball, cankerwort, gray-haired grandmother, lion's tooth, priest's crown, and wild endive. Dandelions are perennials, native to Europe and Asia, but have become naturalized everywhere, much to the chagrin of people who are fussy about their lawns.

Dandelion flowers can be an ingredient in homemade wine and herbal beers. In the spring, young leaves can be picked for use in salads, particularly Pennsylvania Dutch salad, where the leaves are tossed with warm bacon dressing. Older leaves can be cooked as a potherb, sometimes seasoned with nutmeg and lemon. The dried taproots are sometimes roasted as a coffee substitute.

Nettle, *Urtica dioica*, is also known as common nettle, great nettle, great stinging nettle, and stinging nettle. Nettles are perennials, native to Europe and Asia, but naturalized in the United States. Young nettles are used as potherbs, especially in areas of this country inhabited by the descendants of immigrants from France, Ireland, and Scotland. The leaves have been used to brew herbal beers, usually in combination with other wild herbs, such as burdock, chamomile, dandelion, herb bennet, and meadowsweet.

Purslane, *Portulaca oleracea*, is also known as continental parsley, French pusley, hog parsley, miner's lettuce, pusley, pigweed, pursley, pussley, pussly, and summer purslane. It is an annual, originally from India, but is now a common wild plant, or weed, found in waste places, roadsides, and abandoned lots. Purslane's tart and crunchy young leaves are eaten in salads. When cooked as a potherb, purslane thickens liquids, much as okra or filé does.

Ramps, *Allium tricoccum*, are also known as bear's garlic, hill onion, and wood leek. Ramps are broad-leafed perennial wild onions, native to the mountains of eastern North America. Ramps are a traditional sign of spring in the Appalachians. Ramps festivals are held each spring all over the region, especially in North Carolina, Tennessee, and West Virginia. Ramps are eaten raw in salads or on sandwiches, or they are cooked like leeks, only more sparingly, since their garlic-onion flavor is more intense than that of leeks.

Sorrel, *Rumex scutatus*, is also known as buckler-shaped sorrel, French sorrel, garden sorrel, little vinegar plant, meadow sorrel, red top sorrel, and sourgrass. It is a perennial that is native to Europe and Asia. Sorrel is rarely found in ordinary markets, although it is sometimes seen in the spring, before its leaves have become too strongly astringent. Sorrel is used in salads, sauces, and stews, or as a cooked potherb. It is traditionally used to stuff bony fishes, such as shad or pike, because its oxalic acid is alleged to soften the small, forked bones of those fishes.

The unrelated **Wood Sorrel**, *Oxalis acetosa*, also known as cuckowes meat, fairy bells, hallelujah, lady's sorrel, sour trefoil, stickwort, stubwort, surelle, three-leaved grass, and wood sour, also possesses sorrel's pleasantly sour tang and has been used as a substitute for *Rumex scutatus*.

Watercress, *Nasturtium officinalis*, is a perennial that is native to Europe but will grow in cool moving water in any temperate climate. Watercress appears in salads, as a garnish on soups, and, of course, on sandwiches.

[*See also* Flavorings; Flowers, Edible; Garlic; Pepper, Black; Ramps; Sassafrasses; Sorrel; Vanilla.]

BIBLIOGRAPHY

Bailey, L. H. *Hortus Third: A Concise Dictionary of Plants Cultivated in the United States and Canada* New York: Macmillan, 1976.

Elias, Thomas S., and Peter A. Dykeman, eds. *Edible Wild Plants: A North American Field Guide*. New York: Sterling, 1990.

Facciola, Stephen. *Cornucopia II: A Sourcebook of Edible Plants*. 2nd ed. Vista, CA: Kampong, 1999.

Ortiz, Elisabeth Lambert. *The Encyclopedia of Herbs, Spices and Flavorings*. New York: Dorling Kindersley, 1992.

GARY ALLEN

Hero, *see Hoagie; Sandwiches*

Hershey Foods Corporation

Hershey's, the brand named after the company's founder and longtime leader, Milton Snavely Hershey (1857–1945), is synonymous with American chocolate. Known as the "Henry Ford of chocolate makers," Milton Hershey introduced mass-manufacturing to solid chocolate, bringing to the general public a once-luxurious product.

After an initial foray into candy manufacturing, Hershey was inspired by state-of-the-art chocolate-making machinery he saw at the 1893 World's Columbian Exposition. He purchased the machinery after the exposition's close. A year later, the Hershey Chocolate Company was born, operating alongside his Lancaster Caramel Company (founded in 1887). Hershey sold his caramel company in 1900 for $1 million, but kept the chocolate

manufactory, making it the center of a new business, which produced solid chocolates, breakfast cocoa, and baking chocolate. In 1902, Hershey purchased land in rural Derry Township, Pennsylvania, and began erecting a utopian community. By 1904 the chocolate business was in full production, aided by ready supplies of fresh milk, local limestone for building, and a reliable labor force in the hardworking Pennsylvania Dutch.

Until Hershey offered an affordable product, edible chocolate was only available to the very wealthy who frequented elite confectioners. Streamlined production technologies decreased the price of chocolates and increased their availability. Hershey's signature nickel bar, while ever changing in size, remained the same price from its introduction in the mid 1890s to 1969. The incorporation of milk transformed chocolate's bittersweet taste and dark complexion, creating a sweeter, mellower product that was more suited to the American palate. Hershey's earliest product lines included chocolate novelties, such as cigars and cigarettes, and milk chocolate bars, plain and with almonds. Introduced in 1907, Hershey's famous chocolate kisses, bite-sized pieces wrapped in foil, gained their so-called identification plumes (slips of tissue paper emblazoned with the company name) in 1921. The company expanded its own lines and acquired other confectionery companies, eventually producing Reese's Peanut Butter Cups, Twizzlers, Jujubes, Good & Plenty, and Milk Duds, among other candies.

Milton Hershey's philanthropy motivated the development of his chocolate empire. His unified company town and community, a utopian vision, was completed in 1904, effectively insulated from urban ills such as poverty and crime. In addition to the factory, Hershey built modern workers' housing, an amusement park, community center, golf course, department store, bank, public garden, and entertainment center. When Milton's wife, Kitty, died in 1918, Hershey donated the entire estate, including all the company stock, to the Hershey Trust in order to maintain the Hershey Industrial School, a school for orphan boys founded by the couple in 1909. During World War I, Hershey set up a nearly identical factory town in Cuba that produced sugar in response to American supply shortages. During the Depression, he instituted private public-works initiatives within Hershey, Pennsylvania, resulting in the building of, among other things, a stadium and community center.

Until the end of the twentieth century, when it was overtaken by Mars, Hershey's remained the most successful

American chocolate company, and the town's other attractions, like Hershey Park and Chocolate World, helped sustain its earnings. In the late 1990s, the Hershey Trust was worth more than $5 billion. Prospects of selling the trust in the early twenty-first century stirred national controversy, indicating the degree to which people well beyond the region cared about the Hershey legacy.

[*See also* Amusement Parks; Candy Bars and Candy; Chocolate; Chocolate, *subentry on* Later Developments; Mars.]

BIBLIOGRAPHY

Bongartz, Roy. "The Chocolate Camelot." *American Heritage* 24, no. 4 (June 1973): 4–9, 91–99.

Brenner, Joel Glenn. *The Emperors of Chocolate: Inside the Secret World of Hershey and Mars.* New York: Random House, 1999.

Snavely, Joseph R. *Milton S. Hershey, Builder.* Hershey, PA: J. R. Snavely, 1934.

Winpenny, Thomas R. "Milton S. Hershey Ventures into Cuban Sugar." *Pennsylvania History* 62, no. 4 (1995): 491–502.

WENDY A. WOLOSON

Highball

This classic American drink is half whiskey, half carbonated water. There are two stories about how it got its name, both related to the metal ball that railroad stationmasters would hang high on a pole in the station to signal "full speed ahead" to locomotive engineers. Patrick Gavin Duffy, the barman at the Ashland House in 1890 and the author of *The Official Mixer's Manual* (1934), claimed that he named his highball after the speed with which it could be assembled. Another story from around the 1890s says the highball was created by John Slaughtery, a barman at a Saint Louis railway saloon, whose railroad employee customers had only a short break, during which they wanted a drink they could consume quickly.

At the time of its invention, the highball was a remarkable novelty. People had not mixed cocktails, probably because no one wanted to dilute good liquor when plenty of bad liquor already came their way. Although the classic drink itself is no longer very popular, the glass named after it, the tall, narrow-mouthed highball glass, which holds eight to twelve ounces of liquid, remains the most common shape in American barware.

[*See also* Bars; Cocktails; Whiskey.]

LIZA JERNOW

Hines, Duncan

Now best known as a cake-mix brand name, Duncan Hines was once the most widely recognized name in American food. Hines's importance for the latter half of the twentieth and early twenty-first centuries is twofold: as the author of immensely popular guides to American restaurants, which were the forerunner of all the dining guides that would appear in succeeding decades, and, more significantly, as the name on cake mixes and related products. Hines was a prototype for one of the most effective and widely used marketing ploys in the period—branded food celebrity.

Born in 1880 in Bowling Green, Kentucky, Hines began his paid professional life as a traveling salesman for a printing firm in 1905. His avocation was the kind of home-style cooking he recalled from his boyhood on his grandparents' farm, while his passion was cleanliness. Over the next thirty years, Hines and his wife, Florence, collected notes detailing the best of the restaurants they encountered on the road. Word of mouth gave him a reputation as an expert on good eating with exacting standards. His often-quoted remark was to the point: "The library paste served as gravy in some short-order places was a personal insult." And if a restaurant was not scrupulously clean, he would not even enter it. Besieged by callers after a newspaper article on his efforts appeared in the Chicago press, he created cards listing his 167 favorite restaurants across thirty states for the 1935 Christmas season. That led to even more requests, which he answered by publishing the first edition of his guide, *Adventures in Good Eating*, in 1936, which sold for one dollar. Sales from this, together with *Lodging for a Night*, and two cookery books, were such—one half million copies a year—that Hines retired from his traveling salesman's route to take up full-time restaurant reviewing and writing.

Hines's reviews were about places on America's roads. These were mostly small-town eating establishments—tearooms in the South, diners, and, later, a restaurant chain he lauded constantly as a model of cleanliness and good food, Howard Johnson's. Hines promoted well-cooked, down-home American regional food. The "Recommended by Duncan Hines" sign became a valuable marketing tool for lodgings and restaurants and at the same time forwarded Hines's agenda of promoting well-made American dishes and sanitary restaurants. While to later commentators

Hines's tastes might appear to have been provincial, his ideas of regional cookery have come full-circle among American chefs in the early 2000s.

In 1949, Roy Park, a friend and public relations director for a farmers' cooperative that would become Agway, persuaded Hines, then sixty-nine years old, to allow the company to use his name as a brand. Within a short time Hines-Park foods had licensed two hundred products to some ninety manufacturers. Soon, Duncan Hines's name and face on packaged foods were ubiquitous on America's food-store shelves, in advertising, and on television. From fancy preserves to cookware and appliances Hines was the arbiter of good cooking because of his "discriminating" taste. The cake mix is a prime example of his marketing power. Unlike other mixes, it did not contain dehydrated eggs. Eggs had to be added because, as Hines said, "strictly fresh eggs make a bigger, better cake." All the major cake-mix makers followed suit. Hines died in 1959, a famous man, now largely unremembered save for a logo bearing his name, but he was the immediate progenitor of all the Martha Stewarts, Emeril Lagasses, and Wolfgang Pucks who have followed.

[*See also* Cakes; Howard Johnson.]

BIBLIOGRAPHY

Hatchett, Louis. *Duncan Hines: The Man Behind the Cake Mix.* Mercer, GA: Mercer University Press, 2001.

Hines, Duncan. *Duncan Hines' Food Odyssey*. New York: Crowell, 1955.

Levenstein, Harvey. *Paradox of Plenty: A Social History of Eating in America*. New York, Oxford University Press, 1993.

Schwartz, David M. "Duncan Hines: He Made Gastronomes out of Motorists." *Smithsonian* 15 (November 1984).

BRUCE KRAIG

Historical Overview

This entry contains ten subentries:

For a discussion of pre-Columbian foods, *see* Native American Foods.

The Colonial Period

From the beginning of European colonization, the population of eastern North America included numerous culturally, linguistically, religiously, and racially diverse groups. There were hundreds of Native American groups as well as British, Dutch, Swedish, German, and French immigrants. Slaves were brought from Africa to the North and the South. By the early seventeenth century, Africans outnumbered English and French settlers in South Carolina. Although each of these groups contributed to colonial life, English culture put down the deepest roots in America. English settlers not only were the most numerous but also maintained connections with England, unlike other immigrants, many of whom wanted no connection with their countries of origin.

Throughout the colonial period, most Americans lived on farms, which were generally self-sufficient. Those who lived in small towns acquired their food in public markets and occasionally maintained their own gardens. The few colonists who lived in cities, such as Philadelphia, Boston, and New York, had fairly sophisticated foods available, both from the hinterlands and from abroad.

In addition to rural and city differences, diverse climatic and soil conditions created different culinary regions, which roughly divided the colonies into New England (New Hampshire, Massachusetts, Rhode Island, and Connecticut), the middle colonies (New York, New Jersey, and Pennsylvania), and the southern colonies (Delaware, Maryland, Virginia, North and South Carolina, and Georgia). A fourth culinary region was the frontier, which during colonial times began approximately one hundred miles inland from the Atlantic Ocean. Those living on the frontier were largely dependent on hunting, fishing, and trapping,

Colonial America began with the founding of the first permanent English colony in North America at Jamestown, Virginia, in 1607. The provisions that the first English colonists brought with them were scant, and most colonists were unskilled in farming, fishing, and hunting. In addition, the colonists lacked proper equipment, such as fishhooks, nets, traps, and farming implements. Some of the Old World seeds that English colonists brought with them did not thrive in the New World at first. As a result, hunger, malnutrition, and starvation took their toll on the early settlers. Lives were saved by the timely arrival of supply ships from England, but the settlers owed much more to the Native Americans who supplied them with food and taught them how to hunt, fish, gather wild foods, and cultivate New World plants.

Other European settlers, such as the Dutch in New Amsterdam in 1624 and along the Delaware River in 1630 and the Swedes in Delaware in 1638, were better provisioned, skilled, and equipped than the English, but they, too, initially depended largely on the cultivation of American plants, fishing, and hunting for their survival. Within a decade of the beginning settlements, however, food was plentiful, as was remarked upon by many observers, who compared the availability of abundance of food in America to the lack of food in Britain and Europe. Domesticated animals, particularly pigs and chickens, were common throughout the colonies. Agricultural staples, such as corn, wheat, and later, rice were produced in abundance, and a variety of vegetables and fruits were available everywhere.

American Vegetables

By far the most important plant food in pre-Columbian America was maize. It had originated in Central America in prehistoric times, and knowledge of its cultivation slowly spread eastward and northward, arriving along the east coast of North America a few hundred years before the arrival of European explorers. Native Americans taught English colonists how to grow, harvest, dry, store, and prepare corn, and it quickly became a staple food of the colonial diet.

Early colonists consumed corn in many ways. They boiled ears of corn or roasted them in hot ashes, as the Indians did, and then flavored them with salt and butter. Corn was also ground into cornmeal, which was cooked in dishes such as samp, which was coarsely ground corn boiled with vegetables and meat. Other corn dishes were mush and hasty pudding, which was frequently served with milk and flavored with whatever was available, such as milk, cider, or syrup.

Various versions of cornbread, also called "pone" and "johnnycake," were made from cornmeal and served at most meals throughout the colonies. In New England bread was made from cornmeal mixed with rye flour to make "rye 'n' injun," or "thirded" bread, which was made of corn, whole wheat, and rye and evolved into Boston brown bread. Hominy (corn hulled by boiling with lye)

Pilgrims' Dinner. *The Pilgrims' Dinner Interrupted,* nineteenth-century print. *Culinary Archives & Museum at Johnson & Wales University, Providence, R.I.*

was almost as common as cornbread. Coarsely ground hominy, later called grits, was cooked to make starchy side dishes, puddings, and porridges.

The second most important New World vegetable was beans (genus *Phaseolus*). Pre-Columbian Indians had domesticated numerous types of beans, many of which were widely distributed throughout the Americas before the arrival of Europeans. The lima bean (*Phaseolus lunatus*) most likely originated in South America but was commonly cultivated in Florida and the southern colonies. The kidney bean (*Phaseolus vulgaris*) was disseminated widely through North America in pre-Columbian times. Native Americans typically planted beans with corn, and the bean runners climbed the corn stalks. Many Native Americans boiled beans with corn. One Indian name for this combination, succotash, survives. Native Americans slow-cooked beans by burying them in fire pits with water in earthen pots. Colonists adopted this method, adding new ingredients to suit their tastes. Later colonists in Boston, for example, added molasses and meat to the baked beans, a dish that evolved into Boston baked beans.

Members of the genus *Cucurbita*, such as the pumpkin (*Cucurbita pepo*) and numerous varieties of squash, were the third important group of vegetables given by Native Americans to the colonists. Pumpkins were solid enough to be stored through the winter, whereas squash was more fragile and was usually consumed in the late fall or early winter. Native Americans dried slices of pumpkins and squash, which could be kept for years. In eastern America, pumpkins, or "pompions," were easy to cultivate. Colonists roasted, boiled, stewed, and mashed both pumpkins and squash. Winter squash was mixed with cornmeal and baked into bread and cakes. It was also used in making puddings, pies, tarts, and pancakes and was eaten as an accompaniment to meat.

Native Americans introduced colonists to a variety of New World plants. Cranberries, which resembled English barberries, were an instant success, particularly in New England, where the berries were baked into tarts or mashed into a sauce for poultry and game. Groundnuts (*Apios americana*) and Jerusalem artichokes were boiled and served as vegetables. Sunflower seeds were consumed as a snack and later were used to make oil. Nuts, such as American chestnuts, filberts, hickory nuts, and black walnuts, were gathered and served after meals. Some colonists occasionally added nuts to bread. Colonists, particularly in frontier areas, also gathered wild foods, such as acorns, elderberries, grapes, leeks, onions, plums, pokeweed, and strawberries. Blackberries, blueberries, and huckleberries were sun-dried Indian-style and substituted for currants and raisins. For those who could afford it, sugar was used in preserving these fruits as jams and conserves. By 1776 the price of sugar had dropped such that the middle class could afford it.

Many vegetables from Africa and South America were brought to colonial tables by slaves. Slave traders, protecting the health and lives of their investments, brought African foods on the Atlantic Middle Passage to America. Some Africans were indentured and were freed after their term of indenture, and many grew foods that were familiar to them. In the southern colonies, many slaves were permitted to have their own gardens, which supplemented their basic food rations, so vegetables that had been little used in England became popular in the American South in the eighteenth century. For example, okra, which originated in Africa, was used in soups and was served in side dishes. Cassava (*Manihot esculenta* and *Manihot dulcis*), which originated in South America, was used for making bread and pudding. Sweet potatoes (*Ipomoea batatas*) were served in numerous ways and sometimes were inaccurately called "yams." Yams (genus *Dioscorea*), which originated in Africa, were prepared similarly to sweet potatoes and cassava. Peanuts were consumed in stews and soups and were pressed for their oil. Sesame, or benne, seeds yielded cooking oil. Chilies and tomatoes were used as ingredients in sauces and soups and were used as flavorings.

Game, Fowl, and Seafood

Before sufficient stocks of domestic cattle and poultry had been raised, the colonists harvested the abundant game, fowl, fish, and seafood they found in their new land. European settlers quickly became proficient at trapping, hunting, and fishing. Game and fish were extremely important food sources throughout the colonial period.

Three game animals predominated in the colonial diet: deer, bear, and buffalo. Deer were by far the most important. They were plentiful throughout the colonies and relatively easy to hunt. Venison was served freshly killed; the meat also was preserved by drying over fires in the Indian manner. Deer were so abundant that some families, particularly in frontier areas, lived wholly on venison for months at a time. Bears were numerous, and their meat was an important food source in the east. More important was the bear fat, which colonial Americans prized because it was as good as lard and much less expensive than scarce olive oil, which was then imported and largely used for dressing. Buffalo roamed through most of the English colonies from New York to Georgia, although never in the quantities found on the plains. Buffalo were a substantial food source simply because of their size. Buffalo were hunted with such skill and intensity that by the time of the American Revolution, they had disappeared from the continent east of the Mississippi River. Other game included beaver, muskrat, rabbit, raccoon, and squirrel.

Colonists ate wild birds, such as turkeys, cranes, and swans, which were easily caught. The birds were hunted to such an extent that by the late eighteenth century, these wildfowl were rare in populated areas of the colonies. Migratory ducks and geese were plentiful, and early colonists ate them often. Colonists also ate an astonishing array of smaller birds, such as blackbirds, blue jays, crows, grouse, herons, larks, orioles, partridges, pheasants, pigeons, plovers, quail, reedbirds, robins, sandpipers, snipes, turtledoves, and woodcocks, just as they had in Europe—roasted over a fire or boiled and baked in savory pies.

Early colonists feasted on fish and seafood taken from rivers and coastal waters. The favorite fish included freshwater bass, catfish, saltwater flounder, and migrating salmon, shad, herring, perch, pike, sturgeon, and trout. Fresh fish had to be promptly prepared and consumed. More frequently, fish was salted and dried or smoked for future use. Although fishing was important throughout the colonies, it was particularly so in New England. By 1665 more than one thousand vessels were regularly engaged in fishing in Massachusetts. Some of the abundant catch was salted and dried, and before 1700 the preserved fish was traded with the middle colonies for grain, with the Caribbean for rum, and with South Carolina for rice.

Shellfish also was plentiful. As in England, oysters were so common in coastal areas that they were considered food for the poor, but they were enjoyed by all. Oysters were eaten raw, boiled, baked, and broiled. Pickled oysters were shipped to the West Indies (the shells were saved and burned to make lime, which was used in construction and later as fertilizer). Next in importance were crabs, which were particularly favored in the Chesapeake Bay area and along the New England shores. Clams were consumed throughout the colonies in various ways. New England became famous for its quahog clam chowder but also enjoyed razor and soft-shell clams. American lobsters were large and abundant. During the colonial period, lobsters were not considered a delicacy but were mainly used to stave off hunger when other foods were unavailable. Turtles were taken for food in the area from the Florida Keys to Chesapeake Bay. They were usually made into soup. Prawns and shrimp were eaten in pies and soups.

Domesticated Animals

The English colonists liked mutton and lamb, but the sheep initially brought to the New World fared badly. When they finally did thrive, sheep were mainly raised for wool, not meat. The most important meat animal in colonial America was the pig. Pigs had been imported into the New World by the Spanish, who introduced them into Florida and the American Southwest. Pigs and hogs thrived throughout the English colonies, but particularly in the South, owing to the mild winters. Pigs were generally turned loose in the woods, where they fed on mast and other food sources and rapidly multiplied. Pork was easier to preserve by salting, pickling, and smoking than was mutton, which did not store well. Southerners gloried in their hams, and ham and various types of sausages became breakfast staples. Pigs' feet were pickled, and pig intestines were used for making sausages. German immigrants added pork to their dumplings and scrapple. In addition, pigs provided lard. Lard had been the most highly regarded fat in European frying, sautéing, and pastry preparation. Because it was produced in abundance in the colonies, lard was prized and used everywhere in the colonies as well. Frying in lard became the most typical medium for heating food in colonial America. Lard also became the preferred shortening for pie crust.

The colonists imported cows, which supplied milk, butter, cheese, and, occasionally, meat and hides. The settlement at Jamestown had cows before 1611, and by 1634 large plantations in Virginia were producing plenty of dairy foods. In New England the Pilgrims had imported cows by 1624. Colonists drank milk, converted it into butter and cheese, and consumed it with maize-based dishes, such as hasty pudding and samp. A favorite dish during the colonial period was baked pumpkin filled with milk and eaten with a spoon. Curds and cream, a mixture of coagulated milk and cream, was rated a delicacy. By 1650 dairy farming was so successful that the Massachusetts Bay Colony exported butter and cheese, although many well-to-do colonists often continued to import these products from England and Holland. The Dutch settlers who colonized Manhattan in 1625 were even more committed to dairy farming than were the English. The Dutch imported cows and recruited dairy farmers to settle in New Netherland. The Dutch colonists drank tea with milk, breakfasted on bread and butter or bread and milk, favored sour tarts, drank buttermilk, and served cheese at all meals. It was not until after the American Revolution that New Englanders flocked to central New York and established a dairy industry based on English traditions.

During the colonial period, oxen were used for plowing and transportation. Dairy cows were so important as dairy producers that they were not slaughtered until they were unable to produce milk or beef cattle herds. Dairy cows eventually became a mainstay of New England and the middle colonies. In the South, milk spoiled quickly in hot weather, and it kept better in the forms of buttermilk, butter, and cheese. When cattle herds became large enough, during the summer cattle were driven through city streets to butchers located near the market stalls, because fresh meat had to be sold within a few hours of slaughter. In the countryside, where most people lived, beef cattle were butchered in early winter. The coldest weather was needed for chilling the meat quickly after killing and for preserving the desirable fresh meat as long as possible. Meat not immediately consumed was preserved by salting, brining, drying, or smoking. Slabs of beef had to be soaked in brine for weeks before they could be hung for drying or smoking.

Domesticated poultry, particularly chickens, ducks, geese, guinea hens, and turkeys, were important food sources during the colonial period. Fowl generally foraged for themselves and were fed kitchen scraps and corn, but they needed protection from predators. Hens provided eggs, and when old, they provided meat for the stew pot. Unlike beef, lamb, and pork, chicken or goose could be eaten in one or two meals, so preserving poultry was not an issue. Fowl also provided feathers for pillows and bedding. In colonial America, poultry was abundant but expensive, because the chief value was in the eggs. Capons and tender hens were great luxuries.

Grains

The colonists were fortunate in that Europe and New England and the middle colonies had similar climates, making possible the transfer of many Old World plants to America. Rye and oats were introduced into North America by early European explorers even before English colonies had been established. For example, in 1602, the English explorer Bartholomew Gosnold planted barley, oats, peas, rye, and wheat on the Elizabeth Islands, off the coast of Massachusetts. Rye was successfully grown by the Pilgrims during their first year in Plymouth, and it quickly became an important grain in New England. Rye was mainly used to make bread. Oats were grown in New England, Maryland, New Amsterdam, and Virginia by the mid-seventeenth century. When wheat began to be successfully cultivated, oats were mainly grown for animal feed, although colonists from northern England and Scotland continued to enjoy their traditional oat puddings, porridges, bannock, and other baked goods. Buckwheat was successfully grown in the Mid-Atlantic area, especially western Pennsylvania and New Jersey, where buckwheat cakes became a common breakfast dish.

Wheat was introduced by early colonists. With the exception of the Connecticut River valley, wheat never flourished in New England, where it remained a marginal crop throughout the colonial period. Wheat did grow in the middle colonies from New York to Virginia. By the mid-seventeenth century, these colonies became known as the "bread colonies," because they sold crackers to ships for provisions and exported wheat to other colonies as well as the Caribbean and England. Wheat did not grow well in the warm southern colonies, but rice, introduced from Africa in the latter part of the seventeenth century, become the most important grain in the Southeast and was used to make bread, puddings, and many other foods. Slaves from West Africa who were familiar with rice cultivated it in low-country South Carolina and Georgia and helped to incorporate the grain into American colonial cuisine. Dishes such as hoppin' John were the result. Although England had previously imported rice from Portugal and had experimented with it, rice from the colonies flooded into England, as did American ways of preparing it.

The word "pancakes" is believed to have originated in America, but it derived from English "flat jacks" or "slapjacks." Pancakes were eaten everywhere in the colonies, although they were made from different grains, depending on what was easily available. In Virginia and elsewhere the English custom was observed of eating pancakes on Shrove Tuesday, or Pancake Day. The Germans and Dutch encouraged the eating of waffles and wafers, which were also generally consumed throughout the colonies by the eighteenth century.

Vegetables

Colonists successfully transplanted many common European vegetables, such as beets, cabbage, carrots, onions, peas, and turnips, to their American settlements. Colonists also planted asparagus, chives, cabbage, cauliflower, cucumbers, endive, garlic, leeks, lettuce, shallots, and spinach in kitchen gardens. Vegetables not consumed fresh were preserved for future use by drying, canning, pickling, and cellaring.

In colonial times sweet potatoes were cultivated in Virginia, Georgia, and the Carolinas. They had originated in central South America but were introduced into the Caribbean and perhaps Florida in pre-Columbian times. At an early date, sweet potatoes were introduced into Africa, where they thrived. Sweet potatoes most likely were introduced into colonial America through the slave trade, and slaves commonly grew them in gardens in the South. Because they served as cooks on plantations, slaves probably introduced sweet potatoes into the diets of English colonists. The white potato, a native of South America, was introduced by the Spanish to Europe and was brought back across the Atlantic to the English colonies during the late seventeenth century but did not become an important food until the following century. The colonists prepared sweet and white potatoes in similar ways: boiled, broiled, baked, roasted, fried, stewed, and mashed, and they used them in savory pies, breads, pancakes, and puddings.

Fruit

Old World fruits thrived in the American colonies. The colonists established orchards at an early date, and within twenty years of initial settlements, orchards were in full production in all colonies. Depending on climatic conditions and the region, colonists grew apples, cherries, currants, peaches, pears, plums, pomegranates, and quinces. Fruit was eaten fresh, made into tarts and

Copper Preserving Pot. Such pots were used in the eighteenth century for making fruit preserves. *Collection of Alice Ross*

pies, fermented and distilled into alcoholic beverages, and dried for use during winter. At first fruit was rarely preserved, because sugar was too expensive to be used for making preserves. By the mid-eighteenth century sugar was available and was used by the middle class to preserve small quantities of fruit.

Apples and pears were grown throughout the northern colonies, and peaches thrived in all the colonies. Apples were eaten fresh, dried for winter use, cooked into applesauce or apple butter, and pressed for cider, which was the most common American beverage. Peaches were crushed to a paste and dried; they were also used in breads, cakes, and even a type of brandy called "peachy." Pears were treated like apples and pressed into "perry," a pear cider. Blends of dried and fresh fruit were preserved in mincemeat by those who had enough sugar.

Colonists planted melon and watermelon seeds soon after colonization, and these fruits proliferated throughout America. Figs, nectarines, oranges, and pomegranates grew on the coastal plain from South Carolina to Florida. Citrus fruits were imported from the Caribbean. Because they traveled with difficulty, citrus fruits were expensive and were mainly used by those of means for special occasions. The fruits were consumed fresh and were juiced for various beverages. They were also used in puddings and tarts and were preserved in jams and marmalade. Pineapples were imported from the Caribbean beginning in the seventeenth century. The pineapple became a symbol of hospitality in the colonies, and pineapple motifs were common on furniture, gateposts, and silverware.

Herbs, Spices, Salt, and Sweeteners

The early colonists used caraway, cinnamon, cloves, coriander, curry, ginger, nutmeg, mace, allspice, and pepper, all imported, for most purposes. Ginger was commonly used in gingerbread, and anise, coriander, and caraway were used to flavor cakes and cookies. The colonists grew other seasonings, such as horseradish, marjoram, mustard, parsley, rosemary, sage, savory, and thyme, in kitchen gardens.

The most important preservative in the colonies was salt, which was needed to preserve meat and fish. The English colonies never produced enough salt from seawater, inland salt springs, salt licks, and mining of small deposits of salt, so much salt had to be imported. Native Americans sold or traded salt to colonists. Better-quality salt sometimes was imported from Europe. Salt was available in many grades depending on the source; marsh salt was of lesser quality, for example, than mined salt.

There were few natural sweeteners in North America. Dried pumpkin was used as a sweetener, but it was a poor substitute for sugar. More successful as a sweetener was maple sap and later maple syrup and sugar, which by the eighteenth century were used in limited quantities as sweeteners in the northern and middle colonies. Because maple sap was converted into sugar at a ratio of forty to one in the sugaring-off process, the supply was limited and largely seasonal. Wild honey was collected, but New World bees were not proficient at producing honey. During the 1630s and 1640s Dutch and English settlers imported European bees, which were much more efficient at producing honey, and honey became more common. The most common form of sweetening was dried fruit. The most common dried fruits, plums and apples, were used as sweeteners in puddings, pancakes, pies, and bread. Because they were unaccustomed to large amounts of sugar, colonists were satisfied with fruit as sweeteners.

Colonists imported refined sugar from Holland. The Dutch produced it in Brazil and later on Barbados and other sugar islands in the Caribbean when sugar production began there in the mid-seventeenth century. Sugar remained expensive throughout the colonial period. It was found mainly in well-to-do homes in the form of large white cones or loaves, and it was used sparingly. A less expensive alternative was molasses, an end product of sugar refining. Molasses was used to sweeten many foods, including meats and mush but mainly desserts and baked goods.

When sugar was available, colonists enjoyed sweet, creamy desserts such as floating island, trifle, and syllabub (cream whipped to a froth with wine and spices). Puréed fruit was folded into whipped cream to make a "fool." Ice cream, though known in Europe from the late seventeenth century, first appeared in the American colonies in the mid-eighteenth century.

The Colonial Kitchen

The kitchen was often the center of the colonial farm home. Kitchens initially had crude furniture, which was replaced with carpenter-made tables, chairs, cupboards, and shelves. At first, kitchen utensils and equipment were minimal, but as colonists became more established, the equipment expanded to include colanders, choppers, griddles, kettles, mortars and pestles, skillets, spits, tongs, and trivets.

The kitchen was dominated by a large brick or stone fireplace. Chimneys had built-in lug poles—usually an iron bar set into the masonry—from which were hung trammels that held cooking kettles. Lug poles eventually were replaced by moveable iron cranes, which swung out from the fireplace, making it easier, safer, and more efficient to move kettles on and off the hearth. One or more fires had to be tended, and the temperature was regulated by the use of air flow to make the fire hotter or by moving the pot away from the fire if it became too hot. Food also was cooked over modest piles of coals shoveled onto the hearth for gentle heat.

In the hearth it was possible to use most of the traditional methods of cooking. Soups and porridges were heated in kettles suspended from trammels that were raised,

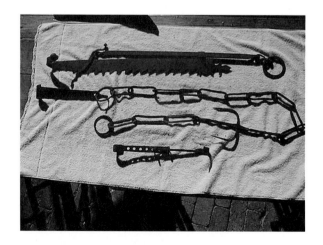

Eighteenth-Century Forged Iron Trammels. Trammels, which were adjustable, were hung in the fireplace; the terminal hook that held the cooking pot could be raised or lowered to regulate the heat. *Collection of Alice Ross*

lowered, and removed. Meat and fish were roasted on a spit and had to be basted and turned, a task frequently assigned to a child. In a tin reflecting oven, a roast was secured in a series of positions so no one needed to be in attendance full time. Meat also was broiled on metal grids mounted on short legs that could be moved with a long handle. Some foods were fried in a pan over coals. Ovens were built either freely standing or into the back walls of fireplaces—usually at the back during the seventeenth century and on the side wall in the eighteenth century. Ovens also were constructed outside of the kitchen in a brick, stone, or clay enclosure, which was heated by a wood fire built inside. When the oven reached the correct temperature, the fire was removed, the food was placed inside the oven, the door was set in place, and the heated brick radiated the necessary heat. Outdoor baking ovens reduced the danger of a fire and lowered household heat in the summer. Outdoor ovens were inconvenient in bad weather, however, and were not favored, except for large communal ovens in Pennsylvania, for example.

Except among those wealthy enough to have a dining room, meals were eaten at a table in the kitchen. In the earliest decades the table was small, possibly a barrel top, and only the man of the house sat to eat. Others stood or sat on the floor. As furnishings were constructed, tables were made large enough to serve as work surfaces and eating areas. On the frontier, foods such as mush, porridge, and stew were served in wooden bowls from which all ate directly with spoons of wood, horn, or hollowed gourd. In later years colonists replaced wooden dishes with vessels of earthenware. The more prosperous used pewter or even silver. Everyone carried a small working knife throughout the day and used it at table for dining. The rich also had sharply pointed knives for spearing food, but forks remained a curiosity for all but the most wealthy during the colonial period.

English colonists usually ate three meals a day. These meals varied by region and season, by the religion and social station of the diners, and by whether the family was farming or urban. Breakfasts frequently consisted of a choice of leftovers, bread and butter, or porridge, oatmeal, or mush; occasionally eggs, smoked or pickled beef, pork, fish, or cheese; and fruit. The English drank tea, the Germans coffee; beer and cider were common. Chocolate was occasionally drunk by the wealthy. Dinner was served at midday and included a buffet-like series of dishes that included meats, fish, side dishes, bread, and perhaps butter and jam. The meal was concluded with fruit and nuts

Pewter Plates. Pewter was used in the colonial period and was considered a step up in staus above the more common and inexpensive ceramic redware. *Collection of Alice Ross*

or cheese. Sweet dishes were not ordinarily served but rather were offered at afternoon tea or on special festive evening occasions. Served with the meal were several alcoholic beverages, such as beer, cider, and wine, depending on the wealth of the host. Supper was a light meal served in the early evening. It frequently consisted of porridge or soup and a dessert, usually cheese, fruit, nuts, or pastries. The well-to-do had complicated menus, whereas the poor ate whatever was inexpensive and at hand.

Colonial Drink

Because its quality was wholesome, water was the most important beverage in the colonial period, particularly in rural areas. As small cities developed in the eighteenth century, water was usually supplied by public pumps placed at intervals along the streets. However, contamination of the water supply by sewage became a serious problem as cities grew. Common solutions to this problem were boiling water before consuming it, adding alcoholic beverages to water, and drinking other beverages.

As cows became common, milk became an important beverage in colonial America. Milk was consumed fresh by young and old alike. Milk was added to many dishes, such as porridge, coffee, tea, chocolate, and alcoholic beverages. Milk punch, composed of egg yolks, sugar, rum and grated nutmeg, was common for festive occasions.

The English, Dutch, and German colonists were partial to beer, and breweries were set up in New Amsterdam, Virginia, and Massachusetts soon after the colonies were established. Light alcoholic beverages were made from elderberries, persimmons, pumpkins, nuts, bark, roots, and leaves. Porter, a dark, sweet ale brewed from malt, was common in America by the time of the Revolution and was a favorite drink of George Washington.

As apples became plentiful, hard cider and applejack quickly became the most important alcoholic beverages

in New England and the middle colonies. Horse-powered cider mills were established throughout New England by the end of the seventeenth century, and the cost of cider decreased so that almost everyone drank it, including children. Mulled cider, a festive drink composed of warmed cider, sugar, egg yolks, and spices was sometimes mixed with rum to give it greater strength. In the southern colonies, where apples did not grow, cider was imported from the northern colonies, and perry (pear cider) and other wines and brandies were made from cherries, currants, black raspberries, peaches, and many more fruits.

Native New World grapes were abundant. Colonists such as Thomas Jefferson tried to use New World grapes for wine making but were unsuccessful. New World grapes simply did not have the characteristics needed for wine making. Old World grapes were imported but did not survive, mainly owing to infestation with phylloxera (*Daktulosphaira vitifoliae*), an insect that originated in eastern America and destroys unprotected grapevine roots. Wealthy colonists imported shipments of wine, such as canary, claret, Madeira, port, and sherry. These fortified wines traveled well, but for the most part, most colonists did not drink wine and considered it pretentious.

Rum was introduced into North America from the West Indies around 1651. When importation of inexpensive molasses began, New Englanders began to distill their own rum. The first Boston rum distillery was founded in 1657. Because rum was inexpensive, its use quickly spread among all classes. Rum was served in a variety of ways, including punches and toddies. Rum was a common drink at taverns, where people of all levels dined. Sailors also drank rum combined with water, called "grog," and grog shops were common in port areas.

Whiskey was commonly made from corn and other available grains. At first these distilled spirits were made for home consumption. As grain harvests increased, it was often easier to convert grain into alcohol with its smaller bulk than it was to transport the grain over the poor roads that existed in colonial America. This issue was particularly important for those living in isolated rural areas, such as western Pennsylvania. When Congress tried to tax such industries in the 1790s, after the colonial period, the result was the Whiskey Rebellion, which was suppressed by George Washington.

Colonists favored mixed drinks, of which there were many types. Flips—sweetened beer strengthened with rum—had become popular by 1690; buttered toast frequently was placed in a flip. Posset, made from spiced hot milk and ale or beer evolved into eggnog and other beverages. Shrubs, composed of citrus juice and various spirits, were popular before the Revolutionary War, as were hot toddies, which were made of liquor, water, sugar, and spices, and cherry bounce, which was made from cherry juice and rum. Punch, the most popular mixed drink, was composed of rum, citrus juice, sugar, water, and spices, although myriad variations existed. During the summer, punch was served iced; hot punch was served in winter. Sangaree was made of wine, water, sugar, and spices and evolved into sangria.

Boston Tea Party

To cover the costs of the French and Indian War (1755–1764), the English Parliament tried to raise money from colonists through a series of taxes, including the Stamp Act of 1764, which was repealed the following year. The Townsend Acts passed in 1767 taxed everything from beer to tea. Many taxes subsequently were rescinded, but an exception was the tea tax, which the colonists largely evaded, but the British decided to enforce. On December 16, 1773, Boston colonists dressed as Indians dumped 340 boxes of tea into the harbor. The Boston Tea Party, as this event became known, led directly to the Revolutionary War and the end of the colonial period.

[See also Beans; Beer; Cider; Corn; Dairy; Fish, subentries on Freshwater Fish, Saltwater Fish, Saltwater Shellfish; Fruit; Hearth Cookery; Herbs and Spices; Kitchens, subentry on Early Kitchens; Milk; Native American Foods, subentries Before and After Contact, Technology and Sources; Potatoes; Rice; Rum; Salt and Salting; Squash; Sugar; Sweet Potatoes; Tea; Vegetables; Wheat; Whiskey.]

BIBLIOGRAPHY

Acrelius, Israel. *A History of New Sweden.* Ann Arbor, MI: University Microfilms, 1966. Translated from the Swedish with an introduction and notes by William M. Reynolds. The original edition was published in 1874.

Booth, Sally Smith. *Hung, Strung, and Potted: A History of Eating Habits in Colonial America.* New York: Potter, 1971.

Brown, Alice Cooke. *Early American Herb Recipes.* Rutland, VT: Tuttle, 1966.

Brown, John Hull. *Early American Beverages.* Rutland, VT: Tuttle, 1966.

Carlo, Joyce W. *Trammels, Trenchers, Tartlets: A Definitive Tour of the Colonial Kitchen.* Old Saybrook, CT: Peregrine, 1982.

Carson, Jane. *Colonial Virginia Cookery.* Williamsburg, VA: Colonial Williamsburg Foundation, 1942.

Conroy, David. *In Public Houses: Drink and the Revolution of Authority in Colonial Massachusetts.* Chapel Hill: University of North Carolina Press, 1995. Published for the Institute of Early American History and Culture, Williamsburg, VA.

Crawford, Mary Caroline. *Social Life in Old New England.* New York: Grosset and Dunlap, 1914.

Earle, Alice Morse. *Home Life in Colonial Days.* Stockbridge, MA: Berkshire Traveller, 1974. The original edition was published in 1898.

Gardiner, Anne Gibbons. *Mrs. Gardiner's Family Receipts from 1763.* Boston: Rowan Tree Press, 1984.

Hess, Karen, ed. *Martha Washington's Booke of Cookery.* New York: Columbia University Press, 1981.

Hooker, Richard J. *A History of Food and Drink in America.* Indianapolis and New York: Bobbs-Merrill, 1981.

Hooker, Richard J., ed. *A Colonial Plantation Cookbook: The Receipt Book of Harriott Pinckney Horry, 1770.* Columbia: University of South Carolina Press, 1984.

Miller-Cory House Museum and the New Jersey Historical Society. *Pleasures of Colonial Cooking.* Newark: New Jersey Historical Society, 1982.

Pinckney, Eliza Lucas. *Recipe Book.* Charleston: Committee on Historic Activities of the South Carolina Society of the Colonial Dames of America, 1969.

Rice, Kym S. *Early American Taverns: For the Entertainment of Friends and Strangers.* Chicago: Regnery Gateway, 1983.

Rubel, William. *The Magic of Fire: Hearth Cooking—One Hundred Recipes for the Fireplace or Campfire.* Berkeley, CA: Ten Speed, 2002.

Salinger, Sharon V. *Taverns and Drinking in Early America.* Baltimore: Johns Hopkins University Press, 2002.

Spruill, Julia Cherry. *Women's Life and Work in the Southern Colonies.* New York: Norton, 1972.

ANDREW F. SMITH

The Revolutionary War

Food commodities played their part in the political upheaval that characterized British North America in the 1760s, 1770s, and 1780s. Taxes and tariffs on these commodities went to replenish British government coffers. The most notorious duty, the 1773–1774 Tea Act, was levied to prop up the East India Company and became a crucial catalyst for rebellion when it inspired the Boston Tea Party. Less militant citizens engaged in political action by refusing to drink tea. Some friends of the American cause, however, could not give up the "pernicious weed" and purchased it under the table rather than using ersatz tea or other substitutes. Wartime mobs seized tea or threatened merchants who charged exorbitant prices for it, but tea, along with coffee and chocolate, remained popular with Americans during the Revolutionary War (1775–1783).

Wartime Shortages and Soldiers' Rations

Occasional wartime shortages caused difficulties, and food riots, long a fact of life in England and France, occurred more than thirty times in America. Causes ranged from local hoarding to inflated prices. Molly Gutridge of Marblehead, Massachusetts, circulated a broadside poem (ca. 1779) that mentioned many foods connected to rioting, as well as trouble with dietary staples. One verse states, "It's hard and cruel times to live" and goes on to lament,

> For salt is all the Farmer's cry,
> If we've no salt we sure must die.
> We can't get fire nor yet food,
> Takes 20 weight of sugar for two foot of wood,
> We cannot get bread nor yet meat,
> We see the world is nought but cheat . . .
> All we can get it is but rice
> And that is of a wretched price . . .
> We now do eat what we despis'd . . .
> We must go up and down the Bay.
> To get a fish a-days to fry.
> We can't get fat were we to die.
> Were we to try all thro' the town,
> The world is now turn'd up-side down.

Soldiers too had to eat, and cultural considerations, actual or ideal, affected the components and quantities of Continental Army rations. In February 1778 Timothy Pickering noted that less meat would be necessary if troops ate more soups, but, he reflected, "No people on earth eat such quantities of flesh as the English," and "nothing but the example of the [American] officers would possibly avail to effect this matter, and perhaps the attempt [to reduce the meat ration] could not be made without the danger of mutiny." The original ration, which was based on that of the British, illustrates what foods were considered necessary to sustain American soldiers and provides insight into society's staples. The hoped-for per diem allotment included one pound of beef or fish or three-quarter's of a pound of pork, one pound of bread or flour, one pint of milk per day, one quart of spruce beer or cider. Each man per week was entitled to three pints of peas, beans, or other vegetables, one-half pint of rice or one pint of Indian meal, and nine gallons of molasses for one hundred men. Meat and flour, with occasional vegetables, became army staples, while supply difficulties caused milk, beer, cider, and molasses to be dropped.

Other foods, more often seen in civilian life, were sometimes issued. For seven months in 1780, New Jersey soldiers stationed in their home state received extraordinary state stores consisting of rum, sugar, and coffee in substantial quantities, and small amounts of chocolate, tea, pepper, and vinegar. After a winter of reduced rations at Valley Forge, in April 1778 fish, bacon, and peas or beans were added to the daily allotment. Four months later soft and hard breads, as well as butter, were being issued. When flour rations were reduced in November 1779, additional portions of meat, beans, potatoes, and turnips were issued.

Foraging and Feasting

Although scarcity was hardly an everyday occurrence Revolutionary soldiers' suffering is popularly synonymous with food dearth. Colonel Josiah Harmar wrote about shortages on August 22, 1780, "Provisions extreme scarce; only half a Lb. Meat in three days." Three days later he wrote, "This movement of our . . . [troops] is occasioned through dire necessity, the Army being on the point of starving." In hard times soldiers often subsisted on fire cake, the "sodden cakes" described by one man as "Flower . . . Wet with Water & Roll[ed] . . . in dirt & Ashes to bake . . . in a Horrible Manner." As hardtack later became a symbol connected to Civil War service (1861–1865), so fire cake was for the Continental soldier.

Soldiers' narratives also provide insights into civilian foodways. Near Woodbridge, New Jersey, Colonel Israel Shreve wrote, "I Rode All over this Village through the Gardens in search of Asparigas [but] found none, All the Beds being Cut that Day by the soldiers." General George Washington authorized foraging for wild "vegetables" at Middlebrook, New Jersey. His list included common and french sorrels, lamb's-quarters (or goosefoot), and watercresses. He went on to recommend to the soldiers the constant use of greens, "as they make an agreeable sallad, and have the most salutary effect."

During 1776 at Fort Ticonderoga, New York, a soldier wrote of having chocolate, "Milk Porrage," and supawn (boiled corn meal and water) on different days. Joseph Joslin served as a wagon driver for the Continental army in Connecticut. His diary lists foods eaten at local taverns and private homes in and around Danbury in 1777 and 1778, including Indian pudding, milk porridge, johnnycake, potatoes, fried pumpkin, codfish, scallops, and "a good Supper Pork beef turnips tators Bread Sider Butter Cheese Puden appelpy nuts & milk."

General George Washington's rather elegant meals at West Point in August 1779,

> had a Ham (sometimes a shoulder) of Bacon, to grace the head of the table; a piece of roast Beef

adorns the foot; and a small dish of Greens or Beans . . . decorates the center. When the Cook has a mind to cut a figure . . . we have two Beef-stake-Pyes, or dishes of Crabs in addition. . . . Of late, he has had the surprizing luck to discover, that apples will make pyes.

Regional foods could pose problems for outsiders. Colonel Henry Lee remembered that in South Carolina, "Rice furnished our substitute for bread, which . . . was very disagreeable to the Marylanders and Virginians, who had grown up in the use of corn or wheat bread." Luigi Castiglioni, traveling through the United States from 1785 to 1787, wrote,

Ordinarily, edible rice is given no other preparation except to boil it in water and take it this way to the table, where it is mixed with fresh butter. In the country it is used boiled in this manner at lunch and dinner. However, certain thin cakes are also made of it, which are served in the morning with tea or coffee, and it is also prepared in many other ways. The cracked rice serves as food for the negroes.

Food-related taxes had instigated the eight-year struggle for independence and it was another food trade issue, American access to the Newfoundland Banks fisheries and the right to dry the catch onshore, that held up the peace negotiations in 1782 and 1783. Hostilities ceased when those rights, and other concessions, were won.

[See also Combat Food; Cookbooks and Manuscripts, subentry From the Beginnings to 1860; Hardtack; Supawn; Tea sidebar on Boston Tea Party.]

BIBLIOGRAPHY

Cometti, Elizabeth. "Women in the American Revolution." *New England Quarterly* 20, no. 3 (September 1947): 335–337.

Commager, Henry Steele, and Richard B. Morris. *The Spirit of 'Seventy-Six.* New York: Harper & Row Publishers, 1975.

Fitzpatrick, John C., ed. *The Writings of George Washington from the Original Manuscript Sources 1745–1799.* Vols. 8, 16. Washington, DC: Government Printing Office, 1933.

Force, Peter. *American Archives*, series 5, vol. 1. (Washington, DC, 1837–1853): 865.

Gutridge, Molly. "A New Touch on the Times. Well Adapted to the Distressing Situation of Every Sea-port Town. By a Daughter of Liberty, Living in Marblehead." In *American Broadside Verse from Imprints of the 17ᵗʰ and 18ᵗʰ Centuries*, edited by Ola Elizabeth Winslow. New Haven, CT: Yale University Press, 1930.

Harmar, Josiah. Lieut. Colonel Josiah Harmar's Journal. No. 1. November 11, 1778, to September 2, 1780, p. 79. Josiah Harmar Papers. William C. Clements Library. Ann Arbor, MI.

Joslin, Joseph, Jr. "Journal of Joseph Joslin, Jr., of South Killingly, a Teamster in the Continental Service, March 1777–August 1778."

Collections of the Connecticut Historical Society. Vol. 7 (1899): 301, 305, 306, 320, 334, 344.

Middlekauff, Robert. *The Glorious Cause: The American Revolution, 1763–1789.* New York: Oxford University Press, 1982.

Morgan, Kenneth. "The Organization of the Colonial American Rice Trade." *William and Mary Quarterly*, 3rd ser., 52, no. 3 (July 1995): 432–452.

New Jersey State Archives. Department of Defense, Military Records, Continental Army, Quartermaster General and Commissary General's Records, Account Book of the Jersey Brigade, Box 1. Account book of state stores delivered to the 1st–4th Regiments [January–July?] Trenton, NJ, 1780.

Pace, Antonio, ed. and trans. *Luigi Castiglioni's Viaggio: Travels in the United States of North America 1785–87.* Syracuse, NY: Syracuse University Press, 1983.

Pancake, John S. *This Destructive War: The British Campaign in the Carolinas 1780–1782.* Tuscaloosa, AL: University of Alabama Press, 1985.

Rees, John U. " 'The Foundation of an Army Is the Belly.' North American Soldiers' Food, 1756–1945." In *ALHFAM: Proceedings of the 1998 Conference and Annual Meeting.* Vol. 21. Bloomfield, OH: Association for Living History, Farm and Agricultural Museums, 1999. http://revwar75.com/library/rees/index.htm. Also contains Continental and British army ration lists.

Shreve, Israel. To his wife, April 18, 1777. Israel Shreve Papers. Buxton Collection. Prescott Memorial Library. Ruston, LA: Louisiana Tech University.

Smith, Barbara Clark. "Food Rioters and the American Revolution." *William and Mary Quarterly*, 3rd ser., 51, no. 1 (January 1994): 3–38.

Todd, Jonathan. Surgeon 7th Conn. Regt., to his father, November 9, 1777. Revolutionary War Pension and Bounty-Land-Warrant Application Files. National Archives Microfilm Publication M804, reel 2395, Washington, DC.

Wickman, Donald, ed. "The Diary of Timothy Tuttle." *New Jersey History* 113, nos. 3–4 (Fall–Winter 1995): 69.

JOHN U. REES

From the Revolutionary War to the Civil War

As America emerged from the Revolutionary War to become a new nation rather than a disparate set of colonies, the task before its citizens was both daunting and undefined. A first imperative was to create a social and political order that would ensure the peace and prosperity of the new nation yet also remain true to revolutionary ideals. As the eighteenth century ended and the nineteenth century began, Americans turned their attention from separating from Britain to creating a national government and the institutions and rituals that would contribute to a civic identity The contesting sectional interests and the ideal of national unity were not the only challenges the young country faced: from the Revolution to the eve of the Civil War, the United States coped with industrialization, westward expansion into Indian territory and former French and Spanish colonies, Indian wars and relocation, a second war with Great Britain, increasingly repressive slavery and active abolitionism, the beginnings of public education, the arrival of new groups of refugees and immigrants from Europe, and the development of political parties. While food and eating were everyday, mundane occurrences, they also became a part of each of these debates.

What Did Americans Eat?

Americans in this period had many styles of eating. For many average farm families, pork and grain along with dried beans composed most of the diet for much of the year. However, wealthy slave owners were able to sustain a luxurious, British style of dining little changed from colonial times. Urban workers had access to a variety of foods, although they might not have been able to afford them every day. Merchant families in port cities were able to participate in a global food economy that brought them occasional access to tropical fruits, European wines, curry spices from India, and varieties of coffee and tea. Americans did not politicize class differences in eating until the 1840 presidential election, when the Whigs successfully contrasted cider-drinking William Henry Harrison with President Van Buren's fine dining in the White House.

The notion that early Americans ate unseasoned food and avoided milk, fruits, and vegetables is actually a late Victorian one that got wrongly attached to early Americans after the nation's centennial in 1876. The detailed recipes of Eliza Leslie are lavish with nutmeg, mace, cinnamon, pepper, and lemon juice where contemporaries wrote "spice to taste." Tomatoes, broccoli, and new varieties of vegetables and fruits enjoyed popularity in a vogue for experimental farming in the 1830s. But poor Americans took advantage of the foods local to their areas, and some rural families were still living on very few seasonal foods, eating the same thing until it ran out, during the late winter-to-spring lean period. Regional variations persisted; in New England, for instance, wheat was difficult and expensive to grow and thus barley, rye, oats, and corn were substituted, even after the opening of the Erie Canal brought western wheat to market in the 1820s. In coastal regions, Americans ate oysters and lobsters as well as other fish. While lobsters were not yet regarded as a luxury, an oyster frenzy hit the nation in the mid-nineteenth century when those living inland clamored for them. The delicacy was shipped by rail to the heartland to be served in oyster houses and sold by street peddlers. All over the country, shellfish was served raw, baked, fricasseed, in soups, and in pies. The railroads also lengthened the seasons for urban cooks and made for more reliable supplies of strawberries and other delicacies.

Class also dictated diet. Wealthier Americans of course ate better and more varied diets than members of the working classes. Many tried to emulate European tastes, eating a wider range of foods, which required more complicated preparations. The presence of servants to cook for wealthier families made cooking and eating more pleasurable. Working-class Americans favored cheap and easily prepared foods. A popular dish among laborers was blood pudding, a mixture of pork or beef blood mixed with chopped pork stuffed into casing. Pigs were especially cheap and easy to raise; they did not require feeding or other care. When New York City banned pigs from roaming the streets, housewives protested the ban by fighting back with their brooms.

Americans of every stripe enjoyed a great variety of sweets and beverages. Access to sugar for American refineries had been an issue in the Revolution, and cheap rum, sugar, and molasses were among its victories. Pork and beef were often cured with molasses. Americans developed a sweet tooth. A wide variety of desserts were popular in America. Gelatin—or gelatine, as it was spelled in the nineteenth century—(prepared with calf's-foot jelly, isinglass from sturgeon, and increasingly faked with arrowroot or cornstarch) was a popular pudding. Yeasted cakes and pound cakes began to yield to the taller, layered cakes as baking powders became more widely marketed, sometimes with a temperance endorsement. Pies were still popular for their durability and ease of baking, but the most popular and exciting dessert was ice cream. This delicacy offered an opportunity to display one's access to the improved ice cutting and distribution developed in this period in New England, especially on the Fourth of July holiday. During and after the War of 1812, when the price of British-monopoly tea rose and coffee from Brazil and the Caribbean became more affordable, the traditionally British drink fell out of favor. Nineteenth-century housewives produced a large variety of drinks at home: beers from barley, ginger, spruce, sassafras, maple syrup, and molasses; and wines from local and imported grapes and berries, as well as cordials and punches.

Food on the Frontier

With the Louisiana Purchase in 1803, millions of new acres were opened up. To accommodate a growing population and to find new land to replace what was becoming exhausted from nearly two centuries of use, the U.S. government encouraged citizens to settle the western lands, sending Lewis and Clark on an expedition to see just what it was that Thomas Jefferson had bought. While Lewis and Clark did not find the new foods the gourmet president had hoped for, their expedition was useful in guiding future pioneers in what foodstuffs to bring and what to leave at home. Westward migration was planned with the climate in mind. Pioneers brought food with them and found foods along the way as much as they could. When men traveled alone, they subsisted on salt pork and beans, wild game, and what they could trade with the Indians, as well as great quantities of whiskey. When families traveled together, women prepared meals as best they could amid the dusty, rocky conditions It was difficult to make a home on the road, as much as they tried; no doubt familiar foods eased their loneliness.

Once settled in the West, Americans found fertile virgin soil, plains rich in livestock, and rivers and streams overflowing with fish. The new territories (and later states) produced great amounts of cattle for beef—and milk, corn, sugar beets, oats, and fruit. Women took full advantage of the selection, even if it meant preparing meals in primitive frontier kitchens. A California settler described her experiences in 1852: "I am making mince pie and Apple pie and squash pie. . . . and now and then Indian jonny cake . . . and Indian Bake pudings [sic]. . . . and then again I am scareing [sic] the Hogs out of my kitchen and Driving the mules out of my Dining room" (Fischer, p. 44). While confronting unfamiliar situations and homesickness, women could take pride in preparing meals in their new homes.

Drink in American Life

Drink was as much a part of American life as food was, and in the late eighteenth and early nineteenth centuries, alcoholism was regarded as a great problem in America. Liquor, most often whiskey and cider, was a regular part of everyday meals and social gatherings. No election, militia mustering, or quarterly session of a court would be held without drinking to accompany it. The amount of alcohol consumption peaked in 1830 with the rate of four gallons per capita. Such levels rose after the American Revolution for several reasons. New production technology coupled with the opening of new farmlands in the West meant that whiskey was more easily and cheaply distilled from surpluses of corn. Steamboats provided an inexpensive, quick way to transport the spirits. Attitudes changed as well; the upper classes no longer held their bias against distilled spirits. What increased among all classes was the belief in the unhealthfulness of milk and water. The temperance movement of the 1830s and 1840s was begun not by self-righteous women and men searching for a cause as much as by the recognition that liquor in excess amounts was causing violence, disruptions in family life, and agricultural and industrial accidents. So successful was the temperance movement that President Andrew Jackson switched the military ration from rum to coffee, and after 1830 the per capita consumption rate dropped.

Food and the Industrial and Transportation Revolutions

Changes in technology and transportation changed American foodways. Refrigeration, in particular improvements in icehouses, allowed meat, poultry, and fruit to be kept longer. Machinery that cut ice more easily, better insulation techniques (such as packing ice in sawdust), as well as falling ice prices made keeping food cold a more viable option. By the mid-nineteenth century, icehouses were common on farms. The ice chest was

Wood and Iron Sausage Grinder. A hand-made grinder typifies the pre-industrial implements that would be superseded by cast-iron equipment of similar design that was made industrially after the Civil War. With its lid removed, the wooden core set with iron "pushing nails" guided the meat into small knives embedded in the frame, eventually pushing the completed sausage meat out onto a place below. *Collection of Alice Ross*

patented in 1803, and cold storage warehouses appeared in 1858. Americans began to consume different foods as a result of refrigeration; perhaps the best example is fresh milk, which had become a health hazard because it spoiled so quickly.

It also became possible to transport foods greater and greater distances. Before the period of the early Republic, food had to be consumed within a few miles of where it had been produced and also within a short time of its harvest or slaughter, unless it had been dried or salted. Late winter and early spring were especially difficult times (these had been the "starving times" in seventeenth-century America). The appearance of steamboats beginning in 1807 meant that foodstuffs could be transported long distances; by 1830 they were widely in use. Roads and canals also facilitated the exportation of food. Prices dropped as a result of new transportation methods. Flour, which had been scarce along the eastern seaboard, became cheaper and more readily obtainable. Railroads had an even greater impact. The rails brought a wider variety and better quality of foods to Americans. Different types of grain were transported to different regions to be fed to cattle, which in turn produced a higher quality of beef. Beef became more tender as cows no longer walked to the slaughterhouse, walks that had made their meat more muscular and tough. Once-exotic or limited-season fruits and vegetables (especially peaches) were more commonplace in the middle of the country. The appearance of clipper ships at mid-century meant that pineapples, bananas, and coconuts, if not eaten every day, were available to middle-class consumers along the eastern seaboard.

New Trends in America: Immigrant Foodways

The 1840s and 1850s witnessed a wave of immigration. Crossing the Atlantic from Europe (primarily from Germany and Ireland) were 4.2 million newcomers. They brought their own foodways. The Irish came in large part as a result of the potato famine that had reduced their country's population from just over 8 million to 6.5 million. They had relied upon the potato as the mainstay of their diets because it was cheap and filling. Despite their limited national cuisine, the Irish became kitchen servants, grocers, hoteliers, saloon keepers, and restaurateurs in America, reinforcing the Anglo-American taste for meat and potatoes and dairy products. The Germans brought a more distinctive national cuisine with them and included more urban families with experience as butchers, bakers, brewers, wine merchants, and restau-

rateurs. Because both groups used the saloon as a social center, nativist movements raised intemperance as an issue against immigrants.

New Trends in America: Natural Foods

Between the 1830s and 1850s, many Americans became involved in reform movements. They endeavored to perfect themselves and society as a whole. While some people became involved in movements such as abolitionism and temperance, and others sought solace in utopian movements such as Brook Farm at West Roxbury, Massachusetts, still others used the consumption of food as a way to achieve the ideal state. This was true on the "reform" left, and also among the many religious revivalists and founders of new denominations and sects in the 1830s and 1840s. Perhaps the best-known food reformer was the Reverend Sylvester Graham. He was disgusted by gluttony and the pleasures of the flesh. The man who gave his name to graham crackers espoused eating "natural foods," especially raw fruits and vegetables and whole wheat bread, and abstaining from meat. Graham found pork and shellfish most abhorrent. Even adding spices— salt was a culprit—might cause insanity and would offend God, who had created foods in a particular way. Despite (or perhaps because of) the fact that his ideas contradicted contemporary American notions of diet and food, they became very popular. In 1838, Graham "boardinghouses," in which his theories were put into practice, appeared all over the nation. Recipes for whole-wheat "dyspepsia" bread began to appear in mainstream cookbooks. Other nutritionists advocated vegetarianism as the healthiest diet. Women such as Mrs. Horace Mann and Catharine Beecher joined the chorus of those calling for a healthier diet, although the vast majority of Americans ignored their suggestions and consumed pie for breakfast, fatty puddings with every meal, and alcoholic beverages daily.

American Cookbooks as American Culture

In the colonial era, Americans remained loyal to English cookbooks. The appearance of native cookbooks suggests that Americans recognized the need for their own cuisine or the need to document that it already existed. The first to answer this need was Amelia Simmons, whose *American Cookery* was first published in Hartford in 1796. Calling herself "an American orphan . . . circumscribed in her knowledge," Simmons noted that she "calculated" her "treatise . . . for the improvement of the rising generation of *Females* in America" (Simmons, p. 3). Simmons's volume made use of English recipes, but with the twist of American ingredients. She baldly plagiarized from British cookbook authors, especially Susannah Carter and her *The Frugal Housewife* (1772). Simmons's work was, however, original in her inclusion of foods native to America and in her use of American vocabulary. Her recipes called for New World ingredients, such as corn, squash, and pumpkin. She included recipes for Jerusalem artichokes, which Americans favored but the English did not. Simmons called for potash as a leavening ingredient in baking; it did not become known in England until 1799. Where the English referred to "treacle," Simmons called for the more American "molasses." Simmons's gingerbread recipes produced a cakelike product while English recipes made thin cut cookies.

American Cookery became an enormously popular work. The volume was reprinted in 1800 with new recipes that reflected the attempt to Americanize food, including such titles as Election Cake, Independence Cake, and Federal Pan Cake. Its popularity left it open to plagiarism. In America, the book was republished under different, disguised titles, the new "writers" sometimes even keeping the "orphan" references in the introduction.

Simmons's work was not the only published cookbook in antebellum America. Published cookbooks proliferated in the South, especially as compiled by white women of the planter class. The best known, Mary Randolph's *The Virginia House-wife* (1824); Mrs. Lettice Bryan's *The Kentucky Housewife* (1839); and Sarah Rutledge's *The Carolina Housewife* (1847), offered both recipes as well as a glimpse into the culinary culture of the American South. They did, however, represent, primarily the small slice of southern life that was enjoyed by the wealthy white woman who was assisted by slaves as she entertained in the lavish, gracious style of the plantation. Northern women also published cookbooks. Eliza Leslie's *Seventy-Five Receipts* (1828), contains several recipes that call for abundant amounts of lavish foods. Leslie went on to write two larger cookbooks and to translate a French cookbook in a literary and culinary career of more than thirty years. In contrast, Lydia Maria Child's *American Frugal Housewife* (first published as *The Frugal Housewife* in 1829) contains everyday foods including the first published recipe for baked beans. The next generation of cooking writers— Catharine Esther Beecher, Mary Cornelius, Mrs. Putnam, and Mrs. Crowell—spanned the Civil War and revised their books to reflect the transition from hearth to stove cooking, and the newer, taller cakes.

Cast Bronze Preserving Pot. Preserving increased in the nineteenth century as glass fruit jars began to replace earlier preserving methods. *Collection of Alice Ross*

Mrs. J. Chadwick's *Home Cookery* (1853) offers a combination of simple and economical dishes, with variations to make them more elaborate and appropriate for members of the upper class. She also includes a variety of foreign and American regional dishes that suggest the widening horizons of some cooks in northern seaports. The variety and sophistication of recipes given in early American cookbooks suggest that Americans were adventurous and curious in the kitchen and in the dining room. Perhaps the recipes were for special occasions or for company; perhaps they were meant to encourage Americans to step beyond their regular eating habits.

Unpublished works were more common in American households. These private documents were mundane objects in many households. Women often assembled manuscripts with recipes and other household notes. Extant in every region of antebellum America, they offer a glimpse into local cuisines and preferences. Manuscript cookery books also demonstrate the division of classes in the United States. For instance, the manuscript of Elizabeth Randolph, a member of a wealthy Philadelphia Quaker family, delineated the differences in tasks assumed by servants (such as preparing daily breakfasts and baking bread) and by mistresses (such as planning parties). Women also included recipes in letters and on scraps of paper. They traded ideas with family and friends, and women often showed favor to others to whom they gave their most prized recipes.

Not only cookbooks were intended to assist "the rising generation" in the kitchen; household manuals appeared in the nineteenth century to help women create an

"American" household also. As labor patterns shifted because of new forms of industrialization and men often went off to work (as opposed to laboring in more home-based workshops), two separate spheres, men's and women's, emerged. White middle-class women (most often living in the Northeast) were now regarded as the keepers of the homes. As members of the "Cult of True Womanhood," they were charged with the crucial task of making the domestic realm one of piety and purity, a sanctuary for their husbands and children. Manuals—most notably the *Treatise on Domestic Economy* by Catharine Beecher (1841; revised after the Civil War as the *American Women's Home* written by Catharine Beecher and Harriet Beecher Stowe) and *The Mother's Book* (1831) by Lydia Maria Child—taught nutrition and domestic practices, extolling the virtues of women who took pride in their homes. By providing their husbands and children with food of both the literal and spiritual varieties, women would not only be making happy, peaceful, and Christian homes, they would also contribute to the strength of the nation. Such views were reiterated in popular women's magazines and other literary treatises, and were common to an antisuffragist and antiabolitionist like Miss Beecher, and to a Garrisonian abolitionist and suffragist such as Mrs. Child.

Food as Ritual: Feasting on the Fourth

The framers of the Constitution quickly realized the need to surround it and other symbols with celebratory rituals. On July 4, 1788, the Grand Federal Procession was held to commemorate the nation's independence and celebrate the ratification of the Constitution. Members of every occupation and every class marched in the parade, and floats, horses, and ships traveled down Philadelphia's streets. From highest to lowest—dignitaries, tradesmen in every industry, clergy, and students—all joined together in the holiest day of the American civil religion. After the procession a great feast was held. A cold lunch was served along with American beer and cider—no foreign spirits were allowed. No expense was spared for this celebration, and all were invited to dine. The inclusiveness of the day was made evident by the presence of a kosher table. Jews, who by their dietary laws were usually excluded from eating with non-Jews, saw themselves as Americans on that day. While unable to break their kosher laws, they still desired to be part of the celebration. Their table was next to the others, and they partook in the feast, too.

Fourth of July celebrations in other cities and other years included food and drink rituals. In Boston, several private dinners were held. The most famous was that hosted by the governor, who offered a cold lunch of food and (imported) canary wine to his guests before the procession to the State House. Other groups, especially members of the militia, held their celebrations in taverns and hotels. After dinner, orations were given and toasts were offered, at first thirteen and then more as new states joined the Union. In other cities, light meals and toasts characterized the day. Newspapers offered detailed accounts of what foods were eaten and of the toasts. Even as different political parties developed, differences could be set aside for a time to sit down to a Fourth of July meal. In 1810, the Democratic-Republicans served leftover lemonade to six hundred takers without regard for their political affiliation. As serving food on Independence Day became associated with their rivals, the Federalists ended ritual dining. Average Americans developed their own rituals: popular foods included turtle soup—turtles were in season in the summer—and ice cream. (Free African Americans stopped celebrating July 4 as the abolition movement grew. They either celebrated July 5, or West Indian Emancipation Day, August 1, 1834.)

Food as Ritual: Christmas Feasts

As Christmas began to be celebrated more and more throughout America in the eighteenth and nineteenth centuries (the New England Puritans and Pennsylvania Quakers had frowned upon it in the seventeenth and eighteenth centuries), food became a part of the festivities. Along with sentimental images of Santa Claus, sweets were part of Christmas culture. Philadelphia confectioners competed for customers beginning in 1840 with elaborate cakes. Candies in unusual shapes—animals, loaves of bread, and insects—also graced the shop windows. Christmas dinner, a grand meal, became custom; another British Christmas custom was lavishing the poor with food and gifts. (New Englanders had transposed the meal and the gifts to the poor to Thanksgiving, which was often declared for early December.) In the early nineteenth century, more in the South than in the North, consuming great quantities of alcohol also became common. Southern planters often held open houses in which they served eggnog; they sometimes hosted two gatherings, one for friends and one for the "lower orders."

Feeding the Slaves

The amount and types of food that masters allotted to slaves differed from that which slaves prepared and ate.

Their owners were concerned with providing only enough nourishment to enable slaves to work as much as possible. The mainstays of the slave diet were pork and corn, both of which were plentiful in the South. The typical ration, set in the eighteenth century, was a peck of corn per slave per week. This was varied locally with broken rice, sweet potatoes in season, and other starches. The diet of pork and corn allowed the adult slave to consume approximately 4,500 calories per day. While this amount seems excessive in a modern diet, surviving photographs of African Americans, who were, with little exception, slim, suggest that this intake was necessary to sustain them as they worked "from sun-up to sun-down." The typical diet was both monotonous and not especially healthful, because pork and corn, while providing protein and carbohydrates, lack many vitamins. To vary their food choices (and to a lesser extent to provide more nutrition), slaves hunted, fished, trapped, stole, and grew their own foods whenever possible. This was allowed by some masters, since it was less expensive to give slaves the freedom (and sometimes the arms) to provide for themselves. Other masters, especially as plantations evolved and became larger, thought that it was inefficient to have slaves working to feed themselves and so provided a better ration, or delegated certain slaves to cook in the fields or in communal kitchens for the children. When and where they could, slaves added okra, cabbage, squash, peas, and rice, as well as grouse, squirrels, raccoons, possums, fish, alligators, turtles, and groundhogs. Some of these foods were regarded by the masters as farm pests or beneath notice, while others were actually sold to masters or on the open market, providing slaves with a cash income. This was more prevalent in the early part of this period than in the later years of slavery. Fathers took pride in teaching their sons to obtain their own food, thereby providing the opportunity to assume some of the familial responsibilities that were frequently denied to adult male slaves.

Some female slave cooks, and a handful of males, reigned supreme among the house servants and were able to assert some authority. Some slave cooks had other slaves to assist them in the kitchen, as meals were often elaborate productions. The cook alone had access to exotic and expensive supplies, and she alone helped the plantation mistress entertain in grand southern style, thereby solidifying the reputation of both. Masters and their families liked French and English food, and were forced to embrace local dishes only with the naval blockade of the Civil War. The stereotype of the skilled slave cook also seems to have developed mostly after the Civil War, when African Americans could compete for paid positions in the fewer wealthy southern families, and when more white southerners had developed a taste for African-derived dishes and seasonings.

The exception to the normal corn and pork diet for slaves came at special occasions such as Big House weddings and the week between Christmas and New Year's Day. Slave masters often threw parties at the end of the year and provided food and drink. This was the only time in which slaves were permitted to consume alcohol. A former slave recalled many years after emancipation that his masters "give us everything you could name to eat: cake of all kinds, fresh meat, lightbread, turkeys, chickens, ducks, geese, and all sorts of wild game. There was always plenty of pecans, apples, and dried peaches too at Christmas." Such feasts were held certainly less to indulge the slaves' tastes than to create enough goodwill to last until the following year's holiday season. Weddings, the other great occasion for slave feasts, were held at the end of the year and were often combined with Christmas festivities. As slaves were increasingly denied access to legal and religious marriage, the ironies of such occasions must have multiplied.

[*See also* African American Food, *subentry* To the Civil War; Alcohol and Teetotalism; Beecher, Catharine; Child, Lydia Maria; Cookbooks and Manuscripts, *subentry* From the Beginnings to 1860; Cooking Manuscripts; Fourth of July; Graham, Sylvester; Ice; Jewish Dietary Laws; Kitchens; Leslie, Eliza; New Year's Celebrations; Randolph, Mary; Simmons, Amelia; Temperance; Thanksgiving; Transportation of Food.]

BIBLIOGRAPHY

Breedon, James O., ed. *Advice Among Masters: The Ideal in Slave Management in the Old South.* Greenwich, CT: Greenwood, 1980.

Bryan, Mrs. Lettice. *The Kentucky Housewife.* Cincinnati: Shepard and Stearns, 1839. Facsimile, Paducah, KY: Image Graphics, n.d.

Bushman, Richard. *The Refinement of America: Persons, Houses, Cities.* New York: Knopf, 1992.

Child, Lydia Maria. *The American Frugal Housewife.* 12th ed. Boston: Carter, Hendee, 1832. Facsimile, Worthington, OH: Worthington, Ohio, Historical Society, 1965.

Cott, Nancy. *The Bonds of Womanhood: "Woman's Sphere" in New England: 1780–1835.* New Haven, CT: Yale University Press, 1977. Discusses women's new roles in industrializing America.

Fischer, Christiane, ed. *Let Them Speak for Themselves: Women in the American West, 1849–1900.* Hamdon, CT: Archon, 1977. Women's accounts of their experiences on the frontier.

Fogel, Robert William, and Stanley L. Engerman. *Time on the Cross: The Economics of American Negro Slavery.* Boston: Little, Brown, 1974. Contains an analysis of the slave diet.

Fox-Genovese, Elizabeth. *Within the Plantation Household: Black and White Women of the Old South*. Chapel Hill: University of North Carolina Press, 1988. Includes a discussion of slave women's roles as cooks.

Leslie, Eliza. ["A Lady of Philadelphia"]. *Seventy-Five Receipts for Pastry, Cakes, and Sweetmeats*. Boston: Monroe and Francis, 1828. Facsimile, Cambridge MA: Applewood, 1988.

Morgan, Philip D. *Slave Counterpoint: Black Culture in the Eighteenth-Century Chesapeake and Lowcountry*. Chapel Hill: University of North Carolina Press, 1998. Although mostly set before this period, the most detailed summary of slave nutrition across the Atlantic south.

Nissenbaum, Stephen. *The Battle for Christmas: A Cultural History of America's Most Cherished Holiday*. New York: Knopf, 1996. Includes a discussion of ritual foods and slave feasts.

Randolph, Mary. *The Virginia House-wife*. Washington DC: Davis and Force, 1824. Facsimile with notes and commentaries by Karen Hess. Columbia: University of South Carolina Press, 1984.

Rorabaugh, W. J. *The Alcoholic Republic: An American Tradition*. New York: Oxford University Press, 1979. Includes a discussion of the types of alcohol Americans drank and why the rate increased in the early Republic.

Rutledge, Sarah ["A Lady of Charleston"]. *The Carolina Housewife*. Charleston, SC: Babcock, 1847. Facsimile with introduction by Anna Wells Rutledge. Columbia: University of South Carolina Press, 1979.

Simmons, Amelia. *American Cookery*. Hartford, CT: 1796. Reprint, New York, 1958. The first American cookbook.

Simmons, Amelia. *American Cookery*. Albany, NY: Webster, 1796. Facsimile with an introduction by Karen Hess: Bedford, MA: Applewood, 1996. The second edition, with corrections and additions by the author, of the first American cookbook.

Sklar, Kathryn Kish. *Catharine Beecher: A Study in American Domesticity*. New Haven, CT: Yale University Press, 1973.

Theophano, Janet. *Eat My Words: Reading Women's Lives Through the Cookbooks They Wrote*. New York: Palgrave, 2002.

Travers, Len. *Celebrating the Fourth: Independence Day and the Rites of Nationalism in the Early Republic*. Amherst: University of Massachusetts Press, 1997.

Welter, Barbara. "The Cult of True Womanhood: 1820–1860." *American Quarterly* 18 (1966): 151–174.

RACHELLE E. FRIEDMAN

The Civil War and Reconstruction

The Civil War (1861–1865) and Reconstruction (1863–1877) eras bridged old and new pathways. Western expansion, industrial innovation, and foreign immigration all had their effects. Large-scale immigration into the West began in the 1840s, exposing Native Americans to Anglo foods, and vice versa. Native cultures suffered and European foodways gradually prevailed. The Lakota Sioux medicine man Sitting Bull referred to this when advising against assimilation in 1867: "The whites may get me at last . . . but I will have good times till then. You are fools to make yourselves slaves to a piece of fat bacon, some hard-tack, and a little sugar and coffee."

Soldiers' Food

Society's idea of the daily food needed for basic sustenance was reflected in the U.S. Army Civil War ration (1861–1864):

> . . . twelve ounces of pork or bacon, or, one pound and four ounces of salt or fresh beef; one pound and six ounces of soft bread or flour, or, one pound of hard bread, or, one pound and four ounces of corn meal; and to every one hundred rations, fifteen pounds of beans or peas, and ten pounds of rice or hominy; ten pounds of green coffee, or, eight pounds of roasted (or roasted and ground) coffee, or, one pound and eight ounces of tea; fifteen pounds of sugar; four quarts of vinegar; . . . three pounds and twelve ounces of salt; four ounces of pepper; thirty pounds of potatoes, when practicable, and one quart of molasses.

Whenever possible, troops supplemented government rations with found or purchased foods, such as ripe or unripe fruits and vegetables, or pies, cakes, and canned goods bought from sutlers (mobile storekeepers). Civil War soldier-cooks tried to imitate homemade fare, making soup, stew, hash, pudding, flapjacks, fried cakes, corndodgers, boiled or roasted corn, succotash, baked beans, lobscouse, and applesauce. How close these dishes came to the home-cooked original is open to question. In 1862 Private Wilbur Fisk from Vermont voiced a theme common to soldiers' cooking: "These . . . boys . . . out-Graham Sylvester Graham himself, in his most radical ideas of simplicity in diet. . . . Coarse meal, cold water and salt have been the ingredients composing many a meal for us, which a thanksgiving supper, in other circumstances, will scarcely rival."

Soldiers' humorous epithets signaled the importance of food: "dough bellies" (infantrymen), "chicken thieves" (cavalrymen), "Soft Breads" (Army of the Potomac soldiers), "pound-cake brethren" (easy-living soldiers), "coffee coolers" (stragglers), "Virginia rabbits" (pigs), "desecrated" (dessicated) vegetables, and a "square meal" (hardtack). Hardtack came to symbolize the soldier's life. Some men thought it inedible at first, but most came to agree with Lieutenant Fred Chapman, Twenty-ninth United States Colored Troops: "two pieces of hard-tack with a slice of raw, fat salt pork between—not a dainty meal, but solid provender to fight on." Major Frederick Hitchcock of Pennsylvania described a popular hardtack preparation. " 'Lobskous' . . . consisted of hardtack broken up and thoroughly soaked in water, then fried in pork fat."

Front-Line Restaurant. A sutler's bomb-proof "Fruit and Oyster House" on the front line in Petersburg, Virginia, 1864–1865. *Prints and Photographs Division, Library of Congress*

Cornmeal was a southern staple, and "cush" was a dish associated with Confederate troops. Sergeant William W. Heartsill from Texas described it in October 1863: "Well dinner is ready . . . prepared in this manner, chop up a small quantity of fat bacon into a frying pan, get the grease all out of it, put in a quart of water, when it boils crumble in cold corn bread and stir until dry, and you are ready for a dinner of 'CUSH.' " Another Texan, Second Lieutenant Robert M. Collins, added that " 'cush' . . . with some of the corn-bread burned to a black crisp, out of which we make coffee, was fine living." Real coffee, a prerequisite of Federal fare, having replaced the alcohol ration in October 1832, was often traded to southern soldiers for tobacco.

Alcohol was occasionally issued, and both officers and men continually sought other sources. Cornelia Hancock, a Quaker nurse from New Jersey, alluded to its widespread use in July 1864, "I introduced [brother William] to all my friends. They, of course, invited him to drink some whiskey which he refused to do . . . a very rare thing in the army." Sergeant Cyrus Boyd, Fifteenth Iowa Volunteers, told of soldiers' behavior in Tennessee in January 1863, "I took a ramble thro' Memphis. . . . Whiskey O Whiskey! Drunk men staggered on all the streets. . . . The streets were full of *drunk* men. The men who had fought their way from [Fort] Donelson to Corinth and who had met no enemy able to whip them now surrendered to Genl *Intoxication*."

Widespread alcohol consumption fueled the temperance movement. The Prohibition Party was founded in 1869, and the 1873–1874 Woman's Crusade resulted from years of female activism against alcohol consumption and traffic.

Civilians' Food

For wartime southerners, deprivation and make-do were the order of the day. Game animals, fish, and eggs replaced beef and pork, one wag remarking that a "hundred ways of cooking an egg became well-known in the Confederacy." Preserves made with sorghum instead of sugar "had a twang." Rice bread was called secession bread. And rye and other coffee substitutes were used. Occasionally meals were reminiscent of prewar plenty. Mary Chestnut of Charleston wrote in April 1861, "The supper was a consolation—*pâté de foie gras* salad, *biscuit glacé* and *champagne frappé.*" She wrote from Richmond, "*Christmas Day, 1863* . . . We had for dinner oyster soup, besides roast mutton, ham, boned turkey, wild duck, partridge, plum pudding, sauterne, burgundy, sherry, and Madeira. There is life in the old land yet!"; and on "*February 1st.* [1864]—Mrs. Davis gave her 'Luncheon to Ladies Only' . . . Gumbo, ducks and olives, chickens in jelly, oysters, lettuce salad, chocolate cream, jelly cake, claret, champagne, etc."

The nurse Cornelia Hancock's letters home to New Jersey show the variety of dishes possible in an 1864 Virginia army hospital. From Brandy Station, dated February 11, "Today the men had for their breakfast oysters, meat and breads. For dinner, soup, Turkey broth, corn and lima beans. For supper oysters, farina, bread, and butter. So you see, although out of the world we are of the world." She continues on March 2, "We had what is called here a splendid dinner—Ham, Eggs, Oyster pie, Roast Beef and Potatoes, peach tarts and cup custards." From City Point on July 4, "a real Fourth dinner, potatoes, beef, onions, canned peach pie, and corn starch pudding." And on July 18, "Twice have I given ice cream to my patients."

Canned Goods and Meatpacking

Large city-centered populations needed quantities of long-lasting, easily stored foodstuff. Armies on the march had the added requirement of portable, compact comestibles. While not an army-issue item, canned foods began to fill those needs. In 1870 Captain T. J. Wilson, tasked by the army to study the quality of American canned goods, wrote:

> Ten years ago Baltimore . . . cou'd boast no more than half a dozen packing establishments (there are now, December, 1867, at that place, from twenty-five

to thirty). . . . Hermetically sealed goods at that day sold for fabulous prices, and were consumed by a few only. The outbreak of the Rebellion, in 1861, brought about a sudden and remarkable change. Manufactories sprung up everywhere, and the demand for the supply for the army, through sutlers, became enormous.

A 1924 study noted that at the war's onset in 1861: "Probably five million cans of everything [was annually produced]. . . . In 1870 . . . the output reached thirty million cans. . . . Factories could not be built fast enough to supply customers. . . . Canneries were started inland for the first time, at Cincinnati, Indianapolis, and other places."

Wartime demand for meat fueled the growth of the western beef business. As a major rail-hub, and because of the Mississippi River blockade, Chicago benefited. By 1865 the new 320-acre Chicago Union Stock Yards were operating, attracting to the city the large meatpacking firms of Armour, Swift, Morris, and Hammond. According to the Chicago Historical Society, by 1900 Chicago's meatpacking industry employed more than 25,000 people and produced 82 percent of the meat consumed in the United States. The 1872 institution of meat coolers allowed year-round meatpacking, and the adoption of refrigerated rail cars in 1882 meant that processed meats could be transported over long distances.

Canned goods and refrigerated beef had become commonplace items at the supper table by the century's end. The U.S. Army subsisted on both in Cuba, Puerto Rico, and the Philippines in 1898.

[*See also* Armour, Philip Danforth; Canning and Bottling; Coffee Substitutes; Combat Food; Cookbooks and Manuscripts, *subentry* From the Civil War to World War I; Graham, Sylvester; Hardtack; Southern Regional Cookery; Swift, Gustavus Franklin; Temperance; Transportation of Food.]

BIBLIOGRAPHY

Acken, J. Gregory. *Inside the Army of the Potomac: The Civil War Experience of Captain Francis Adams Donaldson.* Mechanicsburg, PA: Stackpole Books, 1998.

Collins, James H. *The Story of Canned Foods.* New York: Dutton, 1924.

Connell, Evan S. *Son of the Morning Star: Custer and the Little Bighorn.* San Francisco: North Point Press, 1984.

Donald, David Herbert, ed. *Gone for a Soldier: The Civil War Memoirs of Private Alfred Bellard.* Boston: Little, Brown, 1975.

Jaquette, Henrietta Stratton. *Letters of a Civil War Nurse: Cornelia Hancock, 1863–1865.* Lincoln, NB, and London: University of Nebraska Press, 1998.

Martin, Isabella D., and Myrta Lockett Avary, eds. *A Diary from Dixie, as Written by Mary Boykin Chestnut.* New York: Appleton, 1905.

Massey, Mary Elizabeth. *Ersatz in the Confederacy: Shortages and Substitutes on the Southern Homefront.* Columbia: University of South Carolina Press, 1993.

Ohio State University. *Temperance and Prohibition.* Available at http://prohibition.history.ohio-state.edu/Contents.htm

Rawlings, Kevin. *We Were Marching on Christmas Day: A History and Chronicle of Christmas During the Civil War.* Baltimore: Toomey Press, 1996.

Rees, John U. "'The Foundation of an Army Is the Belly.' North American Soldiers' Food, 1756–1945." In *ALHFAM: Proceedings of the 1998 Conference and Annual Meeting,* vol. 21. Bloomfield, OH: Association for Living History, Farm, and Agricultural Museums, 1999. Also contains Continental and British army ration lists.

Strong, Robert Hale. *A Yankee Private's Civil War.* Edited by Ashley Halsey. Chicago: Henry Regnery, 1961.

Thomas, Samuel N., and Jason H. Silverman, eds. *A Rising Star of Promise: The Civil War Odyssey of David Jackson Logan, 17th South Carolina Volunteers, 1861–1864.* Campbell, CA: Savas, 1998.

Throne, Mildred, ed. *The Civil War Diary of Cyrus F. Boyd, Fifteenth Iowa Infantry, 1861–1863.* Baton Rouge: Louisiana State University Press, 1998.

Trudeau, Noah Andre. *Like Men of War: Black Troops in the Civil War, 1862–1865.* Boston: Little, Brown, 1998.

Wilson, T. J. *Notes on Canned Goods (Prepared Under the Direction of the Commissary General of Subsistence U.S.A.).* Washington, DC: Government Printing Office, 1870.

JOHN U. REES

From Victorian America to World War I

As the Industrial Revolution brought America into the machine age, its impact on agriculture transformed the way food was produced, purchased, and consumed. In the years from 1880 to the beginning of World War I, the American public began to change from a nation of producers to a nation of consumers. Everything from the way that food was grown, processed, and packaged to the manner in which it was distributed, purchased, and consumed was affected, as the marriage of science and agriculture created a more efficient, mechanized, and industrialized food system.

In the beginning of this period, the main processed foods available to consumers were items such as crackers, white flour, and refined sugar, produced locally and sold in bulk at the general store. For the most part, food processing was done in the home, with canned and preserved foods. It was during this era, however, that many of the commercially processed foods that have become mainstays of the American diet were developed by large food corporations that burst onto the landscape to become permanent fixtures of the American food industry.

The transition from the local and regional foodways of Victorian America to the national and international

New Appliances. Advertisement for the New Empire stove, c. 1875. *Collection of Kit Barry*

markets of the modern food system was made possible by advances in agriculture, transportation, and food processing, as well as the marketing and advertising revolutions of the era. By the time World War I began, nationally branded, mass-produced products that were individually wrapped, packaged, and canned were being purchased on a cash-and-carry basis from markets stocked with a wide array of processed goods—a far cry from the way that Americans were buying food just a few decades earlier.

In the years immediately following the Civil War, America was still very much an agrarian nation. The majority of the nation's workforce was employed in farming or farm-related activities, and local agriculture was a major factor determining one's diet. This meant that food was seasonal, and diets did not vary to a great degree. A family produced food to sell for a living, as well as for its own consumption. Traditionally, the men tended to the fields, and the women baked bread, canned fruits and vegetables, and otherwise processed, preserved, and prepared food for the household.

Goods the household needed were purchased at the local general store, where an array of barrels, bins, and jars greeted customers, and large slabs of products like cheese and butter sat on the counter. Patrons requested the desired amount of these bulk items, and the clerk skillfully cut off a piece of butter or cheese from the slab, scooped flour from the bin or crackers from the barrel, and wrapped the items or placed them into a receptacle supplied by the customer. Next, a price was determined. The day of fixed prices for goods had not yet dawned, so the cost of these items was left to the bargaining skills of customer and clerk. The totals were then added to the

customers' credit account, and at the end of the week, month, or year, depending on the retailer, they were tallied up for payment. It was a simple system that would soon be rendered a relic of the past.

Advances in Agriculture

The union of science and agriculture is one of the defining characteristics of this period. An era of research and testing in the agricultural sphere dramatically increased production on American farms, increased the nation's food supply, and hastened the movement from the local food system to the industrial model. The starting point of this development was the federal Hatch Act of 1887, which provided that agricultural experiment stations be established in every state, administered by the land grant colleges and universities that had been created by the Morrill Act of 1862. The annual grants provided by the Hatch Act strengthened the curricula at land grant institutions and funded agricultural research. The work of these institutions reached an even larger audience as extension programs disseminated the results of the experiments to farmers and other rural groups. This system led to widespread efficiency in farming methods and hardier strains of hybrid seeds for wheat, corn, soybeans, and other crops.

As a result of this research, the time between planting and harvesting crops decreased, along with the costs of the farming. Between 1875 and 1915, U.S. production of most staple crops doubled, and wheat production tripled. Dairy farming also increased, as ranchers developed ways to produce stronger animals, and the corn and hog belts expanded as larger tracts of farmland were purchased farther and farther west. This increased production also served to lower prices on agricultural products, making more items affordable to all Americans. However, farmers were now receiving lower prices for their goods, necessitating even greater output to make the same profits. The movement toward larger acreages, mechanization, and crop specialization was underway.

The huge farms established in the 1870s and 1880s in Minnesota, Nebraska, Kansas, and the central region of California foreshadowed the future of American agriculture. These farms advertised the abundance of land available in the west, and they were called bonanza farms, the name suggesting the potential lucrative benefits for those willing to take the risk on such a venture. Bonanza farms consisted of enormous tracts of land, organized and mechanized, each with its own manager and staff of farmhands. In the Red River Valley of the

Dakotas alone, 34 million acres were dedicated to bonanza farming. Settlers were lured westward by the image of seemingly limitless land, money, and the employment opportunities that these farms displayed. However, years of wheat farming eventually exhausted the land and grain prices dropped. By World War I, the era of bonanza farming was over, although the ideas it introduced remained.

In addition to their size, these farms were noted for their use of farming implements like ploughs, grain drills and combines. As agriculture became more commercial and farms grew larger, the increased workload created a need for more mechanical equipment. Many, like the mechanical reaper and the steel plough, had been invented several decades earlier. Between 1870 and 1920, the value of farm equipment in use went from $271 million to $3.6 billion. Grain elevators and silos began marking the new rural landscape, made possible in part by the ability to transport goods produced on commercial farms in the West to cities and urban centers in the East.

Transportation and Distribution

With the completion of the first transcontinental railroad in 1869 and the increased use of the refrigerated railroad car, which had first been used in 1867 to transport fresh produce, railroads became a key factor in the industrialization of food. Railroads enabled food to be shipped across the country and lessened the importance of local and regional markets. The system opened up competition among food producers and helped entice settlers to the huge expanses of inexpensive land in the West, from which the goods produced could now be easily transported to consumers and processors. Railroads helped make large-scale agriculture more economical. As farms grew bigger, farmers and the railroaders became more dependent on each other.

Everything from the way meat was brought to market to the selection of vegetables available in different areas of the country was dramatically affected by the railroad, particularly by the refrigerated car. The improved transportation system transformed the meat industry and increased the availability and affordability of meat products. Gustavus F. Swift, a Chicago meatpacker, perfected the system of transporting midwestern meat to markets in the East in 1879. Before that time, cattle were shipped east on the hoof, to be slaughtered close to the markets where they would be sold. Swift fattened, slaughtered, and dressed the beef in Chicago and brought it to market in refrigerated rail cars. This method yielded fresher, less expensive meat, available to a broader population.

Refrigerated shipping also allowed fruits and vegetables from warm climates to be marketed far from the farms, and made it possible for dairy products to be carried to market without spoilage. Fresh fruits, vegetables and milk became available all year, even to those living in urban areas. Furthermore, as crops grown in California could now be shipped to New York, season and locale were no longer determining factors in the American diet. As a national market for food became a reality, efficient production and distribution gave Americans a wider variety of agricultural products at lower cost.

Another result of the shipping of fresh vegetables around the country was the creation of new types of crops designed to withstand the journey to market. Georgia growers, for example, developed a new strain of longer-lasting peaches that could be shipped to distant markets before perishing. Lettuce was another item that was very delicate and difficult to ship until a strain of lettuce called "iceberg" was developed in 1903, transforming lettuce from an expensive and rare treat to a food product for the masses.

Food Processing

The increased agricultural output and ever-growing food supply could not be handled by the traditional methods of processing food. New technologies were created to capitalize on agricultural advances and by the end of this period, food processing would account for 20 percent of the nation's manufacturing, mostly dominated by several large companies. The changes in food processing methods during this period can be illustrated through the example of flour milling. Before the 1880s neighborhood and regional millers ground wheat into flour by crushing the grain between two stones and then passing it through a cloth to remove the outer bran shell. When wheat was being produced on a large scale, more efficient methods of milling were sought out. Steel rollers that could remove the outer shell more completely and efficiently became the preferred method of milling. Since these rollers were expensive, only larger companies could afford to purchase them, thus pushing the smaller millers without sufficient capital out of business. In the two years between 1884 and 1886, more than six thousand flour mills went out of business, and large companies like Washburn and Pillsbury competed to become national brands.

As mass production spread through all areas of industry, production methods were broken down into routine tasks designed to reduce the time and the expense required to make each item. The ideas expressed by Fredrick

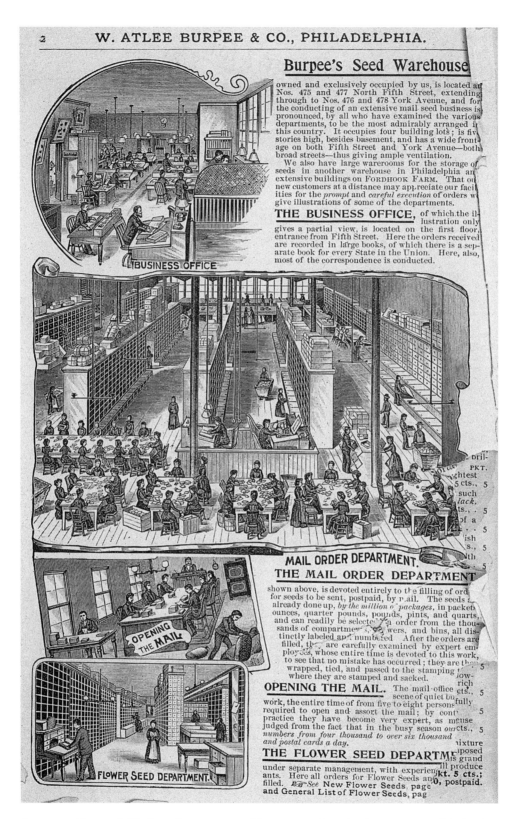

Serving a National Market. Interior views of Burpee's seed mail-order operation, Philadelphia, 1893.

W. Taylor in his writings on scientific management in 1911 represented dominant themes in American business during this era. "Maximum prosperity can exist only as a result of maximum productivity," Taylor wrote. Saving time became the prevailing business goal, machinery replaced skilled labor, and the quest for profit replaced respect for traditional production methods. Corporations that could afford to mechanize sought to exploit the economies of scale in mass production, and the techniques of mass production enabled the processed food industry to flourish. Although the tin can was first used to preserve food in 1810, canned products were not able to supply a mass market until after 1880, when a process for mass producing cans from tin plate was invented. By 1910 it was possible for one machine to produce 35,000 cans a day. Companies such as the Van Camp Packing Company, Franco American, and the Joseph P. Campbell Soup Company emerged during this period, taking advantage of these and other methods of making food processing profitable.

As food companies sought to create demand for their product, they realized that one way to do this was by replacing items traditionally produced in the home with those mass-produced in factories. In 1870 the technology for packaging under steam pressure made large-scale glass jarring possible. Combined with the availability of inexpensive cans after 1880, this enabled firms such as the H. J. Heinz Company to mass-produce foods that were usually canned or preserved at home and sell them for a low enough price to entice consumers to try them. By 1900 Heinz was the nation's largest food processor, selling over 200 different food products. Heinz also worked on improving seeds, developed contracts with farmers, and had its own railroad cars. The Heinz model of vertical integration was emulated by competitors, and soon many companies not only controlled the processing stage of the food system, but a portion of the entire industry, from seed to grocery shelves.

Meanwhile, the Joseph P. Campbell Soup Company, one of Heinz's biggest competitors, was making breakthroughs of its own. In 1897 the company introduced condensed soups. With the water removed, the soup could be packaged in smaller cans, shipped for less, and stored in less space. The company passed on the savings to the consumer, lowering the cost of a can of condensed soup to ten cents, while competitors were charging at least thirty cents for a can of noncondensed soup. It was not long before the Campbell's label was one of the most recognizable on the shelves.

Packaging, Branding, and Advertising

Before the period of mass production and shipping, packaging was not a necessity in the food industry, but the shipment of food outside of local areas required some kind of package in which the product could be protected from damage. The paper bag came into wide use after the Civil War, and was the first kind of packaging used for food. The first cardboard packages were round or oval in shape and took up too much space when they were empty to make them acceptable for many companies. The year 1879 brought a solution to this dilemma when Robert Gair, a paper-bag manufacturer in New York, invented machines that produced flat, foldable cardboard boxes.

As food processing technologies created products that were similar to each other, branding and labeling were developed to advertise and differentiate one company's product from the next. Packaging of food became increasingly widespread after 1900, even in general stores where food that had once been sold in bulk was now being packaged and branded. A classic example is provided by the National Biscuit Company (Nabisco), founded in 1898. The cracker barrel had been a mainstay in general stores across the country well into the Victorian era. This changed when the National Biscuit Company started to ship its product and came up with the name Uneeda Biscuit. A national brand was born, and its five-cent product in patented moisture-proof packaging ended the reign of the cracker barrel. By 1900 Uneeda's sales were over 10 million packages a month, while other brands were selling about forty thousand packages.

Part of the success of Uneeda Biscuit can be attributed to Nabisco's large expenditures for advertising in newspapers, in magazines, and on billboards and streetcars. The food industry was a major factor in the rise of the U.S. advertising business during the period, as national brands wielded enormous budgets to make their products household names.

An outstanding advertising success story was dry breakfast cereal. One of the original convenience foods, dry breakfast cereals were made from highly processed grains, could be purchased in neat, tightly sealed packages, and required no cooking. In 1906 the Battle Creek Toasted Corn Flake Company was incorporated and spent two-thirds of its budget on advertising. Corn flakes had never before been part of the American diet, but as a result of its packaging, advertising, and promotion, the product was embraced by Americans. The cereal companies like the C. W. Post Company, the Kellogg Company

Advertising Canned Foods. Advertisements for Van Camp's soups and Durkee salad dressing that appeared in *The American Montly Illustrated Review of Reviews,* November 1899. *Collection of Georgia Maas*

and their imitators advertised their wares as nutritious, a claim that was becoming more of a selling point during this period. Cereals were also promoted as clean and more sterile because of their packaging, an idea that was equally compelling. The success of the breakfast cereal industry prompted many other companies to note the effectiveness of packaging and advertising.

As the cereal industry proved, advertising can create a demand where none had existed before. To take full advantage of the economies of scale of mass production, farms and factories needed to operate at full capacity, often producing more goods than consumers actually needed or demanded. In order to remain profitable, corporations relied on advertising to create a demand. It was during this period that Americans saw the rise of national brands and big corporations with enormous advertising budgets.

In 1892 Heinz adopted its 57 Varieties trademark and slogan and promoted its product in many ways, including a money-back guarantee, free samples, and enormous signs. In 1894 Van Camp became the first company to take out a full-page advertisement for a food product in a national magazine. Campbell's became particularly adept at using print advertising to promote its products. Advertising and mass production made skill in selling food more important than skill in producing food in determining a product's success.

The increased availability of individually packaged goods, the growth of national brands, and improved distribution systems dramatically affected the way that food was sold and purchased once it got to market. The independent general store of the Victorian era gave way first to the grocery chain stores, where individually packaged goods with fixed prices replaced the need for clerks to dole out bulk items and determine their price. Still later, the arrival of self-service markets would further reduce the need for sales clerks. With the dawn of the packaging revolution, markets were no longer just selling food, they were selling appearance as well.

Grocers realized that attractively packaged, nationally advertised brands increased their sales. The Great American Tea Company (later renamed the Great Atlantic and Pacific Tea Company, or A&P) in New York City is often credited with introducing modern merchandising methods. The owners, George Huntington Hartford and George F. Gilman, were able to undersell their competitors by purchasing food close to the source and in large quantities in order to eliminate the middleman. The company rapidly grew into a national chain.

There were sixty-seven A&Ps in 1876, nearly five hundred in 1912, and one thousand by 1915.

Purchasers for chain stores such as the A&P had much more buying power than the owners of individual groceries because one purchaser acquired goods for several stores at a time. These buyers sought out larger producers, further encouraging large-scale mass production. As agribusiness prospered, small farmers who could not compete were forced to take factory jobs in urban areas, thus becoming part of the industrial economy. Between 1870 and 1920, the number of people living in cities increased from 10 million to 54 million. In 1850 approximately 85 percent of the U.S. population was engaged in farm-related work, but by 1900, because of competition and falling agriculture commodity prices, this number had fallen to 60 percent, and it continued to drop throughout the twentieth century. This shift stimulated the food industry, creating more demand for quantity and diversity of products in urban areas. Every facet of the industrial food system thrived as more people depended on the industry for what they ate.

Food Purity

Promoting products as pure and healthy became a major strategy in the advertising of processed food. The discovery of bacteria in the 1880s raised awareness of food safety issues and created a demand for food that was free of germs. Sterile foods such as refined sugar and flour, goods tightly packed and sealed, and canned goods seemed more attractive than brown sugar, goods sold in bulk, or even fresh fruits and vegetables.

Yet the processing of food far from the source of its production also raised concerns about food safety. In the early 1900s the United States government recognized the need to regulate the food industry. Demands for pure, clean food were set off by a growing awareness of how little was known about what went on in the nation's factories and processing plants. As pure food laws were being passed in the U.S. Senate, the publication of Upton Sinclair's *The Jungle* in 1906 awoke consumers to the unsanitary conditions in meat processing plants.

The Pure Food and Drug Act of 1906 called for the labeling of ingredients in packaged food and prohibited the sale of mislabeled or adulterated products. These regulations favored large corporations over the long term, as smaller processors could not afford to comply with the new laws. Capitalizing on consumer demand for pure products, Kellogg's, Heinz, Franco-American, and even the Armour meat packing company turned a potential public-relations catastrophe into a marketing strategy by opening their doors to the public and demonstrating the cleanliness of their facilities.

Concern over infant mortality rates led to increased regulation in the milk industry. In 1908 the nation's first compulsory pasteurization law was passed in Chicago, but it was not until 1914 that commercial pasteurization was made possible by mechanization and pasteurized milk could be sold at competitive prices. Again, the equipment required for this process was too expensive for small manufacturers, and they suffered the same fate as their counterparts in other industries.

As the nation's food supply became more industrialized, there was a growing disconnection between Americans and the food they consumed. In these decades, many Americans went from producing their own food, or at the very least consuming food produced locally, to purchasing food from places they had never even visited. No longer restricted to seasonal foods, grocery stores from the East Coast to the West began selling identical products, and the food industry became increasingly consolidated. The remarkable changes in the food production and distribution system permanently affected the nation's eating habits and eventually wreaked havoc on the environment.

[*See also* Advertising; Armour, Philip Danforth; Campbell Soup Company; Canning and Bottling; Cookbooks and Manuscripts, *subentry* From the Civil War to World War I; Food Marketing; Grocery Stores; Heinz Foods; Kellogg Company; Nabisco; Pillsbury; Post Foods; Pure Food and Drug Act; Transportation of Food.]

BIBLIOGRAPHY

Coppin, Clayton A., and Jack High. *The Politics of Purity: Harvey Washington Wiley and the Origins of Federal Food Policy.* Ann Arbor: University of Michigan Press, 1999.

Cummings, Richard Osborne. *The American and His Food: A History of Food Habits in the United States.* Chicago: University of Chicago Press, 1940. Rev. ed., 1970.

Harper, Charles L. *Food, Society, and Environment.* Upper Saddle River, NJ: Prentice Hall, 2003.

Levenstein, Harvey. *Revolution at the Table: The Transformation of the American Diet.* New York: Oxford University Press, 1988.

Magdoff, Fred, John Bellamy Foster, and Frederick H. Buttel, eds. *Hungry for Profit: The Agribusiness Threat to Farmers, Food, and the Environment.* New York: Monthly Review Press, 2000.

Norris, Frank. *The Octopus.* New York: Doubleday, 1901. Set in California's Central Valley, this book offers insight into bonanza farming and the railroads during this period.

Root, Waverly, and Richard de Rochemont. *Eating in America: A History.* New York: Morrow, 1976.

Schlereth, Thomas J. *Victorian America: Transformations in Everyday Life. 1876–1915.* New York: Harper Collins, 1991.

Shapiro, Laura. *Perfection Salad: Women and Cooking at the Turn of the Century.* New York: Farrar, Straus & Giroux, 1986. A look

at domestic science and how what happened in American kitchens encouraged the acceptance of industrialized food.

Sinclair, Upton. *The Jungle.* New York: Doubleday Page, 1906. The conditions in meat packing plants in Chicago.

Smith, Andrew F. *Souper Tomatoes: The Story of America's Favorite Food.* New Brunswick: Rutgers University Press, 2000. Information on the canning and soup industries.

Strasser, Susan. *Satisfaction Guaranteed: The Making of the American Mass Market.* Washington: Smithsonian Press, 1995. A history of the advertising industry.

Taylor, Fredrick W. *The Principles of Scientific Management.* New York, London: Harper, 1911.

Trager, James. *The Food Chronology: A Food Lover's Compendium of Events and Anecdotes, From Prehistory to the Present.* New York: Holt, 1995. When and where it all happened.

Williams, Susan. *Savory Suppers and Fashionable Feasts: Dining in Victorian America.* Knoxville: University of Tennessee Press, 1996.

ALISON TOZZI

World War I

By the time the United States entered World War I in April 1917, the war had been raging for three years and food was desperately needed to supply America's European allies. American civilians were urged to conserve food by increasing production, cutting waste, and substituting plentiful for scarce foods in their diet. President Woodrow Wilson placed exports of foodstuffs, fuel, iron, and steel under government control as war matériel. Congress passed the Food and Fuel Control Act (Lever Act), and the future U.S. president Herbert C. Hoover, who had served as chairman of the Commission for Relief in Belgium, was appointed to head the U.S. Food Administration in 1917. Hoover exhorted U.S. farmers with the slogan, "Food can win the war."

The government instituted limited control over the production and distribution of food during the war but did not ration food for civilians at first. For example, the government limited sugar purchases by industrial manufacturers, wholesale producers, and retailers, while encouraging domestic consumers to use sugar in home canning to preserve as much food as possible. Consumers were entitled to purchase sugar in twenty-five-pound quantities for that purpose, and to minimize waste. Rather than rationing, Hoover's early mandate was to persuade Americans to cut back voluntarily on consumption of beef, wheat, and other foodstuffs that were needed by U.S. and Allied troops in Europe.

U.S. wheat prices rose precipitously in the spring of 1917 as Allied governments, American millers, and speculators bid up prices on the Chicago Board of Trade. The Grain Corporation, part of Hoover's U.S. Food Administration, bought, stored, transported, and sold wheat and fixed its price at $2.20 per bushel under the terms of the Lever Act.

Although certain areas of Europe, most notably Belgium, suffered from food shortages throughout "The Great War," the United Kingdom was hit harder by labor shortage than by food shortage in the early years. Although luxury goods such as alcoholic beverages, sugar, cheese, and butter were scarce and expensive, staples such as bread, milk, and beef were still relatively available thanks to generous subsidies. It was not until late 1917 and early 1918—in retrospect, the period deemed to be the height of distress for Europe—that rationing was instituted. Prior to 1918, British civilians were encouraged to conserve foodstuffs, but institutionalized rationing began in January 1918, beginning with sugar and continuing with meat and butter.

The United States only began its conservation measures after the country entered World War I. During wartime, a greater effort became necessary in order to feed U.S. citizens, send provisions to soldiers in Europe, and supply much of the food of U.S. Allies, both civilian and military. U.S. sugar rationing began in mid-1918, with each citizen allowed eight ounces per week. Sugar prices soared, and the black market for consumer goods proliferated. Hoover established special conservation days, urging Americans to eat no wheat on Mondays and Wednesdays, no meat on Tuesdays, and no pork on Thursdays and Saturdays. He also asked citizens to eat whole wheat "victory bread" in place of white bread. To replace the factory-canned vegetables that were sent overseas to feed soldiers and the Allies, people were urged to raise vegetables in vacant lots or yards, called "Liberty gardens," in order to bring fresh, home-canned, and dried produce to the table. For many Americans, the wartime restrictions resulted in a more nutritious diet of whole wheat bread, less sugar, and more fresh vegetables than usual.

World War I helped move the baking of bread from the home to commercial bakeries as more women took work outside the home, leaving less time for baking. Besides, the government asked both bakers and the public to bake with flours that combined several grains, mixtures that were difficult for householders to obtain. Home cooks developed new and imaginative ways of using low-grade war flour and wheat substitutes in their recipes. They used syrup and molasses instead of sugar and found substitutes for lard, butter, and meat to feed their families; the relatively new vegetable shortening, Crisco, became a substitute for butter or lard, and peanut butter emerged as a protein substitute for meat.

Hoover's Food Administration sponsored a major education campaign to familiarize people with calories, vitamins, proteins, carbohydrates, the values of fruits and vegetables, and the best means of canning, preserving, and drying foods. A multitude of pamphlets, posters, advertisements, and other documents were produced to help teach the rules of substitution and persuade Americans that eating less would not harm their health and might even improve it. Even the press, schools, and clergy pitched in to preach what became known as "the doctrine of the clean plate."

World War I gave many Americans their first taste of vegetarian meals as home cooks introduced dishes like bean loaf to the dinner menu to replace meat loaf. Soybeans, later a staple of vegetarian diets, also gained space in Americans' awareness, if not yet on most dinner tables. For example, in 1918 U.S. Secretary of Agriculture David F. Houston issued a circular entitled, "Use Soy-Bean Flour to Save Wheat, Meat, and Fat." It included recipes for "victory bread," soybean "meat loaf," and soybean "mush croquettes." However, few U.S. farmers produced soybeans, few facilities existed to process the beans, and few stores carried soybean products. Soybeans were produced more widely starting in 1920.

While U.S. consumers observed voluntary rationing, or "conservation," during the war, consumers in some Western European countries were subject to compulsory rationing. Some scholars, such as Amy Bentley, in her book *Eating for Victory*, suggest that voluntary rationing during World War I did not work for everyone. Better-educated and more affluent Americans observed no-wheat and meatless days, but immigrants and those in the working classes were less likely to do so and in many cases ate more meat as their incomes rose. These inconsistent conservation habits also contributed to rampant price inflation, panic about food supplies, hoarding of food, and black-market sales of scarce food items.

On November 11, 1918, World War I ended in an armistice. "Hunger does not breed reform; it breeds madness," said President Wilson in his Armistice Day address to Congress. All food regulations were suspended in the United States by December 1918 but remained in effect in Britain and Europe for several months thereafter.

[*See also* International Aid; Kitchen Gardening; Nutrition; Peanuts; Soybeans.]

BIBLIOGRAPHY

Archer, Mary, comp. *Belgian Relief Cook Book*. Reading, PA.: Ladies of the Belgian Relief Committee, 1915.

Bentley, Amy. *Eating for Victory: Food Rationing and the Politics of Domesticity*. Urbana and Chicago: University of Illinois Press, 1998.

Clymer, Dr. R. Swinburne. *The American Volunteer Cook Book*. Quakertown, PA: The Rosicrucian Aid, 1918.

Elizabeth, Mary. *Mary Elizabeth's War Time Recipes*. New York: Stokes, 1918.

Handy, Amy L. *War Food: Practical and Economical Methods of Keeping Vegetables, Fruits and Meats*. Boston and New York: Houghton Mifflin, 1917.

Haskin, Frederic J. *War Cook Book for American Women: Suggestions for Patriotic Service in the Home*. Washington, DC: U.S. Food Administration, 1917.

Hiller, Elizabeth O. *The Corn Cook Book*. War ed. Chicago: Volland, 1918.

Women's Central Committee on Food Conservation. *Patriotic Food Show: Official Recipe Book*. St. Louis, MO: Wilson, 1918. Containing all demonstrations given during Patriotic Food Show. St. Louis, February 2–10, 1918.

U.S. Army. *Extracts from Manual for Army Cooks*. Washington, DC: Government Printing Office, 1917.

KARA NEWMAN

From World War I to World War II

Changes in American food from roughly 1915 to 1945 must be seen in the context of larger demographic and cultural changes.

Demographic and Social Changes

The increased entry of women into the work force, for example, affected the number of hours spent preparing meals in the home; the emergence of children and teenagers as a recognizable market segment contributed to the spread of soft drinks, candy, candy-coated bubble gum, and ice cream–based treats. A long-standing trend of rural depopulation with a shrinking farm-labor pool (attested in the watershed 1920 census, when urban residents first outnumbered rural) was hastened by an approaching farm-price crisis (see below). Its effects were accentuated by the 1924 National Origins Act, which all but ended immigration from anywhere except northwestern Europe and the British Isles. For many rural areas, shutting off the flow of immigrants from Italy, other "undesirable" parts of Europe, and Japan meant shutting off supplies of new farm workers. As the rural population struggled to hold on, city dwellers ironically came to have access to a better, more varied supply of fresh foods than farmers.

To some extent, the drying-up of immigration made earlier interethnic tensions less visible (though this certainly did not happen with Japanese farmers in California). From a culinary viewpoint, the 1924 cutoff allowed at least some assimilation to proceed in a fairly amicable way for the next forty years. Well before 1930, the elements of the great 1880–1920 immigrant waves that had been widely viewed as most alien to American culture—southern Italians and eastern European Jews—were grafting American food habits onto their own traditions in varying degrees. In the 1920s and 1930s, a few already somewhat familiar ethnic dishes entered mainstream foodways in versions—often canned—acceptable to everyone: chop suey, spaghetti, chili con carne, and goulash. Meanwhile, general American cookbooks were including other quasi-ethnic items like "Spanish rice" (probably a bastardized version of a Spanish-descended rice dish like *arroz a la mexicana*), "tamale pie" (also considered Mexican), ravioli, and "Swedish meatballs."

Culinary fads and fashions blossomed with the aid of mass communication developments like national radio networks, news wire services, syndicated newspaper features, movies, expanded "lifestyle" coverage in newspapers and magazines, and highly visible national advertising campaigns (often presented in several media at once). After World War I, Americans became increasingly aware of brand names. This partly mirrored a growing "consumerist" view that national productivity directly depended on getting the public to adopt purchasing/using-up/repurchasing habits on the largest possible scale. It also reflected a major shift away from foods sold in bulk and toward prepackaged goods distributed to the new self-service stores. Criteria other than those fostered by ads and package labels became less visible to shoppers while the range of shopping choices grew explosively. New, catchily titled cold breakfast cereals, nickel candy bars and frozen snacks, and bottled sauces appeared in profusion. Products like prepackaged cheese (Kraft, ca. 1915) and bread (Wonder Bread in the 1920s), instant puddings (My*T*Fine, 1918), mixes (Bisquick, 1930), and canned or bottled fruit juices (successive introductions, mostly in the 1920s) were aggressively brought to public notice. As coverage of food-related topics expanded in print media and on the radio, food journalists helped consumers keep up with food "discoveries" and shopping opportunities. Clementine Paddleford's food-news column in the *New York Herald-Tribune*, starting in 1936, showed the degree of public eagerness for trend-spotting. Journalists also aided in the quest—often spearheaded in manufacturers' test kitchens—to expand the uses of existing products in unexpected contexts, as in "mystery cake" made with canned tomato soup or "mock apple pie" made with Ritz crackers.

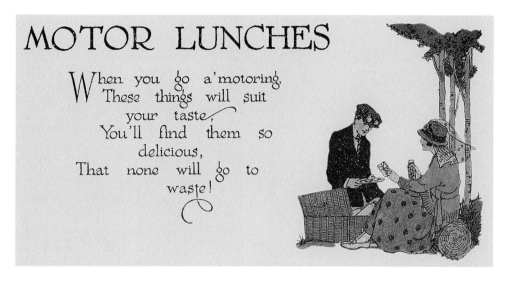

Impact of Motor Travel. Cover of a packet of recipe cards with picnic foods suitable for transportation by automobile, 1920s. *Collection of Alice Ross*

Multiplication of discretionary spending choices, the hallmark of the post-1915 consumer culture, transformed not only food shopping but public eating. In the interwar era, eating out became permanently understood as not just a pleasure for the wealthy or a convenience to office workers and travelers, but a recreational activity open to all classes in different forms. In any mid-sized town, the citizenry could expect several choices—particularly for casual meals or "a quick bite"—suitable to different pocketbooks, age groups, social ambitions, occasions, and even moods. By 1930, vast numbers of middle-class and working-class people were familiar with coffee shops, drugstore or five-and-dime lunch counters, luncheonettes or lunchrooms, cafeterias, diners, cheap ethnic eateries (usually Chinese or Italian), "tea shoppes," hamburger joints, drugstore soda fountains, pushcarts, candy stores, and places devoted to some regional specialty like "shore dinners." Except in large cities, the only upscale choice was likely to be a hotel dining room.

The impact of motor travel on American food habits was nowhere more striking than in the national restaurant landscape. Inexpensive popular restaurants accessible by road—drive-ins, roadhouses, ice cream or frozen-custard stands, chili shacks, and visual-gimmick establishments like restaurants in the shape of giant hot dogs—owed their existence to the automobile. By the late 1930s, American drivers could consult Duncan Hines's regularly updated coast-to-coast restaurant guide *Adventures in Good Eating*. Automobiles made shorter hops feasible—

for example, day trips from city to picnic site or roadside farm stand (one of the few remaining direct-sales options for farmers)—and helped expand home-delivery routes for milk, meat, bakery products, and fresh produce. Increased mobility helped awaken American curiosity about regional cuisines, which had, however, never been as prominently developed as journalists imagined (with the exception of the South). On the whole, however, cars speeded up the obliteration of regional differences more than they illuminated them and also played a large role in the effacement of farmland in the orbit of cities.

Packaged Foods

Meanwhile, the act of retail food shopping had also been profoundly altered. On the eve of World War I, most families filled everyday food needs at several different places carrying different specialties: butcher shop, bakery, grocery (for provisions like flour, sugar, and coffee), and greengrocer's shop or public market for fresh produce—though the markets were already in decline. Most items were either loose, stored in bulk, or (in the case of meat and cheese) cut to order; the proprietor or a clerk filled customer requests. The advent of self-service stores, starting in 1916 with the first Memphis store of the eventually huge Piggly Wiggly chain, aided in a transition to packaged retail goods, which as noted above supported the new consumerist mentality by increasing the visibility of brand names. The change tended to blur consumer understanding of food's innate variability, which a generation or two back knowledgeable retailers could have pointed out to customers. When the self-service idea was carried to the next logical step in the giant supermarkets that sprang up during the Depression (heralded in 1930 by King Kullen on Long Island), the hold of prepackaged foods on American shopping habits became overwhelming.

Manufacturers, bottlers, and packagers assured the public that food and drink in sealed containers was purer and more hygienic than that exposed to human touch, and they pointed to the merit of labels printed with the exact amounts of the contents. As loose and bulk goods lost ground, customers came to value a high degree of sameness in the foods they bought, regardless of place or season.

As an increasingly urbanized America learned new habits of consumption, it also turned to new models of kitchen organization made possible by the spread of public utilities—electricity, gas, expanded water systems. By about 1915, household-engineering experts were successfully arguing for small, compact kitchens that combined modern gas or electric stoves with a new use of space involving ingeniously designed built-in shelves and cabinets. The disappearance of kitchen ranges that required building and maintaining an actual fire for a day's cooking made quick-cooking foods like steaks, chops, hamburgers, and canned vegetables more practical meal options. The new flip-of-a-switch stoves contributed to impulse cooking and helped boost the rising importance of canned prepared sauces, soups (which multiplied swiftly in the 1920s and 1930s), and entrees (ready-to-heat ham, meat stews, chicken à la king, tamales, enchiladas, and ravioli, among other items). Cheap lightweight pots and pans of aluminum or enameled steel, suitable for can-opener cookery, became many households' preferred cookware. Better-insulated iceboxes and (after about 1930) mechanical refrigerators encouraged larger purchases of fresh (usually pasteurized) fluid milk, which by now had become a necessity urged on all families by nutritionists, though canned milk retained a role in infant formulas.

Between the wars, many kitchens acquired electric toasters, waffle irons, and coffee percolators. Electric mixers (introduced in home versions in the 1920s) and blenders (popularized in home-bartender versions by the bandleader Fred Waring in the late 1930s) gained more slowly. Ovenproof borosilicate glass baking dishes like the Corning Glass Company's Pyrex line were introduced before 1920; pressure cookers of manageable dimensions with saucepan-like handles became widespread after the

mid-1930s. Disposable paper goods like absorbent paper towels and waxed paper grew in importance, foreshadowing the expanded role of throwaway products after World War II.

The actual content of meals was now surrounded by ceaseless, often intimidating dietary advice reaching the public from two different directions. On the one hand, the fetish of a pencil-slim female body type after about 1910 drove many affluent and middle-class women to an obsession with pound-shedding that was continually nourished by a burgeoning weight-loss literature. Professional dietetics experts, meanwhile, had attained a remarkable pinnacle of authority from which, during and just after World War I, they launched aggressive public education campaigns chiefly aimed at schoolchildren and parents.

The usual eat-to-lose strategies, inspired by journalistic treatment of calories as a kind of scientifically validated sin index, urged the avoidance of "fattening foods" and touted the benefits of various low-caloric or low-fat items, often in supposedly magical combinations. Butter, lard, cream, potatoes, and bread were to be

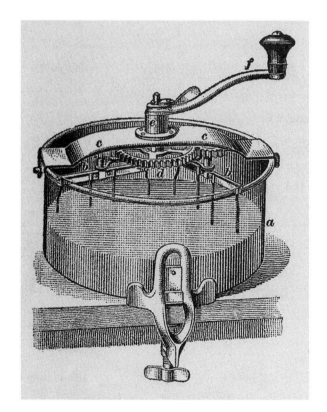

Cake Mixer. From *Woman's Institute Library of Cookery: Essentials of Cookery, Cereals, Breads, Hot Breads* (Scranton, Pa., 1924), sec. 2, p. 6.

shunned; among the foods periodically hailed as reducers' secrets were grapefruit, melba toast, spinach, cottage cheese, and skim milk, which orthodox dietitians considered a poor substitute for whole milk.

The nutritional experts went along with the slimmers' agenda up to the point of wanting people to distinguish between adequate and excessive intakes of different foods. But their real concerns were shaped by the great wave of vitamin discoveries that began in 1912 (being amplified by other breakthroughs in the 1930s), and the nutritional-patriotism initiatives of World War I. These events had helped spread the knowledge that in time of need, cheap, plentiful foods could sometimes be substituted for more prestigious scarce ones (e.g., fish or eggs for beef) with no nutritional disadvantage, and that fresh fruits and vegetables were supremely vital to health—a major break with earlier experts' priorities.

During the 1920s, American eating habits came to reflect parts of these new scientific or cosmetic beliefs. By the early 1940s, some general-purpose cookbooks included calorie charts and a few reducers' recipes. Meanwhile, the experts' advice about calcium propelled fresh fluid milk sales upward, and praise of vitamin C made orange juice ubiquitous on breakfast tables. Carrots and leafy green vegetables were regularly added to family regimens; cold breakfast cereals came to be thought of as rich sources of B vitamins or aids to "regularity"; canned fruits and fruit juices found a large sales niche; grapefruit overcame an earlier reputation for unpalatability and became nearly as familiar as oranges. The experts' praise of raw fruit and minimal processing of some foods inspired a school of faddists who urged eating everything possible raw, often in the form of machine-squeezed juices.

Generally speaking, the diet of the American working and middle classes probably broadened in variety and improved in vitamin content during most of this period. Certain advances in understanding found practical application during World War I and the Depression, when dietetics experts tried to teach consumers to stretch food dollars further by using beans and grains as alternative protein sources. In another dietary initiative, flour to be used under federal purchasing programs in World War II was required to be enriched with B vitamins and iron. The proliferation of dubious or exaggerated health claims on behalf of commercial products, however, suggested a fairly weak public grasp of nutritional preaching, while a simultaneous surge in weight-loss nostrums presaged unfortunate future trends in popular dietary priorities.

Farming Changes

Shifting dietary emphases and food fashions between the wars dictated corresponding shifts in some kinds of farm production. But from the early 1920s on, American agriculture was wracked by a series of crises first triggered by large wartime production increases. The face of regional agriculture changed in ways reflecting both the overall decline in rural population and the advent of "factories in the field," as the labor-partisan journalist Carey McWilliams called the new array of large-scale, capital-intensive farms dedicated to single cash crops. The greatest growth opportunities were for horticultural crops, the new nutritional stars, fruits and vegetables. These opportunities in turn mirrored the decline of small local farms in the near neighborhood of cities. The three Pacific coast states quickly filled the gap, becoming huge fruit growers; California farmers also began looking for specialized niches (for example, vegetables popular among Italians) and broadening their sales appeal. Items that thus started becoming familiar to a cross-section of American shoppers included zucchini, broccoli, bulb fennel, artichokes, avocados, and canned olives. California growers' cooperatives also popularized seedless raisins (under the trade name "Sun-Maid") and other dried fruits as nutritious high-energy snacks or breakfast aids to digestion.

Despite the enlarged volume of produce, the period was not one of notable fruit and vegetable cookery or connoisseurship. Two obvious reasons are that the culinary qualities of tomatoes, apples, spinach, and so forth did not matter to food authorities as much as their supposed health benefits, and that in the shift to intensive, mechanized farm production, growers were obliged to concentrate on factors like hardiness, high yield, disease resistance, and transportability. Thus the genetic diversity of American crops generally shrank between the wars. A few hybridized corn strains replaced open-pollinated seed saved by farmers; a few high-yielding cultivars came to dominate the table-fruit industry. In a society of consumers becoming more familiar with brand names and trademarks than with built-in variations in the products of the soil, the emergence of fresh fruits and vegetables as uniform in taste, texture, shape, color, and cooking properties as their canned counterparts was logical.

In the years spanning the two world wars, no influence on American farming and food was more powerful than that of the federal government. Through initiatives ranging from the U.S. Department of Agriculture Bureau of Plant Industry's tropical expeditions in quest of superior avocados or passion fruits to the first federal food-stamp program in 1939, it played an ever-expanding role in determining what people put on their tables.

The first major federal innovation during this period was the World War I attempt—through the Food Administration under Herbert Hoover—to conserve strategically vital food supplies by expanding production and encouraging civilians to substitute more plentiful foods for meats, white flour, and sugar. While encouraging the nation's farmers to expand crop production, the Food Administration drew on improved knowledge of nutrition and food chemistry to propose healthful substitutes for certain foods—meat (meaning beef and pork), refined white flour and sugar, butter—that citizens were asked to voluntarily conserve by forgoing them each in turn one day of the week. This effort gave a strong boost to whole wheat and other grains and helped launch several corn derivatives (oil, syrup) on commercial careers.

The Volstead Act of 1919, which took effect in 1920, remains the government's most drastic regulatory intervention to date into private consumption habits—and despite the long and broadly based grassroots effort that led the nation to ratify Prohibition through the Eighteenth Amendment, the act was an eventual disappointment even to many of its supporters. It drove liquor sales underground and put some old-style luxury restaurants out of business, Delmonico's in New York being the most famous casualty. To some extent, it encouraged the soft-drink industry—which was, however, able to recover handily from the repeal of Prohibition in 1933 by promoting the use of ginger ale and colas as mixers for hard liquor. Prohibition probably contributed to the rise of eating places like luncheonettes, cafeterias, and diners that did not depend on alcohol sales and were suited to daily work and travel schedules. It also helped propel hard-liquor consumption (by both sexes in public) into private homes as well as illegal night spots. Repeal, which coincided with the worst misery of the Depression, set free a huge hunger for at least the fantasy of giddy indulgence, as shown during the next few years in a profusion of lavish bon vivant journalism (culminating in the 1941 launching of *Gourmet* magazine), a big crop of night clubs and chic wining-and-dining spots populated by what came to be called café society, and new American chapters of international gastronomic associations like the Wine and Food Society or *Les Amis d'Escoffier*.

Government intervention in a series of farm crises brought on by gigantic surpluses (the result of chronic overproduction since the war) and slumps in prices was resisted by several successive presidents until 1933. In that year, the worst price collapse yet coincided both with the vast soil-erosion catastrophe known as the Dust Bowl, precipitated by overcultivating areas of marginal rainfall, and with pandemic unemployment. The nation was horrified by the spectacle of farmers—unable to pay shipping fees for harvests—burning mountains of grain or burying thousands of slaughtered hogs while desperate city-dwellers literally raided garbage cans for food.

The corrective measures enacted by the Franklin D. Roosevelt administration brought Washington more forcefully than ever into the food-policy and rural-lifeline business. They included farm price supports, acreage-reduction and soil-conservation measures, the Rural Electrification Act of 1936 (which eventually allowed modern technology to reach virtually all American kitchens), attempts to transfer food surpluses to state and local relief agencies, and the 1939 food-stamp program—which came, however, when recovery was well underway.

World War II brought further federal food initiatives, even before America was officially at war. In 1941, moving beyond the applied-nutrition lessons of the Food Administration in World War I, the administration commissioned a panel of nutritionists to draw up nutrient recommendations to assist the wartime food-planning effort. These were published in 1943 as the Recommended Dietary Allowances of the National Research Council. The rationing measures instituted in 1943 and enforced through the Office of Price Administration differed from those of 1917 in being compulsory. Restrictions were placed on the use of metal; the resulting shortage of canned produce helped encourage "Victory Garden" plantings and home-canning efforts. Once again potential meat substitutes and protein boosters were urged on the public by nutrition experts; this time they included various soybean and peanut products as well as powdered nonfat milk, which had not been seriously investigated for home use before the Depression.

The immediate aftermath of World War II was a chaotic tug-of-war between a civilian population rejoicing at the end of rationing restrictions and major food interests looking to the end of price restrictions. The resulting inflation of some food prices—most dramatically and controversially, meat prices—at a time when the government was diverting much food to massive foreign-relief programs, touched off great anger among middle-class consumers and proved a serious political liability for the Truman administration.

Stable meat prices returned in several years. But the episode of meat-price protests evinced a difficult legacy from the sustained crises of Prohibition, the Depression, and World War II. Cumulatively these events had left Americans eager to demonstrate recovered morale and prosperity through ample indulgence of appetite and more able to do just that than any prior generation. The same events, however, had also left the public and the producers of the nation's food viewing the American table as a battleground of nutritional, economic, cultural, and moral interests, as well as a potential counter in international politics.

[See also Alcohol and Teetotalism; California; Delmonico's; Department of Agriculture, United States; Diets, Fad; Farm Subsidies, Duties, Quotas and Tariffs; Grocery Stores; Piggly Wiggly.]

BIBLIOGRAPHY

Bentley, Amy. *Eating for Victory: Food Rationing and the Politics of Domesticity*. Urbana: University of Illinois Press, 1998.

Cummings, Richard Osborn. *The American and His Food: A History*. Chicago: University of Chicago Press, 1940. Facsimile reprint, New York: Arno Press, 1970.

Hooker, Richard J. *Food and Drink in America: A History*. Indianapolis and New York: Bobbs-Merrill, 1981.

Hurt, R. Douglas. *American Agriculture: A Brief History*. Ames: Iowa State University Press, 1994.

Hurt, R. Douglas. *The Dust Bowl: An Agricultural and Social History*. Chicago: Nelson-Hall, 1981.

Levenstein, Harvey A. *Paradox of Plenty: A Social History of Eating in Modern America*. New York: Oxford University Press, 1993.

Levenstein, Harvey A. *Revolution at the Table: The Transformation of the American Diet*. New York: Oxford University Press, 1988.

Marchand, Roland. *Advertising the American Dream: Making Way for Modernity, 1920–1940*. Berkeley: University of California Press, 1985.

Mariani, John. *America Eats Out: An Illustrated History of Restaurants, Taverns, Coffee Shops, Speakeasies, and Other Establishments That Have Fed Us for 350 Years*. New York: Morrow, 1991.

Poppendieck, Janet. *Breadlines Knee-Deep in Wheat: Food Assistance in the Great Depression*. New Brunswick: Rutgers University Press, 1986.

Rasmussen, Wayne David and Gladys L. Baker. *The Department of Agriculture*. New York: Praeger, 1972.

Schwartz, Hillel. *Never Satisfied: A Cultural History of Diets, Fantasies, and Fat*. New York: Free Press, 1986.

Seid, Roberta Pollack. *Never Too Thin: Why Women Are at War with Their Bodies*. New York: Prentice-Hall, 1989.

Strasser, Susan. *Satisfaction Guaranteed: The Making of the American Mass Market*. New York: Pantheon, 1989.

Strasser, Susan. *Waste and Want: A Social History of Trash*. New York: Metropolitan, 1999.

ANNE MENDELSON

World War II

During World War II (1941–1945) the mandatory rationing of food in the United States was a vital part of the war effort. While rationing ensured a sufficient, if at times unexciting, diet for Americans, it also helped instill for many a sense of public commitment to the war. By complying with rationing, conserving food, and even producing and preserving their own food, Americans increased their initial commitment, making it easier for them to support an extended and devastating world war. Though Americans managed to modify their food consumption to the strictures of wartime rationing, such changes were short-lived. After the war's end a booming postwar economy helped to hasten the return to familiar eating patterns, and Americans increased their consumption of such high-status foods as expensive cuts of red meat even beyond prewar levels.

As the United States thrust itself full force into World War II, the tremendous volume of goods required to wage war in both the Pacific and European theaters meant shortages of food as well as shortages of steel, nylon, tin, wool, cotton, and soap. Additionally, domestic consumption of food was rising. As the United States geared up for war, the ensuing substantial economic growth created more employment and higher wages, allowing people, for the first time in years, to relax and enjoy the fruits of their hard labors. After a decade of the Depression, Americans eagerly spent more on food—a luxury almost impossible to relinquish voluntarily.

Government officials immediately recognized the need for rationing programs and price controls, especially for food, to offset the possibility of spiraling inflation, ferocious black markets, and inequitable distribution of goods. Price controls and rationing would keep prices down, allowing all, not just the wealthy, to afford food that otherwise would demand exorbitant prices. Distributing food equitably—especially those foods in greatest demand—was important politically. Mandatory food rationing was needed to ensure an equitable distribution of food across the country, across socioeconomic boundaries, and beyond national borders. Rationing thus helped maintain a needed check on Americans' eating habits.

The phenomenal increase in agricultural production during the war might have rendered food rationing unnecessary, except that increasing consumption and commitments abroad subsumed any surplus food produced. During the war, U.S. farmers, largely in response to government requests and monetary incentives, produced 50 percent more food annually than they had during World War I. With 10 percent fewer workers, farmers managed to produce 10 percent more food per capita for a population that had grown by a third since 1919. The percentage of grains and vegetables produced as well as the number of livestock raised and slaughtered had grown tremendously. Yet much of this prodigious output was earmarked for wartime distribution; to the U.S. military, Allied countries, and formerly Axis-occupied territories, the government sent twice as much food annually as had been distributed in World War I.

Rationing Implemented

Days after the bombing of Pearl Harbor on 7 December 1941, the U.S. government enacted its first measures to control the country's resources by putting restrictions on the purchase of tires and other products made from rubber. By May 1942 sugar was rationed, with meat and other foods soon to follow. People picked up booklets of coupons at neighborhood schools, where schoolteachers were asked to volunteer their time to distribute the ration books. The

Office of Price Administration (OPA), as the overseer of rationing, sought a system that would curb Americans' consumption but would still allow people choice and control over their food. While sugar and eventually coffee were rationed according to the stamp method, under which consumers would relinquish a stamp to purchase an allotted amount every few weeks, the government introduced a more complicated point system for rationing meat, fats, and processed foods (which included juices as well as canned, frozen, and dried fruits and vegetables).

The point system maintained government control over rationing but at the same time allowed the consumer a reasonable amount of control over the family's diet. Every month the OPA issued each person five blue stamps and six red stamps worth ten points each, a total of fifty blue points for processed foods and sixty red points for meat, fats, and some dairy products. Each item—canned pineapple or pork chops, for instance—was assigned a point value determined by both availability and consumer demand. The point values were periodically reevaluated. For example, the OPA lowered the point value of canned peaches to encourage consumption during the 1943

Food Rationing during War. Harold B. Rowe, director of the Office of Price Administration's Food Rationing Division, indicates the point values of various processed foods, February 1943. *Prints and Photographs Division, Library of Congress/Alfred T. Palmer*

Food in Wartime. Chefs in the U.S. Senate restaurant prepare a luncheon of dehydrated foods, December 1942. *Prints and Photographs Division, Library of Congress/George Danor*

summer bumper crop of the fruit. With such a system, a consumer could choose to spend some of the family's points on more highly desired and scarcer items with high point values, such as beefsteak, knowing that fewer points would be left that month to buy other meats and fats. Not surprisingly, officials found it difficult to assign the proper point value to many foods, often because they were unfamiliar with certain groups' food habits. A couple of weeks after meat rationing had gone into effect, for example, it was discovered that the point value per pound of chitterlings, popular among African Americans, had been set much too high. OPA officials did not realize that several pounds of chitterlings cook down to a much smaller amount.

The War on the Kitchen Front

Government propaganda and commercial advertising declared the homemaker's kitchen a war zone, turning it into a public arena. Cooking and shopping for food became, according to the media, political and patriotic acts and thus subject to public scrutiny. Numerous popular writers and advertisements used war metaphors when discussing women and their kitchens. The National

Livestock and Meat Board's wartime pamphlet proclaimed, "The American homemaker has an important part to play in the war effort. Her uniform is the kitchen apron and she may wear it proudly; for there is no more important responsibility than hers." The booklet went on to provide an array of tempting recipes women might use when cooking the less appealing (and thus more patriotic) cuts of meat: French Fried Liver, Creole Kidney, Jellied Tongue, Tongue Rolls Florentine, and Tripe à la Maryland, the last made with cherries, bay leaf, and lemon. Even stretching meat loaf became part of women's war effort.

Because women were the traditional family food procurers, part of their patriotic duty was to avoid hoarding food or buying on the black market. Yet women felt the pull of competing interests: their allegiance to the larger American family, which called them to resist hoarding and black markets, versus a heightened concern for the well-being of their immediate families, stimulated in large part by powerfully seductive advertising. Ads told women that by cooking nutritious food, they could create a place of refuge, a haven in which to provide nurture, love, and security that would help family members survive in the outside world.

Home and kitchen thus served not only as a public battle-front but also as a refuge from battle. Nurture equaled food, which equaled good health, which equaled winning the war.

Home Front Food Production: Victory Gardening and Canning

By calling food production "the first line of defense," the government hoped to encourage millions of Americans to grow and eat their own fruits and vegetables. This effort would free up the bulk of the commercially grown and canned produce for the "boys overseas," the Allies, and newly liberated countries while at the same time seeing to the health and thus productivity of the home front workforce. In 1943, the peak year for home front food production, 20 million households, constituting three-fifths of the population, produced more than 40 percent of vegetables Americans consumed. In addition, 4.1 billion jars of food were preserved at home and community canning centers. From a half-acre garden to a window box planted with tomatoes, from a well-stocked pantry to a few jars of peach preserves, Americans on farms and in big cities embraced victory gardening and canning as quintessential symbols of home front sacrifice and patriotism. While evidence suggests that official numbers of gardens planted and food produced were inflated, there is no doubt of the program's effectiveness in allowing citizens to feel they were making a real contribution to the war effort. Further, victory gardening and canning, in addition to rationing, functioned as community builders. The notion of people working together to produce wholesome and much-needed food inspired a spirit of communalism. Home front food production was touted as a way to renew or strengthen community ties during this global crisis.

Setting Official Standards for Healthy Eating: The Basic Seven

During the war, the Food and Nutrition Board (FNB) of the National Research Council first established recommended daily allowances (RDA), dietary requirements and guidelines for good eating to remedy Americans' insufficient knowledge. The FNB established daily allowances of calories and nutrients according to the differing needs of men, as factory workers or soldiers; women, including those who were pregnant or nursing; and children of different ages. In addition it suggested adding vitamins to refined white flour, bread, and milk; devised nutritional plans for communal cafeterias; and determined the amount of nutrients lost through cooking vegetables. The FNB's recommended daily allowances have since been criticized as being wildly inflated for most Americans' needs.

To promote knowledge of healthy eating, the government established an educational campaign called the Basic Seven. The Basic Seven, a forerunner of the later pyramid guide to nutritious eating, outlined the different foods Americans should eat daily for optimum health. They consisted of green and yellow vegetables; oranges, tomatoes, and grapefruit; raw cabbage or salad greens; potatoes and other vegetables or fruits; milk and milk products; meat, poultry, fish, and eggs, or dried beans, peas, nuts, or peanut butter; bread, flour, and cereals; and butter and fortified margarine. Government officials regarded the Basic Seven as a way in which housewives could learn about proper nutrition without having to know much about specific nutrients. Vitamin C was the dominant vitamin in the second group, for example, and foods high in the B vitamins dominated group six. Those consuming foods from each group every day, Americans were told, would receive all the necessary nutrients. The Basic Seven accurately assessed the need for different vitamins but gave no clues about the amounts of fat, for instance, that one should consume daily. That butter had a category of its own is telling.

Effects of Food Rationing

While during the war Americans cut down on their consumption of sugar, coffee, butter, and choice cuts of red meat, wartime food rationing did not significantly alter Americans' long-term eating habits or the structure of their meals. What clearly changed during wartime, however, was Americans' perception about food and its abundance during wartime, a perception that in the realm of politics and symbols often substituted for reality. Especially early on in the war, Americans worried that food rationing, combined with tight domestic supplies, could lead to severe food shortages and hence inadequate nutrition. The perception of shortages added to the anxiety already created by the war's effect on society in general, and it did, in fact, help to create shortages by spurring the hoarding of coffee, sugar, and red meat; when word came of a new shipment of coffee at the local grocery store, people rushed to purchase as much as they were allowed.

Americans' fears of shortages and the actual reduced availability of certain high-status food compelled the government and private advertisers to portray meals in idealized terms. This idealization was particularly true of dinner, the most symbolic and ritualized of the three daily meals. The iconographic ordered meal of a large cut of red meat with accompanying smaller servings of vegetables was held up in the government-sponsored media as an ideal, connoting the stability, familiarity, and abundance Americans had long believed their country symbolized. While food rationing compelled women to serve many meatless and one-pot meals, it was tacitly assumed that once the war was over, life—and consumption patterns—could and would return to normal. To counter the notion that such one-pot meals were inferior, dietitians, food writers, and cookbook authors did their best to infuse recipes with the same kinds of symbolic connotations of security, love, and abundance that traditional meat-and-potatoes dinners contained. Cookbooks and newspaper articles urged women to go back to one-pot soups and stews, even though the busy wartime woman would have to make them from scratch. Serving such a homemade meal, writers explained, would hearken back to the old-fashioned one-pot meal, providing a warm and comforting (though, it is implied, perhaps inferior) substitute for the idealized meat-and-potatoes dinner.

Despite the urging by some to consume more soybeans, casseroles, and so-called variety meats, these messages promoting meat substitutes paled next to the plethora of posters, advertisements, films, and pamphlets regularly featuring reassuring images of the (high-status) meat-dominated ordered meal. For example, the *Saturday Evening Post* carried for Dow Chemical Company a full-page advertisement featuring a woman in her kitchen preparing the traditional dinner: a platter barely accommodating a huge roast accented by serving bowls of potatoes and green beans. Thus messages to the public were at odds: some told Americans to downsize their accustomed meals, while others suggested that an abundant meal with a huge cut of meat still symbolized the American way of life.

Despite such mixed messages, on the whole, food rationing seemed to work: food was distributed relatively equitably, and Americans had surprisingly full larders, given rationing restrictions. As the economist John Kenneth Galbraith, the first "price czar" of the OPA, wryly remarked, "Never in the long history of human combat have so many talked so much about sacrifice with so little deprivation as in the United States during World War II." In a public opinion poll taken in May 1943, almost two-thirds said their meals had been no different since extensive rationing had gone into effect; three-fourths indicated that the size of their meals had remained the same. In

1944 surveys showed that 90 percent of women felt rationing provided all the meat they and their families needed; 75 percent felt their sugar rations were adequate. More than one-third of Americans could not use up their allotment of canned goods stamps before they expired. Americans could not get as many choice cuts of red meat as they could before the war, but they did have other, less desired cuts from which to choose, as well as unrationed though more limited supplies of chicken, fish, eggs, and cheese. Moreover, while quantity remained fairly consistent, the quality of foods that Americans consumed during wartime declined only moderately. There is compelling evidence that the wartime diet of many Americans, including those with low incomes, actually increased both in quality and in quantity. This is not to say, however, that World War II rationing was not needed, as some have argued. With up to 50 percent of some foodstuffs being sent overseas to the military and the Allies, combined with military priorities that made it difficult to distribute foodstuffs across regions of the United States, mandatory food rationing assured Americans that they would get their fair share of the nation's food supply.

Food and Beverage Products Prominent in World War II

In addition to vitamin-enriched flour and bread products, recipes for sugarless desserts, and the tepid promotion of soy products and "variety meats" as substitutes for the more familiar steaks and chops, World War II also spurred the consumption of such manufactured products as Spam, margarine, and Coca-Cola. Though developed in the 1930s by the Hormel meatpacking company, Spam was catapulted into the American and international spotlight during World War II. An unrationed, easily transportable meat product high in fat and salt that had an indefinite shelf life, Spam was popular both at home and abroad. Americans stocked their cupboards with Spam, and the government shipped it by the ton to its allies. Nikita Khrushchev later commented that, despite the jokes, Spam tasted "good," and he credited American exports of Spam with saving the Soviet Army. As a result of the war, Spam became a common and desirable ingredient in Hawaiian everyday cuisine. Margarine, created before the war, rose to prominence as a result of wartime rationing of butter. First produced in France in the 1870s, margarine was available in the United States by the end of the nineteenth century. Because of strong lobbying by the dairy industry, however, margarine was heavily taxed and severely restricted in terms of production. Some states, for example, prohibited the manufacture and sale of yellow-colored margarine that resembled butter. Instead consumers kneaded capsules of yellow dye into the white-colored fat. As margarine gained popularity during World War II because of butter shortages and rationing, some states repealed taxes on margarine as well as color restrictions as a benefit to consumers. Coca-Cola similarly acquired national and international fame as a result of World War II. Strategic product development—the Coca-Cola Bottling Company was allowed to set up bottling plants wherever soldiers were deployed around the world—and acclaimed advertising campaigns that cleverly cultivated the relationship between Coca-Cola, Americanism, and patriotism, cemented its popularity both at home and abroad. By the end of the war, Coke had become an international symbol of the United States.

[*See also* Advertising; Coca-Cola; Cookbooks and Manuscripts, *subentry* From World War I to World War II; Food and Nutrition Systems; Kitchen Gardening; Spam.]

BIBLIOGRAPHY

Anderson, Karen. *Wartime Women: Sex Roles, Family Relations, and the Status of Women during World War II.* Westport, CT: Greenwood, 1981.

Bentley, Amy. *Eating for Victory: Food Rationing and the Politics of Domesticity.* Urbana: University of Illinois Press, 1998.

Blum, John M. *V Was for Victory: Politics and American Culture during World War II.* New York: Harcourt, 1976.

Jeffries, John W. *Wartime America: The World War II Home Front.* Chicago: Dee, 1996.

Leff, Mark H. "The Politics of Sacrifice on the American Home Front in World War II." *Journal of American History* 77 (March 1991): 1296–1318.

Hartmann, Susan M. The *Home Front and Beyond: American Women in the 1940s.* Boston: Twayne, 1982.

Hayes, Joanne Lamb. *Grandma's Wartime Kitchen: World War II and the Way We Cooked.* New York: St. Martin's Press, 2000.

Spang, Rebecca. "The Cultural Habits of a Food Committee." *Food and Foodways* 2, no. 3 (1988): 359–391.

Ward, Barbara McLean, ed. *Produce and Conserve, Share and Play Square: The Grocer and the Consumer on the Home-Front Battlefield during* World War II. Portsmouth, NH: Strawbery Banke Museum, 1994.

Weiner, Mark. "Democracy, Consumer Culture, and Political Community: The Story of Coca-Cola during World War II." *Food and Foodways* 6, no. 2 (1996): 109–129.

Westbrook, Robert B. "Fighting for the American Family: Private Interests and Political Obligation in World War II." In *The Power of Culture: Critical Essays in American History,* edited by Richard Fox and T. J. Jackson Lears, 195–221. Chicago: University of Chicago Press, 1993.

Wilcox, Walter P. *The Farmer and the Second World War.* Ames: Iowa State College Press, 1947.

AMY BENTLEY

From World War II to the Early 1960s

For the United States, the period after the end of World War II to the early 1960s was a dazzling time. The economy boomed, and a powerful consumer culture flourished; millions of Americans purchased new cars, new appliances, and new houses. There was an unprecedented rush to the suburbs and a new celebration of family life in the form of the nuclear rather than the extended family as well as a consequent baby boom. During this era of rapid change and rising personal wealth, American eating habits, indeed the very food that Americans ate, changed profoundly.

Before the war Americans had been in the middle of the Great Depression; unemployment was high, and budgets were tight. During the war unemployment went down dramatically, but rationing—both of food and of goods, such as refrigerators, cars, stoves, and washing machines, not to mention new houses—suppressed demand. After the war that demand was unleashed.

Returning GIs and their wives needed housing desperately, and the government weighed in with the GI Bill, which not only helped with higher education costs but also covered home loans for up to two thousand dollars at 4 percent interest. Industry responded with a huge burst of building—over 5 million homes went up after the war, including the first Levittown on Long Island, New York. The new homes all needed washing machines, lawn mowers, refrigerators, and stoves. Most of the families buying the homes also required cars because most of these new homes were in the new neighborhoods called suburbia, and former GIs needed cars to get to work. With family income double what it had been before the war and with new babies on the way, many of the wives decided to give up their wartime jobs and stay home.

Postwar Appetite for Meat

Demand for houses and goods was not the only thing that was unleashed after the war. During the lean years prior to and during the war, Americans had had to be careful about what they ate. After the war Americans seemed to indulge in everything they had been missing for so long, particularly meat. Demand for meat was so high that farmers depleted their grain stocks to fatten their animals, while some even went so far as to butcher their breeding stock. In 1947 Americans set a forty-year record for meat consumption—155 pounds per person. But rising incomes coupled with the rising demand caused prices to soar, so much so that a nationwide boycott of butcher shops was organized in 1948. As a result, prices dropped as much as 20 percent, and some meat markets even closed temporarily.

While pork was always popular, the preferred meat by far was beef. Roasts, of course, were considered to be luxurious fare, perfect for special occasions or Sunday dinner, yet still prized for their leftover possibilities. But the most prestigious meat was steak, thick T-bones and porterhouse for no-nonsense good eating, and tender filet mignons for gourmet dining.

Yet with meat prices rising and demand so high, families sometimes had to make do with lesser cuts. One dish that became popular after the war was Swiss steak, made from less expensive and tougher beef cuts such as round, chuck, or shoulder. Adding to its popularity was the advantage that Swiss steak could be cooked in the new Reynolds aluminum foil, introduced in 1947. Reynolds promoted its foil with a recipe for the dish, highlighting the fact that the baking pan could be lined with foil, thereby making cleanup much easier, and also, perhaps more significantly, that the steak could be baked with frozen vegetables and potatoes for an "all-in-one meal for today's busy lifestyles."

Even less expensive than the meat for Swiss steak was ground beef, which had become a popular, stretchable, and low-ration-point protein source during the war. A favorite way of serving ground beef was as meat loaf. Although this humble dish was usually reserved for family suppers, it could be dressed up. Two of the most popular "gourmet" versions were stuffed meat loaf, usually featuring a line of hard-boiled eggs baked in the middle of the loaf, or frosted meat loaf. Frosted meat loaf, covered in mashed potatoes, was a huge hit all through the 1950s and was considered entirely suitable for informal entertaining. Plain old meat loaf, with tomato sauce, was reportedly the favorite dish of President Harry Truman (1945–1953).

Another use for ground beef was as "emergency steak," ground beef shaped into steak form with a cooked carrot inserted to represent the bone. Equally odd was the popularity in the 1940s of "faux chicken." At that time chicken was very expensive, so cooks resorted to using others meats, particularly veal, as a substitute. Veal, never particularly popular with the majority of Americans, was cooked on skewers as "mock drumsticks," and the wildly popular *Picture Cook Book* (1950), published by Betty Crocker, includes a recipe for mock chicken loaf, made from veal, with the claim that "it's hard to tell it from the real thing."

Of course, one of the most common ways to serve ground beef was as hamburgers. One of the most popular places to get a hamburger was the drive-in. Drive-ins had been popular before the war, but after, with plenty of money in their pockets and plenty of gas in their V-8 cars, Americans wanted to get out and enjoy themselves. Gerry Schremp, in *Kitchen Culture* (1991), attributes this love affair for eating in a car to the need for family privacy in a public space, combined with the ease of eating in the car with the kids and the entertainment value of the carhops. Americans flocked to drive-ins in record numbers, gobbling up burgers, fries, shakes, and floats while watching the carhops run, or sometimes skate, from car to car. The very prosperity that was making drive-ins (as well as other restaurants) so popular, however, was also what doomed them in the end: there were too many better paying jobs available after the war, and it was hard for the drive-ins to find reliable employees who would work for the relatively low wages involved. Two drive-in owners who thought a lot about this problem and then came up with a remedy were Richard and Maurice McDonald of San Bernardino, California. In 1948 the McDonald brothers got rid of their carhops, cut their menu drastically, and opened service windows where customers had to walk up to order. They also cut the price of their hamburgers. Although their idea was slow to take off at first, by 1952 they were selling over 1 million hamburgers a year. They began franchising with Ray Kroc in 1955, and by the time Kroc bought them out in 1961 for $2.7 million, the McDonald brothers' restaurants had sold over 500 million burgers.

Many other self-service fast food restaurant chains got their start in the 1950s as well. Church's Chicken and Kentucky Fried Chicken both opened in 1952; Jack in the Box and Burger King opened in 1951 and 1953 respectively; Shakey's Pizza opened in 1954; Gino's opened in 1957, and Pizza Hut in 1958; and the first Dunkin' Donuts opened in 1950.

Backyard Barbecue

Many of the suburban homes into which Americans moved after the war were modeled after the California ranch house, with a prominent patio in the backyard. What better accessory for that patio than the outdoor grill? Of course, what was cooked on that grill was meat.

But while we tend to think of the 1950s as the big years for the backyard barbecue, as indeed they were, the

1940s were also rife with grilling fever. In 1941 the American cooking icon James Beard published *Cook It Outdoors*, with instructions for cooking on the outdoor fireplace or "the portable charcoal grills which may be folded and stored in the automobile." The hibachi was also very chic, if still somewhat exotic, in the 1940s. Heatrola Gas and Electric Estate Ranges even advertised what they called the Bar-B-Kewer oven in 1945.

In 1951 the Kingsford Chemical Company took over the production of Ford charcoal briquettes, the same year that George Stephen made his first kettle-shaped covered grill, which would become the number-one grill in the country under the name Weber Kettle. In 1953 Sears, Roebuck started selling the Big Boy grill for the then fairly princely price of seventy-nine dollars. Still, the home-built outdoor brick fireplace was a prominent feature of many patios. The *New York Times* gave instructions for building one in 1952. Cornell University and the University of Connecticut both came up with instructions for building barbecues as well as recipes for cooking on them. A favorite episode of *I Love Lucy* centered around Lucy and Ricky Ricardo's problems with building their backyard barbecue in their new suburban Connecticut home.

Many of the barbecues featured rotisserie spits, another popular method of open-air cookery in the 1950s. Rotisseries and grills were considered so essential to home cooking and entertaining that many high-end homes had them built in during the period, and both were part of *House Beautiful*'s 1953 Pace Setter Kitchen.

All through the 1950s Americans consumed on average seventy-four pounds of beef per year, rising to eighty-five pounds by 1960. Hot dogs also saw a tremendous rise, from 750 million pounds per year in 1950 to over 1 billion pounds per year in 1960. Much of the increase was due to the popularity of the backyard barbecue.

While women occasionally did the honors at the grill, men were the primary backyard cooks. Better Homes and Gardens published the *Barbecue Book* (1956), which touts grilling as a primarily male activity: "Tie on your aprons, men! You're boss of the barbecue when steak's the special attraction." For highbrow entertaining and manly gourmet eating from the barbecue, nothing beat a good steak, well aged, well marbled, and at least two inches thick. One of the specialties deemed particularly suitable for men was a special sauce to top off their steaks—herbed butters; spicy, tomato-based sauces; or the garlicky mustard sauce favored by

Armand Hammer, the international businessman and bon vivant.

When women did get into the backyard barbecue act, it usually involved the side dishes. Side dishes of choice included garlic bread, especially easy now that aluminum foil was available; three-bean salad made with canned beans; baked beans, also mostly made with canned beans that were doctored with ketchup, mustard, and molasses; corn on the cob; and potato salad. Another popular item was the baked potato—often wrapped in foil and cooked on the side of the grill—topped off in the new California style with sour cream and chives. Women were also likely to contribute to the feast by frying chicken or corn dogs (frankfurters fried in a cornmeal batter and served on a stick) in the new portable electric skillet, introduced by Presto in 1953.

Kebabs, or skewer cookery, on the barbecue was also a passion of the age. The noted *New York Times* writer Craig Claiborne said that the "shish kebab craze was second only to the national rage for pizza" after World War II. Although meat, with the occasional vegetable thrown in for color, was the primary ingredient of kebabs, fruit was also frequently skewered and grilled, both as a side dish and as a festive but easy dessert. Kebab cookery was fun and relatively simple, but it was also glamorous. Shish kebab was considered entirely suitable for a somewhat exotic dinner party, to be served not with old-fashioned American potatoes but with the newly fashionable rice or even more fashionable wild rice.

Glamorous Cookery and the Instant Epicure

One of the prime movers of American taste in the postwar era, particularly into the 1950s, was the urge to become a gourmet cook, without having to undergo any fuss or spend any time. The food columnist Poppy Cannon epitomized this trend with her best-selling *Can-Opener Cookbook* (1952), which promised to turn "the use of convenience foods into an art." American cooks rushed to prepare such fashionable items as "beer-rich" beef flambé, which Cannon said could be made in "less than fifteen minutes from a tin of beef stew and a can of onion soup"; brandied pâté, made from canned liver pâté mixed with mushroom bits and brandy; cheese soufflé, made with Velveeta cheese and canned white sauce; or borscht, made from jars of strained baby food beets (using baby food as a base for adult "gourmet" food was a fleeting fad in the 1950s). Many recipes from the time reflect ingredients no longer on supermarket shelves, such as one for salmi of duck, made with canned cooked duck and canned wild rice, or another for a salad made with canned celery hearts and canned tomato aspic. (Tomato aspic, canned or homemade, was a chic item in the 1950s, as useful as "a simple black dress," according to *House Beautiful* in June 1951.)

Of course not all hurry-up cooking was on the same gourmet level as salmi of duck. More everyday food was also chock full of canned and processed ingredients. Campbell's soup was in high demand, especially as part of one of the many casseroles taking the country by storm. Indeed, President Truman's second favorite dish (after meat loaf) was tuna noodle casserole, which most people made using Campbell's undiluted cream of mushroom soup as the sauce.

Manufacturers were only too happy to help this phenomenon along. Campbell's home economists came up with their famous "green bean bake" in 1955, featuring not only their own cream of mushroom soup, but also frozen or canned beans and a can of french fried onions. Another multiproduct, cross-company recipe was for a "buffet party loaf" concocted from Del Monte fruit cocktail, Spam, Miracle Whip salad dressing, and gelatin. Pillsbury offered its Tuna Lima Bake, featuring Pillsbury's own refrigerated biscuit dough, along with canned soup, frozen lima beans, canned tuna, and shredded processed cheese. Pillsbury also had recipes for the popular bubble loaf (sometimes known as monkey bread), both in savory and sweet varieties, made from canned biscuit dough.

Quick Salad Seasoning. Jell-O box, 1950s. *Culinary Archives & Museum at Johnson & Wales University, Providence, R.I.*

So accepted was the idea of quick-cook meals by the mid-1950s that *Good Housekeeping* presented an entire dinner menu that came out of cans or the freezer in its July 1956 issue, featuring Spam, instant mashed potatoes, frozen peas, and a dessert made from fruit cocktail, purchased sponge cake, and instant pudding.

America Goes Gourmet

With the combination of new wealth, frequent and increasingly more affordable intercontinental airline flights, and America's new position as an outward-looking world power, it was no wonder that Americans flocked overseas in record numbers in the 1950s. When they came home, they wanted to re-create the delicious dishes they had tasted abroad. They were encouraged in this trend by writers and cooks like Beard; the New York–based French chef Dione Lucas; M. F. K. Fisher, who was writing about the food of France so winsomely; and the highbrow *Gourmet* magazine, which had gotten its start in 1941 and seemed to focus almost entirely on international cuisine. But even less chic magazines like *Look* furthered the trend, saying in 1955, "From the home base of an American kitchen, you can eat your way around the world. You can lunch in Mexico, dine in Italy . . . or journey still farther to the steamy forests of Equatorial Africa."

The most popular cuisine, or at least the one considered the most sophisticated, was French. French onion soup became a popular restaurant dish, usually garnished with a raft of toasted french bread sporting a load of melted Gruyère-type cheese. Duckling à l'orange, coq au vin, and boeuf bourguignon were three popular dishes, frequently made at home by ambitious cooks. Other cooks, a little less sure of themselves, might nevertheless perk up a familiar American beef stew with a slightly daring flick of garlic or an even more daring splash of wine. The most adventurous eaters might try frogs legs or escargots on a trip to a French restaurant.

Gourmet clubs sprang up around the country, and earnest oenophiles collected wine labels, consulted vintage charts, and spoke knowingly of "nose," "finish," and other mysterious terms. Beard, understanding that many Americans were not only unused to wine drinking but were intimidated by it, tried to reassure his readers. "Cooking with wine is not fancy cooking," he said in 1959, "just good cooking."

Some of the most popular "gourmet" dishes of the period were not necessarily French, but they sounded sophisticated. Beef stroganoff first became chic in the

1940s, and by the 1950s it was considered an essential party dish, helped along by the fact that it could be made in the fashionable chafing dish. (Hamburger stroganoff, often made with canned soup as a sauce, came along in the mid-1950s and was considered good enough to serve at more casual company get-togethers.) Chicken divan—made with chicken, broccoli, béchamel sauce, and hollandaise sauce—was also a favorite party dish. Although it definitely was not French, having been devised sometime in the 1940s at the Divan Parisien restaurant in New York City, it sounded French, and it was definitely fancy enough for company dinner. For the very best company dinner, however, a hostess might want to pull out all the stops and serve either lobster thermidor or tournedos Rossini, two rich and expensive dishes usually reserved for momentous occasions. Tomato aspic, although not at all French, continued its vogue as a necessary adjunct to many a fancy meal. Three desserts that might finish up a gourmet dinner in the 1950s were baked Alaska, crêpes Suzette, and zabaglione. All three had been popular in the 1940s as well but reached their zenith after the war.

Besides French and quasi-French cookery, Italian cooking—meaning mostly spaghetti and meatballs and fettuccine Alfredo—was considered quite gourmet. But there was also a long-lasting fad for Scandinavian cookery, just as there was a fad for Danish modern furniture. Scandinavian restaurants were extremely fashionable, and home cooks delighted in giving smorgasbord parties. One of the most enduringly popular of the foods to come out of that period was Swedish meatballs, often cooked or at least served in the chafing dish.

Exotic

Whether it was because of the country's new outward-looking attitude, because of American soldiers' and sailors' sojourns in the Pacific and Japan, or because of the interest in Hawaii that culminated with its admittance to statehood in 1959, there is no doubt the country went mad for anything connected with the South Seas in the 1950s. Thor Heyerdahl published *Kon-Tiki*, James Michener put out *Hawaii*, the movie *South Pacific* came to theaters, Wham-O introduced the hula hoop, and people flocked to restaurants like Trader Vic's, Don the Beachcomber, or the Mai Kai to dine on exotica such as *rumaki*, pupu platters, chicken luau, *haupia*, mai tais, and zombies. Hawaiian parties, or luaus, were popular and fun ways to entertain during the 1950s. *Sunset*

magazine even went so far as to suggest correct attire for one of these parties—muumuus or pedal pushers for the ladies, "aloha" shirts and slacks for the men.

Exotic cuisine included Chinese and Japanese dishes as well, as befitted a style that owed a great deal to the fascination with Hawaii. Teriyaki and sukiyaki were big fads in the 1950s, the sukiyaki often being cooked table side in the new electric skillets. Cantonese Chinese food enjoyed a huge boom, helped in part by the new wave of Chinese immigrants who came to the United States following the easing of immigration laws in 1943. Egg foo yong, barbecued pork (*cha sui*), Chinese spareribs, almond chicken, sweet and sour pork, and Chinese-style duck were all fashionable and ubiquitous dishes in the 1950s. Chinese food was especially popular when accompanied by pineapple or pea pods, not to mention an exotic drink served with a little paper umbrella perched on the edge of the glass.

Cocktail Parties

Since the repeal of Prohibition in 1933, Americans had had an uneasy relationship with alcohol. There were many teetotalers, as reflected in the midwestern Betty Crocker's *Picture Cook Book* (1950), which contained not an ounce of potable alcoholic drink; even its Christmas plum pudding was flamed with the use of a sugar cube soaked in lemon extract rather than brandy. At the same time, drinking, and often drinking to excess, was considered amusing and perhaps even desirable, so long as it was done by society's upper echelons and did not involve anything more dangerous or embarrassing than wearing a lampshade on one's head. So while many Americans were serving milk with dinner (for adults) and punches made from ginger ale and lime sherbet for adult parties during the 1950s, a large group was going all out for home cocktail parties.

So popular were cocktail parties that a whole industry grew up around gag gifts related to drinking. There were cocktail glasses with bent stems; if guests thought the glasses were straight, they had had enough to drink. There were giant, three-foot-high highball glasses with "I Bet You Can't" or "Did You Think You Could?" printed on the side; bottle openers that looked like false teeth; cocktail shakers shaped like fire extinguishers; and bar accessory sets that included "open all night" signs that could light up.

Cocktail party drinks were the standard Manhattans, whiskey sours, rickeys, fizzes, Collinses, and old-fashioneds, but particularly popular was the martini. By the end of the 1950s one San Francisco bar was serving nearly three hundred martinis per day. The period also saw the cult of the dry martini, with such amusements as a vermouth atomizer that would blow a mist of vermouth over a martini glass; for an even drier martini, the drink maker could omit vermouth entirely and simply salute in the direction of France, according to Lowell Edmunds in *The Silver Bullet* (1981).

Food at a cocktail party was primarily of the "nibble" variety; it was calculated that in 1953 over $200 million worth of pretzels alone were consumed at home parties. For hosts and hostesses who wanted to serve their guests more than pretzels, other popular items were Swedish meatballs, sweet and sour meatballs, Vienna sausages, *rumaki*, crackers with fancy cheeses, celery stuffed with cream cheese, salted nuts, cheese straws, and cocktail canapés. Potato chips and dips were extremely popular, especially clam dip, which had been around for a while but got a huge push when the recipe for it appeared on the *Kraft Music Hall* television show in 1951. According to a number of sources, stores sold out of canned clams within twenty-four hours of the show's airing. Also wildly popular was California dip, which apparently got its start in 1954, when an unnamed California cook took Lipton's dried onion soup mix, which had come out in 1952, and mixed it with sour cream. Another ubiquitous feature at cocktail parties—indeed nearly any party featuring grown-ups—was the cheese ball. These were usually made out of a mixture of "nippy" cheeses, which was then rolled in chopped nuts and served with crackers or small breads. Appetizers featuring rolled up salami or bologna, spread with cream cheese, were also popular.

The Changing American Home

Not only were many of the new American homes in the postwar period ranch or split-level homes built in suburbia, many of them also dispensed with the formal dining room altogether and expanded the kitchen. This change occurred not only because a study of American habits indicated that most meals were eaten in the kitchen, but also because as television became more central to home life, meals and entertaining often centered around the "tube."

As American families gathered nightly around the television to watch *The Adventures of Ozzie and Harriet* or invited guests over to watch a Saturday football game, the need for dining areas that were adjacent to the television became apparent. Food that was easily eaten while watching television also became important. Swanson

introduced its frozen TV dinners in 1953, with a box that was designed to look like a television. The first dinner consisted of turkey and dressing and cost ninety-eight cents, but Salisbury steaks and fried chicken followed swiftly, accompanied by mashed potatoes, gravy, and slightly rubbery frozen vegetables. But even before Swanson had introduced frozen meals, *Sunset* magazine had given directions to homemakers for freezing meals in individual metal trays that could be reheated and served to guests on lap trays. The TV tray, a folding tray table, followed swiftly so that the family without a dining area near the television would not have to miss a single episode of their favorite show during mealtime. Another food that seemed to come about as a result of the need for something easy to "grab and gulp" was TV mix, a mixture of various popular cereals, pretzels, and nuts that was baked with lots of butter or margarine and salt.

Entertaining with television, or the newly popular hi-fi (high-fidelity record player), was not only for lowbrow football games or family sitcoms. An evening of listening to the latest LPs (long-playing, high-fidelity records) or of

1950s Food Icon. Campbell advertising piece distributed in Canada, 1950s. *Culinary Archives & Museum at Johnson & Wales University, Providence, R.I.*

watching a challenging drama on one of the popular and serious television "playhouse theaters" was also a common way of entertaining. That sort of evening called for more sophisticated fare, such as boeuf bourguignon, stroganoff, or chicken divan, along with cocktails (clam juice cocktails were popular for nondrinkers), and often one of the most popular deserts of the 1950s, ice cream or sherbet topped with a liqueur.

Big changes were occurring in the contents of the kitchen as well. In 1954 General Electric brought out appliances in bright colors, such as turquoise, pink, blue, yellow, and brown. Freestanding home freezers were popular, eventually overtaking the rented lockers that families had used during the 1940s to hold large quantities of frozen foods. Corning developed its "pyroceram" dishes, which could go from the freezer to the oven and introduced America to the white ceramic pots with the trademark blue cornflower in 1958. Tupperware parties, begun in 1951, brought a whole new way of storing leftovers—and of carrying food to picnics and parties—to the American family. Also useful for leftovers and for making food portable was Saran Wrap, introduced in 1952. In the late 1940s melamine plastic dishes, designed by the noted modernist Russel Wright, became fashionable, and by the mid-1950s nearly every family had a set of colorful and unbreakable Melmac dishes, at least for use at barbecues and picnics. Unfortunately for Melmac, the new user-friendly dishwashers that Americans were buying in the 1950s were very hard on the surface of the melamine. The under-sink garbage disposal became popular in the 1950s (at least in municipalities that allowed them), and wall-mounted stoves also made their appearance. Electric carving knives became common, and the electric can opener was introduced in 1956. At the beginning of the 1960s the Salton Hottray came out and almost instantly became an absolute necessity for any type of entertaining.

A New Era Dawns

As the Eisenhower postwar era ended, a new era was getting under way with the young President Kennedy and his chic wife. The Kennedys' "Camelot" presidency was widely credited with bringing a new sophistication, particularly French sophistication, to the American culinary landscape. With all their international traveling and gourmet clubs in the 1950s, Americans were ready to embrace this new lifestyle. Other forces besides the Kennedys and their French chef in the White House kitchen contributed as well.

In 1956 the popular cookbook writer, product endorser, and television show host James Beard opened his cooking school. The following year Craig Claiborne joined the *New York Times* as a restaurant reviewer, startling his readers with his detailed and frank reviews. In 1961 Claiborne produced *The New York Times Cook Book*, a massive, authoritative, and hugely popular compendium of mostly sophisticated recipes. That same year the first *Mastering the Art of French Cooking*, written by Julia Child with Simone Beck and Louisette Bertholle, debuted. In the following year Child's cooking show, *The French Chef*, premiered and would nearly single-handedly revolutionize American home cooking.

But not everyone wanted to spend time in the kitchen. While many American homemakers (no longer housewives) were interested in expanding their cooking repertoire to include fancy new dishes, there were many who had neither the time nor the inclination for anything requiring a whisk or a roux. The wildly successful *I Hate to Cook Book* (1960), by Peg Bracken, contains one of the country's most popular dishes, which Bracken dubbed "sweep steak" because of the way the recipe had swept the country. It consists of a pot roast topped with a package of dry onion soup mix, which is then wrapped in a sheet of aluminum foil and baked. The dish was easy, tasted good, was economical, and if the foil was wrapped properly, involved no dirty pans.

As the 1950s ended and the 1960s began, the split between those who were willing to cook complicated dishes from scratch and those who preferred to whip up family meals from processed ingredients was widening. In 1950 only 23 percent of married women worked outside the home. By 1960 that number had risen to nearly 32 percent. The feminist movement was also gaining momentum. In 1963 the housewife and mother of three Betty Friedan published *The Feminine Mystique*, which examines what was missing from women's, especially suburban women's, lives. Lack of time for working women was an important factor in the ready acceptance of convenience foods, but there was also a mid-century fascination with the very idea of modernity, exemplified especially at the end of the 1950s by the very modern space race between the United States and the Soviet Union.

While the American housewife of the early 1960s was just as likely to prepare easy "sweep steak" for her family one day and then whip up a complicated duckling à l'orange when her husband's boss was coming to dinner the next, there was no question that the new decade would bring many changes.

[*See also* Barbecue; Beard, James; Child, Julia; Chinese American Food; Cocktails; Cookbooks and Manuscripts, *subentry* From World War II to the 1960s; Dips; Drive-Ins; French Influences on American Food; Frozen Food; Hawaiian Food; Japanese American Food; Tupperware.]

BIBLIOGRAPHY

Anderson, Jean. *American Century Cook-book*. New York: Potter, 1997.

Lovegren, Sylvia. *Fashionable Food: Seven Decades of Food Fads*. New York: Macmillan, 1995.

Mariani, John. *America Eats Out: An Illustrated History of Restaurants, Taverns, Coffee Shops, Speakeasies, and Other Establishments that Have Fed Us for 350 Years*. New York: Morrow, 1991. Thorough, well-illustrated source for American restaurant history.

Schremp, Gerry. *Kitchen Culture: Fifty Years of Food Fads*. New York: Pharos Books, 1991. An excellent and entertaining source for twentieth-century kitchen information; somewhat hard to find but well worth searching out.

SYLVIA LOVEGREN

From the 1960s to the Present

From 1960 to 2000, the American food scene changed radically. It went from primarily home-based food preparation, with less than 40 percent of women working outside the home, to the widespread custom of buying premade food for home consumption, with nearly 70 percent of women working outside the home. Simultaneously, as people were less and less likely to cook at home on a regular basis, the complexity of the recipes that they did cook went up, and the appliances in the underused home kitchen began to resemble those in a restaurant. The types of foods available, whether ready-cooked or not, changed dramatically as well.

The 1960s

Although homemakers had been using canned and frozen convenience foods for years by the 1960s, a new idea began to creep in during that decade: canned or frozen food was better than homemade food. It was faster, more modern, and more space-age. After all, weren't canned and frozen goods made from the best ingredients, in the most spotless and scientific of conditions, by trained chefs? In her *Instant Haute Cuisine* (1963), Esther Riva Solomon describes a painstaking velouté she was learning to make at the Cordon Bleu School in France as "just like a good canned gravy I'd bought from time to time." If the French chef at the very chic Kennedy White House could use canned mushroom soup to make his beef

Rushed for Time. Busy consumers too tired to cook were encouraged to use Veg-All canned vegetables. Cookbooklet issued by the Larsen Company, 1980s or 1990s. *Collection of Andrew F. Smith*

Stroganoff—and he did—then surely it was not only acceptable but smart for the home cook to do the same.

The idea that gourmet, or at least pretty good, meals could be whipped up on a moment's notice with canned or frozen ingredients took off like wildfire. Books poured out of publishing houses promoting this new and improved idea. In addition to Solomon's *Instant Haute Cuisine*, there was *The Instant Epicure*, which features frozen lobster in a sauce of mayonnaise, A1 Steak Sauce, chili sauce, and canned tomato paste; *Easy Gourmet Cooking*, which features the recipe One Man's Poisson, made from frozen fish and canned soup; *The Fast Gourmet Cookbook*, which combines canned chicken, canned gravy, and canned grapes to make chicken moutarde with grapes; and *Cooking from the Pantry Shelf*, which includes yet another recipe for beef Stroganoff that calls for not only canned mushrooms and canned gravy but instant onions and canned roast beef as well).

Not everyone approved of this hurry-up gourmet trend, of course. The well-known food writer Joseph Wechsberg, in the October 1961 issue of *Esquire*, likens the instant gourmet "chefs" to piano students trying to play Chopin after five lessons. But genteel naysayers were in the minority. Quiet good taste was not a particularly valuable cultural commodity in the 1960s, either in fashion or in food.

If quick-cooking instant food was good in the 1960s, an even better and newer idea was that of eating nonfood, or artificial food. General Foods introduced an artificial orange juice called Awake in 1964. Although Awake was not a huge hit, Tang, the orange-flavored crystals in a jar, which was introduced nationwide in 1965, was. Because it was modern and scientific, mothers felt comfortable giving it to their children. "Whipped toppings," or fake whipped cream, became popular in the 1960s as well. Although tubs of Cool Whip "in the dairy case" would come along in the 1970s and become the best-known of these whipped toppings, the first types were boxed mixes that required added water and beating. One of the best known was Dream Whip. These toppings were initially touted as healthier to eat than real whipped cream with its saturated fat and cholesterol. Yet, a great deal of their appeal probably came from the fact that they were modern and that they could be stored for extended periods, unlike real cream.

Cooking as a glamorous leisure-time hobby was also a 1960s idea. One favorite of cooking hobbyists was flaming food, which was considered to be almost unbearably gourmet. All the standard flambéed dishes were trotted out and fine-tuned—the crêpes Suzette, the café brûlot, the cherries jubilee. But enthusiasts flamed virtually everything else they could get their hands on as well. *The Pyromaniac's Cookbook* includes the recipe Baked Beans au Glow-Glow, which was just canned baked beans topped with flaming rum before serving. Restaurants outdid themselves in the flambé department as well, and the fancier and more expensive the restaurant, the more diners expected huge trolleys of flaming food, often pushed by serving personnel in fancy dress.

Gourmet food hobbyists did not eat only flambéed food, of course. Some of the other favorite elegant dishes of the time were green beans amandine—often canned or frozen green beans topped with almonds browned in margarine—and beef Wellington. The latter became so ubiquitous that it eventually devolved from its initial incarnation as an expensive cut of beef coated in fine pâté, mushroom duxelles, and exquisite pastry to a quick dish made out of hamburger baked in an envelope of store-bought pie dough. Gazpacho was another favorite gourmet dish, as was paella, which the *New York Times* food writer Craig Claiborne said was one of the most requested recipes of the period.

In the 1960s came fondue. First, of course, there was cheese fondue, served in a pot that looked like the space-age Sputnik satellite. Then came beef fondue, introduced by the pacesetting Konrad Egli of the Chalet Suisse restaurant in New York City. Also invented and introduced by Egli, in conjunction with Toblerone chocolates, was chocolate fondue. *Look* magazine called Egli's creation the "new hip dip."

Partly a result of, partly a cause of, the interest in gourmet cooking was Julia Child. Although her first cookbook came out in 1961, it was not until Child's television show aired in 1963 that her fame really took off. Because of her popularity, cooking schools blossomed overnight across the country, and chef's knives, wire whisks, and copper bowls became best sellers. It would be difficult to find anyone who cooked in the late 1960s who did not spend hours in preparation for an elegant dinner party, carefully following one of the lengthy and detailed recipes in Child's books.

Last, the 1960s brought America the hippie health food movement. A great deal of this movement was directed against parents and the society in general, but it was also aimed squarely against the "instant gourmet" mentality. Hippies tried their hand at "back to the land" farming and opened food coops to share—or proselytize—their organic produce. These "flower children" baked bread, grew sprouts on their kitchen counters, and tried desperately to reclaim the tastes they suspected had been lost when canned and frozen food took over the kitchen.

JULIA CHILD ON AMERICAN FOOD

American food. What is it? Talk to a New Englander and it's fish chowder, to a Southerner and it's fried chicken, or it's Tex-Mex or what ever the local speciality happens to be. Americans are for more gastronomically adventurous now that so many of us have enjoyed eating different foods abroad. But, no matter where you eat in this great country of ours, American food is characteristic of the people who prepare it.

The 1970s

Following the 1960s, gourmet cooking was still very popular, but it was being taken over by baby boomers who were coming into their own as young adults. Particularly after the hippie movement at the end of the 1960s and the somber mood of the nation at the end of the Vietnam War, young adults seemed to want to just enjoy themselves. One food trend that definitely started with baby boomers was silly names for food or food-related items. A popular sweet boxed snack was called Screaming Yellow Zonkers. Two sweet but heavily alcoholic drinks favored by the disco crowd were the Elmer Fudpucker and the Harvey Wallbanger. A popular sandwich made with peanut butter and Marshmallow Fluff was known as a fluffernutter. Restaurants even came up with silly names for themselves, like Boondocker, Sundecker, and Greenthumb or the Frog and Nightgown.

A restaurant with a long and silly name was likely to be a "fern bar." This designation indicated a particular type of restaurant decoration that became popular in the 1970s, which involved hanging Boston ferns along with faux-Tiffany stained glass and Victorian-style furniture and accessories. Many of the fern bars operated at night as true bars (usually singles' bars), but in the daytime many of them served brunch. Although brunch was not invented in the 1970s, it became an extremely popular way to socialize over food during that period. Two of the most common foods at a brunch were quiche and crepes.

Crepes, of course, had been around long before the 1970s. But coincident with the popularity of French and gourmet cooking, crepes really took off. A restaurant called the Magic Pan, which served primarily crepes, opened in San Francisco in 1965, and by the early 1970s the company had opened branches all across the United States. Crepes stuffed with everything imaginable were served, but it was almost certain that the filling would be creamy and high in fat. One typical recipe for chicken and mushroom crepes contained cream sauce, whipping cream, gruyère cheese, sour cream, and parmesan cheese.

Quiche was also hugely popular, both at brunch and as an easy, easy-to-serve, gourmet item for buffets. Although it had appeared occasionally in the United States in the 1940s and 1950s, it was Julia Child who made quiche part of everyone's vocabulary in the mid-1960s on episode eighty-seven of her television show. Part of the dish's popularity came from the ease with which it accepted improvisation and leftovers. By the end of the 1970s, hostesses were making quiches using such things as canned Welsh rabbit with a sprinkling of Baco Bits, and quiche's popularity waned.

In addition to brunch, one of the fashionable items usually found at a fern bar was the salad bar. Predictably, one of the first restaurants to offer a salad bar was one of those with a silly name: R. J. Grunts in Chicago, which opened in 1971, featured forty different items.

Americans continued to be interested in gourmet cooking during the 1970s, but increasingly their gaze turned from France and French cooking to the foods of Italy, China, and Japan.

Italian food had long been considered quite chic and just a tad daring in the United States, but by the 1970s tomato-based sauces and traditional dishes like spaghetti and meatballs were considered a little old-fashioned. But pasta dishes with rich and creamy white sauces became all the rage. Spaghetti carbonara with a sauce of butter, cheese, cream, and bacon was one rich dish that was very popular, as was fettuccine Alfredo, made with butter, cheese, and sometimes cream. But one of the most fashionable dishes was pasta primavera, which Craig Claiborne said was "by far the most talked about dish in Manhattan" in 1977. Although exactly who first made pasta primavera and when is not totally clear, this dish of cream, butter, cheese, and fresh spring vegetables seems to have been invented by one of the cooks at Le Cirque restaurant in New York City in the mid-1970s.

Although Chinese food had been available and popular at restaurants in most towns across the United States for years, it became very fashionable for Westerners to cook Chinese at home during the 1970s. Tofu was just becoming widely available, and frozen pea pods were in all the supermarkets. At the same time, the wok came out of import stores and started appearing in mainstream kitchen shops. Taylor & Ng was a West Coast design group that did much to make the wok a necessary part of Western kitchen equipment. Two Chinese restaurant items that everyone seemed to want to order in the 1970s were moo shu pork and the Chinese brunch specialty dim sum.

Japanese cooking also rose in popularity during the 1970s. The first Benihana of Tokyo opened in New York City in 1964, and by the middle of the next decade Japanese steak houses had appeared across the country. With their comfort level with Japanese food rising, young Americans started venturing into sushi bars, and by 1980, when the TV movie *Shogun* aired, sushi had become not only a huge national fad but an accepted, if exotic, part of American cuisine.

JEREMIAH TOWER ON AMERICAN FOOD

It is generally believed that in the last fifty years as goes California, so then, sooner or later, goes the East Coast of the United States, then the rest of them, if they cannot resist.

They did not for the Gold Rush of the 1960s and '70s of which an important part was fresh flowers in Berkeley. First they were put down the barrels of rifles, and then onto plates of mixed greens cultivated so perfectly that the cooks could be accused of reading England's John Evelyn. I had. And so the circle with Europe's perfectly fresh ingredients was once more completed.

One of the most important developments in the 1970s was the American counterpart to the French nouvelle cuisine revolution. American nouvelle owed some of its existence to French reforms, but it was as much a product—or by-product—of the organic health food movement of the 1960s as well. Alice Waters opened Chez Panisse in Berkeley, California, in 1971, with the revolutionary idea of showcasing fresh, seasonal, and local ingredients. Deborah Madison's luminous cooking at the Greens restaurant in California did much to push vegetarian cuisine into the American mainstream. Chefs who highlighted this new American cooking, such as Jeremiah Tower, Wolfgang Puck, Michael McCarty, Larry Forgione, and Paul Prudhomme, all first came to prominence in the 1970s.

The 1980s

The Reagan boom of the 1980s brought heretofore unheard-of wealth to many American families—and heretofore unheard-of lack of time. Not only was the economy booming, but for the first time the number of women working outside the home exceeded 50 percent. Predictably, eating at restaurants became more popular, but so rushed for time and so hungry to move up the economic ladder were many Americans that "power breakfasts" and "power lunches"—fast meals in which business was conducted among the crockery—became buzzwords. Fads started turning over faster as well. In the 1960s the fondue fad lasted nearly the whole decade, but in the 1980s fads for things like pink peppercorns or blue potatoes lasted for weeks or months rather than years. "Foodie" became a word, used to describe someone who was passionate or knowledgeable about cooking or eating.

The 1970s interest in nouvelle cuisine and health food coalesced into "new American cuisine," which was the umbrella term that encompassed all the regional cooking styles, or ingredients, that became popular.

"California cuisine" was the cooking that had really set off the trend, with Alice Waters and Jeremiah Tower of northern California leading the list. Michael McCarty and Wolfgang Puck had opened popular and extremely chic restaurants in Los Angeles. This style was characterized by fresh ingredients, often with a Mediterranean or Mexican slant, light sauces, grilling (often over mesquite), beautiful yet informal presentation, and usually high prices as well. Some of the items that were characteristic of California cuisine were warm goat cheese salad, cream of corn soup (both Tower and McCarty claimed first to have popularized the dish), roasted whole heads of garlic served on toasts, and designer pizzas (Tower first served them at Chez Panisse in 1974, but Puck made them a household word in the 1980s).

Also coming out of California was Frieda's Finest Specialty Produce. Started by Frieda Caplan in the late 1960s, Frieda's introduced and named the kiwi fruit. Kiwi became a star attraction in new American cooking, and consumption of the fruit increased sevenfold from 1980 to 1985. Other exotics that became popular during that period were the passion fruit, mango (also introduced to national distribution by Frieda's), star fruit, radicchio, blood oranges, enokidake mushrooms, blue potatoes, mesclun, arugula, Tahitian vanilla, lemongrass, and green peppercorns.

The next trend to hit was southwestern cooking. This style included Cal-Mex, Tex-Mex, and Santa Fe styles, and it became so popular that the revered food writer M. F. K. Fisher complained in 1987 that all the talk about Tex-Mex made her feel like throwing up. Beans, corn (especially blue corn), chilies, cilantro, jicama (introduced by Frieda's), limes, and squash blossoms all become fashionable ingredients, and everyone seemed to have a special recipe for fresh salsa. Two of the "great- youngchefs," as the writer Paula Wolfert called them, who were cooking southwestern came out of Chez Panisse: Jeremiah Tower served cornmeal "blinis" in San Francisco, and Mark Miller opened the Coyote Café in New Mexico in 1986, serving such dishes as smoked chili pasta with duck. In Texas two famous chefs were Dean Fearing of the Mansion on Turtle Creek and Stephan Pyles at his Routh Street Café, which opened in 1983. Fearing's specialty was a warm lobster taco with yellow tomato salsa and jicama salad; Pyles was known for a lobster enchilada with red pepper crème fraîche and caviar.

In addition to the California and southwestern food crazes, foodies went wild for Cajun cuisine in the 1980s. One of the reasons was the Louisiana chef Paul Prudhomme, who in March 1980 created his signature dish, blackened redfish. The fish was coated with a complex mixture of herbs and spices and cooked in a white-hot skillet until it was nearly, but not quite, burnt. So popular did blackened redfish become that the redfish was actually placed on the endangered species list. Cajun-style restaurants opened across the country, and other restaurants offered such dishes as duck gumbo or spot prawn jambalaya, but the fad had disappeared by the end of the decade, a casualty of overexposure and mostly not very good cooks.

Italian food, so long as it was not old-fashioned spaghetti and meatballs, became even more popular than it had been in the 1970s. Particularly chic were colored pastas—tinted with tomato or spinach, or even such exotics as beets, saffron, herbs, or squid ink. Pasta with vodka sauce became extremely popular after it was introduced at Joanna's Restaurant in New York City in the early 1980s. Pasta salads, which seem to be more an American than an Italian invention, also became a huge fad. The culinary historian Betty Fussell credits Craig Claiborne with starting the craze when he repeated his sister's recipe for cold spaghetti with mustard-mayonnaise in the *New York Times*. Overexposure, mediocrity, and a penchant for throwing everything but the kitchen sink into these salads had made pasta salad unfashionable by the end of the decade.

Freshly made pesto became popular in the 1980s, and some of the trendier chefs introduced pestos made from herbs other than basil; cilantro was an herb commonly used in southwestern-influenced dishes. Polenta cast off its humble beginnings as food for poor people and was served at nearly every trendy restaurant in the 1980s. Its more upscale cousin, risotto, also became popular.

For dessert, fruit tarts filled with raspberries, star fruit, and kiwi were very popular. Also very fashionable in the eighties were ices and gelati, both of Italian origin and both usually served in small, exquisite portions for high prices. Ices made with exotic fruits were especially popular. By the end of the decade, an Italian dessert that took the United States by storm was tiramisu. This *semifreddo* (chilled) pudding made with chic mascarpone cheese, espresso, ladyfingers, and chocolate was soon on virtually every restaurant menu coast to coast.

RAYMOND SOKOLOV ON AMERICAN FOOD

There is no such thing as American food, only food that Americans eat. Like Jewish food, American food is a special interpretation of dishes and ingredients borrowed from other people. The difference is that Jews emigrated to their cuisine(s), while Americans took what came to them from immigrants. The fundamental exception to this, the one that proves the rule, is the American food that developed in each new place where settlers came to terms with unfamiliar New World ingredients and the cuisines of people who had been living here before Columbus.

None of the earliest of these hybrid dishes was invented in what is now the United States. North American settlement started more than a century after the Spanish and Portugese overran the Americas south of what is now our border. So the well-established mestizo cooking of Mexico percolated north into our Southwest, while black slaves influenced all the foodways of the West Atlantic coast from Pernambuco to Newfoundland.

Also on the dessert cart was anything made with chocolate. Chocolate decadence cake was extremely fashionable, as were chocolate truffles, fruits dipped in chocolate, and tortes and cakes covered in chocolate ganache. White chocolate also became popular, particularly after the chef Michel Fitoussi served a white chocolate mousse in New York City in 1977. At the more "mommy food" end, double-chocolate brownies were a common treat, even at expensive restaurants. Debbi Fields shocked the business world when she opened a shop selling only cookies in Palo Alto in 1977, but by the end of the 1980s, Mrs. Fields' giant chocolate chip cookies were the model for hundreds of imitators, and home cooks started making extra-large cookies as well.

As Americans grew to love these rich desserts, they also grew to fear the effects that rich foods could have on their bodies. The 1960s had produced the organic health food movement, but by the 1980s the young hippies who had espoused health food were aging baby boomers who had discovered that they could not only get old but could also fall prey to disease.

Oat bran, which was supposed to help clear clogged arteries, was so much in demand that stores ran out of the product. Americans became so obsessed with getting fiber into their diets in the 1980s that some manufacturers actually fortified bread with ground wood. It was reported that omega-3 fish oils were heart-helpful as well, and many people started taking fish oil supplements. Beta-carotenes were supposed to be extremely protective against disease, so Americans tried to eat more broccoli, although President George Bush hated the vegetable so much that he ordered no more broccoli on White House menus shortly after his 1989 inauguration.

In the 1980s it was discovered that the monounsaturated fats were much better for the heart than the polyunsaturated fats Americans had been eating. In 1985 the Food and Drug Administration (FDA) approved the sale of canola oil in the U.S. market, and because of canola oil's high proportion of monounsaturated fats, sales of canola skyrocketed. Olive oil also was promoted for its high monounsaturated fat content, and Americans were encouraged to eat a "Mediterranean diet"—high in olive oil, carbohydrates, and fiber.

At the same time, many Americans developed a fear of eating certain things. Fears about antibiotic residues in milk and meat caused a surge of organically grown animal products to hit the shelves. Fear of red meat caused the consumption of beef to drop from over one hundred pounds per person per year in the early 1970s to under seventy pounds by the end of the 1980s.

Significantly, whether they were afraid of their food or were gorging on sumptuous chocolate desserts, fewer and fewer Americans were eating food cooked at home from scratch. The microwave oven was finally becoming a real presence in the American kitchen, and over 760 microwavable food products were introduced in 1987 alone. By the end of the 1980s over 40 percent of American families reported bringing home a complete meal twice a month or more.

The 1990s

The end of the 1980s brought a stock market recession and with it a reduction of conspicuous consumption, at least for a while. Staying home to eat, even if that meant eating a microwaved Lean Cuisine meal—as one popular brand of frozen food was called—became so fashionable that the term "cocooning" was coined to describe it. Expensive restaurants either closed or scaled back their menu prices from about eighty-five dollars per person to under thirty dollars per person.

During the recession, chic cooking magazines featured what they called *cuisina povera*, or the cooking of the poor. Italian food, particularly peasant Italian food,

became more popular than ever. The simple foods of Tuscany were very fashionable, and recipes for Tuscan beans—featuring nothing more than beans, salt, and olive oil—seemed to be on every magazine cover. Beans also fit very well into the high-fiber, high-carbohydrate lifestyle that was considered so important for health—never more so than when the U.S. Department of Agriculture (USDA) revised its "Four Basic Food Groups" into the "Food Pyramid" in 1992. Because red meat was still considered not only unhip but dangerous and because fish was considered ecologically and nutritionally superior, the combination of fish and beans was a high-profile but short-lived trend of the early 1990s.

American *cuisina povera* was also fashionable, but it was called "comfort food" or "retro food." Old-fashioned American favorites like fried chicken, mashed potatoes and gravy, meat loaf, Jell-O salads, grilled cheese sandwiches, lemon meringue pie, and chocolate cake started showing up not only in people's homes but in trendy restaurants. These dishes were usually fiddled with a bit—the fried chicken would probably have herbs or hot spices in the batter, and the mashed potatoes would contain potato skins and a clove or two of garlic. Famous chefs were known to show how down-to-earth they were by claiming a penchant for eating Oreos while making their fanciest dishes.

Two fads that coincided in the 1990s were the extreme popularity of chilies and the interest in the cooking of South America and the Caribbean. The fad for hot chilies seemed to grow out of the popularity of salsas in the 1980s. Soon "mouth surfing," as eating the hottest chilies was known, became something of a sport, and men in particular liked to show off their ability to take those chilies at the highest range of the Scoville heat index. The incendiary habañero chili, over one hundred times hotter on the Scoville index than the jalapeño, became extremely fashionable, but not everyone was able to eat it.

Hot chilies appeared in salsas, curries, chutneys, and sambals, all of which became ubiquitous relishes. In the 1980s tomato-based, Mexican-style salsa had been the most fashionable, but ten years later it was eclipsed by salsas based on black beans, mangoes or other fruit, and corn. Still, salsa of any stripe was popular, and in the early 1990s salsa sales outpaced those of America's former king of condiments—ketchup.

In the 1990s one of the hottest cuisines, both in Scoville index units and in popularity, was Jamaican cooking. Extremely spicy and aromatic Jamaican "jerk" chicken seemed to take the country by storm, and

Jamaican restaurants seemed to pop up everywhere for a while. A number of cookbooks featuring Jamaican cuisine also appeared. Although most of them have gone by the wayside, *Jerk: Barbecue from Jamaica* (1990) by Helen Willinsky was still in print at the beginning of the twenty-first century.

Other Caribbean foods were also in favor, although few of them were as hot as the popular jerk chicken. Still, Brazilian *feijoada*, a mighty and traditional bean-based feast dish, became fashionable for a while, as did many recipes for pork roast flavored with orange or lime and chilies.

One of the most controversial fads of the 1990s was so-called "fusion cuisine." Americans had always been fusion cooks, melding the techniques and recipes they brought from the old country with the ingredients they found in the New World and adapting their neighbors' recipes to their own taste. But in the 1980s chefs in Los Angeles and Hawaii started blending French and Japanese ingredients and techniques to produce intentionally shocking tastes. By the 1990s the idea of deliberately blending cuisines was taking hold with many chefs. One fairly representative fusion dish was calamari steak with orange cascabel chili cream sauce over sun-dried tomatoes and artichoke ravioli

BURT WOLF ON AMERICAN FOOD

If there is something that could be called American food, I have not been able to find it. What I have discovered is a 500-year-old history of talented cooks taking the traditional ingredients and cooking techniques of almost every culture in the world and adapting them to their New World kitchens and their own sensibilities.

I have seen the ingredients of an ancient Basque soup separated and served as a vegetable side dish. I have watched chiefs take classic French produce and prepare it with Japanese techniques. Our cookbooks are filled with dishes we think of as "American" but are actually basic West African recipes with a twist.

These days, the driving force behind our most skilled cooking appears to be the desire to be free . . . free of the constraints of any culinary tradition and free of the arbitrary and often idiotic regulations of our U.S. Customs Bureau. Our chefs have formed their own gastronomic Immigration and Naturalization Service and I, for one, feel more secure. It's good to have a taste of freedom.

tossed with spinach, eggplant, and artichoke hearts. Another was warm chocolate ganache with salty caramel ice cream and Szechuan peppercorn foam ("foams" were also fleetingly popular in the late 1990s). The merits of fusion cooking were debated on the editorial pages of many food magazines and on food websites. People who liked fusion stressed that it was a natural outgrowth of the number of immigrants flowing into the United States and the increasingly international food supply, and that it was a counterpart to the popular "world music" that was so popular. Whether they wanted to or not, Americans became so used to fusion food that a chain restaurant put a dish called Szechuan shrimp Alfredo on its menu in the 1990s.

Along with the trend for fusion cooking was that of "cosmopolitanizing" ethnic or peasant cuisines. Humble Greek dishes such as *pastitsio* (a lasagna-like dish of pasta with meat sauce) or the intensely flavored *skordalia* (a paste of garlic and bread or potatoes) had its strong tastes and textures diluted and smoothed out. This was not a particularly unusual event in the old days of American cooking. What was new was that highly trained chefs were deliberately attempting to take low dishes and make them upscale and "haute," as had been done in France years before. As a corollary, unabashedly peasant-style dishes such as beef cheeks and entrails *en daube* showed up at expensive restaurants with correspondingly high prices.

One trend that appeared for a while was "vertical food"—food presented in such a way so as to resemble skyscrapers. Gotham Bar and Grill in New York City was a leader in this fad. Although vertical presentation still occurs occasionally, diners found it inconvenient, and it has faded away at most places.

Another 1990s fad was for "crusted" dishes, as in pistachio-crusted sea bass with lemongrass, hazelnut-crusted sturgeon with blackberry barbecue sauce, and walnut-crusted halibut with oregano asparagus and zebra tomatoes. Most of these dishes were fish, but occasionally poultry and meats were "crusted" as well. As was shown with these particular dishes, dishes with extremely long names were popular during the 1990s.

Health concerns remained high on Americans' radar screens during the 1990s, but the focus seemed to shift to the fat content of foods. In 1992 the California Prune Board started promoting the use of prune puree in baked goods to reduce fats. In 1993 Snack Well's low-fat and nonfat products were introduced, and in 1996 Frito-Lay introduced potato chips made with olestra, a fat substitute that caused great controversy because of the way the body metabolized it. While people seemed to be obsessing over the amount of fat they were eating, the USDA reported that the average school lunch contained 25 percent more fat than dietary recommendations, and the reasons for the growing American obesity became a hot topic of discussion.

One of the most visible trends of the 1990s, particularly during the Clinton economic boom, was the fad for expensive, designer kitchens. Handmade tiles, expensive granite or cement countertops, handcrafted cabinets, and high-end appliances, such as Viking stoves, Gaggenau ovens, Sub-Zero refrigerators, and Miele dishwashers, became extremely fashionable. Many of these extraordinarily expensive kitchens were used only by the caterers hired by the homeowners for parties; otherwise the six-thousand-dollar stove top was likely to be used only to boil water.

By the end of the 1990s nearly 70 percent of women were working outside the home. The number of households using microwave ovens grew from 8 percent to over 80 percent. Many grocery stores cut back on the actual "groceries" they stocked and expanded their lines of ready-to-eat foods. And although 74 percent of grocery shoppers in 2001 indicated that they had a home-cooked meal at least three times a week, a rising proportion of "home-cooked" food was really "home-heated" convenience food. If the trends continue, it seems likely that the number of from-scratch, homemade meals will only decline as Americans move through the twenty-first century.

[*See also* Cajun and Creole Food; Caribbean Influences on American Food; Child, Julia; Chinese American Food; Cocktails; Diets, Fad; Fast Food; Fats and Oils; French Influences on American Food; Italian American Food; Japanese American Food; Jell-O; Kitchen Gardening; Kiwis; Mexican American Food; Microwave Ovens; Organic Food; Organic Gardening.]

BIBLIOGRAPHY

Lovegren, Sylvia. *Fashionable Food: Seven Decades of Food Fads.* New York: Macmillan, 1995.
Mariani, John. *The Dictionary of American Food and Drink.* New York: Hearst Books, 1994.
Schremp, Gerry. *Kitchen Culture: Fifty Years of Food Fads.* New York: Pharos Books, 1991.

SYLVIA LOVEGREN

Historic Dining Reenactment

Making history come alive is the goal of the living-history museums and historical-reenactment groups that sprang up throughout America in the twentieth century. The practice began in the 1890s in Sweden, when the folklorist Artur Hazelius introduced costumed people performing traditional crafts into the exhibits at Skansen, the outdoor museum of Stockholm. At roughly the same time, the historic John Ward House in Salem, Massachusetts, began outfitting its guides in period attire. But the living-history movement really flourished in the late 1920s, when John D. Rockefeller Jr. underwrote the restoration of the historic buildings of Williamsburg, Virginia; soon thereafter, the town was populated with costumed interpreters who demonstrated or discussed different aspects of Williamsburg's eighteenth-century culture with visitors. Colonial Williamsburg became a popular alternative to traditional academic courses as a way for Americans of all ages to learn history.

Popularity had its price. Until the emergence of social history as a respected academic discipline in America in the 1960s, scholars condescendingly, but accurately, accused living-history museums of catering to the public's appetite for a sentimental, sanitized reinforcement of national myths served up as entertainment. (The charge was still being levied at the end of the century, but with less justification at the preeminent sites.) In the late 1960s, historians, archaeologists, anthropologists, and other academically trained specialists moved into the living-history museums, transforming them from antiquarian curiosities to laboratories for testing theories about quotidian past life.

While much of the behind-the-scenes scholarship has been rigorous, many of the public programs at these largely not-for-profit sites depend heavily on well-meaning volunteers or nonacademics to interpret the history to a public that expects both education and entertainment.

Historic Dining Reenactment. Lafayette, Indiana. *Tippecanoe County Historical Association, Lafayette, Indiana/ Photograph by R. Woods*

This interpretation can be done either in the first-person mode, in which the interpreters assume an historic persona (real or composite) and talk to visitors as if they were all in the past, or in the "third-person" approach, in which interpreters consciously act as a liaison with the past but do not assume character roles. The success of the experience depends on the interpreters' historical knowledge and on their ability to address the public's expectations. Visitors enjoy observing research first hand, but they sometimes have difficulty appreciating authentic historical foods, such as a baked calf's head or a "forced," that is, stuffed and larded, tongue. Even the best living-history museums peddle anachronistic food-stuffs as so-called regional foods, such as cranberry ganache truffles, to keep the public happy and to raise money for continuing research and operations.

Foodways Programs

Most living-history museums belong to the Association for Living History, Farm and Agricultural Museums (ALHFAM). These institutions have contributed to the academic and popular appreciation of the old foodways by establishing historically based gardens and agricultural plantings, using preindustrial horticultural techniques, researching and raising so-called rare or heritage breeds (defined as animals that have fewer than one thousand animals registered in North America and that could have been found in a particular location before the twentieth century), cooking in restored period kitchens, and brewing according to ancient recipes.

Colonial Williamsburg re-creates the late seventeenth- and eighteenth-century Virginia capital and is the best-known of all living-history museums in America. In 1983 it created a Department of Historic Foodways and set up demonstration kitchens at the Governor's Palace and the George Wythe House. Using the reconstructed kitchens and period recipes from books and manuscripts known to have reached Williamsburg by the middle of the eighteenth century, such as Hannah Glasse's *The Art of Cookery* and Eliza Smith's *The Compleat Housewife*, third-person interpreters prepare and display colonial-style foods. The department has also offered specialized programs in butchery and curing, brewing, hearth cookery, and chocolate. Less authentic, however, are Williamsburg's historic taverns that provide what they promote as a taste of the past: menus are based on historical records and recipes, but the dishes served are thoroughly adapted to suit modern equipment, service

constraints, and the customers' expectations and palates. With advance arrangement for special groups, the Shields Tavern can take reenactment one step closer to historical authenticity by serving meals in a formal eighteenth-century style, à la française, that would be impractically expensive for most visitors.

Behind the scenes at Williamsburg are various archaeological programs that produce scholarly papers shared primarily among academics and living-history professionals. These include investigations into slave foodways based upon digs in the Chesapeake area and studies of white colonial cooking and dining habits based on ceramics and other material finds. In 1986 Williamsburg started a rare-breeds program with several breeds of chickens and sheep that could have been found in eighteenth-century Williamsburg.

Plimoth Plantation, a living-history museum near Plymouth, Massachusetts, has rebuilt the historic Plymouth as it is believed to have existed in 1627—but two miles from the original site. Archaeologist James Deetz and vernacular architectural specialist Henry Glassie pioneered the reconstruction of the village using seventeenth-century techniques and tools, with appropriately attired interpreters providing the labor. Plimoth also opened its stockades in 1972 to Jay Anderson, an expert in the yeoman foodways of the Stuart era. Anderson and a colleague lived for several weeks within the confines of the stark plantation, brewing "Shakespeare's" beer according to seventeenth-century East Anglian receipts and dining on boiled salt fish and sour porridge. Anderson started the foodways program at Plimoth, bringing cookery into virtually all of the houses, so that Plimoth Plantation's air is perfumed with a pungent mix of cooking aromas and barnyard fragrances from free-ranging livestock. Plimoth also has a "rare" breeds program.

Visitors to Plimoth can fare better than Anderson in the museum's public eateries. Plimoth understandably focuses on the Thanksgiving mythology that is inescapable at the home of the *Mayflower*. Thanksgiving dinners are sold out months in advance and include modern adaptations of seventeenth-century foods (forks discouraged) as well as out-of-period Victorian menus (forks encouraged).

In the early 1970s Plimoth Plantation also launched an ambitious and controversial Native American program, which included slash-and-burn land clearing, growing flint corn, and cooking roadkill by indigenous techniques. Questions were raised about the appropriateness of Native Americans' affiliating with a museum project that represented the ultimate destruction of the indigenous culture. There were fears of being viewed as animals in a zoo, and a desire to maintain the privacy and dignity of native culture. Although interrupted during the 1980s, the program as later reconfigured represents Wampanoag life and agriculture. It is staffed and directed by Native Americans but does not use the role-playing found in the 1627 village.

Other famous New England living-history museums include the Hancock Shaker Village, located in Pittsfield, Massachusetts, and affiliated with the New England Heritage Breeds Conservancy, and Old Sturbridge Village in Sturbridge, Massachusetts. Both present dining experiences in period settings, with Old Sturbridge also offering lessons in 1830s table manners, such as conveying food to one's mouth using the flat blade of the knife rather than the awkward, two-tined forks then popular in New England. In the 1950s Old Sturbridge published some of the first well-researched essays on early nineteenth-century foodways and material culture relating to the table.

Beyond colonial America, other regions' presentations of living history focus on different time periods, ethnic groups, and cultures. The Conner Prairie Settlement in Noblesville, Indiana, re-creates a frontier village of around 1836 with a mixed population resettled from New England, the Hudson River Valley, and Kentucky. Conner Prairie visitors can assist first-person interpreters in preparing a hearth-cooked dinner using recipes from works such as Lettice Bryan's *The Kentucky Housewife*.

Although rare in comparison with museums that focus on (colonial) immigrant foods and cooking, museums that explore Native American foodways do exist. Under the aegis of the National Park Service, Arizona's Coronado National Memorial encourages school groups to experiment with the foodways of the Zuni, grinding corn with a stone mano and metate and tasting other indigenous foods. Unfortunately, many of the sites are more concerned with entertainment than education and have not incorporated serious scholarship on Native American foodways; some of them offer recipes for fried "Indian Tacos" made from sugar, milk, self-rising wheat flour, and canned corn.

Amateur Reenactments

Reenactments of historical events are mainly conducted by groups of amateurs with a keen interest in a particular historical era. Members of these groups attempt to reenact life as it might have been during their period of interest, donning period-style dress; utilizing period technologies, engaging in period activities, and preparing and consuming food and beverages according to period recipes and cooking techniques. Food is a highly important component of these events, its preparation and presentation often based on considerable research.

One such group is The Society for Creative Anachronism, Inc. (SCA), an international organization with more than 28,000 members. Founded in Berkeley, California, in 1966 by a group of science fiction and fantasy fans, the organization researches and reenacts events in pre-seventeenth-century Europe. The group is organized on a feudal structure, with seventeen different kingdoms, each composed of localized baronies, cantons, and shires. These units gather regularly to select and re-create elements of medieval culture that interest and attract the members. Although there is a heavy emphasis on arms and warfare, all aspects of medieval and Renaissance life are fair game. The SCA welcomed female members from its inception.

Feasts in the various SCA locales are run by a "feasto-crat" who is selected on the basis of demonstrated cooking experience within the organization, but who is sometimes chosen after political infighting. Yet despite the organizational imbroglios, some members of the SCA have produced meaningful research on pre-1600 foodways, translating and sharing medieval and Renaissance cookery texts, adapting period recipes, discovering sources for hard-to-find ingredients, or reenacting feasts using technologies that fairly re-create centuries-old cookery methods. The SCA has advanced the popular understanding of premodern eating and drinking. The SCA sells pamphlets on herbs, brewing, and cookery, and various members have assembled compendia of recipes and suggestions for cooking from primary sources. Its website links to a number of scholarly resources for period information. Yet with few peasants on hand to eat only porridge and wild greens, and fully utilizing modern transportation to obtain out-of-season (but period-type) foods, the SCA readily admits that its feasts usually present an unabashedly skewed picture of pre-1600 dining.

Most other reenactment groups in the United States focus on either the Revolutionary War or the Civil War. They generally reenact battles and initially attracted a largely male enrollment, although more women joined as the cultural play expanded beyond the battlefield. These groups can be quite accurate in their simulations of soldiers' foodways during various campaigns. Civil War groups use records of the actual rations prescribed for soldiers, with mess officers requisitioning foodstuffs from a commissary and setting up field kitchens comparable to those that would have been found under battle conditions. Although the mess officers give more food to modern reenactors to adjust for larger modern body frames, the bills of fare are generally well grounded in the historical record and frequently prepared according to period recipes.

The sophistication of the Civil War reenactments is reflected also in the distinction between officers' and enlisted men's tables: officers had to pay for their food and so their reenacted meals focus on more elegant comestibles, again using period recipes. Experienced reenactors conduct seminars and other educational programs to train participants in foodways specifics. These include recommendations on the safe handling of food after it leaves the anachronistically refrigerated commissaries and practical advice on protecting rations from animals and the elements when the armies decamp for battle.

The Past Masters in Early American Domestic Arts is a group that interprets domestic skills and processes in English colonies from 1681 to 1783, with a special emphasis on the Revolutionary War period. A main activity is period cooking from the Delaware Valley, with frequent demonstrations and classes. The *Past Masters News*, a quarterly publication, contains many food-related articles; several members regularly speak at ALHFAM events and have published well-researched books and articles on colonial gardening and household receipts.

[*See also* Chesapeake Bay; Corn-Preparation Tools; Historiography; Kitchens, *subentry on* Early Kitchens; Pioneers and Survival Food; Thanksgiving.]

BIBLIOGRAPHY

Anderson, Jay. *Time Machines: The World of Living History.* Nashville, TN: The American Association for State and Local History, 1984.

Association for Living Historical Farms and Agricultural Museums. http://www.alhfam.org. A very detailed website with many helpful links for living history professionals; extensive bibliographies and ties to most of the living history sites

Brandau, Rosemary. "A Taste of the Past." *Journal of the Colonial Williamsburg Foundation* 9, no. 4 (Summer 1987): 28–32.

Deetz, James, and Patricia Scott Deetz. *The Times of Their Lives: Life, Love, and Death in Plymouth Colony.* New York: W. H. Freeman, 2000. The concluding chapter explains the reconstruction history of Plimoth Plantation after Deetz joined as assistant director in 1959.

Glassberg, David. "Living in the Past." *American Quarterly* 38 (1986): 305–310. A telling review of Jay Anderson's *Time Machines.*

Gode Cookery. http://www.godecookery.com/. Medieval cookery by serious reenactors; often with photographs of events; see especially the Hatherleigh Fire Festival Medieval Dinners.

Heart-to-Hearth Cookery. http://www.hearttohearthcookery.com. Native American and seventeenth-century foodways in Pennsylvania.

Kruger, John D. "Behind the Public Presentations: Research and Scholarship at Living History Museums of Early America." *William and Mary Quarterly*, 3d ser., 48 (1991): 347–385.

Leon, Warren, and Margaret Piatt. "Living-History Museums." In *History Museums in the United States*, edited by Warren Leon and Roy Rosenzweig. Urbana and Chicago: University of Illinois Press, 1989.

Living History News: A Common Passion Connecting Reenactors and Living Historians of All Time Periods. Available at http://www.heritagebooks.com/ An electronic newsletter offering practical advice to reenactors.

Past Masters in Early American Domestic Arts. http://www.past-masters.info/.

Rawlings, Kevin. *We Were Marching on Christmas Day.* Baltimore, MD: Toomey Press, 1995. A Civil War reenactor's careful assembly of hundreds of primary sources documenting meals and food provisioning at Christmas.

Sussman, Vic. "From Williamsburg to Conner Prairie: Living History Museums Bring Bygone Days to Life, But Not Always Accurately." *U.S. News and World Report* 107, no. 4 (July 24, 1989): 58–62.

Theobald, Mary Miley. "Sampling 18th-Century Fare at Shields Tavern." *Journal of the Colonial Williamsburg Foundation* 15, no. 2 (Winter 1992–1993): 47–50.

The Society for Creative Anachronism, Inc. http://sca.org/welcome.html. The website includes many informative links for food and drink before 1600.

CATHY K. KAUFMAN

Historiography

Through trial and error, early humans collected wisdom as to what foods could safely be eaten and how they could best be prepared. Throughout most of human history, this storehouse of life-or-death information was passed down orally from generation to generation. Because of the universal importance of food, it comes as no surprise that humankind's earliest writings attempted to record this culinary heritage. Sumerians, for instance, recorded recipes on clay tablets, and Egyptians registered divers recipes in hieroglyphics on the walls of their tombs and temples.

The ancient Greeks may have been the first to compile recipes into cookery manuscripts. While many such manuscripts are known to have been written in ancient times, only one—*Artis magiricae, Libri X*, attributed in part to the first-century Roman chef Marcus Apicius—is known to have survived. This manuscript was considered so important that it was copied for centuries after it was written and long after the Romans themselves had disappeared. During the Middle Ages, additional cookery manuscripts were compiled in the Middle East and western Europe: these, too, were copied centuries after their origin. The importance of cookery is reflected in the fact that a cookbook, *De honesta voluptate* (Concerning honest pleasure), was published a mere twenty-five years after Gutenberg's initial publication of the Bible in 1450. The importance of historical cookery is reflected in the fact that Apicius's ancient manuscript was published but a few years later. It was subsequently translated into several European languages, and has been reprinted ever since, including three major English translations since 1936.

Since 1500, thousands of articles and books have been published related to food history. Europeans were particularly interested in what the ancient Romans and Greeks ate. Richard Warner, for instance, compiled and published historical cookery manuscripts and other culinary curiosities in his *Antiquitates Culinariae* (1791). Similarly, *The Pantropheon; or, History of Food* (1853), attributed to Alexis Soyer, attempted to describe the "greatest gastronomic marvels of antiquity." It was published in England and subsequently in the United States, making it the earliest known culinary history published in America.

Bibliographers

In the late nineteenth century, a second direction emerged: cookbook collectors began assembling and publishing bibliographies, a tradition that has continued into the twenty-first century. Although an absolutely complete list of cookery works from any geographical location has yet to be published as of the early 2000s, bibliographies provide a base for work in culinary history. Waldo Lincoln's *American Cookery Books* (1929) attempted a systematic bibliography of American cookbooks published prior to 1861. It was revised and enlarged by Eleanor Lowenstein in 1954 and again in 1972. Lowenstein was a New York book dealer, and several other important cookbook dealers, such as Jan Longone of the Food and Wine Library, and Joseph Carlin of Food Heritage Press, have made major contributions to the field of culinary history.

Eleanor and Bob Brown's *Culinary America: Cookbooks Published in the Cities and Towns of the United States of America* (1961) picked up chronologically where Lincoln left off, beginning in 1861 and ending in 1960. Other bib-

liographers focused on specific themes in cookbooks, such as Margaret Cook's *America's Charitable Cooks: A Bibliography of Fund-Raising Cook Books Published in the United States (1861–1915)* (1971).

Other frequently cited American cookbook bibliographies have focused on specific collections, such as Elizabeth Robins Pennell's *My Cookery Books* (1903) and Katherine Bitting's posthumously published *Gastronomic Bibliography* (1939). The surviving collections of Pennell and Bitting are now in the Library of Congress. Others have focused on particular collections at libraries such as G. A. Rudolph's *Receipt Book and Household Manual* (1968), based on the cookery collection at Kansas State University, and William R. Cagle and Lisa Killion Stafford's *American Books on Food and Drink* (1998), based on the cookery collection at the Lilly Library at Indiana University.

Other American bibliographies concentrate on particular geographic areas or on specific culinary topics. For instance, Barbara Ketcham Wheaton and Patricia Kelly's *Bibliography of Culinary History* (1987) focuses on all cookbooks and food books in libraries in Massachusetts; the John C. Pace Library in Pensacola published *A List of West Florida Cookbooks and Random Selection of Early Recipes* (1984); Dan Strehl, a senior librarian at the Los Angeles Public Library, published *One Hundred Books on California Food and Wine* (1990).

American Historians

Since the nineteenth century, Americans have been writing about culinary history. Food topics do appear in historical works. For instance, Alice Morse Earle's *Home Life in Colonial Days* (1898) included several chapters on food. Mary Tolford Wilson's essay "Amelia Simmons Fills a Need: *American Cookery*," first published in the *William and Mary Quarterly* in 1957, placed American culinary history into context. It was later reprinted as the preface to the facsimile edition of Simmons's *American Cookery* (1958), which was the first cookbook published by an American. Wilson was followed by many others, including Jane Carson's *Colonial Virginia Housewife* (1968), which looked seriously at aspects of American culinary history.

One observer has claimed that the modern field of American culinary history was created by Karen Hess. This may be an exaggeration, but not by much. With her husband, John Hess, she coauthored *The Taste of America* (1977). She edited Martha Washington's *Booke of Cookery* (1981), a facsimile edition of Mary Randolph's *The Virginia House-wife* (1984), and other works. She served as a critic and an encourager of others who have come into the culinary history field.

For academics, food history was generally considered trivial and it did not fit easily into the traditional historical topics related to politics and important events that most historians were concerned with. It was mainly journalists, magazine writers, and cookbook authors who took on the burden of examining the cultural, social, and historical aspects of cookery. As there were few authoritative works on culinary history, much of what was written about culinary subjects in the popular press was based on "fakelore" or undocumented food stories. Myths gain reality through repetition, and unfortunately most food writers have colluded by repeating them: Marco Polo did not introduce the Italians to Chinese noodles, which then emerged as pasta; Catherine de Médicis did not introduce the French to Italian cookery, which then became the base for the French gastronomic advances in the eighteenth century; Robert Gibbon Johnson did not introduce the tomato into the American culinary repertoire; and the African American scientist George Washington Carver did not invent peanut butter—and neither did John Harvey Kellogg.

British Contributions

Some popular British writers revolted against lightweight scholarship. They include Elizabeth David, whose works, from her 1950 *Book of Mediterranean Food* to the posthumously published *Harvest of the Cold Months: The Social History of Ice and Ices* (1995), offered elegant writing coupled with a clear attempt to locate appropriate support for her historical statements. Another outstanding exception is Reay Tannahill, whose book *Food in History* (1973), an ambitious work that tapped into extensive sources, offered an overview of culinary history throughout the world. While some scholars have rightly criticized specifics in Tannahill's work, her book legitimizes a global approach and provides a fresh framework for understanding culinary history. A third influence is Alan Davidson, a former British ambassador, who produced several extraordinary culinary books, including editing *The Oxford Companion to Food* (1999). Other important contributions have been his founding of Prospect Books, his editing of the journal *Petits propos culinaires* (PPC), and his participation in and encouragement of the Oxford Symposium on Food and Cookery. Prospect Books is the

single largest publisher of British cookery facsimiles and other scholarly works related to food. PPC includes essays on culinary topics and reviews of cookery books. The Oxford Symposium serves as an annual meeting place for those interested in culinary history. Both PPC and the Oxford Symposium are major communications hubs for individuals interested in culinary history throughout the world. David's, Tannahill's, and Davidson's works were all published in the United States and influenced many American culinary historians. In addition, American culinary historians were published in PPC and gave presentations at the Oxford Symposium.

American Journals, Newsletters, and Reenactors

Sparked by these successful British works, several American culinary history newsletters and journals have been inaugurated since 1984. In that year, American culinary historians were assisted by the publication of the *Journal of Gastronomy* by the American Institute of Wine and Food in San Francisco. The journal served as an outlet for articles on culinary history and provided a communication mechanism among those working in the field. Unfortunately, this periodical was discontinued in 1991. However, by that date, culinary history was firmly rooted in the United States. As the twenty-first century opened, journals with culinary history content were emerging, the most important of which were *Gastronomica: The Journal of Food and Culture* published by the University of California Press; *Food History News* published by Sandra Oliver in Isleboro, Maine; and *Flavor and Fortune*, a quarterly publication of the Institute of the Science and Art of Chinese Cuisine. Likewise, culinary history organizations had begun to thrive in many American communities, such as Ann Arbor, Boston, Chicago, Houston, Los Angeles, New York, Philadelphia, and Washington, D.C.

Yet another segment of the culinary history field are the "practitioners" and "reenactors" who participate in culinary history programs, such as those sponsored by members of the Association for Living History, Farm and Agricultural Museums (ALHFAM). They engage in preserving the culinary heritage of the past by attempting to duplicate recipes or food practices of different historical periods.

Food museums have opened throughout the world, such as the Wyandot Popcorn Museum in Marion, Ohio. Some museums have taken to the Internet and have become virtual museums, such as the Food Museum founded by Tom Hughes and Meredith Sayles Hughes of

Albuquerque, New Mexico, and the New York Food Museum. Food has also become an important topic for many traditional museums. Several major television series focusing on the history of food and drink have been aired, generating wide popular interest.

Theories and Syntheses

What has emerged is a broad-based, interdisciplinary, diverse field of culinary history that counts scholars from a variety of disciplines, such as sociology, anthropology, women's studies, religion, political science, geography, environmental studies, culinary arts, psychology, ethnobotany, literary criticism, food technologists, and those sciences related to health and nutrition. In addition to academics, the field embraces professional chefs, food writers, librarians, independent scholars, historical reenactors, cookbook authors, and just plain old foodies.

The eclectic nature of the food-studies field brings with it many strengths, but one weakness is that practitioners have approached their work from very different perspectives, used diverse methodologies, employed different vocabularies, attended different conferences, and read different books and journals. It comes as no surprise that diverse conceptual models have been presented to explain different aspects of food studies.

Because preparing, serving, and eating food are common features of all human societies, anthropologists and sociologists have always been concerned with the role food plays in society. However, few early conceptual models developed in anthropology or sociology are directly applicable to examining or comparing food systems over longer durations. This began to change with K. C. Chang's *Food in Chinese Culture*, published in 1977, which combined anthropological and historical approaches to the study of food. Likewise, Sidney W. Mintz combined these two approaches in his *Sweetness and Power: The Place of Sugar in Modern History*, published in 1985. This classic work recounted the relationships between slavery, sugar production, and sugar consumption.

A more comprehensive study was conducted by Jack Goody. In his *Cooking, Cuisine and Class: A Study in Comparative Sociology* (1982), Goody argued for an examination of all aspects of food, including processes (growing, allocating, or storing, cooking, eating, and cleaning up), phases (production, distribution, preparation, consumption, and disposal), and locations (farm, granary, or market, kitchen, table, and scullery). He then applied this model to culinary practices throughout history from ancient Egypt, imperial Rome, and medieval China to early modern Europe and modern Africa. He was particularly interested in how food reflects socioeconomic structures.

A History of Culinary History

Some historians have examined the influence of food products on broader historical themes; one example is Richard S. Dunn's *Sugar and Slaves: The Rise of the Planter Class in the English West Indies* (1972). Other historical works have examined foodways within national contexts, such as Richard Osborn Cummings's *The American and His Food: A History of Food Habits in the United States* (1946) and Richard J. Hooker's *A History of Food and Drink in America* (1981), both of which remain excellent general resources for American culinary history.

Since the 1950s, a major change has emerged in the approach to food history. In France, the *Annales* school (named after the journal *Annales: économies, sociétés, civilisations*) criticized traditional historians who focused only on high politics and events at the expense of long-term historical structures and dynamics. The *Annales* school also believed that historians should supplement traditional historical methods with those from the social sciences. Their emphasis on material culture meant that food was an appropriate and significant topic for historical investigation. The *Annales* school influenced American historians and several American historians have focused specifically on food. For instance, Robert Forester and Orest Ranum collected eleven such articles and reprinted them in *Food and Drink in History* (1979). In the United States, an academic journal, *Food and Foodways*, launched in 1985 by Steven L. Kaplan at Cornell University, has provided an extremely valuable outlet for scholars working on food history.

This latter cultural approach to food history has expanded rapidly since the mid-1990s. Individual professors have incorporated culinary topics into traditional courses and scholars have formed groups, such as the Association for the Study of Food in Society, to examine particular aspects of food. Several academic newsletters and journals, such as *Digest: An Interdisciplinary Study of Food and Foodways*, published by the Foodways Section of the American Folklore Society, have emerged. Regional food studies programs have been initiated, such as the Center for the Study of Southern Culture and its affiliated institute, the Southern Foodways Alliance, whose mission is to celebrate, preserve, promote, and nurture the traditional food culture of the American South.

FOOD HISTORY ORGANIZATIONS

Before 1975, roughly, there were few organizations, associations, or venues where professional chefs and others interested in the serious study of food could meet and discuss ideas. This changed in large part because of the explosion in the number of people needed to manage an expanding food-service industry, which in turn led to the growth of a national network of professional cooking schools to meet the demands of that industry. As a result, professionals found a need to form a variety of associations with a variety of purposes. Some of them are listed below.

American Culinary Federation
10 San Bartola Drive
St. Augustine, FL 32086
904-824-4468
800-624-9458
Fax: 904-824-4758
http://www.acfchefs.net

Culinarians dedicated to promoting their profession through education, apprenticeship and certification. Local chapters throughout the country.

The American Institute of Wine and Food (AIWF)
304 West Liberty Street, Suite 201
Louisville, KY 40202
502-992-1022
Fax: 502-589-3602
http://www.aiwf.com

Educational organization devoted to improving the appreciation and understanding of food and drink.

American Personal Chef Association
4572 Delaware Street
San Diego, CA 92116
800-644-8389
Fax: 619-294-2436
http://www.personalchef.com

The Association for the Study of Food and Society (ASFS) is a multidisciplinary international organization dedicated to exploring the complex relationships between food, culture, and society. Its members, who approach the study of food from numerous disciplines in the humanities, social sciences, and sciences, as well as in the world of food beyond the academy, draw on a wide range of theoretical and practical approaches and seek to promote discussions about food that transgress traditional boundaries. Search the Internet for current address and membership information.

Association for Living History, Farm, and Agricultural Museums (ALHFAM)
8774 Route 45 NW
North Bloomfield, OH 44450
http://www.alhfam.org

ALHFAM is the museum organization for those involved in living historical farms, agricultural museums, outdoor museums of history and folklife, and those museums—large and small—that use living history programming.

Food and Culinary Professionals (FCP)
P. O. Box 46998
Seattle, WA 98146
http://www.foodculinaryprofs.org/index.htm

FCP is a Dietetic Practice Group of the American Dietetic Association whose members are committed to developing food expertise throughout the profession of dietetics. *Tastings*, a newsletter is published quarterly.

Foodways Section of the American Folklore Society
American Folklore Society
4350 North Fairfax Drive, Suite 640
Arlington, VA 22203
703-528-1902
http://www.afsnet.org

Publishes *Digest: An Interdisciplinary Study of Food and Foodways*.

International Association of Culinary Professionals
304 West Liberty Street, Suite 201
Louisville, KY 40202-3011
502-581-9786
Fax: 502-589-3602
http://www.iacp.com

Association provides continuing education and development for its members who are engaged in the areas of culinary education, communication, or in the preparation of food and drink. This organization has a food history section.

The James Beard Foundation
The Beard House
167 West Twelfth Street
New York, NY 10011
212-627-2308
http://www.jamesbeard.org

Continued

FOOD HISTORY ORGANIZATIONS (Continued)

James Beard is recognized by many as the father of American gastronomy. The foundation celebrates the country's culinary artists, provides scholarships and educational opportunities, serves as a resource for the industry, and offers members the opportunity to enjoy the delights of fine dining.

Radcliffe Culinary Friends.
Schlesinger Library
10 Garden Street
Cambridge, MA 02138.

Publishes *Radcliffe Culinary Times*, which often has articles by and appealing to food historians.

Research Chefs Association
5775 Peachtree-Dunwoody Road
Building G, Suite 500
Atlanta, GA 30342
404-252 3663
Fax: 404-252-0774
http://www.culinology.com

This is the leading professional community for food research and development. Its members are the pioneers of the discipline of culinology, the blending of culinary arts and the science of food.

San Francisco Professional Food Society (SFPFS)
268 Bush Street, Number 2715
San Francisco, CA 94104
415-442-1999
Fax: 415-358-5960
http://www.sfpfs.com

A forum for food and beverage professionals to come together to exchange information and promote social interaction.

Slow Food U.S.A.
434 Broadway, Sixth Floor
New York, NY 10013
212-965-5640
Fax: 212-226-0672
http://www.slowfoodusa.org

Slow Food U.S.A. is an educational organization dedicated to stewardship of the land and ecologically sound food production; to the revival of the kitchen and the table as centers of pleasure, culture, and community; to the invigoration and proliferation of regional, seasonal culinary traditions; and to living a slower and more harmonious rhythm of life.

The Italian association was founded in 1986 and the international movement was founded in Paris in 1989.

Southern Foodways Alliance
Center for the Study of Southern Culture
Barnard Observatory University of Mississippi
Oxford, MS 38677
662-915-5993
http://www.southernfoodways.com/index.shtml

Established in 1977 at the University of Mississippi, the center has become a focal point for innovative education and research by promoting scholarship on every aspect of Southern culture.

CULINARY HISTORY GROUPS

Until the Culinary Historians of Boston was founded in the early 1980s, there were few opportunities for those interested in the history of food or the culinary arts to meet. Some of these early food historians were chefs, such as Louis Szathmary, who operated the Bakery Restaurant in Chicago, and Barbara Ketcham Wheaton, the author of *Savoring the Past*, who worked outside the food field but had an abiding interest in all things culinary.

During the early 1980s, word spread about this new Boston group, which held their monthly meetings in one of the residence halls at Harvard University in Cambridge. Other groups soon sprang up around the country and outside the United States. In 2004, the Culinary Historians of Tasmania announced their formation.

The following is a list of known organizations in the United States. Because these groups are locally organized the contact name and phone number is likely to change frequently. For that reason only the name of the organization and the city and state in which they generally hold their meetings is listed. If they have a dedicated website it is also listed. The Internet is the best place to start a search for a current contact person or one can go to www.foodhistorynews.com for an up-to-date list of culinary history groups.

Culinary Historians of Ann Arbor
Ann Arbor, Michigan

Founded in 1983 by Jan Longone, a well-known food historian and dealer in antiquarian culinary publications. The group also publishes a quarterly newsletter.

Continued

FOOD HISTORY ORGANIZATIONS (*Continued*)

Culinary Historians of Boston
Cambridge, Massachusetts
http://www.culinary.org/chb/index.htm

A bimonthly newsletter is published; meetings are monthly.

Culinary Historians of Chicago
Chicago, Illinois
http://www.culinaryhistorians.org

Founded in 1993 as a nonprofit educational organization committed to the study of the history of food and drink in human cultures. The members are from a wide range of competencies: from everyday cooks or amateur historians to those in academia.

Foodways Group of Austin
Austin, Texas

Founded by the food writer Alice Arndt, cofounder of the Houston Culinary Historians, and Glenn Mack of the Culinary Academy of Austin. The purpose of this group is for local food lovers to explore food and foodways of the past and present, in Texas and around the world.

Culinary History Enthusiasts of Wisconsin (CHEW)
Madison, Wisconsin

New Orleans Culinary History Group
New Orleans, Louisiana
http://www.tulane.edu/~wclib/culinary.html

Culinary Historians of Connecticut
Various locations

Culinary Historians of Hawaii
Honolulu, Hawaii

Historic Foodways Society of the Delaware Valley
The society began in October 1994 with a gathering of more than thirty people interested in preserving the rich foodways culture of the communities along the Delaware River. The organization is devoted to exploring the rich, diverse culinary heritage of the region including southeastern New York, Pennsylvania, New Jersey, Delaware, and Maryland's Eastern Shore.

Houston Culinary Historians
Houston, Texas

Culinary Historians of New York
New York, New York

Culinary Historians of Southern California (CHSC)
Los Angeles, California
http://www.lapl.org/central/science.html#Culinary

CHSC was founded in 1995 for scholars, cooks, food writers, nutritionists, collectors, students, and others interested in the study of culinary history and gastronomy.

Culinary Historians of Washington, D.C.
Washington, District of Columbia
http://www.chowdc.org/index.html

Their newsletter, ChoWLine, is published nine times each year. It contains monthly reports on the organization's meetings and provides information on upcoming meetings, food-related events, publications, and films.

Mediterranean Culinary Historians of Houston (MCHH)
Houston, Texas

MCHH was founded to merge the growing academic field of culinary history with popular interest in Mediterranean cuisine and diet.

JOSEPH M. CARLIN

The result of this activity has been the rapid expansion of culinary history as an academic topic. This growth is reflected in the increasing number of culinary courses and interdisciplinary programs, such as those offered by the Radcliffe Institute for Advanced Study at Harvard University, the Department of Nutrition and Food Studies at New York University, the Culinary Arts Program at New School University in New York, and Boston University's Master of Liberal Arts in Gastronomy. In addition, hundreds of professional culinary arts schools, most of which have courses on culinary history, have blossomed around the world. These centers, organizations, programs, and conferences have encouraged academic research into food and drink, and numerous articles have appeared in academic journals. Likewise, the number of food-related theses and dissertations has increased and the number of books published on related topics has mushroomed. Several university presses, such as those at Oxford, Cambridge, the University of Iowa, University of South Carolina, University of Illinois, and University of California, have developed extensive lists of scholarly works on food. In England, Prospect Books is devoted almost entirely to food history.

In the early 2000s hardly a week went by without a university or commercial press releasing yet another academic work on some topic related to culinary history. Some culinary historians have focused on culinary ingredients or products, for example, Virginia Scott Jenkins's research into the history of bananas. Others, like Ken Albala in *Eating Right in the Renaissance* (2002), have examined particular historical periods, while others have focused on histories of national cuisines. Still others have focused on topics, such as Alison J. Clarke's *Tupperware: The Promise of Plastic in 1950s America* (1999). In addition, several reference works have been released: *The Cambridge World History of Food* (2000), edited by Kenneth F. Kiple and Kriemhild Coneè Ornelas; *Food: A Culinary History from Antiquity to the Present* (1999), edited by Jean-Louis Flandrin and Massimo Montanari; and the *Encyclopedia of Food and Culture* (2003), edited by Solomon H. Katz. All reflect a broader approach. Despite this growth, or perhaps because of it, diversity reigns within the emerging culinary history field. Culinary historians, like other scholars exploring the broader field of food studies, have focused on different contents, explored different culinary processes, and employed different methods. Little attempt has been made to link these diverse works together.

Methods of Culinary History

The methods used in culinary history include the traditional academic ones of observation, text analysis, linguistics, botany, zoology, and DNA studies, travelers' putative eyewitness reports, self-reports of individuals from within a culture, historical records, and archaeological evidence among others. But there are also methods unique to culinary history, such as actually preparing the recipe, whether written, orally communicated, or inferred from archaeological, literary, and other primary sources. The cookbook, a collection of written recipes, is an important manifestation of culinary history, but until recently it was rarely mentioned in traditional academic discourse. In many ways, the recipe itself is a means by which to explore the past. Much is to be learned from the past by trying to re-create it. Culinary historians must be able to analyze, reconstruct, and evaluate the results of the recipes. This includes preparing, serving, and consuming food. The proof is in the tasting, and understanding what tastes good is yet another ability needed by culinary historians. By using their understanding of tastes, researchers can discover how foods and flavors were combined in earlier times, and this in turn reveals information about the larger cultural context in which the food was consumed.

The purpose of writing about culinary history is not just to describe what happened in the past. It is also to discuss the historical consequences of culinary activity. These consequences include the nutritional health of individuals, groups, and civilizations, as well as the environmental and ecological effects of preparing and consuming food, such as the loss of biodiversity through overharvesting, the destruction of agricultural land or the rain forests, or the failure to properly dispose of waste, which might lead to illness or environmental degradation. In addition, culinary history should tell us where humankind has been and perhaps suggest directions for the future.

[*See also* Bitting, Katherine; Culinary Historians of Boston; Culinary History vs. Food History; Historical Overview; Historic Dining Reenactment; Library Collections; Lowenstein, Eleanor; Randolph, Mary.]

BIBLIOGRAPHY

Bitting, Katherine. *Gastronomic Bibliography*. San Francisco: Halle-Cordis Composing Room and Trade Freeroom, 1939.

Brown, Eleanor, and Bob Brown. *Culinary America: Cookbooks Published in the Cities and Towns of the United States of America during the Years from 1860 through 1960*. New York: Roving Eye Press, 1961.

Bullock, Helen. *The Williamsburg Art of Cookery; or, Accomplish'd Gentlewoman's Companion*. Williamsburg, VA: Colonial Williamsburg, 1938.

Cagle, William R., and Lisa Killion Stafford, *American Books on Food and Drink*. New Castle, DE: Oak Knoll Press, 1998.

Cook, Margaret. *America's Charitable Cooks: A Bibliography of Fund-Raising Cook Books Published in the United States (1861–1915)*. Kent, OH: np, 1971.

Katz, Solomon H., ed. *Encyclopedia of Food and Culture*. 3 vols. New York: Scribners, 2003.

Lincoln, Waldo. *American Cookery Books 1742–1860*. Worcester, MA: The Society, 1929.

A List of West Florida Cookbooks and Random Selection of Early Recipes. Pensacola, FL: The John C. Pace Library, 1984.

Lowenstein, Eleanor. *Bibliography of American Cookery Books, 1742–1860*. Worcester, MA: American Antiquarian Society, 1972.

Pennell, Elizabeth Robins. *My Cookery Books*. Boston and New York: Houghton Mifflin, 1903.

Rudolph, G. A., comp. *Receipt Book and Household Manual*. Bibliography series, no. 4. Manhattan: Kansas State University, 1968.

Smith, Andrew F. "Everything You Wanted to Know About Culinary History, But Didn't Have the Time to Find Out." *Culinary Historians of Boston Newsletter* 18 (November 1997): 11–17.

Smith, Andrew F. "False Memories: The Invention of Culinary Fakelore and Food Fallacies." In *Proceedings of the Oxford Symposium on Food and Cookery 2000*, edited by Harlan Walker. Devon, UK: Prospect Books, 2001.

Wheaton, Barbara Ketcham, and Patricia Kelly. *Bibliography of Culinary History: Food Resources in Eastern Massachusetts*. Boston: G. K. Hall, 1987.

ANDREW F. SMITH

Hoagie

Sandwiches based on Italian rolls or French bread and filled with multiple layers of ingredients are known by various names throughout the United States, including hoagie, hero, submarine, Italian sandwich, grinder, bomber, torpedo, rocket, spuckie, wedge, and zeppelin. These made-to-order sandwiches originally consisted of cold cuts, cheese, and lettuce garnished with a choice of tomatoes, onion, pickles, or peppers and dressed with mayonnaise, oil, or mustard. Fillings were later expanded to include other choices, such as tuna, meatballs, sandwich steaks, and various vegetarian options.

The hoagie is the earliest sandwich of this type. Legend credits its creation to the Philadelphia sandwich shop proprietor Al De Palma, who introduced the sandwich as the "hoggie" in 1936. De Palma reportedly chose the name after witnessing a friend devour a large sandwich and thinking that he was a hog to eat it all once. As competitors in the Philadelphia area copied his sandwich and sold it under various names, including hoagie, hogie, and horgy, De Palma responded by proclaiming himself "The Original Hoggie Man." By 1950 the various spellings started to disappear, and the sandwich became commonly known as the hoagie. It was declared the "Official Sandwich of Philadelphia" in 1992.

Meanwhile, word of the hoagie spread, and by 1939 New York had its own version of the sandwich. Known as the hero, it was popular among visitors to Coney Island. Around 1940 the submarine became the local rendition of the hoagie in restaurants along the mid-Atlantic coast.

As the popularity of these large, multilayered sandwiches increased throughout the United States during the 1950s and 1960s, they became known by different names on a regional basis. Hoagie is used in Pennsylvania and New Jersey, while in New York City they are referred to as heroes. In Maine they are known as Italian sandwiches, and in Massachusetts, Rhode Island, Connecticut, and Vermont they are usually called grinders. Spuckie is a term for the sandwich unique to the Boston area. Submarine is commonly used throughout the United States, while other names, including bomber, rocket, wedge, zeppelin, and torpedo, can be found in various areas throughout the country.

[See also Italian American Food; Sandwiches.]

BIBLIOGRAPHY

Mercuri, Becky. *Sandwiches That You Will Like*. Pittsburgh, PA: WQED, 2002.

BECKY MERCURI

Home Economics

In the late nineteenth century, industrialization and urbanization placed the American home in a state of flux. As the production of household items became centered in shops and factories, the economic function of the home shifted toward the buying of goods and the rendering of services. To guide homemakers through this transition, a group of middle-class women—and a few men—launched an educational reform movement. Widely known as "domestic scientists" in the last few decades of the nineteenth century, in 1899 they organized a meeting in Lake Placid, New York, to propose the term "home economics" for a new field of study that would enable homemakers to perform domestic work more efficiently and manage household budgets more economically.

For the next ten years, a diverse group of educators, writers, and scientists gathered annually to formalize an academic discipline to teach these principles in the nation's schools and universities. The discipline they created reflected a shared moral conviction of the superiority of white Anglo-Saxon Protestant culture, a belief in scientific and technological progress, and an optimistic faith in the ability of experts to improve social conditions—a faith that was characteristic of many Progressive Era reform initiatives. In 1909 they established the American Home Economics Association (AHEA) to promote a vision of private family life that was predicated on a public role for this new group of women professionals. Food was a central, but not exclusive, concern for home economists. All household activities—including cleaning, managing the family budget, and even child rearing—represented opportunities for these women to model the home on the new industrial order and infuse it with moral ideals. Still, the selection, purchase, and storage of foodstuffs, and the preparation and serving of meals, received special emphasis in home economists' quest for "right living" based on rationality. In part because food occupied the single largest expense in all but the most generous family budgets, the movement's founder, Ellen Swallow Richards, and her colleagues understood the American diet as a focal point for reforming American domestic life and, by extension, the nation at large.

What to eat and why were questions of great import for early home economists. New findings in chemistry, physiology, and bacteriology provided not only reassuring answers but also opportunities for many of these women to pursue scientific careers. Although the specific instruction varied according to the individual teacher and her audience, most home economists emphasized the quantifiable aspects of foods and their constituent parts rather than taste and pleasure. Efficiency in fueling the human body, economy in purchasing ingredients, and sanitation in preservation were thus the main goals of the home economists' lessons about food. By incorporating these values into a new understanding of a homemaker's responsibility for her family's food consumption, home economists helped ordinary women navigate the expanding body of scientific and technological information about food.

In their campaign to make sense of American meals within the context of a growing consumer society, home economists succeeded in carving out academic and professional niches for themselves as food experts in the first quarter of the twentieth century. Thousands of girls and women received classroom instruction in home economics at all levels of the educational system, lessons that were reinforced by home economists' activities inside institutions that manufactured and studied food products. Through the early 1970s, home economists worked as elementary and high-school teachers, college professors, government researchers, agricultural extension agents, representatives of consumer-products companies, women's magazine editors, and recipe and cookbook writers—and thus served as the primary educators on food and nutrition for several generations of Americans. In less visible but equally significant ways, home economists influenced the diet of ordinary families by contributing to the development of processed foods and of public policy related to food. Collectively, these women used the traditional idea that food is women's work to perform a public role in shaping new understandings of food and its management.

Scientific Cookery and Social Reform

The movement got its start after the Civil War, as surveys among the urban poor revealed that many families spent as much as one-half of their overall budgets on food. In response, reformers fastened on diet as the means of combating the social problems of the day: poverty, crime, intemperance, and labor unrest. Convinced that workers were ill-fed because of ignorance as much as for lack of money, domestic scientists established cooking schools in many northeastern cities to promote more economical and healthful ways of preparing food. The primary targets of these schools—which opened in New York, Philadelphia, and Boston in the 1870s and 1880s—were

immigrant women. The cooking instructors viewed the mixed foods of eastern European and Mediterranean cultures as too spicy and thus difficult to digest. In the place of traditional ethnic foodways, they held up New England Yankee cookery as the cultural ideal that would elevate foreigners—as well as African Americans and Native Americans—to a higher standard of living and thereby transform them into true Americans.

These urban cooking schools taught women to consider food in scientific terms. At the Boston Cooking School, founded in 1879, Mary Lincoln lectured about systematic measurements, kitchen procedures, food value, and the process of digestion. In addition to encouraging women to cook by the book, the classes urged students to regard the kitchen as a laboratory for the study of foods and their composition. Lincoln and her colleagues at other schools took as their jumping off point the scientific findings of Ellen Swallow Richards, the first female graduate of the Massachusetts Institute of Technology (MIT). Richards devoted much of her career to the chemical analyses of food adulteration and water contamination, and to studying the chemical processes involved in cooking and digesting food. At the Women's Laboratory she directed at MIT, and at the New England Kitchen she helped launch in Boston, Richards trained a cohort of younger women in an array of scientific methods for preparing healthy and economical meals under sanitary and efficient conditions.

The new science of bacteriology also attracted the attention of Richards and her generation of early home economists. By 1900 they were teaching women to understand the domestic environment in terms of the germ theory of disease. Concerns about the cleanliness of the milk supply and the contamination of processed foods led them to encourage consumers to buy packaged foods rather than purchase foodstuffs from open containers in markets. A desire for food safety also drove a number of early home economists to campaign for regulation by state and local governments and to lobby for the passage of the Pure Food and Drug Act of 1906.

Already predisposed toward the rational and the modern, domestic scientists welcomed the emerging science of nutrition with open arms. By the 1890s this new field presented a coherent vision of how the human body uses foods. Pioneering nutritional scientists in Germany had analyzed the components of food as carbohydrates, proteins, fats, minerals, and water and had demonstrated that each nutrient performed specific physiological functions.

Wilbur O. Atwater, a professor of chemistry at Wesleyan University, had studied with these leaders, and he initiated the first major investigations into food and human digestion in the United States. In mapping out the American diet in quantitative terms, Atwater generated a comprehensive set of food composition tables and popularized the calorie as a unit of measurement; both of these advances became building blocks for home economists' research and teaching in later decades. Atwater welcomed women into his laboratory as students and researchers, and he enlisted a number of Ellen Richards's protégés in an ambitious survey of the nation's eating habits. The participation of Isabel Bevier, Caroline Hunt, Martha Van Rensselaer, and others in these investigations did much to legitimize them as scientists; their role in preparing recipes and government bulletins based on Atwater's findings established them as important interpreters of nutritional science to the general public.

Simultaneously, in the 1890s, domestic scientists found an attentive audience for their cooking instruction. Working-class women had rejected their high-minded calls for dietary reform. The New England Kitchen, which served cheap, nutritious meals for workers to take home in Boston's North End, was a failure with the neighborhood's Jewish, Portuguese, Italian, and Slavic residents. The cooking schools proved popular, however, with white women who sought to identify themselves as members of a new, urban middle class. Domestic scientists' critique of the overindulgent eating practices of the rich appealed to their sense of bourgeois gentility. College-educated women who came of age in the Progressive Era were accustomed to seeking advice from experts and embraced the home economists' rational approach to food. The widespread success of scientific cookery—and the myriad of cookbooks, recipes, schools, and clubs it inspired—placed food and nutrition at the center of the new discipline of home economics after 1900.

World War I was a watershed for home economists and their authority as experts on nutrition and food. The United States Food Administration (USFA), established to send food to the American military and the Allied civilian population in Europe, and directed by the engineer and business manager Herbert Hoover, enlisted home economists to promote food conservation and popularize new ideas about nutrition. "Food will win the war" was the USFA's rallying slogan. Determined not to ration, Hoover brought Martha Van Rensselaer, director of home economics at Cornell University, and Sarah Field Splint,

editor of *Today's Housewife*, to Washington and placed them in charge of teaching homemakers throughout the country how to prepare healthy meals without wheat, meat, sugar, fats, and other scarce foodstuffs.

The war emergency allowed home economists to bring scientific cookery into the cultural mainstream. In the name of patriotism, home economists translated the findings of nutritional experts into practical explanations and recipes that homemakers could understand and use. Home economics professors, teachers, and students developed recipes that gave precise definitions of meatless meats, sugarless sweets, and bread without wheat. The food conservation drive provided a context for home economists to teach the concept of food value and the principle of substituting one food for another. By emphasizing each food's contribution to an individual's diet, they showed homemakers that substitutes were not only possible, but also healthy. The wartime cookbooks they produced encouraged women to embrace eggs, cheese, and fish as alternate sources of protein and to consider the potato as nutritious as bread. Although researchers still had only a vague understanding of how vitamins functioned in the diet, home economists heralded the healthful effects of fruits and vegetables and promoted them as "meat extenders." Having recently revised canning methods in accordance with the latest bacteriological findings, home economists disseminated these techniques as a way to ensure the year-round availability of fruits and vegetables.

Through the USFA's organizational and publicity apparatus, hundreds of cookbooks, pamphlets, newspaper and magazine articles, and lesson plans offered homemakers practical instruction in conserving food while eating according to scientific principles. Dozens of home economists prepared these publications behind the scenes while others wore official USFA aprons and caps as they demonstrated cooking and canning techniques to communities throughout the nation. Although the food conservation campaigns were not universally popular, they did expose an unprecedented number of Americans to the idea that there was a close relationship between food and health and that home economists were the experts to turn to for advice on the subject.

Status and Expertise

The home economists' enhanced wartime reputation as food experts enabled them to secure postwar places in higher education, in agricultural research establishments, and in industrial corporations. In the Midwest, state land-grant colleges had supported women's education in home economics as a counterpart to the education of male farmers as early as the 1870s, and after 1910 federal legislation provided additional funding for the expansion of home economics departments at these schools. Intended to train home economics teachers, agricultural extension agents, and a new generation of modern homemakers, the expansion of home economics in the land-grant colleges and some private universities also created opportunities for ambitious women to serve as professors and administrators. Within the United States Department of Agriculture (USDA), the establishment of the Office of Home Economics in 1915 and a Bureau of Home Economics in 1923 further supplied home economists with an institutional context for building a research program around consumption, with a considerable emphasis on food.

From within these institutions, home economists converted the subjects of food and nutrition into an academic study. Many home economics researchers made contributions to new knowledge in the nutritional sciences and published regularly in technical journals and the *Journal of Home Economics*. But as a group home economists concentrated their efforts on defining an *applied* science of nutrition that they could call their own. This broad field injected an element of empirical study and science into just about every aspect of food and its use in the home. Nutritional food values, food preservation and storage, dietary planning and budgeting, and recipe development—investigated according to the principles of chemistry, bacteriology, and physics—all had a place in home economists' nutritional research agenda.

The USDA's Office of Home Economics, and then the Bureau of Home Economics, played a leading role in defining food and nutrition as a research field for home economists to have to themselves. Beginning in 1915, home economists in the department used an experimental kitchen to investigate such topics as vegetable canning methods and techniques for the efficient use of gas ranges. When Louise Stanley was appointed director of the new bureau in 1923, she discontinued the costly respiration calorimetry work that Atwater had begun. Representing a second generation of scientifically trained home economists, Stanley had earned a doctorate in biochemistry from Yale University where she studied with Lafayette Mendel.

Throughout her tenure as the first woman director of the federal home economics research program, which continued through the early 1940s, Stanley encouraged

investigations by women scientists and hired female nutritional chemists to lead the USDA's continued studies of the composition and preparation of foods. While male nutrition researchers in the 1920s and 1930s took charge of cutting-edge investigations to identify and isolate new vitamins and understand their effects on the human body, bureau chemist Hazel E. Munsell and her colleagues pursued the labor-intensive laboratory work required to determine the precise vitamin content of foods. These studies revealed how vitamin content varied with conditions of production and handling, and bureau staff thereupon developed recipes and instructional literature to help homemakers maximize the vitamin benefits. On the basis of this vitamin content work, in the 1920s most government home economists advocated waterless cookery, the practice of cooking vegetables in their own juices for a limited period of time so as to preserve their vitamin and mineral content.

At the Bureau of Home Economics, home economists also studied kitchen design and equipment from the user's perspective. Many of these investigations, such as one into the size variation of measuring cups on the market, were directed at improving and standardizing manufactured goods. Bureau home economists also worked with the bacteriologist and chemist Mary Engle Pennington and with manufacturers to define and optimize healthful and efficient specifications for refrigerator design, and to promote safe and sanitary methods of refrigerator use. This project resulted in a publicity campaign that defined the refrigerator as a public health necessity and emphasized the importance of maintaining standard, constant cold to prevent food from spoiling. In another research project in the 1930s and 1940s, bureau home economists evaluated the quality of commercial canned goods with the intention of developing a system of grade labeling.

At colleges and universities, home economics researchers pursued similar lines of research. A number of them—such as Mary Swartz Rose at Teachers College, Columbia University, and Agnes Fay Morgan at the University of California, Berkeley—built up solid reputations as professors of nutrition. Most of Rose's publications, including *Feeding the Family* (a popular book for mothers first issued in 1916 and revised several times after that) dealt with the practical applications of nutrition research. Morgan was a leading contributor to the nutritional sciences, and she used her position to develop Berkeley's home economics department. At Iowa State University in the 1920s, Eloise Davison established a specialty in the study of household equipment; her successor, Louise Peet, developed this area of investigation and wrote multiple editions of the standard college textbook on the subject. As a whole, home economists' food research programs made them the experts to consult for definitive answers to such questions as the nutritional value of spinach, ideal roasting temperatures for meat, and the best kitchen designs.

Nutrition Education as Social Service

By 1940 home economics had acquired a distinctive place in the curriculum at four-year and junior colleges, high schools, and elementary schools. While many of these courses were aimed exclusively at girls and young women, younger boys were also exposed to home economists' ideas about food by the lunch programs that home economists implemented in many schools. Mature homemakers in rural areas received informal instruction from home demonstration agents through the agricultural extension service. In addition, the Bureau of Home Economics disseminated many of the results of its studies

Home Economics. Researcher at the Home Economics Department, Iowa State College, Ames, Iowa, May 1942. *Prints and Photographs Division, Library of Congress/Jack Delano*

directly to women through government bulletins, written correspondence, and *Aunt Sammy's Radio Program.*

Home economists related meal preparation to the homemaker's role not only as cook but as the manager of household consumption. Using nutrition as a jumping-off point, home economists taught students to understand foodstuffs as material goods to be efficiently consumed and effectively managed. Through their textbooks, classroom instruction, and home demonstrations, they taught American homemakers rational methods for selecting ingredients, preparing dishes, and preserving perishable foods. By defining family meals according to the principles of intelligent buying, home economics professors and teachers spoke in an alternative voice that challenged the cultural stereotypes of women as passive victims of manipulative advertisements.

Home economists' persistent faith in technological progress was embedded in their instruction, particularly in their efforts aimed at modernizing life on the farm. Home economists shared the concerns of male agricultural reformers about the population drain from the rural areas to the cities. Seeking to keep native white families tied to the land, home demonstration agents drew on science to improve the standard of living on American farms according to urban ideals. Just as the agricultural extension service encouraged farmers to apply science to growing crops and raising animals, home economists embraced laborsaving technologies to ease the lot of the overworked farm woman. From the 1930s through the 1960s, female extension agents were particularly active in promoting rural electrification and encouraging rural women to adopt domestic appliances and streamlined kitchen design. By helping to integrate this large group of women into the market economy as consumers, home economists acted as agents of social change.

National emergencies gave home economists the opportunity to provide important social service in times of need. During the Great Depression and World War II, food was a public issue. Economic hardship and national preparedness triggered renewed interest in healthy eating and food conservation on the part of government leaders as well as many homemakers—particularly middle-class women who had the time and money to do the planning and work required. Soon after the 1929 stock market crash, the Bureau of Home Economics launched the *Market Basket*, a weekly press release with suggestions for canning methods and low-cost recipes using "protective foods" to help families avoid malnutrition in hard times;

many newspapers reproduced it as a regular feature. To support President Franklin D. Roosevelt's New Deal relief programs, bureau food economists developed a set of diets appropriate to four levels of income as a guide to making careful dietary choices. At Cornell University, home economics professor Flora Rose devised emergency food budgets to help families eat healthily while spending less on food. Publicized by First Lady Eleanor Roosevelt, and distributed widely throughout the 1930s, these diets and budgets served as the primary standards for social service and relief agencies in urban and rural communities.

When the military draft during World War II revealed that many potential soldiers suffered from malnutrition and had to be rejected, the National Research Council established committees to determine dietary needs and to explore ways of adjusting food habits to meet those needs. Leading home economists and nutrition experts served on these committees. At the Bureau of Home Economics, Hazel K. Stiebeling played a key role in developing the first official recommended dietary allowances (RDAs) of vitamins, carbohydrates, and calories. Others at the bureau translated these dietary guidelines into terms that homemakers could understand and use. With leadership and encouragement from the AHEA—whose members totaled fifteen thousand in 1942—home economists also planned menus for the military, helped set up canteen services for workers in the defense industries, and stepped up their nutrition education activities. Through these initiatives, home economists promoted the notion of a balanced meal based on seven basic food groups, while also upholding the icon of the wartime homemaker as a guardian of family health and stability.

Product Development and Promotion

An elite group of home economists found jobs in the 1920s working in business. Commercial work for home economists was nothing new; as early as the 1880s domestic scientists had provided consulting services for a number of companies. Many food processors relied on home economists during World War I to ally their brand-name products to the patriotic cause of food conservation. After the war corporate managers created a more permanent place for home economists because they saw them as a means of getting closer to female consumers. Home economists' dual identity—as women and as scientists—perfectly suited the needs of these managers. By 1940 the AHEA's business section included more than six hundred members working as permanent employees

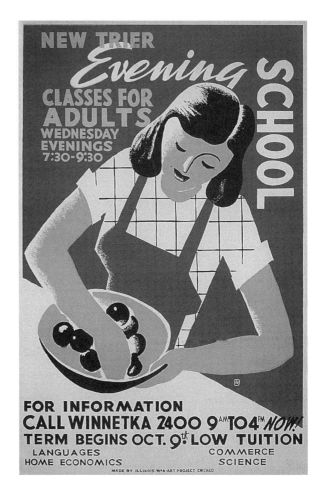

Home Economics Classes. Poster publicizing classes at New Trier Evening School, Winnetka, Illinois, 1941. The poster was produced by the Illinois WPA Art Project. *Prints and Photographs Division, Library of Congress*

in more than four hundred private enterprises, including utility companies, women's magazines, restaurants, manufacturers of household equipment, and retail firms. These women helped to correlate supply and demand for many elements of the modern kitchen.

The corporate home economics department became a hallmark of the progressive food company in the interwar period and remained a standard channel by which managers communicated with homemakers through the early 1960s. Several dozen large, vertically integrated firms had achieved mass production by 1900; investing in home economics was part of a broader effort to control demand, while also demonstrating the purity of their products in the face of increased government regulation. At most of the leading companies, the home economics department expanded rapidly from a one-woman show to a staff of dozens. The work varied from firm to firm, but one standard function was instructing homemakers how to use a company's processed or packaged foods. Some home economists traveled around the country demonstrating products to public audiences in company-sponsored cooking classes. Others worked more anonymously behind the scenes, within such corporate identities as Betty Crocker, developing recipes in company kitchens.

Just as modern advertising and packaging presented brand-name foods as grocery staples, company cookbooks treated a whole new array of products—including leavening agents, processed cheese, and factory-made sauces—as standard ingredients for a homemaker's pantry shelves. Thin recipe booklets such as *The Complete Jell-O Recipe Book* (1929) and more comprehensive volumes such as the 370-page *General Foods Cook Book* (1932) inspired women to cook with the featured products and taught them how. Through these publications, home economists promoted the idea that the proper American diet depended on the daily consumption of processed foods. By infusing these publications with the principles of scientific cookery and nutritional science, home economists furthered their educational agenda while at the same time instilling confidence in their employers' products. Whether given away for free or sold at minimal cost, such books proved widely popular. Companies typically printed millions of copies at a time, and multiple reprints and revised editions were common.

Home economists also helped corporate managers to understand consumers' views of their products. Before marketing and market research emerged as distinct functions of business management after World War II, home economists gathered information about consumer preferences and shared them with corporate managers. By testing products from the user's perspective, home economists also contributed regularly to the development of the products themselves. As home economics director at the Procter and Gamble Company for almost twenty-five years, Eleanor Ahern handled a wide spectrum of responsibilities. Her test kitchen, located at the soap and shortening company's factory, reported to both the advertising and chemical divisions. As such, Ahern generated new knowledge about homemakers' preferences and how Crisco vegetable shortening and other Procter and Gamble products actually performed in contemporary home kitchens. Her perspective proved critical when the company sought to improve its shortening in the face of competition from another firm.

While the largest number of business home economists were employed by food companies, others worked with retailers and manufacturers of household equipment. At gas and electric utility companies, demonstrations by home economists became fundamental to a strategy of encouraging homemakers to adopt the new power sources for cooking. Women and men considering the purchase of a new appliance could attend demonstrations by home economists at a company's downtown headquarters. When the Peoples' Gas, Light, and Coke Company in Chicago established branch offices in the city's neighborhoods, the structures included large auditoriums designed to accommodate cooking lessons. While hundreds of home economists touted the benefits of cooking with gas and electricity in public settings like these, smaller numbers of home economics–trained women helped engineers at such firms as Servel Manufacturing Corporation, Westinghouse Electric Company, and Corning Inc. design appliances and cooking utensils.

Expertise under Fire

Home economists' status as food experts began to diminish in the 1960s. Although home economics instruction remained a mainstay of public school education, the home economists themselves lost their foothold in the institutions that had afforded them their earlier cultural authority. On college campuses throughout the country, home economics departments faced attacks by university administrators who discontinued their programs or put men in charge of them. Home economists in the consumer products industries confronted challenges to their professional status from male business-school graduates specializing in marketing and from new specialists known as food engineers and "food technologists." Although they remained on board, the home economists' duties became limited to recipe development, and many adopted new titles such as "consumer affairs specialist." After a brief period of expansion and emphasis on human nutrition during World War II, the USDA reorganized the Bureau of Home Economics and virtually dismantled it.

Simultaneously, home economists came under fire from a wide range of social critics. Feminists accused the movement of chaining women to the domestic sphere; consumer advocates accused its members of selling out to corporate powers. Food writers criticized home economists for overemphasizing nutrition and neglecting the taste of food and blamed them for the poor state of the American diet; a home economist is not a cook, declared John L. Hess and

Karen Hess in *The Taste of America* (1977). Indeed, home economists had explicitly worked to distance their field from mere "cookery" since the earliest years.

Although college home economics programs (renamed human ecology on many campuses after 1970) still included cooking instruction, the curriculum on most campuses broadened to include so many topics that the early emphasis on food was lost on many of those who graduated in the post–World War II years. For those home economists who did study food, much of the instruction they received tended to reinforce a national consensus about nutrition. This consensus centered around getting the right biochemical nutrients in whatever form they were available, and it accepted the processed, packaged products and convenience foods that most home economists regarded as a labor-saving help to the busy homemaker. As the 1960s and 1970s counterculture challenged this assumption, home economists debated among themselves about how closely to ally themselves to commercial interests. But together with many other nutrition professionals—dietitians, agricultural scientists, and many food writers—they generally resisted the calls of "health food" advocates for organic, unprocessed, and natural foods. Home economists similarly steered clear of the era's consumer advocacy initiatives, steadfastly struggling to maintain a professional identity based on scientific objectivity even as the surrounding culture no longer considered it valid. In stark contrast to their predecessors' campaign for pure food at the beginning of the century, home economists were no longer in the progressive vanguard in regard to food. Although a newer generation of home economists eventually joined the new trends and in 1994 adopted a new name—the American Association of Family and Consumer Sciences—to reflect the altered priorities, the failure of the profession to keep up with changing values in the 1960s and 1970s left an indelible mark.

Throughout the twentieth century, home economists wielded their authority as food experts to make their ideas part of the dominant culture. Although they failed to achieve their ultimate, idealistic goals of rational consumption and the eradication of ethnic cooking practices, they did have a strong influence over what families ate. Through education, research, and the development and promotion of manufactured food products and appliances, home economists ushered in many of the elements that make up the modern kitchen and articulated a set of cultural values that made it meaningful for American homemakers. By framing food in terms of health, economy,

efficiency, and cleanliness and by teaching women how to achieve these goals, they made nutritious eating—along with packaged food products, gas and electric cooking, mechanical refrigeration, and cooking by the book—a symbol of middle-class identity. Insofar as Americans have internalized these values, the home economists' legacy persists. Processed foods—and recipes for such quintessentially American foods as California Dip (made with Lipton's Onion Soup Mix) and Rice Krispie Treats (made with the Kellogg Company's cereal)— remain standard to many a home cook's repertoire. Many Americans have come to understand food in more sensual, aesthetic terms, and the specific definition of a nutritious, balanced meal has changed, but the scientific value of foods in terms of calories, nutrients, and vitamins is still fundamental to the ways that professionals and ordinary Americans think about eating.

[*See also* Betty Crocker; Cookbooks and Manuscripts, *subentry* World War I and World War II; Department of Agriculture, United States; Ethnic Foods; Food and Nutrition Systems; Health Food; Historical Overview, *subentry* From Victorian America to World War I; Lincoln, Mrs.; New England Regional Cookery; Radio and Television; Richards, Ellen Swallow; Vitamins.]

BIBLIOGRAPHY

Barber, Mary I., ed. *History of the American Dietetic Association, 1917–1959.* Philadelphia: Lippincott, 1959. Written by the director of home economics at the Kellogg Company, this organizational history documents the participation of home economists in the dietetics profession.

Belasco, Warren J. *Appetite for Change: How the Counterculture Took on the Food Industry.* New York: Pantheon, 1989.

Bentley, Amy. *Eating for Victory: Food Rationing and the Politics of Domesticity.* Chicago: University of Illinois Press, 1998. This cultural history of food rationing during World War II includes discussion of home economists as leading advocates of the "ordered meal" and symbols of the iconic "wartime homemaker."

Cravens, Hamilton. "Establishing the Science of Nutrition at the USDA: Ellen Swallow Richards and Her Allies." *Agricultural History* 64 (Spring 1990): 122–133.

Cowan, Ruth Schwarz. *More Work for Mother: The Ironies of Household Technology from the Open Hearth to the Microwave.* New York: Basic Books, 1983.

Ehrenreich, Barbara, and Deirdre English. *For Her Own Good: 150 Years of Expert Advice to Women.* Garden City, N.Y.: Anchor, 1978.

Hess, John L., and Karen Hess. *The Taste of America.* New York: Grossman, 1977. By blaming home economists (along with other nutrition professionals) for the poor state of the nation's diet, this entertaining diatribe signaled the downfall of the group's cultural authority over food.

Levenstein, Harvey. *Paradox of Plenty: A Social History of Eating in Modern America.* New York: Oxford University Press, 1993.

Levenstein, Harvey. *Revolution at the Table: The Transformation of the American Diet.* New York: Oxford University Press, 1988.

Marling, Karal Ann. *As Seen on TV: The Visual Culture of Everyday Life in the 1950s.* Cambridge, Mass.: Harvard University Press, 1994. Includes a chapter on *Betty Crocker's Picture Cook Book,* written by home economists at General Mills and published in 1950.

Pundt, Helen. *AHEA: A History of Excellence.* Washington, DC: American Home Economics Association, 1980.

Rossiter, Margaret W. *Women Scientists in America: Before Affirmative Action, 1940–1972.* Baltimore: Johns Hopkins University Press, 1995. Places home economists' struggles after World War II in the context of increased discrimination against women in academia, government, and industrial corporations in the 1950s and 1960s.

Rossiter, Margaret W. *Women Scientists in America: Struggles and Strategies to 1940.* Baltimore: Johns Hopkins University Press, 1982. This pathbreaking synthesis demonstrates the importance of home economics as an avenue for women scientists to direct their abilities at a time when they were excluded from most male-dominated fields.

Rury, John. *Education and Women's Work: Female Schooling and the Division of Labor in Urban America, 1870–1930.* Albany: State University of New York Press, 1991.

Shapiro, Laura. *Perfection Salad: Women and Cooking at the Turn of the Century.* New York: Farrar, Straus, and Giroux, 1986.

Stage, Sarah, and Virginia B. Vincenti, eds. *Rethinking Home Economics: Women and the History of a Profession.* Ithaca, N.Y.: Cornell University Press, 1997.

Strasser, Susan. *Never Done: A History of American Housework.* New York: Pantheon, 1989.

Tomes, Nancy. *The Gospel of Germs: Men, Women, and Science in American Life.* Cambridge, Mass.: Harvard University Press, 1998. This cultural and medical history of the "germ theory" includes an analysis of home economists' efforts to teach household bacteriology as a means of disease prevention, including overcooking foods and the hygiene of food storage.

Weigley, Emma Seifrit. *Sarah Tyson Rorer: The Nation's Instructress in Dietetics and Cookery.* Philadelphia: American Philosophical Society, 1977. A biography of a leading late-nineteenth-century domestic scientist who founded the Philadelphia Cooking School.

CAROLYN M. GOLDSTEIN

Homemade Remedies

Until concrete scientific advances began to occur in the late nineteenth century, professional medical treatment in America was frequently unavailable and when available was ineffectual and occasionally brutal and dangerous. By necessity and choice, many Americans preferred to treat illnesses and injuries at home. Many home medical practitioners were women who concocted remedies and potions with herbs from their gardens. Knowledge of such preparations and their proper administration was considered an essential part of a girl's overall education. The first settlers from England and the Continent were well versed in herbal remedies, with recipes handed down from mother to daughter, or found in popular household books, such as Culpepper's *Complete Herbal and English Physician* (1652). Healing herbal plants were cultivated alongside vegetables in kitchen gardens and considered just as important to a family's survival, harvested to be brewed into teas and soups; mixed in with oats for fortifying gruels; and steeped for use as medicinal soaks and first-aid ointments.

Invalid Cooking

The reality of American life, whether in the fast-growing cities, or out across the vast plains, was that for rich and poor alike, disease was rampant. In addition to published books, family household accounts and individual diaries often listed remedies. A fine example of these personal records are those left behind by the wealthy New York Van Rensselaer family women, who wrote out cures for everything from sore throats (rue steeped in rum) and earaches (a roasted onion pressed, still warm, to the afflicted ear), to frozen limbs (rub with warm goose grease). Other common household remedies included black cherry bark, blackberries, allspice, and rhubarb to alleviate diarrhea and dysentery and turpentine, camphor, laudanum, and peppermint to battle cholera.

Separate from these cures, however, was a repertoire of recipes, often known as "Invalid Cooking," that were expressly used to feed and restore the sick and convalescent and were listed in almost every cookbook printed throughout the nineteenth and early twentieth centuries. Examples of these recipes include wine whey (white wine mixed with boiling water to form curds); lightly spiced oatmeal gruels, saps (milk toast), and beef teas (essentially the bloody drippings of a flank steak); Irish moss puddings, wine-infused jellies, and flavorful broths. Directions for making and serving these dishes were precise. To lessen any chance of contamination, these dishes were made in small batches from the freshest ingredients available. Patients were served small amounts at regular intervals, and the tray upon which the dishes were brought to the sick room was to be arranged, as one author noted, as "a dainty Dresden watercolor of delicate hues and harmonious tints."

The Invasion of Quackery

While invalid cooking, in itself, may have been beneficial to patients, most homemade remedies were not. This, however, did not stop the creation (and incredible prosperity) of an industry whose purpose was to promote dubious—and often dangerous—patented medicines to the gullible public. What was particularly American about this development was its convergence of commercialism, democratic individualism, entertainment, and even religious fervor.

Medicine and tent shows crisscrossed the country, providing the populace with lively entertainment in the form of instant cures for everything from baldness and lameness to cancer—all by drinking a potion or submitting to electric shocks. Drug preparations could be bought at general stores or from mail-order catalogs. Some were even prescribed and dispensed by doctors who found them convenient and certainly no less damaging than common medical procedures. Many of these preparations were a corruption of old recipes—mixtures of herbs and roots—fortified with hefty measures of alcohol or narcotics (and sometimes both). While users certainly felt better for a time, these elixirs produced their own ills—poisoning, addiction, and even death. And yet patented medicines proliferated, encouraged by outlandish advertising campaigns, and by the fact that they were often cheaper and less invasive than a doctor's visit. With no laws to hinder them, medicine companies made vast fortunes promoting such brands as Lydia Pinkham (for female complaints), Parker's Tonic (which claimed to cure consumption and asthma as it rejuvenated blood), and Belle tablets (for dyspepsia).

Pure Food and Drug Act of 1906

The regulation of patented medicine came about through the efforts of muckraking journalists who called attention to the dangers of these potions, which resulted in public pressure on Congress. In 1906, a reluctant Congress passed the landmark Pure Food and Drug Act, giving birth to the Food and Drug Administration (FDA) and to laws requiring the strict governance of the food and drug industries. The act also forbade anyone from obtaining prescriptions except from a licensed doctor and required warning labels on all habit-forming medicines. In addition, all medicines had to be certified by the FDA, a certification that most patented medicines failed, and consequently most were banned from the market.

Homemade remedies, and even some patented medicines, survive in the twenty-first century, protected by cultural and ethnic preferences. Since 1960, there has been renewed interest in natural and Native American medicines, and various ethnic groups, especially those from the Caribbean, China, and Asia, have brought to America their ancient reliance on medicinal herbs. Many of these are gaining increasing respect and acceptance from the established medical communities.

[*See also* Food and Drug Administration; Health Food; Pure Food and Drug Act.]

BIBLIOGRAPHY

Anderson, Ann. *Snake Oil, Hustlers, and Hambones: The American Medicine Show.* Jefferson, NC: McFarland, 2000.

Food and Drug Administration. "The Story of the Laws Behind the Labels." http://vm.cfsan.fda.gov/~lrd/history1.html. A good and clear overview of how the Food and Drug Act of 1906 came about.

Kett, Joseph. *The Formation of the American Medical Profession.* New Haven, CT: Yale University Press, 1968.

University of Toledo Libraries. "From Quackery to Bacteriology: The Emergence of Modern Medicine in 19th Century America: An Exhibition." http://www.cl.utoledo.edu/canaday/quackery/quack1.html. A particularly interesting and concise document recounting the background influences on the rise of patented medicines.

Willard, Pat. *A Soothing Broth.* New York: Broadway Books, 1998.

PAT WILLARD

Hominy, *see Corn*

Honey

Honey is the fragrant, thick, syrupy creation of honeybees (*Apis mellifera*) that can be flavored by the type of bloom growing most profusely where the bees gather their nectar. Consumers can find honeys flavored with the blossoms of wildflowers, sage, thyme, rosemary, lavender, heather, apple, orange, clover, grapefruit, tupelo, buckwheat, and alfalfa. Buckwheat honey is one of the darkest, in both color and flavor; grapefruit is one of the lightest. Artisanal honeys are available in limited quantities. Blueberry and cranberry are popular in the Northeast. Sage and mesquite rule in the West, while eucalyptus and manzanita are prized in California.

Orchardists who keep domesticated bees to fertilize fruit blossoms net a second crop, honey, from the hives set out among the fruit trees. Over the course of a worker bee's lifetime, the bee makes less than one-twelfth of a teaspoon of honey. Bees store honey in combs, collections of six-sided wax cells. Honey can be purchased in combs but is much more expensive than bottled honey, which has been separated from the wax by heat and centrifuge. The wax is recycled in candles, cosmetics, furniture polish, and in sewing applications.

Honey is mentioned as an ingredient in the earliest Roman cookbooks. From ancient times until the eighteenth century, honey was the main form of sweetener in Europe and the American colonies. (Molasses, maple sugar, and maple syrup were also used in America.) Clarified sugar from sugarcane was so expensive that it was sold by the ounce, by apothecaries. A German chemist discovered beet sugar in 1747. Barley sugar was common into the 1940s but is seldom manufactured in the early twenty-first century.

Honey's virtues are many. It has greater sweetening power than sugar. It combines levulose and dextrose, both quickly absorbed by the bloodstream and thus is a source of quick but lasting energy. Unlike white sugar, honey contains vitamins and minerals. Its antimold enzyme is useful in canning and preserving, and it can also be used as an antiseptic on minor cuts. Finally, it helps to keep yeast breads and pastries moist longer than those baked with other sweeteners.

In medieval times, honey was fermented with water to make a drink called mead. In colonial America and through the nineteenth century, honey was commonly used in switchel, a haymaker's drink, and as a base for homemade vinegar. Honey is pleasant added to a cup of hot tea, smeared on toast, scones, or biscuits, or drizzled over morning oatmeal. Salad dressings and vinaigrettes are the better for it.

Honey can be substituted for white sugar in any recipe by using about half the quantity. However, honey in a recipe can cause the cookies, cakes, or breads to brown more quickly than if beet or cane sugars were incorporated, and bakers must be vigilant so that sweets do not burn. Should honey crystallize, it can be reliquefied by setting the honey jar in a pan of warm water, or briefly heating the jar in a microwave.

Children under a year of age should not be fed honey or soothed with nipples dipped in honey, because it may contain bacterial spores that could cause infant botulism—a rare but serious disease. Adults and children over one year of age are routinely exposed to, but not normally affected by, botulism spores. Honey is slightly laxative, and some people find it indigestible. For most people, however, it is an aromatic addition to the daily diet.

[*See also* Sugar; Sugar Beets; Sweeteners; Switchel.]

BIBLIOGRAPHY

Albright, Nancy. *The Natural Foods Epicure*. Emmaus, PA: Rodale, 1977.

Montagné, Prosper. *Larousse Gastronomique: The Encyclopedia of Food, Wine and Cookery*. New York: Crown, 1961.

Rombauer, Irma S., and Marion Rombauer Becker. *The Joy of Cooking*. Indianapolis, and New York: Bobbs-Merrill, 1975.

Rosenbaum, Stephanie. *Honey: From Flower to Table*. New York: Chronicle, 2002.

ANN CHANDONNET

Hot Brown Sandwich

The Hot Brown is an open-faced sandwich based on toasted white bread upon which thin slices of turkey or chicken, ham, crisp bacon, and sliced tomato are layered. A rich cheese sauce, usually made from cheddar, is spooned over the top. Sprinkled with grated parmesan cheese, the sandwich is quickly broiled until bubbling hot. Fred K. Schmidt, chef at the Brown Hotel in Louisville, Kentucky, created the Hot Brown to serve famished guests following the nightly dinner dances featured at the hotel after it opened in 1923. The sandwich was so popular that it was added to the hotel's luncheon menu along with a cold version, composed of rye bread, chicken or turkey, lettuce, sliced tomato and hard-boiled egg and served with thousand island dressing. Long revered as a favorite sandwich of the upper South, the Hot Brown, or one of the many variations on the original, is found on menus throughout the United States.

BIBLIOGRAPHY

Mercuri, Becky. *Sandwiches That You Will Like*. Pittsburgh, PA: WQED Multimedia, 2002.

BECKY MERCURI

Hot Dogs

Hot dogs are smoked, cooked sausages composed of pork, beef, chicken, or turkey, singly or in combination. Most hot dogs are made from emulsified or finely chopped skeletal meats, but some contain organs and other "variety" meats. Water, fat (roughly 30 percent), and seasonings, such as salt (about 1–1.5 percent), garlic, sugar, ground mustard, nutmeg, coriander, and white pepper, are other ingredients. Hot dogs can be made in natural gut casings, but most are skinless, stuffed in a cellulose wrapper that is stripped off after cooking. But the hot dog is more than just a sausage.

From the end of the nineteenth century and well into the second half of the next, the hot dog was America's chief iconic food item. Originally an ethnic food, it may have been America's first industrially produced, portion-controlled, and mass-marketed meat product. Widely sold in public venues such as ballparks, boardwalks, and fairs to consumers from every social and economic strata, its mythic attributes might best be summed up in the phrase, "America's great democratic food."

The real and legendary histories of the hot dog are tied to the history of modern America. Wieners and frankfurters, as their interchangeable names reveal, are descended from European sausages: Viennese (Wiener) sausages are slim, white, finely ground, or emulsion-made sausages, usually containing at least 30 percent veal. Frankfurters contain some beef, are spicier, heavier, and more coarsely ground than wieners. Both were brought to America in the nineteenth century, by mainly German-speaking Central European immigrants. German beer gardens became common in American cities by the 1860s as did their staple foods: sausages, bread, and potatoes. Sausages served with bread took to the streets with pushcarts in that decade and soon became Americanized as sandwiches. Charles Feltman's sausages, sold with rolls and sauerkraut at his famous Coney Island stand in 1871, were an early example. Nathan's, serving hot dogs in buns with french fries, founded in 1916, is the most famous of all stands.

What went into the casings had always been a subject of wry speculation. Ditties such as, "Oh Hagenbeck [the name changes according to the singer], oh Hagenbeck, how could you be so mean to grind up all those doggies in your hot dog machine?" The earliest known joke of

Hot Dog Stand. Nathan's hot dog emporium, Coney Island. *Culinary Archives & Museum at Johnson & Wales University, Providence, R.I.*

this type dates to 1860. That German butchers kept sausage-shaped dogs—dachshunds, recognized by the American Kennel Club in 1885—might have added to the legend. From these associations, German-style sausages came to be called hot dogs. In the mid-1890s students at Yale and Princeton were using the term. Apparently applied first to young dandies, or perhaps good athletes, at Yale, it migrated to sausages by 1894 or 1895. One sausage wagon was even called "The Kennel Club." The term "hot dog" was certainly popularized by such originators of slang phrases as the sports cartoonist T. A. Dorgan (TAD) early in the twentieth century.

Chopped or encased ground pork products (for example, hot links) were already staples of the American table, but the rising popularity of German-style sausages attracted major meat packers, such as Swift, Armour, Wilson, and Cudahy. Before the Pure Food and Drug Act of 1909 and later labeling laws, sausages had often been convenient ways to use scraps and offal. Rising technology permitted mass-processing: power meat choppers appeared in the 1860s (in 1868, the first steam-powered one); mixers, improved choppers, powered sausage stuffers, and linkers in the 1890s; and in the early twentieth century more potent grinders and mixers that could handle large amounts of meat. Mechanically operated smokers simplified and increased production. So popular had sausages become that, in the late 1880s, companies, such as John Morrell in Cincinnati sent hog casing to Chicago to be processed and then returned for stuffing. Chicago and New York sausage companies began importing large amounts of sheep casings in the 1890s, mainly from Australia. Today natural-cased sausages account for only 5 percent of the market.

Small-scale butchers—such as Oscar Mayer, founded in 1883 in Chicago and later headquartered in Madison, Wisconsin—grew into large local and regional producers. A niche-market producer before World War II, Oscar Mayer emphasized purity and quality. Its products were made exclusively from skeletal meats. Other local producers, such as the Jewish packers of New York and Chicago, emphasized meaty all-beef products with an aura of purity from their kosher associations. The latter makers, like many bratwurst producers in the upper Midwest, geared their production to the food-service industry. Sabrett in New York and Vienna Beef in Chicago were the main suppliers of urban hot dog carts and stands in the early 2000s, while large-scale companies, Bryan in the South, Oscar Mayer, Hygrade (Ballpark), Armour, Swift, and others, had considerable presence in supermarkets. These hot dogs differ greatly from the older varieties in formulas and usage.

The hot dog was marketed largely as a fun food, playing its role in cookouts, amusement parks, and ballgames. Marketing campaigns carried out by large centralized food producers before World War I made the hot dog the great American fast food. By the 1920s, the phrase "weenie roast" had passed into common usage. Oscar Mayer in the 1930s exemplified such marketing. The company hired a small person to bring Little Oscar, a cartoon character created for print advertising, to life. Little Oscar drove "the famous wienermobile," a car designed to look like a wiener as a way of publicizing hot dogs. Little Oscar, intended to appeal to families, was a newly minted myth devised to sell a food product. After World War II campaigns pitching hot dogs as a convenience food were directed toward the home market, especially children. Jingles, such as "I wish I were an Oscar Mayer wiener" and "Armour hot dogs, the dogs kids love to bite," became imbedded in American popular culture.

The rise of national hamburger chains, and to some extent, pizza and taco purveyors, after World War II eclipsed hot dogs as the Americans' fast foods of choice. Hot dog stands remained local, mainly in urban areas such as Mobile and Birmingham, Alabama, Chicago, New York, and Los Angeles. Nevertheless, by the turn of the twenty-first century, hot dog sales were strong with more than 1.25 billion pounds of all types sold in retail stores alone. The hot dog remained an icon of American life as commemorated in the advertising slogan: "Baseball, hot dogs, apple pie and Chevrolet."

[*See also* Amusement Parks; Armour, Philip Danforth; German American Food; Street Vendors; Swift, Gustavus Franklin.]

BIBLIOGRAPHY

Barnhart, David K., and Metcalf, Allan A. *America in So Many Words: Words that Have Shaped America.* Boston: Houghton Mifflin, 1997.

Cohen, Gerald, ed. "Compiling Material for a Book on *Hot Dog*—Part I: Bibliography." *Comments on Etymology* 33, no. 3 (December 2003).

Graulich, David. *The Hot Dog Companion: A Connoisseur's Guide to the Foods We Love.* New York: Lebhar-Friedman Books, 1999.

BRUCE KRAIG

Hotel Dining Rooms

Hôtel means "town mansion" in French. When Americans began building grand public accommodations in the nineteenth century, these hotels were called "palaces of the people." More than feeding guests, the hotel dining room showcased upwardly mobile, status-conscious, public leisure in a uniquely egalitarian, American context. As the editors of the *Weekly Mirror* observed about the Hotel Astor, "The distinguished, the fashionable, the dressy and handsome may all dine without peril of style *in the public table*. But,—since so *may* the opposites of all these, and anybody else who is tolerably dressed and well behaved,—*the public table* is the *tangible republic*."

Taverns, inns, and "ordinaries" had fed and sheltered travelers along colonial thoroughfares, but these spots catered primarily to the community and often accommodated transients indifferently. These establishments would lay copious dishes of the house's choosing on communal tables at fixed hours. The cost of these meals was included in the room charge—what came to be known as the "American plan." To the extent that one toured for pleasure or required extended lodging, one might sojourn at a boardhouse, taking meals in comparatively modest surroundings with limited public access.

Hotels were different. The largest hotels sported imposing architecture, billiards rooms, theaters, shops, and capacious dining rooms that seated hundreds at a time. Although many early hotel dining rooms copied the tavern model, the most elegant hotels, including the Tremont House, which opened in Boston in 1829, offered guests the choices of when and what to eat. The Tremont grouped guests into small parties of six or eight, delicately serving individual dishes from a sideboard. Similarly, the Astor House in New York boasted that although its dining room kept regular meal hours in the traditional style, it also would serve, "Dinners for one or more at any hour. In short, we take pleasure in providing for the wants of our patrons, regardless of the hour." The Astor even had its own press for printing menus, novelties in themselves but necessary for this individual service. The European plan, whereby room and food charges were separate, had evolved by the middle of the 1840s. Use of the European plan slowly spread through the nineteenth century, but the American plan remained common.

Nineteenth-century hotel dining rooms filled four distinct niches. First, hotels like the block-long City

Hotel Dining Room. Hotel dining scene, nineteenth century. *Culinary Archives & Museum at Johnson & Wales University, Providence, R.I.*

Hotel, which opened in New York in 1794, sprouted in the commercial districts of larger cities and served emerging business communities. Well-heeled businessmen who could not travel home for the midday meal dined on the hotels' original "businessman's lunch."

Second, the grandest hotels were entertainments in themselves and had a near-monopoly as sites for banquets and elegant dining. Often staffed by European chefs and waiters, the hotels broadcast sophistication. Dinners were choreographed with military precision. A gong summoned guests for dinners at which waiters in unison removed silver domes covering the various dishes, creating a public spectacle akin to the most opulent dinners in private homes. The great expense of the food generally was compensated by liquor sales. Prohibition effectively killed the hotel dining rooms, and in the changed economy of the 1930s, restaurants, rather than hotels, became the sites of culinary excellence.

Third, hotels great and small were long-term residences. Before America's first apartments were built in the 1870s in New York, the cost of elegant urban homes and housekeeping increased dramatically. Well-to-do, permanent boarders, single persons and families alike, accounted for one-half of the hotel occupancy in the mid-nineteenth century and often took meals in the public dining rooms.

Fourth, hotel dining rooms were a progressive public venue for ladies, who generally were not welcome in restaurants, particularly unescorted, until the late nineteenth century. Hotel etiquette and service differed from that in private homes, as detailed by authors such as Eliza Leslie and Tunis G. Campbell. Both of these authors emphasized the egalitarian nature of the hotel

tables. Leslie observed that, "Nobody 'sits below the salt'. And every one has an equal chance of obtaining a share of the nicest articles on the table."

On the other side of the social coin, hotels were a battleground for fledgling labor unions in the early twentieth century. Carefully timed walkouts by waiters at the most elegant establishments left bewildered patrons in dinner jackets to serve themselves. When cooks joined the fray, shutting down the immense kitchens, management was forced to negotiate. Labor unions continue to organize vast hotel staffs. Hotel dining rooms no longer command their extraordinary place in the pantheon of American eateries. For the cost of a nineteenth-century dinner, they allowed old and new money, women, and the socially aspiring to "rub elbows and pick their teeth at a public table."

[*See also* Boardinghouses; Restaurants; Taverns; Tschirky, Oscar.]

BIBLIOGRAPHY

Batterberry, Michael, and Ariane Batterberry. *On the Town in New York: The Landmark History of Eating, Drinking, and Entertainments from the American Revolution to the Food Revolution.* New York and London: Routledge, 1999.

Campbell, Tunis G. *Hotel Keepers, Head Waiters, and Housekeepers' Guide.* Boston: Coolidge and Wiley, 1848.

Hamilton, Thomas. *Men and Manners in America.* New York: Kelly, 1968. Reprint of the 1833 edition with additions from the edition of 1843.

Josephson, Matthew. *Union House, Union Bar: The History of the Hotel and Restaurant Employees and Bartenders International Union AFL-CIO.* New York: Random House, 1956.

Kimeldorf, Howard. *Battling for American Labor: Wobblies, Craft Workers and the Making of the Union Movement.* Berkeley, Los Angeles, and London: University of California Press, 1999.

Leslie, Eliza. *Miss Leslie's Behaviour Book.* Philadelphia: Hazard, 1853.

Veblen, Thorstein. *The Theory of the Leisure Class.* New York: New American Library, 1953. The original edition was published in 1899.

Weekly Mirror (New York). 7 December 1844, vol. 1, no. 9, p. 131.

White, Arthur. *Palaces of the People: A Social History of Commercial Hospitality.* London: Rapp and Whiting, 1968.

Williamson, Jefferson. *The American Hotel.* New York: Arno, 1975. The original edition was published in 1930.

CATHY K. KAUFMAN

Hot Toddies

To many Americans, who know the toddy only as a steaming après-ski pick-me-up, the term "hot toddy" may seem redundant. Yet it makes a legitimate distinction, for the cool toddy does exist. Both of these drinks reflect the climate of their birthplace; indeed, toddies may even be defined by their usefulness in countering the effects of extreme temperature.

The cool version has its origins in the tapped and fermented sap of certain tropical palms, for which British colonialists in India developed a taste and a name, toddy, derived from the Hindi word *tārī*. The word traveled from the outposts of the British Empire to sultry plantation-era America, where Dixie gentlemen adopted it for their own combination of rum, sugar or molasses, and nutmeg, which was mixed with hot water and then cooled. It was also known as bombo, or, on occasion, bimbo.

The hot toddy hails from eighteenth-century Scotland, where a similar mixture of spirits (namely malt whiskey), hot water, sugar or honey, and lemon, plus spices, such as nutmeg, cinnamon, cloves, or mace, was touted as a cure for colds—although its application was, not surprisingly, far more general. The name, in this case, is said to refer to Tod's Well in Edinburgh from whence the water came. Scottish affection for the drink is particularly evident in the gadgetry contrived specially for its preparation, including kettles, ladles, and lifters. (The lifter, which was usually made of glass, resembled a decanter but functioned like a ladle, transferring the beverage in question from punch bowl to drinking vessel.)

The hot toddy's popularity must have spread fast, if the lore that would-be American revolutionaries took courage from rounds of toddies (which were often heated by pokers straight from the tavern hearth) holds any truth. Certainly Americans adopted the drink wholeheartedly, down to the toddy-stick (an implement akin to a muddler, flat at one end and knobbed at the other) with which it was stirred. In colonial New England, however, rum or brandy often replaced the whiskey—and the punch bowl itself often precluded glassware, since drinking from a common vessel was considered properly sociable among tavern patrons. Although for all the democracy of the gesture, it should be noted that toddy contained two ingredients—citrus and sugar—that commanded high prices at the time. It was thus not quite the drink of the people. New Orleanians, for their part, boast of their favorite French-born son Antoine Peychaud's experiments with bitters-laced toddies as leading to the invention of the cocktail around the turn of the nineteenth century.

Meanwhile, a few variations on the theme help stretch the definition of a hot toddy, from the blazer—a toddy that is not merely heated but actually ignited—to hot buttered rum, which floats a pat of butter on its surface.

Such drinks are typically served in a short-stemmed glass with a handle that is itself known as a toddy.

[*See also* Cocktails; Homemade Remedies; Taverns.]

BIBLIOGRAPHY

O'Hara, Christopher B. *Hot Toddies*. New York: Clarkson Potter, 2002. A definitive collection of recipes.

Rice, Kym S. *The Early American Tavern: For the Entertainment of Friends and Strangers*. New York: Fraunces Tavern Museum in conjunction with Chicago: Regnery Gateway, 1983. A thorough look into the space, as well as the occupants and activities therein.

RUTH TOBIAS

Howard Johnson

Howard Johnson was a mid-twentieth-century phenomenon, an American company that pioneered concepts of food service and hospitality still in use in the twenty-first century. Super-premium ice cream, restaurant franchises, turnpike service stops, commissary-based restaurant production, quality control, and customer service were concepts formulated by the founder, Howard Deering Johnson, beginning with one corner drugstore in the oceanside Wollaston section of Quincy, Massachusetts, south of Boston. In 1925, the twenty-seven-year-old businessman turned his newsstand into a thriving delivery service, then set his sights on improving the soda fountain. He developed the first super-premium commercial ice cream using natural flavoring and cream with twice the butterfat content. Depending on the source, the story goes that Johnson either improved on his mother's recipe or purchased the formula from a pushcart operator. In any event, his new, larger portions were distinctively sculpted with a specially designed ice cream scoop.

Johnson sold his ice cream cones for a nickel from a growing series of wooden stands situated directly on the beach. By 1928, sales grossed $240,000 and the original flavors, vanilla, chocolate, and strawberry, gradually increased to twenty-eight. A high-quality hot dog was added to the beachfront menu. Clipped at either end, notched down the center, and cooked in butter, it was presented in a buttered, toasted roll, cradled in a cardboard holder with scalloped edges, and renamed a "frankfort."

In early 1929, Johnson opened a full-service restaurant in a new ten-story building in downtown Quincy. The menu included typical New England fare, such as fried clams, chicken potpies, and baked beans, in addition to the popular frankforts and ice cream and huge sodas that

Howard Johnson Restaurant. *Culinary Archives & Museum at Johnson & Wales University, Providence, R.I.*

were topped with an oval cookie embossed with the company logo.

The Franchise

Just as the fledgling company was poised for expansion, the stock market crashed. Banks were not lending, but Johnson conceived of the idea of a franchise. In return for an initial investment, Johnson would provide the design, menu, standards, and food products while the investor-franchisee-property owner reaped most of the profits. The first franchise opened in Orleans, Massachusetts, on Cape Cod in the depths of the Great Depression. A simple white clapboard colonial house, trimmed in turquoise, it featured three dormers, multipaned windows, a cupola with a clock and weathervane in the shape of Simple Simon and the Pieman, the company logo. A bright orange roof ensured maximum visibility.

Johnson outlined in the "Howard Johnson Bible" hitherto unknown standards of cleanliness and service that ranged from procedures for scrubbing to staff comportment." He enforced these standards strictly during personally conducted surprise inspections. In an era when roadside-dining facilities consisted of diners, teahouses, and small eateries of questionable quality, Johnson stressed dependability.

By 1940, the established company, with two hundred roadside eateries in the eastern United States, bid on and won, in rapid succession, exclusive rights to build restaurants on the Pennsylvania, Ohio, and New Jersey turnpikes. When World War II brought a halt to leisure motor travel, most of the outlets closed. The company kept solvent by providing meals for war workers and educational institutions.

At the war's end America was poised for travel: gas rationing ended, cars rolled off assembly lines, and a baby boom filled new housing tracts and suburbs outside city limits. A system of interstate highways was under construction, and although the highways were business-free, Howard Johnson built restaurants at the exits. The company claimed the road, adopting the slogan "Landmark for Hungry Americans" and the family-friendly nickname "HoJo's."

With a shortage of trained chefs, the company established the large central commissary to produce and portion food, thus ensuring standardization throughout the franchises. As the U.S. economy and family travel flourished, the turnpike restaurants reaped great profits. The company added motor lodge franchises with a restaurant on each property.

The Next Generation

In 1959, Johnson turned operations over to his son, Howard Brennon Johnson, remaining as chairman and treasurer, and in 1961 the company was publicly traded on the New York Stock Exchange. Jacques Pépin, formerly personal chef to the French president Charles DeGaulle, oversaw the central commissary from the 1960s to 1970. Applying his French training, he learned the work of every station, beginning by flipping burgers in the largest restaurant in the chain on Queens Boulevard, New York City. Pepin recalled that era as "my American apprenticeship, learning about mass production and marketing." Pepin, along with his fellow French chef Pierre Franey, worked on product development. Under their leadership simple macaroni and cheese bubbled in pre-portioned oval casseroles; vats of creamy clam chowder were tasted and tested; and mass-produced fried clam strips, without the highly perishable bellies, were developed to maintain fresh Cape Cod seafood flavor. Home convenience products were developed for sale in supermarket freezers.

The company opened Red Coach Grills for the business traveler and the casual Ground Round. But after Howard Deering Johnson died in 1972, the company began to fail. In the late 1970s, an energy crisis, oil embargo, and inflated fuel prices brought the automobile travel that made up 85 percent of the company's business to a standstill. New competing food outlets, such as McDonald's, Burger King, and Kentucky Fried Chicken, streamlined Howard Johnson's concepts and were able to feed the population faster and cheaper. Holiday Inn, Ramada Inn, and Marriott built newer, more comfortable hotels. Inside the company, unsupervised, and unscrupulous franchisees cut corners. According to Pepin, "after Johnson's death in 1972, the company lost its raison d'etre. The restaurants became obsolete; the food quality deteriorated."

In 1979, Imperial Group of Great Britain acquired both the company-owned and independent operations, a total of 1,040 restaurants and 520 motor lodges, for $630 million dollars, then sold them, except for Ground Round, to Marriott, which in turn sold off the company-owned franchises to Prime Motor Inns. The independent franchise owners incorporated and hired the former U.S. Attorney General Griffin Bell to negotiate with Marriott and Prime Motor Inns.

In the early 2000s, Franchise Associates Inc. retained ownership of the original recipes. The company produced Howard Johnson's signature products for retail sale, such as Macaroni and Cheese, TenderSweet Fried Clams, Chicken Croquettes, and Toastees at Fairfield Farm Kitchens in Brockton, Massachusetts, and bulk ice cream at The Ice Cream Club in Boynton Beach, Florida. Cendant Corporation operated the midprice hotel chain under the name Howard Johnson (without the "'s").

The last original Howard Johnson's Restaurant in Massachusetts closed in March 2002. Fewer than a dozen restaurants remained in the twenty-first century, one in New York City's Times Square. A number of websites are devoted to Howard Johnson's lore and memorabilia.

[*See also* Burger King; Clams; Ice Cream and Ices; Johnson, Howard; McDonald's; Roadside Food; White Castle.]

LINDA BASSETT

Humor, Food

"Waiter, waiter! Bring me a crocodile sandwich, and make it snappy!"

Food humor probably has as long a history as food. What passes for humor, however, has changed over the years. A kind of humor modern Americans would find strange or even unnerving marked the banquets of the Romans and continued through the Middle Ages. From ancient Rome came "flying pies" immortalized in the nursery rhyme about "four and twenty blackbirds baked in a pie." These pies consisted of empty shells with lids baked separately that, after baking and cooling, had birds put inside them to be released in the banquet hall for the amusement and entertainment of the guests.

In Renaissance Italy, Ascanio Sforza invited his fellow cardinals to a banquet where there were bones sculpted from sugar and the drinking cups were shaped like skulls. Another frequent joke was to have a sculpture at a wedding feast of the bride in childbirth. Perhaps mercifully, no pictures survive of such sculptures, although frequent references to them exist in old writings.

In colonial America, there was "grinning for cheese," a popular contest at fairs and markets in which, in what would seem a cruel joke, people would grin widely. The contestant with the fewest teeth would be the winner and given cheese as a prize—perhaps the source of "say cheese" for photographs.

Food humor has often taken the form of jokes, songs, and skits. Consider the song "Yankee Doodle" with its humorous reference to a dandy with a feather in his hat as a "macaroni." Many songs mention items of food and drink, like "mountain dew" with its moonshine reference or "red beans and rice" with its New Orleans flavor.

In contemporary America, food humor falls into several loosely defined and often overlapping categories. The two-story story, the tall story, wordplay including the pun, and the essay. "There are two laws in the universe: The law of gravity, and everyone likes Italian food," said Neil Simon. This is a two-story story. The setup implies a certain kind of conclusion, an expansion on the beginning, but the punch line delivers a different and contrasting one. Most of the "waiter, waitress" jokes fall into this category. "Waiter, waiter, what's this fly doing in my soup?" "The backstroke, I believe, sir." There are countless variations on that theme: "Waiter, there's a dead fly in my soup." "What do you expect for a dollar, a live one?" A variation: "Waitress, there's a fly in my soup!" "Well, keep quiet about it or everyone will want one." And yet another variation on the concept: "Waitress, I'll have my bill now." "How did you find your steak, sir?" "Oh, I just moved the potato and there it was."

A tall tale is a story that has a larger-than-life situation and exaggerated details that describe things as greater than they really are. The classic tall stories are exemplified by tales about Paul Bunyan and his blue ox, Babe, Johnny Appleseed, or Pecos Bill. One such tells about watermelons growing so fast that they were "drug round the garden and had their skins wore off" by the friction "so when the vine decided to rest, they done sat there all red and ready to eat."

Wordplay is pivotal in many types of humor. For example: "The new chef from India was fired a week after starting the job. He kept favoring curry." Or: "A Zen Buddhist walks into a pizza parlor and says, 'Make me one with everything.'" Puns are a form of wordplay. A famous one transforms the observation, "The pun is the lowest form of wit" into, "The bun is the lowest form of wheat." There are riddles that use plays on words: What was green and a great trick shooter? Annie Okra. And there are true puns: "Waiter, there's a hair in my honey." "It must have dropped off the comb, sir!"

Longer food-related stories featuring puns and wordplay have been making the rounds on the Internet. An excerpt from one of the more popular ones is:

PILLSBURY DOUGH BOY DEAD AT 71

Veteran Pillsbury spokesman Pop N Fresh died yesterday of a severe yeast infection. . . . The graveside was piled with flours as longtime friend Aunt Jemima delivered the eulogy, describing Fresh as a man who "never knew how much he was kneaded.". . . Fresh is survived by his second wife; they have two children and one in the oven. The funeral was held at 2:25 for 20 minutes.

The following essay usually appears as an article for a newspaper or magazine and runs to several hundred words. An edited excerpt from one example (which appeared in the *Waynesboro News-Virginian*):

SPOILAGE SIMPLIFIED

Many people ask me how to know how long to keep food in the refrigerator. A good question. Something we should all know for maximum safety and to prevent the need to use power tools to clean the veggie crisper.

Let's list a variety of things to consider in the specific cases of the most common foods we all have. There are some commonsense things you already know. Even the most hardened kitchen-avoider will know much of this stuff. But it's good to have reminders, don't you think?

FOOD SPOILAGE INDICATORS

THE GAG PROTOCOL—Anything that makes you gag may safely be considered spoiled. Except for leftovers from what you cooked for yourself within the past 48 hours. Or if it contains okra. Or if you're watching an old Jerry Lewis movie.

DAIRY PRODUCTS—Milk is spoiled when it looks like yogurt. Yogurt is spoiled when it looks like cottage cheese. Cottage cheese is spoiled when it starts to look like beige spackle. All cheese is just spoiled milk anyway, so don't get too strange about that whole idea. It can, however, grow pretty green fur. Once I saw pink fur. I controlled my desire for cheese that day.

EGGS—When something, anything, is pecking its way out of the shell, the egg is probably past its consumption ideal. You'd better hope it's a chicken working so hard if it came from your fridge and came with 11 kindred ovals.

[See also Literature and Food; Myths and Folklore.]

BIBLIOGRAPHY

Jillette, Penn, and Teller. *How to Play with Your Food*. New York: Random House, 1992. Zany magic tricks and illusions generally involving the dining table and, often, food.

Lileks, James. *The Gallery of Regrettable Food*. New York: Crown, 2001. Humorous observations about the foods and habits of Americans.

Steingarten, Jeffrey. *The Man Who Ate Everything*. New York: Vintage, 1997. An often-humorous collection of essays from *Vogue*.

BOB PASTORIO

Hunger Programs

Historically efforts to alleviate hunger in the United States have been initiated and supported by both private and public sectors of society. Nearly every faith-based organization in America provides funds or direct services for feeding the hungry. The Salvation Army, for example, began providing food aid with its first mission to the United States in 1880. Other major, nonprofit charitable groups include Meals on Wheels, begun in 1954 to provide food to the country's homebound residents, and Second Harvest, the nation's largest domestic hunger-relief organization, which operates as a network of over two-hundred food banks and food-rescue programs.

Prior to the 1930s, most food aid came from community-based charitable groups and local government support. Unable to meet the enormous demand imposed by the Great Depression, when breadlines and soup kitchens for the destitute and unemployed witnessed unprecedented need, such aid was supplemented through several New Deal programs providing temporary relief. The largest of these was the National Social

Security Act of 1935, which, in addition to providing a supplementary pension to retirees, included a provision for Aid to Dependent Children (ADC), later Aid to Families with Dependent Children (AFDC), a major program in what became known as welfare. Various food-distribution programs were also put into place. Although many federal programs had their roots in the Depression years and shortly thereafter, most of those specific to food aid did not gain much momentum until the War on Poverty began during President Lyndon Johnson's administration in the 1960s.

Federal programs include those that came into being with the Food Stamps Act (1964), the most extensive hunger-prevention initiative. The National School Lunch Act (1946), later expanded to the Summer Food Service Program (1968), and the School Breakfast Program (1975) were meant to provide nutritional security for America's youth. The Supplemental Food Program for Women, Infants, and Children (WIC) (1974), a voucher program, provided health benefits and nutritional education to low-income mothers and children up to age five. The Child and Adult Care Food Program (CACFP) provided nutritious meals and snacks to those in need. The Emergency Food Assistance Program (TEFAP) (1990) was another form of aid, this coming through distribution of surplus commodities to individuals and community agencies. In the early 2000s, an additional federal hunger program was administered by the U.S. Department of Health and Human Services' (USDHHS) Office of Community Services (OCS). The Community Food and Nutrition Program (CFNP) provided funding to a number of antihunger organizations for food distribution and nutrition education.

Hunger Program. Unemployed miner with food from surplus commodities corporation, Ziegler, Illinois, January 1939. *Prints and Photographs Division, Library of Congress/Arthur Rothstein*

The U.S. government's responsibility for monitoring hunger in America was redefined in 1999 with the implementation of the USDA's standardized measures of food security and hunger in conjunction with the U.S. Census Bureau. A report titled "Household Food Security in the United States, 2001" by the USDA Economic Research Service found that almost 11 percent of American households were food-insecure at some time during the year and that in 3.5 million households, at least one member went hungry because there was not enough food to go around.

The key issue permeating the history of hunger programs in the United States relates to whether these programs should function as emergency food relief or as entitlements. This has set up a debate, much like that concerning welfare generally. One side sees food assistance as a form of charity that should be provided on a temporary basis and then only to the neediest. Any kind of entitlement, or anything beyond emergency assistance, under this argument, is ripe for fraud and abuse and provides no incentive for leaving the program. Therefore, nonprofit charitable organizations and local governments, not the federal government, should provide all additional needed support. Because of such reasoning, the governmental programs that have traditionally gained strongest bipartisan support are those targeting children and the elderly.

The other side of the debate believes that structural inequalities continue to contribute both to poverty and hunger in America. Unless these underlying concerns are addressed, hunger and poverty will never decrease. In this argument, public assistance is not a matter of charity but a matter of social justice: individuals have a right, or entitlement, to a minimum standard of living, including food assistance, in a civilized society.

The nongovernmental voluntary programs that continue a tradition of soup kitchens, food pantries, and food banks are under constant pressure to bridge the gap left by government programs. This is especially true for feeding the homeless, who, without a permanent address or phone number, often find it difficult to secure federal food aid. The ultimate contradiction for hunger programs in the United States is that as nongovernmental programs increase in size and number with the growing demand for hunger relief, many lawmakers feel justified in making cuts in federally funded initiatives. While large numbers of the U.S. population are not starving, millions do go hungry. Given the affluence of American society, that this should be the case, especially for children, raises basic issues of human rights.

[*See also* Department of Agriculture, United States; Food Stamps; Meals on Wheels; Soup Kitchens.]

BIBLIOGRAPHY

Eisinger, Peter K. *Toward an End to Hunger in America.* Washington, DC: Brookings Institution Press, 1998.

Food and Nutrition Service: Nutrition Assistance Programs. http://www.fns.usda.gov/fns. Run by the Food and Nutrition Service of the USDA, this site describes the various nutrition assistance programs, eligibility, the level of benefits, aggregate demographics of participants, and how to apply, among other things.

Food Research and Action Center. *State of the States: A Profile of Food and Nutrition Programs across the Nation.* Washington, DC: Food Research and Action Center, 2003.

Nord, Mark, Margaret Andrews, and Steven Carlson. *Household Food Security in the United States, 2001.* Food Assistance and Nutrition Research Report, no. 29. Washington, DC: USDA Economic Research Service, 2002.

Poppendieck, Janet. *Sweet Charity? Emergency Food and the End of Entitlement.* New York: Viking, 1998.

BARRETT P. BRENTON AND KEVIN T. MCINTYRE

Hunt's

In 1888, Joseph and William Hunt launched a small preserving business in Santa Rosa, California. Two years later, it was incorporated as the Hunt Brothers Fruit Packing Company. During their first year, they canned thirty-thousand cases. They expanded in the following years and outgrew their canning facility. In 1896, the brothers moved their operation to Hayward, California. At the turn of the century, they produced an extensive line of fruit and vegetable products. However they did make one major mistake: shortly after Hawaii was acquired by the United States, Hunt Brothers was offered exclusive importing rights for Hawaiian pineapple but passed up the opportunity, because they did not think that pineapples would be popular with the American public.

The Hunt Brothers chose not to join the California Fruit Canners Association, a cooperative that later marketed Del Monte brand foods. They did, however, join the Pure Food Manufacturers Association, along with the Beech-Nut Packing Company, H. J. Heinz, and Charles Gulden, in an attempt to raise the standards of the canning industry.

By the early 1940s, Hunt Brothers was a regional canner known mainly in the West. The Hunt Brothers sold their operation to Norton Simon in 1943. Simon had previously acquired Val Vita Food Products, a small orange juice–canning factory in Fullerton, California. Through advertising, he had increased Val Vita's sales dramatically within a few years and he hoped to do the same with Hunt Brothers. In 1945 Simon merged Hunt Brothers with Val Vita to form Hunt Foods.

To promote his new company, Simon targeted tomato sauce for major promotion. The slogan, "Hunt—for the best," appeared along with color illustrations of Hunt's Tomato Sauce in major women's magazines in 1946. These advertisements also featured recipes for dishes with tomato sauce as the key ingredient. Simon also printed tomato sauce recipes inside millions of matchbook covers. This campaign propelled Hunt Foods from a regional business into a national brand. Coupled with the company's campaign featuring tomato sauce, Simon also began promoting Hunt's Tomato Catchup, later changed to "Ketchup." Precisely when Hunt's began producing ketchup is unknown, but it took off after Hunt Foods acquired the E. Prichard Company in Bridgeton, New Jersey, in 1948, which had manufactured Pride of the Farm ketchup. Hunt Foods was extremely aggressive in their ketchup marketing during the 1950s. In addition, Simon introduced new lines of convenience foods, including Manwich, Skillet dinners, and snack packs.

By the 1950s the company claimed to be the largest processor of tomato-based products in the world. It increased its tomato products to include spaghetti sauce and barbecue sauce. To promote its tomato products, Hunt Food, published advertising cookbooklets, such as *Hunt's Complete Tomato Sauce Cookbook* (1976).

Simon merged Hunt Foods with the Wesson Oil and Snowdrift Company to create Hunt-Wesson Foods in 1960. Eight years later, Hunt-Wesson Foods became a major group of Norton Simon, Inc., which in turn was acquired by ConAgra, based in Saint Louis. By the twentieth-first century, ConAgra was the second-largest U.S. food conglomerate behind Kraft Foods. By the late twentieth century, Hunt Foods manufactured only tomato products, such as barbecue sauce, ketchup, sauce, paste, and puree, as well as diced, stewed, and crushed tomatoes.

[*See also* Canning and Bottling; ConAgra; Ketchup; Tomatoes.]

BIBLIOGRAPHY

Hunt's. http://www.hunts.com/A01AboutHunts.jsp?mnav=about.

Mahoney, David J. *Growth and Social Responsibility: The Story of Norton Simon Inc.* New York: Newcomen Society in North America, 1973.

Smith, Andrew F. *Pure Ketchup: The History of America's National Condiment.* Columbia: University of South Carolina Press, 1996.

ANDREW F. SMITH

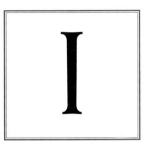

Iberian and South American Food

Although it is easiest to trace the very early and the very recent influences of Iberian and South American foodways on North American food, the influences have been continual and often have come along several vectors at the same time. There were exchanges of foodstuffs and possibly techniques between ancient South America and Mesoamerica, although these were accelerated by the arrival of the Europeans. It is also important that even before the first Iberian voyages to the Western Hemisphere, Spanish, Portuguese, Basque, and Catalan cuisines were multicultural. They had been built with layers of Celtic, Roman, Gothic, Arab, and North African influences and were experiencing an infusion of new foodstuffs from navigation around Africa, direct contact with South Asia, and the beginnings of the African slave trade. Within a few decades of discovering the Caribbean islands, Spanish and Portuguese voyagers had colonized them as well as Mexico and South America, charted both coasts of what became the United States, and may have reached Hawaii. Native American foodways were affected by early-sixteenth-century contacts with Iberians as far north as Maine and Newfoundland, where the Portuguese had a colony at the turn of the sixteenth century, and in what became the southern and southwestern states, where early Spanish expeditions introduced horses, pigs, and fruit trees, and African slaves introduced watermelon—all before 1550.

South American Connections

Some South American foodstuffs had reached Mexico and the Caribbean before Columbus. Cacao, peanuts, and chilies had been domesticated in South America, and there may have been exchanges of maize, squash, beans, and tomatoes between Mexico and South America. The Caribbean islands had been populated from the South American mainland, and thus the maize, chilies, squashes, sweet potatoes, cassava, peanuts, and pineapples presented to Spanish explorers were South American or Central American domesticates. Mexican foodstuffs such as maize, tomatoes, haricot beans, turkeys, and localized varieties of peppers, cacao, and peanuts quickly followed, again entering Europe through Spain and Africa via Portugal. Native slaves from Brazil and the north coast of South America were brought to Europe and may have assisted with these crops. The plants were altered across the Mediterranean, selected for more northern climates, and returned to North America with colonists from Spain, France, Holland, England, and even Sweden and Finland.

With the Spanish conquests in South America came white potatoes, lima beans, and other strains of maize and haricot beans. These crops also came to North America through Europe. Because they were grown at high altitude in Peru, these crops were more suited to northern Europe and the northern colonies in America. The white potato may have been brought to Florida or Virginia in the sixteenth or seventeenth century, but it appeared in most American colonies with the eighteenth-century influx of the Protestant Irish ethnic group known as the Scotch-Irish. This group is most identified as the antecedents of the Appalachian mountaineers but lived throughout the English colonies. The Scotch-Irish were growing "Irish potatoes" in their settlement of Londonderry, New Hampshire, by the 1720s.

African-Iberian Connections

Portuguese explorers and colonists introduced maize, cassava, sweet potatoes, and peanuts to Africa, and thus many African slaves arrived in North America with a taste for and a knowledge of these originally South American foods. The narrative of Olaudah Equiano (Gustavus Vassa), an American slave, noted that although in the 1750s he had never seen a white person in his home in what became Nigeria, the villagers ate "Indian corn." Because the Cape Verde islands were settled as a station for the Portuguese slave trade, many similar dishes are found in Brazil, Cape Verde, and the Cape Verdean immigrant communities in southern New England, which date to the 1780s.

The Portuguese colonists of Brazil, like the Spanish Caribbean colonists, traded Native American slaves north, some of whom reached the British colonies in the Caribbean and North America. Some combination of Native American and African slaves acquired a Brazilian Indian technique of molding maize meal mush, to which they gave the African name "couscous." Related dishes are still eaten as *cuscux* in Brazil, *cou-cou* in Barbados (the way station of the British slave trade), and "coush-coush" in Louisiana. During and after the Civil War it spread from Louisiana throughout the American South as a Confederate soldier's dish.

Although it is difficult to sort out the origins of African American foods, the early Iberian contact with Africa and primary involvement in setting up the transatlantic slave trade left enduring influences on African American food. Iberians probably reinforced African techniques such as deep-fat frying, marinating foods in vinegar, and making rice into pilafs. These techniques may have been reinforced in both Iberia and West Africa by the centuries-old trans-Saharan trade. It is certain that Iberians introduced Africans to the precursors of American cornmeal mush, corn bread, hoe cakes, sweet potato pie, and roasted peanuts. The Iberian slave trade also introduced African plants, such as coconut palm, cowpeas, rice, and watermelon, and animals, such as guinea hens, to Florida and the Caribbean. From there these foods diffused to the British American colonies. Well before Jamestown and Plymouth, Native Americans had acquired peaches, watermelon, hogs, wheat, and horses from Iberian colonists and spread them so rapidly that explorers sometimes mistook them for native species. Iberian foods were introduced directly to Native Americans by Spanish explorers and colonists. It is possible that Navajo fry bread was influenced by sopaipillas made by New Mexico Hispanics.

The North American colonies were not self-contained units but part of global trading networks that brought many Iberian foods to them—peacefully during periods when England, Holland, or Sweden was allied with Spain or Portugal; through privateering in times of war; and often by illicit trade or smuggling to northern colonies with their own ships. Samuel Sewall, a judge in Salem, Massachusetts, gave a sense of this culinary globalism in a diary entry in 1697: "I wait upon the Lieut Governor at Dorchester [Massachusetts] and there meet with Mr. Torry, breakfast together of venison and chocalatte; I said Massachusetts and Mexico met at his Honour's Table" (Coe and Coe, *True History of Chocolate*, p. 25). Within

fifteen years chocolate was a regular breakfast drink at the table of the wealthy Virginia planter William Byrd.

Basques in America

Basques may have been fishing and whaling in Newfoundland before the time of Columbus and were well established there by the early sixteenth century, when the fishery was dominated by Iberians. (Basques are still approximately one-third of the population of the tiny French colony of Saint-Pierre and Miquelon, off Newfoundland.) Spanish and French Basques were so prominent in Newfoundland cod fishing that Mi'kmaq and other Algonquian Indian languages absorbed Basque vocabulary. When his English expedition reached central Maine in 1602, Bartholomew Gosnold found Native Americans trading out of a Basque shallop. In Maine and on Martha's Vineyard, Gosnold's men saw Iberian clothes and copper kettles used by the Native Americans. The sailors on fishing vessels—dozens and sometimes hundreds of vessels annually for more than a century before the Plymouth colony—traded so many copper kettles and iron hatchets for furs and local foods that Indians in New England were abandoning their traditional ceramic pots and stone tools, altering the ecology by exterminating beavers, and probably accelerating the development of maple syrup and clam chowder.

Basque names are prominent in all Spanish colonization in the Americas, but Basque-speaking shepherds began coming to the Americas as contractors in the mid-nineteenth century. Although many returned to Europe after periods of work, communities formed around boardinghouses in California, Nevada, and Idaho. In the twentieth century, some of the boardinghouses became public restaurants, providing ethnic flavor to the Rocky Mountain states, where few other ethnic restaurants exist even in the early twenty-first century. Hearty Basque soups and lamb stews have become popular outside the 100,000 members of the Basque American population. The French Basque omelet called *pipérade* may have been an influence on the western omelet and the Denver sandwich made from it.

First Spanish American Towns

The best-known Spanish colonies in what became the United States are Saint Augustine, Florida (founded 1565), and Santa Fe, New Mexico (founded 1608). The Spanish had an earlier colony near what became El Paso, Texas, and had influential missions in Georgia and

Alabama in the sixteenth and seventeenth centuries. Most of the California missions date from the mid- to late eighteenth century.

Saint Augustine was turned over to the British in 1765, but the population of Catalan-speaking Minorcans recruited by the British (who had taken over their Mediterranean island homeland at the same time) remain and retain a few words of Catalan origin. A number of Saint Augustine recipes also remain, including Easter cheese cakes, chowders of local shellfish, and dishes that make extensive use of *datil* chilies. The Minorcan *pilau* of Saint Augustine may have been an influence on rice cookery up the coast.

The New Mexico colonies had to be abandoned for almost twenty years after the Pueblo Revolt of 1680 but then developed a considerable Iberian identity that has persisted for more than three hundred years. Descendants of the original settlers consider themselves Spanish rather than Mexican because the colony was remote from Mexico City and part of independent Mexico for only a few decades. New Mexico Hispanics enjoy Mexican food but preserve many old Iberian foodways, such as noodle soups and wheat breads baked in beehive ovens. The Spanish dominion over Louisiana (1765–1803) likely introduced pralines (from similar Mexican sweets), possibly jamba-laya, possibly the empanada-shaped turnovers that survive as "Nacogdoches meat pies," and the mild, Central American–style "hot tamales" sold by African American youth from 1880 to 1910. The Spaniards encouraged colonization by French-speaking Acadians in Louisiana and by Canary Islanders in Louisiana and Texas. The San Antonio Canarios may have introduced the characteristic cumin to Texas chili. Spanish Louisiana had a trading network into the Tennessee valley. This trade may have introduced Mexican-style breakfast chocolate to the Appalachians, where it is called "chocolate gravy." (Another possibility is that the very old population of mixed-race Appalachian Melungeons has preserved the dish from the sixteenth- and seventeenth-century Spanish colonies on the East Coast.)

Although the Spanish missions and colonies in California (which included many Basques) and Arizona date from the mid-eighteenth century, Iberian influence in early California was reinforced by gold seekers and ranchers from South America, some only a generation or two out of Spain. Descendants of Spanish colonists of Texas, Arizona, and California later tended to exaggerate their Spanish roots and understate the influence of their Mexican and Native American ancestors, but some old Iberian noodles (*fideos*), meatballs (*albondigas*), and fish dishes persisted. Encarnación Pinedo, who wrote the first California cookbook in Spanish, had an Ecuadorian father and included in her book a group of Argentine dishes that were popular in nineteenth-century Hispanic California.

In the mid-nineteenth century, Iberians and South Americans came to California on the same ships that brought the Anglo-American gold seekers. Communication between the two coasts of North America was primarily by ship around South America. There was exchange of people and foods at ports of call in Brazil, Uruguay, Argentina, Chile, Peru, Colombia, and what was then the Pacific coast of Bolivia (lost to Chile in the 1923 war). In the early part of the nineteenth century, gentleman farmers and progressive seed merchants visited South America in search of seeds. The first real popcorn in the United States probably came from Chilean seed, and most of the beans grown in the United States have primarily South American DNA. Before and after the Spanish-American War, the United States acquired a number of immigrants from Cuba, Puerto Rico, and the Philippines, some of whom were Iberian born and all of whom brought Spanish food, such as rice dishes and egg-rich sweets, along with the Creole foods of their native regions.

Portuguese Americans since the Seventeenth Century

Although Portugal did not successfully colonize North America, there was a notable minority of Portuguese, mostly Jewish, refugees from the Inquisition in Brazil and Surinam, in the New Netherlands colony. A later and even larger colony of Iberian Jews settled in Charleston, South Carolina. Both of these colonies, along with a group of Spanish Jews in London, helped to introduce deep-fried fish and what came to be called "French toast" to the Anglo-American table. Some Portuguese were involved in Spanish exploration and colonization, and a community of Portuguese and Cape Verdean immigrants developed in the whaling ports of Massachusetts in the 1780s. This community was reinforced by continual immigration, especially after the earthquakes in the Azores in the 1950s and 1960s.

The recipe for a Cape Verdean bean pilaf called *jagacida* was published as a regional Massachusetts dish in English as early as 1939. The dish became a regional specialty, along with kale soup, linguica and chorizo sausages, and eggy sweet bread. The Cape Verdean national dish is a stew of corn, beans, and mixed meats called *cachupa*. Cape Verdeans and Brazilians share a rice porridge called *canja*, which is similar to the African Puerto Rican *asopao*. The sausages and sweet bread have become regional dishes in Hawaii, where Portuguese were among the earliest contract workers on the sugar plantations. Spanish and Puerto Rican contractees arrived later. Portuguese communities of fisherman and dairy farmers were founded in the nineteenth century in northern California.

Later Immigrants from Iberia and South America

The results of the ancestry survey of the 1990 U.S. census suggested that approximately 1 million Americans claimed Spanish descent and that approximately the same number considered themselves Portuguese Americans. Since the loosening of immigration restrictions in the late 1960s, South American immigrants have come to the United States to escape civil strife or to work, often in restaurants. The largest group is probably Brazilians, who gather in their own communities for the complex black bean stew *feojada*. They also have started restaurants of mainstream appeal based on the *parilladas* of Rio de Janeiro, where assorted grilled meats are carried on swords and carved at tableside. Colombians, Peruvians, and Ecuadorians have gathered in American cities on both coasts, but their hearty mountain cuisine has tended to stay in small restaurants patronized by immigrants, often on Sunday. Argentine steakhouses have opened periodically in New York and Los Angeles. Later immigrants from Argentina most often opened mainstream Italian restaurants.

"Neuvo Latino" fusion food has had some success in New York and Los Angeles, as well as at its center in Miami, Florida. Enterprising chefs have made elaborate dishes out of Peruvian seviches and stews, the Ecuadorian potato stew *locro*, Venezuelan Christmas bread, and newly available ingredients such as passion fruit, cherimoya, plantain, and yucca.

[*See also* African American Food, *subentry* To the Civil War; Appalachian Food; Cajun and Creole Food; Caribbean Influences on American Food; Chocolate; Pinedo, Encarnación.]

BIBLIOGRAPHY

Coe, Sophie D., and Michael D. Coe. *The True History of Chocolate.* New York: Thames and Hudson, 1996.

Equiano, Olaudah. "From the Interesting Narrative of the Life of Olaudah Equiano, or Gustavus Vassa, the African." In *Early American Writings*, edited by Carola Mulford, 913–927. New York: Oxford University Press, 2002.

Forbes, Jack D. *Apache, Navaho, and Spaniard.* 2nd ed. Norman: University of Oklahoma Press, 1994. The original edition was published in 1960. The definitive account of Spanish encounters with southern Athabascans, in what became the American Southwest, from the 1530s to the end of the Pueblo Revolt, in 1698.

Quinn, David B. *North America from Earliest Discovery to First Settlements: The Norse Voyages to 1612.* New York: Harper and Row, 1977.

Sauer, Carl Ortwin. *Sixteenth-Century North America: The Land and the People as Seen by the Europeans.* Los Angles and Berkeley: University of California Press, 1971. Sauer revived colonial studies on a global basis.

Steele, Ian K. *Warpaths: Invasions of North America.* New York: Oxford University Press, 1994. Colonial America from the native point of view, with a fine history of early St. Augustine. Inexplicably omits New Mexico.

Thomas, Hugh. *The Slave Trade.* New York: Simon and Schuster, 1997.

Weber, David J. *The Spanish Frontier in North America.* New Haven, CT: Yale University Press, 1992.

West Kauai Community Development Corporation. *West Kauai's Plantation Heritage: Recipes and Stories for Life from the Legacy of Hawaii's Sugar Plantation Community.* Waimea, Kauai, HI: West Kauai Community Development Corporation, 2002. Very good ethnic history, with recipes.

Wright, Louis B., ed. *The Elizabethans' America.* Cambridge, MA: Harvard University Press, 1965. Excellent collection of original documents on visits from 1565 to 1630.

MARK H. ZANGER

Ice

Ice has been used to preserve food and cool beverages for thousands of years. Wealthy Europeans brought their appreciation of icy desserts and iced drinks with them to the New World. Archaeologists at Jamestown, Virginia, found ice pits dating from as early as the seventeenth century. The colonists cut ice from ponds, lakes, and rivers during the winter and stored it in caves and underground cellars to last through the hot summer months.In the eighteenth century, icehouses, which were more efficient than cellars, provided cold storage, as well as preserving ice for chilling food and drink and making ice cream. Ice was advertised for sale in Philadelphia newspapers as early as 1784, and Europeans visiting Philadelphia and Baltimore in the 1790s reported that Americans drank water with ice and that containers of ice were used to cool hotel rooms.

The first recorded cargo of ice was shipped from New York to Charleston, South Carolina, in 1799, and between 1805 and 1860 Frederick Tudor, a Boston merchant, grew rich shipping harvested ice from Massachusetts ponds overseas. Tudor, known as the Ice King, promoted the construction and use of ice chests, sent agents to help establish businesses selling ice cream, extolled the virtues of ice for preserving food, and promoted the sale of carbonated water, which he thought tasted better cold. He even offered bar owners free ice for a year if they agreed to sell iced drinks at the same price as warm ones. In spite of Tudor's enthusiasm for cold drinks, some customers resisted because they believed that ice disguised bad liquor or diluted the effects of alcohol.

By the 1850s ice was available in most urban places that were near rivers or served by railroads, and the widespread availability of ice at a reasonable price allowed the middle classes to use large quantities. By the 1880s every well-equipped kitchen contained a patented icebox or ice chest, which was supplied almost daily by local refrigeration plants. In 1895 more than fifteen hundred ice wagons served customers in Brooklyn and New York City.

Seafood and dairy products packed with ice were transported in refrigerated railroad cars from the 1840s to the 1860s. The refrigerated transport of meat came later. Until the late 1860s local butchers had slaughtered their own animals and chilled the meat in walk-in cold-storage boxes supplied with lake or river ice. Frozen meat was common in colder climates, where farmers and ranchers butchered their cattle and sheep in early winter, then packed the meat in outside cold boxes filled with ice and snow. The first shipload of commercially frozen beef was transported in 1869 from Indianola, Texas, to New Orleans, Louisiana, where it was served in hospitals, hotels, and restaurants. However, not everyone was in favor of frozen meat. Many considered it unsanitary, dangerous, or even poisonous, and some states attempted to put the new cold-storage warehouses out of business.

In 1867 J. B. Sutherland of Detroit, Michigan, patented an insulated railroad car with bunkers for ice at each end, with the result that food was no longer packed in ice. This development made it possible to regulate the temperature by adding ice or by putting heaters in the bunkers in the winter. Gustavus F. Swift, who had founded a meatpacking business in Chicago in 1875, is generally credited with having commercialized the system of shipping fresh meat in refrigerated railroad cars. By 1892 over 100,000 refrigerated railroad cars transported dairy products, fruit, vegetables, meat, and fish.

Harvesting Ice. Cutting ice in Lehigh County, Pennyslvania, in the 1920s. *Collection of Georgia Maas*

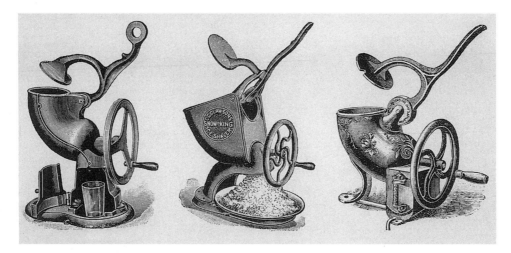

Ice Shavers. From the 1922 catalog of the Crandall Petite Co., New York, p. 63.

The natural ice harvest peaked in 1886 at 25 million tons, and then began to decline as mechanical refrigeration took the place of natural ice. In 1911 the United States boasted nearly two thousand artificial ice plants serving the general public, in addition to the dedicated plants supplying meat packers, breweries, ice cream manufacturers, and other businesses requiring large quantities of ice. Despite advances in mechanical ice making and refrigeration, the natural ice trade between Maine and southern ports lasted well into the twentieth century.

The invention of small electric refrigerators was fatal to many large, established ice companies. In 1914 Fred W. Wolf Jr. invented a refrigerating machine, the Domestic Electric Refrigerator (DOMELRE) with an ice cube tray, and in 1918 Frigidaire became the first affordable, mass-produced electric household refrigerator. The first flexible metal ice cube tray, which fit the small freezer compartments of the new electric and gas-powered refrigerators, was invented by Guy L. Tinkham in 1933. The rural electrification movement that began in the 1930s brought electricity to rural as well as urban dwellers and made it possible for small businesses to make their own ice and to run their own freezers. The mass production of modern refrigerators with large freezers began after World War II, and automatic ice makers appeared in the 1960s. Nevertheless, commercial ice companies continue to provide ice for the fishing industry, as well as ice cubes for parties and the coolers of campers, sailors, and picnickers.

[*See also* Iceboxes; Refrigerators; Swift, Gustavus Franklin.]

BIBLIOGRAPHY

Anderson Jr., Oscar Edward. *Refrigeration in America: A History of a New Technology and Its Impact.* 1953. Reprint, Port Washington, NY: Kennikat Press, 1972.

Funderburg, Ann Cooper. *Chocolate, Strawberry, and Vanilla: A History of American Ice Cream.* Bowling Green, OH: Bowling Green State University Popular Press, 1995.

Woolrich, W. R. *The Men Who Created Cold: A History of Refrigeration.* New York: Exposition Press, 1967.

VIRGINIA SCOTT JENKINS

Iceboxes

Ice was the original refrigerant and at one time was big business. During the nineteenth century, thousands of Americans made their living in the ice industry. Some cut ice from ponds and lakes to sell. Others manufactured equipment for the industry. Some shipped ice all over the world, and others delivered it from door to door. Still, ice had its drawbacks. It was often scarce or expensive, and worst of all, it melted. To slow the melting, people mixed it with salt, layered it with straw, covered it with sawdust, or wrapped it in old blankets or carpets. They built ice pits and icehouses in which to store it, and they bought iceboxes, which were also called "refrigerators."

Many iceboxes were handsome paneled, hardwood cabinets fitted with brass hinges and locks. Others were of a plainer design. The interiors were lined with zinc, galvanized metal, or porcelain and were insulated with charcoal, cork, or fiber. One compartment held large blocks of ice; the others were for food. The ice could last for a day or more if the door to the ice compartment was not opened too often. Iceboxes for home use were made in a variety of sizes, from three to five feet high and from two to three feet wide or even larger. Horizontal ice chests were from two to three feet high and from two to three and one-half feet wide. Larger iceboxes were made for grocers and restaurateurs.

Iceboxes kept foods cold but not frozen, so chefs, confectioners, and cooks for the elite had a special, smaller icebox for ice cream and other frozen treats. The French term for this smaller icebox was *cave*; it was also known as an ice safe, freezer box, freezing box, or (confusingly) an icebox. The *cave* was a simple oblong box made of metal and lined with sheet iron or zinc. The space between the box and the lining was filled with charcoal, sawdust, or fibers for insulation. The *cave* had movable tin shelves to allow for the storage of several small ice cream molds or a few tall ones. It also had holes near the bottom to allow the melted ice to drain out. *Caves* were available in a variety of sizes and held from one to several quarts of ice cream.

Caves were intended to keep items frozen for a few hours or even overnight, provided they were not opened frequently during that time. They allowed cooks and confectioners to make and even decorate fancy molded ice creams ahead of time without having them melt before being served or sold. After filling the molds with ice cream, cooks placed them in the *cave*, heaped salted ice over and around them, and left them until it was time to unmold and serve the ice cream. Some small *caves* had handles and could be used to transport ice cream to picnics and garden parties.

Electric refrigerators were introduced in the early part of the twentieth century. By the end of World War II, *caves* and iceboxes had become obsolete, and the demand for ice was melting away. By the end of the century, the industry still supplied ice to supermarkets and convenience stores, and consumers occasionally bought bags of ice for a party, but ice was no longer a big business.

[*See also* Freezers and Freezing; Ice; Ice Creams and Ices; Refrigerators.]

BIBLIOGRAPHY

Jones, Joseph C., Jr. *America's Icemen: An Illustrative History of the United States Natural Ice Industry, 1665–1925*. Humble, TX: Jobeco Books, 1984.

Israel, Fred L., ed. 1897 *Sears Roebuck Catalogue*. New York: Chelsea House Publishers, 1968.

Selitzer, Ralph. *The Dairy Industry in America*. New York: Dairy and Ice Cream Field and Books for Industry, 1976.

Wheaton, Barbara Ketcham. *Victorian Ices & Ice Cream*. New York: Metropolitan Museum of Art, 1976. A reprint of the 1885 edition of *The Book of Ices* by Agnes B. Marshall, with an introduction and annotations by B. K. Wheaton.

JERI QUINZIO

Ice Creams and Ices

Americans eat twenty-three quarts of ice cream per person per year, more than people in any other country. Ice cream, like apple pie, is not just a dessert; it is a national symbol. Although Americans cannot claim to have invented ice cream, they can take credit for democratizing it.

Ice cream's origins go back to the sixteenth century, when Italian scientists discovered they could intensify the natural coldness of ice by mixing it with salt. Inspired by these scientists, confectioners experimented with freezing drinks and cream desserts and created the first ices and ice creams. Freezing was fraught with difficulty in an era that lacked refrigeration. The earliest printed recipes listed quantities of snow or ice and salt among the ingredients, and they included more detail about freezing than they did about creating the ice or ice cream mixture. In fact, some recipes called for the cook to use an existing drink or cream recipe, and then follow freezing instructions. After making the drink or cream mixture, the cooks poured it into a covered pot called a *sorbetière*. Next they mixed ice or snow with the correct proportion of salt in a large pail. They put the covered *sorbetière* into the ice-and-salt–filled pail and banked the ice up around it to begin the freezing process. Cooks soon learned that to make smooth ice cream, they had to stir the mixture frequently while it was freezing. So from time to time they took the *sorbetière* out of the pail, opened it, and stirred the mixture thoroughly. Then they put the cover back on and put it back in the pail. They had to turn or shake the closed *sorbetière* while it was in the ice mixture, and they needed to drain the freezing pot as the ice melted. It was cold, hard, time-consuming work.

Despite all the difficulties, by the eighteenth century confectioners were making ices and ice creams in every conceivable flavor and presenting them in every imaginable shape, with flavors that ranged from orange blossom to artichoke, from apricot to parmesan cheese. They were molded, turned out, and tinted to imitate bunches of asparagus, fuzzy peaches, and delicate roses. Walnut ice cream was served in walnut shells; fruit ices were embellished with fresh leaves and branches. They were royal desserts, enjoyed by royalty.

America's first families were ice cream fans. George Washington bought "a Cream Machine for Making Ice" in 1784, and Thomas Jefferson's papers include his own handwritten recipe for vanilla ice cream. Americans could also buy ice cream from confectioners. An ad in the May 12, 1777, *New York Gazette* stated that "Philip Lenzi, Confectioner from London" had ice cream available "almost every day." Most confectioners offered a few standard flavors and made others to order. Until the mid-nineteenth century, the average person could not afford ice cream, whether made at home or bought from a confectioner. Ice was not always affordable or available nor was cream. Sugar was costly. Most important, making ice cream was so labor-intensive that, unless they had servants or slaves, most people could not afford the time.

Ice Cream for All

Ice cream became more democratic when Nancy Johnson, an American, invented an ice cream freezer suitable for home use in 1846. Johnson's freezer featured a crank and a dasher, or churn, inside the freezing pot, which meant that the ice cream mixture could be stirred without taking the freezing pot out of the pail and opening it. With Johnson's new freezer, home cooks could make ice cream much more easily. At around the same time, the price of sugar went down and ice became more accessible, so ice cream making became more affordable.

The cost of buying ice cream also went down as wholesalers went into the business. In 1851, Jacob Fussell, a Baltimore dairyman, became the first ice cream wholesaler in America. He set up a factory in a small Pennsylvania town, packed the ice cream in ice, and put it on the train to Baltimore. Eventually Fussell opened factories in Baltimore, Washington, Boston, and New York. Others followed his lead, and after the Civil War ended, the ice cream business expanded rapidly. Confectioners found it difficult to compete with wholesalers, who could easily undersell them. The *Confectioners' Journal* of 1883 described the wholesalers' products as "frothy, watery slop and slush and still viler 'flavorings,' whose make up is only known to the devil's chemical emissaries."

From the earliest days, medical opinion was divided over the merits or dangers of eating ice cream. Some physicians thought it was unnatural and dangerous and blamed it for everything from colic to paralysis. Others countered that ices cured diseases, especially scurvy, emaciation, and paralysis. In the nineteenth century, writers warned that eating ice cream after meals would reduce the temperature of the stomach and thus stop digestion. People continued to eat ice cream. In fact, it was becoming a mass-market product. In 1859, national production was estimated at 4,000 gallons. Ten years later, it was 24,000 gallons. By the turn of the century, despite the fact that it was still mostly a summertime treat, Americans were gobbling up 5 million gallons a year.

Ice cream was served at home and in restaurants. It teamed up with cake at birthday parties. Specialized ice cream forks, knives, spoons, and dishes all became fashionable. Hostesses served ices as palate cleansers between dinner courses or as accompaniments to the meat or fish course. Cucumber sorbet accompanied boiled cod, gooseberry sorbet went with goose, and ginger ice was served with roast beef. At the other end of the social spectrum, vendors on city streets screamed "ice cream," and kids came running, pennies clutched in their hands.

Ice Cream Originals

Drugstore soda fountains made their debut early in the nineteenth century. At first they served carbonated water, which was thought to have health benefits, at a simple counter. Before long, fruit syrups and other flavorings were added to the waters, and the fountains became architectural fantasies made of marble and mirrors. Ice cream sodas were initially made with soda water, flavored syrup, and cream, but no ice cream. During the 1870s, someone—accounts vary as to exactly who and exactly where—ran out of cream as he was making a soda. He substituted ice cream for the cream and created a true ice

Ice Cream Truck. *Culinary Archives & Museum at Johnson & Wales University, Providence, R.I.*

cream soda. It became such a success that, in 1893, a magazine called it "our national beverage."

The invention of the ice cream sundae is also the stuff of legend. One version has it that preachers thought it was sinful to sip sodas on Sundays, which led an enterprising soda jerk to invent the sundae. Another says it was invented when someone ran out of soda water. The sundae was hugely popular, and other ice cream innovations followed.

Eskimo Pies, Popsicles, Creamsicles, Fudgsicles, ice cream sandwiches, and Good Humor bars were among the successful ones. Harry Burt, of Youngstown, Ohio, invented the Good Humor Ice Cream Sucker, the first chocolate-covered ice cream bar on a stick, in 1920. He was also the first to sell ice cream from trucks, which he painted white and decked out with jingling bells.

Perhaps the most popular ice cream innovation was the ice cream cone, which is reputed to have been invented at the 1904 World's Fair in Saint Louis. Supposedly a vendor selling ice cream in small glass dishes could not wash the dishes fast enough to keep up with demand. Ernest Hamwi, a vendor selling wafers, solved the problem. Hamwi rolled his wafers into cone shapes and filled them with ice cream. Before long, everyone at the fair was eating the ice cream cones he claimed to have invented. Nearly a year earlier, however, Italo Marchiony, who sold lemon ices from a pushcart in New York, had applied for a patent on a mold that turned out ten cones at a time. He also claimed credit for the invention. However, long before, European confectioners rolled wafers into cones and filled them first with flavored whipped creams and then ice creams. But these were ice cream cones on a silver platter, eaten at a table with fork and spoon. America popularized the ice cream cone that is licked outdoors on a summer day.

In 1920, America prohibited alcohol and started an ice cream boom. Consumption went up by more than 100 million gallons when the United States went dry. Soda fountains and ice cream parlors took the place of corner saloons. Anheuser-Busch and other breweries switched from producing beer to making ice cream. "I scream, you scream, we all scream for ice cream!" was a popular song lyric as well as a kids' rhyme.

The repeal of Prohibition and the Great Depression of the 1930s caused a downturn in ice cream consumption. Ice cream makers fought back with inexpensive novelties like the Twin-Popsicle and the Side-Walk Sundae. They tried to sell ice cream for breakfast. "Serve it over your cereal in place of cream," suggested one ad. Celebrities including Babe Ruth and Charlie Chaplin endorsed ice cream, and President Franklin D. Roosevelt claimed he ate ice cream at least once a day.

A New Era for Ice Cream

By the end of the 1930s, ice cream was back and selling better than ever. New manufacturing and refrigeration methods changed the business. Ice cream was produced in a continuous stream instead of separate batches, making it possible to turn out more of it faster than ever. Grocers began installing refrigerated cabinets that kept ice cream frozen, and householders started replacing their iceboxes with refrigerators complete with tiny freezer compartments. Packaged ice cream would not gain significant market share until after World War II, but the trend had begun.

During the war, the government deemed ice cream a necessity for U.S. fighting forces. It was easy to digest, nutritious, and great for morale. The Navy launched a floating ice cream parlor in the western Pacific, and the Army supplied the troops with enough ingredients to make 80 million gallons a year. In 1943, the U.S. military was the world's largest ice cream manufacturer. Ice cream played a role on the home front, too. Ice cream cup lids featured pictures of planes, tanks, and guns, and kids collected and traded them. Their parents happily paid an extra ten cents for Victory Sundaes because each one came with a war stamp. The stamps were saved and converted to bonds to raise money for the war.

When the war and gas rationing ended, Americans took to the road. They drove to Dairy Queen, Carvel, and Tastee-Freez for the new soft-serve ice creams, and they stopped at Howard Johnson's for ice cream cones. Howard Johnson had opened his first ice cream stand in 1925 with three flavors of old-fashioned, hand-cranked ice cream—vanilla, chocolate, and strawberry. By the 1950s, he had four hundred restaurants and twenty-eight flavors. Later, Baskin-Robbins would come up with thirty-one flavors, one for every day of the longest months. Neighborhood ice cream parlors and drugstore soda fountains could not compete with the chains. The ice cream parlor became a museum piece in 1955 when one opened at Disneyland.

In the 1950s, Americans began shopping at supermarkets, buying packaged ice cream and storing it in their new home freezers. Supermarket ice cream was cheap and readily available, but much of it was not very good. Before the war, the butterfat content of ice cream was about 14 percent. Manufacturers lowered it to 10 percent during

Ice Cream Paraphernalia. *Culinary Archives & Museum at Johnson & Wales University, Providence, R.I.*

the war, and most kept it there. They made ice cream with artificial colors and imitation flavors, and they whipped a lot of air into it.

In 1960, the American ice cream maker Reuben Mattus created a high-fat, super-premium ice cream he named Häagen-Dazs for its European sound and gourmet appeal. The ice cream was made without preservatives and without much air. It came in three flavors: vanilla, chocolate, and coffee. Mattus discovered that consumers who were starved for rich, high-quality ice cream were willing to pay more for it. He ushered in the premium ice cream market.

At the turn of the twenty-first century, Americans could choose from light, reduced-fat, low-fat, nonfat, regular, premium, and super-premium ice creams as well as sherbets, sorbets, gelati, frozen yogurts, and innumerable novelty frozen desserts. Ice cream eaters no longer worry about health issues like colic and cold stomachs. They are concerned about fat and cholesterol instead. As a result, manufacturers are replacing saturated fats with oat bran

and soy flour and fortifying ice cream with fish oils for their healthful Omega-3 fatty acids. More appealingly, they have created floral ice creams, including orange blossom, jasmine, and rose. The same flavors eighteenth-century confectioners made for royalty are blossoming again for everyone, thanks to the democratization of ice cream.

[*See also* Birthdays; Dairy Industry; Desserts; Flowers, Edible; Freezers and Freezing; Howard Johnson; Ice; Iceboxes; Ice Cream Makers; Ice Cream Molds; Ice Cream Sodas; Jefferson, Thomas; Johnson, Howard; Milk; Milkshakes, Malts, and Floats; Myths and Folklore, *sidebar* The Ice Cream Cone and the Saint Louis World's Fair; Refrigerators; Soda Fountains.]

BIBLIOGRAPHY

David, Elizabeth. *Harvest of the Cold Months*. Edited by Jill Norman. New York: Viking, 1995.

Emy. *L'Art de bien faire les glaces d'offices*. Paris: Chez Le Clerc, 1768.

Funderburg, Anne Cooper. *Chocolate, Strawberry, and Vanilla: A History of American Ice Cream*. Bowling Green, OH: Bowling Green State University Popular Press, 1995.

Garrett, Theodore Francis. *The Encyclopaedia of Practical Cookery*. London: Upcott Gill, 1898.

Gilliers. *Le cannameliste française*. Nancy: Chez Jean-Baptiste-Hiacinthe Leclerc, 1768.

Jarrin, G. A. *The Italian Confectioner*. London: John Harding, 1823.

Kelly, Patricia M., ed. *Luncheonette: Ice Cream, Beverage, and Sandwich Recipes from the Golden Age of the Soda Fountain*. New York: Crown, 1989.

Liddell, Caroline, and Robin Weir. *Ices: The Definitive Guide*. London: Grub Street, 1995.

Lincoln, Mrs. D. A. *Frozen Dainties*. Bedford, MA: Applewood, 2001. A facsimile of the booklet published by the White Mountain Freezer Company, 1889.

Randolph, Mary. *The Virginia House-wife*. With notes and commentaries by Karen Hess. Columbia: University of South Carolina Press, 1984.

Rorer, Sarah Tyson Heston. *Ice Creams, Water Ices, Frozen Puddings, Together with Refreshments for all Social Affairs*. Philadelphia: Arnold, 1913.

Selitzer, Ralph. *The Dairy Industry in America*. New York: Dairy and Ice Cream Field and Books for Industry, 1976.

Wheaton, Barbara Ketcham. *Victorian Ices and Ice Cream*. New York: Metropolitan Museum of Art, 1976. A reprint of the 1885 edition of *The Book of Ices* by Agnes B. Marshall, with an introduction and annotations by B. K. Wheaton.

JERI QUINZIO

Ice Cream Makers

In the eighteenth century, ice cream was a rare and expensive treat in the United States, enjoyed only at the most genteel gatherings. However, there was nothing elegant about the process by which it was made. Home cooks and professional confectioners alike faced the same difficulties. First, they had to obtain ice, chip it into manageable pieces, and mix it with salt. They put the ice-and-salt mixture into a large wooden tub or bucket. Then they mixed the ingredients for their ice cream; poured the mixture into a metal freezing pot with a cover, called a *sorbetière*; secured the cover; and set the pot in the tub. *Sorbetières* made of pewter or even silver could be purchased, but some cooks simply used any pot with a cover.

To make creamy—rather than icy—ice cream, the pot had to be shaken and turned continuously by hand. In addition, every now and then the person making the ice cream had to stop, open the pot, scrape the frozen ice cream off the sides, blend it into the mixture, close the pot, and begin turning it again. This process was repeated until the ice cream was ready. It was cold, difficult work—the task of slaves, servants, or lowly confectioners' helpers.

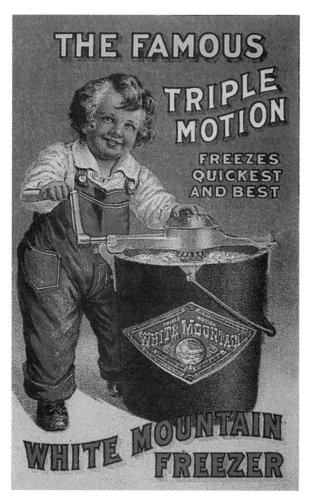

Ice Cream Maker. Advertisement for White Mountain freezer, c. 1885. *Collection of Kit Barry*

In 1843 an American, Nancy M. Johnson, revolutionized ice cream making. She invented (and patented as U.S. patent 3254) an ice cream freezer with a crank outside the tub that was attached to a dasher, or paddle, inside the freezing pot. The person making the ice cream turned the crank, and the dasher churned the ice cream mixture, automatically scraping the sides of the pot. Johnson's invention involved less work and made better ice cream. Best of all, it democratized ice cream, since it allowed even those who lacked servants and helpers to make it.

Johnson's invention led to others, and both home and commercial ice cream making expanded rapidly. Commercial ice cream makers used horse-powered treadmills, steam engines, and finally electric motors to churn ever-larger quantities of ice cream. Eventually, home cooks switched to electric ice cream makers, although hand-cranked models remain the stuff of nostalgic memories. Thanks to the ice cream maker, by the twentieth century, ice cream was an everyday treat enjoyed by all.

[*See also* Ice; Ice Creams and Ices.]

BIBLIOGRAPHY

David, Elizabeth. *Harvest of the Cold Months: The Social History of Ice and Ices*. Edited by Jill Norman. New York: Viking, 1995.

Lincoln, Mrs. D. A. *Frozen Dainties*. Bedford, MA: Applewood Books, 2001. A facsimile of the 1889 booklet published by the White Mountain Freezer Company.

JERI QUINZIO

Ice Cream Molds

A bowl heaped with ice cream was enough to dazzle dinner guests in early eighteenth-century America. But once the novelty of having ice cream wore off, American cooks began to emulate Europeans by sending ice cream to the table in disguise. In the nineteenth century, they molded and decorated ice creams to resemble anything from a wedge of cheese to a melon with a slice cut out to contrast its green exterior with its pink center, and from a bouquet of flowers to a stalk of asparagus.

The ice cream molds themselves were crafted from pewter, copper, or tin and shaped to resemble fruits, vegetables, animals, and flowers. They were made in single-serving, quart, and banquet sizes. Home cooks could buy simple molds at the general store or from catalogs. Confectioners and caterers used elaborate, often multipart, molds.

Ice Cream Molds. *Culinary Archives & Museum at Johnson & Wales University, Providence, R.I.*

To mold the ice cream, cooks chilled the molds, packed them full of ice cream, and put them in a small icebox, called a *cave* from the French (as in *cave à glace*), on a bed of salted ice. Then they heaped up more ice around the molds inside the *cave* and left the molds to firm up. After removing the molds from the *cave*, wiping off the ice mixture, and dunking the molds in warm water, they turned out the ice cream. It could be served immediately, put back in the *cave* to be served later, or decorated.

While home cooks molding ice cream for a special occasion might line a fluted mold with vanilla ice cream and fill the center with strawberry, professionals went to far greater lengths. After they unmolded the ice cream, they embellished it. They tinted ice cream "lemons" with yellow coloring made with saffron and painted ice cream "cucumbers" with green coloring made from spinach. They tucked real leaves and stems into the tops of ice cream "fruits" and served them in baskets sculpted from sparkling ice. They wrapped ice cream "asparagus" in ribbons and brushed colored sugar over ice cream "peaches" to give them a delicate fuzz. The practice of molding ice creams, if not the attention to fine detail, continued throughout the twentieth century, as large-scale manufacturers offered both ready-made and custom ice creams molded into a variety of shapes for holidays, birthdays, and banquets.

[*See also* Desserts; Ice; Ice Creams and Ices.]

BIBLIOGRAPHY

Funderburg, Anne Cooper. *Chocolate, Strawberry, and Vanilla: A History of American Ice Cream.* Bowling Green, OH: Bowling Green State University Popular Press, 1995.

Ranhofer, Charles. *The Epicurean.* New York: Dover Publications, 1971. An unabridged republication of the 1893 work by Ranhofer, chef at Delmonico's, the famed New York City restaurant.

JERI QUINZIO

Ice Cream Sodas

By the early nineteenth century, cold carbonated waters that imitated waters from famous spas were sold in the United States on street corners in major cities and towns, in drug store soda fountains, and in lush surroundings such as those of the Tontine Coffee House in New York City. While they were initially drunk as curative beverages, ice cream sodas rapidly came to be viewed as refreshing treats.

Flavored syrups were added to carbonated waters beginning in the early 1800s. These flavored beverages caught on quickly, and the number of flavorings grew from a handful early in the century to hundreds by the end. Sweet cream or sweet cream syrup could also be added, creating what were called "ice cream sodas" or "iced cream sodas," although they did not actually contain ice cream. That these beverages were considered healthy is indicated by Gustavus Dow's 1861 advertisement promoting his soda fountains: "to preserve your health during the warm season, drink from two to five glasses of Dow's Ice Cream Soda Water Daily!"

The man most often associated with the creation of the ice cream soda as it is known today is Robert Green, who operated a small soda fountain at the semicentennial celebration of the Franklin Institute in Philadelphia in 1874, selling soda water flavored with various syrups and sweet cream. When Green ran out of cream, he purchased some vanilla ice cream from a nearby confectioner to use instead. Returning to his stand, Green found customers waiting and instead of melting the ice cream, he scooped it into the beverages.

In Green's own account of the origin of the soda, which he provided years later, he recalls that when he realized that his small fountain could not compete with a more elaborate one, he decided that he had to come up with something new, a soda with ice cream. He offered young people free sodas to try his creation. They did, loved it, and spread the word. A number of other people laid claim to the creation of the soda, but it was Green who popularized it. He even directed that "originator of the ice cream soda" be engraved on his tomb.

Sipping ice cream sodas had become a national pastime by the 1890s, though not without initial opposition. Soda fountain proprietors worried that the ice cream soda took too long to assemble and too long to consume. However, sodas became so popular that the soda fountain industry soon promoted them vigorously, providing formulas and diagrams of new creations. A few religious leaders initially viewed sipping sodas on Sunday as sinful, but temperance advocates saw the soda as a good alternative to alcoholic beverages, and church opposition faded.

Ice cream sodas in endless variety were soon sold in every soda fountain in the country. They ranged from simple chocolate and strawberry sodas to the black cow, made from root beer syrup, vanilla ice cream, soda water, and whipped cream, to the fancifully named Minnehaha and Floradora Brandy sodas. Ice cream sodas represent a simpler time in America's history, when families, dating couples, and neighbors gathered at the local soda fountain to sip and socialize.

[See also Chocolate Drinks; Soda Drinks; Soda Fountains.]

BIBLIOGRAPHY

Funderburg, Anne Cooper. *Sundae Best: A History of Soda Fountains.* Bowling Green, OH: Bowling Green State University Popular Press, 2002. Well-researched and well-documented, with a good bibliography.

Kelly, Patricia M., ed. *Luncheonette: Ice-Cream, Beverage, and Sandwich Recipes from the Golden Age of the Soda Fountain.* New York: Crown, 1988.

PATRICIA M. KELLY

Iced Tea, *see Tea*

Indian American Food

There are two kinds of Indian American food. One is the type cooked at home by expatriates and the other is available in Indian restaurants. Most obviously, there is much diversity in terms of the former and substantial standardization in the case of the latter. But the difference between restaurant cuisine and domestic Indian American cooking is more substantial than the usual differences between banquet food and everyday cooking seen in every culture.

Restaurant Cuisine

There is a common saying in northern India, "*Kosa kosa pai pani badale chara kosa pai bani,*" meaning "Every two miles the water doth change and every four the dialect." This Hindustani proverb hints at a popular geography of taste and language where *pani*, water, is a metonym for taste. Contrary to this natural dispersal of taste, food in most Indian American restaurants is stringently limited to aggressively spiced, exceptional foods (exceptional by Indian standards), such as large cuts of meat cooked in the dry heat of the tandoor. Why this limitation?

In most societies there are numerous sites where cooking—the rule-determined preparation of comestibles—develops. Three of the more important locations of culinary creativity are imperial courts, commercial eating establishments, and domestic households. Each of these institutions puts food to a different use. For instance, the essential point of court cuisine is to display power through the consumption of elaborately prepared foods using expensive ingredients, such as sugar, ice, spices, and meats. These foods are typically prepared by formally trained male chefs who invariably write down their recipes. Feasts and banquets are an important part of this system of power. Power is often displayed literally as foods acquire height, breadth, and aromatic range. In the case of India, court cuisine is one of rich curries using ghee, cardamom, clove, saffron, and other ingredients and represented quintessentially by kebabs, *koftas*, and *biriyanis*. It is typically the cuisine of Delhi in northern India or Hyderabad in the Deccan, called Mughlai food after the Moguls (Mughals), that reflects these qualities. In India in the twenty-first century Mughlai cuisine is one of the four sources of fine dining, which also include Continental (a colonial reprise of Anglo-French restaurant food), Chinese, and Brahmin cooking.

The next site of culinary creativity is the marketplace, which feeds itinerant pilgrims, shopkeepers, migratory workers, and those of the traveling business castes. There are two kinds of market foods: cheap snack foods that can be bought from vendors and shopkeepers, and expensive cuisines in fine dining restaurants. The market for street foods was, until recently, relatively underdeveloped in India because of the upper caste taboo against buying cooked food. Brahmanic normative thought, as R. S. Khare (1976) and Arjun Appadurai (1988) have argued, gives short shrift to cooking against which royal practices, temple cuisines, and commercial eateries have labored through much of Indian history. Hindu India lacked a distinctly gustatory approach to food as separate from its moral and medicinal implications. To the somewhat austere Brahmanic dining ambience the Muslims, since the thirteenth century, brought a refined and court-ly etiquette. Hence it is no surprise that Delhi and Hyderabad, the two major loci of Islamic power, developed a remarkable reputation for culinary elaboration, especially in the realm of nonvegetarian Mughlai cooking. Taking some inspiration from this courtly culture, a new cuisine developed in the marketplace: on one hand, fried, pickled, and highly salted and sweetened foods that have a relatively long shelf life, typically sold by vendors; and on the other hand, highly spiced meat cuisines sold in relatively exclusive restaurants.

If courtly cuisine was a contribution of Delhi-centered regimes, then street food was marked by four regional variations: savory samosas in the north, sweet and salty fried legumes in western India, sour and savory crepes (*dosa*) in south India, and desserts made from farmer's cheese in the east. In India today these foods dominate street eating.

Beyond the court and the marketplace, the final site of culinary creativity is the domestic hearth. This is where food exhibits the least flamboyance. This is also where spices, salt, and sugar are used much more sparingly, partly due to poverty and partly because there is no need either to impress vassals and patrons or to extend shelf life. In addition it also may be that women, who are usually responsible for the family budget, enforce a more restrained logic on domestic cooking. Eastern India, which has been neither the center of Indian politics as has Delhi in the north, nor so highly urbanized as the western region around Surat and Mumbai, is almost exclusively the realm of domestic cooking. It is quite difficult for instance to get Bengali food in any restaurant even in the preeminent Bengali city of Calcutta.

Historians, such as Hermann Kulke and Dietmar Rothermund, have argued that the course of Indian history, especially its regional patterns, was shaped both by physical geography and strategies of warfare. Indo-Aryan warriors relied on swift chariots, which were superior to the military technology of the indigenous peoples but inadequate for the centralized monopolization of power. Centralization came with the superiority and expense associated with war elephants. Kulke and Rothermund noted that the upkeep of an army of war elephants required a "regional stronghold of sufficient dimensions . . . an area about 100–200 miles in diameter." This strategic pattern remained more or less the same for more than two thousand years, thereby decisively determining India's cultural geography.

The Hindustani proverb about water and dialect describes a world from the local perspective where a *kosa*, or the metaphoric mile, is a long distance, and in all probability taste does change every mile. But viewed from the imperial heights of national geography, it might be more appropriate to draw the shifts every one hundred to two hundred miles. The one-hundred-to-two-hundred–mile limits of Indian regional economies are generally confirmed by language distributions. Most major linguistic states in India span about two hundred miles. In line with this linguistic regionalization, Indian cuisine also changes about every two hundred miles, normatively pulled toward a centralizing metropolitan center typically located in a river valley. Each of the subregions in the north, south, east, and west, such as Punjab and Uttar Pradesh in the north and Tamilnadu and Andhra Pradesh in the south, has its own cuisine with its distinctive spice mix, fat base, cooking methods, utensils, cutting and grinding implements, complex carbohydrate core, protein fringe, and legume.

The variety of Indian regional cuisines is not reflected in the cooking of Indian American restaurants. Most serve a version of northern Indian Mughlai cuisine. There are hardly any foods from southern or eastern India on their menus. Typically the main courses are Mughlai, such as *rogan josh* or chicken *dopiazza*, while some of the appetizers are from western India, such as *bhel puri* and various kinds of *chats*. These restaurants appear to confine themselves to one or two kinds of food, much as Italian American restaurants did until the last decades of the twentieth century.

Most Indian restaurants in the United States are entrepreneurial ventures of Punjabis and Gujaratis. And that is because they come with fewer professional credentials and much more sweat capital than other South Asians, such as Bengalis from West Bengal and Telugus from Andhra Pradesh. Hence Punjabis and Gujaratis are more likely to use small ethnic businesses as routes of upward mobility. Thus it is the northern (Punjabi) and western (Gujarati) aesthetic that dominates Indian restaurant cuisine. In addition, many Bengalis from Bangladesh (not from West Bengal) also work in these restaurants run by Punjabis and Gujaratis, because they come with even fewer professional credentials. Thus (as the Taiwanese have come to dominate sushi restaurants) Bangladeshi sojourners cater Mughlai food in Punjabi restaurants to Americans seeking Indian food presumably because they believe that Americans will not know the difference and their bosses will not know any better.

Domestic Cooking

To say something about Indian American domestic cooking, it is necessary to abandon the category "Indian" and look more closely at the linguistic subsets, such as Punjabi American, Gujarati American, or Bengali American. What is happening to domestic cookery among Bengali Americans is probably similar to other groups.

Bengalis come from a linguistic region that is divided between two political units: Bangladesh with about 125 million inhabitants occupying the eastern two-thirds of a delta formed by the Ganges and Brahmaputra rivers, and West Bengal in India with about 70 million people inhabiting the western third. There are about 100,000 Bengalis in the United States in the early 2000s.

For most of the approximately thirty-thousand Bengali American households, breakfast eaten at home is either milk and cereal or toast. Lunch, consumed at or near the workplace, is a salad or a slice of pizza, sometimes a sandwich. For restaurant workers, lunch is rice, *dal*, and some curried vegetables or meats. It is dinner that remains the realm of "tradition," where there is still a literal truth to the question asked by a Bengali: "Have you eaten rice?" when what is meant is, "Have you eaten?" Rice, *dal*, and fish cooked in a sauce with *panch phoron* (a Bengali five-spice mix of fenugreek, onion seed, fennel, cumin, and mustard seed) is eaten for dinner, more often in the United States than in Calcutta.

It is of course an exaggeration to say that dinner remains wholly "traditional" in any meaningful sense. It would be more accurate to argue that dinner is perceived to have remained traditional while in reality it has changed. Take, for instance, the appetizer for a typical Sunday dinner: ground turkey croquettes (called *pokora*) cooked with chopped garlic, ginger, onion, and fresh cilantro. Turkey is hardly a traditional Bengali ingredient. Yet it is cooked in a typically Bengali form, with ground turkey replacing ground goat meat. Any meat in Bengali cuisine is usually cooked with the trinity of wet spices: onion, ginger, and garlic. It is so in the case of the *pokora*.

Then there is the more explicit intermingling of what are self-consciously defined as American and Bengali cuisines when the menu might be roast chicken, steamed rice, American-style salad, sautéed bittermelon, grapes, and apple juice. Or a truly typical Bengali repertoire, typical, that is, with the exception of strawberry shortcake for dessert and grape juice as an accompaniment. Or a family night out at Red Lobster, hardly a classic Bengali option.

Nonetheless, there is a pervasive "Bengaliness" in all this mixing up. Rice continues to be the core of the evening meal. The animal protein is important but remains a fringe item in terms of the caloric contribution to the meal. It is usually two small pieces of fish or a few bite-size portions of meat. The complex carbohydrate core and the animal-protein fringe is paired with the third defining element—*dal*. *Dal*, or legume soup, is sparsely spiced, often with only a few roasted cumin seeds. The animal-protein fringe, in contrast, is highly spiced as is typical in Bengali cuisine. The spices and herbs are drawn mostly from within the Bengali repertoire and the cooking processes are typically limited to sautéing, stewing, and braising, which are the basic Bengali notions of "cooking."

Further, the greatest change can be seen in the elements that are peripheral to the Bengali conception of the "meal," that is, turkey replacing goat meat in the appetizer, juices and soda replacing water, and strawberry shortcake simulating a Bengali dessert. It is perhaps because the most radical changes are confined to the accompaniments—the drinks, the dessert, and the appetizer—that the "meal" as such can still be defined as Bengali. Hence, in spite of rampant creolization of ingredients, dinner is perceived as the realm of traditional Bengali cuisine.

Further, what might encourage the perception of the Bengaliness of dinner is that it is truly so, almost in an exaggerated manner. Middle-class Bengalis consider rice and fish to be the most distinctive ethnic ingredients of their meal. About 60 percent of Bengali American households serve rice for dinner almost every day. In contrast only 31 percent of comparable Bengali households in Calcutta serve rice for dinner on a typical day. An equally dramatic sign of change is the rate of consumption of fish. Up to a third of comparable households in Calcutta serve fish for dinner on a typical day. In contrast, almost one-half of Bengali American households eat fish at dinner on an average day in a week. Thus expatriate families have become even more Bengali in their food habits in exile.

In addition, rice and fish have migrated from lunch to dinner, and dinner has become more important in defining a Bengali culinary identity in the United States. Heightened valorization of dinner as the only cooked meal is in itself a product of modern work schedules. Although in this case that modern transformation is being used to strengthen a tradition: a dinner of rice and fish. Further, the size of the fish portion has almost doubled from about four ounces on the outside in Calcutta to about six to eight ounces in the United States. This is also a development that can be seen either as Westernization (because of the valorization of the protein component of the meal) or as a traditional carryover (because of the stress on fish, which is a self-conscious marker of Bengaliness).

Thus dinner has changed in two directions: new ingredients, such as turkey, are absorbed into old culinary paradigms; and the use of old constituents, such as rice and fish, is insisted upon. One absorbs change and the other accentuates tradition in a new context. With breakfast and dinner, it is as if Bengalis have divided up the day into what they characterize as moments of "modernity" and moments of "tradition," both perceived as good and necessary in their separate places. This complementary duality toward the "modern" and the "traditional," the former imagined as embodied in something as mundane as industrialized breakfast cereal and the latter with traditional rice and fish, is central to the identity of the Bengali *bhadrasamaj* (literally, respectable society). The Indian middle class has long been both threatened and seduced by the promise of modernization, and it has acted on those concerns in organizing food practices in the United States.

[*See also* Ethnic Foods; Herbs and Spices; Muslim Dietary Laws; Rice; Vegetarianism.]

BIBLIOGRAPHY

Achaya, K. T. *Indian Food: A Historical Companion.* Delhi: Oxford University Press, 1994.
Appadurai, Arjun. "How to Make a National Cuisine." *Society for the Comparative Study of Society and History* (1988): 3–24.
Khare, R. S. *Culture and Reality: Essays on the Hindu System of Managing Foods.* Simla: Indian Institute of Advanced Studies, 1976.
Kulke, Hermann, and Dietmar Rothermund. *A History of India.* London: Routledge, 1996.

KRISHNENDU RAY

Insects

Lobsters, crabs, and shrimp are esteemed foods in the United States, but grasshoppers, termites, and caterpillars are not. All are arthropods with tough, segmented exoskeletons and high-protein muscle tissue. Yet many Americans define ocean-living shellfish as edible and land-dwelling insects as inedible. Just the mention of eating "bugs" can prompt the gag reflex.

This aversion to insects as food is not shared globally. Entomophagy, meaning "insect eating," is widespread,

providing approximately 10 percent of protein consumed worldwide. Baby bee appetizers in Japan, mopane worm casserole in South Africa, scorpion soup in China, and grasshopper tacos in Mexico are examples of specialties. The American attitude toward entomophagy has its roots in Europe, when during the Middle Ages (1000 to 1400) meat, especially beef and pork, became so abundant that even the poor had plenty of protein without foraging for insects. It is theorized that only regions of the world with scarce or difficult-to-hunt protein sources and a geography unsuited to raising domesticated animals developed extensive entomophagy. In Europe and the United States, where protein is ample, insects are usually associated with dirt, disease, crop destruction, decomposition, biting or stinging, teeming, and other attributes that bring forth loathing and disgust.

In the United States, nineteenth-century ethnographic data demonstrate that entomophagy was important in certain Native American groups, especially those living in the Great Basin and southwestern desert areas. Locusts and grasshoppers were particularly popular. The Shoshone formed a large circle called a surround and beat the ground with sticks, herding the grasshoppers into a large pit. The Ute used a similar technique, driving them toward hot coals. The Washo would set the prairie grasses aflame to collect locusts. Both insects were enjoyed roasted with salt (likened to shrimp) and pulverized to make a flour used in porridge or bread. Pandora moth caterpillars were commonly smoked out of trees and roasted for immediate consumption, or air-dried for future use. Shore fly larva collected from alkaline lakes, crickets beaten out of bushes, and larva scooped from anthills were other insect favorites.

In this same period, some Plains settlers consumed grasshoppers following destruction of crops by swarms of the insect, but others starved due to entomophagy prejudice. A few U.S. authors began to question the rationality of ignoring insect protein sources, especially during food shortages. In 1885, a small book titled *Why Not Eat Insects?* by Vincent Holt suggested that the addition of insect dishes to the diet was a matter of common sense and of reason conquering fashion. Anticipating deprivation during World War I, some scientists recommended that research on insect palatability be undertaken by college departments of home economics and by the U.S. Department of Agriculture. Concern that the world's food supply was running out popularized Ronald Taylor's book on entomophagy *Butterflies in My Stomach* (1975) and his booklet *Entertaining with Insects; or, The Original Guide to Insect Cookery* written in 1976 with

Barbara Carter. Increasing interest in a unique dining experience resulted in a number of late-twentieth-century publications, including the *Eat-a-Bug Cookbook* by David George Gordon (1998) and *Man Eating Bugs: The Art and Science of Eating Insects* by Peter Menzel and Faith D'Aluisio (1998).

Canned insects are sometimes available in ethnic markets. However, American entomophagy in the twenty-first century is primarily limited to tequila-flavored lollipops with mealworms, chocolate-covered ants, other candied insect novelties, and the occasional instructional menu created by entomologists for their students. Unintentional insect eating is more common. The Food and Drug Administration regulates the amount of whole insects, fragments, and larva or eggs allowed in food, such as ten aphids in five hundred grams (about one pound) of raspberries that are frozen or canned, three hundred fragments in that same amount of chocolate, and five fly maggots in that amount of tomatoes used for tomato paste, pizza sauce, or juice. In most cases, the insects are processed and become an undetectable addition to the product.

Pound for pound, edible portions of insects provide high-quality protein that is typically lower in fat and higher in other nutrients, such as calcium and iron, than protein from meat, poultry, or fish. Entomologists note that some insects convert their feed to body tissue more efficiently than vertebrates, at rates nearly double those of chicken and five hundred times higher than cattle. It has been suggested that mass production of insects could ease world hunger. Entomophagy should be limited to commercial insects because of the potential for contamination by pesticides and toxins; people sensitive to shellfish may also be allergic to insects.

[*See also* Adulterations; Aseptic Packaging; Gibbons, Euell; Native American Foods, *subentry on* Technology and Sources; Pioneers and Survival Food; Pure Food and Drug Act.]

BIBLIOGRAPHY

Bodenheimer, Friedrich S. *Insects as Human Food: A Chapter in the Ecology of Man.* The Hague: W. Junk, 1951.

De Foliart, Gene R. *The Human Use of Insects as Food: A Bibliographic Account in Progress.* Available at http://www.food-insects.com. 2002.

Harris, Marvin. *Good to Eat: Riddles of Food and Culture.* New York: Simon & Schuster, 1985.

Lindroth, Richard L. "Food Conversion Efficiencies of Insect Herbivores." *Food Insect Newsletter* 6 (March 1993).

Sutton, Mark Q. *Insects as Food: Aboriginal Entomophagy in the Great Basin.* Menlo Park, CA: Ballena Press, 1988.

PAMELA GOYAN KITTLER

International Aid

Signed into law in 1954, Public Law (PL) 480 has served as the most significant instrument of food aid in U.S. foreign policy. The program has three parts. Title I, overseen by the U.S. Department of Agriculture, makes government-to-government sales of agricultural commodities (such as wheat, rice, corn, and soybeans) on long-term credit to developing countries. Title II, administered by the Agency for International Development (AID), makes donations by the U.S. government of agricultural commodities for international humanitarian food needs to other governments, intergovernmental agencies, and public and private nongovernmental organizations. Title III, also administered by AID, supports economic development by donating agricultural commodities to governments, which then sell them on the domestic market, and use the proceeds for development programs.

Public Law 480 arose from the poor economic conditions in Europe following World War II. American agriculture had produced large surpluses sufficient to supply U.S. domestic needs and those of European countries. As European agriculture recovered in the early 1950s, overproduction in the United States created economic uncertainty and the consequent need to expand markets in lieu of curtailing U.S. agricultural production. The Agricultural Trade Development and Assistance Act of 1954, which authorized PL 480, was designed to dispose of federal surplus agricultural commodities, expand international trade, and create new foreign markets via economic development in developing nations. The act also furthered the U.S. geopolitical interests of the Cold War. Congressional desire to use "food as a weapon" of foreign policy to stop the global spread of communism was explicitly reflected in debate on S. 2475, which became PL 480.

An overt emphasis on humanitarian food aid did not emerge until 1958 when Senator Hubert Humphrey (D-MN) sought revisions to the law in a report entitled "Food and Fiber as a Force for Freedom." Humphrey sought to rename the law the Food for Peace Act, a name that remains current in the early 2000s, and to redirect the focus from economic support of the agricultural sector in the United States, toward the promotion of international welfare, peace, and freedom. With Cold War objectives still in place, PL 480 played an unambiguous role in helping those countries considered politically friendly to the foreign policy interests of the United States. For these

International Aid Poster. Poster created by the National Association of Ice Industries for the United States Food Administration during World War I. *Prints and Photographs Division, Library of Congress*

reasons critics refer to PL 480 as the "Food as a Weapon" program. Congress later redefined the program's goals, directly linking food aid to countries demonstrably affected by food shortages. Public Law 480 continued, as the twenty-first century opened, to be defined in part by commitments to development and expansion of export markets for U.S. agricultural commodities, as well as by promoting political goals.

In its initial years, the Food for Peace program accounted for one-quarter to one-third of all U.S. agricultural exports. Largely through PL 480, the U.S. by the early 1960s had come to supply over 95 percent of all international food aid, a figure that declined by nearly half in the following decade. PL 480 continues to serve as a major source of humanitarian food assistance. In fiscal year 2002, the program provided 2.7 million metric tons of food valued at nearly $595 million, making the United States the single largest government contributor of international food aid.

Critics of PL 480 have pointed to several, sometimes contradictory, concerns with the program. Some stress the tendency of PL 480 to flood the markets of less-developed countries with large surpluses of U.S. agricultural commodities, thereby threatening the indigenous agricultural base and economy. Others argue that certain recipient governments have relied heavily on PL 480 contributions to insulate and support local agricultural sectors that in some cases actually could benefit from greater modernization. Still others note that PL 480 has served as a major governmental subsidy for U.S. agricultural interests. Concerns over genetically modified U.S. food aid have also been raised in some recipient countries.

Supporters of the program, including the World Food Program, CARE, and the Coalition for Food Aid, view PL 480 as vital in the continuing effort to feed populations facing serious threats to food security. For them, compassion fatigue and declining American support in the 1990s for foreign food aid signal troubles for ongoing humanitarian efforts.

[*See also* Department of Agriculture, United States; Hunger Programs; Nutrition.]

BIBLIOGRAPHY

Cathie, John. *The Political Economy of Food Aid*. New York: Palgrave Macmillan, 1982.
FASonline. http://www.fas.usda.gov/food-aid.html. Describes food aid programs under PL 480 and other initiatives of the U.S. government.
United States Congress. House. Committee on Agriculture. Subcommittee on Department Operations, Nutrition, and Foreign Agriculture. *Review of Public Law 480, The Food for Peace Program*. 104th Cong., 1st sess. 1995. H. Doc. 104-16.
United States Congress. Senate. Committee on Agriculture, Nutrition, and Forestry. Subcommittee on Foreign Agricultural Policy. *Food for Peace, 1959–1978—Major Changes in Legislation*. 96th Cong., 1st sess. 1979.

KEVIN T. MCINTYRE AND BARRETT P. BRENTON

Irish Coffee

Although people have been lacing coffee with alcohol for years, Irish coffee, a drink of slightly sweetened hot coffee that is fortified with Irish whiskey and served with a blanket of whipped cream floating on top, was supposedly invented in the winter of 1943 by Joe Sheridan, chef at Foynes Airport in Limerick, Ireland. The story goes that

Sheridan, after hearing that a flight bound for New York had turned back owing to bad weather, mixed up a special drink to warm the exhausted passengers. Among the travelers was the writer Stanton Delaplane, who liked the concoction so much that he brought the recipe back to Jack Koeppler, bartender at the Buena Vista Hotel in San Francisco. Koeppler and Delaplane tried to recreate the drink, but the whipped cream kept sinking to the bottom. Koeppler eventually visited Sheridan in Ireland and learned the threefold secret of floating the cream—the coffee must be lightly sweetened, the cream must be both fresh and softly whipped, and the cream must be poured into the hot coffee over the back of a spoon.

Irish coffee became a staple after-dinner drink in the United States in the 1950s. Its popularity peaked in the 1970s, when seemingly endless variations using sweeter liqueurs came into vogue. Although it is no longer a huge fad, Irish coffee remains a classic cold-weather drink.

[*See also* Coffee.]

BIBLIOGRAPHY

Lovegren, Sylvia. *Fashionable Food: Seven Decades of Food Fads.* New York: Macmillan, 1995.
Mariani, John F. *The Dictionary of American Food and Drink.* New Haven: Ticknor and Fields, 1983.

SYLVIA LOVEGREN

Irradiation

Irradiation is a process in which food is exposed briefly to a radiant energy source in an effort to kill harmful bacteria, eliminate insect pests, inhibit further maturation of fresh foods, extend shelf life, and sterilize packaging materials. Similar to sending luggage through an airport scanner, the food is passed in containers quickly through a radiation field. Commercial irradiation equipment uses gamma rays, electron beams, or X-rays. Federal rules require irradiated foods to be labeled as such. Irradiating food does not eliminate all risk of food-borne illness, and proper handling is still required.

Scientists first studied radiation in the 1930s, but shortly after World War II research efforts increased as the U.S. Army sought a means of reducing field troops' dependence on refrigeration. By the 1950s, research took a new turn when the Eisenhower administration's Atoms for Peace program explored irradiation as a way of killing insects on fruits and vegetables.

Combined with simultaneous studies in other countries, the research found the most important benefit of irradiation to be the control of harmful food pathogens. It was not until 1963 that the FDA approved the first commercial use of irradiation for wheat and wheat flour. As is still true in the early 2000s, the approval came with strict guidelines for the maximum amount, or dose, of radiation allowed, as measured in kiloGrays, or kGy.

It took another twenty years for the FDA to approve additional commercial uses of the process. In 1983, irradiating spices and dry vegetable seasonings became permissible for the purpose of decontaminating and controlling insects and microorganisms. Two years later, dry and dehydrated enzyme preparations were added to the list of products approved for irradiation, and, in 1986, the FDA approved pork for irradiation in an effort to control *Trichinella spiralis* parasites. It took six more years for approval to be granted for use on poultry, and it was not until 2000 that the federal government added raw meat and meat products to the list of foods that could be irradiated to control pathogen microorganisms.

Consumer understanding and acceptance of irradiation has by no means kept up with the government's approval of the process, although consumer acceptance has increased. In 1993 a national Gallup poll found that over 60 percent of consumers were extremely concerned that

Radura Symbol This symbol on a package means the food has been subjected to irradiation. *U.S. Department of Agriculture, Food Safety and Inspection Service*

irradiated food might cause cancer or other illness. By 1998–1999, a survey of adult consumers by the Foodborne Diseases Active Surveillance Network (FoodNet) showed 50 percent of their participants were willing to buy irradiated foods. But the study further showed that the percentage decreased greatly when the cost of irradiated food was higher than that of nonirradiated food.

The amount of food irradiated in the United States will be limited, according to the U.S. Department of Agriculture's *Food Safety Economics,* by manufacturers' perception of public attitude toward irradiation. As the twenty-first century began, irradiation equipment was very costly, and food manufacturers were unlikely to make the investment as long as they perceived consumers were unwilling to buy irradiated products.

[*See also* Aseptic Packaging; Food Safety; Microwave Ovens.]

BIBLIOGRAPHY

Frenzen Paul D., Alex Majchowicz, Jean C. Buzby, and Beth Imhoff. "Consumer Acceptance of Irradiated Meat and Poultry Products." *Issues in Food Safety Economics.* USDA/ERS Agriculture Information Bulletin no. 757. Washington, D.C.: Department of Agriculture, August 2000. Available at http://www.ers.usda.gov/publications/aib757/aib757.pdf.
U.S. Food and Drug Administration. *FDA Consumer.* Available at http://www.fda.gov/fdac/fdacindex.html. See especially the issues for May–June 1998 and January 2000.

MARGE PERRY

Italian American Food

Among the six largest ethnic groups in modern America, Italian Americans were the last to arrive in substantial numbers, had the most difficult transition from rural to urban life, faced a great deal of discrimination as immigrants, retained the most of their traditional foodways, and have the most popular ethnic cuisine by every measure: restaurant meals, supermarket sales, published cookbooks, and recipes in contributed cookbooks. Contemporary American youth of all backgrounds love pasta and pizza; the most refined gourmets seek out exotic Italian regional specialties like *ventresca tuna, farro,* and fennel pollen. Americans have embraced Italian food to the extent that many other ethnic cuisines are described in Italian culinary terms: Jewish delicatessens sell kosher salami, Chinese potstickers are called "Peking ravioli," and Greek and Korean restaurants feature fried calamari.

All of this would surprise the typical Italian immigrant family of the early twentieth century, who might well know none of the foods mentioned above, nor even think of themselves as Italian. Like Germany, Italy did not become a unitary country until late in the nineteenth century. Southern Italy and Sicily, the origin of most Italian Americans, were actually part of Spain for most of modern European history, or semi-independent as the Kingdom of Naples or the Kingdom of the Two Sicilies. They did not join the Kingdom of Italy until 1861. Differences in dialect also ensured that many immigrants thought of themselves as coming from a particular village or province. For many immigrant groups, urbanization within their country of origin had begun a nationalizing process in them before they reached the United States. Even the Anglo-American colonists had often spent some time in London. This was substantially less true of Italian immigrants, who seemed to come directly from rural villages to American port cities, mostly between the years 1900 and 1924—when most of the farmland in the United States had been taken. Thus people of peasant background were crowded into "Little Italy" urban neighborhoods and may have learned that they were "Italian" instead of Sicilian or Abruzzese from immigration officials or social workers. The large numbers of immigrants and the concentrated period of migration for southern Italians did tend to throw them together, and their local dialects began to alter into a distinctively American dialect. Had they arrived at an earlier time in American history and settled outside large cities, they might well have developed a uniquely American dialect like the Pennsylvania Dutch dialect of German.

Early Italian Influences on American Food

Although it is generally known that Italians in service of Spain, Portugal, and England were the first to lead expeditions to the Americas, it is less widely understood that Iberian exploration and colonization were also partially financed by Italian capital and that reports on the new continents—including significant botanical information and samples—went directly to Venice, Florence, and Genoa. The continents were named after Amerigo Vespucci (and not Columbus, Verrazano, or Giovanni Caboto) not because he put his name on an early map, but because his Florentine associates relayed his information to a German mapmaker.

Less prominent Italians were sailors and soldiers in Iberian service in the "New World." There were also some scattered Italian artisans in the British colonies, including

Italian Bread. Bread peddlers, Mulberry Street, New York City, c. 1900. *Prints and Photographs Division, Library of Congress*

Philip Mazzei, who came to Virginia in 1773 and became a close associate of Thomas Jefferson. Although Mazzei's attempts to grow wine grapes in Virginia failed, he became a Revolutionary diplomat in Italy and sent Jefferson seeds and plants. Mazzei also dispatched to Jefferson the first of a series of Italian sculptors who worked on the U.S. Capitol building. Jefferson himself traveled in northern Italy in 1787 and sent his associate William Short to Naples a year later to collect a pasta mold (among other things) and to study cheese making and possibly ice creams. Some of this activity may have resulted in the recipes "To Make Polenta" and "To Make Vermicelli" in *The Virginia Housewife* (1824) by Jefferson's friend and relative-by-marriage, Mary Randolph. However, Randolph's recipe for macaroni and cheese (boiled then baked) is more likely based on pasta dishes introduced by French chefs, who had fled the French Revolution a generation earlier and established imports of macaroni and a pasta factory in Philadelphia. This kind of soft, baked macaroni and cheese became a standard on southern tables and is loved by American children, but it is far from being Italian food.

Of the American foodstuffs sent to Europe, tomatoes, bell peppers, and zucchini were significantly improved in Italian gardens before returning to North America with colonists. Maize had probably replaced millet in Tuscan polenta by the early seventeenth century, but North American colonists from England, Holland, Sweden, and France did not know that, so they had to work out cornmeal mush all over again. A number of European vegetables and some identifiable recipes that did come with early colonists originated in Italy, though sometimes as long ago as Roman times. On the other hand, heading broccoli (also known as "cauliflower broccoli") was not widely eaten in the United States until marketed in the 1930s by Italian American growers, and arugula—a weed in Italy—did not become part of the American gourmet vocabulary until the 1990s.

There was an unknown number of Italians among the eight hundred or so predominantly Catalan colonists of New Smyrna, Florida, in 1768. But the first lasting Italian American communities were founded by northerners in the nineteenth century. Most were miners, stonemasons, stone carvers, or other skilled artisans. The largest groups, including some Italian-speaking Swiss and Croatians, settled in northern California, where they were involved in the early Napa Valley wineries, the San Francisco fishing fleet, and the developing agriculture of a Mediterranean climate region in which they could grow artichokes, cardoons, olive trees, and familiar herbs. Nineteenth-century Italian immigrants also worked in the New Orleans and Florida fisheries and established wineries in upstate New York. Northern Italians were early restaurateurs on the East Coast, especially in New York City, but the restaurants, such as the famous Delmonico's, served predominantly French food for most of the nineteenth century, introducing pasta and tomato sauce only in the last quarter of that century and probably keeping polenta, risotto, pesto, espresso, and gelato to themselves. In contrast, out West, Italian Americans were able to produce and popularize cioppino, a classic seafood stew. It was only when reinforced by the millions of southern Italian immigrants who arrived in the first two decades of the twentieth century that Italian restaurateurs were able to advance their own food to its present level of esteem.

Italian Background of Southern Italians

One of the most remarkable things about Italian American food, with its origins in southern Italy, becoming the favorite ethnic delight of the United States is how seldom the new Italian immigrants had eaten most of those dishes in their homeland. The late dissolution of feudal property relationships in Italy had left millions of rural people without direct ties to the land, impoverished, and in debt to middlemen known as "padrones." Many immigrants recalled eating meat only three times a year: at Christmas, at Easter, and at the *festa* of the local saint. These celebrations, with food preparations beginning well ahead of time and food shared among all members of society, were so significant that Italian American immigrants were able to restore an entire cuisine from memories of those few days.

In America, Easter and Christmas remained ethnic, but local traditions were both Americanized and made pan-Italian. Peasants who had always had a roast kid at Easter accepted lamb, and if a northern Italian–style panettone (tall raisin-egg bread) was in the market, it went onto a southern family's table as well. The Christmas Eve dinner with seven courses of seafood persisted, even if some of the fish and shellfish were basically unfamiliar, or one of the courses had to be spaghetti with canned tuna.

The *festas* for local saints, with a brass band and parade behind an image of a saint bedecked with donations of money and jewelry, remained a rallying point for regional identity in immigrant neighborhoods. Some groups sent back to Italy for valued images of locally venerated saints, such as Cosmas and Damian from Gaeta in

Campania (which went to Cambridge, Massachusetts). At the same time, the *festas* were increasingly becoming street parties that served as meeting points for people from different parts of the old country. The Italian sections of New York, Boston, Newark, Philadelphia, Baltimore, Chicago, and St. Louis had mutual associations for many Italian provinces and church circles devoted to the saints of particular Italian cities and towns. A *festa* was fun and a chance to get out of the house, and in America one could afford to honor all of the saints of Italy. More than three hundred such *festas* survive in the United States, joined by more secular Italian festivals in smaller communities.

Thus in the early 2000s, St. Paolina is celebrated by descendants of Nola in Campania, now settled in Brooklyn. St. Rocco gets the biggest parades in Chicago, brought there by immigrants from Valenzano in Bari. St. Sebastien is important to people whose ancestors came from Curami, Sicily, to Montclair, New Jersey. St. Gabriel, especially dear to the Abruzzese, has a *festa* in Baltimore. In Boston's North End, one of the oldest *festas* is that of the Madonna del Soccorso, venerated in Sciacca, Sicily. And the *festa* of San Gennaro, patron of Naples, in New York's Little Italy can draw 1 million visitors, with much of the street food being Sicilian, Roman, and even American (hot dogs, cotton candy, pretzels).

Not all of the saints are so localized. St. Joseph's Day (March 19) was and is important to all Sicilians, and many other Italian Americans join in, creating elaborate altars hung with fruit and symbolically shaped breads. Because his day is during Lent and requires sharing with the poor, St. Joseph's breads, traditional fish dishes, pasta and chickpeas (the original form of "pasta fazool"), and traditional fried sweets are widely distributed.

In addition to the saints, the old padrone system was also imported but was never fully accepted by American employers and political leaders, although aspects of it were incorporated into Italian American fraternal organizations and even some organized crime groups.

How Italian Immigrants Kept Their Own Food

Although most immigrant groups followed a consistent pattern of Americanization, with language and food substantially assimilated in approximately three generations, Italian Americans were and are different in more than just their greater numbers. As late arrivals, they appeared more alien to mainstream Americans than other immigrants did and were stigmatized for their accents, their appearance, and—remarkable as it may seem—their use of herbs and garlic in cooking. Unsupervised Italians were known to gather apparently inferior foods, such as mussels and dandelions, from the urban wild. Settlement houses and public schools were intent upon improving the immigrants by teaching them to overcook vegetables, eat in a genteel fashion, and embrace the white sauces and bland flavors of the late Victorian Anglo-American table. Unwittingly abetted by urbanization, Italian families resisted with imported foodstuffs, rooftop gardens, and multigenerational Sunday dinners.

Settlement houses that had been giving cooking and sewing classes to newly arrived women found that Italian American women did not want the cooking classes. They knew how to cook and preferred their own food. American home economists, who thought that bland food, with the ingredients separated on the plate, was more healthful and would combat sexual excess and even political extremism, were frustrated. When they visited Italian American homes and found small quantities of expensive olive oil and cheese, intended to flavor masses of pasta, they thought that this was poor budgeting. They also thought that Italian immigrants were not buying enough milk and meat, although the Italian Americans themselves considered a Sunday roast chicken or pork roast luxurious compared with eating meat three times a year in the old country. Italians had invented béchamel sauce but would not immerse their vegetables in it in the approved manner of the American domestic science movement.

In Boston, the North Bennet Street School in 1894 had thirty-eight women in dressmaking classes. None showed up for cooking. By 1936 the Anglo-American board finally caved in and published a cookbook of "137 Tested Recipes of Famous Italian Foods," most taken from "neighborhood friends," and "many of which they have inherited from other generations." Domestic science hints and a recipe for béchamel sauce had to be tucked in toward the back of the book. But the board of directors had come to understand that Italian women would cook their own food and that that food was appealing and practical enough that their cookbook could be sold in the wider community as a fund-raiser. By 1975 Marguerite Dimino Buonopane of the nearby North End Union began collecting recipes from senior citizens for a fund-raising cookbook and was asked to give cooking classes to the younger generation, but in Italian-style cooking, thus completing the circle. Nevertheless, Italian American women who went to public school in Boston as late as the 1960s still remember, "They made us cook everything white."

Celebrity Cookbook. Cookbook with recipes attributed to the opera singer Luisa Tetrazzini (1871–1940), distributed by the *Sunday American. Culinary Archives & Museum at Johnson & Wales University, Providence, R.I.*

Although meal plans changed in America, most of the changes were shifts in the employment of essentially Italian recipes. Many immigrant groups quickly lost traditional foods during the week but held fast to a Sunday dinner that served as a reserve of ethnic foods. The Italian American Sunday dinner, now legendary and multicultural, began as a typical Italian multicourse meal, only with Christmas levels of meat. One of the clearest contrasts between Italian meals and American meals was that Americans had evolved into quick eaters, collapsing traditional courses into one platter with meat, staple starch, and vegetable or salad, with a sweet for dessert. By Early American times, this was how Americans ate all three meals, and on Sundays the plate was larger. In contrast, Italians, when they could, were used to an opening course of antipasto, a soup course, a first course of pasta or rice, a second course with meat and vegetables, and a salad course, usually followed by cheese (or sometimes a sweet instead) and possibly fruit or a few nuts. All of the portions were smaller in Italy; however, in America the first way this meal changed was to become larger and more complex. The antipasto grew into a large platter of cold cuts, cheeses, pickles, and olives. The soup was rich with meat. The pasta was now purchased—factory-dried pasta was a rare luxury in Italy—and the quantities were unlimited. (Handmade pasta persisted for Christmas and *festas*.) The meat was not just a small pot roast that had been cooked in the spaghetti sauce; now that piece was larger, and there was also a roast, initially chicken or rabbit, but eventually a real steak or Italian Christmas pork roast. In America pork was so cheap that the *porchetta* became what Italian Americans brought to a potluck supper or to a funeral or wedding. The salad also got bigger. As generations multiplied, desserts were added, as in the American model, but generally taken from the Italian festival cookbook, such as *cassata*, the Sicilian Easter cheesecake.

One reason Italian Americans kept these dinners going and getting larger and larger was that many cooks could participate. The presiding matriarch could train daughters-in-law or let them add dishes of their own regional origins. Men also made parts of the dinner—Italian men were not ashamed to cook or bake, and the earliest migrants had done so on all-male work crews. This made the Sunday dinner both a refuge of ethnic solidarity and, over time, a pan-Italian melting pot.

What is more remarkable is the preservation of a weekday meal plan in such changed circumstances. Most immigrant groups adopted American foods for the quick breakfasts and lunches needed to suit the more organized and urbanized workdays in the United States. Weeknight dinners also had to be truncated and typically were either American or ethnic, with the ethnic dinners narrowed to meals that could be cooked the most quickly. Italian American families were already used to a quick breakfast of bread and coffee, like many poor Americans. For lunch they were able to produce and commercialize American sandwiches with Italian flavors and to retain Italian foods for weeknight meals. As recently as one study in the 1980s, Italian American families in Philadelphia alternated "gravy meals" and "platter meals." The "gravy" meals were American in that they were one-pot suppers, but Italian in that the pot was meat cooked in tomato sauce ("gravy") and eaten over pasta, with salad. Baked lasagna

Dried Pasta. Advertisement for La Cosechera Italian Macaroni Company. *Warshaw Collection of Business Americana, Archives Center, National Museum of American History, Behring Center, Smithsonian Institution*

and ravioli, more typical of Sundays, were also counted as gravy meals. The platter meals resembled the American three-way plate in form and could include American foods such as hamburgers, quasi-Italian hot sandwiches, vegetables with or without Italian herbs and sauce, and so on. Friday night dinner, traditionally a fish meal, was generally a platter meal. Wednesday or Thursday, difficult midweek nights, were almost always designated as gravy meals, perhaps to reassure on the level of ethnic belonging. (Yes, Wednesday really was Prince Spaghetti Day in Boston, as the commercial announced.)

Italian American Restaurant Foods and Pizza

Men and women working outside the home at first carried what they could approximate of the Italian fieldworker's ration of chunks of hard bread, sausage, and cheese. Groceries, little more than peddlers or sutlers could carry in the nineteenth-century mining camps, arose to provide imported foods, and bakeries quickly followed. In large cities people working in or near their own neighborhoods could buy the components of an Italian fieldworker lunch each day. Inevitably they were made up into sandwiches. These sandwiches became known by a variety of regional names, in part because they were developed as convenience foods in the United States, although they are related to panini (pressed sandwiches) from Italy. The names may vary even within an American metropolitan area, as Italian sandwiches are known as "submarine sandwiches" or "subs" in most of Boston, but as "spuckies" (possibly from a pointed roll called a "spuccadella") among older people and across the harbor in East Boston. On either side, an "Italian" has salami, mortadella, and *capicolla* with provolone and salad, all in a long bun. An "American" sub, or spuckie, substitutes American cheese, and American salami, bologna, and ham—almost literal deracinated equivalents.

Elsewhere in southern New England, the long sandwiches are "grinders." In New York they are "heroes"; in Philadelphia, "hoagies" (probably after a harbor work-site, Hog Island). Round ones (again named after the roll) are muffalettas in New Orleans, where they contain a Sicilian olive salad. In southern Wisconsin, you can order a "Garibaldi sandwich." In Portland, Maine, an Italian grocer claims to have invented something known locally as an "Italian sandwich." Submarine is the most common name nationally and may have originated in Paterson, New Jersey, or in Chicago; the name most likely refers to the shape, as does the occasional "rocket," "torpedo," "bomber," and (formerly) "zeppelin." In some localities they are Americanized as "Dagwoods," after the skyscraper sandwiches made in the 1930s comic strip *Blondie*. Although Dagwood Bumstead piled everything in the refrigerator into a tall sandwich, a restaurant Dagwood is usually shaped like a submarine. Not all of these sandwiches have Italian names, but most are understood as Italian American food, even when purveyed by Greek Americans (who have also moved into pizza parlors in some parts of the country) or when made of tuna salad. This widespread ethnic victory at the level of workingmen's lunches is almost unprecedented in American food history, with the only comparable example being the restricted regional importance of Cornish pasties in northern Michigan and around Butte, Montana.

Ethnic foods tend to rediversify as they go into mainstream use in America, so Italian sandwiches now come with dozens of hot and cold fillings, although the default is generally still cold cuts and cheese with salad. Some of the hot fillings have been adapted from Italian restaurant main dishes, such as meatballs and eggplant or veal parmigiana.

Other Americanized names or translations for Italian foods are surprisingly consistent across the United States. Skewered meats, a popular barbecue in Italian restaurants and bars, are "speedies" (from *spiedini*) to most Italian Americans. Tomato sauce cooked with meat or sausage is almost everywhere "gravy," and the pot roast made in it is "gravy meat"—apparently a direct translation.

Italian American sandwiches crossed over quickly to mainstream use not only because they fit American rapid lunches but also because there were numerous Italian street vendors and restaurateurs to sell them. Immigrant youth were pressed into service as peanut vendors, so much so that Italian Americans founded the Planter's Peanut Company to supply them. Italians sold Italian sauces, American hot dogs, Italian ices, American ice cream bars, Italian sandwiches, American sandwiches, espresso, cappuccino, and American coffee from push-carts, market stalls, luncheonettes, candy stores, coffee shops, bakeries, groceries, and eventually restaurants, supermarkets, and shopping malls (arguably invented by the DeBartolo brothers).

To cross over, Italian home cooking had to be transformed, but even in its most Americanized version it has always been recognizably Italian. A particular problem of serving Italian food to other Americans was that the multicourse pattern of Italian meals did not fit into the rapid pace of American dining. Americans also expected more meat, were shy of garlic, and ate a lot more dessert than southern Italian immigrants did. Each of these difficulties had to be answered—and was answered so well that it is easy to assume that the answers were there all along. To get everything onto the table at one time, Italian American restaurants put the meat course into or next to the pasta course, with a salad on the side. Thus was born spaghetti and meatballs, but also seafood *fra diavolo* and the unfortunate, limp side-dish pasta with meat entrée. To get more meat on the table, a Lenten dish like eggplant parmigiana was redone with what was then the cheapest meat in the market to become veal parmigiana. Rapid-cooking dishes were favored, their names suggesting occupations in which one did not really have time to cook a proper sauce: chicken cacciatore (hunter's chicken), pasta *alla puttanesca* (prostitute's macaroni), and pasta marinara (as made by sailors).

American customers always had white bread and butter with their meals, and so it was served in Italian American restaurants. Americans were shy of garlic, and so garlic butter was added to the soft white bread to make "garlic bread" for *paesani*, who might have had something like foccacia at home. It turned out that Americans would pay extra for garlic bread.

Northern Italian restaurateurs had already set useful precedents. Most nineteenth-century northern Italian restaurateurs served French or Continental food. They were perhaps a little ashamed of polenta and risotto, but they had introduced spaghetti and other forms of pasta, less mushy than Americans made it themselves, and to some extent they had also blazed a trail for tomato sauce, the Bolognese

Sicilian Restaurant. Ferdinando's Focacceria in the Italian neighborhood of Carroll Gardens, Brooklyn, New York. *Photograph by Joe Zarba*

form of *ragu* as a meat-tomato sauce. The northerners had also introduced minestrone, a catchall soup from Genoa, cioppino from the west, and an identification of Italian food with cheap red wine that survived even Prohibition. They also brought forth the idea of a restaurant as a romantic place decorated with oil paintings and sculpture, with violinists and waiters at one's command.

Southern Italian immigrants were employed as waiters and cooks at northern Italian establishments and soon branched out on their own. By the 1930s there were an estimated ten thousand Italian restaurants in New York City, perhaps one-third of all restaurants there. Many of these were small cafés that catered only to other Italian Americans. Pizza bakeries, which had appeared to sell this Neapolitan flatbread at the turn of the nineteenth century, were still exotic even to most Italian Americans and did not spread into the American mainstream until after World War II, when the long campaign for Italy had familiarized many servicemen with the food of Naples, the main liberty port. As with many ethnic foods, pizza was first constricted from the many versions of Naples down to a standard red-sauce-with-cheese version and then rediversified to embrace a variety of toppings. Some local American variations derived from different Neapolitan recipes, such as the clam-based white pizza

of New Haven, Connecticut. Other local varieties, such as deep dish Chicago pizza or New York Sicilian, may derive from other Italian flatbreads, such as foccacia. As pizza has become a main dish, it has diversified outside of ethnic tradition, with such topping combinations as pineapple and ham (Hawaiian). It is unclear if such pizzas will continue to be understood as Italian food, or whether they will enter a post-ethnic zone alongside square bagels and Chinese chicken salad.

Espresso bars, daily meeting places for Italian American men, had few non-Italian customers until they became gathering places for beatniks in San Francisco's North Beach in the 1950s. However, by the early 2000s American teenagers of all backgrounds knew the difference between cappuccino and caffe latte.

From the 1930s until well into the 1980s the stereotypical Italian restaurant had red-and-white checkered tablecloths and candles stuck into straw-covered empty Chianti *fiaschi*; they served cheap red wine and pasta with red sauce. The Italian antipasto course was codified into a platter, typically of cold cuts, cheeses, olives, a few vegetables, and salad, which was one of a number of French-style appetizers served by Italian American restaurants. Many of the other appetizers were taken from other parts of the long Italian feast, such as escarole soup with meatballs, or were confected in the United States, such as stuffed clams casino, an enlarged version of an Italian dish of stuffed mussels. By the late twentieth century the antipasto had again diversified and become a chef's choice of cold tidbits, a fancier version of the original course.

Italian American restaurants have been remarkably resistant to serving desserts, though Italian sweets have a long history. In many cities and towns the only desserts served well into the 1970s were two kinds of ice cream: spumoni, sometimes with red wine sauce, and bisque tortoni. Big city restaurants that could purchase baked goods from nearby bakeries eventually added Sicilian cannoli and sometimes *cassata*, a lemon-flavored ricotta cheesecake that was originally an Easter treat. These ricotta-based desserts may reflect an underlying nostalgia for the Italian bit of cheese to end a festive meal. In the 1990s tiramisu, a kind of layered trifle flavored with coffee liqueur, became the dessert of choice. Italian American restaurants away from the large immigrant communities serve American pies and cakes for dessert, but in the small restaurants of the original Little Italys it is not uncommon for a restaurant to serve no dessert at all and for patrons to walk to a nearby bakery or espresso bar after dinner.

Gourmet Acceptance of Italian American Food

One of the remarkable reversals of Italian American food history is the rise of a despised immigrant cuisine to gourmet status. The crossover decade for Italian food in America was the 1980s, when a previous consensus about elaborate French-style food that had held for almost two hundred years collapsed of its own cream-and-butter-stuffed weight. The baby boomer generation of Americans, reared on pizza and taken out to suburban spaghetti houses, cooked pasta and sauce in their first apartments, preferred the price to value ratio of Italian restaurants when dining out, and—as French haute cuisine went through the expensive excesses of nouvelle cuisine—accepted upscaled Italian food as the new standard for special occasion dining. It helped to see Julia Child, the revered "French Chef" of public television, describe shopping at Italian butchers and grocers. It helped that the electric blender and the newly introduced Cuisinart food processor made excellent pesto. But quite quickly no one was cooking Julia Child's lengthy coq au vin recipe, and everyone was making pasta with a new pasta machine, frothing cappuccino with another shining appliance, making gelato from cream with still another imported machine, stirring stock

into risotto for an hour, pounding veal, and dreaming of Tuscan villas and Roman holidays. The French Chef omelet pan was good enough for frittatas. And it turned out that the once-despised pressure cooker made risotto without all that stirring.

But the immediate attraction of Italian food for the postwar generation was the unmistakable burst of flavor, whether it was the raw garlic and hit of fresh basil in blender pesto, the nutty cheese flavors of imported parmesan or gorgonzola in a slow-cooked risotto, or the citric accents of fennel seed and lemon peel in a Sicilian tomato sauce. In Italian restaurants sharper flavors also came to the fore, with more red pepper in tomato sauce *all' arrabiata*, the capers and anchovies of sauce *alla puttanesca*, or the bitter essence of strong espresso.

Italian restaurant dishes, which had grown ever more abundant and complicated, became refined and expensive. As the yuppies invested in better clothing, the red sauce dishes were superseded by a restaurant category openly described as "white-sauce Italian" or "northern Italian." Although some Venetian (pasta *alla puttanesca*) and Bolognese (creamy sauce) dishes joined the Roman-southern menu of the old "red-sauce Italian" restaurants, and bruschetta topped with lots of tomato salad replaced the old soggy garlic bread, much of the change was cosmetic. (One 1980s dish that was novel in Italy as well was carpaccio, thin slices of raw beef, invented by some accounts at Harry's Bar in Venice.)

Proud Italian Americans had always considered their food the peak of world culinary culture and as much the property of the working-class epicure as the operas of Verdi or the sculptural and oil painting traditions of the old masters. Italian cuisine, like serious French cuisine, had always respected its roots in the kitchens of peasant grandmothers. The difference was that the concentrated Italian mass migration had brought grandmother food to America from the first, whereas French cuisine in America had always been the product of male professionals isolated from a supportive community. Cookbook authors eventually came back to French food in its most Mediterranean forms: Provençal and Catalan food. And Italian cookbook authors responded with explorations of the vivid, North African–influenced food of Sicily. But Sicilian food has been eaten in Italian American homes for more than a century.

At the turn of a new millennium, Italian Americans can laugh comfortably at the stereotyped and neurotic mafiosi of *The Sopranos*, reconstruct great-grandmother's recipes with modern appliances, or even accommodate a low-carbohydrate diet with Tuscan meats and vegetables. Like many third- and fourth-generation immigrants, they have lost the dialect and many of the customs of their ancestors and now attend language classes in standard Tuscan Italian or cooking classes to make Italian foods their provincial ancestors never tasted. They can reclaim the "Italian eye" in the decorative arts or in the kitchen, or choose to advance in professional life, business, and politics. And—in part because earlier generations opened fewer such doors out of whatever combination of family loyalty, guilt, and discrimination—they can do so with a confidence that their ethnic identity and large helpings of food are still there for them. For much of the twentieth century, Italian Americans and their food were at the exotic extreme of the white ethnic spectrum, but what came out of the melting pot at the end was a lot like spaghetti and meatballs.

[*See also* California; Dagwood Sandwich; Ethnic Foods; Gallo, Ernest and Julio; Garlic; Hoagie; Italian Sausage Sandwich with Peppers and Onions; Mondavi, Robert; Mondavi Wineries; Muffaletta Sandwich; Panini; Peanuts; Pepperoni; Pizza; Pizzerias; Salami; Settlement Houses; Tomatoes; Waffle, Wafer, and Pizelle Irons; Wineries.]

BIBLIOGRAPHY

Barr, Nancy Verde. *We Called It Macaroni: An American Heritage of Southern Italian Cooking*. New York: Knopf, 1990. Food by a third-generation Italian American with roots on the island of Ischia (off Naples), from Providence, Rhode Island. The best single cookbook for tracing the evolution of Italian food in the United States.

Buonopane, Marguerite Dimino. *The North End Union Italian Cookbook*. 2nd ed. Chester, CT: Globe Pequot Press, 1987. Ironically, the North End Union had stopped giving cooking classes when the neighborhood turned Italian in the early twentieth century, because no one would come. Buonopane's career there began in 1975, collecting recipes from senior citizens for a fund-raising cookbook, which led her to give classes and rewrite this book twice. As of the early 2000s a third edition was in print.

The Cookbook Committee of Youth Education Services, Humboldt State University, Arcata State University. *A Taste of Humboldt: An Historical and Ethnic Cookbook of Humboldt County, California*. Arcata, CA: Humboldt State University, 1987. A predominantly northern Italian and Italian Swiss community in a place where they actually can grow cardoons and artichokes.

Diner, Hasia. *Hungering for America: Italian, Irish, and Jewish Foodways in the Age of Migration*. Cambridge, MA: Harvard University Press, 2001. Very good summary of conditions around the time of most southern Italian immigration to the United States and of the first generation here.

Esposito, Mary Ann. *Ciao Italia*. New York: Hearst, 1991. Recipes from Companese (Avelino) and Sicilian grandmothers in Buffalo, New York, mixed with Esposito's own training in the

cooking of Sorrento and Umbria to make a wonderful pan-Italian American cuisine.

Goode, Judith, Janet Theophano, and Karen Curtis. "A Framework for the Analysis of Continuity and Change in Shared Sociocultural Roles for Food Use: The Italian-American Pattern." In *Ethnic and Regional Foodways in the United States: The Performance of Group Identity*, edited by Linda Keller Brown and Kay Mussell. Knoxville: University of Tennessee Press, 1984. Crucial examination of daily and weekly meal patterns.

Litrico, Helen Gordon. *Recipes from Amelia Now*. Jacksonville, FL: Progressive, 1991. Mrs. Litrico married into a Sicilian American fishing family in Florida that actually eats spaghetti and meatballs at home, although usually made from shrimp.

Specialità culinare Italiane: 137 Tested Recipes of Famous Italian Foods. Boston: North Bennet Street Industrial School, 1936.

Tusa, Marie Lupo. *Marie's Melting Pot: Sicilian Style Cooking*. New Orleans, LA: Spielman, 1980. By the daughter of the founder of the Central Grocery, where the muffaletta was invented. Mirlitons were stuffed with pine nuts, but Tusa's family also called meat sauce "gravy."

MARK H. ZANGER

Italian Sausage Sandwich with Peppers and Onions

Grilled Italian sausage, served in an Italian roll and topped with fried peppers and onions, is found throughout most of the United States, but it is especially popular in the Northeast and Chicago areas where Italian immigrants originally settled. Preserved meats in the form of sausages have a long history in Italy, so the Italians naturally brought their sausage-making skills to America. Initially, Italian sausage, composed of pork flavored with garlic and anise or fennel seed, was made for home consumption or for sale within Italian communities. American troops returning home from World War II brought with them a taste for many foreign foods, including Italian, and in the 1950s and 1960s the taste for both mild and hot sausages spread to a wider public. Soon, Italian sausage sandwiches, topped with peppers and onions, were being sold at many church and public events and at amusement parks. That tradition continues, and the sandwich is a featured food at festivals, fairs, and ballparks.

[*See also* Amusement Parks; Ethnic Foods; Food Festivals; Italian American Food; Sausage.]

BIBLIOGRAPHY

Mercuri, Becky. *Sandwiches That You Will Like*. Pittsburgh, PA: WQED Multimedia, 2002.

BECKY MERCURI

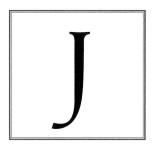

Jack Daniels, *see Bourbon*

Jams and Jellies, *see Preserves*

Japanese American Food

In the history of Japanese immigration to America, food-ways have represented both stable identity and economic, political, and cultural change. Foods are most commonly related to family rather than national identity. Particular dishes are emblematic of Japanese American historical experiences. Nineteenth- and early-twentieth-century Japanese communities in Hawaii and on the West Coast of the mainland, the internment camps during World War II, and postwar dispersals across mainland America demonstrate the maintenance, adaptation, and innovation of diet. The influence of cultural conservatism on the one hand and assimilation on the other led to culturally mixed menus. These adapted and acculturated dishes often are more significant for expressing ethnic identity as it has evolved than are "home country" foods.

Generation, Class, and History

Chief among the factors complicating the story of Japanese American food and identity is generation. The issei, or first-generation Japanese Americans, were born in Japan and immigrated to America with or without their families in the mid-nineteenth century. The first to come were those who came as *dekasegi*, temporary migrant workers whose goal was to return to their families in Japan. These workers included twenty-four samurai who came to America as farmers in 1867. Most of the migrants, however, were of peasant origin and began to arrive in Hawaii, in 1880. Their numbers increased after 1882, when Japanese immigrants began to replace

Chinese laborers, whose numbers were reduced by the Exclusion Act of 1882. In Hawaii the Japanese worked under contract on plantations; on the mainland they worked on the railways and in mines. These workers did not see the overseas sojourn as a new beginning for themselves but as support for those left behind.

As diverse as the situations of individuals who came to America—stowaways, contract laborers, picture brides, farmers, shopkeepers, and professionals—were the experiences of their descendants. Some third- and fourth-generation Japanese Americans look for their roots, while others demonstrate assimilation and its complexities. Tradition, however it may be embodied in Japan, is less important than the way the grandmothers cooked. Food is about the ordinary, the familiar, and the familial. The stories told of issei life on California and Texas farms, of nisei (second-generation) youth spent in internment camps, of family gatherings with intermarried young, of leaving home for college or work all refer to food at home in America and only rarely that distant place of historical origin, Japan.

Japanese arriving in America were more concerned with survival than with preserving a national heritage. Social class and economic conditions affected the experience of food and identity. Where preservation of old-country ways did matter was in maintenance of the culture of village and region, which were more meaningful than being Japanese. Over time one's identity became tied to memories of life in America and not to Japan. Adaptations became the way—a young person's making sushi from brown rice or a grandmother's including shreds of fresh ginger in lasagna. Traditional dishes were adapted to local ingredients and methods.

Some nisei wanted Americanization—a wholesale adoption of American ways that meant conscious or unconscious denial of Japanese roots. Sometimes culinary adaptation preserved elements of cultural heritage. The pressure from American social institutions and communities to assimilate, a force exerted heavily on

European immigrants on the East Coast at the beginning of the twentieth century, was less relevant to Asian populations on the West Coast, which were more segregated. Although American foodways were promoted as markers of acceptability (white bread, large amounts of meat, and long-cooked vegetables, for example), passing into mainstream society was difficult for Asian immigrants regardless of what they ate.

Family foods such as shoyu hot dogs and Spam *musubi* became objects of nostalgia among second- and third-generation Japanese Americans. Shoyu hot dogs—hot dogs seasoned with brown sugar and shoyu (soy sauce) and sautéed with onions and bell peppers—were created out of necessity by families with few resources. Spam *musubi*, a large block of sushi rice with a slice of Spam, might have been the only sushi some families could afford. The immigrant families traveled from difficult lives in Japan to difficult lives in America and would scarcely have been able to taste such iconic Japanese foods as sushi or elaborate *kaiseki* (tea ceremony foods), meals rich in diversity and expensive ingredients. An issei grandfather serving up *dango jiru* (a thin soup with flour dumplings) may recall to his grandchildren the difficulties of the past and encourage gratitude for present comfort. The foods that mark identity are in almost all instances foods of relative deprivation and shared hardship. Inexpensive "comfort foods" invoked the safety and sustenance of family. Ideas of the "authentic" had to wait until relative affluence gave a family the means to aspire to authentic Japanese food, such as rice every day. By the time a family could afford such foods, local foodstuffs and adaptations to local diet likely had altered the family's supper.

Adaptation, Acculturation, and Assimilation

Rearing the second generation in America meant adaptations spurred by children's experiences in schools. Grandmother's pickles or a basic miso soup recipe would remain in the cook's repertoire, but for the sake of children who wanted to fit in at school, lunchboxes would often contain a mix of foods. By packing an *inarizushi* (rice stuffed into a fried tofu skin) in the lunchbox or by stuffing a Thanksgiving turkey with rice, shiitake mushrooms, and burdock root, parents supported a blending of ethnicity. Wanting to be approved, children might ask for an American lunch from home that did not contain "smelly pickles" and "attempt a *hanbun, hanbun* [half and half] life" that included foods they might be able to

trade at lunchtime (Kendis, p. 23). Some children, however, found Japanese foods highly tradable.

In all generations, at least on the West Coast, Japanese Americans usually try to have rice on the table. For most older Japanese Americans, a meal is not a meal without rice. Intermarriage and geographic assimilation in the third and fourth generations may have changed tastes, but an electric rice cooker is an essential appliance in most Japanese American homes. Rice is not necessarily the short-grain rice of the homeland. It may be American fried rice or two scoops of rice on a Hawaiian mixed plate, but rice is almost always on the table.

Hawaii

Between 1885 and 1895, more than thirty thousand Japanese came to work in Hawaii. The first were *yatoi-dohi* (menial workers) who came *toshu kuuken* ("empty-handed") with a dream of striking it rich or at least of working hard and, through self-denial, sending money home to their indigent families in Japan. Japanese contract laborers first came as *gannenmono* (casual workers) and then as *kanyaku imin* (contract workers) from Kumamoto, Hiroshima, and Yamaguchi to Hawaii. By 1893, 70 percent of the 32,000 plantation workers (mostly in sugar cane) were Japanese. By 1900, the plantation populations included Portuguese (often the foremen), Chinese, Koreans, Filipinos, Okinawans, and Puerto Ricans. Okinawa was then (as it is again) part of Japan, but Okinawan Americans remained a distinct group in Hawaii. On the mainland they were assimilated into the Japanese American community and were interned during World War II. By 1924, when the Oriental Exclusion Act was passed, the total number of migrants from Japan was 220,000. Only in 1952 were Japanese residents allowed American citizenship; many by then were second- or third-generation residents. *Kenjinkai* (prefectural associations based on the prefect of origin of members) were formed as protective and mediating agencies for immigrants.

The early immigrants were men, but after 1900, picture brides (women introduced through go-betweens in Japan and known to the men in America only through letters and photographs) came to marry workers. Once they had been released from contract bonds, these families began to see themselves as rooted in Hawaii. They had plans for farming or, often, ownership of a shop or restaurant. Picture brides often arrived with no cooking skills, and their husbands, who had themselves been taught by Chinese workers, instructed the women in the use of local ingredients.

The Mixed Plate

Plantations and other communities in Hawaii were mixing bowls of races and cultures in which people shared meals across ethnic lines. Children traded lunches at school: a *musubi* for a jelly sandwich, *char siu* (Chinese roast or barbecued pork) for chicken stew, Korean kimchi for salt fish and rice, or a native Hawaiian *laulau* for toasted *mochi*. Their parents working in the fields did the same.

The first Japanese-owned restaurants in Hawaii did not prepare Japanese food. They served standard American food such as meat and potatoes and some "ethnic" foods, which meant rice, with a bottle of shoyu on the table. Two "traditions" were evolving. The first was a version of mainland food transformed by Japanese and Chinese restaurateurs. The second was a mixture of traditions of the Asian cooks that made up the classic mixed plate. Lunch wagons, food stalls, and *okazuya* (Japanese Hawaiian delicatessens selling a variety of prepared foods) serve continually changing versions of the plate. The following typical menu served through the side window of a lunch wagon reflects the meals shared on the plantations in the past:

> Rice (pan-Asian)
>
> Kimchi (chili-flavored pickle, Korean)
>
> Takuan (radish pickle, Japanese)
>
> Stir-fried vegetable with noodles (Chinese)
>
> Teriyaki chicken or beef (Japanese)
>
> Beef stew (Portuguese)
>
> Pigs feet (Portuguese)
>
> Chorizo (Portuguese)
>
> Chicken long rice (Chinese noodle dish)
>
> Pork chops (Chinese or Portuguese)
>
> Saimin (Chinese)
>
> Hamburger (mainland)
>
> Spam (mainland)
>
> Hot dogs (mainland)
>
> *Lumpia* (Philippines)

In larger communities of Japanese who settled in Hawaii and on the mainland, foods referred to regions rather than to Japan as a whole. In an interview, one woman reared in Hawaii remembered her mother saying, "You better learn to cook as we do—not like those people down the street from Kumamoto: they mix their foods all up, it's messy!" Debates over the Tokyo style of dashi [stock]—heavy on the *konbu* (kelp) and *katsuobushi* (dried, grated bonito), versus the lighter Kyoto *iriko no dashi*—delineate subcultures. Brands of shoyu have their strong adherents as well.

Sweetness characterizes many transformed foods in Hawaii, such as Portuguese breads, Chinese honey walnuts and shrimp, Filipino *lumpia*, and Vietnamese dipping sauces for spring rolls. One example of a highly sweetened dish is teriyaki chicken, an emblematic mixed-plate food lacquered with a baked-on glaze of sugar and soy. Substitution of local ingredients and use of local methods yield transformations. Brown sugar replaces mirin (sweet rice wine for cooking) in the marinade. Chinese garlic and ginger also are added.

To many, the ultimate merging of Japanese and Hawaiian foodways is Spam *musubi*. More than other transformations, this dish is supremely local. Larger than a *nigiri* or *musubi* sushi in Japan, the dish consists of a slice of Spam (grill marks prominent) placed on top of a large rectangular slab of rice and then banded with a large belt of nori (black pressed seaweed). Spam *musubi* sits wrapped in clear plastic in piles next to cash registers in groceries and convenience stores, in large stacks in supermarkets, and in gas stations across the islands. It is a snack food, a lunch food, and the object of ironic nostalgia, genuine longing (haiku odes), and disgust (at the high fat content). Spam also is cooked with miso into a sort of Spam *dengaku* (in Japan, a preparation of meat, fish paste, and tofu or eggplant typically spread with a miso paste mixture) and prepared with daikon as a kind of *oden* (winter hot pot). Spam becomes Chinese in stir-fries, in fried rice, and in *chow fun*. It is a malleable foodstuff ready to take on cultural flavors.

Mainland Laborers: *Dango Jiru* as Survival Food

In the 1880s, large numbers of Japanese workers arrived on the West Coast of the mainland United States. Chinese workers acted as mentors and, as in Hawaii, taught the Japanese men who worked alongside them in mines, railroads, and farms how to cook. The association between Chinese and Japanese workers produced the "Japanese chop suey" and "Japanese chow mein," which later became emblems of acculturation. For employers, these workers were neither Japanese nor Chinese—they were foreign migrant labor. Although the Chinese were the first Asian laborers, the model for their work was established by earlier Mexican laborers. Landowners and construction foremen treated their minority workers as one ethnic group. The Spanish-based pidgin the supervisors had created to communicate with Mexicans became even more creolized with words first from Chinese and then from Japanese, like the foods these laborers cooked and ate, and "chow" became the word for food.

The food invoked most by issei in the early years of hard labor was *dango jiru*, a thin dumpling soup. After families established themselves on farms and in Japanese American communities, the men often made *dango jiru* to teach their children about the character-building "bad old days." The dumplings floating on the greasy thin soup were made with flour and bacon, sometimes with only flour and water (Iwata, p. 124). With the end of contracts and the arrival of women, major hubs of urban Japanese American activity developed, particularly along the West Coast, including settlements in Canada.

Communities: Urban Centers in Los Angeles, San Francisco, and San Jose, California, and Seattle, Washington

In the urban communities, a common issei culture formed that was soon challenged by children and grandchildren. The foods reflected the generational divide: One meal did not suit the tastes of both grandchildren and grandparents, the latter complaining that the former would be unhealthy from eating too much meat or from straying into what they considered snacks (pizza, sandwiches, and hamburgers) substituting for meals.

Japanese American communities were more meaningful, and Japan less, with each generation. Parents tried to maintain cultural norms, and such things as the quality of soy sauce reflected a family's adherence to these norms. As one Los Angeles resident said in an interview, "We used Chinese shoyu for our restaurant but saved the Japanese shoyu for the family." Harumi Befu, in an interview, remembered that an easy way of identifying a *nikkei* (the first four generations of Japanese immigrants) house was the Kikkoman soy sauce barrels in front adorning both sides of the entrance, often serving as containers for box trees. A family meal remembered by Harry Kitano in his 1980 sociological study of *nikkei* family life epitomized the interaction of generations:

> All family members are present. The issei mother announces that she has made a very simple dinner (*kantan no mono*) but the children understand that she would say this even if she had been cooking for days beforehand. . . . The food is a mixture of

CALIFORNIA ROLL

CALIFORNIA ROLLS, consisting of avocado, imitation crabmeat, and mayonnaise encased in rice with sesame seeds on the outside, are an excellent example of Japanese American food. The rolls were invented by Japanese chefs in Los Angeles during the 1970s for Americans who were squeamish about eating raw fish. California rolls became a popular addition to Japanese restaurant menus in the United States during the 1980s, and they were eventually exported back to Japan, although many sushi purists eschew them, as they were not a traditional Japanese food.

ANDREW F. SMITH

Japanese and American dishes. The main dish is thinly sliced meat cooked with mixed vegetables, but yesterday's leftover spaghetti is also available as filler. . . . The food . . . includes large quantities of rice and Japanese pickles. . . . Father is served first, then sons in descending order of age, sisters, and finally, mother. . . . The children attempt to ignore the slurping noise father makes when he drinks his soup, but they find it intolerably embarrassing on the rare occasions when non-Issei guests are present. . . . The girls, who are counting calories, suffer in silence. . . . Discipline is carried on throughout the meal—sister spills milk and is firmly warned against sloppy, lower-class behavior. . . . Occasionally the good conduct of other Japanese children is introduced to serve as an example or model to follow. (Kitano, pp. 72–73)

At festivals and social events, as long as issei women were cooking there was rice, however localized by its accompaniments. Remembering her days as a nisei child in Seattle before World War II, Monica Sone recalled the many forms of rice that were served at the nisei picnics held for the annual *undokai* (sports day) for Japanese American children:

> I was amazed with the variety of ways in which rice appeared at the picnic. One woman served rice mixed with bits of abalone, carrots, mushroom, shreds of egg omelet and slivers of green beans. Mother had made king-sized hors d'oeuvres with her various rice balls, giving each a different flavor by combining it with vegetables, placing thin slices of vinegared smelt on top, or wrapping it in thick green kelp. Mrs. Matsui had turned rice into

a dessert by making *botamochi* (rice rolled into balls and covered with sweetened crushed red beans). (Sone, p. 77)

The Fourth of July became a big event for Japanese American families—not as an indicator of patriotic assimilation but as an occasion when everyone was free to gather together. The most important holiday meal among Japanese American families, however, was New Year's, and most Japanese American families tried to create something "really Japanese" for this day. New Year's involved hospitality for all who came to one's home, and for this occasion, a scrupulously cleaned home and food prepared ahead were required. It was not only women who cooked, but it was usually men who visited homes, because the women and children stayed at home to welcome visitors. A typical postwar family in Oregon prepared baked fish, chicken, rice curry, *osake* (the honorific form of sake), and *onishime* (a kind of stew), but eventually the work became communal. Families in the area prepared a potluck New Year's meal at a community hall and included large steaks for grilling on the spot. This type of celebration released the women for card playing, which itself became a New Year's tradition. One observer noted in an interview that anything happening on New Year's Day in America became a New Year's tradition immediately.

Internment: Family and Foodways inside the Barbed Wire

At the beginning of World War II, issei on the West Coast found their exile doubled. On February 19, 1942, President Franklin Delano Roosevelt issued executive order 9066, which eventually placed more than 120,000 West Coast Japanese (64 percent of whom were U.S. citizens) in internment camps in the western interior. Japanese residents in the territory of Hawaii were not interned because there were too many, but they did have to dissolve certain organizations. Taken from their homes, Japanese Americans had to make a home life in very restricted conditions, and often food became emblematic both of home and of deprivation. Kazuko Itoi said:

> The menfolk loaded the truck with the last boxes of household goods. . . . [Our friend] held up a gallon can of soy sauce, puzzled. "Where does this go?" Mother finally spoke up guiltily, "Er, it's going with me. I didn't think we'd have shoyu where we're going." . . . "But mama, you're not supposed to have more than one seabag and two suitcases. And of all things, you want to take with

you—shoyu!" . . . But mother stood her ground. "Nonsense. No one will ever notice this little thing. It isn't as if I were bringing liquor!" (Dublin, p. 255)

Almost all accounts by interned Japanese Americans referred to the loss of a sense of family in the communal mess halls. Randomly housed together, people of different social classes, immigrant generations, urban or rural background, and occupation tried to preserve family integrity against "others." Parents would tell children to stay close to them in the mess hall lines and at the long trestle tables, soon marking out a "home" spot at a table that they would try to claim meal after meal, protecting children from contact with unsuitable others. But soon adolescent children would bolt and leave their parents. One woman said in an interview that it was wonderful to be bold enough to say to her mother, "You didn't make this food; I don't have to sit with you to eat it!" and go off to eat with her peers, leaving her parents fearful and shamed. "Nothing was like family anymore" (Masumoto, p. 227). Several internees later commented guiltily that as adolescents they had had good times with friends and romances but had quarreled with family. Teenagers paradoxically were perhaps the only ones who found freedom in camp life.

There were stories of filial respect and solidarity in the camps as well. One told of a woman who sank into a depression in the camp that was caused by her inability to be a good food provider for her family. What she missed most was *unagi* (eel). Her son headed out into the barren desert zone just inside the barbed wire perimeter of the camp and managed to kill a rattlesnake. As a surprise, the family skinned and grilled the snake in a rough approximation of an eel preparation to lighten the sadness of the mother.

Men were the mess hall cooks and were not particularly good at it. The cooks were hired for brawn more than culinary skill, because lifting the huge kettles was seen to be more difficult for women. One woman remembered that she and other women used to laugh at the men, who could not manage to make a good pot of rice: "When it came out too soft or too hard, we women would complain to the men, [who would reply], well, if you don't like it, you do it!" (Tamura, p. 184). An ordinary worker in the camps received sixteen dollars a week, but cooks received nineteen dollars. There was competition for the job among men whose family status and self-esteem were very low because they no longer were family breadwinners. Women worked on the farms attached to some camps, such as Tule Lake, California, where they grew green onions, radishes, beans, potatoes, and later, more "Japanese" foodstuffs such as *gobo* and daikon.

The food in the camps was barely palatable. People tried to improve it with condiments, but the basics were dull at best, inedible at worst. A typical evening meal consisted of a boiled potato, and canned Vienna sausage and bread and margarine. One young girl in the camp near Poston, Arizona, wrote her former teacher a cheerful set of letters describing the conditions:

> In the dining rooms, we have to take our own spoons and forks. They provide knife, cups and plates and food. Yesterday I ate rice, weenies and cabbage with a knife. . . . If Emily Post saw me then she would throw a fit. . . . The dining rooms are one to each block. There are 16 barracks to a block. In each barrack there are four units for four families. . . . A friend who was sent to Lamar California wrote me that they had fried chicken, cookies cakes and fruit on the train. . . . I certainly envied them! . . . If I can only eat fried eggs and fried chicken once more. . . . maybe. . . . if I am a nice girl my wish will soon be granted. . . . this evenings meal was the best we ever had here: ½ sweet potato, 1 piece of steak, lettuce, rice, salad and catsup. If you are interested, I will keep the menu for one week and send it to you. (Louise Ogawa, letter to Clara Breed, August 27, 1942)

Yoshiko Sakurai, who was interned in the camp in Manzanar, California, remembered having *mochi* (pounded rice cakes) sent from the camp in Topaz, Utah, because "we didn't do *mochitsuki* (rice pounding) in Manzanar." Camps such as Tule Lake, where Japanese ingredients were grown, engaged in trade for the produce of other camps. This cultural self-reliance was officially encouraged toward the end of the war, when rations became less available to superintendents of camps. In some camps, Japanese of Okinawan descent attempted to recreate some of the dishes of Okinawa, such as pigs foot soup and other pork dishes. But few internees could have a sense of family or regional food in the camps.

The mimeographed menus from the Tule and Gila River camps in Arizona in the archives of the Japanese American National Museum in Los Angeles showed variation over time and season. Notes on the menus written by the superintendent of the camp to the cooks showed attempts to provide sufficient and suitable food—to avoid unrest and rebellion, not always successfully, because food riots and resistance occurred in several camps. Late in the war, rice was scarce, and penciled notes read, "serve rice to older people, bread to younger people" and "after October 15, the rice harvest will be in: tell people there will be rice." Rice began to dwindle—from twelve servings per week to seven in 1943. Breakfasts often were fried rice with leftovers from the previous evening's meal. Pork, cabbage, and carrots were standard, and ketchup was the main condiment and seasoning. Every menu contained a reference to *tsukemono* (pickles), along with canned string beans, rolls, and marmalade.

Attempts to create a Japanese New Year's meal in camp varied. In 1943, camp menus revealed that mulligan stew was the festive centerpiece. By 1944, a more elaborate menu was prepared. In 1945, several days of Japanese menus appeared. January 4, 1945, was the fourth day in a row that year that midday dinner was almost completely Japanese, although it was a meatless tempura vegetable meal with nori, rice, *tsukemono*, and a dish of boiled daikon with dried shrimp.

Postwar Cultures and Kitchens: Diversity and Identity

After World War II, and not only because of the experience of internment, family power structure and authority tended to decline—as it has among middle-class families in Japan. Children rarely inherit a family business, and parents instead invest more in schooling than in family training, shifting children's point of reference outside the home. The issei, themselves poorly educated for the most part, felt the gap acutely: children and grandchildren had a new language and new measures of success. The spread of Japanese families to the eastern United States produced diversity and attenuation of community identity as families moved farther from the hubs of Japanese American ethnicity on the West Coast. Japanese Americans raised on the West Coast feel that they are a completely different breed from East Coast Japanese Americans. In the West, being Japanese American is "just like breathing" while in the East, "you're always conscious that you're different!" In the East, Japanese Americans tend to be marked as Asian, and their foodways confused with Chinese, Vietnamese, and Korean cuisines.

Japanese American families in the United States for up to four generations found that assimilating was not enough and chafed under discriminatory language during and after World War II. Those who had experienced internment began to speak out, and their descendants fought for reparations. For many, eating Japanese American food became a political statement. A preference for Japanese foods among some third- and fourth-generation Japanese Americans may even perplex their assimilated parents and grandparents.

[*See also* Hawaiian Food; New Year's Celebrations; Rice; Soy Sauce; Soybeans; Spam.]

BIBLIOGRAPHY

Chan, Sucheng. *This Bittersweet Soil: The Chinese in California Agriculture 1860–1910*. Berkeley: University of California Press, 1986.

Dublin, Thomas. *Immigrant Voices*. Urbana: University of Illinois Press, 1993.

Fugita, Stephen. *Japanese American Ethnicity: The Persistence of Community*. Seattle: University of Washington Press, 1997.

Hosokawa, Bill. *Out of the Frying Pan: Reflections of a Japanese American*. Niwot: University Press of Colorado, 1998.

Iwata, Masakazu. *Planted in Good Soil: A History of the Issei in United States Agriculture*. New York: Peter Lang, 1992.

Japanese American National Museum. *From Bento to Mixed Plate: Americans of Japanese Descent in Multicultural Hawai'i*. Los Angeles: Japanese American National Museum, 1997

Kendis, Kaoru Oguri. *A Matter of Comfort: Ethnic Maintenance and Ethnic Style among Third Generation Japanese Americans*. New York: AMS, 1989.

Kimakura, Akemi. *The Kona Coffee Story: Along the Hawai'i Belt Road*. Los Angeles: Japanese American National Museum, 1995.

Kitano, Harry H. L. *Asian Americans: Emerging Minorities*. Englewood Cliffs, NJ: Prentice Hall, 1988.

Laudan, Rachel. *The Food of Paradise: Exploring Hawai'i's Culinary Heritage*. Honolulu: University of Hawai'i Press, 1996.

Masumoto, David Mas. *Country Voices: The Oral History of a Japanese American Family Farm Community*. Del Ray, CA: Inaka Countryside, 1987.

Masumoto, David Mas. *Harvest Son: Planting Roots in American Soil*. New York: Norton, 1998.

Sarasohn, Eileen Sunada. *Issei Women: Echoes from Another Frontier*. Palo Alto, CA: Pacific Books, 1998.

Sone, Monika. *Nissei Daughter*. Boston: Little, Brown, 1953.

Tamura, Linda. *The Hood River Issei: An Oral History of Japanese Settlers in Oregon's Hood River Valley*. Urbana: University of Illinois Press, 1993.

Yanagisako, Sylvia. *Transforming the Past*. Stanford, CA: Stanford University Press, 1985.

MERRY WHITE

Jefferson, Thomas

Thomas Jefferson was born on April 13, 1743, at Shadwell, Albemarle County, Virginia, and died on the Fourth of July 1826 at Monticello. He penned the Declaration of Independence, championed the cause of separation of church and state, served as ambassador to France from the United States (1785–1789), and became the third president of the United States, serving two terms (1801–1809). He was also a most illustrious epicure and may be said to have introduced elements of eighteenth-century royalist cuisine to America, this by two paths: During his years in Paris (1784–1789) he had the enslaved James Hemings trained as a chef, who in turn trained his brother Peter. Further, during his terms of presidency, Étienne LeMaire and Honoré Julien served Jefferson in their respective capacities as maître d'hôtel and chef de cuisine; Edy, described as Mr. Jefferson's "favorite cook," learned her craft in the kitchen of the President's House. Recipes attributed to LeMaire and Julien "turn up" in the culinary manuscripts kept in later years by Jefferson's granddaughters and great-granddaughter. Those attributed to LeMaire, in particular, confirm Jefferson's detailed descriptions of many dishes, these in his own hand. What is remarkable is the fact that these recipes came into the hands of Mrs. Mary Randolph, a cousin of Jefferson and a sister of Thomas Mann Randolph, the husband of Jefferson's daughter Martha Jefferson Randolph. They show up in her work *The Virginia House-wife* (1824), those attributed to LeMaire in particular—some with long, identical telltale phrases. Thus Mrs. Randolph may fairly be described as the amanuensis of the French cuisine at the President's House during Jefferson's terms of office. The imprint of royalist French cuisine is especially strong in Virginia because of the vast and continuing influence of *The Virginia House-wife*.

Jefferson's passion for French cuisine was such that Patrick Henry accused him of forsaking his "native vittles," but in a note to his daughter Martha Jefferson Randolph he wrote: "Pray enable yourself to direct us here how to make muffins in Peter's method. My cook here cannot succeed at all in them, and they are a great luxury to me." This in 1802, when he was ensconced at the President's House with a French chef in the kitchen.

But Jefferson's real passion was gardening. His copious and meticulously kept notes in his *Garden Book* and *Farm Book* serve as the bible of all those who would know about gardening and food in eighteenth- and early nineteenth-century Virginia. He cadged seeds and cuttings from acquaintances far and wide, including France, Italy, and England, cultivating rare varieties like radicchio di Pistoia, recently re-introduced to the United States. He devoted a great deal of effort to acclimating the olive and benne (*Sesamum orientale*) to

Virginia, but was unsuccessful. All this was in addition to his passion for wines. Further, LeMaire's records, kept in his capacity as maître d'hôtel during Jefferson's terms at the President's House in Washington, take careful note of all purchases at the public market in Georgetown, day after day, purchase by purchase, complete with prices. These records are invaluable in showing the extraordinary breadth of choice of vegetables and other foodstuffs that were available at a public market in the first decade of the nineteenth century.

[*See also* French Influences on American Food; Heirloom Vegetables; Randolph, Mary; Southern Regional Cookery; White House; Wine, *subentry on* Eastern U.S. Wines.]

BIBLIOGRAPHY

Manuscripts in Jefferson's hand, or in the hand of various members of his immediate entourage, or in response to his letters. In addition to those listed below, multiple sources and locations exist, chief among them the Library of Congress and the Coolidge Collection in the keeping of the Massachusetts Historical Society.

Betts, Edwin Morris, ed. *Thomas Jefferson's Farm Book.* Charlottesville: University of Virginia Press, 1987.

Betts, Edwin Morris, ed. *Thomas Jefferson's Garden Book 1766–1824: With Relevant Extracts from His Other Writings.* Philadelphia: American Philosophical Society, 1944.

Betts, Edwin Morris, and James Bear Jr., eds. *The Family Letters of Thomas Jefferson.* Columbia: University of Missouri Press, 1966.

Burke, Martha Jefferson Trist. *Receipts and Gardening Notes.* Manuscript, in various hands, ca. 1857 to ca. 1889. Alderman Library, University of Virginia.

LeMaire, Étienne. *Market Accounts of Étienne LeMaire (1801–1809).* Manuscript (HM1253). Henry Huntingdon Library, Huntingdon, CA.

Malone, Dumas. *Thomas Jefferson: A Brief Biography.* Preface by Merrill D. Peterson. Monticello, VA: Thomas Jefferson Memorial Foundation, 1986.

Randolph, Mrs. Mary. *The Virginia House-wife. Method Is the Soul of Management.* Washington, DC: Davis and Force, 1824. Also in facsimile with additional material from the editions of 1825 and 1828 and historical notes by Karen Hess. Columbia: University of South Carolina Press, 1984.

Randolph, Thomas Jefferson, ed. *Memoir, Correspondence, and Miscellanies, from the Papers of Thomas Jefferson.* 4 vols. Charlottesville, VA: Carr, 1829.

Receipts in the Hand of Septimia Anne Randolph Meikleham. Manuscript, ca. 1849 to ca. 1864. Monticello Memorial Foundation, Monticello, VA.

Receipts in the Hand of Virginia Jefferson Randolph Trist. Manuscript, ca. 1850s and 1860s. Alderman Library, University of Virginia, Charlottesville, VA.

KAREN HESS

Jell-O

Jell-O is the brand name of a dessert mix of colored and flavored sugar and crystallized gelatin, made by Kraft Foods Inc. When mixed with water and chilled, it becomes a food that wobbles like rubber, looks like translucent plastic, and tastes like fruit. Although Jell-O sales peaked in the 1960s and some gourmets consider it déclassé, most hospitals, diners, school cafeterias, church potlucks, and holiday tables in America offer Jell-O, either alone or in one of thousands of recipe variations featuring fruit, nuts, miniature marshmallows, and any number of real and imitation dairy products.

Jell-O was invented in 1897 in LeRoy, New York, by a carpenter named Pearle Wait. Wait also made and sold patent medicines, so he knew how to add colorings and flavorings to prettify products of unsavory origins—such as the boiled calves feet used to make gelatin. He was also undoubtedly familiar with the powdered, unflavored gelatin products that had entered the market in the mid-1800s as recipe ingredients. Wait was the first to add color and flavor to the crystallized gelatin to create a stand-alone dessert mix.

Wait's wife, May, named the product Jell-O by attaching to the word "jell" the "O," a popular ending for product names at the time. In fact, another patent medicine maker in LeRoy, Orator Woodward, had become wealthy selling a cereal-based coffee substitute called Grain-O.

Wait peddled raspberry-, lemon-, orange-, and strawberry-flavored Jell-O door to door not very successfully for less than two years and then sold the business to Woodward, his patent medicine competitor, for $450. At first Woodward had little more success than Wait. Woodward was so discouraged that one day in 1900 he offered to sell the whole Jell-O business to his plant superintendent for $35. The employee refused, and that turned out be a lucky break for Woodward, because he soon identified and solved the problem that was hindering sales.

Recipe for Success

At the time, virtually all dishes were prepared from basic ingredients; homemakers did not know what to do with a food that was almost ready to serve and needed no recipes. So Woodward gave them recipes. In 1902 Woodward's Genesee Pure Food Company produced the first of a subsequent flood of Jell-O recipe booklets. Woodward's nattily dressed salesmen, driving spanking new rigs drawn by dappled gray horses, delivered the new recipe booklets to every house in a town. Then, and only then, would the salesmen approach the local grocer to tell him about a new dessert mix that would soon be in great demand.

These direct sales were then supplemented by print ads featuring a little girl, whose image conveyed how much kids loved Jell-O and how easy it was to make. The Jell-O Girl appeared in ads and recipe books for almost twenty-eight years—at first in photographs and later, after the model grew up, in illustrations by Rose O'Neill, the artist who designed the Kewpie doll. Norman Rockwell and Maxfield Parrish also created Jell-O ads at the height of their artistic careers. Magazine illustrators of that era were well-paid celebrities who moved freely between commercial and noncommercial work. The Jell-O domestic scenes and still lifes they painted in the 1920s rival fine art in beauty and technique and were often displayed in magazines as museum oil paintings with the word Jell-O appearing discreetly in the plaque on the frame.

By 1923 Jell-O sales so dominated the Genesee Pure Food Company that the firm's name was changed to the Jell-O Company. In 1925 the company was sold to a former rival in the coffee substitute business, Postum, for an exchange of stock valued at $84 million. Postum reduced Jell-O's price and scored record sales, but not record profits. Jell-O was then in direct competition with cheaper brands, including Royal, which by 1934 was sponsoring a popular radio show featuring Fanny Brice, the singer. Jell-O fought back with Jack Benny, whose Sunday night radio comedy show became an immediate hit. Within a few months, Jell-O sales soared to the highest level since the company, which by then was marketing more than 150 different products under the name General Foods, bought the business.

Jell-O Jingles and Jokes

For the next eight years as many as 40 million Americans tuned in to hear Benny's "Jell-O again" greeting, the five-note ascending "J-E-L-L (pause) O" jingle, and jokes about announcer Don Wilson's "wiggly waist" and "six-delicious-flavors sway." Show skits also frequently mentioned Jell-O. Benny's January 1935 spoof of the French classic *The Count of Monte Cristo* was called "The Count of Monte Jell-O," for instance. General Foods took Benny off the Jell-O campaign in 1942 because wartime sugar shortages restricted Jell-O pro-

duction. Nevertheless, Jack Benny and Jell-O were inextricably linked to each other in the minds of many Americans for decades.

Jell-O sales at the time also benefited from the newly popular electric refrigerators with their more consistent cooling abilities, and from Jell-O's growing popularity as a salad ingredient. During the Depression, a Jell-O salad was considered an elegant and inexpensive way to stretch leftover foods.

When World War II and its sugar shortages ended, American housewives resumed their Jell-O cooking with renewed enthusiasm and unprecedented creativity. In fact, there was hardly anything a 1950s hostess could do that would impress her guests more than to serve a beautiful molded Jell-O dish. Popular molds included Under-the-Sea Salad (layers of lime Jell-O, pears, and cream cheese), Sunshine Salad (lemon Jell-O, crushed pineapple, and shredded carrots), Cranberry Waldorf Salad (cherry Jell-O, jellied cranberry sauce, apples, celery, and nuts) and Crown Jewel Dessert (colored cubes of Jell-O set against a backdrop of real or artificial whipped cream to resemble stained glass).

In 1963 the best of the 1950s Jell-O recipes were collected in *The Joys of Jell-O*, a 250-recipe cookbook that came out again and again, in eleven editions. The 1960s also produced the famous slogan "There's always room for Jell-O." It was featured in a series of ads that showed families eating dinner, and it positioned Jell-O as the perfect light ending to the huge meals common in those prosperous times.

Those ads helped propel Jell-O to its late 1960s sales peak of four boxes per person per year. Jell-O sales declined after that, mainly owing to competition from more convenient snack cakes and frozen desserts and because of the huge increase in the number of women working outside the home who had less time to make elaborate molded gelatin desserts. The gourmet and natural-foods movements also made mainstream America wary of processed convenience foods like Jell-O. In addition, Jell-O's image suffered from twin bar fads of the 1980s: alcohol-spiked portions of Jell-O; and Jell-O wrestling, scantily clad women tussling on a Jell-O "mat."

Bouncing Back as a Snack

In 1990 Jell-O did come up with a big sales success, a recipe for a gummy, candy-like snack called Jigglers. The recipe requires four times the usual amount of Jell-O, and the result can be cut into shapes like cookies, thus making it a perfect means of cultivating young Jell-O fans. Jell-O sales increased by 7 percent the first year of the Jigglers promotion; that banner year also saw the first Jell-O gelatin ads by Bill Cosby, the comedian and longtime Jell-O Pudding spokesman. Even more important at a time when dessert eating was in decline and on-the-go snacking was on the rise, Jigglers could be eaten by hand.

The Smithsonian Institution honored Jell-O with a day-long mock academic conference held on April Fool's Day 1991. In 1997 the historical society in Jell-O's birthplace of LeRoy, New York, opened the world's only museum dedicated to Jell-O facts and artifacts. As the twenty-first century began, Jell-O sales were highest in the Midwest and Utah. Food experts attribute Jell-O's popularity in Utah to the state's extensive Mormon population with large families, low alcohol consumption, and compensating high sugar intake. Whatever the reason, a pin depicting a bowl of lime gelatin proved to be one of the most popular souvenirs of the 2002 Salt Lake City Winter Olympics.

New flavors and mold giveaways remained at the core of official company promotional efforts. In 2002 Jell-O expanded its line of already-made Jell-O gelatin snacks in supermarket refrigerator cases to include tubes of gelatin that can be eaten without a spoon. In fact, Jell-O marketing efforts are clearly aimed at the many Americans who have more room for Jell-O in their hearts and stomachs than time in their schedules to make it.

[See also Advertising Cookbooklets and Recipes; Coffee Substitutes; Desserts; General Foods; Jell-O Molds; Kraft Foods; Radio and Television.]

BIBLIOGRAPHY

The Jell-O Gallery. http://www.jellomuseum.com. Website of the Jell-O museum in LeRoy, N.Y., features early history, trivia, and historic recipes.

Jell-O. http://www.jello.com. Official Kraft Foods website includes a decade-by-decade history, historic ads, and a searchable recipe database.

Kraft Inc. *The Magic of Jell-O: 100 New and Favorite Recipes Celebrating 100 Years of Fun with Jell-O.* New York: Sterling Publishing Company, 2001. Company-tested Jell-O recipes.

Shapiro, Laura. *Perfection Salad: Women and Cooking at the Turn of the Century.* New York: Holt, 2001. Chapter four of this social history explains why domestic scientists like Fanny Farmer loved gelatin.

Wyman, Carolyn. *Jell-O: A Biography: The History and Mystery of America's Most Famous Dessert.* San Diego: Harcourt, 2001. An unofficial, illustrated, comprehensive look at the dessert, including advertising campaigns, festivals, media references, and information on how it is made.

CAROLYN WYMAN

Jell-O Molds

Aluminum molds produced and stamped by the Jell-O Company have become kitchen collectibles, more often hung on walls than used for the salads they were designed to shape. The prototype dates back to fourteenth-century England, where noble households fashioned flavored "jellies" in copper molds. In early America, copper molds lined with tin to prevent food poisoning were commissioned from the local tinsmith. In 1902 the Jell-O Company distributed instructions for having "your tinner" fashion a "mould."

At about that time, however, the need for mass production of Jell-O molds became apparent. The domestic science cooking movement decreed that salads—so naturally unruly—should become neat and contained, and the best way to accomplish that was to encase the salad in gelatin and the gelatin in a mold. Although it is not known when or where the first Jell-O mold of stamped aluminum was made, the Jell-O Company began offering free molds to consumers around 1908. Aluminum had the advantage over copper because it was lighter, cheaper, and did not require periodic retinning. Between 1925 and 1930, as the molds gained in popularity, Jell-O sold about a million at a nominal price.

The next big boost came in the 1930s when gelled or "congealed" salads—savory and sweet—achieved staple status. About one-third of all cookbook recipes of the time were gelatin based. Studded with bits of vegetables, canned fruit, marshmallows, nuts, cottage or cream cheese, and other foods, the molded concoctions were promoted during the Great Depression as an elegant way to package leftovers. This trend continued into the 1940s, and the *Joy of Cooking*, published in 1946, contained sixty-nine recipes requiring molds.

During the 1950s the most impressive food a hostess could serve was a towering, molded Jell-O salad, but by the 1960s culinary fashions had changed. Women hung up their molds, perhaps because the pouring of colored layers of Jell-O and the placing of bits of food in a pre-ordained design were tedious chores, and the unmolding precarious and challenging. Sales of Jell-O fell off during the 1970s and 1980s. In 1995, however, the company introduced a successful new mold, the plastic Jiggler Egg form, to make snacks for children. Collectors covet such classic molds as Jell-O's Bridge Set, but most of the company's aluminum forms are worth not much more than five dollars.

[See also Desserts; Jell-O; Salads and Salad Dressings.]

BIBLIOGRAPHY

Editor, Better Homes and Gardens. *The Joy of Jell-O Molds: 50 Festive Recipes from the Classic to the Contemporary.* Des Moines, IA: Meredith, 1998.

Franklin, Linda Campbell. *300 Years of Kitchen Collectibles.* Florence, AL: Books Americana, 1997.

Wyman, Carolyn. *Jell-O: A Biography, The History and Mystery of America's Most Famous Dessert.* San Diego, New York, London: Harcourt, 2001.

LINDA MURRAY BERZOK

Jelly Rolls

Jelly rolls, also known as Swiss rolls or jelly cakes, consist of a sponge cake coiled around a jelly filling. They are usually sliced crosswise to reveal an attractive spiral pattern and are occasionally used as the decorative exterior for a charlotte (a molded cake filled with custard or fruit or Bavarian cream). The spiral cross-sections of jelly roll line a handsome exterior for this gelatin-set mousse. The earliest reference to them has been found in several cookbooks published immediately after the American Civil War, but they are thought to have arisen at the same time the genoise sponge cake appeared, in mid-nineteenth-century France. Common fillings include currant jelly, pastry cream, apricot preserve, and raspberry jam. Baking pans designed for cooking the thin sheets of batter used for jelly rolls have flat bottoms and one-inch-high straight sides. Called "jelly-roll pans" by consumers, they have become standard baking equipment in commercial kitchens, where they are referred to simply as "sheet pans." "Jelly roll" and "honey pot" were popular slang euphemisms for female genitalia at the turn of the twentieth century, and it is likely that the famous jazz pianist Jelly Roll Morton acquired his nickname from playing in bordellos.

[*See also* Cakes; Creams, Dessert; Desserts; Preserves.]

JAY WEINSTEIN

Jennie June

Jane Cunningham Croly (1829–1901), the journalist and cookbook author known as "Jennie June," was born in Market Harborough, Leicestershire, England. Her family emigrated to the United States in 1841, settling first in Poughkeepsie and afterward in or near Wappingers Falls, New York. She married David G. Croly, a reporter for the *New York Herald*, in 1856.

Under her nom de plume of Jennie, Mrs. Croly was a pioneer woman in the workplace. She was a prolific writer, the first woman journalist to have her articles syndicated, and also invented the syndication of readers' responses. Despite having to run a lavish household and bring up five children, her output was enormous, and she contributed to almost every important publication of the time. She edited *Demorest's* magazine for twenty-seven years and was both editor and owner of *Godey's Magazine* and *The Home-Maker. The Cycle* was her own creation and property. Many of her writings were collected into book form.

Jennie June wrote almost exclusively on homemaking subjects, which found a large audience among the women of the emerging American middle class of the post–Civil War era. Her manual of needlework and stitchery was published in 1885. As a founding member of Sorosis, one of the first organizations in the American Women's Club, Jennie June wrote a history of the movement in 1898.

Jennie June's main contribution to American cooking was the publication in 1866 of *Jennie June's American Cookery Book*, described on the title page as "containing upwards of twelve hundred choice and carefully tested receipts; embracing all the popular dishes, and the best results of modern science, reduced to a simple and practical form." The book is modeled on contemporary British cookbooks (though it is fairly short by their standards, consisting of only 399 pages), including hints on general household management, with separate chapters "for invalids, for infants [and] one on Jewish cookery." There are also separate chapters of contributions from Sorosis and from the Oneida Community, a religious community in Oneida, New York, that practiced a form of free love. Another section of the book is entitled "Favorite Dishes of Distinguished Persons," from which we learn that "President Grant is very fond of scrambled eggs and fried ham" and that Queen Victoria (referred to simply as "Victoria") "loves boiled mutton and caper sauce and is also very partial to a cup of tea." In the preface to a new edition in 1878, Jennie June wrote: "All that I have to beg of young housekeepers is that they will try [the recipes] with their own hands, and not turn them over to the tender mercies of Bridget. It is not the personal extravagance of American women that is sapping the foundation of American homes. It is the disintegrating quality of our domestic service."

[*See also* Cookbooks and Manuscripts, *subentries* From the Civil War to World War I *and* Community Cookbooks; Periodicals.]

BIBLIOGRAPHY

Woman's Press Club of New York City. *Memories of Jane Cunningham Croly, "Jennie June."* New York: G. P. Putnam's Sons, 1904.

JOSEPHINE BACON

Jewish American Food

With nearly six million Jews, the United States is the major cultural center of the Jewish world outside of Israel—known collectively as the Diaspora. In many ways, it is also the culinary center of the Diaspora. America not only has welcomed Jewish immigrants from all over the world but has also incorporated their food into the American diet. Because this country's culinary traditions are always evolving, Americans are equally at home with Italian pizza, Chinese wontons, and Jewish bagels.

Throughout their wandering history, Jews have adapted their lifestyles to the local cultures within which they have lived—and food has been no exception. But because they have lived in so many places, there is no single Jewish food other than matzo, *haroseth* (the Passover spread), and *cholent* and *chamin* (the Sabbath stews that surface in different forms in every land where Jews have lived). Instead, Jews have relied on local ingredients, developing regional dishes in accordance with their dietary laws.

Immigrants to America adapted most of their foods to the culture of their new home, just as they themselves adapted. In doing so, they enriched their adopted homeland. Sweet challah, overstuffed deli sandwiches of pastrami and corned beef, bagels filled with cream cheese and lox, New York cheesecakes, and even "bagel" sushi—rice enclosing wasabi, lox, and cream cheese—are today as American as apple pie.

But not all foods that Americans consider Jewish are Jewish in origin. More than two-thirds of the six million Jews in America today can trace their roots to greater Poland, which includes parts of Austria and Hungary (Galicia), the Ukraine, Lithuania, and Russia. Jewish food, as we know it, came into its own with the arrival of these immigrants. Jews brought with them many dishes from these countries, like herring in sour cream, rye bread, gefilte fish, borscht, and bagels. Despite being identified

here as Jewish, none of these dishes would be labeled "Jewish food" in European countries; everybody ate them. Because Jewish immigrants introduced them to America, though, in America they have been labeled Jewish.

Like other immigrants to this country, Jews went through several stages in the preservation and adaptation of their culinary culture. The first generation brought the traditions of the past with them. Depending upon how they felt about their Jewishness and the degree to which they wanted to assimilate, they cherished, rejected, or modified their cuisine from home, along with their dietary laws.

For second- and third-generation American Jews, what was once daily subsistence became special-occasion foods. For example, in Europe, knishes, like kugels and latkes, provided the poor with a way to vary the daily monotony of potatoes; and here, during the sweatshop era on New York's Lower East Side at the turn of the twentieth century, knishes, a portable food like pasties—lunchtime potato- and meat-filled small pies for Welsh ironworkers—were eaten for lunch every day. Thereafter, these foods disappeared as daily fare—but now they are in vogue again, reappearing in miniature form as hors d'oeuvres at weddings and other ceremonial events, and as fast food snacks.

As "scientific" vegetable shortenings and shortcut foods like phyllo dough have became available to the Jewish housewife, and as "healthy" has replaced "hefty" as a cultural ideal, some traditions, like rendering schmaltz (chicken fat) or stretching strudel dough by hand, have become obsolete even within the Orthodox Jewish community.

Often the members of later generations want to return to their roots, questioning elderly relatives or tracking down cookbooks in search of original recipes. In the 1990s, for example, *ba'alei teshuvah*, or returnees to the faith, began to transform Jewish food. These Jews, often from nonobservant homes, study Orthodox Judaism and are creating a new kosher cuisine mindful of new health guidelines.

Early Sephardic Cuisine in America

The story of Jewish food in America begins in 1654, when twenty-three Sephardic Jews arrived in New Amsterdam. After being expelled from the Iberian Peninsula in 1492, Sephardic Jews fled to Greece, the Middle East, England, the Netherlands, and the Americas. This small New Amsterdam band first sought haven from the Spanish Inquisition in Recife, Brazil.

Kosher Butcher Shop. East Side Glatt Kosher Butcher on Grand Street in New York City. *Photograph by Joe Zarba*

While there, they discovered and adopted exotic and unfamiliar foods, such as sugar, molasses, rum, vanilla, turkeys, chocolate, peppers, corn, and tomatoes along with kidney and string beans.

Sephardic cuisine set the tone for Jewish food in America during colonial America's early history. Because many of the colonial Jews' foods were holiday foods, bound for centuries to traditional observances, they were the last to change during cultural and culinary assimilation in America. Allspice or hot pepper might have been added to a fish or meat stew by Jews in Brazil or the West Indies, but the basic recipes of stew and fish fried in olive oil, beef and bean stews, almond puddings, and egg custards came directly from the Iberian Peninsula and represent the most authentic Sephardic foods we know in the United States. *Jewish Cookery Book* by Esther Levy, the first kosher cookbook in America, which appeared in Philadelphia in 1871, included many of these old recipes.

At the same time that Sephardic Jews were setting the tone on the East Coast, the descendants of crypto, or hidden, Jews who had fled the Inquisition were settling in the Southwest. They had come from Mexico even before the New Amsterdam group, in the sixteenth century. Anthropologists are now discovering that crypto Jews

retained many of their three-centuries-old cultural and culinary traditions, which they continued to practice in secret. Many of their present-day descendants have no idea of the origin of their customs.

Once in America, most Jewish colonists observed the laws of kashruth in their homes. Some of their dishes, like cod or haddock fried "Jewish style" (that is, in olive oil, not lard), soon became popular among non-Jews.

Before Jewish communities developed, most Jewish men learned how to slaughter meat according to the dietary laws; if they did not learn, they went without meat. As opportunities arose, some of these kosher butchers, who lived on the Atlantic seacoast, expanded their businesses and became merchants.

German-Jewish Immigrants and Their Foods

Between 1830 and 1880 many Jews from Germanic lands arrived in the United States. Whereas early American Jewry settled along the Atlantic Coast, after 1830 the second wave of immigrants forged westward, crossing the mountains to the Ohio and Mississippi Rivers. Many, like Levi Strauss, strapped packs on their backs and traveled all the way across the continent to San Francisco, peddling as they went. Jews have always been peddlers, selling wares that could easily be packed up when they were expelled from a country. In America they were a familiar sight in the countryside, until mail-order catalogues, like the Jewish-owned Sears, Roebuck, put them out of business.

Food, especially kosher food, posed a problem for Jewish peddlers when they were traveling. They would often roast herrings, wrapped in newspaper, over an open fire or subsist on preserved or hard-boiled eggs and kosher sausage, as long as those supplies lasted. On Saturdays the men created Sabbath communities in little towns where they met to pray. Often, once they made a little money peddling, they would buy a wagon and eventually settle in these communities, sending for their families in Europe or back in New York.

Of the 10 million immigrants to this country between the years 1830 and 1880, 3 million were German Christians and 200,000 were Jews from German-speaking lands. The most important German-Jewish center of commerce, culture, and cuisine was Cincinnati, Ohio. By 1872 Cincinnati had nine *shochtim* (kosher slaughterers), five Jewish restaurants, sixteen abattoirs for kosher meat, and three matzo bakeries.

Until World War I, German immigrants—Jews and non-Jews alike—thought of their native culture as superior to that of America. By the end of the nineteenth century these Jews had become American-German-Jewish, and this triethnicity, as it were, played itself out in both culture and cuisine. In Jewish homes, foods like chicken noodle or vegetable soup, roast chicken, and goose graced tables for Friday-night dinner or Sunday lunch when the entire family gathered together.

Because baking had reached a more sophisticated level in Germany than it had in the United States at that time, these immigrants brought with them marvelous kuchen, breads, and tortes. In addition, as entire Jewish communities from Bavaria emigrated, they carried their own German regional recipes such as *Lebkuchen* or *Dampfnudeln*, a wonderful brioche-like cake soaked in caramel and served with a vanilla sauce. Surely it was no coincidence that Cincinnati became the home of Fleischmann's yeast and Crisco, a vegetable-based shortening for which, according to Procter and Gamble's advertisements, the Jews had waited four thousand years.

Changes in American Jewry and Its Cuisine

In nineteenth-century America, traditional Jews and those wanting a more "enlightened," more American, Judaism were having a hard time. Since laws prohibited shops from being open on Sunday, Jews usually had to

מלאכת הבישול בדרך נכון וכפי מצות דתנו הקדושה

A COOKERY BOOK PROPERLY EXPLAINED, AND IN ACCORDANCE WITH THE RULES OF THE JEWISH RELIGION.

JEWISH COOKERY BOOK,

ON

PRINCIPLES OF ECONOMY,

ADAPTED FOR

JEWISH HOUSEKEEPERS,

WITH THE ADDITION OF MANY USEFUL MEDICINAL RECIPES,

AND

Other Valuable Information,

RELATIVE TO HOUSEKEEPING AND DOMESTIC MANAGEMENT.

BY MRS. ESTHER LEVY,
(*Neé Esther Jacobs.*)

PHILADELPHIA:
W. S. TURNER, No. 808 CHESTNUT STREET.
1871.

Jewish Cookbook. Title page of Esther Levy's *Jewish Cookery Book*, 1871.

keep their shops open on Saturday (the Jewish Sabbath) and often either postponed their Sabbath meals to Sunday dinner or had a Friday evening get-together of some kind.

Isaac Mayer Wise, the leader of the Reform movement in Judaism, called for many changes in the old order as defined by Orthodoxy: for women to come down from the balcony, for skullcaps to come off in the synagogue, and for the dietary laws to be recognized as an archaic relic of the past. He started eating oysters.

Wise's ambivalence toward the laws of kashruth, and the growing gap within the Jewish community with regard to the dietary laws, contributed to an event that has become known as the "Treif Banquet"; it led to the final schism between traditional and Reform American Jews. On July 12, 1883, the graduation of the first class of

American rabbis was celebrated with an eight-course dinner for two hundred people at the Highland House in Cincinnati. Terrific excitement ensued when two rabbis rushed from the room: littleneck clams had been placed before them as the first course.

While Reform Jews were tasting American produce, their family recipes were becoming regionalized. In Mississippi and Alabama, pecans replaced almonds in tortes and cookies; in Ohio, molasses or brown sugar replaced honey in *schnecken*; in Washington State, salmon appeared instead of carp in gefilte fish on Sabbath tables; and in Louisiana, hot pepper and scallions were used instead of mild ginger in matzo balls. Crossover foods were already beginning to affect the non-Jewish public as well, appearing with greater frequency in mainstream American nineteenth-century cookbooks. The introduction to *Smiley's Cook Book and Universal Household Guide*, published in 1901, notes: "Jewish cookery is becoming much like that of their Christian neighbors, as, except among the more denominationally strict, the old restrictions are melting away."

Eastern European Jewish American Cuisine

Between 1881 and 1921, approximately 2.5 million Jewish immigrants from Eastern Europe entered the United States. Faced with pogroms, forced military conscription, lack of civil rights, periodic expulsion from towns and villages, and displacements due to the industrialization of the 1870s, millions of Jews sought a freer life in America. Not surprisingly, even on the journey over, food became a major issue for Orthodox immigrants. Not all passengers, of course, observed the dietary laws; many were radicals who rebelled against Orthodoxy.

Often entire Jewish communities were transplanted, including the rabbi and the *shochet*, or ritual slaughterer. They crowded into New York's Lower East Side, Chicago's West Side, Boston's North End, and South Philadelphia; at one time there were almost four thousand kosher butcher shops in New York City alone. The immigrants were successful at finding work and housing and became a part of a network of familiar social and cultural institutions, such as *landsmanshaftn*, the Jewish mutual aid societies that were formed by immigrants originating from the same village, town, or city in Eastern Europe.

As the immigrants adjusted to new food habits, they quickly forgot some of the foods of their poverty, like *krupnick*, a cereal soup made from oatmeal, sometimes barley, potatoes, and fat. If a family could afford it, milk would be added to the *krupnick*; if not, it was called "*soupr mit nisht*," or supper with nothing. (Today, *krupnick* is considered a health food.) Bagels, knishes, or herring wrapped in newspaper were taken to the sweatshop, providing a poor substitute for the large midday lunch the immigrants were used to having in Europe, where the midday meal was the biggest of the day.

To combat all these changes—as well as the rise of Reform Judaism in America, which for the most part abandoned kashruth—Orthodox Jews, sometimes with some difficulty, clung to their old traditions, including kashruth. Because most eastern European immigrants were so concerned with the kashruth of their food, the United States gave them great opportunities in the food business. The butchers, bakers, and pushcart peddlers of herring and pickles soon became small-scale independent grocers, wine merchants, and wholesale meat, produce, and fruit providers.

Not only did these immigrants go into the business of food, but they also adapted their eastern European food customs to the new environment. Sunday, for example, as in effect a second day of rest, provided them with new gastronomic opportunities—like a dairy brunch, an embellishment of their simple dairy dinners in Europe.

Innovations in Jewish American Food Inspired by the Second Wave of Immigrants

Cooking, as well as women's roles in the kitchen, changed dramatically from the 1880s to the 1930s. Not only did women gain the right to vote, but the first national Jewish women's organization, the National Council of Jewish Women, was founded in the fall of 1893 as an outgrowth of a national Jewish women's congress. By 1900 its 7,080 members in fifty-five cities helped support the rights of women; mission and industrial schools for poor Jewish children; and free baths in Kansas City and Denver—along with cooking classes in the settlement houses. Council cookbooks, like *The Settlement Cook Book*, were put out nationwide, with proceeds helping to support their projects. These books often had a German slant and included many goose recipes along with other American dishes such as chicken chow mein, often made from leftover chicken soup, and Saratoga chips, a turn-of-the-century potato chip.

Other organizations followed suit. In September 1905, for example, the Montefiore Lodge Ladies Hebrew Benevolent Association of Providence, Rhode Island, published the following in its newsletter: "It was voted that 'this lodge publish and sell a cookbook of favorite recipes.' Two separate committees were appointed, one for the cooking recipes and the other to solicit advertising."

While the women's organizations were working to help the less fortunate, another revolution was taking place— that of food technology and scientific discovery. Slowly the kitchen was transformed, liberating women from time-consuming chores. Not only was Heinz producing its bottled ketchups and fledgling companies making kosher canned foods, but companies were manufacturing a white vegetable substance resembling lard—the shortening that would change forever the way Jewish people cooked. The inventions of cream cheese, rennet, junket, gelatin, nondairy creamer, pasteurized milk, phyllo dough, and frozen foods would all affect the amount of time spent in the kitchen and, as a result, the way Jews cooked in America.

With the growth of food companies, delicatessens, school-lunch programs, and restaurants, both American food and American-Jewish food became more processed and more innovative. In 1925 the average American housewife made all her food at home; by 1965, 75 to 90 percent of the food she used had undergone some sort of factory processing. Today even observant Jewish women can buy almost everything prepared.

As Jews became more Americanized, notions of "Jewish food" changed with the availability of regional ingredients; taste buds adjusted to local spices as well as to new dietary guidelines. While Jews in Burlington, Vermont, ate potato latkes with maple syrup, Californians preferred theirs with local goat cheese. Gefilte fish was made with whitefish in the Midwest, salmon in the Far West, and haddock in Maine. The matzo balls and gefilte fish—even the Passover desserts—that American Jews eat today are certainly very different from those eaten in Europe or in this country a century ago.

Kashruth and American Jews As the latest wave of eastern European Jews became more Americanized, they began trying new dishes, like macaroni and cheese and canned tuna-fish casseroles. Jewish cookbooks included recipes for Creole dishes, for chicken fricassee using canned tomatoes, and for shortcut kuchen using baking powder. Many of these Jews cared little about the import of scientific discoveries on kashruth—but others cared deeply. At the turn of the century, the Union of Orthodox Jewish Congregations, the umbrella organization for Orthodox Jews, was established as a means of bringing cohesion to the fragmented immigrant Jewish populations. In 1923, the year it created its women's

Kosher Beef. Butcher at work in East Side Glatt Kosher Butcher on Grand Street in New York City. *Photograph by Joe Zarba*

branch and three years after women won the right to vote, the Union's official kashruth supervision and certification program was introduced.

At about that time, a New York advertising genius named Joseph Jacobs encouraged big companies to advertise their mainstream packaged products in the Yiddish press. Jacobs's mission was to change the way Americans thought about Jewish dietary practices. The chains and the big food companies did not know how to attract the Yiddish-speaking population, since they employed no Jews.

One day he approached Joel Cheek, the founder of Maxwell House Coffee. Mr. Cheek, who had started selling his coffee from saddlebags off a horse in Tennessee, was searching for ways to expand his eastern market; Mr. Jacobs suggested to him the Jewish Passover clientele. For some reason, eastern European Jews thought that coffee beans, like other beans, were forbidden during Passover.

Mr. Jacobs consulted a rabbi, who told him that coffee beans were technically berries and, therefore, certified kosher for Passover. After the rabbi certified Maxwell House kosher for Passover, Jacobs hired men to go into independent stores with the coffee. The merchants were delighted to sell the coffee, which became such a success that in 1934 the company started producing a Maxwell House Haggadah (the book Jews read from during the Passover Seder, which tells the story of the Exodus from Egypt), another Jacobs idea.

Jewish Food Goes Mainstream — American Food Goes Jewish When canned products like the Heinz Company's baked beans and pork came on the market, an inventive advertising man named Joshua C. Epstein, an Orthodox Jew, thought it would be useful and lucrative if Heinz made kosher vegetarian baked beans. Company officials liked Epstein's suggestion, but they balked at the idea of writing the word "kosher" in Hebrew or English on the package. "Heinz wanted something identifiable, but not too Jewish: they didn't want to antagonize the non-Jewish population," recalled Abraham Butler, the son of the late Frank Butler, Heinz's first *mashgiach* (kashruth supervisor). Thus was born the Orthodox Union "Circle U" symbol, today the best recognized of the some 120 symbols for kosher certification.

Jews went into the packaged food industry, too; in this land of opportunity, some food merchants struck it rich. One Chicago baker named Charley Lubin made a luscious cheesecake; it was the beginning of the age of frozen food, so he tried freezing his cake. It worked, and he named it "Sara Lee," after his daughter. Another Jew in the advertising business, faced with a bumper crop of oranges, invented frozen orange juice.

The fast-growing influence of radio and television affected how Americans saw each other and how products were sold. *The Goldbergs*, a program about a fictional Bronx family, reached a radio audience of 10 million in the 1930s and at least 40 million two decades later on television. Just as *I Remember Mama* taught us about Scandinavians, *The Goldbergs* familiarized non-Jews with a simple, everyday Jewish family. Sometimes Molly Goldberg just cooked throughout the program, cutting up a chicken or chopping fish or herring as the problems of her family paraded through her kitchen.

After World War II another "cooking lady" stepped onto television. Her name was Edith Green, and her popular *Your Home Kitchen* ruled the airwaves in the San Francisco

Bay area from 1949 to 1954. Although this "queen of the range" was Jewish, her cooking was American—and it was "gourmet." A week's recipes might include veal scaloppine, coffee chocolate icebox cake, coconut pudding, or frozen tuna mold. She showed her viewers how to use new gadgets such as electric mixers and electric can openers, all products of the postwar period of affluence.

Jewish Food from World War II Onwards

New Jewish immigrants in the United States from other parts of the world helped shape Jewish food in America. When Sephardic Jews from Syria and Turkey came to the United States at the beginning of the twentieth century, most American Jews already knew about knishes and pierogi. But as new immigrants came, they taught the "old" immigrants about other "Jewish" finger-food pastries. Syrian Jews brought cheese *sambousek* and date *adjwah*; Turkish Jews brought eggplant *burekas*.

Later, with the rise of Hitler, refugees from Germany and Eastern Europe fled to America, and they brought with them updated versions of recipes that had come to this country one or two generations before. We sometimes forget that food in the "old country" was evolving, just as it was in the United States. Many old immigrant recipes experienced a "culinary lag" once they got to this country. Because they were handed down and brought out only for special occasions, they were not changed. In the old country, these dishes were constantly evolving.

Most Hasidim, adherents to an eastern European religious renewal movement of Jews, arrived after the war, following their leaders. In 1940, the story goes, the State Department intervened with the Nazis to allow the (sixth) Lubavitcher rebbe (spiritual leader), Rabbi Yosef Yitzchak Schneersohn, and his followers to leave in a train from Germany to Switzerland. Other Hasidim came by harder routes, carrying their belongings in kerchiefs and cardboard boxes. In Brooklyn they resettled in their own shtetls, American style. Now, a generation later, their numbers are expanding; Lubavitcher Hasidim, in particular, engage in aggressive outreach to assimilated second- and third-generation American Jewish youth and maintain religious centers in cities coast to coast. Hasidic influence has increased in many areas, bringing with it an increased demand for strict adherence to kashruth.

Political and economic upheavals in the decades after World War II brought to the United States more Jews who had been persecuted in other countries by regimes unfriendly to them. In a sense, too, the creation of Israel inspired a worldwide awareness of Jewish food—and now some of the children of immigrants to Israel are coming to the United States. These Mediterranean Jews have enriched the tapestry of Jewish cuisine here, contributing such new "Jewish" dishes as Syrian tamarind-flavored meat pies, fresh cumin-accented carrot salads from Morocco, and Israeli falafel. Americans are attracted to their cuisines because of the many vegetable-based dishes—the kind of cooking that is in keeping with American's new dietary trends.

While masses of Jews came to the shores of the United States during pogroms and the Holocaust, others went to Mexico, Cuba, China, Australia, and Argentina. As political problems swept through these lands, many of these Jews then moved to America or stayed on when they visited relatives here. And they brought still more new dishes with them.

With upheavals in the former Soviet Union, a new kind of Russian Jew arrived—one who knew very little about Jewish customs and the Jewish religion, which had mostly disappeared during the Communist regime. Settling in large cities, converting places like Brighton Beach, Brooklyn, into a new kind of shtetl, they are learning quickly about Jewish foods.

The end of the twentieth century saw a small transformation in Jewish food. Since the 1980s, kosher food has enjoyed an astonishing revival from coast to coast. People respond to an advertisement for a kosher hot dog "answering to a higher authority" or identify with "You don't have to be Jewish to love Levy's." To many Americans the word "kosher" is synonymous with better and safer. But 90 percent of Americans do not even know—nor do they care—that they are "buying kosher" when they pick up a box of Pepperidge Farm cookies or a bottle of Heinz ketchup, only two of the thousands of kosher products that are on the market today.

A shot in the arm to kosher food has been the *ba'alei teshuvah*, returnees to the faith. *Ba'al teshuvah* restaurateur Sol Kirschenbaum of New York's Levana restaurant, for example, has introduced his kosher clientele to rare beef and kosher bison. These formerly nonobservant Jews, who are returning to their Jewish roots, observe the laws of kashruth but are anxious to enjoy the new tastes and dishes that they knew before they became kosher. They have welcomed new look-alike products such as mock shrimp and lobster made of pollack, and enjoy radicchio with shiitake mushrooms without the prosciutto.

Although Jews have long been in the food business, only recently did they start becoming chefs. Today many second- and third-generation American Jews are cooking professionally. Some cooks, although not observant Jews, swear by kosher chickens. Many non-Jewish chefs have become intrigued with Jewish customs, preparing Roman Jewish menus and even catering seders in their restaurants. Not only are there many Jewish chefs and Jewish cookbooks today, but whole chapters in mainstream cookbooks are devoted to cooking for the kosher market.

Jewish chefs often express their "Jewishness" in their preferences for kasha, potato pancakes, kosher chickens, chicken soup, or a good New York cheesecake. There are also increasing numbers of kosher restaurants, where the word is taken seriously—not just metaphorically, as in "kosher-style" delis, a term coined in the 1950s. You can eat kosher Hunan, Indian, Italian, Moroccan, and French cuisine—whatever you want—in New York, Los Angeles, and many cities in between. The latest trend in Jewish cooking in America, as in American food generally, is that home cooks are watching the chefs for new recipes, as opposed to the chefs watching home cooks.

The days of heavy, time-consuming traditional Jewish foods are gone. First-class kosher wines are being produced in California and Israel, kosher meals are prepared for all airlines and cruise lines, and the kosher product market is expanding rapidly.

American Jewish Foods—Or What Passes for Them

Babka Babka is an eastern European-style cake made from an egg-and-butter yeast-based dough, often filled with raisins, chocolate, or cinnamon sugar and nuts. It is sold in most bakeries today, and is served as a dessert and as a coffee cake at brunches.

Bialys Bialys, similar to bagels but without holes, are made with only water, yeast, salt, and flour—the same ingredients as New York bagels, but in different proportions. The soft bialy dough is formed into small rounds, which are patted down. Bialys need a long, slow rising period. Later a thumb indents the center and fills it with diced onions and sometimes poppy seeds before it is baked in a very hot oven.

The bialy's origin is not clear, but bialys are suspected to be from the Middle East. In Poland and Russia, Jews ate a Bialystoker *tsibele pletzel*, a flat onion bread originally from the city of Bialystok, Poland. One hypothesis as to how bialys got their name is that Jewish bakers in the United States made these *pletzel*, and their bosses, perhaps thinking that "*pletzel*" sounded too much like "pretzel," decided to name the bun "bialy," after its place of origin. Bialys, unlike most bagels today, are still made by hand, although a roll maker, invented in the 1930s, has increased production tremendously.

Blintzes Thin pancakes filled with cheese and traditionally eaten at the springtime holiday of Shavuoth, blintzes are of Russian-Polish origin. Suspiciously like French crêpes or Chinese egg-roll wrappers, blintzes, or *blinchiki*, were sometimes filled with shredded leftover brisket to make a complete meal for Russian Jews or to serve as an accompaniment to chicken soup. They were also filled with farmer's or pot cheese for a dairy meal. In this country, many people add richer cream cheese.

Borscht Borscht is a soup, served hot or cold, that uses fermented or fresh red beet juice as a foundation and often includes meat, cabbage, onions, parsnips, and potatoes. Sour cream or sour milk is added to a vegetable-based soup; for a meat-based version, eggs are whipped in at the last minute to whiten it. Borscht is Polish, but it was introduced to the American public by Jewish restaurants.

Brisket Brisket is a cut of beef from the breast muscles and other boneless tissues from the forequarter. It is often braised in liquid and covered, or it can be cured in salt water and spices and served as corned beef. Almost every country has its own variation of brisket.

Burek *Burek* or *burekas* are turnovers of Turkish origin, often filled with cheeses or other savory mixtures.

Challah Challah, originally thought of as the portion of bread thrown in the oven as an offering in the Temple of Jerusalem, is now known as the special bread reserved by Jews for the Sabbath. In biblical times, however, the Sabbath bread was probably more like our present-day pita. Through the ages and as Jews moved to different lands, the loaves used for the Sabbath varied geographically. Eastern European immigrants put challah on the gastronomical map in the United States.

Sugar was added to challah in the late nineteenth and early twentieth century, when all breads were sweetened in the United States; sugar was a sign of affluence. Some restaurants in the United States today, Jewish and non-Jewish, serve challah french toast as a breakfast or brunch dish.

Cheesecake Cheesecake is a rich, dense cake made from soft creamy cheeses. The American version of cheesecake is often made with cream cheese, baked and served cold. Traditional European cheesecakes are often made with ricotta, soft curd cheeses, and flour. Reuben's Restaurant, in Manhattan, claims to have made the original cream cheese (as opposed to cottage cheese) cheesecake; in 1929, Reuben's won the gold medal at the World's Fair for their version. Because of a Kraft promotion, Philadelphia Supreme Cheese-cake and possibly Reuben's Cheesecake became known as "New York Cheesecake," which came to mean "Jewish Cheesecake." Now cheesecake has become an American favorite in a big way: Eli's Cheesecake of Chicago gave away slices of a two-thousand-pound red, white, and blue cheesecake to the eager crowd gathered on the National Mall in Washington, D.C., for Bill Clinton's 1993 inauguration.

Cholent Call it *cholent, chamin, sk'eena,* or *adafina,* this Jewish Sabbath luncheon stew made from beans, meat, and onions is a dish that has distinguished Jewish cooking since the fourth century because it is cooked before the Sabbath begins and heated in the oven throughout the Sabbath. Every wave of Jewish immigration to the Americas has its own form of this Sabbath dish, adding rice, barley, potatoes, and the like.

Cream Cheese Invented in 1872 by a dairyman from upstate New York, cream cheese was an instant hit with the Jewish community; it was sold in (Lithuanian-Jewish immigrants) Isaac and Joseph Breakstone's first dairy store on New York's Lower East Side. James Lewis Kraft's company later bought both Breakstone and Philadelphia Cream Cheese brands and, through a vast marketing campaign, popularized cream cheese among Jews and non-Jews alike.

Delicatessen More than anything else, "delicatessen" came to denote *the* Jewish eating experience in this country. "A deli was a little restaurant with a counter, a few stools and smoked beef, pastrami, frankfurters, potato knishes, rye bread, club bread, mustard, and pickles," recalls Norman Podhoretz, editor of *Commentary* magazine.

Until the late nineteenth century, delicatessens in this country were primarily run by Germans and Alsatians. Eventually Jews, too, went into the business. The word "delicatessen" derives from German and means "delicacies"; it is used to describe both a shop and the products sold there.

Delis were especially attractive for observant Jews because they were usually open on Sundays, selling canned and packaged goods and often duplicating the services of grocery stores.

As Jews became more affluent, two distinct types of delicatessens emerged. The first was an offshoot of the kosher restaurant: a kosher delicatessen and lunchroom. These kosher delis have always closed on the Sabbath and serve strictly meat meals. The other type of delicatessen was the carryout, "kosher-style" deli; it emerged as Jews became assimilated and moved out of downtown Manhattan. Though it looked and smelled like a kosher delicatessen, the coffee was served with cream and over-stuffed pastrami and corned beef sandwiches were followed by a piece of New York cheesecake. The three-decker rye bread sandwich, made famous at Reuben's Resaurant in New York, is a takeoff on the three-decker American club sandwich.

Egg Cream   A drink created in New York that included neither eggs nor cream; the froth on the top just happened to resemble whipped egg whites. Jewish by association, this chocolate-and-seltzer mixture was drunk in Jewish neighborhoods. Egg creams today come ready-made in the supermarket.

Ethrog   An *ethrog* is the fruit of a citron, a citrus fruit similar in appearance to a lemon but less round and more oval-shaped. It is used with the *lulav*, a traditional festive palm branch, in celebrating Sukkoth, the autumn harvest festival.

Gefilte Fish   Gefilte fish, basically a poached fish ball with filler (composed of bread crumbs or matzo meal), was served on the Sabbath and holidays by eastern European Jews; it is traditionally made from whitefish, pike, and carp. Gefilte fish can also describe a stewed or baked whole fish stuffed with a mixture of the fish flesh, bread or matzo crumbs, eggs, and seasonings. Today, gefilte fish mixings are often sold frozen. Gefilte fish is commonly eaten by American Jews today on the Jewish New Year and Passover and still, often, on the Sabbath.

Hamantaschen   Hamantaschen are filled triangular-shaped cookies eaten at Purim, a holiday that usually falls towards the end of the winter and that celebrates the Jews' salvation from the clutches of an evil Persian minister. The cookies, made with either yeast-based or butter-based dough, are often filled with sweet fruits, poppy seeds, or nuts.

Haroseth   *Haroseth* is a paste-like mixture of fruit, nuts, cinnamon, and wine eaten during the Passover Seder; it is often spread over matzo. Traditionally, this mixture represents the mortar that the Israelites used in building during their slavery in Egypt. In this country it is usually made with walnuts or pecans, apples, sweet wine, sugar, and occasionally cinnamon.

Kasha Varnishkes   *Kasha varnishkes* was a dish made with sauteed onions, buckwheat groats (kasha), and square, shell, or bow tie–shaped noodles (*varnishkes*), it is often eaten on Purim. Kasha is usually made from coarse cracked buckwheat but can also be made from barley, millet, oats, or wheat or from a mush made from one or more of those grains. Kasha was the common staple food for poor Jews in Rumania; buckwheat is the grain most indigenous to Russia. Whole buckwheat groats, when they are cooked with water, milk, or broth, make a hearty, nourishing porridge.

Kishke   *Kishke*, literally a stomach casing from beef or fowl, is a delicacy when filled with a savory stuffing, usually composed of matzo meal or flour, chicken fat, and onion. The stuffed casing is then roasted. Nowadays the casing is made from plastic.

Knaidlach   *Knaidlach*, or matzo ball dumplings, are composed of matzo meal, eggs, chicken fat, and sometimes ground almonds. They are served in soups.

Knishes   Knishes are round or square pieces of leavened dough that are folded over a savory meat, cheese, or potato filling. They can be baked or fried. Potato, kasha, liver, or cheese knishes may once have been a celebratory food in the Ukraine, where the potatoes were encrusted in a flaky pastry. But on New York's Lower East Side—specifically on lower Second Avenue, nicknamed "Knish Alley,"—the knish became a convenient hot finger food that sweatshop workers could buy and take to work for a filling snack or lunch. Knishes were often sold outside, so they became visible Jewish food. Today's knishes have gone mainstream, come in a variety of flavors, and are even available at "kosher-style" delis in shopping-mall food courts.

Kreplach   Kreplach, similar to Chinese wontons or Italian tortellini, are triangular pockets of noodle dough filled with chopped meat or cheese. They are boiled and eaten with chicken soup, or fried and eaten as a side dish. Kreplach arrived in Europe either when the

Khazars brought it to Polish lands or Jews brought it from trading expeditions in China.

Kugel Kugel, meaning pudding, is the Sabbath "extra" food that goes along with stew or *cholent*. Kugels are made from bread crumbs and flour, potatoes, vegetables, noodles, and other ingredients and can be sweet or savory.

Latke Latke means pancake in Yiddish, but most commonly it refers to a potato pancake eaten during the wintertime holiday of Hanukkah, when fried foods are served to commemorate the miracle of the holiday. Potatoes, inexpensive and easy to grow, were and are a common food in Europe, where Jews celebrated by eating latkes made from grated potatoes. Although some people take shortcuts, buying dehydrated or frozen grated potatoes or even frozen latkes, freshly made potato pancakes have become popular in chic restaurants as well as in kosher and "kosher-style" delis.

Lekakh *Lekakh* is the Yiddish word for honey cake, traditionally served on Rosh Hashanah (the Jewish New Year), and during the fall holiday season and eaten throughout the year as well. *Lekakh* often appears as a sweet treat on happy occasions, such as a birth or a wedding.

Lokshen *Lokshen* is Yiddish for egg noodles, often eaten with stews or in kugels.

Lox Lox, meaning salmon, comes from the German word *Lachs*. In the late nineteenth century in the United States, "lox" referred to salt-cured salmon from the Pacific Ocean. In this period, before refrigeration, lox was not smoked but cured—in a heavy salt brine as a preservative—and then placed in large wooden casks. A large portion of this lox was shipped to Europe; some remained in New York, where it was soaked in water before eating. It was enjoyed largely by the Jewish community of the Lower East Side. With the advent of refrigeration and freezing, salmon came both frozen and in a mild salt cure before being smoked.

Smoked or cured salmon is not of Jewish origin but has come to be thought of as such because so many Jewish immigrants ate it, especially with cream cheese and bagels. Nova (Nova Scotia) salmon, cured in a wet brine of sugar and salt before being smoked, is available throughout the United States. Smoked salmon from other parts of the world, such as Ireland, Scotland, and Denmark, is frequently dry-cured with rubbed salt before it is smoked.

Mamaliga *Mamaliga* is a Romanian version of polenta, a very thick cornmeal mush. Corn was brought back to the Old World by explorers after they discovered America. Apparently, only Italy and Romania showed any interest in this versatile food; they turned it into polenta and *mamaliga*, respectively. *Mamaliga* is often served with various kinds of cheese on top. Because of the Jewish prohibition against mixing milk products with meat, *mamaliga* could not be served at a restaurant that served meat. Without cheese it can be served, dipped in gravy, with pot roast as a side dish.

Matzo Matzo is an unleavened, crackerlike bread that symbolizes both oppression and freedom. It is eaten by Jews at Passover, the springtime festival of freedom celebrating the Exodus from Egypt. Matzo is made without yeast and is quickly baked, as a reminder that the Jews fleeing from Egypt had no time to let their bread rise or to bake it properly. Originally matzo was round and a lot thicker than the crispy, machine-made matzo sold in stores today.

There are special rules involved in making matzo. No yeast can be used, and the unbleached flour is carefully monitored for impurities, from the time the wheat is reaped (for handmade, so-called *shemurah*—or specially guarded—matzo) or from the time it is brought to the mill (for regular, machine-made matzo). The water used for baking matzo must sit for twenty-four hours, with no foreign elements allowed to contaminate it.

Certain mills are designated and carefully cleaned so as to be suitable for grinding Passover flour, and special blessings are recited by the workers as the flour is ground. According to Jewish law, the mixing of the flour and water, the kneading on one side so no rising occurs, the piercing of holes, and the baking must take no more than eighteen minutes to the emergence of the finished product from the oven. If any more time is taken to make the matzo, the bread will rise, rendering it unsuitable for Passover.

Matzo is eaten at the seder, the ceremonial dinner eaten on the first night of Passover (on the first two nights, among traditional Jews in the Diaspora). On the seder table three pieces of matzo are placed one above the other—to symbolize, according to one interpretation, the division of the Jewish people into *kohanim* (priests), *levi'im* (Levites), and Israelites (everyone else). At the beginning of the seder, the middle matzo is divided; the larger part, or *afikomen* (meaning "dessert" in Greek), is put aside and hidden. The *afikomen* should be the last food eaten at the meal. Matzo is also one of the first foods eaten at the seder, and a matzo sandwich is eaten shortly thereafter.

Petcha *Petcha,* calf's-foot jelly, is a Sabbath afternoon dish. The custom of eating jelly reflects the idea that in the time of redemption even the feet will be elevated; the Sabbath is said to give the faithful a taste of the world to come, so "food made of feet" was eaten in anticipation. In fact, the calf's foot, like the African American delicacy made from hog heads and feet called "head cheese" or souse, is an inexpensive cut of meat, and for poor eastern European Jews, like their poor African American counterparts, this jelly was another way to stretch what meat was available.

Pierogi Pierogi are small pastries stuffed with savory fillings, frequently potatoes. Most countries have a version of these, variously called empanadas, *burekas,* pasties, or turnovers.

Rugelach Rugelach are horn-shaped rolled cookies that have been eaten for at least the last century. They are made in both a pareve (nonmeat, nondairy) and a buttery fashion. Rugelach usually of a dough with a cream-cheese-and-flour base, rolled with a sweet fruit, cinnamon, or chocolate filling. Cream cheese was an American addition to the rugelach dough, as are many of the innovative fillings used today. The cream cheese dough may have been developed by the Philadelphia Cream Cheese Company because the dough is often called "Philadelphia cream cheese dough." Cookbook writer Maida Heatter put rugelach on the culinary map with her grandmother's recipe; Heatter's is the rugelach most often found in upscale bakeries nationwide. Rugelach are often served at Hanukkah, as it is traditional, then, to eat sweets with cheese or sour cream. These cheese sweets represent the cakes that Judith allegedly fed the evil general Holofernes before she killed him.

Sambusak *Sambusak* are crescent-shaped pastries of Middle Eastern origin, filled with savories. Sambusak, along with *burekas,* are among the many finger foods that Middle Eastern Jews brought with them to the United States. These pastries, originally filled with Syrian goat cheese, can also be made with muenster cheese, Balkan kashkeval cheese, or any other type of hard cheese that can be grated. Indian, Iraqi, and Persian Jews also eat *sambusak,* filling them most often with potatoes or chicken.

Schmaltz *Schmaltz* is rendered poultry fat, obtained from the bird by frying the solidified fat until it is liquefied. Traditionally used for frying, schmaltz has been replaced, in large part, by modern conveniences like vegetable-based shortenings.

Schnecken *Schnecken* are cakelike sweets served as desserts or at brunches. They are composed of a buttery yeast or cream-cheese dough rolled with nuts, sugar, cinnamon, and sometimes raisins. The dough is sliced and then baked, usually in a honey or brown-sugar-and-butter syrup. *Schnecken,* when made with yeast, have become the American pecan roll, caramel cinnamon roll, or sticky bun. Pecans and brown sugar have replaced almonds, walnuts, and honey.

Sufganiyot *Sufganiyot* are doughnuts, often filled with jelly, which are an Israeli Hanukkah tradition. *Sufganiya,* a modern Hebrew word, comes from the Greek *sufgan,* meaning "puffed and fried."

Taiglach or Teyglakh *Taiglach* are pieces of fried dough coated in honey, traditionally served at festive holidays and events such as Rosh Hashanah Sukkoth, Simchas Torah, Hanukkah, Purim, weddings, and births.

Tsimmes *Tsimmes* is a sweetened, baked combination of carrots, sweet potatoes, and meat, often made with dried fruits and sometimes with carrots alone. It is stewlike and often eaten on the Sabbath and Sukkoth. In Yiddish, *tsimmes* means a big fuss made over something.

[*See also* Bagels; Bialy; Cheesecake; Delicatessens; Egg Cream; Ethnic Foods; Jewish Dietary Laws; Matzo; New York Food; Passover; Sara Lee Corporation.]

BIBLIOGRAPHY

Braunstein, Susan L., and Jenna Weissman Joselit, eds. *Getting Comfortable in New York: The American Jewish Home, 1880–1950.* With contributions by Jenna Weissman Joselit, Barbara Kirschenblatt-Gimblett, Irving Howe. New York: Jewish Museum, 1990.

Da Silva, Cara. "Cookbook of Dream Recipes: A Collection from a Tragic Past." *Newsday,* 15 April 1991.

Gaster, Theodor H. *Customs and Folkways of Jewish Life.* New York: Sloane, 1955.

Glazer, Ruth. "The Jewish Delicatessen." *Commentary,* February 1946.

Kanfer, Stefan. *A Summer World: The Attempt to Build a Jewish Eden in the Catskills, from the Days of the Ghetto to the Rise and Decline of the Borscht Belt.* New York: Farrar, Straus & Giroux, 1989.

Karp, Abraham J., comp. *The Jewish Experience in America: Selected Studies from the Publications of the American Jewish*

Historical Society. 5 vols. Waltham, MA: American Jewish Historical Society, 1969.

Kisseloff, Jeff. *You Must Remember This: An Oral History of Manhattan from the 1890s to World War II.* Baltimore: Johns Hopkins University Press, 1999.

Kraut, Alan. "The Butcher, the Baker, the Pushcart Peddler: Jewish Foodways and Entrepreneurial Opportunity in the East European Immigrant Community, 1880–1940." *Journal of American Culture* 6, no. 4 (1983): 71–83.

Levy, Esther. *Jewish Cookery Book.* Philadelphia: W. S. Turner, 1871.

Nathan, Joan. *Jewish Cooking in America.* New York: Knopf, 1994.

Nathan, Joan. *The Jewish Holiday Baker.* New York: Schocken, 1997.

Nathan, Joan. *The Jewish Holiday Kitchen.* Rev. ed. New York: Schocken, 1988.

O'Neill, Molly. "Where Seltzer Once Thrived, Few True Fizzes Remain." *New York Times,* July 11, 1991.

Schoener, Allon. *The American Jewish Album, 1654 to the Present.* New York: Rizzoli, 1983.

Shosteck, Patti. *A Lexicon of Jewish Cooking: A Collection of Folklore, Foodlore, History, Customs, and Recipes.* Chicago: Contemporary Books, 1979.

Sperling, Abraham I. *Reasons for Jewish Customs and Traditions.* Translated by Abraham Matts. New York: Bloch, 1975.

JOAN NATHAN

Jewish Dietary Laws

Kashruth, the Jewish dietary laws, shapes the everyday life of those who observe it. Observance of the dietary laws separates Jews from non-Jews and is intended to imbue the most mundane activities with holiness and significance. (The English word "kosher" reflects the western, Yiddish pronunciation of the Hebrew word *kasher,* meaning fit or suitable.)

The cryptic and complicated prohibitions of Leviticus regarding animal food have been expanded by centuries of rabbinic commentary to apply to almost any food one might encounter. Any food that has been handled, processed, or packaged must be subject to strict rabbinic supervision; even some raw vegetables must be meticulously examined for bugs and dirt.

The laws of kashruth as outlined in the Hebrew Bible fall into three basic categories: prohibition of the consumption of blood, prohibition of the consumption of certain categories of animals, and the prohibition(s) regarding combinations of milk and meat products.

Blood. Consumption of blood is prohibited in Leviticus 17:14 on the grounds that an animal's blood is its life. In practice this requires that meat must be thoroughly soaked and salted to remove any blood before it can be cooked, and eggs must be examined for blood spots before they may be added to a recipe.

Forbidden animals. Certain categories of animals are forbidden in the Hebrew Bible. Among sea creatures, only fish with fins and scales are suitable for consumption (Leviticus 11:9–12 and Deuteronomy 14:9–10). The Hebrew Bible provides a list of prohibited birds in Leviticus 11:13–19 and Deuteronomy 14:11–18; because the forbidden birds are scavengers and birds of prey, all such birds came to be regarded as unclean, and prohibited. Among land creatures, only ruminants, animals that split the hoof and chew the cud, are suitable (Leviticus 11:3–8 and 20–27 and Deuteronomy 14:4–8 and 19–20).

The combination of milk and meat. A most important facet of the observance of kashruth, and the one that most distinguishes a kosher kitchen, is the separation of milk and meat products. This practice is traced to the three instances in the Pentateuch (Exodus 23:19, Exodus 34:26, and Deuteronomy 14:21) in which the children of Israel are forbidden to cook a goat in the milk of its mother. Whether these verses are the source of the prohibition remains a matter of dispute. In practice, meat and milk products are never cooked or prepared together and never served at the same meal. Kosher kitchens have completely separate sets of cookware, dishware, and cutlery for handling meat and milk products.

The details of the observance of the dietary laws cannot all be inferred from the Hebrew Bible itself nor from the Talmud, a multivolume elaboration on the commandments of the Torah or Pentateuch completed in the sixth century. The immediate source upon which *poskim,* rabbis who decide questions of Jewish law, base Jewish practice is the *Shulkhan Arukh* (or "Set Table"), compiled in the middle of the sixteenth century by Rabbi Joseph Caro (published 1565), and expanded with the commentaries of Rabbi Moses Isserles.

The Jewish Dietary Laws in America

Jewish immigrants to the United States in the seventeenth, eighteenth, and nineteenth centuries attempted with varying degrees of success to re-create the infrastructure that had enabled supervision of kosher food in Europe. By the late nineteenth century many American Jews had shrugged off the strictures of kashruth entirely. In 1887 Rabbi Moses Weinberger wrote that *shokhtim* (ritual slaughterers) in America were entirely unsupervised, and while there were some *shokhtim* who were honest in their work, in general the kashruth of meat in America was not to be trusted.

In 1888, in an attempt to allay the anarchic situation present in the kosher meat business, Rabbi Jacob Joseph, the first and only Orthodox chief rabbi of New York City, instituted a stamp system under which all poultry that had been subject to proper rabbinic supervision would be certified kosher and stamped with a lead tag, or *plumba*. The intention was to assure Jewish consumers that they could trust their butchers, but the cost of the tags—one cent apiece—caused outrage. The Yiddish press compared the stamps to the *karobka*, punitive taxes levied on kosher meat in czarist Russia.

In 1902, in response to a 50 percent increase in the wholesale price of kosher beef (raising the retail price from twelve cents to eighteen cents per pound), Fanny Levy and Sarah Edelson, Jewish homemakers perhaps inspired by the resistance of Jewish women in the labor movement, went from door to door to persuade their neighbors not to buy kosher meat. On May 15 of that year, thousands of Jewish women broke into kosher butcher stores on the Lower East Side and threw meat onto the sidewalks, doused it with gasoline, or otherwise made it inedible. Two weeks later religious authorities formally endorsed the boycott—which finally ended in mid-June, when the retail price of kosher beef fell to fourteen cents a pound.

Coca-Cola received kashruth certification from an Atlanta rabbi in 1915 after the Coca-Cola company agreed to remove tallow-derived glycerin from its formula. (In order to be made privy to the list of ingredients in the Coca-Cola secret formula so that he could certify Coca-Cola as kosher, the rabbi had to swear that he would never reveal them.)

In the United States, the Union of Orthodox Jewish Congregations, commonly called the "OU" and represented by a letter U inside a letter O, is the most well known certifier of kosher foods. The Orthodox Union created the "OU" symbol in 1923; this trademarked symbol unobtrusively marks prepared and packaged foods that have been certified as kosher by the Union. (The first product to be graced with the symbol was Heinz vegetarian baked beans.) It was to be many years, however, before the "OU" symbol caught on.

In 1933 the Orthodox Union instituted a newsletter with a "kashruth column" to respond to the queries of Jewish homemakers trying to make sense of the staggering abundance of foods to be found in America. Today the Orthodox Union certifies as kosher a quarter of a million products manufactured in sixty-eight countries. About 20 percent of kosher foods are certified by smaller organizations or local rabbinical associations.

[*See also* Jewish American Food; Passover.]

BIBLIOGRAPHY

Cohn, Jacob. *The Royal Table: An Outline of the Dietary Laws of Israel*. New York: Bloch Publishing Co., 1936.

Joselit, Jenna Weissman. *New York's Jewish Jews: The Orthodox Community in the Interwar Years*. Bloomington: Indiana University Press, 1990.

Karp, Abraham. "New York Chooses a Chief Rabbi." *Publications of the American Jewish Historical Society* 44 (1955): 129–198.

Weinberger, Moses. *People Walk on Their Heads: Moses Weinberger's Jews and Judaism in New York*. Translated and edited by Jonathan D. Sarna. New York: Holmes & Meier, 1982.

                                      EVE JOCHNOWITZ

Johnson, Howard

Howard Deering Johnson (1897–1972), the only son of a Boston tobacconist, was born in Quincy, Massachusetts, a small industrial city bordering Boston on the south. The family lived in the middle-class, seaside Wollaston neighborhood. After serving in France during World War I, Johnson returned to take over his deceased father's failing shop. Three years later, in 1922, Johnson liquidated its assets, assumed the debt, and purchased a small corner drugstore that sold patent medicine, newspaper, tobacco, and candy. To make the business viable, he expanded the newspaper section to include a delivery service employing seventy-five boys. Then the self-professed ice cream aficionado, who consumed a cone every day of his life, turned his attention to the marble-topped soda fountain. He improved on the commercial ice creams of the day by manufacturing a product with twice the butterfat content. Different sources state that the formula was based on his mother's recipe or one that Johnson purchased from an elderly street vendor.

The ice cream became the cornerstone of the business, and he gradually expanded from the standard chocolate, vanilla, and strawberry to twenty-eight flavors. To make purchase convenient for sunbathers, he built small wooden stands along the beachfront where he sold ice cream cones for a nickel. By 1928, the Johnson's ice cream business alone was grossing $240,000 in sales.

With the profits, he opened a restaurant featuring New England family-style specialties, such as clam chowder and chicken potpie, in a new ten-story granite building that still stood in downtown Quincy in the early 2000s.

During the Great Depression when banks were reluctant to give loans, Howard Johnson continued to expand his company by creating the concept of the restaurant franchise. For a small investment, he supplied every aspect of the business from facility design to food products, including the use of his name on the logo. The first was in Orleans, Massachusetts, on Cape Cod. Operating investors reaped large profits and the enterprise grew rapidly, numbering two hundred restaurants by 1940.

All but twelve of the restaurants closed with the advent of World War II, but Johnson kept the company alive by providing meals for the military and educational institutions. After the war, Howard Johnson continued to apply the central commissary concept to the restaurant business ensuring quality and uniformity. Many products, including Tendersweet Clam Strips and HoJo Cola, were trademarked.

Anticipating highway expansion, he bid on and won exclusive rights to build the restaurants on the Pennsylvania, Ohio, and New Jersey turnpikes. He recorded a code of quality and cleanliness in the "Howard Johnson Bible" and upheld it through surprise inspections. He continued expansion by building motor lodges beside his restaurants located nearby new interstate highway exit ramps, bringing travelers the same standards in lodging that they had come to expect in the restaurants.

Johnson and his wife, Marjorie Smith, had two children, Dorothy Johnson Weeks and Howard Brennon Johnson. His son succeeded him in 1959 and took the company public in 1961. Although Johnson Sr. remained as chairman and treasurer, he devoted increasing time to acquiring art and sailing aboard his sixty-foot yacht. At his death in 1972, he maintained residences in Boston, Miami Beach, and Manhattan.

[*See also* Burger King; Clams; Ice Cream and Ices; Howard Johnson; McDonald's; Roadside Food; Sanders, Colonel; Soda Fountains; White Castle.]

LINDA BASSETT

Johnson and Wales

Johnson and Wales University was founded as a business school in 1914 in Providence, Rhode Island, by Gertrude I. Johnson and Mary T. Wales, but it soon attained full-fledged associate degree–awarding status. In 1973 the university opened the College of Culinary Arts. Four campuses—in Norfolk, Virginia; North Miami, Florida; Denver, Colorado; and Charlotte, North Carolina—were added over the next thirty years. Associated sites include Vail, Colorado, and Göteborg, Sweden, the latter for programs in business and hospitality.

With more than five thousand students enrolled at its various campuses, the College of Culinary Arts is the largest food-service educator. In 1993 Johnson and Wales became the first school in America to offer a bachelor of science in the culinary arts. In addition to the associate degree and the bachelor of science in culinary arts and in baking and pastry arts, the university offers undergraduate degrees in culinary nutrition, food marketing, food-service entrepreneurship, and food-service management. Master's degrees are also offered in accounting, financial services management, hospitality administration, international trade, marketing, organizational leadership, and teaching.

The private, nonprofit, accredited coeducational institution trains restaurant chefs and professionals in all areas of the food-service industry. Students learn industrial, contractual, and resort food-service operations through a combination of general academic, professional skill, and career-focused courses. The practical curriculum of laboratory classes and academic studies is augmented by the Distinguished Visiting Chef Program, designed to expose students to the techniques and philosophies of internationally recognized chefs who visit the university to lecture and demonstrate.

In 1989 one of the visiting chefs, the late Louis Szathmary of Chicago, donated to the university his entire collection of priceless culinary memorabilia. The collection is housed in the Johnson and Wales University Culinary Archives and Museum at the Providence campus.

[*See also* Celebrity Chefs; Cooking Schools; Culinary Institute of America; Restaurants, *sidebar on* The Rise of Restaurants; Szathmary, Louis.]

ROBIN M. MOWER

Jolly Green Giant

The Jolly Green Giant towers over most other advertising icons. The original giant dates to 1925, when the Minnesota Valley Canning Company wanted to sell a new kind of pea that was tender, sweet, and tasty. But it was also wrinkled, oblong, and huge, and small June peas were popular at the time. To overcome market resistance, Minnesota Valley cleverly capitalized on the size of the peas by calling them Green Giant and putting a symbolic giant on the label.

The first giant looked quite different from the one that the world now knows. Based on a character in a Grimm fairy tale, the original figure sported a bearskin and a scowl. He was white and hunched over, and seemed more like a dwarf than a giant. In 1935 Leo Burnett's Chicago advertising agency provided a much-needed makeover and created a giant with better posture, green skin, a leafy outfit, and a big smile. Accompanying the smile was the addition of "Jolly" to the Green Giant's name.

Burnett also invented a valley for the giant to preside over and gave him a responsibility to rule it well. Part of his job there is quality control, to ensure that only top-notch vegetables are grown and marketed under his watch. Although all he ever says is "Ho, ho, ho," he is positioned as the authority figure, as befits someone of his stature. The supporting characters, or Valley Helpers, quote him in commercials and convey his knowledge and concerns to consumers. He has explained, for example, that peas must be picked at the fleeting moment of perfect flavor, that beans should be cut on a slant, and that niblet corn needs to be vacuum-packed.

The Jolly Green Giant's role has changed over the years. After his makeover, he appeared more often in print ads. He came to symbolize not only the pea but the company as well, and in 1950 Minnesota Valley Canning Company changed its name to Green Giant Company. In 1959 the giant made his TV advertising debut, and, soon after, spoke his first "Ho, ho, ho." In 1972 he was blessed with an enthusiastic and outgoing apprentice, Sprout, a giant in training. The Jolly Green Giant has instructed Sprout in the ways of vegetables and the ways of the valley, nurturing the little fellow just as he nurtures the vegetables in his care. In 1993 the giant tried semiretirement, quitting all ads and appearing only on labels. But on his seventy-fifth birthday, in 2000, the advertisers brought him back to work in print ads with slogans like "Give peas a chance" and "I stand for goodness (In fact I haven't sat down since 1925)."

The Jolly Green Giant represents a successful and enduring advertising campaign. *Advertising Age* considers the giant to be the third most recognized ad icon of the twentieth century, after the Marlboro Man and Ronald McDonald. Green Giant has become the largest vegetable brand in the world. Its vegetables are marketed in twenty-six countries, and the giant appears in such far-flung places as Greece, China, Japan, Israel, and Saudi Arabia.

[*See also* Advertising; Canning and Bottling; Corn; Peas; Vegetables.]

BIBLIOGRAPHY

McGrath, Molly Wade. *Top Sellers, U.S.A: Success Stories behind America's Best-Selling Products from Alka Seltzer to Zippo.* New York: Morrow, 1983.

SHARON KAPNICK

Juice Bars

Juice bars, a billion-dollar business, began modestly in 1926 in Los Angeles when Julius Freed opened a shop selling fresh orange juice. His real estate agent, Bill Hamlin, a former chemist, suggested an all-natural mixture that gave the orange juice a creamy, foamy consistency. It contained orange juice, water, egg whites, vanilla extract, sugar and ice. When Freed and Hamlin started selling the new beverage, sales soared from twenty dollars to one hundred dollars a day, and a name for the product arose from the way customers asked for the drink: "Give me an orange, Julius." By 1929 Orange Julius had grown into a chain with one hundred stores in the United States.

The macrobiotic vegetarianism fad in the mid-1960s stirred up the juice-bar business with the creation of smoothies, originally a mixture of fruit, fruit juice, and ice sold in the back of health-food restaurants and stores. Steve Kuhnau started a health-food store in 1973, offering nutritious, energy-packed smoothies as an alternative to the ubiquitous high-fat food of New Orleans and to help resolve his own health problems. In 1987 Kuhnau and his wife, Cindy, co-founded one of the major smoothie companies, Smoothie King Franchises Inc. A competitor, Jamba Juice Company, began in 1990 in California as a store that offered fresh-fruit smoothies, fresh squeezed juices, bread, and pretzels.

By the end of the twentieth century, regional and independent juice bars had sprouted up across the country, often selling coffee, tea, sandwiches, bagels, soups, and salads as well as juice. Juice bars became prominent at the front of many health-food restaurants and stores, health clubs, and chains such as Wild Oats Markets Inc. and Whole Foods Markets Inc. Mobile smoothie stations in carts and kiosks make the drinks even more available and less expensive to purvey.

Changes in American culture increased the growth of juice bars. With a faster pace of life consumers look for nutritious, convenient, portable snacks or meal replacements, and the aging population searches for an energy elixir as zealously as athletes seek fast replenishment after exercise. Beverages sold in juice bars are a good source of both dairy products and the recommended five-a-day servings of fruit and vegetables. They are often high in calories, ranging from 250 to over 500, many of which are from sugars. They also have a different nutrient combination than a complete meal does.

Juice bars try to make their drinks appealing with names such as Kiwi Berry Burner, Jamba Powerboost, and Bounce Back Blast. Juice bars serve beverages that may contain exotic fruit juices, organic juices, unusual Russian winter wheatgrass, seaweed, or vegetables. Many dessert-style smoothies contain milk; ice cream or ice milk; yogurt or frozen yogurt; sorbet; or soy, rice, or nut milk. Nutritional supplements may be added. Even tea and coffee are sometimes mixed with juice, fruit, and supplements.

In 2002, as the juice and smoothie business surpassed $1 billion in sales for the first time, there were about 3,500 juice bars in the United States. Smoothie King and Jamba Juice dominate the industry, but Orange Julius, owned by International Dairy Queen Inc., survives, with more than 370 franchises nationwide and internationally.

[*See also* Counterculture, Food; Desserts; Diets, Fad; Fruit Juices; Health Food; Orange Julius; Vegetarianism.]

BIBLIOGRAPHY

Wilbur, Todd. *Top Secret Recipes: Creating Kitchen Clones of America's Favorite Brand-Name Foods*. New York: A Plume Book, 1993.

Titus, Dan. *Smoothies! The Original Smoothie Book: Recipes from the Pros*. Chino Hills, CA: Juice Gallery Multimedia, 2000.

ELISABETH TOWNSEND

Juicers

In order to remove as much juice as possible from citrus fruit, a ridged rounded cone that fits inside the halved fruit can be used. From the outside of the fruit, pressure alone, or pressure and rotation combined, squeeze out the juice, seeds, and some of the pulp. Such a ridged cone is called a "reamer"; it is usually fitted with a raised slotted rim to separate seeds from juice and is either positioned over a receptacle or is designed as an all-in-one saucer with handle and pouring lip. Most are molded glass or plastic; the first patented one dates to 1889.

Old juicers are usually levered or cranked. Simple levered types have two hinged handles and date to about 1870. On one side is a convex dome; opposing it is a cavity with drip holes. When the handles are closed, the fruit is squeezed and juiced. In more complex levered juicers, half a citrus fruit is placed on a convex reamer and is squeezed with a levered concave presser. In others, a quarter of citrus fruit is put into a hopper and a levered presser folds and crushes it—much as it would be in your hand. Some cranked juicers move the reamer around the inside of the fruit while it is tightly held by a levered presser. Electric juicers have been used since the 1930s. There are small wedge squeezers for lemon, used at the table or bar, that also date from around the 1930s.

Nineteenth-century juice presses for berries or raw meat were essentially metal boxes with holes in the bottom and a heavy screw-levered pressing plate. Meat juice—that is, blood—was used as food for invalids until the early twentieth century.

BIBLIOGRAPHY

Franklin, Linda Campbell. *300 Years of Kitchen Collectibles*. 5th ed. Iola, WI: Krause, 2003.

LINDA CAMPBELL FRANKLIN

Juices, *see Fruit Juices*